Sylvia Porter's
MONEY BOOK

Sylvia Porter's

MONEY BOOK

How To Earn It, Spend It, Save It, Invest It, Borrow It – And Use It To Better Your Life

AVON
PUBLISHERS OF BARD, CAMELOT AND DISCUS BOOKS

AVON BOOKS
A division of
The Hearst Corporation
959 Eighth Avenue
New York, New York 10019

First Avon Printing, October, 1976
Fourth Printing

AVON TRADEMARK REG. U.S. PAT. OFF. AND
FOREIGN COUNTRIES, REGISTERED TRADEMARK—
MARCA REGISTRADA, HECHO EN CHICAGO, U.S.A.

Printed in the U.S.A.

To G. Sumner Collins
My Husband

FOREWORD

The American market place is an economic jungle. As in all jungles, you easily can be destroyed if you don't know the rules of survival. You easily can fall into dangerous traps from which you cannot escape unharmed if you aren't alert and do not know how to avoid them. But you also can come through in fine shape and you can even flourish in the jungle—if you learn the rules, adapt them for your own use, and heed them.

This book's entire purpose is to prepare you to win in every sphere of your economic life. You may approach its contents in any way you wish, depending on your economic needs or desires at the specific time. Do you want a quick course in consumer economics? Scan the book from cover to cover, for it is designed to be your basic book in personal and family finance. Do you want help on buying or renting, furnishing or financing a home? Turn to Chapter 13, "A Roof Over Your Head," and I am confident you will find the information you are seeking. Are you concerned about investing your nest egg? In Chapters 20–25, on "How to Invest," you will find the fundamental guidelines on investing or speculating in stocks, bonds of all types, mutual funds, commodities, and even in the "far out" fields ranging from rare books and prints to art and antique cars. Do you need to know how to borrow money? Or plan your future financial security? Or finance a college education? Or do you want to know what are your rights in the market place and how to go about getting them? Out of a lifetime of dedicated study, I have tried to give you the fundamentals in each area.

Of course, all I—or anyone else—could give you in any book, no matter what its size or how great its goals, are the basic facts, the most accurate and complete guidelines available, an informed selection of subjects, and, in my case, a lifelong bias in favor of the consumer. You must carry on from here and translate all of it into whatever is right for you to do. In Chapter

6, "The Everyday Necessity of Food," for instance, you will find simple rules for using unit pricing to slash your food costs. But what help will unit pricing be if you ignore this technique when you go food shopping? In Chapter 11, "Your Job, Career, or Business," you will find the telltale signs of this era's most vicious "business opportunities" traps. But what purpose have I served if you refuse to heed the warnings? All of us must decide what and how much responsibility we will accept for the protection of ourselves and our families.

It was more than five years ago that I began this book with great confidence. It is with humility that I finish it. And it is with the hope that it will help make your own life as a consumer more rewarding in these closing decades of the twentieth century in America that I now submit it to you.

October 1974

Leading all acknowledgments must be mine to Lydia Lawrence Ratcliff, my associate for twelve years. She and I worked together on this book from start to finish. Whatever success it earns, I share with Lydia.

Also, my deep gratitude goes to:

Sylvia (Sally) Rosen, my executive secretary and friend for twenty-one years, who supervised the production of the book throughout;

Richard C. Andrews, who researched and reviewed thousands of facts with a reassuring respect for accuracy; and

Mary B. Williams, who organized and kept the files, thereby holding back chaos for five long years.

In the course of writing this book many organizations and individuals— all authorities in their respective fields—helped with essential research and correction of the manuscript. Their contribution has been enormous, and I acknowledge this too with profound gratitude. Among them:

American Automobile Association, American Bankers Association, American Dental Association, American Hospital Association, American Institute of Architects, American Legion, American Medical Association, American Movers Conference, American National Red Cross, American Psychiatric Association, American Society of Travel Agents, American Telephone & Telegraph Co., American Youth Hostels, Inc., Air Conditioning and Refrigeration Institute, Amtrak, Associated American Artists, Association of Home Appliance Manufacturers, Avis Rent-A-Car System, Inc.

The Bride's Magazine, Better Business Bureau of Metropolitan N.Y., Inc., Bicycle Institute of America, Blue Cross, Blue Shield, Bureau of Building Marketing Research, Car Tours in Europe, Inc., Celanese Corp., Chase Manhattan Bank, Chris Craft Industries Inc., College Entrance Examination Board, College Scholarship Service, Commodity Research Bureau, Consumer Education—Extension Service, Consumer Federation of America, Consumers Union, Credit Union National Association, Inc., Edmund Publications Corp., Electronics Industries Association.

Greyhound Lines, Inc., Group Health Association of America, Health Insurance Institute, Health Research Group, H. R. Harmer, Inc., Household Finance Corp., Institute of Life Insurance, International Association of Chiefs of Police, Inc., Insurance Institute for Highway Safety, Insurance Information Institute, Jewelry Industry Council, H. P. Kraus.

Litton Industries, Lightning Protection Institute, Manfra, Tordella &

Brooks, Inc., Merrill Lynch, Pierce, Fenner and Smith, Mobile Homes Manufacturers Association, *Modern Maturity Magazine,* National Alliance of Television & Electronic Service Associations, National Association of Home Builders, National Association of Realtors, National Consumer Law Center, National Family Opinion Research, National Fire Protection Association, National League of Insured Savings Associations, National Live Stock & Meat Board, National Parking Association, National Safety Council, National Society of Interior Designers, New York State College of Agriculture and Life Sciences, New York Stock Exchange, No-Load Mutual Fund Association, Northeastern University, Planned Parenthood—World Population, Public Interest Research Group, Recreational Vehicle Institute, Research Institute of America, Rhode Island Consumers Council, Small Claims Study Group, Sotheby Parke-Bernet Inc., The Conference Board, The National Association of Food Chains, The Singer Corp., Village Music Studio, Vintage Cars of Rockland, Yale University, Zero Population Growth.

The United States Departments of Agriculture, Health, Education and Welfare, Housing and Urban Development, Transportation, and Treasury; the Internal Revenue Service; the Federal Housing Administration, General Services Administration, National Highway Traffic Safety Administration, Occupational Safety and Health Administration, Social Security Administration, and Veterans Administration; the Federal Bureaus of the Census, Customs, Labor Statistics, and the Women's Bureau; the Civil Aeronautics Board, Consumer Product Safety Commission, Federal Trade Commission, Food and Drug Administration, and the Interstate Commerce Commission; the Federal Deposit Insurance Corporation, the Federal Reserve Board, the Federal Savings and Loan Insurance Corporation, and the National Credit Union Administration; the Office of Education and the Office of Consumer Affairs.

Robert H. Bethke, Judith Burbank, Herbert Denenberg, Carol Brandt, L. W. Erickson, Karen Ferguson, Dave Gammill, Herbert Gilman, Dr. Eli Ginzberg, Leon Gold, Robert E. Harper, Richard Hesse, Dr. Milton J. Huber, Richard Huyler, Eugene Emerson Jennings, William L. Jiler, Walter Kolodrubetz, Ken McCormick, Ferris Mack, Harold I. Meyerson, Eugene Miller, Ernest Morgan, Franz Pick, Judge Morris Ploscowe, Walter Polner, Riva Poor, Betsy Rollason, V. Henry Rothschild, Larry Rothstein, Peter M. Sandman, Milton A. Schiff, Brooke Shearer, Elsa Sydorowich, Kacy Tebbel, Barbara Donovan Tober, Stan West, Graham V. Whitehead.

CONTENTS

Part III MANAGING YOUR MONEY

Part IV YOUR RIGHTS AND HOW TO GET THEM

Part I

EVERYDAY MATTERS

1

YOUR PERSONAL
MONEY MANAGER

The Characteristics of Class

Where does your income rank?

Are you rich?

You are if you have a household income of $50,000 and over. This is the class of the rich and there are only about half a million homes in it. But while you make up less than 1 per cent of our nation's population, you get 5 per cent of our entire personal income.

Are you affluent?

You are if your household income is $25,000 to $50,000, and if so, you are also in a skinny minority of 7 per cent of our households. But if you are in this class you have at your disposal some 18 per cent of our nation's total earnings and your per capita income is more than twice the nationwide average.

Are you upper-middle?

Your household income is $15,000 to $25,000 and some 15.5 million— or about one out of every four of the nation's homes—are in this class. Your per capita income exceeds $5,000, which is a third again as much as the national average.

Are you average?

Then your household income is $10,000 to $15,000 and you join nearly a quarter of all America's homes. What's more, in contrast to the affluent and the rich, many of you are thirty-four years of age or younger and less than 25 per cent of you are over fifty-five.

Are you below par?

That's you, if your household income is $5,000 to $10,000, and you represent one of every four homes. Your per capita income is only $2,600 a year and, despite the size of your group, only 14 per cent of all spending power flows to you.

In the United States in the mid-seventies, you qualify for this bottom class if your household income is under $5,000. In this bracket, including one of every six households, lie many of our social problems. Here are the retired, the widowed, the lone female, often over sixty-five years old, the less educated. But happily the importance of your "class" continues to shrink.

Where do you belong? In the past quarter century the distribution of incomes has undergone a dramatic upheaval and realignment. Each year more than a million of our households are moving from the middle into the upper income brackets, a process which has been fundamentally altering our social and economic life styles.

There are two characteristics of class inherent in this realignment which shout a direct personal message to you:

The first is that the higher the income class the higher the education. Among the below-average, only about 20 per cent of all household heads have had any exposure to college. In the $15,000 to $25,000 bracket, some 40 per cent of all household heads have had at least some college training. In the $25,000 to $50,000 bracket, this is up to 45 per cent with college degrees and an additional 15 per cent with some college training. In the class of the rich, an exceptionally high 54 per cent of all household heads have college degrees and 90 per cent are white-collar workers. You can't miss it! The tie is undeniable. The message is clear.

The second is the high incidence of the working wife in the upper-middle bracket—and in fact in well over half of all the $15,000 to $25,000 homes the wife is employed. There are relatively few working wives among the below-average; they rise to 45 per cent among average households and then up again.

The U.S. economy was an income "pyramid" a few generations ago, with most in the below-middle classes, a tiny few at the top. It has become "diamond-shaped," with most people in the middle, fewer at the bottom, still fewer at the top—and if incomes continue rising merely at the annual rate of the past twenty years, the average family income in the United States will top $15,500 by 1985. It remains, though, a far cry from the ideal "reverse pyramid," with most of us at the top and middle, virtually none at the bottom.

"ERA OF ASPIRATIONS"

You're a young family in the $10,000 to $15,000 income range—striving for the "surplus income" family status but still well below it. You have a couple of elementary-school-age kids, you live in the suburbs, and the family breadwinner commutes to work in his car. Are two cars a luxury or a necessity?

Your children are in high school and you, their mother, want to go back to a full-time job to help finance their future education. Is a household employee, at least part time, a luxury or a necessity?

Is home air conditioning, for you who live in the very hot states, a luxury in this era? Is automatic transmission in a car still just an option or has it become "basic equipment"? Does anyone today consider a TV set an unqualified luxury?

We are into an "era of aspirations" in our economy. In this era, most of us will spend a shrinking share of our income on the traditional necessities of food, clothing, shelter, and transportation while we spend a steadily increasing share of our income for goods and services which reflect our hopes and wants.

The implications for our economy and for you are profound.

Even now, the proportion of our total buying power available for spending on the "aspirations" rather than the necessities of life is estimated at a record high 15 per cent. Every year our total "discretionary spending"—defined as "purchases resulting from decisions relatively free of pressure of necessity or force of habit"—soars to new peaks.

As Dr. Ernst A. Dauer, a consumer credit authority, put it, "The typical family no longer purchases only what it needs, it purchases what it would like to have, and its aspirations are continually expanding as rapidly as its income."

As Dr. George Katona, author of *The Mass Consumption Society*, elaborated: ". . . not just a thin upper class, but the majority of households have acquired discretionary purchasing power. In the new wants-or-aspirations economies, in contrast to needs-economies, many consumer expenditures may be postponed or may be bunched at a given time. Therefore, in addition to consumers' ability to buy, consumers' willingness to buy also exerts a great influence on economic trends."

But . . . does our ever rising capacity to buy most of the things we want, over and beyond the things we actually need, make us happier? Not by any means. Again, in Katona's words:

"If what you have today appears insufficient tomorrow, disappointment and frustration may become frequent occurrences. Stress, tension and anxiety may even grow far beyond what has prevailed in less affluent societies. Moreover, because of the persistent gap between the well-being of the affluent to very-affluent 85–90 per cent of our society and the other 10–15 per cent who remain outside the mass consumption society, deprivations are felt more strongly than ever before."

And the ironic clincher: "The higher the aspirations, the more chance that people will be disappointed."

WHY BUDGET?

As the previous analysis surely hinted, it's a virtual certainty that if you're a young couple in our country today you quarrel about money. How to finance not only your day-to-day needs but also your aspirations—that's the objective of people everywhere, in every income group, in every circumstance. And many of you are seeking help because you have an uncomfortable feeling that you ought to be able to manage better than you do.

You may be the rare one who does not need a budget at all, for you may have an instinctive sense of money management within the limits of your regular income. Or you may manage comfortably with only a loose outline of your living expenses and anticipated earnings.

But for the first time in a full generation, budget-keeping is coming back into style—as a result of the oppressively rapid rate of rise in living costs during the early 1970s and skyrocketing prices of many necessities and semi-luxuries. If, therefore, you feel you want or need a budget, you should have one. And if this is you, get this fundamental point straight now: your family's budget almost certainly will be radically different from that of families living near you. And it will without question differ in many key respects from any "average" spending-saving pattern of any "average" American family. The average family exists only on paper and its average budget is a fiction, invented by statisticians for the convenience of statisticians.

The shape of your own budget will depend directly on your own or your family's individual goals and priorities. Would you prefer to spend $4,000 on a new car or on a year of postgraduate education? Would $500 worth of color television mean more, or less, to you than $500 worth of, say, guitar lessons? There is no sense in attempting to fit into a ready-to-wear financial pattern which ignores your own personal wants and desires.

The budget you draw also will depend heavily on the composition of your family. A young working couple without children may have relatively low housing costs, relatively high entertainment and clothes costs, and a good opportunity to save substantial amounts toward future family goals. Drastically different will be the spending-savings blueprint of the young couple with growing children and a heavily mortgaged house.

In essence, there is no such thing as an average budget and you should not even look for a standardized format. Search instead for a simple, flexible financial outline to help you achieve the goals you truly want.

WHICH SYSTEM OF MONEY MANAGEMENT FOR YOU?

You can get your first basic guidance from the experience and methods of others. The shopkeeper on your corner has part of the answer in the way he handles his store's income and outgo and fits the two together with a margin left for "reserve." Your parents had part of the answer in the way they measured their earnings and their prospects for earnings, then divided their spending into so much for essentials, so much for savings, so much for luxuries. The giant corporation has much of the answer in the ways it keeps its books, prepares for bad as well as good times, and provides a cushion for the unexpected and unpredictable.

You may now be handling all your income and outgo on a basis of "Here's what's in my pocket, here's what has been spent." Income, in short, is what you actually have in your hands; outgo is what you are paying to other people. What's coming to you later isn't important this minute. What you owe later isn't important either. The big thing is what you have and what you spend now. Accountants call that operating on a "cash basis"— but, as millions discover, it doesn't go far enough.

It is obvious that what most people need is a system of money management which will:

(1) tell you what money is coming in during the next several weeks or months;

(2) tell you what has to be put aside today for future security and independence and for those big unavoidable bills due in the next several weeks or months;

(3) tell you what is left over for the day-to-day expenses, ranging from food to a new household gadget;

(4) tell you too how much is left, if any, for luxuries and semiluxuries;

(5) relate your income and expenses to a reasonably long period of time so that you can avoid fumbling along from minute to minute and day to day;

(6) show you how to run your personal affairs the way most successful businessmen run their affairs;

(7) achieve your financial priorities.

This system, incidentally, is what accountants call operating on an "accrual" basis, but dismiss that fancy-sounding word right here. The important point is that no business can get anywhere unless it knows what money is coming in tomorrow as well as today and unless it knows also what is to be done with tomorrow's as well as today's cash.

A family or person cannot get far without this type of planning either.

Money is earned to be spent. When you spend, you buy more than material things such as bread or shoes; you make decisions which determine your whole way of life. Your decisions bring you closer to—or perhaps send you further away from—your ambitions, your aspirations, the things and non-things which are really most worth while to you.

Money never remains just coins and pieces of paper. It is constantly changing into the comforts of daily life. Money can be translated into the beauty of living, a support in misfortune, an education, or future security. It also can be translated into a source of bitterness.

It may seem that so many of your decisions are forced by circumstances that you have very little chance to control your own money. Perhaps, however, your income appears too small to go around only because you did not take into account the "nibblers"—the little items that nibble away at your income until there is nothing left. Perhaps you have debts left at the end of the year only because you ignored the "bouncers"—the big expenses that turn up a couple of times a year and make giant dents in your income. Or perhaps you're in trouble only because you haven't considered the "sluggers" —the unexpected expenses, such as sickness and major household repairs, that can throw even a good spending plan way off balance.

Start from the premise that no income you will earn will ever be large enough to cover *all* your wants. Accept the theory that the more income you have the greater will be your desires. Make up your mind that if you want something badly enough you will sacrifice other things for it.

Take the trouble to think out your own philosophy of living and your ambitions for the future. Develop a plan of control over your spending. Then you will make progress toward the kind of living which means most to you.

THREE PRELIMINARY NOTES ON BUDGETING

Although no system in itself can completely eliminate your money problems the following preliminary notes will certainly help:

(1) You must work together if you are married. Your plan must be a joint project and you must talk about a wide variety of things before trying to put down a single figure about income or outgo.

(2) You must provide for personal allowances in your plan—and let each person decide what to do with his or her own allotment. None of you should have to account for every cent of your allowance; that is a personal matter. Similarly, if you're a wife at home, you should not be asked to submit an item-by-item explanation of what happened to the food money. Never permit a budget to become a strait jacket—or it will surely fail. And most important, I repeat, do not try to fit yourself into other people's budgets or try to make the spending averages of other families solve your own problems.

(3) You must keep your records simple. Then they will be fun to maintain as well as helpful. All that is required from your records is a blueprint for each month's spending, a history of where money goes each month, and an over-all picture to help you whenever a financial emergency arises. You can get vital information from simple records, and the simpler the records, the more they will reveal.

Four Simple Forms to Create a Personal Money Manager

You are about to create a personal money manager that, no matter what your income, will do four things:

(1) tell you where your money is coming from—and when it is coming;

(2) provide for the necessities first, then the comforts and self-improvements, then the luxuries—when you have the money to spend for them;

(3) give you a means for saving—a plan to pay off debts or to keep out of debt;

(4) build good habits for spending—for today and tomorrow.

You can do this job very successfully if you, as a family, will learn to complete four simple forms.

Form I. Here is how I get my income.

Form II. Here is what I must put aside to cover my unavoidable expenses and my savings.

Form III. Here is where I find how much I have available for my day-to-day expenses.

Form IV. Here is how I will spend the money available for my day-to-day expenses during this period.

FORM I—FAMILY INCOME

The mistake most people make in beginning a money management plan is that they don't start at the beginning. The *beginning* surely is to find out how much money you have coming in to spend for all purposes during the year.

To reach this vital figure, take a sheet of paper and write down every item of income you expect during the year. Convert each total to a monthly basis. If you are a husband-and-wife working couple or are just living together under one roof, include the earnings of both.

(1) List not only the amounts of your regular take-home pay, translated into equal monthly totals, but also any income you anticipate from stock dividends, commissions, interest on bonds or savings accounts, yearly cash gifts from relatives, rent, bonuses, tax refunds due you, amounts owed to you by others. Also include profits from any sales of securities, your car, real estate, your home, assuming, of course, you sell any of these at a profit. Anything else? List it.

(2) Estimate each item of income as accurately and realistically as you can. When in doubt, put down the *minimum*.

(3) List only the net amounts of your regular pay checks—after subtracting withheld income taxes, your Social Security contributions, union

dues, company pension plan payments you make, any group insurance or other payments which your company automatically deducts from your pay check, etc.

(4) If your income is irregular—as it well may be if you are an artist, writer, teacher, small businessman, work part time or on a commission basis —divide the total you expect for the year by 12. Always keep your estimates low.

(5) If you are not certain how much your income will be for the entire year, list only the amounts you can accurately predict for a shorter period— again, converted to a monthly basis.

(6) If your income increases, don't get carried away: a pay raise always looks bigger than it really is. Before you start even to touch your raise, revise your budget income sheet to place the addition in accurate perspective. Add only the extra *net* (take-home) total—not the amount before taxes and other deductions.

(7) By the same token, if your income takes an unexpected dive, revise all your monthly totals downward as soon as the drop occurs. Remember, the amounts of money you'll have to spend will be based on the amounts actually coming in at any given time.

Your inventory of income must reflect *facts*. On this sheet, there is little room for flexibility and *none* for fuzziness.

You have now broken down your income into 12 spending periods. You have taken the first step away from the "feast or famine" cash basis.

Knowing what you have available to spend each month, you will know how your expenses must be divided to match that real monthly income. When you have set up this kind of money manager, you'll be amazed how different your over-all income-expense picture will appear!

FORM II—FIXED EXPENSES

Now let's consider expenses.

There are three classes of outgo: (1) the unavoidable expenses—the big items such as insurance premiums, repayment of personal debts, real estate taxes—which must be paid no matter what the inconvenience; (2) savings and rainy-day reserves; and (3) day-to-day living expenses.

The key to a good system of money management lies in spreading your big expenses and your savings so that each month bears a share of them. When you put aside $20 every month to meet a $240 yearly insurance premium, for instance, you will not risk spending that insurance money on an unnecessary luxury.

Take a second sheet of paper. On it list all of your fixed expenses during the coming year and convert each of these to a monthly basis.

Form 1 Family Income

WHAT WE WILL GET FROM	JAN.	FEB.	MAR.	APR.	MAY	JUNE	JULY	AUG.	SEPT.	OCT.	NOV.	DEC.	YEARLY TOTAL	NOTES
Husband's job														
Wife's job														
Business interests														
Interest														
Dividends														
Rent														
Gifts														
Company bonus or bonuses														
Tax refunds														
Moonlighting or jobs														
Profits from sales														
Alimony														
?														
?														
?														
Totals for the month														

Among the more obvious fixed expenses to include on your monthly list are:

(1) Rent or mortgage payments.

(2) Predictable, regular household bills for such items as electricity, gas, fuel, telephone, water, garbage collection, cable TV, lawn mowing.

(3) Installment payments you make regularly for your car, washing machine, Christmas or Hanukkah Club, charge or credit card accounts, personal or education loan, etc.

(4) Big once- or twice-a-year obligations such as real estate taxes, payments for tuition and fees, auto, life, and homeowners insurance premiums, dues to your professional society, pledged contributions.

(5) Medical and dental expenses which can be accurately pinpointed for the year (e.g., costs of annual checkups, eye exams, orthodontia); health insurance premiums; predictable drug and vitamin bills.

(6) Federal and state income taxes which have not been withheld.

(7) Automobile and commuting expenses which you can accurately estimate, such as commuter train tickets and car pool costs, monthly parking bills, car registration and inspection, average gas and oil bills for your car or cars.

(8) Membership dues—e.g., union, club, or professional association.

Among the less obvious fixed expenses to include are your monthly personal allowances for each family member. The amount of allowances you allot to each will depend partly on what expenses each person is expected to meet out of the allowance. Is the allowance supposed to pay for gifts? Lunches? Clothes? Music lessons? Charitable contributions?

Without a money management plan, if you have to pay a life insurance premium of $240, a property tax bill of $96, and a personal loan of $600—all in January—you would have to dig up $936 somewhere. And that might be tough indeed. But you probably know beforehand that in January you must meet those payments. When your money management plan is in full effect, you would set aside $78 out of each month's income and then you would be able to take the financial blows in stride.

Of course, when you start your plan, you might find it impossible to provide for those big expenses. For example, let's assume that the $936 is due in January and it is now November. You might have to get a loan or make the November, December, and January income bear the full brunt. But once that hurdle has been passed, you would divide the expenses by 12 to find out how much of the burden each month's income should bear.

Some of your large debts, such as loans from a member of the family, may be past due. Try to pay these as soon as possible and clear your slate.

INCLUDE YOUR SAVINGS!

At this point, let me back up and assure you that item (2) under the above "classes of outgo" was not a misprint. Rather a savings reserve is the least obvious—but still vital—expense you must include in your monthly list.

Put down a total you can reasonably expect to save each month. *Treat savings as an expense and budget for savings as you budget for rent or mortgage payments, and you will discipline yourself into building a nest egg.* "Pay yourself" first—as soon as you get your pay check—and your small monthly totals will become big totals over a period of time.

Include in your savings total an emergency fund equal to at least two months' income, to cover you should you be hit by big unforeseen expenses such as illness, unexpected home repairs, moving expenses. Note: The emergency part of your savings fund should be kept in a readily accessible ("liquid") form—for instance, a savings account.

As a starter, earmark 5 per cent of your total monthly income for savings, and boost the percentage from there if you can swing it.

If you have already saved the recommended equivalent of two months' income, freeze this amount as your emergency reserve. While you may want more or less than two months' income in reserve, be guided on this basically by the size of your other financial cushions: the amount of unemployment compensation for which you are eligible in the event that you are laid off or fired from your job and cannot find another one; the amount of your disability benefits which would be paid under Social Security or by your employer or through your health insurance policies; other health insurance benefits due you in the event of a medical crisis; your non-working wife's ability to take a job if an emergency arises or, if she has a job, to carry the family for a period; your credit-worthiness.

If you haven't the fund on hand now, figure how much more you will have to save before you reach the total. Then decide how long a time you'll need to save the amount necessary to lift your fund to the proper level. Don't try to save the extra amount too fast. Decide what you can put aside each month until the fund is assured and enter that amount on Form II as a fixed expense until your emergency fund is equal to the suggested level. Once it is there, keep it at that comfortable mark.

As for *how* you will save, you have many alternatives today.

(1) An automatic deduction plan from your checking account is offered by many banks. Under this plan, you authorize the bank to transfer to a simple savings account your specified sum at fixed intervals. You will receive the bank's stated interest rate on the amounts you accumulate in your savings account.

(2) Payroll savings plans are offered by many corporations under

Form II Fixed Expenses — Including Savings

WHAT WE MUST SPEND AND SAVE	JAN.	FEB.	MAR.	APR.	MAY	JUNE	JULY	AUG.	SEPT.	OCT.	NOV.	DEC.	YEAR'S TOTAL	NOTES
Rent or mortgage														
Fuel bills														
Telephone														
Electricity, gas														
Water														
Installment payment A														
Installment payment B														
Education (or other) payment														
Real estate taxes														
Income taxes														
Home and life insurance														
Auto insurance														
Medical, dental														
What we must set aside for savings alone														
Other														
Totals for each Month														

which a portion of your pay check is automatically deducted (by your authorization) and also is deposited in a savings account.

(3) Under other corporate employee savings plans now available to millions, a corporation may add its own contribution to the amount you authorize to be deducted regularly from your pay check. Your savings then may be invested in U.S. savings bonds, mutual funds, or company stock.

You'll find many other intriguing and important guides in Chapter 2, "Your Checking and Savings Accounts," pages 64–65, and in Chapter 22, "How to Invest in Bonds," pages 904–41.

Whatever method you choose, these fundamentals will remain unaltered:

The "secret" to saving is to put aside little amounts regularly and let the little amounts mount up to big totals.

The great value of your emergency reserve is protection for you against the unexpected and thus preservation of your peace of mind when the unexpected comes.

FORM III—WHAT YOU HAVE LEFT FOR DAY-TO-DAY EXPENSES

Now that you have taken care of your inflexible expenses—which you must regard as already spent from each pay check—you are ready to begin work on budgeting for day-to-day expenses.

Take a third sheet of paper for Form III. As illustrated, put down your total income divided into 12 equal parts. Put down your unavoidable expenses and your savings, divided into 12 equal parts. The difference is what you have available for day-to-day living expenses.

This much is easy.

Form III Day-to-Day Expenses

	JAN.	FEB.	MAR.	APR.	MAY	JUNE	JULY	AUG.	SEPT.	OCT.	NOV.	DEC.
From Form I, your monthly income	$											
From Form II, the total of your unavoidable expenses and savings for the year, divided by 12.	$											
What you have available for your day-to-day living expenses	$											

FORM IV—BUDGETING YOUR DAY-TO-DAY EXPENSES

Form IV will show you whether you will have to do some major juggling to make ends meet. You can't argue with the fixed figures on Form II, but you can juggle the items you will list on Form IV.

This is important: on Form IV, don't try to figure ahead for a full year. That's too difficult. Simply plan your regular day-to-day living expenses for a month or two ahead.

These will vary considerably but they are a substantial and crucial part of your budget. They also are expenses over which you have the most control.

Because you probably won't even be able to remember many of the little items when you begin your list, keep a detailed record of *all* your living expenses just for a couple of weeks. From this, you'll get an accurate idea of how much you're spending and for what. After you've obtained this guide, stop keeping records in such stultifying detail.

Here are the main categories of day-to-day expenses:

(1) *Food and related items:* the amounts of your regular grocery bills; what you spend to eat out in restaurants (including tips); candy and snacks from vending machines; soft drinks, beer, wine, and liquor; cigarettes; pet foods and supplies; personal and household items such as toothpaste and cosmetics which you buy at the supermarket.

(2) *Household services and expenses:* home repairs and improvements; any maintenance costs not counted in your fixed expenses; cleaning supplies; household help.

(3) *Furnishings and equipment:* what you buy outright for cash and down payments for large and small appliances, glass, china, silverware, curtains, rugs, upholstering, accessories, other items.

(4) *Clothes:* everything, ranging from repairs and alterations through laundry and dry cleaning to the seemingly insignificant accessories which can mount up to alarming totals.

(5) *Transportation:* car repairs, tune-ups, oil changes, new tires; bus, train, taxi, and air fares, parking charges; bridge tolls.

(6) *Medical care:* doctor and dentist bills not listed under your fixed expenses; drugs; eyeglasses; hospital and nursing expenses not covered by medical insurance; veterinary bills for your pets.

(7) *Personal care:* the barber and hairdresser; toilet articles; cosmetics and other items not paid for by each family member's personal allowance and *not* in your supermarket bills.

(8) *Education and recreation:* books; theater, movie, and concert tickets; entertaining friends; newspaper and magazine subscriptions; musical instruments and music lessons; hobby equipment; vacation and holiday expenses; the upkeep of your pleasure boat, swimming pool, or riding horse; tuition and fees not included on Form II.

(9) *Gifts and contributions:* what is not paid out of personal allowances.

(10) *Other things and non-things:* Only you can fill out this item.

Form IV Budgeting Day-to-Day Expenses

WHAT WE WILL SPEND FOR DAY-TO-DAY LIVING THIS MONTH	JAN.	FEB.	MAR.	APR.	MAY	JUNE	JULY	AUG.	SEPT.	OCT.	NOV.	DEC.	NOTES
For food and related items	$	$	$	$	$	$	$	$	$	$	$	$	
For household services and expenses													
For furnishings and equipment													
For clothes													
For transportation													
For medical care													
For personal care													
For education and recreation													
For gifts and contributions													
For other things and non-things													
TOTAL													
Total available for the month (from last line of form III)	$	$	$	$	$	$	$	$	$	$	$	$	

DON'TS TO GUIDE YOU

Just a glance at the list on Form IV shows why it is futile to attempt a precise budget at the start. Unless you are the exception who always has kept exact records of your spending, you will have to estimate the totals. Later it will be possible to be more accurate.

Don't set spending limits which are impossible to meet. It may be hard to fix a range until you've tried this money management system for a few months. That's expected. You'll learn by experience what the limits are and what they should be.

Don't start out by slashing one classification arbitrarily, "on paper." A major expense category cannot be cut just because the figure appears so big when listed. "Food" is the category that most of you will try to slash first. But if you cut this too low, you'll discover you've set an impossible limit.

Don't forget that the big expenses are on Form II. The classifications on Form IV cover only the usual day-to-day expenses. Major costs, such as orthodontia for your child, may be spread over a whole year of income periods. If "spreading" is easier for you, transfer other big items from Form IV to Form II.

Don't ignore your wants and don't try to kid yourself. When you're setting your allocations, be realistic. If your menu says steak, don't put down a figure for stew.

Don't fail to leave room for unexpected expenses. These are certain to arise and you never know in advance what they will be. They may range from a flat tire to an office contribution for a wedding gift.

Don't underestimate the importance of detailed records during the first month of your money management plan. When the next period rolls around and it turns out that your guesses weren't right, cross out the inaccurate estimates and put down what was really spent for each item.

With these hints to help, you can fill out Form IV, marking down your estimates, adding them up for each month, and comparing them with the total amount available. The result easily could be a big minus, indicating that you're spending or planning to spend more than your projected income. If your expense total, including savings, comes out way above your income total and the tally indicates you're heading into a flood of red ink, some items here must be cut.

But you can't cut unless you vow to make the cuts good. This money management plan is more than a pencil-pushing game.

WHAT ROLE DO YOUR CHILDREN PLAY?

TEN RULES ON ALLOWANCES

In any successful family spending plan, your children must play some part—especially when the things *they* want are to be considered. Although the responsibilities to be given children will undoubtedly vary from family to family, here are ten widely accepted rules:

(1) Begin giving your child an allowance just as soon as he or she understands the use of money for getting the things he or she wants.

(2) Have an understanding on what the allowance is to cover. At first it can relate only to such things as toys and special treats, but adjustments should be made from time to time in the size of the allowance and hence in its use. Many teen-age boys and girls can handle allowances that cover their clothing. By the time they are mature, they will have had some experience in looking ahead and in saving for special things.

(3) In addition to having a clear understanding with your child on just what an allowance is or is not supposed to cover, renegotiate the contract at least once a year to take new obligations into account.

(4) Make your child's allowance a fair share in terms of your family's consumption in general.

(5) Take into account what your child's friends and schoolmates have. The allowance should certainly not be so markedly less that the child feels constantly deprived; but it should also not be greatly in excess of what others get; that's just as bad.

(6) As your child gets older, give him a voice in deciding what his allowance should be. Let him share in a family round table on the spending plan. He will thus gain a greater appreciation of fair sharing.

(7) Give your child full responsibility for spending his allowance, although your advice may be required for some things and should be available at all times. If he makes mistakes, he should come to recognize his responsibility for them and put up with the results. In unusual situations you might, perhaps, help him out by an advance from the following week's allowance.

(8) While your child is learning to plan ahead, give him the allowance only for short periods. Perhaps give first for the day, then for the week, and only later for somewhat longer periods. Very early in their lives, your children should learn where the family's money comes from and the effort that goes into earning it. A child's spending should, therefore, be made in part dependent on his own efforts. Children often can be taught the simple lessons of earning and spending by being paid extra for special household tasks. But *do not* carry this too far; your child may acquire the habit of putting all helpfulness on a "pay me" basis. Pay only for exceptional—and not for routine—household chores. Do not confuse this sort of payment with the allowance.

(9) As for saving, teen-agers are notorious non-savers. They tend to spend income as fast as possible and often on apparently frivolous things. But at the same time they are deeply attracted by such big-ticket items as motorcycles, autos, stereos. Once a teen-ager sets an expensive item as a goal, the message usually seeps through that the purchase requires saving over a long period. Encourage your youngster to keep a savings goal within reasonable limits and not to make it prolonged drudgery. Encourage your youngster also to learn how to manage a checking and/or savings account.

Here are some rough guides, developed by Household Finance Corporation, on what children in various age brackets might be expected to buy and pay for out of their allowances:

Under 6: candy, gum, ice cream, small toys, gifts for others, books, playthings, paints, crayons, blocks, and dolls

Ages 6–9: movies, amusements, toys, books, magazines, hobbies, club dues, special savings for sports equipment, carfare and lunches at school, school activities and school expenses, gifts for birthdays and holidays, and contributions

Ages 9–12: fees for skating rinks, pools, etc., club dues, hobby materials, sports equipment and repairs, games and special events, carfare and lunches at school, gifts for birthdays and holidays, contributions, trips, school supplies, clothing and upkeep

Ages 12–18: the above, plus money for dates, grooming, cosmetics, jewelry, clothing, school activities, savings for special purposes such as travel and a future education

Finally, on charge accounts, expert opinion divides violently—with one side warning that it is extremely reckless to give a teen-ager a charge account and the other arguing that, since charge accounts are so much a part of American life, a youngster should learn early how to buy on credit.

My compromise rule would be to teach your teen-ager to use credit modestly and wisely and to pay bills promptly. As an allowance is "learning money," so installment buying is vital financial education. The crucial point is that the earlier a youngster learns to live within a fixed income the better prepared he or she will be to manage money soundly as an adult.

These guides may seem no more than simple common sense—but isn't that fundamentally what proper money management always is?

In Case You're Curious . . .

HERE'S WHAT OTHER PEOPLE SPEND

I repeat: an "average" family living on an "average" budget does not exist. Even if you and your neighbor lead very similar lives on very similar incomes, your budgets may be radically different. Your own ages, your children's ages—not to mention your hobbies or jobs or dozens of other aspects—would make this so.

But, if you're merely normal, you're still curious about the spending patterns of others.

So to start with, here's what the *average* Americans were spending in the mid-seventies of each after-tax dollar in each major category:

FOR	AMERICANS WERE SPENDING OF EACH DOLLAR
Food, alcohol and tobacco	22.3¢
Housing	14.5
Household operation	14.4
Transportation	13.6
Clothing	10.1
Medical care	7.7
Recreation	6.5
Personal business	5.6
Private education	1.7
Personal care	1.5
Religious and welfare activities	1.4
Foreign travel	.7

HOW MUCH CHEAPER ARE LARGE FAMILIES TO FEED THAN SMALL ONES?

In a family of five, it costs 5 per cent less to feed each person than it costs to feed each person in a family of four.

In a family of six, it costs 10 per cent less to feed each person than in a family of four.

In contrast, it costs 20 per cent *more* to feed an individual living alone than it costs to feed each member of the four-person family.

Budgeting if You're in College

Now let's assume you're a college student living—or trying to live—on an allowance. How can the money management plan help you?

Some of you are at home during school years and are on weekly allowances; many others of you live away and receive your checks every month. But for all of you the problem is identical: college years are a constant—and usually losing—battle to make financial ends meet.

Halfway through the week or month, most of you are either broke or on the brink. Some of you live high the first few days you get your money, then scramble for help toward the end. Some of you have only far-apart intervals when you are out of debt. The vast majority of you are either flush or frantic.

But your allowance is a pay check. It deserves the respect and care you will give a pay check after graduation. Just as your parents get the most for their dollars by living by certain financial rules, so you in college can get the greatest satisfaction out of your allowance if you live by certain financial rules.

Whether you live at home or away from home, whether you're at the fanciest of schools or on a scholarship or working your way through, the fundamental principles of money management apply equally.

Here are your "Allowance ABCs." Try them for size.

(1) Plan the spending of your allowance with your parents before you leave for college, and then keep planning on your own from the day you arrive at school.

It's nonsense to say that $20 a week will be fine when $20 a week won't do at all for what you have to cover. Plan realistically and with a clear understanding of what your allowance is to take care of. Then, when you arrive at school, work out your day-to-day budget to cover your necessities and luxuries. Be honest with yourself. (If Cokes and coffee are going to cost X cents a day, plan for X cents a day.) If your allowance is supposed to cover such items as new panty hose, dry cleaning, shoe repair, oil, gas, auto maintenance, and so forth, budget these costs—don't ignore them. This is *your* budget; it should fit *you*.

(2) Deposit your money in a bank account and draw on it only as you need the money. If you carry a wad of cash with you, you'll risk being mugged and the temptation to spend it recklessly may become irresistible. Discipline yourself via your bank account; the lessons you learn now will be valuable throughout your life.

If your school has banking facilities, use them. If not, a nearby bank will accept your deposit even if it's just a few dollars. While you may be slapped with service charges, the bank's advantages could far outweigh the disadvantages; check it out. And while you are learning how to make deposits, to draw checks, to balance a checkbook, etc., you are getting excellent training in personal financial management.

(3) If you and your parents can manage it, also start an account in a nearby savings bank, or try to build one through the term.

There always will be large extra expenses—a special event or a crisis—for which you'll need or want to spend money. Your savings account should be earmarked for your tuition, rent, and extraordinary expenses only. If you can't start with this savings nest egg, try to juggle your seven-days-a-week spending plan so you can save a bit and build one yourself.

(4) Don't figure down to pennies. No money plan ever should be that precise. For your protection and pleasure, give yourself a margin of safety.

(5) Keep some simple records to show you where your allowance is going and why. A record for one week alone would be enough to reveal your errors of omission and commission. For one week, list on a sheet of paper what you spend and where and when you spend it. See how this week's total fits into the monthly total allotted to you. If need be, push your spending around to make it fit. When you've found the right pattern, stick with it. Keep your list in a convenient spot where you will see it from day to day.

(6) Stretch your dollars by learning how to buy items you must have (toiletries, for instance) during special sales or in economy sizes, etc. If you're buying your own wardrobe, stretch your dollars further by buying simple basic styles which will last longer and cost least in upkeep. Also investigate ways you can save by pooling purchases with your friends as you can buy in bulk at bargain prices.

(7) If your evidence is clear after a trial that your funds are too limited, renegotiate your allowance. Your records will be your evidence.

WHERE SHOULD YOU KEEP YOUR MONEY?

You have established a budget to make sure your income covers your expenses each month. You are now ready for your next step in money management: a system to control your money in real life as well as on paper.

For your careful plans can easily blow up into chaotic confusion unless you do have a system to help you put your money where it is supposed to be. There are six basic systems from which you can choose:

(1) the joint checking account;
(2) separate checking accounts;
(3) the savings account;
(4) the combination of savings and checking accounts;
(5) the allowance method;
(6) the broken sugar bowl method.

Whichever control system you choose, it must be:

Efficient. Your "control" should direct your cash where you want it to go.

Easy to operate. This is a "must." The major objection to most financial advice is that it is too complex. If a method is complicated or burdensome, you will abandon it in less than a month.

Suited to your income. How much money you have to manage should guide you on how to control the management.

Your problem is not simply a question of managing your income and outgo "on paper"; it is also a matter of controlling your cash income and cash outgo so that the money goes where it is scheduled to go.

The four budget forms can be of immeasurable help in showing you how to match your income to your outgo but they cannot give you the complete control over your actual spending which will come from intelligent use of one or more of the following six systems.

THE JOINT CHECKING ACCOUNT

If you're a young husband-and-wife team and you decide on the joint checking account method, you'll establish a checking account at a neighborhood bank in both your names. Into that account will go all your earnings. Each of you may write checks on that account to meet your expenses. When this system is adopted, the husband usually writes the checks for the big fixed expenses and for the savings (Form II). The wife writes the checks for the day-to-day and week-to-week expenses (the items on Form IV).

Advantages

Since each of you has a definite responsibility to meet specific expenses you develop a co-operative spirit. Similarly, since each of you has a sense of "owning money," you develop a keener understanding of the value of money.

With a *joint* checking account your average monthly balance will be higher than the balances in two *separate* checking accounts and thus you will have a better chance of avoiding or minimizing bank service charges.

With only one checkbook, you'll find it easier to keep records and file your income tax returns. (If you do have two checkbooks, be sure you tally your stubs every month to prevent overdrawing.)

In an emergency, either of you can sign checks and get money.

Disadvantages

This method can be a success only if both of you are careful about drawing on the joint account. And even then you may get into trouble unless you constantly watch the balance in your account and keep each other thoroughly informed about the checks each is drawing. Monthly tallies of stubs are important.

SEPARATE CHECKING ACCOUNTS

The separate checking account method is fairly satisfactory if you have a moderate to high income and many expenditures. When you use this control system, all the salary or income of the family will generally be deposited in one account in the husband's name. He then will deposit an agreed-upon sum in the second account, which will be in the wife's name.

The husband's account will be used to meet the major, fixed-expense items and to cover savings (Form II). The wife's account will be used to pay for the day-to-day or week-to-week expenses (the items on Form IV).

The main control in this system is the husband's account—for from it will come not only the amounts for fixed expenses and for the wife's account but also the totals for savings.

Usually the wife will cash a check on her account each week or at another regular interval to pay for food and household operation expenses. Expenditures for food and for operation of the house will thus be controlled automatically by the amount of money deposited in her account.

Advantages

The portion of your income determined as necessary for food and clothing expenditures is automatically separated from other funds. Also, by cashing weekly, semimonthly, or monthly checks for food expenditures, you, the wife, automatically control the family's food costs for the period.

Since clothing allowance will be regularly deposited in the wife's account, you'll allow funds to accumulate as desired and this will permit you to take advantage of special sales and bargains. You might leave the clothing allowance mostly untouched for two or three months, then use the funds at a pre- or postseason sale to achieve important savings. The money will be available: that is the key point.

Your checkbooks will contain all the information necessary for a complete summary of your purchases and expenditures, assuming you fill out the stubs conscientiously.

Control of your income is divided between the two of you. Each of you has responsibility for your portion of your income and expenditures. Your separate accounts can give you better control of your income and outgo than a joint banking account.

Disadvantages

The separate account control system isn't practical unless your family income is fairly large. You must have sufficient money at your disposal to permit the establishment of separate bank accounts and justify what service fees may be involved.

Unexpected expenditures may cause considerable mix-ups in your accounting. In fact, a key difficulty with this system—and, indeed, with the joint account method, too—is in the handling of miscellaneous expenditures.

A reasonable solution to this problem is a petty cash fund to meet the "extras" that arise in every household. This fund should be operated on the same principle as the petty cash fund in a business office. A specified amount

—say $100—might be deposited in the fund. Each time you have to draw on this fund—as when you have to buy extra food for guests—you'll put a slip of paper with a notation describing the expense into the cash box in place of the money taken out. If you, the wife, take out $25, you'll put in a chit: "Entertainment—$25." Thus the total of cash in the fund plus the total of notations on the slips always ought to equal the amount of the original fund.

The chits furnish a record to show where the money went, so that if the petty cash fund is being used to stretch the other funds, the situation can be remedied—either through stricter control of your expenditures or by revision of your spending plan to raise the inadequate fund to the necessary level. Each month or pay period, refill the emergency fund and bring it back to its original mark.

THE SAVINGS ACCOUNT

If you don't have a fairly substantial income and you don't write many checks each month, the savings account method may be the best spending control for you. Savings accounts can serve you best if:

(1) You deduct from your monthly income or your regular weekly pay check the totals needed for your fixed major costs and for savings—Form II of your record—and place them in a savings account for safekeeping.

(2) You deduct for your monthly allowances out of your remaining cash and keep those funds at home or in another account. Savings accounts pay interest, and since these accounts can be set up to permit joint withdrawals, either of you can use them freely. Many institutions will help you pay large bills by giving you bank checks made out exactly the way you want them for the now-and-then expenses.

Some savings institutions also will help you control your spending and savings by encouraging "special purpose" accounts—for vacation funds, travel funds, insurance funds, tax funds, etc. The purpose of each fund will be marked on the deposit books, and these books will give you a complete picture of your savings for each objective. A combination of these "special funds" with a rainy-day savings account for unexpected expenses thus can provide both a system of control and a detailed record of your savings.

This idea of using separate accounts for special purposes is becoming increasingly popular, though it is really nothing more than an extension of the long-used Christmas Club plan. The value of these special funds lies simply in the fact that they encourage setting aside a stipulated sum each week (no matter how small) so that the regular saving of little amounts builds toward the stated goal.

Advantages

Like any form of "forced savings," the scheme has the great advantage of earmarking your funds before you receive them—and before you are tempted to spend them elsewhere. It can be an excellent control over the money that must be set aside to meet the items on Form II.

Your money is placed in a thrift account on which interest is paid and compounded. As the account grows, there is a real psychological spur to save more.

Disadvantages

The savings account method is not suitable if you must write many checks every month.

You must have sufficient savings funds to justify the opening of several "special purpose" accounts.

You may earn next to nothing in interest if you keep depleting your account or accounts. Also some of the special savings accounts may pay little or no interest.

Although you may deposit funds by mail to your savings account, you must visit the bank personally each time you make a withdrawal. Another inconvenience is that you must pay many bills with cash if you make a savings account the sole "home" for your income.

THE COMBINATION OF SAVINGS AND CHECKING ACCOUNTS

Or your best method of spending control may be a combination of several methods. One such combination is:

(1) the establishment of a checking account from which you draw funds each week or month to pay for all regular and recurring expenditures (some of the items on Form II and all on Form IV); and

(2) the establishment of a savings account in which you accumulate cash for the major expenses that come up only occasionally during the year and for savings (the rest of the items on Form II). You'll maintain your "emergency fund" in this separate savings account.

Advantages

Your income is divided and your day-to-day expenses are separated from your other expenses. Through your checkbook stubs, you can keep an accurate and up-to-date record of your spending.

Through your savings account, you can accumulate cash to take advantage of sales and other bargains when they are available. Also the savings account part of this system will help you develop the savings habit which is so essential to achieving financial security. You will take pride in watching your nest egg grow and, hopefully, will make a real effort to meet more of your expenses from your regular checking account.

Disadvantages

Fees well may be charged for maintenance of a no-minimum account or for a regular checking account if the balance falls below the bank's established minimum.

Separation of your savings from your checking account may push your average balance in your regular account way down.

THE ALLOWANCE METHOD

The allowance method of money management is used by millions of couples in America, many of them, probably, having adopted it automatically when they married.

Admittedly, it is a simple system. The husband of the non-jobholding wife usually controls the distribution of the money. Every payday he makes an allowance to his wife for the day-to-day living expenses—the items that are primarily on Form IV. After making this allowance, the husband uses the balance to meet all the major items—those on Form II.

The wife may deposit the allowance in a separate account or draw checks on a joint account up to the limit of the allowance—or just keep the money in a strongbox at home.

Advantages

The allowance method is simple, involving merely the distribution of a set allowance to the wife every payday or week or month.

Disadvantages

The allowance made to the wife is often too small, and she takes only a minimum of responsibility for management of the family income. She is often forced to ask for more money to cover essential or luxury expenditures. Such an arrangement discourages co-operative management.

If the allowance is not carefully calculated to cover all the items on Form IV, the control will be too loose.

THE BROKEN SUGAR BOWL METHOD

Many young couples—particularly those still in school or just out of school—use envelopes, marking one "for rent," another "for clothing," a third "for food," and so forth. Or they may have a cash box at home which is divided into compartments labeled "rent," "clothing," "food," and the like. Or it may be that they label small glass jars.

This is nicknamed the "broken sugar bowl method" because many older people remember that when they were children there were always a few old sugar bowls hidden behind the other dishes in the kitchen closet or pantry in which there were always a few dollars for specified expenses.

But the name applied to this money management arrangement doesn't matter. The point is that under this system you'll divide your cash income into fixed amounts to meet the regular and now-and-then expenses. Into each labeled bowl, jar, envelope, or compartment you'll put the dollars agreed upon as necessary to meet that particular living expense.

Both husband and wife will have equal access to the bowls or jars or envelopes. Generally, as in other systems, each will take on the responsibility for meeting certain expenses. This method is designed for very small incomes.

Advantages

When you use the sugar bowl method, presumably the money is always where it is supposed to be—and in cash to cover any specific expense. The system may be used just as separate bank accounts are used to apportion responsibility. And how simple can you get?

Disadvantages

Obviously, it is a risk to keep money in the house—even comparatively small amounts. While the cash is conveniently available for easy spending, it may be too available. When the money is there, the temptation to use it carelessly also is there. And when a sudden shortage develops, the obvious short cut is to shift money from one bowl or envelope to another. While the utter simplicity of the broken sugar bowl method of spending control may be commendable, it is hardly a "control."

HIS-AND-HER BUDGETS

America is a land of working couples. Tens of millions of you who are and will be brides will continue working long after the wedding. Millions of you will quit working for pay only during the years your children are babies. Most of you will return to work when your children go off to school.

Money management takes on a special aspect in today's two-pay check American homes. For with both of you earning salaries, specific questions are bound to come up:

How do you divide the money you bring in? Who pays for what around the house? If you had an ideal partnership, who would pay for what—how and why?

Here are ten basic rules I've worked out over years of discussions with experts on family finance, interviews with husbands and wives in every income bracket across the country, my personal experience as a working wife through my entire adult life. These are *my* rules, no one else's, but I'm sure all of you can benefit from some of them, some of you can benefit from all of them, and any one of them can be revised to fit your individual circumstances.

(1) Make your marriage a *financial partnership;* discuss your income and plan your spending as a husband-and-wife team.

The wife who insists she should pay for only the part-time housekeeper and put the rest of her pay check in her savings account is selfish and wrong. If you're a team in other ways, be a team financially as well. If your mutual decision is that the wife's pay check should be saved, excellent—but make the decision as a couple. Otherwise, deceit and suspicion are virtually inevitable. This is a fundamental rule.

(2) Pool part of your individual pay checks in a family fund which is to be used to cover essential household expenses.

In many households, the pooling will be automatic, for both pay checks are being used to buy things and non-things the family wants. *It should be automatic.* How much of the wife's pay checks will go into the pool may vary from home to home, depending on the wife's income and the family's circumstances, but the key point is that there should be a pool.

(3) Decide which of you will be responsible for paying specific bills out of the pool. As a husband you might take over payment of the "big bills"—rent, mortgage, insurance, taxes, the like. As a wife, you might take over management of the "household bills"—food, entertainment at home, ordinary household overhead. To me, this is a logical division of responsibility. It's entirely okay if you have other ideas, but talk them out to your mutual satisfaction.

For instance, some experts say a woman who has been accustomed to her independence for a long period may be actively unhappy unless, as a working wife, she continues to have "my" telephone, "my" bank account, etc. So be it—as long as she and her husband agree on the division and there is no secret resentment of the situation.

(4) Use the combination savings account and checking account method as your money control.

If you don't carefully separate your savings from your regular checking account, your savings easily can dribble away without your knowing just how or why. For most couples, the two-account "control" works best.

(5) If the wife's job necessitates the added expense of household help, the wife's pay check should cover it. This is a rule I came to instinctively, for in most homes, if the wife did not hold an outside job, she could, if she had to, get along without any extra help. Thus, this is "her" expense which she should handle. If the expense is to be paid out of the family pool, the wife should directly make the payment. Or the wife may withhold a specified part of her earnings for this expense. Whatever the details, it should be understood that this expense is in the wife's department.

(6) Extra expenses for entertainment at home should be handled by the wife, but when you go out, it's the husband's deal. Again, this is my viewpoint only.

(7) If you're a young couple planning to have children, the husband's pay check should cover all basic household expenses, and part of the wife's earnings should be earmarked for the initial expenses of a baby. You must be prepared for the time when, for a while at least, you'll scale down to one pay check. You may decide to share this planning by earmarking funds out of each pay check—but at least *plan*. A couple without the financial responsibilities of children obviously has more leeway to shift spending and saving.

(8) Follow faithfully the budget rules for Form II. With both of you earning money, you'll really benefit from spreading payment of your big bills so that each month bears a share.

In addition, plan your installment buying as a team and with caution so that even if you're hit by an emergency your total monthly bills will be well within your capacity to repay. Under no circumstances take on *any* installment debt without a joint agreement.

(9) The rules on personal allowances are particularly vital for you. If you want to do something absurd with your personal allowance, that's your business. Your allowance is yours alone.

(10) Make a pledge to each other today that when you get into a squeeze in the future—which you will, for nearly everyone does—you'll choose a quiet evening alone to argue it out and decide how to escape from it. And when you talk about it, call it "our" squeeze, not "yours."

A superficial point? Oh no. The wife who in the heat of a money fight says, "We wouldn't have any savings at all unless I worked," is begging for resentment and the retort that she wouldn't have any home unless he paid for the rent or mortgage. It's imperative to avoid discussing your money mess when you're both frantic. If you can't figure a way out, take your problem to the service department of your bank or savings institution and ask for guidance on where and how you might get help.

Here is a chart which you can use as a starter for building your own his-and-her budget. Add to it as you wish; switch it around as you see fit; make it yours.

A BUDGET IF YOU'RE JUST LIVING TOGETHER ("MINGLES")

What if you're among the millions of young Americans who today are just living together under one roof ("mingles")—with no legal ties, no established rules for behavior except those you and your peers agree are okay, and certainly no guidelines for management of your individual incomes and expenses?

You could easily and successfully follow the rules in the preceding pages for a working man and wife. But you may be far more fascinated by the following real-life system of budgeting created over the past two years by a young technical consultant and his schoolteacher living companion. The two insist that, once their system was perfected, it ended two years of destructive

WHO PAYS FOR WHAT?

WHO PAYS FOR:	HE	SHE	BOTH
Rent or mortgage, home repairs, utilities			
Food at home			
Clothing			
Household help			
Auto loan, repairs, maintenance			
Recreation (outside)			
Entertainment (at home)			
Entertainment (outside home)			
Life and health insurance			
New baby			
Education (adult, college)			
Gifts and contributions			
Vacations, recreation			
Income and property taxes			
Savings			
Other expenses			

fighting about money (an even more brutal cause of split-ups among the non-married than among the married).

"Basically," says Dick, "the system consists of four (yes four) checking accounts which we call 'yours,' 'mine,' 'ours,' and 'car.'

"In addition, we have savings accounts. We keep a minimum balance of $100 in each checking account to avoid service charges, which would run between 12 and 18 per cent for us, but higher for frequent check writers. To reduce the temptation to dip into the $100 minimums, we delete the balances from our records and pretend they don't exist."

Here are details which are provocatively similar in many ways to the his-and-her budgets:

• All income from both individuals goes into the "ours" account. Each has a checkbook and the money deposited is arbitrarily split in half between each checkbook as a hedge against overdrawing. If either book runs dangerously low, temporary transfers are made. Then, at the end of each month, the books are balanced and the joint bank statement reconciled.

• Out of this "ours" account come virtually all living expenses—food, rent, utilities, etc.—which these two have agreed to share on a regular basis.

• Once a month, $50 is transferred from the "ours" account to each individual account ("yours" and "mine") as each person's personal allowance. "This figure was chosen arbitrarily and is still experimental," says Dick. "We expect to adjust it after we have had more experience with it." The personal allowance covers clothes and other items "which have a large potential for conflict over what is or is not extravagant" and for "simply spending as we please." Neither accounts to the other for what happens to each month's personal allowance.

The special account for the car is an ingenious twist. "This is the largest single expense we have, costing more than rent and food combined," says Dick. "And we feel that it's important for us both to be conscious of what cars really cost." They are making a vital point. Also, watching the real costs of their car tends to discourage excessive driving.

A simple record is kept of the number of miles driven and deposits of 10¢ per mile are regularly transferred from the "our" account. The 10¢ covers all operating expenses, plus a margin of 5¢ a mile for depreciation. (This figure is subject to revision upward as costs dictate.) The "car" fund includes forced savings for a new car in the future.

Another ingenious system for food shopping involves the initialing of all store register tapes or chits and periodic checking and reconciling of the records.

There are many gaps in this couple's system—but if you add their hints to all you've read in "Your Personal Money Manager," you will be way, way ahead of the vast majority of budget-keepers.

Without any difficulty, you can shift the details to fit your own situation. You, for instance, may prefer to contribute equal amounts—rather than all—of your income to your joint checking and savings accounts. Whether you're a married couple or merely living together, you may feel it's unfair for both of you to bear an equal share of the food costs if the man regularly eats far more food and far more expensive food than the woman. Or you may argue that it's unfair for both of you to bear an equal share of the phone bills if the woman does most of the long-distance talking.

Whatever your own decisions, I guarantee that personal budget-keeping will help you curb your living costs—and help bring you peace of mind.

(Like the working husband and wife, use the chart "Who Pays for

What?" as a basic guide and switch it around to fit your own needs and desires.)

How Much Are You Worth?

You easily may feel flat broke or, at a minimum, painfully squeezed when you are creating a budget and a system to manage your money. But I'll wager that if you figure your "net worth" even at this sticky stage you'll be happily surprised by the outcome. Try it right now—and see if you don't discover you're richer than you think in many ways!

Here's a simple method to put a specific figure on your worth. Take a pencil and three sheets of paper. Mark the first sheet "Assets" and list:

(1) The amount of money you have in checking and savings accounts, in savings and loan associations, in credit unions, in time deposits, in cash on hand, in a strongbox at home or elsewhere.

(2) The cash value of your life insurance. This is the amount you actually could borrow back on request.

(3) The cash value of your United States Savings Bonds. This is not the maturity value but the amount you would get if you turned in your bonds now.

(4) The amount of cash or its equivalent you could withdraw tomorrow from profit sharing employee savings, retirement programs, etc. A rough calculation will do.

(5) The current market value of stocks and mutual fund shares you may own. Not the purchase price, but what you'd get if you sold the stocks tomorrow.

(6) The current market value of other securities you may own—marketable federal government, municipal, or corporate bonds—and the market value of other investments you may have, such as mortgages you have extended to others.

(7) The price you would get if you put your house and land, summer house, or other real estate on the market this week. Get a conservative estimate from a reliable real estate agent.

(8) The price you would get if you offered your car (or cars) to a used-car dealer or sold it privately for cash right now. Be cold-blooded about it. Also, your boat, motorcycle, airplane, trailer, snowmobile, the like.

(9) The market value of your household goods—furniture, rugs, appliances, TV, stereo, linen, silverware. Make your own *conservative* estimate, then *slash* it by 75 per cent and you'll be on safe ground.

(10) The market value of your other personal assets, such as jewelry, paintings, furs, rare books, art objects, coins, stamps, antiques, clothes, etc. Cut your own conservative estimate here, too, by 75 per cent.

(11) The price you'd get if you sold out your investment in any unincorporated business, farm, or other ventures.

(12) Amounts of money other *responsible* people owe you.

(13) A conservative estimate of the value of any other asset you can think of.

Add the totals.

Take a second sheet, mark it "Liabilities," and list:

(1) The total amount you owe on your mortgage or mortgages and on your car, boat, motorcycle, etc.

(2) The amount you owe on other installment debts, charge accounts, credit cards, other personal debts and bills.

(3) The amount you owe for taxes which have not been withheld.

(4) Sums you've committed for college education, etc.

(5) Any other liability you can think of.

Add these totals.

Take a third sheet, mark it "Net Worth," and:

simply subtract the total on your second sheet from the total on your first. *The difference between what you own and what you owe is your net worth.*

You should be unexpectedly pleased by the outcome, for you are only average if your net worth runs into many thousands of dollars. You are part of the vast majority of Americans if you have some cash in the bank and in savings accounts and own a car. And while you have debts, you also have substantial assets to offset the debts. This is the norm in no other nation in the world.

HOW DOES YOUR NET WORTH COMPARE?

When you have tallied your net worth, break it down into the ratio of your assets to your debts. Now, just for fun, compare your balance sheet to that of the mythical "average" American consumer.

As the mid-1970s neared, John Doe had $11.40 in assets for every $1.00 of debt—not counting his home mortgage.

If you included his mortgage, John Doe's ratio was $5.70 in assets for every $1.00 of debt. And for every $1.00 of his mortgage debt, John Doe had $2.40 in equity in his home.

IF YOU'RE STARTING TO KEEP TAX RECORDS: QUESTIONS AND ANSWERS

Q. *What records should you keep?*

A. Preserving the right kind of records for tax purposes can be vitally important if your income tax returns are examined later and if you're to be able to prevent a budget-busting disallowance of your deductions because you can't prove their validity. Here, therefore, are key record-keeping points from the Internal Revenue Service:

• Keep a permanent record of your earnings—including W-2 forms provided by your employers and precise statements from others contributing to your income. Vague estimates of income are *not* acceptable. Also, keep copies of all previous tax returns.

• If you use your car for business purposes and intend to deduct a part of the expenses, keep records of the original cost of the car, annual total and business mileage, gas and oil, repair costs, garage rent, license and registration fees, tolls, chauffeur's salary.

• If your job involves travel for business purposes, keep a diary of all expenses involved—including hotel bills, transportation costs, taxi fares, meals, tips, telephone and telegraph charges, stenographer fees. Also keep receipts, paid bills, and canceled checks to document all lodging expenses and any other sizable expenses. However, says the IRS, you are *not* required to keep receipts for transportation costs, such as taxi fares, bus fares, "if they are not readily available."

• If you use your home as an office keep a full record of costs attributable to the office space alone, including the percentage of depreciation on the house or rent paid, of utilities, and of household maintenance costs that can be allocated to the office space. If business entertainment is done in your home, keep records of entertainment expenses such as catering costs and food and liquor bills. Also keep guest lists and other evidence to show that the entertainment was for business rather than social purposes.

• If you have made charitable contributions, keep records of the cash or fair market value of any contributions of property as well as to whom and when made.

• If there is any chance your annual medical expenses will exceed the per cent of your adjusted gross income stated in the tax law, keep copies of all doctor and hospital bills and other allied costs.

All these records should be kept at least five years.

For longer periods:

• If you buy or sell securities, keep full records of the purchase date and price of each stock or bond you buy, the number of shares bought at each price, amounts of commissions, and records of any and all stock splits, swaps, and dividends along the line. Also, keep records of dates, prices, commissions, etc., at which you sell each block of securities. Otherwise, when you sell a batch of stock at a profit, IRS will assume you sold the first batch you bought—for which you probably paid the lowest price, and on which you would be liable for the biggest capital gains tax.

• If you buy a home, keep full records of the date and purchase price, plus all other costs such as commissions, legal fees, etc. Also keep full records of major improvements or additions to the house. When you sell the house, keep records of all costs involved in the sale.

Q. *How long should you keep your tax records?*

A. If you ask the Internal Revenue Service how long you should keep various records for tax purposes, here is the answer you will get: "As long as their contents may become material in the administration of any internal revenue law." Period.

Does this mouthful of mush translate into "You must keep piles of tax records indefinitely?" Generally no, says the IRS. But there are important exceptions. And although there are no hard rules, there are rules of thumb which, for all practical purposes, apply to the majority of ordinary taxpayers. Here they are:

Ordinarily, the statute of limitations for the IRS to demand additional taxes from you or for you to demand additional refunds from the IRS is three years after the return was due or was actually filed, whichever was later. In cases of substantial omission of income or fraud, the statute of limitations may be longer or there may be no limitations at all.

2

YOUR CHECKING
AND SAVINGS ACCOUNTS

GETTING THE MOST OUT OF YOUR CHECKING AND SAVINGS ACCOUNTS

When you start looking for a financial institution in which to open your checking account or savings account—or both—you may not be able to escape the extraordinary gift-gimmick war waged in recent years by our nation's financial institutions via newspaper ads and radio commercials for your checking and/or savings dollar. Never has the competition among financial institutions, for your savings dollar particularly, seemed so frantic. All the institutions are in it: commercial banks, savings and loan associations, mutual savings banks, other lesser ones. All are using lures which can befuddle as well as bewitch you.

Obviously it would be utterly senseless for you to channel your family's entire banking business to institution A simply because it offers you a pair of free football tickets while B offers no such gimmicky prize.

Before you even start shopping for a financial institution, familiarize yourself with the basics about today's array of bank services, different types of savings and checking accounts, varying charges for each service. Before you even consider changing institutions, make sure you're using your present one to its very best advantage.

Let's say you have just moved to a new home in a new town. You urgently need the services of a bank so you can get checks cashed, pay bills, start a savings account, arrange for a small loan to buy a needed household appliance. Where do you start shopping? How do you weigh the virtues of bank A against those of bank B?

Or let's say you're not sure you are now getting the most economical deal with your present bank, in terms of services offered, service charges, or the frequency with which interest on your savings is compounded. How do you compare the services offered by other local banks in these areas?

In short, how do you find your way around the financial market place?

By comparing institutions on each of the following points and then deciding which are the most important to you.

Savings: Does the bank offer a range of various savings plans? Does it offer time deposit plans and savings certificates in addition to the straight passbook account? Will it automatically transfer funds from your checking to your savings account if you choose?

Interest: Is the institution's rate of interest on savings competitive? How frequently is interest compounded and credited? What about the grace periods at the beginning and end of each quarter during which you can make deposits or withdrawals without losing full interest for the quarter? Most banks today compound interest at least quarterly: the more frequently interest is compounded, the greater your financial advantage. Also, it's to your advantage if interest is paid on your average balance instead of on your minimum balance during the interest period.

Availability: Are there any restrictions on withdrawals in case you require your money in a hurry? Could your deposit be "frozen" without your being aware of it? What are the legal restrictions on withdrawals—if any?

Insurance: Are your deposits federally or state insured? With more than 99 per cent of all deposits in commercial banks covered by the FDIC, for example, they almost surely are. But make certain.

Checking: Is the minimum required balance on regular checking accounts about as low as you can get in your area? Also, what are the service and maintenance charges, the fees for checks? Does the bank offer an automatic line of credit with checking? What are the charges on special checking?

Charges: In addition to charges on checking accounts, what about the exact charges on such other bank services as safe deposit boxes? In these charges is a key to saving—and so here, compare each institution with extreme care. Many banks offer safe deposit boxes at a low monthly rate as part of a package of services.

Loans: How does the bank compare on availability of installment loans —ease, lack of red tape, speed? And how does it compare on interest rates, other terms, and availability of auto and similar loans?

Mortgages: Are mortgages easy to get? On what terms? Are mortgages available for co-ops, condominiums, summer homes?

Trust Department: Has this department a good junior as well as senior staff so that there will be continuity of trust services you want? Can you check the department's record with investments to find out how it has performed for clients over a long period?

Proximity: Is the bank—or at least a branch office—convenient to your house or office or both? If you're in business and much on the move, a bank with lots of branches might be the best, provided its other services measure up.

Banking Hours: Are they convenient for you—late on Friday or early Saturday, for instance? If the hours are limited, does the bank provide off-hour services to assist you?

Teller Service: Courteous? No congestion and long waiting times? If you want to bank by mail, does the bank supply stamped, self-addressed envelopes? Are there automated teller services?

Extra Services: Do you need or want these? Comprehensive monthly statements? Superchecks? Charge cards? Interest-paying Christmas Clubs? Help with your income tax forms? A travel service? Automatic bill paying?

Continuity: If you do stay with the institution with which you've banked a long time, will you receive preferential treatment—mortgage money when mortgages are tight, other special and valuable favors of this nature?

What Each Financial Institution Is

As the second half of the decade of the 1970s began, the trend among America's financial institutions was clearly toward over-all similarity in services offered. Savings institutions and credit unions were finding ways to provide checking accounts in mounting numbers; commercial banks also were finding ways to become directly competitive with other institutions in both the interest rates they paid and in the forms they offered on savings mediums. It appeared increasingly probable that by the start of the 1980s, an entirely overhauled and unprecedentedly "homogeneous" financial system would be serving the United States. However, in mid-decade, the following is the way the institutions were still set up and these were the major services each type offered.

FULL SERVICE BANKS

(also known as commercial banks, trust companies, and community banks)

Structure: Federally or state chartered corporations owned by stockholders, organized for profit.

Deposits Insured By: Federal Deposit Insurance Corporation (FDIC) in Washington. (Virtually all banks are insured.)

Services: The widest range, including:

Checking accounts

Savings and time deposits

Mortgage and home improvement loans

Consumer credit loans for automobiles, appliances, the whole range of big-ticket and small-ticket items

Personal, farm, and business loans

Student loans

Trust, investment, estate, and custodian services

Financial counseling

Letters of credit

Safe deposit boxes

Travelers checks

Christmas and vacation clubs, many of which now pay interest

A variety of travel and miscellaneous financial services

Sale and redemption of U.S. savings bonds

In mid-seventies, paid, in general, the lowest interest rates on savings accounts, but the situation was changing

SAVINGS AND LOAN ASSOCIATIONS

(also known as building and loan associations, co-operative banks, savings associations, and homestead associations)

Structure: Specialized financial associations, either federally or state chartered, operating in every state. Mainly mutually owned by their shareholders. When you open an account, you become a member of the association and thus a shareholder. Dividends paid on the money you put in your account.

Deposits Insured By: All federally chartered associations insured by the Federal Savings and Loan Insurance Corporation (FSLIC). State-chartered associations also insured by FSLIC and most of them are. Some other state-chartered associations are insured by state-chartered savings account insurance organizations.

Services:

Savings accounts and time deposits

Finance home building, home buying, and remodeling and thus play a key role in the housing field

Passbook loans to customers with money on deposit

Personal loans

Sale and redemption of U.S. savings bonds

Guaranteed student loans

Provide safe deposit boxes, sell money orders, travelers checks, etc.

In mid-decade, in general, did not offer checking accounts and did not make business loans, but the situation was changing

Also, in mid-seventies, paid in general, higher interest rates on deposits than full service banks. (In mutually owned savings associations, share owners receive "dividends," not "interest.")

MUTUAL SAVINGS BANKS

(operate in 18 states)

Structure: Non-profit specialized savings institutions, organized and operated for their depositors on a mutual basis with no stockholders; administered by trustees.

Deposits Insured By: Federal Deposit Insurance Corporation (FDIC) or by state deposit insurance funds.

Services:

Savings accounts

Home mortgage loans and home improvement loans

Safe deposit boxes

Student loans

Personal money orders

Passbook loans

Travelers checks

Sale and redemption of U.S. savings bonds

Low-cost life insurance policies in some states

In mid-decade, began offering checking account services in increasing numbers

Generally paid higher interest rates on deposits than full service banks, but gap was closing in mid-decade. (Since savings banks are "owned" by their depositors, savings also actually receive "dividends," not "interest.")

CREDIT UNIONS

Structure: Co-operative associations of people with a common bond, such as place of employment, professional association, place of residence, membership in a union, religious group, etc. Governed by the member-users on a one-member-one vote basis, they basically accept savings from the members and make loans at low cost to the members. The member is a "shareholder," not a depositor, and holds "shares" rather than makes deposits.

Deposits Insured By: National Credit Union Administration (NCUA) in Washington; various state insurance programs; some private insurance programs too.

Services:

Savings accounts

Loans (mortgage and home improvement, student)

Credit counseling

Travelers checks, money orders

Payroll deductions

Interest refunds

Check cashing

Sale and redemption of U.S. savings bonds

Borrowers' protection insurance and life savings insurance

Group discount buying

Consumer education

On checking accounts the trend in recent years has been for more and more credit unions to offer accounts, in collaboration with commercial banks, with the balance kept in such accounts earning the regular rate of interest.

SHOPPING GUIDE TO BANKS

You probably take for granted such "routine" bank services as free parking, conveniently located branches, evening or Saturday banking hours, stamped banking-by-mail, personal money orders, night deposits, drive-in banking facilities. Some banks are even open twenty-four hours a day, frequently using "robot tellers," capable of dispensing cash, making deposits, and transferring funds at any hour.

Increasingly, banks are offering such services as automobile rentals and computer leasing and are even serving as part-time employment agencies.

If you are a doctor, many banks will take over all your patient billing and fee-collecting problems.

If you are a landlord, you might find your bank is set up to serve as your rent collector.

If you are a share owner, you may find that you can have your dividend checks sent directly to your bank to be deposited and acknowledged—via a receipt to you—without charge.

If you wish to reinvest your dividends in the same company's stock, automatic reinvestment-of-dividend plans also are available.

If you want to invest in stocks, many banks offer monthly stock investment plans which are automatic and which can be tailored to meet a limited budget.

If you are planning a vacation, you may discover that your bank offers you a wide range of travel services—from hotel and airplane reservations to travelers checks—in addition to a savings plan or a special loan to pay for your holiday.

But let's say you are *not* a doctor or a landlord or a stockholder, you *don't want* to rent a computer, and you are *not* planning a vacation. What types of special services does today's *typical* bank offer you, a typical customer?

Here's a sampling (in alphabetical order) of 11 increasingly common bank services, including some which go way, way beyond the traditional savings and checking account.

(1) *Automatic Bill Paying.* Many banks today will pay at least a few of your routine bills and some will, if you authorize them to do so, automatically deduct your insurance premiums, your monthly automobile installment loan payments, and a variety of other types of regular payments from your checking account. Hundreds of banks will allow customers to pay such regular monthly bills as utilities, telephone, and water directly at the bank—thereby saving cost of writing and mailing out checks. In mounting numbers, savings institutions too permit automatic deductions from accounts to pay certain bills—such as insurance premiums, mortgage payments, the like.

(2) *Automatic Line of Credit.* On your application, a specified maximum amount of credit (depending on your credit rating) will become available to you either through your regular checking accounts or through a separate checking service which goes by various names, such as Executive Credit. In cases where the credit line is pinned to your own checking, you are able to write checks for more than your balance, up to a certain specified level. With the Executive Credit-type plan, you receive a special book of checks to write against a predetermined credit maximum. As you write the checks, you will receive notices from your bank as to when you must start repaying the total in monthly installments. This is one way to take advantage of special sales on big-ticket items, and the amount you may save may more than offset the high interest charges you'll have to pay on this type of loan. But beware! "Tap credit" also is an invitation to overspend, so if you're the type who is constantly tempted to live beyond your means, steer clear of all types of revolving loan accounts.

(3) *Automatic Savings.* On your request, the bank will transfer at regular intervals given amounts of money from your checking account to your regular or special savings account. Or the bank will invest such funds every month or quarter in U.S. savings bonds or specified mutual funds. Or, if you have a trust account with the bank, you can have any dividends or interest from your investments automatically deposited to your savings account.

(4) *Bookkeeping Services.* A few banks are beginning to expand the automatic bill-paying idea into a full range of accounting and other financial services for their customers. Included among these services are tax accounting, financial counseling, bill paying for purposes ranging from credit card accounts to parking tickets to taxes and health insurance premiums—plus detailed record keeping for all of these expenses. Of course, any bank offering this type of personally tailored service will charge you for it. However, as one appealing alternative, some banks keep an adding machine in the lobby for customers to use.

(5) *Comprehensive Checking.* A few banks are trying out a comprehensive checking technique which one institution calls Phase II checking. In one package, the customer gets a cash reserve, automatic monthly payments on consumer loans and the mortgage, automatic monthly transfer of funds to savings or the Christmas Club account.

(6) *Investment Services.* Many commercial banks offer across-the-board investment counseling for specified fees and also handle the details of purchases, sales, reinvestment of dividends in selected stocks and safekeeping of securities.

(7) *Money Substitutes.* .

(a) *Cashier's checks.* Also called "official checks," these are bank-guaranteed checks written against the bank's own account which you buy by giving the bank the amount of the check plus a small service fee. Cashier's checks are a far safer way to transfer major amounts of money from one place to another than cash itself and, since they are bank-guaranteed, will be accepted by a stranger. You may ask the bank to give you a cashier's check when you withdraw a relatively large sum from your savings account or when you borrow a sizable sum of money which you intend to turn over to another individual or company.

(b) *Certified checks.* These are simply regular checking account checks which the bank stamps to certify that the amount of the check has been deducted from your checking account and that the bank guarantees the payee that the check is good. Banks will make a small charge for this service.

(c) *Traveler's checks.* Probably the most familiar form of money substitute, available from most banks in denominations of $10, $20, $50, $100, and more, and widely used by travelers because they can be cashed throughout the world. You pay the total amount of the checks you want to buy, plus a small fee (except for the Barclays Bank checks, sold in some major cities at no fee), and establish your identity by signing the checks when you buy them and again when you cash them. With most types of traveler's checks, you are protected in the event you lose any checks—so long as you report the loss promptly to the issuing company. (Incidentally, you lose money if you hold your unused traveler's checks after you have returned from your trip, for you get no interest on the money the checks represent until you cash in your checks, redeposit the money in an interest-bearing account, and put your funds to work for you.)

(d) *"Do it yourself" traveler's checks.* Some banks will give you a supply of "free" do-it-yourself traveler's checks which you can write anywhere in the country instead of regular checks. Like traveler's checks, these checks are accepted far more readily than ordinary checks because the issuing company—your bank—guarantees them. You pay a small service charge only on the checks you actually write and, if you write a check for more than the amount of your account balance, this automatically becomes a loan. The key advantage of this type of check is that you don't tie up a large sum of cash in purchasing the checks, as you do with regular traveler's checks.

(e) *Letters of credit.* Similarly, banks will issue to you letters of credit, along with letters of identification which you can present to the bank's branches or correspondents elsewhere in the United States or abroad, to open up reserves of cash for use in your travels.

(f) *Bank drafts.* Banks also will issue "drafts" transferring funds from your account to someone else in another state or country in a matter of hours. You can, in effect, overnight wire your cash to any payee you wish and have it converted into the currency of the country—a tremendous help in an emergency.

(8) *No Checks at All.* In areas throughout the United States, banks are experimenting with the ultimate in checking sophistication—no checks at all. Funds are electronically transferred via computer terminals among consumers, merchants in giant shopping centers, and the banks. Look, Ma, no hands.
. . .

(9) *One-check Payroll System.* Corporations across the country are sending their banks lists of their employees with the amount of salary due each, the amount of each individual's federal income and Social Security taxes to be withheld, plus all other regular deductions. The corporation issues one check each pay period for the entire operation. Then the bank takes over, deposits each employee's check to his or her own account at the bank or to his or her account at another bank.

The employee receives no pay check—only a deposit slip indicating the money has been credited to his account. The company receives a periodic statement showing the cumulative pay to each employee, his total tax and other deductions.

The success of the one-check payroll system in reducing a company's payroll department costs and in assisting employees has encouraged a few banks to go beyond this to a "no-check payroll" system. Here payroll funds are simply deducted by the bank from a company's account and credited directly to each employee. Thus payday becomes just a computerized paperwork transaction. In sum, "the modern pay check is rapidly becoming as obsolete as the old pay envelope stuffed with bills and coins," says one banking official.

(10) *One-statement Banking.* This is an expansion of your monthly checking statement to include your savings account balance, cash reserve, the balance of any installment loan and any mortgage you have outstanding. Some banks today also list your checks not in the order they clear but in the exact order you wrote them, thereby giving you a great assist in keeping your checkbook records in order.

(11) *Superchecks.* More and more banks are offering the monthly "multipurpose check" or "supercheck"—an oversized check which you can use to pay as many as 45 regular monthly bills. Some 500 banks from coast to coast offer this service, usually for 50 cents a supercheck—which amounts to a substantial saving considering the number of individual checks and stamps you'd use otherwise. On that one check, you write the figures you want the bank to pay each of several merchants, up to 45, attach the bill stubs, send the whole thing to the bank to handle.

Imaginative as some of these innovations are, they are just a sampling of the changes under way.

In the offing is an "electronic fund transfer system" in which you will be able to pay your bills simply by inserting a plastic card coded to identify your checking account in a special slot in your home telephone, dialing the bank's computer number, and then dialing also the amount of the check you wish to "write." Within seconds, an electronic voice informs you, let's say, that $18.43 has been transferred out of your checking account into the payee's account—and that is that. Ultimately, banking by telephone could mean the elimination of as much as 75 per cent of all your check writing.

And what if the computers spin out more "checks" than you have money in your account to cover? The overdraft total would simply become a loan—until you replenished your account—at the going interest rates, of course. The extent of the damage would become evident only when you received your comprehensive computerized monthly bank statement.

Even farther out—but still *not* off the edge of the horizon—is your future "shop at home" plan. In this scheme, you would tune in a supermarket display on your home Picturephone and dial, for example, "vegetables." The store's current stock of spinach, beans, carrots, etc., would then be displayed on your home phone screen, along with prices and identification numbers. You would next punch numbers on your telephone to indicate exactly what you wished to order. The supermarket would then assemble your order and dispatch it to you in a delivery truck. As for paying? Why, of course, the store—via a telephone hookup with the bank—would just automatically charge your bank account for the total you owed.

YOUR CHECKING ACCOUNT

I remember—and I'm sure you do too—when a checking account was just that and nothing more, so basic that about your only option was to choose between a regular and a special account. But now the alternatives have become so numerous that it's actually unfair to compare today's checking account with that of as recently as the 1960s.

The reasons are apparent: our rising pay checks, the ever continuing uptrend of American families into middle-income ranges where checking accounts are commonplace, our increasing familiarity with financial services, the banks' hard sell, and the steady growth of the two- or three-checking-account family.

Visibly, the checks are different, too. For ladies, the pattern may be several shades of tweed or herringbone. Many banks offer checks with scenic illustrations across the check's face. A few have special left-handed checkbooks for southpaws.

The purpose of a checking account, of course, is to give you a convenient and safe way to handle relatively large amounts of cash and to transfer money to other people. Your checkbook serves as an excellent personal financial record and your canceled checks are among the best forms of proof of to-whom-you-have-paid-how-much-and-when.

As of the mid-1970s, well over 24 billion checks worth more than $12 *trillion* were clearing annually through the U.S. banking system and the number of checks we write is due to cross the 50-billion mark during this decade. This despite all the talk about our becoming a "checkless society"!

Four out of five American families have at least one checking account. Today, more than 90 per cent of payments in this country are by check. In some states, you must be at least eighteen, or twenty-one, to open an individual checking account. Otherwise, you may open a joint account with a parent or relative.

To open an account, you simply go to your bank's New Accounts Department, fill out a signature card, decide what type of checking account you want (or can afford) to open, and make your initial deposit.

There are two main types of checking accounts—regular accounts and special accounts.

In a regular checking account, you normally must keep a certain cash minimum—which usually is at least $100 and quite possibly $200 or more. As long as you maintain the required minimum at all times, many banks will permit you to write as many checks and make as many deposits as you please without paying any monthly service charge.

However, as of the mid-seventies, generally if the amount in your regular checking account falls below the minimum, you may have to pay a monthly charge of $2.00 to $3.00. Or the bank may levy a maintenance charge for your account each month, in addition to the required minimum balance. Or still other banks will let you write a certain number of checks each month before any service charge is made. And in many parts of the country banks in the mid-seventies were offering free checking accounts requiring no minimum balance.

A regular checking account will be the best for you if you write a relatively large number of checks during the month and you are also able to maintain the required minimum balance in your account. But the key point about *any* checking account involving a required minimum balance is that this money is not earning interest. So before you decide which type of account is best suited to you, make at least a rough calculation of the interest you would not earn on whatever minimum balance is required over the span of a year.

One calculation is to count your checks for the last year. The average person uses 22 checks per month. Multiply the total by the figure the bank charges per check on special checking. Multiply the monthly maintenance charge by 12 and add this to the check charges. The total shows the *annual cost of special checking.*

Then take 5½ per cent of the minimum balance required by the bank for regular checking, which is about the least interest a person would earn by keeping that amount in a savings program rather than tying it up in a minimum balance. On a $300 minimum, for example, it would come to $16.50 a year. Multiply by 12 the bank's monthly maintenance charge on a regular account. Add any charges the bank makes for deposits on regular checking. Add the interest total, maintenance total, and any per check and deposit charges on regular accounts to get the annual cost of regular checking.

In a special checking account (or "economy account") you do not have to keep a minimum balance. However, you usually must pay a flat monthly service charge plus another 10¢ or 15¢ charge for each check you write.

This type of account is probably the more economical for you if you are a young individual or couple whose balance tends to dip way down at the end of each pay period and if you write only a few checks during the course of a month.

A third type of checking account which has exploded onto the banking scene in recent years is the automatic line of credit or overdraft account—or whatever its name—mentioned in the previous section, "Shopping Guide to Banks." Some banks simply tack the "overdraft" feature on to your existing regular checking account; others will issue a special set of overdraft checks.

In recent years, more and more banks have begun offering free checking accounts with no minimum balance. Assuming other bank services are generally equivalent, of course it makes sense to take advantage of free checking if a bank in your area is offering it.

To repeat and emphasize: the type of checking account you choose will depend on the cash balance you are able to keep in the account, the number of checks you normally write, and whether you have the discipline to avoid the temptation of instant loans at relatively stiff interest rates.

RULES FOR WRITING AND ENDORSING CHECKS

Millions of Americans do not know the basic rules for writing, endorsing, and depositing a check. Do not permit yourself to be among them—for you may be unwittingly courting the bank's refusal to honor your checks—or even inviting costly check-doctoring by a professional earning a living in this craft.

Heed these main do's and don'ts on writing checks:

Do date each check properly. A bank may refuse to accept a check which is dated ahead, or hold it until its date is reached. The bank's reasoning is that, if the check were charged to your account before you expected it to be, it might cause other checks you wrote to bounce.

Don't leave any spaces between the dollar sign and the amount of the check you are writing, or between the amount you spell out in the middle line and the word "dollars" at the end of that line. Or, if you do leave such spaces, draw lines across them.

Do make sure each check is numbered properly—for your own book-keeping purposes.

Don't alter the way you sign your checks (e.g., by adding your middle initial) once you have decided on a standard signature.

Do, if you are a married woman, sign checks with your own first name, plus your married name—"Mary Dowd," *not* "Mrs. Jack Dowd."

Don't use "Mr.," "Miss," or "Mrs." as part of your signature.

Do fill out the middle line ending with the word "dollars" in this format: "Five and 50/100," or "One hundred and fifty and no/100." If you write a check for less than $1.00 be sure to put a decimal point between the printed dollar sign and the amount of the check—followed by the word "cents." On the line where you write out the amount of the check, write, for example, "Only 95 cents," and cross out the word "dollars."

Don't use somebody else's check unless you cut out the special magnetic code number which usually appears at the lower left-hand corner of the check. Inking it out won't do the trick with today's electronic check-"reading" devices; if you don't actually cut out this account number, you risk having the check charged against your friend's account. (Technically, you can write a check on any surface from a paper bag to an eggshell, but banks shudder at this sort of eccentricity for obvious reasons.) For the identical reasons, don't lend anyone one of your checks. Because of the indelible symbols, your pre-imprinted check will be sorted according to its magnetic coding and charged to your account even if someone else, with no dishonest intentions at all, has crossed out your identifying number and name and written in his own.

Do endorse a check only on the back of the left-hand side (the perforated side, in one type of checkbook), *exactly* as your name appears on the front of the check. If this is not your usual signature, add the correct signature below your first endorsement. Of course, if your address is on the check too, you need not include this—or the "Miss," "Mrs." or "Mr." which may also be included.

Don't ever underestimate the importance of your endorsement or forget that your endorsement on someone else's check means you would be willing to cover the check yourself should the bank for any reason refuse to honor it.

A blank endorsement—your signature only—means you transfer the ownership of the check to the person holding it at the time. This person may then cash it.

An endorsement in full—or special endorsement—means you sign a check over to someone else by writing on the back of a check "Pay to the order of" this person or organization.

A *restrictive endorsement* should be used on checks you wish to deposit by mail. You write "For deposit only" over your signature. Or, if you give someone a check which has been made out to you or cash, you write "Pay to the order of ————" and sign your name beneath this.

Do deposit all checks you receive as soon as you get them. Not only is it a big bookkeeping nuisance for the person who has issued the check if you keep it for a month or more, but many banks refuse to honor checks which are two or three months old—unless they are "reauthorized" to do so by the payer.

Don't write checks out to "cash" unless you yourself are cashing them at a bank, supermarket, or elsewhere. Such checks are negotiable by any bearer and leave you with no record of how the money was spent.

Do record on your check stub the key facts about every check you write. This includes the date, check number, payee, amount, and the purpose of the check if the "payee" notation doesn't make that evident. The best way to make sure you don't forget to record this information is to do so *before* you write the check itself.

And *don't* ever, ever give signed blank checks to anybody whom you do not trust completely; blank checks are as good as cash—unlimited amounts of it, for that matter. As a matter of fact, it's risky to ever sign a blank check!

KEY QUESTIONS ABOUT WRITING CHECKS

Now here are additional questions you almost surely would like to have answered—leading logically from the rules covered in the preceding pages.

Q. *When you deposit a check from another bank, how long should you wait for it to be cleared before you can safely draw checks against your deposit?*

A. If the other bank is in the same city, allow two or three more days for the check to be collected. If the bank is out of town, allow five to ten days depending on its location. When it's important for you to know exactly when a check will actually be credited to your account—so you won't risk having any of your own checks returned—ask one of your bank's officers about the particular check.

Q. *Is it legal to write a check in pencil?*

A. Yes. But it's obviously dangerous since anyone could erase the amount and substitute a larger one. Write all checks in ink.

Q. *May a check be dated on Saturday, Sunday, or a holiday?*

A. Yes. The folklore to the contrary is wrong. However, since some people who believe the folklore may refuse to accept the check, it's generally safer to date it on a previous day.

Q. *What happens when you make the mistake of writing one amount in words and another amount in figures?*

A. Most banks pay the amount which is spelled out. If they don't pay this amount, they return the check.

Q. *Should you ever erase or cross out anything on a check?*

A. No. Even if you initial the change, the bank will not honor an altered check. And knowing this, you should never accept or cash an altered check yourself.

Q. *How long does a check remain valid?*

A. Technically, a check is good for six years. In actual practice, though, most banks consult with the payer before honoring a check which is more than six months old and many, I repeat, do this after only two or three months.

Q. *Will your bank give you a new check if you spoil one for which you've already paid?*

A. Yes.

Q. *How do you stop payment on a check?*

A. You can, for a small fee of about $1.00, stop payment on any check you have written simply by *telephoning* your bank's stop payment department and giving the details, including: the date, amount, name of payee, check number, and the reason for stopping the payment. Then immediately confirm the order in writing. The bank will issue a stop payment form which you must complete and which the bank will keep on file—to be sure your intention *not* to have the bank honor your check is properly carried out.

When you stop payment, be sure you notify the payee—the person, company, or organization who was to have received the amount of money you specified on the check.

As a general rule, *don't* send a check in payment unless you are willing to have it honored. Stopping payment may damage your credit rating.

GUARDING AGAINST CHECK FORGERIES

What would you do if you suddenly discovered your checkbook had been stolen and that a professional forger was using *your* name to write check after check against your account?

Do not dismiss the question, for check forgeries have been climbing at an alarming pace in recent years. As a simple precaution against becoming another victim, you should at least be aware of a few of the forger's favorite techniques.

Typically, the forger will find out when your bank mails out monthly statements and will loot your mailbox at that time. Armed with samples of your signature, a good idea of the amount of money you keep in your account, and the number of checks you usually write during the month, he will start raiding your account. You may not discover the damage until *his* canceled checks start coming home to you.

Or the forger may simply "raise" a carelessly written check of yours, by hiking the amount from "one" dollar to "one hundred" or "six" dollars to "sixty," or "twenty" to "seventy"—at the same time subtracting this amount from your account.

Here are a few key rules to protect yourself against check forgery:

• Guard your checks as if they were cash. I re-emphasize, in many ways, they're *better* than cash, since they can be written out for any amount.

• Notify your bank *immediately* if you lose even a single check, not to mention your entire checkbook. Note: Forgers frequently will steal checks from the *back* of your checkbook to postpone detection, so flip through your whole checkbook now and then as an added precaution.

• Notify the bank if you fail to receive your bank statement within a couple of days of the usual time.

• Reconcile your bank statement promptly each month and glance at each returned check for evidence of any tampering or forgery.

• Report any such evidence to the bank immediately. Banks normally are insured against such losses.

• Learn and obey the rules I've already given you for writing checks.

• Destroy all old checks if and when you change your name, address, account number—or become formally separated or divorced.

• Avoid the sweeping illegible "executive" signature—or a hand-printed signature. This is much easier to forge than a clear, freely written two-name signature with connected letters.

HOW TO BALANCE YOUR CHECKBOOK

As Chapter 1, "Your Personal Money Manager," stressed, the monthly ritual of checkbook balancing should be assigned to whichever member of the family is the more deft at it and the more willing to do it *as soon as possible* after each bank statement comes in. An arbitrary decision that this chore should automatically go to the man in the family is downright foolish—if he has neither a flare for nor an interest in it. Whoever of you gets the job can use the chart illustrated to guide you on the key steps to balancing a checkbook.

1. Your own checkbook balance	
2. Minus service charges appearing on your bank statement	
3. Your own new checkbook balance	
4. Balance in the bank's statement	
5. Plus recent deposits not yet recorded in bank statement	
6. Minus value of all outstanding checks — those not appearing on bank statement	
7. New bank statement balance	

This last total—item 7—should agree with item 3, your own "new checkbook balance." If it does not, go back and follow these steps:

(1) First compare the amount of each canceled check with the amount appearing in the bank statement. Make a notation after each check on the bank statement as you go.

(2) Now arrange the stack of checks in order of check numbers—which will permit you not only to recheck the amounts against those appearing in your own check records but also to tell immediately which ones are missing.

(3) Compare the amount of each check with the amount you have written on each appropriate stub—and check off each entry in your record as you go.

(4) Compare, and verify with a notation, all the deposits you have made and recorded with the deposits recorded on the bank statement.

(5) Add up, in the appropriate space provided on your bank statement, the amounts of all checks you have written which have not yet appeared on your statement and subtract this total from the balance appearing at the end of your bank statement. Make sure the amounts on the checks agree with the amounts recorded on your check register.

(6) Add to the statement balance the total amount of deposits you have made to your account which do not appear on the bank statement.

(7) Subtract any bank service charges appearing in your statement from the balance which appears in your checkbook. Do this in your checkbook as well.

The revised totals for the bank statement and for your checkbook balance should agree to the penny.

But don't panic if they still don't agree. Here's what to do:

Recheck your original math in your checkbook. The bank's math is usually correct since it was probably done by a machine. However, errors of other sorts are entirely possible.

Recheck the balances you carried forward from page to page in your checkbook.

Double-check to be certain you have subtracted *all* outstanding checks from your bank statement balance—including those still missing from previous statements.

Double-check to be certain all of the canceled checks which came with your statement are included in your checkbook record—and that you haven't forgotten to note *any non-checkbook checks* you may have written during the period of the statement.

If your accounts *still* don't balance, and you're completely stymied as to why, take the whole business to the bank and ask for help. You'll almost surely be given this help freely and without charge—but don't delay. There is always the possibility, although remote, of sleight of hand with your bank balance—and the sooner any type of thievery is pinned down, the better your chance of avoiding financial losses. Most banks expect to be informed of a possible error within ten days.

Your Savings Account

HOW MUCH SHOULD YOU KEEP IN A SAVINGS ACCOUNT?

How much money should *you* keep in a savings account?

• The average amount of money kept in a regular savings account in a U.S. financial institution in 1975 was close to $2,000.

• The rule of thumb I gave you in Chapter 1, "Your Personal Money Manager," is that your emergency fund should equal at least two months' income.

• Many of the major financial institutions of the country would call my total far too low, would recommend your reserve in the form of "liquid assets" —cash or its equivalent—should total three to six months' income.

• But the vital point which erases any apparent disagreement is that your own special financial circumstances must be the crucial factor deciding whether your emergency reserve can safely be as low as two months' income or should properly be equal to six months' earnings.

So how much should *you* keep in an emergency fund? Let me answer by asking you these questions:

How many circumstances can you think of in which you might require really large sums of cash, literally at overnight notice?

What types of unexpected financial emergencies might conceivably befall you or your family? (A disabling accident, job layoff, big auto repair job.)

What share of the estimated costs of such emergencies would be covered by your other forms of financial protection such as major medical insurance, life insurance, other types of insurance, disability and survivor's benefits under Social Security, U.S. saving bonds you might have stashed away, stocks, mutual fund shares, bonds, other investments, benefits from your employer?

What emergency financial help could you realistically expect from parents, other relatives, or your employer?

Could you, the non-working wife, move into a paying job fairly readily —if need be?

If the family breadwinner should lose his or her job tomorrow due to a layoff, merger, or other development, how long would it probably be before he or she could find a comparable job in his or her field of training?

How big a financial nest egg in cash do *you* need to *feel* financially secure?

Are you preparing for big-ticket expenses and purchases in the months ahead—e.g., a down payment on a house, a new baby, a long-planned vacation, a big outlay to go into business for yourself?

The amount you really need as an emergency reserve will depend on your honest answers to these questions.

It well may be that *if* you're a young couple with no children and a modest income, the *maximum* you should keep is $1,000 to $1,500 in a regular savings account. And in some cases even less would be realistic if you have other safe financial reserves which you could readily tap.

For your emergency cash reserve—whatever its amount or wherever you deposit it—should be precisely what its name implies. It should be protection against unexpected financial emergencies. It should be no more nor less than that.

KEY FORMS OF SAVINGS ACCOUNTS

Within any single financial institution, you may choose between a variety of savings accounts, each one tailored to fit particular needs, each account with special advantages, and each with disadvantages. You must select the one which best fits your requirements.

In general, these will be offered to you:

Passbook Savings Accounts

Have complete flexibility. Your money is always instantly available. You may deposit or withdraw any amount at any time.

Interest you earn on this type of "liquid" savings will be the lowest among the major types of accounts. Commercial banks by law paid the lowest rates on passbook savings accounts in the mid-1970s—one of their key disadvantages.

"Liquidity" of this type of account is the highest, the best of all types of savings outside of your checking account or cash in your hand. Liquidity denotes the ease and speed with which you can convert your funds into cash, and the amount of interest you can earn on your savings tends to be lowest where the degree of liquidity is highest.

Interest is usually compounded annually, semi-annually, or quarterly and in some cases daily.

Federally insured or state insured in almost all cases up to $40,000 for each account held in a different name (a joint account can be insured separately from the individual accounts of those sharing the joint account).

Funds in this type of account can be used as collateral for personal bank loans.

Tally of your savings balance may be kept in a passbook or reported periodically to you in computerized statements mailed by the financial institution holding your account. The passbook itself is being gradually phased out.

Time Deposit Open Accounts

Form of savings account in which you must leave your savings with the institution for a specified period of time in order to obtain the higher interest rate offered on these deposits. (Has many names. The trick name depends on the institution.) Note: you can withdraw the interest but not the principal.

Minimum initial deposits required, usually ranging from $500 to as much as $5,000.

While you can add funds to this type of account or withdraw interest at any time, notice of thirty to ninety days frequently required for withdrawal of the principal, with the actual interest you receive depending on how long you maintain your account.

Insurance features the same as for Passbook Savings Accounts.

Consumer Certificates of Deposit

• These are the certificates of deposit for individuals with savings of under $100,000. They are a medium for your most liquid funds—assuming you are confident you will not need to cash in your certificates before they mature.

• In the mid-1970s, consumer CDs were available in denominations from $100 to as high as $5,000 to $10,000.

• Maturities ranged from two to four years or more with the interest rate the highest paid on any savings account.

• Notice of withdrawal was required and penalty imposed—in form of reduction of interest—in event of prior withdrawal.

• Insurance features and all the rest identical with other forms of savings accounts.

On top of these basic forms of savings accounts, financial institutions are developing new savings programs or variations of older ones. As a banker remarked, "In my Midwestern youth, our small-town bank had only two different devices to help me save. Today, that bank has nine variations and larger banks have still more." Just to indicate the scope, ponder these variations:

• Monthly memo savings. The full service bank lets you set a goal in total dollars, then it develops a savings plan to fit and determines what monthly deposits you need to make to meet the goal. Every month the bank sends a statement to the depositor reminding him that he "owes" the account a deposit of X dollars. The top of the statement can be detached and used as a deposit slip, with an attached prestamped envelope.

• Assorted interest. On many savings accounts, especially higher-interest time accounts, larger banks offer several options on payment of interest: interest can be credited to the time account, the regular savings account, the checking account, or mailed out on a quarterly basis.

• Special savings withdrawal. In one Midwestern city, several banks have together installed a special-purpose computer system to provide instant savings withdrawal transactions for customers. Through an on-the-line system of 90 keyboard terminals, the teller keys in a savings account number and dollar amount any time a customer wants to make a withdrawal and gets a green, yellow, or red light response for Yes, Maybe, or No.

• Quick deposits. More and more banks have quick deposit boxes for savings so customers needn't stand in the teller line. There also has been great improvement in teller line traffic, drive-in and walk-up windows, expresslines, etc.

• Safe deposit boxes. Some banks give customers free use of safe deposit boxes if their savings accounts run a certain size. Other special promotions are widespread.

• Insurance. Based on the depositor's age and the size of his account, this program makes term insurance available at what amounts to a group policy rate or less.

The mutual savings banks in New York, Massachusetts, and Connecticut also sell low-cost life insurance over the counter. It is inexpensive insurance because it is sold directly to you—at the bank itself or by mail—and there are no salesmen's commissions to add to its price to you. Many savings banks now also sell shares in a no-load, no-redemption-fee mutual fund. (See Chapter 21, "How to Invest in Mutual Funds," for details on no-load funds.)

Most credit unions provide life insurance without charge to you if you put your savings in the credit union.

WHICH TYPE OF SAVINGS ACCOUNT IS BEST FOR YOU?

You can decide which savings account is best suited for your personal needs and goals only when you know the variety of accounts available. In brief, you may choose among these major types:

(1) *An individual account.* This may be opened by only one person—adult or minor—and you are the sole owner, the only person who can draw on the account. You can open this type of account with a small deposit.

(2) *A joint account.* Two of you may open this type—usually a husband and wife. Either of you may deposit funds in the account and either of you may withdraw funds from the account. In the event that one of you dies, the balance will be payable to the survivor.

(3) *A voluntary trust account.* You may open this type in trust for your child or another person. You will control the account during your life—after which it will be payable to the person you name as beneficiary. You have the right to change the beneficiary of this account at any time.

(4) *A fiduciary account.* If you are appointed an administrator, executor of an estate, or a guardian of another person, you may open a fiduciary account for the funds entrusted to you.

(5) *An organization account.* If you belong to an organization which collects dues or fees and which therefore has funds to safeguard and if you are in charge of the funds, you can open an organization account. The organization might be a club, your church, your lodge, a mutual benefit society, or any other non-profit organization.

(6) *A school savings account.* Your child may open a regular school bank savings account with insignificant deposits—and as he or she learns how to save and the virtues of saving, this tiny account may grow to become your child's regular savings account with a respectable deposit balance.

HOW CAN YOU FORCE YOURSELF TO SAVE—GRACEFULLY?

One way to save money is through a "loose money" system. Put aside at the end of each day all the change you have left in your pocket—or only all your quarters, or even all your single dollar bills. Once every week, faithfully deposit your little hoard in a nearby bank or savings association. In just over eighteen months, the dollar-bill approach helped one family make the first payment on a piece of land in the exurbs for a weekend cabin.

Another way to build a nest egg is to save all windfall money—dividends, inheritances, bonuses, cash gifts, tax refunds. Put this money in your savings account the instant you get it. Don't even cash the check or do more than peer at the amount of cash in a gift envelope. Don't give the temptation to spend the windfall the slightest edge.

A third excellent way to save is to authorize your bank to deduct a specified percentage from your pay check automatically when you deposit the pay check in your checking account and to transfer this percentage to your savings account. Make it 10 per cent, if you can manage, or 5 per cent—but make the transfer automatic and regular. The automatic, regular feature is the secret, as I stressed over and over again in Chapter 1, "Your Personal Money Manager."

Or maybe you will decide the best approach for you is an automatic deposit of X number of pay checks each year entirely in the savings account. For instance, you might decide to save every tenth weekly pay check or the first check of every quarter of the year. Or if you're paid on a semi-monthly basis, you might decide you can manage to put away two or three full pay checks a year.

Or you might find a periodic "Nothing Week" is your best deal. During this week you would not spend any money on dinner out or stop at the bar on the way home from work or go out to the movies or go bowling—or whatever. You would eat inexpensive foods at home, read books, or look at TV—and add at least $25 to your nest egg.

Or surely you could save the money you formerly used for, say, cigarettes. I, for one, am saving more than $300 a year on this item alone since I quit.

And there are all sorts of tricks, of course. You might put, say, $50 in your savings account on every national holiday or family birthday. Or you might add an agreed-upon amount whenever you break a family rule. Or add that agreed-upon amount whenever you enjoy a particular pastime.

You can easily figure out your own approach, once you make up your minds to adopt one.

You'll save if you force yourself to by some method. Then you'll build your nest egg if you'll put the program on an automatic basis. You can't lose by trying this. You can only win.

WHAT IS "HIGHEST" INTEREST ON SAVINGS?

By law, banks and other financial institutions must state clearly in their advertisements the *true* annual interest rate they pay on savings—if they make any reference at all to interest in their ads—as well as any special conditions for getting the full interest rate.

But clear as this seems, it still leaves plenty of room for befuddlement. In fact, in this area of interest earned on savings, "highest" may not be highest at all—and the institution which advertises the top stated rate of interest on your funds may not be actually paying you the top total of dollars on your funds.

So much more than the stated rate of interest is involved. Far more revealing than the percentage which stands out in the ad may be what is not even included in the ad. For instance, how often is the interest promised you compounded—so that your interest earns interest? When does your deposit start to draw interest? Is there any penalty for frequent withdrawals or any bonus for no withdrawals for a specified period?

To underline my point, a while ago, as an experiment, I surveyed a couple dozen of employees in my newspaper office who had savings accounts nearby. With two exceptions, all were fuzzy about every aspect except the stated interest rate.

This ignorance is self-defeating. You may think you are getting the best interest deal but you might be able to do significantly better at another institution a block away. You may think you are handling your savings sensibly, but you actually may be cutting your own return by the way you deposit and withdraw funds. Here are five questions you should be able to answer:

(1) What is the institution's policy on the compounding of interest? The more frequently interest is compounded the more interest your savings earn. A rate of 6 per cent paid once a year is a straight 6 per cent—or $60 per $1,000 of savings. But a rate of 6 per cent paid to you every quarter is higher, because the interest credited to your account is added to your original amount every quarter and then the stated rate is paid on the bigger sum. A rate compounded every month comes out to still more and a rate compounded every day is most. The larger your savings and the longer you maintain your account, the more the factor of "compounding" matters.

(2) When does your savings account start to earn interest (or dividends)? Under a policy most favorable to you, the institution will pay interest on your account from the day of deposit to the day of withdrawal. Also, under a most favorable policy, the institution will pay interest on all funds you keep in your account during the interest period. Under a least favorable policy, the institution will pay interest only on the smallest balance you have in your account during the interest period.

(3) When is interest credited to your account? On the first of each month? At the end of each quarter? At the end of June and December? Or just at the end of December? This is of major importance, for under the policies of many institutions, if you withdraw funds before the stated interest payment date, you will lose all the interest owed to you on these funds, for the interest period. When you withdraw funds, try to schedule the withdrawal immediately after the date for crediting interest.

(4) Is there any "grace period" during which you can withdraw funds around the interest payment date without being penalized by loss of interest? If so, how many days of grace are you allowed in which to withdraw funds and still be entitled to the interest the funds had earned? Also find out if there is a grace period after each interest payment date during which you can deposit funds and have them earn interest from the payment date. Pertinent too is whether the period of grace includes every calendar day or just business days. A period of grace which includes only business days will be longer than it appears offhand.

(5) What about penalties for frequent withdrawals? And what about payment of an interest bonus if you make no withdrawals for a specified period—say none for one year? Both penalties and bonuses are fairly commonplace.

Any reputable financial institution should automatically answer these questions (and others which may bother you). With the answers, you then may make an intelligent decision on where to keep your cash nest egg.

HOW DOES A SAVINGS ACCOUNT GROW?

Compound interest means that you are earning interest on the interest paid to you as well as interest on your own deposits.

Say you deposit $5.00 a week in your savings account at a local bank and you earn 5 per cent interest from the day of deposit. Say your bank compounds your interest quarterly.

Here is how much your account would grow *without* the compound interest and *with* compound interest—at 5 per cent.

$5.00 a Week at 5%

NUMBER OF YEARS	SAVINGS WITHOUT COMPOUND INTEREST	SAVINGS WITH COMPOUND INTEREST	SAVINGS INCREASE REPRESENTED BY COMPOUND INTEREST
1	$ 260	$ 266.45	$ 6.45 (2.5%)
2	520	546.48	26.48 (5.10%)
3	780	840.77	60.77 (7.8%)
5	1,300	1,475.10	175.10 (13.5%)
10	2,600	3,366.23	766.23 (29.5%)
15	3,900	5,790.74	1,890.74 (48.5%)
20	5,200	8,899.04	3,699.04 (71.1%)

Or say you can deposit $5.00 to $50 a month. How will your savings grow at 5 per cent a year interest, compounded semi-annually? Here's how much:

How SAVINGS GROW	$5 MONTHLY	$10 MONTHLY	$15 MONTHLY	$20 MONTHLY	$25 MONTHLY	$50 MONTHLY
6 months	30.44	60.88	91.31	121.75	152.19	304.38
1 year	61.64	123.28	184.90	246.54	308.18	616.37
2 years	126.40	252.81	379.17	505.57	631.97	1,263.94
3 years	194.44	388.89	583.26	777.71	972.15	1,944.30
4 years	265.93	531.85	797.69	1,063.62	1,329.55	2,659.10
5 years	341.03	682.06	1,022.98	1,364.01	1,705.04	3,410.09
10 years	777.58	1,555.16	2,332.48	3,110.06	3,887.64	7,775.28
15 years	1,336.40	2,672.80	4,008.76	5,345.15	6,681.55	13,363.10
20 years	2,051.73	4,103.47	6,154.53	8,206.26	10,257.99	20,515.99

Or say you have $5,000 in cash to deposit in a savings account. How much will this sum grow at varying interest rates over the years, if compounded quarterly?

Here's that answer:

How a $5,000 Deposit Will Grow

INTEREST RATE	AFTER 1 YEAR	AFTER 3 YEARS	AFTER 5 YEARS	AFTER 10 YEARS
4.50%	$5,229	$5,718	$6,254	$7,822
4.75	5,242	5,761	6,332	8,018
5.00	5,255	5,804	6,410	8,218
5.25	5,265	5,848	6,491	8,425
5.50	5,280	5,890	6,572	8,636
5.75	5,294	5,934	6,652	8,851
6.00	5,306	5,978	6,734	9,070

Or say your objective is to save a specific sum—anywhere from $2,000 to $20,000. If you save X dollars a month, how many years will it take you—at Y interest compounded continuously—to achieve your goal?

The following compilation answers this one.

Start by setting your savings target in total dollars and years (the left-hand column). Follow across to one of the other columns and see how much you should save each month in order to reach your goal—at varying interest rates.

Or start with a rough idea of how much money you can put aside every month. Then look in the left-hand column to see what size nest egg you're aiming for.

Savings Time Table

If you want this amount:		Save this much each month at the interest rate of:		
		4½ %	5%	5¼ %
$ 2,000 in	1 year	$162.64	$162.20	$161.53
	3 years	51.79	51.39	50.78
	5 years	29.67	29.28	28.70
$ 4,000 in	1 year	$325.28	$324.40	$323.06
	3 years	103.58	102.78	101.56
	5 years	59.34	58.56	57.40
$ 6,000 in	1 year	$487.92	$486.60	$484.59
	3 years	155.38	154.17	152.34
	5 years	89.00	87.84	86.10
$ 8,000 in	5 years	$118.67	$117.12	$114.80
	10 years	52.69	51.28	49.21
	15 years	31.06	29.78	27.93
	20 years	20.51	19.36	17.72
$10,000 in	5 years	$148.34	$146.40	$143.50
	10 years	65.86	64.10	61.51
	15 years	38.83	37.23	34.91
	20 years	25.64	24.20	22.15
$12,000 in	5 years	$178.01	$175.68	$172.20
	10 years	79.03	76.92	73.82
	15 years	46.59	44.67	41.90
	20 years	30.77	29.04	26.58
$14,000 in	5 years	$207.68	$204.96	$200.90
	10 years	92.21	89.74	86.12
	15 years	54.36	52.12	48.88
	20 years	35.89	33.88	31.01
$16,000 in	5 years	$237.35	$234.24	$229.60
	10 years	105.38	102.56	98.42
	15 years	62.12	59.56	55.86
	20 years	41.02	38.72	35.44

If you want this amount:		Save this much each month at the interest rate of:		
		4½%	5%	5¼%
$18,000 in	5 years	$267.01	$263.52	$258.30
	10 years	118.55	115.38	110.72
	15 years	69.89	67.01	62.84
	20 years	46.15	43.56	39.87
$20,000 in	5 years	$296.68	$292.80	$287.00
	10 years	131.72	128.20	123.03
	15 years	77.65	74.45	69.83
	20 years	51.28	48.40	44.30

NOTE: This table was prepared by the Continental Bank of Chicago. It is based on three assumptions: (1) Deposits monthly are made at the first of the month; (2) periodic deposits are monthly and are the same amount as the initial deposit; and (3) interest is compounded continuously.

How to Save on Bank Service Charges

Do you know how much you are now paying in bank service charges to maintain your checking and savings accounts? Probably you don't. But these charges often run $35 to $50 or even more a year, depending on the number of services you use. This is a possible leak in your budget which you should not ignore—particularly in view of the fact that you're using an unprecedented variety of bank services today, are likely to use more and more in the future, and the long-term trend of charges for these services is relentlessly up.

Here, therefore, are guides on the amounts you well may be paying without realizing it and ways to reduce your charges. At one Midwestern bank, the service charges on a regular checking account with a minimum balance of $300 are 5¢ for each bookkeeping entry, 4¢ for each deposit, 75¢ a month for maintaining a regular checking account, and $3.00 for each overdraft. Thus, this bank's typical net monthly charge is $1.00 to $2.00.

Some banks charge you for any checks you write over a certain maximum number as well as the monthly maintenance charge. Typical charges in the mid-1970s on a special checking account with no minimum balance were 50¢ to 75¢ a month plus 10¢ for each check you wrote. Some banks charge less per check but add a charge for each deposit. But using this example, if you wrote 20 checks a month, the service charge would run $2.50 to $2.75 —or $30 to $33 a year.

Most banks also impose a "late charge" if you fail to make a payment on an installment loan within five to ten days of the due date. This "grace period" is not advertised, but most banks which extend home mortgages provide for several days of grace on loan repayments. A typical charge is 5 per cent of the payment, up to a maximum of $5.00 in any one month and $25 over the life of the loan—or 2 per cent of the original loan amount, whichever is less.

Usually there is no service charge on savings accounts. However, many banks charge "activity fees" for frequent withdrawals.

If a bank pays no interest on Christmas Club or Vacation Club accounts, this adds up to a "hidden" service charge of sorts. Even banks which do pay interest on such accounts generally pay less than the going rate for regular savings accounts. (A few do pay full savings rates.) Similarly, on regular savings accounts, some banks pay no interest on balances below a certain amount.

Here are basic rules to help you save on bank service charges:

• Generally, a regular checking account is the most economical type, for on this type of account, you can often eliminate *any* service charge simply by keeping the required balance in the account—and as I reported in the section "Your Checking Account," many banks now offer completely free checking accounts.

But keep in mind that if you maintain a large minimum balance you are losing a substantial amount of interest on these funds. A $500 minimum, for example, translates into a loss of about $25 in interest during one year.

• If you have a regular checking account and there is a minimum balance requirement, make sure you don't dip under the minimum balance and invoke a monthly penalty charge.

• If you are being regularly charged for drawing beyond the minimum balance in your checking account, consider transferring money from your savings account. You might be able to save more in charges than you'll lose in interest.

• If you, a young couple, have two separate accounts (one individual and one joint account), consider consolidating them—to increase your combined minimum balance and thus shave service charges you might be piling up for dipping below this minimum.

• If yours is a special checking account and you find that you are writing a rising number of checks, perhaps it would be cheaper to switch to a regular checking account. Normally, a special checking account is the more economical only if you write fewer than ten checks a month.

• In either type of account try to limit the number of checks you write. Just by writing a single check for $60 in cash instead of six checks for $10 each, you could save 50¢ or more in service charges. Or hold out a fairly large sum of cash when you deposit your pay check. Also, pay as many little bills in cash as you conveniently can unless you need the canceled checks for your tax records—and find out if you can pay your utility bills at the bank, without using any checks.

• Check your bank statements immediately when you receive them to make sure that you're not about to make a costly overdraft. And *don't* get into the habit of sending out a deposit in the same mail as you send out a slew of checks drawn against that deposit. An out-of-town check you deposit may not be credited to your checking account until it is actually cleared—which may take from a day to a week. On the other hand, the amount of each check you write is deducted from your balance the minute your bank receives the check. In this era of erratic postal service and computerized check-clearing techniques, what this means is that your checks easily might beat your deposits to the bank. Quite aside from the fact that this practice is illegal, it could leave you with both a fistful of rubber checks which reached the bank before your deposit got there and overdraft penalties of $2.50 to $5.00 or more *per check*.

• Make installment loan payments within the period of time your bank specifies in order to eliminate late charges.

• Avoid asking for a statement of your checking account balance. A growing number of banks are now making extra charges if you ask for such statements before they are automatically sent to you. Charges range from 25¢ to $4.00 for an itemized supplementary statement, and the typical cost of a simple verbal report on your balance is 50¢.

• And try to avoid requesting a special search for a "lost" deposit you may have failed to record properly. You may find that your bank makes a charge of $1.00 or more for such a search.

How "Safe" Is Your Money?

It is almost impossible for most Americans to conceive of what it must have been like before federal government insurance of bank and savings association deposits—to imagine the tragedy when an innocent family's lifetime savings disappeared in the crash of the trusted bank on the corner.

But ponder what it is like now:

In recent years a fair number of banks have failed—several of them frighteningly large but *in no case did a depositor lose a single penny of his or her insured deposits.* The system has worked superbly well, there has been no worry—much less panic.

In recent years a fair number of savings and loan associations also have failed—*but not one depositor in an institution federally insured lost one penny of his or her insured funds either.*

Today, 98 per cent of our banks are insured by the Federal Deposit Insurance Corporation in Washington. The insurance fund, paid in by nearly

14,000 member banks throughout the nation, totaled an awesome $5 billion-plus in the mid-seventies. On top of that, the FDIC has authority to borrow as much as $3 billion additional from the U. S. Treasury.

As for us, 99 per cent of all bank depositors' savings and checking accounts are FDIC-insured, and as of the mid-1970s most of the funds we had on deposit in insured banks were covered up to a $40,000 limit.

In a recent year, too, about 4,200 federal and state-chartered savings and loan associations—out of a total of roughly 5,400—were insured by the Federal Savings and Loan Insurance Corporation in Washington. The FSLIC's fund totaled $3.1 billion and covered more than 96 per cent of the savings in insured associations. The vast majority of associations not covered by the FSLIC are backed by state insurance funds.

In 1974, all federally chartered credit unions were insured by the National Credit Union Administration—a total of approximately 12,700—and 1,705 of the 11,000-plus state-chartered credit unions were also federally insured. Many of the credit unions not protected by federal insurance have opted for other insurance alternatives and some states have mandatory laws for federal insurance.

It's not a perfect system for depositors, but it's coming close, and the performance record has been great.

Q. *What are the chances your bank might fail?*

A. Very slim indeed. In contrast to an average of 588 bank failures a year in the 1920s and an average of 2,277 in the 1930–33 period, bank failures averaged only 5 a year between 1943 and 1973 among all banks, and only 3 a year for insured banks. The record has been similar for insured savings and loan associations.

Q. *Are only savings and checking accounts insured?*

A. No. These other types of deposits also are insured: Christmas savings and other open-account time deposits, uninvested trust funds, certified checks, cashiers' checks, bank travelers checks, and all other deposits "received by a bank in its usual course of business."

Q. *If you have both a checking and a savings account, is each insured up to $40,000?*

A. No. All deposits under your own name are added together and this total is insured up to $40,000.

Q. *What if you have, in addition to your own accounts, a joint account with your husband?*

A. Your joint account, with your husband or your child, is insured separately for up to $40,000.

Q. *Are accounts kept at different banks insured separately?*

A. Yes. However, if you keep separate accounts at separate branches of your bank, all of these are considered as a single bank for the purposes of deposit insurance.

Q. *Are certificates of deposit covered?*

A. Yes. But they are not insured separately if they are held in the same bank at which you have other deposits in the same name.

Q. *How and when would you be paid in the event your bank failed?*

A. You might be paid, probably within a week of the date your bank closed, by an FDIC check which you could then either cash or have deposited in your name in another insured bank. Or, more likely, your funds would be transferred to a new bank under new management, and become available to you within a few days. The payment period might be more prolonged in the case of a savings association failure but the payment period of the FSLIC has generally been comparable to that of the FDIC.

Q. *Who pays for the insurance coverage on deposits?*

A. FDIC member banks, which are assessed approximately 1/30th of 1 per cent of their total deposits. Savings and loan associations pay higher assessments.

Here's a brief table to give you an idea of how much money you, a couple with one child, could keep in a single bank or savings and loan association, fully insured:

INDIVIDUAL ACCOUNTS

Man:	$40,000
Wife:	40,000
Child:	40,000

JOINT ACCOUNTS

Man and wife:	40,000
Man and child:	40,000
Wife and child:	40,000

TESTAMENTARY REVOCABLE TRUST ACCOUNTS

Man (as trustee for wife):	40,000
Man (as trustee for child):	40,000
Wife (as trustee for husband):	40,000
Wife (as trustee for child):	40,000

IRREVOCABLE TRUST ACCOUNTS

Man (as trustee for wife):	$40,000
Man (as trustee for child):	40,000
Wife (as trustee for husband):	40,000
Wife (as trustee for child):	40,000
TOTAL	$560,000

It's most unlikely anyone would keep this total in cash in a financial institution, but you can actually have *insured* savings of as much as $560,000 in one institution!

To get 100 per cent protection against the remote possibility of a bank failure, follow these two fundamental rules:

1. *Don't* keep more than the legal maximum in your individual accounts of all types in any one financial institution or its branches.

2. *Do* bank only with a federal- or state-insured institution. All insured institutions advertise this fact, so take the time to make sure your institution is properly insured.

But be reassured. Banking is among the most tightly regulated and closely scrutinized industries in the nation. And legal steps are continually being taken by federal and state regulatory agencies to make the system ever more failureproof.

SHOULD YOU RENT A SAFE DEPOSIT BOX?

You almost surely own a collection of records and valuables which *should* be stored in a bank safe deposit box—particularly in this period of soaring numbers of home burglaries and in view of the fact that many types of documents are very difficult if not impossible to replace.

Today, it costs only $5.00 to $15 a year to rent the small (typically 2 or 3 by 5 by 22 inches) safe deposit box most people find adequate. In some areas the cost is under $5.00. And, assuming you use the box to store such income-producing property as stocks or bonds, the rental charge is deductible from your federal income tax.

To be specific, you *should* rent a safe deposit box and put into it your valuables, hard-to-replace or irreplaceable items, including:

Any stock or bond certificates or bank savings certificates which you do not keep at your bank or with your stockbroker.

Insurance policies—except life insurance policies, which should be kept in a more accessible place in the event of your death.

Property records, including mortgages, deeds, titles.

Personal documents such as birth certificates, marriage licenses, divorce papers, citizenship papers, adoption papers, diplomas, business contracts and agreements, important legal correspondence and income tax records, passports, military discharge papers, and trust agreements.

An inventory of all household items of any value, giving the cost and purchase date of each item as a reference in case of fire or theft. This inventory should include photographs of furs and jewelry and fine pieces of art and furniture; serial numbers of TV sets, stereo sets, etc.; details about valuable coin or stamp collections you keep at home; jewels, collections of stamps or coins, heirlooms which you seldom wear or use or refer to.

A copy of your will—but *not* the original, which should be filed at your lawyer's office, kept in the hands of an executor, or in some similar protected but accessible place. Frequently a bank safe deposit box is sealed by state law for a specified period after the box owner's death.

Should you, as a married couple, own a safe deposit box jointly? How do you arrange for someone besides yourself to get in the box if need be?

The advantages of joint ownership of a safe deposit box are strongly offset by the disadvantages. You may squabble—when it comes to removing the box's contents—over which of you owns what. Or if a lawsuit is brought against one of you, this would tie up the property of the other—if it's in a jointly owned safe deposit box. As for what happens when *one* of two joint renters dies, ask your lawyer what are your own specific state laws covering this aspect.

Instead of joint ownership, you might authorize the other (or a lawyer or trusted relative) to serve as his or her "agent" if necessary. The first spouse keeps the keys and, technically at least, owns the entire contents of the safe deposit box. If the second spouse has valuables or important records of her or his own, there is no reason why this partner shouldn't have a separate box.

Once you make the decision to rent a safe deposit box, here are further rules for you to follow:

Make a list of what is in your box and put the list in a safe place at home. Your list should include: an identification of each valuable in the box; serial numbers and dates of stock or bond certificates, insurance policies, etc.; written appraisals of jewelry; the date you put each item in the box; the date you remove any item; the date of your most recent inspection. Keep this inventory up to date.

Collect receipts or other papers which prove you own the items in the box and put them in a safe place outside the box. Then you will have the essential papers should the box ever be destroyed or burglarized (most unlikely but possible).

Check your homeowner's insurance coverage to find out if it covers the contents of your safe deposit box and, if so, to what extent it insures you against loss. Also, check the agreement you sign or have signed with the institution from which you rent your box to find out if the agreement includes clauses which limit your protection. For instance, are you prohibited from putting cash or diamonds in the box?

Keep each other (husband and wife) informed about the location of your safe deposit box, the number of the box, the contents of the box, the place you keep the keys.

Of course, the odds are overwhelmingly against any loss of the contents of your safe deposit box due to a robbery or some other catastrophe. This is obvious from the way boxes are built and the location of the vaults. And remember, *nobody* but you, the box holder (and any agent you may name), has keys which can open the box.

3

HOW TO BORROW CASH
AND USE CREDIT WISELY

INTRODUCTION

Should you borrow money NOW?

Of course you should—*if* you have sound (to you) reasons for doing so.

Is this the RIGHT TIME *for you to borrow money?*

Of course it is—*if* your reasons for borrowing are sound and your chances of repaying your debt within a tolerable period of time are good.

"Of course" always will be the answer to both these questions assuming your debt is for goods or services you feel you need or want, your loan is in line with your income, you have a plan for regular repayments.

There are two distinct sides to the possession of money: one is saving it, the other borrowing it. In our economy, both sides are crucially important to our financial health as a nation and as individuals. And both sides make vital contributions to our financial well-being as a nation and as individuals.

It is no exaggeration to say that almost uninterrupted buying on the installment plan has become a way of life in American homes to a point where a hefty percentage of the families we consider as representing the "ideal" in our nation are never out of debt and another hefty proportion seldom are.

That was, in fact, one of the most provocative findings which emerged from a survey I made a few years ago of the finalists in the "Mrs. America Pageant"—all outstanding women, bright, talented, good-looking, superb homemakers. What leaped first from their answers was how knowledgeable the women were, how acutely aware they were of money management, how devoted they were to budgeting, even "strict" down-to-the-penny keeping of the household accounts. And what leaped next from their answers and impressed me even more was the extent to which installment buying was an essential part of their family lives.

As one contestant put it to me: "We find that the best way to obtain major items is to maintain planned debt, purchasing one major item at a time for a cost which will fit into our budget and including interest as part of that cost." In the words of another, "We consider it worth the interest cost to use someone else's money and have earlier use of a product."

The statistics underline this further. More than one out of every two U.S. families today owes installment debt. And it's a virtual certainty that you have installment debt *if:* you are married and the head of a family; you are between eighteen and thirty-five years of age; you have children, teen-agers or younger; your income is between $5,000 and $25,000 a year. Nine of every ten families with these four basic characteristics have installment debts.

I do not find the modern attitudes toward debt any cause for alarm. I see nothing wrong with paying money to use "someone else's money." I approve of "planned debt" which really is a kind of thrift. And, to an important degree, payments on an installment loan are merely replacing many old-time cash payments—like the money Americans used to dole out to the ice man or the cash we paid to the corner laundry.

In fact, I'll go beyond this and submit that the fundamental reason Americans have been borrowing so much today is precisely because they have had so much. This has intensified your desire to satisfy your aspirations rather than simply to finance your needs. And this in turn has led to unprecedented borrowing to achieve your aspirations at once.

Another factor is your increased financial security—through health insurance, Social Security, unemployment compensation, retirement pensions, employee savings and stock plans, ownership of stocks and mutual funds, life insurance, etc.—and, very importantly, the income of the working wife. All these economic cushions are helping to make obsolete the traditional goal of protection against a "rainy day." (See Chapter 1, "Your Personal Money Manager," and Part III, "Managing Your Money.")

A third similarly subtle factor is the increased *regularity* of your income, which strengthens your capacity to take on responsibility for repaying installment debts. This development stems from the fundamental fact that our economy is now dominated by the service industries—and employment is much steadier in a service-oriented economy than in a predominantly industrial society.

Other factors include: the huge amounts of financial assets you as families are building up, primarily in your homes; the dramatic extension of credit to include unsophisticated as well as sophisticated borrowers; the youthful hunger to acquire, instantly, all the things that other families have; and finally, the tendency of lenders to extend credit to borrowers at much younger ages than ever before.

And, of course, behind all the factors is the basic change that inflation has created in your attitudes toward being in debt and toward the goods and services which you appropriately may buy on time.

Perhaps as fundamental as any point is this: You, today's American, are far less interested than past generations in your legal total ownership of your toasters or automobiles or refrigerators. Instead, you are far more interested in the toasting services of that toaster, the transportation services of that automobile, the cooling services of that refrigerator. You are less and less impressed with *owning things,* more and more interested in the proper *use of things.*

The Right and Wrong Reasons for Borrowing

The cheapest way to buy any thing or non-thing is to buy it for cash. You *always* save money when you do this, for there are no extra charges added to your purchase price. As a buyer for cash, you can shop around for the best buy. Also, as a buyer for cash, you don't tie up future income, you are well aware of how many dollars you actually are spending, and you are not tempted to overbuy. The reason that retailers dangle the lure of "easy credit terms" before you is that the lure does work. It does encourage you to buy more. It does increase the retailer's sales.

But when you borrow to buy some things or non-things, you get the privilege of enjoying the purchase while you pay for it. You can start using at once something you need or want instead of being forced to wait until you can accumulate the savings to finance its purchase. Your buying on credit can teach you thrift. The discipline forced on you by your installment payments can spill over and encourage you to develop excellent saving habits. Many types of credit charge accounts are more convenient than cash or checks. Credit can be a crucial assist in a financial emergency.

To me, the advantages of buying on credit far outweigh the disadvantages of the cost of credit and the possible extravagance.

THE RIGHT REASONS FOR BORROWING

Regardless of whether you are equally convinced at this point, for the moment assume you agree that borrowing money is right for you if your reasons are right.

What might those reasons be?

(1) You are establishing a household or beginning to have a family. Either of these major events in life will take a lot of money—and it's in these, your early years, that you should learn how to use credit wisely and to the best advantage for yourself.

(2) You must make some major purchases. Few Americans can buy a car out of cash on hand and few can buy furniture or appliances that way either. These big-ticket items are traditionally bought with credit. As for a

house, virtually all of us borrow to finance that key purchase of our lives. (See Chapter 13, "A Roof Over Your Head," for details.)

(3) You are faced with a genuine emergency and have not as yet had the opportunity to accumulate a sufficient emergency cash fund. Borrowing to meet emergencies is about as valid a reason as there can be.

(4) There are attractive seasonal sales or specials on which you can save money if you can use a charge account or a time-payment plan or get a low-cost loan from a financial institution. This assumes that the items on sale are ones you really want or need.

(5) You need money for college or other education expenses. This also is a top-notch reason for borrowing either by the student or by the parents. In fact, borrowing for college is the normal thing in America in this era. See Chapter 10, "A College Education and How to Finance It," for details.

(6) The price of an item you will need in the future is heading sharply higher and it is ridiculous for you not to try to beat the price rise by borrowing the money to buy it now.

THE WRONG REASONS FOR BORROWING

(1) You haven't a reasonable prospect of repaying the loan but you are going ahead anyway and borrowing because you need the money or want the goods or services. Or you are borrowing to the very hilt of your capacity to repay, which means that even a minor miscalculation on your part could force you to default.

(2) You are buying something impulsively and are primarily attracted to the purchase, not because the product is of good quality and reasonably priced, but because the payment terms seem so easy and you are offered a long time to pay up. This is self-deception of the most dangerous kind from your personal financial point of view.

(3) You are charging purchases solely to boost your morale. Some individuals try to beat the blues with an extravagant shopping spree. Doing this on credit can bring on an even bigger attack of melancholy when the bills—with interest—finally come due.

(4) You are using credit to increase your status. Charging a purchase does allow you to pay for things while you're enjoying them. But credit alone can't raise your standard of living. Over the long run, if you "can't afford" certain items on your present income, you can't afford to buy them on credit.

(5) You are overusing credit generally and failing to maintain an adequate cash reserve. People who do this also tend to live hand to mouth with their cash. They build up little or no savings fund to use during medical or other emergencies. So even if they are able to repay regular debts on schedule, any unexpected financial reversal can be their complete undoing.

(6) You are using credit against the expectation of future salary increases or windfall cash. When your income is on the rise, it's tempting to

figure that your next raise is a cinch. But if you go ahead with major credit expenditures and then don't get the extra money, your budget can get very, very tight in a hurry.

(7) You are borrowing to gamble on some exceedingly risky venture—as distinct from borrowing to invest in a worthy enterprise you have thoroughly investigated. Borrowing to buy stocks or real estate or invest in a small business deal is entirely in order, particularly if you are young enough to recoup if you lose. But borrowing to gamble is begging for trouble—and the very fact that you have to borrow means that this is not extra money you can afford to lose.

(8) You are living so far beyond your income that you have to borrow to meet your current bills. In Chapter 3, in the section entitled "How Much Debt Is Too Much Debt?" you'll find several guidelines on the safe limits for borrowing. Suffice it to say here that when you must pile up debts just to manage your day-to-day living you are headed for financial disaster.

(9) You are borrowing to buy something that will be used up or worn out long before you have made the final payment for it. This caution is exceedingly flexible, though, and you must use your common sense in applying it to yourself.

For instance, it might make sense to take out a twelve-month installment loan to pay for this year's vacation, for even though you would still be paying off the loan after the vacation is a memory, it could be worth it if you wouldn't have any vacation otherwise. But it would not make sense to take out a two-year loan for this year's vacation, for in this case you would still be paying off this year's vacation when next year's vacation time rolls around.

Another illustration of this point (9) is borrowing to pay for college education or special training courses. You well may be paying off a loan years after you've completed your education but the value of your education will endure years and years after that. In this case, the value of your purchase is without time limit and cannot be measured by the yardsticks which we use for material goods. But precisely the opposite is borrowing to pay for an exceedingly expensive gown. Buy this sort of gown for cash if you have it, and if this is your deep desire. But *borrowing* to buy it? That's financial stupidity.

THE BASIC DO'S AND DON'TS OF CREDIT

No matter where you go for credit and no matter how many different types of loans you take out in the years to come, the basic *do's* and *don'ts* of credit will remain the same. Below you'll find them in the form of a simple check list to which you can refer again and again to make sure you are obeying these most fundamental of all credit rules.

Do always keep in mind that credit costs money. When you borrow you are, in essence, renting money—and just as you must pay when you rent an apartment or a car, so you must pay when you rent money. Anything you buy on credit will cost you more money than the identical item bought for cash.

Do shop for credit as you shop for any other important purchase and buy your credit on the most advantageous terms to *you*. You can compare credit terms much more easily today than before the Truth in Lending law went into effect in 1969. Compare the price of any item bought for cash or bought on the installment plan. Find out whether it's cheaper for you to borrow from a bank or credit union and then buy the item you want for cash—or whether it's better for you to finance the purchase at the store or dealer's.

Do check with care the maximum amount of credit you can soundly and safely carry. You can do it against the guidelines you'll find in this chapter and you also can check your credit status with a responsible loan officer at your local bank, consumer finance office, credit union, other lending source. This officer is in the business of "selling" money—and nothing else—and he will want to make sure the person to whom he is selling the money is in a sound position to pay back.

Do ask lots of questions about the credit deal you are being offered, if you have any doubts at all. Insist on a written statement from the salesman showing you all charges plus the cash cost *before* you decide on buying.

Do ask yourself: would you buy the item for this amount of money in cash if you had the cash in your wallet or purse right now? Would you buy as expensive an item as the one you are considering if you had to put down the entire sum in cash now? In short, have you taken the proper *time* to make sure that this is a good purchase for you in view of the *time* it will take you to pay for it?

Do study your installment contract with utmost care and be sure you understand it before you sign it. When you sign, get a copy of the contract and keep it in a safe place.

Do keep receipts of your payments in a safe place.

Do pay off one major installment debt obligation before you take on another. Stagger your debts; don't pile them one on top of another.

Do make sure that, in the installment deal you sign, all your monthly payments are roughly equal and make sure this applies particularly to your last payment. Avoid the danger that you'll be faced with a very big final installment ("balloon" payment). (See "The Great Pitfalls of Credit" later in this chapter.)

Do have the courage to say *No!* to an installment deal if any of the above warning signals are flying—any of them.

And *do* continue saving regularly as you buy on credit. Even if you can save only a small amount each week, save it. For it's the regularity of savings and the discipline of the installment payments which will be the foundation of your own and your family's wealth.

Don't buy any item or service from any seller unless you have checked his reputation and have confidence he is a responsible retailer or dealer or whatever. Before you pledge to pay a specified part of your earnings for a protracted period, use your common sense and make sure you are dealing with a reputable businessman conducting a reputable business at a reputable place and that you can come back to him should your purchase turn out to be a lemon.

Don't buy anything you don't need or want—certainly not for credit. Learn how to handle high-pressure selling.

Don't carry several charge accounts which are seldom or never paid up. Revolving accounts make it very easy to maintain a permanent debt. But pay off each account periodically, for without this kind of self-discipline, revolving balances tend to grow ever larger (and more expensive) over periods of time.

Don't use your debts to establish your budgeting "system." Although some people would have no financial system at all if it weren't for their stack of bills, wise use of credit means month-by-month planning—not this sort of upside-down method.

Don't ever buy any thing or non-thing on credit without consulting your spouse or other person with whom you may be sharing financial responsibility and making sure that the two of you think the purchase is worth while. You must agree on any major purchase or you'll have great difficulty meeting the discipline of installment payments.

Don't be in any hurry to sign any installment contract or agreement.

Don't make the mistake of thinking you can get out of an installment debt simply by returning the merchandise you bought to the seller. What you almost surely have done when you bought the item is sign two contracts: one for the actual purchase and the second for the money to finance the purchase. In most cases, your loan contract will be sold by the retailer at once to a bank or finance company and it is to this bank or finance company that you will have to continue making your payments in full—even though your TV set may not show a picture or your dishwasher may not wash a dish or your automobile may not move a mile.

Don't rely on verbal warranties or pledges of the salesman or his boss. Get the warranties and pledges in writing.

Don't buy any item on credit which does not have a value that will outlast the installment payments. This is an extension of the flexible wrong reason No. 9 for borrowing. The key word in this rule is "value."

Don't buy anything on credit of which you will tire before you finish the installment payments. You might really ponder this "don't" when buying your four-year-old an expensive and easily breakable toy game on a twelve-month payment plan.

Don't ever borrow money from a loan shark—even if you are desperate for the cash. In fact, the more desperate you are for the money, the more insane it is for you to commit yourself to pay back interest rates ranging to 1,000 per cent a year and more for the money. This way lies financial disaster.

Don't sign any loan contract which contains blank spaces that could be filled in to your disadvantage.

And *don't* co-sign a loan for anyone unless you have complete faith in that person's ability and willingness to repay the loan. For, if the borrower whose note you co-sign defaults on the loan, *you* are responsible for paying off the entire indebtedness.

How Do You Establish a Credit Rating?

A young Army veteran, with a wife and two babies, was recently turned down for an FHA mortgage which he needed to buy a new home in eastern Texas. The reason: information at the local credit bureau showed him to be a bad credit risk. Astonished, the veteran visited the credit bureau and discovered that the reason for his credit troubles was that his former wife had run up a lot of unpaid bills just prior to their divorce. The veteran explained that under the separation agreement his estranged wife had signed a full year before she ran up the bills, she was legally responsible for all her debts and his credit record had been wrongly damaged. His credit record was cleared and he got the mortgage he needed.

The ease with which Americans can open a charge account, get a new credit card, or take out a bank loan is directly dependent on the voluminous dossiers in the files of 2,500 credit bureaus throughout the United States and of large numbers of local merchants' associations on virtually every borrower. The bureaus freely exchange this information. They sell it to retailers, banks, other lenders, credit card companies, corporations, etc.—and a credit report almost surely will be obtained on you when you apply for a job or insurance or credit.

The consumer credit reporting industry processes from 125 to 150 million credit reports each year. Just one computerized credit reporting company says it maintains 30 million files, enters 4 million "pieces of information" on individuals each month, services 14,000 subscribers, and maintains on some individuals as many as 35 to 40 open accounts on which credit performance is reported.

Credit bureaus do *not* "rate" how good or bad a credit risk you are. They simply collect, from merchants with whom you have credit, public records, other sources of information on you which can be used in turn by banks, merchants, etc., to decide whether to grant you credit. The information ranges from your name, address, occupation, employer, and earnings to your former employment and earnings record, your marital history, your moving habits, your repayment patterns on previous loans, and records of any court proceedings against you.

The lenders then decide, on the basis of information provided by the credit bureau, whether or not you are a good credit risk. The guidelines vary from lender to lender, of course. A department store may be satisfied if you are in the habit of repaying charges within thirty to sixty days, while a bank may demand that, with very few exceptions, you repay bank loan installments on the due dates.

Or lenders may summarize their policies by telling you they are rating your application in terms of the "Three C's" of Credit. These Three C's are your:

Character: Your personal characteristics, revealed through factual records, which indicate how you are likely to perform as a borrower. These would include your honesty, sense of responsibility, soundness of judgment, your trustworthiness.

Capacity: Your financial ability to repay your loan. Your capacity would be judged on the basis of the job you hold, the amount of money you earn, the length of time you have held this or a previous job, your prospects in this or another job.

Capital: Your assets which can serve as backing—collateral—for your loan. These assets would include your home, bank accounts, stocks and bonds, a car or cars, jewelry, valuable paintings, other tangible property.

These three qualities of Character, Capacity, and Capital form the foundation of any credit rating for you, as an individual or as a family.

To get even more specific, here are points which every lending officer will tick off when considering your application for a loan and your rating as a credit risk.

Your Employment Record: How long have you worked for the same company—although not necessarily in the same office or plant of the company?

A prime consideration is the stability of your employment. It is up to you to prove your trustworthiness by showing you have not been a job-hopper who might once again leave for a job far away from your present one when, say, less than half your loan payments have been made.

Your Previous Loans: Have you ever paid off a loan before? The theory is that, if you have repaid a loan on time before this one, you will repay this loan too. If you have defaulted on any previous loan, the danger is you'll default again. You'll almost certainly have a poor credit rating if you have any record of defaults or of repossession of items you have bought because you didn't maintain your payments or of suits for being delinquent in payments.

Your Home: Do you own your own home? Or have you lived in the apartment in which you now live for some time? If the answer is "yes" to either question, it's a sign that you probably are trustworthy.

Your Charge Accounts: Have you a record of paying your charge accounts regularly? If so, this will be a plus mark for you because it will indicate your sense of responsibility and your ability to repay.

Your Checking or Savings Accounts: Do you have either? If so, and particularly if they are at the bank to which you may be applying for a loan, this will be a great help.

Now here are six potential black marks on your credit rating:

(1) If you can't identify yourself. Surely you will have one or more of these: a driver's license, birth certificate, Social Security card, draft card, union card.

(2) If you have a "floating" address. This might be a furnished room in a rooming house or a transient hotel, a post office box number, a mail address in care of a friend. You might offset this, however, if previously you had lived in one place for a long time.

(3) If your employment is in an exceedingly unstable industry or profession and your own job is also basically volatile. If you're a ballet dancer . . . have a strictly seasonal job . . . are in a very restricted field. . . .

(4) If, in some states, you are under twenty-one or eighteen and have no adult to co-sign for you. However, many stores do extend credit to teens without a co-signer anyway, for as a group they have turned out to be good credit risks.

(5) If you apply for a loan at a bank or small loan company or other financial source far from your residence or if you have a record of dealing extensively with numerous small loan companies.

(6) If you are planning to go into the armed services before your loan is repaid. Under these circumstances, the lender almost surely will demand that a co-signer guarantee your loan repayment.

HOW TO MAINTAIN OR RESTORE A GOOD CREDIT RATING

How do you keep up a good credit record? Or *restore* one if it has gone bad? Here are the key rules:

• Avoid overloading yourself with installment debt. Note those guidelines on how much debt is too much debt for you and abide by them!

• Aim for and maintain a rainy-day fund in cash or its equivalent equal to two to three months' pay.

• Be truthful when you apply for credit and repay all your debts as agreed. But if you find you are unable to meet one or more payments on time, go to the creditors involved, explain your circumstances, and try to work out a more practical repayment schedule. The problem could be merely that payments on a loan or a purchase fall due on the twelfth of the month, though your pay check doesn't arrive until the fifteenth.

• Do everything possible to avoid such extreme measures as repossession, litigation, or having your account turned over to a collection agency. However, if any of these is threatened, go to your credit granters first, explain what happened, and in many cases they will be willing to extend your payment schedule. Or they may refer you to a reliable local credit counseling service.

But what if you are turned down for credit and believe the turndown is unwarranted? Turn to Part IV, "Your Rights and How to Get Them," Chapter 27, for details on what to do.

WHAT IS THE DIFFERENCE BETWEEN CREDIT REPORTS AND INVESTIGATIVE REPORTS?

A regular *credit report* is compiled and maintained by a credit bureau for the purpose of helping consumers obtain credit. The credit bureaus do not make use of outside investigators, who are sometimes used in insurance reporting.

The information normally accumulated in your credit record consists of identity information, including your name, address, marital status, and Social Security number; present employment, which includes the position you hold, length of employment, and income; your personal history, such as date of birth, number of dependents, previous address, and previous employment information; credit history information including your credit experiences with credit granters; and public-record information which credit granters feel is important to know.

An *investigative report* consists of much more information—including data about a consumer's character, general reputation, personal characteristics, or mode of living. The information usually is obtained through personal interviews with the consumer's neighbors, friends, or associates or with others with whom the consumer is acquainted.

Credit bureaus do not normally compile this type of report, although an employment report made by a credit bureau will often contain some investigative information.

THE BASIC TYPES AND MATURITIES OF LOANS

THE SINGLE-PAYMENT LOAN

This is precisely what its name implies: a loan you must repay in one lump sum. A single-payment loan may be a demand loan, meaning there will be no set time when you must repay but you will be obligated to pay back what you owe when the lender asks you to. Or the single-payment loan may be a time loan, meaning your loan will have a fixed maturity date and you'll have to pay back every penny on that prefixed maturity date.

A single-payment loan is usually made against collateral, meaning that you must put up certain valuable assets, such as your stocks, bonds, insurance policies, etc., to guarantee the loan repayment. The primary drawback of the single-payment loan is that you do not have to make periodic payments on it and thus you are not disciplined into reducing the loan month after month until it is all paid off. Instead you are faced with the entire repayment on a single date.

THE INSTALLMENT LOAN

This also is precisely what its name implies: a loan you must pay off in specified amounts at periodic intervals.

Usually you repay an installment loan in equal amounts every month over a period from twelve to sixty months. Usually, too, the interest cost is figured on the total amount of your loan.

In addition to these two basic types of loans, there are three major *maturities* on loans.

A SHORT-TERM LOAN

This is the type of loan you use most frequently either to buy goods or to obtain cash or to finance everyday services.

For instance, you're using short-term credit when you buy a big-ticket appliance on the installment plan and promise to pay off within twelve to thirty-six months. You are also using short-term credit when you get a cash loan—single-payment or installment payment—and promise to pay off within three years. Whether it's "cash" credit or "sales" credit, whether it's "installment" credit or "non-installment" credit, whether it's a "demand" loan or "time" loan, you're using short-term credit if you pledge to repay within a period ranging from as little as thirty days to three years.

AN INTERMEDIATE-TERM LOAN

This is the type of credit you use most often when you are financing major improvements or major repairs on your home. The maturity of this type of loan ranges from five to seven or even to ten years.

A LONG-TERM LOAN

This type is implicit in its name. A familiar example is the real estate mortgage, extended over a period ranging from twenty to thirty years or even more—and repayable in regular installments at fixed intervals, usually monthly, during the life of the loan. Of course, you may get a long-term loan for other purposes but the mortgage is the best illustration of this category.

YOUR SOURCES OF LOANS IN CASH

If you want to buy a new TV set you don't just walk into the first TV store you pass and buy it. You look around, decide which model you prefer, then shop for the dealer who offers the set you want at the most favorable price to you.

Okay, *you* want to buy *money*.

Whatever the reasons why—whatever goods or service you want to buy or whatever you want to build or finance—you need more money than you're earning each week or are able to commit for this single purpose. Whatever the amount—$500 or $2,500 or $5,000 or whatever—you are about to borrow (buy) money and pay the interest rate (price) asked by the lender (seller).

You live in a highly competitive economy, though, and the price of money in this competitive economy, like the price of everything else, will vary considerably. There are many sources for cash loans. Many compete for your patronage on the basis of price, convenience, service. Many also compete by specializing in specific types of loans. Many of them—such as your parents, other relatives, or friends—are simply "there." But never forget this key point: you easily can pay a price (interest rate) hundreds of dollars a year *more* than you need to pay by going to a lender who is not the best for you. You easily can cheat yourself disgracefully by not shopping for your money.

Let's approach this vital aspect of your financial life in the simplest way possible. To begin with, here are your sources of loans in cash.

PARENTS OR OTHER RELATIVES

Your parents or other relatives could be your best, easiest source of low-cost or no-cost loans. Assuming they have money available and are eager to help, your search for a cash loan may end right here.

Typical maximum you may borrow:

That depends on your relatives' affluence, their attitudes toward lending you money, your needs, your relationships, etc. In short, obviously there is no "typical" maximum.

Typical annual interest rate:

Yours could be a no-interest loan or you could insist on paying the same interest rate you would pay another lender (say, what you would pay the bank on the corner). I opt strongly for paying an interest rate and also for matching at least the minimum you might be charged by an outside source of credit. But this is your loan negotiation and again the obvious point is there is no "typical" charge.

Typical maximum maturity:

There is no typical maximum maturity and, just because most loans made by the parents would have no maturity date, the loan might drag on and on. This lack of a definite maturity can be both an advantage and a disadvantage.

Advantages:

There is no legal pressure on you to meet regular monthly payments, even if you do have a moral, if not contractual, responsibility to try to pay back the loan as soon as you can.

Your parents may have a sympathetic understanding of the reasons you are borrowing and be eager to help you.

Disadvantages:

The embarrassment of having to ask your parents or other relatives for financial help.

The very lack of pressure on you to repay may make you lazy about repaying and the debt could continue hanging over your head much longer than it need to or should.

The amounts you borrow may be too large or too small, because the personal relationships will affect your judgments on both sides.

FRIENDS

A loan from a close friend or a group of close friends with sufficient extra cash and interest in you to be your loan source is in the same general category as a loan from your parents or other relatives.

This applies even though your friends may be backing you in a venture they think is as exciting and promising as you do and even though there is a stated or implied pledge on your part to let them share liberally in any profits you make, for presumably you are also making the same explicit or implied pledge to share the profits with your own relatives. And if you aren't, you should.

Typical maximum you may borrow:

None. See above.

Typical annual interest rate:

Also none. But I repeat it's only common sense to insist on paying roughly the same interest rates you would pay the local bank.

Typical maximum maturity:

None. However, again I suspect your friends will work out a maturity date of some sort—and if they don't, *you* work it out.

Advantages:

In general, the same advantages that apply to a loan from parents or other relatives apply to loans from close friends. But I warn you: a loan from friends easily can corrode your friendship even if you pay it off promptly.

Disadvantages:

The same disadvantages apply to these loans as to loans from relatives.

ADVANCE AGAINST SALARY OR LOAN FROM EMPLOYER

Most employers are reluctant to advance a salary pay check or to make a personal loan. This generality, though, by no means applies to all employers, and in fact many corporations have special departments through which employees may borrow money with a minimum of red tape. Also your boss may be an acceptable loan source for you if yours is a close friendly relationship in a small office.

But an advance against your future salary—say your next two pay checks delivered right now—means you will face two empty pay periods some days hence.

Typical maximum you may borrow:

This varies so widely from corporation to corporation and small business to small business that it would be a disservice to be specific. Also, in a small business, the maximum will depend on the business' profit picture, the employer's financial position, your relationship with the employer, your reasons for borrowing, and on and on.

Typical annual interest rate:

Usually the same interest rate that you would be charged if you went to a bank for a loan. However, I know of no employer who charges interest on a salary advance. Other conditions of the salary advance are subject to private negotiation between the employer or the corporation personnel manager and the employee.

Typical maximum maturity:

Usually six months to a year although, again, this maximum varies widely among both large and small businesses.

Advantages:

The money is there.

Your employer may be a most sympathetic lender if he knows and approves the reasons you are borrowing.

The interest rate and repayment period will be among the best available from all sources.

An advance on your salary is simply borrowing in advance money due you in the future and involves no more than that.

Disadvantages:

Borrowing money from your boss can hurt your relationship with him and place you in a sticky position.

This loan may permit him to ask and find out things about your personal financial life which you would prefer he not know.

If you take an advance on your salary, you may not be able to swing the payless pay periods and you may have to go to outside sources for cash after all.

FULL SERVICE COMMERCIAL BANK

For most of you a commercial bank will be the most convenient loan source of all. For at this bank, which is probably a mere city block or two from where you live in town or only a couple miles away if you live in the suburbs, you may get the widest variety of loans including:

Personal loan

You may apply for a personal loan, repayable in one lump sum at its due date, or you may apply for an installment loan repayable in regular monthly installments over a period of twelve, eighteen, twenty-four, or thirty-six months.

Automobile loan

You may apply for an automobile loan to finance your new or used car. These loans usually are repayable in installments ranging from twelve to forty-two or even forty-eight months. Many automobile dealers as well as other merchants help the customer arrange for bank installment financing right in their showrooms.

Check loan

You may get money simply by writing a check, assuming you qualify. Your bank automatically enters the "loan" on your monthly statement of checking account transactions.

Mortgage and home improvement loan

You may get home improvement loans with intermediate maturities under which you can repair, remodel, expand, and generally improve your home. And you may get a long-term mortgage through which you may finance the purchase of your home in the first place.

Secured loan

You may get a loan quickly and comparatively inexpensively simply by putting up collateral to back your pledge to repay the loan. You can arrange to repay this loan in monthly installments. Your collateral may include your stocks or bonds or mutual fund shares or savings account passbook or the cash surrender value of your life insurance policy.

Student loan

Banks offer several types of student loans—some government subsidized, some not.

Credit card loan

You, the owner of a bank credit card, may use your card to buy goods at stores participating in the bank's credit card plan. The bank bills you monthly, and you, the borrower, pay interest on the unpaid balance you owe on your purchases. There is no interest charge, typically, for the first twenty-five or thirty days of your unpaid balance.

Or you may use your bank credit card to borrow a limited amount of cash.

Typical maximums you may borrow:

$5,000 on a personal loan; auto loan.*

$50,000 on a mortgage loan.*

$10,000 on a home improvement loan.*

$2,500 a year on a federal-state-guaranteed student loan.

$1,000 on a check loan.

$500 to $750 on a bank credit card plan.*

Up to the amount in your savings account on a passbook loan and up to a specified proportion of the estimated value of the collateral you put up to back a secured loan.

Typical annual interest rates:

So flexible and variable from year to year and loan to loan and area to area that no "typical" figure has meaning to you for long. However, here were typical rates as of 1974.

Personal loan:	10.5 to 13%
Automobile loan:	
New car	9 to 12
Used car	11 to 16

* Although these are typical amounts in most cases, banks are *not* in any way limited to making loans in these amounts.

Check loan:	12	to 18
Mortgage loan:	8	to 11
Home improvement loan:	10	to 15
Passbook loan:	9	to 10
Secured loan:	10	to 13
Federal-guaranteed student loan:		7
Credit card loan:	12	to 18
Education loan:	9	to 12

Typical maximum maturities:*

Three to four years on personal loans, auto loans, secured loans.

Five to seven years on home improvement loans.

Up to thirty or thirty-five years on first mortgages and three to ten years on second mortgages.

Up to twenty-five to thirty years on refinancing mortgages.

By regulation, up to ten years after graduation on student loans.

Advantages:

Simplicity: you fill out an application and a financial statement, have an interview with the bank loan officer, and quite likely your cash loan is approved within twenty-four hours.

Objectivity: you can get a loan whether or not you are a depositor at the bank and, although of course bank practices vary widely, generally you will qualify for a loan if your credit rating is okay and your income will enable you to handle the monthly payment.

Relatively inexpensive: rates on bank loans compare favorably with rates from most other loan sources and so do bank loan maturity terms.

No extra or hidden fees or charges; under the law, there must be full disclosure of terms.

Since co-makers are not usually required, you need not appeal to friends or business acquaintances to endorse your note.

When you have fulfilled the terms of the loan, as prescribed, you have established a valuable credit reference.

The insurance the bank may take out on your life protects your family, for should you die before the loan's repayment the insurance will repay the loan. (Note: This insurance may be comparatively costly, though.)

Even in instances where the insurance is optional, banks generally make it most convenient for you to obtain credit life insurance plus health and accident insurance at the time the loan is made.

* Typical but actual maximums set by bank policy.

Disadvantages:

The requirements—your personal financial standing, credit rating—are sometimes more rigid than other lenders may demand.

You will be penalized if you take out an installment loan and don't meet your monthly installments on schedule. The penalty is often a flat fee of 5 per cent, plus interest, for each delinquency. State laws generally prescribe allowable charges for delinquency.

How to use "ready credit":

How does this form of credit work? Who qualifies for it? When is it economical to use it and when not?

Ready credit is an automatic line of credit offered by your bank. In some cases its reserve is an extension of your checking account. In others the reserve may be kept in a separate account involving special checks. Usually the reserve is between $500 and $1,000, but it may run up to $5,000.

In either case, the overdraft check or special check you may write becomes a loan as soon as it reaches your bank. In either case also, the typical interest rate, including credit life insurance, is 1 per cent a month on the basis of the daily outstanding balance, which works out to a true annual interest rate of at least 12 per cent. Typically, no interest charge is made unless and until you actually use your special line of credit, and the interest charge stops when you repay the amount you have withdrawn from your reserve.

"Ready credit" is granted by a signed agreement to qualified customers and the requirements for eligibility are generally stricter than those for ordinary bank loans because it is unsecured credit and, once granted, is available year after year to the responsible borrower.

As an illustration of the costs involved at 1 per cent a month interest, let's say you overdrew your checking account by $100. If you repaid the amount one month later, the cost to you would be $1.00. If you repaid the total after one week, the cost would be 23¢. If you repaid it in one day, the cost would be 3¢.

Under what circumstances is it to your advantage to use this type of credit and when is it a disadvantage? Here are the answers:

• If you spot a major bargain, an appliance selling at a big discount, for example, you probably would save by using the overdraft plan. Here, the amount of interest you would pay would be comfortably covered by your savings on the appliance, assuming you repaid the special loan within a few weeks or even a few months.

• If an emergency arises on a weekend, or when you are far from home, a reserve credit line may be the easiest and surest way to raise emergency funds.

• If you are a chronically bad bookkeeper, the interest on a reserve credit line might be less costly to you than a pile of service charges for department stores or for overdraft checks. It might also save you the tremendous embarrassment of bouncing checks.

• If you are self-employed or if your income goes into sharp but temporary dips, this credit may provide you with enough peace of mind to make it worth the interest you pay.

To save on interest expense, a fundamental guide is that your line of ready credit should be strictly for short-term purposes and your overdrafts should be repaid as quickly as possible. Thus, "ready credit" is *not* usually the right type for you when you're paying longer-term debts—financing a car, a planned home improvement, your college education. Banks offer other types of loans more appropriate for these purposes and generally at lower interest rates.

LICENSED SMALL LOAN COMPANY

Over the years, leading small loan companies the nation over have spent countless tens of millions of dollars to advertise their willingness and readiness to extend financial aid to you, the little fellow. They have boasted that they exist to help solve your emergency problems and the littler you are the more welcome you are. Their very name—small loan company—inspires the trust of the would-be borrower. (Other well-known names are "consumer finance company" and "personal finance company." All have the same appeal.)

There is no doubt that these companies have filled and do fill an important place in our financial structure. You will note from the interest rate range below that the small loan companies charge a comparatively high rate of interest—but there are explanations. For one thing, they borrow part of their own capital from banks so they themselves are paying a high rate of interest to get the money to lend in turn to you. For another, small loan companies lend to individuals who do not have top credit ratings and who well might receive a flat "no" from a local bank. Inevitably, they have to write off a number of these risky loans or spend considerable money and time collecting the money due them.

Small loan companies specialize in personal and automobile loans and offer both single-payment and installment loans. As for security, the usual requirement of the small loan companies is nothing more than your promise to pay: i.e., your signature. Under certain conditions, they also ask additional security in the form of a chattel mortgage on your household furniture, to make sure that you will honor your debt.

If, though, you have a questionable credit rating and do not have a regular source of income, the small loan company may demand that a qualified friend co-sign for your loan. If you, the borrower, then fail to meet your payments, your co-signer will become responsible for the unpaid balance of your loan.

Typical maximum you may borrow:

$500 to $1,000—with the actual limits (some are higher) depending on state law.

Typical annual interest rate:

State laws generally prescribe interest rate ceilings but rates often are two to three times higher than bank interest charges.

Typical maximum maturities:

One to three years.

Advantages:

Frequently you can obtain a smaller loan from a small loan company than from a bank. You may even borrow just a few dollars if that is all you need.

The small loan companies are not as selective as banks. They can take greater risks just because they charge higher rates.

As the charge is based on the unpaid balance of your loan, you pay only for the credit you actually use.

Suits for collection are relatively infrequent and lawyers' fees are rarely imposed on a delinquent borrower.

If you have a grievance against a small loan company, you may take it to the state banking department and get advice and help at no expense.

You also may take a gripe about a small loan company to the Consumer Affairs Center of the National Consumer Finance Association, 1000 16th Street, N.W., Washington, D.C. 20036. Telephone (202) 638-1340.

Disadvantages:

The interest rates are much higher than those charged by full service commercial banks.

The maximum amount you can borrow is often less than you can get from banks and less than you need.

You may not be able to get the loan without a co-signer.

CREDIT UNION

A credit union may be the ideal answer to your borrowing problem if you have access to one and the union is efficiently managed.

Few, if any, regular lending agencies have the credit union's advantages of low operating costs, tax exemption, and often free office space, clerical and managerial help too. Thus naturally no other type of lender can afford to make loans at the low rates credit unions charge or can compete with the credit unions on service to borrowers.

Credit unions usually are formed by members of a closely knit group—such as employees of a business firm or members of a labor union, club, or lodge—and their purpose is implicit in their name. The union extends credit to its members when the members need the help.

There are now more than 22,500 credit unions operating in offices, churches, professional organizations, and communities across the country, chartered under federal or state laws. Moreover, if there isn't one around and you are part of a well-defined group, it is not too difficult to form one of your own. You can get help and precise rules for creating a credit union with either a federal or state charter by writing to CUNA International, Inc., P.O. Box 431, Madison, Wis. 53701.

Credit unions specialize in small personal loans, particularly to a member faced with a sudden emergency. Credit unions also make automobile and home improvement loans.

Typical maximum you may borrow:

Up to $2,500 on your personal signature.

Typical annual interest rates:

Maybe as little as ¾ of 1 per cent per month. Usually the lowest of any major category of lender.

Typical maximum maturities:

Two to three years.

Advantages:

The interest rates may substantially undercut rates charged by other lenders. A credit union is probably the cheapest borrowing source available to you.

You pay no extra fees and credit life insurance usually is automatically included in the stated interest rate.

You are dealing with fellow workers or friends or lodge members who have in common a special interest in the financial welfare of all credit union members.

Disadvantages:

You must be a member to borrow. This means not all of us have the opportunity to borrow through one of these co-operatives.

You may hesitate to reveal your borrowing needs and financial problems to the committee of fellow workers who must approve your loan request.

SAVINGS BANK OR SAVINGS AND LOAN ASSOCIATION

Savings banks exist in only seventeen of our fifty states, mostly in the Northeast. Savings and loan associations exist in all states, but in most they are given power to lend primarily for the purchase of home and for home improvements.

Both types of savings institutions specialize in mortgages and home improvement loans. (Savings and loan associations are authorized to make mobile home loans and educational loans too.) Savings banks also frequently make personal loans.

Typical maximum you may borrow:

Up to 90 per cent of your passbook savings total for passbook loans.
Up to $3,000 for personal loans.
Up to $30,000 for mortgages.
Up to $10,000 for home improvement loans.

Typical annual interest rates:

Slightly less than a commercial bank for passbook loans and home improvement loans; about the same for other types of loans.

Typical maximum maturities:

One year for passbook loans and up to three years for personal loans.
Up to twenty-five to thirty years for mortgages.
Up to ten years for home improvement loans.

Advantages:

Although you are borrowing your own money when you make a passbook loan, your net cost is far less than on any regular installment loan and you are disciplining yourself into maintaining your savings.

Savings institutions specialize in mortgage and home improvement financing. Their rates are competitive and their services superior.

Disadvantages:

Really none.

LIFE INSURANCE COMPANY

This may be your indisputably number *one* source for money. In fact, it is a source I suggest you check *before* you turn to any other. After a period of two or three years the premiums you have paid on a regular life insurance policy (not a term policy) become a prime cash asset. Your insurance company will then lend you your cash surrender value directly at a specified and relatively very low interest charge.

Typical maximum you may borrow:

Generally up to 95 per cent of your life insurance policy's cash surrender value. And since every year the cash value of your policy increases, every year the total you may borrow increases too.

Typical annual interest rates:

Five per cent simple interest in New York, 6 per cent simple annual interest in other states; only 4 per cent on a veteran's life insurance policy. The interest rate will be specified in the policy.

Typical maximum maturities:

None.

Advantages:

The loan is a cinch to get. You merely ask your company to send you the loan forms, fill them out, return them, and the cash is yours.

The interest charged is very low by today's standards—a flat rate on the unpaid balance of your loan without any extras or hidden charges. Usually the company will collect the interest you owe at the time you pay your premiums: quarterly, semi-annually, or annually.

You are not held to any specified time for repayment. This may be an advantage if you cannot take on the burden of regular payments right away.

Disadvantages:

The amount of your loan decreases the face value of your life insurance policy—which means, of course, that you're temporarily undercutting the protection of your family.

The absence of a specified time for repayment might lull you into maintaining the loan indefinitely, thus continuing to pay interest indefinitely and decidedly increasing the over-all cost of your loan.

INDUSTRIAL LOAN COMPANY

The "industrial" part of this source's name stems from the fact that the companies make loans mostly to industrial workers—not to the industrial corporations employing them.

Industrial loan companies fill a gap between the commercial bank and the small loan company. They make a wide variety of loans, ranging from a regular personal or auto loan to a second mortgage on your home.

Typical maximum you may borrow:

Up to $5,000 on personal loans.
State laws prescribe limits on second mortgages.

Typical annual interest rates:

Comparatively high compared to banks but the companies *may* make loans at lower interest rates than small loan companies.

Typical maximum maturities:

One to three years on personal or auto loans.
Ten years on second mortgages.

Advantages:

They can make larger loans than small loan companies and might charge lower interest rates.

They will accept a wide variety of your possessions as collateral, ranging from your home to pieces of your furniture.

They might lend you money when you do not have a sufficient credit rating to get a loan from a bank.

Disadvantages:

Interest rates are higher than charged by banks.

Industrial loan companies frequently insist on co-signers—which means you must ask your friends or business acquaintances to guarantee the repayment of your loan and this you well may hate to do.

BANK CREDIT CARD

With your bank credit card you may not only charge items ranging from hotel bills and air travel to TV sets and fur coats; you also may get "instant" cash loans. At a few banks you even can get an instant $50 to $100 loan simply by slipping the bank's magnetically coded plastic card into a machine.

Typical maximum you may borrow:

$400 to $5,000 at any bank honoring the card.

Typical annual interest rates:

Interest is not charged on any balance if paid within normal cycle from purchase date-billing date to repayment time—usually a span of twenty-five to thirty-five days from the date of billing.

Then interest accrues only on balances "rolled over" or unpaid after fee billing time allowance.

Annual rate of interest charged at that time ranges from 12 to 18 per cent (as of 1974).

Typical maximum maturities:

One to two years.

Advantages:

It's quick, "easy" convenient credit.

You don't have to ask anyone directly for a loan; you just use your own previously established line of credit and get it.

Disadvantages:

That interest rate of up to 18 per cent a year if you are not careful about paying.

The temptation to overuse this source of credit just because it's so easy.

SECOND MORTGAGE COMPANY

These companies do precisely what their name implies: lend you money against your home on a second mortgage so you can meet your pressing obligations. On top of the first mortgage you are carrying to finance your original home purchase, you take out a second mortgage for a given period of time and then use the money raised from the second mortgage for purposes which may have nothing whatsoever to do with your home.

But this can be an exceedingly expensive source for money—and an unsound borrowing method too. The interest stated on your mortgage may not seem high but the extra charges can multiply the actual rate you are paying. At the same time, your second mortgage may run for years—meaning you'll be paying for the money long after you have forgotten the purpose for which you borrowed. And this, you will recall, breaks one of the cardinal rules for borrowing.

Typical maximum you may borrow:

Up to $10,000.

Typical annual interest rates:

The legal maximum in the state plus "charges" which, I repeat, can build up to startlingly high percentages.

Typical maximum maturities:

Three to ten years.

Advantages:

Quick way to raise funds for just about any purpose.
Repayment can be strung out over a number of years.

Disadvantages:

A second mortgage can add a financial burden undermining your entire investment in your house in bad times.

You take on a relatively long-term debt—three to ten years—to purchase a product or service which may have a much shorter life.

You could, without realizing it, commit yourself to paying an excessively steep rate for the money.

YOUR OWN HOME MORTGAGE

You may get a second mortgage on your home and raise substantial sums from other lenders besides a second mortgage company, of course. Or you may refinance your mortgage, take out a new mortgage with a new long-term life and new interest rate, to raise hefty sums. This you may do through the institution which gave you your first mortgage or through another bank, savings association, or an individual investor.

The trend toward borrowing on your own home to raise money for non-home purposes exploded in the 1960s and the trend is apparently here to stay. What this represents, in effect, is the dramatic development of a *twenty-to thirty-year installment loan* as against the familiar *two- to three-year installment loan*. The long-term mortgage is the vehicle through which money is raised for everything from college costs to pleasure boats.

Typical maximum amounts you may borrow:

Depends on your deal.

Typical annual interest rates:

The going rate for first mortgages.

Typical maximum maturities:

From ten years up to original life—twenty, twenty-five, thirty years—of first mortgage, depending on age of the property.

Advantages and disadvantages:

This trend toward using the home mortgage for purposes far removed from the original purchase of the home is so powerful that it demands more than a few short sentences stating the pros and cons. Thus read the following real-life illustration with care:

Mr. H.B.A. is a successful lawyer in his forties who bought a $50,000 house in a suburb near New York fourteen years ago with the help of a 6 per cent mortgage. H.B.A. now has one son in college, another entering this fall, and an extremely popular teen-age daughter. In addition to tuition fees, he therefore has suddenly developed a wallet-emptying list of new "necessities": a car for the boys, a swimming pool, new terrace furniture, etc.

So H.B.A. recently refinanced his mortgage and raised $12,000 in new cash to be repaid over a twenty-year period. He has bought the car for his boys, he is decorating the terrace, and he is about to build the swimming pool. To him, this is an excellent deal—a way to borrow "instant cash" on the most painless repayment terms.

But right as the deal seems to H.B.A., it's wrong from a strictly dollars-and-cents viewpoint. For H.B.A. is breaking that fundamental rule of sound finance: he is "borrowing long to buy short." Years after his son's auto will have been junked, he'll be paying interest on the loan to purchase it. By committing himself to pay interest over a twenty-year period, he'll end up paying far more on this loan than he would have paid on a two- or three-year loan at twice his borrowing rate.

That's H.B.A. Now let's take *you* as an illustration. Say you borrow $3,000 on a conventional installment loan, pay 6 per cent interest in advance, agree to repay over a two-and-a-half-year period. Your true interest rate is roughly double 6 per cent. Your monthly repayment will be $115. Your total interest cost will come to $450 ($3,000×.06×2.5=$450.)

Or say you borrow $3,000 by refinancing your mortgage over a twenty-year period. Your interest rate is a simple 6 per cent a year. Your monthly repayment will be only about $21.50. But over the twenty years the 240 monthly payments will total $5,160—an out-of-pocket interest cost to you of $2,160. In addition, you'll pay at least $250 for closing costs.

In the first case, your interest cost is $450. In the second, it's $2,285 to $2,410—about five times more.

Now I can summarize the pros and cons, confident that you grasp the nuances. The easy appeal of refinancing a home mortgage to obtain cash for non-home equity purposes is undeniable but it glosses over the tremendous difference in interest costs. Like other financing methods which on the surface seem easiest and least expensive, this one turns out to be among the hardest and most costly.

RURAL FAMILY LOANS

If you are a farm family living in a rural area, you may be able to get a rural family farm or home loan at a comparatively low interest rate through a nearby production credit association. These are co-operative associations created to assist in providing credit for people living in rural regions—and you also may be able to get a loan to finance your farm or farm-related business or other enterprise.

You'll get details on these loans and your possible eligibility for them from the production credit association serving your area or from the Farm Credit Administration, 490 L'Enfant Plaza, N.W., Washington, D.C. 20578.

PAWNBROKER

The pawnbroker is not the worst of all loan sources but he's close to it. He certainly must be classed as a source of last resort for the desperate borrower. You'll not only pay an enormous annual interest rate on small loans; you'll also be able to borrow only a fraction of the auction value of the asset you pledge as collateral. And to get your funds, you'll have to turn over your property (which you may badly need) to the pawnbroker for the life of the loan.

Your loan usually will have a very short life and in many parts of the country you must redeem your collateral within thirty to sixty days or it becomes the property of the pawnbroker, who may then offer it for sale. A pawnbroker's terms underscore how limited are the options of the desperate borrower. The person least able to afford horrendous interest rates always is the one who pays them.

Typical maximum you may borrow:

Up to 50 per cent (but possibly 60 per cent) of the auction value of the asset you pledge.

Typical annual interest rates:

Three to four times higher than rates on personal loans charged by most major lending institutions.

Typical maximum maturities:

180 days, possibly with the privilege of a 180-day extension.

Advantages:

You have complete privacy, need not give any information about yourself or your financial circumstances. The pawnbroker doesn't care who you are so long as he's assured the asset you are pledging isn't stolen property.

You can borrow money at once against your possession and, if you need the cash in a matter of hours, this can be a crucial factor.

If you are in a very volatile profession—the theater, say—you can get periodic loans by pawning and redeeming the same asset over and over again.

Disadvantages:

It's an excessively expensive way to borrow.

You do not have the use of your asset while the loan is outstanding—and you might need that asset to earn an income. (A musical instrument, for instance, or a typewriter or special tools.)

You can borrow only a small percentage of the value of your assets.

LOAN SHARK

Absolutely at the bottom of any list of loan sources is the loan shark—in every way an evil source, lending money to the desperate, innocent, and ignorant at sinfully high and openly illegal rates. He is a racketeer charging usurious rates for money and threatening punishment if the repayment is not on schedule.

A typical deal might be "7.50 for 5"—$7.50 for $5.00 borrowed until payday next week. That may seem only $2.50 in interest on your $5.00 loan, but it's actually 2,600 per cent a year, and that's a hellish rate by any yardstick. Moreover, the loan shark usually will try to keep you from repaying the entire sum you owe, for if part of your loan remains outstanding at all times, he can build up the interest you owe to ever higher totals. At the same time, he threatens you with punishment ranging from broken bones to death itself for failure to repay.

Yet the brutal fact is that the loan shark continues to thrive. Even though the Truth in Lending law forbids the collecting of debts by violent means, loan-sharking is a multibillion-dollar business dominated by organized crime. Even though there are many alternative sources for loans, these crooks can and do get away with charges running 1,000 per cent, 2,000 per cent, or more a year and a conservative estimate is they are bilking the poor out of more than $350 million each year.

How do you spot a loan shark? Be suspicious *if* he:

does not show his state license prominently;

dates a loan prior to the time you get the money;

asks you to sign the papers before the figures are filled in;

requires more than one note for one loan;

refuses to give you a copy of the papers you signed or receipts for payments;

requires you to buy expensive insurance.

Get legal advice immediately if, when you attempt to repay part of a debt, the lender says you must repay the entire principal or none.

Appeal to local or state legal authorities at once if, when you admit to the lender that repayment is difficult, he sends you to someone else who seeks another fee in addition to the interest owed.

If a reputable lender's plan for repayment seems too difficult for you, turning to a disreputable lender will only intensify your problems.

Typical maximum amount you may borrow:

None.

Typical annual interest rates:

500 to 2600 per cent.

Typical maximum maturities:

None.

Advantages:

None.

Disadvantages:

Endless. The loan shark as a source for money is truly unspeakable.

YOUR SOURCES OF CREDIT FOR GOODS AND SERVICES

When you have a telephone installed in your apartment or house, make a number of phone calls, receive a bill, and pay the bill *after* you have used the phone, you have been using credit. Only instead of a loan in the form of cash, you are getting credit in the form of the service provided to you by the telephone company. The same goes for an electric light bill or a gas bill or doctor bill or dentist bill.

You receive the service. The service is unmistakably, indisputably worth money. You do not, however, pay for the service until usually thirty days or more after you've taken advantage of the service. This is credit.

When you open a charge account at a local store, buy goods you want or need, use the goods, receive a bill the month after your purchase—and pay the bill usually at least thirty days later, you have been using credit too. This time the credit is in the form of the goods provided to you by the store. This is credit just as much as a loan in cash is—with the vital distinction that the loan comes via goods given to you with the clear understanding that you will pay later under an agreed-upon schedule.

When you sign a charge account agreement, you have applied for credit. When you have filled in the lines of the application form asking about your income, outstanding debts, assets, family responsibilities, etc., you have in effect done the same thing you do when you fill out an application for a cash loan.

Similarly, when you sign a retail installment contract to buy an important product—TV set, furniture, kitchen appliances, a car—this too is a loan in the form of credit for the merchandise you are buying on time. The contract spells out the terms you, as buyer, and the merchant, as seller, agree upon. You, the buyer, do not own the goods until *after* you pay for them and if you do not meet the terms of your contract the seller may take back (repossess) the goods.

After you've signed an installment contract, you may receive instructions in the mail that you are to make your payments not to the merchant who sold you the TV set or auto or furniture, but instead to a bank or finance company. This means simply that the merchant has sold your contract or "paper" to the financial institution named in order to replenish his cash so he can continue offering installment contracts to other customers. That's all it means—just that you must make your payments to the financial institution which took over your contract.

Here are the types of credit you can get today in the form of goods and services and examples of these credit sources.

SERVICE CREDIT

Sources: Utility companies; physicians; dentists; hospitals.

What it is: This is the free credit you use to get vital services such as utilities and professional help. You pay for the services only after you have taken advantage of them. Your debt is usually payable within thirty days after the service has been rendered.

CHARGE ACCOUNT

Sources: Department stores; other types of retail stores.

What it is: An *open* (*thirty-day*) *account* is an account in which the store accepts your promise to pay for the goods you buy, usually within thirty days of your purchase.

A *revolving account* is one in which the store states a maximum amount of money you may owe the store at any one time. The limit is decided when you open the account and is based on your income and credit rating. You in turn agree to pay a stated amount on your balance every month and to pay interest on the unpaid balance you owe.

A *budget account* or *flexible account* is an account in which your monthly installment payments to the store are based on the size of your account balance and interest is charged on the unpaid amount. For instance, if your account balance is $100 you might be expected to make monthly installment payments of $25 each.

A *coupon credit plan* is an account in which you are given "credit coupons" which you may use in the store as cash while you pay for the coupons over, say, six months. This eliminates a monthly billing to you and the nuisance of detailed bookkeeping by the store.

RETAIL INSTALLMENT CREDIT

Sources: Department stores; appliance stores; furniture stores; automobile dealers; hardware stores; sales finance companies; door-to-door salesmen of big companies selling books, magazines, cosmetics, hardware items, etc.

What it is: This is the credit you use when you buy such big-ticket items as automobiles, vacuum cleaners, other household appliances, encyclopedias, the like. You usually make a down payment and then sign a contract to pay off within a period ranging from a few months to as much as five years in regular weekly or monthly amounts which you and the seller agree upon and which are stated in your contract. The retailer adds a finance charge to the cash price of the article and you, the buyer, do not own what you have bought until you have completed your payments.

Sales finance companies specialize in auto loans but also finance such big items as boats, mobile homes, major home appliances.

CREDIT CARD

Sources: Issuers of travel and entertainment cards; airlines; oil companies; banks.

What it is: This is an identification card permitting you, the holder, to charge a wide variety of goods and services simply on your signature. You agree, in most cases, to pay for all you charged once a month. If you make only a partial payment on your account, your account is automatically treated as a revolving account and interest is charged accordingly.

If you have an airline card, you use it to charge air trips; an oil card, to charge gas and other purchases at a gas or service station; a travel and entertainment card, to charge travel and all sorts of hotel, restaurant, and entertainment bills the world over. This card is an automatic charge account at all the participating businesses in the plan to which you belong and may give you charge accounts at thousands of places.

If you have an all-purpose bank credit card, you also have automatic charge accounts at all the businesses participating in the bank's plan, which can include thousands of places all over the world.

The card issuer gets a record of what you have charged from the business at which you have charged a purchase of goods or services. The issuer then bills you, the holder of the card, once a month for the total of your charges. You write one check a month covering what you owe. If you don't pay off within twenty-five days on a bank credit card, your account also is automatically treated as a revolving account and interest is charged accordingly. You are expected to pay for charges on travel and entertainment cards upon receipt of a bill unless it is a major item which may be paid for in installments set up at time of purchase. If you haven't paid your debt within sixty days after receipt of your bill, you must pay a late charge and your card may be revoked.

INTEREST RATE CHARGES SIMPLIFIED

The primary purpose of the Truth in Lending law is to help you understand just how much it costs you to borrow money either in the form of cash or in the form of goods and services.

That is why the law makes it mandatory for the lender or merchant to provide complete information to you. For the theory is that, once you have this information and you know how much the credit costs, you will be in a position to judge whether or not it is worth while for you to borrow—and if you decide it is, you will be able to compare the costs at various sources.

Despite the law, though, most borrowers are still in an interest rate labyrinth. Even sophisticated borrowers admit they are still befuddled by the various ways interest charges are stated. As for most amateurs, they readily confess they are lost in the maze. Shockingly, a study made years *after* Truth in Lending became law disclosed that only two out of three borrowers knew what interest rate they were paying on their used car loans. Even more shocking, one in seven didn't even know the rate of interest they were being charged on their home mortgages! This is something like buying a house without bothering to inquire about the price.

Thus, I think the easiest way to guide you through this labyrinth is to pretend the law doesn't compel disclosure and to take you through a series of fundamental questions and their answers.

Q. What is the annual percentage rate?

A. The annual percentage rate (APR) is the key yardstick by which you can measure and compare the costs of all types of credit. It is the basic interest rate you pay when you borrow—essentially a simple annual rate which relates the finance charge to the amount of credit you get and to the amount of time you have the money. With this information, you can compare financial terms offered by competing lenders, regardless of the terms of the loan or the amounts of credit offered or the difference in state laws.

When you know the annual percentage rate and the finance charge, you know the cost of borrowing money.

Q. What is the finance charge?

A. This is the total of all charges you are asked to pay to get credit. Among the charges which must be included in the finance charge are interest, loan fees, finder's fee, service charge, points, investigation fees, premiums for life insurance if this is required, amount paid as a discount.

Some costs are *not* part of the finance charge, though: for instance, taxes, license fees, certain legal fees, some real estate closing costs, other costs which you would pay if you were using cash instead of credit.

Q. If I borrow $1,200 for twelve months at a dollar cost of $6.00 per $100, or $72 for the year, what rate of interest am I paying?

A. That depends on your terms of repayment. If you repay the total amount of $1,200 plus $72 at the end of the year, your interest rate is a simple 6 per cent.

But if you repay in twelve monthly installments of $106 each, your interest rate is almost double 6 per cent, or 11.08 per cent, to be precise.

Your dollar cost is still $72 but, because you are paying off steadily throughout the year, you don't have the use of your $1,200 for the full year. In effect, you have the use of only about half the original amount for the full year.

This table explains it clearly:

DETAILS	SINGLE PAYMENT LOAN	INSTALLMENT LOAN
Amount of loan	$1,200	$1,200
Term of loan	1 year	1 year
Charge for loan	$72	$72
Dollars per $100	$6.00	$6.00
Monthly payments	None	12 @ $106
Simple annual interest rate	6%	11.08%

It is the very easy payment method of an installment loan which increases an apparent 6 per cent interest rate to an annual percentage rate of almost 12 per cent.

Q. What is an "add-on" rate?

A. It is one of two major ways (the other is directly below) you may pay interest on an installment loan. When you pay the *add-on* rate, your finance charge is added to the principal at the time you take out the loan and you pay the total of the two. In the preceding illustration, for instance, you borrow $100; 6 per cent is your add-on finance charge; you pay back $106; your true annual interest rate is 11.08 per cent.

Here is a further translation of the add-on rate:

IF YOU'RE CHARGED		THE TRUE ANNUAL INTEREST RATE IS
$4.00 per $100	or 4% per year	7.4%
$4.50 per $100	or 4½% per year	8.31
$5.00 per $100	or 5% per year	9.23
$5.50 per $100	or 5½% per year	10.15
$6.00 per $100	or 6% per year	11.08
$8.00 per $100	or 8% per year	14.8
$10.00 per $100	or 10% per year	18.5
$12.00 per $100	or 12% per year	22.2

Q. What is the "discount" rate?

A. Under the discount method, the second major way you may pay interest on an installment loan, the finance charge is deducted from the principal of your loan at the time you get the money. Again using the preceding illustration, you borrow the $100; 6 per cent is your finance charge discounted in advance from the loan; you receive $94; your true annual interest rate is 11.58 per cent.

In this case you also begin paying back your loan within a month and don't have the use of your $94 for the entire year.

Here is a further translation of the discount rate.

IF YOU'RE CHARGED	THE TRUE ANNUAL INTEREST RATE IS
$5.00 per $100 per year	9.57%
$6.00 per $100 per year	11.58
$7.00 per $100 per year	13.61
$8.00 per $100 per year	15.68

Q. Is a 6 per cent interest rate ever a simple 6 per cent annual rate (or 8 per cent or 9 per cent)?

A. A 6 per cent annual rate is 6 per cent simple annual interest if you borrow the $100 for one year and repay it one year later with the $6.00 added on—or a total of $106 in a *single payment*. (Or $108 or $109.)

A 6 per cent mortgage also is a true 6 per cent a year, for you are paying the 6 per cent on the *declining balance* of your mortgage, not on the original total.

Q. What if I'm charged interest monthly on my unpaid balance?

A. If you're charged monthly on the unpaid balance you owe, then:

¾ % per month	is 9% simple annual rate
⅚	is 10
1	is 12
1¼	is 15
1½	is 18
2	is 24
2½	is 30
3½	is 42

Q. How can I compare the dollar cost of different ways of charging interest?

A. Take as an example a $500 loan to be repaid in twelve monthly installments. If the rates charged are:

• 1 per cent per month on the unpaid balance, the dollar cost will be about $32.

• 6 per cent annual interest on the unpaid balance, the dollar cost will be about $16.

• 6 per cent annual interest "add-on," the dollar cost will be about $30.

If the payments are spread over eighteen months, each payment would be smaller, but the total dollar cost would of course be higher. For example, at 1 per cent per month on the unpaid balance, the cost over eighteen months would be about $47 compared to $32 for twelve months.

Q. Why does the percentage rate on an installment loan for twelve months sound so much higher than the dollar charge?

A. Because the dollar charge is applied to the total amount of money you borrow, but on an installment loan you do not have the use of the money for the twelve months and this increases the percentage rate charged.

Q. If I pay back a twelve-month installment loan in six months, will I get back half the interest added to my loan?

A. No. You will get back less because in the first six months you've had the use of most of the loan funds, so it is only fair that you pay more of the interest in the first six months than in the last.

To illustrate, in the first month of your twelve-month loan, you have the use of 12/12ths of the money. In the final month of your twelve-month loan, you have the use of only 1/12th of the money.

Your rebate of interest on your installment loan will be figured on the basis of the "Rule of 78s" formula. In this formula, the total of the number of months for the loan equals 78: 100 per cent of the interest due on a twelve-month loan thus equals 78/78ths.

In the first month of your twelve-month loan, you pay off 12/78ths of the interest; in the second, 11/78ths of the interest; in the third, 10/78ths of the interest and so on to the last month, when you pay 1/78th of the interest.

Now say you pay off your twelve-month loan at the end of the sixth month. You have already paid off 12/78ths, 11/78ths, 10/78ths and on through 7/78ths. The total of 12+11+10+9+8+7 equals 57. What's left is 21/78ths—or about 27 per cent of the interest initially added on to your loan. And that 27 per cent, not 50 per cent, is what your rebate would total.

It *is* a complicated formula and you need not puzzle over it. But should you ever ask for a rebate of loan interest and question why it is less than you think is due you, refer to the "Rule of 78s" for the explanation.

Q. What about the charges on bank credit card and revolving credit accounts?

A. Finance charges on these accounts are usually expressed as a percentage of the unpaid balance per month, as of the billing date. This is a simple monthly rate, which is then multiplied by 12 to give you the annual percentage rate. Thus:

A monthly rate of 1½ per cent becomes an annual percentage rate of 18 per cent.

A monthly rate of 2 per cent becomes an annual percentage rate of 24 per cent.

A monthly rate of 2½ per cent becomes a yearly 30 per cent.

3 per cent becomes 36 per cent.

And so it goes. . . .

Q. Why is the rate on credit card accounts higher than the rate on a simple installment loan?

A. The main reason, say the banks, is that the amounts are smaller and the monthly processing expenses are higher. Generally, the monthly processing on a regular installment loan involves only one operation—recording the monthly payment. With a credit card account, the bank or retailer, etc., must make a record of the charge every time the card is used, total the charges at the end of the billing period, compute the interest on any unpaid balance, make up a bill, mail it, and record your payment.

Q. How are mortgage rates quoted?

A. Mortgage rates have been traditionally described in terms of simple annual interest rates. However, if points, a finder's fee, or certain other charges are required, these now—under the Truth in Lending law—must be included in the finance charge. These "extras" make the true annual rate appear slightly larger than before the law went into effect.

Q. Why are mortgage rates lower than rates on installment loans?

A. The average cost to the lender per dollar loaned is lower for a mortgage loan because mortgage loans are substantially larger than most other types. Their sheer size helps to offset the monthly processing expenses, permitting the lender to pass the saving on to the borrower in the form of a lower interest rate.

Q. What can I do when no credit charge is quoted at all?

A. This is illegal. But, for illustration, let's say a sewing machine is offered to you at $100 and you can pay for the item in twelve monthly installments of $9.00 for a year. Multiplying the monthly payment by twelve will give you $108. You are therefore paying $8.00 or a 15.8 per cent true interest rate for the equivalent of an installment loan of $100.

CREDIT CARDS

DIFFERENCES BETWEEN TYPES OF CREDIT CARDS

You can now use credit cards to pay for:

tooth extractions, tombstones, and taxi rides;

driving lessons, diamonds, and dog kennel fees;

ambulance service, apartment rent, and auto license fees;

music lessons, movie admissions, and marriage costs;

and savings bonds and scuba diving instructions, church tithes and college tuition, garbage removal and psychiatric care . . .

In 1975 nearly 12,000 banks were participating in credit card plans and more than 65 million bank credit cards alone were in circulation. About

6 million travel-entertainment cards are in use. So it goes, for we are far into the era of plastic credit.

If you know how to handle your credit cards, they can be a tremendous convenience. They can help you keep detailed tax records for your travel and entertainment expenses. They can allow you to charge these costs anywhere in the world—without paying any interest. They can be a magnificent substitute for cash everywhere, a major benefit if you travel a lot. (And Americans lose more than $2 billion a year in cash, says the American Express Company.)

Or if you are among the millions who have all-purpose bank charge cards, you can greatly simplify your budgeting problems by paying for hundreds of dollars' worth of purchases of every kind with a single check at the end of the billing period. You can achieve substantial savings by buying an item on sale even if you're low on cash. You can order goods easily by mail or telephone—and also return merchandise with a minimum of trouble. And *any* arrangement which can give you the use of big amounts of cash for as long as twenty-five days without interest (from date of billing), as with bank charge cards, is advantageous to you.

To use credit cards to your maximum advantage, you must first learn the differences between the various types in use. There are:

Single-purpose cards issued by all kinds of businesses—oil companies, motel chains, telephone companies, car-rental agencies, department stores, and the like. You pay nothing for them, and they allow you to charge merchandise or services, paying when billed. If you don't pay promptly, you will be charged interest, typically amounting to 1½ per cent a month. The aim of this kind of card is to encourage you buy only from the company that issued the card to you.

Food, travel, and entertainment or multipurpose cards, like Diner's Club, Carte Blanche, and American Express. These are used mostly by businessmen, although anyone may apply. Holders of these cards pay a yearly fee—usually $15 to $17—to the issuer, and can then use the card in thousands of business places. Bars, restaurants, hotels, and expensive shops are this kind of card's best customers. Usually cardholders are billed within thirty to sixty days and are expected to pay on receipt of the bill. No interest is charged if payment is prompt.

Bank credit cards, of which BankAmericard and Master Charge are the best known. All operate in much the same way. The bank issues you a card after checking your credit rating. There is no fee. You may then use the card in place of cash at any shop, restaurant, service station, or other business participating in the plan. The shop will turn the charge slips over to the bank, which will accumulate them until the end of the billing period. If you pay the bill within the time specified—usually twenty-five days from the date of billing—the use of the credit card is free. After that a service charge of 1 per cent to 1½ per cent a month is levied against the balance.

HOW DO YOU USE CREDIT CARDS?

Do you have at least three credit cards, most of them good only at a particular store or chain of stores?

Do you use at least one of these cards regularly?

Do you think of your card or cards primarily as a source of credit, and in only a secondary way as a convenience?

Do you write more checks than you used to, despite your use of the cards too?

Do you have a basic, nagging fear that credit cards make it too easy for you to buy things you do not really want or cannot honestly afford?

Do you, as a result of this basic fear, tend to think of your cards as an evil—a necessary evil, but still an evil—and not as a good thing?

If you answered yes to every one of these probing questions, you are typical of today's credit card user, according to "Credit Card Use in the U.S.," the first comprehensive study of the subject ever made, published by the University of Michigan Institute for Social Research. "Few Americans tend to think of credit cards as a good thing, whether they use them or not," says Dr. Lewis Mandell, who directed the ISR study. "Fully 75 per cent of all respondents said that credit cards made it too easy to buy things."

Now check where you, a credit card owner, fit in the wide range of users analyzed.

• If you have a higher-than-average income and higher-than-average education, you're more likely to be a card user than those with lower incomes and educations. Income is the major determinant of credit card use.

• If you are a young family and have children, you are more likely to use cards than other groups and more likely to incur debt on your cards than other groups. Another determinant of credit card use is related to the age of the family head.

• If you live in the suburbs, it's probable that you are an active credit card user, while families living in central cities or rural areas are least likely to use such cards.

• If you use your cards to buy clothing more than any other category of goods, you're typical. On both bank and store credit cards, clothing is the most frequent type of purchase.

• And if you're in any income group below the very top, you use your card to obtain credit, and this is the most important use you make of the card. You see your card as another instrument for taking on installment debt and you treat your card debt like an installment loan—paying a little each month, generally the minimum allowable monthly payment.

• But if you're in the highest income group you use your card as a convenience—and whatever debt you incur on the card you attempt to pay off as quickly as you can.

• And no matter what your special group, you write more checks than families who do not use cards.

What are some of the fundamental implications of all this? One prime implication is that, although all credit cards are substitutes for money or checks in transactions, they are *not* pushing us toward a "checkless society" —as was so widely forecast and is still so widely believed.

Another prime implication is that our consumer debt pattern is being changed by the addition of credit card debt to other types of consumer debt.

The use of credit card debt is most pronounced among higher-income families, who often have no other consumer debt and certainly could borrow at less than an 18 per cent annual rate. But these families aren't taking on long-term debt; they're using the cards as convenience and they pay off the debts quickly.

And a third implication is that most of you are using your eminent common sense in handling your credit cards—recognizing their dangers as well as their allure. Most Americans are indeed their own best money managers.

SHOULD YOU USE A CREDIT CARD?

As a general rule, you should—at any income level—if you have shown in the past that you can handle credit responsibly and that you will use your card as a convenient budgeting and record-keeping tool rather than a license to overspend.

As a general rule, though, you should not use cards *if* you're a habitual impulse buyer who frequently buys unnecessary things; *if* you're habitually late in meeting payments; *if* you've never managed to live comfortably within your income. And you should certainly shy away *if*, on top of all these characteristics, you do not have a steady income.

Here are the ways to use any credit card to *your* best advantage.

• Accept only those cards which you actually need and want and will use fairly regularly. For most of you in the middle-income bracket, one bank charge card and maybe a couple of oil company cards for gas are enough—although if you are in business you may find a travel-entertainment card helpful as well.

• Treat every purchase you are planning to charge as you would a cash purchase. Ask yourself: Do you really want and need the item? Can you really afford it? Can you repay the charge comfortably and on time?

• At the beginning of each month, decide on a maximum total of charges you'll be able to repay easily. Stick within that limit and repay the charges promptly to avoid any finance charges.

• Keep all your receipts until you receive your statement to check your spending and your totals against the statement for errors, which can easily occur (due, say, to no more than a clerk's bad handwriting).

HOW TO PROTECT YOUR CREDIT CARD

In just a matter of days a while ago:

• Three Long Island housewives went on a shopping spree, billed $16-000 worth of merchandise to stolen credit cards.

• A Pittsburgh gambler was arrested with $10,000 in his pocket—most of it refunds from airline tickets he had bought with other people's credit cards.

• A credit card thief posing as a health center operator ran up bills of more than $10,000 at gas stations by promising attendants health courses in his non-existent health center if they would make out phony bills against the credit card and give him cash.

These are *not* extreme examples, and the warning to you is implicit if you own a credit card or department store charge plate. Criminals have invaded the credit card field. Millions of cards are now being lost or stolen each year and are being used by thieves and other fraudulent operators to run up millions of dollars in unauthorized charges.

Fraudulent use of credit cards on sizable amounts is now a federal crime and the Truth in Lending law forbids the mailing of unsolicited credit cards.

The Truth in Lending law now also provides that a cardholder is not liable for charges on a stolen or lost card if the issuer has failed to inform him that he is otherwise liable for up to $50 per card, or has failed to supply the holder with a self-addressed, pre-stamped notice to use if a card is lost or stolen. Your maximum liability in the case of unauthorized use of any credit card which has been stolen from you is $50 for each card. This maximum holds even if you fail to discover the loss for a considerable period of time and even if you fail to notify the issuer promptly. The law also provides that all cards must bear your signature, photograph, or similar means of identification.

But you also must take steps on your own to protect yourself. Here's what to do:

• As soon as you've finished reading this, go over every card you own. Make sure you have destroyed all you do not need. Cut unwanted cards in half and throw them away.

• Make a list of all credit cards you decide to keep with the names and addresses of the issuers and the account numbers. Keep this list in a safe place but *not* in your wallet.

• Sign each new card you decide to keep this minute. This will force anyone trying to use the card fraudulently to forge your signature on store bills, restaurant checks, etc.—no problem for the professional card-abuser, admittedly, but a definite deterrent to an amateur.

• Check your credit card collection every couple of weeks. If any card is missing, inform the issuer immediately—first by phone, then by letter or telegram in which you refer to your call. Some issuers now have twenty-four-hour answering services for just this purpose. Although there is a federal $50 limit on your liability, it applies to *each card* you own.

• Never lend your card to anyone else. This is a violation of your contract with the issuer.

• Make sure your card is returned to you each time you use it. Among the major suppliers of credit cards to fraudulent users are dishonest employees of legitimate establishments.

• Don't leave your credit card in the glove compartment of your car. This is one of the first places a professional credit card thief looks.

• Don't underestimate the value of your card because it's made of plastic. Consider it the equivalent of cash and at least as tempting to a thief as cash.

• Don't leave credit cards lying around in your office or hotel room any more than you would leave a stack of cash lying around. Instead, keep your cards securely in your wallet or purse.

In sum, either give up the advantages of owning credit cards and return to cash-check living or treat these cards with the respect which they—as the equivalent of cash in your wallet or purse—deserve.

How to Hold Down Your Borrowing Costs

How can you, an attractive credit risk, hold down your cost of borrowing?

Throughout this section I have dropped in rules on this and you will find more hints for mortgages in Chapter 13, "A Roof Over Your Head," and more rules for automobile loans in Chapter 9, "Your Transportation." But the guides below are the most fundamental of all and go across the board for all types of credit. Whatever repetition you note can only help underline their value to you.

(1) On any type of purchase on time, always keep in mind that the most expensive way to borrow money is to make a small down payment and to stretch out the life of the loan for the longest possible period.

(2) Thus, to save interest on any type of loan—from appliance to auto or mortgage—make the largest down payment you can manage and repay in the shortest period that's feasible for you. Unless you buy the pessimistic argument that we're in for a never ending period of galloping, utterly ruinous inflation, in which the only way to protect yourself is to borrow as much as you can so you can pay back in dollars of dwindling value, you cannot dispute this rule's logic.

(3) Try to include a clause in any long-term loan contract giving you the privilege of prepayment of your loan at no penalty to you or at the lowest

possible penalty. This will give you leeway to renegotiate your loan at more favorable rates when and as interest rate levels decline or to pay it off entirely. (Note, though: Refinancing costs must be considered and minimum loan charges are often set by policy and sometimes law.)

(4) On the other hand, don't pay off loans you might have outstanding at dramatically lower rates than now prevail. Just keep up your regular required payments and invest your extra cash so it earns more money for you than you're paying out on your old loans.

(5) Beware of ads for big-ticket items on "easy" repayment terms, and if the ads are befuddling despite Truth in Lending law requirements, use the formulas I've given you for determining how much you are paying on a true annual basis.

(6) Always keep in mind that any "instant cash" plan will be comparatively *expensive* to you. Whether it's a multipurpose credit card or an automatic line of credit at your bank, or any newer plan, the point is you'll almost surely end up paying *more* for this instant cash than you would for a traditional loan.

(7) In general, during periods of high interest rates, borrow only the exact amount you need. Borrowing more will mean paying peak interest rates for the extra cash. Borrowing too little will mean returning for another loan and paying extra processing costs.

(8) Offer the best security you can. A loan secured by top-notch collateral almost always may be obtained at a cheaper rate than a loan backed only by your signature. You lose nothing. You get back full possession of your asset when you pay off your debt.

(9) Before you borrow or buy on time, use whatever free credit you can get. For instance, use your regular thirty-day charge account as much as you can. If you buy at the start of the billing cycle, you won't be billed for about thirty days, and then you have another thirty days to pay.

(10) In shopping around for bargain credit, don't overlook the occasional "money sales" or similar features offered by full service banks. For regular bank customers who already have savings, checking accounts, and the bank's charge card, installment credit may be offered at a full per cent less than the normal interest rates. And if you have a number of small loans outstanding, ask your bank whether you would qualify for a "cleanup" type of loan at a lower rate. If so, by all means take advantage of the lower rate.

THE GREAT PITFALLS OF CREDIT

Truth in Lending has not eliminated the credit tricksters and racketeers —and the likelihood is no law ever will wipe them out. As for us, it would be ridiculous to claim that even an excellent education on credit would be sufficient protection for the vast majority of Americans—particularly since eight out of ten Americans admit they are unable to find their way through what one observer once called the "wonderland of credit where percentages multiply and divide at will, where finance charges materialize on command and fees are collected on the way out."

Do you know how to read the fine print on a complicated installment sales contract? Do you even understand the bold-type statement of interest charges required under the Truth in Lending law? How, then, can you, the ordinary borrower, detect hidden interest charges, protect yourself against unsuspected loan costs? One very good way is by becoming aware of the great pitfalls of credit—and, by this awareness alone, learning how to avoid these yawning traps.

"DEBT POOLING"

No matter what your plight, avoid commercial debt poolers, who simply lump your debts together, collect one regular payment from you—then charge you as much as 35 per cent of your debts for this "service."

Debt pooling, or "pro-rating" or "debt adjusting" or "debt liquidating," for profit is now barred in a majority of our states and the District of Columbia. But it still thrives in many parts of the country, and you must be on guard.

Specifically, a "debt adjuster" may say to you: "If installment payments or past-due bills are troubling you, let us consolidate and arrange to pay all your bills, past due or not, with one low monthly payment you can afford." If you accept this offer, you will turn over part or all your income to a firm and your debts supposedly will be paid out of the income on a pro-rated basis. The basic difficulty with the arrangement is the fact that almost never is the plan carried to fruition. Either the creditors won't accept the plan or you, the debtor, find it impossible to live with the expected payments. Some "consolidators" simply pocket the money and never pay your creditors. As a consequence, the only thing you, the debtor, obtain is an expansion of your original debt because of the fee you must pay to the adjuster. The service charges are steep in debt consolidation and, typically, your whole first payment may be taken by the company for these charges— without a penny going to your creditors.

Debt adjusting or debt pooling has nothing to do with legitimate credit counseling services—nor should it be confused with legitimate bank or credit union debt consolidation loans. The debt adjuster merely takes the debtor's money with the understanding that he will make the payments to the creditors—after absorbing a substantial portion of the debtor's funds as payment for his services. He adds to the debtor's problems with excessive charges and makes no effort to offer financial counsel or budget guidance. In some cases, he leaves the debtor with far too little money to live on.

"SEWER SERVICE"

Let's say that you, a consumer committed to periodic payments on an installment loan, lose your job and subsequently default on a payment. Under the law, if a creditor wishes to sue you for payment, he is required to serve you a formal notice of the impending lawsuit.

But let's say you never receive the notice—quite likely if you are among the nation's millions of unsophisticated borrowers. If so, the next blow well may be a "default judgment" against you, the equivalent of a decision that you, the debtor, are at fault before you consult a lawyer and find out your rights, not to mention go to court.

"Sewer service" is the colloquial name for this technique, which is widely used by unscrupulous debt collectors to deprive the gullible low-income borrower of his or her legitimate rights. To summarize what happens: the summons or other legal document which the creditor is supposed to deliver to the debtor is simply chucked into any dead-end receptacle (thus, "sewer" service). Unless you manage to get the judgment set aside, you are automatically stamped as liable and may be legally bound to pay whatever the creditors say you owe and you may lose your right to defend yourself in court, no matter what the facts may be.

Sewer service is the least expensive way for an unprincipled creditor to force payment of a debt. It is used not only to collect payments on installment debts but also to deprive tenants of their rights to contest eviction by landlords.

This is a flagrant attack on your most basic rights. If it happens to you, complain immediately to a law enforcement agency and also to the court where the judgment was entered. Get a lawyer to move to set the judgment aside. If you can't afford a lawyer, tell the clerk of the court you want to make a motion to set aside a default judgment for lack of service and ask him for advice on how to file the necessary papers.

Don't take this lying down!

"INCONVENIENT VENUE"

"Inconvenient venue" is another technique designed to deprive debtors of their legal rights. Under this procedure, the creditor simply files suit against his victim from a branch, affiliate, or lending institution hundreds of miles away from the debtor's home. Again, the victim has no feasible means of defending himself against the suit.

Pressure is now mounting steadily for state and federal laws to ban inconvenient venue as a means of obtaining default judgments against debtors, guilty or not guilty.

"CONFESSION OF JUDGMENT"

Ranking with the most vicious of all ways in which debtors are being trapped is the "confession of judgment" clause appearing in so many installment sales contracts. In effect, this clause is a built-in confession of guilt should the borrower miss a single monthly payment unless, in many instances, he can come up with the entire amount he still owes. By signing the contract he has waived whatever legal rights he otherwise may have had in advance—and the creditor can move in to collect at once. Frequently, too, the first a debtor knows that such a judgment has been made against him is when he receives a notice that his property is being put up for a sheriff's sale within days.

Confession of judgment is legal in only a few states, but this technique is still being illegally used to some extent against consumers in many other states as well.

Of course, it is reasonable for lenders to insist that they be protected against default and, of course, there are explanations for each of these clauses. But this technique is an outrageous deprivation of the rights of the individual.

Even if you signed a confession of judgment, under recent Supreme Court decisions you may be able to have it set aside if you can show that you didn't understand the clause when you signed it and didn't have legal advice.

HARASSMENT

Harassment is the "normal" means, in countless cases, of collecting small debts and past-due installment payments. And you need not be a ghetto resident to come up against this: it can happen to you, whoever and wherever you are.

• A typical cornered debtor may first receive a flood of dunning notices from debt collection agencies with names which sound in some cases very like those of government agencies. The letters will threaten legal action and serious damage to the debtor's credit rating.

• In addition, the debtor may be subjected to repeated telephone calls at all hours of the day and night, not only at his home but also at his job.

• The caller may falsely represent himself as a lawyer, a policeman, a private detective. Or he may hint that he works for a government agency.

• He may call a debtor's neighbors, relatives, wife, even his children. He also may call the debtor's employer, a tactic which easily can lead to the debtor's losing his job.

Whatever the tricks, the harassment usually succeeds in frightening a debtor into "settling" his debt—even though the debt may have been imposed on him through fraudulent, illegal means and even though he may have a sound, legitimate, legal defense against the creditor who is harassing him.

As you might expect, laws are being passed to control this sort of viciousness. The Federal Trade Commission has proceeded against some unfair debt collection methods. In Massachusetts debt collectors are licensed by the state and a collector may lose his license if he calls you late at night, informs your employer that you owe money, or indicates on an envelope that you have not paid your bills. In New York City a regulation forbids creditors (or their lawyers or collection agencies) to "communicate or threaten to communicate with an alleged debtor's employer" without first obtaining a court judgment against the debtor. And the Federal Consumer Credit Protection Act makes it a federal crime for a creditor or his representative to use violence or threats of violence to collect debts.

But none of it is enough. Neither the new laws nor regulations are curbing, much less wiping out, the problem of debtor harassment.

REPOSSESSION

You buy a slightly used car loaded with options for $3,600, including 18 per cent interest on your auto loan, fees, insurance, etc. You pledge to pay $100 a month for three years.

After one year and $1,200 in payments, you fail to meet a due date. A while later your car disappears from your driveway. A lending company which bought the note for your car from your used car dealer has simply sent his "repo" man to your home. He has crossed the wires of your car to get it going and has driven off.

Repossession of automobiles, as well as of many other personal items, is a widespread and entirely legal practice used against the delinquent—particularly low-income—debtor in the U.S. today.* It also may be only the beginning, for the lender may then turn around and sell your repossessed car back to the original dealer for an amount to be credited to you. This resale price, if the participants are unprincipled, may be a rigged bargain sum of, say, $500 for your car. You are now sued for the remainder you still owe: $2,400 minus $500, or $1,900. You're also liable for extra charges.

You thus not only have no car but you also have a debt equal to nearly two more years of payments. And now the used car dealer may in turn resell your repossessed car to another buyer for $1,500. Of course, cars are repossessed without such tactics—but a shocking number do involve deceit, fraud, perjury too.

* However, the U. S. Supreme Court recently ruled that certain repossession practices which have been widely used violate constitutional guarantees. The Court ruled that no item may be repossessed unless the buyer is notified that the matter is in court and given a chance—in formal hearings—to tell his side of the story.

Automobiles are only one category of consumer goods subject to repossession today. Another not untypical situation is repossession when the consumer buys a set of furniture on time, then defaults on a single payment. The seller or the holder of the installment loan contract may confiscate the entire set and then sue to collect the remainder of the debt, plus charges and fees. Many corrupt ghetto merchants, in fact, make a living selling goods over and over in this manner. Their profit depends on default in payment and a chance for resale—not on the original sale itself.

To crack down on these practices, laws are being urged at both federal and state levels which would permit creditors either to repossess their goods or to sue for payment of the debt—but not both. Meanwhile, the only protection you, the debtor, have is your own awareness of the pitfall.

"HOLDER IN DUE COURSE"

An elderly woman bought a hearing aid for her son, involving a fat down payment and an installment loan for the balance of her purchase. When the device failed to work, she took it back to the seller, who agreed to send it to the factory for repair. But when she returned again to pick up the hearing aid, she found that the seller had gone out of business—and had sold her installment loan contract to a local lender.

Incredibly, this woman remained under legal obligation to repay the loan plus stiff interest charges—despite the fact that her son still had no hearing aid.

This legal quirk—called the "holder in due course" doctrine—was, until May 19, 1976 one of the biggest and costliest loopholes remaining on our consumer lawbooks, with "literally millions of dollars lost every week because of this doctrine," said the Consumer Federation of America in Washington.

Under the holder in due course doctrine, an unscrupulous used car dealer or other retailer could lure naive consumers into buying a long list of products or services on time. He would then immediately sell the contract to a finance company. The product might have turned out to be a lemon, badly damaged, or have needed servicing under the warranty, or it might not even have been delivered. And the seller might have flatly refused to replace or repair the product. Nevertheless, the financial institution which owned your loan contract would sternly remind you that he was "in the business of financing, not repairing furniture or cars." If you refused to make payments as they came due, you might be sued for the remainder of the loan, payable at once. Or, as an alternative, the finance company might have repossessed not only the item in question but also other personal goods. It was indisputably one of the most vicious of all consumer traps.

Among the goods and services most frequently involved in holder in due course problems were: vacuum cleaners, furniture, carpeting, sewing machines, "lifetime" series of dancing or judo lessons or health spa visits, major appliances, home improvements.

But now as the result of a '76 Federal Trade Commission rule, the holder in due course loophole has been plugged. You have the right to assert claims and defenses against a creditor as you might against an unscrupulous seller. You may, for instance, stop payment to a creditor on a defective dishwasher or a car that turns out to be a lemon. You may refuse to pay a financing company for a set of encyclopedias that doesn't arrive or may sue for refund of payments already made to a health spa that has gone out of business.

Furthermore, all consumer contracts now must carry a notice informing you of your rights of action against creditors as well as sellers. The rule applies to merchants who offer you installment sales contracts or arrange direct loans with finance companies or engage in "referral" schemes in which you are led to believe you will get a product free if you refer a specified number of other customers to the seller.

You no longer must bear the burden of a seller's wrongdoing; your lender must either absorb the costs of unfair or fraudulent practices or take the seller to court and force him to pay up. At last, this utterly unfair credit practice that in the past has compelled so many consumers to pay for broken or worthless merchandise has been outlawed. But be on guard! Some sellers still will try to pull you into the trap.

AND ALSO BEWARE THESE TRAPS!

The *add-on clause*. Avoid the contract in which the seller keeps title to a whole list of items you are buying on credit until all payments have been completed (for instance, a 14-piece set of furniture). A single delinquent payment could permit the seller to repossess the entire set, even though you have paid all but a few dollars of the total. This gimmick also permits the installment seller to add purchase after purchase to your original installment contract. Then just one delinquent payment could permit the seller to repossess your whole collection of purchases.

The *balloon contract*, which provides for a final payment which is considerably larger than the previous monthly payments. If you are not aware of this and are not prepared to meet the final payment, your purchase may be repossessed before you can produce the money. Or you may be compelled to refinance at disastrously disadvantageous terms to you. Balloon payments are illegal in some states today because they are widely used to trick you into buying—at low initial monthly costs—things or services you cannot afford.

An *acceleration clause*. In this case, default in one single payment—or in some instances, the fact that you have lost your job—can make all other payments due at once. If you are unable to pay the total balance, your purchases could be carted away for resale and you still may not be absolved of all future liability.

Obscure provisions in your credit contract which stipulate you must buy extra items you may not want. These clauses are frequently buried in the contract so you don't realize they are there until after you have signed.

Exorbitant extra charges and "processing fees," adding substantially to your borrowing costs. A lender might list such charges separately to deceive you with seemingly very low loan rates.

HOW MUCH DEBT IS TOO MUCH DEBT?

Who are the individuals and the families who get caught in an intolerable debt squeeze? Can we draw a fine but critical line between a healthy, bearable load of loans and an unhealthy, unbearable load?

The overextended credit individual is usually a faceless vexation in our society, according to a revealing study by a University of Wisconsin professor some years ago, who then drew this detailed portrait of the overextended credit family:

• The family is young, has more than the average number of children and an average income.

• The parents are easygoing, carefree, and impulsive, have "limited pleasure postponement mechanisms" and rubber wills when confronted with high-pressure salesmen.

• Although the husband, in most cases, is satisfied with his job, one in three wives is dissatisfied with her husband's pay.

• The family doesn't read anything, not even the daily newspaper. TV is the major communications medium in the family's life and TV disproportionately influences the couple's buying decision.

• The parents tend to blame their plight on vague, unavoidable "circumstances" or superficial backbreaking straws such as pregnancy, temporary loss of job, buying a car—and thus they feel their troubles are not really their fault.

• Neither husband nor wife assumes clear responsibility for managing the family's finances. Even among the couples who think they are sharing money management responsibilities, there is little indication of joint decision making. As one husband remarked, "We don't quibble about it. If either one of us wants to buy, we buy!"

• The family moves from house to house more often than the average U.S. family.

Most consumer debts are adequately cushioned by our incomes and savings, our financial assets, and our earnings potentials. But there is a minority always in deep financial trouble—in the eighteen-to-twenty-four age bracket, and in the under $10,000 bracket, particularly.

The crucial difference between sound and unsound borrowing is whether or not *you* are carrying too much debt at any one time. Okay, then, *how much debt is too much debt?*

Deep and prolonged study has gone into this question—and there is considerable disagreement on the conclusions. However, the following are clear warning signals that you're moving dangerously close to the debt borderline and may be crossing it.

• You are continually lengthening the repayment periods on your installment purchases and putting down smaller and smaller initial payments. At the same time, your interest charge load is mounting just because you are sinking deeper and deeper into debt for longer periods.

• What you owe on your revolving charge accounts also is climbing steadily. You're never out of debt to the local stores at which you have revolving charge accounts.

• Before you have finished paying last month's bills this month's are piling in. You're always behind these days in your payments and you're now regularly receiving notices that you're delinquent. You might even get an occasional notice threatening repossession or legal action against you—something that has never happened to you before.

• Slowly but unquestionably, an ever increasing share of your net income is going to pay your debts.

• You are so bedeviled by so many separate bills coming at you from so many sources each month that you turn to a lending institution or lending agency for a loan to "consolidate" and pay off all your debts and leave you with just this one big consolidation loan to meet. But you continue to buy on credit—thereby adding more new bills on top of your one big debt you must pay each month.

Here are more specific guidelines on how much debt is too much debt:

Do not owe more than 20 per cent of your yearly after-tax income (not including your home mortgage, though). This means that if you earn $800 a month in take-home pay or $9,600 after taxes a year, your debt limit would be about $2,000.

Do not owe more than 10 per cent of the amount you could pay for out of your income within the next eighteen months. Again, say your take-home pay is $800 a month; that gives you 10 per cent or $80 for debt repayments each month. With this monthly sum you could pay off $1,500 over eighteen months. Your safe debt limit would be about $1,500.

Do not owe more than one third of your discretionary income for the year—meaning the income you have left after you have paid for the basic needs of food, clothing, and shelter. Once again, say you earn $9,600 in take-home pay a year and you spend an average of $200 a month for shelter, $280 a month for food, $50 a month for clothing. Your basic living costs are $530 a month or $6,360 over the year. Your discretionary income is, therefore, $3,240. By this measurement, your debt limit is $1,080—or one third of your discretionary income of $3,240.

Also, in deciding how much debt your family can handle, ask yourself: How stable is your family breadwinner's job and income?

What is the chance of a layoff in his occupation and in your area? Is he eligible for unemployment compensation? How much? How long would this finance your needs? How many protections does your family have against other disasters besides unemployment—insurance coverage for your home, health and life pension credits, savings and investments, equity in your home, etc.?

BUT WHAT IF YOU FIND YOU'RE OVER YOUR HEAD IN DEBT?

In South Bend, Ind., a young couple with three children accumulated debts of $4,200. This couple's monthly take-home pay amounted to only $328, and monthly payments on installment debts to eighteen creditors amounted to $148.73, nearly half their take-home pay.

The couple finally appealed to a Consumer Credit Counseling Service, which advised them to trade in the expensive new car they were buying for a lower-priced car involving lower monthly payments. The service also arranged for the couple to make small monthly payments to two hospitals and seven doctors to whom they owed substantial amounts. Within nine months the couple had reduced their debt by nearly $1,400, and within eighteen months all of their debts had been completely paid off. This case history is just a single illustration of how one family out of hundreds of thousands was saved from personal bankruptcy.

It's estimated only about one in six families cannot be helped by credit counselors, because their problems are psychological or legal or because they are "credit drunks" who simply are not willing to try to solve their problems. However, without counseling service, today's huge annual personal bankruptcy toll easily might be 50 per cent higher than it is.

The fact is, says the Family Service Association of America, "People do want help—desperately—but they don't know where to go, and until recently there hasn't been anywhere to go."

So what if *you* find you are over your head in debt?

Start at your local bank: more and more banks are offering formal or informal debt counseling to overburdened customers.

If your bank (or credit union or consumer finance company) can't or won't help, write to the National Foundation for Consumer Credit, 1819 H Street, N.W., Washington, D.C. 20006, for the address of one of the 150 Consumer Credit Counseling Services nearest to you. These non-profit organizations, backed by local banks, merchants, educators, and others, are set up to provide financial counseling to anyone, but offer special help to over-extended families and individuals in an effort to find ways to get them out of trouble.

Check the nearest Family Service Agency. Hundreds of Family Service Agencies across the nation offer either financial counseling or can refer you to some agency offering such counseling. If you don't know which agency offers such help in your area, write the Family Service Association of America, 44 East Twenty-third Street, New York, N.Y. 10010.

Another good source of help could be your church. Other sources from which you may get some form of debt counseling include:

> legal aid societies;
>
> your labor union's community services counselors;
>
> your employer's personnel department.
>
> The Army and Navy also maintain debt counseling services to assist servicemen and their families.

Above all, heed this warning: If you find your payments, when added to your necessary living expenses, are more than your pay check, don't try to hide out from your creditors! Instead ask for help!

How to Go Bankrupt

But let's say all efforts and plans to bail you out have failed. The debt counseling service hasn't been able to come up with a plan your creditors will accept. No consolidation loan is available. The only option left seems to be bankruptcy.

If so, here are your final two "outs":

(1) "Chapter XIII." This method of debt reorganization is provided for under Chapter XIII of the Federal Bankruptcy Law. Under Chapter XIII, debtor, creditors, and a referee—all supervised by a federal judge—get together to work out a way for the debtor to pay his debts on an installment basis.

This is known as the wage earner plan, because it protects the wages and essential property of a debtor who wants to stay away from straight bankruptcy by repaying his or her debts from future earnings.

Whether rooted in puritanism, pride, or ego, the general attitude toward bankruptcy is negative and you well may find it difficult to live with. But there are other than social aspects to be considered. Co-signed loans become the debts of the co-signers; the cost of going into bankruptcy may reach $300 to $500 or more; bankruptcy almost invariably is the blackest possible mark on a credit rating.

Here's how the wage earner plan works.

Either you, the debtor, get a written extension of your debts, with more time to pay them off in full; or, less commonly, you arrange a "composition" in which you pay off only a certain percentage of the amount you owe each creditor.

One half of your creditors must approve your filing of the Chapter XIII petition, at which time all interest charges usually stop. Your wages, personal property, your home and furniture, secured loans, particularly mortgages on real estate, usually are not included in the plan for distribution of your assets to creditors.

In addition to legal fees, which a Chapter XIII petitioner must pay to the lawyer who files the petition, there are filing fees of about $15 and a trustee's fee of up to 5 per cent of the debts, plus expenses.

You, the debtor, make your required payments, spread over three years, to the trustee, who then pays your creditors—thus making the federal government, in effect, a collection agency. An employer may agree to deduct the payment from a debtor's salary and forward it to the trustee.

There is no uniformity of application of Chapter XIII, and top legal experts deplore the fact that it is not more widely used.

Important Note: If you successfully complete this plan, it will be considered a "plus" on your credit rating.

(2) Voluntary bankruptcy. Finally, there is the voluntary petition for straight bankruptcy. To do this you must put together a list of all your assets and liabilities and pay a $50 filing fee. Ordinarily, the rest is routine. Except for clothing, tools, a selected list of household goods, and other items depending on the exemption laws of your state, all your assets will be collected by the court and liquidated—and the proceeds will then be distributed among your creditors. Once you, the debtor, have been discharged by the court, your financial slate is clean—except for the bankruptcy record, which, no matter what you are told, will dog your footsteps for years.

THE BAFFLEGAB OF BORROWING

Many of the most crucially important terms to you in the sphere of credit already have been exhaustively explained in the immediately preceding pages. But many other words which you'll hear or read have not yet been put into simple language. You'll come across them frequently enough, though, and they are of sufficient meaning to you to demand that they be as clearly explained as possible.

ACCELERATION CLAUSE: See page 127.

ADD-ON RATE: See page 112.

ADD-ON CLAUSE: See page 127.

ANNUAL PERCENTAGE RATE: See page 111.

ASSETS: Everything you own which has monetary worth.

BALANCE: The amount you owe on an account or loan at any given time.

BALLOON CONTRACT: See page 127.

BORROWER: The person who borrows cash or who buys something on time.

CARRYING CHARGE: The charge you pay a store or any other lender for the privilege of having a period of time in which to pay for the goods or services you have already bought and which you may use in advance of payment.

CHARGE ACCOUNT: See page 109.

CHARGE OFF: To declare a loss and remove a loan from the assets of a lender because the loan cannot be collected from the debtor.

CHATTEL MORTGAGE: A legal document in which your personal property (chattels) is put up as security for payment of your debt but generally is left in your hands so long as you keep up the payments as contracted.

CHECK CREDIT PLANS: Consumer loan programs similar to credit lines businesses have under which the loans are approved in advance and funds are available when needed. The consumer who has been approved for check credit may borrow up to a stated amount at any time simply by writing a check. As the loan is repaid, the credit limit returns to the stated maximum. See "How to Use Ready Credit," pages 96–97.

CLOSING DATE: The day of the month on which credit accounts and monthly bills are calculated. Payments made after the closing date—or new charges or returns of merchandise—will not show on the bill you receive until the following month, when the next closing date will show subsequent payments, charges, and returns.

COLLATERAL: Anything of value which you have against which you may borrow money—for example, equity in an automobile, real estate, stocks and bonds, savings account passbooks, the cash-surrender value of life insurance policies. If you fail to repay your loan, the lender can take possession of whatever you have put up as collateral. Note: Not *all* loans must be secured by collateral.

CO-MAKER OR CO-SIGNER: The other signer of a note when two people jointly guarantee to pay a loan. Parents often co-sign loans taken out by their minor children. Minors may not legally execute contracts.

CONDITIONAL SALES CONTRACT: Form of installment contract under which you do not legally own the product—say a car—until you've made the final payment. And you must make your payments even if you are not satisfied with the purchase. You cannot cancel your obligation by just giving back the product (car). Term no longer in common use in many areas.

CONSOLIDATE: To bring together several financial obligations under one agreement, contract, or note.

CONSUMER: Any person who uses goods and/or services for personal, household, or family purposes.

CONSUMER CREDIT: Credit offered or extended to a person primarily for personal or family purposes, for which a finance charge is imposed and which is repayable in installments. All consumer credit transactions divide into two types (1) *open-end credit*, which includes *revolving charge accounts* and transactions through *credit cards;* and (2) *installment credit*, which is used by consumers to buy big-ticket items such as automobiles and appliances.

The one fact that consumer credit is used by *individuals* for *personal* and *family* needs distinguishes it from credit used for business, agricultural, or government purposes. Consumer credit usually refers to short-term and intermediate-term debt, thus excluding long-term home mortgage debt.

CONSUMER FINANCE COMPANIES: State-licensed companies which make installment cash loans to consumers.

CONSUMER LOANS: Loans to individuals or families, the proceeds to be used for personal consumption, as contrasted to loans for business or investment purposes.

CREDIT APPLICATION: A form which you must fill out when you want to use consumer credit. It usually contains questions concerning your present and previous places of residence, work history, present earnings, other credit transactions, and loans outstanding.

CREDIT CARD: See pages 110, 115–20; 121–27.

CREDIT CHARGE: See Finance Charge.

CREDIT CONTRACT: Usually a written agreement that says how, when, and how much you will pay.

CREDIT INVESTIGATION: An inquiry undertaken by a prospective lender or creditor to verify information you give in your credit application or to investigate other aspects about you which the creditor considers relevant to your credit-worthiness.

CREDIT LIFE INSURANCE: A type of term life insurance policy, required by some lenders, which pays off a loan in the event of the borrower's death.

CREDIT LINES (See Check Credit Plans): Pre-approved loan privileges made available by banks to big businesses which qualify and maintain specified minimum checking account balances.

CREDITOR OR LENDER: The person, store, company, bank, dealer, credit union, or other organization that lends money or sells things or services on time. Creditors are those to whom you owe money.

CREDIT RATE: The ratio—expressed as a percentage—between credit charges and the average principal amount.

CREDIT RATING (also Credit Standing): An evaluation of your qualifications to receive credit based, in large measure, on your past record of meeting credit payments.

CREDIT RISK: The chance of loss through non-payment of debt.

CREDIT SALE: Any sale in which you are given time to pay for the goods you buy. There's usually an extra charge for the privilege of buying on time, and you usually pay for the goods in a series of installment payments which come due to regular intervals.

CREDIT SALE DISCLOSURE STATEMENT: The form a dealer must fill out giving you the essential details of your financing costs when you buy any product or service on the installment plan. This is required under the Consumer Credit Protection (Truth in Lending) Act.

CREDIT-WORTHY: Given a favorable credit rating and therefore entitled to use credit facilities.

DECLINING BALANCE: The decreasing amount which you owe on a debt as you make your monthly payments.

DEFAULT: Failure to pay a debt when due or to meet other terms of the contract.

DEFERRED PAYMENT: Future payment or series of future payments on a contract entered into sometime before the payment or payments are made.

DELINQUENT: A credit account which is past due and for which the debtor has made no satisfactory arrangement with the lender.

DISCOUNT (OR CASH CREDIT DISCOUNT): Deduction of finance charges from the total amount of your loan before you, the borrower, receive the balance in cash.

DISCOUNT RATE: See pages 112–13.

DOLLAR COST: A way of stating the cost of credit. It is the difference between what you receive as a loan or in merchandise and what you must pay back.

DOWN PAYMENT: Cash required at the outset of an installment sales credit transaction. Sometimes a used car, piece of furniture, or other durable goods will be accepted in place of part or all of the down payment.

DURABLE GOODS: Usually big-ticket things which are useful to you, the consumer, over an extended period of time, such as automobiles, furniture, appliances.

FACE AMOUNT: Total amount of your loan before deduction of finance charges.

FINANCE CHARGE: See pages 111–15.

FINANCIAL COUNSELING: Expert advice on money and credit management.

FORFEIT: Lose or let go—as giving up to a creditor some security when you, the borrower, have failed to meet a contractual obligation.

HIDDEN CLAUSE: Any obscure provision in your credit contract which may stipulate requirements that may be against your interests—for instance, purchase of extra items you do not want.

HOLDER IN DUE COURSE: See pages 126–27.

INSTALLMENT: One of a series of payments to pay off a debt.

INSTALLMENT CASH CREDIT: Cash loaned directly to an individual and repaid in periodic payments (usually monthly) within a specified period of time.

INSTALLMENT SALES CREDIT: Credit through which an item of durable goods (a car, appliance) is bought and paid for in installment payments within a specified period of time.

INTERMEDIATE-TERM CREDIT: Credit which is extended for a period ranging from three to ten years.

LOAN RATE: The rate you are charged for borrowing money at a specific date for a specified period of time.

LENDING INSTITUTION: A bank, loan company, or other organization which lends money and which makes money by advancing funds to others.

LICENSED LENDER: A lending organization authorized by license to conduct business in the state in which it is located.

LOAN SHARK: See pages 106–7.

LONG-TERM CREDIT: Credit which is extended for a period of ten years or more.

MARKET PLACE: Any place where a transaction is made or prices are quoted on goods or services.

MATURED: Fully paid up, fully carried out as to terms, completed as to time or as to contract.

MATURITY DATE (also Due Date): Date on which final payment on cash loan or installment purchase is due.

MORTGAGE: A written pledge of valuable property to assure payment of a debt, providing automatic transfer of the item (e.g., a house) pledged the creditor in case of default.

MORTGAGE CREDIT: Money owed for those borrowing for the acquisition of land and/or buildings (frequently, homes) and which is paid back over an extended period of time.

NON-INSTALLMENT CREDIT: A financial obligation which is repaid in a single lump sum.

NOTE: A written, signed promise to pay which lists details of the repayment agreement: where, when, and in what size installments, etc. A note can be transferred to a third party.

OBLIGATION: An amount of money one is morally or legally bound to pay.

OPEN-END CREDIT OR REVOLVING CREDIT: See page 109.

OUTSTANDING: The still unpaid part of a loan.

PAPER: Nickname for a loan contract.

PERSONAL INSTALLMENT LOAN: Money borrowed by an individual for personal needs which is repaid in regular monthly installments over a period of time.

PREPAYMENT PRIVILEGE: The privilege, stated in loan contract, of repaying part or all of a loan in advance of date or dates stated in contract—with or without interest penalty for the prepayment.

PRINCIPAL: The amount of money you borrow or the amount of credit you receive.

PROCEEDS: The actual amount of money handed to a borrower—after deductions for interest charges, fees, etc.

PROMISSORY NOTE: A paper you sign promising to repay the total sum you owe on specified terms.

REBATE: Return of a portion of a payment. For instance, you receive a rebate when you pay off your debt in advance instead of in the monthly installments you agreed upon. It then costs you less to borrow your money, because you are paying off in a shorter period.

REFINANCE: Revision of a payment timetable and, often, revision of the interest charges on the debt also.

REPOSSESSION: The reclaiming or taking back of goods which you have purchased on an installment sales contract and for which you have fallen behind in your payments.

REVOLVING CHARGE ACCOUNT: See page 109.

RIGHT OF RESCISSION: Your right, guaranteed by the Consumer Credit Protection Act or various state statutes, to cancel a contract under certain circumstances (including cases in which you have put up an interest in your home as security) within three business days—without penalty and with full refund of any deposits you may have paid. The right to a "cooling-off period" is most frequently used in home improvement contracts and the home improvement contractor must provide you with written notice of this right. It also applies, under a Federal Trade Commission rule, to sales made by door-to-door salespeople.

SHORT-TERM CREDIT: Credit extended for a period up to one year.

SOLVENT: Ability of the individual or group or organization to pay all of the debts owed. What the debtor owns is more than the total of the debts.

TERM: The prescribed time you have in which to make installment or other payments, under your loan or credit contract.

TERMS: Details and conditions of a loan (or other) contract: cash price, payment schedule, due date, etc.

THIRD-PARTY TRANSACTION: A three-way business transaction involving a buyer, a seller, and a source of consumer credit.

TITLE: Legal ownership.

TOP CREDIT: Ready credit. See Check Credit Plans.

TRADE IN: Practice of trading in an old product for a new one. Trade-in allowance is the amount of money allowed for the article traded in as against the total purchase price of the article being bought.

TRUTH IN LENDING: Popular name for the historic Consumer Credit Protection Act of 1969. The law applies to virtually all consumer borrowing transactions to individuals which involve amounts up to $25,000.

UNPAID BALANCE: On a credit purchase, difference between purchase price and down payment or trade-in allowance. On cash loan, difference between total loan made and amount still owed (with charges included, of course).

UNSECURED LOAN: Loan extended solely on basis of borrower's ability and pledge to repay.

WAGE ASSIGNMENT: Clause in installment contract under which an employer may be requested to collect part of an employee's wages to pay off the employee's debt to the wage assignment holder.

WAGE EARNER PLAN: See pages 131–32.

WAGE GARNISHMENT: Classic legal procedure which creditors have used for generations to collect debts. Under "income execution" (its other name) a creditor gets a court order instructing the employer of the debtor to withhold a specified portion of his employee's wages until his debt is repaid.

4

HOW TO SHOP
AND SAVE ON EVERYTHING

The Real Reasons You Find It So Hard to Make Ends Meet

You know how fast prices have been rising for everything. You also know that never have you earned so much money as now, never have you had such good prospects.

You feel confident that you are an excellent money manager. You also feel poorer than a year ago, more pinched than ever.

Why?

I am sure this question is echoed in tens of millions of homes in every area of the land and in every income bracket. I am sure too that most of you are not prepared for the complexities of an honest answer. Thus, as an introduction to this chapter on how to shop and save on everything, here are the *real* reasons you find it so hard to make ends meet on the biggest income of your life.

REAL REASON NO. 1

At every level of government, taxes have been rising along with the cost of living and therefore you mislead yourself into thinking you are richer than you actually are when you say your income is what you gross.

Your income is not your gross: it is your net after taxes and after allowing for a continuing high rate of inflation, even though price increases may be only modest in some years.

Say you're the sole support of a family of four who earned $10,000 just a few years ago and say you've had increases of 30 per cent since. Do you have $13,000 to spend? *No.* Your new high pay is actually worth *less* in the market place than your $10,000 was worth because of the erosion in your dollar's value due to inflation and to the bite of soaring Social Security taxes as well as higher income tax rate on your rising earnings.

Or let's say you are the breadwinner who earned $30,000 and now earns $39,000. Do you have $9,000 more to spend? *No.* Your new pay buys *less* than your former pay. And so it goes through all income categories.

Look at Chapter 19, "Planning for Your Financial and Personal Security," and you'll find more starkly dramatic illustrations of the extent to which your dollar's value has been eroded by increases in the cost of living and by climbing taxes in recent times. And I have not included by any means the entire bite in your dollar taken by all types of taxes. If this total "gobble" were included, you would have to be running even faster just to stand still.

If you had put $100 of your wedding present cash in your jewel box in 1967 to have handy "just in case" and you took it out in 1975, this sum would buy you less than $67 worth of food, shelter, clothing, and other necessities and non-necessities of life. If your parents had put the $100 away back in 1939 and you took it out in 1975, you could buy only about $28 worth of the essentials that $100 would have bought in '39.

What I am trying to smash home to you via these figures are the realities of taxes and inflation, for only when you face these realities will you stop kidding yourselves and start adopting the money management policies which will help protect your family.

REAL REASON NO. 2

You are using far more services than ever before and all services cost far more than ever before. You have, in short, chosen to live in a "service society" and you must pay the price demanded by that society.

Let me illustrate this with a list of my own activities on two long work-play days in the country one recent fall day. I took an early morning golf lesson; called the typewriter repairman to fix my new electric portable; paid the piano tuner for his regular quarterly visit; phoned our broker to confirm a decision on our stock account; arranged to have my teeth cleaned and to get my annual physical checkup; had lunch in a nearby restaurant with two economics professors; had my hair and nails done, and dropped off the laundry and dry cleaning on the way; had a lengthy talk with my housekeeper about the need to call the plumber, the electrician, and the exterminator to check the house; took my car to the local garage for its New York State inspection; made notes about what I was doing as I went along.

What was the characteristic which linked each of my activities? Each was or each involved a *service.* Each was a service clearly reflecting our affluent society. And each was a service costing more than ever before. My family's use of so many services to this unprecedented degree is a fundamental reason our cost of living is climbing so fast—and it's a fundamental reason for your pocketbook pinch too.

If you will just stop to think right now about your own activities, you will realize that never have you used so broad a variety of services to such an extent in your own daily life. The rise in your demand for services has far outpaced the rise in your demand for goods. You also will realize that never have virtually all services cost so much. In recent years the upsurge in the cost of services has dwarfed the rise in all consumer prices—with the most severe pinches in the huge areas of education, hospital fees, and interest rates.

Putting it even more succinctly, the average cost of sending your soiled clothes to a laundry has jumped much faster than the cost of a washing machine, while the cost of having a daily household worker do your laundry has zoomed. Again, the rise in the cost of buying a new car is modest compared to the rise in the cost of taking a city bus or subway. The cost of going out to a movie has jumped, but the cost of buying a TV set on which to see a movie at home has hardly moved.

What's more, there is no doubt about the uptrend of service costs in general. The only question—the *only* one—is the degree of rise.

And though you may resent the upward pressures, you are not in a good position to resist them, for when you need most services you need them at once. All I have to think of when I would like to make a peep of protest is that I can't cure an illness or fix an electric typewriter or tune a piano or repair a car, etc.

Even economists who are confident that over the long span the over-all rise in consumer prices will go back into the 4-per-cent-a-year range expect that the rise in service costs will beat that average.

REAL REASON NO. 3

For years you have been continually upgrading your demands—turning the luxuries of yesterday into the necessities of today. You have come to feel entitled to fairly sharp year-to-year increases in your living standards and have become accustomed to boosting your spending budget to new records each year, even though there may be a year now and then when the boosts are unwarranted. Because of this attitude, you are inclined almost routinely to overspend and then to feel pinched when you wake up to the fact that you have spent more than the amount of your raise.

To be even more specific, in your new homes you have been buying more built-in major appliances, more carpeted or linoleum-covered floors, more easy-care counter tops, more recreation rooms, sewing rooms, central air conditioning. The appliances themselves are being steadily upgraded—to self-defrosting refrigerators, eye-level ovens, etc. New homes bought with FHA insured mortgages in 1974 had an average 5.8 rooms; nearly 63 per cent had two or more bathrooms; nearly 54 per cent had garages; 30 per cent had carports.

In the great majority of your new cars you're paying for automatic transmissions and for air conditioning. Moreover, the auto insurance liability limits you're buying are increasingly likely to be in the $100,000 to $300,-000 range against the previous $10,000 to $20,000 range of coverage. In your food baskets, the upgrading is unmistakable, as Chapter 6, "The Everyday Necessity of Food," dramatically illustrates.

You have been indeed translating the pipe dreams of the 1950s into the tangible possessions of the 1970s—and translating pipe dreams costs money.

You well may feel you're going broke on the highest income of your lives, but if you will look honestly at how you live, you might ruefully conclude that you're at least going broke in style.

YOUR KEY WEAPONS AGAINST RISING COSTS

It could be that you are an extraordinarily perceptive shopper. Even so, I'll wager that I can show you how to become a far more perceptive shopper. In fact, I'll go further and wager that in the following pages—and despite my preceding analysis—you'll find ways to shave your costs from a minimum of 5 per cent to as much as 50 per cent or more in *every area* of your family budget.

Behind the over-all increases in your living costs each year, there always will be sharp variations of which you can take advantage. There always will be moves you can make to cushion the impact of inflation on your own budget. Your fundamental safeguards are awareness of the trends and understanding of the ways to protect yourself against the trends. Now here are your four key weapons:

(1) *Substituting* for these items, wherever and whenever you can, others of a similar nature on which prices are holding the line.

(2) *Switching* to less expensive versions of increasingly costly goods and services.

(3) *Shopping* harder than ever for the best possible deal on items you must have and on which prices are soaring.

(4) *Eliminating* items which are of no real value and even are of harm to you.

For instance, contributing tremendously to the increases in food prices have been climbing costs of meat. But within this food category, you can make many delicious substitutions. You also can choose a vegetable in season for one that isn't. And you have great control over how often you eat out, even greater control over what you eat when you are out.

Again, to illustrate, over-all transportation costs have been climbing steadily—but among the real "villains" behind this inflation have been soaring parking charges and public transportation costs. You can't do much but you can do some things to save on public transportation costs—and you can do plenty to curb your parking charges.

You can switch forms of entertainment for activities which are going out of sight. You certainly can save on cigarettes simply by quitting smoking. You have a wide variety of choices in clothing. I could go on and on but there is no need.

With the basic guidance in these pages, you can use your own imagination and carry on superbly from here.

A Dozen Wise Rules for Shopping for Everything

(1) Shop around. Prices do vary even from day to day on items ranging from food to furniture, from cars to cosmetics. Comparison-shop at stores in your area. Keep an eye on the ads. Know which stores have built their reputations by offering values on certain types of merchandise.

(2) Watch for genuine sales and specials and study the "calendar for bargains" which is provided in this chapter. Not everything advertised is at a better price today than it will be tomorrow. Hunt out the real bargains. There always are some around. Stock up on things you need when prices are seasonally reduced, as at semi-annual clothing sales or inventory clearance sales. Watch and learn which stores put what things on sale and when—particularly on big-ticket major things.

(3) Watch for differences in quality. It well may be that the extra luxury or utility of the higher-priced items is really worth the extra cost. But don't spend unnecessarily for quality; buy only the grade of the item you need. Grades A and B tomatoes, for instance, look best—but Grade C, the lowest in price, will be just as good in stews and casseroles.

(4) Hold periodic family councils to discuss money matters. You can cut back on costs better in an atmosphere of co-operation and understanding.

(5) Keep control of your credit purchases, make sure your monthly charge account balances are at a reasonable minimum, and shop for credit with utmost care (see Chapter 3, "How to Borrow Cash and Use Credit Wisely.")

(6) Be careful about impulse buying. Supermarket shoppers consistently buy more than they put down on their shopping lists. Don't permit impulse to trick you into buying things you don't need or even want.

(7) Buy what's right for *you*. In clothing, for example, classic styles may be more appropriate for you (and last longer) than the latest fashion craze. And many combinations of the same basic garment may be a far sounder purchase than any spectacular outfit. Let your own experience guide you.

(8) Buy in bulk but only when you'll use it *all*. All things are not necessarily "cheaper by the dozen." Spoilage and discards can eat up your apparent savings on quite a variety of bulk and "economy" purchases. Check whether the bulk price really is more attractive than what you would pay for a smaller size or amount before you stock up on things you buy regularly.

(9) Investigate the private brands in food, clothing, and appliance lines which may be priced more favorably than national brands. Test the quality, learn which private labels you can rely upon. On major purchases, be sure service facilities are available.

(10) Read the label information. Clothing labels will tell you essential facts about materials used and proper cleaning methods. Even the fanciest packages often carry important data that you will neglect to your sorrow.

(11) Give a plus to low maintenance. Many product improvements in recent years have concentrated on easy care—ranging from permanent-press fabrics and stain repellents to extra-durable furniture. They're worth the slightly higher price tags that may be attached. But don't pay more for convenience than it is worth to you—the other side of "easy care."

(12) Consider service and "returns." Deal with retailers and manufacturers who stand solidly behind what they sell and who never balk at servicing or replacing a product. If they go out of their way to serve you, they want your business, and they deserve it.

QUIZ YOURSELF INTO BUYING WISELY

When you're wondering whether you should or should not buy, give yourself this quiz, prepared by the Council for Family Financial Education, and find out.

1. Do you really need this item? . . . . Yes No
2. Is the price reasonable? . . . . Yes No
3. Is this the best time to buy the item? . . . . Yes No
4. If this is a bargain, is it a current model
   (if that matters to you)? . . . . Yes No
5. If "on sale," is the price a true sale price? . . . . Yes No
6. Are you sure no less expensive item can be
   substituted? . . . . Yes No
7. Are you sure there are no major disadvantages? . . . . . . Yes No
8. If excessive in price, will it truly satisfy an inner
   need? (If not excessive, just check "yes.") . . . . Yes No
9. Have you checked and researched the item? . . . . Yes No
10. Do you know the retailer's reputation? . . . . Yes No
11. Does this retailer offer any special services
    with the item? . . . . Yes No

Score your answers as follows:

9–11 yeses—buy the product:
6–8 yeses—think again:
Fewer than 6 yeses—forget it.

CALENDAR FOR BARGAINS

February is an excellent month in which to buy air conditioners, used cars, rugs, and lamps. Do so—and you can save 10 to 30 per cent or even more on each item's cost.

August is a fine month in which to buy furs, fans, gardening equipment and men's coats. Do so—and you also can easily save 10 to 30 per cent or more.

Buy refrigerators in January . . . Buy millinery in July . . . Buy toys during the post-Christmas clearances . . . And bathing suits during the post-July 4 markdowns . . .

These are the seasonal savings—and they are and will continue to be available throughout the years. Merely by planning your spending to take advantage of the seasonal sales the year round, you can easily slash your spending by hundreds of dollars! Just by ignoring the seasonal "bargain calendar" I submit below, you can "waste" hundreds of dollars.

There are three major periods for store-wide clearance sales: after Easter, after July 4th, and after Christmas. These are excellent times to pick up clothes, linens, dozens of other items, although you may run into shortages of styles, sizes, and colors if you don't shop early in the sales. There also are the well-publicized August white sales; specials for George Washington's birthday, for Columbus Day, Veterans' Day, similar holidays.

And this applies just as strongly to foods. Again to illustrate: If you can manage to resist buying fresh strawberries until June or July—when prices drop sharply from their peaks at the beginning of the strawberry season in April—you will save money on this delicacy. On the other hand, if you are unable to resist buying watermelons as they begin to appear on supermarket shelves in June—instead of waiting until August when watermelon prices will have dropped sharply—your indulgence will cost you plenty.

Do not let the simplicity of the following calendars for foods and non-foods mislead you into downgrading their importance to your pocketbook! These bargain guides alone can put you well on the way to beating any foreseeable price spiral in the future. This *strategy of timing your buying* alone can more than offset any apparent annual rise in the cost of living.

IF YOU WANT TO BUY	GOOD MONTHS TO BUY ARE
Air conditioners	February, July, August
Appliances	January
Art supplies	January, February
Bathing suits	After July Fourth, August

If You Want to Buy	Good Months to Buy Are
Batteries and mufflers	September
Bedding	February, August
Bicycles	January, February, September, October, November
Blankets	January, May, November, December
Books	January
Building materials, lumber	June
Camping equipment	August
Carriages	January, August
Cars (new)	August, September
(used)	February, November, December
Car seat covers	February, November
Children's clothing	July, September, November, December
China	January, February, September, October
Christmas gifts	Any time but Christmas
Clothes dryers	January, February, March, April
Clothing (spring)	March
Coats (women's, children's)	April, August, November, December
(men's)	January, August
(winter)	March
Costume jewelry	January
Curtains	February
Dishes	January, February, September
Drapes and curtains	February, August
Dresses	January, April, June, November
Fans	August
Fishing equipment	October

IF YOU WANT TO BUY	GOOD MONTHS TO BUY ARE
Frozen foods	June
Fuel oil	July
Furniture	January, February, June, August, September
Furs	January, August
Gardening equipment	August, September
Glassware	January, February, September, October
Handbags	January, May, July
Hardware	August, September
Hats (children's)	July, December
(men's)	January, July
(women's)	February, April, July
Home appliances	July
Home furnishings	January, February, August
Hosiery	March, October
Housecoats	April, May, June, October, November
Housewares	January, February, August, September
Infants' wear	January, March, April, July
Lamps	February, August, September
Laundry appliances	March
Linens	January, May
Lingerie	January, May, July
Luggage	March
Men's clothing	August, December
Men's shirts	January, February, July
Paints	August, September
Party items	December

IF YOU WANT TO BUY	GOOD MONTHS TO BUY ARE
Piece goods	June, September, November
Quilts	January, November, December
Radios, phonographs	January, February, July
Ranges	April, November
Refrigerators and freezers	January, July
Rugs and carpets	January, February, July, August, May, September
School clothes	August, October
School supplies	August, October
Shoes (boys' and girls')	January, March, July
(men's and women's)	January, July, November, December
Silverware	February, October
Skates	March
Ski equipment	March
Sportswear	January, February, May, July
Stereo equipment	January, February, July
Storm windows	January, February, March
Suits (men's and boys')	April, November, December
Summer clothes and fabrics	June, July
Summer sports equipment	July
Tablecloths	January, May
Television sets	May, June
Tires	May, end of August
Toiletries	January, July
Toilet water and colognes	July
Towels	January, May, August
Toys	January, February
Water heaters	January, November

"Scraping by" on $40,000 a Year

Billy, a bright young executive with three teen-age children, boasted in 1974 that his family had adopted these moneysaving measures:

• adjusted the engine on their fancy foreign car to run on regular gasoline;

• instructed the local druggist to cut by 20 per cent the number of pills in all prescriptions filled for the family;

• found a factory outlet store where the family can buy underwear at a saving of 20 to 25 per cent;

• switched to trains for all relatively short hops and pledged to use trains instead of planes for other trips whenever possible;

• stopped home milk deliveries (at premium prices);

• started using cold-water detergents in laundering to save on hot water;

• vowed to buy all ski equipment at bargain prices at season's end;

• pledged also to buy all swimming pool-purifying chemicals in bulk to save $20 a year.

What's fascinating is not the variety of angles for saving. What's fascinating is the family, for the executive is a $40,000-a-year man—an income bracket inhabited by a tiny per cent of U.S. households.

The plain fact is that the wealthier among us are feeling the pinch of climbing living costs and soaring taxes just as the less affluent are. Admittedly, the wealthier live on a more luxurious scale and are cutting *their* costs on skiing, pools, and high-test gas, but that doesn't make their pinch any less real to them. Here's a rough breakdown of Bill's $40,000 budget:

ITEM	YEARLY COST
Food, incidentals	$ 9,700
Car depreciation and upkeep	1,440
School tuition, transportation	5,472
Home mortgage; improvement loan	4,800
All insurance	1,788
Medical and dental bills	1,500
Social Security and pension contribution	1,500
Property taxes	1,440
Federal and state income taxes	12,360

Immediately, three points jump out of this breakdown:

First, "school"—for three youngsters in private day school—is one of this family's biggest expenses. Reason: "The public schools in our area simply don't offer quality education." This family, like millions of others, pays increasingly steep school taxes—*plus* steep private tuitions. Private schooling has become a necessity rather than a luxury to many parents across the U.S.

Second, all types of taxes, totaling $13,800 a year, amount to a fat 35 per cent of the budget. The importance of taxes in today's middle-upper income squeeze cannot be exaggerated.

Third, the budget makes *no* special provision for the costs of vacations (this family has simply stopped taking them), restaurant eating, gifts, clothes. And the omission of any savings is appallingly dangerous.

In addition to finding "exotic" cost-cutting devices, what are other upper-income families doing to ease the squeeze? They're taking on more and more moonlighting jobs—in anything from teaching to consulting; demanding bigger and bigger raises from their employers; urging their wives to go back to work. Many, too, are simply using for day-to-day living the capital they had accumulated toward college costs or retirement.

And of course they are seeking and welcoming every moneysaving hint they can find. Which explains why I tell this tale of the $40,000-a-year family. Like them, search out every cost-cutting suggestion in every section of this book. Use each and all in the confidence that no matter what your income bracket—how high or how low—countless others are using them too.

5

THE EXTRA COST
OF BEING BROKE

As I've emphasized as hard as I could in this section, a superb way to save money on your food budget is through shopping the specials at the supermarkets and loading up on bargain-priced foods which you can store in your home freezer.

But let's say you're a young man and woman just starting out together and you're already straining your pay check or checks to finance your day-to-day purchases of food. Where will you get the extra cash implicit in use of this moneysaving hint? Even assuming you have a freezer in good working condition—quite an assumption—how can you afford to take advantage of this indisputably sound advice?

As I've also stressed as hard as I could, a top-notch way to save money on your clothing budget is through buying staple, basic items at out-of-season sales and always being on the lookout for things you know you'll have to buy during the year. November is a traditional month for sales on women's and children's coats; December is a traditional month for sales on men's and boys' suits; January is the prime month for sales on a wide variety of clothing ranging from lingerie to shoes.

But how can you—already limiting yourself, let's say, to a minimum of new clothes so you will have the money to finance your education—take advantage of this moneysaving hint? Just my suggestion that you shop these traditional sales has more than a touch of arrogance about it.

Again, a major way to save money on items ranging from big-ticket appliances to minor cosmetics is through shopping a discount store in the area. Savings can easily range 25 to 30 per cent.

But to repeat the refrain once more, how will you get to a discount store located many miles away? The bus or train fare will be an obstacle by itself—and I surely can't take for granted that you have a car at your disposal and can afford the gas and oil—as well as the ready cash to finance major purchases at the discount stores.

It is obvious when I put it this way, isn't it? And I could continue to place virtually every one of my major moneysaving guides in this context. In blunt and honest summary, my sound pocketbook advice is cruelly unrealistic to those of you who are broke.

And that goes whether you are living on an exceedingly limited budget while you are in school . . . or are just married and living to the hilt of your income . . . or are single, spending all you can earn on non-things and things more important to you now than the goods and services I've discussed in these pages . . . or whatever. . . .

In an excellent analysis entitled "The Extra Cost of Being Poor," Trienah Meyers of the Department of Agriculture zeroed in on these points at a Washington conference a while ago:

"While the buying habits of the more affluent members of the buying public are determined at least partially by convenience," she said, "those of the poor are dictated almost exclusively by an existing need. 'Poor' is buying when you can. . . . 'Poor' is buying in the neighborhood, at whatever the prices happen to be. . . . 'Poor' is buying in amounts you can afford, usually one at a time. . . . 'Poor' is buying whatever quality of brand or item you can manage on your time payments. . . ."

Enough. Surely the points are painfully apparent. The poor not only have less money, they also have less economic freedom on all purchasing fronts: time, place, amount, type, quality.

BUT!

You are not *doomed* to poverty: *you* are just in a transition stage.

You are not among the unskilled, the underprivileged, the ignorant: *you* are in the process of becoming skilled, of earning your right to privileges, of gaining the knowledge that you need to move into a more satisfying and rewarding world.

So! Learn and remember the guides in these pages for your maximum benefit when you have enough money to use them. These rules have been tested by time. They will always help you when you can take advantage of them.

6

THE EVERYDAY NECESSITY
OF FOOD

FOOD PRICES IN PERSPECTIVE

HOW MUCH DOES YOUR FAMILY COST TO FEED?

The amount *your* family spends on food depends on:
- the size of your family pay check (the lower your income bracket, the higher the proportion of your budget goes for food);
- the age of each family member (teen-agers are the most expensive to feed);
- the amount of entertaining your family does;
- the types of foods you eat—and don't eat;
- the importance of food as compared to your other needs and wants;
- food price levels at a given time and in a given place;
- how much time and effort various members of your family are able and willing to spend on food preparation;
- the area of the country in which you live;
- how much you eat out in restaurants, fast food places, etc.;
- whether or not you have a family vegetable garden or raise other foods, and whether your family preserves or freezes significant amounts of home-grown foods.

DO SMALL FAMILIES PAY MORE?

And what if yours is a smaller- or larger-sized family—how much does yours cost to feed? Here are key guides:

For each $1.00 a six-person family spends on food, a four-person household spends $1.03, a two-person household spends $1.07, and a single individual living alone spends $1.11.

On a per-person basis, the large family always pays less than the small family—a point which is becoming increasingly important as food prices continue spiraling ever upward. In fact, the one-person household in the United States pays fully 11 per cent more for the same list of foods than the family consisting of two parents and four children, according to a study by the U. S. Agriculture Department.

NON-FOODS IN FOOD STORES

How complex is the story of your rising food budget? Merely to suggest the ramifications:

• Part of your higher grocery-supermarket bills can be traced to your ever rising preference for gourmet foods and relatively expensive condiments.

• Part can be traced to your ever rising fondness for snacks, which have become a kind of "fourth meal" in the American home.

• Part of the bigger bills can be traced, as you all admit, to your ever rising preference for convenience foods and to the huge wave of big-eating teen-agers moving through our population.

What's more, the tremendous strides we have made in food distribution have made possible nationwide availability of foods grown thousands of miles away.

The modern distribution system also is providing year-round availability of most seasonal foods. This, too, adds to costs. Clearly, anyone who buys fresh corn on the cob in Maine in February is going to pay a lot more for the corn than in Kansas in August.

A huge volume of the food we eat is imported from nations as distant as Brazil and Ghana. So weather and other factors affecting the whole food supply-demand picture in other nations also bear on the prices we pay in our supermarkets for such items as coffee, tea, cocoa, bananas, spices. And all of us, all consumers, pay for the cost to the manufacturer of developing an estimated 5,000 new food items each year—of which only 1,500 reach food store shelves and only 500 last as long as one year.

But the big surge in spending has been in *non-foods*—and these now represent about one fourth of our total store bills.

Item: Among the fastest sale gainers in the nation's supermarkets and grocery stores in recent years have been non-foods ranging from paper towels and greeting cards to dishwasher compounds, furniture polish, and deodorant soaps. Also among the fastest gainers have been cat food, canned soft drinks, and dietetic soft drinks.

Item: More than half of all the toothpaste we buy in the United States is from supermarkets and grocery stores, not drugstores. We now buy more than half of all our aspirin in food stores, and nearly half of our shampoo and shaving products. In addition, we get one third of our first aid equipment in supermarkets plus an astounding one in ten of our phonograph records and more than one in ten of our comic books and magazines.

One less obvious force propelling the non-food upswing in food stores is the domestic do-it-yourself trend in our land. You are spending sharply increased amounts in supermarkets for such things as home spot cleaning fluids, self-polishing floor waxes, shoe polishes, housewares.

Another force is the steady upgrading in our health and sanitary standards. This explains the huge increases in supermarket sales of aerosol household deodorizers and disinfectants, plastic film wraps for food storage, garbage can liners, drain cleaners, deodorant soaps, personal deodorants, all types of first aid equipment.

Here is how you divided up a $20 bill in the supermarket-grocery in 1973. The relationships have not changed and this breakdown will clinch the tale of your spending for non-foods as well as foods in the supermarket in the mid-1970s.

CLASSIFICATION	TOTAL
Perishables	
Baked goods, snacks	$ 1.14
Dairy products (including eggs and margarine)	1.29
Frozen foods	1.06
Meat, fish, poultry	4.69
Produce	2.19
TOTAL FOR PERISHABLES	$10.37
Dry Groceries	
Beer	$ .91
Wine and distilled spirits	.13
Baby foods (excluding cereals)	.09
Cereals and rice	.27
Candy and chewing gum	.20
Canned foods	
Fruits	.18
Juices and drinks	.18
Meat and poultry	.22
Milk	.05
Seafood	.13

CLASSIFICATION	TOTAL
Dry Groceries (CONTD)	
Soups	$ .12
Vegetables	.28
Coffee and tea (including instants)	.52
Dried fruits, vegetables, milk	.22
Jams, jellies, preserves	.07
Macaroni, spaghetti, noodles	.09
Puddings (packaged gelatin and instant desserts)	.03
Soft Drinks	.45
Sugar	.15
All other foods	1.07
TOTAL FOR DRY GROCERIES	$ 5.36
Other Groceries	
Paper goods	$ .42
Soaps, detergents, laundry	.43
Other household products	.37
Pet foods	.27
Tobacco products	.75
Miscellaneous	.14
TOTAL FOR OTHER GROCERIES	$ 2.38
General Merchandise	
Health and beauty aids	$ .76
Prescriptions	.08
Housewares	.19
All other general merchandise	.86
TOTAL FOR GENERAL MERCHANDISE	$ 1.89
GRAND TOTAL	$20.00

THE HIGH COST OF CONVENIENCE FOODS

If you serve your family a store-bought pizza pie, it will cost you about 60 per cent more than if you put the ingredients together yourself. Or if you serve prepared hashed brown potatoes, it'll cost nearly twice the amount per serving it would cost if you had hashed them at home. And the cost of one slice of store-bought apple pie also may be double the cost of a home-baked pie.

Your willingness to pay extra for expensive maid service built into the foods you buy is a well-known force behind rising food prices, but you persist in underestimating how much your own demands for convenience foods are adding to your own food budgets. You don't *have* to buy the ready-made pizza at almost twice the price of making the pie at home—but you do.

As you wheel your cart through today's fantastic selection of supermarket foods, you are increasingly apt to choose the package of frozen beans with butter already added, the box of breakfast cereal coated with sugar or mixed with freeze-dried fruit over the box of plain cereal, the just-add-milk pancake mix over the half dozen separate ingredients which go into pancakes.

The Department of Agriculture calculates that your per capita consumption of fresh fruits and vegetables has been dropping steadily and your consumption of canned fruit has remained fairly stable. But your consumption of canned and frozen vegetables has been climbing steeply. Most dramatically, your purchases of frozen potato products and processed items like instant mashed potatoes have skyrocketed while consumption of fresh potatoes has declined.

A full 10 per cent of the eggs you now consume are pre-emptied and preprocessed, and by the end of this decade, says the Agriculture Department, the proportion of eggs in forms ranging from cake mixes to "instant" scrambled eggs will soar to one third of your total egg consumption.

• Today, about half of all supermarkets have a delicatessen department, and almost every new supermarket has one. Many also have their own kitchens in which 60 to 100 different items are prepared—most of them higher-priced convenience foods.

There's absolutely no basis for expecting any of these trends to slow, much less reverse. And now you are moving to the convenience of the *whole take-home meal*—the carton of chicken or fish and chips or whatever, bought at the fast food, limited-menu store—and this meal certainly costs more than the made-from-scratch version.

OTHER "HIDDEN" FORCES PUSHING UP FOOD PRICES

What I have described so far are only the obvious factors. There also are many other "hidden" forces which may not appear of significance when considered separately but which do add up to real pressure on your food budget when considered as a group. To illustrate with a sampling:

Pollution controls: The steps that farmers, food processors, and others take to reduce runoff of chemical fertilizers into water supplies, to curtail use of dangerous pesticides, to dispose of by-products in ways that won't pollute the air and water.

Tightened food inspection rules: Regulations which have raised the food standards in this country to the highest in the history of man and made our current food supply the safest ever—despite admitted gaps still remaining.

Rising skepticism about food additives, colorings, etc.: Our questioning the safety of these substances—including preservatives—is forcing food processors to stiffen their standards for using the substances, to increase their spending on research, to risk higher losses from spoilage.

Better labeling: This improvement for us has added to the costs of some foods.

Import quotas: These restrictions cost us literally billions of dollars each year.

Then there's the weather (droughts, killing frosts), always a factor. There are periodic, costly dock strikes. There are numerous labor practices which limit productivity and raise labor costs. And there is the organic farming boom which may swell food budgets by hundreds of millions of dollars.

YOUR CHANGING EATING HABITS

"My daughter, fourteen, loves all food. My son, sixteen, likes oriental, kosher, and Italian. He is a gourmet. He likes chocolate-covered ants and grasshoppers. My son, nineteen, will eat anything that won't eat him first."

This was a Los Angeles housewife speaking in a recent survey of U.S. homemakers. Her colorful words illustrate today's complete breakdown in the traditional patterns of which foods go together with which other foods. They highlight the development of one new trend, what might be called a new "ethnic" jumbling together of foods: Italian, kosher, Chinese, soul food, etc., and suggest our billion-dollar-a-year stampede to exotic, gourmet foods.

In addition to this development, here are other key trends and changes in your eating habits:

(1) From a nutritional viewpoint, you are eating less well than in the mid-fifties. Only half of all American households are eating a good diet today, according to a massive and alarming Agriculture Department study. Nearly one family in ten in the $10,000-and-up income bracket has a diet rated as poor, and over all, one in five families has a diet rated as poor. Our per capita national consumption of such nutritional cornerstones as milk, fresh fruits, and vegetables has been declining steadily—replaced to a considerable extent by sweet snacks, sweet soft drinks, etc.

In the past two generations the proportion of calories we as a nation eat in the form of starches has dropped from 68 to 48 per cent, while the proportion in the form of sugar and other sweeteners has soared from 32 to 52 per cent. The old-fashioned fresh potato, one of the richest sources of key vitamins and minerals if you eat it in its skin, is being shunned, although potatoes actually contain fewer calories on an ounce-for-ounce basis than lima beans, prunes, rice, bran flakes, and most fruits canned in heavy syrup.

Our per capita consumption of fresh potatoes in 1973 was 82 pounds a year, versus 97 pounds in 1960.

(2) "Isolated eating" is in a strong uptrend. Breakfast, for millions of Americans, has become nothing more than a foraging expedition through the refrigerator and food cupboards, with each family member gulping down whatever foods are at hand and then hurrying off to work or school. Or it's "instant" breakfast made up of hopefully nutritious imitations.

Lunch also, for millions of children and jobholders, has become an institutional meal, served in school cafeterias or company restaurants. Only the homebound mother and her preschool children may eat lunch together. In fact, for a startling number of families, even sitting down to dinner is now strictly a weekend affair. The kids eat when they come home from school; if the father hasn't eaten downtown, he eats when he comes home hours later; the mother eats whenever.

This haphazard eating is blurring the old demarcation lines between meals. And increasing part of what is eaten is in the form of snacks.

(3) You are often skipping meals altogether, in most cases in your efforts to lose weight. According to a recent study, about one in five Americans in the nineteen- to twenty-four age bracket regularly skips lunch; 16 per cent skip breakfast; one in ten forgoes the evening meal.

(4) Eating out is on the increase—in restaurants, snack bars, fast food stores and stands. The proportion of our food dollar going for eating out (as contrasted with eating at home) is now 20 per cent.

(5) There has been a steady expansion of the office and factory coffee break. With orange juice or some similar food, pastries or rolls, and coffee now included, the coffee break has become a substitute for breakfast at home for workers at every level across the land.

This is not nearly as farfetched as it may appear, for as today's housewife finds she is little more than a short-order cook for her family, she will channel her culinary efforts into special meals for special occasions. She will do her short-order cooking as efficiently and quickly as possible, simultaneously investing ever larger amounts of her time and money in cooking schools, gourmet food guides, chafing dishes, barbecue pits, hibachis, etc. And, incidentally, the evidence is that she is teaching her daughter to cook this way too—to prepare foods on a piecemeal basis rather than systematically as a full meal.

BASIC RULES FOR SAVING ON FOOD

If you make an error in buying furniture, you're almost surely stuck. It may take you years to correct your mistake and you'll probably come out with a painful loss. But *if* you make an error in buying fruit, you can quickly learn from your mistake and only days later come out ahead when you again go shopping for food.

Food is among the biggest items in our cost of living and it is among the most expensive items in the budgets of low- and low-middle-income families. Yet, in contrast to the big-ticket items you buy only from time to time—furniture, automobiles, appliances—you buy food at least once or twice a week. Food is virtually the only major cash-and-carry item left in the typical budget. Thus, food is the one area where you can correct costly errors easily and start saving substantially from the day you determine to concentrate on so doing.

TWENTY KEYS

To be specific, here are twenty keys to saving:

(1) To begin with, plan before you go shopping. Always have a pad handy so you can note food items you need as your supplies run low. Group together the same kinds of foods and supplies to simplify your shopping in any store. Inspect your refrigerator, freezer, and cabinet or pantry shelves to see what you have on hand and what you need. Consult the store ads as you make up your shopping list and group the items on your list into the following categories:

> Groceries and canned foods
> Bakery products and cereals
> Dairy products
> Fresh fruits and vegetables
> Frozen foods
> Meat, fish, and poultry
> Non-foods (cleaning products, paper, etc.)
> Other

When your shopping list is ready, go over it to be sure you have chosen foods on the basis of their nutritional value—the amounts and proportions of protein, viamins, minerals they contain—rather than strictly on the basis of their "taste appeal." Spend your money first for those items, then go on to other foods that you merely want.

Use your list as you shop, and also take along whatever throwaway shopper ads might lead you to the bargains. Glance too at the price specials advertised in store windows—for clues to items you might want to add.

(2) Avoid snacks—among the most expensive food extras you can buy. They easily can add 10 per cent to your weekly food bill but will be among the least valuable nutritionally. Or, as an alternative, stick to snacks and beverages which have some nutritionally redeeming value—i.e., orange juice versus orange pop, fresh fruit versus candy, and whole-grain crackers, oatmeal-raisin-peanut-butter cookies versus chocolate or cream-filled ones.

(3) Keep in mind—as you make out your food lists and as you actually shop for food—what you'll do with inevitable leftovers. If you plan to make split pea soup using a hambone, for example, buy the split peas when you buy the ham. Also use the little leftovers in your refrigerator—bits of cheese, a dab of tuna fish or chicken, a slice or two of salami or ham—to make a smorgasbord that can serve as a complete lunch or supper. Or use the leftovers in a soup. Or make them the basis for a delicious platter of hors d'oeuvre. That's how hors d'oeuvre came into being, you know—out of bits of leftovers.

(4) If you possibly can, shop in person in the store: this will *always* give you the best value for your money and there is no real or comparably inexpensive substitute for this practice. You select the foods, you pay cash, you carry your purchases home. If you shop by telephone, have food delivered to your home, and charge these food purchases, you will pay for these conveniences—and the costs over a year will add up to whopping totals.

Do not—if you are a wife and can avoid it—let your husband come along on the weekly supermarket shopping trip (unless your husband routinely does the shopping). Husbands are notorious impulse buyers and almost inevitably overload the shopping cart with non-essentials and badly chosen brands and varieties of needed items.

Do not go shopping for food on an empty stomach, if you can help it. Shopping hungry is another way to boost your impulse buying. Surveys reveal those who shop after meals spend up to 17 per cent *less* than those who shop when hungry.

(5) Keep records of prices you're paying—particularly for such big items as meat—and shift your menus as prices dictate.

(6) Shop the specials and stock your freezer and pantry with foods you need or want when they are marked down.

(7) Consider quality in relation to your use of the food. If corn on the cob is the heart of your meal, of course you will buy the best quality you can afford. But if you're using corn as part of another dish, you'll do just as well with a much less expensive form of corn.

(8) Check the prices of private versus nationally advertised brands of foods you use frequently. Every food chain and many independent stores sell private-label foods, at savings running to as much as 20 per cent. The reasons: no advertising expenses are built into the private brands; no salesmen or promotion campaigns are pushing up the costs; and in many cases transportation is a smaller expense on private than on nationally advertised brands. The quality of many private-label products compares favorably with that of nationally advertised brands. And many brands are of identical quality because they're packed for retailers by the processors of the nationally advertised brands. Buy the brand you like best but try the less expensive private-label product at least once.

(9) Check the containers with care when you buy frozen foods and never buy an item that is covered with frost. Select only food that is stored below the freezer line at 0° or below. Under *no* circumstances buy a can of food that is bulging—and if you uncover such a can in your own pantry, toss it out.

(10) Buy such foods as meat by cost per portion rather than by over-all price. To find this cost, divide the price of the amount you purchase by the number of portions the amount will supply. More on this later.

(11) Buy such foods as bread or cereals by cost per ounce or pound. There is no waste involved here, so see which package offers the most weight for the identical price. More on this later, too.

Buy bulk items such as flour and sugar in bags rather than in boxes. By so doing, you're likely to save an average of nearly 20 per cent.

(12) Compare package sizes in relation to how quickly you will consume the contents. The "family economy size" is no bargain to you if you end up throwing out a lot of leftovers.

(13) Analyze the real cost of cooking from scratch versus buying "built-in maid service." It's not usual, but the cost of ingredients to prepare something at home may sometimes be *more* than the prepackaged convenience equivalent—especially if staples are left over.

(14) Compare different forms of food. More and more foods are sold in today's market in different forms—fresh, canned, frozen, chilled, and dried. Save money by comparing costs between different forms. As just one illustration of possible savings, per-serving costs of condensed soup run as little as one third the cost of water-added varieties. Before buying a particular item, check to see whether it's cheaper *to buy it fresh, canned, or frozen.* Relative costs change with seasonal patterns. Taste well may be your deciding factor; the difference in nutrition may be insignificant.

When you shop for low-calorie foods, stick to ordinary foods as much as possible—fresh celery, carrots, and radishes, plain beef consommé or chicken broth, fresh fruits and vegetables, regular canned tuna fish, low-fat milk— and avoid higher-priced items on the special diet shelf.

(15) Always remember the seasonal specials. Many of the fruits and vegetables which come to market in abundance in summer, cost 50 per cent less than in winter. But don't buy the *first* of a crop; prices will go down as the supply increases. Also time buying of canned and frozen fruits and vegetables to take advantage of the end-of-summer surpluses after new packs come in. And when these specials are advertised, stock up.

(16) Weigh the cost of gasoline—and time—in choosing a supermarket. The least expensive supermarket in your area almost surely won't be the cheapest for you if you have to drive twice the distance to reach it.

As a general rule, small convenience stores which stay open long hours seven days a week charge the highest prices. Next come small neighborhood "Mom and Pop" stores. Then supermarkets and the food discount stores.

(17) Substitute among protein foods as prices dictate. Try beef or pork liver instead of calf's liver; poultry instead of red meats; bean, cheese, and egg dishes instead of meat dishes. Among today's best protein bargains: chicken, hamburger, eggs, cottage cheese, peanut butter, dry beans, American process cheese.

(18) Use the recipes and food-buying tips offered to you by the Department of Agriculture, your local consumer organizations, and your local newspaper's food editor.

(19) Also use the Agriculture Department's publications, which are designed to help you. The department is loaded with booklets and pamphlets on how to buy, raise, store, cook, and combine food of all kinds—available from the Superintendent of Documents, Washington, D.C. 20402.

Among the key titles:

Your Money's Worth in Foods (Home and Garden Bulletin No. 183)

Family Fare: A Guide to Good Nutrition (Home and Garden Bulletin No. 1)

Beef and Veal in Family Meals (Home and Garden Bulletin No. 118)

Family Food Buying, A Guide for Calculating Amounts to Buy and Comparing Costs (Home Economics Research Report No. 37)

Toward the New, A Report on Better Foods and Nutrition from Agricultural Research (Agriculture Information Bulletin No. 341)

The Food We Eat (Miscellaneous Publication No. 870)

Conserving the Nutritive Values in Foods (Home and Garden Booklet No. 90)

Composition of Foods, Raw, Processed, Prepared (Agriculture Handbook No. 8)

(20) Hunt for the nutrition bargains and *don't* overbuy meat. Use the following guides, developed by the U. S. Department of Agriculture on the minimum amounts of each major type of food we at various ages should consume daily for proper nutrition:

Milk: children under 9 years, 2 to 3 cups; 9 to 12 years, 3 or more cups; teen-agers, 4 or more cups; adults, 2 or more cups; pregnant women, 3 or more cups; nursing mothers, 4 or more cups. (Note: Cheese, ice cream, and milk used in cooking count as part of the day's milk.)

Meat: 2 or more servings of either beef or veal, pork, lamb, poultry, fish, shellfish, eggs—with dry beans, peas, nuts as alternates.

Vegetables and fruits: 4 or more servings with a dark green or deep yellow vegetable at least every other day; a citrus fruit or other fruit or vegetable rich in vitamin C daily; other vegetables and fruits, including potatoes.

Bread and cereal: 4 or more servings—whole grain, enriched, or restored —of breads, bakery foods, cereals, crackers, grits, macaroni, spaghetti, noodles, rice.

STILL MORE SAVINGS VIA "TRADING DOWN"

Do you realize how much you could reduce your food bill by "trading down" in the supermarket today—by choosing the least expensive version available of each item on your grocery list? You're surely generally aware that you could achieve big savings simply by doing this instead of trading up to the highest-quality, most convenient, fanciest-label foods. But would you have guessed that the savings I recorded in a recent shopping experiment of my own amounted to 88 per cent?

For the experiment, I asked an eagle-eyed young housewife-friend to wheel two shopping carts through a huge supermarket in my area of the country; first she would load cart number 1 with the most expensive possible items and then load cart number 2 with the least expensive.

In the milk category, it was regular fresh milk in cart number 1 and powdered milk in cart number 2. And "potatoes" meant fancy Idahos for cart number 1 but plain old Maine spuds for cart number 2. And so on down the line. . . .

When she checked the two carts for me, the bargain cart came to $22.54 less than the most expensive assortment. I won't give you the complete breakdown on the carts, because prices for specific items vary so widely from time to time and area to area. But the total is representative—and if you multiplied it by fifty-two weeks, you would have savings amounting to $1,172.08 a year!

Here is my full shopping list, with the dollar difference *and* the percentage savings between high- and low-priced items:

ITEM	$ DIFFERENCE	% SAVING
Frankfurters (2 lbs.)	$ .49	22%
Hamburger (3 lbs.)	1.62	39
Liver (2 lbs.)	1.80	64
Bacon (2 lbs.)	1.00	42
Steak (3 lbs.)	5.40	69
Eggs (2 doz.)	.12	8
Butter (2 lbs.)	.06	3
Milk (8 qts.)	1.57	61
Coffee (2 lbs.)	.08	5
White bread (2 loaves)	.48	49
Frozen peas (6 pkgs.)	1.41	52

ITEM	$ DIFFERENCE	% SAVING
Pears (2 large cans)	.20	17
Mayonnaise (large jar)	.06	9
Vegetable soup (4 cans)	.44	44
Cat food (3 cans)	.24	41
Frozen orange juice		
(4 6-oz. cans)	.39	33
Tomatoes (2 large cans)	.19	22
Salad oil (1 qt.)	1.26	62
Beer (6-pack)	2.60	72
Cookies (1 box)	.70	71
Onions (3 lbs.)	.49	42
Spaghetti (2 boxes)	.10	18
Potatoes (10 lbs.)	.89	41
Liquid detergent (1 qt.)	.50	56
Flour (5 lbs.)	.45	49

The rundown speaks for itself. In some cases, splurge items cost twice to three times as much as non-splurge items. In some cases, too, the shopper has obviously sacrificed quality (although probably not much nutritional value). In other cases, though, there's no significant difference between the cart number 1 item and the cart number 2 item.

Convenience, too, was ignored in cart number 2—e.g., no pre-peeled vegetables, no butter added to frozen foods, no pre-pattied hamburgers, no individual servings of this or that. But, of course, convenience is part of the sacrifice a careful shopper must pay to reap the maximum savings from trading down.

I'm not suggesting you stick strictly to the cheapest available foods or other items. Most of you don't want to nor do you need to. But even though you can afford to splurge and trade up, not down, is it not fascinating to see how much you could save if your tried to trade down? And you need not go this far. All you really need to do is to buy essentially the same foods in less expensive form.

Here, for instance, are two menus which reveal that you can almost double the cost of your meal by choosing the more expensive variety of meat, fruit, or vegetable or, conversely, you can cut it nearly in half by choosing the less expensive variety.

LESS EXPENSIVE	MORE EXPENSIVE
Grapefruit half	Cantaloupe
Chuck steak	Sirloin steak
Baked potato with sour cream	Frozen creamed potato with chives
Frozen peas buttered at home	Frozen peas in butter sauce
Tossed salad	Salad with tomatoes, avocados
Rye bread	Garlic bread
Chocolate pudding	Frozen éclairs

These two menus were priced in 1974. For four persons, the less expensive menu came to $3.80; the more expensive totaled $6.60.

SHOPPING THE DISCOUNT STORES

Discounting has become the biggest, hottest trend in food retailing today. And you are shouting your preference for this no-frills, big-scale, moneysaving method of food buying.

How much do you save by shopping in discount food stores? According to a major study by A&P, weekly savings run around 11 per cent. Other studies indicate over-all savings generally at from 5 to 15 per cent.

There are two key types of discount operations: general merchandise discount stores which include a food department, and separate stores devoted solely to food.

If you shop in discount stores you'll probably have to travel some distance—and in view of fuel costs, have to space your shopping trips more widely to reap in full the bargains they offer. You'll probably forfeit many of the usual supermarket amenities—ranging from carry-out service to Muzak. You probably won't find trading stamps in these places. You may even have to pick some of your foods out of cut cases instead of neat shelf displays—and in some cases you may have to make do with a smaller variety of products.

But if none of these aspects bothers you and if you have the gas, oil, and use of a car at least once a week, try out the local discount stores. Ask friends about their experience with these stores. Read newspaper ads and compare prices. Then see how much money *you* can save.

START YOUR OWN FOOD BUYING CLUB

If food co-operatives, food warehouses, and other wholesale outlets are operating in your area, by all means use them too. You'll buy staples such as rice, sugar, flour in 25- or 50-pound bags; you'll bag your own purchases and you'll pick the produce you want to buy straight out of packing cases.

You'll also achieve savings ranging from 20 per cent up.

Or you can join with other families to start your own food buying club.

HOW THE CLUBS WORK

Here are tips from New York City's Department of Consumer Affairs on how these clubs work and on how to make a success out of this type of arrangement:

• A buying club may consist of as few as ten to twelve families. Clubs often sell items to members practically at cost. Their small size eliminates the need for the usual supermarket overhead—such as trucks, large distribution centers, hired helpers.

• Members must be compatible—both in personality and in food tastes. Each member must be willing to do his or her share of the work load, to avoid having to hire the outside help which raises costs and defeats the purpose of small-group buying.

• There must be several people for each job: driving, simple bookkeeping, distributing, and buying. This system permits rotation of tasks and prevents any one member from being too heavily burdened.

• Members must be willing to do as much shopping as possible through the club.

• Buying is usually done by two or more buyers going once a week to wholesale markets, which are generally listed in the Yellow Pages. Each week, one buyer who has gone the week before accompanies a novice, to lend his or her previous experience (for example; a and b, then b and c, then c and d). The general shopping list for produce is: two types of fruit, one cooking vegetable, salad vegetables, potatoes, and onions. Meat is often ordered in advance from a distributor or a reliable local butcher who will give discounts.

• After the food is purchased, it is taken to a prearranged point for distribution, often a member's house or apartment. The food is sold at a price to cover the purchase price plus gasoline, oil, other incidentals.

• Buying clubs do *not* compete with each other. In fact, small clubs find it beneficial to co-operate in exchanging names of stores, recipes, and new ideas. Several buying clubs may co-operate on large-scale purchases for which an individual club would not receive a discount.

• A key problem for the clubs may be losses resulting from spoilage of unsold goods. This leftover food might be sold to outsiders via a "leftover list" of names of people who may be called after members have shopped.

• Another problem might arise when members feel that small children prevent them from participating. Some buying clubs have successfully added a baby-sitting system to their operation on buying days.

• Members should pay for their food not later than the day before the next week's buying. Members who regularly fail to pay on time, refuse to help, or do little buying harm the club. It is often best for the club to drop such members.

There must be open discussion of disagreements in order to reach constructive answers to the club's problems, whatever they turn out to be.

• Buying clubs of this type report big savings. The clubs find, moreover, that the quality of their food improves as well. And they have more bargaining power since wholesalers try to please large purchasers.

WHOLESALE UNITS

Here are the wholesale units in which food is boxed or weighed for wholesale:

Dairy and Produce

1. American cheese—5 lbs.
2. Eggs—30 doz.
3. Rice—25, 50, 100 lbs. (bags)
4. Lettuce—24 (box)
5. Tomatoes—20 lbs. (box)
6. Potatoes—50 lbs. (bag)
7. Onions—50 lbs. (bag)
8. Apples—36 or 40 lbs. (box)
9. Oranges—48, 56, 64, 72, 80 (box)
10. Bananas—40 lbs. (box)

Meats (may vary from place to place)

1. Chicken—per head
2. Ground chuck—10 lbs. or more
3. Bacon—12 lbs. (box)
4. Frankfurters—12 lbs. (box)
5. Flank steak—15 lbs.
6. Stew beef—10 lbs.
7. Pork chops—16–20 lbs.
8. Spare ribs—30 lbs.
9. Liver—8–11 lbs.

WHERE TO GET INFORMATION

An excellent source of further information on food buying clubs and co-ops and on shopping for wholesale foods is: The Cooperative League of the U.S.A., Suite 1100, 1828 L Street, N.W., Washington, D.C. 20036.

How to Read Food Labels

Q. *What is the difference between chicken "patties" and chicken "burgers"—in terms of the amount of chicken each contains?*

A. Chicken burgers must consist of 100 per cent chicken. If cereals or other fillers are used, they must be labeled patties.

Q. *How much meat must spaghetti with meatballs contain?*

A. Twelve per cent or more meat.

Q. *What's the difference between "beef and gravy" and "gravy and beef"?*

A. In beef and gravy, the primary ingredient is beef. With gravy and beef, it's the other way around.

These and other vital details, which are at least implied by the labels of hundreds of food products you buy regularly—or which may be stated among our many federal food standards—are key clues to how much of a bargain you are getting for your food dollar. Many labels tell you, too, how much of major nutrients, especially protein, are contained in each can or package.

The true value of what you are buying lies in what amounts of basic ingredients you are getting—not simply in the net weight of the food. Thus, by knowing something about food standards and some of the rules for reading food labels, you can consistently stretch your food dollar.

Here is a valuable rundown on labels and standards* to use to compare products and prices in the supermarket:

• Under federal law as of 1974, every package of food, drugs, or cosmetics must contain the following information on its label in plain English: name of the product; name and address of manufacturer, packer, or distributor; net amount of contents or weight in pounds and ounces and in the total number of ounces; details of dietary characteristics, if appropriate; note of whether the product contains artificial coloring, flavoring, or chemical preservatives; a list of the ingredients, except for certain products (e.g., mayonnaise, macaroni, bread, jams, ketchup, canned fruits and vegetables) for which federal "standards of identity" defining basic ingredients have been established.

• Next, certain descriptive details are required for certain products, primarily canned fruits and vegetables: the variety (white or yellow corn, for instance); style of pack (whole, diced); material in which packaged (sugar, syrup, water).

• Ingredients must be listed in *descending* order of their volume (if a beef stew list shows beef way down and potatoes way up on the list, this is your clue that you are buying mostly potatoes).

• If the food is an imitation, this fact must be stated, and if there is a picture of the product within, it must be accurate.

• Baby food labels must state the nutritional elements they contain—proteins, vitamins, minerals—plus, in the case of strained baby foods, a list of the ingredients.

• Meats and other foods to which special vitamins and minerals have been added or which are claimed to have special nutritional properties ("enriched") must carry labels telling their calorie content, amounts of proteins, and amounts of key vitamins and minerals.

* 1974.

• On the major cuts of the carcasses, meats may carry the U. S. Department of Agriculture's inspection stamp. Federally inspected poultry—fresh or frozen—carries a stamp "inspected for wholesomeness."

• Then there are federal standards covering a host of prepared and convenience foods, especially those containing meat or poultry, that are not stated on the label.

• In addition, you may or may not find on a food package a brand name; directions for storage or suggestions for cooking; a food quality grade set by the Department of Agriculture.

LABEL STANDARDS FOR WELL-KNOWN FOODS

Many labels will undergo marked improvements as the Agriculture Department and Food and Drug Administration continue to revise their labeling rules and its standards. But you can use the following list of standards right now to help you shop for a variety of well-known products and to stretch your food dollar at least a bit more:

Baby Food (High Meat Dinner)—At least 30 per cent meat.

Baby Food (Vegetable and Meat)—At least 8 per cent meat.

Barbecue Sauce with Meat—At least 35 per cent meat.

Beans with Frankfurters in Sauce—At least 20 per cent franks.

Beef Burgundy—At least 50 per cent beef.

Beef Sausage (*raw*)—No more than 30 per cent fat.

Beef Stroganoff—At least 45 per cent fresh uncooked or 30 per cent cooked beef.

Beef with Gravy—At least 50 per cent beef.

Gravy with Beef—At least 35 per cent beef.

Breaded Steaks, Chops, etc.—Breading can't exceed 30 per cent of finished product weight.

Breakfast (*frozen product containing meat*)—At least 15 per cent meat.

Breakfast Sausage—No more than 50 per cent fat.

Cannelloni with Meat and Sauce—At least 10 per cent meat.

Chili con Carne—At least 40 per cent meat.

Chili con Carne with Beans—At least 25 per cent meat.

Chop Suey (*American Style*) *with Macaroni and Meat*—At least 25 per cent meat.

Chow Mein Vegetables with Meat—At least 12 per cent meat.

Deviled Ham—No more than 35 per cent fat.

Dinners (*frozen with meat*)—At least 25 per cent meat.

Egg Rolls with Meat—At least 10 per cent meat.

Enchiladas with Meat—At least 15 per cent meat.

Frankfurters, Bologna, Other Cooked Sausage—"Beef" hot dogs may contain beef only. Hot dogs made of other animals must be so labeled. Foods labeled "frankfurter," "bologna," and the like may contain only skeletal meat (the muscle part of beef). Up to 15 per cent poultry meat, water, sweeteners, and curing agents are allowed too. Any binders such as cereals, non-fat dry milk, or soy protein must be clearly listed on the labels —for instance, "franks, non-fat dry milk added." The maximum for binders is 3½ per cent. Non-skeletal meat, such as tongues and internal organs, may be included if the term "with variety meats" or "with by-products" appears on the label.

Gravies—At least 25 per cent stock or broth, or at least 6 per cent meat.

Ham (canned)—Limited to 8 per cent total weight gain via juices after processing.

Ham (not canned)—Must not weigh more after processing than the fresh ham weighs before curing and smoking; if contains up to 10 per cent added weight, must be labeled "Ham—Water Added"; if more than 10 per cent, must be labeled "Imitation Ham."

Hamburger or Ground Beef—No more than 30 per cent fat; no extenders.

Ham Spread—At least 50 per cent ham.

Hash—At least 35 per cent meat.

Lasagna with Meat and Sauce—At least 12 per cent meat.

Liver Sausage, Liver Paste, and similar liver products—At least 30 per cent liver.

Meatballs—No more than 12 per cent extenders (cereal, etc.).

Meatballs in Sauce—At least 50 per cent meatballs.

Meat Pies—At least 25 per cent meat.

Meat Ravioli—At least 10 per cent meat in ravioli filling.

Meat Ravioli in Sauce—At least 10 per cent meat.

Meat Soups (ready to eat)—At least 5 per cent meat.

Meat Soups (condensed)—At least 10 per cent meat.

Meat Spreads—At least 50 per cent meat.

Pâté de Foie—At least 30 per cent liver.

Pizza with Meat—At least 15 per cent meat.

Pizza with Sausage—At least 12 per cent sausage (cooked basis) or 10 per cent dry sausage.

Pork Sausage—Not more than 50 per cent fat.

Sauce with Meat or Meat Sauce—At least 6 per cent meat.

Scrapple—At least 40 per cent meat and/or meat by-products.

Shepherd's Pie—At least 25 per cent meat; no more than 50 per cent mashed potatoes.

Stews (Beef, Lamb, and the like)—At least 25 per cent meat.

Stuffed Cabbage with Meat in Sauce—At least 12 per cent meat.

Swiss Steak with Gravy—At least 50 per cent meat.

Gravy and Swiss Steak—At least 35 per cent meat.

Tamales—At least 25 per cent meat.

Veal Parmigiana—At least 40 per cent breaded meat product in sauce.

Breaded Poultry—No more than 30 per cent breading.

Canned Boned Poultry—At least 90 per cent poultry meat, skin, and fat.

Poultry à la King—At least 20 per cent poultry meat.

Poultry Chow Mein, without Noodles—At least 4 per cent poultry meat.

Poultry Dinners—At least 18 per cent poultry meat.

Poultry Fricassee—At least 20 per cent poultry meat.

Poultry Pies—At least 14 per cent poultry meat.

Poultry Salad—At least 25 per cent poultry meat.

Poultry Soup—At least 2 per cent poultry meat.

Poultry Tetrazzini—At least 15 per cent poultry meat.

Corned Beef Hash—At least 35 per cent beef; also must contain potatoes, curing agents, and seasonings; no more than 15 per cent fat. Nor more than 72 per cent moisture.

Chopped Ham—Must contain fresh, cured, or smoked ham, along with certain specified kinds of curing agents and seasonings.

Oleomargarine or Margarine—Fat in finished product may not exceed 80 per cent; label must indicate whether product is from animal or vegetable origin or both.

These standards signify progress. Far more meaningful disclosures will come when we also have information in the following areas:

Nutrition: Information on just how much of each vitamin and mineral a package contains surely would be a boon to all of us.

Calorie counts: I cannot exaggerate the frustration I feel when I buy a food labeled "diet" and then cannot find how many calories there are in a slice or cup or tablespoon. This should be mandatory on at least the diet foods. We also should be able to tell how much lower in fats the so-called lower-fat foods are.

Drained weight: If we knew the net weight of soups, minus water, for instance, we could compare the volume of real food—meat, vegetables, etc. —in various soups. In many cases, we would find a concentrated, thick meaty soup is a much greater value at 45¢ a can than a watered-down equivalent at 30¢.

Key ingredients: Labels should tell us much more clearly what proportion of "beef stew" actually is beef, what proportion of fruit is in a fruit drink.

Recommended food storage conditions: Labels should specify how long a package of frozen beans may be kept in the freezer, for instance.

A universal simple "ABC" grading system: Such a system for foods would eliminate our confusion because of the variety of federal food grading systems (especially important in meat).

"TRUTH IN MEAT" LABELING

Look carefully in your supermarket meat counter. Has the piece of beef you've known as "California roast" been transformed into a "Beef Chuck—Under Blade Roast"? Has the old-time "London broil" been renamed a "Beef Flank Steak"? Or the traditional "Delmonico steak" reappeared as "Beef Rib—Eye Steak"?

Starting in late 1973, a whole new system of meat labeling was introduced in supermarkets, meat markets and grocery stores from coast to coast. The "Truth in Meat" program is voluntary but it is the meat industry's big push to let you know not only what you're getting for your money but also how to cook it.

Thus, here's what to look for in the stores where you do your meat buying:

• Each package of meat labeled with the name of the animal species (beef, veal, pork, lamb); the "primal cut"—breast or brisket, shoulder (chuck) arm, shoulder (chuck) blade; rib, loin, sirloin (hip), and leg (round); and one of its more than 300 common, standardized retail names. (In addition, if it wants to, a store may add its own fanciful name—such as "his and her" steaks or "Paradise roast." Hamburger, though, is "ground beef" or "ground sirloin" or "ground chuck." T-bone steak is beef loin T-bone.

• The lean meat ratio of ground meat labeled, with the maximum percentage of fat set at 25 per cent.

• A variety of booklets and meat identification charts available next to meat counters—giveaways detailing both the "what you're getting" and "how to cook it" angles.

The system has been hailed by the meat industry as "the most significant meat-counter improvement since the introduction of self-service nearly four decades ago." But it is just one step toward real consumer information protection at the meat counter. There's a long way to go.

"OPEN DATING"

"Open dating" means the clear marking on all packages or containers of perishable or semiperishable foods with a date "pull" after which they should be removed from sale to you. These products are guaranteed to have a normal period of use in the home after the date. As a result of this form of labeling, disappearing from store shelves are the cryptic grocery codes that tell store managers the condition of the foods on sale but make a secret of the same information to us.

To get the maximum benefit:

(1) Learn the basic fact that the date on a package or container of perishable foods is frequently the "pull" date—the last permissible day of

sale for that item from its normal shelf position in the store. After that day the product must be removed from regular sale.

(2) If you see an item on sale after that date, it should be in an off-shelf special display position and be offered at a greatly reduced price. It also must still be safe for consumption, of course.

(3) If you find cryptic codes on some items, ask the store for an explanation or for a free explanatory booklet and be sure you understand.

(4) If you do discover that you have bought an out-of-date item that was not on special sale as such, take it back at once and demand a refund.

(5) Use your own head about the proper storage and refrigeration of perishables. According to a Rutgers University study, temperature is seven times as important as time in maintaining freshness—and that applies whether you have the food in hand or whether it is still in the store. Don't buy perishables and then stop on the way home to have lunch or pick up your children or whatever.

How to Compare Unit Costs Per Pound of Food

WHICH IS THE BIGGER BARGAIN?

Q. *Which is the bigger bargain: $4.77 for a box of powder to make 20 quarts of non-fat dry milk or $3.27 for a box to make 12 quarts of the same brand of dry milk?*

A. The 20-quart package works out to 24¢ a quart and is therefore a bigger bargain than the 12-quart package, which works out to 27¢ a quart.

Q. *Which is cheaper: a 1-lb. 2-oz. jar of peanut butter costing 53¢ or a 12-oz. jar of the same brand costing 35¢?*

A. Neither. In both cases, the per pound cost is 47¢.

Q. *Which is more economical: a 1-lb. 14-oz. can of sliced pineapple costing 47¢ or an 8½-oz. can costing 21¢?*

A. The larger can—by far. The pineapple costs 25¢ a pound in the larger can, but 40¢ a pound in the small can.

These illustrations underline the extent to which you, the manager of the family pocketbook, can make errors in your purchases if you do not know the price per measure as well as the total dollar price.

At the same time, the comparisons indicate the enormous savings which you can achieve by buying large versus small packages. You don't have to be a mathematical genius to figure out, just from these few examples, that you could save hundreds of dollars per year—without necessarily sacrificing any quality in any item—just by buying the large package sizes instead of the small.

But there are infuriating exceptions. In one study of one major dry detergent, the per ounce cost of the *largest* available size (more than 16 pounds) was significantly *greater* than the cost of either of the next two smaller sizes.

The trend across the land is relentlessly toward new laws requiring retailers to provide shelf labels under each item with a price per ounce, quart, pound, or other unit as well as with the total retail price for the package. Most of the major retail food chains now use some kind of unit pricing system. In almost every major city the pricing system has become available. Increasing numbers of states have laws requiring unit pricing on a state-wide basis.

In this era of record and rising food prices, unit pricing could be the U.S. food shopper's biggest moneysaving weapon. For it is virtually your sole means of comparing the true unit cost of what you buy in the supermarket.

HOW TO USE UNIT PRICING

Next time you go to the food store, look on the edge of the shelf under the article you are considering buying. If the store uses unit pricing, you will find a label which tells the cost per measure (pound, pint, number, etc.) of the item. That's the unit price. This breaks down the total cost of the particular package or can into a simple standard so that you can now choose between brands and sizes on the basis of price.

You'll find other numbers on most labels, but they'll be inventory numbers which you need not bother about.

For instance, say you are buying tomato juice.

A 46-ounce can of a store brand is priced 2 for 65¢, the unit price is 23¢ a quart; a 1-quart bottle of brand A sells for 35¢, the unit price is 35¢ a quart; an 18-ounce of brand B sells at 2 for 35¢, the unit price is 31¢ a quart; a 6-pack of 5½-ounce cans of brand B sells at 51¢, the unit price is 49¢ a quart.

If you look at the unit prices, it will be easy to find the best buy. And surely it's worth while to discover that you can buy more than two quarts of the first for the price of one quart of the fourth. With prices given per quart, all you need do is look and compare.

Or to give you another illustration—how "pretty" do you like your olives?

A 2-ounce jar of "thrown" olives (those put in the jar at random) costs seven cents less than a jar of "placed" olives (those put in the jar in a pattern with the pimentos nicely facing out and lined up). On this week's grocery bill the difference may seem small, but on a cents-per-pound basis the gap really grows.

Of course, you will shop for quality and in terms of your personal preferences too—but why not use unit pricing to save money when quality is not of prime importance and when you have no special preferences? *Why not use the weapon now that you have it?*

UNIT COST TABLE

Unit pricing is not yet universal—not by far.

And, a recent survey revealed, shoppers make the "wrong" choices a shocking 40 per cent of the time on which can or bottle or package is cheapest—on a per-ounce or per-pound basis—*when the packages are not unit-priced.* These errors translate into an average cost of 10¢ on every $1.00 spent in the grocery store. Thus, on a food bill of $100, $10 may be going down the drain simply because you are not choosing the most economical food.

So until unit pricing is in every store, here's a "Cost Weight Table" which you can translate on your own into extraordinary savings. Copy it and put it into your purse to refer to when you shop from now on.

To calculate the unit cost of a product, no matter what size or shape package it comes in, first locate the net weight of the food package in the left-hand column. Then locate the total price of the package along the top of the table. These reference points will lead you directly to the price per pound in the appropriate middle column. By comparing the unit cost of one package with another size, you can discover which is the better bargain.

PACKAGE WEIGHT (IN OUNCES)	COST PER POUND IF THE COST PER PACKAGE IS:				
	5¢	10¢	15¢	20¢	25¢
1	$ .80	$1.60	$2.40	$3.20	$4.00
2	.40	.80	1.20	1.60	2.00
3	.27	.53	.80	1.07	1.33
4	.20	.40	.60	.80	1.00
5	.16	.32	.48	.64	.80
6	.13	.27	.40	.53	.67
7	.11	.23	.34	.46	.57
8	.10	.20	.30	.40	.50
9	.09	.18	.27	.36	.44
10	.08	.16	.24	.32	.40
11	.07	.15	.22	.29	.36
12	.07	.13	.20	.27	.33
13	.06	.12	.18	.25	.31
14	.06	.11	.17	.23	.29
15	.05	.11	.16	.21	.27
16	.05	.10	.15	.20	.25
17	.05	.09	.14	.19	.24

PACKAGE WEIGHT (IN OUNCES)	COST PER POUND IF THE COST PER PACKAGE IS:				
	5¢	10¢	15¢	20¢	25¢
18	.04	.09	.13	.18	.22
19	.04	.08	.13	.17	.21
20	.04	.08	.12	.16	.20
21	.04	.08	.11	.15	.19
22	.04	.07	.11	.15	.18
23	.03	.07	.10	.14	.17
24	.03	.07	.10	.13	.17
25	.03	.06	.10	.13	.16
26	.03	.06	.09	.12	.15
27	.03	.06	.09	.12	.15
28	.03	.06	.09	.11	.14
29	.03	.06	.08	.11	.14
30	.03	.05	.08	.11	.13
31	.03	.05	.08	.11	.13
32	.03	.05	.08	.10	.13
33	.02	.05	.07	.10	.12
34	.02	.05	.07	.09	.12
35	.02	.05	.07	.09	.11
36	.02	.04	.07	.09	.11
37	.02	.04	.06	.09	.11
38	.02	.04	.06	.08	.11
39	.02	.04	.06	.08	.10
40	.02	.04	.06	.08	.10

PACKAGE WEIGHT (IN OUNCES)	COST PER POUND IF THE COST PER PACKAGE IS:				
	30¢	35¢	40¢	45¢	50¢
1	$4.80	$5.60	$6.40	$7.20	$8.00
2	2.40	2.80	3.20	3.60	4.00
3	1.60	1.87	2.13	2.40	2.67
4	1.20	1.40	1.60	1.80	2.00
5	.96	1.12	1.28	1.44	1.60
6	.80	.93	1.07	1.20	1.33
7	.69	.80	.91	1.03	1.14
8	.60	.70	.80	.90	1.00
9	.53	.62	.71	.80	.89
10	.48	.56	.64	.72	.80

PACKAGE WEIGHT (IN OUNCES)	COST PER POUND IF THE COST PER PACKAGE IS:				
	30¢	35¢	40¢	45¢	50¢
11	.44	.51	.58	.65	.73
12	.40	.47	.53	.60	.67
13	.37	.43	.49	.55	.62
14	.34	.40	.46	.51	.57
15	.32	.37	.43	.48	.53
16	.30	.35	.40	.45	.50
17	.28	.33	.38	.42	.47
18	.27	.31	.36	.40	.44
19	.25	.29	.34	.38	.42
20	.24	.28	.32	.36	.40
21	.23	.27	.30	.34	.38
22	.22	.25	.29	.33	.36
23	.21	.24	.28	.31	.35
24	.20	.23	.27	.30	.33
25	.19	.22	.26	.29	.32
26	.18	.22	.25	.28	.31
27	.18	.21	.24	.27	.30
28	.17	.20	.23	.26	.29
29	.17	.19	.22	.25	.28
30	.16	.19	.21	.24	.27
31	.15	.18	.21	.23	.26
32	.15	.18	.20	.23	.25
33	.15	.17	.19	.22	.24
34	.14	.16	.19	.21	.24
35	.14	.16	.18	.21	.23
36	.13	.16	.18	.20	.22
37	.13	.15	.17	.19	.22
38	.13	.15	.17	.19	.21
39	.12	.14	.16	.18	.21
40	.12	.14	.16	.18	.20

NOTES: *Change the weight on a package to ounces if necessary:*

1 pound=16 ounces
1 pint=16 fluid ounces

This will help you figure out weights which are in between a single pound or pint. For instance, 1 pound 10 ounces or 1 pint 10 ounces may be translated into 16 ounces plus 10 ounces, or 26 ounces. Thus, if a product weighs 26 ounces and is priced at 35¢, the price per pound is 22¢.

You can use this table if a package weighs more than 40 ounces or more than 50 cents. Just divide the weight and price of any package weighing more than 40 ounces by 2 and, with the resulting figures, use the table above. Or just divide the price and weight of any package priced at more than 50¢ by 2 and also use the table above.

How to Save on Meat

CLASSIC DEMAND-PULL INFLATION

In food prices—and especially in meat prices—we saw in the post-World War II period a classic illustration of demand-pull inflation.

When *you demand* more and more meat, when you steadily increase your purchases of higher-quality meats across the board, when you stand in line at the supermarket counters, your relentless buying *pulls* up the prices of all the meats in your market basket. This is what economists call *demand-pull* inflation.

Although the blow-off in meat prices generally and in beef prices in particular in 1973–74 interrupted the long-term upsurge in our consumption of meat, the fundamental remains: as our family incomes rise, so do the proportions of our budgets allocated to meats. In three days out of five, we eat red meat and that meat usually is beef. Between one fourth and one third of your annual food bill is spent on meat, poultry, and fish—making these the biggest items in your food budget.

GENERAL MONEYSAVING HINTS

The retail price you pay for meat is not necessarily a reliable guide to its quality, nutritive value, *or* tenderness. Meat prices, instead, depend on such factors as the popularity of a given meat cut or brand or grade; the season of the year; the type of store in which the meat is sold; the type and amount of handling and processing.

As a general rule, beef prices are lower in winter and higher in late summer. Steak prices tend to be highest during the summer "cookout" months and roasts cost more in the late fall and early winter "oven-cooking" months. In contrast, veal prices tend to be lowest in the spring and summer and highest in the winter.

Now here are vitally important general hints for saving money on meat —including "old" ones which a surprising number of Americans have been pulling out of their memories and "new" ones recently put together by consumer economists:

• Shift your family to less expensive cuts of each type of meat. Since nearly four fifths of the beef we buy is *not* naturally tender enough to broil, barbecue, or roast, in this area you will find your biggest meat bargains. With a little special handling, the less expensive cuts can be made virtually as tender and tasteful as the costlier cuts.

Important note: The nutrient content of these cuts is at least as great as that of the more expensive cuts while the fat content in most cases is significantly lower. (See Protein Bargains chart, p. 186, for details on this point.) For example, you can buy good chuck steaks and roasts at bargain prices. Short ribs are another delicious cut of beef which you can barbecue indoors or out. So are beef shank, brisket, and short loin. Lamb chops cut from the shoulder often cost 20 to 40¢ less per pound than rib or loin chops.

Among the other less expensive cuts and types of meat are: ground beef, stew meat, pot roast, beef shank, brisket, short loin, heel of round roast, pork shoulder and rump, lamb shanks, ground lamb.

Among steaks, some of the least expensive cuts are blade and arm chuck steaks, flank steak, sirloin tip, and bottom round. The "broiling steaks"—sirloin, porterhouse, etc.—rarely are bargains except as occasional sales features.

• Experiment with the help of your gourmet cookbook, preparing such "variety" meats as liver, heart, sweetbreads, tripe, kidneys, tongue, brains. Most of these rank high in nutrition. They also are among the "great" foods in Europe and are served in the finest French restaurants everywhere.

• Save simply by learning the cooking rules in your cookbook. You will save an impressive amount on meats, for instance, if you roast them at no more than 300° to 325° F. They will shrink less; be tenderer; be easier to carve. Remember, the higher the temperature of your oven, the more your meats will shrink.

• Check what "family packs" are available—such as bulk hamburger, chops, chicken. Meat in larger quantities is almost invariably offered at lower prices than in smaller packages. You can always do a bit of home butchering—e.g., cutting your own rib steaks from an extra-thick roast beef or cutting a whole pork loin three ways. (An inexpensive hack saw with a good blade will substitute for a butcher's saw when you have to cut through bone.) You can then use the center section as chops, which will cost you considerably less than if you buy the chops in a package by themselves. Or, if you buy bologna, buy it in a chunk. By slicing it at home, you may cut as much as 10¢ a pound from the piece.

• Try buying 2- or 3-pound boxes of bacon "ends and pieces." It may be slightly less lean than regularly packaged bacon and it's not cut uniformly. But it comes from the same animal and may cost only one third or one half what regular bacon costs. Also, consider bacon a condiment rather than meat in view of its high cost per serving and try to serve only two pieces per person instead of three or four. Typically, a pound of bacon dwindles to 3 to 5 ounces and some brands yield as little as 18 to 20 per cent of their original volume.

• Study and compare prices of canned meats—ham, beef roast, corned beef, chopped beef, luncheon loaves, meat in barbecue sauce, turkey, and chicken, to name just a few. Every ounce of these is edible. Canned-meat meals tend to be even greater money- and timesavers for small families.

• Don't overfeed your family with meat, a definitely concentrated source of calories. Overweight is one of our country's leading health problems, and the top cause for overweight is overeating. Meat also tends to be high in cholesterol. There is no reason to feed any family member more than 6 to 8 ounces of meat in one meal. Or try experimenting with even smaller servings (e.g., 3 ounces per meal) for a week—and see who, if anybody, screams.

• When you buy ground beef, try the least expensive forms first and "work your way up" if these don't satisfy your tastes. In a major study of hamburger, Consumers Union found that the price difference from hamburger grade to grade—e.g., from ground beef to ground chuck to ground round—was as much as 40¢ a pound in the same store, although analysis showed that the differences in amounts of fat, water, and protein were "indistinguishable."

• Try buying meat at local discount stores, where you frequently can achieve significant savings over supermarkets (though they may not offer the convenience of the supermarket).

• Shop for meat in terms of meals—and consider, as you buy, what you'll do with the leftovers. Plan to use all the meat you buy. Melt down fat trimmings for drippings; simmer bones and lean cuttings for soup stock and gravy.

• If scales are available for you to use in the supermarket in which you shop, *use them* to reweigh prepriced meat packages. And if you find any discrepancy, point this out immediately to the store manager.

• Read labels with care. Also remember that 3½ pounds is not 3 pounds 5 ounces but 3 pounds 8 ounces.

• Check and compare prices of prefrozen and imported meat. For example, you'll almost surely save by buying frozen lamb which has been imported from Australia or New Zealand.

THE TRUE COST OF A SERVING OF MEAT

Buy according to the true value of any type or cut of meat—as measured in terms of the true cost of a given portion of the final cooked product.

As a rule of thumb, you get two to three cooked servings from each pound of roast beef, pork, lamb, or veal, whole ham, chicken or turkey, trimmed fish, certain types of steaks and chops. And you get only one or two servings from each pound of meat loaded with fat, bone, and gristle—such as rib chops, spareribs, short ribs, plate and breast of veal, lamb shank, chicken wings and backs, T-bone or porterhouse steaks.

Here is a rundown of servings per pound of various meats. Fill in the current cost of each item in your area. Then figure the cost per serving by dividing the per-pound price by the number of servings. This is your key guide to where the bargains are.

MEAT	APPROXIMATE SERVINGS PER POUND	RETAIL PRICE PER POUND	COST PER SERVING
Beef			
Hamburger	4	———	———
Sirloin steak	3	———	———
Round steak	3	———	———
Rump roast, boneless	3	———	———
Chuck roast	3	———	———
Rib roast, with bone	2	———	———
Pork, fresh			
Pork chops	2½	———	———
Loin roast	2½	———	———
Pork smoked			
Canned ham, boneless	4	———	———
Cooked ham, with bone	3½	———	———
Picnic shoulder, with bone	2½	———	———
Poultry			
Turkey	2	———	———
Frying chicken	2	———	———

PROTEIN BARGAINS

Compare meat prices by finding out how much of a "protein bargain" you are getting.

To illustrate: here is a rundown on three key price categories of beef you can buy today—showing the relative amounts of protein, fat, and calories in one lean 3½-ounce cooked serving of each cut:

	PROTEIN (GRAMS)	FAT (GRAMS)	TOTAL CALORIES
Most Tender Cuts			
Standing rib roast	22	21	285
Tenderloin	26	13	224
Porterhouse steak	25	15	242
T-bone steak	25	15	247
Club steak	26	19	280
Rib steak	25	17	262
Top sirloin steak	26	11	208
Medium Tender Cuts			
Standing rump roast or rolled rump roast	32	11	235
Sirloin tip roast	30	4	168
Sirloin tip steak	27	6	166
Heel of round	33	5	189
Full cut round steak	38	8	229
Top round steak	39	7	229
Bottom round steak or roast	36	10	238
Eye of round steak or roast	38	6	219
Stew meat—round	33	13	260
Flank steak	34	7	209
Less Tender Cuts			
Short ribs or cross ribs	32	15	272
English cut or boston cut	33	14	263
Blade chuck pot roast, blade chuck steak, or boneless shoulder steak	35	17	298
Arm chuck pot roast, arm chuck or boneless shoulder steak	35	8	219
Rolled shoulder roast	33	14	263

Just divide the prevailing price by the number of calories or amount of protein in any of these cuts. The resulting figure will tell you how much of a calorie bargain or protein bargain each cut is.

An even more direct route to the best protein bargains is knowing the cost of various forms of protein—meats, fishes, and meat alternatives. To calculate the price per gram of protein, divide the current price per pound (or quart or dozen) being charged in your area for the foods listed in the table below by the number of grams listed.

FOOD	GRAMS OF PROTEIN PER POUND	FOOD	GRAMS OF PROTEIN PER POUND
Lima beans	78.9	Fish sticks	78.7
Peanut butter	72.0	Chili con carne	39.3
Pork and beans	27.5	Whole ham	58.2
Beef liver	88.9	Frankfurters	56.0
Chicken	72.3	Beef chuck steak	43.0
Eggs	71.0 (per dozen)	Round steak	79.6
Cottage cheese	64.0	Pizza	41.7
American cheese	107.0	Bologna	48.7
Tuna fish	118.5	Bacon	42.8
Hamburger	86.4	Rib roast	47.4
Milk	33.8 (per quart)	Sirloin steak	63.6
Ocean perch	69.9		

For example: if peanut butter costs 48 cents per pound, divide 48 cents by 72 grams per pound and you get a total of two-thirds cent per gram of protein. At 71 cents per dozen, eggs would cost one cent per gram of protein and thus, would not be as good a buy as peanut butter.

Of course, protein is by no means the only key nutrient. It's vitally important to know that pork is rich in thiamin, that cheese is rich in calcium, that beans contain large amounts of vitamin B6 and magnesium. Probably your best source of nutritional details is the U. S. Department of Agriculture's Handbook No. 8, entitled *Composition of Foods, Raw, Processed, Prepared.*

HOW TO USE BEEF "GRADES"

• Learn the U. S. Department of Agriculture grades of meat and use them not only to compare price and quality (tenderness, juiciness, and flavor) but also as a guide to the best meat for a particular type of meal.

The five top USDA beef grades are: prime, normally available only in restaurants, fancy meat stores, and from specialty mail-order houses; choice and good, the two grades most commonly found in supermarkets and butcher shops; standard and commercial, definitely inferior as far as your palate is concerned.

The top veal grades are: prime, choice, good, standard, and utility.

The top lamb grades are: prime, choice, and good. Spring lamb should bear the U. S. Government certification "Genuine Spring Lamb."

Choose lower meat grades. For instance, with beef, good versus choice; with lamb, choice versus prime. They may be less tender, but they are also leaner and equally nourishing. Using anything above U.S. good for chopped beef or stew meat is a waste of money, because in these cuts you do not need to worry, for example, about how tender the meat is.

Lower grades should cost even less. However, the taste may be equal if you cook them right—e.g., as pot roast—or if you apply such tenderizing techniques as grinding, pounding, marinating, pot-roasting, using commercial tenderizers, and cubing.

• As another guide to quality, study meat color and texture.

For general freshness, beef should be somewhere between light and dark red. Roasts and most steaks should be at least lightly "marbled" with fat.

Veal should be very pale grayish pink in color; the flesh should be firm and smooth. It should have almost no fat—just a thin coat outside.

Pork, too, should be pale pink and should have only a thin layer of fat.

Lamb should be a dull pink. Spring lamb should be colored somewhere between pink and red—not too dark—and it should have a velvety texture. The bone should be pinkish and there should be a slight amount of marbling.

BUT NUMBER 1: SHOP THE MEAT SPECIALS!

Your number 1 way to save on meat is to shop regularly and seriously for meat specials and stock your home freezer with your purchases. *You can save as much as one third on your meat bills* simply by buying meat at special rather than regular prices. See preceding pages for table dramatizing the point.

Thursday, Friday, and Saturday remain the big days for meat specials, but also watch for specials on such off days as Monday, Tuesday, and even Sunday. (Try to shop as early in the day as possible.)

When you shop for advertised meat specials, make sure the price marked on the package reflects the advertised special. And if you can't find any packages left at the special price, remind the supermarket manager that a Federal Trade Commission rule requires that advertised specials be adequately stocked *at* or below the advertised special prices. At the very least, you should get a rain check.

Watch closely to see whether more fat has been left on the meat that's on sale—particularly on beef and pork chops.

Important note: On any given day you'll probably find only a limited number of items on special, and you'll also find that many if not most stores in your area will offer a very similar set of specials—particularly on weekends.

SAVINGS BY BUYING BEEF IN BULK

How about saving money by buying beef in bulk? Okay. No matter how casual a shopper you are, it's increasingly likely that you will try to curb your meat costs by buying beef in bulk and storing it in your home freezer.

But it's a good way to go—only *if* you are on guard against the estimated hundreds of "bait and switch" beef swindlers in the United States today . . . *if* you instead patronize one of thousands of entirely ethical freezer meat operators situated all over the country . . . and *if* you know and scrupulously obey the rules when you buy beef or other types of meat via the wholesale route.

Below you will find 11 specific rules for this type of buying:

(1) Do not buy a side of beef in hasty response to a tempting ad. If you really want and need as much beef as this and if you can arrange to store it properly, plan your purchase ahead, then shop intelligently for the meat.

(2) Before you buy, decide whether you will want a large quantity of steaks or whether your family will be happy with less fancy cuts or whether you would prefer to have a wide variety of cuts, including lots of stew meat and hamburger.

(3) To help yourself reach these decisions, study the beef-cut charts posted in your butcher shop or available from the U. S. Department of Agriculture in Washington.

(4) Use the following guide to tell you what proportion of what cuts you are likely to find in bulk beef.

In general, if you want more steaks and roasts, you'll probably want a hindquarter. A typical, trimmed beef hindquarter originally weighing about 200 pounds consists of 58 per cent steaks and oven roasts.

Here's the breakdown:

HINDQUARTER

Round steak	20.6%
Boneless rump roast	6.0
Sirloin steak	13.0
T-bone, porterhouse club steak	10.1
Flank steak	.9
Total lean trim	17.1
Fat, bone, and shrinkage	32.3
TOTAL	100.0%

If you want a lot of stew beef and hamburger, you'll probably be best off with a forequarter. A typical, trimmed forequarter, originally weighing 215 to 220 pounds, breaks down into 37 per cent stew and ground meat. Here's the breakdown on this:

FOREQUARTER

Rib roast	13.5%
Short ribs	6.4
Blade chuck	20.9
Arm chuck	12.5
Boneless brisket	4.1
Total lean trim	23.9
Fat, bone, and shrinkage	18.7
TOTAL	100.0%

If you want a wide variety of cuts, a half carcass will probably be the purchase for you. The usable meat from a whole beef carcass breaks down into approximately 25 per cent steaks, 25 per cent roasts, 25 per cent ground beef or stew, 25 per cent waste.

More specifically, a typical U.S. choice beef carcass weighing 300 pounds is likely to break down this way:

RETAIL CUTS	PER CENT OF CARCASS	POUNDS
Round steak	11.0%	33.0 lbs.
Rump roast (boneless)	3.3	9.9
Porterhouse, T-bone, club steak	5.1	15.3
Sirloin steak	8.3	24.9
Rib roast	6.1	18.3
Chuck blade roast	8.9	26.7
Chuck arm roast (boneless)	5.8	17.4
Ground beef	11.1	33.3
Stew meat	10.3	30.9
Brisket	2.1	6.3
Flank steak	.5	1.5
Kidney	.3	.9
Total usable retail cuts	72.8	218.4
Waste (fat, bone, shrinkage)	27.2	81.6
TOTAL	100.0%	300.0 lbs.

And here are a few more important guides on other meats:
A lamb with a carcass weight of 50 pounds trims out to about 75 per

cent legs, chops, and shoulders, 15 per cent breast and stew, 10 per cent bones and waste.

The breakdown for a typical lamb is:

Retail Cuts	Per cent of Carcass	Pounds
Loin and sirloin chops	16.5%	8.25 lbs.
Rib chops	8.2	4.10
Legs (short cut)	20.5	10.25
Shoulder roast	22.3	11.15
Foreshanks	3.1	1.55
Breast	7.9	3.95
Flank	2.9	1.45
Stew meat	1.9	.95
Kidney	.5	.25
Total usable retail cuts	83.8	41.90
Waste (fat, bone, shrinkage)	16.2	8.10
TOTAL	100.0%	50.00 lbs.

A hog carcass weighing 175 pounds or so divides up into about 50 per cent hams, shoulders, and bacon, 20 per cent loins, ribs and sausage, and most of the rest lard.

(5) Don't overlook the importance of "yield grades" in helping you avoid waste! In addition to the basic guides given you above, do you know that typical amounts of waste vary from beef side to beef side—from a minimum of about 20 per cent to as much as 34 per cent—a fact which greatly influences the real-life price you might pay for and the value you get from this beef?

For example, if a quarter of beef weighing 125 pounds ("carcass weight") is advertised at 69¢ a pound and if this quarter trims out to a typical 87 pounds, the effect of this "shrinkage" is to push the price back *up* to 99¢ a pound.

And this is merely the *average* price—which hides the fact that you have bought a hefty percentage of such cheaper meats as stew and hamburger.

The "yield grade," I repeat, is among your best yardsticks of value if you are trying to save money by buying beef in bulk—for it gives you the vital clues on the percentages of the various boneless retail cuts you'll get after fat and bone have been trimmed away.

There are five yield grades, numbered 1 through 5, with 1 the highest, 5 the lowest.

The typical difference in amount of meat yields is 4.6 per cent between grades.

Here are the percentage yields of each grade level for a 600-pound beef carcass:

Grade	Fat trim	Bone	Edible meat
1	7.5%	10.5%	82.0%
2	12.6	10.0	77.4
3	17.7	9.5	72.8
4	22.8	9.0	68.2
5	27.9	8.5	63.6

And here is a more detailed comparison of the percentages of beef carcass weight of USDA yield grades 2 and 4. It's assumed that the meat is trimmed to ½ inch of fat.

Cut	Yield Grade 2	Yield Grade 4
Rump, boneless	3.5%	3.1%
Inside round	4.5	3.7
Outside round	4.6	4.2
Round tip	2.6	2.4
Sirloin	8.7	7.9
Short loin	5.2	5.0
Rib, short cut (7″)	6.2	6.0
Blade chuck	9.4	8.4
Chuck, arm, boneless	6.1	5.5
Brisket, boneless	2.3	1.9
Flank steak	.5	.5
Lean trim	11.3	9.3
Ground beef	12.2	10.0
Fat	12.7	22.9
Bone	9.9	8.9
Kidney	.3	.3
TOTAL	100.0%	100.0%

With these statistics in mind when you are shopping for a side or a quarter of beef, you can get a good idea of the amounts of meat various grades will yield you after cutting and trimming. This will permit you to make sound comparisons with prices charged on beef cuts during the supermarket specials in your area.

And this in turn will tell you how much of a bargain—or non-bargain—each side of wholesale beef really is to you.

(6) When buying in bulk, figure not only what you are paying per pound for the actual meat minus fat, bones, etc., but also what price you are paying for cutting, packaging, and quick freezing. These procedures can easily add 8 to 10 cents a pound to the net cost of your meat if they are not included in the basic price.

(7) If the ads include such terms as "beef order," "steak package," or "steak bundle," find out precisely what these terms mean and cover.

(8) If unbelievably low-priced extras or "bonuses" are thrown in to sweeten the deal—say, 10 pounds of frying chickens for 50¢ or five pounds of hot dogs for $1.00 or 30 pork chops for free—use your head. No butcher could afford giveaways such as these.

(9) And never forget for a minute that the bait-and-switch racketeers use this sort of lure—for instance, ads for sides or quarters of beef at fantastically low prices—in order to bait you and then switch you to a much higher-priced carcass.

(10) If the deal involves payments by you on time, check whether the terms are spelled out as required under the Truth in Lending law—the total finance charge, the yearly percentage interest rate, the number and schedule of payments. Also, which bank or finance company will actually hold the paper you sign?

(11) Learn well the key signs of fresh, good-quality beef and other meats. For example, with beef, the bone should be ivory white, the sign of a young steer, not yellowed; the fat should be white as against yellow and there shouldn't be an excessive amount of fat; the tenderest beef is well marbled, meaning it has streaks of fat throughout the meat, but marbling also means calories and saturated fat.

HOW TO USE YOUR HOME FREEZER FOR TOP SAVINGS

THE RULES

To take the maximum advantage of meat and other specials, and to have the convenience of a "supermarket" in your own home, you must have a home freezer.

To illustrate the savings in just one purchase:

If you could buy 100 pounds of meat on sale at $1.79 per pound against the "regular" price of $2.01, your savings on this purchase alone would be $22.

These savings must, however, be compared to the costs of owning a home freezer—including depreciation, repairs, and electricity.

And there are disadvantages—in addition to annual costs summarized in the preceding paragraph. They include: the possibility of spoilage due to a power failure; the certainty of electricity rate rises in the years ahead; the nuisance of defrosting; the need to plan meals well in advance because the frozen food must be brought to room temperature or will need longer cooking time; the need to have space in which to keep the freezer; other minor annoyances.

But to millions, the advantages seem to win—which leads to the rules for getting the utmost benefits from your freezer:

• Package the meats to be frozen in sizes your family is likely to use and make sure each is tightly wrapped before freezing.

• Set your freezer at the lowest possible temperature the day before you intend to put in any large amount of meat to be frozen and, once frozen, hold the temperature at below 0° F.

• Don't add too much "warm" meat at a time—not more than two pounds per cubic feet of storage space. This means that large purchases, like the 100 pounds of meat, should be prefrozen by the meat packer in his large, high-powered freezer.

• Date and label with its contents each package of food you put in the freezer and consume your frozen food on a "first in, first out" basis.

• Stock your freezer as full as feasible for you: use the food frequently and restock; the higher the turnover of food, the lower the per pound cost to you.

• Keep all foods covered. Clean interiors regularly, including the defrost drainage tubes. Vacuum and wipe down coils and other mechanisms; dirt accumulation makes for inefficient operating.

• Open doors as little as possible to cut down frost. Defrost as often as necessary to keep no more than a fourth to a half inch of frost from accumulating. Don't place unit in a warm area—such as near the furnace. Check the gasket frequently to make certain it seals the door tightly.

• If you live in an area where your electricity goes off for as long as a day or so, set your freezer thermostat at 10° to 20° below zero or as low as it will go. If the power stays off longer, either take your frozen food to a freeze locker or put blocks of dry ice in your freezer. A 25 pound block should be enough to keep the contents of your freezer below zero for two to three days.

• Make sure your frozen food packages are firm, clean, and well sealed.

• Buy frozen foods at the last stop on your shopping trip.

• Keep foods in your freezer only for the recommended periods of time.

• And once you buy a freezer, *USE* it.

FREEZERS

HOW MUCH WILL YOU USE ONE?

Whether a freezer will be a money saver for you will depend on how much you use it, but the odds are it will *not* save you money—unless you live on a farm, or must drive a long distance to shop.

In 1974, it cost $123 a year to own a 480-pound capacity manual defrost freezer (about 16 cubic feet), including depreciation, electricity, and average repairs. If you stored and used only 480 pounds of food in your freezer during the year, costs worked out to an average of 26¢ per pound. If you stored 540 pounds, the cost dropped to 23¢ a pound and if you stored and used 900 pounds of food, down to 14¢. With a 480-pound capacity freezer, you would have to use more than 900 pounds of frozen food a year and save more than 14¢ a pound on the food you buy for the freezer before it would begin to break even. Your bargains would have to average at least 22¢ a pound less than prices at the time you eat the food to come out ahead with a frost-free freezer.

Here are a few more clues to the key costs of operating a home freezer today:

Depreciation. Figure this annual cost as one-fifteenth of the initial purchase price, including any finance charge.

Electricity. If your local electric rates are, say, 4¢ per kilowatt hour, costs are about $54 a year to keep a 450 to 500 pound freezer 80 per cent full.

Repairs. Freezers are among the least troublesome appliances and repair costs normally average well under $5.00 a year.

Packaging. Typical costs of materials run 3¢ to 4¢ per pound of food you package and freeze yourself.

Lost Interest. On the purchase price of the freezer and also on your outlay for the food you buy to fill it.

HOW TO BUY

Now here are the basic points to ponder when you are considering the purchase of a home freezer:

• Decide in advance whether an upright or chest model is best for you. The chest type requires more floor space, and it is less convenient because much unloading and rearranging are required to get food in and out on a proper rotation plan designed to eliminate spoilage. However, this type gives you extra counter space on which to work, accumulates less frost, maintains more even temperatures for longer storage times, and uses about half as much electricity as an upright freezer. The upright takes less floor space and is easier to defrost, but may cost $10 to $30 more than a chest-type freezer.

• Decide also what size freezer is adequate and appropriate for your family. Today's freezers come with capacities ranging from three to thirty-one cubic feet, but the most popular models have twelve to seventeen cubic feet of storage space. The general rule is you'll want three to four cubic feet for each member of the family and five or six per person if you have a vegetable garden and thus do a lot of home freezing or if you shop only every ten days or two weeks.

• Be sure to have adequate space for—and a sturdy floor under—your freezer. When full, this appliance can weigh as much as half a ton.

• Set a budget for your freezer: In the mid-1970s, price tags ranged from about $175 for a no-frills 12-cubic-foot freezer to $250 to $270 for a 16- to 17-cubic-foot model, and $300 to $400 for a luxury 17- to 18-cubic-foot, frost-free model.

• Decide which "extras" you really want and need. Frost-free (self-defrosting) freezers are considerably more convenient than models you must defrost yourself. But you'll pay $50 to $60 more for this feature. A self-defrosting freezer also costs substantially more to operate than a standard upright model, and nearly three times as much as a manual defrost chest. Similarly, a "flash defroster" feature may cut defrosting time to 15 minutes but you'll pay $30 or so extra for this time saving.

Among the other extras you can get—at a price—when you buy a freezer today are:

an interior light;

a special fast-freezing compartment;

a warning signal showing a dangerous temperature rise or power cut-off;

special baskets, trays, and racks for storage;

a built-in door lock.

• Finally, find out—*before* you buy a freezer—whether there is a warranty and exactly what it covers. Does it cover just repairs for the freezer? Or your losses in food spoilage as well if and when the freezer breaks down? And who will honor the warranty?

• Take special care to investigate the reliability of the dealer before you buy—for if and when a freezer breaks down, it must be repaired within twenty-four hours if you are to avoid losing your entire investment in its contents. Your dealer is of critical importance at that time.

BEWARE: THE DISHONEST "FREEZER FOOD PLAN"

There are two major traps associated with buying and owning a home freezer: the dishonest "freezer food plan" and the "bait and switch" in bulk beef buying.

Under the freezer food plan, you buy a freezer and also sign up for regular purchases of bargain-priced foods to put in it. The savings on the food, the ads say, actually will pay for the freezer itself. In effect, you'll get the freezer "free."

But if you commit yourself to such a deal and it turns out to be a come-on, you well may discover that you are obligated to pay a grossly inflated price for the freezer as well as grossly expensive finance charges on the installment loan you use to make the purchase.

The freezer you get may be much larger (and more expensive to operate) than your family really needs.

The seller may fail to deliver the promised food on the promised timetable. Or he may substitute inferior varieties of meats and other items for which you've signed up. Or he may welch on providing the "bonuses" or "free gifts" he used to lure you into the deal.

The guarantee may turn out to be worthless.

What the freezer plan salesman has done is to dazzle you with a promise of whopping savings on future food purchases—to the point where you fail to notice that he has jacked up the price of the freezer part of the deal as much as $200 to $300 over the price of a regular freezer.

Then, after you have signed a contract for the deal, he, in turn, sells it to a finance company and simply fades out of the picture—leaving you quite possibly badly stuck.

Your obvious ways to avoid the freezer plan trap are:

• Compare prices of the freezer you'd buy through regular retailers with those charged by the freezer plan salespeople.

• Also compare costs of the food offered through these plans with the costs of food you buy on special at the local supermarket.

• Be suspicious of any deal in which the food to be provided is advertised vaguely as "enough food for a family of four."

And once you have decided that you want to buy a certain food freezer plan, check the following points in the contract before you sign:

(1) Does the contract state clearly that you have to pay for the freezer?

(2) Does it state the price of the freezer, the total price of the food you are buying, the finance or carrying charges, and any other additional charges?

(3) Does it state the model, year of manufacture, and cubic capacity of the freezer?

(4) Does it state that food prices change and thus the price offer in the present plan will not remain the same?

(5) Does it state the quantity and types of food you will receive, their exact weights, and the grades of the food?

(6) Does it state that the food, should it spoil, is covered by insurance but that you have to pay for this insurance?

(7) Does it state the minimum and maximum quantities of food you must buy?

(8) If the salesman tells you he is making an introductory offer, is this specified in the contract?

(9) Is there a guarantee on the freezer? If so, does it clearly state what

is guaranteed and for how long? (Don't believe unreasonable statements like "lifetime" or "unconditional" guarantees.)

BEWARE: "BAIT AND SWITCH" IN BULK BEEF BUYING

A while ago an inspector for the Virginia Department of Agriculture and Commerce visited a bulk-meat retail plant in northern Virginia which had advertised a side of beef at less than half the price the beef, in suitable cuts, was quoted in the supermarkets. On making a test purchase, the inspector (who didn't identify himself as a VDAC agent) was told that the bargain-priced beef was old, tough, and wouldn't be satisfactory for general cooking. He was also advised that the cutting and trimming loss on the meat would be high, as much as 70 per cent of the gross weight. He was then guided to a more expensive meat—USDA choice—and told this beef would be much better and the cutting loss would be less than 20 per cent.

After indicating that he would take a quantity of the higher-priced meat, the inspector began bargaining with the meat dealer. He finally bought 188 pounds of choice beef at a "reduced" price.

Back at the VDAC laboratory in Richmond, the inspector weighed the beef and found he had received a little over 120 pounds—a 36 per cent cutting loss against the guarantee of less than 20 per cent.

Thus, the 120 pounds of meat actually cost much more than the original quoted price for the hanging, uncut beef. And on top of this, more than half of the 120 pounds delivered represented hamburger!

This test purchase of bulk beef also revealed that close to $100 could have been saved on the same quantities of the same grade and cuts at a simultaneous local supermarket sale. The bulk dealer was charged and convicted of "advertising without intent to sell" and "delivering less than the quantity represented." He was fined $1,000 and costs on each count.

In meat, the dangers are very real that you'll be caught in a "bait and switch" racket. Your warning signals of deception will include:

• The ads will fail to disclose that as much as half of the weight will be lost in cutting, dressing, and trimming—in effect, doubling the price per pound. Or the operator's "estimated" trimming loss will turn out to be a "mistake"—costing you, the consumer, a painful sum.

• The low advertised prices will not be honest offers to sell beef but instead will be lures to bring you into the stores. Here, salesmen will downgrade the advertised meat in order to sell you higher-priced beef.

• The advertised "sale" or "special" prices will be the regular prices, not temporary bargains. The ads will place heavy emphasis on the scary aspects of soaring prices and potential food shortages.

• Credit disclosures required under the Truth in Lending law on installment purchases will be omitted altogether from the ad.

• Even if you agree to buy the better meat at a higher price, the seller may still deliver inferior meat—and you have no way of knowing exactly what has been delivered to you. (In one case reported by the Federal Trade Commission, a "bait and switch" operator sold a single "model" carcass of beef ten times during a single day!)

• Although there may be a money-back guarantee if you're dissatisfied, you may have a hard time actually getting either a replacement of the meat or a refund of your money—because of fine-print conditions and limitations which didn't appear in the advertised guarantee.

• You may discover, when your order of beef is delivered to you, that the stated maximum of ground beef (e.g., 12 per cent) is exceeded.

• The operator's definition of a "half of beef" may turn out to be the two forequarters or front half of the beef—where the steaks and other choice cuts *aren't,* but where much of the waste and bone *are.*

• The advertised "Heavy Western Beef" may turn out to be *cow* meat which is just as laden with yellow fat as beef under some other label.

Here are guidelines that will protect you:

• To find an honest freezer meat provisioner who may be able to lead you to a real meat-in-bulk bargain, ask about dealers who are well-established in your community and whose services your friends can recommend personally. The honest dealer will *not* advertise sides of beef at prices you know are unrealistically low. He will not try to lure you into a deal in which you're persuaded to buy beef at sky-high prices.

• Do not sign up for any bulk meat deal until you have exhaustively checked the reputation of the dealer. Do not permit any meat dealer to use high-pressure sales tactics on you. Give yourself plenty of time to think and to figure out what you are getting for your money.

• Find out whether the meat has been graded and what grade it is. If it is graded utility, it is likely to be tough and stringy and the net yield after cutting also may be low. Meats sold in most supermarkets are usually USDA choice.

• Have the dealer tell you how much trimming loss there will be and what net amount of meat you will receive. Then you can calculate exactly what you will be paying per pound for the meat.

• Once you have calculated the real net costs of the meat *after* trimming and cutting, compare these costs with prices of meats sold on specials.

• Know what cuts of meat—and how much—you will get in your delivered package. It is ridiculous for you to pay for a lot of stew meat when you really want steak, or vice versa.

• If you think you have been gypped, complain and complain loudly to the dealer. If you are not satisfied, do not hesitate to complain to local or state authorities.

The "bait and switch" racket is old and tenacious. It is particularly widespread and particularly vicious in meats because most of us are so ignorant about the rules for judging what is or is not a bargain. Heed these warnings well.

HOW TO SPOT BARGAINS IN POULTRY

A KEY IS FORM IN WHICH YOU BUY

Although poultry is among the least costly and most popular of main-dish foods, the form in which you buy it often will determine how big a bargain it is.

For example, chicken sold whole generally will be a few cents cheaper per pound than chicken cut up. Whole chicken also will usually be a better buy than chicken breasts and legs.

You also can achieve dramatic savings by buying specials on 5-pound boxes of chicken legs or breasts. Compared to the same quantity in smaller packages, you can save as much as $1.00 on this single purchase.

Here's a table showing the price per pound of a fryer, ready-to-cook, and of several chicken parts that would give you equal amounts of edible chicken for the money:

If the price per pound of whole fryers, ready-to-cook is:	BREAST HALF	DRUMSTICK AND THIGH	DRUMSTICK	THIGH	WING
33¢	44¢	35¢	34¢	37¢	27¢
35	46	38	36	39	28
37	49	40	38	41	30
39	52	42	40	43	31
41	54	44	42	46	33
43	57	46	44	48	35
45	59	48	46	50	36
47	62	50	48	52	38
49	65	53	50	55	39
51	67	55	53	57	41
53	70	57	55	59	43
55	73	59	57	61	44

Chicken parts are an equally good buy if price per pound is ——

A chicken should be neither too white nor too yellow but rather a creamy color. Figure about one pound per person for whole chicken.

WAYS TO SAVE ON BUYING TURKEYS

Turkeys are inexpensive, too, and now come in quarters, in the form of legs only, breast slices, rolled roasts, etc. Turkey can be barbecued as easily and as quickly as chicken.

You'll get more meat for your money from whole ready-to-cook turkey than from boned, rolled turkey roast. The bigger the bird, the more meat it will have in proportion to bone. A turkey weighing less than 12 pounds is one half waste. Thus, half of a 20-pound bird may cost less than a whole 10-pound one. Look for a plump, squarish turkey for maximum meat yield. And check the label for a note of "parts missing."

Buy prepared turkey roasts or rolls on the basis of cost per serving.

Other Guides:

• If you invest in the convenience of a self-basting turkey which has had oil, water, flavors, fats, phosphates, and other materials injected into it to make it tenderer and more flavorful, you are paying the same price per pound for these ingredients as you're paying for the gobbler.

• "Turkey loaf" may, by law, contain as little as 35 per cent turkey.

• In other products, such as turkey and gravy, the proportion of turkey also is 35 per cent if *"turkey"* is the first word mentioned on the label. However, if the label says, for example, "giblet gravy and sliced turkey," the proportion of turkey may be as small as 15 per cent.

• The turkey label may or may not tell you what grade the bird is (A, B, or C) since grading is not legally required. There probably will be an indication of the turkey's "class," though—for instance, "young hen," "mature," "broiler," etc.

ORGANIC FOODS

THE BOOM TAKES OFF

In 1972 a volunteer shopper for New York's Department of Consumer Affairs found these gaps between prices of regular goods and their "organically produced" counterparts:

ITEM	REGULAR	ORGANIC
Apple juice, qt.	$ .37	$ .80
Grape juice, qt.	.37	.80
Peanut butter, lb.	.99	2.05
Honey, lb.	.53	.90
Eggs, doz.	.53	1.15
Dried prunes, lb.	.49	1.00
Cider vinegar, qt.	.33	1.00
Wheat bread, lb. loaf	.43	.95

The same shopper found these gaps between prices of regular vitamins and their "natural" counterparts:

VITAMIN	REGULAR	NATURAL
C 500 Mg., 100 tabs.	$1.98	$3.50
B-complex, 100 tabs.	1.79	2.60
E 100 I.U., 100 caps.	2.55	3.30
Multivitamins, 100 tabs.	3.45	9.95

• "Organic living"—at markups ranging to 30, 40, even 50 per cent!—has taken off. Our purchases of organic foods are skyrocketing. The organic foods list has ballooned far, far beyond wheat germ, Tiger's Milk, and blackstrap molasses. It now includes fresh fruits and vegetables, seaweed, organic bakery products, herb teas and coffees, spaghetti and macaroni, milled grains and whole grains of many types, seeds, oils, peanut butter and jelly, breakfast cereals, meats, a dizzying range of snacks.

Thousands of organic food stores from coast to coast also are selling organic food cookbooks and gardening guides, biodegradable soaps and cleaning compounds, home yogurt makers, untreated organic seeds for planting. Among the newer organic food customers are colleges, universities, communes, religious organizations, bakeries.

• Supermarkets are setting up special sections for organic foods. Newspapers are printing organic food columns. Some schools and colleges are offering courses on "organic living." Some towns are launching community organic gardens—for commercial as well as conservation purposes.

Countless thousands of you are now regularly gulping the vitamins and foods. Organic gardening clubs are multiplying and *Organic Gardening and Farming* magazine, published in Emmaus, Pennsylvania, had in 1974 more than 750,000 subscribers—a number which certainly brings this once far-out publication into the big leagues.

• One of the nation's biggest organic food wholesalers, Erewhon Trading Co. in Boston, has farms with more than 25,000 acres under contract and tight quality controls to produce seeds, grains, fruits, and other foods. Erewhon's product list includes more than 150 items and new ones are being added each month.

Theoretically, at least, there could be an organic equivalent of virtually every food product you now find on supermarket shelves.

WHAT IS "ORGANIC" FOOD?

Exactly what constitutes "organic" food? According to the National Farmers Organization in Iowa, it is "food grown without pesticides; grown without artificial fertilizers; grown in soil whose humus content is increased by the addition of organic matter" and "food which has not been treated with preservatives, hormones, antibiotics, etc."

Organically grown beef and other meats are raised on organically managed land; are fed with foods which are free from pesticides and herbicides, antibiotics, feed additives, growth and other medicinal hormones; and tend toward grass grazing over grain feeding.

How do organic foods differ from "natural" foods and "health" foods?

There are no legal definitions, but here are guidelines which are widely agreed upon:

• Natural foods contain no preservatives, emulsifiers, or artificial ingredients. They are sold to provide consumers with an alternative to conventional foods which may contain such additives and preservatives.

• Organic foods are more or less the same as natural foods, except that "organic" implies greater care of soils and plant environment to exclude pesticides and artificial fertilizers.

• Health foods are different from the other two categories. They include dietetic, vegetarian, and other products not necessarily free of chemical additives.

But what could possibly be the advantage of chewing on desiccated liver when you can buy—and probably eat with pleasure—regular fresh liver at far lower cost? Are such products as dulse and kelp, soybean flour, rose hips, sesame seeds, and safflower oil really necessary for *your* good health? Is it honestly worth it to pay 30, 40, even 50 per cent more for specially grown "organic" foods—in terms of their purity and nutritional value to you, the consumer?

You well may be among the millions of us who feel caught between the cross fire of claims and counterclaims by organic food buffs, food faddists, the Food and Drug Administration in Washington, nutritionists on both sides of the organic food argument today.

On one side are the organic food supporters who are (1) issuing dire warnings that we are being poisoned en masse by additives, preservatives, emulsifiers, pesticides, chemical fertilizers, other foreign substances which are routinely added to so many foods we eat, and who (2) point out quite persuasively, that many food manufacturers and processors first remove most or all key nutrients and perhaps put back only a few of them in certain "fortified" foods.

On the other side are many of the world's top nutritionists who (1) insist that most foods on today's supermarket shelves are just as safe, healthy, and nutritious as their more expensive organic counterparts and (2) argue that the only difference between "natural" and synthetic vitamins is that the natural ones cost more.

The FDA lists some 600 different food additives—artificial colors and flavors, monosodium glutamate, synthetic sugar and salt substitutes and preservatives, emulsifiers, and other chemicals—as GRAS (Generally Recognized as Safe). However, the FDA admits that few of these additives have been extensively tested. In the past, the FDA's over-all approach has been to consider an additive safe unless and until it is proven to be otherwise. However, adamant consumer advocates have been increasingly challenging that attitude—and the rules have been steadily tightened.

Somewhere in between are the majority of us who are legitimately worried about the questions raised in recent years concerning pesticides and additives and about our national case of malnutrition. And there's no doubt, as one New York City expert remarked, some labels "read like a qualitative analysis of the East River."

In sum, the dilemma is that most of us just don't know whether we're being ripped off by organic food stores or whether organic foods are really better for us and are worth paying twice the price for them.

And a final touch: we simply have no way of knowing whether the "organic" foods we do buy actually were produced without chemicals or were processed without either removing important nutrients or adding forbidden substances.

TEN RULES FOR BUYING ORGANIC FOODS

If *you* are sold or even partially sold on the idea of organic foods, here are ten basic guidelines on how to buy them and how to get the most for your money:

(1) Start by patronizing the biggest and best established organic food store in your area, then explore others and compare products and prices as you go. Check knowledgeable friends for hints. Stick to stores that appear neat and clean. Stay away from the ill-kept ones with open flour, grain, and seed bins into which all of you are invited to dip your hands to get what you want. Also avoid stores which offer an obviously kooky line of products along with the organic foods: vibrators, fountain-of-youth products, hair restorers, etc.

(2) Interview the proprietor and listen with care. How much control does he keep over the product he sells? What proof (such as certification from known food growers) can he offer you that the foods he sells actually are organically grown? Does he personally know his major suppliers and the farmers? Since there are relatively few large-scale growers of organic foods, it's no great chore to be acquainted with them all. Or if he doesn't know his suppliers and growers personally, does he at least require them to provide affidavits on the authenticity of their organic foods? Can you see these affidavits?

(3) Study organic food labels for details on: ingredients; where, who, and by whom grown (you can easily get to know the names of reputable growers, processors, and distributors); conditions under which the foods

were grown and processed, including types of soil, water, and fertilizers used; appropriate disclaimers on pesticides, additives, herbicides, commercial fertilizers; recipes.

(4) Check with care the contents of breakfast cereal products—consisting of rolled oats, soybean oil, brown sugar, perhaps a few other items. Many varieties on the market are neither organically grown nor particularly nutritious. Note whether the contents of other products—such as juices—are not precisely the same as the contents of their regular supermarket counterparts.

(5) On vitamins, study the source of their "natural" components, as well as the proportions of each substance. Be sure the amounts of ingredients listed are for one tablet or capsule (not five or six).

(6) Comparison-shop, especially on high-priced items. An excellent way to do this is to compare prices of staple items.

(7) Ask yourself: will your family eat the foods? You won't improve your health—and certainly not your budget—by buying foods which end up in the garbage pail (or even the compost heap). Also will you really invest the necessary time to prepare meals from organic "raw materials"?

(8) Be skeptical of exorbitantly priced "organic" toothpastes, shampoos, facial creams, raw sugar (chemically identical to refined sugar), similar products. Certainly be wary if salesclerks tout any of those wares as "wonder foods."

(9) Buy such items as whole grains, wheat germ, cereals, soy beans, lentils, and other beans in bulk.

(10) Write, if you have any questions about various foods and how they're grown, to their producers or suppliers. The top producers and suppliers will respond to your legitimate inquiries. Be wary of any firm which gives you a runaround or no reply at all.

BEWARE! ORGANIC FOOD TRAPS

As you might suspect, the deceivers and gypsters have been crowding into this exploding field and making a mockery of the very definition of organic food. All kinds of packagers have been buying up ordinary foods, labeling them "organic," and passing them off on naïve retailers and an innocent public.

Says the president of one of the nation's largest organic food wholesalers: "Ninety per cent of the 'organic' apple juice now being sold in California is not made from organically grown apples. At least half of the organically grown rice now being sold on the East Coast, isn't."

How, then, can you, a food shopper who buys this type of product, protect yourself against the profiteering charlatans? By using this rundown of current traps in the field:

Deceptive labeling: Probably the biggest trap is using an "organic," "natural," "nature's own," etc., label when this is not the case. In the most flagrant cases, unscrupulous retailers simply paste an "organic" label over the brand name of a non-organic product or its package. Or the "organically grown" food may be merely food which hasn't been sprayed with pesticides —but which fails to meet other generally accepted criteria for organic foods.

Many unscrupulous suppliers, for instance, sell "natural organic" honey (a major health food product), although they have had no control over the antibiotics which may have been used in bee feed or over what types of sprays are used around the bees' base.

Non-organic foods: Often mixed in with organic products in organic food stores, leading you to believe they're somehow special and worth paying extra for.

Small type: Frequently dried fruits which are labeled "natural organic" have preservatives listed in tiny type in an inconspicuous section of the label.

Exaggerated claims: Some protein supplements are being sold with the promise that they'll improve not only your physical fitness but even your appearance.

Sheer misinformation: This is often aimed at innocent older people who are constantly worried about their health. Some health food store operators, once they've sold a customer one bottle of vitamins or minerals, will then try to sell another to "balance" the first one.

Overpricing: The 50 per cent markups on vitamin pills and protein supplements are common. Moreover, most of the vitamin C now being sold as "natural" consists almost entirely of ascorbic acid—the same stuff you find in "unnatural" vitamin C.

Nutrition nonsense: Almost everybody is trying to climb on the health food bandwagon and make a healthy profit in the process. Of questionable nutritional value surely are "organic" variations in toothpaste, refined oils, refined sea salt, syrup.

Low calorie fruits and vegetables: These may be labeled as "natural organic" but actually they're the same as all diet foods.

Your best—and most obvious—safeguards are to know the proprietor of the store you patronize and study carefully the labels of each product you buy. And if you feel you've been deceived or cheated, report the details to your local Better Business Bureau and your Consumer Protection Agency.

WHISKEY AND WINE

HOW TO CUT YOUR LIQUOR BILLS

When did you last add up your liquor bills and face up to how much this one item contributes to your pocketbook pinch?

If you're merely moderate drinkers, spend only $10 a week on liquor, and throw only three cocktail parties a year involving liquor bills of only $50 each, your annual liquor bill amounts to $670. If you're heavier drinkers and entertain lots of friends and neighbors, your annual bill easily may be in the $1,000 to $2,000 range.

Okay. How can you save on liquor without going on the wagon?

• Sample "house brands" of liquor sold locally—especially at delicatessen-type stores (whose house brands often are made by the nation's top distillers). If the house brands taste at least as good to you as the more expensive names you have been buying, adopt them for regular use or at least for large cocktail parties.

• When you throw a cocktail party, offer some "house special," building interestingly on one of the less expensive liquors—gin, vodka, rum. Of course, if you use fruit juices and mixers extensively, it's less important to have expensive, top-quality brands than if you're serving martinis or scotch on the rocks, or Bourbon and branch water. Or try something like a May wine punch with fresh strawberries; you might find that many of your guests actually would prefer this lighter and less costly drink.

• Shop for bargains in cocktail mixers as well as in the cocktails themselves. To me, many of the large-size, lower-cost mixers taste as good as the well-known brands costing 20 to 25 per cent more. But in any event, stick to the larger-size bottles when you're shopping for a party.

• Consider the premixed bottled cocktails (martinis, manhattans, etc.) —*if* they will eliminate your need to hire a bartender. Otherwise they're no bargain since you pay a premium of 25 per cent or so for the convenience. (A homemade 1½-ounce martini costs about 30¢ versus 35¢ to 40¢ for the premixed equivalent.)

• Consider less expensive Virgin Island rum as an alternative to Puerto Rican rum.

• Try out imported whiskey which has been bottled in the U.S. rather than abroad.

• If you happen to be fans of "B & B," save 20 per cent on this liqueur by buying a bottle of Benedictine and another of inexpensive French cognac and mixing your own B & B.

• Unless higher proof (e.g., 100 proof) liquor is far more expensive than its lower proof counterpart (e.g., 86 proof), the higher proof is probably the better deal. You simply dilute it yourself.

• Look for liquor sales. Although liquor prices often tend to be controlled in any given area by state laws and other factors, sales *do* happen in some places, and bargains can be found. The best time to find liquor sales —and to stock up—is after a big holiday.

• Finally, consider the liquor cost on a *per ounce* basis. If a quart of Brand X costs $3.20, the cost per ounce is 10¢, and a fifth of the identical liquor would have to cost less than $2.56 to be a better value (which it almost never is). If a fifth costs $6.40, a quart of the identical liquor would have to cost less than $8.00 to be a bargain.

There are 32 ounces in a quart and 25⅗ ounces in a fifth (four fifths of a quart). Here's a chart to give you *per ounce* equivalents in the typical price range for hard liquors.

QUART	FIFTH	COST PER OZ.
$3.20	$2.56	$.10
3.84	3.07	.12
4.48	3.58	.14
4.80	3.84	.15
5.12	4.10	.16
5.44	4.35	.17
5.76	4.61	.18
6.08	4.86	.19
6.40	5.12	.20
6.72	5.38	.21
7.04	5.63	.22
7.36	5.89	.23
7.68	6.14	.24
8.00	6.40	.25

HOW TO CUT YOUR WINE BILLS

It's scarcely a secret that drinking of wine is in a great boom all over the world—very definitely, even spectacularly, including millions of us in the United States. As it has been with meat, so it has been with wine: this is another classic case of "demand-pull" inflation. To translate, the demand for wine is outrunning the supply of wine and, as a result, prices are being "pulled" relentlessly upward.

Meanwhile, wine collecting and wine "talk" have become among the most "in" of hobbies. "Wine" has joined the great leisure activities.

What should and can you—an amateur wine drinker and collector—do to hold down your costs in this area?

• Become adventuresome and seek out wines that please you at prices that please you. In this process, you must abandon the big names "just as," say the wine experts, "the art collector must stop buying Picasso and Chagall if he wants to pay a reasonable price."

• Develop a relationship of trust with a knowledgeable, established wine merchant and seek sound advice on labels to buy, what wines to store and not to store, etc. You will discover personal favorites at a fraction of the prices of well-known, best-selling trade names that have priced you out of the market. And you'll have fun as well on your odyssey in wines.

• Consider joining an established wine-buying club which buys its wine in large batches and also is backed by professional advisers who are trying to help you save money.

• Buy wine by the case for savings of up to 10 per cent.

• Buy wine on sale for savings of another 10 to 20 per cent.

Before you make a major commitment in wine, try to taste a single bottle of the exact type and vintage; in many cases, small "splits" are available to buyers.

Learn and stick to the great wine years for the bordeaux and burgundies.

If you have no storage area, see if you can arrange storage with a wine dealer (usually at a monthly charge of 50¢ a case).

• As for table wines, try out a variety of the type which sells by the half gallon or gallon—starting with the least expensive you can find. Be your own "wine taster" and trust your own judgments. Remember, in most European families, this is the category of wine consumed day in and day out—at a per-liter cost which is about the same as the cost of milk. Of course, the better domestic U.S. wines are more expensive—but there are less expensive ones, too, which are well worth a try.

Sample, also, wines now being imported from regions and countries other than the famed wine-producing ones—e.g., Chile, Switzerland, Greece, Portugal, the Eastern European countries, and, within France, the Loire and Rhone valleys, the Alps, Alsace.

How to Save on Parties

If you have given parties you must be aware that costs easily can run double or even triple the amount you have budgeted. Yet there are many ways to save substantial sums on your party without compromising its gaiety or quality. Here are the fundamental rules.

• Whatever type of party it is—whether it's a cocktail or a dinner party —set a per-person budget and stay with it. Liquor, hors d'oeuvre, and other trimmings probably will cost between $2.00 and $6.00 a head; a dinner party can cost from $3.00 to $5.00 up, but it's possible to put on a fairly elegant spread for around $10 a person. How much can you *really* afford to spend? How many people do you *really* want to invite?

• Consider one big party—which would undoubtedly be cheaper (and easier)—rather than a smattering of medium-sized parties throughout the year. But if your home cannot take a large number of guests, try parties on successive days—or a brunch and a cocktail party on the same day. By so doing, you can take maximum advantage of mass cooking, flowers, whatever party equipment you've rented, other extras you're paying for.

• As suggested earlier, buy the larger sizes of liquor—quarts over fifths, and half gallons over any of the smaller sizes. A case almost always is cheaper than the purchase of individual bottles, of course. A quart serves 16 two-ounce drinks, so if everybody drinks an average of three drinks, one quart will serve about five people. Ask your liquor dealer if he will take back unused bottles; many will.

• When mixing drinks, use a measure and follow a recipe if the drink requires this. Don't overpour.

• Don't overprepare. It's false economy to prepare a pitcher of some drink and then find you'll serve only a couple of drinks during the entire party. Plan your ingredients, have them ready, then prepare your drinks as you are asked for them.

• Buy the largest available bottles of mixers and the least expensive varieties of soda, mix, tomato juice, etc. Have ginger ale and other non-alcoholic beverages available; some people do prefer these.

• Serve wine and punches at a fraction of what cocktails would cost. You'll be delighted to discover how many of your guests will be grateful. Also try Irish coffee, Café Diable, such non-alcoholic drinks as espresso and cappuccino. These are far less expensive than liqueurs. And if yours is a dinner party, try the European custom of serving a predinner apéritif—such as a glass of champagne or a white wine or vermouth.

• Instead of hiring a bartender, have your husband mix the first drink for everybody and then suggest that everybody mix his own after that. People tend to drink less, incidentally, if an overgracious host doesn't plunge for empty glasses the instant they are drained. Or hire a college student to tend bar with the help of a few notes and advance lessons on how to mix what. If it's a dinner party try to hire a reliable, mature teen-ager in your area (or your own daughter) to help with preparations and cleaning up afterward.

• Place the bar where people aren't apt to congregate, and set the food in another corner. This will help distribute your guests and, incidentally, draw them away from the bar and toward your food.

• Even if you're the type who insists on flowers for every table in the house, consider buying just a dozen or so well-chosen ones, plus a bundle of pretty greenery. One or two flowers in the right-size vase can look just as good as a profusion, if you arrange them right.

• In summer, take everything you can from your garden, and from friends and neighbors. Don't order florist flowers over the telephone. Find out if any neighborhood florists offer a special of the week. Take advantage of these.

• Save on hors d'oeuvre by serving only made-in-U.S. items. Don't feel you must offer a full-scale delicatessen. One beautifully presented wheel of good domestic cheese or a platter of well-chosen cold cuts surrounded by a variety of crackers will be economical and will avoid the inevitable waste of a big variety.

Save on more elaborate food by making your foods from scratch and substituting your time for more expensive packaged convenience foods.

• Also save by serving cold foods. Buckets of ice for cold snacks are far less costly than renting or buying the necessary equipment for hot foods.

• And give a break to the millions of us who are struggling to keep trim figures. All we want is the simplest, lowest-cal crackers and rabbit food.

You probably can dwarf my list. The point is that real savings *are* possible. All *you* need do is plan.

THE HIGH COST OF EATING OUT

TREND: UP, UP, UP

If you are among the tens of millions of us who must or want to eat out regularly, you are acutely aware that the cost of restaurant meals has been skyrocketing. Just between 1967 and 1975 the cost of eating out jumped more than 65 per cent nationally.

And no relief appears in sight. The long-range outlook for restaurant meal prices is up, up, up—with the estimate that as of 1975, we are spending $2.00 out of every $10 of food dollars for food outside our homes.

RULES FOR CURBING COSTS

But you *can* hold down your eating-out costs and not sacrifice the quality of the food you get. Here are the rules which will slash your restaurant bills 10 to 25 per cent.

(1) Avoid restaurants where you must give individual tips to a large staff: headwaiter, maître d'hotel, doorman, hat check girl, rest-room attendant—as well as your own waiter. These tips alone can add up to $10 to $15.

(2) Have a couple of drinks at home before you go and restrict yourself to one (or no) drinks at the restaurant. Today, three drinks each for a couple typically costs $9.00 to $12 in a good restaurant—plus the 15 per cent or more you tip on this total.

(3) Look for good new restaurants which do not yet have their liquor licenses but which may permit you to bring your own bottle of wine—with savings depending on the amount of wine and liquor you normally drink.

(4) Keep in mind that the typical markup on wine in restaurants is around 100 per cent; so do your fancy wine drinking when you have dinner at home.

(5) Favor restaurants which have relatively short, simple menus. You save because food is not wasted in the kitchen and you can get a far more

elegant meal for your money if the chef and his staff can concentrate on a few menu items.

(6) Steer clear of purely snob appeal restaurants—unless it's really worth cash to you to sit across the room from a celebrity or a tycoon.

(7) Patronize restaurants in neighborhoods where you can benefit from the fact that rents and other overhead costs may be 30 to 50 per cent lower than in midtown. If you're trying to save money, this alone can do it for you.

And a final note: don't be mesmerized by exotic, fanciful adjectives or the writing on a menu. You're not eating the menu.

The trend of prices for food at restaurants will still be up, but with these guides you can maneuver nicely within that trend to eat out and actually save.

7

THE NOW-AND-THEN
NECESSITY OF CLOTHES

Finding Your Way Around the Clothing "Supermarket"

Most clothing stores in this era are something like supermarkets. It's up to *you* to plan what you want in your wardrobe yourself, to search the shelves and racks for sizes and styles to suit you and your budget, to determine the quality of everything you buy from socks to suits. Salespeople (if you can find them) are frequently untrained and inexperienced, and far more concerned with making a sale than with helping you to dress properly and attractively.

Modern fabrics and finishes are also a maze in which you can find your way only if you know the hieroglyphics of acrylics and modacrylics, wovens and non-wovens, furs and fake furs, polyesters and foam-bonded materials, and on and on. Today, there are *more than 700* trade names for various manufactured fibers. A clothes label, as one wag put it, often looks "like an inventory list of a chemical factory."

On the minus side is the blunt fact that, if you choose wrong or misjudge quality and a dress or suit falls apart after a few wearings, you almost surely will not be able to get your money back. And you well may not be able to get the item repaired or get a replacement for it.

But on the plus side are the far more important facts that:

A greater variety of clothes styles, fabrics, finishes, is available to you today than ever before in our history.

The price range also is the broadest ever.

Federal laws protecting you against mislabeling never have been so numerous or strict.

And you can draw on an unprecedented wealth of information sources to help you shop for the very best and most suitable wardrobe for you and your family.

In the following pages you'll find this "wealth" broken down into the most valuable nuggets that *you* can use to plan your wardrobe and shop for clothes to fill it.

THE FUNDAMENTALS

SHOP FOR WHAT'S RIGHT FOR YOU

Simple, classic clothing styles may be more suitable for you (and also may last longer) than the latest, most alluring fashion craze. Basic clothes, which never go out of style, are real bargains. And the chance to wear many combinations may be a better addition to your wardrobe than a wild, utterly unforgettable outfit.

If you must buy or cannot resist a way-out style (and this includes shoes), buy the least expensive you can find. Try to establish a simple color theme—perhaps building on one or two basic colors which can be mixed and matched as you choose.

BUY ONLY CLOTHES THAT FIT YOU PROPERLY

This will add to the life of your suit, dress, or coat as well as to your comfort and good appearance.

Don't make the common error of buying sizes that are *too small* for you on the assumption that you are about to lose ten or fifteen pounds! If you cannot get a really good fit, buy a size which is slightly *too large* rather than one that is slightly too small. It's usually possible to alter a dress or a coat from a large size to a smaller size, but often impossible to do the opposite.

Use the following table, prepared by the Money Management Institute of Household Finance Corporation, Chicago, Illinois, and included in the Institute's booklet "Your Clothing Dollar," as a guide to size ranges used by most clothing manufacturers for women's clothes. Note that, in addition to regular sizes, some type of clothing may be marked "tall," "medium" or "average," and "short" or "petite."

SIZE CLASSIFICATION	SIZE RANGE	FIGURE TYPE
Junior Petite	3–15	For figures 5'1" or shorter. The neckline and armholes are smaller and length from shoulder to waist and from waist to hemline is shorter than a Junior.

SIZE CLASSIFICATION	SIZE RANGE	FIGURE TYPE
Junior	3–17	For figures 5'1½" to 5'5½" with a higher, smaller bust, narrower shoulders, and a shorter waistline than the Misses.
Misses Petite	8–18	For figures 4'11½" to 5'2" with a longer waist and a fuller bust than a Junior Petite. Smaller neckline and armholes than a Misses.
Misses	6–22	For the well-proportioned figure 5'2½" to 5'6½". Hips moderately larger than bust and normal to low waist.
Misses Tall	10–22	For the well-proportioned figure over 5'7½".
Half Sizes	12½–26½	A mature Junior. Fuller throughout the bust, back, and shoulders and shorter waisted than the Junior.
Women's Sizes	34–52	The mature, more developed Misses figure. Fuller in the back and shoulders and longer waisted than the Misses.

And use the following chart, also published in "Your Clothing Dollar,"* as your guide to standard children's sizes, corresponding to body weight, height, and other measurements:

* Money Management Institute, Household Finance Corporation, Chicago, Illinois, Copyright 1972.

	SIZE	WEIGHT	HEIGHT	CHEST	WAIST	HIP
Infants' and Babies'	(mos.)					
	3	13	24	17		
	6	18	26½	18		
	12	22	29	19		
	18	26	31½	20		
	24	29	34	21		
	36	32	36½	22		
Toddlers'	(Years)					
	1	25	31	20	20	
	2	29	34	21	20½	
	3	34	37	22	21	
	4	38	40	23	21½	
Children's	2	29	34	21	20½	21½
	3	34	37	22	21	22½
	4	38	40	23	21½	23½
	5	44	43	24	22	24½
	6	49	46	25	22½	25½
	6X	54	48	25½	23	26½

STUDY CLOTHES LABELS

You are protected in the United States by the Federal Textile Fiber Products Identification Act. Under this law, clothes and other textile products must contain the following information on their labels:

• the *generic name* of the fibers (cotton, polyester, etc.), listed in order of the weight of each fiber;

• the percentage weight of each fiber weighing 5 per cent or more of the total;

• the *name* or registered number of the manufacturer or seller;

• the *country* from which an imported item comes.

In addition, wool products must be labeled, under the Wool Products Labeling Act, with the percentage of wool contained, the type of wool (e.g., wool, reprocessed wool, etc.), the percentage of non-wool fibers included, and the identity of the manufacturer.

This information can be more important—and a better clue to quality —than a brand name on natural fibers. For example, the satisfaction you get from a properly made shirt of preshrunk combed cotton can be the same—whether the shirt is a national brand, carries the store's name, or bears no brand at all.

Save the tags from any new garments which do not have permanent care labels, and mark them for identification so you'll know how the clothes should be cleaned. Index and file them in a box you can keep in the laundry area.

Learn at least the basics on the major fabrics and finishes in clothes today—and what each type implies in upkeep, durability, cleaning, laundering, and looks.

The International Fabricare Institute has put together 78 "Facts About Fabrics" leaflets. You can get any of the 78 from member cleaners or by writing the Institute, Doris and Chicago Avenue, Joliet, Illinois 60434, enclosing a postage-paid, self-addressed envelope. Be as specific as you can about the type of fabric (fiber content, woven, knitted, etc.) on which you need information.

Here are some of the key clothing finishes now available. Most of them will boost the price of an item of clothing but will increase its convenience too:

Wash and wear (needs little or no ironing after washing).

Permanent press (can certainly be a savings if you're in the habit of sending your shirts to a hand laundry or your slacks to a dry cleaner, and material stays unwrinkled and fresh-looking all day long, too; bed linens continue to look newly laundered from one bed change to another).

Sanforized (fabric will not shrink more than 1 per cent in either direction; there are other similar finishes).

Water repellent (fabric sheds water but allows air to go through; won't work in a downpour without an umbrella, however).

Stain and spot resistant (fabric resists water and oily stains easily).

Look for clues to these finishes on the label—along with clues to the proper care of the particular item.

Look also for details on:

• Whether or not the fabric is "vat-dyed" or "sun-fast"—assurances (though not guarantees) that the fabrics will not fade in sunlight or with normal laundering. Man-made fibers are almost always totally color-fast. But, as with natural fibers, check the labels for a non-fade statement before you buy.

• Whether or not it is a stretch fabric. (Comfort stretch for everyday use, action stretch for ski wear, etc.) Labels won't tell you how much stretch to expect in a stretch fabric. A test at the store is some help, but it can't guarantee that changes won't occur later. Your best safeguard is to buy from a reputable retailer and clothing manufacturer, both of whom will heed your complaints and, if justified, will make refunds or exchanges.

PLAN YOUR WARDROBE WITH MORE THAN ONE PURPOSE IN MIND

For instance, in men's clothes, a top-notch buy is a raincoat with a detachable lining. Without lining, it can double as a topcoat in mild weather.

With lining, it can get you through the coldest weather. Women's raincoats with detachable linings can be equally good buys.

Another bargain is a tweed suit with a coat which can double as a good-looking jacket to wear with slacks.

And either a man or a woman can buy a flannel suit with pants that can be worn with other jackets or jackets that can be worn with other pants.

LOOK FOR GOOD WORKMANSHIP

Consumers Union, the most prestigious consumer testing laboratory in the field, publishes in its monthly *Consumer Reports* and its annual Buying Guide issue excellent reports of controlled tests on standard clothing brands—from diapers to dinner jackets. You'll benefit from these reports on durability, color-fastness, appearance, laundering ease, quality of workmanship, etc., and learn exactly what to look for when you shop.

Specifically:

Seams should be smooth (no "puckering"), wide enough to let out if necessary, properly finished to prevent fraying.

Hems should be even, properly bound with tape, securely fastened, invisibly stitched, deep enough to permit lengthening.

Stitching should be even and close together.

Buttonholes should be sewn through on both sides of the cloth.

Linings—of the fabric and pockets—should be firm, closely woven, and made of a material which will not stretch or shrink.

Zippers, snaps, and decorative trim should be firmly attached and properly placed.

AVOID IMPULSE BUYING

If you need a spring raincoat, don't stop off at the section reserved for bathing suits and buy a bikini at top price. (And don't laugh, I've done this sort of thing plenty of times and I'll bet you have too!) The same goes for "bargains" which have no place at all in your wardrobe. They are *not* bargains to you if you don't need or really want the items.

And this applies equally to a variety of clothing accessories which you may find tempting in the store but which you didn't even dream of wanting until you spotted them.

MAKE A CLOTHING BUDGET—AND STICK TO IT

Clothes are among the most flexible of all your budget items but, as a general guide, below are a few national "averages" from the Bureau of Labor Statistics in Washington:

• On average, out of each $1.00 a U.S. family spends on everything, about 9¢ goes for clothes and shoes. The share rises to more than 10½ ¢ when the cost of clothes upkeep is included.

• Our annual national clothes-and-shoes bill now runs about $333 a year for each man, woman, and child.

• Typically, clothing costs triple to quadruple between the ages of one and eighteen.

• On average, women spend $3.00 out of every $5.00 of the family's clothing dollars.

• The average adult American woman owns four to five dresses, two to three suits, two to three coats, five skirts and five sweaters, three to four pairs of pants, two knit dresses, and two knit suits.

• The average teen-age American girl owns similar numbers of each item of clothing, plus a couple of extra skirts and sweaters, but fewer knit dresses and suits.

But these are merely averages and almost certainly they do *not* apply to you.

Only *you* can set your own clothing budgets, priorities, and preferences.

In *your* clothing budget:

Make room for luxuries as well as for necessities.

List all the items you *must* have and then the luxury items you'd *like* to have. Ask yourself what kind of clothing you need: for the office; for sports and leisure-time activities; for social occasions. Just the listing will help you pinpoint the necessities you can appropriately buy at minimum prices and you then can apply whatever amounts you have saved to your luxury purchases.

TEN WAYS TO SLASH YOUR CLOTHING BUDGET

You can truly slash your clothing costs—and be better dressed than ever!—by learning and following these ten specific guides:

(1) *Buy clothes off season*—and achieve savings running to a sensational 30 to 50 per cent. March is the best time to buy ski outfits, for instance. January and August are good months to buy furs.

There are three major periods for store-wide clearance sales: after Easter, after July 4, and after Christmas. These are excellent times to pick up clothes as well as a long list of other items—although you may run into shortages of styles, sizes, and colors if you don't shop as early as you possibly can in the sale (if possible, the day it begins).

List the clothing items of standard styles which you know you will need during the next six to twelve months. Study and use the clothing bargain calendar which follows.

Budget your cash and your credit so you have the funds to buy the items you need and want during the clothes-buying bargain seasons.

Your Calendar

Back-to-school clothes—August, October
Bathing suits—after fourth of July in July and August
Children's clothing—July, September, November, December
Coats (women's, children's)—April, August, November, December
Coats (men's)—January, August
Costume jewelry—January
Dresses—January, April, June, November
Furs—January, August
Handbags—January, May, July
Hats (children's)—July, December
Hats (men's)—January, July
Hosiery—March, October
Housecoats—April, May, June, October, November
Infants' wear—January, March, April, July
Lingerie—January, May, July
Millinery—February, April, July
Men's shirts—January, February, July
Men's and boys' suits—April, November, December
Piece goods—June, September, November
Shoes (boys' and girls')—January, March, July
Shoes (men's and women's)—January, July, November, December
Sportswear—January, February, May, July
Toiletries—January, July

Of course, bargains also turn up at odd times through the year because of special circumstances—a store going out of business or into business or moving, an anniversary celebration, an unusual holiday, etc. You can always use these opportunities to buy items you know you'll need later.

A warning is necessary at this point, though: Watch out for those "going-out-of-business" sales on clothes. They can be phonies—and you can spot one if the sale has been going on for months or even years.

(2) *Buy certain items in quantity*—and save 10 to 30 per cent.

If, say, you buy one pair of stockings or panty hose or one pair of socks, a single run or hole can mean a total loss. But if you buy six pairs of the same type and color, you can match what is left and prolong the useful life of each item. (You can cut one leg out of a pair of panty hose when it runs, then one leg out of another pair, and wear both "good legs.") Buying in quantity is particularly practical if yours is a large family. Much clothing is sold on a "three for X dollars" basis.

(3) *Buy standard sizes*. If you're buying a man's sport shirt you will save by buying a small, medium, or large size. The price goes up when you

buy shirts in more detailed neck and sleeve sizes. This principle holds for socks, gloves, and many other types of clothing—men's and women's.

(4) *Find and patronize economical clothing stores.* Chain stores and mail-order houses are excellent for such "staples" as jeans, underwear, shirts, athletic socks, sneakers, boots, pajamas and nightgowns, scarves, belts, and work clothes.

Discount stores vary and stocks within individual discount stores also vary but they are worth a very serious check—particularly Army-Navy stores and "factory discount stores" which are outlets for slightly irregular items or oversupplies at drastic markdowns. Savings run approximately 25 per cent at the typical self-service, cash-only discount store, and often more.

Your key questions in shopping at a discount store should be: How does quality compare with other stores? How does each store handle customer complaints on defective or unsafe merchandise?

Look carefully, too, into local thrift and consignment shops, where you may buy next-to-new well-made and high-fashion secondhand clothes at very low prices.

And before you splurge on a high-fashion, high-priced dress or coat or suit, find out if the city in which you live (or a city nearby) has a high-fashion discount store. Two of the best-known stores of this type are Loehmann's in New York (and several other cities), and Filene's Automatic Bargain Basement in Boston. Typical reductions at this type of store: a minimum of 25 per cent and often 40 to 60 per cent.

(5) *Learn the various departments of your stores.* Within a given department store, check into the different departments and what type and price merchandise each carries. The bargain basement *may* carry designer clothes as well as bottom-of-the-line seconds, but this department usually specializes in high-volume, low-overhead, low-markup business. Durability is stressed more than style.

Although low-priced irregulars and seconds are often available in bargain basements, don't assume that prices are always lower in the basement than upstairs. Check the prices as well as the quality carefully.

Upstairs, you'll find a wide price range as well. If you can find a dress you like in the department store's sportswear department, it may cost less than one of comparable quality in the dress department. If clothes from the teen-age department are appropriate for and fit you, they'll probably be less expensive, too.

(6) *Look without prejudice at clothing seconds.* As a general rule, the bigger the flaws in clothing seconds, the greater will be the price cut. The key point you must consider before buying seconds is whether the flaw is "basic" or simply on the surface. Will the blemish significantly reduce the item's usefulness, attractiveness, or durability? Can the defect be easily and

inexpensively repaired? If the answers are favorable to the purchase, it could be an extraordinarily good one for you.

(7) *Steer away from frills,* especially on utility items. As an illustration, a sweater with a lavish belt or fur collar will be far more costly than the same sweater without the extras. The simple sweater also will be more useful, for the simpler it is the more occasions you'll be able to wear it (and the more you'll be able to dress it up or down on your own).

(8) *Match prices against utility.* For instance, if you have young children, the mortality rate on play clothes will be exceedingly high. Thus it's smart to get them at rock-bottom prices. You can extend this rule to a wide range of clothing purchases for every member of your family, particularly in sports clothes. And, incidentally, remember this rule when you're shopping for your husband. Don't push him into the latest "peacock revolution"—wild frills, rainbow-colored shirts, newfangled shaped suits—if that's not where he's at.

(9) *Buy children's clothes by size, not age.* Buy according to *your* child's height and weight. Buy clothes which have room for growth as your child grows (i.e., deep hems and pants cuffs, adjustable straps on overalls and jumpers, elastic waistbands, raglan sleeves). Buy clothes which are durable and don't show wrinkles and dirt too readily. And don't impose *your* adult tastes on your child.

(10) *Use credit plans with caution.* You can easily overspend with easy charge plans. You also may miss sales opportunities in other stores because you're still paying off old bills to the store in which you have the revolving charge account. But if you have charge accounts at various stores you'll often get *advance* notice of special customer clearances—and you can use those clearances to get bargains.

Many department stores and clothing shops hold private "courtesy days" sales for charge-account customers a week or so before advertising them widely to the public. If you have charge accounts, you'll be on the stores' mailing lists and you'll have first pick of the sale items.

When you are fully aware of the advantages as well as the pitfalls of store credit plans you can use them for your own benefit. See Chapter 3, "How to Borrow Cash and Use Credit Wisely," page 109, for details on department store charge accounts.

Six Rules on Dressing for the Office

During the attempt of the dress industry to force us into the midi at the start of the 1970s, mini skirts remained very much in evidence. Most young office workers simply would not junk their wardrobes—and they didn't. Pants became far more acceptable attire for the office as women turned some of their minis into tunics, combined them with pants, and created instant "suits."

For millions of us, wardrobes became multiple-length collections from which we chose whatever we liked to fit an occasion. No dress length appeared truly out of place at any social occasion. This was a rebellion. It is now an accepted way of life.

Do not underestimate its dollars-and-cents importance to you this very day, though, for what this phenomenon of fashion underlined was one of the most basic rules on dressing for work.

(1) It is: *avoid* imprisoning yourself in the latest fashions or even being in the advance guard of any new clothing trend.

Here are other rules on clothes for the office:

(2) Never buy a new wardrobe all at once.

(3) Wait until a new fashion trend has caught on before you make any significant investment in it (for the office or elsewhere).

(4) Test the wearability of any garment you choose for a full day's wear in the office by crinkling part of it in your hand to see if it returns to its original shape. If it doesn't, pass it up.

For the office, the most practical fibers and fabrics are alpaca, camel's hair, cashmere, crepe, flannel, foulard, piqué, sharkskin, tweed, wool, jersey, and any of the man-made, stay-press fabrics.

Almost all fibers can be suitable for office wear, though—depending on the fabric construction. Silk and linen are the least practical because they wrinkle. Air conditioning and central heating have sharply expanded the usefulness of the widest variety of fibers and fabrics.

(5) Be sure any garment you intend to wear in the office all day long is comfortable. Thus, when you try on clothes, sit down, raise your arms, bend over in front of a mirror.

(6) And when you find two dresses equally becoming, one costing, say, $100 and the other $50, buy the better-quality dress for economy every time.

SAVE MORE CLOTHING DOLLARS BY SEWING

THE BOOM THAT KNOWS NO BOUNDARIES

For Ann-Marie's seventeenth birthday, her wealthy mother offered her a present of a new wardrobe: daytime dress, dinner dress, pants suit, skirt, shirt, sweater, all to be selected by her at the store of her choice. I was tucked into a corner chair in my friend's living room when she announced the lavish present and I turned eagerly to see her daughter's response.

"Thanks, Mom," said she, "but do me a favor, huh? Outside of the sweater, use all the money you expect to spend on the clothes to buy me the materials instead. I'll make what I want. You buy the fabrics because you always spend more than I would. Thanks."

"But, Ann-Marie, it's your birthday," protested my friend. "I want you to use your time studying, not sewing for your present."

"Mom, please do like I say," was the answer. "I'll come out with much better clothes than I would buy in any store and I'll end up with a lot more to wear too."

• Some 52 million American women and girls are now involved in making apparel at home. Over 8 million of them are teen-age girls. More than half of the women who sew learned to sew in home economics classes in junior and senior high schools. About 6 million girls a year study home sewing in school. Among teen-age girls, the vast majority know how to sew.

• Literally hundreds of millions of pieces of apparel are sewn at home each year. And the number of garments sewn at home continues to soar year after year.

• Retail fabric sales—a direct reflection of home sewing, of course—are now running to more than $2 billion a year. In addition, the sale of sewing notions such as thread, buttons, zippers, and pins runs into the hundreds of millions of dollars. Thousands of outlets now sell fabrics.

Enough. The centuries-old home sewing story has been completely rewritten in our land in recent years. The boom knows no boundaries—crosses all income levels, all age categories, all regions, all color and ethnic groups.

Why? This has to be much more than another do-it-yourself offshoot, and it is. A key point, which Ann-Marie hit herself, is that you can save as much as 50¢ out of every $1.00 spent on clothes by making them yourself. A second major point is that, if you are at all competent, you can get far superior workmanship.

Another factor is that home sewing has turned from a "square" to an "in" activity. Many are sewing in order to reproduce at acceptable cost some creation of a high-style designer. Moreover, the pattern companies are aggressively educating millions of youngsters in home sewing.

And men are learning how to sew—and becoming sewing enthusiasts—in ever mounting numbers too.

HOW TO BUY A SEWING MACHINE

With roughly 44 million home sewing machines already in use and with millions being added in our homes each year, let's assume *you* are now in the market for a sewing machine—either a new one or one to replace your aging model. How should you shop? What type of machine should you buy?

• Make up your mind how you will use your machine before you buy. If you'll be doing only utilitarian sewing, then you'll need only a basic, inexpensive machine, without many frills. If you love to create fancy things with a lot of embroidery, you may want a machine with all today's built-in features, which can cost hundreds of dollars.

• Decide what you want your new machine to be able to do. Take a sewing course first if you do not know and rent a machine while you do it.

• If you are a beginner, you might start with a basic portable machine that has straight, reverse, and zigzag stitching capabilities and which may be available for less than $100. These are neither heavy-duty machines nor do they have a long anticipated life span. They are basic models, so try several before deciding which machine suits your needs. As an alternative, you might buy a secondhand or reconditioned machine from a dealer you are sure you can trust and learn on that one. (You may even decide to keep it indefinitely.)

Most sewing machine dealers will give basic operating instructions for your new machine even if it is a less expensive brand. Both the manufacturers and authorized dealers of the European machines are especially eager that you learn to take advantage of every feature on your new machine. One manufacturer even has a learn-by-doing instruction book. The new owner, under the supervision of the dealer, makes her own samples of each sewing technique and puts them in the instruction book for future reference. The fabric for the samples, also provided by the manufacturer, comes with the machine.

• Stick to a well-known brand sold by a company which has an extensive network of sales and service dealerships throughout the country. If properly used and cared for, even a medium-priced sewing machine will last your lifetime.

Off brands, or "private labels," are a particular problem in the sewing machine business. If you buy an off brand in Los Angeles, and later move to New York, you probably will find that you are unable to locate a dealer who handles that brand; therefore, service and parts are for all practical purposes unattainable. A dealer in New York may handle exactly the same sewing machine you have but sell it under his own name. He is reluctant to accept your machine for service because he cannot tell from the outside whether he has the parts or can get them.

The simplest way out, and the usual answer, is "This cannot be repaired," even though in reality the parts are often interchangeable.

• The two most wanted features in more sophisticated sewing machines are the zigzag and stretch stitches. There are zigzag attachments available for less expensive machines: these attachments, though, move the fabric back and forth (as opposed to the built-in zigzag where the needle moves back and forth), they cannot handle all fabrics, and they are inconvenient and inefficient. The zigzag feature is invaluable for mending, sewing with elastic, making buttonholes, overcasting, and reinforcing that might otherwise have to be done by hand. It also permits some basic embroidery.

Don't be pushed into a decision beyond your needs and budget. Buy a machine with a zigzag or stretch stitch only *if you really intend to use them.* Start basic and trade up as your needs and skills increase.

• A portable sewing machine will save you $30 or more over a cabinet model, assuming you have a permanent surface—possibly an old desk or kitchen table—so the machine will always be easily available. The salesman may tell you a cabinet is a must so that dust won't get into the machine. But the dust argument is nonsense, because if the portable doesn't come with a cover, all you need do to solve the dust problem is to whip up a simple dust cover as your first project—something like the covers used for office type-writers or your toaster. It's a lot less expensive than purchase of a bulky cabinet.

• However, though a sewing machine cabinet does add to the original investment, it can save money in the long run.

First, by making the set-up task easier, you well may sew more often—especially mending and maintenance sewing. Or may use an available hour rather than wait for a full evening or day for sewing.

Second, a cabinet will add to your comfort—less eye strain, tension, aggravation—and thus tend to produce better results.

Third, a cabinet is safer—less danger of dropping, knocking over—and thus protects your machine.

• With either a portable or a cabinet model, be certain:

    It is a comfortable height for you to work on.
    You sit with center of your body in front of the needle.
    Leg room is adequate for you.
    Controller comfortably positioned.
    Table leaf is well supported.
    Cutout holds machine level.

• Most sewing machine manufacturers suggest to their dealers a demonstration technique—and the better ones include the demonstrations of how the machines work on various commonly used fabrics. By all means, take advantage of the demonstrations; ask for them.

Be suspicious if your sewing machine dealer demonstrates a machine *only* on the very stiff cotton fabric that all dealers use. This fabric cannot show the shortcomings or the advantages of the various machines you may be considering. Remember that you will probably be sewing on many different fabrics from soft nylon tricots (many dress fabrics are nylon tricot) to bulky wools, corduroys, or fake furs.

The most convincing sales demonstrations are those that show the performance of a machine on many different types of fabric, such as sweater knits, double knits, lycra, nylon tricot, bulky wool or corduroy, leather, various stretch fabrics, and also problem fabrics. You may think you won't use all these, but how can you be certain now what fabric you will wish to sew on next year or the year after?

• If your sewing machine dealer does not have any "real fabric" bring some of your own (bring some anyway!) and try the machine yourself. First, stitch on three or four layers of closely constructed synthetic knit. If the machine skips stitches, you may have a problem when you want to top-stitch a synthetic knit fabric.

Now work with medium heavy fabric, fold to create at least four layers, and stitch across the folds in a perpendicular direction. If you need to push the fabric, or the stitch length varies from very short to very long, you can count on the same trouble almost every time you stitch a seam where two seams meet (such as neck facing). Next, take two pieces of almost any fabric (say, cotton), that are of *exactly* equal length. Stitch a seam about 12 inches long. If the top piece comes out longer at the end, this is what will happen when you try to match plaids on this machine. One more test requires two layers of soft fabric. Cut them in a curve, like a neckline curve, then stitch a ⅝-inch seam around the curve. How easy is it to guide your stitching accurately around the curve? There are vast differences between the way various machines can handle this. *Tests such as these are especially important when purchasing any relatively inexpensive machine.*

• If you're planning to buy a medium- or high-quality brand, look for these features:

> automatic tension adjustment for any weight of fabric
> clip-on presser feet (no screws!)
> one-motion threading
> wide comfortable foot control
> two-speed motor
> built-in cams (nothing to insert)
> built-in buttonholer
> streamlined free arm (for tubular sewing) with slide on table
> rich, full-looking embroidery patterns
> pattern indicator for matching embroidery
> knee lever to raise presser foot (a true convenience!)
> feed-dog lowering at the touch of a knob
> tailor tacking, basting, and various stretch stitches

When your sewing machine is delivered, make sure it is the same model —and sews as well—as the one demonstrated to you. If it isn't—or doesn't— go right back and demand that the dealer make the proper exchange or adjustments.

• After each use clean away thread and lint, and clean and oil the machine regularly as directed by the manufacturer. Always keep your dust cover on your machine when it's not being used.

• Once you buy, use the machine. Your complaints will be handled more equitably early in your ownership than later. Don't grumble to yourself or your friends for a year before you tell the dealer of your dissatisfaction.

BEWARE: SEWING MACHINE TRAPS

Be particularly wary of the gypsters who operate on a grand scale in the area of sewing machines. A dealer, for example, may pass off inexpensive foreign-made machines as American-made by stenciling the names of well-known American machines on them, or by obliterating foreign-origin markings. Others may misrepresent old, well-known machines as being rebuilt by the manufacturer when actually they've only been given a once-over-lightly cleaning by some back-room mechanic. Some imply in their ads that a sewing machine is zig-zag equipped—but not, as you later discover, at the advertised price.

Some insist that their fabulous sewing machine offer is "good for today only"—to keep you from going out and comparing prices. Some give you (or send you) a discount in the form of a "check" for, say, $150—made payable to you but as yet unsigned. However, the price of the sewing machine well may have been jacked up so that it more than covers the discount. Or you may be a second prize winner in a contest—entitling you to receive a sewing machine *only* if you buy an overpriced cabinet. Or you may be given the "opportunity" for a "free" sewing machine—and pay *"only"* $79.50 for a 10-year service contract. But the catch here is that most machines don't need much—if any—servicing within the first five years and you are still paying $79.50 for the machine, no matter what the disguise is.

Or it may be a "repossessed" sewing machine which has not actually been repossessed. Or the claim may be that the price charged is only the very low amount of the "unpaid balance"—which, by no coincidence, turns out to be just about what the machine is worth.

Beware these traps. And if you unluckily fall into any one, check your nearest consumer protection agency at once to find out your rights under federal and/or state law or regulation.

CUTTING YOUR CLOTHES CARE COSTS

Buying (or making) clothes is only part of your investment in your wardrobe. Over the long run, an even larger chunk of your money may go to the cleaning, washing, storing, and repairing of many items in your wardrobe.

How do you keep *these* costs to a minimum—and at the same time make your clothes last as long and look as good as possible?

THE TIME-TESTED TIPS

When you buy clothes, check the manufacturers' tags carefully for details on fabrics and finishes. Try to buy clothing made of fabrics that can without danger of damage be laundered at home or cleaned in self-service machines.

Keep your clothes in a dry, airy, cool place.

Brush your clothes frequently. Once dirt is permitted to set in the material, it gets harder to remove and increases the need for frequent dry cleaning or washing. Dirt also may attract moths and insects.

Mend small rips before they become large ones.

Use proper spot-cleaning solution. Nail polish remover, perfume, or cologne applied directly may seriously damage certain fabrics.

Use shoe trees for your best shoes and keep others in shoe bags.

Wear waterproof shoe covers when it rains to protect your shoes (or wear boots and carry your shoes).

Hang up your clothes on a suitably shaped hanger immediately after each wearing. Don't hang clothes in a closet when they're wet.

Always clean or launder seasonal garments before putting them away in the off season (although it may be a good idea to wait to iron summer clothes until summer arrives). Don't store dirty clothing.

In home washing and drying permanent-press fabrics and clothes with stain-resistant finishes, load your washer only to about 80 per cent capacity and remove the clothes from the dryer just as soon as they are dry.

Slash your dry cleaning bills by using self-service dry cleaning machines for the appropriate garments. These machines are especially valuable for children's winter jackets, woolen sweaters, and most of a long and varied list of items for which delicate hand pressing and steaming aren't necessary.

Follow clothes care labels when you iron. And remember that letting clothes simply steam awhile in the bathroom while you take a shower often will do the ironing for you.

Also study the care labels on washing stretch fabrics. While most of these fabrics can be washed, the kind of fiber, the weave or knit, the color, and the finish may dictate the method and temperature to be used—and this will be indicated on the labels. (Be particularly careful with your stretch ski wear, which often can't even be washed, much less machine-dried.) Dry your stretch fabrics in a tumbler dryer, set at the correct temperature for the fabric. If you don't have a dryer, lay the garment flat and block it if necessary to insure that, when dry, the garment comes back to the correct size. Never hang a garment to dry if it has lengthwise stretch. Never wear a damp stretch garment; it will lose its shape. Don't hang stretch garments for long periods even if dry. Store the garments flat in a drawer or on a shelf.

HOW TO USE CLOTHES CARE LABELS

You are protected by a 1972 Federal Trade Commission ruling requiring permanent clothes care labels or tags to be affixed to most types of clothes you now buy.

Specifically, the labels on clothes must now (1) fully inform the purchaser about regular care and maintenance procedures, (2) warn the purchaser of care methods that should not be used, (3) remain legible for the useful life of the article, and (4) be made readily visible to the user. Key exceptions: gloves, shoes, hats, furs, stockings.

Here are illustrations of the phraseology suggested by the FTC:

"Machine wash in sudsy water at medium temperature."

"Machine wash warm. Gentle cycle. Do not use chlorine bleach."

"Hand wash cold. Do not twist or wring. Reshape. Dry flat. Do not dry clean."

"Dry clean only."

TWELVE WAYS TO REDUCE YOUR SHOE BILLS

Each year we buy an *average* of three to four pairs of shoes per person. Sneakers, slippers, galoshes, other footwear push the total to more than one billion pairs of shoes a year. Our annual footwear bill averages about $175 per family.

With the guides that follow, though, you can spectacularly reduce your shoe bills—and you'll also find you're enjoying your shoes far more.

(1) Obey the rules for a proper fit: make sure that your big toe doesn't reach the tip of the shoe when you're standing, that your little toe lies flat in the shoe, that the heel fits snugly, and that the sides don't yawn. (Poorly fitting shoes can impose the "hidden" extra cost of podiatrists' bills.)

(2) Don't buy shoes by size alone. A size 8 may fit perfectly in one style but not in another. Have each pair fitted.

(3) Shop for shoes in the middle of the day. Typically, the human foot swells 5 per cent with exercise and this swelling can obviously make a big difference in how a shoe fits.

(4) Economize on shoes you won't wear frequently, such as women's shoes dyed to match an outfit. Don't economize on work shoes or hiking shoes: the savings won't be savings if the shoes aren't comfortable or if they wear out quickly.

(5) Save money in men's shoes by buying those with rubber-type soles, usually less expensive and more serviceable than leather.

(6) Choose simple, traditional styles. A simply styled shoe may cost one third less than its high-style counterpart. And stick to darker colors which look better for a longer time than lighter colors.

(7) Buy children's shoes at least a half size larger than is indicated by the measurement. But sturdy, well-fitting shoes are vital for children, so economize only on style. Use the following chart to guide you on how rapidly children's shoe sizes change as they grow up.

Rate of Change: Children's Shoe Sizes

Age of Child	Size Changes Every:
1–6 years	1–2 months
6–10 years	2–3 months
10–12 years	3–4 months
12–15 years	4–5 months
15 years and older	6 months or more

(8) Don't misuse shoes by, say, wearing them out in the rain. Polish shoes regularly to protect them against dirt and bad weather. And note: few shoes can survive a washing machine.

(9) If your shoes become wet, stuff them with paper, dry them away from direct heat with a soft cloth, and rub them with a light film of mineral oil.

(10) Change your shoes at least once a day to give them a chance to "rest" and dry out from foot moisture. If you do this, two pairs of shoes will outlast three which are not alternated during a day.

(11) When buying, look for: smooth, soft linings and smooth inside seams; stitching which is not too close to the edge of the shoe sole; flexible "uppers" and evenly trimmed edges; good material; reputable brand from a reputable retailer.

(12) Buy shoes for yourselves and children during the seasonal sales— using both the winter and summer sales for maximum savings.

8

THE HIGH COST OF GOOD HEALTH

What You Can Expect Your Health Bill to Be

FASTEST-RISING OF ALL PERSONAL EXPENSES

The high cost of personal health in the United States had become a major economic factor in the lives of most American families by the mid-seventies.

• Our spending on health care goods and services ranging from Band-aids to open-heart surgery and cancer research was passing $100 billion a year. For each of us, this represented an average health bill of close to $450 or nearly $1,800 for a family of four.

• The cost of health care services had increased in the late sixties and early seventies faster than any other type of personal expense—one and one half times the rate of rise for our over-all cost of living.

• Hospital bills accounted for the lion's share of our total national health spending. By the mid-seventies it cost an average of more than $105 to spend a day in a community hospital and at a growing number of hospitals the cost was $150 to $200 per day. Some luxury private room costs went even higher.

• Physicians' and dentists' bills, nursing home costs and drug costs—all were soaring.

HEALTH INSURANCE: CAN YOU AFFORD NOT TO HAVE IT?

A widow in Missouri is hospitalized with pneumonia. She needs round-the-clock nursing care for four days until she is out of danger. There are no complications and no surgery is required. She remains in the hospital for three weeks. Total cost: $2,400.

A New York executive has a moderately severe heart attack. The result is three weeks in the hospital, including one week in the intensive care unit. Total cost: $4,700.

A fifteen-year-old Pennsylvania boy is severely injured in an automobile accident requiring more than four months' hospitalization, plus extensive skin grafts and cosmetic surgery. Total cost: $19,880.

How many, even in affluent America, can afford medical bills as astronomical as these?

Just because medical care today is so overpoweringly expensive and because we do not yet have a system of national health insurance, you must regard some form of health insurance as absolutely imperative. What form you choose will depend on the organization from which you buy, the size and age of your family, where you live, where you work, a variety of other factors.

As a general rule, the simplest way to plan the best insurance package for your family is to decide which hazards are the greatest threat to you and to cover these with insurance. Then, to the extent you can afford it, begin to cover the less likely risks.

For instance, if you are a couple beyond childbearing age it would be silly to buy a health insurance policy with maternity benefits. On the other hand, young people would be wise to include in their health insurance package a major medical policy to guard against the big medical bills which could result from automobile accidents that constitute a major hazard for this age group.

FIVE KEY TYPES OF COVERAGE

Here is a rundown on five key types of coverages available today whether you are covered under a group plan where you work or by an individual or single-family policy:

(1) *Hospital Expense Insurance.* This is the best-known and most widely held form. It provides benefits for varying periods of time, usually ranging from 21 days to 365 days or longer. It is offered by Blue Cross plans and by commercial insurance companies.

Benefits under these policies are used to pay for in-hospital services such as room and board, routine nursing care, and minor medical supplies.

In recent years, many Blue Cross plans have been offering coverage for such outpatient and out-of-hospital services as home care, pre-admission testing, nursing home care, dental and vision care, prescription drugs, and a variety of diagnostic and preventive services.

(2) *Surgical Expense Insurance.* This coverage, offered by Blue Shield plans and commercial policies, is used to defray the cost of operations. Policies contain listings of surgical operations and the maximum benefit they will pay for each.

(3) *Physicians' Expense Insurance.* This coverage is almost always combined with hospital and surgical expense insurance, and the three form what

is referred to as the "basic" coverage. Physicians' expense benefits usually cover a specific number of in-hospital visits to you by your doctor. Some policies provide benefits for home and office visits as well.

(4) *Major Medical Insurance*. This type picks up where basic coverage leaves off. It pays for most types of care in or out of hospital, with benefit maximums ranging to $250,000 and up. Blue Cross plans offer this coverage too. These policies use a deductible, which is the amount you must pay before benefits start, and a co-insurance factor, which is a percentage of the total bill you also must pay.

(5) *Disability Insurance*. This type is used to replace earnings lost because of disability. Maximum benefits during disability can go up to $1,000 or more a month, although the maximum is usually about 60 per cent of your gross earnings.

How to Shop for Health Insurance

HOW MUCH COVERAGE DO YOU NEED?

The most economical way to buy health insurance is to insure yourself and your family against the most serious and financially disastrous losses that can result from an illness or an accident. Your minor medical expenses should be met as part of your family's over-all financial plan.

A general rule of thumb is that your basic benefit package should cover at least 75 per cent of your anticipated expenses from any illness or injury.

Other guidelines when you're shopping for health insurance are:

• If you are buying health insurance for the first time, look into the possibility of getting the coverage through a group—a union, an employer-employee plan, a fraternal organization. Group insurance costs 15 to 40 per cent *less* than the same coverage bought on an individual basis. Other advantages of group coverage: Your coverage can't be canceled—unless and until you leave the group. You don't have to take a physical examination to qualify for coverage. And a pre-existing illness does not disqualify you, although it may mean a waiting period to qualify for maternity benefits.

• Find out how many days in the hospital each policy you are considering buying will cover. This is one of the most frequent selling points used by insurers and prepayment plans—and one of the most *misleading*. All basic hospital policies, whether issued by Blue Cross plans or commercial insurers, express benefits in terms of days, with benefit periods of from 21 days to 365 days. But is it really necessary to buy 365 days of basic coverage? Government statistics show that the average length of stay in a hospital is just under 8 days, and that only 3 per cent of all hospital confinements in the country last beyond 31 days.

• Also find out how much each policy pays per day and how the benefits are paid. Basic benefits are paid in two ways: Blue Cross makes payments directly to the hospital for services rendered to you; commercial insurers pay a specified dollar amount either to you *or* to the hospital. The Blue Cross arrangement is generally regarded as preferable to you as a policyholder because Blue Cross plans have direct contractual arrangements with hospitals which grant them (as bulk purchasers) discounts which are passed along to you. The service benefits offered by Blue Cross cover virtually all costs, whereas the specified dollar amount in the indemnity policies offered by the commercial insurers generally represent only a fraction of the costs incurred. There are, though, many exceptions in which both plans offer comparable benefits at comparable costs.

• If you already are covered by health insurance, be sure to keep this coverage updated. If your basic benefits are paid on an indemnity basis (i.e., the commercial insurers' approach), check *frequently* on the current medical and hospital costs in *your own area*. The rates for a hospital in, say, Mississippi, will be substantially less than for one in New York or California. If you have a policy which will pay $40 a day and you live in an area where the average hospital cost is $100, you'll pay the difference. Another point: in recent years hospital charges have been increasing sharply. Thus, if you had an indemnity plan that paid 80 per cent of the hospital charges in the year in which you bought it, chances are there has been steady "slippage" ever since. A mere two years later, your policy will probably cover only 50 per cent of the hospital charges.

THE MEDICAL CATASTROPHE: DO'S AND DON'TS

At today's medical prices, most of you would be plunged deeply into debt in the event of a really serious accident or illness. Every day throughout the country, newspapers carry horror stories telling of the enormous costs faced by families who have suffered this type of misfortune.

The insurance designed for this contingency is called the major medical plan, and if you are about thirty years old and if your family can afford the $175 or so per year it costs in premiums, it can certainly add to your peace of mind.

This type of insurance, like the others, is complex. In the thicket of terminology are such unfamiliar phrases as "inside limits," "co-insurance," "deductibles." Here are do's and don'ts which will make it easier to hack through this jungle.

Don't be dazzled by big benefit maximums such as $250,000 and the like. Even with today's soaring medical costs, it's highly improbable that you'll ever have expenses at this level for a single illness or injury. Keep benefits such as these in perspective, just as you would if someone tried to sell you a policy covering undulant fever or being run down by a herd of buffalo at noon on Main Street. A more realistic ceiling for major medical benefits would be somewhere between $20,000 and $50,000.

Do look into the possibility of getting this coverage through a group. As with your basic coverage, you can achieve big savings by insuring this way.

Do study the deductible and co-insurance features. For example, the usual co-insurance ratio is 75-25 or 80-20, with the 25 or 20 per cent being your share of the medical expenses. If you're willing to take the higher co-insurance percentage offered by one company over another, you may find your premiums proportionately lower.

Do study with care, too, what benefits you get from the way you set up your major medical coverage. You can do this in one of two ways: either as a supplement to your basic coverage or as a single-plan or "comprehensive" major medical plan.

As a general rule, the supplementary type of major medical insurance starts paying at the point where your basic hospital-surgical coverage stops. The "single-plan major medical" covers both basic and catastrophic expenses. Sometimes your deductible is absorbed by your basic coverage in one policy.

Other types of major medical insurance utilize what is known as a "corridor" deductible. That is the amount you must pay above your basic coverage before your major medical takes over. This is available on group health insurance only.

The deductible *applies separately to each family member* (in most cases, up to an annual maximum) for each illness covered by the policy.

Do choose the highest deductible your budget can take. Deductibles usually range from $100 to $1,000. If you feel you can afford to pay the first $1,000 toward medical bills out of your own pocket, the premiums will be lower than if you want to cover everything but the first $100.

. And, by hiking your deductible, you can apply the savings you get through lower premiums to building up extra coverage in other areas that will give you an added dimension of protection.

MONEYSAVING TIPS ON HEALTH INSURANCE

ELEVEN BASIC GUIDES

The following tips on health insurance could save you great aggravation *and* money:

(1) Hold onto any old disability policy you might have if your health is impaired. If you want to expand your disability insurance, keep your old policy and supplement it. Why not replace it? Simply because your present policy undoubtedly carries a lower premium, reflecting your younger age when you bought it. If your health is good, you may be able to get cheaper coverage, even though you are now older.

(2) Check whether a group or family policy has a conversion privilege, so that you can, if necessary, transfer your coverage to an individual basis—

if, say, you leave an employee group for a new job, or you marry—without having restrictive waiting periods reimposed on you.

(3) At the same time, be sure you check whether any refund is owed to you on your previous policy.

(4) Investigate carefully how maternity benefits are paid, if you are a single woman and plan to remain so. Important changes are being made in response to changing attitudes about morals and sex discrimination. Some insurers are altering their hospital and medical coverages to keep up with the new attitudes: more plans, for instance, are providing payments for unmarried women, including maternity benefits for babies born out of wedlock.

(5) Don't waste your money carrying duplicate coverage. It's possible you'll be able to collect on both policies—and maybe even make a profit on an illness—but many insurers are co-ordinating their payments to prevent this. Usually one policy, the first or primary one, is given preference by the company and the second policy will pay only that part of the medical bill not covered by the first. You'll find it increasingly difficult to beat the computers on this.

(6) Health insurance coverage for mental illness is becoming more readily available. Much of the time this condition is covered by major medical policies on a full-payment basis while the patient is hospitalized and with limited payments outside the hospital. But if you have a disability policy you may be able to collect under it. You're entitled to full payment of these expenses under many policies if you are totally disabled as the result of a mental condition—say, a nervous breakdown. If your disability is only partial, your payments will normally cover up to half of the out-of-hospital costs. Another approach to this type of benefit is a sort of "share-the-cost" plan for psychiatric treatment, either through a stated number of visits you make to the psychiatrist or psychologist or through a stated benefit ceiling for psychiatric treatments.

Many Blue Cross policyholders have some mental illness coverage, but in most cases it is sharply limited.

(7) Look into a little-known benefit now available in some disability insurance policies called "income insurance for the breadwinner's wife." This covers the cost of household help if she becomes ill or disabled.

(8) Although this may not be your problem, alcoholism is sufficiently widespread for you to become aware that many insurance policies cover alcoholics and will provide personal medical and social aid, often sending the alcoholic to a specialized rehabilitation center. And even those insurers which do not pay for such specialized treatment almost always cover treatment for alcoholism in their hospital and disability policies.

(9) Note at what age your policy covers your children. Children should be covered from birth and *not,* as some policies state, from the age of two

weeks. It's the first two weeks in the life of your baby that are very often his or her most expensive medically.

(10) If you pay your own premiums directly, try to arrange to pay on an annual or quarterly rather than monthly basis. You'll save money by so doing.

(11) And one final reminder. Although it's important to know just what is covered under your health insurance policy, it's even more important to know what is *excluded* from coverage. Frequently excluded services include psychiatric care, extensive periodontal surgery, foot surgery by podiatrists, cosmetic surgery, care for pre-existing conditions. Knowing what's excluded won't help you pay for the condition if it arises, but at least you won't be in line for an unexpected shock at the worst possible time—when you're flat on your back.

HEALTH INSURANCE BAFFLEGAB GUIDE

ACCIDENTAL DEATH AND DISMEMBERMENT BENEFIT: Payment to a beneficiary, usually through a disability income policy, when an insured person is killed or loses his sight or a limb in an accident.

BENEFICIARY: Person who is designated in an insurance policy to receive a specified cash payment if the policyholder is killed by accident.

CLAIM: Demand by a person covered by health or other insurance for financial benefits provided in his or her policy.

CO-INSURANCE: Special condition, usually found in major medical insurance, in which you and your insurance company share costs. Typically, the insurer pays 50 to 80 per cent of hospital and medical expenses, and you pay the rest.

DEDUCTIBLE: Share of the hospital and medical expenses which you, the insured person, must pay before your insurance policy starts paying.

DISABILITY (OR "INSURED SALARY CONTINUANCE") INSURANCE: Coverage (often group) providing regular weekly or monthly cash benefits to help replace earnings you have lost if you become disabled from just about any cause. In some cases, payment is made for only a limited number of years, and in others, for life.

ELIMINATION PERIOD: Waiting period before benefits (e.g., disability benefits) begin.

FAMILY EXPENSE POLICY: Type of health insurance policy covering you, your wife, and your children.

HOSPITAL EXPENSE INSURANCE: Insurance providing reimbursement of hospital care costs—usually including room and board charges, routine nursing care, anesthesia, surgical facilities, special diets, the like—for illness or injury.

INDIVIDUAL (OR "PERSONAL") INSURANCE: Protection of individual policy-holders and their families, as distinct from lower-cost group insurance which may be offered by employers, labor unions, or professional associations.

MAJOR MEDICAL EXPENSE INSURANCE: Protection against the huge expenses implied by a catastrophic injury or illness. This type of insurance usually pays 75 to 80 per cent of physicians' and hospital bills, after a deductible paid by the insured, up to a maximum from $10,000 to $100,000 or more, and $250,-000 for Blue Cross coverage. "Supplementary" major medical insurance builds on top of basic protection through an ordinary hospital and medical expense policy. A "comprehensive" policy provides both basic and major medical insurance coverage, usually has a low deductible amount.

MEDICAL EXPENSE INSURANCE: Payment, usually partial, of doctors' fees for non-surgical care in the hospital, but sometimes also at home or at the office. Medical expense benefits are sometimes included in hospital expense policies.

SUBSTANDARD HEALTH INSURANCE: Policies issued to those who cannot meet normal health requirements of standard health insurance policies, usually involving a higher premium.

SURGICAL EXPENSE INSURANCE: Benefits to help pay surgeons' fees and other costs of surgical procedures.

YOUR MEDICARE BENEFITS

In the mid-seventies, tens of millions of older Americans—most of them age sixty-five or over—were getting billions of dollars in annual Medicare insurance benefits.

Tens of millions were participating in Medicare's voluntary Part B insurance which covered doctor bills—representing all but a tiny fraction of the elderly. For millions of elderly Americans—plus younger disabled people—Medicare spelled the difference between economic peace of mind when illness struck and instant destitution.

YOUR BASIC BENEFITS

What are your Medicare benefits today under the two separate categories of insurance? Here, first, were the basic Medicare benefits as of 1976:

Medicare Hospital Insurance (Part A) covers, after the deductible, completely or in part, when medically necessary:

• The first 90 days in a hospital or skilled nursing facility for each "benefit period." A "benefit period" begins when you enter a hospital and ends when you have been out of a hospital or any facility providing mainly skilled nursing or rehabilitation care for 60 consecutive days—after which a new benefit period begins if you must go into a hospital again.

• Up to 60 more days of a "lifetime reserve" of extra hospital days.

• Up to 100 days of care in a skilled nursing facility in each benefit period, after you have been hospitalized for at least 3 days in a row.

• Up to 100 home health visits from a participating home health agency within the one-year period after you have been in a hospital for at least 3 days in a row or have received covered care in a skilled nursing facility. Home health services include part-time skilled nursing care, physical or speech therapy, services by home health aides, occupational therapy, and medical supplies and appliances furnished by the agency.

Medicare Medical Insurance (Part B) pays, after the deductible, completely or in part:

• Physicians' services, no matter where you receive them in the United States—in the doctor's office, the hospital, your home, or elsewhere—including medical supplies usually furnished by a doctor in his office, services of his office nurse, and drugs he administers as part of his treatment and which you cannot administer yourself.

• Outpatient hospital services for diagnosis and treatment in an emergency room or an outpatient clinic of a hospital.

• Up to 100 home health visits in each calendar year from a participating home health agency, when prescribed by your physician because you need part-time skilled nursing care or physical or speech therapy and are confined to your home. (These visits are in addition to the post-hospital visits covered under hospital insurance.)

• Outpatient physical therapy and speech pathology services—whether or not you are homebound—furnished under supervision of participating hospitals, skilled nursing facilities, home health agencies, or approved clinics, rehabilitation agencies, or public health agencies under a plan established and periodically reviewed by a doctor.

• Other medical and health services prescribed by your doctor such as diagnostic services; X-ray or other radiation treatments; surgical dressings, colostomy supplies, splints, casts, braces; artificial limbs and eyes; and rental or purchase of durable medical equipment such as a wheel chair or oxygen equipment for use in your home.

• Certain ambulance services.

MEDICARE BENEFITS FOR YOUNGER AMERICANS

Full Medicare health insurance benefits also are available to Americans under age sixty-five who suffer from chronic kidney disease which requires them to undergo regular kidney dialysis or a kidney transplant. Moreover, some 2.3 million disabled Americans under the age of sixty-five are now eligible for *full* Medicare hospital and doctor bill benefits.

What are the rules covering these two key categories of benefits? What must you do to be sure you'll receive the benefits due you (or your parent or relative or friend who might be eligible)?

Q. Who are the disabled persons eligible for medicare benefits?

A. People who are (or have been) entitled to at least twenty-four consecutive months of Social Security disability benefits because they are disabled. Included are:

disabled workers at any age;

disabled widows;

disabled dependent widowers between the ages of fifty and sixty-four;

women aged fifty or older who are entitled to mother's benefits who, for twenty-four months prior to the first month they would have been entitled to Medicare protection, met all the requirements for disability benefits except for actual filing of a disability claim;

people aged eighteen and over who receive Social Security benefits because they became disabled before reaching age twenty-two.

Medicare for the disabled provides precisely the same protection as Medicare offers others when they reach age sixty-five.

Q. When does this protection begin?

A. In the twenty-fifth consecutive month after you originally became entitled to Social Security disability benefits.

Q. What do you have to do to be sure your new Medicare disability insurance goes into effect?

A. You will be automatically notified by the Social Security Administration prior to the first time you are entitled to this coverage. You will also be automatically signed up for the special Part B doctor bill insurance *unless* you specifically inform the Social Security Administration that you do not want this coverage.

This premium will be automatically deducted from your Social Security or Railroad Retirement disability check—starting with the check you receive in the month in which you first become eligible for Medicare coverage.

Caution: If you *don't* accept this Part B coverage (for which the federal government pays at least half the cost) now, but later change your mind, your monthly premium will be hiked 10 per cent for each one-year period you let go by without signing up.

Of course, if your disability ceases before you reach age sixty-five (when you become eligible for regular Medicare benefits), your eligibility for Medicare also ceases.

To be eligible for kidney disease coverage you must be fully insured *or* be receiving Social Security benefits (e.g., as a widow or as a disabled person) or be the spouse or dependent child of a person who meets the above criteria.

Not only hospital services in the treatment of kidney disease will be paid for, but also treatment in approved special kidney treatment centers or "limited care centers," and also the cost of home dialysis equipment and supplies. In addition, persons covered under this provision are eligible for all other Medicare benefits.

Actual Medicare coverage begins on the first day of the third month after the month in which dialysis begins or, if earlier, the month you are hospitalized for a kidney transplant. To illustrate: If your dialysis begins on June 15, Medicare coverage starts on September 1.

Coverage continues a full year after the month you have a kidney transplant or your dialysis treatment ends—and resumes in the third month after treatment begins again.

These are extraordinary valuable benefits for younger Americans who are suffering from grave disabilities.

OTHER MEDICARE BENEFITS

Here, next, is a rundown on other Medicare benefits which went into effect in 1973:

limited services by chiropractors;

services by physical therapists in an office *or* at your home;

payment by Medicare of your capitation premium for covered services if you join a Health Maintenance Organization (see later, this chapter) or a prepaid group medical practice or a medical foundation or a neighborhood health center;

elimination of co-insurance for home health benefits under Part B;

non-emergency and emergency services in a foreign hospital (e.g., in Canada or Mexico) *if* it happens to be closer to your home or more easily accessible than the nearest suitable U.S. hospital and emergency services for beneficiaries traveling between Alaska and another state.

Also, elderly Americans who before mid-1973 failed to qualify for Medicare hospital coverage (e.g., because they hadn't worked long enough under Social Security to qualify) can now buy into the system at a moderate monthly cost. But they also *must* buy the "voluntary" Part B medical insurance, also at a moderate cost.

HOW MUCH YOU MUST PAY

Here are costs you, the Medicare beneficiary (or your parent or relative or friend who is a beneficiary), must pay under the law as of January 1, 1976:

• the first $104 of your hospital bill for each "benefit period";

• $26 a day in "co-insurance" for *each* day you have to stay in a hospital from your sixty-first day through the ninetieth day you are in the hospital;

• the first $52 a day in costs for each day you use of your additional 60-day "lifetime reserve" of hospital coverage;

• $13 a day between the twenty-first and hundredth day you spend in a skilled nursing facility or up to a total of 100 days covered by Medicare in such a facility;

• costs of the first three pints of blood you may need during each "benefit period" under hospital insurance, or the first three pints in a calendar year under medical insurance;

• costs of any private-duty nurses you may need, and costs of any "personal comfort" items for which you sign up in the hospital—e.g., telephone, radio, TV;

• the per month cost of Part B Medicare insurance covering doctor bills —a premium which is being hiked periodically as costs of medical services rise;

• the first $60 of your doctor bills (or other expenses covered by your Part B insurance each year), except for hospital inpatient lab and radiology services performed by doctors for which Medicare pays 100 per cent of the "reasonable charges";

• 20 per cent of your remaining medical bills after you have paid this $60 deductible—plus any charges above and beyond the amounts approved, unless an assignment has been taken by the doctor;

• expenses of physical therapy services in your home or the therapists office over $100 a year.

Among the key items which were *not* covered at all by Medicare as of 1976's law were: routine physical exams and immunizations; out-of-hospital prescription drugs; routine eye exams for eyeglasses; hearing aids; dentures; routine dental care; orthopedic shoes custodial nursing home care; most cosmetic surgery; services furnished free or payable under government programs; services furnished by the members of the patient's household or immediate relatives; and, of course, any services not considered reasonable and necessary for the diagnosis and treatment of an illness or injury.

WHAT TO WATCH OUT FOR IN MAIL ORDER HEALTH INSURANCE

NOT THE BEST HEALTH CARE INSURANCE

Americans are now investing hundreds of millions of dollars each year in mail order health insurance—lured by aggressive advertising, no-strings-attached benefits, low monthly premiums.

Most experts, however, do not regard this type of insurance as the best way to finance your basic health care.

As just one illustration, one survey disclosed that companies which sell this insurance return only 40¢ of each premium dollar in the form of benefits —compared with an average of close to 92¢ on group Blue Cross policies. Even the better state lotteries return more: about 45¢ on the dollar.

KEY GUIDES

If, therefore, you are thinking of buying a mail order policy, obey the following guides:

Consider this coverage as strictly *supplementary*. Most of these companies advertise benefits of $100 to $125 a week. But if you don't have an adequate basic health insurance plan, $100 a week will provide picayune protection in an era when your hospital costs alone can come to more than $100 *a day*. Also, though they may offer benefits for as long as 100 weeks, and this may unduly impress you, remember the average hospital stay is only around eight days.

Study the advertisements carefully. Sometimes enthusiastic copy writing implies that the policy can deliver more dollars than it actually will. For instance, one major company in the mail order health insurance field has an ad which contains this paragraph near the beginning of the text:

"How long could you stay in the hospital without worrying about the pile-up of daily expenses? Who will pay for the expenses of costly X-rays, doctor bills, drugs and medicines? And how about the expenses at home— rent, food, telephone and others that just go on and on? With expenses like these could you avoid having your savings wiped out and your family life upset?"

Then the following paragraph makes the statement (italics added): "Wouldn't it be comforting to know *these problems* could be solved by your Extra Cash Income Plan . . . the plan that gives you $100 a week IN CASH. . . ."

The implication is that this plan, which offers approximately $14.29 per day, will solve the problems of X-rays, drugs, medicines, doctor bills, rent, food, telephone, and all the rest when, in actuality, such an amount would not even pay for more than a fraction of the hospital bill itself, let alone all the other bills.

Be wary of direct-mail pieces which contain approaches such as: "Dear Friend: I know that YOU DON'T DRINK. Because of this I can offer you the Blue Chip (Green Comet; Silver Bullet) brand new hospitalization plan that will pay you $100 a week EXTRA CASH. . . . As a non-drinker, why should you be forced to pay as much for health insurance as people who drink? Our actuaries say that non-drinkers take better care of themselves, so doesn't a non-drinker like you deserve a lower rate? . . ."

A mail order piece such as this is a mass-merchandised catchall unrelated to actuarial realities, for there is no way for the company issuing the piece to know whether you, the addressee, are in fact a non-drinker. In addition, there has been no study by the nationally known Society of Actuaries to support the contention that non-drinkers are better health insurance risks. In many instances the premium charged may even be higher than for a policy from a company which does not use this type of gimmickry.

Buy whatever insurance you do decide to take only from a company licensed to do business in your own state. This is a fundamental rule.

Because the mails and mass-circulation advertising cross state lines, the ads you see easily may be those of a company which is unlicensed in your particular state. This can increase your difficulty of collecting in the event of claims. By purchasing this insurance you not only deprive yourself of the protection of your own state laws but also, if a dispute arises over a claim, you may have to go to the state where the company is based to bring suit. You can find out whether or not a company is licensed in your state simply by phoning or writing to your state insurance department.

Since premiums are usually paid monthly, take the trouble to learn how much leeway you have should you inadvertently permit a lapse in payment. The usual grace period is ten days, or, if you pay the premium weekly, seven days. Remember: Since companies usually do not issue reminder notices, you are obligated to keep track of your payments yourself. If a policy lapses because of non-payment, a new round of waiting periods may be reinstalled.

Analyze the exclusions and waiting periods. Many policies, for example, exclude coverage if the hospitalization results from mental illness. Some policies use large type to state NO WAITING PERIODS, but in the smaller type use a phrase which restricts this significantly.

Another key point: there's nothing special about the advertised tax-free benefits of the payouts. Most health insurance payments are tax-free. And, unlike regular health insurance policies, *premiums* on this type of policy may not be tax-deductible.

CHECK LIST FOR READING MAIL ORDER ADS

There are no direct federal controls over mail order health insurers and until recently most state regulatory insurance departments have been grossly understaffed and reluctant or unable to crack down on misleading ads that could conceal loopholes or exaggerate benefits. Use this check list to your own advantage when you read an ad:

What's covered: Are illnesses as well as accidents covered? What illnesses are excluded? Many policies exclude payments for treating such conditions as alcoholism, pregnancy, miscarriage, mental disorders, and some policies exclude cancer, tuberculosis, or heart disease. Most will cover you only if you are actually confined to a hospital, but not if you are being treated in the hospital's outpatient department.

Waiting periods: When do you begin to receive benefits? If you've had an accident, you can probably collect from the first day you're in the hospital.

In the case of illness, however, the waiting period may be from three to eight days, with an average wait of six days. Moreover, eligibility for sickness benefits often does not begin until the policy has been in force for thirty days. And there is usually also a six-month waiting period for coverage of certain specific diseases such as tuberculosis, diabetes, hernia, cancer, or heart disease.

"Pre-existing" conditions: Among the most agonizing loopholes in many of these contracts are the provisions covering "pre-existing" conditions. In one policy, this small-print clause reads:

No claim or loss incurred after two years from the date of this policy shall be reduced or denied on the ground that a disease or physical condition not excluded from coverage by name or specific description effective on the date of loss had existed prior to the effective date of coverage of this policy."

At first glance, this may look like a helpful provision aimed at protecting *you*, the insured. But what it really says is that for the first two years your policy is in force you can't collect for any condition you had when you first took out the policy—even if you weren't aware of the condition at the time. Incidentally, one factor helping to hold down the cost of these policies is the high number of claims rejected because of pre-existing conditions. Some companies routinely reject from one half to four fifths of policyholders' claims for this reason.

Benefits paid: Don't be dazzled by the advertised lump-sum figures of $100 a week or $600 a month: Instead, figure what the policy would pay you *per day.* A payment of $100 a week comes to $14.29 a day; $600 a month works out to $20 a day.

And what would be your chances of collecting the sums advertised? Say an illness keeps you in the hospital for the eight days and your policy has a six-day waiting period before you can begin collecting benefits. You collect for only two days or, in the case of the $600-a-month policy, a total of $40 for your eight-day hospital stay.

And to collect the maximum $39,000 over a five-year period some ads promise, you would have to be virtually a basket case.

Premiums: A 25¢ or $1.00 "introductory premium" may look inviting but that's just for the first month and typical premiums are $5.00 or so a month thereafter. Rates also may be sharply hiked later or the contract may call for higher premiums at age sixty-five. So, if you're in doubt, write the insurance company and ask for a complete schedule of premium payments.

Enrollment period: Is there a deadline for applying? Often a "limited enrollment period" is advertised and this may create a sense of false urgency. The deadline also may serve to prevent you from making inquiries, since it may leave you only two or three days to enroll. (One company's ads, published on January 3, specified an enrollment period ending midnight, January 6. The company advertised again on February 22, again specifying a three-day enrollment period.)

Renewability: How long will the policy stay in force? Under what conditions can it be renewed—or canceled? You well may get the impression that policies may be renewed indefinitely. But the catch here is that rate changes or policy cancellations may occur as long as they are made state-wide or apply to all policyholders of your "classification." This is subject to wide interpretation: it could for example, mean people of your age group. Raising premiums state-wide is by no means uncommon. If the rates are raised to prohibitive levels, that alone could in effect force many to drop their policies.

This is merely a brief sampling but surely it warns you to read a health insurance ad with healthy skepticism and to check with your state insurance department, if you have any doubts or questions.

And I emphasize again the first guide: *Never* buy this type of policy as a substitute for the broader types of hospital policies which pay virtually your entire bill and which can be supplemented by extra coverage available at moderate additional cost.

WHAT IF YOU'RE DISABLED?

SOURCES OF HELP

What would you do if you became, through some tragic accident, permanently and totally disabled? Could *your* family survive on the average Social Security disability benefit?

Long-term disability insurance, like major medical coverage, also is being overlooked by the vast majority of Americans. Only about one in three of us has any private disability insurance protection. And even in the cases of those who have the insurance, the monthly benefit is often inadequate and the term that benefits are paid is too short to be meaningful. (The average disability lasts five years.)

Disability insurance (often called loss-of-income insurance) pays cash benefits designed to help replace earnings you have lost because of disability up to a maximum of about 60 per cent of your gross earnings. The policies begin paying benefits anywhere from a week following the start of the disability to six months later. They pay benefits from as few as thirteen weeks to as long as a lifetime.

There's little point in trying to insure yourself privately against the loss of your entire gross income because you will have other sources of disability income which will make up much of the difference.

For example, your employer well may have some form of wage-continuation policy which will keep income flowing in for a number of weeks or months after you have become disabled.

Or your union contract may include certain sick-leave benefits.

There also are state workers' compensation payments for job-connected disability.

There's Social Security: you're eligible for benefits in the sixth month of disability, so long as the disability is expected to last at least twelve months.

Look into all these sources plus any veterans' benefits for which you think you might be eligible.

WHAT YOU SHOULD KNOW ABOUT SOCIAL SECURITY DISABILITY BENEFITS

HUGE NUMBERS COLLECTING BENEFITS EACH YEAR

"How bad must my husband's blindness be to qualify him for Social Security disability benefits?" the letter began in a handwriting which wiggled with emotional distress. "My husband has been laid off because of his failing eyesight. He isn't even trying to get another job and he says he can't get disability benefits." Then the letter continued with an urgent plea for guidance.

The answer to this question of the understandably distraught wife is this:

Blindness is defined in the Social Security law as either central visual acuity of 20/200 or less in the better eye with the use of corrective lenses, or visual field reduction to 20 degrees or less.*

In 1974 more than 2 million disabled Americans plus more than 1.6 million of their dependent wives and children were collecting about $5 billion in Social Security disability benefits each year. A full four out of five men and women in the age brackets from twenty-one to sixty-four are "insured"; that is, they are covered under Social Security.

In all likelihood, *you* can count on monthly cash benefits in the event that a severe and prolonged disability keeps you from working. And, in addition, disabled workers who have been collecting Social Security benefits for at least twenty-four months also are eligible for Medicare hospital and doctor bill benefits (see preceding section, "Medicare Benefits for Younger Americans," for details on this coverage).

FACTS ABOUT BENEFITS

Because so many of you do not understand the requirements that may qualify or disqualify you, the need for greater knowledge is enormous. Here, therefore, are key facts about these benefits:

Q. *How do you qualify for disability benefits?*

A. In addition to qualifying as "disabled," you must have earned twenty quarters (five years) of coverage during the ten years before you were dis-

---

* If a worker's visual impairment falls short of this test, consideration may be given to his age, education, training, and work experience to determine whether or not he is disabled.

abled and be fully insured. If you become disabled before age thirty-one, you will need less work credit—only half the quarters between the age of twenty-one and the time you are disabled, with a minimum of six quarters. Payments begin with the sixth full month of your disability. You must provide the names and addresses of doctors and hospitals involved with your medical treatment and you must accept rehabilitation.

Q. *At what age can you start collecting benefits?*

A. At *any* age under sixty-five if you qualify as disabled. A disability can be mental or physical, but it must be "medically determinable" and it must be expected either to result in death or expected to last (or have lasted) at least twelve months. Also, with few exceptions, it must make you unable to do any substantial gainful work anywhere in our economy.

Q. *What about wives and children of disabled workers?*

A. While you are receiving benefits as a disabled worker, payments to your dependents can be made as follows:

Each unmarried child can get a monthly benefit if he or she is under eighteen; (this is in addition to your benefit); if he or she is a full-time student age eighteen through twenty-one or suffering from a disability which began before age twenty-two. Stepchildren and adopted children similarly qualify.

Your wife can get up to 50 per cent of your full benefit too if she's caring for a child eligible for benefits (except that she can't collect if the child is a full-time student between eighteen and twenty-two). Or she can collect, if she is sixty-two, a reduced benefit, even if there are no children entitled to benefits. At sixty-five, she can collect 50 per cent.

A dependent husband sixty-two or older also can qualify for benefits— 50 per cent benefit at age sixty-five, less if benefits begin earlier.

Q. *How much of a benefit would you get?*

A. Disability benefits are based on your average monthly wages and are the same as the full retirement benefits you would get if you had reached sixty-five at the time you became disabled. If you are under sixty-two, though, the total benefits paid to you and your dependents may be reduced if you are receiving workmen's compensation.

Q. *What if a disabled worker with an impairment not expected to improve wants to try going back to work? Does he continue getting benefits for a transition period?*

A. If you return to work, your benefit may continue to be paid during a trial work period of up to nine months—although these need not be consecutive months. If, after these nine months of testing your ability to work, it is decided that you are able to hold a substantial job, your benefit will be paid for an "adjustment period" of three more months. After that, you're on your own.

Q. *Why is there a waiting period of five full months before a disabled worker can begin to receive benefits after applying?*

A. Because usually there are payments made by the employer, a group insurance plan, a private health insurance policy—or, if the injury occurred on the job, by workers' compensation.

Q. *What are the key types of disability for which workers are now receiving benefits?*

A. In the mid-seventies, diseases of the circulatory system (heart disease) ranked first. Emphysema was next and schizophrenia was third.

Check any questions with your nearest Social Security office. You'll find the address under "Social Security Administration" in the phone book. If you can't leave the house, a Social Security representative will come to you. Telephone or write or have a friend do this for you. These are your rights.

WHAT'S YOUR WORKERS' COMPENSATION WORTH?

THE HIGH COST OF WORK ACCIDENTS

When a coal mine disaster hits the front pages, as one does with heartbreaking frequency, our attention is riveted on the tragedy of fatal on-the-job accidents. Yet headlines such as these touch only the tip of the accident iceberg.

Each year, about 14,000 Americans lose their lives in on-the-job accidents. Each year, workers suffer a startling 10 million injuries on the job.

Merely in economic terms, the cost of work accidents and injuries was approximately $10 billion a year in the mid-seventies, double the total for 1962. This included lost wages, medical costs, damages to equipment and materials, delays in production, insurance, etc.

Injuries are a daily fact of life in today's most hazardous industries: coal mining, longshoring, roofing and sheet metal work, meat and meat products (especially cutting and handling), mobile home manufacturing, lumber and wood products, construction.

Workers' compensation, formerly known as workmen's compensation, for job-related accidents, illnesses, and injuries is the oldest form of social insurance in the United States—dating back to 1908 when Congress set up a program under the Federal Employees Compensation Act to cover certain federal employees in hazardous occupations. State after state followed with its own workmen's compensation law until, today, all fifty states have programs of their own, with the coverage paid for competely by the employer and employees getting these free benefits through private insurance, self-insurance, and state insurance funds.

Today the yearly dollar outlay of workers' compensation benefits is in a neck-and-neck race with the massive Social Security disability program.

However, the rules vary widely from state to state and there also is a wide variation in the proportion of lost wages which are replaced.

The states are, therefore, now facing a federal take-over of their workers' compensation systems if they are not brought up to much higher standards. As a result there is a solid trend toward liberalization of the laws across the land.

Among the significant liberalizations:

Employees of smaller and smaller firms are being brought under the workers' compensation umbrella. The number of states with compulsory coverage is rising and the trend in more and more states is toward including at least some farm and domestic workers. More states are providing benefit limits which increase along with the state-wide wage scale.

Limitations on the amount of reimbursable medical, surgical, and hospital expenses are being eliminated. Compensation periods for permanent disabilities—such as loss of limb—are being stretched out. More states are providing complete coverage for occupational diseases. Injured employees are often being given a free choice from a panel of recognized physicians and specialists. There has been a steady succession of hikes in benefits. Every state now has a retroactive pay provision covering the waiting period before normal workers' compensation benefits begin.

The potential importance to you of this coverage must not be downgraded: glance back at those figures on how many workers are injured and killed in on-the-job accidents.

QUESTIONS AND ANSWERS ON BENEFITS

But do *you* know what your workers' compensation coverage is worth to you? Are you aware of how much this insurance would pay if a serious accident befell you while were working?

Q. *How many of us are covered?*

A. Between eight and nine out of ten workers.

Q. *Who's eligible?*

A. Covered workers who are partially or totally disabled as a result of an accident or injury on the job—regardless of blame. The interpretation of "on the job" varies, but in California the state Supreme Court recently ruled that the widow of a worker killed in an auto accident at night after attending a job-related class was still eligible for workers' compensation benefits.

Q. *Who isn't covered?*

A. It varies from state to state but among the occupations with large numbers of non-covered workers are agricultural work, domestic work, work for religious, charitable, and non-profit organizations, "casual" labor, self-employed, workers in small firms.

Q. *How much do benefits run?*

A. Normally, maximum benefits are between 60 and 80 per cent of the pre-disability wage and often there's a dollar ceiling on benefits. In several states there's an extra allowance for workers who have dependents, which brings typical benefits to 60 to 65 per cent of the amount of take-home pay.

Q. *What types of benefits does the program pay?*

A. Three types. The biggest chunk goes to make up for income loss due to disability incurred on the job. The next biggest chunk goes for medical costs. The rest goes for death benefits paid to the worker's survivors. Included in the program are hundreds of millions of dollars in "black lung" benefits paid by the federal government to coal miners suffering from pneumoconiosis —a serious lung disease which comes from inhaling coal dust—and to their dependents.

Q. *How long are benefits paid?*

A. Most state programs pay benefits as long as the disability lasts. Note: More than one in six of our civilian working-age population has some kind of limitation on his or her ability to work because of a chronic disability or health condition.

Q. *Who pays for the workers' compensation program?*

A. In most cases, employers pay insurance premiums either to state insurance programs or to private health insurance carriers or they insure employees themselves. The average cost to employers in covered employment is about 1 per cent of payroll, although costs range in some states up to nearly 3 per cent. Generally, the costs of administering workers' compensation come out of the state's general revenues instead of from employers.

Q. *Can you collect both Social Security benefits and workers' compensation benefits at the same time?*

A. Yes, if the combination does not exceed 80 per cent of your pre-disability monthly earnings. Beyond that, Social Security payments are trimmed to keep the total at the 80 per cent mark.

Q. *What about private health insurance benefits?*

A. There's usually a provision that private health insurance won't pay for any medical conditions covered by the compensation law. But if your employer has "long-term" disability insurance for employees this will make up the difference if workers' compensation provides a smaller amount.

Use the above guidelines to help you find out whether the *total* amount of benefits you and your family would get if you, the breadwinner, became disabled would or wouldn't be adequate to meet your family's needs. Also include company insurance, Social Security, your savings and investments.

PRIVATE DISABILITY INSURANCE COVERAGE

WHAT WOULD IT COST YOU?

Let's say you use the guidelines in the preceding section, check your various benefits, and come to the firm conclusion that your benefits would be seriously inadequate in case of need.

How much would it cost you to buy supplementary private disability insurance—to add to your protection from Social Security, workers' compensation, and other sources?

If you get a private individual policy providing $100 a week for up to two years, it'll probably cost you $76 to $115 a year. If the coverage lasts up to five years, your annual premiums probably would be between $128 and $180—with office workers generally paying less. And there is usually a thirty-day waiting period before any private disability insurance benefits may begin.

With this as a yardstick, you can compute what the coverage you need will cost, keeping in mind that the longer the waiting period the less your premium cost will be. Also, the longer the benefit continues, the more your cost will be.

CHECK LIST FOR COVERAGES

Check with care these points about private disability coverages:

(1) How is "disability" defined in your policy or the policy you are considering buying? Generally, these policies state that you must be "totally" disabled before benefits are paid.

Your policy may have a variation of this definition:

"Unable to engage in any gainful occupation for which the policyholder is suited by education, training, or experience."

(2) What is the difference in benefit periods for an accident and for an illness? For instance, the same policy might provide benefits for two years for sickness and five years for an accident.

(3) What waiting period is appropriate for you? Take into account the length of time your regular earnings would continue, as well as all the other sources of income, then decide whether you should accept a seven-, fourteen-, thirty-, ninety-day waiting period—or longer.

MAKING DEDUCTIBLES WORK FOR YOU

As in major medical insurance, the best way to save money in your disability coverage is to select the highest deductible your budget can stand. In this type of insurance, the deductible amount is expressed in terms of the waiting period. By extending the waiting—or, as it is called, the "elimination"—period before benefits start, you can cut your costs and either save the money or use it to build up your protection. Since you're less likely to have major medical and disability coverage than you are to have basic protection, it's probable that you'll work out some combination of these.

Here's how you can juggle the deductible to your advantage:

One major medical policy offered by a large insurer would provide a twenty-eight-year-old man with $10,000 maximum coverage for himself, his wife, and two children, with a $250 deductible, at a cost of about $225 per year.

If he raised this deductible to $750 he could get a policy which would cut his annual premium to about $182. Then, with the money saved, he could buy a short-term disability policy which would pay him $200 a month for two years after a thirty-day waiting period. Both policies would have a waiting period before benefits are payable—three months for a disability and six months for illness.

Now, to dramatize for you the effect of lengthening the disability policy waiting period, consider this typical policy from another insurer. His policy provides benefits of $200 a month for sixty months and costs $66.40 per year if the waiting period is only fourteen days. But the cost of the same policy providing the same monthly benefit to age sixty-five—roughly thirty-two years more than the first policy for a twenty-eight-year-old man—is only $44.80 a year if the waiting period is upped to ninety days.

How to Slash Your Medical Bills

There's no hope for anything more than a slowing of the pace of rise in medical expenses in the decade of the 1970s.

But there are many ways you can cut your own costs. Below you will find fundamental rules that you could translate into big savings for yourself and family—without in any way jeopardizing your health.

SHOP FOR A HOSPITAL

In shopping for health services, perhaps the most difficult area is the hospital. You can't merely pick out one and walk in. Invariably, unless you're an emergency case, you must be admitted by a physician who is affiliated with the hospital.

Few of the one out of every seven Americans admitted to a hospital each year, I'm sure, ever even thinks about "shopping" for a hospital. But it can be done.

The easiest way would be to telephone each hospital in your city or nearby area until you found the one with the lowest daily rate. But the trouble with this approach is that the hospital you pick in this manner may not be on your doctor's affiliation list, so you'll have to get another doctor. And chances are the institution with the lowest rate is a municipal or "city" hospital. You may not regard municipal institutions with the same esteem you have for private voluntary community hospitals. Private health insurance usually does not cover any tax-supported hospital where no charge is made for service.

You'll find that your physician is probably affiliated with more than one hospital. If he doesn't have strong feelings about admitting you to a particular institution for a particular reason (if the hospital to which your physician wants to send you is the only one in town with a cobalt radiation unit and you need cobalt radiation treatment, you have little choice in the matter), then bear these points in mind:

• *Do* select the hospital on your physician's list that is a teaching institution and also has a strong research program. If a hospital has affiliations such as these, it has sources of revenue and talent not normally open to other community hospitals which are supported almost exclusively by taxes and patient charges. This is also the facility that will give you the greatest range of diagnostic and treatment resources.

• *Don't* confuse bigness with best. Depending on your condition and the type of treatment you need, maybe a smaller hospital would provide you with less hurried and more personal tender loving care—a difficult item to put a price tag on.

• *Do* check whether your state regulatory agencies can help steer you toward a lower-cost hospital. For instance, in Pennsylvania a few years ago, the state's insurance department published a "Shopper's Guide to Hospitals." This guide compared costs charged by the 101 hospitals in the Philadelphia area—and found that the *daily* charges varied by as much as $50.

• *Don't*, unless it means a big sacrifice to you, go into the hospital on a Friday. A large-scale study a while ago showed that the day of the week you go into the hospital is the single largest factor in determining how long you'll stay there. Admissions on Friday, the study disclosed, resulted in longer stays than admissions on any other day. The reason: the hospital is not fully staffed on weekends and if you go in on a Friday you'll have to wait until Monday before all the necessary laboratory and other diagnostic tests can be performed. Meanwhile, you well may be paying $100 or more a day for your "hotel room."

The study also revealed that the *shortest* average length of stay was found for patients admitted on a Tuesday.

If you have an indemnity-type health insurance policy which leaves you with part of the hospital bill to pay out of pocket, getting out just a day or two earlier can be a considerable relief to your budget. In fact, it has been estimated that, if we could cut the average hospital stay by just one day from its 7.9 days in the mid-seventies, the nation could save $1 billion annually.

• *Do* ask your doctor if it's possible to have some of your routine lab tests done *before* you're admitted to the hospital. An increasing number of hospitals participate in pre-admission testing programs of this type. More than one out of every three Blue Cross plans will pay benefits for this type of visit to the outpatient department, and many insurers also pay through diagnostic riders to their contracts.

• And finally, *do,* unless you feel you absolutely must have complete privacy, take a semi-private room, for it is far less expensive than a private room. Many hospitals will charge less for a four-bed semi-private room than for a two-bed room and it's becoming easier to get exactly what you want. Also, semi-private accommodations are usually paid for in full by Blue Cross and also by commercial insurance company indemnity policies.

HAVE A FAMILY PHYSICIAN

Choose him (or her) carefully—for his reputation in the community, the type of practice he has developed, and his availability. If you are a newcomer in the area, the local county medical society will supply you with the names of physicians from whom you can make a choice. You may want to become acquainted with several before deciding.

But don't make your selection solely on the recommendation of a local medical society. Membership in these organizations tells you only that a doctor is licensed to practice and has paid his dues. Also don't assume that because a doctor is well known in his community he is good. He may be prominent for reasons other than medical skill.

One clue to his competence will be his membership on the medical staff of a good hospital, especially a hospital affiliated with a medical school. If so, you can be well assured that he's above average.

Your doctor may practice medicine alone, in a group, or in a large clinic, but he should be a person who knows you and your family and is interested in your *health,* not just your illnesses.

He will keep a permanent record of your medical history.

He will know your background and be better able to tell promptly if anything is wrong.

He will control a key portion of your medical spending, simply because he will determine what drugs you will buy, whether or when you must go to a hospital, whether or when you must see a specialist. And when you must consult a specialist or go to a hospital, he will save you money by making sure you do not repeat costly, time-consuming tests. He also may save you money by referring you to a nurse practitioner for routine health problems.

DON'T WAIT TO SEE YOUR PHYSICIAN UNTIL YOU'RE ILL

If you try to save money on medical bills by not seeing the doctor until you are seriously ill you will defeat the purpose of preventive medicine—the *only sound way* to preserve your health. And it will be more expensive in the long run, for once a disease process has started, it often lasts longer, costs more to cure.

Emergencies are always more expensive, whether the crisis involves the family car, the household plumbing, or your health. And if you are rushed to a hospital emergency room, you really may compound your misfortune—financial as well as physical.

HAVE REGULAR CHECKUPS

A complete physical examination each year is really a must. Try to schedule your exam during your birthday week if possible. Early detection of a disease obviously gives you a better chance to control and cure it. By one estimate, it costs nine times more to cure a disease than to prevent it in the first place. Moreover, your past medical record in your physician's hands will help you should you be hit by a severe accident or illness. Typical cost range in the mid-seventies for a comprehensive physical, including lab fees: $40 to $180. And part of this cost well might be covered by your health insurance or offered as a special employee benefit.

ALWAYS DISCUSS YOUR PHYSICIAN'S FEES WITH HIM

Fees are not inflexible, and physicians frequently adjust their charges to meet your financial situation. Be sure, though, to discuss fees at your first meeting; do *not* wait until after you receive the bill. If you decide a medical fee is unreasonable after a service has been provided, the first step is to negotiate directly with the doctor.

Be particularly careful to discuss fees at the start with a specialist, who may be very expensive but who also may reduce and stretch out payment for his charges to fit your budget.

GO TO THE DOCTOR'S OFFICE

House calls are not only more expensive but also less efficient. Without office equipment and a trained staff, your physician cannot perform a complete examination. (Of course, chronically ill, confined patients can be seen only at home.)

What's more, a house call may not be adequate for the doctor and he'll ask you to come to his office for further consultation. Result: two fees instead of one.

Reserve house calls for real emergencies.

USE THE TELEPHONE

This saves money and also makes good medical sense. A family doctor who has examined you regularly is familiar with your health history. Consequently, he often can advise you over the phone about minor health problems. For anything that seems to be serious, he will ask you to come to his office to be examined.

But call the doctor only when you have adequate reasons—and confine discussions of your appointments and other routine matters to his nurse.

FOLLOW YOUR DOCTOR'S ORDERS

Just as a commonplace illustration, have you ever been told to take off ten pounds and get more exercise? Did you do it? If you refuse to follow the expert advice you solicit and pay for, you are throwing your money away.

YOUR COMMUNITY HEALTH RESOURCES

DON'T OVERLOOK THEM!

All around you are a great number and variety of community health services. They are available to you, and they could mean considerable savings to you over the long term. Don't overlook them!

These resources range from your public hospitals and clinics to volunteer ambulance services, local blood banks, visiting nurse service, rehabilitation and mental health counseling, vocational rehabilitation and retraining programs. In addition, there are special services, such as free screening and immunization programs, especially if you live in a highly populated area. The list of these services is almost endless, combatting health problems ranging from deafness to drug abuse, and fighting illnesses ranging from alcoholism to venereal disease.

On top of your community resources are other facilities backed by labor groups, private foundations, business organizations, and social service agencies. And don't forget government programs. As one illustration, the Veterans Administration conducts a large-scale national program of medical care and rehabilitation services.

Your Department of Health is the place to go to start finding out just what services you might use. Every state has one, and so do many cities and counties, although in some areas you may find this function is fulfilled by a health officer instead of a department. In any event, the Department of Health or the health officer will be able to refer you to the health services that are available through the department or through private agencies.

SAMPLING OF SERVICES

Here are some of the areas of special services you might need or want which are there for your asking:

Abortion	Blindness
Adoption	Blood banks
Aging	Birth defects
Alcoholism	Cancer
Ambulance service	Cerebral palsy
Arthritis	Child placement

Chronic illness	Kidney disease
Convalescent care	Leukemia
Day care	Maternity care
Deafness	Medicare and Medicaid
Dental services	Mental retardation
Diabetes	Nursing and homemaker services
Drugs	Prescription emergency services
Family Planning	Rehabilitation
Food Stamps	Speech handicaps
Handicapped children	Unmarried parents
Heart disease	Venereal disease
Hemophilia	Welfare services

How to Slash Your Drug Bills

NINE BASIC HINTS

(1) Take only the drugs and medications prescribed or recommended by your doctor.

(2) Urge the pharmacist filling a prescription to follow your doctor's instructions at the lowest possible cost. But *do not* decide on your own to substitute a generic equivalent for a trade-name drug—assuming you are now taking one of these drugs or one is prescribed for you. Let your physician make the decision.

(3) Ask your physician to steer you to drugstores in your area which offer quality drugs at the lowest cost. The American Medical Association is now urging physicians to do this as a matter of course.

(4) Shop the drugstores recommended to you, for the variations can be astounding. As a general guide, discount drugstores will fill prescriptions at lower cost to you than regular drugstores. Co-op pharmacies are scarce, but if you can find a co-op, it will be an excellent place to patronize.

(5) Don't buy non-prescription drugs in large quantities unless they are really needed. A 1,000-tablet aspirin bottle may seem more economical than a small size, but aspirin—and many other medicines—deteriorate with time. On the other hand, if you suffer from a chronic illness that calls for the use of prescription drugs over a long period, your doctor may prescribe in relatively large quantities and this may result in some savings.

(6) Get "starter" supplies of drugs from your physician. Most doctors are deluged with samples from drug firms and here you save in two ways: you get your initial supply free and you can try out the medication for its effectiveness before you buy a larger supply.

(7) Make sure you're not paying a professional charge for a non-prescription over-the-counter drug. Sometimes physicians recommend drugs

which can be sold without prescriptions. But if the drugs are handled as regular prescriptions, the pharmacist will charge his usual fee. Ask your physician if the drug is a prescription item at the time he gives you the slip from his pad. If there's any doubt in your mind, look for the legend on the label. Any drug that does not have this legend: "Caution: Federal law prohibits dispensing without prescription" on the label can probably be sold without a prescription.

(8) Buy the cheapest brand of aspirin, as it is a specific chemical compound. (Aspirin tablets are required by law to meet the standards of strength, quality, and purity set forth in *Pharmacopoeia,* a book of drug standards recognized by the Federal Food, Drug and Cosmetic Act as an official compendium. Aspirin must be packaged and labeled in the manner prescribed in this book.)

(9) If you are over age fifty-five, join the American Association of Retired Persons (1909 K Street, N.W., Washington, D.C. 20049) and save through this association's non-profit mail order pharmacy service.

How to Shop for Dental Services

FUNDAMENTAL APPROACHES

Despite the enormous sums we spend for dental services alone, only 20 per cent of us are estimated as receiving proper preventive dental care.

Are you getting this care? Most likely you can't tell. In fact, it is virtually impossible for the average person, lacking professional training, to distinguish between good, adequate, and poor dental service.

There are some basic guides, though, and here goes.

The key to proper dental care is to find a good dentist. One widely used obvious route is through the recommendations of your friends or relatives. Odds are that if a dentist has proved satisfactory to someone whose opinion you value he or she probably will prove satisfactory to you as well.

A second, if you move, is to ask your previous dentist to recommend a practitioner in your new home town. Or call the local dental society, which will usually recommend three names of dentists in the area and supply such information as their schools, graduation dates, and specialties. Keep in mind that about 10 per cent of all dentists are specialists.

Among the specialties:

orthodontics, concerned with aligning teeth;

periodontics, treatment of gums;

prosthodontics, denture work;

endodontics, a new and growing specialty of root canal treatment, saving teeth that fifteen years ago might have been extracted;

pedodontics, also a relatively new specialty devoted entirely to the treatment of children's dental problems;

oral surgery;

oral pathology;

public health dentistry.

• Try to find a dentist in a group practice. Such a dentist is under the direct and constant scrutiny of other dentists in the group. This tends to keep all of them on their toes, since their reputations rest on the excellence of one another's work.

• Call the nearest university dental school; ask for the name of a dentist for your family who maintains a private practice near the school and who is interested in preventive dentistry. Or ask the name of a professor who maintains a private practice near the school. Being a professor doesn't necessarily make him a good dentist, but chances are better than even that he's a top-notch practitioner.

TELLTALE SIGNS

Despite the difficulties of distinguishing between good, adequate, and poor care, there are telltale signs to look for that can alert you to the bad dentist, to the one who overcharges, or to the one who does overly fast work and uses too many short cuts.

• Expect a moderate amount of discomfort, particularly if you have neglected your teeth. If nothing ever hurts, you may not be getting quality work. Beware of the dentist who zips you in and out of the chair with a quick drill and fill. It may indicate a perfunctory job.

• Be on guard if he seems to emphasize extractions. Pulling a tooth is one of the easiest jobs in dentistry, but often is not necessary. No replacement is ever as good as your own tooth. A good dentist will extract only as a last resort.

• At your first meeting, note whether the dentist takes time to discuss fully your dental problems; whether he asks if you are seeking emergency care or are looking for a family dentist. And most important, find out if he is willing to discuss fees frankly and determine in advance a method of payment. Don't patronize a dentist who is not willing to discuss his fees at your request.

• Finally, seriously consider these factors before deciding whether this is or is not the right dentist for you:

Is the general appearance of the office and the dentist and his staff neat, clean, and orderly?

How available is he, both in location and appointment schedule?

Is he prevention-oriented?

Does he use X-rays in his diagnosis? Dental X-rays are one of the most valuable diagnostic tools in modern dentistry. A good dentist will probably have a full-mouth set of X-rays taken, unless suitable X-rays are available from your previous dentist.

HOW CAN YOU TELL IF THE FEE IS FAIR?

This isn't easy, since charges vary from dentist to dentist and depend on such factors as location and complications involved in a specific case. However, it is becoming somewhat easier to get information on dental fees.

One way to check the fee for a particular service is through the local dental society.

A good dollars-and-cents guide on dental fees is included in "A Shopper's Guide to Dentistry" published by the Pennsylvania Department of Insurance. Pennsylvania residents can get a copy by sending a self-addressed 9- by 12-inch envelope with 16¢ postage to "Shopper's Guide," Pennsylvania Insurance Department, Harrisburg, Pa. 17120. Out-of-staters can get a copy by sending $1.00 plus a self-addressed 9- by 12-inch envelope with 16¢ postage to "Consumer Insurance," 813 National Press Building, Washington, D.C. 20045. (See Part IV, "Your Rights and How to Get Them," page 991, for details on other shoppers' guides published by the Pennsylvania Insurance Department.)

IF YOU NEED A PSYCHIATRIST

According to the National Association for Mental Health, about one in ten persons in the United States will at some time develop a form of mental or emotional disorder requiring psychiatric care. On any given day of the year, nearly 400,000 persons are in state, county, and private mental hospitals.

The American public spends literally billions of dollars each year on the treatment and prevention of mental illness; the economy loses many more billions because of the decreased productivity of mental patients. Over all, it's a problem costing more than $20 billion a year in our country alone.

HOW DO YOU GO ABOUT FINDING ONE?

First, if you believe you need such help, consult your primary personal physician. He knows what kind of person you are and which psychiatrist might be of most benefit to you. He probably also will know which particular psychiatrists are highly regarded by his own medical colleagues.

Or you might turn to your county medical society or your local mental health association for the name of a qualified psychiatrist in your area. Or if you have a local community mental health clinic or center, you might find these a source of service—no matter what your ability to pay.

HOW MUCH MONEY AND TIME ARE INVOLVED IN TREATMENT?

How much you can expect to pay and how long your treatment will last will depend on your condition and the treatment chosen for you.

The most typical charge for a psychiatrist's time in 1974, according to the American Psychiatric Association's Hospital and Community Psychiatry Service, was about $40 an hour. The fee for your initial psychiatric consultation would depend on the time involved and might be slightly more than the hourly therapy charge. A majority of patients will be treated for less than 20 sessions. For some, longer-term psychotherapy will be needed. For a few in psychoanalysis the number of sessions may range from 300 to 500 although this depends on the patient and the progress, and the span for you could vary considerably from these totals.

WILL HEALTH INSURANCE HANDLE PART OF THE TREATMENT?

The daily costs of psychiatric hospitalization are often less than the cost of hospitalization for any other reason. Most health insurance plans today will cover the cost of treatment of mental conditions while the person is confined to the hospital, although there is a wide variation as to the extent of the coverage. Many will pay for treatment as an outpatient, but the per cent of the bill covered is usually less than in the case of other illnesses. Outpatient benefits are being written into an increasing number of group policies, including those of Blue Cross and Blue Shield plans.

IS IT POSSIBLE TO SHOP FOR THESE SERVICES?

Yes, it *is* possible to shop for psychiatric services.

By checking with your local health and welfare departments, religious leaders and others, by the simple expedient of checking in the telephone directory, you will discover the range of low-cost psychiatric services available in your community. And they may be of great moneysaving value to you.

How to Beat Our $15 Billion Hangover

THE STAGGERING BURDEN

The United States today is suffering from a national alcoholic hangover which claims thousands of lives and is costing a staggering $15 billion a year.

Of this, the National Institute on Alcohol Abuse and Alcoholism estimated in a special report to Congress, $10 billion is the price our economy pays for lost work time and $5 billion the cost of welfare payments and of the damage to the alcoholic's health and to property.

More than 9 million Americans (one in fifteen of us over the age of eighteen) are alcoholics and alcohol abusers. The yearly cost of the estimated 4 million on-the-job alcoholics, according to the National Council on Alcoholism, is at least $8 billion, translating into a drain of $32 million on business and industry *each working day*.

Absenteeism is two and a half to three times as great for alcoholics as for non-alcoholic workers. Alcoholics average three times as much sick pay as others, and their accident rates also are much higher. Many alcoholic workers lose a full month of working days each year.

Even more devastating is the towering problem of "on-the-job absenteeism"—where an alcoholic employee may fritter away hours each morning recovering from a hangover or sleep off a multi-martini lunch in the local movie house.

Moreover, alcoholism is everywhere and does not respect corporate names or job descriptions. An estimated 45 per cent of the alcoholics in this country are professional or managerial workers; the typical alcoholic has been at his job twelve years; he is between the ages of thirty-five and fifty-four, the key productive years; his alcoholism has been present but unrecognized for years.

If you are the typical alcoholic, you are almost surely spending tremendous time and effort trying to disguise your problem so cleverly that neither you nor your company will become aware of its seriousness. Yet the cost of your illness to you *and* your company (and, of course, also your family) may be enormous—in terms of loss of time, mismanaged business deals, bad decisions, missed promotions, etc. And continued drinking not only can get you fired from your present job but also can become a towering barrier in your search for another.

Whether or not *you* admit you are an alcoholic, you have at least one enormous incentive to seek help—and that incentive is your desire to hold your job.

WHERE DO YOU FIND HELP?

A first step is to inquire whether your employer offers counseling and/or rehabilitative services to employees. Hundreds of companies do, although most of these programs reach only a small number of alcoholics.

Your best single source of help is Alcoholics Anonymous, which for years has been carrying the alcoholism problem almost singlehandedly—and, incidentally, very successfully. Today AA is available to virtually all who wish to use its services, with 16,500 local groups in 92 countries. AA's key resource is an army of 500,000 recovered alcoholics who stand ready, around the clock, to give free help to anyone with a drinking problem. AA meetings are now being held not only in churches and regular meeting halls but also in such places as airplane hangars and at state reformatories.

Other sources of help have been proliferating too. To be specific:

• Since the National Institute on Alcohol Abuse and Alcoholism was set up in 1970, dozens of community action programs and neighborhood health centers have, for the first time, allocated funds to treat alcoholics.

• More and more general hospitals are now treating alcoholics. A few have set up special alcoholism services.

• City after city has been setting up a variety of alcoholism programs.

• Blue Cross and other insurers have begun to add hospitalization benefits for alcoholics.

• The military services, too, are beefing up their programs for alcoholic servicemen.

CARING FOR OUR ELDERLY

WHAT WOULD YOU DO?

What would you do if this problem came before you—or a member of your family?

You, one of your parents, a grandparent or other close relative or friend is over sixty-five;

faces increasingly severe medical, nutritional, living, and other problems;

knows that something has to be done—but is uncertain as to just what;

and is worried about the costs as well as terrified about the unspoken agony of change.

Even today, a full 10 per cent in the United States are over sixty-five and that number may double in less than a decade from now. *Even as early as 1974, 24 cents out of every $1.00 of federal spending was going for Social Security, Medicare, federal retirement, and other benefits.*

"Once, it was conventional wisdom that elderly persons no longer able to live alone or with families should enter a safe, decent place to live where medical care was available," explains William I. Riegelman, president of the board of trustees of the Jewish Home and Hospital for the Aged, a non-profit member of the Federation of Jewish Philanthropies of New York. "That wisdom is no longer enough and one reason is that the cost of nursing home care now runs into five figures annually per person."

"Parents and children are caught in the struggle of the elderly for independence and survival," adds the Rev. Richard Thomas of the Division of Aging of the Federation of Protestant Welfare Agencies in New York. "The greatest thrust now is in independent and congregate living with assistance."

"A planned program of medical, social, and environmental care supports a relatively independent way of life," emphasizes a recent report from Manhattan's Mary Manning Walsh Home, operated by the Carmelite Sisters for the Aged and Infirm. The home offers a "total package" under one roof.

Throughout the United States an increasing range of services is being made available for elderly people—and an urgent search is on for better services at less expense.

The shocking estimate is that perhaps 10 per cent of the elderly are institutionalized too soon because of lack of knowledge of available alternative facilities.

What, then, are the alternatives available if you are facing the problem?

THE ALTERNATIVES AVAILABLE TO YOU

Home care program: An elderly person remains at home, receiving homemaker assistance, outpatient medical care—and, if and when needed on a temporary basis, emergency admission to a full-care institution. Sponsoring organizations may allocate $250 and more a month for each individual served.

Day hospital and treatment centers: a new concept, which enables older people to remain at home with all the advantages of geriatric and general medical facilities. The trend is growing. Cost, as of 1974, around $250 a month per person.

Apartment residences: There are several throughout the United States. JHHA operates Kittay House in the New York area, a pioneering experiment in independent living with a service package including two daily meals, weekly maid service, other assistance. Efficiency apartments plus the service package at institutions such as this ranged in the mid-seventies from $375 for an individual to $650 a month for a couple.

Proprietary or profit-making residences: These provide similar services to apartment residences operated by institutions—rooms, meals, programs. Such homes usually do not provide medical services. As a result, their costs often are less.

Homes and hospitals for the aged: These are run by voluntary, non-profit agencies, with the largest institutions offering the broadest range of services. All residents share the high overhead, in part, but not every resident needs all the services available. Costs in the mid-seventies ran from $8,700 to $17,000 annually.

Even though Medicaid and Medicare pay the bills for a majority of nursing home residents, it is essential that you become aware of your alternatives. For instance, in recent experiments, this thought-provoking pattern has emerged:

First, the elderly person uses the home care program; then the apartment residence; then, as required, he or she moves to intermediate or extended nursing care. Ask yourself:

Can this person truly benefit from institutional living; Is he or she capable of adjusting to special requirements?

SHOPPING FOR NURSING HOMES

Good nursing home care isn't cheap. As a rule you can expect to pay about one third of the cost of maintaining a patient in a nearby hospital—with basic monthly charges in the mid-seventies $500 or so for a semi-private and $800 to $1,000 for a private room. Find out what services are included in the basic fees and what extra charges are. Most homes charge extra for patients requiring feeding and incontinence care. Find out how drug costs are handled and whether you can bring in medicine. Routine services—haircuts, shampoos, personal laundry, linen charges, room TV rental, etc.—may be listed as extras. Charges of your personal physician are never included.

By all means, visit a nursing home before selecting it. Spend at least a couple of hours inspecting the staff; standards; physical, recreational, and occupational therapy facilities; safety devices. Ask about special diets, meal schedules. Spot-check for cleanliness, odor, maintenance, the general atmosphere.

Check what recreational facilities there are and whether the home is a member of professional organizations devoted to professional care.

Look for a nursing home offering rehabilitation services and periodical re-examination of patients to determine whether their needs have changed, for better or worse.

Discuss what financial help you may get with the home's administrator, your Social Security and/or welfare office.

MEDICARE'S YARDSTICKS

Here are the yardsticks Medicare uses in deciding whether or not a skilled nursing care facility is eligible for Medicare payments.

Each skilled nursing facility must:

• have physicians admit patients and supervise their care;

• maintain an organized nursing service, directed by a full-time professional registered nurse, with at least one licensed practical nurse on duty at all times and with enough attendants and nurses' aides to assure each patient adequate care;

• keep a current, separate medical record and patient care plan for each patient;

• assure that each patient is visited by a doctor at least once every thirty days;

• have an active program of restorative nursing care;

• assure that drugs and medications are properly administered;

• provide for promptly obtaining needed X-ray and lab services;

• be able to identify medically related social and emotional needs;

• have a dietary service that meets the institutional needs of patients, including special diets;

• provide for adequate medical attention to patients during medical emergencies, including possible transfer to an accredited hospital;

• assure compliance with state and local fire protection codes, availability of fire extinguishers on each floor, and unobstructed doorways, passageways, and stairwells;

• maintain hygienic conditions, proper lighting levels and ventilation, heating and air conditioning facilities, a hot water supply, and laundry services;

• carry out utilization review of services provided, at least to inpatients.

WHERE TO COMPLAIN

If you have a complaint about a nursing home, for whatever reason, you can tell it to:

(1) The nursing home administrator.

(2 Your local Social Security district office. It functions as a clearinghouse for complaints about all nursing homes, whether or not they receive government funds.

(3) The patient's case worker or the county welfare office if the patient is covered by Medicaid.

(4) The state Medicaid Agency if the home is certified for that program.

(5) The state Health Department and state licensing authority.

(6) The nursing home ombudsman if such an office has been established in your community.

(7) The state board responsible for licensing nursing home administrators. (Get address information from the welfare department.)

(8) Your congressmen and senators. (Address congressmen at House of Representatives, Washington, D.C. 20515; senators at United States Senate, Washington, D.C. 20510.)

(9) Your state and local elected representatives.

(10) The Joint Commission on Accreditation of Hospitals (875 North Michigan Avenue, Suite 2201, Chicago, Ill. 60611) if the home has a JCAH certificate.

(11) The American Nursing Home Association (1200 15th St., N.W., Washington, D.C. 20036) if the home is a member.

(12) The American Association of Homes for the Aging (529 14th Street, N.W., Washington, D.C. 20004) if the home is a member.

(13) The American College of Nursing Home Administrators (8641 Colesville Road, Silver Spring, Md. 20910) if the administrator is a member.

(14) Your local Better Business Bureau and Chamber of Commerce.

(15) Your local hospital association and medical society.

(16) A reputable lawyer or legal aid society.

Health Maintenance Organizations:

PREVIEW OF THE FUTURE

The Blue Cross Association defines a Health Maintenance Organization as "an organized health care delivery system which promotes early detection and continuity of care through an arrangement holding a single organization responsible for assuring delivery of an agreed set of institutional and physician services to an enrolled population for a stipulated period of time in exchange for a fixed and periodic payment."

Mounting millions of Americans are now getting the opportunity to join these Health Maintenance Organizations—which, to put it in plain English, are organizations of doctors, hospitals, and others offering enrolling members a wide range of health services in exchange for a flat fee paid in advance, usually monthly or quarterly.

AN HMO FOR YOUR COMMUNITY?

The federal government is now actively pushing the development of HMOs via the 1973 Health Maintenance Act. Federally supported family health centers also are being transformed into HMOs, providing prepaid health care to people in areas where adequate health care is unavailable. The hope is that these centers will develop into self-supporting comprehensive-care HMOs. On the private front, many Blue Cross plans and private insurance companies are promoting HMOs or tying in their coverage with existing organizations.

What might you expect?

Services. Virtually all you might need—with such exceptions as dental care, long-term psychiatric care, rare and expensive types of care for the few at the expense of the many. Or you might be asked to pay nominal fees for each visit to the doctor or for outpatient prescription drugs. Also excluded are medical services covered or provided by others—such as workers' compensation (see earlier, this chapter), employment physicals, and accident insurance.

Fees. If you're a family of four, a monthly payment ranging between $40 and $80. If you're an individual, a monthly cost ranging between $15 and $30.

HEALTH BAFFLEGAB GUIDE

Do you know the difference between a Health Maintenance Organization, a Health Co-op, and a Health Maintenance Plan? What "capitation" payments are as opposed to "fees for services?" The meaning of a "prepayment plan" for health services? This is the jargon of our unfolding system of health care—soon to become a language you must be able to understand.

CAPITATION FEES: Payments to anyone providing health care of a certain amount of money per month, for each patient for whom the practitioner provides a certain specified range of services.

CATASTROPHIC COVERAGE: Health insurance with a high deductible—payable by you—but also a high ceiling ($50,000 to $250,000) so catastrophically costly care would be paid by the plan.

COMPREHENSIVE HEALTH CARE: Generally includes, both in and out of hospital, the whole works. Specifically:

   preventive care—e.g., periodic physical checkups, immunizations, various diagnostic tests at appropriate intervals; counseling, e.g., diet, exercise, etc.;

   primary care—or medical care by a family doctor or general physician, aimed at maintaining or restoring good health, up to the limits of the physician's capabilities;

   specialty care—by board-certified specialists for complicated illnesses;

   rehabilitation for patients who have suffered from disabling accidents, strokes, mental breakdowns (plans usually exclude illnesses and injuries which require permanent medical maintenance);

   extended care—in nursing homes and other facilities—for non-permanent chronic conditions needing medical attention, geriatric problems and adjustment.

DUAL CHOICE: Setup in company offered plans in which you are allowed to choose between two alternative plans (typically, fee for service or a prepaid group practice plan).

FEE FOR SERVICE: A sum of money paid by the patient for each individual service performed by a practitioner.

GROUP PRACTICE: Organized delivery of health care, by a group of two or more physicians with a prearranged system for sharing income. Some groups are highly specialized (representing a single specialty); others cover a variety of specialties. Most groups charge a fee for each service rendered.

HEALTH CARE PROVIDER: A physician-hospital or other institution, such as an HMO or prepaid group practice plan, providing health care services.

HEALTH CO-OPERATIVE: A health plan involving ownership and board participation in the plan by the members of the plan.

HEALTH MAINTENANCE ORGANIZATIONS: Typically prepaid group practice with dual goals of comprehensive continuous health care and more health care per dollar and with stress on early disease detection and prevention.

More than 5 million Americans now enrolled, getting high-quality care at a cost as much as one third lower than traditional forms.

MEDICAL INDIGENT: Person not legally poor but likely to become poor instantly if hit by expensive illness.

MULTIPHASIC SCREENING: Battery of tests and exams to determine person's state of health and detect signs of illness. Tests usually performed by specialists in lab work, with interpretation by doctors.

PEER REVIEW: Ideally, formal review of medical decisions or procedures by an outside doctor or group of doctors with equivalent training and experience *and* in possession of essential data in each case. Typically, peer review covers quality and appropriateness of care, and charges for medical service.

PREPAYMENT: Health plan concept pioneered by unions—via Blue Cross—in which the subscriber pays a given sum in advance in the event that insured health benefits are needed. Payment is made in advance and limits the individual's liability as against paying for each separate service after it has been performed with unlimited liability.

Millions of Americans belong to some type of prepaid group practice plan. The cost of health care in these organizations has been less because doctors and hospitals maximize the use of facilities, personnel, etc. There are built-in incentives for preventive health care (immunizations, physical checkups) and against overuse of costly hospital facilities. Many problems are handled on an outpatient basis rather than by admission to a hospital where care is extremely expensive. The frequency of elective (non-obligatory) surgery tends to be far less in prepaid group plans since surgeons do not have any financial incentive to perform operations.

KEY QUESTIONS TO CONSIDER

Let's say a group in your community is considering setting up an HMO. What basics should the plan include? Here are key questions you—and everybody else involved in launching an HMO—should ask:

• Is there strong emphasis on such aspects as primary preventive care and health education?

• Are you, a consumer, involved along with health practitioners in determining the planning and delivery of services?

• Is the HMO co-operating with state and local planning agencies to avoid duplicate facilities and services and, thus, unnecessary costs?

• What mechanisms are there to permit continual assessment of the system as a whole, to tell how well it is working?

• What review-evaluation techniques are there to maintain a high quality of service—e.g., peer review by doctors and others? The new problem oriented patient record system? One of the key requirements under the 1973 HMO Act is an "ongoing quality assurance program."

• Are there open enrollment periods at least once a year—also required under the 1973 HMO Act?

• Are there provisions for hospital and doctor emergency services both inside and outside the area? Is there referral to specialists and super-specialists? Who pays how much for the costs of these services?

• Are there incentives to cut health care costs to patients?

SHOULD YOU JOIN AN HMO?

Let's say that a local medical group, hospital, university, or other organization is setting up an HMO. Or the Blue Cross plan to which you subscribe is offering an HMO-type plan as an alternative to your regular coverage.

Costs and coverages vary all over the place—but costs easily can run $500 to $1,000 or more a year for a family. Should *you* join an HMO under these circumstances? How can you tell whether or not it is a bargain for you? Here's your guide:

• Read with utmost care all the literature on the plan, what's covered and what's excluded, how long the coverage lasts.

• Check the monthly premiums and the extra costs you'll be required to pay for non-included items, deductibles, etc.

• Compare these totals with the amounts you've been paying in health insurance premiums, doctor bills, out-of-pocket cash, costs of services not covered or only partially covered in your present insurance, including that provided by your employer.

• Find out the arrangements for choosing and keeping a physician.

• Investigate the provisions for prescription drugs outside the hospital. Does the plan cover these or offer a way you can save when you buy? (Some HMOs have their own pharmacies.) And what about prosthetics and appliances?

• Check other subscribers' opinions. If they are already in a plan, are they satisfied with the medical attention?

• Find out what hours full HMO services are available and what the procedure is for care in evenings and over weekends.

• Ask whether the outpatient services and facilities you use most—physcians' offices, lab facilities, pharmacy—are under a single roof. Is this roof located conveniently for your family?

• Make sure preventive care services are stressed—early disease detection via diagnostic screening, periodic physical checkups, appropriate immunization.

• Investigate what hospital accommodations are provided—private, semi-private? Are such extras as special-duty nursing and private room included if your physician thinks they are essential?

• Are there age limits in the plan—such as when a son or daughter reaches age nineteen? Or marries?

• What medical facilities are included in the hospital to which you would go—such as coronary care, radiation therapy? What exclusions, if any, are there for health handicaps?

CHECK LIST FOR HMO SERVICES

Here is a check list of "basic" services, most of which an HMO is required to offer under the 1973 HMO Act. Use it to judge the comprehensiveness of any HMO, but also weigh it against your own list of health priorities:

physician services (including consultant and referral services by a physician);

inpatient and outpatient hospital services;

medically necessary emergency health services;

short-term (not to exceed twenty visits), outpatient evaluative and crisis intervention mental health services;

medical treatment and referral services (including referral services to appropriate ancillary services) for the abuse of or addiction to alcohol and drugs;

diagnostic laboratory and diagnostic and therapeutic radiology services;
home health services; and

preventive health services (including family planning services, infertility services, preventive dental care for children and children's eye examinations conducted to determine the need for vision correction).

TEST YOUR CHANCES OF STAYING ALIVE

REVEALING QUESTIONS

How often do you exercise? Daily, three times a week, weekends only, rarely or never?

How much do you smoke? Not at all, five cigarettes a day, one half to a pack, two packs or more?

What's your weight as against your height and age?

What are your cholesterol and triglyceride levels? Your blood pressure?

Do you drink an average of more than three ounces of alcohol daily?

Have such between-meal snacks as potato chips, peanuts?

When was your last physical checkup?

The medical bill for circulatory diseases in our country is now an almost

unbelievable 10 per cent of our national bill for all illnesses. At the top of all killers in the United States are diseases of the heart and blood vessels.

The loss to the nation in terms of income and productivity from deaths caused by heart attacks tops $1 billion a year, with half of it lost in the top-productive age group of forty-five to sixty-four. The bulk of the loss to the nation in terms of income and productivity from persons becoming ill of heart conditions and unable to work also is in the most productive age group of forty-five to sixty-four. The convalescence period can stretch to many months.

The economic costs involved in heart and blood vessel diseases alone—not to mention the emotional and other costs—are vast. What's more, our costs are jumping instead of sinking. We are actually falling behind other nations in keeping our men alive longer.

You surely are aware of the danger of a high cholesterol level, although this is not the terrible bugaboo it has been pictured. New discoveries in another blood fat—triglycerides—have added a second warning device, with the two comprising what are called blood lipids. In some patients, cholesterol is found to be relatively normal, while blood triglyceride count is dangerously high. (Question to you: Has your physician ever had your triglyceride count checked? Interpreted it with your cholesterol level?)

During the German occupation of Scandinavian countries, when butter, milk, and cream became scarce, the incidence of coronary artery diseases went way down. But the disease rate went way back up after World War II when these foods again became abundant—"pretty good proof on a large scale," say physicians, "that there is something to dietary control."

Stress aggravates high blood pressure and circulating blood fats—high-risk factors in heart diseases—but exercise lowers them.

And sex is also a very good exercise.

We can't do anything about any adverse family histories we may have, but we can do a great deal about every life-shortening activity or life-lengthening hint. Just by honestly answering the few revealing questions in the quiz alone, you're helping yourself to stay alive.

YOUR BLOOD BANK ACCOUNT

If you are unfortunate enough to have a serious accident or illness requiring extensive blood transfusions, your total needs could amount to 50 to 100 pints of blood. If you must pay (as some do) $25 to $50 per pint, your cost of blood alone could come to $2,500 to $5,000. If you must use a heart-lung machine in the course of surgery, it may take between 12 and 15 pints of blood just to prime the machine for you. And if you happen to have a very rare blood type, you could pay astronomical sums.

Even if you are able to find donors to replace the blood you use, you'll probably have to pay the cost of processing this blood—and this can run $20

a pint or more. To date, the typical blood transfusion involves three pints of blood.

Each year our need for blood rises relentlessly. To meet our civilian needs alone, we needed to collect more than 8 million pints a year in the mid-seventies.

HOW TO PROTECT YOURSELF

How can you protect yourself and your family against the prospect of crippling high costs should you need a large amount of blood for a transfusion?

• Contribute blood periodically through a union, your employer, fraternal club, church, or other organized group which has an agreement with a community blood bank or the Red Cross. Merely by being a member of a group which meets a prescribed quota you will become eligible to receive blood—and there is no limit on the amount of blood which you or members of your family may receive if and when necessary.

• Or set up your own individual blood plan simply by giving blood to the Red Cross, to your local hospital blood banks, or to community blood centers. By donating once a year, you too may achieve the same eligibility status.

To give blood, you must be at least seventeen and not past your sixty-sixth birthday; must weigh at least 110 pounds, be reasonably healthy and free of conditions and diseases such as high blood pressure, jaundice, anemia, malaria, diabetes, and syphilis. You may give up to a maximum of five times a year and at intervals of at least eight weeks. In some blood banks, you may withdraw only the blood you donate, and it must have been donated within a period specified by the blood bank—typically, one to two years. A member of your family elsewhere can withdraw from your account with your permission—through the American Association of Blood Banks' National Clearinghouse Program, run in collaboration with the Red Cross.

QUESTIONS AND ANSWERS

Q. *What about getting blood via your health insurance?*

A. Coverage varies from company to company and plan to plan. But many plans cover processing fees only—and many hospitals require a "replacement fee" to encourage volunteer replacement.

Q. *What about commercial "blood insurance" plans?*

A. One such plan charges $5.00 a year for an individual and $7.50 a year for a family. This may seem welcome protection but most plans draw exclusively on blood from paid donors who may fail to report serious diseases to the collector—an obvious risk to you. You also may find important exclusions, and commercial blood plans unfortunately reduce the incentive for voluntary donations.

Q. *Is blood covered under Medicare for older people?*

A. Yes, under Part A—Medicare's hospital coverage—the full cost is covered after the first three pints used in each "benefit period" (spell of illness). Under Part B, which covers doctor bills, 80 per cent of blood costs subject to the yearly $60 deductible are covered after the first three pints.

Q. *How else can you save on costs of blood?*

A. If you are scheduled for elective surgery involving transfusions, ask friends and relatives to donate blood in advance to the bank with which your hospital is associated. If this hospital has a policy requiring blood replacement, find out in advance just what the terms are. Ask whether friends and relatives in other areas may help you replace blood you use via the Clearinghouse Program.

If you are among the one in 100 of us with a rare blood type, register with the rare donor registries operated by the AABB and ARC. In the Red Cross rare donor registry, for instance, there are now more than 7,000 donors whose names and blood types have been computerized: these rare donors include only those whose blood types are found less than once in 200 persons. The extremely rare types are collected regularly, frozen, and made available to anyone. Extremely rare types are frequently sent to hospitals for use without charge by specific patients.

HEALTH HOAXES

Down through the ages mankind has been plagued by the charlatan with his claim of being able to heal the sick, rejuvenate the aged, to make that which is drab a thing of beauty forever. In fact, health hoaxes extend so far back into history that they appear on the first known written medical record, the Ebers Papyrus (circa 1500 B.C.), which contained a prescription for preventing baldness. This ancient Egyptian remedy included, among other things, fats of the lion, hippopotamus, crocodile, goose, serpent, and ibex.

It didn't work—and not because anything was left out.

Things have not changed so much in the 3,475 years since this old Egyptian gyp. Today, we are still under a constant bombardment of come-ons, exaggerated advertising, gimmicks of dubious value, and pure-and-simple fraudulent claims, ranging over a wide area of products which affect your health.

Following is merely a sampling of what to watch out for. If it serves only to put you on guard against a hoax in the health sphere, I will have accomplished my aim.

DIET COME-ONS

You are young, you are in normal health, you want to look attractive—and you are overweight. It is to you that ads such as these are directed:

"I lost 54 pounds of ugly, dangerous fat!! . . . in only THREE short months!! without a doctor, a diet or calorie counting."

"A definite weight loss of 10–20–50 pounds, even 100 pounds or more may be accomplished in a short time."

The ads go on to claim that you, the overweight person in normal health, may continue to enjoy such foods as cream of mushroom soup, malted milks, spaghetti, pizza, and french toast—and still lose significant amounts of weight in "a short time." A key to these amazing achievements is a "miraculous formulation" involving pills for which you pay "only" $20 for a 120-day supply.

Then comes the fine print, along with the pills for which you have already paid a substantial sum. As it turns out, the spaghetti isn't really spaghetti, the pizza contains no pastry, and the malted milk must be made with skim milk or buttermilk.

Thus it is to you that this warning must also be directed:

Any claim of a cure for overweight which does not even mention dieting is fraudulent. No type of diet pill or program available today can achieve significant, permanent weight loss within a specified period unless the user takes strict dieting measures as well.

Tens of millions of overweight Americans are spending hundreds of millions of dollars a year on an unprecedented array of gadgets, gimmicks, pills, and potions to help them lose weight. Thousands of U.S. physicians are now devoting part or all of their practices to the problem of obesity. No one knows just how much money is being wasted on useless weight reduction schemes or how many of the obesity doctors actually manage to achieve major long-term weight reduction for their patients.

But it is known that the Food and Drug Administration in Washington has year after year seized millions of doses of multicolored "rainbow pills" used in weight reduction schemes on the grounds that they are either useless or dangerous. And the FDA and the American Medical Association have declared over and over that many of today's so-called diet pills may cause serious side effects.

You cannot lose weight on a diet of whiskey and whipped cream.

You cannot expect reducing pills to have any long-term effect—without the usual dietary restrictions and change in your eating habits.

You cannot "melt away fatty tissue" by wearing special tight-fitting plastic belts, blouses, and slacks.

To be blunt: there is no such thing as "effortless" reducing. Loss of pounds is directly dependent on using up more calories by exercise than you consume in food and drink.

Calories *do* count. For any major weight reduction program, you should enlist the help of a physician.

If you are among the millions with a problem of overweight, here are four fundamental rules for facing your problem and avoiding the many useless weight reduction programs now available:

(1) Avoid all "miraculous" formulas and high-powered pills recommended by *anybody*.

(2) Stay away from all gimmicks such as "slimming underwear" and vibrating machines if they are advertised as capable of achieving a permanent loss of X number of pounds in X number of days, weeks, or months.

(3) Be suspicious of any weight reduction schemes involving special pills, "diet cocktails," or self-hypnosis if they do not also involve a lowering of your calorie consumption.

(4) In sum, if you have an overweight problem, consult your physician or your psychiatrist and follow your doctor's advice—which easily might include the suggestion that you join a respected local weight-reduction club or organization operating under medical supervision.

"STOP SMOKING"

A three-day supply of a new product which is supposed to help you stop smoking costs close to $3.00 a package at my local drugstore. If you complete the entire four-week program recommended in the directions, your total investment might add up to $20 or more.

This is a big bargain if you manage to quit smoking, of course. If you are a three-pack-a-day addict, you will spend many hundreds of dollars a year to support your habit—and you can add hundreds of dollars more to this if your spouse chain-smokes too. Also, today's non-smoker may be eligible for non-smoker life insurance at considerable savings in premiums.

But the estimate is that, of the millions of adult U.S. smokers who try to stop smoking each year, only a fraction succeeds. Would-be non-smokers are now spending tens of millions of dollars to buy the products of today's "Stop Smoking Industry"—ranging from pills to gum, lozenges, "pacifiers," stop-smoking books, etc.

Are you among the majority of U.S. smokers who, according to the U. S. Public Health Service, have made at least one serious attempt to quit smoking? How much money have *you* spent on the stop-smoking products —or on losing bets with other would-be non-smokers?

If you are gulping sugar pills and concoctions of ordinary spice such as ginger, licorice, clove, coriander—as well as pharmaceutical preparations —to stamp out your cigarette craving . . .

If you are taking up fake cigarettes—dubbed "smokes" or "adult pacifiers" which contain such non-nicotinic ingredients as menthol crystals, cabbage, lettuce, or just flavored cigarette paper—to keep your nervous hands busy and permit you to "smoke without fear" . . .

If you are falling for suggestive stop-smoking phonograph records . . .

If you are devouring no-smoke tablets and how-to-stop-smoking pamphlets . . .

Here are a few straight guides for you:

Despite the welter of new labels, there are no really "new" substances on the market to help you stop smoking. Old ones simply have been dressed up or combined to appear new.

The three standard types of anti-smoking medications now available are the nicotine substitute (e.g., lobeline sulfate), which alleviates cigarette craving; substances which make smoking taste unpleasant (e.g., silver nitrate); and local anesthetics (e.g., benzocaine), which numb the mouth and reduce desire for the puffing part of the smoking ritual.

Many of these products do, in fact, help you quit smoking temporarily. But none does the job permanently without a generous dose of will power on your part. Most are harmless, but a few cases of nausea, stomach pain, and loss of appetite have been reported as side effects.

A far more effective and more economical approach could be the Stop Smoking clinic. The programs at the better clinics are drawn up by physicians and psychologists. Most conduct regular meetings and seminars, some patterned on the highly successful Alcoholics Anonymous concept. You may or may not pay a small fee to attend the meetings.

QUACK MEDICAL DEVICES

If you have a naggingly painful disease or if you become seriously ill, you could well join the millions of Americans who each year spend billions of dollars for all forms of medical quackery—most of it for worthless and possibly dangerous gadgets and machines.

To illustrate with one horror story, tens of thousands have fallen for a contraption claimed capable of diagnosing and treating conditions ranging from cancer to chicken pox and jealousy—on the basis of a single drop of blood from the patient. When federal officials ran their own test, the machine failed to detect the fact that it was being fed blood samples from a turkey, a pig, and a sheep rather than from three children. Nevertheless, once a "diagnosis" had been made, the practitioner arrived at a special "vibration rate" for each patient and treated the patient's disease by radioing back into the patient the supposedly "normal" vibration rate. For those unable to visit the practitioner's office it was said that healing vibrations could be broadcast to reach anywhere on earth.

To illustrate with another equally shocking tale, suffering Americans have paid as much as $475 for an elaborate machine claimed to be able to cure cancer, diabetes, heart disease, and a wide variety of other serious conditions by "attuned color waves" shined on parts of the body. The primary medical qualification of the machine's inventor was an "honorary M.D."

To illustrate with still another, desperate Americans have paid important sums to another practitioner who claimed he could diagnose and cure anything from double vision to a "bone" in the colon—simply by using an elaborate-looking radio device.

Then there are devices—for which trusting (or despairing) souls among us have actually spent money—which "charge" your body with electrical energy and determine the "wave length" of your cells so that the wave length can be rearranged to restore your health and magnetize or demagnetize you depending on your needs.

There's even a machine which can, in the words of its inventor, "straighten out people who walk lopsided." Most quack devices are fitted with impressive-looking dials, switches, buttons, flashing lights, other space-age trimmings.

Why do countless thousands of Americans, including the intelligent and well educated, fall every year for this unbelievable array of quack gadgets and machines?

The victim of a devastatingly painful, progressive, or fatal disease often will find a quack cut-and-dried diagnosis and sure "cure" completely irresistible—and the very fact that we are living in an era of such medical "miracles" as laser surgery, heart transplants, cardiac pacemakers, nylon arteries, and artificial kidneys has made the machines of the quacks believable. What's more, federal regulation of medical devices has not kept pace with the proliferation of the devices—even legitimate ones.

Thus, basically, it comes down to this: you must protect yourself and your friends and relatives (particularly if they are aged) from the medical quacks.

And your basic protections are:

Stick with a legitimate, trained, medically qualified physician.

Avoid any quick, easy "secret" machine.

Be acutely skeptical of any electronic wonder or formula advertised by a practitioner who claims that the medical establishment is afraid of the "competition" of his sure cure.

CANCER QUACKERY

Today, more than half of all cancers can be cured if they are diagnosed in time and treated properly by surgery, radiation, chemotherapy, or a combination of these. In many types of cancers, such as skin or cervical cancer, the odds are even better: the vast majority of cases can be cured if they are detected early and correctly treated.

Yet thousands of cancer victims continue to refuse or postpone to a fatal degree legitimate treatment and to seek instead the services or elixirs of the cancer quack. Too frequently huge sums are spent by frightened elderly citizens who are already on the brink of bankruptcy and who may not have the disease to begin with.

Why? The key reasons, says the American Cancer Society, are the cancer victim's fear of incurability, fear of the high cost of treatment, fear of the prospect of radical surgery, fear of radiation treatment. In view of the number who develop cancer in our country and the odds on survival, many people are quite understandably quick to suspect its dread presence.

The cancer quack can be a devastatingly expensive economic drain as well as a devastatingly dangerous physical threat. Thus, here are the key guides to spotting the quack.

First, you must know that any qualified specialist will invariably conduct standard tests for any cancer at a recognized hospital or clinic and he will plan a course of therapy according to the results of these tests.

But the quack will:

• Neither perform recognized tests nor be associated with a recognized hospital or clinic—although the tests he does perform will invariably produce a diagnosis of cancer. He very well may advise against biopsy to verify cancer, using the excuse that "it will only spread the cancer."

• Boast that he has many well-known patients, including politicians, lawyers, movie actors, writers, etc. (This, incidentally, may be perfectly true.)

• Produce testimonials from former patients who claim he has cured their cancer. No reputable doctor advertises accomplishments or boasts in print about his famous patients. And, if you look behind the testimonials carefully, you may find those quoted died shortly after they authored the glowing accounts of their cures.

• Claim, when challenged to put his treatment to a scientific test, that he "won't get a fair trial" because the medical establishment is prejudiced against his method. Or he may challenge the medical establishment to test his product—then either fail to deliver a sample or insist on designing the test conditions himself.

• Insist, perhaps to help justify the high cost, that his cancer cure is "secret"—something no reputable member of the medical community would do for obvious reasons.

Until a universal cure or cures for cancer are found, our most potent—and also least expensive—weapons against this dread disease are regular medical checkups and awareness of the seven widely published cancer warning signals.

THE PSYCHOQUACK

If you are a relative or friend of one of the nation's 5 million mentally retarded citizens, you are acutely aware of the heartbreaking, frustrating search for effective treatment of this most widespread and debilitating of all medical problems. You also must be aware of the extent to which parents of the retarded are tempted by the mental health quack, both here and abroad.

There are no hard figures on how many tens of millions of dollars

Americans are spending each year to line the pockets of quacks, unqualified psychotherapists, and untrained marriage counselors. But in the past, parents of retarded children have been reported to be laying out $1,000 apiece to have their children injected with worthless serum. In other forms of pseudo-professional treatments by fringe practitioners, ex-mental patients have been recruited as "adjunctive therapists" to treat other patients, "nude psycho-therapy" has been practiced by borderline psychotherapists, and any num-ber of quacks have managed to persuade parents that their retarded child's problem actually was an allergy, a vitamin deficiency, a low blood sugar level, or some other condition which could be treated relatively easily.

The mental health quack today is often difficult to detect by an average citizen, who probably doesn't know the difference between a psychologist, psychiatrist, psychoanalyst, and psychotherapist. Many of the fringe prac-titioners are forming quasi-medical organizations, adopting scientific jargon, and using a smattering of accepted therapeutic techniques.

Why the upsurge in this form of quackery? How can you tell a quack from a non-quack in this field?

A first reason why mental health quackery (and particularly quackery aimed at the retarded) is thriving now is the simple fact that there is a growing market for the treatment of retardation. Every year in our country an estimated 3 per cent of all babies born are retarded babies.

Another is that the rate of spontaneous "cures" ranges up to two thirds for some types of mental disturbances. Thus, even the quack can claim a high percentage of successes which would have occurred anyway.

Still another reason is the severe shortage of qualified mental health professionals in the nation. Waiting lists at mental health facilities are fre-quently long; treatments are often stretched out over months or years and seldom result in what could be termed complete "cures." This frustration alone may easily translate into an open invitation to the fringe practitioner to move in.

Finally, state laws today are grossly inadequate in the regulation of practitioners in this field. There are still many areas of the United States in which an utterly unqualified person can legally hang up a shingle designating himself a psychologist, psychotherapist, or marriage counselor.

To protect yourself against the psychoquack, *beware of anybody who:*

• offers services for which his or her training is obviously inadequate;

• makes exaggerated claims, not backed up by the medical literature, about their treatments;

• uses articles in the popular press, frequently written by the person himself, as advertisements for his treatments;

• touts his treatments as more "natural" than other kinds of treatment;

• turns directly to threats and lawsuits rather than debate in professional circles as an answer to criticism;

• offers to administer various treatments outside the United States because the "cures" are banned in this country.

In sum, always deal only with qualified physicians and other trained mental health personnel.

ARTHRITIS "CURES"

Would you pay $200 or more to sit in a "uranium tunnel" at an arthritis "clinic" in the Midwest (actually an abandoned uranium mine)?

Or would you buy a "magic spike" containing less than a penny's worth of barium chloride for over $300 and wear it as an arthritis cure?

Or attempt to treat your painful joints by bathing them in colored light with a $50 gadget consisting of a light bulb and a plastic lampshade? Or try to help your arthritis simply by attaching a metal disk to a joint, then placing a cylinder, connected by a cord to the disk, into cold water? Or would you risk taking a powerful drug developed in another country and banned in the United States because its side effects include internal hemorrhaging and mental derangement?

Perhaps you would, if you were suffering enough from this often excruciatingly painful disease. For the fact is that today's extraordinary array of nostrums and devices promoted as capable of curing or relieving arthritis seems to be as tempting as ever to the victims, who include the well educated and well to do as well as the ignorant and poor.

Unproved "bootleg" drugs and devices are coming into this country via a thriving underground network of quackery, dispensed sometimes by the patients themselves. Americans are traveling, by the planeload, to other countries for arthritis "cures" banned here.

In some cases, potentially useful and legitimate treatment is delayed because the arthritic sufferer is so involved with quacks. Also the quacks are aided by the fact that in rheumatoid arthritis, the most serious form of the disease, pain comes and goes intermittently, so over the years the quack can frequently claim success.

The copper "arthritis bracelet" has staged a spectacular comeback—with countless hundreds of thousands of Americans spending from $1.00 to $10 to $100 for this form of copper jewelry on the claim that it will help prevent and/or cure this disease. Although precise statistics are unavailable, this single slice of the "anti-arthritis business" now accounts for tens of millions of dollars in annual sales and covers copper jewelry ranging from tie clips to cuff links, from bracelets to anklets.

And this is occurring in the face of the fact that the Post Office Department, the Federal Trade Commission, and the Food and Drug Administration have repeatedly condemned as fraudulent any claims that copper bracelets would cure arthritis (although admittedly, in most cases, no written claims are actually made). Also utterly phony are any claims that two copper bracelets, one worn on each wrist or each inner sole, create a special therapeutic "circuit."

Nevertheless, just because arthritis now affects one out of every twelve Americans and the number of sufferers is growing by 250,000 a year, any suggestion of relief is immediately seized upon by millions and immediately mounts into big-time money.

The total economic cost of arthritis is approaching a record $10 billion a year, estimates the Arthritis Foundation of New York—in the form of medical care costs and wage losses, lost homemaking services, and premature deaths. On top of this, the "hidden" costs—in the form of spending on worthless arthritis "clinics" and treatments—are approaching $500 million, almost double yearly costs in the 1960s.

As you would expect, financial outlays for fake cures and phony treatments swell with the number of arthritis sufferers. Worthless cures tagged by the Arthritis Foundation now cover white metal and plastic "electrogalvanic" bracelets; expandable "magnetic" bracelets; special electrical vibrators; hyper-immune milk; high-priced "magic spikes" containing a few pennies' worth of various vitamins, laxatives, and ointments; bootleg drugs illegally imported here from Mexico and Canada.

I will not downgrade one tiny bit the anxiety of a person suffering from great pain or a terminal illness to try anything at any cost in the hope of relief or cure. But the tragedy is that you might delay legitimate diagnosis and treatment, you might waste the most precious time as well as money in your commitment to quacks.

The bright fact is that we are at a moment in medical history when nearly three out of four cases of crippling arthritis can be headed off by early detection and proper treatment. The merciful prospect is that we are near major breakthroughs in drugs to treat arthritis.

Thus, if you are among the 17 million sufferers or close to an individual who is, heed these warnings:

• Be wary of any person who uses "testimonials" from former patients as a lure and avoid "home cures" not prescribed or at least approved by your own physician.

• Don't postpone conventional treatment or abandon an ongoing program to patronize an unconventional course of therapy.

9

YOUR TRANSPORTATION—
BY WHEELS, WINGS, AND WATER

Americans of all ages today are carrying on a love affair with mobility. And our love affair goes way beyond the obvious automobile. It also embraces airplanes, buses and trains, motorcycles, campers and snowmobiles, boats and bikes, even horses!

In the mid-1970s we owned at least 112 million cars, trucks, and other vehicles—more than one vehicle for every other man, woman, and child in the United States. More than two out of five families owned two or more cars. Fewer than one in five American families today are without a car.

Every year Americans drive more than *1 trillion* miles, the equivalent of more than 5,000 round trips between the earth and sun. For many, a car is almost a "second home."

Moreover, transportation—notably cars—is the second biggest item in today's American family budget. In fact, if you match merely the *average* moderate-income U.S. family right now, you are earmarking a fantastic 14¢ to 15¢ out of every spending dollar just to buy transportation—primarily by auto and plane. You are spending more than $70 billion a year just to buy fuel, insure, park, and care for your automobile.

I'm taking for granted, therefore, that you know something about buying and insuring a car.

But no matter what the extent of your car dealing has been, I'll also wager you are not fully aware of the great savings you can achieve in your car buying, insuring—and repairing.

How to Buy a New Car

You are in the market for a new car. How do you choose a reliable car dealer? When is the best time of the year to buy? Which accessories are worth the extra cost? How can you tell whether or not you are getting a fair deal if you're trading in your old car?

WHAT TO DO FIRST

(1) In advance, set a maximum price you are willing and able to pay for the car—everything included.

If you are a family with average income and expenses, plan to hold your monthly payments on a car you are buying over a period of three years to one half or less of your monthly housing costs (mortgage and taxes *or* rent). The average amount paid for a new car in the mid-1970s was more than $4,400, and after deducting trade-in allowances, the average dropped to $3,000.

Here was the general price range of most models in various car sizes:

Subcompact (or mini-compacts): between $2,800 and $3,200 (subcompact station wagons cost $150 to $300 more than sedans).

Compacts: between $3,200 and $3,600.

Intermediates: between $3,400 and $4,100, an average of $400 to $500 more than compact cars.

Big four-door sedans: between $4,400 and $6,500.

Station wagons: between $3,600 and $6,000, or $400 to $700 more than a comparable four-door sedan.

Specialty cars, primarily "sporty" cars: between $3,500 and $8,500, with some of the super muscle cars now up to $9,000 to $10,000.

(2) Also in advance, decide in some detail what kind of car you want.

This includes make, size, body type, engine, transmission. Will the size you choose meet your actual family needs, including those of growing children? Is the price within your automobile budget? Are you looking for an all-purpose family first car? Or one mainly for your job? Or mainly for long trips? Or just to go back and forth from the railroad station? What kind of weather will you be driving in? In what kind of traffic conditions? How much cargo room do you regularly need—honestly? (Roof racks or rented trailers are more economical for very occasional cargo hauling than an investment in a station wagon.)

(3) Do your homework before you buy.

Among your best sources are: the "Annual Roundup for New Car Buyers" issue of *Consumer Reports,* which includes frequency-of-repair records for popular makes and models, published in April and available at newsstands; the yearly "Buying Guide" issue of *Consumer Reports,* published in

December and available at newsstands or from Consumers Union of U.S., Inc., 256 Washington Street, Mount Vernon, N.Y. 10550; *Edmund's New Car Prices* (American makes) or *Foreign Car Prices,* from Edmund Publications Corp., 295 Northern Boulevard, Great Neck, N.Y. 11021; Car/Puter's *Auto Facts—New Car Prices,* from Davis Publications, Inc., 229 Park Avenue South, New York, N.Y. 10003; such auto and motor journals as *Car and Driver, Road and Track, Motor Trend, Road Test,* which compare performance and other aspects of each new model; the results of the Union 76 Performance Trials held early each year. Ford Motor Company publishes "Car Buying Made Easier," which is full of easily understandable information on car buying. For a free copy, write: Ford Motor Company Listens, P. O. Box 1975, The American Road, Dearborn, Mich. 48121. (The box number usually is the year in which you write.)

(4) Use the following abbreviated chart to rate various new cars you are considering buying, and to compare costs:

	CAR 1	CAR 2	CAR 3
Net cash price:	_____	_____	_____
Taxes:	_____	_____	_____
Preparation costs:	_____	_____	_____
Cost of other extras:	_____	_____	_____
Cost of options you want:	_____	_____	_____
Key warranty coverage:			
Miles	_____	_____	_____
Years	_____	_____	_____
Parts	_____	_____	_____
Labor	_____	_____	_____
Other	_____	_____	_____
Expected gas mileage:	_____	_____	_____
Safety features:	_____	_____	_____
Convenience of seat belts	_____	_____	_____
Passing ability	_____	_____	_____
Stopping distance	_____	_____	_____
Tire reserve load	_____	_____	_____
Space:	_____	_____	_____
Ride:	_____	_____	_____
Frequency-of-repair record:	_____	_____	_____
Handling:	_____	_____	_____
Luggage space:	_____	_____	_____
Passenger space:	_____	_____	_____
Ease of getting in and out:	_____	_____	_____

	CAR 1	CAR 2	CAR 3
Looks:	_____	_____	_____
Dealer's reputation:	_____	_____	_____
Availability of parts, service:	_____	_____	_____
Efficiency of service:	_____	_____	_____

(5) Be honest with yourself about how important status is to you, as expressed by an automobile.

If you had to make a trade-off, would you prefer a more expensive model with almost no extras? Or the best of the lower-priced models, with budget room for the extras you want?

(6) Ask yourself how long you intend to keep the car you buy.

If you plan to trade it in after only a couple of years, the traditional summer-fall car bargains (available just before the new models are introduced in the autumn) are probably not a good deal. A car you buy in September will be considered a year old in only a month or so, and its market value will depreciate by one fourth in just a few weeks.

However, if you plan to drive the car into the ground, August and September are definitely the best months to find a bargain. You'll often be offered 5 to 35 per cent below regular prices. Also, if you are hunting for discounts, look at the year's less popular models which the dealer may have had a hard time selling. These may sell 20 to 40 per cent below regular prices. Of course, an ugly duckling may be more difficult to trade in, but if you intend to keep your car for several years that won't be a problem.

(7) Make up your mind what "extras" you really want.

A radio (FM or regular?), air conditioner, white-wall tires, an adjustable steering wheel, power seats and windows, automatic transmissions, speed regulator, vinyl-covered roof, remote control outside mirrors, rear window defogger? If the dealer does not have a car with precisely the options you want, he might be willing to give you a good buy on another car with only the options most important to you. Many accessories are simply frills on which you will get no return when you sell or trade.

(8) Consider not only the purchase price of various makes and models but also your probable future gas and maintenance costs. Starting with the 1977 models, new cars must carry stickers listing their gasoline mileage and comparing their costs of fuel per mile with costs of other cars in the same class.

The range of gas mileage on popular cars in the mid-1970s ran all the way from 8 to 30 miles per gallon. A weekly savings of only $5.00 on gas would add up to an average saving of $260 every year you own the car. Check the sticker in the window of the car you may buy, or a sticker like it, for an estimate of the gas mileage you will get. As a general rule, the fewer the number of cylinders, the lower the fuel and upkeep costs—as well as the lower the original price tag.

(9) Time your shopping to get the best deal.

No matter who or where the dealer, there are certain prime times for getting a car bargain. Among them:

Three to four months after the announcement date for brand-new models (generally late September). By this time, winter sluggishness has set in and car buying is at a low ebb, but cars are still rolling off the assembly lines and inventories start to bulge all along the line.

On the last business day of a month, when there is a special promotion (such as "Spring Cleaning Days") which may involve a sales contest among dealers. Cars sold during promotions often produce for a dealer an extra bonus of $100 or even $200, and he may be willing to share part of this bonus with you in the form of a discount to make the sale.

During a blizzard, or after a spell of rotten weather which has reduced traffic in the showroom. Often, dealers find they are short of working cash at these times (business falls off in the service department, too) and will offer big discounts to boost sales.

Of course the very best time to shop would combine *all* of these characteristics. At such a time you might be able to get a car practically at wholesale cost.

SHOPPING FOR A DEALER

Now you have done a reasonable amount of homework. You are ready to start shopping for a dealer.

• Ask your neighbors and friends for guidance on local automobile dealers. Find out not only whether a dealer has a reputation for offering a fair deal but also whether he follows through by delivering the car when he promises to, by reliable servicing, by honoring warranties. How long must his customers wait for routine servicing and for emergency repairs both in and out of warranty? What days—and hours—does the repair shop operate? Saturdays? Any evenings? Will the dealer pick up and/or return your car if you need this type of convenience? Is his advertising honest or does he claim "fantastic savings"?

• Stick to dealers in your own neighborhood. You can reach them easily and they can't duck you easily. If, though, you choose to buy a new car from a dealer some distance from your home, try to estimate what it would cost in fuel alone to go back and forth for repairs, servicing, warranty work. Don't ignore the cost of time lost from work.

• Also, stick to members of the National Automobile Dealers Association and dealers·who are franchised by the major automobile manufacturers (the auto manufacturers will give you the names and addresses of such dealers in your area if you ask for them). The key advantage of dealing with a franchise dealer is that you can ask the manufacturer to put the screws on him if he fails to honor the warranty he gives you, fails to make repairs he has promised, etc.

• Read and compare the warranties offered by each dealer. What does each cover and not cover? Parts? Labor costs? And how long does each warranty last? Warning: If problems crop up after you have bought a car, you'll need your warranty to back up your demands to your dealer for repairs. So have the warranty *in hand* before you close any deal.

• Explore with care how much of a discount from the car's suggested list price the dealer offers. Cars rarely sell at or even near their "sticker" prices, although the law requires that stickers be affixed to every new car which itemize the manufacturer's suggested list price, special preparation charges, sales taxes, transportation costs from the factory as well as the costs of already installed extras.

This sticker is not to be removed or altered in any way until the car has actually been delivered to you. Insist on seeing the sticker. It's the major point of price reference you have.

As one guideline on discounts, the dealer's typical markup is $300 to $800 from the wholesale cost of a medium-priced car (to which he already has added taxes, shipping costs, a "preparation" charge, and sometimes a "clerical" or "documentation" charge of questionable legitimacy). This is the "band" within which he'll bargain with you.

A way you can decipher a dealer's discount offer is by figuring out how much the new car actually cost the dealer. Here's a rough guide to the dealer's cost:

Find the total cost (including transportation) from the price sticker on the car window. Subtract the transportation charge. Then take either: 80 per cent of the balance (for a full-sized car); 81 per cent (for an intermediate-sized car); or 85 per cent (for a compact-sized car). Add back the transportation costs. The result comes very close to the dealer's actual cost.

• Inquire about a computerized auto buying service. One called Car/Puter (1603 Bushwick Avenue, Brooklyn, N.Y. 11207) can provide you with either:

(1) An itemized computer rundown on what any given car you are considering buying cost your local dealer, along with basic costs of the options in which you are interested and the "fixed" cost for transportation, taxes, preparation, etc. This analysis could well be worth its minor cost as you negotiate retail prices from dealer to dealer.

(2) Or the particular car you want to buy at a fixed cost of a modest $125 above the dealer's cost, delivered through a participating local dealer.

Among other computerized services are: United Buying Service (1855 Broadway, New York, N.Y. 10023); Masterson Fleet Auto, Inc. (1957

Chestnut Street, San Francisco, Calif. 94123); Nationwide Purchasing, Inc. (14411 W. Eight Mile Road, Detroit, Mich.)

A most important point in going this car-buying route is to nail down firmly—both by direct discussions with the dealer and by inquiries among other people who have bought their cars this way—how the dealer will handle warranty work which he is obligated to perform and future repairs.

• Be sure the dealer gives you a pamphlet containing full details on safety aspects of the car you are buying, now required by federal law. Among the facts you should receive: the car's acceleration and passing ability, measured in the number of feet and seconds it takes the car to pass a 55-foot truck; stopping distance in feet, from 60 miles per hour, both with a light load and with a maximum load; tire reserve load or safety margin (the capacity of tires, expressed as a percentage, to carry excess weight safely, beyond the maximum number of pounds suggested by the manufacturer).

• When you have made your decision to buy, get a written sales agreement which has been approved by the sales manager, and read it with utmost care before you sign. Have all blank spaces crossed out or marked *void* by the dealer. On extra charges for such services as "preparation" or "undercoating" of the car, keep in mind that preparation (an item usually costing between $35 and $150) is included in the advertised retail price of all U.S. cars and undercoating should not cost much more than $30.

And make sure any oral promises the salesman has made to you regarding special servicing or adjustments to the car are included in the sales contract before you sign it.

THE TRADE-IN

If you want to sell your used car on your own, you'll save the cut of $100 or more a car dealer would tack on as his profit. But you'll have to do your own advertising and selling. And you'll have to find out, too, what is a fair price for the car—considering its make, model, warranty status, age, looks, and mechanical condition.

Consider the fact that you may have to pay a higher finance charge on your new car if you sell your old car on your own. If, for instance, you keep your $1,200 used car for a time-consuming sale to a private individual, you'll raise the amount of the new car loan by $1,200. This could boost the finance charge by more than $200 over a three-year period.

Also, if you live in a state where trading an old car for a new one reduces the sales tax on the new one (you pay sales tax only on the cash amount you pay the dealer), recognize that you'll have to get a higher price from an individual to make up the loss of this saving. For instance, the sales tax saving from trading a $1,200 car in a 6 per cent sales tax state would be $72; you would have to get $1,272 for the car on the open market to get a deal equal to a trade-in.

Do not depend on one dealer or two, or the man at your local service station, to quote you an accurate asking price for your car.

Do not regard a dealer's proposed trade-in allowance toward the new car he wants to sell you as necessarily a reliable guide to the market value of your old car.

Use the information sources listed in the following section, "How to Buy a Used Car," to help you arrive at an objective evaluation of the car you want to trade.

Before you even discuss a trade-in, follow this procedure: first check the approximate market value of your old car; next, ask the new car dealer how much the car you want would cost if you paid cash; *then* ask him what it would cost with a trade-in of your old car. Get both quotations in writing.

If the *trade-in is less* than you would get from a used car dealer, you probably will want to sell the old car on your own and take the cash deal. What's important is *not the "allowance" off the new car's list price that the dealer will give you* for your old car, but the *balance* you have to pay. Repeat the process with other nearby dealers and compare the total package offered by each for *total* charges on the same (or similar) car, the same options, and the same warranty.

If you do decide to trade your car or sell it on your own, these do's and don'ts will help you get a better price.

Do:

wash the car;
polish it;
touch up paint and chrome;
clean stains from upholstery;
vacuum the interior;
wash floor mats;
clean out trunk, glove compartment, and other storage areas;
check all fluid levels (gas, water, oil, transmission and brake fluid) to insure proper operation during a test drive;
check tires and adjust pressures;
replace any burned-out light bulbs.

Take off equipment that might arouse the suspicion that you have used the car for racing or have abused it in other ways: special hubcaps, decals, fender skirts. These racy accessories may tend to drive away instead of bring in buyers.

In addition to using the obvious classified ads in local or regional newspapers or shopping throw-aways, try all free or inexpensive methods of advertising when you put your car on the market: word of mouth, notices on bulletin boards, classified ads in company newspapers, a prominent sign on the car, a "trading post" announcement on your local radio station. Be sure to include times and telephone numbers at which you can be reached by prospective buyers.

When you arrange meetings with possible buyers, try to accommodate their preferences for times. Be honest, but not apologetic, about your car. Do not permit a demonstration drive if your car is not insured for other drivers or if the prospective buyer cannot show you his driver's license.

Be firm about the price, assuming it is in the "book value" range. You may come down to a lower price if the buyer looks right, but don't begin by indicating the price is flexible.

If a buyer needs time to arrange financing, insist on a binder payment of 5 to 10 per cent of your asking price before you agree to hold it for him. And accept payment only in the form of cash or a cashier's check.

Don't:

invest in a new paint job—it will only cost money and raise suspicions in a potential buyer's mind of what you may be trying to hide;

invest in major repairs—it's too late for them, and you will be able to recover only a small fraction of their cost;

spend money on little details a potential buyer well may shrug off: a clock that doesn't run, a window that sticks, that sort of thing.

How to Buy a Used Car

CONSTRUCTIVE RULES FOR BUYING

The used car business in this country is loaded with frauds and misrepresentations—as well as with a wondrous array of entirely legal ways to inspire you to spend a lot more money than you had planned or can afford in order to put yourself on wheels. Just how loaded and how wondrous you'll glimpse in the following section on used car traps and guides for side-stepping them.

To begin with, though, here are the constructive rules for buying a used car:

• Choose a used car dealer only after thorough investigation. Look for one who is a member of a local, state, or national car dealers' association. Query friends on their experience with local dealers and follow their recommendations. Don't go too far from home, or servicing problems could become a real nuisance. Study dealers' ads in your local newspapers and on local TV programs. Are the ads *reasonable* and *believable* to you? If not, don't deal. Also, check with your local Better Business Bureau, which is likely to have a bulging file of complaints on certain local used car gypsters and deceivers.

• Check your local new car dealers to see whether they also have their better trade-in cars for sale—frequently backed by warranties they are prepared to honor in their service shops (they usually sell their lemons to used car dealers).

• Avoid, if possible, shopping for a used car during the peak summer season when millions of other Americans are competing against you to buy a used car for vacation travel.

• Consider as *part* of the purchase price the total finance charges, immediate repairs for which you know you must pay, optional equipment, sales and other taxes, insurance. But *don't*, when you approach a dealer, announce that you have, say $750 and want to know what he has in that price range.

• Choose—if you are trying to find the best bargain in strictly dollars-and-cents terms—a relatively recent compact or other lower-priced model with comparatively few complicated extras over an older, higher-priced model with a lot of extras. The latter well may mean stiff repair costs later.

• Consult the National Automobile Dealers Association's *Official Used Car Guide* or, on the West Coast, *The Kelly Auto Market Report* (*Blue Book*), listing current average retail car values for most U.S. and foreign models, makes, and years. These guides, which your dealer or the loan department of your local bank should be willing to show you, dramatize the fact that prices for a given car can vary as much as $500, depending on whether its condition is "extra clean," "clean," "fair," or "rough."

• Consult, also, *Consumer Reports*, which regularly rates used cars as well as new ones and can serve as a valuable guide to used car bargains. Get a copy both of Consumers Union's pamphlet entitled "How to Buy a Used Car," which gives details on 20 tests you should run on any used car you are considering buying and of *Edmund's Used Car Prices*, available from Edmund Publications Corp., 295 Northern Boulevard, Great Neck, N.Y. 11021. Also get Car/Puter's *Auto Facts—Used Car Prices*, available from Davis Publications, Inc., 229 Park Avenue South, New York, N.Y. 10003. And look over *Motor Trend* magazine's yearly issue devoted exclusively to used car buying.

• Don't fall for the salesman's well-worn come-on, "I'm losing money on the deal." How could the dealer stay in business if he does that?

• Take into consideration the fact that a new car's value drops about 50 per cent during the first two years of its life owing to depreciation—although on certain imported cars the rate of depreciation tends to be lower because of less drastic year-to-year style changes. This suggests that a well-cared-for two- to three-year-old car may be a good buy.

• Test-drive any car which seems to meet your needs—or get a trusted mechanic to test-drive it for you. Try it out in a variety of traffic conditions; on a dirt road as well as a paved superhighway; on a hill as well as on the level.

• Hire a mechanic or diagnostic clinic to check the motor, brakes, clutch, transmission, other vital parts, and expect to pay $15 to $25 for this service —well worth it, even if the check results in your *not* buying the car.

• Ignore the odometer reading—despite the fact that turning the odometer back to zero or otherwise tampering with it is against the law. *A better gauge* of how many miles a used car has been driven is to multiply its age by 10,000 to 15,000 (miles per year). Check the driver's seat for wear. Does the mileage on the odometer equal interior wear? If not, be suspicious of the odometer.

• Heed these guidelines and clues to how much a used car has been used:

The original tires on a car which has been driven 15,000 miles or less will still have good tread. But by 25,000 miles the tread will probably be well worn. As a clue to whether or not the tires are the originals, check to see if all four are of the same brand and similar serial numbers.

At 25,000 miles, the battery may have been replaced. Look for a sticker with a guarantee date.

At 30,000 miles you'll see considerable wear on the brake pedal, and if this or the floor mat has been replaced the car probably has gone more than 40,000 miles. Also at 40,000 miles you may be able to detect a brake pedal wobble.

Another clue to a car's age is its most recent service stickers, giving the mileage at the latest lubrication and oil change. If these have been torn off, that alone should beg the question: "Why?"

• Although most used cars are sold "as is," try to get a guarantee that the dealer will pay in full for all necessary repairs within thirty days of the time you purchase the car. Or perhaps you can get a written guarantee that will protect you against major repairs, or a pledge that the car will pass state inspection. If you do settle for the more typical fifty-fifty deal in which the buyer and seller share the repair costs for the first thirty days, keep in mind that a wheeler-dealer might try to double the repair charges so that you would end up paying the full cost instead of half.

• Ask a dealer if he will give you the name and address of a car's previous owner (some will)—and query this person on possible problems, defects, or advantages of the car. If the former owner turns out to be a traveling salesman, this could serve as a warning to you that the car may have been driven an unusually large number of miles. Or it could turn out to be the proverbial "little old lady."

Important note: In some areas, a contract to buy a used car is not binding if you are unable to move it off the lot—even if you have bought a car "as is."

• Do not assume that because a used car bears an inspection sticker it's in good mechanical fettle. Normally, state inspection laws cover brakes, steering, tires, horn, windshield wipers, headlights, brake lights, etc.—but the laws do *not* cover in any sense the condition of the engine or transmission. And in many states it is easy for a dealer to get a sticker from a friendly mechanic who has made only a cursory inspection. The dealer himself may even have an inspection license in states where private mechanics hold state inspection licenses.

• If you buy a used car from a private individual, try to pay no more than $100 over the wholesale price. And try to get a money-back guarantee to cover you if the car fails to live up to the way in which it was represented to you.

• See if you, as a buyer of a recent-model used car, can have the warranty transferred to you. You can *if* there is documentation of the date of delivery to the car's original owner.

• Make notes on each car which interests you—including the year, make, model, and vehicle identification number—so you can identify it if you return to the dealer. Take a notebook along when you inspect cars on each lot and when you test-drive.

• Compare the deals offered on a comparable car by several local dealers and choose the best for you.

• Then shop among local lenders for the best financing terms as carefully as you shopped for the car itself. The rules on financing follow later in this chapter.

CHECK LIST FOR BUYING A USED CAR

The following check list for buying a used car is exhaustive. With it at hand, it would be difficult for you to go wrong! The guide is adapted from *Family Financial Education for Adults* and was prepared by L. W. Erickson of the Graduate School of Education, University of California.

I. Preliminary Check on the Lot (Exterior)

   A. Paint
      1. Is it faded, scratched, pitted, or peeling? Does it need repainting?
      2. Pry up rubber on door edges; look for difference in paint. Check for accidental paint spray on moldings. If car has been repainted, look for other signs of overhaul.

   B. Body
      1. Look to see if sheet metal is dented or scratched in several places.
      2. Probe door bottoms and fender joints for signs of rust. A "rusted-out" car has little value.
      3. Look for paint overspray or damaged metal on underside of trunk lid. (Lid may have been wrecked.)
      4. Open and close all doors to see if they are sprung or sagging.
      5. Check fit of hood and trunk lid to see if they latch easily.
      6. Check door handles for looseness, indicating hard use.

C. Glass

    1. Is windshield cracked or scratched by wiper blades? A damaged one may fail state inspection.

    2. Work windows. Note whether excessively loose or stiff.

    3. Check vents and windows for cracks.

D. Chrome

    1. Are bumpers and molding rusted or pitted?

    2. Molding missing or loose?

    3. Bumper bent, crooked, or loose?

    4. Grille badly damaged or rusted?

E. Tires

    1. If car's mileage is said to be less than 20,000 all tires should be of the same make, similar serial numbers—and evenly worn. If they are not, mileage is probably over 20,000.

    2. Measure tread depth. New tires have 9/16 inch, worn-out tires, less than 1/16 inch.

    3. Note chafes, tears, and bulges: all indicate replacement is needed.

    4. Look for front tires showing uneven wear: means front end is out of alignment.

    5. Heavy wear on rear tires could mean "rubber burning" by dragster.

F. Suspension

    1. Does car sag on level ground? Could mean one or more weak or broken springs.

    2. Bounce front of car. If it continues to bounce when you release it, shocks are worn.

    3. Stoop directly in front of car about 20 feet away. If front wheels lean inward at top, they need alignment.

    4. Grasp the top of a front tire and vigorously push it in and out. Clunking sound means worn parts in the front-end assembly.

G. Leaks

    1. Look under the car near the engine and transmission. Oily spots on the ground indicate leaks that may be costly to repair.

    2. See if ground or frame beneath radiator is wet with water.

    3. Inspect the inner side of all wheels. Dark areas indicate leaking brake cylinders or grease seals.

H. Chassis

    1. Look at the frame for weld marks or heated areas—indicating repairs made after an accident.

II. Preliminary Check on the Lot (Interior)

A. Upholstery
1. Generally dirty?
2. Seats or back rests torn or frayed?
3. Springs in seats sagging?
4. Armrests missing or frayed?
5. Door panels torn or frayed?
6. Overhead lining torn or frayed?
7. Sun visors missing or frayed?

B. Dash
1. Paint scratched or pitted? Car had hard use.
2. Dash freshly repainted? Car may have been a taxi or police car. Reject such cars.
3. Glove compartment door loose, sprung, or won't latch?
4. How is oil pressure gauge? It should read high on starting, then drop to middle of dial at a fast idle as engine warms. If indicator type, light should go out on starting. If gauge isn't normal, engine bearings may be worn.
5. Does fuel gauge register?
6. Check ammeter. It should show charge at fast idle or, if indicator type, light should go out on starting. If not operating there may be trouble in generator or regulator.
7. Is water temperature gauge working?
8. Are light switches broken? Check dome and backup lights.
9. Does ignition switch stick?
10. Are heater and vent controls stiff or inoperative?
11. Is windshield wiper control stiff or inoperative?
12. Check radio, if any. Working?
13. Check clock, if any. Working?
14. Are knobs missing on any dash controls?

C. General
1. Is horn working?
2. Are directional signals working?
3. Is steering wheel safe? Gently rotate it. More than two inches of play before the wheels respond is unsafe.
4. Is seat adjustment stuck or broken?
5. Are floor mats torn or worn?
6. Are pedals worn more than mileage indicates? Or are they new pedals?
7. Is foot switch for dimming headlights working?

8. Does brake pedal sink slowly under steady foot pressure? This indicates a leak in the hydraulic system or worn master cylinder. Check leaks again as previously suggested. Spongy feeling means air in system, needs attention.

9. Open door and look to rear of car while you race the engine. Blue smoke from exhaust means a ring job is needed.

III. Preliminary Check on the Lot (Engine)

A. Engine idling

1. Examine engine for oil leaks or rust on block. Look closer for cracks in such areas. Be wary of a "steam-cleaned" engine. A dirty one will at least show you what might be leaking.

2. Is head cracked or welded? If so, new one is probably needed.

3. Are manifolds cracked or warped? Repairs needed.

4. Is engine idling too fast? Have idle speed reduced, as fast idle can cover irregular engine operation or tendency to stall.

5. Is throttle linkage bent or worn, keeping engine from returning to normal idle after being raced? (Can be dangerous.)

6. Is there sputtering sound when engine is raced? Often indicates clogged jets or worn accelerator pump in carburetor.

7. Is air cleaner missing or damaged?

8. Are there sounds of knocking, grinding, squealing, or hissing? All are potentially expensive.

9. Are there regular clicking noises in engine with hydraulic valve lifters? Could be tip-off that lifters may have to be removed, cleaned, or replaced.

10. Is generator noisy? Signals worn bearings.

11. Are there traces of gas or oil on fuel pump? Diaphragm may be worn.

12. Is water pump leaking or noisy?

13. Is radiator hose leaking?

14. Are there rusted areas on radiator? Or is it leaking?

15. Do you see oil or bubbles in coolant? Could be internal crack in block.

16. When you kneel beside car, do you hear sputtering sounds? Could indicate dangerous pinholes in muffler or loose connection to exhaust pipe.

17. Is tail pipe rusted or kinked?

B. Engine off

1. Is oil level very low? Car may be an oil burner or a leaker. Recheck for blue smoke in exhaust and oil drippings under car.

2. Are there water droplets on oil dipstick? May indicate internally cracked block.

3. Is oil pan dented? Look carefully under recent-model low cars.
4. Is fan belt worn or frayed? On a low-mileage car, a worn belt suggests the mileage has been set back.
5. Is distributor cap or case loose or cracked? If so, replacement is needed.
6. Are ignition wires brittle or cracked?
7. Look for bulging battery case or cell tops, loose or cracked terminals and cell connectors that mean battery is about finished.
8. Remove wire from center of coil and crank engine for ten or fifteen seconds. Starter should turn engine over quietly and smoothly.
9. Listen for clanking sounds or broken teeth on flywheel gear while cranking engine as above. Entire flywheel may have to be replaced.
10. With coil wire still removed as above, crank engine. Uneven cranking may indicate unequal compression caused by a burned or sticking valve.

IV. Road-testing the Car

A. Brakes
1. Is pedal low? Brakes need relining or adjustment.
2. Do brakes pull car to one side when applied?
3. Do brakes grab or chatter, squeal or scrape?
4. Does hand brake hold on hill?

B. Steering
1. Does car wander or drift from side to side on straight, flat road?
2. Is there a loose, uncertain feel of steering wheel?
3. Make a series of "S" turns on a quiet road. Is it hard to steer on quick turns or when parking? Could be a defective pump or merely a slipping drive belt.
4. Does steering wheel bind on tight turns?
5. Do front wheels shimmy above 40 mph on smooth roads? Wheels need balancing.
6. Do front wheels shimmy on rough roads at low speeds? Front end needs work.

C. Standard Transmission
1. With hand brake set and transmission in second gear, slowly release clutch pedal and depress accelerator. Engine should stall, or clutch is slipping.

2. Check clutch pedal free play. Pedal should move 1 to 1½ inches before it begins to disengage clutch. If it doesn't clutch, facing may be worn.
3. Drive a block or more in each speed range and listen for sounds of chipped gears.
4. Depress the clutch pedal. Lever should move easily into all ranges and there should be no clashing of gears.
5. Check for slipping out of gear while driving. This means transmission is worn.
6. Check on noisy transmission. This means bearings are worn.
7. Check overdrive (if equipped) for operation per owner's manual.

D. Automatic transmission
   1. Is transmission jerky when engaged in low or reverse?
   2. Do shifts take place smoothly?
   3. Does transmission squeal, whistle, or whine? Trouble may be imminent.
   4. Can you hold a park position on a hill?
   5. Does selector lever move easily? If not, linkage may be bent or out of adjustment.

E. Rear axle
   1. Run car at 20 mph and listen for metallic clanking or grinding noises that indicate wear or damage. You will hear these noises better down a narrow street lined with buildings.
   2. Alternately depress and release the gas pedal to jerk the car while in motion. Clicks or thumping sounds mean too much play in power train parts.

F. Engine
   1. Reduce speed to about 15 mph in high gear or drive range, then accelerate moderately—not hard enough to downshift automatic transmission. Sputtering, hesitation, or backfiring indicate poor carburetion, valves, or ignition.

G. Wheels
   1. Open door slightly on your side and listen for crunching sound of chewed-up wheel bearings. Don't confuse the sound with sound of clicking wheel covers. Remove covers if you are uncertain of origin.
   2. Check for bent wheels by watching them while friend or dealer drives car.

H. Frame
Watch car from behind as it is driven; wheels should track.

I. Speedometer
1. Is speedometer working as it should? As measure of speed and mileage?
2. Does needle flutter or vibrate?
3. Is there a ticking or grating sound, indicating a kinked or very dry speedometer cable? If so, it needs oiling or replacement.

V. Final Inspection Back on the Lot

A. Last checks
1. Recheck the engine to see that nothing has opened while on road.
2. Hubcaps missing?
3. Wiper blades missing or deteriorated?
4. Cigarette lighter missing or inoperative?
5. License plate brackets missing or damaged?
6. Spare tire useless, flat, or missing?
7. Jack and lug wrench the correct ones for car?
8. Wheel lugs missing or threads stripped?
9. Radio antenna missing or bent?
10. Keys work in all locks? Check inside door locks.
11. Courtesy lights and switches on door pillars working?
12. Serial numbers agree with dealer's papers? Have dealer rectify any error and prove title before you buy, or you might drive out with a hot car. At a minimum, you will have trouble at state inspection stations.

AUTOMOBILE BUYING TRAPS—AND HOW TO AVOID THEM

Whenever you enter the market for a used car you become a target for one of the slickest groups of high-pressure promoters in our land. And you well may turn into a victim unless you are aware of the pitfalls.

To warn you and guide you, here is a short "dictionary" of today's most widespread car traps, come-ons, and gyps. Read and remember!

Doping. You are told that the used car you want has been completely "reconditioned" and your test drive seems to confirm this claim. But within a few days it develops a host of mechanical problems, for the dealer has used a variety of methods which temporarily—but only temporarily—disguise the car's faults.

The "almost new" car. This may be a bargain late-model "leftover" car which may have been used as a demonstrator. Or it may be a last year's model advertised by mail at the unbelievably low price of, say, $799. The catch with mail order cars is that they often turn out to be repainted taxis, rental, or police cars, etc., which may have been driven 100,000 miles or more. You would not be able to tell this from the odometer reading.

Bushing. Here the new car dealer hikes the price after you have made a deposit—or he lowers the generous trade-in allowance he has offered to keep you from shopping around. You can avoid bushing by insisting on a signed statement promising a refund if the car is not delivered on the specified terms and at a specified time.

Packing. This means heaping extra charges—special fees, exorbitant finance-insurance charges, the like—on top of the purchase price. In some cases the dealer gets a rebate from the finance company. Make sure there is no packing *before* you sign any deal.

The bumper or balloon note. In this deal, you pay relatively low installments at the start and a fat lump sum at the end. Although the only deception here is if the dealer fails to tell you about the "balloon" at the end, you are caught if you cannot meet the final payment.

Bait and switch. Cars are advertised in such tempting terms as "below cost," "below wholesale," etc. *But*—and this will be your warning—when you arrive at the lot you find that the advertised car is not available. The ad has been used as bait to get you to the lot, then switch you to another, costlier deal.

Macing. In this racket, you are the victim of a used car dealer to whom you have sold, on your own, your used car, at a favorable price to you. The dealer pays you a small amount of cash and the rest of your purchase price in notes or a postdated check. At its due date, the check turns out worthless. Or, by the time the notes mature, the fly-by-night operator has flown and the notes also turn out to be worthless paper.

Odometer tampering. Although many states and the federal government have laws turning back odometers, enforcement is difficult. To the expert, it's no problem to crank an odometer back tens of thousands of miles. Use the rules on pages 301–2 to figure out on your own how many miles a car has been driven, and see Part IV, "Your Rights and How to Get Them," or remedies available to you if you have been taken by a dishonest operator.

The highball. This is part of the bushing racket—in which a new car dealer makes a fantastically attractive-sounding trade-in offer and thereby halts your efforts to comparison-shop. However, when it comes time to deliver your new car, the dealer suddenly starts uncovering flaws in your old car—all of which diminish the sum he's actually willing to allow you on it for the trade-in.

The lowball. This is the opposite side of the above trap in which a dealer quotes an unrealistically low price for a new car as "insurance" that a prospective customer will return to his showroom after he has made the rounds of other local dealers. When you return, though, the quote inevitably expands to a more realistic level.

"Would you take . . ." You park your car on a street, go away, and then return to find a card under your windshield wiper which says, "I have a buyer for your car. Would you take $1,500 in trade for a brand-new ————? Call or bring in your car today." If you follow up, you will discover that the price of the new car has been jacked up so it more than makes up for the overgenerous trade-in offer; or the promised trade-in allowance has been somehow diminished to a realistic sum. This one is pure misrepresentation.

The basic rules for avoiding all of these traps are:

1. Deal only with a respected, reliable dealer.

2. Or shop newspaper ads by private owners for low mileage, one-owner cars, other pluses pinpointed in the preceding pages.

3. Resist the temptation of questionable "bargains."

4. Have a qualified mechanic or automotive clinic inspect any used car you are considering buying.

5. Read and understand any contract before you sign it.

6. Shop among several sources of used cars to find the best deal for you.

7. Try to get at least a 30-day warranty with the dealer responsible for paying in full for all needed repairs.

8. Be sure, if reconditioning has been done, that the warranty spells out the details—and whether the car is guaranteed to pass state inspection.

How to Shop for Auto Options

YOU CAN EASILY OVERLOAD

If you load the new car you buy with optional equipment, you can nearly double the car's cost to you. In fact, if you buy just a relatively few "basic" but expensive options, you can raise the price of your car by one third or more.

Do you really understand what options can cost you? Here's a rundown showing you how fast and how far the basic price you pay for a car can rise under two conditions: (1) you add only today's most commonplace options, such as an automatic transmission, air conditioning, tinted glass on all windows, an AM radio, special interior trim, white-wall tires, a remote-control outside mirror, and power brakes; (2) you load the car with every possible extra.

Model	Base Price*	With Typical Options*	"Loaded"*
AMC Gremlin	$ 2,889	$ 3,834	$ 5,932
Ford Pinto	2,976	4,048	6,499
Chevrolet Vega	2,984	4,004	7,804
Plymouth Duster	3,216	4,398	6,648
AMC Matador	3,627	4,824	6,467
Plymouth Fury	3,629	4,669	8,346
Ford Granada	3,797	4,871	9,872
Chevrolet Impala	4,507	5,182	8,080
Chrysler New Yorker	6,641	7,397	10,185
Lincoln Continental	9,277	9,497	17,687
Cadillac Fleetwood	10,586	10,821	17,992

*1976

Which options you choose will depend on the relative importance of each improvement to you, of course—but the vast assortment of alternatives is in itself a major buying hazard. How do you find your way around? Which options are the best buys? In the rundown below, note particularly the high costs of operating and repairing air conditioners.

RUNDOWN ON KEY OPTIONS

Larger engine, costing $70 to $500: Move your car around with much more pep and can improve safety when passing or in other situations where you must accelerate rapidly. But they often make a car more difficult to handle on wet or snowy pavement, they use more gas, and an eight-cylinder engine almost always will cost more to maintain and repair than a six-cylinder.

Note: Although most dealers and manufacturers recommend an eight-cylinder engine for any car equipped with an air conditioner and although most buyers go along with this advice, an eight-cylinder engine is *not* necessary to operate an air conditioner properly. Many four-cylinder cars have air conditioners and get along fine. The engine's *horsepower rating,* not the number of cylinders, is the key here; as a general guideline you'll need 15 to 30 extra horsepower to run an air conditioner on a small car, and 30 more horsepower on a larger car.

Automatic transmission, $250 to $350: Makes driving a lot easier, particularly for non-mechanically minded people and in heavy, stop-and-go city traffic. An automatic can often pay for itself by preventing wear which an indifferent driver might put on the engine, clutch, and gears of a car equipped with a manual transmission. Moreover, part of its cost will be returned at trade-in time. On the negative side: the owner of a car with an automatic transmission will probably pay more in repair bills and slightly more for gas than a skilled driver with a manual transmission. Still, for the majority of car owners, a good buy.

Air conditioner, $425 to $640: Considered virtually a necessity in the South, and also popular in many Northern cities where summertime can be sweltering. "Hang-on" units (not factory-installed) and air conditioners installed in foreign cars are currently considered less satisfactory by buyers, according to Consumers Union surveys of car owners. Many models also offer fully automatic, year-round temperature control (for about $75), but such systems tend to be unreliable. Comfort is the primary advantage of air conditioning, but this option also can help find a buyer at resale time.

On the debit side, air conditioners use a significant amount of extra gasoline and need repairs fairly often—more than one in five within a year. This is by far the single most expensive option most people buy and it tends to beget other options too—such as a bigger engine, power steering, power brakes, heavy-duty suspension, oversize tires, tinted glass. Thus, eliminating it could be a major way to save money—if you can manage without it. With or without air conditioning, consider the newly available synthetic fiber cloth-upholstered seats. They are durable and stain-resistant and more comfortable than vinyl.

Power steering, $120 to $140: Makes handling an intermediate- or full-sized car easier, and safer under some circumstances. Most modern power steering gives good road feel, makes parking nearly effortless, and provides quicker steering response on the highway than non-power steering.

Power brakes, $55 to $100: Probably worthwhile on any large car. They don't make a car stop more quickly but they considerably reduce pedal effort.

Tinted windows, $45 to $70: Make an air conditioner's job easier and improve comfort. However, they do reduce the margin of safety of a driver with poor night vision and should be avoided by this type of driver. Some critics claim tinted glass doesn't even help drivers with good vision.

Remote-control outside mirrors, $10 to $20: Nice, but prone to failure. May become non-adjustable by any means when they fail, and repairs can cost more than the option's price in the first place.

AM radio, $70 to $100: Useful for breaking the monotony of long trips, for listening to music, news, traffic congestion warnings, weather reports. Also of some value when you resell. But fancier sound setups (AM/FM radio, tape deck, stereo) return only a small part of their cost at trade-in and are good buys only if *you* get your money's worth while you own the car. Also, the FM part of an AM/FM radio will do you very little good if you live more than twenty-five miles from a major metropolitan area.

Limited slip differential, $50 to $65: Transfers power to the other wheel when one slips. Will be a great help if you do much driving on back roads in winter or spring, but may be a mixed blessing if you are primarily a highway driver. A more expensive ($105) anti-wheel spin option is available on some luxury cars.

Rear window defoggers, $40 to $100: Most don't work as well as windshield defrosters, but in areas with much cold or damp weather any help at all improves safety considerably. Thus the best rear window defogger you can get is probably a good buy.

A vinyl roof, $75 to $170: May have beauty in the eyes of some beholders, but its practical advantages are nil. A black one makes a car hotter, just about offsetting the effect of tinted windows and increasing the gasoline consumption of an air-conditioned car; may delaminate from the underlying metal; is expensive to repair.

Power windows, $95 to $170: Pleasant luxuries. All are failure-prone and expensive to repair. Power windows also can be a safety hazard with children.

Most *"heavy duty" optional components* such as springs ($20), shock absorbers ($5.00), battery ($15), alternator ($10), radiator ($15), cost relatively little and more than repay their cost if you own a car more than a year or two. The major exception to this might be a heavy-duty suspension, if the ride is stable enough without it and you generally drive with your car lightly loaded. Test-driving cars with both types of suspension will help you determine this.

SIX WAYS TO SAVE ON OPTIONS

Now here are six general tips on how to save money on options when you buy your car:

(1) Have firmly in mind the use to which you expect to put your car and try in your mind to rate the options according to how much each will add to the capacity of *your* car to perform adequately for *you.*

(2) Put together a personal shopping list of options before you go to the showroom. Do not permit yourself to be dazzled by the overwhelming array of improvements available. *Edmund's New Car Prices,* which lists all the options offered on the new cars in the market and roughly what amount you can expect to pay for each, is one good place to do this homework.

(3) When choosing engines, at least specify one that will run on regular fuel. All but a very few models—small or large—offer regular fuel engines. The performance advantage made possible by engines requiring premium fuel is so slight that it is important only in racing; premium gas, though, costs about 10 per cent more than regular.

(4) Choose options which contribute to durability; avoid those which add to complexity.

(5) Be willing to wait until exactly the car you want can be shipped to your dealer—even though the wait may be as long as several months. Don't waste money on taking some overequipped car he may have in stock. Cau-

tion: This may be difficult to do in late summer, early fall, when all the emphasis is on the next model year. But by sticking to your own shopping list and buying only the options you need and you choose to buy for your car, you'll slash the automobile's cost to you.

(6) Be sure to have all options installed by the factory when you buy the car. Later installation can be costly. For instance, say you later decide to install an electric clock, which would have cost $14 at the time of purchase. A dealer might charge you well over $30 for this same clock if he had to install it.

Auto Warranties—and How to Compare Them

Do you, the buyer of a new car, know how long the warranty on the car will last? And whether it covers parts, labor, or both?

Do you know how often you must have the oil changed in order to keep the warranty valid?

Do you know whether or not you must use a certain grade of oil and/or type of oil filter to fulfill your part of the warranty?

You may know the general terms of your warranty, but it's highly probable you know little or nothing about the details, the disclaimers, the exceptions.

Yet the warranty, a promise of quality and safety of a car, can be critically important to you—for better or for worse. It can be worth cash in your pocket: car manufacturers estimate that they spend about $120 per car on warranty work over the life of the warranty. You, the car owner, would spend considerably more than this if you had no warranty protection at all: auto manufacturers pay dealers less for repair work than dealers charge their customers for non-warranty work. And when the time comes to sell or trade your car, you may get an extra $50 to $200 for it if the warranty is still in force: the amount will depend on the make, model, and age of the car.

WHAT IS—AND WHAT ISN'T—A WARRANTY?

Just what *is* an automobile warranty—and, even more important, what *isn't* it?

A *warranty is* a pledge made by a seller of an automobile to a buyer. Legally it is part of the sales contract and if the promise of the warranty turns out to be false this invalidates the entire sale.

A *written warranty,* such as the one you get with a new car, is called an *express warranty.* Usually it describes what the seller is obligated to do for you, in terms of repairs, etc., and also what you, the buyer, must do to keep the warranty valid.

An *implied warranty* is an unwritten (but legally binding) promise the seller makes to a buyer simply by the act of selling. It guarantees "merchantability" and "fitness for purpose." Merchantability simply means that the product being sold is what the seller says it is: what everyone considers a car to be. If, for example, a dealer from whom you agreed to buy a Ford sedan instead delivered a tractor to you, that would be a breach of the "merchantability" aspect of the warranty. Fitness for purpose promises that the merchandise will perform the function that it ordinarily would be expected to perform, or that the buyer and seller have agreed it will perform. A car which just won't go more than ten miles an hour would flunk the "fitness" test.

Many warranties specifically disclaim the implied warranty—with a statement such as "This warranty is expressly in lieu of any other express or implied warranty, condition or guarantee on the vehicle or any part thereof, including any implied warranty of merchantability or fitness, and of any other obligation on the part of the manufacturer or dealer."

A *typical auto warranty* in 1975 covered all parts of the car—except tires and batteries—against defects of materials and manufacturing for 12,-000 miles or twelve months, whichever comes first. Some warranties covered, in addition, the engine and drive train (the collection of parts which transmits motion from a car's engine to its wheels). Specifically, this type of warranty includes the engine block, head, internal engine parts, oil pan and gaskets, water pump, intake manifold, transmission, torque converter, drive shaft, universal joints, rear axle, and internal parts—for 24,000 miles or twenty-four months, whichever comes first.

Some cars equipped with premium batteries carry a battery guarantee for 12,000 miles or twelve months.

Tires are warrantied separately by their manufacturers. The terms of tire warranties vary widely, and you may not even be able to obtain a copy of the warranty on the tires which come with your new car.

Although major improvements are being considered and may be on the way, virtually no warranties cover:

repairs beyond the stated period;

repairs if you have not taken certain specified maintenance measures;

your loss of time while your car is laid up;

additional damage caused by a defective part;

defects which a dealer finds he *cannot* fix (almost certainly he will also refuse to replace your car);

"adjustments";

"normal maintenance items" such as installing spark plugs, points, condenser, fan belt;

your satisfaction: no automobile warranty guarantees that *you* will be satisfied.

Used car warranties, if they exist at all, are even more limited than warranties on new cars. Ordinarily the term of a used car warranty is only thirty to sixty days, and often the buyer must pay 50 per cent of the cost of any warranty repairs.

Watch out for extravagant mileage claims often made in used car warranties. The 10,000-mile part of a warranty advertised as good for 10,000 miles, or thirty days, whichever comes first, is obviously just about meaningless—unless you're planning to crisscross the continent several times just after you buy the car.

However, getting the most out of your warranty protection is primarily up to you. Specifically:

HOW TO SHOP FOR A WARRANTY

Shop for warranties just as you shop for other important features of a car. Most warranties have the same time and mileage limitations, on cars manufactured in any one year, although there may be significant differences if you are shopping among used cars with valid warranties issued in different years.

The majority of manufacturing defects will show up well before the expiration of even the shortest new car warranty, dealers agree. Thus the *exceptions* to the warranty coverage (such as batteries, tires, and "normal maintenance items") and restrictions (such as requirements that you have certain maintenance operations performed at scheduled times in a manufacturer-authorized service shop) are more important than the duration of the warranty.

• Before you buy, find out the dealer's reputation for honoring warranties. This is one of the most crucial "preventive measures" you can take.

• Also before you buy, take a good look at the dealer's service facilities. You may not be able to judge a service shop, but if it is messier or dirtier than others you have seen, this may be a clue that repair work will be sloppy as well. Be prepared for trouble, too, if service facilities comprise less than 60 per cent of the dealer's establishment. Try to see the service manager, even if you don't feel qualified to judge his competence. If he is hard to find now, he will be equally hard to find later.

HOW TO GET YOUR CAR WARRANTY HONORED

If you have a warranty problem, take the steps outlined for you in Chapter 26, "Your Rights as a Consumer," pages 1011–12. These steps will help you get the proper treatment from the car dealer and manufacturer.

How to Finance Your Car

You have located the car you want to buy and arrived at a fair price. Now you are shopping for the best possible deal in financing the car—for I'm assuming that you, like two out of three new car buyers and half of used car buyers, plan to buy on time. On top of today's steep interest rates on automobile loans, financing costs also are being hoisted by the trends toward longer and longer repayment periods (typically, two years on a used car, three to four years on a new car); lower and lower down payments (often only 20 per cent); and larger and larger loans (the other 80 per cent). In the mid-1970s the *average* new car loan was for more than $3,500. The *average* monthly car payment was more than $100.

THE BEST WAYS TO SHOP FOR AN AUTO LOAN

Here, therefore, are your best ways to shop for the best deal in financing your car:

• Ask the dealer from whom you intend to buy the car exactly what financing terms he'll offer. Don't consider *any* deal unless the total financing charges, over the full life of the loan, are spelled out clearly in writing—including the amount of the cash down payment, the unpaid balance to be financed, and the true annual percentage cost. This detailed disclosure is required by the Truth in Lending law: be warned if it isn't made.

• Ignore such slogans as "easy payment terms" until you know exactly what these terms actually mean in dollars and cents.

• Plan to make the biggest down payment you can—if possible, at *least* one fourth to one third of the purchase price—and try to repay in the shortest period you can manage. Of course, your monthly payments will be larger this way than if you stretched out the loan, but you may save hundreds of dollars in interest.

Study this stark table showing what you pay in finance charges on a $1,000 loan extended for twelve, twenty-four, or thirty-six months at various rates.

$1,000 Loan

RATE	12 MONTHS	24 MONTHS	36 MONTHS
8%	$ 43.90	$ 85.50	$128.10
9%	49.40	96.40	144.80
10%	55.00	107.50	161.60
11%	60.60	118.60	178.60
12%	66.20	129.80	195.70

Rate	12 months	24 months	36 months
14%	$ 77.40	$152.30	$230.40
16%	88.80	175.10	265.70
18%	100.20	198.20	301.50
20%	111.60	221.50	337.90
24%	134.70	268.90	412.40
28%	158.10	317.30	489.10
32%	181.70	366.70	568.00
36%	205.50	417.10	648.90
40%	229.70	468.50	732.00

• Once you have the facts on financing a car through your car dealer, visit your local bank or, if you belong to one, your credit union. Ask the loan department what terms the bank or credit union will offer. Make sure such variables as the down payment you intend to make and the period (in months or years) during which you will repay the loan are the same when you compare each lender's terms.

In general, the most expensive sources of automobile credit are new and used car dealers, the automobile finance companies which often work with them, and small loan companies. The least expensive sources are credit unions, which usually charge the lowest rate of true annual interest and which tend to lend relatively large amounts toward purchase of new or used cars; commercial banks, which charge auto loan interest rates generally comparable to those of credit unions; and your life insurance company, if you have a policy with a cash value against which you can borrow at the lowest rate of all.

By all means, put up collateral—securities you own or other assets or a savings passbook—if this will reduce the net cost of your loan to you.

• Find out what provisions are offered by each lender for prepayment of the loan. Will you get a full or nearly full refund of finance charges if you are able to repay the loan more rapidly than you have planned? Is there a penalty for late payments? What are your rights in the event of repossession—such as fair warning before this takes place? Does the contract include an "acceleration clause," making all payments due immediately if you fail to make a payment on time?

• Shop for automobile insurance separately. Don't merely accept the package offered by an automobile dealer, for very possibly you will find that your regular insurance agent will offer the same coverage at a lower cost. Avoid being pushed into a costly credit life insurance provision. This would pay off the car loan in the event of your death, but the cost of credit life insurance tends to be relatively far greater than that of your regular life insurance—which should be sufficient to pay off your smaller debts.

CHECK LIST FOR COMPARING CAR FINANCING COSTS

Here's a check list which will show you how to figure and compare the dollar cost of financing your car:

	Lender A	Lender B	Lender C
Price of the car, including taxes, options, and all other extras			
Minus down payment			
Minus trade-in allowance			
Amount to be financed			
Amount of monthly payment			
Number of monthly payments			
Total amount of monthly payments			
Total dollar cost of auto loan			

THE REAL COST OF CAR OWNERSHIP

YOUR CAR'S COSTS TO YOU

How much does *your* car cost *you* to own and operate?

Here are facts and guidelines to use in making your own personal calculations:

Car ownership costs are basically of two kinds: *Fixed costs,* which are independent of the amount of driving you do; and flexible, *variable costs*— or operating costs—which depend on the number of miles you drive your car. Both depend on the type of car (and trimmings) you buy in the first place. You can figure the real cost, per mile, of running your car by dividing your *total* fixed and flexible costs by the *total* number of miles you drive over any period of time you choose.

Here are your *fixed costs:*

• *Depreciation,* or the amount of value a car loses as it becomes older: As a rough guide, a car depreciates by 30 per cent of its value during the first year you own it; 18 per cent the second; 14 per cent the third; 11 per cent the fourth; 8 per cent the fifth; 6 per cent the sixth; 5 per cent the seventh; and about 2 per cent each year thereafter. Some small imports, though, depreciate only 25 per cent in their first two years.

For non-mathematicians probably the easiest way to find out how much you car actually has depreciated is to look up its wholesale value in the National Automobile Dealers Association's *Used Car Guide*. Simply subtract the figure you find in this guide from the price you paid for your car.

•*Insurance:* These costs may range from less than $100 a year for a good driver of an inexpensive car to $600 or more a year for a young, high-risk driver of an expensive muscle car in a big city.

• *Other fixed costs:*

> Registration
> Purchase taxes (including sales taxes)
> Property taxes
> Financing costs
> Garaging costs

Your *variable costs* include:

> Gas and oil
> Maintenance
> Repairs
> Accessories and parts
> Tires
> Tolls and parking expenses

If you attach a dollars-and-cents figure to each of these categories of car ownership costs, I'll wager that the total will astound you.

AUTOMOBILE COSTS BROKEN DOWN BY SIZE OF CAR

Let's say you are deliberating over what size car to buy. You really need a standard-size car for your size family but don't know how much more it would cost in terms of gas, oil, etc. than a compact or subcompact.

Here is a rundown on the various costs of each size car over a 10-year life of the car by the Federal Highway Administration. The comparisons are for 1975 models.

EXPENSE	STANDARD	COMPACT	SUBCOMPACT
Depreciation	$ 4,864.00	$ 3,830.00	$ 3,189.00
Repairs, maintenance	3,664.13	2,961.00	2,659.97
Replacement tires	448.00	387.20	350.00

EXPENSE	STANDARD	COMPACT	SUBCOMPACT
Accessories added after purchase	$ 91.50	$ 86.00	$ 89.00
Gasoline	3,193.32	2,280.94	1,651.72
Oil	169.60	169.60	154.23
Insurance	1,678.00	1,594.00	1,511.00
Garaging, parking, tolls, etc.	2,208.80	2,108.80	2,108.80
Federal and state taxes and fees	1,561.61	1,143.92	924.63
10-year Total	$17,878.96	$14,561.46	$12,638.35

The standard-size car will cost you 17.88¢ a mile over its 10-year life; the compact will cost you 14.56¢ a mile; the subcompact will cost you 12.64¢ a mile.

HOW TO SLASH YOUR CAR COSTS

How can you slash these costs?

• When you *buy,* choose the smallest car available which will still meet your needs. The annual cost of operating a car is estimated at 35¢ a pound—one good indication of your potential savings.

• Postpone owning a second car as long as possible. Owning two cars can nearly double your over-all automotive expenses.

Although keeping the car you already own for a second car instead of trading it in hardly seems a wild waste of money—you already own it so it's "free," isn't it?—this can, in actuality, be a real extravagance.

Your insurance costs will be considerably higher no matter how you handle it; your maintenance, gas, and repair costs will be way up if only because you just naturally drive two cars more than one; you'll spend more for license fees and other trivial but still real costs, of course. And since you'll not have the old car to trade in, you'll have to use money to purchase a new car that otherwise could be invested to be earning interest or dividends for you.

• Give your new car a gentle breaking-in period. While many manufacturers will tell you it doesn't need it, what they mean is that today's care don't need as much breaking-in care as they did in the past. But by avoiding fast starts, holding your speed down to 55 or 50 mph, and frequently varying the speed at which you drive for the first few thousand miles, you can prolong the life of your engine.

• Read the owner's manual carefully the first time, and reread it occasionally. Particularly important is the list of recommended maintenance measures to improve efficiency in operating your car. Among the moneysaving tips you may find in your owner's manual is how to avoid "overmaintenance."

• Learn the warranty terms well.

• Equip your car properly for trailer towing or carrying heavy loads if you intend to use it this way—including heavy-duty tires, springs, shock absorbers, radiator, and transmission cooler. By thus equipping your car, you'll avoid premature damage to its suspension system and engine.

• Have tune-ups done at regular, appropriate intervals, as suggested in your manual.

At the time of your tune-up, also have your brakes and parking brake checked and/or adjusted or fixed; get a lubrication or oil change; have your automatic transmission fluid checked; have your clutch checked and adjusted; take whatever winterizing or summerizing measures are in order; have your tires rotated; check the list in your owner's manual and warranty for other maintenance moves.

Tune-ups cost from $10 to $50, but since they save you money on fuel consumption and engine wear, they just about pay for themselves. A further payoff is the increased dependability your well-tuned car will provide. The total cost of a good preventive maintenance program usually is less than $75 a year. You can save money by doing tune-ups yourself if you are so inclined. Many of the modern compact cars are designed with this specifically in mind, and their manufacturers offer detailed instructions and inexpensive tune-up parts kits.

HOW TO INCREASE YOUR GAS MILEAGE

You need not be an expert to increase your gas mileage about 30 per cent above the average.

To measure your gas consumption, have your tank filled so you can see gasoline in the filler pipe, record the odometer reading, and drive until the tank is nearly empty. Then refill the tank and again note the mileage reading. Divide the miles you have driven by the number of gallons in the second fillup; this gives you your mileage per gallon. Repeat this process several times to give an accurate result, since variable factors such as head winds can substantially change the mileage you get from a single tankful of gas.

Now:

• Make a habit of driving smoothly and steadily. Jack-rabbit starts gulp gasoline as do high speeds and quick speed changes. The U. S. Department of Transportation measured gas mileage for a typical 4,000-pound car and found that it traveled 11.08 miles per gallon at 70 miles per hour, 13.67 mpg at 60 mph, 16.98 mpg at 50 mph, and 14.89 mpg at 40 mph.

• Keep your tires inflated to two or three pounds above the lowest recommended pressures listed in the owner's manual.

• Don't buy premium gas unless your engine requires it: even some of the fanciest cars today run on regular gas. In fact, except for automobiles with the most powerful engines, all cars will run well on *sub-regular* gas. The average motorist pays $50 to $75 a year on unnecessarily high octane gas. High-test gas costs about 10 per cent more than regular, but it's entirely wasted if the car runs properly on regular. Moreover, using a higher grade than necessary needlessly increases air pollution by lead particles. Your owner's manual tells you what octane rating your car needs.

• In winter, keep your gas tank as full as possible to reduce condensation of water vapor in the tank and the risk of a subsequent freeze-up of the fuel line.

• Instead of wasting gas on prolonged warm-ups in winter, start off slowly and increase your speed as the engine warms up.

• In winter or summer, turn off the engine whenever it is not needed to move the car. A minute of idling uses more gas than it takes to restart. Idling usually uses nearly a gallon of gas an hour, increases pollution, and may clog your engine.

• Don't fall for what one expert calls "additive madness"—the slew of "new," "scientific" products which you simply pour into your gas tank or oil supply or clip onto your motor and which are advertised in glowing phrases ranging from "Run your car half on gas, half on air!" to "Drive up to 700 Miles on a Single Tank of Gas!"

To illustrate, the promoters claimed one typical "mileage booster," costing $3.98, would convert plain air into "high-powered fuel" and save you up to 1,000 gallons of gas a year. The ingenious promotion pointed out that 70 per cent of the gas you put in your car is "wasted" and, to prove it, the ad suggested a simple test: place a wad of cotton on your exhaust pipe and notice how quickly it becomes soaking wet.

But the fact is the moisture coming out of the exhaust pipe is not gas. It's water condensation. The fact also is that, in some cases, independent laboratory tests show the "miracle" additives and gimmicks actually *decrease* the efficiency of gas in your tank. On "gas-saving" products, your best source of advice is your responsible local station service mechanic.

• Aren't there, then, any "aftermarket" items which can really help us get more miles per gallon? Yes:

A first item is a comprehensive shop manual. This will make it possible for you, if you're at all handy, to keep your car in proper tune. Another item is a "vacuum gauge," an accessory which will tell you when you are applying more gas pedal pressure than you need to, consistent with the most economical operation of your car. And one gasoline additive which does have merit in cold, wet winter climates is gas line anti-freeze, which prevents water condensed in your gas tank from freezing and blocking the fuel line.

• Under no circumstances, try to extend your weekend cruising range by having accessory fuel tanks installed in the trunk of your car. A car's trunk is among its most vulnerable areas, and in a rear-end collision a trunk-mounted gas tank might rupture and cause a fire. In addition, Federal Environmental Protection Agency rules make it illegal for an automobile dealer to install an accessory gasoline tank that does not meet present evaporation control standards. The fine could be up to $10,000.

Also, if an auto dealer is found tampering with any of the emission control devices on new cars, the same fine could be the punishment. And if you, the motorist, either remove the devices yourself or have them removed by an independent mechanic you're possibly liable too.

On top of the possible fine, you face a stiff complete engine rebuild bill if you are to gain anything. The reason is that present emission systems are functional parts of the engines and the simple removal of one or two components might actually result in a decrease in mileage or not improve it at all.

WHEN SHOULD YOU TRADE IN?

When is the most economical moment to trade in a car today? This is a crucial but exceedingly difficult question to answer precisely because each of your situations is different. However, if you keep detailed records, here is a way to calculate the answer for yourself:

Each month, total all the automobile expenses you have paid up to that point, including an allowance for depreciation. Divide this total by the total number of miles you have driven. This will give you your average cost per mile to date. Over the life of most cars this average drops steeply at first, then levels off, and finally starts to rise again. The economically "ideal" time to trade in your car is just before your per-mile cost begins to rise.

Normally this point comes between three and six years after manufacture and your purchase of a new car. Other factors, though—such as your car's declining reliability (which can cost you money, too), its appearance and comfort—will enter into your final decision.

Don't make the mistake of trading in your car far too early. As underlined in the section "How to Curb Your Auto Repair Bills," pages 342–50, you probably will not need major repairs until your car has passed the 50,000 milestone—and even then you can slash your repair bills by following the basic rules.

Typically, your heaviest repair bills will come when you have driven 60,000 to 70,000 miles. In the earlier years, your bills mount up to those peaks and in the later years they decline. Because of this decline, it is slightly more economical to keep a car as long as possible—although dependability, comfort, and appearance are important non-economic factors which might lead you to trade in early.

Here are estimates by the U. S. Department of Transportation on annual depreciation, repairs, and maintenance for a car purchased at $4,379 (excluding taxes) and owned over a ten-year period.

Year	Estimated Annual Depreciation	Estimated Annual Repairs and Maintenance	Depreciation, Repairs, Maintenance Combined
One	$1,215.00	$ 157.05	$1,372.05
Two	748.00	199.95	947.95
Three	627.00	414.67	1,041.67
Four	466.00	548.03	1,014.03
Five	340.00	406.52	746.52
Six	306.00	471.46	777.46
Seven	292.00	704.82	996.82
Eight	292.00	280.80	572.80
Nine	291.00	431.20	722.20
Ten	277.00	49.63	326.63
TOTAL	$4,854.00	$3,664.13	$8,518.13

Notice that over the ten-year period the depreciation is close to $4,864—the cost of the car. But also notice that your annual depreciation varies, is highest in the early years of your ownership and lowest in the later years. If you traded in this car each year, your depreciation alone would cost you $12,150 over ten years of automobile purchases or ten times the first year's ($1,215) depreciation. If you traded in this model of car every two years, your depreciation would come to five times the depreciation of the first two years ($9,815).

But while your depreciation costs are declining as your car ages, you will note that your maintenance and repair costs are climbing too.

CHECK LIST FOR ESTIMATING YOUR CAR EXPENSES

Here, finally, is a check list you can use in estimating your annual and per-mile automobile expenses: To get the per-mile total, simply divide your annual expense totals by your annual mileage.

FIXED EXPENSES (ANNUAL)   ANNUAL MILEAGE:————————

Depreciation   ————————
Insurance   ————————
License and registration————————
State property tax   ————————
Finance charges   ————————

FIXED EXPENSES (ANNUAL)   ANNUAL MILEAGE:————————

Garage or parking fees ——————
Auto club dues, misc. ——————

    TOTAL   ——————   Per Mile: ——————

VARIABLE OPERATING EXPENSES
(ANNUAL)

Gasoline   ——————(Annual mileage divided
by miles per gal. times
avg. price per gal.)

Oil   ——————(No. qts. used times price
per qt.)

Tires   ——————(Generally 0.4¢ to 0.6¢ a
mile)

Maintenance   ——————(Generally 0.70¢ to 0.75¢
a mile)

    TOTAL   —————— Per mile:——————

How to Stretch Your Tire Dollar

Our annual bill for tires in this country had reached the $6 billion range by the mid-1970s. We are buying replacement tires for our cars at an annual rate of about 150 million. And this is on top of the 55 million tires with which the new cars we buy already are fitted.

If you drive a not untypical 20,000 miles a year—as many of you who live in the suburbs, exurbs, and rural areas do—your annual tire bill for *each* car in the family easily can amount to $100. If you live in an area in which you go through snow tires at a relatively rapid rate during the winter, your bill easily can be even more.

Your tires, and the air inside them, are your most important single item of armor between you and the road—or the telephone pole, or the pedestrian, or the onroaring trailer truck. Ask any professional racing car driver and he'll confirm that the amount of performance *and* protection you get from your car depend to a very considerable extent on the way in which you choose and care for your tires.

Thus, if you fail to shop carefully and if you fail to take proper care of your tires, you will greatly increase your tire costs, year in and year out— not to mention the risks to your life implied by defective, ill-chosen, or abused

tires. And if yours is a two-, three-, four-, or more car family, you can multiply your extra costs—and your risks—by this figure.

Do not take your tires for granted.

Do not assume that your tires are safe unless and until you have taken
all the steps and precautions reasonably in your power to make sure that they
are safe.

Do not assume that the tires which happen to be attached to the new
car you are about to buy are really suitable for *your* personal driving habits
and needs. These may be fine for the "average" driver but they may not be
fine for *you*. And in many ways greater safety translates into greater economy in the long range.

How do you judge a tire which is on sale for $12 against one carrying a
$65 price tag?

How can you, the amateur tire buyer, plow your way through the complex language of tire sizes and plies, cords and studs, belts and biases, treads
and retreads—to find the best deal? How can *you* cut *your* tire bill without
sacrificing any vital aspect of safety?

TIRE BUYING RULES

• No matter whether you are buying tires as an option on a new car or
as a replacement for tires already on your car, your *best* guide to the *best* deal
is a reputable and conscientious dealer.

This is a fundamental rule in every area of purchasing—as this book
surely has underlined by now. A conscientious dealer will make an honest
effort to sell you the type of tires best suited to your driving needs. He will
make no bones about the cost difference between, say, white-wall tires and
plain black ones. He will not try to sell you super-duper (and super-costly)
sports car tires if "sporty" just isn't your automotive style. He will honor
his tire warranty, which also will save you money in the long run.

In general, the most reliable dealers are franchised dealers of nationally
known and advertised brands of tires, large mail order retailers, and established automobile service stations. Probably your best guide to a satisfactory dealer is a satisfied customer; query your car-owning friends about their
experiences with tire dealers in your area.

• Shop locally among reputable dealers, service stations, etc., and compare prices. Look for legitimate tire sales they may be having.

• Compare prices *and* warranties. Is mounting included? Sales tax? Balancing? How many miles—or months—does the warranty cover? Is there a
lifetime guarantee against road hazards? Today, some manufacturers will pay
part of the price of a new tire, if you accidentally run over an old muffler or a
beer bottle and their tire does not survive intact.

TIRE TRAPS—AND HOW TO AVOID THEM

• Do not, if it's at all possible, buy tires when you're in a hurry. An unscrupulous tire salesman operating along some desolate stretch of the interstate highway system may ask any price he wants to replace your blown-out tire.

• Steer clear of vague, extravagant performance claims which some tire salesmen continue to make. For example, "Stops 25 per cent quicker." (Quicker than what—a train?)

Or "50 per cent more traction." (Again, than what—ice skates?)

Or "Safety tested at 130 mph." (Just what does that *prove?*)

Such claims are utterly meaningless.

• Look out also for the unscrupulous tire dealer who advertises huge but misleading discounts. As with many other types of merchandise sold through this lure, the "original" prices may be pure fiction. Moreover, with tires, warranties are based on list—not sale—prices. Thus, when you get a discount from the advertised list price you must discount the guarantee by a like amount.

• Do not permit yourself to be pulled in by such come-ons as "Buy three tires and get the fourth free!" Real tire bargains do exist, and you may be able to find them by shopping carefully. But use your common sense: no profit-minded businessman is going to give anybody a free tire.

The extravagant claims, the misleading bargains, the fictitious price cuts—the above are the main tire traps in which you easily could lose money. But there are other pitfalls.

• When you buy new tires, insist that the dealer register your name and address and the identification numbers of every tire. This is required by federal law to enable tire companies to recall tires in the event a safety defect is discovered. Many dealers, though, continue to violate this law and, as of now, riding herd on the dealer is your *only* way of being warned if you have a potentially dangerous tire.

Tires which are cosmetically "blemished"—have smudged white sidewalls, for example—are *not* safety rejects if they have the initials "DOT" (for Department of Transportation) on the sidewall. Often, they are a bargain for you too if you can find them. But they may be sold with a reduced warranty or without any warranty at all.

Tire designations such as "first line," "one hundred level," "premium," are strictly subjective claims of tire quality. New national tire quality standards now rate tires according to high-speed performance, traction, and tread wear. The best high-speed tires are rated A, while those of minimum acceptable quality are rated C. Traction and tread wear are rated as a percentage of the values attained by a "control tire" built to DOT specifications. These ratings are molded into the tire and appear on a tag which explains the ratings.

Additional objective information is molded into the sidewall of the tire: size; maximum permissible inflation pressure; brand name and manufacturer's code number; composition of the cord; number of plies (sidewall and tread); tubeless or tube type; the word "radial" if the tire is a radial type; and "DOT" when the tire conforms to federal Motor Vehicle Safety Standards enforced by the U. S. Department of Transportation. Information helpful in choosing tires must be displayed on the glove compartment door of your car or in some other easily accessible place. This includes the vehicle weight, seating capacity, recommended cold tire inflation pressure for the vehicle's maximum loaded weight, and its recommended tire size.

A final point: *do not*, once you have decided which tires you want to buy, automatically permit the dealer from whom you are buying to put the tires on your car—*until* you know what he will charge (if anything) for this service. Exorbitant tire mounting fees can wipe out any savings you may have achieved in the tire purchase—and then some. If the charge is more than a couple of dollars per wheel, simply take the job to another service station.

RUNDOWN ON TIRE TYPES

Now, how do you find the best type of tire for *your* budget and *your* driving habits and *your* car? To help guide you through today's maze of jargon and baffling labels, here is a brief rundown on the major types of tires available today:

Bias ply tires: generally the least expensive available, have cords which wrap around the tire at an angle, tend to ride the most smoothly, and handle well at moderate speeds. Their disadvantage is they may wear out more rapidly than other types of tires.

Belted bias ply tires: cost somewhat more than plain bias ply but, to offset this price disadvantage, they wear longer; have a reinforcing belt of glass fiber or some other material running around the tire beneath the tread, which helps to reduce tread scuffing, and thus permits longer wear but at a cost of a somewhat harsher ride.

Radial ply tires: the highest-quality tire available today; have special plies running straight across the treads, tire-chain style, and a stiff belt (sometimes made of steel) beneath the tread; wear long, handle very well, are capable of improving gas mileage by 3 to 10 per cent. Although one of the most costly categories of tires, their quality, safety features, and the "hidden" gas economy they allow make them the top premium tire.

WHICH IS LEAST EXPENSIVE FOR YOU?

Use this rough guide to make your own price comparisons as you shop:

A radial ply tire will last about 40,000 miles.
A belted bias ply tire will last about 25,000 miles.
A good bias ply tire will last 15,000 to 20,000 miles.

You can figure out the tire cost per mile in each category depending on the going prices in your area but you may be surprised to discover that the "premium" radial ply tires are the least expensive—particularly when you include your gasoline savings over a distance of 40,000 miles.

If you do not intend to drive your car this long, though, you may not want to make such a large long-term investment in expensive tires. Or, if you do not drive a great deal or at very high speeds or with heavy loads, less expensive tires may be the most economical type for you.

The major factors to consider in choosing your tires are: the type of car you drive, the amount of 60 mph (or over) driving you do, the type of roads you ride on, the type of loads you carry in your car, the number of miles you cover during the year, and how you handle your car—in terms of starting, stopping, and cornering.

If yours is a heavier car, if you do most of your driving on superhighways or rough country roads and if you put at least 15,000 miles on your car each year, radial or belted bias tires are probably the most economical choice for you.

If you drive 10,000 miles or less each year and do less than 30 per cent of your driving at high speeds, your best bet probably is a belted bias or a good conventional bias ply tire.

If you are a sports car buff and want optimum performance from your tires, the radial or belted bias types also will be best for you.

If you are driving over rough or rocky roads or carrying heavy loads, you need heavy-duty tires built to take hard treatment. Ask your dealer—and if he cannot or will not answer your questions satisfactorily, go to another dealer who will.

SNOW TIRES

Snow tires are available in all major tire types, and usually cost more than summer tires of comparable quality. In snowy climates, snow tires more than pay for themselves through reduced accident risks and towing charges.

Usually, the open, heavier treads have better traction in snow and mud but build heat and wear poorly on dry pavement, so be guided in your choice of tread style by the prevalence of snow where you drive most.

Most snow tires can be bought with steel-jacketed tungsten carbide studs, usually for $5.00 to $10 extra per tire. Studs significantly improve traction on hard-packed snow or ice but they decrease traction slightly on wet or clear roads or on ice at subzero temperatures. Thus they are *not* a good buy if you do most of your driving in the city or on main roads in a climate where snow does not stay on roads long. Also studs are much more effective on radial ply tires than on any other kind.

FINAL HINTS

You have now decided what general type of tire you want. Your next questions: Should they be tube or tubeless? What size? How many plies? What type cord material?

Buy the size recommended in your car owner's manual or, in the case of snow tires, at most one size larger.

For the majority of uses, two plies of modern cord materials are sufficient. Federal tire standards rate tires according to their load-carrying ability, a far more useful yardstick than a statement of the number of plies. The total load capacity of four tires should be equal to the weight of your car, fully loaded.

Caution: Do *not* combine radial tires with bias ply or belted bias tires on the same axle. If you buy radial tires (or wide tires) buy four if you can; otherwise put a pair on the drive wheels first, and a pair on the rolling wheels later.

Retreaded tires now cost somewhat more than half the prices of comparable new tires. An undamaged casing, properly retreaded, is no more likely to fail than a new tire. And warranties now being offered on retreads are similar to those available on new tires.

How can you buy retreads most safely?

Again, the most fundamental of fundamental rules comes first: *buy from a good dealer, who gets his retreads from a shop which does quality work and inspects used tires carefully before retreading them.*

Have your own used tires retreaded, since you know how they have been used (or abused) to date. Having your own casings recapped costs less than $20 per tire. If you go this route, shop for a good recapping firm. An excellent way to avoid the risks of poor-quality work is to deal with firms which also do fleet work—e.g., for taxi companies or government agencies.

If you deal with a reputable recapper, and *if* the quality of his work is indisputable, you can consider retreads as good as new tires and thus save a substantial amount on your tire bill. Caution: Tires for passenger cars should *never* be retreaded more than once, and a reputable firm will refuse to do so.

Finally, *avoid* the false economy of riding around on near-bald tires—to get the last sixteenth of an inch of wear from them. If you are one of these "economizers," note this warning by the Tire Industry Safety Council: A bald or near-bald tire is far more likely to skid on a wet road than one with adequate amount of tread; *and* a tire with less than 1/16 inch of tread is eighteen times more likely to blow out or be punctured than one with more than this amount of tread. Among the new federal safety regulations covering tires is a requirement that manufacturers include wear indicators which show as smooth, narrow bands across the tread so you can tell when only 1/16 inch of tread remains. Look for this indicator as your tires wear down. After it appears *you are risking your life.*

HOW TO INSURE YOUR CAR

NO-FAULT AUTO INSURANCE IS HERE

At last, our monstrous system of automobile insurance is in the process of a complete overhaul. Many of the inequities—e.g., in the insurance rates *good* drivers pay to make up for the sins of bad drivers—are disappearing. What is emerging is a brand-new system in which every insured accident victim is being paid for lost wages, medical expenses, and other direct economic losses—*whether the accident was his fault or not*. The traditional huge payoff for "pain and suffering," often negotiated in costly liability court proceedings, is being scrapped. Taking its place is a nationwide system of no-fault auto insurance, starting with individual state laws and going on to the clear prospect that these laws will become subject to federal no-fault standards. In essence, our automobile insurance companies are relinquishing their roles as punishers of reckless drivers.

HOW YOU CAN SLASH YOUR INSURANCE COSTS

Go over the following analysis with your insurance agent if you have any reason to believe you are not now getting the full advantage of discounts and reductions available to you.

• Decide first what types and amounts of coverage you need; then check the costs of the coverage you want offered through auto dealers and from reputable insurance agents and firms. One good approach is to solicit bids for your business from several reputable insurers. Reason: rates for liability coverage alone can vary by as much as 50 per cent from one insurer to the next in a given area.

Use this chart to make cost comparisons:

		Rates Quoted		
COVERAGE	AMT. OF LIMITS	Co. A	Co. B	Co. C
Liability	. . . / . . . / . . .	——	——	——
Medical payments		——	——	——
Personal injury protection		——	——	——
Uninsured motorist		——	——	——
Collision	. . . deductible	——	——	——
Comprehensive	. . . deductible	——	——	——

• Find out if such "extras" as towing and temporary car rental costs are included in each package.

• Check the reputations of dealers for financial soundness in *Best's Insurance Reports* and try to stick to dealers with a *Best's* rating of A or A+. This is only a guideline; many reputable dealers have lesser ratings.

• If you are a student, enroll in a recognized driver training course to qualify for a 5 to 10 per cent premium cut. Nearly 14,000 schools in the United States now offer these courses. In addition, the National Safety Council has launched a "Defensive Driving Course" whose graduates in some states are being offered substantial premium reductions.

• If you are a student age sixteen or over with a high (B or better) scholastic average, you'll be eligible for a "good student" discount of up to 25 per cent. You also may get a substantial discount if you attend a school more than a hundred road miles from home or wherever the family car is kept.

• Explore, if you are a young driver, the possibility of getting a "restricted" policy, using your family's coattails as a form of financial security.

• If you change your commuting habits—switch from a car to a train or bus—notify your insurer at once so he can reduce your premium rate accordingly.

• If you are an older person, ask about special policies and discounts offered by most companies based on your age bracket's good driving record. In many states, the typical discount for drivers over age sixty-five is 5 per cent.

• If you drive your car fewer than 6,500 miles a year, check whether you're eligible for as much as a 10 per cent rate cut.

• If you quit smoking or drinking, find out whether your company offers reductions for non-smokers or teetotalers.

• If you work for a large company or are a member of a union, social, or professional group, check whether you can get low-cost group auto insurance. If not, find out whether a local insurance company will develop this low-cost insurance for your group. This *alone* can cut your own premiums 15 per cent or more.

• Check carefully what's offered by a reputable mail order insurer; savings could run to 15 per cent.

• If the dealer from whom you are buying a car offers you collision or comprehensive insurance as part of the deal (to protect himself or the firm which is financing your purchase), find out whether your local insurance company or agent will offer you a lower-cost deal.

• If you already have health insurance, make sure you are not taking on medical payments coverage which duplicates the coverage in your group or individual health insurance policy. Today, more than four out of five Americans are covered by medical insurance, and some auto insurance policies rule out duplicate payment if your health insurance policy already fully covers you. (On the other hand, you might want to *increase* your medical payments coverage if you regularly drive a group of children to school or fellow commuters to work.)

• If you move from one state to another, inquire immediately about auto insurance rates, for these rates vary widely in the United States today. For example, the cost of $50/$100,000 bodily injury liability insurance on a recent-model Chevrolet Impala four-door sedan driven by a thirty-year-old married man with a clean driving record was $34 in Bismarck, North Dakota, against $126 in New York City. Comprehensive coverage for this same man and vehicle was $50 in Bismarck in contrast to $122 in New York.

• If you're a farmer or rancher and use your car or pickup truck only on and around your farm or range, check on your eligibility for a farmer's auto insurance discount.

• If you're buying a new car, keep in mind that rates on a "muscle" or high-performance car may run 20 to 50 per cent higher than average. If you buy an inexpensive or low-powered car, though, you will be charged a lower-than-average premium.

• If you are unmarried and you insure your car in your family's name, stating that you are the principal driver, you are likely to pay a lower insurance premium than if the car is registered in your name and you are listed as the sole driver.

• If you are a family head, insure all the family cars under the same policy: a second family car generally can be insured at a discount of about 20 per cent on the grounds that two cars in one family are likely to be exposed to less risk than two single cars would be.

• And save by paying your premiums annually.

• Inquire about any less well known discounts which your insurance company might offer—for instance, discounts of up to 20 per cent for models with bumpers that meet certain damage-resistance standards.

• Don't file collision claims which are just over your deductible or you may lose your "good driver" discount.

• Leave your car outside the city limits; your rates won't be as high if you can show you don't bring your car into a city. If you park your car in a garage, tell your agent; this could qualify you for lower rates than regular on-street parking.

• *But* over and above all the preceding moneysaving hints is this single best way you, the average automobile owner, can slash your auto insurance premiums on your own: *up all* your present auto insurance deductibles.

Typically, the deductible on collision coverage is $100, but considerably higher deductibles are available—and if you sign up for higher deductibles, you'll save substantially on premiums. To illustrate, if $100 deductible collision coverage costs you $50, your cost with a $250 deductible will be only $30 and with a $500 deductible only $23.

Similarly, if full comprehensive coverage now costs you $50, the cost will drop to $28 if you tack on a $50 deductible and to $21 if you up the deductible to $100.

If your car is more than three years old, or a jalopy worth less than $1,000, you may find it's not worth it to carry collision insurance at all.

You also might simply make your coverage a little less comprehensive. Normally, comprehensive insurance protects you not only against fire and theft but also, if you wish, against a whole list of other perils including flying or falling objects, explosions, vandalism, earthquakes, windstorms, hail, water, floods, civil commotions, riots, and collision with a bird or animal. To illustrate the possible savings, if you are now paying a $30 annual premium for full comprehensive coverage, you might pay only $9.00 a year for insurance against fire and theft only.

The important point to remember about automobile insurance is that it is intended to protect you against a financial catastrophe, especially if you do not have other means of protecting yourself against such a catastrophe.

Automobile insurance (and this also goes for other types of insurance) was *never* intended to help you budget. It was never designed to pay for small repair bills for which you ought to be able to budget routinely. Common sense should urge you to trade off a higher deductible for a higher upper range of liability coverage.

A typical car owner carries at least a minimum "10/20/5" (see "Liability Limits," page 340) auto liability insurance policy—the minimum required under state "financial responsibility" laws. (Some states require 15/30/5 or even 20/40/10.) But if you should be found responsible for a fatal accident, the jury verdict against you easily could amount to $50,000, $100,000 or even $1 million and up.

Here, then, is a table showing you the typical—minor—cost of raising your present bodily injury liability coverage to meaningful levels.

COVERAGE	TYPICAL YEARLY PREMIUM COST
$ 10– 20,000	$50.00
25– 50,000	59.50
50–100,000	65.00
100–300,000	70.50

IF YOUR INSURANCE IS CANCELED

You have not had an auto accident and your driving performance generally has been good—but suddenly your auto insurance policy is not renewed. Or suppose you do have a rotten driving record and you're having trouble getting any insurance coverage at all. What should you do?

Countless millions of you have been exposed to the frustrations of these typical auto insurance problems. If this includes you now or in the future, here's what you should do:

If your policy is not renewed, first contact the agent or salesman who sold you the policy and find out why. In many instances the non-renewal may have nothing to do with your driving record. For instance, the agent may no longer be doing business with that company or the company may have withdrawn from your area. You then may find the agent already has switched your policy and you have no problem at all.

If you learn that the non-renewal was for cause and feel this is unwarranted, write the company. In most states an auto insurer is required to provide an explanation if you, the policyholder, ask for it. If the non-renewal is related to a change in your credit standing, you have the right to know the name and address of the credit rating bureau so you can check your credit file and correct any misinformation that may have crept into it.

If you find erroneous information about you or your driving record in the insurer's files, it is essential for your own benefit that you correct it. If, on the other hand, the non-renewal had nothing to do with your personal characteristics, this information will be helpful when you seek coverage from another company.

IF YOU'RE A BAD RISK

Among the strikes against you when you go to buy auto insurance today in addition to your accident or conviction record—if it's a bad one:

> your age—if you're under thirty;
>
> your race—if you're non-white;
>
> your residence—if it's in a city ghetto.

If you're an American under twenty-five years old, and particularly a single American male, you may be paying a penalty of as much as four times the automobile insurance rates being paid by other drivers.

You pay so much more for automobile insurance simply because your age bracket has the highest accident rate in the nation. Traffic accidents, in fact, are responsible for one half of all deaths of Americans between age fifteen and twenty-five.

If you have trouble getting any auto insurance, shop around. Many insurers have companion companies that specialize in insuring those with a higher-than-average risk exposure. If your insurance agent is unable to get coverage for you, apply to the Automobile Insurance Plan. Every state, except Maryland, has an AIP and any licensed agent can handle your application. (In Maryland, the AIP was replaced in 1973 by a state-run agency called the Maryland Auto Insurance Fund.) States usually require companies in the plan to keep bad risks at least three years. Most drivers can get regular insurance after a three-year good driving record.

The rates charged for insurance in the AIPs are the same as those charged in the regular market in some states and are slightly higher—typically, 5 to 15 per cent higher—in others. Drivers with poor records, though, always pay higher rates whether they are in or out of an AIP.

In shopping for high-risk insurance coverage, watch out for the gypsters. Beware of advertised rates which are suspiciously below those charged by other insurers in your area for your risk category.

If you question the legitimacy of *any* high-risk mail order insurer (and note: *most* are legitimate and do offer insurance below rates charged by insurers with elaborate offices and sales organizations), inquire about the insurer's reputation at your State Insurance Department or State Commissioner of Insurance. And check *Best's Insurance Guide* for the record of financial soundness of any high-risk mail order company with which you're considering doing business.

If all else fails, and if your previous policy has been canceled for reasons you consider to be unfair—send a written complaint to your State Insurance Commissioner, with copies to your local Better Business Bureau and also your congressman. And find out what limitations (if any) your state may put on auto insurance cancellations.

THE BAFFLEGAB OF AUTO INSURANCE

ADJUSTER: Employee or agent of an insurance company whose job it is to help settle auto insurance claims by deciding the extent of financial loss in an accident, and also the extent of the insurance company's liability.

APPRAISAL: Estimate of the amount of loss sustained by a car in an accident —which becomes the basis for a settlement by the insurance company.

ASSIGNED-RISK PLANS (or *Automobile Insurance Plans*): Plans in operation in all fifty states, the District of Columbia, and Puerto Rico, which sell barebones protection to drivers who cannot otherwise get liability coverage.

BAD RISKS: Individuals whom the auto insurance industry labels such bad drivers, with such bad accident records or such poor statistical odds of keeping out of an accident, that they are required to pay extra-high insurance premiums—even assuming they can be insured at all through regular channels.

BODILY INJURY LIABILITY INSURANCE: Pays damages and legal costs if your car kills or injures people in an accident and only if the driver of your car is at fault.

CANCELLATION: Termination—by you or by your insurance company—of your auto insurance policy before it actually expires. Rules for cancellation of auto insurance by the company should be spelled out in the insurance contract.

CLAIM: Demand by an insured individual for the amount of his or her loss insured and covered by the insurance policy. A *claimant* is the person making a claim.

CLASSIFICATION: Categorization of insured individuals according to the extent of risk they represent—statistically—to the company. Taken into account are the individual's occupation, age, similar factors.

COLLISION INSURANCE: Insurance which pays for damage to *your car* if you collide with another car or object, or turn your car over. If an accident is clearly the other fellow's fault and if he has liability insurance, his policy probably would pay to have your car repaired or replaced. However, if there's no way to prove whose fault the accident was, or if the other person involved isn't insured, collision insurance helps cover losses.

COMMISSIONER OF INSURANCE (or *Superintendent of Insurance* or *Director of Insurance*): Key official in your state whose job it is to oversee and enforce the state's auto insurance laws.

COMPREHENSIVE INSURANCE: Insurance which pays for damage to your car from a variety of mishaps other than collision, including not only fire and theft, but also damage from missiles, falling objects, larceny, explosion, earthquake, lightning, windstorm, hail, water, broken glass, flood, malicious mischief or vandalism, riot or civil commotion, and collision with a bird or animal. Comprehensive insurance also covers the cost of renting a car if yours is stolen.

CREAM: The best drivers—statistically speaking—and, therefore, also the best auto insurance risks. These pay the lowest premiums and include Americans over age sixty-five, women over age twenty-five, and middle-aged family men.

DEDUCTIBLE INSURANCE: Coverage under which a policyholder agrees to pay up to a specified sum in each claim or accident toward the total amount of the insured loss. The higher the deductible, the lower your premium.

DOC (Drive Other Cars) INSURANCE: Coverage which protects you, the driver, against liability or bodily injury or property damage while you are driving a borrowed car or a company car.

FINANCIAL RESPONSIBILITY LAWS: State laws under which car owners are required to prove they are financially responsible—a requirement most people meet by owning a certain minimum dollar amount of auto insurance. Such proof is required either to register a car or to preserve your right to return to the road after you have had an accident.

FULL COVERAGE: Coverage for the full amount of covered losses, without any deductibles.

GUARANTEED RENEWABLE: Insurance policy which the covered individual may renew up to a certain age (e.g., sixty or sixty-five) or over a certain specified number of years.

LIABILITY INSURANCE: Protection against claims in the event you injure or kill someone else—or damage his property. This insurance covers legal expenses and also protects others driving your car with your permission, and it protects you and members of your family when you drive someone else's car with their permission.

LIABILITY LIMITS: Maximum amount for which you are covered by a given policy—frequently expressed by a succession of three numbers separated by slashes, designating maximum coverage for bodily injury and for property damage. For example, "10/20/5" means insurance protection of up to $10,-000 payable to any one accident victim in an accident caused by you; up to $20,000 in protection for *all* victims in such an accident; and up to $5,000 in insurance protection against property damage caused by your car to other cars, other people's garages, etc.

MEDICAL PAYMENTS: Coverage of a wide range of "reasonable" medical or funeral expenses within a year of an accident not only for the car owner but also for reasonable expenses of any other people who are injured or killed in his car. Medical payments coverage also applies to the policyholder and members of his family while riding in or being struck by any other car. Payment is made no matter who caused the accident.

NO-FAULT: Type of automobile insurance under which an accident victim is automatically compensated for part or all of his medical costs, wage losses, and other expenses associated with the accident by his own insurance company, without regard to who caused the accident.

NON-OWNERSHIP AUTOMOBILE LIABILITY: Liability coverage for loss or damage caused by you while you are driving a car not owned by you.

PAIN AND SUFFERING: Vague, albeit very real, category of claim in auto liability lawsuits for financial compensation to cover intangible losses such as fright, mental anguish, emotional shock, etc.

PROPERTY DAMAGE LIABILITY INSURANCE: Insurance which protects you if your car damages another person's property, and if driver of your car is at fault. This usually means the other person's car, but it also can mean Japanese gardens, garages, lampposts, telephone poles, and buildings.

RISK: Insured person or thing. In the case of your automobile insurance coverage, you and your car are the principal "risks."

SAFE DRIVER PLAN: Widely used system under which insurance rates are adjusted up or down according to your own driving record.

SCRAP VALUE: Estimated value of a car which has been involved in an accident if it were sold as junk.

TOTAL LOSS: Car which has been so badly damaged that it is not considered to be worth repairing.

UNINSURED MOTORIST INSURANCE: Insurance, sometimes called family protection, which covers you, all members of your family, and any guests in your car for bodily injury losses when an uninsured or flagrant hit-and-run driver causes the accident. This type of insurance also pays medical bills and income loss due to bodily injury if the insurance company of the other driver, who caused the accident, goes bankrupt. And it covers you and all members of your family who are injured by uninsured or hit-and-run drivers, while you are walking or riding on bicycles. Payments are limited to the required liability minimums in your state. In some states, this insurance does *not* pay for bodily injuries.

UNSATISFIED JUDGMENT FUND: An alternative, in a few states, to uninsured motorist coverage, for this is a fund against which you may file a claim if you are hit by an uninsured motorist.

How to Insure Your Motorcycle

FATAL FACTS

If you're among the nation's 3.5 million-plus motorcyclists—or if you are planning to join this expanding army soon—you'll have to face these facts: You are just about the most unloved driver there is. You will be forced to pay big premiums by insurance companies in order to get liability coverage and you will find it is far less comprehensive than similar coverage for an automobile. You will simply be unable to get certain coverages which are typical for cars—at any price.

The reason motorcyclists are getting so cold a shoulder from the insurers is that the danger of a fatal motorcycle accident is four times as great as the chance of this accident in a car. In the mid-1970s, says the National Safety Council, more than 325,000 motorcycles, motor scooters and motorbikes were involved in accidents each year and thousands of them were fatal.

So far as the insurers are concerned, the under-thirty age group is the worst—simply because the highest rate of motorcycle deaths are found in this group. Nearly seven out of ten motorcycle drivers involved in accidents are between the ages of sixteen and twenty-four.

Motorcycle insurance rates, like car insurance rates, vary from state to state and from area to area within the state, and from company to company too. If you can't get this insurance from your regular auto insurance company, you'll probably have to seek out a company in your area which specializes in this type of insurance.

Insurance coverage for a motorcycle may differ radically from ordinary car insurance. Many liability insurance policies for motorcycles, for example, do not cover passengers on the cycle. Under many motorcycle liability insurance policies, coverage is limited to the owner-driver himself—and doesn't cover any other operators. Also, liability coverage may become invalid if a driver is speeding or racing. In addition, many motorcycle policies exclude coverage for medical payments for injuries to the operator.

It is vitally important to check with your insurance agent to make sure you know just what is and what is not covered.

HOW COSTS COMPARE

Just how much more expensive is motorcycle insurance than car insurance? It depends on where you live, how old you are, what your own driving record has been, on a number of other factors. But here are a few general hints on how costs compare and how possible savings stack up:

If your cycle has an engine size under 200 c.c., it will cost relatively less to insure than one with a larger-sized engine.

If your cycle weighs 300 pounds or less, the premium for liability insurance coverage in most states will be about 60 per cent of the basic auto insurance rate. (In a few cases it will be only one half the car rate.)

But, if you are an unmarried man under thirty years of age your cost of insuring this motorcycle will be about 150 per cent of the basic auto insurance rate—about the same rate an unmarried man in his mid-twenties would pay for insurance on his automobile.

If your cycle weighs more than 300 pounds you will have to pay double the rate for the smaller bikes—or about 220 per cent of the basic automobile insurance rate.

If you are an unmarried male under age thirty and you are riding a 300-pound-plus cycle, you will have to pay 300 per cent of the basic auto premium rate in order to insure it. This is approximately what an unmarried teen-age boy would pay for insurance on a car.

And what if you can't find motorcycle insurance through normal sources of auto insurance? As with cars, the insurers operate assigned-risk pools in every state for high-risk motorcyclists as well as high-risk car drivers.

How to Curb Your Auto Repair Bills

A MONSTROUS DRAIN

By one estimate, a monstrous $8 to $10 billion of our $25 to $30 billion annual bill for auto repairs and maintenance goes down the drain—in the form of repairs improperly done, repairs unnecessarily performed, or repairs promised and not done at all.

If you are lucky, you won't need any major auto repairs until your car has gone 20,000 miles or more. And many repair bills will be paid for through your warranty. After that mark, though, you well may face a parade of minor repairs: brake relining; reconditioning of brake drums; possibly an alternator overhaul; replacement of cylinders, hoses, shock absorbers, muffler and/or other parts of the exhaust system, battery and numerous smaller parts of the electrical system ranging from headlights to the voltage regulator and ignition coil. You're also likely to be confronted with a variety of problems involving the various pumps—water, oil, and fuel—that help keep your car running.

If you keep your car past the 50,000 milestone, you almost surely will need some major repairs—a transmission overhaul or even a whole new transmission, a "valve job," involving extensive repair or replacement of your engine's valves and related parts. At this point, too, the likelihood also becomes all too real that you'll have to have your car's engine overhauled or even replaced at a cost of hundreds of dollars. Some of your car's complex options—air conditioning, power windows—also may start to fail.

Or if you are in a costly collision at any stage of your auto's life, you may face big-ticket repairs running into hundreds of dollars.

Larger, more expensive cars tend to cost more to repair than small ones. On the other side of the repair cost coin, though, is the fact that larger cars usually provide more "people protection" in the event of a higher-speed collision.

Now in effect are federal standards requiring certain "safety related" automobile components—such as lights, brakes, and suspensions—to operate "normally" after a car hits a test barrier at specified speeds an hour both head on and going backward. However, the federal standards do not cover damage to such key items as windshields and side and rear windows.

HOW TO SHOP FOR AN AUTO MECHANIC

• Start shopping for repairs *before* you need them. It's too late when your car conks out and you need service at once. Make a plan of action now; have a list of places you would take your car should you need minor repairs, major repairs, simple maintenance, etc.

• Check with your friends and acquaintances on their experiences with local auto repair shops.

• In states which license auto repair facilities, stick to the licensed establishments.

• Make a deliberate choice between your new car dealer, repair boys in local gas stations, independent general mechanics who do not sell gas, and shops in specialties such as brake relining, muffler replacement, or wheel alignment—and recognize you do have these four alternatives.

For instance, if you like the dealer from whom you bought the car and have come to trust him, his shop is probably your best bet. He is apt to give you good, fairly priced service in the hope that you will also buy your next car from him. And he probably will be familiar with your car's quirks and will have an ample stock of the parts the car is most likely to need. But if the dealer from whom you bought seems not interested in servicing, go elsewhere.

Convenience is the key advantage of a local service station—and you easily can establish a valuable relationship with a station if you buy your gas there and take your car to the station for regular servicing. Here too, look for the proprietor who considers his service area a major part of his gas station operation. Many gas stations are not equipped for complex repairs, though, and—as a result—generate customer complaints.

Your third alternative is the independent mechanic whose earnings depend primarily on repairs and servicing, his ability and reputation. The independent, though, may not be as conveniently located as a gas station, may not be able to do repairs on as short notice as an automobile dealer—and may not have as complex a line of special tools and parts as the dealer.

For some types of work—such as muffler replacement or brake relining—you may be able to save money by patronizing a specialty shop which does a large volume of repairs in these areas and which has accumulated all the special equipment, parts, and expertise needed to perform them. But carefully check out the reputation of any outside specialty shop before you turn your back on your regular mechanic. And remember that these shops are sometimes highly skilled at selling you repairs you don't need.

• Whatever type of establishment you choose to patronize for repairs, note whether the mechanic and/or owner solicits your repeat business. The competent, honest shop will want you back. Its mechanics will schedule work with as much regard for your convenience as possible; will explain as much about the repairs your car needs as you seem capable of absorbing. They will take the time to make a careful diagnosis of your car's problem instead of casually informing you, "That sounds like your 'whatzit' and will cost $20 to fix." They even may tell you the work you thought you needed isn't necessary until later—or isn't needed at all.

• Look for a membership certificate for the Better Business Bureau or the Independent Garage Owners of America.

• Try to find a place where you can talk face to face with the man who will actually work on your car. In many shops, the customer sees only a person who writes work orders for the mechanics to follow. This fellow is primarily a salesman, rather than a mechanic. He well may be working on a commission basis, so that the more repairs and parts he sells you the more he earns. If you speak directly with the mechanic, you're less likely to be talked into unnecessary or inappropriate service. Also, two-way communication is much clearer than a few words scrawled on a service order. And the mechanic is likely to feel more responsibility toward the job if he has discussed it with you personally.

If an establishment won't let you speak directly to the mechanic, even when you indicate you're willing to pay for the time he spends talking to you, go elsewhere.

• Consider taking a course on auto mechanics at a local extension college, night school, or similar place. Even if you never work on a car, it will help you to evaluate the mechanical competence of others.

• Be your own mechanic whenever possible, if you're capable and so inclined. First you'll save money—most obviously on simple repairs, for which you pay a skilled mechanic the same hourly rate as for complicated ones. With a little practice, you'll also be assured that what you do is done right. Most important, you'll become better acquainted with your car's workings and will be less easily baffled or intimidated by a serviceman if a breakdown occurs on the road.

In some areas, do-it-yourself auto service centers, which rent repair bays and tools (at $3.00 to $4.00 or so an hour, depending on the equipment you use), make it easier to do at least some of your own work. They may even provide free advice if you run into problems. If there is no such facility in your area, there may be one soon: the idea is catching on fast. Savings, even after rental fees, can run to 75 per cent on some jobs.

• Look for reasonably detailed estimates on repairs which also indicate what work may be optional. A good repair shop will itemize parts on its bill and the parts which mechanics have taken from your car will be available for you to inspect and keep (if you wish). And although labor probably will not be itemized among repairs—very difficult to do and would cost more than it is worth—the mechanic can estimate the proportion of his time devoted to each job.

• Give preference to shops willing to warrant their work. For instance, many dealers will now guarantee repair work for 4,000 miles or 90 days.

• If you suspect you have been overcharged for any parts, demand to see the suppliers' parts price list—giving both wholesale and estimated retail prices on parts of every description. To this you must add labor costs, of course. If a mechanic refuses to show you his copy of this book, be warned. You may have been gypped this time. Start looking at once for another shop to patronize the next time you need service.

• Once you have found a mechanic or service repair station you feel confident will give you honest, skilled, and reliable service, stay put. Many service stations automatically separate their customers into either regular, bread-and-butter business or once-in-a-while customers. And, understandably enough, they tend to provide better treatment for the regulars—a great help when your car won't start on a bitter subzero morning.

• Whenever possible, make an appointment in advance for work you want done. This makes your mechanic's job easier, more profitable, and ultimately more economical for you.

• Try to avoid scheduling work on Mondays or Fridays, the busiest times in any repair shop.

• When you ask for a tune-up, or any other collection of procedures customarily lumped under one term, be sure you and your mechanic know exactly what you mean. There are nearly as many definitions of a tune-up as there are mechanics.

• When you discuss your problems with a mechanic, describe symptoms rather than giving your opinion on what needs fixing. Your view will tend to prejudice even a good mechanic and can lead to a wrong diagnosis.

• If you cannot wait to see the mechanic, leave a note on your windshield, describing what you want done if you have particular services in mind, and problem symptoms if a diagnosis is necessary. Leave your name and phone number, and leave instructions such as: "Call me before making additional repairs."

• Whenever you deal with the service writer in a large shop, make your own list of what you want done, date it, and sign it. The service writer can staple your list to his to have your signature. This will protect you from having additions made to the service order after you leave and will permit you to refuse to pay for work you did not request.

HOW AND WHERE TO SHOP FOR BIG-TICKET REPAIRS

How can you tell if, say, a new transmission or an engine overhaul is really needed?

A transmission overhaul is among the first big, costly repair jobs your car is likely to need—and it's a job that easily could pit you against some of the biggest swindlers in the auto repair business today. This is a reconditioning of the unit which transmits the power that moves your car from the car's engine to its wheels. Among the key symptoms of trouble are: puddles of fluid on your driveway; erratic gear shifting or refusal to shift at all; engine racing between shifts.

But these symptoms do not necessarily mean you need a complete transmission overhaul costing from $100 to $250. Erratic shifting can often be corrected by adding fluid or by quick and inexpensive repairs; leakage of transmission fluid frequently can be corrected for less than $65.

To find out just what kind of transmission work is required, a mechanic *must,* at a minimum, road-test the car and make a close inspection. In some instances, he must disassemble the transmission to determine exactly what is needed. For this diagnosis, you must expect to pay a reasonable fee. Beware, though, of the repair shop that will refuse to reassemble your transmission without being paid a whopping amount. Check into this with care *before* the shop takes apart your whole transmission.

Steer clear of any outfit which advertises a transmission overhaul at a flat rate—especially a ridiculously low rate of, say, less than $75. Don't be misled by claims that your transmission needs only an "adjustment." Most modern automatic transmissions cannot be adjusted at all, and even in older ones little adjustment is possible. Don't be taken in by a mechanic who shows you metal filings in the bottom of your automatic transmission case and says you need a complete overhaul—some metal filings are a normal result of using the transmission.

Also be just as cautious about a "valve job"—another category of big-ticket auto repairs which can cost up to $150 or more. Although a rough-running engine, lack of power, and declining gas mileage are symptoms of poor valves, here too they may be signs of other problems as well. A properly performed compression test is a *must* for a correct diagnosis of sick valves. Be suspicious of any repairman who says you need a valve job without doing this test.

Now, what about an engine overhaul? If your car's performance falls off drastically, a complete engine overhaul may become necessary at a cost of $150 to $800. But as an alternative to an overhaul, you might buy a rebuilt engine. Assuming the engine has been properly rebuilt by a qualified factory, it is virtually the equivalent of a new engine, and factory-rebuilt engines are commonly referred to as "new." The costs of the engine overhaul and the rebuilt engine will be about the same, but the rebuilt engine usually can be installed a lot faster than the repair shop can perform an overhaul. Your old engine will normally be taken in trade, rebuilt, and later sold to someone else—which certainly should warn you to be sure the engine you are buying is actually *rebuilt* and not simply used.

"Motor exchangers" deal in rebuilt engines and some of these offer a worth-while service at fair prices. But the motor exchange business is loaded with unscrupulous fringe operators who resort to just about any lure you can name to get your patronage and your money. Here is a sampling of the myths they use to trap you:

MOTOR REPAIR MYTHS

Myth No. 1: "Your motor can be replaced for a low flat rate." You, the customer, are told over the phone that the cost of a motor for your car will be "$129.80, exchange." The conversation quickly switches to where and when the operator can pick up your car. What he does *not* tell you is that there will be an additional charge of $40 for such items as installation, gaskets, oil, perhaps a "federal tax." Nor are you told of the $30 to $35 charge to be made if your engine block turns out to be damaged "beyond repair." Nor does the dealer mention that the $129.80 price omits a lot more parts you need just to make your car run. Upshot: after the old motor has been removed, you discover you must pay $208 for other parts and accessories, for a new total of $337.80.

Myth No. 2: "Make no down payment; take 18 months to pay." Few motor exchanges extend their own credit. In most cases, you must pay cash for your repairs and arrange your own loan with a financial institution.

Myth No. 3: "We can give you one-day service." Under ideal circumstances, an engine can be installed in one day, but it doesn't happen very often. You must be prepared to wait several days until space becomes available in the shop or while your loan application is being approved.

Myth No. 4: "You get a 10,000-mile guarantee in writing." But nothing is said about the time limit on this guarantee—which may be as short as 30 days.

Avoid repair shops which give you bargain basement estimates on accident repairs; they also may do low-quality work and your insurance company is almost surely willing to pay the cost of a decent job.

Be warned: Once your car is in the shop and is being dismantled, you're over the barrel.

THE QUICK AND DIRTY TRICKS AWAY FROM HOME

What if your car unexpectedly grinds to a halt on a trip, hundreds or even thousands of miles from your home where you know nothing about the local service stations and there's no Better Business Bureau to call?

Although most service stations on the road are no more anxious to swindle you than those near home, some "last chance" stations actually specialize in "skinning the dude"—especially along lonely stretches of the nation's 42,500-mile interstate highway system. They may try to sell you an oil change or a new oil filter by flashing a dipstick covered with "dirty" oil (all oil in a car looks "dirty" after a few minutes of circulation in the engine). Or some swindlers will actually slash your tires ("honking") while you aren't looking in order to sell you new ones. Or they will refuse to remount tires they have removed until you agree to buy a new set (at an exorbitant price, of course).

Or they will tell you your tires have dangerous "flaws" and must be replaced. The gullible itinerant may not only get talked into buying an expensive set of new tires, she or he also will leave the "old" still good tires behind. While your car is jacked up for new tires, they may wobble the front wheels as "proof" you need new ball joints too—but all suspension systems are designed to have some looseness when the weight is off the wheels.

Among their other quick and dirty tricks:

draining the acid out of a battery cell, replacing it with plain water, then "proving" the battery is dead by a hydrometer check;

bending windshield wiper blades and pointing out you need new ones;

"boiling batteries"—putting an alkali such as baking soda or Alka-Seltzer in a battery to make it foam and appear damaged or dead or pouring soapy water on the top to produce the same appearance;

"short sticking"—pouring "oil" from an empty can;

"short thumbing"—or not pushing the dipstick all the way in;

"the liquid smoke trick"—inducing smoke from an engine by spraying it with chemicals;

puncturing radiator hoses;

slashing the fan belt;

switching ignition wires around to make the engine run roughly or not at all;

bending wires on the alternator to make the red warning light glow;

squirting oil on the engine to simulate a leaking fuel pump or oil pump;

filling the gas tank from one pump and charging the higher amount registered on an adjacent pump;

altering amounts or adding sums to the credit card slip after you leave —or imprinting blank bills with your card to be filled in after you have gone.

Then there are "freeway runners"—advance men who hang around exits shouting friendly warnings of wobbly wheels to terrified travelers and thereby forcing them to head for the nearest service station where, of course, collaborating con artists are waiting.

HOW TO AVOID THE TRICKS ON A TRIP

To avoid these fast-buck maneuvers, stand by and carefully watch all operations performed at any service station whose reputation is unknown to you.

If you suspect your oil has been incorrectly checked, ask to have the check repeated.

Watch the gas tank filling operations.

Don't leave your car unattended, and if you must, even for a few minutes, lock your doors.

If you want to use the rest room, lock your car and do so *before* you even talk to the service people about your car's problems.

Check the credit card slip for the correct amount before you sign and save your copies to check your bill at home before paying. Never let your credit card out of your sight.

Have your car checked regularly for possible trouble spots: e.g., tire tread, fan belt, battery, ignition and other electrical equipment, radiator hoses, spark plugs, brake fluid. Without fail, have this checkup done *before* you leave home for a long automobile trip.

Experts, in fact, say that if you're going to put on the miles—6,000 or more round trip—install a complete new or almost new set of tires before you go and take along a spare with as much tread as your regular tires. When you're pulling a camper, another two good spares are a must for the camper, if they're an odd, hard-to-get size.

If all precautions fail and you begin to suspect you are in trouble on a trip, heed the warning signals your car is putting out. *Stop early.* You will save the cost and nuisance of having to be towed off the highway. You'll also have a chance to shop around, rather than being forced to accept the services of whatever shop the tow truck delivers you to.

Make sure your travel budget earmarks at least $150 for automobile emergencies far from home.

Generally, the rules for finding reliable service on the road are the same as the ones you would use at home, but you'll have to substitute advice from the local Better Business Bureau and chapters of automobile clubs for the advice of friends. An additional tip: try to find a repair shop which is a member of the Independent Garage Owners of America. Members subscribe to a nationwide guarantee plan which provides that any member garage will make good on work done improperly by another.

How to Cut the High Cost of Accidents

THE DRIVE FOR SAFETY

Obviously spurring today's extraordinary auto safety drive are our persistently costly accident rates.

The annual death toll from auto accidents was more than 55,000 in the early years of this decade—plus another 5 million injured. The annual economic loss has been running to $20 billion, including car repairs, medical bills, lost wages, other losses related to accidents.

Today, the typical driver on American roads has about one chance in three of having an accident within a year.

HOW TO REDUCE YOUR ODDS ON AN AUTO ACCIDENT

What can *you* do to reduce the odds that you'll have an auto accident?

• At the very beginning, when you are looking for a new or used car, *comparison-shop for safety features*—just as you comparison-shop for options, comforts, economies. Ask car dealers you visit to give you the federally required free rundown on the safety aspects of each car you are considering—ranging from acceleration and passing ability to tire reserve loads and stopping distance.

• Before you buy a car, new or used, check whether the model and make you want has been the subject of a federal safety recall—and if so, for what reason.

• If you receive a recall notice on the car you already own, don't ignore it. Take in your car *immediately* for the suggested repairs and/or adjustments.

• Don't try to side-step your state's motor vehicle inspection laws—e.g., by sweet-talking an inspection station into overlooking such hazardous problems as too worn tires or a burned-out headlight or brakes on the blink. Have the recommended (and, remember, legally *required*) repairs performed promptly—and be grateful the problems have been spotted before they can kill you.

• *Drinking* may account for as many as half of all fatal car crashes today. Although the ideal rule is "If you drink, don't drive," this may be unrealistic for many. Thus, an alternative rule, offered by the National Safety Council, is: take no more than one normal drink per hour—and do not drive until at least one hour after the last drink.

• *Don't* drive when you're overly fatigued or in an angry or depressed mood. These conditions frequently lead to *fatal* accidents.

• At night don't try to guess what may be beyond the reach of your headlights: most cars going at 60 mph cannot stop within this range.

What to Do If You Are in an Accident

HOW INFORMED ARE YOU?

If you become involved in *any* auto accident, report the facts at once to your insurance agent—even if the other driver involved is completely at fault, admits it, and promises to have his insurance company pay for any damage. Do this simply because the other driver's oral promises are worthless to you. He (or she) could change his mind any time—or even turn around and claim it was *you* who caused the accident.

Follow up this call with a registered letter to the company writing your insurance, stating that you have been in an accident and giving your policy number as well as the name of your auto insurance agent.

This rule holds true even in cases in which visible damages are minimal and in which reporting the accident may end up costing you more in hiked premium rates than the expense of just having the car fixed yourself. Reason: should the accident turn out to be more serious than it first appeared (i.e., if the other driver later develops signs of whiplash injury), you may lose the benefit of your insurance coverage because you did not report the accident within the prescribed number of days.

Also in order to *collect full benefits* due you on your automobile insurance, you may be required by the company writing your policy to report any accident in which you become involved within a certain limited period of time. If you don't report, the insurance company may be able to disclaim any and all legal responsibility in the affair.

KEY RULES

Do you know what moves you must make in order to be confident you'll collect the full amount of insurance actually due you? If you're among the majority who don't, here are the key rules to guide you:

• After you have stopped your cars, checked to see if there are any injuries needing medical attention, set up some kind of system to route other vehicles around the accident area, and called the police, exchange drivers' license and registration numbers. Take down the other person's name and address plus the make, model, and year of the other car. Exchange telephone numbers and the names and addresses of your respective insurance companies and/or agents.

• Get names and addresses of:

all other drivers involved in the accident;

the insurance companies of these drivers;

two or three witnesses (if you fail to get their names, at least get their license plate numbers so you can track them down later if you need to).

• Write down the name, badge number, station number, and jurisdiction of the policeman who arrives at the scene of the accident.

• Make accurate notes on the following circumstances surrounding the accident:

The date, place, and time.

Weather conditions—Rain? Snow? Fog? Sleet? Clear?

Road conditions—Icy? Dry? Wet? Slushy?

Any evidence of physical injury to either party.

Whether either or both cars were under—or out of—control.

The car seats in which passengers in the other car were sitting.

How fast you—and the other car—were going at the time of the accident.

Where on the road each car was (e.g., on his own side of the road?).

Whether there is evidence of either driver being drunk (encourage a breath test for *both* of you when the police officer arrives if there's any question about this aspect).

Whether the other person's driver's license lists any relevant restrictions —such as a requirement that he or she wear glasses while driving (obviously particularly important if you noticed that the other driver was *not* wearing glasses when the accident occurred).

• Make your own notes even though the policeman or state trooper also is taking lengthy notes on the same topics.

• Make a sketch of the cars and placement of people and cars involved in the accident in relation to each other as well as to the road. If you have to move your car from the place it was hit, make marks on the road indicating the original position.

• If you should have a camera with you, snap a few pictures of the accident, the people involved, details of the damage.

• *Do not* disclose the extent of your insurance coverage.

• *Do not* confess guilt, even at the scene of an accident you have caused, and do not pledge to "have everything taken care of by your insurance company."

• *Do not* sign any waivers of liability or any assurances that you have not been physically injured. Such injury might not become evident for days or even weeks.

• *Do not* attempt to answer by yourself letters or telephone queries from the other party involved in an accident. Send all along to your insurance agent to handle.

• If the accident is a serious one—particularly one involving injury to others—consult a lawyer. But avoid the services of any lawyer who claims he can win an unusually large settlement, the proceeds of which he might offer to split with you. And if it's a serious or complicated accident resign yourself to staying in the area awhile—even if it's far from home. It'll be cheaper than trying to resolve difficult problems by long-distance phone.

• Go to two or three reputable auto body shops and compare estimates for properly repairing your car. Steer clear of any repair shop which offers to jack up its estimate—and later its bill—to cover the cost of your deductible. The shop which goes in for this type of cheating may not stop short of compromising the quality of its work on your car.

• Keep a record of your substitute transportation costs while your car is being fixed: the costs to you of renting a car, or taking taxis, or whatever.

• Make a copy of these rules and keep the guide in the glove compartment of your car. Otherwise you'll more than likely forget most of the important ones when and as you do get involved in an accident.

• Also keep in your glove compartment the insurance identification card your insurance agent may have given you—listing his office phone number and also the name of the company insuring you. This card may include the addresses and phone numbers of branch offices—most useful information if you smash your car up a few hundred miles from home.

• As a practical alternative, ask your insurance agent and/or state police to give you copies of the accident report form they would require you to fill out in the event of an accident, and keep these forms in your glove compartment to remind you which details to get when you have an accident.

• Or copy the following "composite" form I have put together from several different insurance companies and keep this guide in your glove compartment.

Whichever alternative you choose, just be sure you choose one!

ACCIDENT REPORT FORM

Policyholder and Driver

Name of policyholder_____Policy number_____
If married, name of husband or wife_____
Home address_____Phone_____
Business address_____Phone_____
Occupation_____Employed by_____
Driver's name_____Address_____Phone_____
Driver's license number_____Years driving experience_____
Driver's age_____
Relation to policyholder_____
Who authorized him to drive?_____

Names of occupants of policyholder's car_____
_____

Policyholder's Automobile

Make_____Year_____Body type_____Model_____
State license number_____Motor number_____Serial number_____
Name of holder of auto loan, if any_____
Name of owner if other than policyholder_____
Address_____Telephone_____
Car garaged at_____

Details of Accident

Date of accident_____Time_____
Where accident occurred_____
City_____State_____
Purpose for which car was being used_____
Was driver on errand for owner?_____
Where may car be seen during day?_____
Name of claim representative handling claim_____
Name of insurance firm_____
Direction my automobile was going_____
What side of street?_____How fast?_____Speed limit_____
Were headlights on?_____Signals?_____Condition of street_____
If object collided with was moving, in what direction?_____
How fast?_____Which side of street?_____
Any signals given?_____
If an automobile, were lights on?_____
Was either driver violating traffic regulations?_____
Was accident investigated by police?_____

What department and precinct?_____

Were any charges brought?_____Against whom?_____

Give full account of accident, including direction of all vehicles involved and traffic controls present (draw a diagram):_____

_____

_____

Personal Injuries

Name of injured person(s)   Address   Age   Occupation

_____   _____ _____ _____

_____   _____ _____ _____

Situation of Each Injured Person

Driver_____Pedestrian_____Rider in your car_____

Rider in other car_____

Describe injuries_____

_____

Name, address, and phone number of physician called_____

_____

Where was injured person taken?_____

Were there seat belts in your car?_____

If so, were they in use?_____

Damage to Property of Others

Name and address of owner of damaged automobile or other property___

_____

Home phone number_____Business phone number_____

Name of other party's insurance company_____

Policy number_____

Make of auto_____Year_____Body type_____Model_____

Describe damage_____

Estimated repair cost_____

Name of driver of other car_____Age_____

Address_____

Driver's license number_____State registration number_____

Occupants of other car   Address

_____   _____

_____   _____

Where can other car be seen?_____

What was said between you and other driver?_____

_____

Is claim being made against you?_____

Are you making claim against other party?_____

Damage to Your Automobile

Date of damage_____

Description and damage—itemize parts damaged_____

_____

Estimated cost of repairs (attach estimate)_____
If car was stolen, were police notified?_____
Officer's name and number_____
Give make, size, and mileage of tires stolen or damaged_____

_____

Age of convertible top_____
Purchase date and warranty of battery_____

Witnesses to Accident

Name	Address	Telephone number
_____	_____	_____
_____	_____	_____

Date of report_____Policyholder's signature_____

How to Foil Car Thieves

BASIC WAYS TO PROTECT YOUR CAR

• Be wary of super-bargains in Johnny-come-lately car lots. Be leery of any sale being made in the street. If you innocently buy a stolen car, you will have little chance of recovering your investment: if such a car is traced to you, you'll have to give it up, of course, so it can be returned to its rightful owner.

• *Do not* tempt a car "window-shopper" by leaving suitcases, gift boxes, obvious valuables within sight inside the car. At a minimum, keep your tapes in the glove compartment or elsewhere out of sight. You might also "mark" your stereo player and tapes—and record these "fingerprints" to help you establish your ownership if they're stolen later and traced.

• Mark your engine, transmission, and other valuable accessories not bearing identification numbers with your initials—to help police recover the items if they're stolen and to identify them as yours.

• Identify your car by dropping your business card in the slot between the door and window or by scratching your initials in some hidden place. This will help you particularly if the engine numbers and other identification have been tampered with.

• Park in lighted, well-trafficked areas—preferably near a street lamp or lighted store window. Most thieves won't risk working on a locked car in the light. At home, lock your car in the garage if you have one; many cars are stolen right in their owners' driveways. If you lack garage space for all your cars, put the most desirable ones inside and block the driveway with the others.

• If you leave your car in a public garage or parking lot, do not be definite about when you will pick it up. Dishonest attendants can easily steal new equipment from your car and replace it with the old parts when they know how much time you will be away. Double-check your mileage to make sure it's the same as when you parked the car. This will reveal whether thieves have driven your car while you were away to a spot in which they could switch equipment.

Assuming your state laws do not force you to keep the car's title and registration certificate in the glove compartment, leave them home or carry them on your person. Pro auto thieves steal these documents, then forge them for their own use.

• *Keep your car locked*—both doors and windows. If you're afraid of locking yourself out—with your keys accidentally left inside—carry a second set of car keys with you. Do not "hide" extra keys, though, in what you consider safe places but to which thieves turn at once: under a seat, fender, floor mat, the hood, the like.

• *Always* take the keys out of your ignition. Even when you're on a brief errand, remove your keys. Never leave your engine running. By always removing your keys you'll not only slash the chances of having your car stolen but also eliminate the possible hazard of being faced with liability charges if your stolen car later becomes involved in an accident.

• If your car breaks down or runs out of gas, continue to follow the rules on locking your car and taking out the keys. Just because you can't start your car doesn't mean a thief can't.

IF YOUR CAR IS STOLEN

But let's say that, despite all your defenses, your car is stolen. If or when this happens, you will find out at once that the police, your insurance company, and possibly the National Automobile Theft Bureau will ask you to supply critical information necessary to trace your car.

Will you at that moment have the essential data at hand—some twenty items including detailed information on your car, license, insurance, bank or finance company?

To help you be prepared, here is a form developed by the American Mutual Insurance Alliance which you should fill out *now* so that you will have all the facts on file for ready reference. You might carry a card in your wallet which gives all this information—to speed the search for your car if it is stolen.

Vehicle Information
Make_____Year_____
Model_____Body style_____
Vehicle identification number_____Color (upper/lower)_____
Type and size of engine_____Type of transmission_____

Ignition key number_____Trunk compartment key number_____
Repair work, dents, secret marks, or other peculiarities which would help
identify vehicle

_____

_____

License Information
License number (and state)_____Year license expires_____
City registration number_____

Additional Information
Insurance company_____Policy number_____
    Agent_____
Bank or finance company holding title_____
_____Account number_____
Purchased (new/used) from_____
    Address_____Date_____
Optional equipment or other items usually kept with auto (list serial
numbers)

_____

_____

Now here is another form, also developed by the AMIA, for your use
immediately after the theft. This information will provide a permanent record of the facts surrounding your case and will be helpful in co-ordinating
efforts to find your car.

If Your Car Is Stolen
Date of theft_____Place of theft_____
Time of theft_____Speedometer reading_____
Personal items in auto when stolen_____

_____

_____

Law enforcement agency contacted_____
    Date_____Complaint number_____
    Officer investigating theft_____
Insurance company contacted (date)_____Claim number_____
    Claims representative_____
Auto recovered at_____Date_____
    By (law enforcement agency)_____
Condition of car (list damage)_____

_____

_____

How to Save on Your Parking Charges

PARKING: CAN BE HUGE COST

In New York City, *daily* parking charges at downtown garages in the mid-1970s ran as much as $5.00 to $7.50. For a commuting businessman, this could mean a monthly cost of parking his car in Manhattan as high as $165. Even at less expensive garages, typical monthly parking charges in New York ran from $80 to $100.

Although you probably think of your car primarily as "wheels in motion," the fact is it is *parked,* on average, more than 95 per cent of the time. If you are a regular automobile commuter in a major U.S. city today, your yearly parking costs probably run between $300 and $1,000, your daily charges between $1.50 and $3.00. Parking, in sum, can be a huge part of the cost of owning a car for millions of city and suburban families.

If today's parking costs seem exorbitant to you, tomorrow's charges will be even more so. The reasons are a cinch:

• In virtually every big U.S. city, land costs are soaring—along with demand for space to build offices, stores, apartment buildings, hospitals. City parking lots are being erased by these more lucrative uses of land.

• Parking also has become a major burden at suburban shopping centers, hotels, airports, hospitals, universities. What was once free parking is being replaced by monthly charges to growing numbers of students, doctors, others. As high a proportion as 75 per cent of leading U.S. colleges and universities are now slapping parking charges on students: the argument is that a car takes up the same amount of space as a seminar room for twenty students.

"Free" parking downtown surely is doomed to disappear altogether— along with all on-street parking in densely populated areas. Even in suburban towns, street parking is being banned—and in some cases monthly charges are being assessed for street parking.

TEN WAYS TO SAVE ON PARKING CHARGES

(1) Form a car pool and arrange a monthly contract with a downtown garage under which it won't matter whose car is parked each day. Quite a few garages will do this for you and some will provide movable plastic stickers so car-poolers can take turns during the month. In some cases, a car pool can be less expensive than public transportation.

(2) Shop for a garage a short distance from the central business district. A daily walk of as little as five or six blocks can mean as much as a 50 per cent cut in your parking charges.

(3) When you drive downtown for shopping, find out which of your favorite stores offers free or reduced-rate parking. Merchants of all types

across the country have arrangements with parking companies to provide free or reduced-rate parking for customers.

(4) If you're commuting alone, do so, if you can, with a compact car: these often qualify you for preferential garage rates because they can be slipped into spaces which are too small for the larger cars.

(5) If you are renting a car from a company which also owns parking facilities, check what parking benefits you might get as part of your rental agreement.

(6) Be careful about adding steep charges to your bill by taking your car in and out of a long-term parking garage; taxis might be cheaper.

(7) Compare monthly and daily parking costs. Monthly rates might come out cheaper even if you don't use the garage every day.

(8) Seriously consider parking your car at a low-cost facility at the edge of the city and taking a bus, subway, or train from there to the office. Such facilities are being expanded and made more convenient in response to gasoline shortages.

(9) Avoid all extra charges by obeying the rules of the garage. For instance, if the garage requests you leave your key in the car, do so, and thereby avoid possible penalty charges.

(10) Be sure your brakes are in top-notch condition to avoid damage due to an accident in the garage.

WHAT ABOUT RENTING A CAR?

HOW TO TELL WHICH IS THE BEST DEAL

You get off a plane in a strange city and start shopping for a car to rent. At one rental counter the use of a car will cost you $18 a day, plus 18¢ a mile, plus the cost of gas. At the next booth you can get the same car for $20 a day and 20¢ a mile, but the gas is furnished by the car rental company. And you also read in an ad that just a block from the airport there's an economy car rental outfit offering subcompacts for about half the price charged at the airport offices.

How can you tell which is the best deal in a car rental? What is the most important thing to look for?

Take the example of the $18-a-day versus the $20-a-day car. Your total costs for driving the first car 300 miles are $90, including $18 you must pay for gas. However, the second car would actually cost you $10 *less* —or $80. This example points up how important it is for you to figure total car rental costs on a *daily* basis.

Car rental costs vary widely from company to company. To illustrate, the daily rental rate of a Ford Pinto in one major U.S. city in the mid-1970s ranged from $7.00, plus 10¢ a mile, to $14, plus 14¢ a mile. Thus, if you drive Pinto A 200 miles a day, the daily cost was $27 against $42 a day for Pinto B from another company. Over a five-day period this difference amounts to $75.

From coast to coast, the daily rental rate for various types and sizes of cars in the mid-seventies ranged from $1.00 to $90. Weekly rates typically ranged from $35 to $100. And on a monthly basis the spread is similarly wide. In some cases you get a certain number of miles free; in others you get unlimited mileage; in still others there is a mileage charge of 5¢ to 25¢ depending on the car and the company.

Why pay up to twice the car rental rate and mileage charge from a big-car, big-name company when far less expensive deals might be made around the corner?

Item: Frequently, the biggest companies offer newer cars with newer tires than do the smaller companies. But this does not necessarily mean that the cars rented out by big-name companies are always safer or significantly more trouble-free.

Item: The bigger companies have hundreds or even thousands of offices across the United States—usually in the most convenient places such as airports, downtown hotel lobbies, etc. And you can make car reservations over toll-free telephone lines from anywhere in the country.

But the budget car rental companies usually will deliver a rental car to you quickly if you call them, often on a direct-line telephone from an airport or hotel lobby—or, in some cases, also on a toll-free line from wherever you are. They also are frequently willing to let you drop off a car wherever you want when you are ready to return it, for a small charge or no charge at all.

Item: The bigger companies tend to keep their offices open for longer hours than do the smaller companies, and to offer you a long list of travel assistance. But smaller companies often will make special arrangements for off-hour needs or returns and also will provide you with maps, directions, etc.

Item: The bigger companies will let you drop off a rented car at another U.S. city—either at a small drop-off charge or at no charge. In this case, the smaller companies may not have an office at your destination.

Item: Both small and large companies probably will let you charge a car rental on any major credit card.

Enough. What *is* the most important thing to look for when you rent a car—a low, flat daily charge or a low mileage charge?

Should you pay that "nominal" $1.50 to $2.00 a day charge to waive the first $100 in damage to the car you rent?

At what point does it become more economical to rent on a weekly versus a daily basis?

RULES FOR COMPARISON SHOPPING

Here are your major rules for comparison shopping. If you follow just these, the likelihood is that you'll save hundreds of dollars in the next few times you rent a car.

• Estimate, in advance, how many miles you *realistically* think you'll drive during the rental period. You're typical if you usually underestimate the mileage, so don't just count the number of miles between where you are and your destination. Add at least one third as many more miles to make up for getting lost, making unexpected detours and side trips, etc. If you plan to travel any significant distance, shop for the car with the lowest per-mile charge.

• Figure out, in advance, just how many days you'll need the car. If you'll need it five days or less, the daily rate probably is the best deal. But if you'll need it longer, the weekly (or even monthly) rate is probably better.

• Make up your mind how important are the comforts of big, fancy limousines versus relatively spartan small cars. To show you the differences in costs, a Cadillac costing $23 a day and 23¢ a mile, which you rent for five days and drive an average of 200 miles a day, will cost you a total of $345—an average of $69 a day. But an economy car costing $10 a day and 10¢ a mile over the same period will cost you a total of $150—an average of $30 a day.

Note: If you decide on an economy car, reserve it well ahead of time.

• Ask about the special deals—such as the low-cost "weekend specials" which are usually available from Friday noon to Monday noon, X number of "free" miles, "businessman's specials." See if you "fit" one of them.

• Find out, if you intend to leave the car in another city, whether there is a drop-off charge. Between major cities you usually can find a deal in which you pay only a minimum or no drop-off charge at all.

• Although the ads say there is only a "nominal" charge for waiving the renter's responsibility for damage up to $100, this charge usually is at least $1.50 a day—which amounts to an annual rate of at least $547.50. And this is not for full collision coverage. It usually covers *only* the $100 deductible which most of you could afford to pay if necessary. I suggest rejecting this extra coverage on the basis of its cost. Just be sure to inspect the car you rent and point out any obvious dents or scratches to the agent so they can be noted on the rental contract before you initial the waiver and inspect the rental contract carefully to be sure it is *only* the first $100 of coverage you are waiving.

• Whatever deal you choose, if you don't have any recognized credit cards, expect to make a cash deposit on a rented car of an amount roughly equivalent to your expected total rental charge.

But don't *count* on being permitted to pay for a rented car with cash—

especially during evenings and weekends. Some firms *require* you to show them credit cards, no matter how much cash you have in your pocket. Reason: thefts of rental cars are a major problem for car rental firms and some are understandably hesitant to lend you, say, $5,000 worth of property without first checking whether you have sound credit credentials.

By Air—"It's the Only Way to Go"

If your time is limited and you're traveling a fairly long distance, a plane is the only way to go. If your funds also are limited and you're traveling a long way, a plane can be an economical form of transportation too. But how economical it will be will depend on your knowledge of and ability to take advantage of what has become a fantastic web of air fare bargains, low-cost package deals, and travel discounts.

BARGAIN AIR FARES

The basic fare the majority of travelers pay today is the "Y"—for coach. Every $1.00 on this fare costs $1.37 to $1.63 first class. There are also many special stopover and "circle" deals offered by most airlines. There are lots of angles—such as scheduling your flight at mealtime to save on restaurants, traveling light to save porter's tips.

Be on the alert, though, for major changes in all arrangements under which you now fly. The Civil Aeronautics Board, which regulates the U.S. air travel industry, is making and will continue to make fundamental alterations in the criteria governing all fares in coming years.

Consult a knowledgeable travel agent or inquire at various airlines about the best bargain deals and the rules for taking advantage of them.

Avoid being overcharged by checking the fare for the flight you want with more than one airline or more than one ticket agent.

CHARTER FLIGHT BARGAINS

"Travel abroad" has a lot in common with any familiar consumer product. You can buy it in a wide range of brands, grades, quality, types, and guarantees. You can buy it at list price. Or you can buy it marked down for sale. Or you can buy it "hot" from a fence.

To illustrate: There are the individual fares available on the scheduled airlines which offer you the greatest flexibility in schedules and the highest guarantees of service and responsibility. These are at the very top of the price range.

Then there are the package tours, and special group fares offered by the scheduled airlines and their agents which are subject to limitations that do not apply to normal fares but which still have built-in service guarantees and negotiability (meaning the tickets may be exchanged for other dates and airlines).

Finally, there are the charters which can be bought from a variety of sources in a variety of forms and are the least expensive of all. You can take a three-stop inclusive tour charter (ITC) or a travel group charter (TGC). A recent variation is the One-stop tour charter (OTC) designed for the unaffiliated individual traveler. You must sign up at least 15-30 days in advance, depending on whether your destination is domestic or international, pay for air transportation and ground accommodations, agree to stay a minimum of four-seven days. You need not remain with the group as long as you leave and return on the same plane and pay for the ground package.

Most charter flights are safe, well managed, and compare quite favorably with regular scheduled airline flights.

RULES FOR BUYING CHARTER FLIGHTS

If you buy a bargain charter flight for transportation only, make sure it *is* a bargain. Compare the charter price with the lowest fare on a scheduled flight; consider how much side trips might boost your costs. New York to London on a charter may be a bargain. But short trips elsewhere and back to London could hike your cost above a group fare package on a scheduled flight which usually permits some stopovers at no extra charge.

If you're sharing costs with other passengers, check the costs for accuracy. Ask the tour operator or group that arranged the flight for the facts; they must give them. Beware of last-minute surcharges, dues, or fees which can rise your costs. Exception: the entirely legal price hikes necessitated by rising fuel costs, about which you are warned in tour descriptions.

If you are traveling with children under twelve, check the rules on lower fare rates.

Consider the negotiability or refund value of your ticket if your charter doesn't make the return trip or you can't go back on schedule. You do not get your money back if you change your mind about the return date.

Read all the literature on a tour package to satisfy yourself the trip is well planned. Check prices item by item.

If you have valid complaints, report to an appropriate law enforcement agency, the Better Business Bureau and/or the Civil Aeronautics Board, 1825 Connecticut Avenue, N.W., Washington, D.C. 20428.

And best guide of all: find and use *a good travel agent*. See Chapter 12, "How to Save on Vacations," for details.

"LEAVE THE DRIVING TO THEM"

More than 30,000 towns still depend on the bus for their sole means of scheduled transportation. In countless instances, people can't operate a car or can't afford one—because, say, of youth or old age, location or income level. And even if you have a car, on a short trip you might want someone else to do the driving. Moreover, many buses are now equipped with reclining seats, individual reading lights, and lavatories.

What is a "short" trip? Up to 500 miles is an accepted rule of thumb. Generally speaking, cost aside, a plane might be more comfortable and convenient over a longer trip. But the point is the very turnpikes which have made the automobile so popular also are a boon to the bus. The flexibility of the bus hasn't been approached by the trains or planes because the buses follow the highways and the highways follow the people.

TRAVEL TIPS

Q. *What about valuables and breakables?*

A. Carry them with you. Most companies will insure items up to $50 in value, free of charge, with added coverage available.

Q. *What about reservations and luggage on intercity trips?*

A. A reservation is not vital. During peak periods back-up buses are ready. To avoid crowds, travel in midweek or midday. If you're in a hurry, check on express buses. Check luggage you can't carry on at the terminal about a half hour in advance. Be sure you have your identification tags on all luggage.

Q. *How do I find the right company for a charter?*

A. Ask your local college or athletic team: they use dozens of charters and know the good firms.

Q. *What are guidelines for prices on chartered buses?*

A. Prices are generally quoted in either of two ways, depending on the trip's distance. For local work of up to fifty miles in one direction, the price is quoted on a per-hour basis.

For trips of more than fifty miles in one direction, prices are usually quoted on a per-mile basis. In addition, there is usually an hourly charge if the trip goes over a specified number of hours because the driver must be paid, no matter whether the bus is moving or standing still.

Q. *What are hidden cost pitfalls to look out for?*

A. Does the quoted price include tolls, parking charges, permits? Is the cost of the driver's lodging and/or food included if yours is an overnight trip? Check each of these items in advance.

Prices are usually higher on weekends, so consider scheduling your event during the week.

Order the bus to report as late as possible to reduce unproductive waiting time for the inevitable last-minute arrivals.

Use box lunches and save money.

Also, for your own comfort, make sure the bus you charter has sufficient baggage capacity for your luggage—particularly ski gear—and that the seating capacity of the bus itself is adequate.

AMTRAK: RAILROADS INTO THE TWENTIETH CENTURY

Trains, like buses, are among the least expensive ways for people to travel today—and they also leave the driving to someone else, permitting you, the passenger, to relax, read, look out the window.

Trains also are a far more efficient means of transportation than cars and highways, and therefore are far easier on our fuel supplies: one railroad train can accommodate as many people as fifty cars. One track can replace twenty lanes of superhighway. A train gets twice as many passenger miles from a gallon of fuel as a fully loaded economy car.

The National Railroad Passenger Corporation, Amtrak—created by Congress as a quasi-public corporation early in this decade to help passenger trains stage a comeback—has been making giant strides toward bringing this nearly moribund system of travel into the twentieth century.

Among other moves, Amtrak has:

Placed experimental high-speed turbo trains in service and has ordered more;

Ordered many brand-new cars, including dozens of new Metroliner cars and a whole series of new-style, bi-level long-distance coaches, diners, lounges, and sleepers;

Greatly upgraded the general quality of passenger trains, by picking the best 2,000 passenger cars out of the more than 3,000 formerly on the tracks, then completely refurbishing a considerable number of these;

Installed a nationwide, centralized ticket-and-reservation system;

Begun building a string of "satellite" train stations for suburban travelers;

Started the acquisition and refurbishing of hundreds of old passenger stations;

Reintroduced long-haul sleeper routes throughout the United States—and started a complete redesign of the cars to make them more efficient and comfortable;

Improved connections on long hauls to eliminate many long waits for trains;

Made noticeable improvements on many trains in dining cars and other food service facilities;

Cleaned up the train rest rooms so that, as one official notes, "the whole train no longer smells like a bathroom";

Made moves to ease buying of train tickets. You can pay for your ticket with American Express, a Master Charge, Diners Club, Carte Blanche, BankAmericard, or a Rail Travel card. Thousands of travel agents can help you make arrangements for travel on the Amtrak system. You can order tickets by phone to be mailed to you and billed to your credit card;

Introduced a uniform ticket format across the country.

You can get reservations and information on Amtrak schedules by calling this toll-free number: (800) 523-5720.

RECREATIONAL VEHICLES

WHICH TYPE FOR YOU?

If you are in the market for a recreational vehicle and if you are starting your hunt from scratch, here are the five basic types—a list you can use as a preliminary shopping guide:

Camping trailers: compact folding "cottages on wheels" which you tow with your own car. Typical campers sleep four to six; are equipped with bunks, kitchenette, and portable toilet; cost $500 to $2,500, average $1,500.

Truck-mounted campers: in two variations—the slide-in truck camper which fits into the back of a pickup; the chassis-mount truck camper which is *permanently* mounted on a truck's chassis (with the truck bed and sides removed). "Truck-mounts" have bunks, kitchenette, plumbing; are 6 to 11½ feet long; cost $1,500 to $5,000 for slide-ins, and $4,000 to $10,000 for chassis-mount units.

Pickup covers: simple structures with few, if any, built-in conveniences; attach to a pickup to create a sheltered space; cost $300 to $1,000, average $350.

Travel trailers: up to 35 feet long and 8 feet wide; pulled by your car; come with baths, kitchens, bedrooms; cost $700 to $18,000 or more, average $3,800. Newest and largest travel trailer is the "fifth wheel" unit which is towed by a pickup truck by means of a special swivel hitch located directly above the truck's rear axle, making the huge unit easy to tow. Prices range from $4,500 to $10,000 or more.

Motor homes: most luxurious, are comfortable carhouses in one unit; 20 to 35 feet long; cost $5,000 to $35,000, average less than $10,000.

Then there's a whole new family of "fun" cars and specialty vehicles ranging from jeeps to snowmobiles.

SHOPPING GUIDES

Whatever type you choose, look for one which is convincingly described by the manufacturer as sturdy and stable in winds. If at all possible, test-drive on a windy day before buying. Many, if not most, recreational vehicles are very unstable in winds and so flimsy they splinter in a rollover (frames are often wooden). Consumer advocates are pressing for government safety standards for recreational vehicles but, as of the mid-seventies, they had made little progress.

Don't spend a penny on buying until you have rented the equipment you think you would like best. You might properly rent more than one type before you settle on anything.

Buy a good, *used* unit when you begin: since many campers trade up to bigger units or different types as they go along, lots of good used equipment is for sale. Be sure, though, that an experienced mechanic checks the equipment—particularly the engine and transmission—before you buy. Don't buy a used lemon.

Finally, don't fail to count costs of owning and running a recreational vehicle. These include registration and insurance (which often run more than the costs of registering and insuring an ordinary car); increased fuel costs of towing a trailer or driving a large motor home over costs of fueling a car by itself; extra garaging costs; extra maintenance and repair costs; financing charges and/or the interest you lose on your initial cash investment.

BOATS AND BIKES

The fundamental rules of buying stressed over and over—and over—in this book can easily be translated from area to area, and thus you can without difficulty translate them for yourself into the spheres of boats or bikes or even horses).

BOATS FOR FUN

In our country in the mid-seventies, boats numbered 8 to 10 million—more than double the number of only two decades ago, and boating is now a multibillion-dollar industry with about one in five Americans now counted as a boater. Each spring, literally millions of boats change hands. Outboard motorboats cost from $200 to $5,000, new, are far and away the most popular type, and are familiar sights in every part of our country. Many of today's boats run into thousands of dollars. And with maintenance, repairs, insurance, and a trailer to haul the boat, plus the frequently high cost of winter storage in or out of the water, a boat can become among the most costly possessions of an unwary family.

BUYING A USED BOAT

Buying a used boat can be a particularly tricky thing—and for this purchase, therefore, there are several special rules.

Under a typical cycle, a buyer's interest might first be grabbed by the fanciest styles; his attention would then be heightened by the flashiest accessories; finally, a transfer might be clinched by nothing more than the most colorful "cosmetics" added by an earlier owner (owners).

But this is not the way to buy a used boat. Instead what you, a potential buyer, should do is "kick the tires." What should govern your decisions is the same degree of caution that would be in order when you buy a used car—and that's caution! Specifically:

• Grasp from the start that used boats do *not* depreciate, as automobiles do, by a rule-of-thumb annual percentage and that some late-model boats, in fact, grow in value. So comparison shopping is absolutely essential—after you have listed the basics you really want. Are you looking for a specific construction or type? Do you want the craft for day sailing or fishing? Inshore or offshore? What do you need in accommodations, speed, and size? How much do you want to spend—and no more?

As one general rule, the more experienced a boatsman you are, the less elaborate accommodations you will want.

As another, a boat used inshore may be less sturdy than a boat used offshore or in the Great Lakes—*even once*. The latter must—literally—be strong enough to withstand being dropped into the water from ten or more feet up *without any damage*.

• Check the hull once you have narrowed your choice to a couple of boats, for hulls determine the real value of a boat and you must inspect their safety. On wooden hulls, check that all butts, seams, and joints are tight. Also look carefully for rot—especially in corners where soft spots tend to "hide." With fiberglass boats, check the gel coat for cracking. Also check around the hull for any accumulation of slight cracks, for although this is primarily a cosmetic problem, a concentration of small cracks might indicate an impact area.

• When the boat is out of water, examine the keel and bottom for damage. Small gouges can be repaired easily but a badly mauled keel may have to be replaced. Inside the boat, check that hull fittings are sound, that hoses don't have cracks, that hose clamps fit tightly. Study the fuel connections, for a faulty hookup can cause a fire or even a major explosion. Check, too, the wiring and fuse systems for short circuits and improper insulation.

• Make a list of the approved equipment the Coast Guard requires, under federal and state laws, for the area in which you intend to do your boating. This equipment usually includes fire extinguishers, life preservers, horns, proper lights, and sufficient ventilation. Be sure this equipment is still installed on the boat and is in top condition. Don't try to cut any corners on it.

• Be sure the boat is fitted with whatever anti-pollution devices (e.g., toilet holding tanks) are required locally, or wherever you intend to use your boat.

• Check the installation and ventilation of the engine and fuel tank areas. Look for tank corrosion and leaks. You can get information on current ventilation requirements from your local Coast Guard offices.

• Have the engine checked by a marine mechanic. When the salesman says the boat has "very little running time," does he mean the engine has given the previous owner trouble?

• Check the steering controls by rotating the helm from one limit to the other. Make sure the rudder or outboard motor moves without binding or requiring undue force. Then take a trial run. Does everything work? Does the boat perform as you expected? Is your "crew" satisfied?

• If you're in the market for a sailboat, inspect every inch of sails, spars, masts, and rigging. Check for abnormal wear, evidence of strain and compression cracks in the mast.

• And your personal inspection of these areas may well not be nearly enough. It may be more than worth your time and money to get the advice of a professional marine surveyor—particularly if you are spending more than $5,000 for the boat.

• In fact, if your purchase is into these high dollar ranges, the advice of a professional surveyor whose interest is your interest would seem to me to be mere common sense.

TIPS FOR BUYING BICYCLES

Do you remember (I do) when $20 to $30 was a standard price for a bicycle and $50 meant you were buying "all the extras?" Do you realize that a bike has now become one of the costlier pieces of equipment you can buy and that your spending for bikes is now reaching for the landmark of $1 billion a year?

We are now buying more than 15 million bicycles a year and our bicyclist population by the mid-1970s had crossed the believe-it-or-not peak of 83 million (two in five of us).

Against this background, tips on how to shop for and save on a bicycle seem singularly appropriate for you—and you—and you. Here goes:

• Decide in advance how much a bike is worth to you and what kind is right for you. Your choices are:

Middleweights: weighing 50 to 60 pounds, costing $30 to $40 and rugged. They're one speed only and hard work to pedal.

Touring bicycles: miscalled "English racers," weighing 35 to 40 pounds, costing $50 to $100. Most have three speeds, are good for normal use, are your best buy if you're a casual cyclist.

Lightweights: racing bicycles, weighing less than 30 pounds, costing $80 to $500. Have from 5 to 15 speeds, with 10 typical. Need fairly frequent maintenance, are tops in efficient pedaling for the serious cyclist.

Stores also carry a variety of children's bikes, "high risers" which look like motorcycles, folding bikes, three-wheelers for adults with poor balance, tandems, even unicycles.

• Test-ride any bike you're considering to see how it feels and "fits." A lightweight's turned-down handlebars will feel awkward at first, but it will be most comfortable for long jaunts. A way to test-ride is to rent one or more bikes before you buy.

• Get the correct frame size (distance from pedal crank to point where seat mounts) for you. The range is 17 to 24 inches. To get your size, subtract 9 or 10 inches from the length of your inseam, measured to the floor.

• Be sure your child's bike fits. Do *not* buy a big—but unsafe—bike that he'll "grow into." Just allow a reasonable range of seat and handlebar adjustment for some growth.

• Check the brakes before you test-ride. The bike may have a coaster brake on the rear wheel activated by back-pedaling, or caliper brakes activated by hand levers on the handlebars. A coaster brake takes longer to apply than calipers and is more difficult to service, but it rarely needs service and works better in wet weather. Dual caliper brakes will give you a quicker stop in dry weather, but they will be poor or worse when wet. Self-adjusting caliper brakes are a strong plus. Note: Don't buy a child's bike with caliper brakes unless the child has a big enough hand to use them easily. Even some adults do not have strong enough hands for some caliper brakes.

• Also, while testing, find out how springy the frame is. A more rigid frame means less pedaling wasted. Guard against raw, sharp, or rough edges on any parts, even parts protected by guards and grips. On children's bikes, be wary of gearshift levers placed far back on the horizontal bar, "sissy bars" (high back on seat), small front wheels. The Bicycle Manufacturers Association thumbs-downed all these features some time ago as hazardous. Beware too of elongated "banana seats" (unless you prohibit riding double on them). Look for a red, white, and blue "BMA/6" seal of certification on the post just under the seat of an American children's bike. This indicates that the bicycle meets the most recent standards of this organization. Note: No imported bicycles (even the best) can get this seal, and some excellent American bikes lack it too—so use it primarily as a guide to children's bicycles.

• Bikes, like cars, have options, or accessories. Although the cost of bike accessories is much less than car options, you'll still want to be discriminating in what you buy, for all add complexity and weight. Here are the most popular and useful:

Bell or horn: a bell is more reliable than a horn and doesn't consume batteries. Both will warn pedestrians of your presence, but neither will help you in your interactions with cars, unless you invest in a marine-type freon-powered air horn.

Chain and lock: these are your first line of defense against bicycle thieves, who steal hundreds of thousands of bikes each year. The chain should be long enough to go through both wheels, the frame, and around a fixed object. It also should be hard enough to resist cutting by ordinary instruments. Your lock should be of equal quality.

Light: generator types eliminate the battery hassle but significantly increase pedaling effort when they're on—and go out when you stop. A small battery light which clips to your left leg is also a good idea, since it quickly identifies you as a cyclist by its motion. A taillight is as important for safety as a headlight.

Luggage rack or basket: either makes a bike more useful for small errands and larger outings.

The list of possible accessories you can load onto a bike is long. It includes an odometer or speedometer (some types make a bicycle pedal harder; see a good dealer for recommendations); a tool kit; a tire patch kit; an extra inner tube; a water bottle for long trips; a kiddie seat for taking a small child along; an aerosol can of bike-chasing dog repellent; special cycling clothes; and a protective helmet for areas with dangerous traffic.

• To save money, buy a used bike—but if it's in good condition, expect to pay 75 per cent of the price of a new one. A low price for a good used bicycle is a warning that it may have been stolen. Inspect any used bike with care—or pay a qualified mechanic a few dollars to go over the bike for you.

• Assemble a new bike yourself—a job which will also save money by teaching you how to repair it. Have a competent repairman check your work to be sure you did it right.

• Be prepared to wait until the type of bicycle you want can be shipped to you; do not be talked into a more expensive model on hand. Few bicycle shops have any used ones, and bikes generally are in such demand that your choice may be very limited if you are not prepared to wait. You can, of course, widen your choice considerably by shopping around.

• If yours is a big family, you may be able to save literally hundreds of dollars over the years by letting your children earn the money for their own bikes, rather than providing them as gifts. An earned bike will probably last two or three times as long as a gift bike.

• After you have bought your bike, register it with the local police. Many communities impound unregistered bicycles, and, in any event, registration sharply increases your chance of recovering your bike if it is stolen.

• Check your homeowners insurance to see if it covers a bicycle. If not, you can get a special policy at about $10.50 a year for a $125 bicycle.

• And two final points: Don't set your heart on one bike as an absolute must. Until you get way up in the $200 price range, there is not that much difference between them. And in inexpensive bikes, a good dealer is your key to value, for he, rather than any manufacturer's guarantee, will stand behind your machine.

ENOUGH!

This chapter by no means covers all forms of locomotion. In addition, there are roller skates and pogo sticks, horses, snowshoes and parachutes.

But this is just a book, not an encyclopedia.

10

A COLLEGE EDUCATION
AND HOW TO FINANCE IT

COLLEGE EDUCATION COSTS SOARING

A college education has become close to essential in today's workplace —in fact, a *must* if you are to qualify for many jobs in industry, business, government, education, in the health professions, in hundreds of other occupational areas. But in recent years the cost of college education has soared far beyond even the middle-income family's ability to pay. The scramble for the limited number of scholarships, loans, and on-campus jobs is becoming ever more furious each year. For millions, the dream of college has become a nightmare.

A few revealing points:

The average cost of tuition and room and board at a public college rose 45 per cent in the one decade of the 1960s.

The increase at private institutions was even greater—a whopping 65 per cent.

On average, these costs are mounting 8 to 10 per cent a year, year after year.

The cost of going to a good, private American college for four years, as the mid-1970s approached could run to as much as $30,000.

If you have a brother or sister or two who also are at college age, your family's total expense could be an astronomical $60,000 to $90,000. And this assumes—unrealistically—that college costs will stay at today's levels. Obviously, they won't.

SHOPPING FOR COLLEGE

Let's say you are not poor enough to qualify for a scholarship or grant. What *can* you do to cut the costs of going to college?

A prime way to cut your costs at the very start is through your own selection of a college or university. Your basic guidelines are:

• The least expensive way to get a college education is to live at home and go to a free or low-tuition college or two or four year college, or live at home and participate in an external degree program (see section "Bargain Education" in this chapter).

• Next is the state college in your own state.

• After that is a state college out of your home state.

• The most expensive is the private university—even if you live at home.

Tuition, fees, room and board charges vary widely from college to college, both public and private. A public college will usually charge much less than a private school and, taking other factors into consideration, your savings could amount to as much as $2,000 to $3,000 *per year*.

To illustrate, let's take two well-known universities in one state: the University of Pennsylvania, a private institution in Philadelphia, and Pennsylvania State University, in University Park in the western part of the state. Both are major coeducational institutions; both are highly respected for their faculties and programs.

For the 1976-77 school year, the University of Pennsylvania charged about $4,100 in tuition and fees and $2,200 for room and board—for a total of $6,300 per year.

For the same year, if you were a resident of the state and chose Pennsylvania State University, you would have been charged $1,095 in tuition and fees, and $1,389 in room and board charges—for a total of $2,484.

If you found that two institutions both offered you comparable programs for the purposes of your studies, and you chose the state university, *your annual savings would have been $3,816*.

Here is a sampling of resident charges made around the country in private and public four-year colleges, large and small. It is excerpted from "Student Expenses at Postsecondary Institutions, 1976-77," available for $2.50 from the CSS, College Entrance Examination Board, Box 2815, Princeton, N.J. 08540. This is one of the best guides of its kind; it includes average costs at about 930 two-year institutions and 1,568 four-year institutions.

Private colleges

NAME AND LOCATION	TUITION, FEES	ROOM, BOARD	OTHER EXPENSES	TOTAL EXPENSES
Beloit College, Beloit, Wis.	$3,540	$1,280	$ 500	$5,320
Bennington College, Bennington, Vt.	5,150	1,400	400	6,950

*Indicates data for the 1975–76 academic year.

Name and Location	Tuition, Fees	Room, Board	Other Expenses	Total Expenses
Boston College, Chestnut Hill, Mass.	$3,350	$1,525	$ 925	$5,800
*Brandeis University, Waltham, Mass.	3,550	1,750	650	5,950
*University of Chicago, Chicago, Ill.	3,225	1,775	670	5,670
Colgate University, Hamilton, N.Y.	3,800	1,640	660	6,100
Dartmouth College, Hanover, N.H.	4,230	1,975	1,755	7,960
Duke University, Durham, N.C.	3,300	1,600	650	5,550
Emory University, Atlanta, Ga.	3,150	1,551	1,074	5,775
Fairleigh Dickinson University, Rutherford, N.J.	2,550	1,550	700	4,800
George Washington University, Washington, D.C.	2,750	1,900	850	5,500
Howard University, Washington, D.C.	1,518	1,186	1,150	3,854
Johns Hopkins University, Baltimore, Md.	3,600	2,050	950	6,600
Knox College, Galesburg, Ill.	3,530	1,270	750	5,550
**Loyola University, New Orleans, La.	1,750	1,100	800	3,650
Massachusetts Institute of Technology, Cambridge, Mass.	4,150	2,750	750	7,650
Northwestern University, Evanston, Ill.	3,840	1,570	700	6,110

**Indicates data for the 1973–74 academic year.

NAME AND LOCATION	TUITION, FEES	ROOM, BOARD	OTHER EXPENSES	TOTAL EXPENSES
Oberlin College, Oberlin, Ohio	$3,838	$1,540	$ 450	$5,828
University of Richmond, Richmond, Va.	2,600	1,350	800	4,750
Sarah Lawrence College, Bronxville, N.Y.	4,190	2,100	1,100	7,390
Tulane University, New Orleans, La.	3,330	1,695	575	5,600
Vassar College, Poughkeepsie, N.Y.	3,410	1,500	800	5,710
Wilkes College, Wilkes-Barre, Pa.	2,500	1,300	650	4,450
Xavier University, Cincinnati, O.	2,100	1,460	765	4,325
Public Colleges				
**University of Alabama, Huntsville, Ala.	$ 525	$1,180	$ 820	$2,525
Arizona State University, Tempe, Ariz.	450	1,750	950	3,150
University of Florida, Gainesville, Fla.	660	1,665	780	3,105
*Indiana State University, Terre Haute, Ind.	744	1,139	617	2,500
University of Maryland, College Park, Md.	778	1,600	775	3,153
**University of Michigan, Ann Arbor, Mich.	696	1,236	768	2,700
Ohio State University, Columbus, O.	810	1,500	665	2,975
University of Texas, Arlington, Tex.	370	1,585	890	2,845
University of Virginia, Charlottesville, Va.	750	1,400	650	2,800

*Data for 1975-76 year; **Data for 1973-74 year.

BARGAIN EDUCATION

Other ways to slash your college costs are through a telescoped, three-year degree program; through credit by examination programs, such as the College Level Examination Program (CLEP), or through an "external degree program."

Three-year degree options are offered by an increasing number of colleges. They are ordinarily open only to the ablest students, because you must not only take on a heavier load of courses but you must also, normally, attend classes during the summer. This obviously reduces your ability to earn money to meet college expenses. Nevertheless, the possibility of paying only three years of tuition and living expenses for a college degree, combined with the time saving, make three-year degree programs a very attractive deal financially.

The College Level Examination Program permits you to cut college costs by demonstrating knowledge of a subject in an examination. CLEP exams are given monthly at 650 different locations throughout the United States—and more than 2,000 colleges and universities grant credit toward degrees to those who score high enough on the tests.

For details, write to CLEP, College Entrance Examination Board, Box 2815, Princeton, N.J. 08540, or Box 1025, Berkeley, Calif. 94701. Home study courses which might not by themselves qualify for college credit can help you toward a college degree if they enable you to get a passing score on the appropriate CLEP test.

(Caution: If you are in the market for this type of study, heed the warnings later in the section "Beware: Home Study Gyps.")

In an *external degree program* you do your regular college studies off campus. It's a unique form of low-cost education with particular appeal if you must maintain a job while you study. It also opens up many new opportunities for millions of you—housewives and others—who might never have a chance otherwise to get a degree.

If you, a student, live and study at home, your education may cost only about half as much as the cost of an on-campus education. One large experiment of this kind is New York State's new Empire State College, where costs for New York residents ran only $1,067 for a recent twelve-month year. Another is the New York Regents External Degree Program, which is unique in its willingness to grant a degree to an applicant who has not followed any prescribed program of study—if he can demonstrate his ability in his field.

The degree you get through one of these external degree programs is *not* a cut-rate mail order diploma in any sense. It is the same high-quality, specialized degree granted the normal way by a given institution. Despite the fact that these programs still are experimental, they do offer you great potential—if you are capable of studying independently.

HOW TO COMPARE COLLEGE COSTS

You have made the basic choice of what type of college you want to go to and in what state. Now write the three or four institutions you would like to attend. Ask each for its catalogues and whatever material it has available on local living costs, financial-aid programs, and the like.

Then, using this material and your own estimates of other costs, make out financial work sheets to give yourself an idea of what a year's total expenses will be. If you're careful, you'll come very close to the actual amount.

Two tips: *Add* 7 per cent a year for the second year, 15 per cent for the third year, and 23 per cent for the fourth year to take inflation and other price-boosting factors into account. *Don't* underestimate, and thus invite a rude shock later on.

Use the following college-expense work sheet to estimate and compare college costs:

ANNUAL EXPENSE ITEM*	COLLEGE A	COLLEGE B	COLLEGE C
Tuition			
All fees (student activity, library, application, breakage, etc.)			
Room and board			
Books			
Equipment and supplies			
Laboratory charges			
Travel to and from school			
All other travel			
Recreation and entertainment			
Clothing			
Laundry, dry cleaning, etc.			
Dues for fraternity or sorority			
Grooming (cosmetics, haircuts, etc.)			

* If you are a married couple, see Chapter 1, "Your Personal Money Manager," pages 23–25.

ANNUAL EXPENSE ITEM*	COLLEGE A	COLLEGE B	COLLEGE C
Health expenditure (incl. insurance premiums)	_____	_____	_____
Snacks, cigarettes, etc.	_____	_____	_____
Church and charity contributions	_____	_____	_____
Your capital expenditures, prorated annually (car, bicycle, record player and records, musical instruments, sports equipment, etc.)	_____	_____	_____
Miscellaneous current expenses	_____	_____	_____
Total annual estimate	_____	_____	_____

* If you are a married couple, see Chapter 1, "Your Personal Money Manager," pages 23–25.

WHERE WILL THE MONEY COME FROM?

The essential element in getting a college education is the motivation of you and your family. Despite the enormous price tag, if you *really* want an education, you'll get the funds for it somehow.

Obviously, the first answer to the question "Where will the money come from?" is from family savings built up over many years for precisely this purpose. This is where the motivation of parents comes in, for the savings must be accumulated through long-term planning, periodic investment, discipline, and dedication.

If your children are young enough, it may be possible for you to put away enough in savings to get a head start on college costs. However, unless you're most unusual your savings will not be enough.

A second answer, therefore, must be deductions from current income. This is where the working mother enters the picture in brilliant light—for it is her earnings which have become, are, and will be among the biggest sources for college education funds. Without the contributions of their mothers to their education funds, millions of students simply could not make it.

But neither of these answers is anywhere near adequate.

So we come to the fundamental point that most families trying to get one or more children through school must have help. Here are the other key sources of college education money:

- A student's own savings and earnings, part time and during vacations.
- Loans. These can range from federal and state loans to those arranged

through civic organizations, social clubs, churches, and commercial lending institutions.

• Scholarships. Perhaps the most sought-after single source of aid, scholarships are awarded by the colleges and universities themselves, by corporations, veterans' groups, civic groups, cities, states, private philanthropies and foundations, a host of others.

• Grants. Much of this money goes to the low-income student, and most of the funds come from the federal government—although corporations and foundations offer substantial amounts of grant money as well. For most grant money, academic achievement is not a factor.

You probably will find that you will wind up with some combination of all of these.

SCHOLARSHIPS

THE SCHOLARSHIP SQUEEZE

Every few months a headline in newspapers across the country proclaims "Millions in Scholarships Go Begging." The story usually is released by firms that use computers to search for scholarships, which match the needs, interests, and qualifications of students against huge banks of details on the scholarships actually available to them today.

And there are a lot of specialized scholarships knocking around, for would-be organic vegetable growers, future rodeo ropers, pottery majors, prospective missionaries, direct descendants of Union soldiers who served in the Civil War, etc.

I would never downgrade *any* effective scholarship matching service— computerized or otherwise. I certainly won't claim that every penny of available scholarship money is actually being used, particularly those "funny funds" for students with special interests or special backgrounds. But I *will* quarrel with the cruel implication that huge sums of scholarship money are being wasted because students and parents simply don't know where to find such funds. It just isn't true. The students who are in college now are up against the biggest scholarship squeeze in our history.

Among the facts on scholarships today:

• At a growing number of colleges more than half of the student body is getting some type of financial assistance.

• Federal funds of all kinds to assist college students, which were counted in the millions only a decade or so ago, now are counted in the billions. *But* most federal funds are going today into low-cost publicly subsidized loans and work-study grants, rather than into straight scholarships.

• Scholarships are, as always, by far the most eagerly fought-over source of financial aid, whether the giver is government, colleges, corporations, foundations, cities, states, or civic organizations. If *you* let yourself count on getting one, chances are you'll be bitterly disappointed, for only a fraction of those who apply ever get one. Furthermore, the individual amounts involved often are $500 or less—a sum which barely touches real-life financial needs.

SCHOLARSHIP SHOPPING LIST

Here's a rundown on some scholarships now available.

• *The National Merit Scholarship Corporation,* which hands out millions in scholarships each year, is the largest, best-known, and most widely sought private scholarship source in the United States today. More than a million students take the combined PSAT/NMSQT three-hour test every fall in high schools across the country both for guidance purposes and in competition for one of these scholarships. But only about 3,000 ever get one. The scholarships range in value from $100 to $1,500 a year for four years, with financial need being the yardstick to determine who gets the $1,500. Some winners simply get one-shot stipends of $1,000. Just about every high school in the country takes part, so you might as well try. See your guidance counselor.

There is one added dividend here. Even if you're not one of the lucky finalists, you could be one of the 50,000 who receive special commendations and citations because of your test scores. *These can help you when you look for financial help elsewhere.*

• *State scholarships* number in the thousands, vary all over the lot in size, terms, etc. For information, check with your school guidance counselor or state Department of Education. If you are a handicapped student, check with your state Department of Vocational Rehabilitation.

• *Labor unions* also now award large numbers of scholarships. Check with either your union or the union your parents belong to. Or write for the "Student Aid Bulletin—Scholarships Offered by Labor Unions" ($2.00 prepaid; Chronicle Guidance Publications, Moravia, New York, 13118).

• *Corporation scholarships* are a worth-while source of funds, so don't overlook them. Many businesses now offer scholarships for children of employees. Some companies award scholarships to students who have no connection with the company.

• *Trade associations* often have their own scholarships for children of members.

• *Civic and fraternal organizations* sponsoring scholarships range from the American Legion posts or auxiliary units to the Elks, Lions, Masons, Parent-Teacher Associations, and Daughters of the American Revolution. In most instances scholarships are for young men and women living in the community in which the organization is located.

• *Other sponsors include* the Boy Scouts, 4-H Clubs, Chamber of Commerce, Jaycees, Junior Achievement, a wide range of religious organizations.

• Black students are aided by the National Scholarship Service and Fund for Negro Students (1776 Broadway, New York, N.Y. 10019).

• *Professional associations* are worth following up, and if you already have plans to enter a specialty after you finish college, check with the professional associations in your future specialty for what financial aid they offer. Many try to stimulate young students to enter their fields through scholarships and fellowships.

• *The Supplemental Educational Opportunity Grant Program* is the federal government's key scholarship source. This is not a scholarship program in the usual sense, for the primary criterion is not academic excellence but rather *exceptional* financial need. Still, some 400,000 low-income students (family income less than $9,000) got a total of $240 million in grants in fiscal 1975.

Eligible students received grants for up to four years of undergraduate work and the amounts ranged from $200 to $1,500 per year, up to $4,000 for four years of college, $5,000 for a five-year program. The total may not exceed one half of a student's estimated financial needs. To qualify, students must be exceptionally needy, but need not be academic stars. These grants are matched by the institutions with other forms of aid such as loans and jobs. Nearly 3,400 colleges and universities participated in this program during the 1975-76 academic year, making awards directly to the students. Check with the director of student financial aid at the institution you want to attend for more details.

• *Basic Educational Opportunity Grants,* authorized by the Education Amendments of 1972, are available to half or full-time undergraduate college, vocational, and technical school students.

The grants are designed to add up to half the total costs of attending a school. Theoretically, the amounts go up to $1,400 a year—but the average in 1975 was about $800 per student. To apply, get an "application for determination of expected financial contribution" from your high school guidance counselor, public library, college financial aid officer, or the U.S. Office of Education. Fill out the form and send it to the address indicated. A computer will estimate what your family should be able to contribute toward your education.

When this data is returned to you, report the amount to the financial aid officer at your chosen school.

• *ROTC scholarships* are being awarded to students at hundreds of colleges in most states of the United States. ROTC scholarships gained in popularity after the end of the Vietnam war and during the economic slump of 1975-76.

These scholarships are aimed at students wanting to pursue careers as officers in the military services. In most programs, full costs of tuition, books, and fees—plus a monthly allowance for living expenses—are covered. In return, you, the participant, must commit yourself to a military career. In the Army, though, you can retire after only twenty years of service at one half your base pay. To apply, contact the appropriate military service or the ROTC office at the participating college of your choice. Application deadlines in most cases are in November and December.

• The federal government also has substantial sums available to students going into special fields—particularly health. Scholarships range up to $3,500 per year. To get details, write to the Bureau of Health Resources Development, National Institutes of Health, 9000 Rockville Pike, Bethesda, Md. 20014.

This is only a sampling. Any complete listing of scholarships available in this country today would be so extensive that it would make a book of its own.

WHAT DOES IT TAKE TO GET A SCHOLARSHIP?

How needy must you—or your family—be? What factors, in addition to academic standing, boost a student's chances for a scholarship today?

Generally speaking, a high school student today must graduate with at least a B average and rank in the top half of his class to get into a good four-year college. The requirements are understandably tougher for scholarships.

But high grades are not the sole yardstick for winning a scholarship. Even without a superior academic record these other factors can help tremendously toward a scholarship: a student's outstanding personality, a demonstrated capacity for leadership, an unusual or special talent (say in music, art, sports, foreign languages).

Special consideration is now often given, too, to students from minority groups or candidates who have overcome a severe handicap or misfortune during their lives.

How needy must your family be?

Whether you are merely a better-than-average student or one with a straight A record, your key to getting a scholarship will be *proving need*. You cannot just *plead* poverty; you must *prove* it.

The gifted child of the very needy has the best chances for most scholarships. But some help is also available to students whose families have other burdensome expenses. Or help may be available if college costs are especially high at the institution the child wishes to attend.

For instance, even the $20,000-a-year family may be considered "needy" —if there are three children to support and if the college charges $3,000 to $4,000 or more a year.

Although less needy students and their families are expected to contribute substantial shares of their earnings, savings, and assets toward college costs, a family's total financial picture is taken into account—and the amount the family is expected to pay is measured by what it can "reasonably afford." Today's student financial aid is designed to fill the gap between that sum and total college costs.

How are "total" costs and family "need" figured today?

Here are the basic guidelines of the College Scholarship Service, part of the non-profit service of the College Entrance Examination Board in New York City, which helps major U.S. colleges determine eligibility of students for financial aid.

In calculating total college costs, the CSS includes not only tuition and fees but also room, board, transportation, clothing, books, spending money.

In calculating family need, it takes into account these major factors: family income, number of other children to support, the breadwinner's age and retirement plans, unusual financial burdens such as other children in college at the same time, an expensive illness, whether the spouse works, size of debts.

The CSS also weighs total family assets—cash savings, equity in the home, securities owned, etc.—and applies a share of this total to the amount a family can afford to contribute. This share, though, is comparatively small —12 per cent—and assets up to $10,000 are usually not counted. If the family head is more than fifty-five years old, even higher asset totals are disregarded.

You, the scholarship seeker, are expected to contribute part of your total college costs. Typically, your expected contribution would include 30 per cent of your current savings for each year that you are in college. Also about $500 in summer earnings must be contributed for the first year (before you enter college), and increasing amounts for the following years.

Here is what the CSS believes families should be able to contribute in the 1977-78 academic year toward college costs for one child—at various income levels and with varying numbers of dependent children.

INCOME BEFORE TAXES	ONE CHILD	TWO CHILDREN	THREE CHILDREN
$ 8,000	$ 97	$ 0	$ 0
10,000	410	124	0
12,000	707	419	164
14,000	1,013	724	473
16,000	1,386	1,042	779
18,000	1,832	1,418	1,109
20,000	2,368	1,856	1,484

These are just "suggested" contributions. By no means do they bind any college to provide the balance of the costs. They do give you a general indication of what financial efforts are expected in the mid-1970s from the student and his family. They also indicate what financial help many colleges are trying to provide you or your child via scholarships, loans, and student jobs.

"HIDDEN" SCHOLARSHIPS

Are you aware that Social Security benefits are a major source of income for many students? Could it be that you're among the many qualifying for such benefits today but you don't know it?

All of you who are unmarried full-time students qualify for this Social Security program, which can be a major income supplement to help you meet college costs—*if you are children of deceased, disabled, or retired workers*. Check at once at your nearest Social Security office.

And do you realize that veterans' educational benefits are now being paid to hundreds of thousands of college students—and tens of thousands of veterans' wives, widows, and children are also receiving college benefits? These benefits represent more help to students than all scholarships at all U.S. colleges and universities put together.

Under the Veterans Readjustment Benefits Act of 1966 (the "Cold War GI Bill"), single veterans who have been at some time on active duty since January 31, 1955, were being paid $270 a month in 1974 if they attended an accredited college or other educational institution. Married veterans were getting as much as $321 a month. Married veterans with one child were getting up to $366 a month—and $22 for each additional child. Stipends were reduced for veterans studying less than full time. For example, the monthly benefit for a single half-time student was $135 ($160 for a married student).

You, as a veteran, can get these "scholarships" not only to attend college but also to complete high school if you have not already done so; or to attend business school; or to enroll in a wide variety of vocational training programs. There are provisions for farm co-operative training and 90 per cent reimbursement programs for correspondence school and flight training. If you have difficulty with your studies, the VA will pay for tutoring (up to $60 a month). Veterans in apprenticeship or on-the-job training programs in 1974 were eligible for stipends of $196 per month if single, or $220 per month if married and more if there were children.

In addition, under the so-called "Junior GI Bill," if you are a wife, widow, widower, or child of a veteran who died or became permanently and totally disabled as a result of his military service, you can get similar monthly stipends to attend college.

And if you're already enrolled in a VA educational program, you can get extra allowances if you agree to work up to 250 hours for the VA (up to $625 per semester in 1975).

HOW TO GET A GRADUATE FELLOWSHIP

A single year of graduate study now costs a staggering $4,500 to $8,000. A Ph.D. may cost $25,000 to $30,000 or more, on top of as much as $30,000 for undergraduate schooling.

Obviously the vast majority of you cannot afford such sums, even though you may be acutely aware of the potential long-range return on the investment. You must have financial help. Fellowships, which have jumped to an average of about $3,000 a year today, are a major solution.

However, the number of fellowships is diminishing and competition for graduate fellowships is fierce, particularly in the sciences and particularly for the fattest fellowships. There are only a limited number of fellowships available to the non-genius with a serious interest in higher education. For him or her, the emphasis is on loans and jobs.

So, if you are considering graduate study and need a fellowship to help support it, here are five basic rules for finding and applying for one:

(1) Consult your graduate study adviser and professors in your major department on kinds and sources of fellowships and on institutions you might want to attend. Write the graduate school of each university to which you intend to apply and ask what financial assistance is available. The universities administer not only their own fellowship funds but also many of the government and private foundation funds as well.

(2) Find out all the financial details of each fellowship for which you think you might qualify. Exactly what does it cover: Tuition? Travel? The full year? Or only the academic year? Will the funds be tax-free? Are there special allowances for dependents?

(3) Focus on three or four fellowship sources, and confine your efforts to those for which you think you really qualify.

(4) Fill out application forms neatly, concisely, thoughtfully, and correctly. Pay special attention to your statement on why you want a fellowship and how you intend to use it. Include with your application *all* supporting documents which may be required, letters of recommendation, special tests, academic records, financial information, etc.

(5) Get your application in on time. Deadlines for some fellowships are as early as the fall of your senior year in college. Preparation of your applications can easily take as long as six months before the deadline.

EARN YOUR WAY: IT'S "IN"

COLLEGE CO-OP PROGRAMS

You should be able to earn $5,000 to $13,000 or more during your college years without endangering your college standing. With other financial assistance you can get, you should be able to boost your income to $18,000 over the college period, a major portion of the cost of education at even the more expensive private universities.

It is actually easier to work your way through college than it has ever been. It also is "in" as never before. Even at such institutions as Massachusetts Institute of Technology and Harvard, half or more of all undergraduates hold jobs during the school year. Today literally millions of U.S. students are earning more than half of their total instructional costs at private colleges and one third of these costs at public colleges.

The typical part-time job at college now pays $400 to $800 during the academic year.

Here is a typical four-year income program:

$2,100 for four summers or $525 a year, including a pre-freshman summer;

$240 each year for the Christmas, mid-season, and spring vacations;

$450 each year for part-time work while school is in session.

This approximates $5,000 for the four years.

Meanwhile, co-operative education programs—under which students alternate periods of study with periods of work, frequently in their field of interest—are multiplying. Some 125,000 college students at more than 500 colleges the nation over are now using these work-study programs to earn an estimated $300 million during the school year. Another 400 are considering establishing these programs on an optional basis or in certain departments. At some schools, including Antioch, Wilberforce, and Boston's huge Northeastern University (one of the pioneers in the co-operative education movement), participation in this kind of plan is *mandatory*.

Although the programs differ from place to place, the basic aim is the same: to spread the financial burden so that the student shares part of the loan with parents and/or the college. Most plans also spread tuition costs as well, simply by requiring five years to earn a degree instead of the usual four.

At Northeastern, more than 15,000 full-time students were enrolled in some 46 different degree programs in a recent year and also worked for more than 2,000 employers across the nation. Here's how the five-year Northeastern study schedule works:

As in most plans of this type, the freshman year is spent in regular, full-time, on-campus study. During the next four years the student alternates between three months of school and three months working on a paying job. He is paired with another student so that the job is covered full time throughout the year without a break. At the end of five years the graduate has his degree, plus about two years of relevant job experience—and that's a *priceless* plus these days.

The college usually will find the job for you and, ideally, the position will be related in some way to your field of study. When the job market is tight, you may not be able to count on getting just the kind of job you had in mind and business cutbacks may also temporarily cut down on your choice of jobs. But these cycles run their course in time. Employers also are showing increasing sympathy to the needs of students and willingness to employ them on a temporary, part-time basis.

How much can you earn in a work-study program of this type? The *average* annual earnings of the co-op student in the mid-1970s were approaching $3,000. This was about $1,500 higher than the earnings of the student in the more traditional type of school.

Most students can earn between $60 and $200 per week during work assignments—with the average about $113 a week. Thus, if you live at home during the work periods, you should be able to earn and save about half your tuition.

For example, at Philadelphia's Drexel University the tuition, fees, and room and board in the 1972–73 academic year were $14,288 for the traditional four-year course, and $15,295 for the five-year co-op plan also offered by the school.

A four-year student, working summers and vacations, can earn perhaps $5,000. This leaves a tab of $9,288 to be paid. On the other hand, a co-op student can earn about $12,850 in engineering and about $14,690 in business. This leaves only another $2,445 for the engineer or $605 for the business student to pay over a period of five years.

And don't discount the *intangibles* of co-op education: many students, for instance, find the work experience gives them a heightened sense of responsibility, more confidence in their decisions, and greater maturity.

For a list of colleges offering co-op programs write: National Commission for Cooperative Education, 360 Huntington Avenue, Boston, Mass. 02115.

THE FEDERAL WORK-STUDY PROGRAM

Since 1965 more than a million college students from low-income families have been helped by the federal government's work-study program.

This program, which should not be confused with co-operative education, is strictly aimed at promoting summer and part-time employment of students with great financial need in order to help them get through school. The jobs are *not* necessarily related to the anticipated careers for which the students are studying but in some cases they are career-geared.

Here's how it works: the government provides up to 80 per cent of the salaries of those students who qualify for jobs on campus or by nearby employers; the latter must be non-profit, non-religious, and non-political. Students are paid at least the basic national minimum wage.

You may qualify if you can demonstrate need. You'll probably average about fifteen hours of work while you're attending classes, and work about forty hours a week between semesters and during the summer.

More than half a million students and about 3,000 institutions were participating in 1974. So it's more than likely that the college you prefer participates in this program.

Many governmental agencies are also taking part in the work-study program as employers. There's a whole range of them you should look into. For instance:

• The Civil Service Commission hires students during summer periods in a variety of specialties, including such esoteric fields as oceanography.

• The U. S. Weather Bureau hires students to train in meteorology.

• The Army, Navy, and Coast Guard all have co-operative programs and hire undergraduate technical students in engineering, mathematics, science, and accounting.

Other agencies involved include the Federal Aviation Agency, the Federal Communications Commission, the National Aeronautics and Space Administration, and the Departments of Commerce, Agriculture, and Interior.

The federal "academic apprentice" program is operated very much like other co-operative-education programs in that students alternate study and work periods. It will give you a chance to earn while you learn, and may give you a clue as to whether you would enjoy government work later on.

For information, contact the Civil Service Commission or those government agencies which have departments in your specialty. If you have *any* questions, check with your college placement office.

LOANS

HOW TO SHOP FOR A COLLEGE LOAN

For you, the students with high grades and great financial need, there will be an unprecedented number of scholarships and low-cost student loans to help you through college.

But what about the millions of you who are students with marks which are less than excellent? What about the millions of students who aren't considered needy enough by federal, state, or university standards to qualify for a scholarship or a loan at little or no interest? What about parents in the middle to higher income brackets who suddenly face the staggering drain of a college education for two or more children?

Confronted by the steep and rising costs of college education, mounting numbers of families are turning to commercial banks, savings and loan associations, insurance companies, credit unions, and other lending institutions for college loans. Thousands of private lending institutions are now offering an increasing variety of college loan plans with a wide variety of repayment terms and interest costs.

How can you—a student or a parent—find your way through the maze of college loan plans? This point is as vital in this sphere as in all others: You must shop. You must shop for a college loan as you would for a mortgage or any major personal purchase.

Here, then, are basic rules for finding the best deal—assuming you do not qualify for scholarship assistance or a loan at little or no interest:

• As I urged you at the start of this chapter, first draw up a total budget for all anticipated college costs—including tuition, board, room, books, clothes, transportation, spending money. Divide this amount by the total number of semesters of school attendance.

• Decide how big a debt you can handle and don't exceed your limit.

• Decide how long you will need to repay the loan.

• Present these figures to at least two or three different lenders and ask what monthly payments would be required—including any charges for insurance.

• Compare the bids. The lowest monthly charge will be the most favorable to you—assuming equal repayment periods, equal loan amounts, and equal insurance charges.

THE LOANS AVAILABLE TO YOU: A LIST

Here are the kinds of loans available to you as a student, starting with the least expensive. Look into them in this order:

(1) A college loan involving low interest on the loan, which is repayable starting sometime after graduation.

(2) A federal government loan which is administered by a college.

(3) A loan that is guaranteed by a state and/or the federal government.

(4) A low-interest loan through a civic or religious group.

(5) A deferred-tuition plan offered by a number of schools.

(6) A loan from a credit union, if you're a member.

(7) A bank or insurance company loan.

(8) As a last resort, a finance company loan.

Now, the details . . .

COLLEGE LOANS FROM COLLEGES THEMSELVES

What to Do

Hundreds of colleges and universities are now offering long-term loan programs of their own to you, the student. Almost all of these are bargains in terms of low interest rates and tolerable repayment schedules.

You'll find that the amount of money available through these loans does not begin to compare with the huge sums available from other sources. But if you're lucky enough to borrow through a school's own program, most of your financial worries will be minimized from the very beginning.

Loans made to: Students

Loans made by: College itself. May be short-term emergency loan. Or may be in co-operation with federal government for long-term. Or may be a long-term loan under a postponed tuition plan.

Amount of loans: Varies widely. Can be small if short-term emergency loan or can run into thousands of dollars.

Interest rates: Also vary widely, no fixed rate, but almost always compare *very favorably* with rates charged by others.

Repayment: Starts at graduation or a year thereafter if ordinary college loan; can be stretched out over a very long period. Repayment is likely to be deferred for as long as the student is in graduate school.

How to apply: Go directly to the financial aid officer at your college.

FEDERALLY ASSISTED STUDENT LOAN PROGRAMS

National Direct Student Loans

The 1958 National Defense Education Act established an unprecedented program of low-interest, long-term loans to students with financial need. This legislation literally multiplied the volume of loan funds for higher education. More recently, the National Defense Education Act was superseded by the Educational Amendments of 1972, and the revised program was renamed the National Direct Student Loans. Key facts of this program:

Loans made to: Students who are citizens or permanent residents of the United States and plan to study at a college in this country.

Loans approved by: Colleges on the basis of student's needs. College student aid officers on campus determine which students are eligible and the amount of money to be loaned.

   This is a vital point, for you must demonstrate that you are *in financial need* to get one of these loans if your income is above $15,000. The student financial aid officer may expect you to accept some

Loans approved by: (CONTD)	part-time work to minimize your loan needs and to give the college making the loan an opportunity to spread available funds among a larger number of students. Some colleges also require parents to complete a detailed account of the family's *entire* financial picture as a way of determining how much the parents can be expected to contribute to the student's educational costs.
Who puts up money:	For each NDS loan, the federal government puts up 90 per cent of the money and the college itself puts up 10 per cent.
Amount of loans:	Up to $10,000 for graduate or professional students; up to $5,000 for students who have finished two years of a program leading to a bachelor's degree; and up to $2,500 for all other students. The size of the loan for you will probably *not be these maximums,* though. The amount you get will depend on *your* individual financial need as well as on the funds available at the college you will attend.
Interest rates:	3 per cent a year, paid by the student beginning with the start of the repayment period.
Repayment starts:	Nine months after the student ceases at least half-time study.
Repayment period:	Can be stretched out over a ten-year period.
How to apply:	Go directly to the student financial aid officer on your campus.
Other points:	No repayment is required and no interest is charged for any period up to three years during which you are serving in the armed forces, Peace Corps, or Vista. Up to half your loan may be canceled at the rate of 12.5 per cent for each complete year of armed forces service in a combat zone. Also, if you, the student, become a teacher for the handicapped, or Head Start, or in a school in an unusually low-income area, all of your loan may be canceled at the rate of 15 per cent a year. As part of the application procedure, you must

Other points:
(CONTD)

sign, and have notarized, an affidavit affirming that the loan will be used for educational purposes only.

There are several other direct loan programs for students in special fields, notably health professions and law enforcement. For information on these programs, see your guidance counselor or financial aid officer.

Government Guaranteed Student Loan Programs

Before 1965 a number of states financed programs guaranteeing repayment of college loans to protect private lenders against default by students, in order to make such loans more attractive to the lenders. Since then, the Higher Education Act of 1965, the National Vocational Student Loan Insurance Act of 1965, and the Educational Amendments of 1972 have made federal loan repayment guarantees available in states without programs of their own. The key facts:

Loans made to:

Students who are enrolled and in good standing, or accepted for enrollment, at an eligible school. Some states require full-time attendance, but the federal government and most states accept half-time students for their programs.

Borrowers must be citizens or permanent residents of the United States.

Eligible schools:

Most public and private institutions of higher education. Also eligible: many vocational, business, trade, correspondence, and technical schools, and some schools located in 55 countries abroad—a vital point you should not miss. In the mid-seventies more than 8,000 institutions were eligible. The Accreditation and Eligibility Staff of the Office of Education, Washington, D.C. 20202, can tell you whether or not a particular school is eligible.

Loans made by:

Nearly 20,000 participating lenders—commercial banks, savings and loan associations, credit unions, mutual savings banks, some colleges, insurance companies, and pension plans.

Amount of loans:

You normally may borrow as much as $2,500 per year toward your education, depending on your educational costs. However, some state programs may

Amount of loans: (CONTD)	place a lower ceiling on borrowing than this. And, of course, a lender may be unwilling to lend you the maximum for his own reasons. Your total loan may not exceed $7,500 if you are an undergraduate or vocational student, or $10,000 if you are borrowing for graduate study.
Interest rates:	A maximum rate to you of 7 per cent per year, in simple annual interest. In addition, the federal government pays a "special allowance" of up to 3 per cent, readjusted quarterly, to lenders to make the loans more attractive to them.
	Loans may be available at lower rates at times of very low general interest rates, but you ordinarily should expect to pay the 7 per cent maximum. In addition, there may be a charge for an insurance premium up to ½ per cent a year on the unpaid principal balance (this is limited to ¼ per cent on federally insured loans).
	If your adjusted family income is less than $15,000 a year, you will not face a needs analysis test and the federal government will pay your interest until the start of your repayment period. You may still qualify for these federal interest benefits if your gross adjusted income is above $15,000, but then you must pass a needs test.
Repayment starts:	Nine to twelve months after you leave school.
Repayment period:	May extend to ten years after you leave school—subject to a maximum of fifteen years from the date the loan was made. The minimum yearly payment is $360.
	If you join the Peace Corps or Vista after graduation, or if you go into military service, payments may be deferred for up to three years. Repayment also may be deferred for any time you spend in further full-time study at an eligible school.
	Your federal interest subsidy resumes during the payment-deferral period if you were eligible before.
Prepayment:	Allowed without penalty.
How to apply:	Go to the financial aid officer of the college you plan to attend and fill out the appropriate forms. Then go to one or more lenders in your own town or city where

How to apply:
(CONTD)

you or your parents have accounts or other established business relationships, and find out whether they participate in the Guaranteed Student Loan Program. Visit banks and savings institutions, of course, but do not forget credit unions.

If you do not find a participating lender, write or go immediately to the financial aid officer of your college, or the nearest regional office of the U. S. Office of Education or state guarantee agency (see pages 398–400 for appropriate addresses), and ask for the names and locations of financial institutions near your home which do participate.

Ask the appropriate officer at the lending institution to help you complete the necessary forms. Your college's financial aid office may help you with the forms (and it should analyze your finances to determine your loan needs) to be submitted as a recommendation to the lender. You also will have to sign an affidavit declaring that your loan will be used only for educational purposes. The affidavit must be notarized.

The lender will evaluate your application and the school's recommendation and decide how large a loan will qualify for federal interest benefits and how much it will lend you.

You might find it difficult to locate a lender when money is tight, though the history of the program suggests that if you keep trying you will find one.

By all means, when you apply, check on what restrictions the lender makes on loan recipients. This could save you a lot of time and work as well as the disappointment of getting needlessly involved in the elaborate application process at a balky financial institution.

United Student Aid Funds

The largest private guarantor of student loans today is the non-profit United Student Aid Funds (845 Third Avenue, New York, N.Y. 10022), supported primarily by foundations and private business contributions. The USAF is not only a major participant in the Government Guaranteed Student Loan Programs, in its role as the administrator of a number of state programs; it also has a separate guaranteed student loan program with many hundreds of colleges and universities participating in all fifty states. The key characteristics of these loans are exactly the same as previously described for government guaranteed student loan programs.

Where can you get detailed information on the Government Guaranteed Student Loan Program operating in your state?

Here are the addresses:

ALABAMA
Director of Higher Education
Office of Education, Region IV
50 Seventh Street, N.E.
Atlanta, Ga. 30323

ALASKA
Student Aid Officer
State Education Office
Pouch F, AOB
Juneau, Alas. 99801

ARIZONA
Director of Higher Education
Office of Education, Region IX
50 Fulton Street
San Francisco, Calif. 94102

ARKANSAS
Student Loan Guarantee
    Foundation of Arkansas
Suite 515, 1515 West 7th Street
Little Rock, Ark. 72202

CALIFORNIA (*see* Arizona)

COLORADO
Director of Higher Education
Office of Education, Region VIII
9017 Federal Office Building
19th & Stout Streets
Denver, Colo. 80202

CONNECTICUT
Connecticut Student Loan
    Foundation
251 Asylum Street
Hartford, Conn. 06103

DELAWARE
Delaware Higher Education Loan
    Program
% Brandywine College
P. O. Box 7139
Wilmington, Del. 19803

DISTRICT OF COLUMBIA
D.C. Student Loan Insurance
    Program
1329 E Street, N.W.
Washington, D.C. 20004

FLORIDA (*see* Alabama)

GEORGIA
Georgia Higher Education
    Assistance Corporation
9 LaVista Perimeter Park
2187 Worthlake Parkway
Atlanta, Ga. 30084

HAWAII (*see* Arizona)

IDAHO
Director of Higher Education
Office of Education, Region X
1321 Second Avenue
Seattle, Wash. 98101

ILLINOIS
Illinois Guaranteed Loan Program
102 Wilmot Road, P. O. Box 33
Deerfield, Ill. 60015

INDIANA
Director of Higher Education
Office of Education, Region V
300 South Wacker Drive
Chicago, Ill. 60606

IOWA
Director of Higher Education
Office of Education, Region VII
601 East 12th Street
Kansas City, Mo. 64106

KANSAS (*see* Iowa)

KENTUCKY (*see* Alabama)

LOUISIANA
Louisiana Higher Education
    Assistance Commission
P. O. Box 44095
Capitol Station
Baton Rouge, La. 70804

MAINE
Maine State Department of
    Education and Cultural
    Services
Augusta, Me. 04330

MARYLAND
Maryland Higher Education Loan
    Corporation
2100 Guilford Avenue
Baltimore, Md. 21218

MASSACHUSETTS
Massachusetts Higher Education
    Assistance Corporation
511 Statler Building
Boston, Mass. 02116

MICHIGAN
Michigan Higher Education
    Assistance Authority
309 North Washington Avenue
Lansing, Mich. 48902

MINNESOTA (*see* Indiana)

MISSISSIPPI (*see* Alabama)

MISSOURI (*see* Iowa)

MONTANA (*see* Colorado)

NEBRASKA (*see* Iowa)

NEVADA
State Department of Education
Carson City, Nev. 89701

NEW HAMPSHIRE
New Hampshire Higher Education
    Assistance Foundation
3 Capitol Street
Concord, N.H. 03301

NEW JERSEY
New Jersey Higher Education
    Assistance Authority
65 Prospect Street
P. O. Box 1293
Trenton, N.J. 08625

NEW MEXICO
Director of Higher Education
Office of Education, Region VI
1114 Commerce Street
Dallas, Tex. 75202

NEW YORK
New York Higher Education
    Assistance Corporation
50 Wolf Road
Albany, N.Y. 12205

NORTH CAROLINA
State Education Assistance
    Authority

P. O. Box 2688
Chapel Hill, N.C. 27514

NORTH DAKOTA (*see* Colorado)

OHIO
Ohio Student Loan Commission
33 North High Street
Columbus, O. 43215

OKLAHOMA
Oklahoma State Regents for Higher
    Education
118 Capitol Building
Oklahoma City, Okla. 73105

OREGON
Oregon State Scholarship
    Commission
1445 Willamette Street
Eugene, Ore. 97401

PENNSYLVANIA
Pennsylvania Higher Education
    Assistance Agency
Towne House, 660 Boas Street
Harrisburg, Pa. 17102

PUERTO RICO
Director of Higher Education
Office of Education, Region II
26 Federal Plaza
New York, N.Y. 10007

RHODE ISLAND
Rhode Island Higher Education
    Assistance Corporation
Room 414, 187 Westminster Mall
P. O. Box 579
Providence, R.I. 02901

SOUTH CAROLINA (see Alaska)

SOUTH DAKOTA (see Colorado)

TENNESSEE
Tennessee Education Loan
    Corporation
Cordell Hull Building
Fl. C-3, Rm. 301
Nashville, Tenn. 37219

TEXAS (see New Mexico)

UTAH (see Colorado)

VERMONT
Vermont Student Assistance
    Corporation
191 College Street
Burlington, Vt. 05401

VIRGINIA
Virginia State Education Assistance
    Authority
501 East Franklin Street
Suite 311
Professional Building
Richmond, Va. 23219

WASHINGTON (see Idaho)

WEST VIRGINIA
Director of Higher Education
Office of Education, Region III
P. O. Box 12900
Philadelphia, Pa. 19108

WISCONSIN
Wisconsin Higher Education
    Corporation
State Office Building
115 West Wilson Street
Madison, Wis. 53902

WYOMING (see Colorado)

AMERICAN SAMOA (see Arizona)

GUAM (see Arizona)

TRUST TERRITORY (see Arizona)

VIRGIN ISLANDS
United Student Aid Funds, Inc.
845 Third Avenue
New York, N.Y. 10022

LOANS FROM CIVIC ORGANIZATIONS

What to Do

Sources of college loans which are frequently overlooked but which might be ideal for you are local civic groups. Or perhaps your best bet would be a labor union or a church group.

Whatever the group, before you turn to a commercial lender, check into organizations such as these in your town. You well might find that one or more of them have substantial low-interest loans available to students.

Loans made to:	Students
Loans made by:	Organizations sponsoring the loan program: Rotary, Lions, Kiwanis, PTA, labor unions, churches, employers, etc.
Amounts:	Vary, depending on the financial resources of the organization and the student's need.
Interest rates:	Comparatively low against the money market at the time of loan.
Repayment:	Generally deferred for a while after graduation but also varies, according to the agreement between lender and borrower.
How to apply:	Consult your high school guidance counselor, your community center, your church, similar likely sources for information on what loans are available and your eligibility.

LOANS FROM PRIVATE FINANCIAL INSTITUTIONS

What to Do

If you can't develop other alternatives to finance your college education and must go the commercial loan route, do not hesitate to do so.

If a loan—even a long-term debt of thousands of dollars—is the difference between going to college and not going, consider it among the best investments you ever made.

Loans made to:	Parents, guardians, or students—usually the adults and students of legal majority age.
Loans made by:	Commercial banks, savings institutions, finance companies, credit unions, other financial sources.

Amount of loans: Not specifically limited, if the borrower has demonstrable ability to repay or satisfactory collateral. This is, in short, an ordinary personal loan for education purposes. Maximum, though, is usually $8,000 to $10,000. Funds usually given to borrower in lump sums at start of each semester.

Interest rates: Vary, depending on state of money market, area of country, caliber of borrower, term of loan.

Generally rates are relatively high against levels of the money markets at the time—and a minimum "service charge" may be added.

Repayment: Terms vary and depend on deal agreed upon but a period of six to eight years is fairly typical and repayments often start at the end of the first month of the loan's life.

"Special" College Loan Sources   Then there are private lending companies which specialize in education loans. Some offer special arrangements—"budget" plans, revolving credit accounts under which borrowers may repay loans in installments and prepay whenever possible, etc. The plans might involve a fee for joining, monthly service charge, insurance premium, possibly a cancellation charge, possibly other fees too.

The costs of each and all of these plans should be carefully compared—a chore which you will find made easier by the Truth in Lending law which requires the lenders to disclose all important details of the charges to you.

A major company specializing in education loans is: The Tuition Plan, Inc., 575 Madison Avenue, New York, N.Y. 10022.

Questions to Ask Each Lender

What is the simple interest rate on your loan? Remember, by law, this rate must be disclosed.

What extra charges are involved?

How much may your family borrow for each child?

Can the lender terminate the plan? Under what conditions? Does it have to give you notice before cancellation?

Can you, the borrower, terminate the loan before the expiration of the contract? How much notice are you required to give? Are there any prepayment penalties involved?

Is there an age limit above which a parent will no longer qualify for the loan?

What other restrictions are there?

POSTPONING TUITION—OR "PAYE"

"NEW" IDEA FOR FINANCING HIGHER EDUCATION

When my brother John was going to medical school in the depression years of the 1930s there was only one way he could finance it: through high-interest education loans, co-signed by the most financially respectable friends we had. Those loans were renewed . . . renewed . . . renewed . . . until many years later, when John had graduated from med school, returned from World War II, and was earning money as a physician, he was able to repay the debt out of his current income.

It was a clumsy, monstrously expensive way to meet the costs of his education but it was the best we could do. John got his education and became a physician and surgeon. His loans, although stretched out over a long period, were finally and honorably repaid. Both goals were achieved and that's all any of us cared about.

Now in the 1970s, a "new" idea for financing a college or graduate school education is a revolutionary refined version of John's makeshift plan. The idea has various names: "the Yale plan"; "deferred tuition"; "tuition postponement"; "pay as you earn" (or "PAYE"). But fundamentally the student does in the 1970s what John did in the 1930s; he or she postpones paying at least part of the tuition until the years after graduation, when he is earning money and can manage it out of his own income.

Yale was the pioneer in the experiment and other colleges have developed their own variations. A national tuition postponement option plan, patterned after Yale's program, is very much a possibility, if not a probability, in coming years. But a national tuition postponement plan remains in the future. Here, meanwhile, are the key features you'll find in most of today's plans:

• The schools borrow the funds from private sources such as banks. Because of the caliber of the borrower and because the loan is a single large transaction, rather than a lot of little ones, the interest charges are comparatively favorable. These charges are certainly much lower than you would be charged for a conventional loan at the same institution.

• The student defers tuition by getting a loan from this fund. Then, after graduation, he repays what he has deferred.

• Repayment is geared to the graduate's income. Some will pay back more than the cost of their respective loans; others a bit less, depending on their income level. Essentially, this means that those fortunate enough to earn more money in later life will help pay toward the education of those who earn less. Students can borrow to meet the cost of their education without losing the opportunity to take low-paying but possibly challenging jobs after graduation.

WHERE TO GET ADDITIONAL HELPFUL INFORMATION

Here is a sampling of free or inexpensive publications which should be of extraordinary help to you as you pursue this subject by yourself.

"Meeting College Costs: A Guide for Parents and Students." College Entrance Examination Board, Publications Order Office, Box 2815, Princeton, N.J. 08540. (Free. Updated annually.)

"College Costs Today," Promotion Services, Room 1108, New York Life Insurance Company, Career Information Service, 51 Madison Avenue, New York, N.Y. 10010. (Single copies free with self-addressed, stamped envelope.)

"Information for Students," U. S. Office of Education, Washington, D.C. 20202. (Free.)

"Need a Lift?" American Legion, Attention: Need a Lift, P. O. Box 1055, Indianapolis, Ind. 56206. (50¢.)

"How About College Financing," American Personnel and Guidance Association, 1607 New Hampshire Avenue N.W., Washington, D.C. 20009. (30¢.)

BEWARE: HOME STUDY GYPS

Today more home study courses are available by mail than you could possibly pursue in any single geographic region, or even at any of the nation's largest universities. Home study has truly "come of age" in the United States —a great force in upgrading the educational-economic status of millions, and a potent weapon in our nation's struggle to overcome skill shortages.

But as legitimate, worth-while home study courses have gone into a record boom, the racketeering fringe has expanded too. At last count, nearly one in twenty correspondence schools was granting unearned degrees. Among the many areas in which the gypsters have been "specializing": civil service training, electronics, operation of heavy equipment, real estate appraisal, nursing, and jet airplane mechanics.

For instance, not long ago a trio of gypsters peddled correspondence courses in such subjects as jet engine mechanics and missile design drafting at costs up to $660 with guarantees of jobs with leading U.S. corporations. The "school" failed to place a single student in any paying job. Total loss by the public: $2 million.

In another case, worthless correspondence courses in practical nursing were sold to women high school dropouts. Total take by this team over a ten-year period: about $3 million.

In a third scheme, the exact same "training course," supposedly for the U. S. Civil Service, was sold to different individuals wanting to become a law enforcement officer, a government meat inspector, and a park ranger.

How can you tell the worth-while home study program from the worthless and often exorbitantly priced one? Here are your guidelines:

• *No* legitimate correspondence school will or can guarantee a job after completion of its course.

• *Nobody* can qualify as a practical nurse through correspondence study alone.

• Be suspicious if a correspondence school uses a high-paying job opportunity as a come-on in an advertisement and this is followed by a high-pressure salesman who comes to your door to inform you that further training is needed to fulfill the job requirements (through the course he is peddling, naturally).

• If you have any doubt whatsoever about the value of any home study school or course you have seen advertised, check its reputation with the local Better Business Bureau, Chamber of Commerce, or state Department of Education.

• To find out what legitimate courses are available to you in the field you wish to pursue, consult a high school, college, or guidance counselor.

• Finally, get a free list of accredited, reputable home study schools from the National Home Study Council, 1601 Eighteenth Street N.W., Washington, D.C. 20009.

In the case of correspondence courses offered by *accredited* colleges and universities, a similar list entitled "Guide to Independent Study Through Correspondence Instruction" is available from National University Extension Association, Suite 360, 1 Dupont Circle N.W., Washington, D.C. 20036. ($1.00.)

You'll also find useful information on choosing a correspondence school in "Tips on Home Study Schools," a pamphlet available from the Council of Better Business Bureaus, Inc., 1150 Seventeenth Street N.W., Washington, D.C. 20036. (Single copies free.)

11

YOUR JOB, CAREER,
OR BUSINESS

SHOP FOR FRINGE BENEFITS, TOO! (CONTD)

BASIC ASSUMPTONS

The U. S. Bureau of Labor Statistics is the source of the ten-year projections quoted in this chapter. The Bureau of Labor Statistics, in turn, based them on the following major assumptions:

that we will maintain today's system of government and institutions;

that we will have a relatively low, although fluctuating rate of unemployment in this decade;

that the international climate will improve and our armed forces will be reduced and held at approximately 2 million men and women or below.

Given these basic assumptions . . .

WHERE WILL THE JOBS BE?

TRUE OR FALSE?

• The fastest growth in government jobs in the years ahead will be jobs in federal agencies.

• Most workers in the United States work for companies producing goods.

• In view of the U.S. population explosion, the biggest expansion in jobs for teachers will be in elementary and secondary schools.

• Increasing automation in the office will slash the number of jobs for office workers.

• Good jobs for high school graduates will shrink dramatically as more and more employers demand that workers have college degrees.

• Jobs in agriculture also will dwindle near to zero because of mechanization of farm work along with the virtual disappearance of the small farm.

• Our work force is growing older as our population generally lives longer, and thus more and more key positions are being filled by middle-aged and older employees.

If you answered "true" to *any* of these questions, you were wrong. If you answered "true" to most, you flunked.

Taking the questions one by one:

• There will be considerable growth in the number of government jobs. But the growth will be *much greater at the state and local levels* than at the federal level.

• More than half of the U.S. work force today is producing *services*— medical, teaching, banking, insurance, painting, writing, advising, planning, etc.—making us the first service-dominated economy in all world history. The vast majority of the new jobs now opening up are in the services. By contrast, manufacturing jobs are increasing an average of only a little more than 1 per cent a year during the 1970s.

• The fastest expansion in teaching jobs will be in adult education and at the two-year college level. During this decade the number of elementary schoolteachers is expected to increase only slightly. Our population not only isn't "exploding"; our growth rate has come to a virtual standstill.

• Automation in the office has reduced opportunities for certain types of workers but sharply increased demand for other important categories ranging from business machine operators and copying machine repair people to computer programers, tape librarians, and tape perforator typists.

• Despite the stress on college education in the 1970s, three out of four jobs will still be open to people who have *not* completed four years of college —including high school dropouts as well as high school graduates. More and more training is being required of young people, but it is not necessarily college training.

• The decline of the small farm has been going on for more than a century and by 1980 our entire food supply probably will be grown by a minuscule 3 per cent of the labor force. However, many new agricultural occupations are opening up in big "agribusinesses" which employ large numbers in fields ranging from stenography to surgery. And more and more farmers are going to college to learn biology, soil science, engineering, agronomy.

• Finally, instead of growing older, our work force actually has been growing steadily *younger,* with a majority of new jobs being filled during this decade by Americans in their twenties and thirties. A key force behind this trend is today's relative scarcity of middle-aged workers. (Not many babies were being born in the depression 1930s.) As a result, corporations and other employers are being compelled to reach into the younger age brackets to find executive and other talent—and this is creating major opportunities for many American men and women now in their late twenties and thirties.

REVOLUTION IN THE U.S. WORKPLACE

Can you define the following occupational fields?

Cryogenics
Fiber-optics
Geomagnetics
Pattern recognition

These are some of the job categories and occupational specialties which have just begun to appear on the U.S. job landscape.

Here are brief definitions of each:

Cryogenics: Study and use of super-cold temperatures, ranging from 110° F. below zero (the temperature of dry ice) to nearly 460° below zero ("absolute zero"). Cryogenic temperatures are used today for making liquid air, liquid natural gas, and for fast-freezing certain foods.

Fiber-optics: Use of transparent fibers made of glass or other materials to transmit light along curves and around corners. The technique is now being used to light otherwise inaccessible places such as inside the human body.

Geomagnetics: Study of the earth's composition (geology) through the measurement of irregularities or disturbances in its magnetic field.

Pattern recognition: Study of how to recognize patterns, especially when the patterns are hidden, incomplete, or partially obscured (e.g., in images, facts, concepts, information, etc.).

Just the strange sound of the above job titles underscores the extent to which whole new occupations are emerging under our eyes, while old occupations—ranging from the elevator operator to the railroad foreman—disappear.

KEY TRENDS IN JOBS AND CAREERS

Here are other key U.S. employment trends to watch for in the years directly ahead. Let them guide you not only in your initial career choice (if indeed you make such a "choice") but also in any of your deliberations over a *second* career.

• Demand for *professional and technical workers* will increase twice as fast as demand for all workers.

• Increasingly, *scientists and engineers* will become the heads of U.S. corporations.

• And hopefully, manufacturers, under pressure from consumers and government regulatory agencies, will be hiring workers to attend to *social and environmental* as well as strictly technical considerations—e.g., pollution controls, accident proofing of cars, factories, toys, and homes.

• Physicians also will be moving toward outpatient care and comprehensive, continuous health care for groups of people for whom this care has not previously been available, such as the urban poor and those living in isolated rural areas. (And for the "haves" as well.)

• Today's *"minorities"*—especially women and blacks—will find many new and better jobs as companies vie with each other to eliminate discrimination.

• *Part-time* jobs will open in many fields, creating new work opportunities for students, young mothers, older workers.

• Expanded *vocational rehabilitation* programs will boost job chances for the handicapped, the retarded, and ex-criminal offenders.

What message does this sampling of employment trends shout to you? This above all:

Before you settle on a final career choice you should at least scan the literally hundreds of different occupations which will be open to you in the years ahead. Find out which occupations within each career field seem to interest you. Then check the most promising job opportunities in each occupation. Then, and only then, zero in on the career you want.

CHANGES COMING IN YOUR WORK WEEK

One further vitally important trend in the U.S. work place is a reshuffling of your workday, work week, and work year.

Thousands of Americans are now moving to a four-day, forty-hour week, and unions are pushing for a four-day, thirty-two-hour week. Thousands of companies already are on some kind of rearranged week and this is a trend virtually sure to prevail in the years directly ahead.

The average full-time worker now puts in about 2,000 hours a year. Well within the career span of today's young college graduate—thirty years— trade unions hope the average American will be working as few as 1,600 hours a year, 20 per cent fewer than today.

The variations of work patterns are endless. Workers and employers may come around to "negotiating" their schedules and thus getting far more out of each other than they do now. One trend may be toward the "gliding" workday, with workers arriving and departing when they choose within a twelve-hour day; their only obligation would be to work a certain number of hours a week.

As for the advantages of extended time off, it can be a real antidote to on-the-job boredom—by permitting a worker to recharge his physical and mental abilities periodically. Moreover, many people find they can do things with extended periods of leisure that they cannot manage otherwise.

Experiments in a rearranged work week are, in fact, part of a broader trend toward greater employment flexibility which could well emerge in future years as a major cure for many of today's major sources of on-the-job discontent—particularly, enforced retirement. A shorter work week could meet the need of many older Americans to remain active—and also leave people more time to devote to community affairs and volunteer work.

Since the trend seems relentless, though, it is only common sense to start preparing now for the time when "5-40" gives way to "4-40" and then swings into "4-32." (How have you handled yourself on previous three-day holidays?) Look into the fascinating choices in volunteer work, the absorbing possibilities of second careers in services starving for you, the many deeply satisfying alternatives in the vast expanse of non-work.

Killing time is suicide on the installment plan.

WHERE WILL THE JOB OPPORTUNITIES GROW FASTEST?

First, here are the U. S. Labor Department's projections for growth in major occupational categories during the decade of the 1970s:

FIELD	PER CENT CHANGE 1970–80
Professional and technical workers	+39%
Service workers (except private household), e.g., hospital attendants, policemen, waitresses	+35
Clerical workers	+26
Sales workers	+24
Craftsmen and foremen	+20
Managers, officials, proprietors	+15
Operatives (assemblers, truck drivers, bus drivers)	+11
Non-farm laborers	− 6
Farm workers	−17
All occupations	+21

Here, even more specifically, is a list of occupations with job requirements projected to 1985:

OCCUPATION	ESTIMATED EMPLOYMENT 1972	PROJECTED REQUIREMENTS TO 1985
Business administration and related professions		
Accountants	714,000	935,000

OCCUPATION	ESTIMATED EMPLOYMENT 1972	PROJECTED REQUIREMENTS TO 1985
Clergy		
Ministers (Protestant)	325,000	360,000
Engineers		
Electrical	231,000	330,000
Mechanical	209,000	280,000
Civil	177,000	235,000
Industrial	125,000	190,000
Health service occupations		
Registered nurses	748,000	1,050,000
Licensed practical nurses	425,000	835,000
Physicians, M.D.s and D.O.s	330,000	485,000
Medical assistants	200,000	320,000
Pharmacists	131,000	163,000
Medical laboratory workers	165,000	210,000
Dentists	105,000	140,000
X-ray technologists	55,000	87,000
Dental assistants	115,000	155,000
Teachers		
Kindergarten and elementary schoolteachers	1,274,000	1,590,000
Secondary schoolteachers	1,023,000	1,045,000
College and university teachers	525,000	630,000
Technicians		
Engineering and science technicians	707,000	1,050,000
Draftsmen	327,000	485,000
Other professional and related occupations		
Lawyers	303,000	380,000
Programers	186,000	290,000
Social workers	185,000	275,000
Librarians	120,000	162,000
Home economists	120,000	140,000
Systems analysts	103,000	185,000

OCCUPATION	ESTIMATED EMPLOYMENT 1972	PROJECTED REQUIREMENTS TO 1985
Managerial occupations		
Managers and assistants (hotel)	110,000	160,000
Bank officers	219,000	308,000
Clerical and related occupations		
Stenographers and secretaries	3,074,000	4,950,000
Bookkeeping workers	1,584,000	1,900,000
Cashiers	998,000	1,360,000
Typists	1,021,000	1,400,000
Bank clerks	473,000	665,000
Stock clerks	511,000	750,000
Telephone operators	230,000	232,000
Shipping and receiving clerks	451,000	490,000
Office machine operators	195,000	230,000
Receptionists	436,000	650,000
Electronic computer operating personnel	480,000	531,000
File clerks	272,000	318,000
Bank tellers	248,000	350,000
Sales occupations		
Retail trade sales workers	2,778,000	3,330,000
Wholesale trade sales workers	688,000	860,000
Manufacturers' sales workers	423,000	545,000
Insurance brokers and agents	385,000	450,000
Real estate sales workers and brokers	349,000	435,000
Securities sales workers	220,000	290,000
Service occupations		
Private household workers	1,437,000	1,000,000
Building custodians	1,885,000	2,430,000
Waiters and waitresses	1,124,000	1,300,000
Hospital attendants	900,000	1,360,000
Cosmetologists	500,000	670,000
Police officers (municipal)	370,000	490,000
Guards and watchmen	250,000	320,000
Meat cutters	200,000	198,000
Firefighters	200,000	315,000
Barbers	157,000	147,000
Bartenders	200,000	235,000

OCCUPATION	ESTIMATED EMPLOYMENT 1972	PROJECTED REQUIREMENTS TO 1985
Building trades		
Carpenters	1,000,000	1,200,000
Painters and paperhangers	420,000	460,000
Plumbers and pipe fitters	400,000	500,000
Operating engineers (construction machinery operators)	435,000	570,000
Electricians (construction)	240,000	325,000
Bricklayers	180,000	225,000
Elevator constructors	17,000	25,000
Mechanics and Repairmen		
Automobile mechanics	727,000	860,000
Maintenance electricians	260,000	325,000
Appliance service workers	130,000	175,000
Industrial machinery repairers	430,000	850,000
Aircraft mechanics	123,000	190,000
Air conditioning, refrigeration, and heating mechanics	135,000	265,000
Truck and bus mechanics	130,000	165,000
Telephone and PBX installers and repairers	108,000	120,000
Instrument repairers	100,000	140,000
Business machine service workers	69,000	97,000
Other craft occupations		
Blue collar worker supervisors	1,400,000	1,700,000
Driving occupations		
Truck drivers, local	1,600,000	1,800,000
Truck drivers, over-the-road	570,000	670,000
Power truck operators	300,000	370,000
Other operative occupations		
Assemblers	1,017,000	1,100,000
Inspectors (manufacturing)	725,000	940,000
Welders and oxygen and arc cutters	554,000	770,000
Machine tool operators	546,000	670,000
Gasoline service station attendants	435,000	545,000

OCCUPATION	ESTIMATED EMPLOYMENT 1972	PROJECTED REQUIREMENTS TO 1985
Other		
Construction laborers and hod carriers	876,000	1,000,000
All-round machinists	320,000	400,000
Musicians and music teachers	85,000	111,000
Life scientists	180,000	235,000
Chemists	134,000	184,000

Choosing a Career

Next to choosing a mate, the choice of a career may be the most important one you make in your entire life.

Where do you begin? How do you protect yourself against the ever increasing fickleness of today's job market?

KEY GUIDES FOR YOU

• First and most obviously, study the full range of options and combinations open to you—and the range is vast indeed.

If you were asked to list, in a reasonable period of time, all the occupations you could think of, I'll wager you would name fewer than fifty. Yet the U. S. Labor Department's *Occupational Outlook Handbook* describes more than 800 occupations—many of them not even in existence a few years back. And the U. S. Government's *Dictionary of Occupations Titles* lists approximately 40,000 different job titles!

• *Don't,* though, make the mistake of abandoning a career goal you genuinely want just because your choice isn't among the fastest-growing occupations. Simply accept the likelihood that you will have to face stiff competition—and possibly a certain amount of job insecurity too. Explore the new careers, for you may find there an unsuspected offshoot of your dream career.

• Think of your career as a "black box" *inside you. Your* career is *not* in the minds of your parents or the files of your school counselor or anywhere else. It's *yours* to unwrap and unlock and pursue.

• Understand thoroughly the extent of education and training which may be required—and available—for any given occupation. Today's machinist, for instance, must have a solid foundation in mathematics and numerical controls. Today's top-notch secretary must know how to operate a range of new office machinery, possibly must know a foreign language or have a secretarial specialty (such as law or medicine). Today's plumber needs at least a high school diploma to qualify for a job or for additional on-the-job training. For a majority of occupations, some post-high school education or training has become a minimum.

• Recognize that, whatever occupation you choose, broad general knowledge ranks in importance with the specific education directly related to the occupation. In this era's rapidly changing job market, flexibility is crucial.

• Keep open your chances to change careers throughout your whole working life. The choice of an occupation is *not* a single decision. Rather, it is at least a ten-year process, says manpower expert Dr. Eli Ginzberg, involving a long-term strategy which could include several different careers.

If you are now entering the labor market, you can expect to change jobs at least a half dozen times over your working lifetime. You well may change your entire career at some point; in fact, two or three careers in a lifetime are becoming increasingly commonplace. This holds for the physicist as it holds for the pipe fitter: both can anticipate a continuous process of training and re-education throughout their working lives.

GUIDES FOR PARENTS

As for you, the parents of a young person beginning his or her career hunt, here are five "Do's and Don'ts" to guide you on counseling your children:

Don't force your own occupational choice on your child. The idea that your son must be a doctor because you are or wanted to be is ridiculous. A career choice involves much more than intelligence. It involves the child's values, attitudes toward work and life, emotional maturity.

Do be understanding if your child is in no hurry to choose a career. Even if he or she drops out of college in the second year, it could be a sign of wisdom. Be supportive as your child explores the occupational options open to him or her.

Don't try to drive your child to "get ahead." The young generation has watched their parents become great "career successes"—at the cost of discontent, divorce, alcoholism, absentee fathers. Relax. You've had your chances to make your choices. Let your kids have the same.

Do understand that your home is the single best source of values and that your attitudes toward work generally can be a real and important influence. Stress the values you cherish.

Don't plague a child who does not have the required intellectual equipment to become a professional or even to complete college. You'll only create impossible conflicts for him or her.

YOUR EDUCATION AND YOUR JOB

Today's relentless trend is toward more and more education to qualify for most jobs, higher and higher degrees to aspire to the very top in many fields, lower and lower esteem for the less-than-college-educated individual.

Do these ever rising educational requirements reflect *real* job requirements—or merely "creeping credentialism"?

Some of both. Specifically:

The U. S. Bureau of Labor Statistics estimates that in the 1972–85 period demand for professionals will increase at twice the rate of rise in demand for all other workers. But it also estimates that about 50,000 more college graduates will be entering the job market between 1972 and 1980 than there will be jobs for them; in the 1980–85 period, the "surplus" is due to expand to 700,000. This means that large numbers of college graduates may have to downgrade their expectations. In fact, an increasing number of college graduates even now are entering management and sales rather than the field for which they trained. Moreover, as the demand for paraprofessionals has soared, particularly in the health, education, law, and environmental fields, so has the number of two-year colleges and/or job-training opportunities—points not to be overlooked or underrated.

Meanwhile, the oversupply of Ph.D.s as of the mid-1970s is balanced by real shortages of skilled craftsmen and technical supportive personnel in many areas. As we have pushed back the limits of scientific and academic knowledge, we have tended to undervalue craftsmanship. Dropouts who took up carpentry or pottery were among the first to rediscover that working with one's hands could be deeply satisfying. Now educators and economists realize the urgent need to give status to those who have manual talents. (In pay, many craftsmen, such as electricians, carpenters, plumbers, already more than compete with high-paying white-collar jobs. It's how society views the craftsmen that is different.)

Does this mean guidance counselors will stop encouraging students to go to college? No. But it does mean counselors will increasingly endeavor to persuade overanxious parents of something many young people have long suspected: college isn't for everyone and this is nothing to be ashamed of.

It also means that the educational systems of the future must be designed to turn out fewer specialists and more generalists in both the "humanities" and the sciences so that young people will be able to shift among a number of different professions. For example, a young man or woman interested in children might train simultaneously for child care, recreation, mental health, and education, in order to be able to step into whichever field most needs his or her talents at a given time.

And it means that training programs, apprenticeships—in fact all forms of vocational training—will come in for more serious consideration than ever before. Says a noted educator: "We are going to have to make the same resources available for the would-be hairdresser as we are doing for the Ivy League collegian."

What then will be the new status of education? More than ever, education for its own sake will be a prime concern in this country. Colleges will make their educational facilities available to the community at large, enabling professionals (and paraprofessionals) to keep abreast of change and to enrich all those leisure hours which are coming, as the work week shifts from five to four and eventually three days.

Yes, the pay will remain somewhat higher for the college graduate who can find work, and it will still take a degree to get to the very top. But a college degree is no longer a guarantee of employment, whereas certain crafts, paratechnical and paraprofessional areas are crying for help. Already graduates of two-year colleges who cost less and do a perfectly adequate job are being preferred in many areas where the B.A. had become a bloated requirement.

In essence, what all this says to you is:

Read the projections in this chapter with two points always in mind. First, our society is changing faster than ever before, reacting to technological breakthroughs with unpredictable impacts on the job market. And second, where evidence is unmistakable that work exists to be done, such as in the rebuilding of our cities, the key factor in determining how many jobs will be available for the trained worker will depend on the future reordering of our national priorities.

Against this background, it is no more than common sense to try to start with as broad and sound an education as you can get; to choose your general field of work as late as you can to give yourself as much and as varied a training in that field as possible. Then you will enter the job market supported by the widest range of capabilities from which you can only benefit.

GOOD CAREERS FOR COLLEGE GRADUATES

You will find most of the details on which jobs require which levels of education or training in the current edition of the U. S. Labor Department's *Occupational Outlook Handbook* or in another guide, *Occupational Outlook for College Graduates*. Both of these are well worth the few dollars the government charges for them. Look for them in your school guidance office or library.

Here is a synopsis of some of the careers for those of you who have had at least some higher education—including junior and community colleges, business schools, vocational or technical institutes—in terms of the numbers of jobs opening each year and also in terms of job requirements:

Accountant: College degree required for higher-paying jobs; junior college, business school, or correspondence school courses acceptable for others.

Advertising: Keen competition for beginners. Employers increasingly prefer college training although some jobs go to those without degrees who have other extraordinary qualifications.

Architect: License required. Usually earned by a five-year course leading to a bachelor of architecture degree, followed by three years' experience.

Bank officer: Thousands of openings each year. Management trainee should have a major in business administration. Courses in accounting, economics, commercial law, political science, and statistics also are valuable.

Chemist: Favorable employment prospects. Bachelor's degree with major in chemistry is minimum; graduate training usually necessary for research or teaching.

Clergy: Wide education range. Some religions have no formal requirements but an increasing number require several years of theology after college graduation.

Commercial artist: Usually two or three years of art school required. Training in vocational high school or home study courses helpful. Artistic talent essential.

Counselor (school): Favorable employment opportunities. Most states require both a teaching and a counseling certificate—involving graduate work in guidance plus, usually, one to five years' teaching experience.

Dentist: Four years in dental college preceded by two or three years of predental college work. License is required in all states.

Draftsman: Best prospects for those with post-high school training. Junior college, technical institute, vocational school training usually required. Also good preparation is a three- or four-year apprenticeship.

Engineering or science technician: Demand will be strongest for graduates of post-high school technical training programs. However, some train on the job.

Engineers, all specialties: A bachelor's degree in engineering is minimum basic requirement.

Home economist: Very good employment opportunities, especially for teachers in secondary schools and colleges. Bachelor's degree in home economics necessary. Graduate degree required for college teaching and research work.

Lawyer: Moderate rise in employment. Keen competition for salaried positions. Usually four years of college followed by three years of law school. Must be admitted to the state bar for court practice.

Librarian: Bright employment prospects, particularly in public and special libraries. Required in most cases are four years of college followed by one year of specialized study in library science.

Library technical assistants: Good prospects, especially for graduates of academic programs. Best opportunities in large public and college university libraries.

Life scientist: Severe competition since number of graduates expected to exceed number of openings. Those with advanced degrees will experience the least competition. Best opportunities for medical scientists.

Mathematician: Best opportunities for those with Ph.D. degree. Increasing competition for entry positions as the number of new entrants may exceed openings. Graduate degree required for teaching and research and valuable for advancement in all specialties.

Manufacturer's sales worker: Best opportunities for those trained to sell technical products. College graduates generally preferred, though many successful sales workers have less education.

Medical lab technologists: Usually must have completed three years of college plus a training program in medical technology.

Musician: Stiff competition for performers. Prospects brightest for teachers. For teachers in public schools, a four-year course in a college or conservatory usually required; also a state certificate.

Personnel: Opportunities best for college graduates majoring in this field.

Pharmacist: Usually required are three to four years of professional study in a college of pharmacy following two years of pre-pharmacy college education. License necessary.

Physician: Excellent employment opportunities despite limited capacity of medical schools. Four years in medical school preceded usually by four years of college. At least one year of internship generally required plus a license to practice.

Physicist: Favorable employment opportunities, particularly for holders of advanced degrees. Holders of bachelor's degree will have limited opportunities, but may find openings in other occupations that utilize their training.

Psychologist: Outlook good for clinical and counseling psychologists. Ph.D. degree increasingly vital for advancement.

Public relations: Moderate opportunities. College education best preparation.

Purchasing agent: Moderate employment growth. Greatest demand for business administration graduates who have had courses in purchasing.

Recreation workers: Excellent job opportunities. Bachelor's degree, with major in recreation, social science, or physical education generally preferred.

Registered nurse: Three types of training available: diploma programs (three years), mainly in hospitals; associate degree programs (two years) in junior and community colleges; and baccalaureate degree programs (four to five years) in colleges or universities. License required.

Securities sales worker: Good employment opportunities. College education increasingly important and degree in business administration or economics good preparation. Most states require securities sales workers to be licensed.

Social worker: Excellent employment opportunities for those with master's degree in social work. Bachelor's degree generally the minimum.

Systems analyst: Excellent employment opportunities in this very rapidly expanding occupation. Most employers prefer a college background and experience in computer programing.

Teacher (college or university): Entrants may face keen competition. New doctoral and masters' degree holders, the main source of teacher supply, may exceed the demand for these teachers.

Teacher (kindergarten, elementary and high school): In competitive environment, greater emphasis will be placed on quality of applicant's training and academic achievement. Teaching certificate necessary in public schools and some parochial and other private schools. Certification usually requires a bachelor's degree and certain education courses, sometimes a master's degree.

Technical writer: Beginners with good writing ability and appropriate education should find opportunities. Usually four years of college, including technical and/or writing courses necessary.

Veterinarian: A license, based on four years of professional study in a college of veterinary medicine, necessary—following two years of pre-veterinary college work.

GOOD JOBS FOR HIGH SCHOOL GRADUATES

COLLEGE GRADUATE STILL IN MINORITY

The first fact is that *half* of the young Americans who are now receiving their high school diplomas will *not* be going on to college. The second fact is that only one in five young Americans graduates from college today. The clincher is that millions of young people will be going from high school directly to shopping for permanent careers or looking for extra training in trade schools.

If you (or your son or daughter) are not college bound, you will find hundreds of thousands of good jobs with bright futures and substantial pay checks looking for people to fill them. Growing numbers of employers now are offering extensive on-the-job training and paying trainees substantial wages while they learn. In some cases the high school graduate can expect to be earning $15,000 or more a year within just a few years of entering the job market.

SAMPLING OF OCCUPATIONS

Here is a sampling of occupations in which opportunity is relatively great—all now open to the high school graduate—with a few details on how much education training is needed for each.

Air conditioning, refrigeration, or heating mechanic: Most job openings will be for air conditioning and refrigeration mechanics. Most begin as helpers and learn on the job.

Aircraft mechanic: Most airlines train apprentices in three- or four-year programs. Some train in federal government-approved schools. Mechanics must be licensed to practice. Prospect is for rapid growth through 1980.

Airline pilot or copilot: Must be licensed and meet flight-training requirements. Written and physical exams required. Some airlines require two or more years of college. Training is rugged but pay is excellent.

Animal health technician: "Assistant veterinarians" (both male and female) can now take two years of post-high school training at certain colleges and junior colleges.

Blue collar worker supervisors: Usually must be about forty-five years of age and have spent several years learning skills on the job. Ability to motivate employees, command respect, and get along with people especially helpful.

Bookkeeper: Post-high school education sometimes needed. Courses in business arithmetic and bookkeeping are helpful. Large number of openings anticipated.

Business machine service worker: Outlook bright for work with electronic business machines. Usually trained on the job or in manufacturers' training schools. Basic knowledge of electricity and electronics very helpful.

Composing-room occupations: Technological changes will cause slow employment decline. Most compositors learn trade through six-year apprenticeship. Some learn on the job. Tape-perforating machine operators usually learn typing in high school or business school.

Computer programers and other computer workers: Demand for computer programers is expected to continue growing. Candidates needn't be mathematicians; basics can be learned in high school. Many companies train beginning computer workers themselves.

Cooks, chefs: Shortages of trained chefs in the nation's restaurants and hotels translate into major opportunities and high pay for those interested in this field.

Electrician (construction): A four-year apprenticeship recommended, but possible to learn this trade through job experience.

Electronic computer operating personnel: Very rapid employment increase on way. On-the-job training usually provided. To become a console operator, some college training may be required.

Firefighter: Competition keen because of large number of applicants. Must be at least twenty-one and in good physical condition; also pass a written intelligence test.

Health service workers: Less obvious occupations calling for applicants are medical record technician, laboratory assistant, dental technician, occupational therapy aide, child care attendant for retarded children—in addition to the obvious categories of hospital attendant and licensed practical nurse.

Hotel front office clerk: Clerical skills, including typing and bookkeeping, helpful.

Hotel manager: Increasing emphasis on college education, though successful hotel experience is generally chief requirement.

Instrument repairman: Training may be acquired on the job, in an apprenticeship (usually four years), in a technical institute or junior college, or at armed forces technical school. High school courses in math and science, including electronics, useful.

Insurance agent or broker: A competitive field. Courses in accounting, economics, and insurance useful. All agents and most brokers must obtain state licenses.

Lithographic craftsman: A four- or five-year apprenticeship usually required after high school.

Machine tool setup man: Must be all-round machinist or skilled machine tool specialist.

Machinist, all-round: A four-year apprenticeship best way to learn trade, but many learn on the job.

Medical laboratory workers: There are three different levels, with differences in educational requirements and pay. Assistants usually need only a high school education plus on-the-job training. Technicians usually need one or more years of post-high school training. Technologists usually must have completed three years of college plus a training program in medical technology.

Model: Employment to increase moderately through the 1970s. Most openings, however, will be for replacement, since the work life span of most models is relatively short. Modeling school training usually preferred. Courses in art, speech, drama, fashion design, dancing, and salesmanship also useful.

Office machine operator: Some on-the-job training usually provided. Business school training helpful. Specialized training needed for some jobs.

Operating engineer (construction): Many learn through informal training and experience, but three years' apprenticeship recommended.

Photographer: Employment opportunities relatively limited, but best for industrial photographers. Many train on the job or in three-year apprenticeship programs. For some specialties, post-high school training is needed.

Police officer: Tendency toward specialized assignments. Generally must be twenty-one and a U.S. citizen. Local civil service regulations usually govern appointment. College training often required for women because of their specialized duties.

Printing pressman or assistant: Usually a two- to five-year apprenticeship. Some learn through on-the-job and technical school training.

Radiologic (X-ray) technician: Very good prospects for both full-time and part-time employment. Usually a twenty-four-month, post-high school training program.

Real estate salesperson or broker: Increasing opportunities for women. License necessary; requirements include passing a written test on regulations affecting real estate transactions.

Receptionist: Business courses as well as some college training useful.

Sheet-metal worker: A four-year apprenticeship recommended, though many learn through on-the-job experience. Trade or correspondence school courses helpful.

Stationary engineer: Many learn on the job, but four-year apprenticeship recommended. Large numbers of states and cities require licenses.

Stenographer and secretary: High school courses in typing and short-hand or post-high school course in business subjects helpful.

Surveyor: Usually special training following high school plus training on the job. For some specialties, a college degree is required.

Telephone operator: Courses in English and business arithmetic important. Training in typing and other commercial subjects helpful for PBX operators.

Telephone installers and repairers: Telephone companies provide their own training courses.

Television and radio service technician: Skills acquired through technical or vocational school training, correspondence courses, training on the job, or military service courses. Some learn entirely through experience on the job.

Tool and diemaker: Either a four- or five-year apprenticeship or long-term training on the job needed.

Typist: Must meet fairly high standards of accuracy and speed (generally 40 to 50 words a minute).

Waste water treatment plant operators: Candidates for these jobs are now being offered paid college-level, on-the-job training under the GI bill and under several other programs tool.

Welfare aides, outreach workers, and recreation aides: These workers are often designated "human service workers." Work may be part time. Many jobs are supported by federal and state governments—including the employment service, welfare and social service agencies, and the public school system.

Wholesale trade sales worker: Specialties involving sale of scientific or technical equipment; training beyond a high school education often required.

In addition, the job outlook for high school graduates is bright for appliance servicemen, retail salesmen and -women, truck drivers, welders, and many others.

So if you, the high school graduate, or you, his or her parents, are now discussing a career, study the full range of opportunities. Look beyond a big beginning pay check for a job offering training in a field which interests you. Choose a job which leads in the direction you think you might really want to go.

GOOD JOBS FOR HIGH SCHOOL DROPOUTS

THE BRIGHTER BACKGROUND

You've heard the figures: the unemployment rate for high school dropouts is always way above that for the labor force as a whole in this country; dropouts almost always land—and almost always remain—at the bottom rung of the occupational-wage ladder; when there's a layoff, the typical dropout is usually the first to go, and when the rehiring begins, the typical dropout is usually the last to be rehired.

Of course, there is some truth to this grim blueprint. But the truth also is that the vast majority of high school dropouts either have decent jobs today or could have—if they would seek a relatively small amount of training and preparation. In literally *hundreds* of occupational categories—which pay good salaries—workers are desperately needed and a high school diploma, although it may be preferred, is not necessarily required to move into this work.

In many cases the training is available under a variety of government programs.

WHERE THESE JOBS ARE

And where are the jobs for dropouts today? Here is a sampling of the many opportunities for dropouts:

Appliance service worker: Rapid increase in employment is on the way. Mechanical ability necessary. Skills learned on the job. Courses in electricity, mathematics, and physics helpful.

Assembler: Must have aptitude for mechanical work and be in good physical condition. Most learn skills on the job.

Automobile body repairer: Three- to four-year apprenticeship recommended, but not necessarily a requirement.

Automobile mechanic: Good outlook. Most learn skills on the job, though a three- or four-year apprenticeship is recommended. Requirements are similar for auto body repairman.

Barber: Practically all states require licensing, for which applicants usually must be sixteen to eighteen years old and be graduates of a state-approved barber school.

Building custodian: Most learn skills on the job. High school shop courses helpful.

Bus driver, local transit: Applicant should be at least twenty-one and must be in good physical condition. Chauffeur's license required in most states.

Carpenter: Many openings each year in this very large occupation. Applicant usually must be at least seventeen. Some learn skills informally on the job, but a four-year apprenticeship is recommended.

Cashier: Numerous opportunities for part-time work. Applicants who have taken distributive education or business subjects preferred.

Construction laborer: Little formal training required. Applicant usually must be at least eighteen years old and in good physical condition.

Cook and chef: Excellent employment opportunities. Skills usually learned on the job. Courses in cooking schools an advantage for work in large hotels and restaurants. Some train as apprentices.

Cosmetologist: Job opportunities to be very good for full- or part-time work. License required. Applicant usually must be at least sixteen and have completed a state-approved cosmetology course. Some states require an apprenticeship.

Gasoline service station attendant: Most learn on the job. Must have driver's license and know simple arithmetic.

Hospital attendant: Generally trained on the job, sometimes combined with classroom instruction.

Licensed practical nurse: Candidates must be seventeen or eighteen years old, must have completed at least two years of high school, and must have a state-approved practical nursing course as well as pass a licensing examination.

Machine tool operator: Usually skills learned on the job. Courses in mathematics and blueprint reading useful.

Mail carrier: Slow employment rise expected. Must be citizen, eighteen years of age, and pass civil service and physical examinations.

Painter or paperhanger: Applicants usually must be at least sixteen. Many acquire skill informally through on-the-job experience, but three-year apprenticeship recommended.

Plumber or pipe fitter: Applicants usually must be at least sixteen. A five-year apprenticeship recommended, but many learn on the job. Trade or correspondence courses can be helpful.

Private household worker: General housework, cooking, and care for children are expected. Skills usually learned at home.

Sales worker (retail trade): Many opportunities for full- or part-time work. Distributive education courses useful.

Shipping or receiving clerk: Business courses useful.

Taxi driver: Many employment opportunities, though number of cab drivers is declining. In general, must be over twenty-one, have chauffeur's license and special taxicab operator's license.

Truck driver: Generally, must be at least twenty-one. Some employers prefer two to four years of high school. Must be in good physical condition and have a chauffeur's license.

Waiter and waitress: Majority of jobs for women. Men preferred, however, for jobs in formal dining establishments. Many employers prefer two or three years of high school. On-the-job training common. Ability to do simple calculations needed.

Welder or oxygen and arc cutter: Sharp increase on way in employment. Generally, several years of training on job required. Some less skilled jobs can be learned after a few months of training.

AND CAREERS FOR OPT-OUTS

But what if your goal is a career in farming? Organic gardening? Leather working? Running an organic food store? Weaving or wool spinning? Or a job as a waiter in a Greenwich Village coffee shop? Or driving a taxi in San Francisco? Or delivering newspapers in Denver?

THE IMPORTANCE OF AN "OCCUPATION"

Mounting numbers—maybe millions—of you are rejecting America's long-standing occupational values of money, security, success, challenge, position. You are turning your backs on the standard careers which I have listed in previous pages. You are trading well-paying jobs you could perform excellently for non-paying jobs in conservation, political campaigns, consumer organizations.

Confirming this is a recent study of college students which reveals a startling downgrading of the importance of an "occupation" among life's satisfactions:

SOURCE OF SATISFACTION	1ST CHOICE	2ND CHOICE
Family	55%	35%
Leisure	23%	20%
Occupation	14%	37%
Other	8%	8%

It is conceivable that within twenty-five years working solely to earn a pay check won't even appear on a list of reasons young Americans choose a trade, skill, profession.

If you are a college dropout and especially one who hates competition, computers, machines, executive authority, the profit motive, you well may already have become a revolutionary or an emigrant to the backwoods where the preferred occupations are homesteading and manual crafts.

But there are other alternatives for you, the young humanist, in blending such fields as engineering with social consciousness, technology with ethics.

Perhaps you have seen the old vocational aptitude tests on which you found such questions as "Would you rather read novels to a blind old lady or repair a broken garbage disposal unit?" If you checked the former, you were classed as preferring the social service type occupations; the latter, as a budding scientist. It could be that one of the choices on tomorrow's tests will turn out to be "scientific social service" (that is, repairing a garbage disposal unit for a blind old lady). The tests already are being rewritten to include that sort of option.

How to Look for—and Get—a Job

You have just graduated from high school or college. You are now ready to look for your first full-time, year-round job.

Or you are currently stuck in a dreary, dead-end position. You are yearning to escape to another, more challenging and interesting job.

Or you are a woman with skills which the market place needs but you have been out of the job world for years while you raised your children to school age. You are determined now to return to an outside job.

How do you begin your job hunt? How do you apply? How do you get ready for job interviews? How should you handle yourself during this "ordeal?" How do you write a résumé—and what information should it include? How, in sum, do you sell yourself to prospective employers?

AN INVENTORY OF YOURSELF

Before you even begin to pursue specific job openings, take a good look at yourself—personally and occupationally. Sit down in a quiet corner and, with deliberation, make an honest inventory of your interests, experience, and skills. Write it all down. (This inventory, incidentally, will be a valuable fund of information for you when you later prepare your résumé.)

Here are the key areas to explore and the key questions to think about:

Your Skills, Talents, and Abilities

What are you really good at? Have you special personal qualities which you could bring to a job? Such as an ability to lead? To analyze difficult problems? To organize? To work with children, old people, sick people—or other workers? To be patient with details? Imagination?

What type of education, job training, and general experience do you have which might apply to a new job?

Your Actual Work History

List *all* the jobs—including summer jobs, campus jobs, and volunteer jobs—you have had, along with the nature of your duties at each. What aspects did you like and dislike about each? Why did you take and why did you quit each? Or if you were fired, why, honestly why?

Your Education

Which schools, colleges, and technical training courses have you attended? When and for how long? What were your key courses? What subjects did you most enjoy (and least enjoy) and why? What degrees, scholarships, and special honors did you earn? What were your extracurricular activities? How might these count as job skills?

Your "Outside" Activities

What serious hobbies do you have which might relate in any way to a job? What volunteer jobs have you held? These cannot only serve as a form of work experience and training but also be a key clue to your real interests.

Are you, for example, good at drawing? Painting? Cooking? Caring for children? Can you play a musical instrument? Or sing well? Do you speak a foreign language? Have you traveled widely—within or outside the United States?

Your Physical Condition

Are you in good physical shape or handicapped in any way which might limit your ability to work? If you do happen to have a major handicap, there are many special schools, courses, and rehabilitation programs to help you—and the employment service or the Vocational Rehabilitation Administration can steer you to them.

Your Financial Position

Do you have an adequate financial cushion to fall back on if you are entering or considering a job or career field involving high risks of layoffs, cutbacks, etc.? Can you afford to take the time now to find a job which is really suitable to *you*? Can you manage a period of relatively low, entry-level wages into a new occupation?

Your Career Goal

What types of jobs, activities would you like to be doing now? What type of work do you think you would like to be doing a year or five years from now? Does this long-range goal suggest added training you should consider getting now? Is your present career field truly one in which you want to remain indefinitely? Or is now the time to consider a Big Switch to another field?

Your Interests

What do you really want out of the work you choose to do, the job you choose to take, the career you choose to follow? Money? Security? Status?

Power? Challenge? Fun? Usefulness? Adventure? Social contact? A chance to change the world in some meaningful way? Recognition for your achievement?

Your goals and values may differ greatly from the norms and averages —but whatever they may be, think about them, sort them out, decide what's really important to *you*.

Now *study* your personal inventory. What kinds of jobs can you list which would use *your* talents and skills to their best advantage?

With your completion of your inventory of yourself, you have begun an intelligent job hunt.

YOUR RÉSUMÉ

Your next step in this vital "how to" section is to write your résumé— your key means to get your foot in your prospective employer's door.

From the inventory of yourself you have prepared, select and organize with utmost care the facts which will help most to sell *you*. Keep the résumé concise and uncluttered—no more than two pages long and, of course, have it neatly typed. Include all of the following items of information about yourself, more or less in this order:

your name, address, and phone number;

the date of your birth, your marital status, and number of your dependents, if any;

your physical limitations, if any;

your education—giving data on your highest degree first, and then working backward;

name and location of each school;

major (and minor) courses of study (omit if you are well along in your career);

scholastic standing (if now in school);

honors and activities (include honorary and professional societies, awards, extracurricular activities, college jobs and amount of college expenses earned);

your work experience—listing your last employer first: employer, length of service, type of work performed (including non-paid volunteer work);

other relevant experience such as your special skills and hobbies, a few details on your travels (including ambitious hitchhiking and bicycling trips, community activities);

three or four references whose names or positions or achievements might reflect favorably on you (get the permission of your references to use their names, and give their addresses).

For samples of effective résumé and more pointers on how to write one, get a copy of "Merchandising Your Job Talents," free from the U. S. Department of Labor, Manpower Administration, Washington, D.C. 20210.

SOURCES OF HELP FOR JOB HUNTERS

With your inventory of yourself clearly in your mind and your résumé typed, you are ready to start looking for the best possible jobs in your chosen career field.

Among your sources of jobs and job leads:

Friends and relatives, obviously. If a friend or relative helps you find a job, he or she is automatically giving you a valuable reference. (If you get the job this way, you also take on something of a moral obligation to the friend or relative and employer.)

Help Wanted advertisements in newspapers, professional journals, trade magazines.

The Yellow Pages of your telephone directory (assuming you want a specific occupational category).

Your high school guidance counselor or college job placement officer.

Unions in your field.

Nearby army bases.

The YMCA, YWCA, and other local civic organizations.

Job referral services of professional and trade associations.

The U. S. Civil Service Commission—for U. S. Government jobs of all types both in the United States and abroad.

Professional associations.

A Situation Wanted ad you place in the local paper.

And the U. S. Employment Service—among free job placement facilities, undoubtedly the biggest and best with more job listings in more different occupations than any other single job source in the United States today. The USES has more than 2,000 offices throughout the country offering many new and/or specialized services for job hunters.

If you are a professional, use the many branches of the employment service which have national registers for professional occupations ranging from anthropology to economics and library science.

If you are a young American in a low-income bracket, investigate the USES offices' special programs for high school dropouts, including counseling as well as referral to training and job opportunities.

If you are a worker who is willing to take a job in some other city or state, use the USES' nationwide computerized job bank, which has details on job openings throughout the United States.

If you are interested in training programs, ask the USES to pinpoint programs appropriate for you.

HOW TO USE A PRIVATE EMPLOYMENT AGENCY

In a category by itself goes the private employment agency. There are thousands of licensed employment agencies operating in the United States today—many of them specializing in particular career fields, but most attempting to match almost any type of job hunter with the type of job he's seeking. Some offer you extensive job counseling—ranging from tips on job interviews to guidance on locating the really appropriate career field for you. Others offer no such services.

Employment agencies must be licensed in almost all states. Many states fix legal ceilings on the fees employment agencies may charge, and many regulate their practices. But, typically, fees charged by non-executive employment agencies run about one half of the first month's salary in the $400-a-month range, or 5 to 10 per cent of the first year's salary. Frequently, too, *you* must pay the fee—normally over a period of several months. And the fee is figured as a percentage of your base salary—*not* your take-home pay.

Note: Some employment agencies charge *all* applicants a "registration fee." Reputable employment agencies consider these fees unethical, though they are common for unskilled applicants. State regulations normally require the fee to be refundable on demand if employment is not obtained and specify that the fee must be credited against the total fee if a job is found.

Here are the basic rules to help you get the most benefit from *any* private employment agency:

• *In advance,* find out precisely how much the fees will be and by whom and how they will be paid. Find out *in advance* what the agency's policy is in the event the job falls far short of your expectations within days after you begin working. If the policy is to refund your money if the job goes sour, find out what the time limit is for your eligibility for a refund. *These details should be in writing.*

• No matter how "ideal" the job is portrayed to you, take the time to look it over with the utmost care. Since the typical employment agency earns its fee only if it places you in a job, there's a real "incentive" to sell you on any opening which happens to be available—whether or not it suits *your* career objectives.

• Don't be swayed by scare tactics such as warning you how tight the job market is or implying that, with *your* limited skills and talents, you're lucky to get *any* job.

• Make sure you read and understand any contract before you sign it—and make sure you get your copy of it.

• Be direct and straightforward, and don't attempt to hide adverse aspects of your records (a recent firing, a previous serious physical or mental illness); these facts easily could come out when your references are checked and do you a lot more damage than if you had stated them matter-of-factly in the beginning.

• Communicate and co-operate with the agency as your job hunt proceeds. Let the agency know how each interview went, whether or not you got the job.

• Do not return to any agency which refers you to a company which, it turns out, is not seeking employees.

• Make sure, if yours is a state which requires employment agencies to be licensed, that the agency with which you wish to deal actually is licensed.

• If in any doubt, assure yourself on the credentials of an employment agency with which you're considering doing business by checking whether it's a member of the National Employment Association, the industry's self-policing organization (2000 K Street, N.W., Washington, D.C. 20006).

YOUR LETTER OF APPLICATION

Next, here are the rules on how to write a covering letter of application to a prospective employer:

• Apply for a specific job—not just for "anything that is available."

• Keep your letter to one page; let your résumé (which should be attached to this letter of application) give the details.

• State *what you have to offer* your employer clearly, concisely, neatly —not just what you *want* from the employer. Avoid jargon, gimmicky or flowery language.

• Address your letter to a specific individual—the head of the personnel department, the camp director, the person in charge of the department, or *whomever;* double-check the spelling of his or her name before you make a final copy.

• After you have written a draft and edited it to cut out unnecessary verbiage and to correct any spelling mistakes, etc., retype it neatly on 8½ by 11-inch bond paper. Or, if you can't type, get someone who can to do this for you.

• Do *not* send a duplicated letter to several employers. This is insulting because it suggests an "assembly line."

• Do *not* give details on the former salaries you may have earned.

• Be sure to include a proper return address for yourself—including your telephone number and zip code.

• Make—and keep—a carbon of each letter you write, for reference in the event an employer responds positively to your application.

• Enclose a business-size stamped self-addressed envelope.

• Enclose a passport-size photograph of yourself.

• If you are looking for a summer job, apply early. Christmas vacation isn't too soon.

• Keep in mind that your letter of application is your prospective employer's first impression of you; it's his *sole* initial guide to your sense of neatness, your personality, your capacity for organization of thoughts, plans, etc.

• If the employer sends you an application form in response to your letter, fill it out neatly and completely—and follow all directions on extra documents requested, references, deadlines, etc.

You might use the following as a "model" for your letter of application:

150 W. Ask Street
Anywhere U.S.A.12345
Anytime, 1975

Dr. Timothy Street
Neighborhood Health Center
55 Wentworth Avenue
Seattle, Washington 98107

Dear Dr. Street:

This is my application for a job as a health aide, which I learned about through the employment service office.

My goal is a career in the field of medicine and I am seeking experience in community work—the aspect of medicine which interests me most. I have worked with disadvantaged people in volunteer jobs during the past three summers, both in the city and on an Indian reservation.

My résumé, a picture of myself, and return envelope are enclosed. I am prepared to come for a personal interview at any time. If you wish to know more about my qualifications, please tell me what additional information to submit.

Thank you for your consideration.

Sincerely yours,

Jane Doe

HOW TO HANDLE A JOB INTERVIEW

Your first face-to-face confrontation with your prospective employer—the job interview—will be your best single chance to get (or lose) the job you are seeking. It also will be an excellent opportunity to get real-life impressions of what it might be like to work for his or her company. Heed, then, these guidelines on job interviews:

Before the interview, find out as much as you can about the company—e.g., the goods and services it sells, its business philosophy, its size and financial standing, its markets, its problems, its competition.

Clearly organize in your mind what skills or talents you want to stress, and what you think you can contribute to the company.

Be able to tell the interviewer *why* you want to work for this particular company.

Take along extra copies of your résumé—just in case the copy you have already sent has been mislaid. Also take, if you are, say, an artist or a writer, examples of your work. And take copies of any letters of recommendation you may have.

Pay attention to such amenities as neat appearance, civilized grooming, and punctuality. Whatever generation you belong to, the odds are strong that your would-be employer belongs to an older and more conservative era. At the same time, do not overdress for the interview. *Do not* permit your girl friend, boy friend, relative—*or anybody,* for that matter—to come along on the interview. Your interviewer is interested solely in how *you* act and react *on your own.*

Avoid being vague, overaggressive, or wordy. Understate rather than oversell your qualifications. Listen carefully to the interviewer and follow the conversational directions he or she sets. Answer questions briefly and naturally.

Have a fairly good idea of what salary you expect to earn. But *let the interviewer bring up the subject of money.* And be as flexible as you can when you discuss salary—particularly if you find that your expectations are significantly above prevailing rates in the area or at the interviewer's particular company.

When the subject of pay does come up, be sure you give proper value to fringe benefits such as company-paid health insurance, pension plans, vacation time, year-end bonuses, etc. These easily could add up to an extra 25¢ in pay for every $1.00 you receive.

Do not hesitate to ask the interviewer questions about the company or about the job for which you are applying. Asking good questions not only may get you interesting answers but also will give the interviewer further clues to your enthusiasm for and knowledge of the company and your prospective job.

Don't criticize former employers, discuss your domestic or financial problems (unless specifically asked about them), make promises you can't keep, talk in monosyllables, stare at the ceiling, drag out the interview. And *don't panic.* Your world won't come to an end if you flunk the interview and miss out on this particular job.

Find out, if you can, whether you will be expected to take any intelligence, ability, aptitude, personality, or other tests at the time of your job interview and approximately how long they will take. Leave plenty of time for this procedure. When you are actually taking the tests, carefully listen to (or carefully read) whatever instructions you are given—especially the rules covering time limits. And again, don't panic. The worst you can do is flunk and that, also, is not the end of your world.

Finally, study the following key reasons given by employers for rejecting job applicants—in descending order of importance. Learn from these reasons what to do to help yourself. The list is based on a study by Northwestern University's director of placement, Dr. Frank C. Endicott:

Poor personal appearance.
Inability to express oneself clearly—poor voice, diction, grammar.
Lack of planning for career—no purposes or goals.
Lack of interest and enthusiasm—passive, indifferent.
Failure to participate in activities.
Overemphasis on money.
Poor scholastic record—just got by.
Unwilling to start at the bottom—expects too much too soon.

WHERE TO GET JOB TRAINING

The range of job training opportunities in the United States today is broad and attractive—and in many cases the training is accompanied by very respectable pay checks.

Where will you find these opportunities?

CONSIDER AN APPRENTICESHIP

Consider one of the oldest (at least four thousand years)—but once again rapidly growing—ways to acquire important job skills: apprenticeship. This type of training is open to women as well as men; hundreds of women, in fact, are now being trained in fields ranging from plumbing to aircraft mechanics, auto mechanics, fire fighting, machining, sheet-metal work, carpentry, pipe fitting, shoe repair, jet engine assembly, cheese making, embalming, computer repair, and even as purser-pharmacist mates on oceangoing vessels. In the mid-seventies, hundreds of thousands of apprentices were being trained each year in more than 350 trades ranging from stained-glass window making to musical-instrument repair, photography, and leather working.

As a general rule, apprentice training programs run two to five years. You, the apprentice, learn on the job, under the guidance of an experienced craftsman who probably was an apprentice himself some years ago. You also may spend a few hours a week in a classroom: technical instruction will be an important part of your apprenticeship.

Apprenticeship programs are generally a joint labor-management effort and generally are registered with the U. S. Department of Labor's Bureau of Apprenticeship and Training, or with your state's apprenticeship agency. Such programs are open to you if you are a man or woman of legal working age.

Your best local sources of information on apprenticeship programs available in your area are:

the local AFL-CIO building and construction trades council;

the Urban League;

the Recruitment Training Program, Inc.;

the Apprenticeship Information Center at the local state employment service office;

your state's apprenticeship agency;

a corporation employing workers in your field of interest;

the union which represents the trade in which you are interested.

In addition there are pre-apprenticeship programs, backed by the federal government and geared to meet the needs of those whose qualifications are insufficient to get them into formal apprenticeship programs. These consist of a combination of work training, tutoring, and classroom instruction.

Normally, starting apprentices earn 40 to 50 per cent of the going pay to journeymen (journeymen are those who have satisfactorily completed apprenticeship training). Apprentices also normally are granted pay raises every six months until the end of the training period when the pay scales reach 90 per cent of the current rate paid to journeymen. In addition, there may be valuable fringe benefits—including paid vacations and holidays, health insurance, pension plans.

Here was a typical pay ladder in the mid-seventies for an apprentice who had chosen a trade in which the going rate for skilled workers was $5.00 an hour—after four years of apprenticeship:

TRAINING PERIOD	HOURLY PAY
First 6 months	$2.50
Second 6 months	2.80
Third 6 months	3.10
Fourth 6 months	3.40
Fifth 6 months	3.70
Sixth 6 months	4.00
Seventh 6 months	4.30
Eighth 6 months	4.50

Moreover, if you are a veteran who is eligible for benefits under the Veterans Pension and Readjustment Assistance Act of 1966 and amendments, you will receive from the VA starting monthly training allowances, the size of which will depend on your number of dependents. This allowance decreases as the apprenticeship period progresses—but the sums you receive are *over and above* the amounts you receive from your employer.

SOME OTHER WAYS TO ACQUIRE WORK SKILLS

Apprenticeship is only one of many different forms of job training available today. Another is on-the-job "vestibule" training. You work at the employer's place of business, under the guidance of experienced workers, foremen, or instructors. In some cases you may get classroom instruction in math, reading, or other subjects. In many instances such programs are federally subsidized, but traditionally they are strictly a private industry effort.

Normally, your training period will range from one month to two years. Normally, also, you will receive an allowance which is below going pay scales for skilled workers in your field but still adequate to support you until you have completed the training period. For information on training programs available to you in your field, ask major employers in your area and also the local office of the U. S. Employment Service.

Still another way to get job training is through a *co-operative education program*—a system in which you, a student, attend high school or college for a semester (or other period of time), then work a semester at a paying job in a field related to your study program. The result is a degree *plus* valuable on-the-job experience *plus* a significant amount of pay during the year. Many schools offer this type of program. See "College Co-op Programs," Chapter 10, for more details.

FEDERAL JOB TRAINING PROGRAMS

You also will find a wide range of government job training and assistance programs are now in operation. Most are open only to low- and medium-income applicants. The biggest and best-known federal programs are the packages of job training retraining, and upgrading offered under various federal laws.

For information on federally administered programs, your key source is the local office of your state employment service.

BUSINESS, TECHNICAL, TRADE SCHOOLS

In addition, of course, hundreds of business, technical, and trade schools throughout the United States offer you an unprecedented variety of job training opportunities in an unprecedented number of different fields.

Among the typical courses you can get at junior and community colleges today: accounting, dental hygiene, fashion design, food-service administration, nursing, scientific technology, secretarial specialties—e.g., legal, medical, technical.

Among the typical courses you can get at business, trade, and technical schools: beauty culture, bookkeeping, drafting, medical laboratory work, nursing, office machine work, photography, salesmanship, secretarial skills, technical skills.

Your high school vocational counselor and the state employment service are among the best sources of information on which schools are best for your needs and wants.

A free guide intended to help you avoid wasting time and money on the wrong vocational school is "Pocket Guide to Choosing a Vocational School," available from Consumer Information, Pueblo, Colo. 81009. More extensive and detailed is the New York *Times's Guide to Continuing Education in America* (Quadrangle Books, $4.95). Compiled by the College Entrance Examination Board, it describes more than 2,000 schools in fifty states especially suited to continuing education. Look also at the "Directory of Post-secondary Schools with Occupational Programs," an excellent listing from the U. S. Government Printing Office, Washington, D.C. 20402.

WHY JOIN A UNION?

What are the pros *and* cons of joining a union today? What could a union do for you and not do for you if you joined?

First, a few obvious disadvantages:

• There is the cost: union dues in 1974 ran between $3.00 and $7.00 a month in most cases, but reached to $10 to $12. There is usually also a one-shot initiation fee which ranges from $5.00 to $15 but sometimes is as high as $100. And there may be special assessments to pay for union activities and obligations which aren't covered by the regular monthly dues.

• There is the cost of strikes. Although the overwhelming majority of union workers do not become involved in strikes, huge numbers of workers do go out on strike each year, they usually lose at least some pay, and for some types of workers (teachers or government workers) strikes are getting longer.

But despite these and other disadvantages, there seems no doubt that the pros far outweigh the cons. Specifically:

• Pay scales for union workers are far above those for non-union workers—as much as 40 to 50 per cent above in heavily unionized industries and trades.

• Along with job training, joining a union is one of the surest and fastest routes to higher pay in the U.S. workplace today. The *average* earnings of a full-time worker who belonged to a union in the early 1970s, reports the U. S. Labor Department, were 14 to 16 per cent more than the average earnings of the non-union worker. Union membership has become synonymous with superior pension coverage and with the fatter fringe benefits which now make up 25 to 30 per cent of the wage-fringe cost to the union worker's employer.

• Job training programs tend to be more widely accessible to union members than to non-union workers.

• Grievance mechanisms are another key benefit to union members. If you are summarily fired, laid off, or even treated unfairly, your union contract provides for some procedure you can use to appeal. The typical collective bargaining agreement also provides for some form of impartial arbitration if the problem can't be worked out using regular grievance mechanisms. Non-union employers may not offer these mechanisms.

YOUR SOURCES OF CAREER INFORMATION

A LISTING

Even the preceding smattering of clues to a random sampling of career fields must dramatize the importance of getting a broad background and detailed facts about any area that intrigues you before you even begin to commit yourself.

But where do you get this information?

The U. S. Labor Department's *Occupational Outlook Handbook* heads the list. I repeat, though it is probably available in your school or local library, or high school counseling office, or employment service office, buy a copy from the Superintendent of Documents, U. S. Department of Labor, Washington, D.C. 20402, for $6.25. Also check the two-volume *Encyclopedia of Careers and Vocational Guidance* (J. G. Ferguson—Doubleday).

Here, next, is a listing of trade associations, government agencies, and individual companies which can provide you with career information in specific fields:

ACCOUNTANT

American Institute of Certified
    Public Accountants
666 Fifth Avenue
New York, N.Y. 10019

ADVERTISER

American Association of
    Advertising Agencies
200 Park Avenue
New York, N.Y. 10017

AEROSPACE ENGINEER

American Institute of Aeronautics
    and Astronautics
1290 Avenue of the Americas
New York, N.Y. 10010

National Aeronautics and Space
    Administration
Washington, D.C. 20546

AGRICULTURE AND AGRICULTURAL
    RESEARCH

Office of Personnel
U. S. Department of Agriculture
Washington, D.C. 20250

AIR CONDITIONING AND
    REFRIGERATION MECHANIC

Refrigeration Engineers and
    Technicians
435 North Michigan Avenue
Chicago, Ill. 60611

AIRPLANE MECHANIC

Air Transport Association of
    America
1000 Connecticut Avenue, N.W.
Washington, D.C. 20036

Federal Aviation Agency
Department of Transportation
Washington, D.C. 20553

ANTHROPOLOGIST

American Anthropological
Association
1703 New Hampshire Avenue,
N.W.
Washington, D.C. 20009

APPLIANCE SERVICEMAN

National Appliance Service
Association
1525 Broadway
Kansas City, Mo. 64108

National Appliance & Radio-TV
Dealers Association
318 West Randolph Street
Chicago, Ill. 60606

National Association of Service
Managers
6650 Northwest Highway
Chicago, Ill. 60631

Appliance Service News
5841 West Montrose Avenue
Chicago, Ill. 60634

APPAREL DESIGNER

Fashion Institute of Technology
227 West 27th Street
New York, N.Y. 10001

ARCHITECT

The American Institute of
Architects
1735 New York Avenue, N.W.
Washington, D.C. 20036

ASTRONOMER

American Astronomical Society
211 FitzRandolph Road
Princeton, N.J. 08540

AUTO MECHANIC AND BODY REPAIR

U. S. Trade Schools
500 East Ninth Street
Kansas City, Mo. 64106

Automotive Services Industry
Association
230 North Michigan Avenue
Chicago, Ill. 60601

National Automobile Dealers
Association
2000 K Street, N.W.
Washington, D.C. 20006

AUTOMOTIVE ENGINEER

The Society of Automotive
Engineers, Inc.
Two Pennsylvania Plaza
New York, N.Y. 10001

BANKER, BANK TELLER

American Bankers Association
1120 Connecticut Avenue, N.W.
Washington, D.C. 20036

BIOLOGIST

American Institute of Biological
Sciences
3900 Wisconsin Avenue, N.W.
Washington, D.C. 20016

BOTANIST

Botanical Society of America
Department of Botany
Indiana University
Bloomington, Ind. 47401

BRICKLAYER

Bricklayers, Masons
and Plasterers
International Union
815 15th Street, N.W.
Washington, D.C. 20005

BUSINESS MANAGEMENT

The American Management
Association
135 West 50th Street
New York, N.Y. 10015

CARPENTER

United Brotherhood of Carpenters
    and Joiners of America
101 Constitution Avenue, N.W.
Washington, D.C. 20001

CHEMICAL ENGINEER

American Institute of Chemical
    Engineers
345 East 47th Street
New York, N.Y. 10017

CHEMIST

American Chemical Society
1155 16th Street, N.W.
Washington, D.C. 20036

Manufacturing Chemists
    Association
1825 Connecticut Avenue, N.W.
Washington, D.C. 20009

CHILD WELFARE WORKER

Division of Family and Child
    Welfare Services
Community Service Administration
Social and Rehabilitation Service
U. S. Department of Health,
    Education and Welfare
330 C Street, S.W.
Washington, D.C. 20201

CITY PLANNING

American Institute of Planners
1776 Massachusetts Avenue, N.W.
Washington, D.C. 20036

American Society of Planning
    Officials
1313 East 60th Street
Chicago, Ill. 60637

CLERICAL WORKER

United Business Schools
    Association
1730 M Street, N.W.
Washington, D.C. 20036

COMMUNITY ACTION WORKER

National Association for
    Community Development
Room 106
1424 16th Street, N.W.
Washington, D.C. 20036

Office of Economic Opportunity
    Community Action Program
1200 19th Street, N.W.
Washington, D.C. 20506

COMPUTER OPERATOR, PROGRAM-
    MER, SYSTEMS ANALYST

American Federation of Information
    Processing Societies
210 Summit Avenue
Montvale, N.J. 07645

Data Processing Management
    Association
505 Busse Highway
Park Ridge, Ill. 60068

Association for Computing
    Machinery
1133 Avenue of the Americas
New York, N.Y. 10036

CONSERVATIONIST

The Conservation Foundation
1717 Massachusetts Avenue, N.W.
Washington, D.C. 20036

The Wildlife Society
3900 Wisconsin Avenue, N.W.
Washington, D.C. 20016

The Nature Conservancy
1800 North Kent Street
Arlington, Va. 22209

The Wilderness Society
1901 Pennsylvania Avenue, N.W.
Washington, D.C. 20006

Office of Personnel
Environmental Protection Agency
401 M Street, S.W.
Washington, D.C. 20460

National Wildlife Federation
8925 Leesburg Pike
Vienna, Va. 22180

Scientists Institute for Public
    Information
30 East 68 Street
New York, N.Y. 10021

Natural Resources Council
1025 Connecticut Avenue, N.W.
Washington, D.C. 20036

National Parks & Conservation
    Association
1701 18th Street, N.W.
Washington, D.C. 20009

American Public Works
    Association
1313 East 60 Street
Chicago, Ill. 60637

National Audubon Society
950 Third Avenue
New York, N.Y. 10022

COOK, CHEF

Educational Director
National Restaurant
    Association
One IBM Plaza, Suite 2600
Chicago, Ill. 60611

DATA PROCESSOR

American Federation of
    Information Processing
    Societies
201 Summit Avenue
Montvale, N.J. 07645

DAY CARE WORKER

Day Care and Child Development
    Council of America, Inc.
1401 K Street, N.W.
Washington, D.C. 20005

DENTIST AND DENTAL ASSISTANT

Division of Career Guidance
Council on Dental Education
American Dental Association
211 East Chicago Avenue
Chicago, Ill. 60611

American Dental Assistants
    Association
211 East Chicago Avenue
Chicago, Ill. 60611

DENTAL HYGIENIST

Division of Education Service
American Dental Hygienists
    Association
211 East Chicago Avenue
Chicago, Ill. 60611

Division of Dental Health
Public Health Service
U. S. Department of Health,
    Education and Welfare
Washington, D.C. 20201

DIESEL MECHANIC

International Association of
    Machinists & Aerospace
    Workers
1300 Connecticut Avenue, N.W.
Washington, D.C. 20036

DIETITIAN

The American Dietetic Association
620 North Michigan Avenue
Chicago, Ill. 60611

DIRECT SELLING

Direct Selling Association
1730 M Street, N.W.
Washington, D.C. 20036

ECONOMIST

American Economic Association
1313 21st Avenue, South
Nashville, Tenn. 37212

EDUCATION

American Association of School
Administrators
1801 North Moore Street
Arlington, Va. 22209

National Education Association
1201 16th Street, N.W.
Washington, D.C. 20036

ELECTRICAL CONTRACTING

National Electrical Contractors
Association
7315 Wisconsin Avenue
Bethesda, Md. 20014

ELECTRICAL-ELECTRONIC
TECHNICIAN (RADIO AND TV)

Electronic Industries Association
2001 Eye Street, N.W.
Washington, D.C. 20006

ELECTRICIAN

International Brotherhood of
Electrical Workers
1125 15th Street, N.W.
Washington, D.C. 20005

National Joint Apprenticeship and
Training Committee for the
Electrical Industry
1730 Rhode Island Avenue, N.W.
Washington, D.C. 20036

ENGINEER

National Society of Professional
Engineers
2029 K Street, N.W.
Washington, D.C. 20006

Engineers Council for Professional
Development
345 East 47th Street
New York, N.Y. 10017

FAMILY AND HOME ECONOMICS,
NUTRITIONIST

American Home Economics
Association
2010 Massachusetts Avenue, N.W.
Washington, D.C. 20036

FARMER, AGRICULTURAL RESEARCH
WORKER

Public Information Office
U. S. Department of Agriculture
Washington, D.C. 20250

FLIGHT ATTENDANTS

Air Transport Association of
America
1000 Connecticut Avenue, N.W.
Washington, D.C. 20036

FOOD INDUSTRY WORKER

National Association of Food
Chains Educational Council
1725 Eye Street, N.W.
Washington, D.C. 20006

FOOD SCIENTIST

Institute of Food Technologists
Suite 2120
221 North LaSalle Street
Chicago, Ill. 60601

FOREIGN SERVICE

Director, Foreign Service
Recruitment
Board of Examiners
Department of State
Washington, D.C. 20520

FORESTER

Society of American Foresters
1010 16th Street, N.W.
Washington, D.C. 20036

U. S. Forest Service
U. S. Department of Agriculture
Washington, D.C. 20250

American Forestry Association
1319 18th Street, N.W.
Washington, D.C. 20036

GEOGRAPHER

Association of American
    Geographers
1710 16th Street, N.W.
Washington, D.C. 20009

GEOLOGIST

American Geological Institute
2201 M Street, N.W.
Washington, D.C. 20037

GEOPHYSICIST

American Geophysical Union
1707 L Street, N.W.
Washington, D.C. 20036

Society of Exploration
    Geophysicists
P. O. Box 3098
Tulsa, Okla. 74101

GOVERNMENT JOBS

U. S. Civil Service Commission
Bureau of Recruiting and
    Examining
Room 1416A
1900 E Street, N.W.
Washington, D.C. 20415

HEALTH

Division of Careers and
    Recruitment
American Hospital Association
840 North Lake Shore Drive
Chicago, Ill. 60611

National Health Council
Health Careers Program
1740 Broadway
New York, N.Y. 10019

Health Resources Administration
Bethesda, Md. 20014

Program Services Department
American Medical Association
535 North Dearborn Street
Chicago, Ill. 60610

HOSPITAL ADMINISTRATOR

American College of Hospital
    Administrators
840 North Lake Shore Drive
Chicago, Ill. 60611

HOTEL-MOTEL WORKER

American Hotel and Motel
    Association
888 Seventh Avenue
New York, N.Y. 10019

The Council on Hotel, Restaurant
    and Institutional Education
Suite 534
1522 K Street, N.W.
Washington, D.C. 20005

INSTRUMENT REPAIRMAN

Instrument Society of America
400 Stanwix Street
Pittsburgh, Pa. 15222

INSURANCE UNDERWRITER OR
    CLAIM EXAMINER

Institute of Life Insurance
277 Park Avenue
New York, N.Y. 10017

Insurance Information Institute
110 William Street
New York, N.Y. 10038

American Mutual Insurance
    Alliance
20 North Wacker Drive
Chicago, Ill. 60606

JOURNALISM

Sigma Delta Chi
35 East Wacker Drive
Chicago, Ill. 60601

American Newspaper Publishers
  Association Foundation
Box 17407
Dulles International Airport
Washington, D.C. 20041

Journalism schools at major univer-
  sities (e.g., Columbia, New
  York City; University of
  Missouri, Columbia).

LAWYER AND LEGAL ASSISTANT
  (PARALEGAL)

Association of American Law
  Schools
Suite 370
1 Dupont Circle, N.W.
Washington, D.C. 20036

Pre-Law Handbook
c/o Educational Testing Service
Box 944
Princeton, N.J. 08540

American Civil Liberties Union
22 East 40th Street
New York, N.Y. 10016

Law Students Civil Rights Research
  Council, Inc.
22 East 40th Street
New York, N.Y. 10016

National Lawyers Guild
23 Cornelia Street
New York, N.Y. 10014

LIBRARIAN

Office for Library Manpower
American Library Association
50 East Huron Street
Chicago, Ill. 60603

LICENSED PRACTICAL NURSE

National Federation of Licensed
  Practical Nurses, Inc.
250 West 57th Street
New York, N.Y. 10019

National League for Nursing, Inc.
10 Columbus Circle
New York, N.Y. 10019

LIFE INSURANCE SALES WORKERS

Institute of Life Insurance
277 Park Avenue
New York, N.Y. 10017

MACHINIST

The National Machine Tool
  Builders Association
7901 West Park Drive
McLean, Va. 22101

MASON

Bricklayers, Masons and Plasterers
  International Union
815 15th Street, N.W.
Washington, D.C. 20005

MEDICAL ASSISTANTS

American Association of Medical
  Assistants
1 East Wacker Drive
Chicago, Ill. 60601

American Medical Association
Department of Allied Medical
  Professions
535 North Dearborn Street
Chicago, Ill. 60610

MEDICAL LABORATORY ASSISTANT

National Committee
  for Careers in
  the Medical Laboratory
9650 Rockville Pike
Bethesda, Md. 20014

MEDICAL RECORD LIBRARIAN

American Medical Record
  Association
Suite 1850
875 North Michigan Avenue
Chicago, Ill. 60611

MEDICAL TECHNOLOGIST AND
MEDICAL TECHNICIAN

American Medical Association
Department of Allied Medical
Professions
535 North Dearborn Street
Chicago, Ill. 60610

American Society for Medical
Technology
Suite 200
5555 West Loop
Houston, Tex. 77401

METEOROLOGIST

American Meteorological
Society
45 Beacon Street
Boston, Mass. 02108

MINERAL INDUSTRY WORKER

Chief, Division of Personnel
Bureau of Mines
U. S. Department of the Interior
18th and C Streets, N.W.
Washington, D.C. 20240

MUSEUM WORKER

American Association
of Museums
2233 Wisconsin Avenue, N.W.
Washington, D.C. 20007

MUSIC TEACHER

Music Educators National
Conference
1201 16th Street, N.W.
Washington, D.C. 20036

NATIONAL PARK SERVICE WORKER

Department of the Interior
Division of Personnel
National Park Service
18th and C Streets, N.W.
Washington, D.C. 20240

NURSING

Nursing Information Service
National League for Nursing, Inc.
10 Columbus Circle
New York, N.Y. 10019

American Nursing Association
1200 15th Street, N.W.
Washington, D.C. 20036

NURSE AIDE

American Hospital Association
840 Lake Shore Drive
Chicago, Ill. 60611

OCCUPATIONAL THERAPIST

American Occupational Therapy
Association
6000 Executive Boulevard
Suite 200
Rockville, Md. 20852

OCEANOGRAPHER

International Oceanographic
Foundation
1 Rickenbacker Causeway
Virginia Key
Miami, Fla. 33149

American Society for
Oceanography
Marine Technology Society
1730 M Street, N.W.
Washington, D.C. 20036

National Oceanic and Atmospheric
Administration
Office of Public Affairs
6001 Executive Boulevard
Rockville, Md. 20852

Scripps Institution of Oceanography
La Jolla, Calif. 92037

Woods Hole Oceanographic
Institution
Woods Hole, Mass. 02543

OIL INDUSTRY

American Petroleum Institute
1801 K Street, N.W.
Washington, D.C. 20006

OPTOMETRIST

American Optometric Association
7000 Chippewa Street
St. Louis, Mo. 63119

PAINTER

Painting and Decorating
 Contractors of America
7223 Lee Highway
Falls Church, Va. 22046

PAPER INDUSTRY

American Paper Institute
260 Madison Avenue
New York, N.Y. 10016

PATHOLOGIST

American Society of Clinical
 Pathologists
2100 West Harrison Street
Chicago, Ill. 60612

American Medical Association
Department of Allied Medical
 Professions
535 North Dearborn Street
Chicago, Ill. 60610

PHARMACIST

American Pharmaceutical
 Association
2215 Constitution Avenue, N.W.
Washington, D.C. 20037

American Association of Colleges
 of Pharmacy
8121 Georgia Avenue
Silver Spring, Md. 20910

PHOTOGRAPHY

Eastman Kodak Co.
Rochester, N.Y. 14650

PHYSICIAN

Association of American Medical
 Colleges
1 Dupont Circle, N.W.
Washington, D.C. 20036

American Medical Association
535 North Dearborn Street
Chicago, Ill. 60610

PHYSICIAN'S ASSISTANT

Health Resources Administration
Bethesda, Md. 20014

American Medical Association
Dept., Allied Medical Association
535 North Dearborn Street
Chicago, Ill. 60610

PHYSICIST

American Institute of Physics
335 East 45th Street
New York, N.Y. 10017

PHYSIOLOGIST

American Physiological Society
9650 Rockville Pike
Bethesda, Md. 20014

PLASTERER

Bricklayers, Masons and Plasterers
 International Union
815 15th Street, N.W.
Washington, D.C. 20005

PLUMBER, PIPE FITTER

National Associations of Plumbing-
 Heating-Cooling Contractors
1016 20th Street, N.W.
Washington, D.C. 20036

POLICEMAN

International Association of Chiefs
 of Police
11 Firstfield Road
Gaithersburg, Md. 20760

POLLUTION CONTROL

Water Pollution Control Federation
3900 Wisconsin Avenue, N.W.
Washington, D.C. 20016

Air Pollution Control Association
4400 5th Avenue
Pittsburgh, Pa. 15213

Office of Personnel
Environmental Protection Agency
Washington, D.C. 20460

PSYCHIATRIC SOCIAL WORKER

National Association of Social
    Workers
600 Southern Bldg.
15th and H Streets, N.W.
Washington, D.C. 20005

PSYCHIATRIST

American Psychiatric Association
1700 18th Street, N.W.
Washington, D.C. 20009

National Association for Mental
    Health
1800 North Kent Street
Rosslyn Station
Arlington, Va. 22209

National Institute of Mental Health
5600 Fishers Lane
Rockville, Md. 20852

PSYCHOLOGIST

American Psychological Association
1200 17th Street, N.W.
Washington, D.C. 20036

PUBLIC HEALTH WORKER

American Public Health
    Association, Inc.
1015 18th Street, N.W.
Washington, D.C. 20036

National Health Council
1740 Broadway
New York, N.Y. 10019

Health Resources Administration
Bethesda, Md. 20014

PUBLIC RELATIONS WORKER

Career Information Service
Public Relations Society of
    America
845 Third Avenue
New York, N.Y. 10022

RADIO AND TELEVISION

National Association of
    Broadcasters
1771 N Street, N.W.
Washington, D.C. 20006

RADIOLOGIST

American Medical Association
535 North Dearborn Street
Chicago, Ill. 60610

RECREATION THERAPIST

National Recreation and Park
    Association
1600 Kent Street
Arlington, Va. 22209

RECREATION WORKER

National Recreation and Park
    Association
1601 Kent Street
Arlington, Va. 22209

REFRIGERATION AND AIR
    CONDITIONING MECHANIC

Refrigeration Engineers and
    Technicians
435 North Michigan Avenue
Chicago, Ill. 60611

RESPIRATORY THERAPIST

American Association for
    Respiratory Therapy
7411 Hines Place
Dallas, Tex. 75235

SANITARY ENGINEER

National Environmental Health
   Association
1600 Pennsylvania Street
Denver, Colo. 80203

SCIENTIST

Scientific Manpower Commission
1776 Massachusetts Avenue, N.W.
6th Floor
Washington, D.C. 20036

Occupational Outlook Service
Bureau of Labor Statistics
Department of Labor
Washington, D.C. 20210

SECRETARY

United Business Schools
   Association
1730 M Street, N.W.
Suite 401
Washington, D.C. 20036

National Secretary's Association
240 Pershing Road
Kansas City, Mo. 64108

SOCIAL WORKER

The National Association of Social
   Workers
600 Southern Bldg.
15th and H Streets, N.W.
Washington, D.C. 20005

SOCIOLOGIST

The American Sociological
   Association
1722 N Street, N.W.
Washington, D.C. 20002

SOIL CONSERVATIONIST

Soil Conservation Society of
   America
7515 Northeast Ankeny Road
Ankeny, Ia. 50021

SOIL SCIENTIST

The American Society of
   Agronomy
677 South Segoe Road
Madison, Wisc. 53711

Office of Personnel
U. S. Department of Agriculture
Washington, D.C. 20250

SPEECH PATHOLOGIST

American Speech and Hearing
   Association
9030 Old Georgetown Road
Washington, D.C. 20014

STATISTICS

American Statistical Association
806 15th Street, N.W.
Washington, D.C. 20005

TAX WORK

Chief, Recruitment Section
Internal Revenue Service
Washington, D.C. 20224

TEACHING

National Commission on Teacher
   Education and Professional
   Standards
National Education Association
1201 16th Street, N.W.
Washington, D.C. 20036

TECHNICIAN

National Association of Trade and
   Technical Schools
2021 L Street, N.W.
Washington, D.C. 20036

Engineer's Council for Professional
   Development
345 East 47th Street
New York, N.Y. 10017

454 SYLVIA PORTER'S MONEY BOOK

TELEVISION-RADIO SERVICEMAN

National Alliance of Television and
    Electronic Service Associations
5908 South Troy Street
Chicago, Ill. 60629

TILE SETTER

Bricklayers, Masons and Plasterers
    International Union
815 15th Street, N.W.
Washington, D.C. 20005

TOOL AND DIE MAKER

International Association of
    Machinists and Aerospace
    Workers
1300 Connecticut Avenue, N.W.
Washington, D.C. 20036

Skilled Trades Department, United
    Automobile Workers of
    America
8000 East Jefferson Avenue
Detroit, Mich. 48214

VETERINARIAN

American Veterinary Medical
    Association
600 South Michigan Avenue
Chicago, Ill. 60605

VOCATIONAL REHABILITATION

Social and Rehabilitation Service
U. S. Department of Health,
    Education and Welfare
330 C Street, S.W.
Washington, D.C. 20201

WELDER

The American Welding Society
2501 Northwest 7th Street
Miami, Fla. 33125

X-RAY TECHNICIAN

The American Society of
    Radiologic Technologists
645 North Michigan Avenue
Chicago, Ill. 60611

HOW TO LOOK

The above list is as important in showing you how to look for information as it is in guiding you to specific sources.

Note that, in most cases, a trade association will exist for members of the occupation. Note also that its name will almost always include the identification of the career—so that a check of the telephone books of major headquarters cities (Washington, New York, Chicago, Los Angeles, San Francisco) will probably lead you to a key source. Note, too, that colleges, universities, and big corporations are excellent places at which to seek guidance.

How to Get a Good Summer Job

Competition for summer jobs can be brutal, for this is the time of year when millions of high school and college graduates also are flooding into the labor market.

Thus, the earlier in the year you start your summer job hunt, the better are your chances of landing a good one. And the more you familiarize yourself with the basic rules on summer job hunting, the better off you'll be.

HOW TO SHOP

Here is how to shop for the summer job best suited to *you*.

If your biggest need is to earn and save money to finance your education, concentrate on the lucrative "summer industries." For example: resort hotels and motels; country clubs; drive-in movies; swimming pools and beaches; restaurants on highways; playgrounds; road and other types of construction; air conditioning and boat rental businesses; marinas; landscaping and home maintenance; ice cream parlors and distribution services; parks and playgrounds; moving companies; dude ranches and riding stables; gas stations and car washers; baseball parks; community recreation centers.

If you are looking for a summer camp job, an excellent source of information is the yearly *Directory of Accredited Camps for Boys and Girls,* available either in your library or, for a few dollars, from the Publications Service, American Camping Association, Bradford Woods, Martinsville, Ind. 46151.

Among the jobs open to students and teachers at summer camps: counselors, business managers, nurses, caretakers, dietitians, cooks, recreation specialists.

If you are interested in an office job, you may find work as a spare-time typist, file clerk, or secretary, or you might get temporary work in a library.

If you're a college student with some travel experience, you may get a job as a tour guide. Travel bureaus will give you the names of tour companies.

If you are willing to accept the challenge, try setting up your own enterprise. For instance: washing and waxing cars; baby sitting; operating a typing service; performing lawn or garden chores; arranging parties for small children. Door-to-door selling is worth trying, too.

For the past several years the Youth Conservation Corps has been putting young people to work on important conservation projects in camps across the country, paying them a modest salary, and giving them environmental instruction. For details, contact the Division of Manpower and Youth Conservation Programs, Forest Service, U. S. Department of Agriculture, Washington, D.C. 20250.

The Canadian government recently backed a program entitled Federal Opportunities for Youth Program (OYP), under which young people who came up with worth-while ecological projects were given grants to organize them. Perhaps you can persuade your state or town to do something similar.

A surprising number of students manage to earn $1,000, $1,500, or even $2,000 in the course of a summer.

However, if you have the choice of a job paying $2.50 an hour and one paying $3.00 an hour, don't automatically grab the higher-paying job if the

$2.50-an-hour one offers more challenging work, more responsibility, better job training. Your loss in pay would be compensated by these other benefits.

If economic considerations are *not* top priority for you, use your summer job as a "career proving ground." If you have not decided on a career, use the summer to find out more about your own interests and abilities. Each summer, take jobs in different fields in which you have some interest to get an idea what goes on in each.

If you have already decided on a career, use the summer to explore different aspects of that field. For instance, if you plan to become a social worker, you might take jobs (especially volunteer jobs) that would expose you to the different problems of city slum children, adult illiterates, etc. If you are interested in medicine, consider successive jobs that might acquaint you with allied fields ranging from public health to occupational therapy. If you are interested in archaeology, consider joining a "dig," either in the United States or abroad.

If you think you might be interested in business as a career, find out *now* about "summer intern" programs offered by a growing number of corporations. In these, you are not only well paid but also receive valuable training and, most important, a firsthand view of the business world. Many corporations are now actively trying to attract students—via scholarships and summer job training programs. Their aim, of course, is to line up future employees—but a summer internship by no means commits you to work later for any corporation.

If you are a girl, don't restrict yourself to "women's jobs." You will have more and more opportunity in almost any job field for which you may later qualify.

In sum, give your summer job the same attention as you would a permanent job. Plan enough ahead to give yourself the best possible chance for the best job. Use the summer to broaden your experience, sharpen your skills, and sift your interests.

SOURCES OF JOB LEADS

Here are some of the best sources of job leads, and of guidance generally, to help steer you to a suitable summer job:

- Classified ads in your local newspapers.
- Friends, relatives, and neighbors; local businessmen.
- The state employment service with its more than 2,000 offices throughout the United States, many of them equipped with computerized job banks. In many cases, also the employment service offices have guidance counseling specialists in summer job-finding.
- The YMCA, YWCA, YMHA, and other community service organizations—not only for sources of information and leads on paying summer jobs but also for volunteer positions.

HOW ABOUT A NON-JOB?

What if you just can't find a summer job of any kind? What if you aren't poor enough to qualify for special help and are not eligible for a publicly subsidized job? What should you do?

First answer this question with utter honesty: Can you possibly afford to invest twelve weeks in a project which doesn't pay you a salary? If your answer is "yes," here are just a few of the many valuable possibilities:

• Go to summer school and take courses which will put you ahead during the coming fall semester, help you in a future job, or simply appeal to you. Community colleges, state universities, high schools, and many other institutions offer, at remarkably low or no cost, courses in subjects ranging from remedial reading to typing, foreign languages, art history, and investments.

• Travel in the United States or abroad. Many bargains are available to students. For example: a student identity card, available from American Youth Hostels, Inc., in New York will get you big discounts at student unions, restaurants, museums, etc., throughout Europe. See Chapter 12, "How to Save on Vacations," for more suggestions.

• Get into a political campaign. You may not yet have a vote but your volunteer time and talents could be even more important to a political candidate of your choice than a vote.

• Try your hand at farm work, as an educational switch from whatever you have been doing. The pay is low, but probably not as low as you think. And you might use your creativity to help alleviate the plight of the migrant harvester during the summer months.

• Take a trip within the United States—camping, biking, driving, flying. And if you have the courage, try working your way to your destination.

• Use this summer to cultivate a hobby. Check with your school on tutoring programs in which you may enroll to tutor students who need your skills. Learning to use your leisure time will be almost as important in the future as learning a profession or marketable skill.

If you must earn money, many volunteer jobs will pay you at least a pittance. (See section "Needed: Volunteers," at end of this chapter.)

Volunteer work will not only keep you busy. It also will be experience which can assist you in choosing a future career or getting into college. Admissions officials are showing a growing interest in the extracurricular activities listed by college applicants.

What About Working Abroad This Summer?

What about spending the summer abroad—either working as a volunteer or in a paying job? The key drawbacks to working abroad are: competition is keen; pay is low; many countries have restrictions on employment of foreigners; work permits often are required and these can be difficult to get; language can be a barrier.

Nevertheless, overseas jobs do exist—and your best bet in finding a good one is to work through an established, reputable job-finding organization.

BEST SOURCES OF JOBS

Among the best sources of summer jobs abroad are:

(1) The Association for the International Exchange of Students in Economics and Commerce (AIESEC), Room 1110, 52 Vanderbilt Avenue, New York, N.Y. 10017, which has an internship exchange program in more than 53 countries for undergraduate and graduate business students.

(2) The International Association for the Exchange of Students for Technical Experience (IAESTE), American City Building, Suite 217, Columbia, Md. 21044, which specifically seeks engineering, science, architecture, and agriculture majors who want to work abroad during the summer.

(3) Summer Jobs in Britain and Australia, run by the Council on International Educational Exchange (CIEE), which is qualified to help you find a job in Great Britain and Australia (see below for address).

BEST SOURCES OF INFORMATION

• The CIEE issues low-cost student identity cards and publishes a yearly study-work-travel directory entitled, *Whole World Handbook* ($2.95). Write to the Council at 777 United Nations Plaza, New York, N.Y. 10017, for details.

• The National Student Travel Bureau will refer students to reputable agencies that arrange transportation and jobs overseas. Address: 2115 S Street, N.W., Washington, D.C. 20008.

Excellent publications, too, covering overseas student study and travel programs are:

• "Working Abroad." Free from CIEE.

• "A Word of Caution." Free from the Director of Public Information and Reports Staff, Bureau of Educational and Cultural Affairs, Department of State, Washington, D.C. 20520.

• "Summer Study Abroad." Published yearly by the Institute of International Education, 809 United Nations Plaza, New York, N.Y. 10017 ($2.00).

• *Study Abroad*. Available from the UNESCO Publications Center, P. O. Box 433, New York, N.Y. 10016 ($6.00).

• "Invest Yourself." Available from the Commission on Voluntary Service and Action, 475 Riverside Drive, Room 830, New York, N.Y. 10027 ($1.00).

• "Summer Jobs in Europe." Available from Vacation Work, 266 Ludlow Avenue, Cincinnati, O. 45220.

• *The Directory of Overseas Summer Jobs.* Available from National Directory Service, 266 Ludlow Avenue, Cincinnati, O. 45220 ($4.95).

You also will find the following good sources of information on summer jobs, study, and travel programs abroad:

Experiment in International Living
Kipling Road
Brattleboro, Vt. 05301

American Institute for Foreign
Study
102 Greenwich Avenue
Greenwich, Conn. 06830

KEY QUESTIONS TO ASK

Finally, here are key questions to ask about any private agency whose services you might enlist to help locate a summer job abroad and about any specific programs offered:

Can the organization tell you of and refer you to someone from your campus who has used its services?

What does the organization charge for its services compared with other agencies?

Is the total cost to you, the participant, clearly spelled out?

Does the literature specify what is covered and, more importantly, what is not covered?

What percentage of the total cost goes for administration? Commissions?

Will the fee be refunded should you have to cancel?

Does the organization have an official base in the United States which would be legally responsible in the event of complications?

Does the organization secure low-cost passage and living arrangements for you?

Are special student identification and discount cards offered?

In work-abroad programs, does the organization specify exactly which types of jobs are available to you? The hours? The pay? Whether meals and lodging are included?

"Tailored Pay Checks"

KEY TRENDS IN COMPENSATION

The "tailor-made pay check" is becoming ever more widespread—permitting you, an individual employee, to shape your own pay checks (so much cash, such and such a pension deal, this or that type savings or stock purchase plan) according to your own individual wants and needs. For example:

If you're in your late twenties, at the start of your career, married, with young children and a load of debts, what you need from your employer is all the current cash income and protection against death or disability you can get. What you don't need is a retirement income plan to which you are required to make fat contributions.

But if you're in your late fifties, around the peak of your taxable earnings and free of many of your family burdens, what you need is assurance of a lifetime retirement income for you and your wife. What you don't need is more current cash income on which you'll pay more taxes.

COMPENSATION GEARED TO YOUR AGE

Let's take a more detailed specific example of a middle-income manager called John Jones.

In his late twenties, Jones holds an accountant's position in an industrial corporation which pays him $15,000. Married and with three children, he finds it hard to keep up with his mounting family obligations despite several raises. Though his life insurance program is barely adequate, he complains of being "insurance poor." His requirements at this stage are easily defined.

He needs all the cash income he can command plus protection for his family. Thus, salary compensation, medical coverage, life insurance, and disability income protection are key elements in his pay package, with a minimum of employee contribution requirements.

Consider Jones fifteen years later, in his mid-forties, holding a higher job paying $25,000. Now one son is in college, another is a year away, his teenage daughter is having expensive orthodontal work, his debts and tax obligations are higher, and his auto insurance bill is painful. He still needs all the cash he can command.

But he needs to be able to count on the cash regularly. Thus, bonus dollars in lieu of salary dollars offer little attraction because of their uncertainty. And though various forms of protection continue important, he must start building toward a retirement income in the years he has left at work.

Now consider Jones at fifty-seven, earning $40,000 in a job he'll almost certainly keep until retirement. His expenses have declined but his peak earnings have been cut by peak taxes and he still is far from achieving his retirement fund goal. Social Security (an increasingly important source of retirement income) will help but his most urgent need now is additional retirement income from his company's program.

The idea of "tailored pay checks" (or "cafeteria compensation") is becoming ever more widespread. But as company management explores their use as a powerful and sensible motivating force, you, the middle manager, will increasingly reap the benefits of a personalized pay package custom-designed for you.

AND "PERKS"

On top of all the cash compensation, the fringe benefits, and the tailoring of pay checks to meet the individual's changing circumstances comes a long and lengthening list of "perks"—perquisites—for executives: use of company hotel rooms and resort facilities; use of company planes; company autos; medical care; personal money management, etc.

In many cases the perks are old-fashioned, tax-loophole frivolities. In others they are highly imaginative incentives to executives.

(P.S. One "extra" which virtually no executive enjoys is overtime pay. No matter what the rules for premium pay for overtime work under the federal wage-hour law, these men and women work sixty, seventy, eighty hours a week or more for no extra pay at all. Why? They love what they do, they want to work, that's why!)

SHOP FOR FRINGE BENEFITS, TOO!

ROUTINE DEDUCTIONS

You're not at all untypical today if as much as one third of your pay is "missing" by the time you receive your check. And you're not at all untypical if, aside from the large chunk you pay for taxes, your deductions cover a dozen or more different items, offered by your employer as a fringe benefit at lower-than-usual cost or as a convenience to you.

Here is a partial list of goods and services for which deductions from pay checks are now routinely being made: federal and state income taxes; Social Security ("FICA") and Medicare taxes; life insurance premiums; health and disability insurance premiums; contributions toward company profit-sharing plans, and stock purchase plans; purchase of U. S. Savings Bonds; homeowners insurance premiums; personal catastrophe liability insurance premiums; repayments to credit unions for many types of loans.

A key attraction of fringe benefits rests on our income tax structure. If your employer simply increased your pay so that you could buy your own life insurance, health insurance, etc., you would have to pay income taxes on your fatter pay check. But if he offers these as fringe benefits you get the coverage *without* paying increased taxes. Moreover, your employer can get a better buy on many fringes (such as group health insurance) than you could get as an individual for yourself.

The extent to which increases in fringe benefits have entered and are continuing to enter crucial wage negotiations involving millions of workers dramatizes this fundamental and yet still startlingly understated point: in a mounting number of cases, improvements in fringe benefits are becoming as important as—or even more important than—cash pay hikes themselves.

For the majority of U.S. workers in the economic mainstream fringe benefits are a real blessing. But for the have-nots in our society they are a potent source of discontent. Reason: the "fringe binge" perpetuates the gap between those who are eligible for valuable fringes and those who are ineligible—because they are unemployed, employed part time, or work for marginal employers who cannot finance the extras.

Nevertheless, focusing strictly on the "haves":

• Today, if you're an average U.S. worker, for every $1.00 you are earning in regular pay, you are getting another 25¢ to 30¢ in fringe benefits. That translates into an extra $2,500 to $3,000 in fringes for every $10,000 of yearly pay.

• In the mid-1970s, if you were typical, you were receiving about $1.00 an hour in the form of "hidden" pay which didn't appear on your regular dollars-and-cents pay check, against only 25¢ of "hidden" benefits in the late 1940s.

• Fringe benefits have been increasing in recent years at two to three times the rate of increase in cash wages and salaries; in recent years the growth has been a hefty 10 to 12 per cent a year.

To help you compare your benefits with what others are receiving and to help you shop for benefits as you compare one prospective new job with another, here is a brief rundown on key benefits and trends today:

PAID VACATIONS AND HOLIDAYS

Typical today is a two-week vacation plus at least six to eight paid holidays. But this norm is rapidly becoming three weeks and ten to twelve paid holidays after just a few years of service.

Also the typical employer grants employees the equivalent of another two weeks' "vacation" in the form of a couple of coffee breaks each day.

The trend is toward ever lengthening vacations as well as vacation-splitting—permitting you to divide your vacation into chunks. Moreover, a growing number of companies are switching to the four-day (but still forty-hour) work week—giving you no fewer than fifty-two long weekends during the year. See Chapter 12, "How to Save on Vacations," for more details on how your vacations compare with those other workers get.

GROUP INSURANCE

Nearly all U.S. companies now make at least some contribution toward some type of insurance for their employees. Health and life insurance are the most common but the trend is toward group automobile insurance, and even group homeowners insurance. The typical company-paid policy is canceled when you move to another job, but often you can convert your group coverage to a low-cost individual policy if you do so within a stated period of time.

The new trends in health insurance are toward increasing amounts of major medical coverage for catastrophic illness, outpatient psychiatric care as well as in-hospital care, dental bills and eye care, yearly physical exams. A few employers provide coverage for totally disabled dependents and make prescription drugs available at bargain prices. For more details on health insurance coverage and costs, see Chapter 8, "The High Cost of Good Health."

In life insurance, the trend is toward substantial group coverage not only for workers themselves but also for their wives and children.

EDUCATIONAL BENEFITS

Many employers today will pay the full costs of further education and training—even programs lasting as long as a year. In a few cases employers also are offering college scholarships for workers' children.

MOVING BENEFITS

A growing minority of top U.S. corporations will pay at least part of your mortgage interest costs when you are reassigned to a new post in a new location. Many also will extend a low-cost loan to you to help you with the down payment on this new house. Virtually all companies will pay at least some of your direct moving expenses. For other fringes now being offered to employees on the move, see Chapter 13, "A Roof Over Your Head."

TIME OFF TO VOTE

The overwhelming majority of firms make some time-off arrangements for employees—both hourly and salaried—to vote. The usual thing is to give workers whatever time is needed "within reason." Only a dwindling minority says "no time off," on the basis that their employees have ample opportunity to get to the polls on their own time. Incidentally, most states now have laws providing for time off to vote, and many require that time off with pay be provided.

SPECIAL INVESTMENT PLANS

Under these plans, which vary widely from employer to employer, employees may invest regularly in company stock, in government bonds, in securities of outside companies, or in mutual funds. See Chapter 20, "How to Invest in Stocks," for more details.

DIVIDEND REINVESTMENT PLANS

See Chapter 20, "How to Invest in Stocks," for full analysis.

PROFIT-SHARING PLANS

Today, millions of workers—both white- and blue-collar—participate in private corporation profit-sharing plans often as an alternative to private pension plans, and thousands of new plans are being set up annually. In some, profits are distributed as periodic bonuses to employees. But in the vast majority of plans funds are held in trust until you, the employee, quit or retire. A key advantage of the typical "deferred" profit-sharing plan is that you pay no federal income taxes on your cut until you actually withdraw it from the profit pool. These plans are being set up by smaller and smaller companies. Employees are becoming eligible to participate in them and to withdraw their full funds after fewer and fewer years of service.

To suggest how significant such plans can be, Chicago's Continental Bank has calculated that if an employer of a thirty-year-old, $10,000-a-year man contributed an average of 10 per cent of these earnings to a profit-sharing account each year, if the worker matched this amount, and if the investment grew at 7 per cent compounded annually, the worker would have accumulated $228,000 by the time he retired at age sixty-five.

NEW "EXTRAS"

After reporting its findings in a recent every-other-year survey of fringe benefits in private industry, the U. S. Chamber of Commerce suggested that we stop labeling them "fringe" benefits. The Chamber has a point. For here is a sampling of extras already offered by *some* corporations:
- Free or reduced-price meals in company cafeterias.
- Paid membership in clubs, professional, and trade associations.
- Medical help for alcoholic and drug-abusing employees.
- Discounts on company products and services.
- Free or low-cost day care services for preschool children of employed working mothers.
- Free or nominal-cost use of company vacation and recreation facilities.
- Free retirement counseling to middle-aged workers in such areas as financial planning, Medicare benefits, how to turn a hobby into a part-time job.
- Financial aid for adoption expenses—to parallel maternity benefits.
- Fat bonuses for valuable employee suggestions.
- And free flying lessons . . . paternity leave for expectant fathers . . . time off for working mothers to consult with schoolteachers . . . company-paid legal services . . . taxis to and from work . . . free parking . . . employer-paid funerals (about the last word in paternalism!) . . .

And this is not all.

EXOTIC BENEFITS

Here's an abbreviated list of some of the exotic fringe benefits which knowledgeable students of this type of "pay" are predicting for the decade of the seventies and beyond:
- Free concert and theater tickets at regular intervals.
- Use of company computer facilities for your own purposes.

• Loans via employer credit cards which you'll repay by deductions from your pay check.

• Company-run private schools for your children—particularly if you live in an area where public schools are below average.

• Free financial advice from experts paid by the company for which you work.

Before 1985, many experts think, fringe benefits might include coverage of more than 50 per cent of the costs of home nursing care for employees, maternity benefits for the unwed as well as the wed, and subsidized homes in company-owned retirement communities.

They see sharply expanded protection against increases in our cost of living through escalator clauses in retirement pensions and more and more leeway for you to choose which hours of the day and which days of the week you want to work.

But, of course, towering above all other fringe benefits is the private pension plan—next to your salary, quite likely your most important single point of comparison between Job A and Job B.

It's so important, in fact, that it demands a key place in Chapter 19 on "Planning for Your Future Financial and Personal Security." And that's where you will find full details on pensions.

IF YOU ARE A WOMAN

YOU PROBABLY WORK

If you are a woman between the ages of eighteen and sixty-five, the odds are better than fifty-fifty that you are now holding a job. The chances are nine out of ten that you will work or have worked at some time during your life.

Even if you are married, you are almost as likely to be holding a job as not; more than four out of ten of all married American women are now in the U.S. labor force.

And even if you have children, the chances are good that you're working too. Nearly half of the millions of working wives have children under age eighteen. Even the mothers of very young children work; 4.8 million working mothers in the mid-seventies had children under the age of six.

Of course, if you're not married, it's even more likely that you are working. More than half of all single women are in the labor force—as are two out of three divorcees and one in four widows (many of whom are old and unable to work).

As a general rule, the more education a woman has and the older her children, the bigger the odds she is in the labor force. More than half of the wives who have completed four years of college are in the labor force.

If you're typical, you'll marry in your early twenties, raise your children, and then go back to work. On average, the birth of one child reduces your work-life expectancy by ten years. And the birth of each additional child reduces your work-life expectancy another two to three years.

Children or not, though, you'll probably work in a paying job a total of twenty-five years during your lifetime.

WOMEN WORKERS AND FAMILY INCOME

Like men, women work primarily because they need to earn money. For most working women, the question of working purely for personal fulfillment simply is not the issue. Almost all of the 7 million-plus single working women and the more than 6 million women workers who were widowed, divorced, or separated in the mid-seventies were working to support themselves and—in the latter cases—often their children too. These are all women who must work because they do not have husbands to support them.

But wives and mothers work too; and for a great many of these women, financial need also is the compelling force keeping them in the labor market. These wives—many of them with young children—need to work to keep their families afloat; because their husbands are unemployed; to raise the family's standard of living. On average, wives' earnings contribute 27.5 per cent to family incomes, with the wives' contribution to family income ranging from 39 per cent for those who work full time all year down to 12 per cent for those who work less.

And they need to work because they are what the Labor Department calls "female heads of families"—women with young children to support and no husband to help. There are more than 6 million families in the United States headed by women.

Moreover survey after survey has shown that a very large percentage of the women who are not in the labor force would like to work if they thought they had a chance at a job. These women don't actively look for work (and are therefore not counted as being "in the labor force") because they think racial or sex discrimination would bar them, or they lack skills, or they have family responsibilities that keep them at home. Many would go to work if decent day care facilities were available.

The income level for families with children under age eighteen and headed by women, however, is low. When we talk about the low incomes of families headed by a woman, we are talking about one of the root causes of poverty in our society. Until we can improve the situation of these women— by upgrading their skills, expanding their job opportunities, abolishing sex discrimination in pay levels, and providing adequate child care—our welfare problem will continue to plague us and millions of our children will continue to grow up on a hopeless treadmill of poverty.

For information on how to fight job discrimination on account of sex see Part IV, "Your Rights and How to Get Them."

GET READY NOW FOR THE "EMPTY NEST"

But what if you're among the many, many mothers who *want* to stay at home with your young children, and who are financially able to do so? Fine— but, at the very least, realize now that your children, too, will grow up and leave home. And when they do, you, the full-time mother, will be a still young, vigorous woman. What will you do then?

For the last several years my husband and I have been what economists call an "empty nest"—an economic unit which has become enormously significant in our society, the family in which both parents are alive and the last child has left home. A full one in seven families in the United States are empty nests—families with no children under eighteen living at home.

And now that I have lived this story and learned its true dimensions, I cannot urge you too strongly to start preparing for your empty nest early in your life! Start before you are married and even have a nest of your own.

The empty nest is very much a phenomenon of modern times. At the turn of the century the average American family never knew an empty nest; typically, the father died before the last child left home. A half century ago, if an empty nest did develop, it lasted only a year or so, until one spouse died. But now, as a result of trends toward longer life spans, smaller families, and concentration of childbearing before the age of twenty-six, an empty nest in the United States will last an average fourteen years. Some couples will spend thirty or forty years together between the time when the last child leaves home and the death of either spouse.

The number of empty-nesters is impressive enough and growing rapidly —but the reasons they are so important stretch far beyond numbers alone. Specifically, this unit includes:

• The most affluent of all age groups. When the typical empty nest occurs, the husband is at the peak of his earning years. Although this group represents one tenth of our total population, it gets one fifth of our annual personal income.

• The least debt-burdened of all age groups. By the time the nest empties, most parents have slashed their debts and the overwhelming majority own their own homes. They are financially "free" to an unprecedented degree.

• Consumers who are eager buyers of leisure-time and luxury items of all types. Here are the big spenders for foreign travel, eating out, costly clothes and cars—all the goods and services they had to forgo while bringing up the children.

• Devoted buyers of small packages of almost everything. There are still tremendous gaps in goods and services designed for the small adult family unit.

• And most important, a towering percentage of working wives. Among women in their middle years (in their forties and over) the non-working wife is becoming the *exception!* Of those holding a college degree, more than two out of three are in the labor force, and of those with graduate training it's four out of five.

The economic implications of all these points are clear—and equally unmistakable should be the message to you, as a girl in school, a young bride, a mother of babies or teen-agers. If you are still in school, remain there until you have achieved the education to get and hold a job which interests you. If you are a young bride or young mother who chooses not to work temporarily, keep your education up to date. If you are a mother of teen-agers, actively refresh your training to be ready to go to work part or full time.

Abysmally lost is the wife who does not have something to occupy herself when the nest empties. Don't wait to find out for yourself how true this is; prepare now to avoid the experience.

BASIC CAREER GUIDES

Let's say you are a young woman planning for a career in today's challenging era. What basic guides could I give you to help you fulfill yourself as well as to make a significant contribution to your family and to the national economy?

• Before you decide on your career, study the enormous range of occupations now open to you. You'll find the guides in the previous pages of this chapter.

• Set your career goals as high as you dare, or think about how you might upgrade your goals within a given field you've already picked. For example, if you're thinking about becoming a nurse, ask yourself whether you might qualify for training as a nursing teacher or a psychologist. If you want to become a secretary, consider upgrading to a high-paying specialty such as medical, legal, or bilingual secretarial work.

• Make a long-range plan to meet the requirements for the occupation you choose. Your immediate goal probably will be to complete college; the statistical likelihood is that you'll then get married and raise a family. But you can go on to specialized education-training later, or pick it up on a part-time basis while you're an active housewife. Today hundreds of organizations, and colleges and universities, including community colleges and university extensions, offer "continuing education programs" for adult women. In some cases, class schedules are geared to the hours you're likely to be free from domestic duties. See Chapter 10, "A College Education and How to Finance It."

• If you received professional training or graduate education before you married and left the labor force, do everything possible to keep that training up to date while you're at home. Maintain your membership in professional associations. Subscribe to, and read, technical journals in your field. Attend any seminars or lectures in your field which you can. Keep in touch with other members of your profession. Use your education and practice your skills through part-time jobs or volunteer work in your field.

• Explore the possibility of studying at home—via correspondence courses, adult education programs, educational television, independent study —then taking examinations leading to a high school diploma or giving college credit toward a degree. Ask your local board of education, community college, or state employment service for details on high school equivalency examinations. You'll find information on home study approaches to a college education in Chapter 10, "A College Education and How to Finance It."

An excellent source of information on continuing education programs for women is the Women's Bureau, Employment Standards Administration, U. S. Department of Labor, Washington, D.C. 20210. You can buy a copy for a modest price of the Women's Bureau's publication, "Continuing Education Programs and Services for Women" from the Superintendent of Documents, Washington, D.C. 20402. Also useful are: "Directory of Postsecondary Schools with Occupational Programs," (Superintendent of Documents) and the New York *Times*'s *Guide to Continuing Education in America* (Quadrangle Books, $4.95).

• When you're free to take a full-time job, don't just "take a job." Look for work in the field in which you were originally educated or trained. If it requires more training or retraining, get it. Or if you want to start over on a new career, do that.

MYTHS ABOUT WOMEN WORKERS

Not long ago a young acquaintance who works in a private employment service and who is compensated according to the number of jobs he is actually able to fill received from an employer a request for mechanical engineer specializing in fluid control devices—e.g., heat exchangers, centrifugal pumps, valves; substantial salary for the qualified person. But there was a catch. The employee had to be a *woman*. Although sure that a search would be fruitless, the young man nevertheless called his firm's Chicago office. Within minutes this office produced the names of six eligible candidates and one was promptly hired for this job.

You're in the majority if you never would have considered an engineering specialty in "fluid control devices" a woman's job. You also are in the majority if you continue to indulge in unfair, illegal "job labeling" which arbitrarily insists that one occupation is for men only and another for women only.

Aptitude tests have repeatedly shown that women can perform just about any job as well as men can. Women are now represented in virtually every one of the 400-plus occupations listed in the 1970 census. Yet, in defiance of all equal opportunity laws, job labeling persists—and it continues to bar women from the higher-level, higher-paying jobs.

In defiance of the 1964 Civil Rights Act—prohibiting job discrimination on the grounds of sex as well as race—employers continue to indulge in such flagrant examples of discrimination as: automatic firing of women within sixty days of marriage; refusal to allow women to work overtime, even though state laws permit the overtime; banning women even from training for managerial jobs. And unions, too, continue to engage in such grossly unfair practices as clinging to collective bargaining agreement clauses which reserve certain jobs for men and others, usually at lower pay, for women.

Here, in addition to the "women's jobs" myth are other myths which mock this era of equal job rights.

Myth: Women are absent from their jobs because of illness more than men are, thus cost the employer more money.

Reality: The absenteeism rate due to illness or injury currently averages 5.2 days a year for women, 5.1 days for men. Moreover, these figures ignore the fact that relatively few women work in high managerial positions, which always have been associated with lower absenteeism rates, and thus they may be distorted.

Myth: Women switch jobs much more frequently than men do.

Reality: Labor Department studies show that women's job-changing rates are slightly lower than rates for men if proper allowance is made for the fact that low-paid workers of either sex switch jobs often.

Myth: In any high-unemployment period, women take jobs away from men, the traditional breadwinners.

Reality: There are millions more married women in the labor force than there are unemployed men! Thus, if all married women quit and if all the unemployed men moved into their empty jobs, there would remain tens of millions of unfilled jobs—causing one of the most horrendous economic disasters imaginable. What's more: few of today's unemployed men have the education, skills, or other qualifications to fill jobs held by women as secretaries, nurses, schoolteachers.

Myth: Women work only for "pin money."

Reality: That has been answered. Of all women now in the labor force, nearly half are working because they are single, widowed, divorced, separated, or have very low-income husbands.

Myth: Training women is a waste of money since they quit when they marry or have children.

Reality: The separations are only temporary. Even taking into account her child-rearing, non-working years, the average woman worker has a work-life expectancy of twenty-five years. For a single woman, the average is forty-five years versus an over-all average of forty-three years for men, married or single.

Myth: Men don't like to work for women.

Reality: Notes the Department of Labor's Women's Bureau: "Most men who complain about women supervisors have never worked for a woman."

And an examination of attitudes entitled "Are Women Executives People?" first printed in the *Harvard Business Review,* found that only one man in seventeen was "strongly unfavorable" to the idea of women managers. In contrast, one in ten was "strongly favorable" and the other attitudes ranged from "mildly favorable" to "mildly unfavorable."

WHAT'S A HOUSEWIFE WORTH?

If you are a typical "non-jobholding" U.S. housewife, you fill at least 12 well-defined occupations valued in the open market at a minimum of $300 a week for an actual pay in dollars of $000.

If you are among the tens of millions of American women classified as "married, not in the labor force," you put in 100 or more hours per week working at these occupations—and frequently many, many more—again, for the dollar pay of $000.

You have no set hours and it's normal for you to start early and stop late. You have no specified schedule for rest. You have no assurance of any vacation worth the name at any time for any duration. You get little, if any, recognition for your job performance as such. It's taken for granted that you'll be good.

As a "card-carrying" pioneer in the world of women's lib, I have understandably concentrated on the working women—and our right to equal pay for equal work, equal recognition, equal opportunity, all the rest. But I have also studied the "non-jobholding" housewives among my friends in the exurb where we have a country home. Without their being aware of my scrutiny, I have checked their performance without any help as cook, chauffeur, seamstress, housekeeper, laundress, etc.

I've watched most of them go to work at 6 A.M. to feed their families before sending them off to the commuting trains or school. And I've watched most of them start another cycle of several hours of work involving dinner and cleanup at 6 P.M., a mere twelve hours later.

What's more, a housewife's work is not only non-paid, it's not even counted in our output as a nation. When I turn out something, I'm paid for my production and my pay is included in our nation's Gross National Product. But when a housewife sews a magnificent dinner skirt, all that counts toward GNP is what she spent for the material, the thread, whatever else she bought. Her labor, without which the skirt would not have come into existence, doesn't count one whit. (If she had hired someone to sew the skirt for her, though, and had paid her, what the seamstress earned from her would count.)

Imagine what our GNP would swell to if we counted in just the $300 a week being earned by tens of millions of women!

Use the following chart to figure *your* worth as a housewife in *your* area, at current wage rates:

JOB	HOURS PER WEEK	LOCAL RATE PER HOUR	YOUR "VALUE" PER WEEK
Nursemaid			
Housekeeper			
Cook			
Dishwasher			
Laundress			
Food buyer			
Chauffeur			
Gardener			
Maintenance man			
Seamstress			
Dietitian			
Practical nurse			
TOTAL			

HOW TO FIND A DAY CARE CENTER

If you are a typical young family with small children, an absolute *must* before you, the mother, can take even a part-time paying job is a good nursery school, baby-sitting service, or day care facility at a cost you can afford.

If you could find a top-notch day care center, it could be a boon not only to you but also to your child—for if it's top-notch it will be well staffed, well equipped, well populated with other children, and well supplied with a variety of cultural-educational stimuli.

Where and how do you find good child care arrangements? What are the costs likely to be?

• Start by checking your would-be employer's day care facilities. Many, many companies—ranging from hospitals to factories, baby food companies, and government agencies—have set up day care facilities. In most cases you pay a modest sum each week, for your child.

If you are considering taking a job in a hospital, weigh the presence or absence of day care facilities before you choose a particular institution. Hundreds of hospitals have day care centers today—as a way to attract nurses and other health service workers who otherwise might be housebound.

And hundreds more are in the process of setting up day care facilities. Almost all have opened their doors just within the past few years.

• If you work for the federal government, check with the several agencies which now have day care centers—including the Department of Labor, the Department of Agriculture, and the U. S. Office of Education.

• Make inquiries at local civic and religious organizations about available day care facilities run by these organizations or by other agencies.

• Certainly canvass with care the wide variety of private day care combinations—including nursery schools, baby-sitting services, communal care, informal child care agreements among neighbors.

• Investigate—if you're a college student—whether the college you're attending (or plan to attend) has some type of low-cost day care facility.

• Check, if you're a member of a labor union, whether your union runs a day care center.

• Look among available publicly supported preschool programs—particularly any federally financed programs aimed primarily at preschool-age children from lower-income families, but not always segregated along economic lines.

• Use these sources of guidance and information on child care services for you and in your community: The Day Care and Child Development Council of America, 1025 14th Street, N.W., Washington, D.C. 20005; the federal Department of Health, Education and Welfare's Office of Child Development, Washington, D.C. 20201; also regional offices of this agency; the local chapter of the National Organization for Women.

• Ask your library to help you get a copy of *The Early Childhood Education Directory* (New York, R. R. Bowker Co.)—a descriptive compendium of more than 2,000 nursery schools, federally financed centers, and day care centers throughout the country.

• Order the Office of Child Development publication, *Finding the Best Day Care for Your Children*, from Consumer Information, Pueblo, Colorado 81009.

• If you can't find decent day care facilities at a cost you can manage in your home community, try pooling your own ideas, children, time, skills, with those of other neighbors and friends who are working mothers. Share out-of-pocket costs—and rotate responsibilities among you. Or try to hire, at least part time, someone who has been trained in this field.

• Another alternative is to try to find a conscientious college student willing to trade bed and board, say, for looking after your small children part time. You might even be able to track down an *au pair* foreign student through an agent specializing in making arrangements for such young people to live in your home—for a small sum per week plus room and board.

DAY CARE CENTER QUIZ TO GUIDE YOU

Here are the key questions to ask about any day care center to which you are considering entrusting your child and to which you may be committing yourself to pay substantial fees, charges, or tuitions:

• Is the center a professionally staffed, decently equipped place in which your child is likely to learn something? Or is it merely a baby-sitting service?

• What are the center's hours—and does it operate five, six, or seven days a week? Is this schedule convenient for *you?*

• Will your child be permitted to "try out" the center for, say, a couple of weeks before he or she is committed to sign up for a longer period?

• Do toys, equipment, and the layout of the center itself appear to add up to a safe place to be and play and learn?

• Is a doctor and/or nurse on call—especially if the center is a relatively large one?

• Is the center licensed by the state or some other public agency (most licensed centers are listed in the Yellow Pages of your telephone book)?

• What meals and/or snacks are offered and is their content of real nutritional value?

• Who and how many are on the staff—and what kind of training (if any) have they had in early childhood education?

• What is the child-to-teacher ratio? An adequate ratio would be around 10 to 1.

• How varied are the activities and experiences to which your child will be exposed?

• What are daily or weekly charges? Are there special rates for half days and for second or third children from a single family? Is there a special charge for lunch? If fees are based on your family's ability to pay, just what would that mean?

IS IT REALLY WORTH IT?

Every word in this section surely must shout to you my own profound conviction that "it" is worth it indeed.

Every line in this discussion surely must disclose how intellectually and emotionally I am committed to the *right* of a girl and a woman to have her own career and the importance of this to her own sense of values and dignity. And surely my own life underlines how I have translated my beliefs into reality.

But *you* may want to calculate the advantages strictly in financial terms.

Okay. Let's say your before-tax salary was $150 a week and that deductions for various federal, state, and Social Security taxes and for group health insurance amounted to $35.88. That would leave you $114.12.

Then deduct $1.00 a day for transportation to and from work, $1.50 a day for lunch, and $5.00 a day for the baby sitter or day care services.

Next figure that the extra clothes, personal-care costs, and other personal items will cost you about $5.00 a week.

Then try to estimate the higher household expenses you're likely to have, such as more expensive convenience foods to save you cooking time. Say these come to $15 a week.

The total comes to $57.50 a week, meaning $93.38 will be deducted from your $150 pay check. This leaves you $56.62 a week, or less than half of your before-tax pay. And your husband may argue with even that figure for income tax reasons.

But I cannot say it too strongly: the amount left is *not* the key point! What *is* the key is that, if you want to work, you should. If you want to take extra training to upgrade your job and your pay, you should.

To estimate *your* own costs, fill in this chart—and weigh the total against your own pay check.

Gross Weekly Salary $_____

Deductions:
    Federal income tax   _____
    State income tax   _____
    State disability   _____
    Social Security   _____
    Group life insurance   _____
    Group health insurance   _____
    Pension plan   _____

Total deductions   _____
Amount of take-home pay $_____

Weekly Expenses:
    Transportation $_____
    Lunches   _____
    Child care   _____
    Personal grooming (including extra
      cleaning and laundry)   _____
    Extra clothes   _____
    Dues (professional, union, etc.)   _____
    Household help   _____
    Added household expenses
      (convenience foods, paying for
      things you might have done
      yourself, etc.)   _____

Weekly Expenses (CONTD)
    Office contributions, etc.   _____
    Other   _____

    Total Weekly Expenses $_____

    Take-home pay $_____

    Minus weekly expenses $_____

    Your real pay net $_____

How to Play "Success Chess"

YOUR LIFETIME JOB GUIDE

"At what ages," asked Terry, a twenty-nine-year-old investment banker obviously destined to climb the success ladder, "is it entirely okay for you to change jobs frequently in order to test yourself on what you want to be and do?"

In what age range, both of us then debated, should you be finding the industry in which you want to spend your future years and should you be moving from job to job within that industry in order to build up your skills and experience?

By what age should you have definitely located your own industry, be set to move vertically toward the job goals you have concluded are right for you?

Spurred by Terry's penetrating questions, I went to one of the top executive recruiting and management training firms in the world—charging, for counseling on a single job, fees ranging up to $3,000 for an individual, $30,000 for a corporation.

Since it's highly unlikely you'll have the opportunity—not to mention the fee—to ask such a firm in person for specific advice about jobs, I did the asking for you.

Important note: The advice that follows applies as much to "Theresa" as to "Terry." In fact, the experts at this firm went out of their way to emphasize that the guides are for young women as well as for men.

Now here are six practical guides to job success this firm developed over years of helping to mold the careers of famous industrialists.

(1) In the first five years of your job career—say from age twenty-two to twenty-eight—try to find out what you want to *do*, what you want to *be*. Don't hesitate to make several job changes, for you are testing yourself. As a young man or woman, ask yourself: "What do I want out of life? What do I want to do?"

In these years young men or women who are unmarried are generally more successful than married individuals, because they can more easily move around on their own or more easily be moved by their firms.

(2) Also, in the twenty-two to twenty-eight age range, concentrate on finding the industry in which you want to stay.

The future top leaders are to an impressive extent the ones who were set in their own industry in their twenties and who then moved within it to gain know-how.

(3) At the age of thirty, stop and think hard. Take the time to sit down quietly and write out some answers to yourself on such questions as these: Where do you want to live? Where would you and your spouse be happiest? How much annual pay will you need to earn ten or fifteen years from now to meet the standard of living you want? You'll have a much clearer concept of your goals after you've honestly made this effort to "know thyself"—which well may be among the hardest tasks you'll ever undertake.

(4) For the next ten years—say to age forty—prepare yourself deliberately for what you want to be. Grade yourself on these qualities for success: drive, responsibility, health, good character, ability to communicate, ability to think, ability to get along with people, ability to keep your perspectives (i.e., recognize your responsibilities to society even while you're watching your competitors in business).

(5) In the forty to forty-two age bracket you'll hit a treacherous phase of "cyclical restlessness" when you may mistakenly change jobs because you're looking for the "greener grass." Be on guard: again, quietly check up on your goals.

(6) After age forty-five, start consolidating—use the years to broaden your objectives, achieve fulfillment, lay the basis for a rewarding new life after you leave your company.

Brief as this guide is, it's loaded. And it also has given you one of the most significant job hints of your entire career if it challenges you merely to find your answers to those two deceptively simple questions:

What do you want out of life?

What do you want to do?

WHAT MOVES TO MAKE

Now let's say you are in your thirties—into the decade during which you should be preparing yourself for what you want to do and be.

Let's say, too, that you have found a new job as a well-paid middle executive in an aggressive fast-growing corporation. The promise of rapid promotion into the upper corporate ranks was part of the deal—as long as management believes you deserve a promotion because of your superior performance in your starting position.

What moves can you make at this stage to boost your chances of stepping up the corporate ladder as rapidly as possible? Here are nine—drawn up by a top authority in the field of executive behavior:

(1) *Keep open the widest possible set of options* or of future opportu-

nities to alter your behavior. It is less important to know exactly where you are going than to keep your options open. When you see that you are being stereotyped, make a move either within or outside the company to break the stereotype.

(2) *Avoid loss of career time.* Do not waste this precious commodity by working for an immobile superior. The chances are greater that you will be blocked by such a boss, for a shelf-sitter is more likely to stay than be replaced.

(3) *Become a crucial subordinate to a mobile superior.* When he moves you'll move, since you are as important to him as he is to you.

(4) *Aim for increased exposure and visibility,* and make sure you are traveling the right kind of "route" in your company. If manufacturing men tend to inherit the presidency and you are in sales, think very hard about whether or not you have gone as far as you can go up the management ladder.

(5) *Practice "self-nomination" for top jobs.* Let those who do the nominating for key posts know that you want a bigger job or at least want to learn how to qualify for it.

(6) *Make sure that if you leave your company* you do so on your own terms, and always leave on the best of terms.

(7) *If after long and serious deliberation you decide to quit, rehearse the move ahead of time.* Avoid being counted among the executives who have fired their corporation in the afternoon and rehired it the next day. Instead, write out your resignation, put it in a safe place in your desk, and let at least a week go by before you submit it.

(8) *Look upon the corporation as a market* rather than a place in which you simply work for a living. The market is for skills, and skill is best determined by your real achievements and performance.

(9) *Have faith* that if you can succeed in one thing you can probably succeed in another, even without having climbed a single rung on a corporate ladder.

FIVE CLUES ON PROMOTIONS

Now study the following five clues on promotions offered by other experts on the subject of executive advancement:

(1) The great majority of promotions to top executive spots are made from within the firm; significant numbers of these, however, were employed by their companies for only a relatively few years.

(2) The average age of newly promoted company presidents and chief executive officers is now in the early to mid-forties.

(3) Virtually all newly promoted company executives are college graduates and more than one in three holds an advanced degree. Among those

holding B.A. degrees, most majored in business or engineering and among those with master's degrees, most are in business.

(4) The top four rungs of the corporate ladder from which executives are being promoted today are: operations-division management; finance; marketing; administration.

(5) The least likely corporate specialties from which businessmen are now promoted to top jobs are: public relations; manufacturing; international; research and development.

SHOULD YOU QUIT YOUR JOB?

Here are fifteen questions which will reveal to you your own feelings about your job:

(1) In the last couple of months have you thought that you would like to quit or change jobs because you do not like the work itself?

(2) Do you feel that your work is monotonous, that the work itself provides no basic interest?

(3) Do you like the work itself that you are doing?

(4) Do you feel your work is checked too much?

(5) When you are away from work, do you think of your job as something you look forward to?

(6) Do you feel your job is a dead end as far as a work career is concerned?

(7) Do you find your work interesting enough to talk about it with people outside your work situation?

(8) Do you feel that your job is a place where you can continually learn something worth while?

(9) Do you find your job less interesting than, say, six months ago?

(10) How often are you fed back information about things that go wrong in a way embarrassing or awkward for you?

(11) How often do you feel that putting in effort to do your job well is not worth it because it really won't affect anything in the long run?

(12) How often do you feel that some parts of the job you do really do not make sense?

(13) How often do you find yourself wishing that you could take up another type of work because the work itself is not interesting?

(14) How often do you feel that you are just marking time, just putting in time at your work?

(15) How often do you feel that putting in extra effort is just looking for more problems?

Your answers just to these fifteen questions will indicate the scope of your dissatisfaction with your job.

And will your answers also determine whether you should switch jobs? At the very least, they will give you something to ponder very, very hard.

DO'S AND DON'TS ON QUITTING

Say you are a young middle-management executive earning between $20,000 and $25,000 in a subsidiary of a giant corporation and say three men in your own age bracket are ahead of you. Say you have just made a New Year's resolution to get out of this box *now* and find another job with better prospects for advancement. What should you do?

• *Don't* quit! Keep your present job while you look for another, for in addition to giving you income and a sense of security it will prove to a would-be employer that you are making the move voluntarily.

• *Do* get firmly in your own mind that this job change may be just one link in a lifelong chain of job changes. For if you are a man twenty years old, you can expect to make more than six job changes during the remainder of your working life. Even at age forty you can still expect to make more than two job changes, and even at fifty you can expect at least one more job change.

Of course, these are only averages, calculated by the Labor Department. Some of us will work at one job all our lives, some will make many more than the average number of changes. Nevertheless, the averages underline the extraordinary degree of job mobility in this country—despite the holding power of fringe benefits, pensions, seniority rights. Executive "dropouts" have become almost as commonplace as high school dropouts.

We're changing and upgrading our jobs and careers as never before in history. We're shopping continually not only for higher pay but—often more importantly—for more fringe benefits such as better pension plans and longer vacations; for a better chance to advance; for a more appreciative boss; for a way out of the big city rat race; for greater on-the-job excitement and adventure; for a chance to learn more; for an opportunity to do our bit to better the troubled world in which we live.

• *Don't* answer in your own name any "blind" ad (one giving only a box number and not identifying the company). Instead, have a friend cover for you by signing a third-person letter describing your qualifications to help you remain anonymous if the ad was placed by your own company. Do not have a job counselor, recruiter, or employment agent answer for you, for the recipient may get the impression that money is changing hands and this will destroy your letter's impact.

• *Do* prepare on your own—and with no professional help—a résumé of your career, your qualifications, your objectives. See earlier in this chapter for rules on résumés.

• *Don't* be thrown off base if your employer discovers you are job hunting and in fact *do* accept the fact that you are taking this risk and your employer is likely to find out. This emphasizes the importance of having your campaign planned in advance—so you will be well on your way to something new by the time your plans are discovered.

• *Do,* if you know of employment agencies which others have found responsible and effective, register with them and leave your résumé. The company hiring you probably will pay the fee. If yours is a highly specialized field, you may be able to locate an agency specializing in finding jobs in this field.

• *Do* register too with your nearest state employment agency, which offers free job finding and/or counseling. Many branches of this agency now have specialized job placement services for executives and professionals. They also can steer you to further job training opportunities if appropriate.

And you may find of vital help the U.S. computerized "job banks" listing job openings in your field in many nearby states or even throughout the country. Ultimately the job banks' computers will be linked nationally and the network will be able to provide comprehensive information on all major *national* job markets—for professionals, technicians, managers, and others.

• *Do* also send a covering letter and résumé to executive recruiters who work at your salary level. This is admittedly a long shot but certainly worth the price of a postage stamp. (You can get a list of responsible recruiting organizations from the Association of Executive Recruiting Consultants, 30 Rockefeller Plaza, New York, N.Y. 10020.)

WHAT IF YOU LOSE YOUR JOB?

"My husband is an advertising account executive in his early forties, earning $30,000 a year. We have a daughter halfway through college and a son who is a senior in high school and will be entering college next fall. We have a large house in southern Connecticut and my husband commutes to New York City by his car or train. I am president of the local garden club.

"For the past year or so we have been spending every cent coming into this house and are just barely managing to scrape up $5,000 a year for our daughter's college tuition, fees, and expenses. A couple of months ago we committed my husband's next year-end bonus (usually $1,500 or more) to a skiing vacation in Switzerland in January and made a down payment on a charter flight.

"We had been planning to sell some of our mutual fund shares at a profit to pay our son's freshman-year college costs but the shares are now selling for much *less* than we paid for them and we hate to sell and take the loss.

"Last evening my husband came home and told me that, because of a sharp drop in his agency's profits, this year's bonus is being canceled and all executives are also being asked to accept a 20 per cent pay cut. Moreover, he said it would be only realistic for us to consider his job in serious jeopardy.

"What if he loses his job? Where do we go for help? *What can we do?*"
Answer: *Don't panic!*

INTERVIEW YOURSELF

Many young executives are—or have been—in exactly this same bind. The bind may be in the form of a layoff, outright firing, a pay cut, a "vacation without pay," a merger, forced "early retirement," or corporate bankruptcy.

But in every case it means you (and here I'm writing to both and either of you) must at least think about finding a new job—sooner or later. In every case, also, it should mean taking a penetrating new look at yourselves—as a husband, as a wife, as partners—and at both of your ways of life.

Sure, it may have been years since you've pounded the pavement to find a job.

Sure, the threat of losing your job comes at a moment when you've become accustomed to spending to the hilt and even overspending, and when you're faced with an ever rising cost of living.

Sure, you may be confronted with a job market which is riddled with irrational prejudices against "older workers" in their fifties and even forties.

But why not turn this emergency to your own advantage?

Whether or not this is precisely the moment to make a job switch, at least ask yourself: is your job one which you find truly rewarding? Or do you feel trapped in it? Has it become overspecialized or too narrow in scope? Are you bored? Frustrated? How did you get into your present career in the first place —and do the reasons still make sense to you?

Think hard about *yourself*. Interview yourself: prepare a synopsis of your own past career, your qualifications, your goals. Decide whether or not you like this man who is you. In short, are you "doing your thing"?

A new, second career in mid-life can be a glorious adventure. In fact, many career counselors now are advising young Americans to expect and welcome the prospect of two or even three entirely different careers during the course of their working lifetimes.

For facts on your unemployment insurance *rights,* see Part IV, "Your Rights and How to Get Them."

"HIDDEN" RESERVE

But quite possibly you, the wife and marriage partner, are the biggest "hidden" financial reserve. If you, this non-working wife, are no more than average, you are entirely capable of earning a pay check from a part-time or full-time job. In fact, the threat of your husband's job loss easily could turn out to be a blessing for you, by forcing you to consider the benefits of going outside your home to work, particularly if your children are on their way out of your nest and the need for you to be at home during the daytime hours will soon disappear.

If you are like many of the women I know, you would like to return to work but you don't know how—and you're afraid.

Okay. Use your husband's crisis as your catalyst and with his blessing (if he's an understanding man, he'll be happy to give it) start moving back into the job world.

WHY?

In any event, and whatever financial resources you fall back on to ease the blow of being fired, you, the husband, should make a real effort to find out why *you* were the one (or among those) to be fired, laid off, sent on an unpaid vacation or whatever. Don't be unduly brutal with yourself, but be as honest as you can be. The answers and reasons could be valuable clues to help steer you into a new career direction or toward a different type of employer.

Were you really able to work smoothly and effectively with co-workers as well as your boss and those working under you?

Was your interest in the job really sincere and enthusiastic?

Were you flexible enough to welcome—and use—new facts and techniques affecting your bailiwick?

Were you willing to learn on the job?

Were you up to the demands of your job? And, on the other hand, was the job big enough for your talents and energies?

MERGER!

Or perhaps you were dismissed from your job because your company merged with another company and a certain number of heads inevitably had to roll.

For you who may face this prospect—and millions of men and women will indeed face it in coming years—here are profoundly important warnings which almost surely will startle you:

The more successful you may be as an executive in your present job the *less* likely you may be to advance in a new company created by a merger.

Higher-placed executives are *not* necessarily the ones who will be in on merger discussions *or* the ones who will necessarily come out on top.

Those top executives who have a basic sense of security and who are good leaders and administrators are *not* necessarily the most likely to exercise good business judgment on behalf of themselves when a merger occurs.

Nine out of ten executives are psychologically unprepared to cope with the aftermath of a merger.

A QUIZ TO PROTECT YOURSELF

How do you use this information to help yourself in a merger? Study this quiz. Use the answers to protect yourself against weakness in a future merger.

(1) Did the new owner buy your company for management talent, including yours?

(2) Are you the key executive in a profit center of vital interest to the new management?

(3) Are you flexible enough to: (a) report to a new group of executives; (b) function in a new organization setup; (c) do things "their" way?

(4) Are your executive skills transferable within the new structure?

(5) Was your company acquired for non-management reasons, special financial advantages, manufacturing facilities, distribution structure—of which you are a part?

(6) Is your salary high in relation to the compensation scale of the purchasing company?

(7) Is your salary high relative to the market place for your job outside the company?

(8) Is your function duplicated in the parent company?

(9) Were you publicly against the merger?

(10) Are you in a staff position?

(11) Are you a "self-made" man with long tenure?

If you answer "yes" to the first five questions and "no" to the remaining six, you are in a strong position in a corporate merger. If your answers are off—on even three or four points—*look out!*

GUIDE FOR EXECUTIVE JOB HUNTERS

What's the difference between an "executive search firm," an "executive job counselor," and an employment agency? Who pays for each type of service—you, the executive seeking a new job, or your new employer?

These are vitally important questions to which you must have the correct answers if you are to avoid some perilous traps in the labor market today. To name just one: the unscrupulous "career counselor" who promises a high-paying job which he cannot deliver, but for which he still charges a fee amounting to thousands of dollars.

Therefore, following is your guide to . . .

WHO DOES WHAT IN EXECUTIVE SEARCH

Management consultants: In some cases, find new executives for client companies. The employer always pays for this service, and the fee is often based on the time needed to conduct the search. You, the job seeker, never pay.

Note to executives: Thus, if you are looking for a new or better job, and if you know of a consulting firm which recruits executives, let this firm know that you are available.

Executive search firms: Also are always paid by the companies for which they find new talent. These firms, known too as executive recruiters, search out, screen, and assess the talents of prospective executive employees and charge fees amounting to one fourth or more of the new executive's first year's pay. (Some charge a flat fee.) Although, normally, executive search firms are interested in knowing about qualified executives looking for jobs, they do *not* normally assist in the job hunt.

Executive career counselors: Work for the *executive,* who pays for services ranging from appraisal interviewing to aptitude and pyschological tests. (In some cases, an employer wanting to assist a laid-off executive may pick up the tab.) However, job counseling firms are *not* employment agencies and are not in any position to guarantee you employment.

The fee you pay an executive counselor can range all the way from $50 for a couple of hours of consultation to $1,000 or more. Get this fee spelled out in detail *before* you sign any contract and check all details in advance with your lawyer. Also check carefully the reputation of any job counselor you are considering with your local Better Business Bureau—as a protection against worthless tests, empty mailings to would-be employers, other traps. The "psychological appraisals," for example, may simply be designed to flatter you into buying more services than you want or need.

Employment agencies: Normally are state-licensed, the job placement fees also regulated by the state. The maximum fee for executives may be up to 20 to 30 per cent of your first year's salary, usually payable *after* you get a job. The employer seeking you will often pay the fee, but if he does not you, the executive, must. So get this point clear before you accept a new position.

WHO PAYS—AND HOW MUCH

Here is a summary of who pays—and how much—for key types of executive career and job counseling, prepared by a large New York international management consulting firm:

TYPE OF SERVICE	WHO PAYS?	HOW MUCH
Management consultants	Corporation	Per hour or per diem
Executive search firms	Corporation	25% and up of first year's salary
Executive career counselors	Executive	Per hour, per diem, % or flat fee

Type of Service	Who Pays?	How Much
Manufacturers' representatives search services	Corporation	Per hour, per diem, flat fee
Personnel psychological testing services	Corporation	Per hour, per diem, flat fee
Do-it-yourself career counselors	Executive	Usually flat amount
Employment agencies	Either may pay if job is accepted; if corporation does not pay, executive does	A % of base salary depending on state law

BEWARE: JOB-FINDING TRAPS

You, the job-hunting executive, answer a "career counselor's" newspaper ad which claims there will be no "initial charge." After a brief interview at the firm's office, in which a smooth salesman name-drops you into confiding in him, the salesman says, "Why don't you go home and bring your wife back for the next interview? After all, this is a family affair."

Your wife accompanies you on the next visit and the salesman now aims a special pitch appealing to her desire (blatant or buried) for her husband to earn more money.

"Mr. A., like your husband," the spiel goes, "was fired just a few weeks ago from a $25,000 job. But we managed to find him a $50,000 job in no time."

You, who have just lost your job, now lose your resistance. You're like the victim of an unscrupulous fast-talking funeral director just after a member of the family has died. You sign a lengthy contract. Job interviews are set up—although there is no realistic chance of employment. Expensive résumés are prepared and mailed out indiscriminately to dozens of companies.

The résumés and interviews may—or may not—result in a job or better salary. The "counseling" may be next to useless. In the words of one victim, "The psychological evaluation was a farce. The counseling amounted to bull sessions."

If you do get a job, you'll probably have to get it on your own and it won't be at anything like the salary level you have been led to believe you'll achieve.

But you are presented with a bill for $2,000 or more—far above the typical $500 to $1,000 which most reputable firms charge for job counseling, testing, and referral services.

To avoid such a trap:

Steer clear of any job counseling firm which leads you to believe it is also an employment agency or makes extravagant claims or promises. Use your cold judgment.

Check out the reputations of any firms with which you are considering a relationship and ask for, then follow through on references from former clients similar to yourself.

Do not sign a contract before you have asked a lawyer to read it and before you are satisfied that the firm is reputable and will actually provide you with services you need at a fair price.

Get those definitions and the facts straight on this whole befuddling subject of job assistance so you know where you're going and what to expect.

Shop with care for job advice. Consult friends or others who have dealt with the agency or firm whose advice you would like to buy. Also ask officers of your former employer for guidance.

Write to The Association of Executive Recruiting Consultants, 30 Rockefeller Plaza, New York, N.Y. 10020, for its membership list and/or send $2.00 to the American Management Association, 135 West Fiftieth Street, New York, N.Y. 10020, for its Executive Employment Guide.

TEN QUESTIONS TO ASK

You will protect yourself if you get satisfactory answers to these ten key questions about any career counseling firm with which you are considering doing business:

(1) Just what obligation are you incurring?

(2) How long has the firm been in business?

(3) How competent is its staff in executive guidance—and what are the qualifications?

(4) What is the firm's record of success or placements and what are the names of satisfied client-executives? Can you check them yourself?

(5) What are the names of satisfied employers with whom it has placed personnel? Can you verify this?

(6) Has the firm's advertising been proper and accurate as to the services offered?

(7) Does the contract cover *all* aspects of the agreement?

(8) Are additional promises in writing and signed by an officer of the firm?

(9) What service period is covered by contract?

(10) What provisions are there, if any, for a refund?

JOB-HUNTING TIPS FOR THE OVER-FORTY-FIVE

You're out of a job. You are in your late forties or older. You are being turned down by employer after employer as "overqualified" or "inexperienced" in whatever the specialty is. You're told over and over again that you "shouldn't have any trouble finding a job," as you're ushered out the door of your interviewer. But in your heart you know the towering obstacle is your age alone.

For your rights if you are hit by job discrimination because of your age, see Part IV, "Your Rights and How to Get Them." But always, no matter what, remember these do's and don'ts for improving your job-getting chances.

Don't apologize for your age or for minor disabilities or insignificant physical limitations.

Don't dwell on your need for a job.

Don't underrate yourself in your résumé or interview. Shoot as high as you think reasonable in your pay and status.

Don't hesitate to remind a prospective employer who may throw the old myths at you—for instance, older workers are slower workers, less flexible, weaker, more prone to absence and illness—that numerous objective studies prove precisely the opposite. Older workers' attendance and motivation records are likely to be better than those of younger workers; older workers are less likely to job-hop; the productivity of older workers compares favorably with that of younger workers; the learning ability of an individual in his or her fifties is approximately the same as that of a sixteen-year-old. Do the reminding in terms of your own work history.

Don't fail to register with your state employment office. Many of these offices have specially trained counselors to help those in your position. And even if your local office does not offer such services, it is still required to give you an equal crack at any job opening listed.

Do check the nearest federal Job Information Center (these centers are located in dozens of U.S. cities) for advice and information on federal job opportunities. Another good public source of help: your state Agency on Aging.

Do inquire about any federal government programs through which you might find appropriate training, leading to a good-paying job.

Do check whether there is any private employment agency in your area specializing in helping middle-aged and older workers find jobs. One such agency, Mature Temps, Inc., is backed by the non-profit American Association of Retired Persons, based in Washington with offices in several other major cities. Check into whether there is a "Forty-Plus Club" in your area and whether it has anything to offer you. Also touch base with such organizations as the Chamber of Commerce, YWCA, and private temporary employment agencies.

Do ask your trade association or professional association for job advice, and look into professional journals in your field for job leads. Ask your former business colleagues for guidance.

Do approach *all* employers who you think might have use for your services and go straight to the top people in these companies or agencies or organizations to present your qualifications.

It's easier said, I know. It's even somewhat unrealistic, I admit. But *do*, above all, keep your confidence!

SHOULD YOU GO INTO BUSINESS FOR YOURSELF?

WHY BUSINESSES FAIL

If you go into business for yourself, even when the United States is in a period of major prosperity, the odds that you'll survive for even two years are only fifty-fifty.

Although there were 8.8 million small businesses in the United States in the middle of this decade—the vast majority of them in the black—each year hundreds of thousands of them closed their doors.

Why?

The answer underlying the failure in an overwhelming nine cases out of ten is: the manager's incompetence, inexperience, ineptitude.

The apparent causes may appear entirely different: a slump in sales because of economic recession, heavy operating expenses, a poor location, a rise in competition, excessive fixed assets, etc. But why did sales slump or why were operating expenses so out of balance or why was the firm in a poor location? Because of the boss's incompetence or inexperience. All the other explanations for business failures can be bunched into that minor 10 per cent —including neglect, fraud, disaster.

Should this discourage you from realizing the American dream of going into business for yourself, of being your own boss? *No!* But surely it shouts a warning to you to take all the proper steps in advance to avoid the obvious pitfalls, to make sure that you have prepared yourself to win. That's merely elementary common sense.

A QUIZ TO SUCCESS

As a guide to success, ask yourself and honestly answer these questions:

Have you worked before in a business like the one you want to start and do you want this venture badly enough to keep working long hours without knowing how much money you'll end up with?

Do you know how much money you will need to get your business started and have you a precise idea of how much money of your own you can put into the business?

Do you know how much credit you can get initially from your suppliers, the people you will buy from—and where you can borrow the rest you need to start?

Have you made an educated estimate of the net yearly income you can expect to get from this enterprise (count your salary and your profit on the money you put into the business) and can you live on less than this amount so you can use some of it to help your business grow?

Do you know the good and bad points about going it alone, having a partner, or incorporating your business?

Have you talked to both a lawyer and a banker about legal and financial aspects of your plans?

Have you tried to find out whether businesses like the one you want to open are doing well in your area and elsewhere?

Do you know what kind of people will want to buy what you plan to sell? Do people like that live in your neighborhood and do they need an outlet like yours?

If you're planning to buy a business someone else has started, are you sure you know the real reason why the owner wants to sell?

Have you talked with other businessmen in the area to see what they think of the type of business you want to start?

Are you timing your move right, thus giving yourself every chance to succeed financially—in terms of demand for the goods and services you want to sell, availability and cost of credit, quantity and quality of competition already lined up against you?

Do you have a real interest in people—both the prospective employees who will be working for and with you and the customers who will buy from you?

Are you a good, sensible planner—financially and otherwise—since your profits will depend largely on your capacity for advance planning, timing the introduction of new products, etc.?

Are you capable of delegating authority and responsibility to those capable of handling it?

Do you know the local zoning and licensing rules covering the type and size of business you want to launch?

Have you answered "yes" to every question? If so, okay, you seem a good risk.

If you have answered even one "no," back up and think again. For this suggests you have a lot more preparing to do.

Whatever your answers to this sampling, write for the Small Business Administration's pamphlet, "Checklist for Going into Business." Available from the Superintendent of Documents, Washington, D.C. 20402, or the SBA, 1030 15th Street N.W., Washington, D.C. 20417. (Free.)

Study the pamphlet with great care.

FUNDAMENTAL RULES

Now, ask your friends and objective observers—a lawyer, banker, casual acquaintance at your office—to judge you too, against the following fundamental rules for success in launching any new business:

Know thoroughly the line you're going into and don't kid yourself about your own know-how.

Be sure you have well-rounded experience—in selling, purchasing, producing, whatever—or that you can get others to fill in your gaps.

Provide yourself with ample cash and access to credit to carry your business through the first, most vulnerable years. Be sure to budget ample sums for start-up advertising and promotion costs, for buying stocks, for extending credit to your customers.

If you are buying an existing business, study the "Business Opportunities" section of your local newspaper. See if alternate possibilities to the plan you already have in mind seem worth checking through. Also, compare the prices asked for businesses in the field which interests you with the price being asked for the business you think you want to purchase.

Ask the appropriate trade association in the field in which you want to work for ideas and leads on companies which may be for sale. One catalogue of these associations, which you may be able to find in your library, is the *Directory of National Trade Associations*.

Go to the nearest branch of the Small Business Administration for further guidance on buying a business. The SBA publishes several vitally important booklets, available free or for little cost.

Do not even attempt to buy *or* launch a business without the help of a competent lawyer, a competent accountant—and the appropriate officer at the bank with which you do business.

IS FRANCHISING FOR YOU?

ANOTHER WAY TO GO INTO BUSINESS

By the mid-1970s, the total of franchises in the United States had soared to between 400,000 and 700,000. In 1974 alone, Americans bought local franchises which sold an enormous $140 to $150 billion of goods and services—more than 10 per cent of our country's total yearly output.

Among the hundreds of different areas in which franchises were available in the mid-seventies:

anti-smoking clinics	beauty salons
art galleries	bridal salons
auto transmission and brake repairs	burglar and fire alarms
	campgrounds

computer dating schemes	mobile classrooms
computer programming schools	nursing homes
laundromats	pet grooming establishments
miniature golf courses	portable toilets
	roadside ice cream stands

Among the most rapidly-growing areas of franchising in this decade have been:

automotive products and services	educational products and services
business aids and services	fast food establishments
construction and remodeling businesses	recreational, travel, and entertainment
convenience grocery stores	rental and leasing services
	tax preparation services

Among the most eager and most vulnerable investors in franchises are: financially strapped family breadwinners needing to supplement their regular income; unemployed men in their forties and fifties who are suffering from job discrimination; elderly individuals and couples seeking to boost their meager retirement incomes; college students needing a means to help pay today's high college costs.

Is franchising a business for *you*—the man or woman whose experience has been limited until now to working for others?

The answer is a resounding *"No!"*

unless you realize it's easier to lose money than to make it in a franchise operation;

unless you choose a reputable, solid operation;

unless you have enough capital to cover your initial investment and carry you through at least the first six months;

unless you first do a lot of "homework" about yourself as well as the business;

and *unless* you are on the alert for the fraudulent operators who have in the past infested franchising.

QUESTION AND ANSWER GUIDE FOR POTENTIAL INVESTORS

Q. *Exactly what is a franchise?*

A. A franchise is a contractual right and a license to sell a product or service produced by a parent (usually national) company, and advertised and promoted by that company. For this right you usually pay a fee.

Q. *What type of operation should an amateur choose?*

A. Only one in which you have some experience. If you are a bookkeeper, for instance, don't go into an auto transmission overhaul operation which demands a mechanical skill you probably don't possess. Instead, choose a direct mail business or a personnel service. Also, as an unsophisticated franchisee, choose an area with a proven record of success and avoid areas which play on fads. As one illustration: several years ago, trampoline franchises were hot businesses. But the fad died quickly and most of the franchises flopped.

A key point never to forget: a franchise will *not* magically endow you with abilities you do not already have or are not willing to learn. There's just no way for a retired letter carrier to become an entrepreneur in two weeks. And a degree in physics is *not* necessarily a passport to a successful art gallery or nursing home.

Q. *How failure-prone are franchises—as compared to your own small business?*

A. Statistically speaking, franchising is a lot safer than starting your own independent business—on average, many times safer, in fact, according to the U. S. Department of Commerce.

Q. *What sort of investigation should you make?*

A. As thorough as you can. Check basic sources of information on available franchises—e.g., the *Wall Street Journal* and New York *Times*, journals in your field of interest (you will find the names listed in a directory available in most libraries, entitled Standard Rate and Data).

Get the 1974 *Directory of Franchising Opportunities* (Pilot Books, 347 Fifth Avenue, New York, N.Y. 10016, $2.50).

Collect advice on both the parent company and the type of business from friends, bankers, brokers, trade associations, the Small Business Administration, lawyers, accountants, the local Better Business Bureau.

Get a detailed, certified profit and loss statement from the franchiser on one or more existing firms—and check the figures yourself with the owners of those firms.

Have your bank check the franchiser's bank and its Dun & Bradstreet rating.

Dig out—from other franchisees—full details on weekly sales, selling costs, rent and utility bills, advertising and promotion costs, labor and tax bills, insurance, as well as profits.

Ask each about traffic, hours, seasonal business, personal involvement, and also about one experience each has had in dealing with the franchiser.

Beware of any franchise firm that is unwilling to supply you with the names and addresses of other franchisees.

Take a month to make your decision, and under *no* circumstances sign up under pressure from a franchise salesman.

Have your lawyer go over details of the franchise agreement before you sign anything.

If you decide to engage (and pay for) the services of a franchise consultant, check thoroughly into his or her reputation and make *sure* the consultant is not working with the enfranchiser to whom he may refer you.

Q. *What about the franchise fee?*

A. Virtually all franchising operations require an initial fee, or "front money." The average requirement in the mid-seventies was between $500 and $25,000 (although some ran up into six- or even seven-figure levels).

You *must* have a sufficient pool of liquid capital not only to buy the franchise but also to keep you going for several months. Don't expect to be in the black from the beginning. No new business, franchise or non-franchise, ever is.

Q. *What about the profit potentials?*

A. A franchise operation should eventually give you a net profit of at least $15,000 a year—just to make the investment worth while. But don't expect a big annual income from a small franchise investment. The franchisers have a good idea of what their kind of operation will gross and net and they scale their franchise fee accordingly.

Q. *What will a legitimate franchiser do for you that you couldn't do for yourself?*

A. Give you a name built up by national advertising; proven selling, advertising, and public relations techniques; experts who will help you get started; a line of credit which you may tap or advice on how to establish your own credit; trouble shooters through the year to help you too; guidance on where you should (and should not) locate; equipment at a fair price because the franchiser bought the equipment in volume at discount prices; training you might need to make a success from your franchise; an employee training program.

If a franchiser you're considering doesn't offer you most of these fundamentals in return for the fee, *beware!*

FRANCHISING CHECK LISTS

Here are check lists, developed by the Council of Better Business Bureaus, designed to lead, you, the prudent investor, into collecting sufficient background information on which to base an informed decision and commitment.

The Company

1. How long has the firm been in business?
2. Does it have a past record of accomplishment?
3. Are its principals well regarded? Experienced?
4. What is its financial strength?
5. What are its plans for future development?
6. How does it stand with your Better Business Bureau or Chamber of Commerce?
7. How selective is it in choosing franchisees?

The Product or Source

8. What is the product's quality?
9. Is it a staple, a fad, a luxury item?
10. Is it seasonal?
11. How well is it selling now, and has it sold in the past?
12. Would the franchisee buy it on its merits?
13. Is it priced competitively?
14. Is it packaged attractively?
15. How long has it been on the market?
16. Where is it sold?

The Sales Area

17. Is the territory well defined?
18. Is it exclusive?
19. Is it large enough to offer good sales potential?
20. What are its growth possibilities?
21. What is its income level?
22. Are there fluctuations in income?
23. What is the competition in this area?
24. How are nearby franchisees doing?

The Contract

25. Does the contract cover all aspects of the agreement?
26. Does it benefit both parties?
27. Can it be renewed, terminated, transferred?
28. What are the conditions for obtaining a franchise?
29. Under what conditions can the franchise be lost?
30. Is a certain size and type of operation specified?
31. Is there an additional fixed payment each year?
32. Is there a per cent of gross sales payment?
33. Must a certain amount of merchandise be purchased? From whom?
34. Is there an annual sales quota?
35. Can the franchisee return merchandise for credit?
36. Can the franchisee engage in other business activities?
37. Is there a franchise fee? Is it equitable?
38. Has your lawyer examined it?

Continuing Assistance

39. Does the franchiser provide continuing assistance?
40. Is there training for franchisees and key employees?
41. Are manuals, sales kits, accounting system supplied?
42. Does the franchiser select store locations? Is there a fee?

43. Does he handle lease arrangements?
44. Does he design store layout and displays?
45. Does he select opening inventory?
46. Does he provide inventory control methods?
47. Does he provide market surveys?
48. Does he help analyze financial statements?
49. Does he provide purchasing guides?

SOURCES FOR ADVICE ON JUDGING A FRANCHISE

Here are the names and addresses of the organizations most likely to be able to give you practical advice or assistance in judging a franchise today:

> International Franchise Association
> 7315 Wisconsin Avenue
> Bethesda, Md. 20014

> Council of Better Business Bureaus, Inc.
> 1150 17th Street, N.W.
> Washington, D.C. 20036

> Small Business Administration
> 1030 15th Street, N.W.
> Washington, D.C. 20417—or any of the SBA's field offices

> Small Business Guidance and Development Center
> Howard University
> 1420 N Street, N.W., Suite 5A
> Washington, D.C. 20005

> Office of Minority Business Enterprise
> U. S. Department of Commerce
> Washington, D.C. 20230—or any of the Commerce
> Department's field offices

CRIME INSURANCE FOR SMALL BUSINESSMEN

A PROGRAM TO INVESTIGATE

If you are a small businessman in a high-crime-risk area in city or suburb, you are probably eager for crime insurance at "affordable rates."

But you may not even be aware that low-cost federal crime insurance up to a stated maximum exists. The insurance came into being in mid-1971 under a program of the Department of Housing and Urban Development. The objective of the program is to make crime insurance available at tolerable rates in states where it has been especially hard to come by. Since 1971 the law has been liberalized twice to make it much easier and also cheaper for you to obtain the federal crime insurance coverage. This is a program which you should investigate at once.

To give you key details:

• If you are the owner of a small business (liquor store, jewelry store, grocery store, restaurant, clothing store, beauty shop, etc.) you can buy either burglary coverage or robbery coverage. Burglary coverage pays off on visible signs of entry, while robbery insurance pays for holdups or observed theft.

• There are specific provisions requiring you to use protective devices—ranging from window grates to central and local alarm systems.

• There are favorable provisions on deductibles. The deductible depends on your annual gross receipts.

• If you are interested and eligible, go to any licensed insurance agent or broker, ask for an application, and complete it. Your application will then be forwarded to an insurance company acting under contract with the Federal Insurance Administration. The policies are not available directly from any federal agency but are sold through licensed agents and brokers and through a servicing company designated by the FIA for each participating state. Your policy will go into effect after the servicing company has inspected your premises and approved the protective devices.

Rates vary depending on your geographic location, crime statistics compiled by the FBI, and the amount of your gross receipts.

Beware: "Business Opportunities" Swindles

RACK ROUTES

"PART-TIME/FULL-TIME . . . P/T 5–6 hours weekly nets to $700 monthly . . . F/T 50 hours weekly nets to $7,000 monthly. . . .

"$2,800 part-time investment secured by inventory fully refundable has unlimited growth opportunity with potential earnings to $100,000 per year. This national public company has outstanding success record since 1954 and is seeking reliable individuals to service company secured routes. An opportunity to own your own business and become part of a multi-million dollar market. This is no get rich quick scheme or a pyramid but a solid year-round business. . . .

"NO SELLING, NO OVERHEAD, IMMEDIATE INCOME . . . No experience necessary; we train . . . Simply check stores weekly and restock what has been sold . . . LIMITED OPENINGS AVAILABLE. MAKE THE AMERICAN DREAM A REALITY. OWN YOUR OWN BUSINESS TODAY . . . Write or call. . . ."

An ad of this sort—the above is a composite for a "rack route"—shouts "Fraud!" It has, though, deep appeal to men and women searching for ways to solve their income problems by going into business for themselves. Business opportunities rackets are, in fact, heading into the top ranks of all lists of swindles in the latter half of this decade.

Thus, beware these earmarks of a "rack route" gyp:

• Inconsistencies. The ad says that one can realize an immediate income and advertises that, while no experience is required, earnings can go up to $100,000. How can this be if "no selling is required" and the investor isn't paid a wage or a salary?

A "business" is a going concern, an active enterprise, but what's really involved in this case is a static inventory of goods for resale—and you're the only one to do the selling.

• Appeal to flattery. This usually comes in the initial letter you get from the company in which there are flattering references to "your talent and your experience in your job" plus your capacity to "bring profit to your company way above your own present pay." Few people who have just lost their jobs will stop to consider how presumptuous are these statements by an unknown correspondent who doesn't know them personally.

• Pressure to act quickly. This is evident in the phrases "limited openings available" and "own your own business today."

• Claims of ease of operation of business. All you need do is "check stores weekly and restock." That's ridiculous.

• Exaggeration. The ad is saturated with impressions of instant wealth, and the promotional literature when it arrives also suggests almost automatic acquisition of this wealth. "A few hours each week and you are on your way to a whole chain. . . ."

What's wrong with this operation?

The earnings are simply not there—and it's not because you're not working hard enough. They're just not there.

The product is frequently inferior. For instance, if you're selling cosmetics, you may have been stuck with last year's colors or antiquated packages. While the claim is that no selling is involved, the product doesn't sell itself and your income is dependent on the sale of the product.

The service you get from the promoting company is inferior: late delivery or no delivery, no maintenance when you need it.

The misrepresentations begin to manifest themselves. The implication that the promoter is connected with, or endorsed by, a nationally known company just isn't true.

To avoid being taken in by this racket:

• Ignore the flattery. Be honest about your own qualifications. Do you really know anything about merchandising? Are you really a good enough salesman to develop and maintain successful relationships with twenty or more retail merchants in widely separated, distinct businesses?

• Verify the claims made to you with at least two independent sources.

Call the local Better Business Bureau. Frequently the BBB will have a report on the company.

• Talk to the man behind the operation, not the front man or a salesman. There are hundreds of salesmen for these schemes and they move from one scheme to the next, not caring what they sell or what they say. Give the BBB not only the company's name but the promoter's name. Promotions come and go but the promoters remain the same.

TRAVEL

"Do you want to get into travel? Make money? You can. Right now! . . . No experience necessary. Immediate sales force.

"We are offering an exclusive area and some incomparable advantages including a marketing force of at least 25 travel ambassadors, professionally trained to sell big ticket travel programs in their neighborhoods and bring business to you!

"Our company is organized and operated by experts in every phase of the travel business. We assist you in the operation of your business. In addition you get a bonus—a going advertising and promotional campaign!

"PLUS! Since you must enjoy travel to be in this business, as a franchise owner with us you see the world—premiere classe! . . . If you are interested in PROFITS AND FUN, call . . ."

This too is a composite ad which illustrates a "business opportunities" fraud in the giant travel field.

Here are the earmarks of fraud in this ad:

• Lack of clarity. An "exclusive" area is promised, but how an area could be protected from other travel agencies is not explained. The American Society of Travel Agents, in warning against phony travel agencies that offer "round trips to nowhere," has condemned this very feature as reprehensible.

• Exaggeration. You get a bonus—"a going advertising and promotional campaign." If there really is such a campaign, it's designed to lure new suckers like you, not customers for you. "Operated by experts." Anybody can call himself an expert. "See the world premiere classe." Hardly. "Travel benefits do not flow automatically to travel agents," warns ASTA. As for those twenty-five professionals hunting out prospects for you alone, the promise strains all credulity.

• Inconsistency. The travel business is a highly complex business, as any thoughtful person must realize. It requires years of experience for success. That "no experience is necessary" simply cannot be reconciled with realities in this area.

The pitch is all too simple. You pay the promoters from a few hundred dollars to $20,000 and they'll put you in the travel business. But no matter what you're led to believe, you cannot become a successful travel agent overnight—and this highly competitive business arena is no place for the rank amateur.

As for the training programs, they are often no more than short lectures —as valuable in real life as those "exclusive" territories which may be described but not delivered.

How do you avoid being lured into this racket?

• Before responding to an ad such as this, learn something on your own about the travel business. There are plenty of courses available to you. Also talk to travel agents running their own agencies or employed by airlines and steamship companies to get the facts and a believable appraisal of opportunities.

• Ask the American Society of Travel Agents (360 Lexington Avenue, New York, N.Y. 10017) for literature describing the nature of the industry and for any other literature it says would be of help to you.

• Call the local Better Business Bureau for a report on the company behind this promotion. Give the name of the promoters, too.

• Ask the company itself for substantiation of its claims. For instance, will it show you the advertising campaign that is supposed to be available to you? Say that you want to study it before making a decision. Surely, if the program is so successful, the ads must have appeared in print or been seen on TV or heard on the radio by the time you show up.

• Be honest with yourself in evaluating your own qualifications. If in fact the full "25 travel ambassadors" would become available to you as your sales force, would you have the expert knowledge to use them properly and keep them busy? Have you the qualities essential to run a business of your own?

• Do not underestimate the part that any current unfortunate circumstances—loss of a job, difficulty in getting employment at a level you want, sinking profits in your present business—may be playing in your eagerness to become a "franchise owner" in this glamorous "see the world" industry. Be extra conservative.

PYRAMID SELLING

"Help Wanted Male/Female . . . College Graduate 15 M to 25 M Caliber . . . Executives/Managers On the Way Up . . .

"Our company has openings in mgt. positions recently created through our northeast expansion. Must be self-starter and have leadership capabilities. No exp. necessary. We will train . . .

"For interview, call . . ."

This apparent route to a successful venture of your own sounds so attractive, seems a way to avoid ever again being dependent on someone else's fortunes for a pay check.

But don't fall for it! It's a composite ad that highlights still another "business opportunities" fraud. Here are the major earmarks of this one:

• Inconsistencies. What "college graduate" with "no experience" will be handed a $20,000 pay check? What "management position" requires "no experience"? Any man or woman intelligent enough to have completed college will be unable to reconcile the claims. And any thoughtful person will wonder why any successful company has to advertise this way for executives and managers.

• Incongruities. Legitimate $20,000 management positions usually aren't advertised in the general help-wanted male/female columns but in the business sections of newspapers and specialized business publications.

• Appeal to flattery and to status. That's implicit in the "college graduate" lure and in the "must be self-starter and have leadership capabilities" requirements. Don't we all think we are self-starters and potential leaders?

What are the pitfalls?

The ad is simply bait for a pyramid scheme, among the most vicious and pervasive of all "business opportunities" swindles flourishing in the United States today.

The prospective investor is pressured to invest on the spot. The "opportunity" meeting the investor attends is so emotionally charged that if he hasn't left his checkbook at home he may sign away his savings right there.

The investor can never make the money predicted by the advertiser, because in fact there are never enough people in a community to sustain the pyramid, or the chain-selling method, indefinitely. One would-be investor characterized this ad as "an invitation to cheat my friends" (see Chapter 13, "A Roof Over Your Head," for mathematical proof of the giant pitfall of this scheme—which is the required number of "qualified" prospects).

Millions of dollars have been lost on these pyramid or chain schemes in this decade, and government regulations against certain pyramid operators have been tightened. But the pyramid selling racket continues to flourish and the promoters continue to lure victims through ads that slip into every medium. So, to protect yourself:

• Get the details on this type of ad over the phone, and if the details are sketchy, just forget it. If this were a valid help wanted offer, the person answering the phone would want to discourage unqualified applicants, not intrigue you. Don't even bother going to the personal "interview."

• If you do go to a personal interview, leave your checkbook—and your enthusiasm—at home. Don't sign anything, no matter how pressured you are.

• Be suspicious at once of any help-wanted ad which does not pay a wage or salary, which does not disclose selling is involved, and which does require an investment. This is all wrong! The advertiser is deceiving the medium as well as you.

VENDING MACHINES

"$500 PART-TIME $5,000 FULL-TIME per month . . . Fast growing international company. No selling. Huge profits . . .

"Opportunity for persons looking for good income in field of coin-operated vending machines. Secured investment of $3,000 required. We secure locations.

"Financing available to those who qualify. Call . . ."

Beware! The telltale signs that this is a racket are in the ad:

• Lack of clarity. Again, is this $500 to $5,000 a month a wage, salary, profits, what? Where is that money to come from? The company calls itself "international." What does international mean? In the case of one company, it became international because one investor sent his machine to Madrid.

• Flattery, hint of exclusivity. "Financing available to those who qualify," says the ad. How many, if any, are actually rejected when they apply?

• Inconsistency. The mutually exclusive "no selling required" and "huge profits."

• Exaggeration. The ad mentions a "secured investment." What's the security in an inventory of broken vending machines?

The earmarks of this fraud also show up during the interview—which actually is the focal point of the deception.

• Verbal promises that don't appear in the contract. For instance, the salesman promises help with establishing routes for the vending machines. He also may promise that the company will buy back the machines if the investor changes his or her mind or that the territory is exclusive. None of these conditions and promises appears in the contract, however. Here's the way a complainant described her meeting with a salesman:

"Even before I mailed the card back authorizing a visit from a salesman, one called . . . He did not seem pleased when I told him that my husband and father would be present; he wanted to know if I had authority to close the deal. He arrived an hour early. . . . He evaded our questions, I had to ask some questions two or three times. My husband asked to see the machines in operation at some locations but he wouldn't give specific addresses. When we told him we wanted to check out his company with the Better Business Bureau he became very quiet and nervously put his papers together."

The major pitfalls in this operation are:

The machines are of such poor quality they frequently break down as soon as they are put into use. One disenchanted investor wrote: "I bought two machines at $550 each. They were supposed to vend a toy and play a tune at the same time. I had mechanical problems every other day—the toy would not come out and the music kept on playing. In six months I had to move my machines around to six different locations. I've had virtually no return."

The quality of goods to be dispensed is often very poor. Unknown or inferior brands have frequently been supplied by the promoter, sometimes at exorbitant prices.

You can't get the company to answer your service calls and no local servicing is available.

• To protect yourself, be alert to such claims in the sales pitch as "laboratory tested," "location tested," "non-competitive." What laboratory, what locations, what results? If you're told the machine is "patented," check that out. A patent number touted by one company in its literature turned out to be fictitious; the company supplied another which the Patent Office said had expired. There was nothing at all exclusive about the machine.

• If the company mentions a nationally known manufacturer in its sales pitch, check whether the manufacturer does in fact endorse the company. Probably not. Don't be impressed by such words in names of the companies as "U.S." or "International" or "American" or "Nationwide," "General," the like.

• Ignore the flattery.

• Talk to the people behind the operation.

DISTRIBUTORSHIPS

"Make big profits! Become an authorized distributor. Sell Special Formula gasoline additive—the hottest selling item in the automotive direct selling field. Manufacturer endorsed.

"Guaranteed free luxury motor car if appointed state franchise director . . . Free samples available. Send $10.35 . . .

"Good only for orders received in next 10 days. Bigger discounts if order rushed."

Then appears a table showing that your cost for six units is $24.50, on which you make a profit of $7.00. But if you buy three dozen units at a cost of $92.50, you make a profit of $90.

The telltale signs of fraud, as exemplified by this ad, are:

• "Creative" accounting. That table is very clever, for who's going to buy $24.50 of goods to make a $7.00 profit when he can make approximately 100 per cent if he goes up to $92.50?

• Exaggerations. A "free luxury motor car" if one sells enough cans of gasoline additive? Even a cockeyed optimist should have trouble believing that one. "Manufacturer endorsed"? Who? "The hottest selling item in the field of automotive direct selling"? Hardly. . . .

• Pressure. The implication is that you must act at once or you're barred. The offer will last for only ten days. The pressure is intensified in follow-up letters to the sucker.

• Duplicity. There are "free samples" offered to the skeptical—but the "free" samples cost $10.35.

• Ease of operation. This is not in the composite ad, but it is in the letter the potential investor receives, assuring him that "you don't have to be a salesman in order to rake in those profits. Those unique formulas, together with the endorsement from the luxury motor car, practically sell themselves."

How do you avoid being taken by this business opportunities swindle —as in the others preceding?

• Verify the claims for the product. Check out the endorsements from manufacturers referred to in the literature. Ask the company representative for the name of a person at the manufacturer's office to whom you can talk and with whom you can discuss your doubts. Do not permit yourself to be turned away.

• Ask the promoter for names and addresses of other distributors. Contact them to find out how much money they have made selling these products under current market conditions.

• Find out how many of these distributors have been in operation for more than a year. A year should be long enough to determine whether or not the business can be a success.

• Discuss the investment and operation of the business with your own family, your lawyer, your local banker.

• Never forget that a written guarantee is only as good as the company behind it. If the company offering "full refund" isn't in business, the offer is worthless.

From these five illustrations, you can carry away the guides to protect you from all other variations of business opportunities rackets.

What About Working at Home?

A POWERFUL TREND

Still another way to "be your own boss" is to work at home—even if you're working for some relatively distant employer. And there is now a powerful and grossly underestimated trend in this country toward doing just that.

You well may be among the millions who *could* do so if you really wanted to. The switch could be a real boon if, say, you are a young mother who can't leave the house but still have plenty of spare time; if you are a businessman who could easily switch your office to your home and who detests the daily commute to the big city; if you are a shut-in for any reason; if in your work you spend virtually the whole day on the telephone and could easily use the phone just as well at home as at the office.

Today, millions of Americans work at home, part or full time, and the list of jobs which you can perform without going to an office is lengthening daily. Some work from elaborate home offices, fitted with typewriters, electric calculators, dictating machines, filing cabinets, and other office equipment. Others manage to earn a living from a bedroom card table.

Of course, some people simply can't work at home. Your job, for instance, may involve the use of expensive specialized equipment available only in an office. You may need to confer frequently—and face to face—with others in your office. Or you might be subject to destructive distractions at home from children, social telephoning, visiting neighbors. Or you might not have the essential discipline to set up and stick to a productive work schedule. Or you may be unproductive without the stimulus of a busy office.

But for many of you the advantages far outweigh the disadvantages. Anybody who works at home can save substantial sums of money by not having to pay commuting costs, eat lunches out, keep up an office wardrobe, lose hours of work time battling traffic.

If you are a working mother, a job at home may save substantial sums on baby-sitting fees—which when combined with other typical expenses of working mothers often chew up 40¢ to 50¢ or more of your pay dollar. For pregnant women, there are obvious reasons for working at home.

A further advantage lies in the substantial income tax deductions that can be claimed for the bona fide costs associated with the portion of your house you use as an office, the cost of business equipment, business telephone calls, etc.

SAMPLING OF "AT HOME" CAREERS

Following are some of the jobs which are being performed, at least in part, at home. Study them carefully to see if this could spark a desired new trend in your own life.

In journalism-publishing: foreign language translation, proofreading, copy editing, technical writing, art work, copy writing—and, of course, the usual writing of books, magazine articles, feature stories.

In education: many assistant teaching jobs such as correcting test papers, tutoring in remedial reading and other key subjects, music and art instruction, child day care, vocational counseling, speech therapy.

In scientific and technical fields: inventing, engineering and scientific consulting, computer programing, a wide assortment of individual projects in chemistry, mathematics, and other disciplines, appliance repair.

In health and medicine: physical and occupational therapy, the practice of medicine, dentistry, psychiatry.

In radio and TV: disc jockeying, film editing, film making, script writing.

In advertising: Literally thousands of small ad agencies are operating out of private homes in this country today.

Also: architecture, art, law, insurance and real estate, interior decorating, investment management, sewing, cake baking, public relations, many kinds of research, accounting and drafting. And this is only a random selection. There are dozens of others.

If the idea of working at home appeals to you, analyze your interests and/or your present job. *You* can tell as well as anyone what the potentials are.

Before you decide to go ahead, check the local zoning rules and also any restrictions which may be included in your own deed (or rental lease) against at-home business operations. These limitations could be a temporary obstacle—but that's all they can be *if* "working at home" is what you really want.

BEWARE: "EARN MONEY AT HOME" SWINDLES!

But precisely because so huge a number of you secretly wish you could work at home, the crooks and gypsters can make fortunes exploiting your yearnings.

As an illustration, let's say you are a young mother who is staying at home to care for your infants. Let's say, too, that you're finding it increasingly tough to get by on your young husband's pay check, quarrels about money are starting to undermine your marriage, and thus you're desperately seeking ways to supplement your family's income.

You are now a perfect setup for the "work at home" swindlers.

Here is a sampling of the most common forms making the rounds— along with the catch in each case and rules for spotting outright gyps.

Scheme: Address postcards at home. Promoter furnishes everything. Earn $50 a week.

Catch: Promoter is selling "instructions"—not offering employment —despite the fact that he lures you through the help-wanted columns. If you're a "double victim," you'll pay for postcards as well as instructions. You make money only if the cards you send actually bring in orders. In a typical case, a home worker spent a total of $25 for instruction, 250 postcards, and for postage. Total revenue from two orders: $2.50. Loss: $22.50.

Scheme: Assemble at home anything from bow ties to garters, fish lures to artificial flowers. And reap enormous piecework profits.

Catch: Promoter offers no employment. Again, he's selling instructions and in all probability overpriced equipment and precut materials. He has no intention of buying the goods you make unless they're "up to standards" and, of course, they never are. Often, victims spend hundreds of dollars on heavy equipment at grossly inflated prices in the belief that the promoter will furnish enough work to cover the equipment costs. Such work never materializes and you're left with a heartache and a debt payable to a finance company.

Scheme: Clip newspapers at home. Earn $75 a week selling local press mentions to individuals and companies at $1.00 to $5.00 a piece.

Catch: "Instructions" cost up to $15 (often shoddy, badly mimeographed, unprofessional), and you must subscribe to the newspapers yourself. You also must find your own markets for your clips.

Scheme: Raise animals—bullfrogs, chinchillas, foxes, minks, muskrats, etc.—at home and sell them for fabulous profits. Typical ad says: "There is Big Money in raising bullfrogs. Start in your back yard. We furnish breeders and instructions and buy what you raise."

Catch: Breeders are excessively priced, potential profits are grossly exaggerated, and animals bought back must be "in a healthy and marketable condition." Of course, they never are so judged by a gypster, and frequently the fine print you never read stipulates the animals must be skinned and butchered before they will be bought.

Scheme: Test consumer products in your own home, in your spare time. We pay up to $10 for each opinion you give us on the products we send you.

Catch: To get on this gravy train, you must send in a $10 "registration fee." Legitimate market researchers do not operate in this manner and do not ask you for any "registration fees" in exchange for your supposedly unbiased opinion of their products or services. You're lucky if you get so much as a couple of dollars for whatever opinions you send in—much less a refund of your registration fee.

Scheme: Go into the mail order business at home. Earn huge sums by mailing out, for example, catalogues.

Catch: The cost of such a "distributorship": $10 a year. The point to remember about this gimmick is that any firm wishing to employ your services to help mail out catalogues will not charge you a fee for this privilege.

Scheme: Be a "Personal Shopper." Buy clothes and other products from a list of parent firms, then sell the products to consumers in your exclusive marketing area. Guaranteed: short-term financing, instructions on selling, collection of past due accounts, credit for unsold merchandise, *and* substantial earnings.

Catch: Earnings are *not* substantial. Help for the supplies is minimal. In many cases collection is not possible on delinquent accounts.

OBVIOUS EARMARKS OF A FRAUDULENT SCHEME

There are many, many more—all the frauds feeding on your need and on the fact that there are legitimate deals for making money at home.

Here are the most obvious earmarks of the fraudulent scheme:

• Ads slanted to imply the offer of home employment when in fact the advertiser is selling something, not hiring.

• A promise of huge profits or big part-time earnings.

• A profusion of vague "testimonials" to the deal.

• A requirement that you buy expensive instructions and equipment— even before the promoter gives you details of the deal.

KEY QUESTIONS ABOUT ADS

Here are the key questions to ask about any ad you see in your local newspaper or which comes to you through the mails regarding home work deals.

• Will you be paid by the firm and, if so, how much? If you will not be paid by the firm, where will the promised earnings come from?

• Are you expected to pay any significant sum to buy "instructions"— before you can get into business? (If so, consider this a warning signal to stay away from the deal.)

• Who will be your customers and who will be responsible for lining them up—the company or you?

• Is the product or service in which you are supposed to invest—either time or money or both—one for which you will manage to find a market close to your home?

• If commissions are promised as payments for your efforts, what assurance do you have that such commissions actually will be paid? A vague promise which comes through the mail from a company unknown to you is hardly adequate insurance.

• Is the company willing to give you names and phone numbers of other people who have invested in its instructions or products so that you can query them about their experience in the real market place? How much money did *these* people make on the deal? (Disregard any and all "testimonials" quoted in ads if you cannot check them out personally.)

Finally, and especially if "fantastic profits" for "easy work" are offered, in combination with a requirement that *you* invest substantial sums of money for instructions, materials etc., find out whether the firm is trying to buy your services, or—much more likely—sell you a bill of goods. Get in touch with your nearest Better Business Bureau, Federal Trade Commission office, or consumer protection agency. Do not take one further step toward the deal without informed assurance it is legitimate.

P.S. A good source of legitimate and often original ideas for working at home is the monthly "Home Office Report" published by Leon Henry, Jr. A full list of occupations covered by this publication is available free upon request. Address: 17 Scarsdale Farm Road, Scarsdale, N.Y. 10583.

NEEDED: VOLUNTEERS

THE GREAT NON-PAID PRODUCER

Across the land are close to 2 million of you who are working as American Red Cross trained volunteers in community activities—in the blood and youth programs, in safety, nursing, and health programs, in hospitals, clinics, disaster relief, in helping members of the armed forces and their families, and in raising funds to support all of these services.

On average, you are putting in 150 hours a year at your volunteer jobs. But that's just average: many of you are putting in 150 hours a month. Many of you certainly are contributing twice, three, four times 150 hours a year.

All of you give your time, training, devotion, and dedication for *zero* pay in dollars. All of you fall into one of the enormous categories of non-paid producers in the U.S. economy. On top of this, hundreds of thousands of you also contribute cash and property.

If you were paid merely $2.00 an hour, your contribution of only 150 hours a year would amount to an annual output well over $500 million, an impressive sum by any yardstick.

If you were paid what your skills—as a nurse, a first aid or swimming instructor, a teacher—could easily bring in the job market place, your contribution of only 150 hours a year would easily mount to $1 billion or more. And if there were a more accurate estimate of the number of hours you actually work, the total would go zooming again—would add billions of dollars to our annual output of goods and services, give a far more realistic picture of what is our true Gross National Product.

Of course the contribution of the volunteer goes far beyond this. There are now more than 43 million volunteers working for 22 national and local agencies in the U.S. Put a dollar total on that production, I defy you!

But because I have been so close to the Red Cross in past years I have had a unique chance to see how its volunteers work. And I haven't included in the volunteer total the millions who donate blood each year or the millions of students who participate in the Red Cross programs in schools.

The economic story of the volunteer in America never has been told— and perhaps it never can be. But just because we cannot put a precise dollar tag on the volunteer's contribution must not lead us into downgrading the magnificent size of that contribution.

WHERE THE VOLUNTEER JOBS ARE

"Long hours, hard work, low pay . . ."

"Dirt and rats, crowded rooms . . . headaches, frustration."

"$50 a month."

This was one of the come-ons blared across the nation a few years back to launch Volunteers in Service to America—VISTA, the "domestic Peace Corps." Tens of thousands responded from every age group, background, political stripe, and tax bracket—and tackled some of the hardest, dirtiest, most thankless jobs imaginable.

Most federal voluntary programs have since been merged into an agency called Action, including:

the Peace Corps, which puts volunteer nurses, mechanics, organic farmers, teachers, and many others to work in dozens of countries on every continent; VISTA; the Teacher Corps, part of the U. S. Office of Education —HEW; Foster Grandparents; and the Service Corps of Retired Executives (SCORE) who help small businesses.

And outside Action:

• Boy Scouts, Girl Scouts, Boys Clubs, Campfire Girls, 4-H Clubs, YMCA, YWCA, YMHA and YWHA groups, American Youth Hostels and many other organized youth groups have needed volunteers for years and still do.

• In schools and child care programs, thousands of volunteers of all ages are acting as teaching assistants, helping individual children in music and art programs, tutoring dropouts, taking youngsters on field and camping trips. In poverty areas, more thousands are serving and recruiting in a wide variety of programs, helping in Neighborhood Health Centers and drug addiction centers, working with alcoholics in rehabilitation programs.

• Church-related groups, such as American Friends Service Committee, co-ordinate thousands of volunteers to help other people.

• In Neighborhood Legal Centers across the land, young lawyers and law students are helping to provide free legal advice and services to the poor.

• In consumer agencies, "action lines," and similar organizations, thousands of young volunteers and semivolunteers are answering phones, handling consumer complaints, tracking down the sources of various problems.

• Also across the land, environment-minded citizens—young and old —are investigating complaints on forms of pollution, organizing "pollution tours" for local citizens to view the area's offenders, launching recycling programs, and in a heartening percentage of cases earning money in the recycling process.

• But nowhere can volunteers find a more fascinating array of jobs and responsibility than in hospitals, outpatient clinics, emergency rooms, drug addiction programs, physical therapy programs.

Blood bank aides are needed to call on patients who have received blood to ask them to sign forms for their friends or families to replace the blood they have used and to arrange donations. Translators are needed to interpret for non-English-speaking hospital or outpatient clinic patients. Maternity-room aides are needed to accompany maternity patients to labor and delivery rooms to give aid and comfort.

Other hospital volunteer areas range from assistants in children's wards to recreational therapy helpers. In city hospitals alone, it's estimated that 300,000 additional volunteers are needed right now. Gone forever are the days when volunteers worked only in the gift shop or hospital library. Desperately in demand are volunteers in just about every phase and at every level of health care.

Similarly, there is a relentless demand for volunteers to track down and look after the desperate needs of many elderly Americans: to see that these citizens are fed, make sure they're getting Social Security and welfare benefits to which they're entitled, to run errands, arrange to have plumbing problems solved, just to take them out for a Sunday drive.

As for the kids, here are just a couple of hints on the opportunities which have sprung up for helping youngsters:

In Philadelphia, HELP was launched by the young, for the young, to answer calls around the clock, deal with problems ranging from homelessness to drugs, pregnancy, and suicide.

In San Rafael, California, the YMCA launched a Dropout Prevention Program in which college students work with second- through fifth-graders who show early indications that they might later drop out of school.

Big Brothers of America matches fatherless young boys with male volunteers who stick with their charges (and their problems) year after year, on a one-to-one basis.

And of course, volunteers work in the offices of political candidates and elected officials such as state senators, congressmen, etc.—at many different types of jobs.

Yet broad as this sampling is, it still gives you only an idea of .the variety of volunteer jobs actually open to you today.

"MOST WANTED"

Professionals are among the "most wanted" of all volunteers—for obvious reasons of skills and scarcity.

Semiprofessionals, including just about anybody with specialized education or professional training, are in great demand to help the pros. There are simply not enough professionals to go around, and there won't be enough for years.

Retired citizens with special skills, talents, or training are finding jobs in the Action program, doing everything from helping to clean up city slums to teaching Alaskan Eskimo school children.

Shut-ins are being invited to volunteer for telephone and desk work at home.

The poor are being welcomed as a vital link with other poor.

Even twelve- to fifteen-year-olds are helping in preschool classes. As a former anti-poverty leader remarked: "We need millions of 'extra mothers,' because millions of children simply don't have them. The crying need still is for warm sensitive human beings with a willingness to spend time on another human being, with the diligence and perseverance not to wash their hands of a problem when things get tough and grimy."

HOW DO YOU VOLUNTEER?

Volunteer work no longer is strictly summer, strictly unpaid, or strictly private. Many volunteers just cannot afford to work without pay. Instead, they may be part-time, part-paid, part-reimbursed, part-government-financed.

In contrast to the old concept of "busy work" for volunteers, today you can count on assuming as much responsibility as you are capable of handling and of becoming involved in a broad range of demanding tasks.

Volunteer jobs in recent years have spread to all income, age, and ethnic brackets, and a volunteer job well may be a major assist to you when you apply for a full-time permanent job later.

(1) If you want to volunteer for any of the major federal volunteer programs, get in touch directly with the Washington headquarters of these programs. Or get in touch with the National Center for Voluntary Action, 1785 Massachusetts Avenue, Washington, D.C. 20036, which acts as a referral agency for local volunteer placement organizations.

(2) If you have had training in a field related to environmental protection and if you're interested in working on a volunteer program abroad, contact the Smithsonian-Peace Corps Environmental Program based in Washington (Office of Ecology, Smithsonian Institution, Washington, D.C. 20560). Some of the areas where volunteers were needed in the mid-seventies were fish biology, ornithology, entomology, zoology, marine biology, plant pathology, plant ecology. The program operates in 55 countries, with length of tours ranging from twenty-four to twenty-seven months. All volunteers are paid modest in-country living allowances plus a small stipend per month, held in the United States. Many of the jobs give volunteers an opportunity to carry out research that could be used to complete requirements for an advanced degree.

(3) If you are interested in working through a private charity, you will find that major private charities participating in anti-poverty and other programs have telephone listings in all sizable cities and towns. The Service Corps of Retired Executives, for example, has chapters in cities from coast to coast. To find the closest one to you, contact SCORE's national headquarters at 1030 15th Street N.W., Washington, D.C. 20417.

(4) If you are a student, check the National Student Volunteer Program, which oversees student volunteer efforts now under way at more than four out of five U.S. colleges and universities. Involved are hundreds of thousands of students, many in state-wide student volunteer programs. Simply inquire at nearby colleges for details.

(5) Investigate whether your community is among the cities and communities which have set up Voluntary Action Centers or Volunteers Bureaus

to ease the red tape and to guide volunteers in best applying their talents and individual circumstances to meet the most urgent demands.

(6) Also inquire about volunteer jobs and sources of actual jobs in *your* city at: City Hall; local youth organizations; the public school system headquarters; the welfare department; juvenile court.

(7) Look into a publication entitled *Invest Yourself*. This is a catalog of service opportunities in the United States and abroad compiled by the Commission on Voluntary Service and Action, a council of roughly 150 private organizations in the United States and Canada which sponsor and/or support voluntary service projects all over the world (no connection between this council and the federal Action agency). CVSA's address is 475 Riverside Drive, Room 830, New York, N.Y. 10027.

(8) Or simply pin down your own community's most urgent unmet needs and start up your own volunteer program to help fill these needs.

The central point is that *if* you want to volunteer and *if* you are willing to work you are wanted, you are needed. And your contribution to our economy will run into incalculable tens of billions of dollars a year—helping us as individuals, helping us as a nation.

12

HOW TO SAVE
ON VACATIONS

TIME YOUR VACATION OFF SEASON

If you take a trip to Rome during the Thanksgiving holidays, you well may save 20 per cent on a double room at one well-known luxury hotel as against the price you would pay during the packed, pushy, peak tourist summer days.

If you rent a car for an Irish holiday in October, you'll save even larger percentages as against the sum you would pay for the same car during the summer—and you'd enjoy additional savings on plane and boat fares, hotel rooms, meals, local transportation, entertainment.

If you take a three-week package tour of eight European countries starting in October, you well might pay $100 less than the same tour would cost you in June–August.

And if you are planning a week's skiing vacation this winter, you'll save 20 per cent or more on hotel accommodations just by waiting until late in the ski season, when the snow will be just as skiable, but the influx of skiers and après skiers will have slowed to a snowplow's pace.

Timing is at the very core of saving money on your vacation—either in the United States or abroad. What's more, since millions of you now have the privilege of taking your vacation whenever you wish during the year, this is a major moneysaving weapon you can use at your discretion and to whatever extent you want to.

You even might split your vacation into two holidays, taking advantage of bargain off-season rates at traditional summer resorts, then repeating your move and taking advantage of off-season rates at traditional winter resorts.

A key fact is that in many resort areas across the United States the weather is far more trustworthy in off season than it is at the season's height. May and October are particularly glorious months in many foreign lands.

As a general rule, the expensive "high season" in the Caribbean runs from mid-December until mid-March. In Europe, it's more or less the reverse: the high season begins with June and runs to (or, in some cases and places, *through*) September. A short "shoulder season" with intermediate prices sits between the high and low seasons.

SAVE BY GOING WHERE THE CROWDS ARE NOT

But even if you *must* take your vacation during the peak weeks of summer, you can save by heading for the less-crowded areas and by avoiding the well-known paths.

Don't squeeze yourself into the popular national parks, or visit a jammed resort. Head for one of the less crowded western Canadian provinces, or the wide-open spaces of Montana or Idaho, or a remote section of Upper Michigan. Or go to New York City while New Yorkers are off summer vacationing themselves. Miami and the Florida Keys offer reduced summer rates (though increasing numbers of tourists are discovering the fact). The ski towns of Colorado don't have as many summer visitors as winter skiers, yet their year-round weather and accommodations are delightful.

You also will be extra smart in midsummer if you avoid day-by-day travel, and instead find a single resort or hotel which can accept your reservation for a week or two.

SAVE ON A PACKAGE PLAN

Another key way to save is by buying a vacation "package." Many hotels in resort areas advertise special rates for stays of a weekend or a week or more. Often these are part of a transportation package with the airline or railroad serving the resort. Travel agents can suggest literally hundreds of good, moneysaving packages.

Or if you are buying a tour, consider a package, too, on unescorted standard-itinerary tours sold by tour operators. Included in the flat, low price will be your air ticket, hotel room, and certain sightseeing expeditions. You pay only for meals and extras and *you* decide how you'll spend most of your time.

Here's a sampling of the many other ways you can cut your vacation costs today:

• If you can, hook into an "inclusive tour charter" arranged by a travel agent. By doing so, you'll slash your air fare. For more details on air travel bargains, see Chapter 9, "Your Transportation."

• Inquire about other air fare bargain deals: excursion fares (good for 14- to 21- or 22- to 45-day trips); reserve-in-advance packages (which include a minimum payment for land arrangements); special fares.

• Look into the "stopover." Any time you travel outside the continental United States, your ticket probably entitles you to stop at additional cities (not shown on the ticket) without extra charge or at a very low charge.

• Investigate the Home Exchange Service, affiliated with Pan American World Airways, which publishes an annual directory of thousands of homes around the world whose owners want to exchange with other members in other countries. Members work out their own arrangements, pay a specified moderate total in dues per year. Address of HES: 119 Fifth Avenue, New York, N.Y. 10003.

• Or, as a poor man's alternative, get a copy of the "Travelers Directory," a listing throughout the United States and abroad of hundreds of people and places which will put you up for free (51-02 39th Avenue, Woodside, N.Y. 11377). You must offer your hospitality to others to get the directory, and a "donation" of a few dollars is requested to cover printing costs.

• If you're a student more than twelve years old, get for a small cost an International Student Identity Card from the Council on International Educational Exchange, 777 United Nations Plaza, New York, N.Y. 10017. This card gives you significant price reductions in a wide variety of student (not youth) hotels, restaurants, transportation, and cultural events abroad.

• Buy a cut-rate Eurailpass—giving you unlimited rail travel in thirteen continental countries on Western Europe's vast, subsidized railway system. Cost of a first-class rail pass in 1976: $180 for three weeks, $220 for one month, $300 for two months, or $360 for three months. If you're a foreign student (e.g., American) under age twenty-six, you can get a thirteen-country, two-month second-class Student-Railpass for only $195. (Of course, prices will go up from time to time but the bargain aspects will remain.) No Eurailpasses are available in Europe; all must be bought in the United States.

The Eurailpass in some instances entitles you to steamship or bus travel in addition to rail travel—either to facilitate surface connections or simply as an "extra."

For full details on the Eurailpass, ask you travel agent or write to Eurailpass, c/o French National Railroad, 610 Fifth Avenue, New York, N.Y. 10020, or Box 90, Lindenhurst, N.Y. 11757. (Information also available from the Austrian, German, Italian, Scandinavian, and Swiss railroad offices in the United States.)

• Avoid renting cars or buying goods and services in airports. Prices usually range 10 to 40 per cent above prices off the airport premises.

SHOPPING

Do your Christmas shopping at cut-rate duty-free shops. Take advantage of your quota of duty-free liquor, tobacco, etc. U. S. Customs permits you to bring back to the United States $100 worth of goods* you bought

*1974.

outside the country—retail value—if you were away at least forty-eight hours. (No minimum time applies to Mexico or U. S. Virgin Islands.) If you bring back more than $100 worth, you pay duty on the wholesale value, or about 40 per cent of the retail value. Special rules cover liquor and tobacco. You may include a quart of liquor duty- and tax-free, in your $100 exemption. If you're returning from the American Virgin Islands, Guam, or Samoa a *gallon* is duty-free under your exemption from duty, which increases to $200. Duty on wines, even expensive wines, is low.

You pay no duty at all on original oil paintings, stamps, or coins, books, or on antiques more than a hundred years old. Trademark restrictions limit the number or amounts of certain items you may bring home—particularly watches, perfumes, clocks, and cameras.

If you buy an automobile abroad and want to bring it back with you, you'll have to pay duty, of course—although under most circumstances you and other members of the family may use all your $100 exemptions to reduce the value of the car for duty purposes. In 1974 the rate of duty on a passenger car was 3 per cent of the "dutiable value," as determined by the customs inspector. To use the $100 exemption, the key rules for a returning U.S. resident are that:

the auto is imported for your personal use or for use of members of your household;

the auto has been acquired abroad as an incident of the journey from which you are returning;

the auto accompanies you at the time of your return on the same carrier.

Customs agents normally apply your $100 exemptions to the items with highest duty to give you the maximum savings, but it's wise to check yourself to be sure this is being done.

For more details on customs regulations, request the following pamphlets from the Bureau of Customs, Treasury Department, Washington, D.C. 20226:

"U. S. Customs Trademark Information," "Know Before You Go," "Customs Hints for Returning U. S. Residents," and "Importing a Car."

HOW TO SHOP FOR A VACATION TOUR

In recent years scandal after scandal has erupted across the front pages of the nation about "bargain" vacation tours. If you were a victim, you found many real costs hidden in the small print; or your costs were vastly increased when omitted essentials were included; or your de luxe accommodations were marginal at best; or you, a single, discovered too late that you had been booked into a double room with a stranger. Or many, many times your departure was at an abysmally "off" off hour.

But in strictly economic terms, the package tour *is* the least expensive way to take a vacation, particularly a vacation abroad, today.

Just what is a package tour? It is not, as you might think, always a highly organized, closely time-tabled tour during which the tour members eat, tour, sightsee, practically sleep together, and are herded in and out of places and countries with stopwatch precision.

Some travelers, primarily older couples, single persons, and inexperienced travelers may prefer the security of the traditional escorted group tour. But most of today's tour packages allow you to travel on your own and require only that the relatively small group fly together to and from their destinations.

A tour package does have, though, a predetermined price, number of features, and period of time. Within those limits, you, the traveler, can do whatever you please when you please. The greatest advantage to the traveler is that the cost of the land tour arrangements and air fare in the package is far less than the costs the traveler would otherwise pay for each item separately.

But, how do *you* avoid the traps? How do *you* shop for a tour?

Obviously, the prime rule—which I cannot repeat too often—is to deal only with an airline or tour operator or travel agent you have checked thoroughly and are confident is honest, reliable, and well established.

Obviously, it's no more than common sense to phone a couple of airlines, car rental firms, and the like to double-check whether the price of the tour you want really represents a saving over booking your vacation yourself or through a travel agent.

Now, use this check list to help you decide what you want from a vacation tour, to compare one tour against another, and to alert you to possible hidden costs.

Price: What's the total, including taxes and other extras, for the accommodations you want? If the tag says "from $198," will this minimum give you the comforts you need?

What's included: How many meals are provided each day? Fixed menu —or à la carte? Who pays tips for porters and tour guides? Who pays the hotel bills? For sight-seeing buses and guides? For theater tickets? For transfers between airports, train stations, and midtown? For transportation to your hotel? Is air fare included? If a rented car is part of the package, who pays for gas, a very costly item in most foreign lands? Typical *exclusions:* one or two meals a day, porters' tips, airport taxes, laundry and valet costs, taxi fares, snacks, excess baggage costs.

Accommodations: What type and class of hotel rooms are offered? Are the hotels named? Is there a clause permitting the tour operator to book you into substitute hotels for those named? Is the stated price for double occupancy? If you're traveling alone, is there a supplementary charge for a single room? Are such basic amenities as a bathroom included? Is the hotel's location convenient to where you're likely to be spending your time?

You'll save a lot of money by not bolting from the "package" to higher-cost hotel rooms. But if you prefer fancier surroundings, find out from the airline or tour operator the conditions and costs of trading up, if you so desire.

Terms: When do you have to pay for the tour? Is a deposit required and, if so, how much? What are the conditions for getting a refund if you cancel out or change your vacation plans? If you're paying on the installment plan, what annual interest rate is charged on the outstanding balance and how does this rate compare with the rate you might get on a loan from your bank or savings institution?

Your companions: How many other people will be along? Will they be interesting company for you—if you must be in close quarters (such as a bus) for long periods? Is there a theme for the tour to attract people with interests similar to yours?

Timing: How far in advance must you sign up? Choose a departure date and itinerary? Make a deposit? Pay in full?

Free time: How much will you have in each place you visit? Can you duck out for an afternoon or a day or two without being left behind, if you so wish? What's the likely pace of the tour? Will you be up to it? (As a general rule, if you travel more than nine or ten hours a day or more than 250 miles a day, you well might find your trip exhausting.) Will local guides shepherd you on certain legs of your trip and supplement your regular guide?

Find out these details *before* you sign up!

WHAT A TRAVEL AGENT CAN (AND CANNOT) DO FOR YOU

Let's say you are planning your first major vacation trip—either in the United States or abroad—and you have a general idea where you want to go and what you want to do. But you know absolutely nothing about costs, schedules, hotel accommodations. Just what could a travel agent do for you at what (if any) cost? How and where do you find a suitable travel agency?

A good travel agent should be well supplied with air and boat schedules; rates and costs for various types of travel; details on tours and group arrangements, schedules of festivals and other special events, hotel-motel room rates, cruise information.

A knowledgeable travel agent can:

guide you in applying for a passport and/or visa, alert you on immunizations you'll need for travel abroad, fill you in on customs rules and regulations;

sign you up for almost any kind of group tour (including tours the travel agency itself is putting together and selling);

make almost any kind of reservation or buy any kind of tickets for you

—hotel, motel, plane, train, theater, ballet, bullfight, etc.,—although many travel agencies do not sell bus and train tickets or short-haul air tickets or freighter accommodations;

sell you travelers checks and counsel you on how to get the best deal when you change money abroad;

steer you to bargain vacation packages—including transportation, hotel rooms, car rentals, meals, etc., off-season deals, places which cater to and offer cut rates to families traveling with children;

tell you what are the "on" seasons, the "off" seasons and the "shoulder" seasons in between—in various parts of the world;

advise on tipping customs, what kind of clothes to take, what kind of weather to expect, good restaurants;

"tailor-make" a trip or tour for you and your family—to fit *your* tastes, *your* interests, *your* budget. This type of trip is known in the travel trade as an "Independent Inclusive Tour" (IIT) and this category is further divided into the Domestic Independent Tour (DIT) and the Foreign Independent Tour (FIT).

How much do travel agents' services cost you, the traveler? How and by whom are these costs paid?

The bulk of travel agents' costs are paid by the airlines, steamship lines, railroads, hotels and resorts, tour operators, in the form of commissions. But you, the customer, well may be charged for such extras as:

certain telegrams and long-distance telephone calls;

reticketing;

making reservations in certain foreign hotels;

short-stay hotel reservations.

Many travel agents also charge you for arranging a special, fancy custom-designed trip abroad.

Okay, now that you know what travel agents do—and don't do—how do you find a good one?

Get recommendations from friends and others who have been customers of a travel agency with which you are considering doing business.

Try to find a travel agent who has himself (or herself) traveled in the area where *you* intend to go—and ask just how extensive the travel was.

Take the time to *visit* the travel agency. How thorough and "personal" is the agent's interview with you to discover your travel needs and wants? What "extras" are offered—i.e., a reading list on the countries you intend to visit?

Discuss your budget as well as your travel tastes frankly.

Ask if the agency is a member of the American Society of Travel Agents. (This is only a clue, since many reputable travel agencies are *not* members.)

Do not be misled by the size of a travel agency, for this is *not* necessarily an indication of the quality of its services. Good ones come both large and small.

Note whether the agent seems genuinely interested in steering you to travel bargains or whether he or she tries to push you into more expensive ways to "get there" than you can afford (remember, travel agents are paid commissions based on the cost of the accommodations). If the latter, go to another agency.

If you are booking a tour being sold by the travel agency, nail down details on deposits you'll be required to make, policies on refunds and cancellation fees. Each agency sets its own rules in this area and if the agent fails voluntarily to spell out the rules, *ask* what they are. (You may lose 100 per cent of whatever amount you have paid toward a tour—if this is the written policy of the tour operator and/or travel agency selling the deal. The loss could include even air fares you've paid for overseas tours. Also, when you sign a contract with a travel agent it's a legally binding piece of paper—both ways.)

If a travel agency promises to make refunds for cancellations you have made for valid reasons, find out just what constitutes valid reasons.

If a "slight" penalty is to be imposed in the event you cancel, check just how slight is "slight."

If you ask a travel agent to draw up a special itinerary for you, find out in advance what the costs will be, whether you'll be required to make a deposit, and, if so, how much. The charge for a custom-planned trip can be as high as 25 to 50 per cent of the value of the package—if the planning involves a lot of the agent's time, thought, and expertise.

If you have any suspicions about a travel agent with whom you're considering doing any substantial amount of business, check the agency's reputation with the local Better Business Bureau.

DO-IT-YOURSELF TRAVEL PLANNING

If you are booking on your own into one of the large hotels and hotel chains, use their toll-free telephone reservations number. You'll get an instant answer by phone or a letter more or less by return mail to confirm your reservation.

If you are making your own airline reservations, ask any major airline to advise you on other airline schedules as well as on special rates offered by all airlines. Most will freely do so.

Call Amtrak for most U.S. rail travel. (The toll-free number throughout the United States for reservations and information: (800) 523-5720.) More than 5,000 travel agents around the world also are authorized to sell Amtrak tickets. In Canada, the two key lines are: Canadian National Railways, 630 Fifth Avenue, New York, N.Y. 10020 (or CN System, Rail Travel Bureau, Central Station, Montreal, Quebec); and the Canadian Pacific Railway, 581 Fifth Avenue, New York, N.Y. 10017 (or CP Rail, Windsor Station, Montreal 101, Quebec).

The two best-known domestic bus lines are Greyhound and Trailways. Both have offices located at Eighth Avenue and Forty-first Street, New York, N.Y. 10014 (the New York Port Authority bus terminal).

Most of the key steamship lines have headquarters offices in New York City.

Look into the wide array of overseas travel information available from each major country's government travel office in New York (and, in some cases, in other cities as well).

Write the state Tourist Information Bureaus in the states you want to visit within our borders or the U. S. National Park Service, Department of the Interior, Eighteenth and E streets, Washington, D.C. 20240.

Go to the nearest Passport Office for guidance on how to apply for a passport. In some cities and towns which have no Passport Office, this information is now available at the U. S. Post Office along with passport application forms; elsewhere, get the information and application forms from the clerk of a federal or state court or from your county clerk's office.

For details on international auto registration certificates and International Drivers' Licenses, check the American Automobile Association, 28 East Seventy-eighth Street, New York, N.Y. 10021. And if you're a member of this organization, use its facilities to help plan your trip—including information on roads under construction and speed traps; maps; itinerary recommendations; regional guides to motels, restaurants (with ratings and tourist attractions).

Check your automobile insurance to be sure it covers you in all states you will visit. (Failure to take care of this could be very costly in the event of an accident.) If you will be traveling in Canada, ask your insurance company for a Canada Non-Resident Inter-Province Motor Vehicle Liability Insurance Card, required to prove your coverage to provincial officials. In Mexico, auto insurance laws are very strict. U.S. insurance is usually not valid for more than forty-eight hours after entry and you will need a more expensive Mexican policy for longer stays. *Be sure* to look into the car insurance problem *before* you leave home.

Study at least a couple of travel guides and books which you can borrow from your library or buy at a bookstore. (Some have coupons which will buy you discounts for various tourist services.) Among the best ones:

Fielding's Travel Guide to Europe and many other Fielding guides (William Morrow).

Frommer's *Europe on $5 and $10 a Day* and other "$5-a-Day" guides (Simon & Schuster).

Fodor's *Europe* and other Fodor guides (McKay).

Let's Go: Europe, a Student Guide (Harvard Student Agencies, Inc., distributed through E. P. Dutton & Co.).

The Mobil Travel Guides (Simon & Schuster).

Writers' Guides to the various states of the United States.

Rand McNally Guidebooks: *Road Atlas, Travel Trailer Guide, Guidebook to Campgrounds, Campground and Trailering Guide, National Park Guide, Ski Guide.*

Woodall's *Parks and Campgrounds* (Woodall Publishing).

The Michelin Guides to France and other European countries and Michelin's *Green Guide to New York City* (Simon & Schuster).

A to Z Guides by Robert S. Kane (Doubleday).

Blue Guides (Rand McNally).

AAA Tour Book, one for each region of the United States; also *Eastern and Western AAA Campground Guide*—all available to AAA members only.

The Official Student Travel Guide (International Student Travel Conference, 1560 Broadway, New York).

Whole World Handbook—Six Continents on a Student Budget (Council on International Educational Exchange, 777 United Nations Plaza, New York, N.Y. 10017).

PanAm's New Horizons World Guide and other PanAm guides to the United States, Canada, South America, European countries, Africa, Asia, the Middle East, and the Caribbean.

And finally the most important rule for all do-it-yourselfers: *plan ahead,* just as far ahead as you possibly can.

DO'S AND DON'TS FOR CUTTING YOUR HOTEL BILLS

If you're a typical American today, your spending for hotel and/or motel bills will run into hundreds of dollars a year. So will your spending for food and drink away from home—on long weekends, holidays, vacations.

If you're typical, you'll also "waste" as much as $2.00 of every $10 you spend simply because you do not know the basic do's and don'ts for saving on your hotel and motel bills:

Do, when you make a room reservation, ask for a room by price category. (Most hotels have three categories: economy, standard, and luxury.) If you want the minimum rate, ask for it. Virtually all good hotels now provide radio, TV, phone, air conditioning—and, if the hotel isn't full, many will give you better than minimum room accommodations even though you pay the lowest rate.

Don't underestimate the cost of room service. There usually is a room-service charge added to the bill the waiter gives you and the prices on the room-service menu usually are higher than prices for the same or similar items in the hotel coffee shop. Room service is a luxury which makes sense when you're on a special vacation, but it can add many dollars to your bills if you are a frequent traveler.

Do be careful about check-out time. If you want to stay an hour or two after check-out time, notify the manager or assistant manager directly, and unless your room is needed at once, he'll probably allow you to stay without charge. But if you stay as long as three hours after check-out time, the hotel may charge you $5.00 extra, and if you stay into the evening hours, you may be charged for a full extra day.

Don't, if you're traveling with your family, fail to inquire about the "family plan" that many hotels feature. It's ridiculous to pay for an extra room when—for no charge or for at most a nominal fee—the hotel will provide a folding bed which can be set up in your room. And this rule may apply to kids into their teens. Also, many hotels have special meal-ticket programs which will cut down on your family's dining bills.

Do take advantage of the toll-free electronic reservations systems which most large chains provide. By doing so, you can save the expense of a phone call or of a wire ahead to hotels in other cities you are planning to visit.

Don't, if you are driving your own car, ignore the extent to which overnight parking fees can throw your budget out of line. Make sure the midtown hotel you choose offers free parking either on the premises or nearby. Even in New York City, major hotel chains park cars without charge. Frequently, however, a charge is made each time you take your car out of the garage.

Do find out in advance if the hotel at which you're planning to stay is on the regular route of an airport bus or limousine. If it isn't at one of the regular stops, you'll have the added expense of a taxi to get you to your destination.

Do take another look at famed old downtown hotels which you may by-pass because you assume they're too expensive. To meet the competition of motor inns, airport and suburban hotels, many of these great establishments have cut their rates. You may be concentrating on saving a tip or two by staying in a motel, but as one great hotel man remarked, "I could never understand why anybody would want to spend $2.00 more for a room to save 25¢ on a tip."

Don't pay for the use of a hotel or motel swimming pool, sauna, gym, etc. (which may add $1.00 to $2.00 to daily room rates) if you don't intend to use the facilities.

And *do,* finally, try to plan your travels around the hotel package deals —off-season bargains, weekend plans, family specials—I've underlined in the preceding pages.

WHOM AND HOW TO TIP

The old guideline for restaurants, resort hotels, taxis, etc.—tip 15 per cent of the bill—has been firmly upped to 15 to 20 per cent of the total if you want to be known as generous.

The old rule for *porters* carrying your luggage also has been upped from 25¢ a bag to a minimum of 50¢, and frequently $1.00 is the minimum if you want to avoid scowls and recriminations from the porter.

The minimum tip for *taxi drivers* in big cities is 25¢—which works out to 25 per cent of a $1.00 fare.

Of course, many travelers still tip well below these levels—and a surprising number of skinflints don't tip *anyone any* percentage at all. But tipping remains an economic institution in this land and so:

The hotel doorman: Tip him 50¢ when you arrive, if he carries your baggage to the registration desk, $1.00 if you have three or more bags. Give him 25¢ each time he finds you a taxi—but give him no more than a "thank you" if he does no more than wave forward a cab waiting in line in front of the hotel.

The bellhop: Tip him as you tipped the doorman, increasing your tips if your luggage is especially heavy and/or cumbersome. Whenever he delivers anything you have ordered, give him at least 25¢, even if it is only a newspaper costing 10¢. Of course, if he has paid for the item you requested, also reimburse him.

The wine steward: Tip him 10 to 15 per cent of the cost of the wine, at the end of the meal.

Room service: Tip 50¢ each time an item is delivered. But tip $1.00 if the waiter brings ice and drink mixers and $1.50 to $2.00 if he brings a whole tray full of soda, glasses, ice, and other drinking equipment. When you have a meal sent to your room, tip as you would in a restaurant— 15 to 20 per cent of the check.

Valet: Tip 50¢ per delivery. If you give the valet a rush order, though, or ask for extraordinary service—say a suit pressed and back within the hour—give him $1.00.

Chambermaid: You need not tip her if you spend only a night or two at a regular commercial hotel, but it's increasingly recommended that you leave her 50¢ a day if you stay longer. Leave the money in an envelope addressed "For the Chambermaid in Room—" at the reception desk the last day of your stay and tell the housekeeping department you left it. Tip her $1.00 to $2.00 if you have a cocktail party in your room or suite, involving a big cleanup job for her. In a resort hotel, the standard minimum tip for the chambermaid is 50¢ per day for a single person, $1.00 day for a couple, more for special service.

Travel abroad: Even if a substantial service charge has already been added to your hotel or restaurant bill, the trend today is toward adding another 10 per cent to the total rather than just leaving the small change. The trend also is toward personal distribution of the money to make sure the chambermaid, doorman, waiter, or others who have served you actually get the tips. And the trend too is for tipping above and beyond these percentages for any extra special services—for tips frequently are the sole source of income for service personnel in Europe and elsewhere abroad.

At a resort hotel—including those operating on the American plan (all meals included) or modified American plan (breakfast and dinner included)—a service charge of 15 per cent or more may be added to your total bill. If it isn't, tip your dining-room waiter 15 per cent of your restaurant bill. You'll probably find details on how much of your daily room rate is for your meals in the hotel directory in the dresser drawer of your room but, if not, ask the assistant manager or social director for pertinent facts. Tip bellboys 50¢ for each bag they carry and tip your chambermaid and pool boy 50¢ each per day per person, as you leave. Tip your resort's hairdresser 15 to 20 per cent.

Visiting friends: If there is a housekeeper or cook who helps make your stay more gracious and comfortable, you, as a visiting couple, might properly tip $1.00 to $2.00 a day as a "thank you."

P.S.: Perhaps as you grumble and struggle over whether to tip 10 per cent or 15 per cent or 20 per cent or whatever, you might remember that, by one definition, "TIPS" were originally intended as a means "To Insure Prompt Service." This reminder might help guide you to the right amount for the right persons.

AND TIPPING ON WINTER CRUISES

Let's say you are now making plans for your first winter vacation on a cruise ship. You've read all the brochures on what to wear, what to see, what to do. But one angle I'll wager you've missed is: whom to tip how much. Even if you already have been on every type of winter holiday, I'll bet you have made plenty of inadvertent tipping blunders.

Here, too, tipping expectations are being revised sharply upward in many instances from the old 10 to 15 per cent range to a new 15 to 20 per cent range—and employees who never were considered eligible for tips suddenly are turning up on the lists. Following, therefore, you will find up-to-date rules for cruise-ship tipping:

• Tip your dining-room steward and your room steward or stewardess a minimum of $1.00 each per day per person. Thus, if you are a couple on a two-week cruise, tip a total of about $30. If your cruise lasts a week or less, tip at least $10 for each steward—at the end of the trip.

• Tip the deck steward 50¢ a day or about $2.50 to $3.00 a week. Tip the headwaiter in the dining room a couple of dollars, plus $1.00 or $2.00 each time he performs some special service for you. Tip the bartender 15 to 20 per cent each time you are served a new drink. Tip the telephone operator $1.00 or $2.00 if she puts through complicated ship-to-shore calls for you.

• On shore, tip tour guides 50¢ or 15 per cent of the cost of the tour if it's a half-day tour, $1.00 if it's a full-day tour. Tip the men who carry your luggage in U.S. ports at least 35¢ per bag—even if the dock is plastered with "no tipping" signs.

• Don't tip the cruise's social director; or the person who leads calisthenics; or the purser or other ship's officers; or customs men in port. If you are in doubt, ask for guidelines from your travel agent, the cruise director, or the ship's purser. The excursion agent on board your ship can tell you if tipping is expected anywhere ashore.

SAVE BY HOSTELING

One of the least expensive ways to "see the world" is to use the world's extraordinary network of youth hostels. These are inexpensive dormitory-style accommodations providing shelter, bunks or beds, and often some sort of kitchen facilities. Fees in the United States are typically $2.50 in summer and $3.25 in winter per day for lodging; abroad, fees are lower.

There are some 4,400 hostels today in 48 different countries, and the youth hosteling organizations offer a long list of special bargains to hostelers. You can go hosteling by foot, canoe, bike, public transportation, or car. You can go alone, or with friends, or with a group and trained leader.

Typical cost of a thirty-day American Youth Hostel tour within the United States in 1976 was in the $350 to $400 range and in the $550 to $650 range for tours abroad. Included were: transportation from a specified departure point; all costs of accommodations and food; insurance; leadership; and transportation back to the original departure point. *Not* included in this price were: equipment you must have (generally simple camping gear); spending money; cost of passports; bicycle shipping; transportation to or from trip starting point; AYH membership dues and an emergency fund which must be deposited with the trip leader for unexpected expenses (unused amounts are returned).

Hostelers on a National Group Trip must be at least fourteen years old or must have completed ninth grade. On International Trips campers must be at least sixteen years old or have previously completed a National Trip.

There is no upper age limit, but most trips are intended for young travelers in good physical condition. A few, however, are for adults only.

As an alternative to a youth hostel tour, you can travel on your own, staying at youth hostels along the way. American Youth Hostels also has a bargain car-leasing plan in Europe. Or you can rent a car and tent and camp where there are no hostels.

Your passport to hostels throughout the world is a pass issued by AYH.

A junior pass in 1976 (for people under age eighteen) cost $5.00; a senior pass for older hostelers cost $11; a family membership covering children up to age eighteen cost $12. Only individual passes—junior and senior —can be used outside the United States.

For detailed information on trips and applications for passes, write American Youth Hostels, AYH National Campus, Delaplane, Va. 22025.

BUS PASSES AND BIKE TRAILS

Another way to cover a large territory on your vacation—at very low cost—is to go by bus. You can now get a special type of bus ticket, similar to the well-known Eurailpass, which will give you virtually unlimited bus travel in the United States and Canada for sixty days. Greyhound calls its version Ameripass and Continental Trailways calls its ticket Eaglepass, but in 1976 both cost about $250 for thirty days and about $350 for sixty days. This worked out to $6.00 to $8.00 a day—a clue to how great a bargain the passes really are.

Your only limitations in using either pass are: you may not take more than four round trips between any two points.

More than 150,000 miles of routes in forty-eight states and Canada are yours to choose from, and Greyhound's pass also gives you a variety of discounts up to 20 per cent on hotels, car rentals, tours, and other services. Greyhound's pass may be used on the Trailways system where Greyhound does not provide service and vice versa. But it is most convenient to buy your pass from the line which serves your travel plans best.

An increasingly popular way to go camping—or just to sight-see at your vacation destination—is by bicycle. You can even combine it with bus travel. Bicycle are proliferating and it is becoming easier all the time to find places to combine this sport with camping. The Bureau of Outdoor Recreation, U.S. Department of Interior, estimates that there will be more than 200,000 miles of bike routes in the United States by the end of this decade. Ohio, for instance, has more than a half dozen biking routes running through the most scenic areas of the state, and more are being laid out all the time. The average length of these routes is about 30 miles and all are marked by standard bikeway signs. ("Ohio Is Happening Along Bikeways" from the Ohio Department of Development, Box 1011, Columbus, O. 43216, describes the trails.)

Or you can ride through Indiana's covered-bridge country on a bikeway running through Parke County. A longer trail is the towpath of the old Chesapeake and Ohio Canal from Georgetown, D.C., to Cumberland, Md.—184 miles. Or you can ride 320 miles on the Wisconsin State Bikeway from the Mississippi River to Lake Michigan.

Many more trails are being planned for the future; most spurred locally, but some of them with financial help from the federal government. But you don't have to wait for official designation of trails. With a little help from cycling clubs and friends, plus some practice and experience on your own, you'll be able to choose the most enjoyable routes yourself from highway maps and government topographic maps.

Also, send for "The AYH North American Bike Atlas," which describes 60 one-day trips throughout the United States and 100 one-week to one-month trips in Canada, Mexico, and the Caribbean ($2.45; American Youth Hostels, Inc., AYH National Campus, Delaplane, Va. 22025).

Try combining hostels, state and private campgrounds, perhaps a friendly farmer or two, and even an occasional motel. You'll surely find you can work out literally hundreds of real cycling adventures almost anywhere in the country—at astonishingly low cost. (The rules on how to *buy* a bicycle are in Chapter 9, "Your Transportation," on pages 370–72.)

MONEYSAVING GUIDES FOR CAMPING TRIPS

During most of the summer weeks each summer, tens of millions of you go off on camping trips and in the process spend more than $1 billion on travel trailers alone, plus hundreds of millions on camping equipment, plus millions more on getting to and from the camping grounds, on overnight fees, and on other expenses.

Until recently, camping in the United States meant stuffing a sleeping bag, some warm clothes, a few cooking utensils and first-aid equipment into a rucksack, slinging it over your back, and heading for the hills. But today the typical camper travels in a fully equipped trailer or motor home, cooks on gas stoves instead of campfires, watches TV instead of beavers. Today's typical campsite provides creature comforts ranging from hot showers to hair dryers, clothes washers to canteens.

Obviously, camping has become a significant factor in the outdoor recreation industry and also a potentially whopping expense to the individual camper or camping family.

As one measure of camping's spectacular growth just in this decade, the Rand McNally *Guidebook to Campgrounds* listed more than 15,000 campgrounds in the United States and Canada in 1974 (with more than 550,000 individual campsites), up from only 5,000 campgrounds listed in

1961. Rand McNally also counted thousands of camping areas specifically set up to accommodate travel trailers, with more than 400,000 separate sites for trailers.

If you're the back-to-nature type and really prefer to rough it, you and your family can go on a camping trip by foot or by canoe in any one of thousands of national and state parks for as little as $75 a week,* assuming you don't go too far from home and you already own basic equipment such as cooking utensils, sleeping bags, and back packs. Even if you have to rent these basics, the total cost for a family of three or four needn't run over $100 a week. But if you prefer the "motel in the wilderness" type of camping, involving rented travel trailers, overnight fees at private campgrounds, electricity and gas bills, etc., costs can rise to $300 or more a week.

If you're considering taking your first camping expedition, your best bet is to avoid an outlay of hundreds of dollars to buy trailers, tents, etc. Rent them instead. Buy just as little as possible until you find out whether or not you like the whole idea of camping and, if so, what style of camping you enjoy most.

If you decide to go the recreational vehicle route, you can choose from a wide range of travel trailers, campers, motor homes, etc.—at an even wider array of prices. (You will find the moneysaving guides on buying recreational vehicles in Chapter 9, "Your Transportation," pages 367–68.)

Another possibility is a U.S.- or foreign-made small camper which you can rent for about the price of renting a car at an airport. This type of camper will sleep four people and has the full range of kitchen equipment and other camping gear. The vehicles are available in many major U.S. cities and throughout Europe.

Here are more tips if you prefer to rough it:

• The federal government offers a $10 Golden Eagle Passport card which will admit you and any passengers in your car to all areas of the national park system and give you the use of most facilities and services provided by the National Park Service during the year. (A free version, available to citizens more than sixty-two years old, also gives a 50 per cent discount on all special user fees on all federal lands—not just the national parks.)

Get your pass at any national park, at most national forests, or from any first- or second-class post office. Also write the U. S. Superintendent of Documents, Washington, D.C. 20402, for brochures entitled "Camping in the National Park System," "Fishing in the National Park System" and "Boating in the National Park System" (modest cost for each).

• If you're inclined toward a really "wild" camping experience, full of educational information about the wild areas you visit and the ways to get there, it is hard to beat the package wilderness tours offered on a non-profit

* All of these figures prevailed in 1974.

basis by several large conservation and other outdoor sport associations. Examples:

The Wilderness Society operates dozens of tours ranging from hiking, back-packing, and canoeing to horseback riding in wilderness areas throughout the United States. Emphasis is on getting to know the wilderness in a non-destructive way. (For information, write to the Wilderness Society, Western Regional Office, 4260 Evans Avenue, Denver, Colo. 80222.)

The American River Touring Association runs an extensive program of river touring in many distant parts of the world as well as in the United States. Prices in 1974 ranged from under $100 for weekend trips to up to $2,000 and more for month-long semi-expeditions. (Write ARTA, 1016 Jackson Street, Oakland, Calif. 94607.)

The Sierra Club, the oldest and one of the largest (137,000 members) wilderness conservation club in the United States, sponsors hundreds of wilderness outings each year, including river trips (by raft or canoe), hiking/back-packing trips, and saddle trips. You may be continuously moving or operate in a more leisurely fashion from a base camp. Many trips are specifically designed as family trips. You can write the Sierra Club for a publication describing the entire year's trips at 1050 Mills Tower, 220 Bush Street, San Francisco, Calif. 94104. Chapters also organize a regular schedule of local trips throughout the year at very low cost.

• If you are camping in a national park, choose your campsites carefully. Each year, more than 50 million people somehow squeeze themselves into fewer than a million campsites. In the process, many areas become overused, while some are underused. The name of the game, of course, is to find the latter.

• Be on the lookout for the creation of new national parks on the very edges of major cities. The current proposal of the Interior Department is to make 1 million park acres easily accessible near every city of 250,000 or more people.

• But even before these new areas are created, study the areas close to your home carefully. Often you'll find little gems of wilderness in the midst of urban areas, unfrequented by the crowds whose urge to escape leads them to overlook their immediate neighborhood and to travel as far as possible. If you find one of these, restful camping may be yours for very little money and travel time.

• If your interest extends beyond camping to the more exacting sports —such as mountaineering, rock climbing, white-water canoeing, or scuba diving—you'll need special instruction as well as special gear. First-aid courses are also valuable if you plan to do much camping. You can get this training most economically from experienced friends or from local clubs, who usually share their knowledge willingly and without charge.

Nationally known groups, such as the Sierra Club or the Red Cross, are sound non-profit alternatives though they may charge for direct expenses. There also are dozens of commercial schools, whose reputations and costs are usually easy to check through knowledgeable devotees of the sport.

TOURISM AND ENERGY SHORTAGES

Tourism is defined as travel fifty miles or more one way, in any form of transport, for any purpose other than commuting for work. It is a vital part of our country's life style, employing 4 million people and accounting for $60 to $65 billion of spending each year (food, lodging, public transportation, fuel, auto operating costs, entertainment, sight-seeing). It is a labor-intensive, service industry, and in every state tourism is vital to our economic well-being (we take in each other's washing). In three states—Florida, Hawaii, and Nevada—tourism is the leading industry. In six others—California, Texas, Pennsylvania, Illinois, Michigan, Ohio—tourism brings in more than $1 billion annually. In seven other areas—Maine, Alaska, Arizona, Washington, D.C., the Virgin Islands, Puerto Rico, and Guam—the dependence on the travel dollar is extremely heavy.

Not only for your own physical and mental well-being, but also for your nation's welfare, the thing to do in this era of energy shortages is to plan your vacation so that, with the use of 75 per cent of the energy you consumed before the shortages emerged, you can enjoy 100 per cent of your life style.

Here, therefore, are tips on travel designed specifically to help you conserve energy:

• Investigate with much more care than you formerly did fly/drive, bus/drive, rail/drive, fly/sight-see packages. Be as flexible on dates and routing as you can and use public transportation where feasible.

• Fly/drive vacations now come in all types and sizes, involving rental cars and hotels. Nearly all the airlines have them. Check with a reputable travel agent for pertinent details.

• "Take me along" vacations are booming. For the very simple reason that it saves money, families are planning their vacations around convention and business trips.

• If you like national parks, you'll have no trouble getting to the park by bus these days as well as rail. And buses within the parks have been vastly improved too. There are 200 park systems located within 100 miles of a metropolitan center—involving the use of bus rather than a tankful of gas.

• Hotels and motels are offering minivacations and "escape weekends" to people within 100 miles at up to 50 per cent discounts. Most major attractions are within 100 miles of airports or rail terminals or can be reached by bus.

• When traveling by air, be much more flexible on dates, avoiding Fridays and Sundays if possible. On routing, adjust your schedule if need be and don't insist on non-stop.

• Let your travel agent make one booking, and have a confirmed reservation. Avoid double booking—which means you are depriving someone else of a seat.

• Investigate Amtrak, especially for family travel and short-haul business travel. Railroads and motorcoaches are the most economical users of fuel.

• Discover your own area close to home by motorcoach. Travel in groups. Avoid congested areas by private auto. On these trips, you really waste gas because of traffic tie-ups and idling motors.

• Take buses to the airport, get there early, avoid gas-eating traffic jams, try not to meet friends at airports.

• Forget haphazard touring. Do not plan an auto trip without a plan. Know where you want to go, when. Buy guides, know your wayside itinerary, make reservations.

• Now the universities are trying to lure us with vacation and travel opportunities on college campuses and surrounding areas. Mort's "Guide to Low-Cost Vacations & Lodgings on College Campuses" ($2.95 in bookstores or $3.50 from CMG Publications, Box 630, Princeton, N.J. 08540), describes the great recreational and cultural facilities of 144 colleges in the United States and Canada which formerly have been enjoyed mostly by students but now are open to all of us at a fraction of commercial recreational, food, and lodging prices.

You need only make relatively easy adjustments. Try them, you'll even like them.

13

A ROOF OVER YOUR HEAD

WHAT DO YOU REALLY WANT?

When you start planning to buy, build, or rent a roof to go over your head, you face some of the biggest financial decisions of your life and also an all-time high number of formidable competitors for that roof.

The mere fact that during the decade of the seventies 4 million or more Americans will be marrying each year spells serious shortages of most forms of housing throughout the nation. For this means a 2 million-plus new couples will be created each year, probably exceeding the average number of new houses being built, and of course each year millions of dwelling units disappear because of old age or disasters or other developments.

You are facing historically high rents as well as record high home-buying and home-building costs.

If you are in the market to buy a house and you do not buy wisely, it could be the most expensive mistake of your life. On the other hand, if you do buy wisely, your investment is virtually certain to grow in value over the years.

Thus your first rule is: take plenty of time to hunt for a house or an apartment. Being in a hurry puts you squarely into a sellers' market and it almost inevitably will cost you money. Being at ease will make it more likely that you will find a place truly suitable to your family's needs. The typical U.S. shopper for an old house takes two months and visits five different houses before he finds the right one. For new-house shoppers, the norm is three months and ten different houses. Allot even more time if you possibly can— especially if you intend to settle in for several years.

Before you even begin to shop for a house in which to move your family, sit everybody down and throw out the question: "What do we *really* want?"

An apartment or a house?

A house in the suburbs on a paved street with a sidewalk and lawns?

A house in the country with woods or a field between you and the next house?

A house close to the center of town?

A new one-story house loaded with every convenience, a two-car garage, and an acre of land—or an older, roomier house with elbow room outside as well as in, which needs major fixing up?

A house, if you want to do a lot of entertaining, with a separate dining room? Or one, if you're the type of family which congregates mainly in the kitchen for meals, with ample eating space there?

Do you want a wood house? Or a stucco one? A brick or a precast concrete one? Clapboards or shingles or shakes? Or aluminum siding? Paint or stain or just weathered wood?

How much can you afford to pay?

What type of neighborhood do you want to live in?

What style house do you want? Conventional? Ranch? Split level? One-story or two-story?

How much land do you want? Will you want a garden?

How many rooms do you need?

Do you want a house you can resell quickly?

What kinds of neighbors do you want? Informal, dungarees-on-Sunday, drop-in-for-a-drink types? The mentally stimulating, intellectually inclined set? A wide variety of social-economic-ethnic backgrounds?

Do you want a big rambling lawn to sit on (and mow)?

How highly does each member of the family value privacy?

If you're now under thirty-five, the vast majority of you plan to move to a new home (or a first home of your own) within the next five years. If you're typical, you'd prefer to live in your own house rather than in an apartment, to buy rather than to rent, and you're willing to pay the price of doing so. You would like to live as far away from the city as you conveniently can and an astonishing number of you—about one half of American families today— would like to live in a house in the country complete with a real privacy-protector (such as woods or a field between you and the next house).

The *average* house bought in 1973 had about 1,300 square feet of improved floor space. The *average new* house has more than 1,500 square feet, six rooms (three of them bedrooms), at least two bathrooms, and a garage.

But *no* family is average. Your own needs surely differ greatly from the needs of everybody else. So arm yourselves with the facts and get ready to *shop* for a roof over your head which will really suit *your* individual needs, dreams, and budget.

WHAT TYPE OF SHELTER FOR YOU?

At every age there is a right type of shelter for most of you. For illustration, let's take a more or less typical couple through a more or less typical life cycle. You can identify with whatever group fits you.

You are eighteen to twenty; single: earning a modest income; have a job which very well may be temporary (you might move to a job in another neighborhood or another city).

Rent. Stick to a studio or one-bedroom unit, keep your overhead and responsibilities to a minimum. If your temperament permits, get a roommate and cut your costs still more.

You are under twenty-five; married: both of you are working and your combined pay checks come to more than $15,000 a year. Neither of you likes the bachelor digs you have and you're very tempted to go for a co-op or condominium with all the convenient, comfortable extras.

Don't. Rent a modest two-bedroom place near your jobs. Build a nest egg for use later when you'll have children, your expenses will go up, and the wife wants to stay home for a while.

You are twenty-five to thirty-five; now have one or two children: your income is at a level permitting you to buy, the husband is quite sure to stay with the same company for three years at least. The apartment is far too crowded and you're thinking of a house in the suburbs.

Consider a townhouse—a multiple dwelling with individual ownership, the closest thing to a single-family home with all the ownership advantages but with much less burden.

While you might select other types of homes, the townhouse is an attractive variation at your income level.

You are in your early forties: have just taken a new job at a much higher pay in a new area; your children are at the ages where they will have guests, frequently overnight; you want the house of your dreams.

This time, you buy a four-bedroom house and select the life style you want—in the suburbs or exurbs or whatever. You might have done this at earlier ages when your children were very young—if you (and your wife, with or without a job) had the income to finance it and you were really set in your area. But this age progression arbitrarily assumes that you will take that new job in your forties.

You are into your fifties: the kids have left home, the four-bedroom house is a burden. You sell.

Now your options are very wide. You may slip back into the big city and rent. Or you might go for a small condominium in your same area—enjoying the benefits of ownership and the suburban life without the annoyances of upkeep etc. Or you might put your money into a vacation/retirement home on a lake or golf course. Or you might build a rustic place in ski country.

Qr you might buy a mobile home (a really mobile one!) and follow the seasons when you, the husband, retire.

SHOULD YOU BUY OR RENT?

WHICH IS CHEAPER?

Mortgage interest rates soared to record highs in many major cities in the mid-1970s with the *average* on a new, single family home in 1974 crossing 9 per cent. Home construction costs rose at a yearly rate of as much as 20 per cent in some areas, primarily because of skyrocketing building materials costs. By 1974 the National Association of Home Builders reported the average cost of a new house had spiraled to more than $41,000. During the past decade, added the American Bankers Association, the cost of a plot of land on which a house is built jumped at a yearly rate of 9.1 per cent while the average size of a building lot shrank from 8,202 to 6,990 square feet—resulting in a net average rise in land costs of 13.4 per cent annually since the late 1960s.

Let's say that against this background, you are trying to decide whether to put down $10,000 on a $40,000 house and pay off an 8½ per cent mortgage over the next quarter-century—or to rent a house or apartment of similar size and location. Which is cheaper? How great are the differences?

Let's say both the house you are considering buying and the one you are considering renting can be expected to grow by four per cent a year in value; that the landlord is taking and will continue to take a ten per cent profit each year; that property taxes, insurance, and maintenance costs amount to a total of 5½ per cent of the value of the house at the start of each year.

And let's assume, too, that both the for-sale and the for-rent house (or apartment) have an equivalent amount of space and/or other yardsticks of value (too often, people try to compare the high cost of owning a ten-room house with the much lower cost of renting a five-room apartment).

• Using these assumptions, you'll pay rent of $6,200 the first year, or $516.60 a month—a rent which will grow over the twenty-five years to nearly $16,000 a year or more than $1,300 a month as the value of the house rises and so do property taxes, insurance, etc.

• Your first year costs to buy the house will be $6,960 (adjusted to reflect the amount you would get back if you sold the house). But this yearly cost will drop steadily to about $3,200 after the twenty-five year mortgage is paid, primarily because you are building up equity in your house and because your interest costs will drop steadily as the outstanding balance of your mortgage declines.

• Over twenty-five years the average yearly cost of renting the apartment will be $10,328 or $861 a month. The average cost of buying the house will be $3,196 or $266 per month—or only one-third of the cost of renting.

Here's a rundown of the year-by-year costs, using the above assumptions—including 10 per cent return for the landlord.

Year	Rent Costs	Annual Net Ownership Costs	Ownership Savings (Loss)
1	$6,200	$6,960	$ (760)
2	6,448	4,965	1,483
3	6,706	4,303	2,403
4	6,974	3,975	2,999
5	7,253	3,780	3,473
6	7,543	3,652	3,891
7	7,845	3,561	4,284
8	8,159	3,495	4,664
9	8,485	3,444	5,041
10	8,824	3,404	5,420

Not surprisingly, it's cheaper to rent than to buy if you will live in the house for only a year or so: you save $760 by renting the first year, for instance. But over the ten-year period your savings on owning versus renting come to $32,898 or an average of $3,290 a year.

What if the landlord can't or doesn't take the full 10 per cent profit on the rental. How would that change the picture?

If, say, he took only 6 per cent, your rent in the first year would be $4,600 versus a net ownership cost of $6,960; you would save $2,360 by renting. But at ten years, your rent would come to $55,226 versus net total ownership costs of $34,036. At fifteen years, the comparison would be $92,106 for rent as against $49,349 for ownership; at twenty-five years, you would have paid $191,564 for rent as against $79,889 for total home ownership.

Over the twenty-five-year period, your average yearly rent would come to $7,663 or $639 a month. This would be more than double the cost of owning a home or a total of $111,675 more in rent than in home-ownership costs over this span. It could not be clearer.

IN FAVOR OF HOME OWNERSHIP

Obviously, cost is only one of the key factors to weigh in deciding whether to rent or to buy. Other important factors favoring ownership of your home over renting are:

• Taking on regular home mortgage payments becomes a form of "forced savings" plan in which you build up a long-term asset of prime value.

• There are many emotional-social advantages in home ownership. You may change and improve your house or apartment and its grounds as you wish. Your long-term financial and geographical commitment and the fact that you pay property taxes give you a strong tie to a community and built-in stake in its problems and benefits.

There are *disadvantages* to home ownership too. Among them:

• You will almost surely have to lay out a hefty down payment for a house (possibly as much as 25 to 30 per cent of the purchase price) and also sign a mortgage binding you to regular payments for your house over a period as long as twenty to thirty years.

• You will be committed to the care of your home over this same period— much like the obligation of time, energy, and money in rearing a child. You well may squirm under the burden of home repairs and upkeep for which you, the owner, will be responsible. These can be costly—reaching, particularly on an older house, a full 2 per cent of the average homeowner's take-home pay. You will have to be your own landlord, superintendent, garbage man, fix-it man, etc.

• If you should be forced to move, it might take you months or even years to sell your home for what you consider a fair price.

IN FAVOR OF RENTING

Among the positive advantages of renting:

• Renting gives you much more financial flexibility than home ownership. If your income slumps or your job involves frequent transfers, your commitment lasts only as long as your lease.

• It is probably the best initial course for a young couple with limited financial means. You shouldn't rush long-term decisions until you have children and a definite idea of where and how you want to live permanently.

• Renting holds distinct advantages if you are moving into a new neighborhood, particularly in a fast-growing suburb. If possible, rent for a year or so, and become thoroughly acquainted with the area before making a final decision to invest and settle.

• Renting means that taxes, insurance, major repairs, and often costs of utilities too are the landlord's responsibility.

• In some places it may be simpler for you to find suitable quarters by renting.

YOU WILL BOTH RENT AND BUY

In this era the odds are that you will *both rent and buy*. The odds are that you will own a home over a much greater span of your lifetime than you'll rent. And the odds are that the living space you buy will cost you significantly less than the space you rent.

A NEW OR AN OLD HOUSE?

IN FAVOR OF AN OLD

If you are in the market for a house in the winter months, in most parts of the United States the likelihood is that you will buy one already built—possibly long enough ago to be called an "older" or even an "old" house. What's more, older houses are the only ones available in some areas, so the statistical probability is that no matter when you are looking for a house—summer, winter, fall, or spring—you will be vitally interested in the pros and cons of buying an older house.

Here is your rundown:

• You'll probably be able to buy an older house for about 10 to 15 per cent less than a new one—in terms of the space you get for each home-buying dollar. Also, if you're buying from the owner, he may be willing to bargain on price, for the simple reason that home selling is not his sole business. (The exception is in areas where old-fashioned houses are "in.")

• The rooms—and the house as a whole—probably will be more gracious and spacious, and the house generally will be more comfortable. Try to assign values to such extras as walk-in closets, porches, entrance rooms, basement space, sheds, the like—in terms of dollars and in terms of their intangible value to you.

• Try especially to measure the worth of the character and warmth you'll find in so many older houses. It's up to you to put your own money tag on the "feeling" you get in one house versus another.

• The construction, including materials and workmanship, is likely to be of considerably higher quality.

• Frequently the house will be located in an established neighborhood involving long-established landscaping of the neighborhood as a whole. This will give you a better idea of what it would be like to live there than would a new house in a whole new community. The land surrounding the house itself will have been landscaped too.

• Its kinks and shortcomings—such as a dilapidated porch or peeling wallpaper or exposed water pipes—will advertise themselves loudly to you when you inspect the house. Flaws in a new development house—a badly poured foundation or poorly spaced joists under the floor—may be hidden.

• The variety of shapes, sizes, and designs of older houses from which to choose probably will be greater than the variety of new homes offered by builders or developers. And old house styles, remember, have stood the tests of time.

• Taxes tend to rise less sharply for older houses than for newer ones—and the burden of special assessments for improvements such as utilities and town water systems may be less since many of these amenities will already have been installed and paid for.

AGAINST THE OLD

Of course, the above is merely one side of the older-home-buying tale—and it would be a disservice to you if I were to stop at this. To suggest some of the points against the older house:

• You may find it tougher to get a mortgage on an older house than on a new one, and other terms—down payment, duration of mortgage—also may be less favorable on the older house.

• The older house may need costly repairs and remodeling and the major modernization jobs can run into big-time money unless your family includes devoted and gifted do-it-yourselfers.

• Your upkeep costs may be greater than for a new house, simply because there's more space to heat and light, more surface to paint, more trees to prune, more rooms to clean.

• Older houses tend to be less tight than newer ones, meaning there's greater heat loss.

• You may be offered more space than you actually want—and you may find utterly useless certain types of space: butlers' pantries, libraries, large attics. In the same category might go the lack of scientific design in many older houses, so that traffic may flow awkwardly from room to room.

• Few older houses will have central air conditioning, new built-in appliances and other conveniences which are often part of new homes.

• And you really don't know the full cost of your older house until you have repaired and remodeled—and these expenses may more than offset that 10 to 15 per cent lower cost.

This is a balanced and honest picture which can save you money, time, and headaches as you probe the older house market.

HOW TO SHOP FOR A NEIGHBORHOOD

Let's say your family has agreed that a house is for you and it will be a good investment. You know in general where you would like to live, what type of house you would like to live in, how much house you can really afford.

Your next steps are to find the specific community and the precise neighborhood which will be most comfortable and convenient for you and in which living costs—over and above the costs of the house itself—will be best suited to your budget. The neighborhood you choose is crucial to whether your investment in your house ultimately turns out to be excellent, just fair, or an out-and-out disaster.

To help you shop for a community and a neighborhood, make inquiries in these key areas:

PROPERTY TAXES

Even in the mid-seventies—when our collective, nationwide property tax bill is moving toward $50 billion—the new and naïve home buyer may underestimate what a huge and growing expense property taxes are. In some rural and exurban towns, local taxes pay only for schools, roads, and miscellaneous expenses. In other, larger cities and towns, taxes cover not only these basics but also the costs of an enormous range of services: the town water supply and sewage disposal system, garbage collection and disposal, the fire and police departments, health and welfare, the towering costs of preventing and eliminating pollution.

The tax on a house, in practice, is a *going charge* just as rent is. Next to your mortgage payment, your tax bill is likely to be your second biggest home ownership cost, and property taxes for years have been among the fastest-rising items in your total living costs. Even if your home deteriorates, your property taxes almost surely will continue to rise, for cities rarely reduce the valuation of a home.

Of course, property taxes vary widely from community to community. But the closer you get to a big city, the higher rates tend to be, and the farther out in the rural countryside you go, the lower they tend to be. Consider this factor when you are choosing a place to live and estimating your costs of home ownership. And when you investigate tax rates in a community, find out how land and houses of the type you would like to buy are valued.

Good sources for this information will be a real estate agent, people living in the neighborhood, and officials at the town offices.

Look out too for special assessments. Here you will find a wide range, depending on the project involved and the community.

A new road, for example, may result in an assessment on the homeowners concerned, which can make a mockery of any carefully worked out family housing budget. A neighborhood landscaping project, on the other hand, may not be too costly and also may greatly enhance the value of the property. Special assessments are a variable item, but woe to the family who forgets them! They will always come up sometime!

Ask a real estate agent, a courteous banker, and any other knowledgeable sources you can find, these questions on property taxes in each community and neighborhood in which you are considering buying:

• When a property changes hands, what usually happens to taxes on that property? In many communities new homeowners are routinely sledgehammered by the tax assessors and slapped with tax bills which are far higher than the amounts the former owners were paying.

• What does the community provide in return for your taxes? Low taxes may *not* be a bargain if they mean inferior schools, second-rate police protection, poor snow removal and garbage disposal services. On the other hand, high taxes may be well worth it—if a community is committed to high educational standards, rigid water and air pollution controls, modern sewage disposal systems, water fluoridation, good health and recreational facilities, clean and green roadsides.

• What new bond issues are being debated or scheduled in each community—for schools, sewage treatment facilities, road-building equipment, public parks and playgrounds, hospitals, etc.? What will be the likely impact of the issues on tax rates? Or, if a costly new school is being planned or built, for which a bond issue already has been voted, what tax hikes may already have been announced for the coming year?

• Is a major re-evaluation of properties in the offing—and what will be the likely hike in the valuation of houses in the community and neighborhood in which you wish to settle? In some areas, tax reassessments have doubled or even tripled tax bills for certain homeowners.

Take the time to visit the town hall or county seat. Ask for full details on property and other local taxes in the area in which you think you would like to buy. Get the facts on how fast these taxes have been rising. Ask for estimates on likely future trends—especially if new roads, schools, sewers, and other community improvement projects are in the works.

And listen to local gossip. It can be far more accurate than you suspect.

SCHOOLS

School costs are usually a community's biggest budget item—and thus the local taxpayer's biggest financial commitment. So, wherever you settle, schools are crucially important in your comparisons of one community or neighborhood against another.

If you have or may have children, check the quality of local schools by talking with parents of children already enrolled, by visits with schoolteachers and PTA members. Ask to sit in on a couple of actual classes and, if you have school-age children, take them along.

Judge the quality of education provided not only by the school's physical plant. Judge also by how the teachers are accepted by the children in their classes; by how creative and stimulating the classroom atmosphere is; by what amount of money is spent per pupil as compared to the national and state averages; by the school's special services and facilities such as science and language laboratories; by the library, psychiatric and guidance counseling services; by how open-minded school officials are toward promising new teaching techniques.

Inquire at the school superintendent's office about the district's "achievement test rating" and compare this rating with state and national scores on pupil achievement.

Find out what kindergartens, nursery schools, and day care centers are available—and what costs are involved.

Look into the school bus services and study the bus route.

Investigate what other cultural-educational facilities the community offers, such as libraries, music, theaters.

CONVENIENCE

Ideally, your house should be as convenient as feasible for those who must commute to work.

For instance, if the family breadwinner must commute every day, how great a distance will that be? What forms of transportation are available? What are traffic conditions like? How reliable are the trains and buses?

Try a trial run yourself on the commuters' route during rush hour before you decide on a location. Do not underestimate the fact that almost any kind of commuting implies costly wear and tear—on yourself as well as your car.

Calculate commuting costs for a year—and compare these with commuting costs from houses in other communities in which you are considering buying or renting. These costs can range from $1.00 to $10.00 or more a day, so make the effort to track down specifics. Also, figure on these costs rising fairly steeply in the years ahead. Remember this point: if you could, through the choice of the neighborhood in which you buy a house, eliminate just $1.00 from the daily commutation, this could add up to savings of $250 or more a year.

Ideally, your house also should be near a good shopping district where the prices are within your budget.

It should be near the church you will attend, if you are a churchgoer.

It should be in a location where children can play. Preschool children should be able to play in places within sight of the house. Older children should have parks, playground, or other play facilities within half a mile of the house.

It should be reasonably close to service stations, medical facilities, banks, airports, and theaters.

And if you or your spouse or both of you are likely to want to go back to college in the near future, you should plan to live near a university or community college.

CHARACTER

You almost surely would prefer to live in an area in which you can find people of more or less compatible background and interests. So take the time to drive—and walk—around communities and neighborhoods which appeal to you, either because you know and like people who live there or because you like the area's general appearance.

Look for a neighborhood that is stabilized or, even better, is improving. Make sure it is not deteriorating, for as the value of your neighbors' houses decreases the value of your house will be affected too. Check for signs of deterioration by noting the general state of surrounding dwellings, whether they are well tended or neglected; by counting the number of "for sale" signs and studying the trend of sale prices in the locality; by investigating the encroachment of commercial establishments; by counting the number of dwellings for rent. Experienced appraisers agree that when more than one quarter of the houses in a neighborhood are rented, rather than owned, the neighborhood is declining.

Ask about recent crime trends in the community or neighborhood—especially the record of burglaries and break-ins.

Inquire about how local officials and citizens' groups are going about enforcing laws against polluting the community's air and water—and whether they have a reputation for toughness.

Among the signs of an economically healthy community:

• A record of relatively full employment in periods of recession as well as in booms.

• A slow but steady growth in job opportunities and population—or at least no significant population decline. The town offices will have facts and figures from the 1970 as well as the 1960 Census—and these will spell out the trends for you.

• Steadily rising income levels.

• Steadily rising real estate values.

ZONING AND PLANNING

Make a point of inquiring about zoning regulations affecting the neighborhood and the entire community. You should be able to locate a serious, local planning-conservation commission dedicated to keeping community growth attractive and orderly.

If you envision building a new wing or a guest cottage or a garage in the future, find out *before you buy* whether zoning rules would permit such an addition.

Ask about the zoning rules not only on the property you want to buy but also on nearby tracts of undeveloped land—and other property in the neighborhood. What, for instance, about overnight parking on the street in which you might choose to live?

And ask to see the master land use plan for the community as a whole and its surroundings. (If there is no plan, that in itself is a signal to you to find out why not.)

CHECK LIST FOR SIZING UP A NEIGHBORHOOD

The following abbreviated check list should be useful to you in sizing up a neighborhood—and comparing the merits of one neighborhood with those of another:

	NEIGHBORHOOD A	NEIGHBORHOOD B
Is neighborhood attractive?		
Are good public schools available?		
Are there sound zoning ordinances?		
How much will the yearly property taxes be?		
What is the outlook for special assessments?		
Are there any objectionable noises or smells?		
How many miles (and minutes) to workplace?		
What public transportation is available?		
Is bus or train stop nearby?		
What will monthly commuting costs be?		
Will second car be needed?		
How many miles (and minutes) to shopping center?		
How many miles (and minutes) to nearest grocery store?		
Are there parks and/or playgrounds nearby?		
How far away is the church you'll attend?		
Where are theaters, movies, libraries?		

	NEIGHBORHOOD A	NEIGHBORHOOD B
How far is school bus stop?	_____	_____
Will you be able to keep pets?	_____	_____
Are streets well lighted?	_____	_____
Is adequate police and fire protection provided?	_____	_____
Are pollution controls enforced?	_____	_____

How to Shop for a House

You have decided, within reasonable limits, where you want to live and what kind of a house you want to own. You are now ready to begin your search for a specific house.

WHERE DO YOU BEGIN?

You can get in your car and simply start cruising around whatever neighborhoods you have already checked out and like, looking for the "for sale" signs and querying residents on available houses, prices, and possibilities.

You can, if you're looking for a house in or near the neighborhood where you have been living, simply get word around among friends, acquaintances, and tradespeople of the type of house you're looking for.

You can start merely by studying the local newspaper. You may be lucky enough to spot a good house advertised for sale by its owner and in any event the newspaper real estate ads will give you clues to prices being asked for the category of house in which you're interested.

In fact, it is worth spending a day or two checking out these ways of locating a house, just to see what may be available among properties not listed by real estate agents.

But the chances are you'll begin your serious search by consulting a real estate broker or agent—preferably a Realtor who is a member of the National Association of Realtors and who subscribes to the association's code of ethics. (Realtor is a trade mark registered by the NAR.)

He or she not only has a large bank of information on what types of property are available, where, and at what prices. He also is familiar with the housing market in general. He knows details on zoning and highway building plans. A Realtor can arrange appointments for you to see the type of house you want, inspect these houses with you, give you informed advice on likely costs of maintenance, taxes, repairs, and other matters. He can help you assess the future of neighborhoods, the value of the home as a long-range investment, tell you what is the cheapest kind of mortgage available to you.

Choose a Realtor with care!

Look for one you feel you can trust implicitly. Tell him or her how much you can afford, as exactly as you possibly can, what type of property you would like to own—and where.

Typical Realtors' fees are 6 to 8 per cent of the selling price of a house and 10 per cent of the price of raw land. These fees are paid by the person selling the house or land—not the buyer, although the seller frequently jacks up his price to cover the Realtor's fee.

Most Realtors keep in touch with other Realtors and agents in the area who might have the type of property for which you are shopping. And he or she may also be tied into a new computer system which keeps a huge amount of information on listings throughout the area or even the United States. The largest system of this type in operation today—to which hundreds of Realtors in all states subscribe—is Realtron, a Detroit-based computer service real estate data bank.

WHERE DO YOU FIND THE BARGAINS?

Your Realtor should be able to guide you to housing bargains in the area—if there are any.

You might, for instance, find a bargain on a property on which the mortgage has been foreclosed. This could be a house that a bank or other lender is eager to sell before the house starts to deteriorate from disuse.

Or you might find housing bargains at the outskirts of a suburb, in the path in which the population appears to be moving. You won't find all the conveniences of the suburbs, such as superhighways and shopping centers. But you will find lower property taxes and lower land prices. If this interests you, check out the possibility of employment in the suburb adjoining this exurb—as well as all the commuting angles if either or both of you are working in the central city.

Or you could find house bargains in a neighborhood which is now run down but which was attractive once. Look closely at neighborhoods which seem in line for urban renewal or intensive restoration. Washington's Georgetown district and New York City's Greenwich Village are classic examples of formerly depressed neighborhoods which have become ultrafashionable and ultraexpensive. This area of bargains can be exceedingly tricky and dangerous, though. You must be able to distinguish between a run-down neighborhood in line for rebirth and a deteriorating section doomed by a new superhighway, housing project, factory or other commercial development.

Or your source of bargains could be the house with several unfinished rooms which deter other buyers but which you would be perfectly content to finish off later as your family expands. And if your family includes a do-it-yourselfer, you have a natural money saver built in.

And finally, there's the charming "freak house" or the crazy combination of Victorian and colonial—which has been on the market for months or years and has been knocked way down in price. If you are willing and able to invest the necessary amounts to restore and modernize it, if your family finds it comfortable, and if you plan to live in it for quite a few years, the "freak" you fall in love with may be a perfect answer for you—and available at a real bargain price, too. This goes even though you, in turn, may have a tough time selling your freak at the price you think it's worth years hence.

HOUSE SHOPPING DO'S AND DON'TS

Take a notebook and pencil with you when you go on a house-hunting tour and, if possible, a Polaroid camera as well. Write down the name, address, and phone number of each owner—and the name and number of the real estate agent handling the deal. Make notes on all points of special interest to you—and note also the specific problems which you spot in each. Snap a couple of pictures of each house which tempts you—for later reference and to show other family members.

By all means, use the check lists in this section to help you rate one house against another.

If it is an older house you are inspecting, query the seller on these points:

• Why he wants to sell the house—especially if his reasons have to do with the building's problems.

• What his tax bills are—and are likely to be in the near future, and how fast they have been rising.

• How much the utility bills run each year. (Ask to see actual copies of a year's bills, particularly most recent months.)

• Which major improvements have been made—and specifics on such matters as how deep the artesian well is, the location and type of the septic tank and leaching field, the status of the war against the invading termites.

• Also, if you and your family tend to be away from home a lot—on business trips, vacations—find out whether the house can be easily turned off, closed up, and left to take care of itself.

Don't be swayed because you first saw a house when the dogwood or the lilac bushes were in bloom. You are not buying bushes and trees. You are buying a *house!* Look at the house both during the day and at night, when it's gray and raining as well as bright and shining, when it's cold as well as hot.

Don't stray too far from the original "dream house" your family agreed it wanted. If there are such specialized rooms as family rooms, dens, sewing rooms, tool sheds, "rec" rooms which you did not include in your original requirements, you'll pay a considerable sum for this space. Do you need it? Do you even want it?

Do try to avoid, if possible, shopping for a house or apartment in the spring or fall—the two busiest seasons of the year, and the times when prices also tend to be highest because so many buyers are stumbling over one another in the real estate market place.

And *don't* let yourselves be stampeded into a deal. Many real estate brokers will exert at least some pressure on you—for example, by telling you that another buyer is hot on the track of the house you are viewing. Many a family, in fact, has jumped into a purchase of a not really suitable house just to keep it away from a competitor.

Do consider, as you hunt for a house, its future resale value. The biggest pluses include a good location, in a stable but progressive community; good-sized living spaces; adequate closet and other storage space; good kitchen and laundry facilities; and a convenient arrangement of rooms.

Do, before you buy an older house, have a contractor look over the house and estimate costs of any major, basic repairs in these seven key areas: foundation and basement, roof, heating plant, plumbing, electrical wiring, sewage system, paint on the outside of the house. If you cannot find a qualified contractor, professional engineer, or other consultant to advise you on the structural soundness of the house, the town engineer may be willing to do so.

Do also consult individual specialists such as plumbers, electricians, roofers, and exterminators for advice if you fear other major problems may exist. These people will probably give you their advice free—on the basis that you'll use their services if it turns out that major repairs are needed. Or you may find a consulting firm which specializes in going over a house, uncovering its faults, and estimating costs of correcting them.

APPRAISING THE HOUSE

Surely, in view of the investment you are making, you owe it to yourself to spend a small sum to discover—*before* you buy—whether the house is likely to fall apart, burn down, be ravaged by termites. Surely you will be willing to pay an appraiser a fee to hear whether the house's asking price is fair and reasonable.

An appraiser should assess the design and structural aspects of the house; delve into prices at which comparable properties are being sold; inform you on the quality and character of the neighborhood, zoning regulations, population trends, property tax levels and prospects; estimate the community's economic growth patterns.

Ask the Chicago-based American Institute of Real Estate Appraisers or the National Association of Realtors (155 East Superior Street, Chicago, Ill. 60611) for names of qualified appraisers in your area. Although you have no real yardstick of an appraiser's competence, one guide you can use is whether the appraiser is a member of the American Institute of Real Estate Appraisers or a member of the Society of Real Estate Appraisers which certifies appraisers who can pass an examination in this field and meet other professional standards as well. Look for the designations M.A.I. (Member of the

Appraisal Institute), R.M. (Residential Member), of S.R.A. (Senior Residential Appraiser) following the appraiser's name in the Yellow Pages.

Expect to pay at least $75 to $200 for an appraisal—and make sure you get a written report on the inspector's findings.

Your best sources of names of qualified home appraisers and/or inspectors are:

your Realtor (who may be qualified to make the appraisal himself);

any bank which extends mortgages;

an established builder or local builders' association;

the town engineer;

the Yellow Pages—under either "Appraisers—Real Estate" or "Real Estate Appraisers."

AN APPRAISAL QUESTIONNAIRE

Here's a questionnaire for you and/or your professional appraiser to use as a guide in judging design and structural aspects of a house:

• Are there termites? If termite damage already has occurred, how serious is it and what must be done to correct it? If an underground termite shield has been installed around the outside of the house, is it installed properly? Do other houses in the neighborhood have termite problems—a clue that your house also could be a target?

• What is the condition of the electrical circuits? How many and where are the outlets—and is the number adequate for your needs? How old is the wiring and is it sufficient to carry the load of appliances and lighting your family would put on it? Inadequate wiring is hazardous and shortens the life of your appliance.

• What is the state of the plumbing and water supply? Is the water pure? Soft? What does it taste like? Is there adequate water pressure—especially when several faucets or appliances are running at the same time? Enough hot water? Are the plumbing pipes of brass, copper, galvanized iron, or plastic, and in what condition are these pipes? Is any major plumbing work likely to be needed before you can move in? Do all the faucets, drains, and other plumbing fixtures work well? Is each bathroom complete with all the fixtures and accessories you need?

• What type of sewer system is there—and where are the drainage pipes, septic tank, cesspool, or whatever? If there is a cesspool or septic tank, are drains provided with a grease trap? Is it a proper system in terms of soil types in the area, state and local zoning and/or health codes? Is there any visible seepage above ground? If the owner does not have enough information to satisfy you, see if the local government has a record of the building permit application, which describes the type of sewage system installed.

• What type of hot water heater is there? What are the monthly costs for normal use? How many baths or showers can be taken, one after another, within a given period of time such as one hour? And, once the hot water supply has been depleted, how long does it take to heat another round of baths and showers?

• What is the age and condition of the furnace? Is it capable of heating the house to at least 70° when the outside temperature reaches the lowest point for this area? Has it been well serviced or does it contain fire hazards? What are the yearly costs of heating the house?

• Of what material are the foundation walls and are these walls in good condition? On what type of footing does the foundation sit? If the house doesn't rest on solid rock, does it have, as it should, poured concrete footings *below* the frost line in the area?

• What type of basement is there? Is it properly ventilated? Is it dry— or have any leaking basement problems already been corrected? Is there a drain in the basement? (Check this on a rainy day.) What protection does the house have against invasion by water—from the ground or from flooding resulting from rain? Is there, for example, a heavy plastic "vapor barrier" between your foundation floor and the ground underneath? Do the outsides of the foundation walls have a moistureproof coating? Are there footing drains under the ground outside the house leading away from it at the base of the foundation? Are you likely to have a leaky, wet basement?

• What type of soil is the house built on? Is there any evidence of settlement which could cause damage to the foundation?

Is the house solidly built? Does it meet local zoning laws?

• Of what materials is the house built—especially the "basics" such as girders, columns, sills, joists? Are they of the proper size and spacing?

• Are the floors in good condition—and hard enough for the wear and tear they are likely to suffer? Will they support a heavy load such as a piano or water bed? Are they noisy when someone walks on them? (Jumping up and down on floors may reassure the jumper that the floors won't collapse under such provocation. It also will yield a clue to how rigid (good) or springy (not good) the floor is. But this test might *not* reveal serious decay in the sills or other supports holding up the floor, too narrow or otherwise inadequate joists beneath the floor, termite damage and other problems. Take a flashlight, go down to the basement or crawl space, and examine the ground floor from its underside if it is not covered with plaster or paneling.)

• What is the condition of the attic and is it strong enough for storage purposes or for building extra living quarters if needed? Is it well ventilated? Are the framing and sealing around the chimney tight enough to prevent leaks when it rains?

• In what condition is the garage? Will your car or cars fit in it? Is it big enough to provide the type of storage and work spaces you need? If the garage is on a second floor, are the floor and framing strong enough to support a car?

• Are the plaster or plasterboard walls and ceilings smooth? Or are there cracks which could be evidence of settling of the house? How easily can any cracks be filled? In the case of plasterboard, are the seams neatly sealed?

• Is the inside trim, such as moldings and baseboards, in good condition? What about hardware such as locks and knobs? Do doors close properly and are there good outside door locks? Are the windows weather-stripped? Are the kitchen cabinet doors properly hung?

• If there is a fireplace, does the damper open and close properly—to prevent heat escape when the fireplace is not being used? Is there a heatilator which will cut fuel bills and, if so, is it rusty or is it sound?

• Is the house insulated? What type and how thick is this insulation—especially overhead, but also in the exterior walls? If new or more insulation is needed, how expensive a project is that likely to be?

• What material has been used for exterior walls? What condition are the walls in? Is the exterior of the house attractive-looking? Will walls and/or trim need scraping and painting—and how much of a job is that likely to be? (A new paint job on the outside of an average-size house may cost $500 to $1,500 or more, depending on how much scraping, caulking, priming, and other preparation are needed.)

• In what condition is the roof and will any roofing repairs be needed? How many years will the present roof last?

• If the house—or roof—is shingled, what type of shingles are they? Wood? Asphalt? Some other material? If shingles are wood, are they the chemically fireproofed type? If forest fires or fires generally are a real hazard in the area, how much would it cost to substitute some other type of roofing for untreated wood shingles?

• What about the gutters and leaders? What maintenance is necessary to keep them in workable condition?

• Are the storm windows and doors in good condition? What about screens?

• In what condition is the masonry throughout—such as foundations, basement floor, walkways, fireplace, chimneys? Is mortar tight and solid or loose and flaky? If there are serious cracks or missing bricks, or if chimneys are improperly lined, what would it entail to correct these problems? (Note: cracks in the foundation do *not* necessarily mean a major masonry project is needed—but check this point carefully.)

• Which major appliances are included in the deal, and which will you have to buy? Today, more than half of new homes being built include dishwashers; more than 90 per cent include stoves, and more than one third have a central air conditioning system.

• How easy—or difficult—will the house be to keep clean (Note: a house which is air conditioned tends to be easier to keep clean than one which is not).

• Is there enough light?

• What is the exposure of the house: does it face east, west, north, or south? A northern exposure may mean that a garden will be relatively difficult to cultivate and also may mean higher fuel bills in winter. But it may be more comfortable in summer. As a general rule, a southern, eastern, western exposure or some combination of these is more agreeable than a house facing the north, northeast, or northwest. This is particularly true for kitchens, porches, patios, and living rooms.

For more guidance on checking out a house send for the booklet *Basic Housing Inspection* (U. S. Department of Health, Education and Welfare, Room 1587, Parklawn Building, 5600 Fishers Lane, Rockville, Md. 20852 Free).

Check Lists

CHECK LIST FOR COMPARING SPECIFIC HOUSES

The following abbreviated check list will help you compare and rate one specific house against another.

	House No. 1	House No. 2
Location of house		
Name of owner or builder		
His address and telephone number		
Realtor's name		
Realtor's telephone number		
Price asked		
Down payment required by lender		
Term of mortgage		
Monthly mortgage payments		
Estimated closing costs		
Yearly property taxes		
Deed restrictions, if any		
Estimated cost of immediate repairs		
Type or style of house		
Total floor space (sq. ft.)		

	House No. 1	House No. 2
Number of rooms	_____	_____
Bedrooms	_____	_____
Bathrooms	_____	_____
Dimensions of living room (*Measure.* Empty rooms appear deceptively large.)	_____	
Size of kitchen	_____	_____
Dining room?	_____	_____
Fireplace?	_____	_____
Type of heating system	_____	_____
How many closets?	_____	_____
How big are the closets?	_____	_____
Is there at least one closet for each bedroom?	_____	_____
Is there a linen closet?	_____	_____
Other storage space?	_____	_____
Is there a separate laundry room?	_____	_____
Utility room?	_____	_____
"Mud" room?	_____	_____
Garage?	_____	_____
Size of garage? How many cars?	_____	_____
Does it have electrical outlets?	_____	_____
How much garage storage space?	_____	_____
Is there an entrance from garage to kitchen?	_____	_____
What type of water supply?	_____	_____
What type of sewer system?	_____	_____
Sanitary?	_____	_____
Storm?	_____	_____
Basement?	_____	_____
—or crawl space?	_____	_____

	House No. 1	House No. 2
How big?	————	————
Which appliances are included?	————	————
Stove	————	————
Range hood	————	————
Refrigerator	————	————
Dishwasher	————	————
Garbage disposal	————	————
Clothes washer and dryer	————	————
Air conditioning	————	————
Freezer	————	————
Other	————	————
Is carpeting included?	————	————
Is there a separate entrance hall?	————	————
Are kitchen and living room protected from through traffic?	————	————
Are bedrooms near baths?	————	————
Do the size and layout permit enough privacy?	————	————
How soundproof is the house—especially bedrooms?	————	————
Are there enough outside doors?	————	————
Are they equipped with foolproof locks?	————	————
How difficult would escape be if fire broke out? (High, small bedroom windows a minus.)	————	————
Does house have "character"?	————	————
Notes on other good *and* bad points		

CHECK LIST FOR THE KITCHEN

Now, starting through the house, make notes on these important aspects of the kitchen (the most costly room per square foot) in each house you are considering:

Yes   No

Over-all dimensions
Size of sink
Amount of counter space and other work surfaces
Amount of shelf and cabinet space
Location of sink in relation to stove
Location of refrigerator in relation to stove and sink
Location of counter in relation to stove and sink
Stove vent fan
Overhead lighting
Lighting for work surfaces
Type and condition of appliances
Type of and ease of cleaning kitchen floor
View of outdoor play area
Light from outside
Distance to family room or living room
Size of eating area
Condition of pipes
Wall covering

CHECK LIST FOR THE LIVING ROOM

And note these important aspects of the living room in each house you might buy:

Yes   No

Are floors sturdy, attractive?
If carpeted, what is underneath?
Is there a fireplace and does it work?
Does it include heatilator?
Does chimney draw well?
Is there adequate wall space for furniture? Pictures?
Are views to the outside attractive?
Are there bookshelves?
Are type and color of wall coverings suitable?
If there is a sliding glass door, does it work?
Is it shatterproof?
Do windows and doors permit cross-ventilation?

CHECK LIST FOR THE BATHROOMS

Yes   No

Is grout in tiled areas in good condition?
How handy—and how large—is the linen closet?
Is the medicine cabinet large enough?
Are there outlets for a razor, hair dryer, etc.?
Is lighting, especially near mirror, adequate?

                                                        Yes   No

Is there an exhaust fan?
Can door locks be opened easily from outside in event of an emergency?

CHECK LIST FOR OUTSIDE OF THE HOUSE

                                                        Yes   No

Now, on the outside of each house, explore these questions:
Is siding of good construction and in good condition?
Are windows and doors weather-stripped?
Is there proper flashing over doors and windows?
What is the type and condition of the gutters?
Are storm and screen windows in good condition?
Is chimney masonry in good condition?
Is porch in sound condition?
How up to date is the paint job?
Is the roof in good shape?
Are there enough hose connections?

CHECK LIST TO JUDGE THE LOT

Here, finally, is a compact check list which will help you judge the lot
which goes with a house—assuming you have already jotted down the size
and shape of the lot and the location of the property lines.

                                                        Yes   No

Is lot big enough for your needs?
Is parking space adequate?
Does driveway permit turning around?
Is its length or grade excessive if area is snowy?
Is general topography attractive?
Is there a patio?
Or terrace?
Or back yard?
What dimensions?
How many big trees are there?
Do they appear healthy?
Is there enough privacy from neighbors?
Can garbage cans be concealed?
Is there a garden or room for a garden?
Will the soil type permit a garden?
Are wires or gutters obtrusive?
Are views pleasant?
How much landscaping has been done?

What About Buying a Co-operative Apartment?

HOW A CO-OP WORKS

Today, Americans of all types and *all* income brackets—from millionaires to those existing on poverty incomes, from swinging singles to elderly retirees—are buying and living in co-operative apartments and condominiums. These types of housing, in fact, are now the *most rapidly expanding* of all permanent housing categories in the United States. Of every seven new apartments, one is a co-op or condominium.

Many of the rules for buying a house apply to co-ops and condominiums as well. For if you enter a co-operative or condominium, you are *buying*. But there are significant variations and differences too.

First, here's how a co-operative works:

• A co-operative is a corporation, with shareholders, elected directors, and officers. Each shareholder has a voice in how the entire co-op is managed (usually by a professional manager or management firm).

• When you buy into a co-operative building you are buying stock in the whole corporation which in turn owns and runs the building. The larger your apartment, the larger your "share" will be in the over-all organization. Today's range of co-op prices runs all the way from a few thousands to many hundreds of thousands of dollars.

• In addition to the purchase price of your shares in a co-operative, you pay a monthly *maintenance charge* which covers the mortgage on the entire building, property taxes, and general maintenance of the building as a whole. The amount of the maintenance charge depends on the size and location of your apartment.

• That portion of the maintenance fee which is earmarked to pay for mortgage interest and property taxes is deductible from your federal income taxes—with the exception of publicly subsidized co-ops, where only the non-subsidized portion is deductible.

• As a member of a non-profit co-operative, you are your own landlord. *You* help set the standards for the entire building. *You* help choose your own neighbors and *you* get the "profit" a landlord would otherwise get—in the form of lower monthly maintenance charges.

• Your costs compare favorably with the costs of renting. The Federal Housing Administration estimates that the cost of living in a co-operative is about 20 per cent less than the cost of renting. Also an advantage is that resident-shareholders tend to take better care of their surroundings than do rental housing tenants.

• Unlike the person who rents a house or apartment, the shareholder in a co-operative can benefit from an increase in the value of his share of the project. As the over-all value of the co-operative unit rises—in response to housing shortages and other factors—the value of each family's share rises too.

KEY DISADVANTAGES

• If too few shareholders sign up to share ownership and costs, those who have already bought in must accept hikes in their maintenance charges.

• Or if one or more other occupants default on their payments, *you* must make up for these losses.

• You usually must get the approval of the board of directors before you may sell to someone else or before you may make any major alterations in your apartment.

• Buyers sometimes must have all cash.

• In some areas, prices may be ridiculously inflated.

VITAL QUESTIONS TO INVESTIGATE

Before you buy into a co-operative, investigate these vital points:

How big a loan or, in a few places, a mortgage can you get from a lender on the shares you might buy? Normally the proportion is 50 to 80 per cent of the appraised value of your shares, but sometimes the proportion is far lower.

What interest rate will be charged on the loan? Typically, in the mid-seventies this rate is at least 1 to 2 per cent above regular mortgage interest rates—and sometimes it is more.

What is the neighborhood like? This is an important clue to whether or not an investment in a co-operative is likely to be sound.

What is the record on sale of the other apartments? Have they been sold to financially responsible individuals? Remember, you are, in effect, *going into business* with the other families in the building. You may be financially responsible; your next-door neighbor may not be.

If it is a new building, do you have reason to believe the builder is financially responsible and is in a position to fulfill whatever deal he makes?

What efforts has the builder made, if any, to reduce the risks involved to responsible investors when some default on their payments? It is crucially important to find out the extent of your risk.

Is the price fair? To find out, add up all your monthly costs—including the maintenance charges, utility costs, and debt service—and compare these with the amount it would cost you to rent a similar apartment.

Is the management professional and skilled? How will *your* gripes be handled?

If you had to or wanted to get out of the deal, exactly what would be the mechanics of doing so?

What About Buying a Condominium?

HOW A CONDOMINIUM WORKS

Buying a condominium is very much like buying a house or apartment, since you, the purchaser, get legal title to your own dwelling and are responsible for paying property taxes.

The key difference between a co-operative and a condominium, as one observer put it, is this:

"A co-operative is a batch of people owning one structure. A condominium is a batch of people owning a batch of structures."

• In a condominium, you buy your apartment—or house or second house —outright, with the usual down payment, mortgage, and legal paperwork. At the same time you are buying a share of the condominium's community property and facilities, which may include elevators, laundry rooms, garage, gardens, golf clubs, swimming pool, or a marina.

• You agree to pay monthly maintenance costs (although these tend to be far lower than in a co-operative) and you may deduct that portion of the costs going for mortgage interest and property taxes from your federal tax return.

• Since you have a deed (or "condominium declaration") and are the owner of your condominium, you may resell it or give it to anyone you choose —although the other owners often reserve a right of first refusal. And you usually are permitted to do anything you choose within your own four walls.

• You finance a condominium just as you would a house. Both the Federal Housing Administration and the Veterans Administration now back mortgages on condominiums. A mortgage is usually much easier to get for a condominium than for a co-op.

• An exceedingly important difference between a condominium and a co-operative is that, if others default or the whole condominium project fails, you are *not* held financially responsible for the failure. This becomes the problem of the mortgage lenders involved, not you.

• As a general rule, co-operatives are strictly apartments while condominiums may be "duplexes," "fourplexes" or "sixplexes"; separate "townhouses"—usually row houses and usually built in clusters; apartments or vacation cottages; or facilities at a "condominium campground."

• You have the advantage when you own a condominium of building up equity in the house or apartment as you pay off your mortgage. You also have the use of important community facilities.

• You can, when you own a condominium, particularly in a vacation resort, rent it to others—and, if its primary purpose is to produce income, you can get the added tax advantages of being able to deduct your expenses for repairs, maintenance, depreciation, etc.—with definite limitations on your deductions, though, if, you use the property personally and rent it only when you don't use it.

CONDOMINIUM PITFALLS

The condominium boom, however, is not all joys of tax-sheltered easy living, no lawn mowing or snow shoveling, community pools, health clubs, etc.

But just pointing out that there are weaknesses and that there have been serious abuses is not enough. How do you, a buyer, avoid the pitfalls? Here are several basic guides if you are considering the purchase of a condominium:

• The most fundamental rule of all is a thorough investigation of the seller/developer to be sure he is highly reputable, well financed and experienced in the field. Don't fail to check all resources available to you—including the local real estate board, local Better Business Bureau, banks, friends. Use the same basic rules in shopping for and judging a condominium as you would if you were buying into a co-operative or buying a separate house outright.

• Do not permit your deposit funds to be commingled with other developer funds, and instead, request that they be deposited into an escrow account with interest in your name. Ask, too, that any bank statement related to the account be forwarded to your attention. Don't compromise on this.

• Do not accept the statement of the real estate developer on real estate taxes. Be certain the information given you is accurate, and confirm what you have been told with local assessing authorities.

• Make sure you fully understand all lease situations, for there are increasing instances of developers maintaining fee ownership to the land under the condominium (thus creating a leasehold). Some hold onto the parking garage, others to the recreational amenities. These leaseholds do not necessarily present a problem to you, but they are vital in comparing costs. For instance, if Condominium A is priced at $55,000 with the seller maintaining ownership of the land and leasing it back to you at $500 a year, a comparable Condominium B with the land included is clearly worth more.

• Check whether the common area charge budget is realistic. If a developer establishes an unrealistically low budget to minimize the carrying charges and make the units more saleable, the result can be poor service and inadequate maintenance until the budget is increased and the extra costs passed on to you.

• Investigate the management to make sure it is experienced and well-regarded, for management will have a direct impact on the value of your investment.

• Do not accept mere promises of a swimming pool, clubhouse, tennis courts, etc. These amenities should be available before the developers start marketing their units.

• Find out about provisions for parking—particularly if you have two or more cars. Be sure the space is adequate for you.

• Study with care the condominium association rules, so you understand the meaning of such terms as "right of first refusal," "usage provisions," "rental restrictions," "pet restrictions." Don't risk learning their meaning after you have bought. Each condominium has its own rules on pets. What about children? Many do not allow children under the age of sixteen as permanent residents although they permit children to visit or remain on the premises for temporary periods and under certain regulations.

• If an apartment building is being converted to a condominium ("condo-conversion"), check whether the developer is certifying to the condition of the structure, electrical heat, plumbing, the like. In these cases, additional considerations must be the soundproofing of the building, adequate utilities, a strong structure. Hire a lawyer who knows condominium conversions to manage the transfer of title and definition of your property boundaries. Anticipate the rise in taxes that often follows conversion of an apartment condominium.

If you are now renting, don't overestimate the tax savings in condominium ownership. Your tax bracket is your adjusted gross, not your gross-earnings tax bracket. And whatever benefits accrue will be in the government's hands until receipt of your tax refund.

Finally, the IRS in early 1974 ruled that condominium owner associations *are not exempt* from federal income tax (previously, they had been). This opened up important tax questions which demand your close scrutiny.

Of course, the advantages of condominium ownership remain and the concept is valid in an era of steep and rising maintenance costs. But you must recognize and know how to avoid the pitfalls if you are to enjoy a condominium's benefits.

WHAT ABOUT BUYING IN A DEVELOPMENT?

IMPORTANT QUESTIONS

Millions of American families are now living, either temporarily or permanently, in housing developments—for the very good reason that developments, or tract houses, often offer the most economical deal in housing today. Just because they are developments, professional home builders are able to use mass-produced "modular" segments, computer-standardized designs clustered together, attached townhouses, and other means to control costs. And thus they are able to offer home buyers major financial advantages.

Most development houses sell for amounts ranging from $20,000 to $40,000 but prices can exceed $70,000.

Typically, most major appliances—and often central air conditioning as well—come with the house.

Typically, the home buyer may choose from several basic plans—any of which can be modified to suit his family's individual tastes and needs.

If you are thinking of buying in a housing development, consider these important questions:

• How much open, undeveloped outdoor space has been left for the use and enjoyment of everybody?

• Has the developer built around existing trees and shrubbery—or simply razed everything and superimposed a rigid plan on top of bare ground?

• Is the development planned so that there are cul-de-sacs and dead-end streets which prohibit fast, through traffic from whizzing by your house? Is there planning for parking? Sun exposure? Views from windows?

• Are the houses well constructed, from good-quality wood, paint, and other materials? A few chats with residents who have lived in similar houses in the community should reveal any major shortcomings in the design and construction of the houses. Supplement your conversations with your own close inspection plus the judgment of an outside builder-consultant.

• Are the houses situated on well-prepared building sites? If they were filled in by bulldozers, were they permitted to settle for a year or more before building was begun?

• Is there enough topsoil to plant a lawn and/or garden?

• Is the lot large enough to afford your family the amount of privacy you need and want? Or will you have to spend money to build a fence to separate yourselves from neighbors who are too close or too noisy?

IF YOU BUY ON THE BASIS OF A MODEL

If you decide to buy on the basis of a model, several months before your own house will be completed, discuss your special housing needs and wants as soon as possible with the builder. And negotiate the price you'll actually pay on this basis.

For example, you may want to forgo central air conditioning—at a possible saving of up to $1,000 or more—and use that money for more kitchen appliances. Or if you are planning a Japanese garden you may prefer to have the builder landscape your house with gravel instead of topsoil.

Before you make a decision based on a model home, get a full set of floor plans and specifications for the house you are agreeing to buy in writing—including everything from landscaping promises to wallpaper designs and paint colors.

Finally, *do not* sign any contract to buy a development (or any other) house, or put down the usual $50 to $100 "binder," before your lawyer has exhaustively checked the deal.

HOW TO AVOID "QUESTIONABLE" DEVELOPMENT BUILDERS

The field of development housing is riddled with promoters using high-pressure sales tactics and builders with exceedingly sleazy reputations. Nevertheless, there are ways to recognize the good, honest builder. Before you make any financial commitment on a house which has not yet been built or not yet been completed:

Ask whether he lives within the development—one sign he is willing to listen to his buyers' grievances.

Inquire whether or not he is a member of the National Association of Home Builders—no guarantee of, but definitely a clue to, his ethics.

Visit houses he has built previously to see if they are well built and well landscaped.

Check his reputation with the local Chamber of Commerce, local Better Business Bureau, the bank where he has his accounts, and his major suppliers.

Get a financial statement from the developer.

Try to find a couple of families or individuals who bought their present homes five or ten years ago from the builder-developer from whom you are considering buying. Ask *their* opinions on how the builder rectified construction errors and in general fulfilled his obligations.

Take your time in reaching your decision until *you* are satisfied—thoroughly—that all is well.

NEW TOWNS

Finally, there's the increasingly widespread, entirely *new town*—usually a community planned for a population of tens of thousands of families. Most new towns are situated in the exurbs of big cities. They come complete with shopping centers, parks, playgrounds, cultural facilities—and, often, jobs in offices and factories. And most new towns offer a variety of types of housing—ranging from small, inexpensive apartments to big, expensive individual houses.

The key advantages of new towns are that they:

eliminate the agonies of commuting, assuming the worker holds a job in the new town or nearby;

offer adequately large parks and other open spaces and fewer driving hazards because of their good, large-scale, long-range professional planning;

have the convenience of nearby schools, shopping centers and cultural attractions, a varied population, reasonable nearness to big cities;

generally do not have such big-city problems as high crime rates, filthy air and waterways, embarrassing slums.

However, unlike cities, new towns offer no "roots," traditional "charm," or ties with past history.

AND WHAT ABOUT A MOBILE HOME?

CHEAPEST LIVING SPACE AVAILABLE

Only recently the "Model T" of the U.S. housing industry, mobile homes now account for virtually all new homes in the $15,000-and-under price bracket, more than two out of three new homes in the $25,000-and-under price bracket, and half of all new homes.

So popular has this type of housing become, in fact, that an estimated one in six Americans is expected to be living in mobile homes by the end of the 1970s.

• Next to a tepee, a mobile home is about the least expensive living space you can buy today. And in the last decade prices have dropped while quality has risen. For minimum accommodations, the cost in 1975 could have been as little as $12 to $13 per square foot, or only $11,000 to $14,000 in all. Although the biggest, best-equipped double-wide mobile homes measuring 28 by 65 feet or more could have cost $30,000 or even more, the average new mobile home in the mid-seventies measured 14 by 69 feet and cost about $12,000 furnished. This was about $12 per square foot—or half the cost of a conventional house. Over its lifetime, the cost of owning a mobile home in this period averaged nearly $500 a year less than rental of most low-rent apartments available.

• In addition to the purchase price—assuming you do not own any land on which to put a mobile home—the typical rent charged for space in a mobile home park was in 1976 rarely more than $125 a month, depending on the region, the views, and the facilities offered.

• The personal property tax on a $10,000 mobile home in 1976 was only about $150 to $200 a year—plus, frequently, a small license fee—if the home was not taxed at a somewhat higher rate, as real estate. Generally, mobile homes are not taxed as real estate unless they are on permanent foundations.

• The cost of setting up the home according to a mobile home park's rules ranged between $60 and $600. Monthly maintenance and utility charges usually ran $25 to $50. What's more, when you buy a mobile home you avoid altogether the customary array of closing costs, legal fees, similar charges.

• Here's a dramatic illustration of the difference in costs of owning a mobile versus a conventional home, calculated by Professor Carl M. Edwards of Michigan State University:

The average direct cost of owning a $30,000 home with an 8½ per cent FHA-backed mortgage over thirty years—including mortgage, interest, taxes, insurance, maintenance, furnishings, water and sewer charges, all the rest—approximates $378 a month. But the average direct cost of owning a mobile home over ten years approximates only $180 a month.

Edwards figures the average life of a mobile (also increasingly called "manufactured") home at ten years and depreciation at the rate of 20 per cent the first year and 7 per cent a year thereafter. However, these assumptions are probably conservative: a study commissioned by New York's First National City Bank found the average life of a mobile home to be fifteen years (new, better-built ones may last even longer), and depreciation to be only 10 per cent the first year and 5 per cent each succeeding year. On a desirable site, the value of a mobile home actually may grow. So the cost of owning a mobile home may be even lower than Professor Edwards' estimate.

• To summarize typical mobile home economics in 1976:

Basic home price	$12,000
Down payment (20%)	1,800
Balance to be financed	10,200
Monthly payment 5 years	229
Total financing costs	3,570
Total 60 monthly payments	13,590
Land	1,150
Installation	150

Financing terms on mobile homes also tend to be relatively "easy." In the mid-seventies the required down payment ranged between 10 and 30 per cent of the price of the home or as low as 5 per cent on federally insured loans less than $6,000 (10 per cent on any amount over $6,000), and the balance was repayable over a period ranging from five to fifteen years. Interest rates were high, though—typically 12 per cent on regular loans, and 7.6 to 10.6 per cent on federally insured loans. Under the 1969 Housing Act, the Federal Housing Administration will insure loans up to $10,000 for mobile homes ($15,000 for double-wides) but not the price of the land on which they sit, with repayment over twelve years and thirty-two days (fifteen years for double-wides). And under the 1970 Veterans Housing Act, the VA also will back loans up to $10,000, for up to twelve years to buy a mobile home, and up to $17,500 for fifteen years if a developed lot is included.

• Aside from the basic cost advantage, mobile homes are probably the most convenient form of housing available today—especially for people who intend to stay in one place only a short period of time—e.g., military personnel, college students, engineers on the move, many young married people, retirees. Most mobile housing comes equipped with all basic furniture and appliances.

• Maintenance costs are far below those for conventional housing. To day's mobile homes are fitted with the most modern, easily cleanable surfaces and outside walls which may be periodically washed instead of painted.

• In more luxurious homes, fireplaces, second bathrooms, cedar closets, front porches, and two-car garages also may be included. All you need do is add pots and pans, linens, silverware, a toaster—and you're ready to go.

• You can haul a mobile home from one place to another, anywhere you want if you want to badly enough.

• Mobile home parks often have a stronger sense of community than other areas of housing. Residents have a lot in common; visiting, neighborliness, and informality are the rule rather than the exception.

KEY DISADVANTAGES

However, among the key disadvantages of many of these homes are: smaller living space; inadequate amounts of storage space; lack of privacy from neighbors. They tend to be aesthetically poor. Moreover, some mobile homes have serious safety defects. For instance, few provide exits on both ends as well as in the middle, necessary to allow escape in a fire. Windows may be too small for emergency escape. Wiring is sometimes inadequate, and use of flammable materials is sometimes excessive.

Partly as a result of these defects, the average property loss in a mobile home fire in the past has been four times as high as in a conventional home, and the mortality rate in mobile home fires eight times as high. Consequently, it may cost as much to insure a $6,000 mobile home as it costs to insure a $40,000 conventional house.

Other safety defects which tend to crop up more frequently in mobile homes include the use of gas floor heaters (with grates that get hot enough to cook meat), furnace vents prone to blocking by snow, and poor electrical grounding by the installer.

And while mobile homes are perfectly safe with proper tie-downs, they can be blown over by high winds if they are improperly secured. To guard against this threat, follow the mobile home manufacturer's recommendations for tie-downs. (This alone may reduce the cost of your homeowner's insurance by as much as 10 per cent.)

The whole concept of "mobility" in mobile homes has long since faded. Few are ever moved once they are set in place, and experienced owners advise against it.

CHECK LIST OF QUESTIONS

In view of all the above, if you considering living in a mobile home park —even temporarily—it is important to check into the following questions:

• What recreational and other facilities are offered?

A typical mobile home park today will have paved streets, sidewalks, landscaping, parking facilities, a playground. Some will offer such extras as a swimming pool, community laundry building, clubhouse, fishing pond, golf course. You'll pay for any or all of these, so make sure you at least know what you are getting.

• What is the monthly site rental charge?

Some parks sell lots, but most rent. While the average in 1974 was $60 for a 4,000-square-foot site, the range was generally $30 to $120. Find out if there are any special charges above rent.

• How many sites are there and how big are the lots?

Avoid eyeball-to-eyeball arrangements in which you and your neighbors are just too close for privacy and comfort.

• What are the baby-sitting arrangements?

A tradition of friendly neighbors within a park can be a major fringe benefit to you, financially and otherwise. You can find out about this with just a few discreet questions.

• Is the park socially suited to your needs, your interests, your age bracket?

You might want to consider an "adults only" park or one geared to young couples with young children. Check this out.

• What services and utilities are provided and at what costs?

Include here such services as sewage disposal, water, electricity, gas, phone, TV cable, fire and police protection, garbage collection. Add up the costs of these utilities and services and check on which are not included. If you will be required to buy gas, oil, etc., from the park, how do prices and service compare to those of the local utilities?

• How much are the local personal property taxes?

This assumes you own your home, of course. Find out whether there is a monthly or yearly school tax or assessment.

• What are the rules and regulations of the park?

As an illustration, investigate the rules on pets, parties, gardening and landscaping, sale of your home if you move. In some parks, children are not permitted, but presumably you would find that out at the very start. Also, find out if the rules are enforced. A set of rules you like will not help if they are unenforced; if one or a few are casually broken, others will be too. Get a copy of all rules and restrictions *in writing*.

• What about storage space for bulky belongings?

These might range from big trunks to a boat, and it's a vital point. Your mobile home itself might not have sufficient storage space for anything except small luggage and personal items. What about your oversized packages of important papers? Out-of-season clothes? Skis? The like?

• How well designed and well managed is the park?

An excellent way to check this point is through a frank chat with several residents of the park about their experiences with management—especially how tenants' gripes and grievances are handled. Don't hesitate to go directly to a park's residents and ask questions. And go alone—*not* with the park's manager.

While studying the design, consider the view from the park and whether it appeals to you.

While judging management, use these clues:

Are the concrete slabs on which your mobile home may be located at least 4 inches thick? Is there adequate off-street parking space? Is there a paved walkway? Is the park's wiring underground? Are oil and gas tanks concealed? How well lighted are the streets? What security protection is there against vandalism and intruders? What is the park's general appearance? And finally, would your family feel at home there?

Woodall's *Mobile Home and Park Directory* ($5.95; Dept. 240, 500 Hyacinth Place, Highland Park, Ill. 60035) is considered the best source of ratings of about 13,000 mobile home parks on the market. It is revised annually and includes only those of the 24,000-plus parks in existence which meet basic standards for listing.

SHOPPING RULES

If you are shopping for a mobile home:

• Choose a dealer with the utmost care, since he may not only be selling you a home but also arranging the financing terms for you. Usually the dealer from whom you buy a mobile home then sells your loan contract to a bank or finance company. Also, he is the sole person responsible for honoring the home's warranty or for performing repairs which may be needed.

• Check the reputation of any dealer with whom you are considering doing business with the local banks, local business associations, and the Better Business Bureau. One indication of a dealer's reliability is whether he belongs to the Chicago-based Manufactured Housing Association. You also can go to a local mobile home park, simply knock on a few doors of homes similar to the one which interests you, and ask the occupants about the dealer's reputation.

• Compare what is and is not included in the purchase price. Normally, new mobile homes today are sold complete with kitchen range, refrigerator, water heater, furniture, draperies, carpeting, lamps—and furnace. Normally also, you pay extra for such optional equipment as air conditioning, dishwasher, garbage disposals, clothes washers and dryers, screen and storm windows, shutters, house-type doors and windows.

• Before you sign up for any financing deal offered by the dealer, investigate and compare rates and terms offered by other lenders.

• If you are not a veteran and therefore do not qualify for a mobile home loan backed by the VA, ask your local banks and/or savings and loan associations about mobile home interest rates. If you own the land on which the home will be placed and if it's properly zoned, these lenders may extend a more or less conventional mortgage loan. However, interest rates charged on non-insured mobile home loans by banks and other lenders are usually closer to those charged on automobile loans.

• Collect *all* the facts on the financing terms—including the annual interest rate, the total dollar finance charge over the life of the loan, the amount of the down payment, the repayment period, the amount of any miscellaneous costs related to the deal. Compare these terms—especially the *total* finance charge—on each mobile home you consider buying.

• Get estimates on the costs of all accessories and extras you will want or will be required to have by the rules of the mobile home park. The list of accessories ranges from front doorsteps and skirting to cover the crawl space underneath the home to shutters, and "facia"—panels of aluminum around the roofline, patio cover, and carport to "connect" these accessories visually. These can add 10 or 15 per cent to the price you pay for a mobile home.

• Check all the usual fixtures and equipment of a house—from air conditioning to storm windows—to make sure, first, that *they are there* (assuming you want and need them); second, *where* they are; and third, that they are in good operating condition. See that the furnace has a "gun" burner rather than the obsolete and dangerous "pot" burner. Find out whether the hot water heater capacity is the minimum 17 gallons or a more adequate 30 or 40 gallons.

• Find out whether the front tow hitch is removable—a plus on the better homes.

• Compare the weights of equal-size homes. Generally, heavier ones are better.

• Ask the dealer whether he will pay the costs of setting up and leveling your mobile home at its destination (even if he doesn't agree to do this at first, it may be a good bargaining point for you), along with the installation of the skirting around the bottom of the home. Many provide free delivery and installation anywhere within 75 or 100 miles, and charge only 75¢ or $1.00 per mile outside the free area.

• If a lot is included in the deal make sure a lot number and description of the lot appear in the mobile home sales contract.

• Look for the MHMA-TCA seals (Mobile Homes Manufacturers Association—Trailer Coach Association) near the doorways which tell you that the home meets certain basic building standards, a requirement in order to get FHA- or VA-backed financing.

• Look also for the UL safety seal of approval, which virtually guarantees safe electrical wiring.

• Ask the dealer to show you the "Official Mobile Market Report," the "Blue Book" of mobile homes published and updated every four months by the Judy Berner Publishing Co. of Westmont, Ill. This will help you compare current retail prices for all major models.

• If the furniture appears cheap or shoddy, ask the dealer how much of a discount he would give you if you furnished the mobile home yourself. His response may at least be an indication to you of the quality of the furniture he's offering with the home.

• Be sure a written warranty goes with each major appliance included in the home—including furnace, water heater, dishwasher, refrigerator, clothes washer and dryer.

• Before you sign any contract, also insist on getting the manufacturer's written warranty on the home itself, usually good for one year. Insist too that the dealer correct any defects you detect in it. If you cannot get satisfaction, request a service report from Consumer Action Bureau, Mobile Homes Manufacturers Association, Box 35, Chantilly, Va. 22021 (east of the Rockies) or Consumer Affairs Council, Trailer Coach Association, 3855 La Palma Avenue, Anaheim, Calif. 92806 (west of the Rockies).

• Finally, before you buy a mobile home consider all the alternative types of bargain-priced housing being produced today—including prefabricated permanent homes, homes built of modular units, houses and apartments (mainly in the cities and city fringes) which are being gutted and "instantly" fitted with entire new "packaged" interiors, and publicly subsidized low-cost housing.

The Legal Mechanics of Buying a Home

GET A LAWYER!

If you want to buy a refrigerator or kitchen stove, you can go to a dealer, put down your money, and take the goods home with you. Not so when you buy real estate. If the regulations and laws are not followed, you, the buyer, may lose a considerable amount of money or get a poor title or both.

The first, most basic rule you *must* obey is: get a lawyer! And get a general practitioner with special *know-how* about real estate in your chosen area. Do not enter any agreement—informal or formal—without your lawyer's guidance. And do not retain a lawyer "provided" by the seller: he represents the seller, not you. For more guidance on retaining a lawyer, see Part IV, "Your Rights and How to Get Them."

Do not even put a mark on a piece of paper—much less a check or a contract—without his approval. Consider your lawyer's fee an integral part of the price of the house. And discuss this fee openly before you retain him or her. Let there be no basis for misunderstanding or friction.

Here is a description of the three legal instruments a lawyer usually prepares when you buy a house. Go over them carefully so you will be able to ask intelligently for further information—no matter what type of shelter you are buying and no matter what its price level.

THE CONTRACT FOR SALE

When you have made at least a tentative decision to buy a house, you'll be asked to sign a commitment to buy, at a given price. This is a legal contract and it is called a contract for sale or "purchase agreement" or "contract," "bid," "binder," "offer to buy," "deposit receipt," "memo." You also will probably have to make a "good faith" deposit of a small percentage of the purchase price. This is also called "earnest money."

Some of the items that should be specified in a contract for sale are:

the purchase price;

when and how the purchase price is to be paid;

a brief legal description of the property (not simply a street address);

a description of any other property including furniture, carpets, and appliances included in the sale;

an agreement as to who will pay what portion of property taxes, insurance, water charges, and other costs which become (or became) due during the year;

the date on which the buyer will get possession of the property;

a guarantee that the seller will provide an abstract of title, title warranty, plus details on what type of title;

a statement that the seller will provide a specified type of deed at the time of settlement with details on any deed restrictions and that he also will provide a marketable title;

any other agreements reached between the buyer and seller—for instance, your right to cancel the deal if you can't get a mortgage;

a provision for the return of your initial deposit in the event the sale falls through for some reason other than your own failure to fulfill your part of the deal;

the signature of the seller.

Your lawyer can guide you on other legal points which may be involved in your transaction. Consult him on any questions or doubts you may have on this and all other documents involved in property buying.

Do not rely on verbal explanations from the seller or his agents on what any contract means.

THE TITLE SEARCH (OR ABSTRACT OF TITLE)

The title search is the next step in a real estate transaction. The title to a piece of property you buy represents your right, as owner, to free use of it (within the limitations of laws and zoning ordinances and perhaps also the deed itself)—and therefore also your right to sell or mortgage it later. A title search is a history of the title, showing former transactions affecting the ownership, such as existence of liens and encumbrances and any other factors which bear on the title to the property.

The chief purpose of a title search is to make sure that the title is not "clouded"—that no one other than the present owner has a claim against the property. The abstract also may turn up an earlier mortgagee whose loan has not been released or which has not been paid. This person or his heirs may still have a legal claim against the land. Under such circumstances, the present owner may not be able to give you, the buyer, clear title.

Only through a proper title search can you, the buyer, be reasonably sure you will not be bothered by unexpected claims against the real estate.

THE DEED

After the title has been examined, the seller's lawyer draws up a deed. A deed describes a property in detail and formally conveys title of the property from the seller to you. There are several types of deeds: sheriff's deed, quitclaim deed, warranty deed, etc.

The warranty deed is the most commonplace. It guarantees that the seller will defend the title against anyone who may claim an interest, although this warranty is only as good as the man who makes it. Other deeds—for instance, quitclaim deeds—give the buyer only such rights and interests as the seller may have in the property.

When you, the buyer, receive the deed, make certain that it is properly recorded in the town or county records. Deeds require federal revenue stamps, for which the seller must pay.

TITLE INSURANCE

Title insurance is generally a must for anybody who is buying real estate. In fact, the Federal Housing Administration will not insure a mortgage unless there is title insurance on the property for which the mortgage is intended. And banks often refuse to extend a mortgage unless there is title insurance protecting them.

After your title search has eliminated known risks—such as possible claims against your property or unpaid back taxes—title insurance then protects the bank or other mortgage lender against "hidden" risks and claims which may not have been uncovered by the search. For example: claims by missing heirs, a forged deed, some defect in the records, liens of laborers for work on the property, other obligations of the previous owners. There also may be rights of individuals on the land, called "squatters' rights."

There are said to be some 1,000 different possible claims which *could* be made against your ownership of a given property.

Title insurance, for which you pay a one-time premium at the time of the closing, also covers the costs of legally defending your title in the event it is later challenged, and of paying off any claims which turn out to be valid.

OR SHOULD YOU BUILD?

ADVANTAGES

No house is perfect for everyone. One family will want a bathroom next to each bedroom; another will have a passion for huge hall closets; a third will want a workshop in the cellar; a fourth will want a huge living room and tiny bedrooms. The key reason for building rather than buying is that you may have a new dwelling, with all the advantages of recent inventions and scientific developments, plus a layout tailored to *your* family's living preferences.

It is almost always more costly to build your own house than to buy an existing one—old or new. But for millions of Americans, the advantages of building their own homes still outweigh the cost disadvantages.

To illustrate, if you build your own house, you can:

create something of your own, which expresses your own personality and also the personality of your family;

build it at whatever pace you wish and can afford—room by room or wing by wing—fanning out into new living space as each room or wing is finished;

choose exactly which materials, fixtures, colors you want, including higher-quality materials than those you might find in a ready-built house;

save at least a part of the labor costs by doing part of the building yourself and getting other family members to pitch in;

design the house to meet your own family's specific needs and wants—in terms of arrangement of living spaces, lighting, exposure, decorations;

keep control over construction as it progresses, making changes and undoing errors as needed, having your say, if you want, on every single nut, bolt, and hinge which goes into it;

include only those appliances, conveniences, and labor saving systems that you really want and can afford;

choose any building site you want, in any neighborhood, with any exposure and any surroundings—assuming, that is, the site is for sale;

and clear the land just as you wish—saving whichever greenery and opening up whatever views you wish.

DISADVANTAGES

Of course there are disadvantages when you build your own house— over and above the cost disadvantage. If your dream is a highly unusual, individualistic house, you may risk—when the time comes to resell it—not finding a buyer whose family fits into the house. It may be difficult to retrieve the full amount you laid out for special materials and custom craftsmanship. You must (or should) assume the costs of an architect.

And, despite all the bids and estimates you get, you can never be positive just how the final costs will total up—because the near certainty is that there will be underestimates, that you will expand your ambitions for your new home any number of times during the course of construction and that utterly unanticipated extras will come up (they *always* do).

HOW TO FIND THE RIGHT SITE

Before you invest a penny in your dream house you must find the right property on which to build. Here's how to go about it:

• Find out from the town clerk's office the zoning regulations in the neighborhood in which the property you like is situated.

• Ask for a survey of the lot. Exactly where are the boundaries? (Walk the lines yourself.)

• Plan to invest in a title search, no matter how little the lot costs.

• Find out from local lenders whether they will make home-building loans in your neighborhood. A good source of information is the Federal Housing Administration's nearest branch office. The FHA considers the neighborhood as well as the individual house when it insures loans.

• Inspect the lot after a heavy rain; if possible, after several days of downpour. That will show how rapidly surface water leaves the site. If a plot is filled, the fill may settle and take the house along with it.

• Be wary of land subdivisions still in the "blueprint stage." These always are a gamble.

• Avoid sites which are close to things that will reduce the value of the property or detract from pleasant living—such as city dumps, mortuaries, industrial buildings, railroads, high-tension wires, heavy traffic, garbage incinerators.

• Make sure not only that the lot is large enough for the house you intend to build on it but also that the house and lot go together as a unit and that they relate pleasantly to other properties in the vicinity. What is the view like?

How much privacy is there? You will almost certainly want to sell someday. A house and lot suited to each other and suited to the surroundings will prove far more salable later than ones which stand out and just don't belong together or don't belong where they are.

• Check whether all public services will be available—or can be built—on your property: water, sewer (storm and sanitary), gas, electricity, telephone, street lighting, fire and police protection, trash removal. Don't be satisfied with vague statements such as: "The company will run the lines" or " 'They' will extend the water main." If the services are not already installed, get your information on future plans from residents in the vicinity or go to the town or city hall and find out where to get the facts. And also find out how these services are to be paid for.

Note these key points if you buy in areas in which these services are not publicly provided:

If you must supply your own water and sewage-disposal facilities you will need a much larger lot than otherwise. For an individual sewage-disposal system, the lot must be large enough to permit location of the tank and leaching field at a proper distance from your house and your neighbors' houses.

You must be certain that you can get an adequate supply of safe and potable water at reasonable cost.

You also must consider the nature of the soil: it should be sufficiently porous to assure adequate drainage.

• Satisfy yourself that the price being asked is reasonable—by consulting your real estate broker, your lawyer, and local bank officials. Typically, the cost of an improved lot is about 20 per cent of the total value of the property after your house is built. In 1973 the *average* price of a new homesite was around $5,000, and in some communities it was more than $10,000.

HOW TO CHOOSE AN ARCHITECT

Unless you can find a ready-made house plan which really suits *you,* you must hire an architect. Thousands of such plans *are* now available—many of them drawn up by architects—from shelter magazines, dealers in building materials, mail order houses. But if your dream house is even relatively elaborate you may be better off with an architect.

You wouldn't try to treat your child's first serious illness: you'd call in your doctor. You wouldn't tell a construction crew how to build a highway: you'd hire a highway engineer. It is merely common sense to recognize your ignorance about building a house, just as you recognize it in many other fields. A trained architect will know about new developments in design, building materials, and techniques—and how they may help in building your house.

A competent architect will be prepared to:

study your family's living needs and try to match these to your budget;

advise on your choice of building site and also on where a structure should be located on it;

make rough preliminary sketches of your house-to-be;

put together rough cost estimates;

make detailed drawings and materials lists;

provide whatever technical information is needed to draw up a contract with the contractor;

advise on a choice of contractors, take competitive bids for the job, and choose the most favorable one;

observe construction to make sure it is carried out according to plan;

decide whether and how changes and substitutions proposed by you and your contractor can be carried out;

check and authorize payments to the contractor;

inspect the finished building and arrange for your final payment to the contractor after your building has been satisfactorily completed.

Architects' fees tend to depend on the value of the job and on the amount of designing, supervising, and other work involved. They may be computed as a percentage of total building costs, as a fixed fee plus expenses, or as a multiple of the architect's direct expenses. The figure arrived at is usually between 6 and 15 per cent of the total building costs. Normally, you pay this fee in installments—your payments beginning with an acceptable rough sketch of your house and ending when the house is actually completed.

An architect, however, may be able to save you at least the amount of his own fees by helping you avoid expensive mistakes and leading you to efficiencies in building which neither you nor the builder may have even considered.

These savings, of course, are on top of the sheer convenience to you of having someone else deal with contractors, subcontractors, zoning boards, and health officials.

How do you find a competent, suitable architect?

• Look for an architect who is a member of the Washington-based American Institute of Architects.

• Before you make a deal with any one architect, study other houses he has designed—inside as well as out, if possible. How well does your taste agree with his?

• Ask the architect's former clients, if possible, how well he stuck to his original cost estimates—or by how much he overshot the budget they gave him. You can get an impression whether or not the customers were generally satisfied with the architect's work.

• Talk over your ideas, plans, and costs with at least two architects and ask each to make at least a rough preliminary sketch—to see how each translates your ideas onto paper. Or ask them to show you examples of their work as similar as possible in scope to your project.

• Discuss fees with any architect whose services you might want to use—and find out the minimum percentage of the costs he'll work for. Quite possibly a younger architect who is a little hungrier for business than are his older and busier colleagues will charge less. Consider, too (if the architect's fees seem too high), buying his advice on an hourly basis—at least at the outset. Perhaps he could leave a lot of the supervisory work to you (if you're qualified) or to your builder-contractor.

• Find out from each architect which measures each would take to cut building costs.

• Make sure you *like* and respect the architect you finally choose—and that both of you are able to communicate ideas easily to each other.

HOW TO CHOOSE A CONTRACTOR

Your architect will probably recommend one or more builders after he has worked out plans and drawings which satisfy you. He'll probably get written bids from at least two contractors on the job of building your house.

At this point the following guides in finding a good contractor will be of great value to you.

• Carefully check the reputation of each—with the local bank, the local Better Business Bureau, local building suppliers, *and former customers*. And inspect previous houses each contractor has built.

• Then compare not only the amount of each bid but also the manner in which each intends to do the job, what types of materials each would use, the completion date, and the guarantee of the work.

• Check each builder's addresses, business as well as home. If his home is located near any of the homes he has built, it's an encouraging sign of his reliability.

• Ask about each builder at the local office of the National Association of Home Builders. As a general rule, builders who are members of the NAHB are reliable: however, not all good, reliable builders are members of this organization.

• Ask the local FHA office to see its "DSI list," which is a nationwide list of all contractors the FHA has found unsatisfactory. Also ask to see the local list of workmanship ratings. Both must be made available to you under the Freedom of Information Act, and can serve as valuable guides, though not the last word, on the reliability of contractors you are considering. Among the reasons for the FHA's blackballs are: overpricing, misrepresentation of products, false guarantees, falsifying credit information, fraudulent "model home" comeons. The DSI list, also is available from HUD Printing Office, 451 7th Street S.W., Washington, D.C. 20410.

• Beware of any unusually low bid on the job you want done. If you accept such a bid you are likely to be risking bad workmanship and the use of inferior materials. Good builders use top grades of lumber and other building supplies and hire highly skilled carpenters, masons, plumbers, and others. These costs must be reflected in the builder's bids.

• Make sure the contractor carries adequate insurance protection to cover the men who work for him. Get a statement to this effect in writing from his insurance company.

Beware also of any contractor or supplier who advertises that the FHA endorses his work or products. The FHA does *not* make such endorsements.

• In the case of individual workers who do not carry such protection, make sure the liability part of your own homeowners insurance policy does provide this type of protection against accidents and injuries on the job.

• Study "Your Home Improvement Contractor and Your Contract" later in this chapter. Some of these guides also may help you choose a contractor to build a new house.

HOW TO CUT THE HIGH COST OF BUILDING

In the mid-seventies the cost of building most houses ranged between $10 and $25 per square foot of living space—plus the cost of the building lot, not counting unimproved basement space. For the highest-quality houses, building costs may run $25 to $35 or more per square foot.

According to the National Association of Home Builders, here are the major cost items in a typical new, single family home selling for $38,500 in 1975:

ITEM	% OF COST	AMOUNT
Labor	15	$ 5,775
Materials	33	12,705
Land	22	8,470
Builder's overhead and profit	12	4,620
Financing costs	11	4,235
Miscellaneous	7	2,695

Against this background, these are your fundamental moneysaving guidelines:

• Try to design economies into your house. For example, a two-story house costs less to build, per foot of floor space, than a one-story house. A rectangular floor plan costs less than a U-shaped, L-shaped, or other-shaped house. Standard gable roofs tend to be less expensive than other types of roofs. Using treated wood instead of masonry for the foundation—a technique approved by the FHA—can save several hundred dollars.

• Time your building project, if possible, to take advantage of economic cycles in the area in which you are building. Perhaps you can manage to schedule it during a slack season (such as winter). Or perhaps you are building during a phase of high unemployment in the building trades. If you can take advantage of cycles of this type, you can save thousands of dollars.

• Consider most seriously hiring the largest builder with a good reputation in your area. As an indication of the savings bigger builders are likely to achieve on your behalf for materials alone, here is a comparison of what various types of builders might pay for basic materials going into a $30,000 house, adapted from a study by the College of Engineering and Architecture, Penn State College:

CLASS OF BUILDER	LUMBER, BRICK, OTHER BASICS	HEATING, WIRING, OTHER UTILITIES	HARD-WARE, FIXTURES, MISC.	TOTAL
Do-it-yourself builder	$4,000	$5,000	$6,000	$15,000
Small builder	3,600	4,250	4,800	12,650
Medium-sized builder working on 3 houses at one time	3,400	3,750	4,020	11,170
Large builder who buys in large volumes	3,080	3,000	3,240	9,320

• Also consider building a "manufactured" house. Through this type of construction, homeowners in many cases are achieving savings of 20 per cent or more in over-all home building costs.

Prefab housing covers a broad range. It can be large sections of a wall, pre-assembled at a factory building supply store, an entire side of a house built in some standard size, or a "package" of prebuilt parts which a builder or homeowner can put together into a whole house. One reason for the big savings available on prefabs is that you are spared the architect's fee—plus 10 to 20 per cent in labor costs.

Modular housing units are factory-built rooms, groups of rooms, sections of a house, or even whole apartments (but not whole houses). They are delivered to the construction site on a flatbed or similar conveyance. Usually a builder puts several of these modular rooms or other units together to make a complete house.

The typical price of a prefab house in the mid-seventies ranged from $7.00 to $15 a square foot, and the typical total cost of a prefab house, from $18,000 to $30,000. The range of prices, however, was from as little as $12,-000 to more than $50,000. Normally the dealer who sells you a prefab house puts it up for you. Local builders, building suppliers, and prefab dealers can fill you in on what's available at what cost in your area.

• Or consider as an alternative to the all-prefab house the part-prefab—part-custom-built house which may make many economies possible and also permit individuality. As an illustration: a complete "wet unit" is being sold for about $7,000. This box includes one and a half bathrooms, heating, plumbing, air conditioning, washer and dryer, electrical system, and closet.

• And what about making yours an expandable house, if you cannot afford to build the entire house at one time? The principle of the expandable house is simple: build what you can afford now and what will meet your present needs; postpone building for future requirements and more spacious living. Our early New England houses were built in this fashion—section by section to accommodate expanding families.

If this is an answer to your building problem, plan the complete house first. Then separate it into its logical parts and decide on the sequence of additions. The house should be complete in appearance and function at each stage. The basic unit always should provide all the facilities for the normal life of a small family: living room, bedroom, bath, dining space, kitchen, closet and storage space, lighting and heating equipment, hot water heater, and laundry facilities—even though some rooms may have to serve two or more purposes.

Here are additional guides for expandable houses:

Be sure your lot is big enough and shaped correctly not only for your basic house but also for all future extensions.

Carefully check community restrictions, included in zoning ordinances or restrictive covenants in deeds. These restrictions may control the size and price of a house built in a given locality, ruling out the first unit of an expandable house as a dwelling, even though the expanded house would meet all other requirements.

Plan all stages in the progress of your expansion so that there is no wasted space and there is convenient circulation from room to room.

Design your additions to minimize the disturbance to your family while the building is going on.

Select your materials for their ultimate use. For instance, plywood might be used for an exterior wall which you plan to turn into an interior wall later.

Frame the openings to later additions in the early stages. A window can be installed temporarily in a space framed for a future door.

Rough in from the start pipes, ducts, cables which you will need for later additions to save ripping out and rebuilding walls and floors later.

The expandable house need not be expanded. If your family's needs do not grow, you may not want any expansion. As long as yours is a complete house in function and appearance, you will not endanger its resale value.

Ordinarily the cost of building a house in separate stages would be higher than building it all at once. But by careful planning you can keep the additional costs to a minimum. In general, the greater ultimate cost will be more than offset by savings in maintenance, interest, taxes, and insurance during the period between the building of your basic unit and your later additions.

• Finally, consider building your house yourself. Given the enormous variety of prefab materials and house sections, a dazzling variety of do-it-yourself equipment in hardware and building supply stores, and house building kits complete with instructions as well as alluring materials and drawings, record numbers *are* building their own homes.

You must coldly appraise whether or not you are qualified to build your own house, whether or not you can afford to absorb the cost of mistakes you might make, whether or not you can even dare try to do the tasks normally done by such experts as plumbers and electricians.

You may have trouble getting a bank to extend a mortgage to you—especially if you are not a professional. You also almost surely will have to pay a relatively higher price for the materials you use, since you may not be eligible for the discounts available to builders or for the savings available to development builders. (Refer to the preceding comparison chart on material costs.

But you will, of course, reap big savings on the high cost of labor. Also you pay any labor you hire with your after-tax dollars while the labor you invest yourself may be "worth" 20 or 30 or 40 per cent more, depending on your tax bracket. To illustrate with a rough calculation: if you're in the 20 per cent federal income tax bracket, the $5,000 worth of your own labor you put into your house may translate into real savings of $6,000. (This is the amount you would have to earn in order to pay an outsider $5,000.)

Here are rules for investing in such major, costly components of your house as a roof, heating plant, plumbing system, etc.:

Plumbing: When you get into the plumbing aspects of your house, you're into an area which is hopelessly hamstrung by obsolete building codes, by city or town inspectors who are dead set against modern efficiencies and the newer, less expensive materials for plumbing pipes and fittings, and by deeply ingrained union traditions which dictate against many of the money-saving methods you or your architect might want to try. Still, there are ways you can economize (and *not* economize) on the purchase of plumbing supplies and services and in the general upkeep of your plumbing facilities.

Use plastic, if zoning codes permit, for cold water pipes and also for drainage pipes and save money by using 3-inch instead of far more expensive 4-inch pipes. Use copper for all hot water pipes.

If there is a great distance between the hot water heater and faucets, insulate the hot water pipes to avoid waste of hot water.

Stick, as far as possible, to standard, stock plumbing fixtures and to prefabricated modular bathroom units. Today, moderately priced prefab bathrooms, complete with everything from soap dishes to storage shelves, tub, and toothbrush holders, are on the market and can be installed within a few hours. The deeper you get into custom plumbing, the more expensive it is.

Heating systems: In deciding what type of heating system to install, you will have to weigh both installation and operating costs. If you are reasonably confident you will occupy the house more than just a few years, operating costs, involving expensive fuels, will be more important than installation costs. Nevertheless, here are the approximate costs of building various types of heating systems into a 2,000-square-foot house in the Baltimore-Washington area in 1973:

Electric baseboard	$1,300
Gas-forced air	1,400
Electric-forced air	1,430
Oil-forced air	2,000
Solar	4,000

Operating costs include fuel and maintenance.

Fuel prices vary across the country, but in the mid-seventies piped-in natural gas, where available, usually was the cheapest fuel, followed closely by oil. In the Northeast, however, oil was the cheapest. Electricity is almost invariably the most expensive way to keep warm, in many areas more than twice as expensive as the cheapest available fuel. LP (liquefied petroleum) gas is somewhere in the middle. Sunlight, of course, is free, though most solar heating setups require some back-up fuel.

Here's a formula for comparing current home fuel prices in your area:

(1) Find out the going price of oil (per gallon), of gas (per therm), and of electricity (per kilowatt hour). When you ask about gas and electricity rates, be sure you get the rates applying to home heating.

(2) Multiply the price of electricity by 33 and the price of gas (whatever kind you can buy) by 1.4.

(3) Compare these numbers with the price of a gallon of fuel oil. The smallest number is the cheapest fuel.

Caution: Consult local builders, heating system contractors, and fuel suppliers on prices and known trends in your area.

Do not be swayed by *minor* price differences. Although large differences probably will continue for a long time, small ones could reverse overnight.

As for which type of fuel will increase fastest in price in the long run, the answer is no one really knows. The future is hopelessly befuddled by Middle Eastern policies and politics, conservation issues, world supply-demand balances, the world's capacity to develop the necessary technology to clean up one fuel or convert another fuel into forms that are acceptable, economical, and usable.

The only certainty is that costs of all home heating fuels except sunlight will continue up, up, and up.

Here are other key points, pros and cons, to consider in choosing one type of heating system over another:

• Oil and LP (liquefied petroleum) gas systems require storage tanks on your grounds (or underground). Storage tanks can be minus because they consume space and because they can run dry. They're a plus, though, in that no one can turn off your supply as long as there's fuel in your tank. In contrast, you have no control over your natural gas or electricity supply lines.

• Oil furnaces require some electricity, and thus, if the power goes off, they may shut off altogether and stay off. That's a major disadvantage to you if you're frequently away from home and you live in a cold climate. Certain types of gas heating systems, though, are immune to blackouts and brownouts—a key advantage in an era when these are likely to become ever more widespread.

• Electric heat is relatively inexpensive to install, is very quiet, demands little space—and permits you the flexibility of individual room thermostats. However, the most common types of electric heating systems require thorough insulation of your house if they are to be at all economical, and obviously electric heat is no help to you during a power failure. Also, do not install electric heat strictly on the basis of promises that nuclear power plants will soon lower your electric rates. Serious controversy exists over the possible dangers of many proposed plants and many already under construction are facing long delays before completion. Some plants in operation have actually turned out to be among the least economical sources of electricity.

Finally, do not assume, because today larger-volume users of electricity (industrial users and families with all-electric homes) are now getting more favorable rates in your area, that this practice will prevail indefinitely. *Do not*, therefore, opt for electricity strictly on this basis.

• Do not believe claims that one source of heat is cleaner or safer than others. All heat sources are equally clean and safe if you maintain and properly service your heating plant.

• Do insulate well, no matter what type of fuel you decide to use. Choose double-pane windows (even triple-pane windows in very cold climates) and avoid huge glass areas. If you decide on gas or oil, install large tanks and keep them full. You may even wish to design your new house so part of it can be left unheated at times, particularly if you live in a cold area.

• Do give some consideration to alternative types of back-up heating, such as a heating fireplace, to tide you through temporary shortages of your primary fuel and minimize the danger of frozen pipes. *But,* however romantic and cozy an old-fashioned fireplace may be, it is one of the *least* efficient sources of home heat. Reason: it may take all night for a fire you've enjoyed for only a few evening hours to die down, and during this time more heat goes up the chimney than the heat your fireplace provided while it was blazing.

As for maintenance, electric baseboard systems are virtually maintenance free. Gas furnaces need occasional cleaning, and oil furnaces require somewhat more frequent attention. In any heating system, motors, fans, pumps, and thermostats fail occasionally, so systems with more of these items lose some reliability. Because few solar-heated houses have been built, their maintenance costs are unknown.

For guides on how to save heat once your system is installed, see "How to Cut Your Home Heating Bills," later in this chapter.

The roof: Get advice from your builder and/or architect on the life expectancy of each material you are considering using in your roof. Don't make false economies—for example, by choosing a lightweight shingle when, for only a slightly higher cost, you could get a heavier grade which would last two or three times as long.

The roof is likely to be among the most expensive aspects of any new house. And the price range is enormous between the more expensive roofing materials, such as slate and clay tile, and the less expensive ones, such as asphalt shingles and liquid asphalt topped with gravel. But probably the most important factor to consider is that one roofing material may tend to last only ten years, after which you will need a whole new roofing job, while the next material may be expected to last as long as you will.

The walls: Old-fashioned plaster is almost always more expensive than dry-wall (or plasterboard or gypsum board) construction—a key reason why the latter is the far more widely used of the two today. But plaster is likely to look better and to last a lot longer than dry wall. So again, before you decide beween the two (if these indeed are your only two choices), get time and cost estimates on the *entire* job of installing properly and painstakingly each type of wall.

Sewage disposal: Avoid putting in a too small septic tank or an inadequate leaching field. Most houses today require a tank with a capacity of at least 900 to 1,000 gallons, and local zoning and/or health regulations well may specify requirements for other aspects of your sewage disposal system. So be sure to consult these rules before you start digging. Or, if no rules exist, get the advice of a sanitary engineer.

The floor: Choose your flooring for each room on the basis of the *wear* it actually is likely to get—as well as its looks and cost. Today's three most popular types of flooring are hardwood (e.g., oak, maple, birch); carpeting (frequently directly over a plywood subfloor); and tile (such as vinyl, vinyl-asbestos, and asbestos).

A CHART FOR ESTIMATING YOUR HOME BUILDING COSTS

ITEM	ESTIMATED COST
The lot	_____
Survey fees	_____
Closing costs	_____
Architect's fee (if any)	_____
Materials	_____
Labor	_____
Homeowners insurance	_____
Landscaping	_____
Building permit	_____
Interest on loans	_____
Other	_____
TOTAL	_____

HOW TO SHOP FOR A HOME MORTGAGE

HOW MUCH HOUSE CAN YOU AFFORD?

As your home is likely to be the biggest single investment you'll make in your entire lifetime, so the mortgage you take on to finance it is likely to be the biggest single debt of your life. And the monthly payments you assume on that mortgage are likely to be the biggest single item in your budget.

To find the most favorable terms, you'll have to shop with utmost care among *all* types of lenders and *all* types of mortgages available in your area. The obvious sources to check will be: savings and loan associations; full service commercial banks; savings banks; life insurance companies; mortgage companies. Others are pension funds and individuals. You'll want to ask each source details about rates, points, closing costs, all the other terms highlighted for you in the pages ahead.

Most of you probably consider the amount of the monthly payment the key to the cost of the mortgage. Actually, this is the *least* significant figure to use as your guide to true costs. In fact, a low monthly payment probably means a *long* life for a mortgage and, as a result, the highest possible over-all interest costs to you.

In this high-interest era, it's not at all uncommon to commit yourself to pay more in interest over the lifetime of your mortgage than the total amount of the mortgage itself. As just one example, on a $10,000 mortgage the interest at 8 per cent over a period of twenty-five years would be $13,154.

Before you start shopping for a mortgage you must decide how much mortgage—which really means how much house—you can afford. This goes beyond the down payment and beyond the monthly payment to your entire mortgage obligation over the next twenty to thirty years.

(Incidentally, you borrow money to build your own house in much the same way as you borrow to buy an already built one. Construction loans are made on the basis of your plans and specifications and your schedule for paying building costs and are replaced once the house is completed by a regular long-term mortgage.)

One long-standing rule of thumb for the average American family is:

You can afford to buy a house costing roughly two and one half times your gross (before tax) yearly income. For example, if your gross annual income is $15,000, you can afford a house costing $35,000 to $40,000; if it's $20,000, your range is $45,000 to $50,000.

If your income tends to fluctuate sharply you can use an average of your yearly income over the past few years as a yardstick. If you are in a high income bracket, figure on spending relatively *less* than two and a half times your gross income on a new home.

Even if you are in the lower brackets, the sum you pay for a house should be *less* than two and a half times your gross income *if* you will be carrying a heavy debt load on other purchases; *if* your family is large; *if* you plan to buy an old house requiring a lot of repairs; *if* you will have heavy near-future financial obligations for the college education of your children; *if* property taxes and living costs in the neighborhood in which you plan to buy are high (and likely to rise further as you make improvements); *if* your income is irregular; *if* your down payment is low; and *if* your job may force you to move unexpectedly.

On the other hand, in any income bracket, you can afford to pay *more* for your house *if* you plan and are able to do a lot of the necessary maintenance and repairs on the house yourself; *if* your family is small; *if* your property taxes are low and likely to remain so; *if* you are virtually certain your income will increase at regular intervals; *if* the home you buy involves low upkeep costs; *if* the house is loaded with all the appliances you might otherwise have to buy—and *if* you are able to make a relatively large down payment from your savings.

Another long-standing rule is that you should count on laying out one to one and one half week's take-home pay for each month's *total* housing expenses including all the costs of owning and operating your home—ranging from your monthly payments on mortgage principal and interest, insurance and taxes, repairs and maintenance, heat and utilities, to garbage collection and your commuting costs.

By this yardstick, if you have a take-home income of $450 a month, you could safely carry housing costs totaling at least $120 a month, and if you have a take-home income of $800 a month, you could safely carry costs to-taling in the $300 range.

Your yearly home mortgage costs will probably amount to more than 60 per cent of your total home ownership costs. This will give you an idea of how much to budget for property taxes, insurance, and upkeep—but not in-cluding utilities. These are only approximations and the expenses will vary widely among families and areas of the country.

Admittedly, the formulas above are no guarantee that you'll avoid finan-cial errors in your home purchase and financing. You may, even if you are within the limits, be trying to take on too much too soon. You may be reach-ing for too much house. You may be way off base in other areas—emotional if not financial. And remember this fundamental point about owning a house in the suburbs: the "hidden" cost of car ownership will add substantially to your *home ownership* cost. In the suburbs and exurbs, home ownership often means two cars are a necessity, not a luxury. But at least the formulas give you the bench marks.

Since your home mortgage is such a big part of your financial life, it should be an area in which know-how helps you achieve big savings. And it is. In fact, there are *four* areas in which you can chalk up impressive sav-ings: the amount of the down payment; the number of years the mortgage spans; the interest rate; "points," closing costs, and other "extras" that go along with most mortgages.

WHAT SHOULD YOUR DOWN PAYMENT BE?

How much of your savings nest egg should you put down as an initial payment? The key dollars-and-cents rule is to make the largest down pay-ment that is feasible for you.

The average mortgage on a new home now covers about three fourths of the purchase price—so this is one guide for you on the amount of down pay-ment you are expected to make. But do not fail to leave enough money on hand to cover such extraordinary initial expenses as fees for lawyers, sur-veyors, appraisers, architects involved in the purchase; recording fees, title search, insurance fees and closing charges on the loan; insurance and taxes on your new home; property taxes for the current year; moving costs and immediate repair bills. And there always will be unexpected expenses.

The more you pay down, the lower will be your interest costs over the years ahead and the lower will be the over-all cost of the loan to you. The more you pay down, the greater will be your equity (ownership) in your home, and thus the greater your sense of security and protection should you be hit by an unanticipated financial emergency. The more you pay down, the smaller will be your monthly mortgage payments, permitting you additional leeway to spend on other thing or non-things and to rebuild your savings nest egg. The more you pay down, the easier it will be for you to obtain a mortgage loan on interest terms most favorable to you.

If you can't put down a reasonably solid initial payment for your house, the odds are you can't afford the house. If this is the case, your best bet is to keep renting and building your nest egg until you can.

Here's a table which pounds home the generalities on down payments on home mortgages. Assume you're buying a $35,000 house and can get a mortgage for a twenty-five-year period at 8½ per cent. (The rates will change from year to year and from one part of the country to another, but the relationships between low down payment and high interest costs are what count.)

DOWN PAYMENT	AMOUNT BORROWED	MONTHLY PAYMENT	TOTAL FINANCE CHARGE
$ 3,500	$31,500	$253.84	$44,651
5,000	30,000	241.75	42,525
7,500	27,500	221.60	38,981
10,000	25,000	201.46	35,438
15,000	20,000	161.17	28,350

HOW LONG SHOULD THE TERM OF YOUR MORTGAGE BE?

The second fundamental way you can save on your mortgage is to keep its life span just as short as you can reasonably manage.

Here's a table which pounds home the generalities on mortgage terms. It assumes an 8½ per cent, $30,000 loan over various periods of time:

REPAYMENT PERIOD	MONTHLY PAYMENT	TOTAL INTEREST
15 years	$295.50	$23,190
20 years	260.50	32,520
25 years	241.75	42,525
30 years	230.75	53,069

WHAT WILL THE INTEREST RATE BE?

Although most mortgage lenders in any given city or area of the United States are likely to charge about the same rates at any given time, you still may find a variation of ½ to 1 per cent—a difference which can be highly significant in terms of your total interest costs.

You *must* shop for terms. You cannot fudge this job. Here's a table which translates these generalities. The details are on a $30,000, thirty-year mortgage, at various interest rates:

INTEREST RATE	MONTHLY PAYMENT	TOTAL INTEREST
7½%	$210.00	$45,600
8	220.25	49,289
8½	231.75	53,069
9	241.50	56,940
9½	252.50	60,899
10	263.50	64,860
10½	274.50	68,820

"POINTS," CLOSING COSTS, PREPAYMENT, LATE PAYMENT PENALTIES

And this is not all. In addition to the interest rate, the term, and the down payment on your home, there are less obvious costs which are inevitably tucked into the loan. Here are the key "extras"—and ways you can save on them:

Points: Because of state-regulated interest ceilings, many lenders add "points" to their basic mortgage charges when the general trend of interest rates is up. This holds for FHA and VA as well as conventional mortgage loans. If a lender charges you 5 points, it means he deducts 5 per cent from the face value of your mortgage at the beginning. You must, however, repay the full amount of the mortgage. To illustrate, on a $20,000 mortgage, $1,000 would be deducted, leaving only $19,000 actually available to you. This is the equivalent of adding more than ½ per cent to your basic interest rate.

If the lender charges you 10 points, this is the equivalent of adding an extra 1¼ per cent to the rate you are paying.

Since the number of points you are charged will vary from institution to institution in any given area, be sure to find out how many points each lender in your area would charge you. Also explore the possibility that the seller of the house might share the cost of points.

Closing costs: These, too, can vary quite dramatically from lender to lender and, since they can range today from 2 to 10 per cent of the loan, they represent a major area for possible savings. On a $30,000 house, closing costs alone typically total $150 to $1,200—and you have to pay this amount in cash. There is virtually no room for negotiation on certain closing items: property taxes, fire insurance, title insurance, credit life insurance (if required). There is little room for bargaining over the appraisal fee, credit report fee, and survey fee. But there are other closing costs which may be negotiable, such as the bank's charge for processing your mortgage application and legal fees. You also might ask your own lawyer whether it is possible

that the seller of the house might share the cost of such items as local recording fees, surveys, termite inspection, or even the title search. Shopping among
lenders might help you to minimize closing costs. In any event, get a copy of
the seller's closing costs, to be sure you are not both paying for the same
items.

Note: A large building firm selling you a new house and arranging the
mortgage is likely to offer lower over-all closing costs than a small builder.
Similarly, on VA- and FHA-insured mortgages, closing costs tend to be significantly lower than on conventional mortgages.

Here's a rundown on typical closing costs and related expenses for a
$30,000 house bought in 1974 with a mortgage from a commercial bank:

Legal fees (your lawyer)	$150
Survey, recording fees, and title insurance	300
Property taxes	120
Appraisal and bank attorney	240
Homeowners insurance (first year)	145
Total	$955

Prepayment: Some lenders will not allow any prepayment without forfeit of an interest refund on the amount you prepay. Some exact a penalty for
prepaying more than a fixed amount or for prepaying any amount during the
first year of the loan. Some impose no penalties at all. So try to get the privilege of prepaying your mortgage at no or minimum penalties. Prepayment
could save you hundreds or even thousands of dollars if you get a cash windfall or should mortgage interest rates decline sharply.

Late payment: Also check how long a grace period is provided after each
payment due date before a penalty is applied and find out how big the penalty is. Late charges are typically 4 and 6 per cent of the overdue payment,
but can be even larger.

OTHERS AREAS TO EXPLORE

In addition, here are other areas to explore and in which to make comparisons between one mortgage deal and the next:

• How quickly can you get the loan?
• Can the life of the mortgage be extended at a later date if you choose?
Can you "reborrow" after you've made several payments by increasing your
monthly payment or extending your mortgage's life? If you can, what will be
the deal on interest rates on the new borrowing versus the original mortgage?
An open-end mortgage can be an attractive arrangement for you if the provisions for interest rates and closing costs are in your favor and there is a
minimum of red tape. Check with care.

• What type and how much home insurance must you carry to get the mortgage? Must you deposit funds (probably at no interest) with the lender to pay for this insurance? Are you permitted to arrange your insurance on your own and get the most favorable terms you can? If you do not have this freedom of action, the restriction is a minus. There is no reason why the lender of your mortgage money should also make a profit on the insurance he demands to protect this investment.

• And, if you're buying an older house or apartment, can you work out a private arrangement with the seller in which he would transfer his lower-rate FHA- or VA-backed mortgage to you?

Note: When you get your mortgage, you probably will have to take out a credit life insurance policy which would pay off your mortgage should disaster strike. This is a term policy which declines in coverage as your mortgage loan is reduced.

MAIN TYPES OF MORTGAGE LOANS

Here are the advantages and disadvantages of the main types of mortgage loans available to you in 1974.

Loans Guaranteed by the Veterans Administration

ADVANTAGES: Up to 100 per cent of the appraisal value of a home can be borrowed and thus no down payment is required (although the bank or other lending institution through which the VA loan is made may require a down payment). There is a ceiling on interest charged set by the Veterans Administration. You get the privilege of partial prepayment without penalty. The repayment period runs up to thirty years. The VA makes a special effort to help veterans keep their homes by encouraging lenders to extend forbearance and indulgence to the veteran if he has repayment difficulty.

DISADVANTAGES: This type of mortgage may be hard to find. There is a certain amount of red tape involved. Only eligible veterans qualify. An appraisal is required, and thus an appraisal fee is added to the closing costs. However, the appraisal often serves to lower the buyer's asking price, so it may save more than it costs.

For details on current terms for VA-backed mortgages consult your local VA office or write the Veterans Administration, Washington, D.C. 20420.

Loans Insured by the Federal Housing Administration

ADVANTAGES: The repayment period can stretch as long as thirty years, or even thirty-five years in some special cases. The down payment is very low: 3 per cent of a house appraised at $25,000 (but only $200 for eligible veterans); 10 per cent of the next $10,000; and 20 per cent of the remainder (15 per cent for eligible veterans).

DISADVANTAGES: There may be a lot of red tape involved, and a long wait while the loan is being processed and while the FHA determines whether or not the house meets the FHA's standards of construction, livability, and location.

For details on current terms for FHA-backed mortgages consult the Federal Housing Administration, Department of Housing and Urban Development, 451 7th Street S.W., Washington, D.C. 20410.

Conventional (non-FHA or VA) Mortgages

ADVANTAGES: There is no set maximum amount which can be borrowed. There is a minimum of red tape and the waiting period is usually just a few days. A conventional mortgage is usually the fastest and easiest to get and virtually anybody in good financial standing is eligible.

DISADVANTAGES: The repayment periods are generally shorter than for FHA or VA loans (fifteen to twenty-five years). Down payments, frequently regulated by law, are relatively larger (usually 25 to 40 per cent of the appraised value). Interest rates may be higher, and extra "points" may be tacked onto the stated interest rates.

Important note: The rules are somewhat different and substantially more liberal for mortgages extended by savings and loan associations. Though the typical down payment is 20 per cent, you may be able to borrow up to $36,000 with a down payment of only 5 per cent, and up to $45,000 with a down payment of only 10 per cent. As with commercial banks, savings and loan associations have no set limit on the life span of home mortgages.

"Little FHA" Mortgages

These low-cost loans are available to elderly and low-income rural Americans from the Farmers Home Administration with a repayment period up to thirty-three years. The mortgage interest rate you pay depends on the size of your family and family income.

The only disadvantages of a "little FHA" mortgage is that FHA funds occasionally may be limited and then not all applicants succeed in getting these loans. You can find out what your local situation is by calling your local FHA office, Department of Agriculture. Or write to the Farmers Home Administration, Department of Agriculture, Washington, D.C. 20250.

Purchase Money Mortgage

Finally, there is the purchase money mortgage, in which the seller finances the unpaid balance of the purchase price—at an interest rate and under terms negotiated directly with you, the buyer.

HOW YOUR EQUITY BUILDS

"Mort" means "dead." When you pay off your mortgage, you amortize it or "kill" it and it's "dead." As you put the mortgage to "death," your equity or stake in the house which the mortgage helped you buy or build increases.

But in the early years of your mortgage a giant share of your monthly payments goes just for interest and a picayune proportion goes toward killing your mortgage and thereby building your equity.

Thus your equity increases very slowly in the early years and accelerates only as the mortgage nears maturity.

For instance, after the tenth year of payments on a thirty-year mortgage at 8½ per cent, you will still owe almost 88 per cent of the loan. Even at the twenty-year mark, you will have 60 per cent of the mortgage still to pay. In the twenty-eighth year of your thirty-year mortgage, you will still owe 35 per cent.

THE BAFFLEGAB OF REAL ESTATE

Here, for quick reference, is a guide to the bafflegab of buying and selling real estate.

ABSTRACT: Short legal history of a property tracing ownership over the years and noting such encumbrances as unpaid taxes and liens.

AMORTIZATION: Reduction of a debt through monthly mortgage payments (or some other schedule of repayment in which the loan principal is reduced), along with payments of interest and other loan costs.

APPRAISAL: Estimate, made by the Federal Housing Administration, the Veterans Administration, a private lender, or other qualified appraiser, of the current market value of a property.

ASSESSMENT: Special charge imposed by local government on homeowners to cover costs of special projects such as street paving or new sewer systems from which the homeowners presumably benefit.

BINDER: Tentative agreement, between a buyer and seller of real estate, to the terms of the transaction—usually involving a deposit of a small amount of money.

BROKER: Professional who is licensed by the state in which he works to assist buyers and sellers of property.

CERTIFICATE OF TITLE: Legal statement to the effect that property ownership is established by public records.

CLOSING: The occasion on which the buyer and seller of a property—or their representatives—meet to exchange payment for the deed to a property.

CLOSING COSTS: Costs, other than the basic purchase price of a piece of property, which are imposed at the time a real estate deal is closed. Closing costs can include lawyers' fees, title insurance, taxes, and several other items.

COMMISSION: Fee which a seller of property pays to a real estate agent for his services—usually amounting to 5 to 10 per cent of the sale price.

CONDOMINIUM: Individually owned real estate consisting of a dwelling unit and an undivided interest in joint facilities and areas which serve the multi-unit complex.

CO-OPERATIVE: A form of real estate ownership in which each individual owns stock in a corporation, giving him the right to live in one of the units owned and administered by the corporation.

DEED: Legal, written document used to transfer ownership of property from seller to buyer.

DEFAULT: In this context, failure by a buyer to meet a mortgage payment or other requirement of the sale—which may result in forfeiture of the property itself.

DEPOSIT (OR "EARNEST MONEY"): Sum of money, normally a small fraction of the sale price of the property, which a prospective buyer gives to a seller to secure a sales contract. See "Binder."

DEPRECIATION: Decrease in the value of property due to wear and tear, obsolescence or the action of the elements. Differs from deterioration, which signifies abnormal loss of quality.

EARNEST MONEY: A deposit. See above.

EASEMENT: Right granted to one property owner by another to use the grantor's land for certain purposes—for example, a right-of-way for an access road or for power lines.

ENCUMBRANCE (OR DEFECT OF RECORD): Claim against the title of a parcel of real estate by a third party, other than the buyer or seller (e.g., a lien due to unpaid taxes or a mortgage delinquency) which challenges the property's ownership and tends to reduce its value.

EQUITY: In real estate terms, value built up in a property over the years, in the form of payment of principal as a part of mortgage payments. The amount of equity in a property is the total amount of principal paid minus the debts against the property.

ESCROW: The placing of money or other items of value in the custody of a bank or other third party until the terms of a real estate transaction are fulfilled by the two parties involved.

FHA: Federal Housing Administration, which insures mortgage holders against losses from default on loans made according to the Administration's policies.

FORECLOSURE: Sale by a bank or other lender of a property on which payments are seriously in default—in order to satisfy the debt at least partially.

LIEN: Claim against a property which sometimes is kept as security for the repayment of a debt.

LISTING: Registration of a property with one or more real estate brokers or agents, entitling the broker who actually sells the property to a commission. An *exclusive listing* gives one individual broker the exclusive right to handle the sale of a property; a *multiple listing* permits a special *group* of brokers to handle the transaction.

MORTGAGE: Legal right given by a borrower to the lender of the funds with which the borrower has purchased a property to take back that property if repayment of the loan is not made.

OPTION: Right, often sold by a seller of property to prospective buyer, giving the latter the right to buy the property at a specified price within a specified period of time.

PLAT: Pictorial plan or map of a land subdivision or housing development.

POINTS: Part of the settlement costs of exchanging real estate. One point is 1 per cent of the amount of the mortgage. Points are paid to the mortgage lender, technically by the seller of the property. However, since the price of the house normally is adjusted to allow for this, points effectively increase the interest rate on the loan to the buyer.

PURCHASE MONEY MORTGAGE: Mortgage granted directly by a seller to the buyer of the seller's property, in which the seller may take back the property if the buyer does not pay off the mortgage as agreed. In brief, the seller of the house lends the buyer the money with which to buy the house.

QUITCLAIM DEED: Deed which releases any interest a seller or other individual may have in a given piece of land. (See "Deed," above.)

REAL ESTATE (REAL PROPERTY): Land, and any structures situated on it.

REALTOR: Real estate agent who is a member of the National Association of Realtors. A copyrighted word, always capitalized.

SETBACK: A common restriction provided under zoning ordinances specifying the distances a new house must be set back from a road or from the lot boundaries.

SURVEY: The determination, by means of examination of land records and also field measurements based on these records, of the exact boundaries and location of a property.

TITLE: Legal document containing all necessary facts to prove ownership of a property.

TITLE DEFECT: Fact or circumstance which challenges such ownership.

Insuring Your Home

BASIC GUIDELINES

You have found the house (or apartment) which really meets your needs and fits your budget. You have tracked down the most advantageous mortgage available in your area. Now, before you even set foot in the place, you must have it insured against fire, theft, and any other real threats which exist in your region and your neighborhood. The most widely used way to do this today is through a homeowners insurance policy.

Here are your basic guides:

Deal with an insurance agent who is respected by your neighbors and friends who have been dealing with him over the years. Your bank or lawyer are other good sources of advice on reputable insurance agents.

Sit down with the agent and go over all of the possible types, coverages, deductibles, and other aspects of property-liability insurance which might apply to you and your home.

Ask the previous owners or occupants of your house what kinds and amounts of insurance *they* carried. Use this as a starting point only, though, for it is more than likely they were underinsured. Also ask which major additions or improvements—such as a new garage or a new wing or a new bathroom—have been made since their policy was last reviewed and updated. Then fill your insurance agent in on the details and costs of such additions and request an appropriate upward revision of your basic coverage for the house.

Consider having the house professionally appraised—if you do not have a fairly good idea how much your house or apartment, and its contents, are now worth. A local real estate agent probably can recommend an appraiser who would do this job for you at reasonable cost. See pages 556–57 for guides on how to find a qualified appraiser. As an alternative, ask the contractor who built the house to estimate the cost of rebuilding it should it be totally destroyed.

At an absolute minimum, ask your insurance agent for his appraisal of your house in terms of trends in building and home repair costs in your area. Or ask him for one of the do-it-yourself appraisal kits provided by many insurance companies today. Some of these kits give you only a rough idea of cost trends; others detail building trade wage scales, materials costs, and other items, in various areas of the United States.

Keep in mind that, just between 1967 and 1973, over-all home construction costs soared by more than 50 per cent—meaning that a house which cost $20,000 to build in 1967 would have cost more than $30,000 to replace only six years later.

Insure your house for *at least* 80 per cent of its replacement value— in order to collect in full for loss or damage. If your coverage is less than this (as it is today for the majority of American homeowners), your insurance would pay only for the depreciated value of your house, rather than for the actual replacement cost. To illustrate this important difference:

If a fire in your ten-year-old home causes $10,000 worth of damage and if your house is underinsured, you'll be reimbursed for $10,000 *minus* the amount by which the insurance adjuster decides your house has depreciated during the decade (if any). No matter how well insured your house is, any personal property losses would be reimbursed not for their replacement value but rather for their depreciated cash value—unless you have extra coverage for this personal property.

Here are typical coverages provided by a homeowners policy for a $30,000 house today: $24,000 for the house itself (80 per cent of its value); $2,400 for unattached garages and other buildings on your property; $12,000 for personal property losses; $4,800 for extra living expenses in the event fire forces you out of your house temporarily; $37,500 in personal liability for each instance in which you are held liable (except for automobile liability); $750 in medical payments for each person injured on your property; and $350 for physical damage you cause to the property of others. There also may be personal liability coverage for accidents off the premises if they are caused by the homeowner, a member of his family who lives with him, or his pet. Provisions for legal expenses in the event of lawsuits against the policyholder are included too.

Make an inventory of the contents of your house—including factual descriptions of the appearance, type, and condition of each item of value; snapshots of each room taken from two or more different angles; detailed photographs, descriptions, and professional appraisals of each painting, musical instrument, rare book, or other item of significant value.

Keep a copy of this inventory in your safety deposit box to help support any insurance claim you may make later. Keep all records, photographs, up-to-date appraisals made by qualified appraisers, and other documentation of the value of such items in your safety deposit box.

Note that, as a general rule, the contents of your house and other personal property will be insured automatically for 50 per cent of the amount of insurance on your home. If you have especially valuable possessions such as paintings, sculptures, antiques, furs, stamp or coin collections, stereo equipment or jewelry, make sure their combined value falls within the limits of coverage of personal belongings—$12,000 in the above example—and if not, consider insuring them separately. You probably will find you have to insure them separately anyway, because such property is often classified "high risk" and assigned only nominal coverage unless extra premiums are paid.

Also, if you live in a city or suburb with a high crime rate and if your insurance company refuses to offer you coverage against burglaries, robberies, etc., consider applying through a nearby commercial insurance firm for a federal crime insurance policy issued by the Federal Insurance Administration, Department of Housing and Urban Development. A federal crime insurance policy will be valuable, comparatively inexpensive—and very important to you if you are not able to buy burglary and theft insurance through the normal commercial channels.

Note: If you rent a house or apartment you can get a special tenant's homeowners insurance policy covering your personal belongings and providing liability protection as well.

HOW TO GET THE RIGHT COVERAGE AND SAVE TOO

As a general rule, a homeowners insurance policy covers your home and belongings against a wide variety of perils, including fire, lightning, windstorm, tornadoes, explosions, and riots, on top of the other coverages it provides.

The so-called "broad form" homeowners policy adds to this list such perils as falling objects, building collapse, exploding hot water heaters and heating systems, pipe freezing, weight of ice and snow, and electrical damage to appliances.

The more expensive "all risks" policy covers you against every possible threat to your property except earthquakes, volcanic eruption, landslides, floods, tidal waves, sewage backups, nuclear radiation, war, and a few other possibilities.

Flood insurance is available through the National Flood Insurance Program. It is offered only in communities which have passed and enforce federally approved zoning restrictions on future flood plain development. Your insurance agent can tell you the limitations and other details as well as how to buy the coverage.

Obviously, the more dangers you insure your house against, the more your coverage will cost you. So go over the whole list with your insurance agent. Decide realistically which risks are a significant threat to your home. Buy the coverage which is suitable *for your house.*

Don't, however overinsure your house by basing your coverage on an inflated appraisal of its value or by including the value of your building site, foundation, or underground pipes and wiring in your valuation.

Take advantage of the deductibles now available in homeowners insurance policies. You might save a full 20 per cent in premium costs just by raising the deductible on your basic coverage from $50 to $250.

In some states a $50 "disappearing" deductible is available on homeowners and tenants policies. With this deductible, your insurance company is not required to pay for any losses under $50, but will pay for an increasingly larger proportion of losses between $50 and $500, and entire covered losses of more than $500.

In addition, a $50 deductible is now being offered by many home insurers on full comprehensive coverage (against perils ranging from earthquakes to civil commotion to collision with birds)—which translates into savings of 45 to 55 per cent over first-dollar comprehensive coverage.

If you belong to a professional organization, find out if it offers low-cost group homeowners insurance to members. As just one example, the National Education Association offers such a plan to teachers the nation over—costing considerably less than that of ordinary individual policies. Group homeowners insurance is an increasingly popular employee fringe benefit, offered by both organizations and employers. Check into this possibility.

Finally shop among insurance companies. If you don't have time to shop when you buy your house, do so when it is time to renew your coverage. Rates can vary widely for the same coverage.

HOW TO BOOST YOUR HOMEOWNERS COVERAGE

To expand your home insurance protection, you can:

• Simply increase the current over-all limits of the coverage on your home and/or its contents.

• Add a "floater policy" to give you extra coverage of certain personal effects such as jewelry, art works, professional tools, musical instruments.

• Increase your personal liability coverage. The typical yearly cost of hiking this coverage from $25,000 to $300,000 is only $6.00.

• Add a new "inflation guard endorsement" in your homeowners policy, for which you must pay an extra 5 to 6 per cent in premiums. This feature automatically increases your coverage as home replacement costs increase. This inflation-proofing is now available in most states.

Whatever you do, vow to have your policy updated every two or three years—because this is a vitally important financial protection against the soaring costs of repairing or replacing your house, and also because the values of any fine art works, antiques, stamp collections you may own are likely to soar over the years.

Don't risk finding out the hardest, cruelest, and costliest way, how drastically underinsured your home is.

The Bafflegab of Home Insurance

BURGLARY AND THEFT INSURANCE. Coverage which reimburses you for property which has been stolen from you or your home.

COMPREHENSIVE PERSONAL LIABILITY INSURANCE. Insurance, usually included in homeowners policies, which reimburses you for money you have had to pay for virtually any kind of damage or injury you have caused to other people. Damage caused by your automobile, however, is not covered. Nor are injury and damage associated with your business.

DEDUCTIBLES. Maximum amounts you, the policyholder, are required to pay in each claim or accident *before* your insurance payments begin. The higher the deductible you choose, the lower your premium costs.

EXTENDED COVERAGE. Protection against loss or damage to property caused by windstorm, hail, smoke, explosion, riots, vehicles, and aircraft.

FIRE INSURANCE. Coverage against losses due to fire and lightning and also against damage caused by water in home fires. Fire insurance includes extended coverage.

HOMEOWNERS POLICY. Home insurance "package" of coverages, including fire insurance, burglary and theft, and personal liability coverage.

LIABILITY INSURANCE. Protection against loss resulting from claims or lawsuits brought against you in the event that you cause injury to another person or damage to his property.

MEDICAL PAYMENTS INSURANCE. Type of insurance, often included in your liability insurance policy, which reimburses you as well as others, no matter who is at fault, for medical and/or funeral expenses resulting from certain types of injuries and accidents up to the limits of the coverage.

PROPERTY INSURANCE. Financial protection against loss or damage to your property as a result of theft, fire, smoke, windstorm, hail, explosion, riot, aircraft, motor vehicles, vandalism, malicious mischief, riots and civil commotion, and various other perils. The protection against perils other than fire is called "extended coverage."

UMBRELLA LIABILITY INSURANCE. Insurance against losses above and beyond those covered by your basic liability insurance policies. This type of insurance is often written for sums in the $1 million range. It is used mainly by well-to-do doctors, other professionals, and business executives who may be vulnerable to malpractice suits and other big liability claims.

How to Buy "House Equipment"

A HOUSE IS NOT A HOME

As the illustrious—albeit infamous—house mother Polly Adler put it more than a generation ago: a house is *not* a home.

A house is the shell. A home means furniture, appliances large and small, entertainment equipment, rugs, curtains, and you-name-what-else (not to mention people) it will take to make the shell *your* home.

In all, we spend tens of billions of dollars each year on furniture, appliances, and other "household durables."

Furniture, in fact, ranks among the biggest investments you will make in your lifetime. Yet the danger is that you will go about this purchase in near-total ignorance or innocence.

QUESTIONS AND ANSWERS ON FURNITURE

The following questions and answers will illustrate your basic guides to furniture buying.

Q. *Should you buy a whole houseful (or apartment full) of furniture all at once when you set up housekeeping?*

A. Few Americans, even older ones, are in a position to make an investment involving so much money and forethought. A more realistic approach would be to draw up a two-, three-, or five-year furniture-buying plan to meet your own particular needs.

Q. *How do you accomplish this?*

A. Lay your plan out in advance. You will then know precisely where you stand in your home furnishing from year to year. You also will know what first-year purchases can be switched to other uses as time goes on—e.g., a first-year wrought-iron table and chairs might go from the living room to the terrace or recreation room the second year, or a first-year throw rug for the dining alcove might go to the bedroom the third year, etc. And you will be able to fit the whole plan without difficulty into your personal money manager (see Chapter 1, "Your Personal Money Manager").

Q. *Where should you begin?*

A. Decide what type and size furniture will look the best and then focus on the basic, essential pieces you'll need right away—such as a bed, couch, table and chairs, good portable lamp, bureau, dresser, mirror. Decide in advance what job you want each piece to perform in terms of durability, beauty, practicality, economy.

Fill out the "basics" you can't afford to buy new with good-quality secondhand furniture from secondhand stores, thrift shops, junk shops, auctions, garage sales, Salvation Army and Goodwill Industries, want ads in local newspapers, family and friends. Good-quality used furniture is a better deal in both durability and attractiveness than low-quality new furniture. Seconds or slightly damaged new furniture also can be a bargain, but before you buy, find out how much necessary repairs would cost. Another good investment might be unfinished furniture which you can finish yourself to blend with your other furnishings.

Q. *How can you save in buying new, finished furniture?*

A. Choose basic designs rather than "fad" furniture which may cost just as much but soon go out of style. Select with an eye toward the future: sturdy but inexpensive canvas fold-up chairs, for example, might do now for the dining area and can be used later as porch furniture. Shop during furniture clearance sales, usually in August and after Christmas. Check your newspaper for these sales.

Q. *There's a tremendous price range in beds you see advertised; what's the rule for saving money here?*

A. Spend as much as you can afford for a mattress and box spring that will remain comfortable for a long time. You'll probably spend twenty-five years of your lifetime—if you're average—in bed. Don't skimp, and beware of "drastic reductions" and "fantastic bargains" in beds. Stay away from soft foam or foam flake mattresses—although good foams may be very good and also easier to handle. Make sure there's enough padding in your mattress so that you can't feel the innersprings through the padding. Also be sure the stitching is neat and firm, the ticking is durable. Before buying, lie down on the mattress and test its buoyancy and firmness. Your body weight should be supported equally at every point. The bedspring (box springs, usually) should have the same features as the mattress and should be bought at the same time.

It's a good idea to have a sleeping space 38 inches wide and 6 inches longer than your height (with a ½-inch allowance, plus or minus).

The mattress should have handles so it can be turned easily. It should have a strong outer fabric so that it will last, and ventilation on both sides to minimize dampness. Read the label attached to the mattress to find out if it has been treated to resist stains and whether it meets flammability standards.

Q. *How much should you budget for furniture if you are planning to move relatively soon to another home?*

A. Much depends on your individual priorities and means. But one guide is to avoid a big outlay for any item of furniture which probably wouldn't be appropriate in other quarters.

Q. *What type of furniture is best for a young couple with a small child?*

A. It can be risky to own a lot of really fine furniture while you're raising young children, unless you confine it to quarters which are out of bounds for the children. Otherwise, your best choice would probably be solid, simple furniture which can stand plenty of wear and tear and which can be replaced later.

Q. *How much should you earmark for accessories and strictly decorative items such as pictures, curtains, etc.?*

A. This will be determined by how much is left after you've collected your big items. If you find there's almost nothing left, you can use many attractive but inexpensive decorative items, such as wall posters and blown-up photographs instead of pictures and curtains made of burlap or unbleached muslin. But don't count curtains as "accessories" if you need them to give you privacy in your apartment or house.

Q. *What about the economics of patching up old, badly worn pieces of furniture?*

A. Don't throw good money after bad. When an item is finished, throw it out with no regrets.

Q. *What happens if you decide you don't like a big piece of furniture after it has been delivered to your home?*

A. The store from which you bought it is not legally required to take it back (it's a very costly hauling job for the retailer) so find out store policy on furniture returns, especially sale items, before you buy. Also ask the store to put in writing its policies on damage to furniture in transit to your home, installing and/or servicing items. Finally, is there a written warranty and, if so, exactly what does it cover?

Q. *What about reupholstering an old chair instead of buying a new one? Does this save money?*

A. The cost for reupholstering even a medium-size chair may shock you, for upholstering is largely a hand operation, and labor costs are high. This may be the best reason for replacing an old chair with a new piece of furniture, if the chair frame is of questionable quality. If, however, a chair or sofa is an antique or a sound, old piece of furniture, it's probably well worth the cost of getting it reupholstered.

Before calling an upholsterer, telephone several upholsters for a non-binding, over-the-phone indication of what labor charges would be for a particular type of chair or sofa. Fabric costs usually must be added to labor costs. Ask upholsterers who stock their own fabrics if their labor charge is the same whether their own fabrics are used or you supply them. Try to agree on a firm delivery date with the shop that gets your business. Ask if you can visit the owner's workshops—so you can get some idea of whether the work is sloppy or meticulous.

Prices tend to be somewhat lower in small owner-operated shops but it also may take a small shop longer to complete a job. Department stores near you may have upholstering departments. The work often will be done in your own home and be no more costly than that done by the small shops.

The construction of a chair often dictates the method of restoring. Expect to pay more for reupholstery of tufted or channel-backed chairs or sofas.

Q. *What are the comparative costs of reupholstering and buying a new chair?*

A. It can cost as much as $150 to $200 to reupholster a wing chair. A new one of average quality runs about $200 and up. The key to your choice should be the quality of the frame and springs of your chair or couch compared with that of a new piece. Wood frames in furniture bought a generation ago usually are better quality than the softer woods in upholstered furniture now on the market. A chair bought at a secondhand shop and reupholstered may prove a better buy in the long run than a new one.

Q. *How do you figure costs of fabrics in reupholstering?*

A. Fabric costs are fairly consistent from one upholsterer to another. Fabrics usually come 54 inches wide and range from as little as $5.00 a yard to as much as $75 a yard, with most in the $10 to $20 range. It takes about 6 yards to cover a wing chair and almost twice that for a three-cushion sofa.

Q. *Are there guides for spotting good quality in furniture?*

A. All joinings should be clean, tight-fitting, difficult to detect, and put together with screws instead of nails.

Drawers should slide smoothly. There also should be stops to prevent them from being pulled all the way out.

Backs of the furniture should be attractively finished—and not, as in cheap furniture, made of heavy cardboard.

Furniture doors should be well hung and fitted, and should open and close easily.

Undersides should be sanded and stained to match more visible parts.

The hardware, such as knobs, pulls, and handles, should be firmly attached, tastefully designed, and in keeping with the quality of the piece it adorns. Brass and other metal hardware should be rust-resistant and tarnish-proof.

Federal Trade Commission rules require furniture to be tagged if synthetic materials are used, or if the material is veneer. If such furniture does not have these tags prominently displayed, or if the tags are difficult to decipher, steer clear of the store.

Q. *What about the quality of upholstered furniture?*

A. It is harder to detect quality in upholstered furniture because the upholstery hides the construction. But you can get a good idea of the quality and type of materials used in an upholstered piece from the label, which, by law, must itemize all materials used in it. Ask questions about the quality and type of construction of the piece, the material used in the padding, color-fastness of the outer covering, durability. Look at the material to see if patterns match at seams and if seams and welts are straight.

FTC rules also give you some protection with upholstered furniture, requiring clear and conspicuous labels substantiating special claims for the fabrics.

Deal only with stores which have good reputations.

Also test the pieces you want to buy. Sit in them, see if they're the right height and size for your comfort, as soft or hard as you like your furniture to be. Sit on the furniture in the store the way you like to sit at home.

Q. *Should you buy furniture on time?*

A. Cash is the cheapest way to pay for furniture, of course. Moreover, interest charges by retail stores on furniture bought on the installment plan are higher than interest charges on many other forms of credit. So, if you do buy on time, shop among the various available sources of credit for your most advantageous deal.

Q. *What are the best stores in which to buy furniture?*

A. You'll find this out by comparing prices, quality, and service among furniture stores, chain stores, department stores, discount stores. Look at different price levels for the same item. Compare quality as nearly as you can determine it. Patronize no-frills, low-cost furniture "clearance centers" operated by major furniture stores where you buy for cash and take home your purchases yourself.

Don't be afraid to shop. The honest merchant will want you to look around in his store. Most furniture stores are honest. But there are retailers who will try to take advantage of you and high-pressure you into buying something you cannot afford or may not even want. Before you buy, find out from friends what their experiences with the store have been. Also check on the reputation of a store by calling or writing the local Better Business Bureau.

Q. *Chairs, tables, couches—these can be very expensive items. Where is there room for savings?*

A. Use your own individual skills to finish lower-cost unfinished furniture yourself. Rely on color and arrangement, rather than expensive craftsmanship, to achieve good style.

Q. *What about plastic furniture—is that any bargain?*

A. Some of the best-designed modern furniture available today is made of fiberglass or plastic. Some pieces are expensive, but many others sell at prices well within the budgets of most young Americans.

Q. *What if you love fine old furniture but just can't pay the price for it?*

A. If you're inclined toward antiques—but can't afford the real thing—consider "honest copies" made decades after the originals by lesser craftsmen, often at considerably lower cost than genuine models.

Q. *Are there any special guides for wood?*

A. The leading native woods are: walnut, oak, pine, spruce, redwood, cedar, cherry, pecan or hickory, maple, birch. Each has a distinctive color and grain pattern. The major foreign hardwood is mahogany. It shrinks or swells less than almost any other wood.

Q. *Do you save by buying a complete bedroom or dining-room set, instead of individual items?*

A. You may, if you actually need each item offered in the package. But you won't save any money if the roomful includes things you hadn't intended to buy in the first place.

Q. *What about the bargain specials—lamps, racks—offered free with complete sets?*

A. Don't be misled by stores that toss in lamps, ashtrays, magazine racks, and other accessories to make up a "bargain" room of furniture. Reputable stores try this on occasion too, and it's no bargain. Price the basic furniture so you'll know exactly what you're paying for what.

Q. *What about furniture ads which say "wholesale prices to you"?*

A. Don't be misled by any ads claiming "wholesale prices" or "factory to you." A retailer cannot sell to customers at wholesale prices. How would he make a profit? And if factories sold wholesale to everyone, who would want to be a retailer?

Q. *What about "introductory" discount cards to furniture showrooms?*

A. If you get a "card of introduction" to a furniture showroom, do not buy until you have compared its "discount prices" with the regular prices at other stores. Make sure that the discount cards or cards of admission or introduction really do give discounts. And also make sure that "warehouse" stores are truly warehouses and not retail stores actually charging higher prices than regular stores.

Q. *What about guarantees and warranties on furniture?*

A. A reputable merchant is your best protection, for furniture is seldom guaranteed. Mattresses, however, are usually "guaranteed" by the manufacturer for ten to twenty years. Get a copy of the guarantee, read it with care, and save it for future reference. (See Part IV, "Your Rights and How to Get Them," for details and how to get your money's worth on any type of warranty.)

Q. *How long do you have to wait for furniture to be delivered?*

A. If the furniture you have ordered is available, you will probably get it right away. However, if the furniture is not available and has to be ordered from the manufacturer, you may have to wait from six to twelve weeks or more! Get delivery promises in writing, and put down as small a deposit as possible. Don't get rid of your old furniture until you get the new. Most dealers will tell you if there will be a delay in delivery.

If you have serious late delivery problems, contact the Furniture Industry Consumer Panel, P. O. Box 951, High Point, N.C. 27261, or one of the consumer rights organizations listed in Chapter 28, "Where to Get Help."

Q. *Should you hire an interior designer?*

A. Before you hire a professional designer, find out if your local stores offer, as many now do, free counseling services on home furnishing problems, either at the store or at your home. You also can get good decorating ideas just by studying the variety of furniture ensembles (or model rooms) on display at most large stores. You may soon feel confident to go ahead on your own.

But, if you're planning and can afford a substantial furnishing job and if you have neither the interest nor talent to tackle the job yourself, by all means consider hiring a professional interior designer. Clever designers often can save you money—by buying furniture and materials at substantial discounts, by finding practical uses for unused spaces, by turning inexpensive "raw material" into imaginative and attractive designs, by helping you sidestep the pitfalls—economic and otherwise—of dealing through untrained, unsophisticated retail salespeople, by making sure you avoid costly decorating errors (e.g., dashing colors, oversize pieces of furniture, etc.), by knowing where the best bargains are in the goods you need.

Q. *How do you shop for this type of service?*

A. Ask either the National Society of Interior Designers (315 East Sixty-second Street, New York, N.Y. 10021) or the American Institute of Interior Designers (730 Fifth Avenue, New York, N.Y. 10019) for names of reputable members in your area. Ask friends who have worked with interior designers what their experience—and costs—have been.

Be sure you communicate well, both ways, with the person you choose and that the designer will build on your ideas, tastes, and preferences in whatever job he or she takes on for you.

Insist on sketches and drawings from the designer, showing the plan or scheme to be followed. Such sketches are a crucially important clue to what a room or rooms will look like when finished.

Ask the designer to help you plan if you are furnishing and decorating your first home and if you have to spread out your purchases over several years.

Discuss costs and fees in advance and be sure these details are in a written contract for a given job. Write in this contract what services and which furnishings will be included, what completion date is anticipated, and on what schedule you will pay for the work done.

Q. *What charges should you be prepared for?*

A. Typically, you pay one third of the total agreed-upon price when you sign the contract, another one third when the designer orders the furnishings you want, and the balance when the job is done.

Typical designers' fees for a preliminary consultation in the mid-seventies ran about $25 an hour, with some as high as $100 to $200 for each sixty minutes of consultation time.

Procedures vary, so be sure you check them out. Some designers, including architects who offer interior designing services, charge clients only the difference between the wholesale and retail value of whatever furniture and materials they buy for you. Others charge a flat fee.

QUESTIONS AND ANSWERS ON RUGS AND CARPETING

Q. *What about wall-to-wall carpeting?*

A. That can be very expensive. Before taking on this extra cost and getting involved with some of the disadvantages—for instance, in cleaning and in your inability to turn the carpeting to spread out wear—consider your situation carefully. If you're just starting out, or if you are a family on the move from apartment to apartment or city to city, just buy rugs or carpet tiles for the rooms that absolutely need them, and in colors which will not clash with furniture you may buy later.

Q. *Are the rug-carpet sales any good?*

A. Yes. And you can save from 20 to as much as 50 per cent on carpets and rugs if you wait for the periodic sales which take place in January–February and July–August. Most department stores and long-established rug stores have legitimate sales at least annually, during which you can save up to 20 or 25 per cent. Sometimes, too, you may be able to find an item that is being discontinued by the mill at savings up to 50 per cent. But deal only with reputable stores.

Q. *How do you judge fibers?*

A. *Wool,* the most expensive carpeting material, experts still believe offers the most elegant mixture of qualities in a rug or carpet: ease of cleaning, resistance to fire and soiling, durability, and resilience. However, it must be mothproofed, may be damaged by alkaline detergents, and can cause allergy problems.

Nylon is somewhat less resilient than wool and less springy but it gets less beaten up by abrasion, and water-soluble stains can be wiped out with a sponge very easily. It tends to cause harmless but annoying static electricity shocks unless a small amount of metal fiber is included.

Rayon is cheap but it doesn't hold up well under use and should be avoided.

Acrylics wear at least as well as nylon, resemble wool in looks and performance, resist soil and sun-fading better than any other fabric in use, and clean easily. But there can be a fire danger in 100 per cent acrylics. So examine the carpet label carefully and be sure there is at least 20 per cent modacrylic blended in.

Q. *What about carpet flammability?*

A. Under the Flammable Fabrics Act, all newly manufactured or imported carpets, rugs, and carpet tiles must meet federal flammability standards. If the carpet dealer cannot provide you with the appropriate assurance that a carpet or carpeting is fire-resistant, write to the manufacturer. And if you get no assurance there, shop elsewhere.

Q. *How do you judge carpet construction?*

A. Construction is the basic secret of good carpets. Construction means pile and workmanship. Bend the carpet back to see how thick the pile is. The thicker the individual tuft the better; the closer each tuft is to the next the better. Take a look also at the back of the carpet. Tufts that are well anchored, that have a latex coating to help anchor them even more, are signs of quality. However, the anchoring method is often hidden on modern carpeting; ask to see a diagram of the anchoring method, and give preference to the most informative seller.

Incidentally, the term "broadloom," often associated with quality of a carpet, refers merely to the width of the carpeting.

Q. *What's the best way to clean wall-to-wall carpeting—and the cost?*

A. Use a rug-cleaning establishment which specializes in cleaning carpeting in the home. These companies usually charge about 10¢ a square foot and some offer reduced rates during slow seasons, such as the early part of the year.

For an easily understandable rundown on all aspects of carpeting write for a copy of "Carpets and Rugs," prepared by the U. S. Government's General Services Administration (90¢; Consumer Product Information, Pueblo, Colo. 81009).

HOW TO AVOID "CARPET SHARKS"

"Wall-to-wall nylon carpet . . . two rooms plus hall or stairway. . . . Complete with padding and custom installation . . . $119."

"Three rooms of wall-to-wall carpeting. . . . Free tickets to a Broadway show and a free vacuum cleaner. . . . All for $115."

These and hundreds of similar ads are typical of the "carpet shark," who knows little about carpeting but every trick in the book on making a sale —often at a price many times the carpet's value. And once he has made a sale and the carpet has been installed, there is absolutely nothing a victim can do about it. One victim reported paying $2,064 for a carpet worth $650. Another shelled out $3,000 for a small carpet valued at a few hundred dollars.

To illustrate the pitfalls, let's say you respond to a come-on ad offering rooms of carpeting, completely installed, for $100 or so. A high-pressure salesman arrives at your door and immediately downgrades the carpet his company advertised. Sample remarks made by a fast-buck salesman to a "detective" planted by one Better Business Bureau:

"If you take it up, you will have to resand your floors. Be careful how you vacuum it—it will run like a stocking from the corners. With baseboard heating like you have, it will crumple right up and won't last six months."

The salesman has instructions to sell *not* the low-priced carpet to you but some other, vastly overpriced product. If you insist on buying the $100 carpeting, he simply refuses to sell.

Another type of carpet gypster advertises "industrial" or "commercial" carpeting at bargain prices—claiming that the carpet is left over from a big job in a hotel or office building and that such carpeting wears longer than regular covering. As it turns out, you may end up paying the gypster up to three times the price you would pay at your local store for the same stuff. "The fact is," says one industry expert, "that there is no established commercial standard and seldom is there enough carpeting left over from a commercial installation to cover an average-sized bathroom."

Still another trick is called yardage "jumping" or "stealing." This simply means telling you that you need 30 yards of carpeting instead of the 25 you actually should buy. A variation of this gyp is the phony reference to "factory units" of carpet measurement—another way to induce you to buy more carpet than you need.

Here's how to spot a carpet shark:

• Beware of ads that offer an "astonishingly low" price. You just can't have three rooms of carpeting installed for less than $100. Many reputable dealers figure as a rule of thumb that you'll get one year of wear for each dollar per yard that you spend.

• Beware of the salesman who tries to switch you from his company's advertised special. "Bait and switch" techniques are outlawed in most states, but enforcement of the law is difficult.

• Ask for a sample of the carpet to be installed, or at least make sure the same carpet you ordered is actually delivered.

• Beware of "free" offers along with "bargain" carpeting. The offers *aren't* free.

• Deal only with an established, reputable dealer. Be wary of any carpet ad which gives only a telephone number—but no address—of the carpet company.

YOUR APPLIANCES

AN ENORMOUS HOUSEHOLD EXPENSE

No matter how and where you live in this country—whether as a single person or married and with or without kids or in a house or apartment, in a boat or trailer—you will use appliances and various forms of household equipment. You will spend tens of thousands of dollars to buy these big-ticket items. Then you will spend more thousands (countless thousands) to repair, to power, to modernize, or to remodel these big-ticket items.

This is, in short, an enormous part of your living expense. Here's a Census Bureau rundown on what proportion of American families own which types of appliances today:

APPLIANCE	% OWNING
Refrigerator	99.8%
Television	95.3
Washing machine	91.9
Color TV set	50.0
Clothes dryer (gas or electric)	46.9
Room air conditioner	31.9
Freezer	33.2
Two or more TV sets	29.4
Dishwasher	23.7

We in this country now own more than one *billion* appliances—an average of 16 appliances for each home. Our annual spending for small appliances alone—ranging from electric toothbrushes to electric knives, ice crushers and pencil sharpeners—now tops $2.5 billion. Our outlay for the large appliances now exceeds $8 billion a year.

RULES FOR BUYING APPLIANCES

Recognize the danger of impulse buying of expensive appliances. Ask yourself: Do I need, do I want, can I really use this appliance? Can I afford the addition it will make to my electricity or gas bill?

Unless you are more than usually familiar with the appliance, stick to name brands, for which repair parts are more readily available. But by no means overlook private label appliances sold through major outlets—many of which are made by the big, well-known manufacturers. Repairmen also are more familiar with the major brand-name appliances so your chances of getting the appliance fixed are better.

Consult Consumers Union's ratings, descriptions, and comparisons of the type of appliance you're buying, as well as its "frequency of repair" record—a clue to how much of a lemon (or non-lemon) each brand and model is likely to be.

Start with non-frill models. Every manufacturer has lower-priced models which are the same equipment as the high-priced models, minus frills. Look first at the least expensive model to see whether it will fit your needs, and then decide how many of the refinements in more expensive models you need, and whether they're worth the price. You well may find the de luxe models are a nuisance and all you really want is the basic, least expensive—and least expensive to operate—machine.

Look for model clearance sales where you easily can save money. When old models are being cleared out, you can get an excellent buy. But be sure the guarantee or warranty applies to the old model and you will have no trouble getting service or parts for it.

Be sure before you buy a major appliance that it fits not only through the door but also into the space you have available for it. Many people buy appliances, then find they can't get them into the area they planned to use. Or they find that their landlords won't permit the use of a washing machine or dryer in the apartments. So think it out before you buy. Measure the area where you intend to place the appliance. Be sure the floor is strong enough. Check the manufacturer's directions on how much space you must leave between the appliance and a wall for the safest and most efficient use (typically at least one half inch for a refrigerator or freezer, several inches for a freestanding range).

Consider whether the appliance will be large enough. Will a 10-cubic-foot refrigerator be large enough for your future needs when you have children in coming years?

Comparison-shop, for appliance prices can vary substantially from store to store—and buy only from a dealer whose reputation is good for service as well as sales. Ask the salesmen if their stores service the appliances they sell. Many dealers sell a number of brands and refer customers to factory-authorized shops for service. Be sure such service is available in your area.

Know what the price includes. Will the dealer make free delivery, directly into your home? Will he install those appliances that require it, and will he charge for installation? Are warranty and service included in the price? What is covered and what's not covered by the warranty? (See Part IV "Your Rights and How to Get Them," for a detailed rundown on warranties.)

If you are buying an appliance on time, compare *total* finance charges offered by each dealer—not just monthly payments.

As an indicator of safety, look for the Underwriters Laboratories seal on the body of all electrical appliances, the Blue Star Seal of the American Gas Association Laboratories on gas appliances, or the CSA (Canadian Standard Association) mark of approval. (If the UL seal is only on the plug or cord, that is all that is approved.)

Make sure you have adequate electrical circuits to handle the appliance before you buy. Ask your landlord about this, if you're renting. Or, if you own your home, ask the local utility for a free check on these circuits. If it won't oblige, hire a qualified electrician to do it.

Be sure the type of gas you have (e.g., natural gas, propane gas, etc.)

suits the gas appliances you buy. The gas company and appliance dealer can guide you.

Check your local repair shops to find out what appliance service they offer. The appliance might be trouble-free for months, but when repairs are needed or even the smallest part has to be replaced, it will be costly if you must travel a long distance to get what you need. Find a good repair shop *before* an emergency arises.

If your appliance develops problems after the warranty runs out, deal only with service agencies authorized by the manufacturer or with a reputable local service firm.

In deciding whether to throw away an appliance rather than repair it, consider your time, travel, and inconvenience. Consider also whether the problem is functional or merely one of appearance. And don't waste money trying to repair a too old appliance. If the appliance is much older than the following life-expectancy guide—based on Department of Agriculture findings—put your money into a replacement instead.

LIFE EXPECTANCY OF APPLIANCES

APPLIANCE	AVERAGE LIFE SPAN
Sewing machine	24 years
Vacuum cleaner, upright	18 years
Ranges, electric or gas	16 years
Refrigerator	16 years
Toaster, automatic	15 years
Freezer	15 years
Vacuum cleaner, tank	15 years
Clothes dryer	14 years
Washing machine, automatic and semi-automatic	11 years
Television set	11 years
Washing machine, wringer and spin dry	10 years
Toaster, non-automatic	7 years

HOW TO BUY "BARGAIN" APPLIANCES

When you see a bargain-priced appliance offered "as is," how can you tell whether or not it's likely to fall apart just after you get it home? What do retailers mean when they claim they are selling items at "wholesale" prices? Is a "free home trial" of a major appliance really free?

These are some of the questions you must consider as you venture into today's increasingly complex and trap-ridden appliance market place. In response, here is a short list of money- and nerve-saving rules on appliance bargains and non-bargains:

• Be alert to what you're buying. If it's a "floor model" or "demonstrator"—or a damaged, scratched, beat-up "as is" item—are you getting enough of a discount?

• Similarly, if you're tempted by a bargain appliance advertised as "reconditioned" or "rebuilt," the key question to ask is: by whom? If a gadget or machine is advertised as "factory rebuilt," this *should* mean rebuilt by the original manufacturer. Again, what warranty applies?

• Recognize that claims by appliance retailers of "wholesale" prices are, as the Better Business Bureaus warn, "usually wholesale bunk."

• If a "free home trial" is offered, make sure that you have no obligation to buy. Watch out for the unscrupulous dealer who may attempt to get you to sign a purchase contract which you are led to believe is simply a receipt for the "free home trial."

• One real way to save money when you buy appliances is to buy them secondhand. This obviously can be a gamble, since you usually buy them "as is." But if the dealer is reputable, he may guarantee the used appliance he is selling you or otherwise agree to fix it if problems arise. And one advantage of a slightly used appliance is that its bugs and kinks may already have been discovered—and fixed—before you get it.

• Finally, if you discover you have bought a lemon, or if a dealer fails to live up to a warranty or service contract, gather the facts to support your complaint, and complain—loudly! You'll help not only yourself but also every reliable appliance manufacturer and dealer, and all the rest of us in the market for appliances today. (See Chapter 28, "Where to Get Help," for valuable information on how to complain and get action on appliance agonies as well as other categories of consumer miseries.)

HOW TO CUT REPAIR COSTS

Always somewhere on the horizon is the dreamy promise by one company or another to provide a comprehensive, economical maintenance and repair service for appliances. But so far the dream hasn't materialized. Meanwhile, when you deal with appliance servicemen, you must be on the alert for an array of deep pitfalls—ranging from having to pay for unneeded or unsatisfactory work to losing deposits on work and parts not provided.

This is one reason why U.S. consumers throw away something like $20 *billion* of defective and worn-out household goods each year—in many cases because we do not know how to fix them, we cannot find anyone else to do the job, or the repair costs just aren't worth it.

A basic precaution is to inquire about each model's frequency of repair record *before you buy*. Consumers Union regularly publishes details on how often major appliances break down and require repairs. From this record you can easily calculate the probable repair costs of each brand—and choose the brand which is not only reasonably priced but which also has a record of few needed repairs. To suggest the savings you can achieve by exploring this single point, five $30 service calls after the warranty on your refrigerator has run out can add 50 per cent to the basic cost of this appliance.

Certainly do not fail to take all the preventive maintenance measures you are supposed to take. If the owner's manual calls, for example, for regular defrosting, or periodic cleaning, or removal of lint from appliance screens and filters, do these things on schedule. To remind yourself, compile a special calendar for maintenance measures on your household appliances and post it in a prominent place.

Study from the start the owner's manual which came with the appliance. Keep a file of all these manuals for the lifetime of the respective devices and machines. They are your number 1 source of information on how to operate an appliance properly, what to check if something goes wrong, common errors to avoid, etc. Merely reading each instruction booklet could eliminate the need for half the appliance service calls you are making today.

Before you call in a serviceman, check the electric plug to make sure the appliance is plugged in firmly. Also check dials, buttons, switches, and safety valves, to make sure they haven't been accidentally pushed in the wrong direction. And check appropriate fuses both in the appliance and in the cellar to make sure they have not blown.

These steps alone could save you, the consumer, more than 25 per cent of appliance service costs—and could result in really significant savings after your warranties have run out.

CHECK LIST OF MOST COMMON APPLIANCE PROBLEMS

For quick reference, here's a chart of today's most common appliance problems—and what to do about them *before* you call a serviceman. The chart was prepared by a small consumer magazine, *Everybody's Money,* published by the Credit Union National Association.

APPLIANCE	PROBLEM	DON'T CALL SERVICEMAN UNTIL YOU CHECK
Automatic washer	Motor won't go	1. Fuse—is it in washer fuse box? 2. Plug—is it in outlet?
	Won't fill	1. Is water turned on?
Automatic dryer	Slow drying	1. Overloaded lint screen 2. Insufficient fuse rating 3. Too heavy loads 4. Too wet clothes

APPLIANCE	PROBLEM	DON'T CALL SERVICEMAN UNTIL YOU CHECK
	Runs noisily	1. Dryer resting unevenly on floor 2. Loose belt
Vacuum cleaner	Cleans poorly	1. Clogged nozzle 2. Hose obstruction 3. Very full bag 4. Bag needs replacing
Toaster	Release won't work	Mechanism may be jammed with crumbs, raisins, etc. Clean every two weeks by sliding out trap or turning toaster upside down
Electric range	Oven or elements won't heat	1. Is automatic oven control set back at manual? 2. Main cartridge in house fuse box may be blown; use 40-amp. fuse for older-type range, 45- or 60-amp. for new double ovens
Oil or gas furnace	Won't come on	1. Fuse in house fuse box may be blown 2. Thermostat may be set too low 3. Fuel tank may be empty 4. Pilot light may be out
Dishwasher	Motor won't go	1. Impeller may be jammed with small pieces of food or broken glass 2. The fuse may be blown
	Cleans unsatisfactorily	1. Improper dish stacking 2. Too much detergent 3. Wrong type of detergent
Refrigerator	Doesn't keep food cold	1. Poor door seal 2. Door left open too long, too often

APPLIANCE	PROBLEM	DON'T CALL SERVICEMAN UNTIL YOU CHECK
		3. Shelf paper on refrigerator shelves preventing air circulation
		4. Thermostat set too high
	Food freezes in refrigerator compartment	1. Return air louvres in freezer compartment blocked by loose wrapping paper
		2. Thermostat set too low
Garbage disposal	Doesn't grind	1. Use self-service wrench or push blade-activating button
		2. Jammed with food

TELEVISION

HOW TO GET THE BEST DEAL

More than nine out of ten American households now own at least one TV set, millions of families own two or three sets, and more than one half of U.S. households now possess color TV sets.

With TV ownership as broad as this in our country, you would think we were a nation of pros when it comes to buying TV sets. We aren't. Millions continue to be lured into buying sets at prices and on terms they simply can't afford. Or they get the wrong kind of antenna setup and cancel out the advantages of the extra money they have paid for the basic set. Or they just don't know what to do when the TV set conks out a few months after they've bought it.

What can *you* do to prevent these problems? How can you get the best possible deal for the hundreds of dollars you'll almost certainly spend for TV sets in the years directly ahead?

• To start with, arrive at a clear idea of what kind of—and how much —TV you want. Today's typical black and white TV set has a 19-inch screen (measured diagonally). This, by Federal Trade Commission regulation, is the area in which the picture *can actually be seen*. It's portable— although, weighing in at 35 to 45 pounds or so, not that easy to lug around. Most sets produce a better signal with an outside antenna than with a built-in one. Most have controls for on and off, brightness and contrast in the front of the set.

A few have such sophisicated mechanisms as a "continuously variable" horizontal size control to "expand" a shrinking picture back to normal and another control mechanism which automatically keeps a picture from rolling or tilting—thus eliminating the need for separate vertical and horizontal control dials.

• Decide what price you can afford to pay. Most of today's black and white TV sets cost between $100 and $200. But by all means find out what that price tag does and does not cover. Delivery? Installation? Will the dealer install and adjust (for a fee) an appropriate antenna? Or, if you live in an apartment or on a cable TV line, will he connect up your set to the central antenna?

• Inquire with care into what the warranty provides. Today, a typical black and white TV set is guaranteed for 90 days—*for parts only*—and one year for the picture tube, again not counting labor costs. Color sets typically carry a warranty running one year for parts and labor, two or five years for the picture tube.

However, TV warranty terms vary widely. And a TV dealer is not obligated to give you a new TV set if the one you have just bought turns out to be a lemon. He's required only to get it back into operating condition.

• Study the TV picture. Key aspects which you can check in any large TV showroom are:

Sharpness, resolution (detail), focus (the sharpness of horizontal scanning lines), the interlacing or evenness in the spacing of these lines, nonlinearity (which makes TV actors get fatter as they move toward the edge of the screen), and lack of distortion.

Brightness of the set is governed by the voltage of the picture tube. Modern tubes should have about 1,000 volts for each diagonal inch on the viewing screen.

"AGC"—or automatic gain control—is another important factor in a TV picture; it maintains the brightness and contrast setting when you switch from a strong to a weak signal and vice versa.

• Get the answers to these other key questions:

How does a particular set perform in the location of *your* house—particularly if your house is in an area in which signals tend to be weak or certain stations are hard to get?

How will the set look in your living room?

Does it have a fast warm-up feature which brings on the picture almost instantly when you turn on the set? Is such a feature, which may cost you about $15 a year in extra electricity, important to you?

How are the circuit boards arranged? In some models there are a limited number of plug-in boards fitted with certain key parts. In the event of a breakdown (which will happen to the average set about once a year), you simply remove the ailing circuit board and plug in another—with a minimum of hunting time (and repair costs) to locate the source of the trouble. However, many TV repair shops cannot afford to stock the spare boards and you may be forced to choose a high-priced shop to fix this type of set.

• Finally, does the apartment or area in which you live offer cable TV —providing extra-good reception, especially in areas with formerly poor reception? If CATV is offered, how much will it cost to hook into it—and what monthly fees will you have to pay the company which owns the cable?

EXTRA GUIDELINES FOR COLOR TV

Today, you can purchase a superior color TV with a fairly large screen and improved features for under $400. But the improved features so prominently advertised by manufacturers can confuse as well as benefit you. How, then, do you shop wisely?

• Begin by familiarizing yourself with three basic terms: solid-state circuitry, in-line picture tubes, and automatic tuning.

Solid-state circuitry, now available from every domestic manufacturer, is perhaps the single most important innovation in color TV and there's no reason you should settle for anything less. Solid-state is an important step forward because transistors use far less energy than tubes, produce less heat while operating, and don't burn out the way tubes can.

In-line picture tubes, built into many makes of 17″ and 19″ sets are being used by a large percentage of manufacturers who believe they are fuzzy-free and fiddle-free.

Automatic or one-button tuning is offered by virtually every manufacturer. On most sets, it's a simple control that eliminates the need to fiddle with a handful of knobs to adjust color for each channel. Brightness, contrast, color, and tint are pre-set.

• Look for the number of stages, through which the picture signal is amplified, called IF stages. Most sets push the signal through three stages, though some of the less expensive models have two. But lack of that third stage can mean less resolution in the picture, particularly in areas where the signal is weak. You can determine the number of IF stages by a glance at the set's specifications.

• Check the range of house voltage the set can take. A wider range gives you more protection against future brownouts. Most sets accept 108 to 132 volts, but some will work in as wide a range as 70 to 140 volts.

• Don't skimp on an antenna. A $50 antenna can be worth every penny in terms of improved reception and in helping you get the results you want from an expensive TV set. A color TV requires a better antenna than a black and white model.

• Don't overlook service. Deal only with a reliable store that will offer you the assurance of the services you will need.

• By no means, permit yourself to be rushed into buying. Decide in advance what you want; take time to brief yourself on what you should expect.

Color TV now significantly outsells black and white in the United States—and it can add a whole new dimension to your viewing pleasure, even during summer reruns. But you may regret the day you bought your set unless you know the simple rules that will help you maneuver through the maze of claims and counterclaims.

TV REPAIRS

HOW TO SLASH THESE COSTS

TV repairs are a category unto themselves. For one thing, a TV set—particularly color TV—is by far the most complex and sophisticated device in most households, and the one most likely to need service. One survey even indicated that many new TVs are "dead on arrival" from the store. For another, the field of TV repairs always has been plagued by more than its share of incompetent and unscrupulous repairmen. In fact an estimated $150 million of the $1 billion plus Americans spend annually on TV repairs are wasted through incompetence or fraud. The TV repairman can be among the most frustrating and painfully expensive service people you must deal with.

Still, there are ways in which you can reduce the frustrations *and* the costs. First, to cut down on the over-all number of TV service calls:

• Try using another receptacle. It's possible the problem is with the first receptacle, not the set itself. Of course, make sure the set is plugged in.

• Check the antenna and lead-in from the antenna, which might have been torn by a storm or accidentally disconnected from the back of the set by your child or your dog.

• Try the adjustment controls to make sure they are operating properly, and if they are not, consult your TV owner's manual for guidance on how to get them back in working order.

• If your problem is "ghosts"—or multiple images on a TV screen—this is seldom due to defects in the set. These images are caused by interference or other problems in the location in which you live (e.g., nestled between a couple of skyscrapers), and therefore usually cannot be remedied by a TV repairman. Thus, before you ask a serviceman to lay your TV ghosts to rest, ask your neighbors whether they have been having problems similar to yours. And find out what results they have had when *they* called in professionals to solve them.

Only if these steps shed no light on your problem, call a serviceman. Jot down details on just what happened when the set broke down; these are vital guides for him. Also have your bill of sale ready to show him, so he can check your warranty coverage.

• If you are choosing a TV service firm for the first time, ask your friends where they have found reliable and satisfactory service. If you are in doubt about any company's record, ask the local Better Business Bureau if it has any adverse information on the company. If you are tempted by an estimated low cost of repairs, back up; this is *not* the basis upon which to choose a TV repairman. In states which license TV technicians, stick with the licensed shops and report any complaints to the licensing authority.

• If it is necessary to take your set back to the shop for repairs, get a written estimate of the approximate repair costs—before the repairman takes the set out of your house. Depending on the complexity of the trouble, your bill might vary from the estimate by 20 per cent or so. Whether or not you authorize its removal, you should expect to pay the service call charge for the technician to come to your home and diagnose your set's trouble and sometimes also an extra pickup and delivery charge. Note: You'll probably save money if you take your set to the service shop and have the work done there rather than in your home. Be prepared to pay a charge just for checking over your TV, whether or not any work is done, since the checking ties up costly equipment and manpower.

• Don't underestimate the fact that a good TV technician must maintain thousands of dollars' worth of diagnostic and repair equipment—plus an inventory of spare parts. He may have as much as two to four years of specialized education and training behind him. He can no more afford to make a free house call than a doctor can. According to studies by the Chicago-based National Alliance of TV and Electronic Service Associations, the average cost to the operator of an ethical TV repair service in 1974 was $14 to $27 per hour.

• Insist on and keep itemized bills for any and all repairs—for reference if the repairs fail to hold up properly. As with other appliances, see if you can pay for any repairs within thirty days. In this time, you should find out whether or not the set was repaired correctly.

BEWARE: UNRELIABLE TV REPAIRMEN

Steer clear of the "sundowner" who moonlights in TV repairs—operating out of his home and advertising only a telephone number, often an answering service, but no address. The sundowner accepts any and all work he can get but may take weeks or months to service *your* TV set. It can be defiantly difficult to reach this type of repairman—since you do not know his address and he may pay no attention to telephone messages. He also may simply walk off with your TV set and never show up again.

Avoid the "baiter" who advertises ridiculously low prices for TV service calls, then slaps on extra-steep charges for parts. For instance: "$1 per call, plus parts." This practice is also known as "low balling." Or, once the baiter gets your set in the shop, he may uncover an endless, expensive array of problems, all of which will necessitate new parts and much expensive labor. The baiter may then turn into a "setnapper," demanding a "ransom" in the form of an unreasonable bill before he will release your TV.

Surely you need no further analysis to convince you that the TV service firm which made free service calls or even charged only a couple of dollars for a service call would go broke almost overnight.

Also stay away from the repair outfit that lists itself under a dozen different names in the Yellow Pages to bring in as much business as possible—without regard to whether or not the outfit can handle the repairs. If you get tangled up with one of these firms, you may get neither service nor your set back.

SOUND EQUIPMENT

WHAT'S WHAT IN HOME LISTENING

If you are over age forty, you probably continue to clutch an image of this basic home listening equipment:

One metal box fitted with several knobs, which is a radio; another box with a round turntable on top and an arm fitted with a diamond needle on which you play 12-inch records, singly or in stacks; perhaps a couple of speakers connected to one of these boxes to enrich the sound of the records you're playing. And that's it.

But if you're in your teens or twenties or thirties, you well may speak an entirely different language: of stereophonic or quadraphonic sound; of cartridges, cassettes, and consoles; of tapes and tape decks; of vastly complex, often vastly expensive "component systems" with parts you can string through your house.

Let's, though, ignore age and just assume you're an amateur considering investing in a home listening system. Let's also say you do have some money to spend and you're ready.

Your first step is to familiarize yourself with what's what in the world of home listening:

An *AM radio* receives the standard list of stations, local and distant.

An *FM radio* gives you different stations but a higher quality of sound and, possibly, better programming.

Monaural sound, e.g., in a standard phonograph or radio, comes from a single speaker and generally is the least expensive kind of sound available today.

Stereophonic sound comes from two separate speakers spaced five feet or more apart and hooked up to a phonograph, radio, or tape player, and gives the impression of two-dimensional sound as you might hear it in a concert hall or discothèque. You can listen to the radio, a phonograph record, or a prerecorded tape on a complete stereo hookup.

A *quadraphonic* (quadio, four-channel), system engulfs the listener with music coming from four separate speakers, each with its own channel. This type of system is the "ultimate" in multidimensional sound today and also the most expensive—though basic systems are available for less than $300.

Prerecorded, eight-track tape cartridges are the modern equivalent of phonograph records. They cannot be recorded upon by you, unless you have special equipment. You buy them prerecorded—with music or whatever—and they play nearly as long as a phonograph record. Eight-track tape cartridges also are somewhat more expensive than phonograph records. You play one by slipping it into a cartridge tape deck or "eight-track deck" —a much easier operation than putting on an LP record.

Tape cassettes are small, encased reels of recorded music or words, or blank reels on which you may do the recording yourself. You may play these on a cassette tape recorder or a cassette tape deck which might be considered the modern equivalent of the turntable on a phonograph.

Important note: You cannot play an eight-track cartridge in a cassette tape deck. Nor can you play a tape cassette in an eight-track deck.

Both cartridges and cassettes last far longer and wear far better than phonograph records.

HOW TO SHOP FOR SOUND EQUIPMENT

Now that you have this short dictionary of sound equipment, how and where do you begin shopping for it?

As with all types of home equipment, you must first decide what you want the equipment to do for you and how much you can afford to spend for it.

If you have small children, possibly your best bet is an inexpensive old-fashioned portable record player or inexpensive cassette player permitting them to do their own recording as well as listening. Some players are available for less than $20, although the average price for this type of equipment is more like $40.

If the finest sound reproduction is important to you, you'll certainly want some kind of stereophonic equipment. A good compact stereo system today costs between $300 and $500—but a system can be bought for as little as $140. It may be semi-portable or non-portable. Generally it consists of two speakers, plus a "chassis" containing a turntable and record changer, a receiver and an amplifier to boost the volume of sound coming from both receiver and record player. In some versions, a tape deck may supplement or replace the turntable-record changer.

If you want to create something special which has the advantage of fine stereophonic sound, look into a "component system" which you (or the dealer from whom you buy the system) can put together yourself. A component system consists of a collection of whatever parts *you* want—ranging from turntables to tape decks, tuners, amplifiers, receivers, speakers, antennas, and headphones. Of course, the cost of such a system depends on the type and quality of the components you choose and also on how much of the effort of putting it together you contribute yourself. But typical prices of good component systems range from $350 to $1,000.

If you are gifted electronically, the system you put together yourself well may outperform any other type of home sound equipment you can buy ready made.

But let's say you are an electronic dunce who is loaded with money. The full-scale "console" costing up to $2,000 may be your choice. Consoles are the "whole works"—AM-FM radio, phonograph, tape deck, speakers, etc. A console is also a piece of furniture, though, and this authentic advantage may contribute heavily to its price tag. It tends to be relatively large since the two speakers must be fairly widely separated. It is the ultimate in convenience. You just plug it in and turn it on.

As an alternative, probably the ultimate in versatility is a custom built-in system for *your* house. There are firms specializing in custom-designing such systems—and for fees in the $1,500 to $3,500 range, they'll design and install a sound system throughout your house, with speakers that can play different music in every room—all controlled from a master unit. Options include computer-controlled automatic tape recorders, automatic volume reduction when you pick up the phone, an automatic 50-record player, an automatic 24-cassette player/recorder, a transmitter for reception on a pocket radio so you can even listen outdoors. Needless to say, such extras can jack the basic price considerably higher.

RULES FOR BUYING

Once you have decided what type of sound equipment you want and how much you can afford to pay for it, follow these rules when you actually go out to make the purchase:

• Check carefully into discounts—ranging up to 30 per cent—which are offered widely in this type of equipment since it is a highly competitive field. Obviously a no-name brand with a near-worthless warranty sold at a drastically reduced price may be no bargain. But substantial discounts occur also in the best stores and on the best equipment. Nail down what is covered by the warranty.

• Don't be misled by claims that a machine or system is "portable." Look at it. Would it take a lumberjack to lift it?

• Don't be tempted by bargain "kits" which now come in an enormous variety and from which you are supposed to assemble your own systems or components—unless you are truly qualified to do so. If you're unskilled in electronics, keep this in mind while you're shopping! However, if you are a reasonably skilled hobbyist and can follow directions faithfully, you may be able to save a lot of money by going the kit route.

• Be sure you make room in your budget and your home for adequate facilities in which to store the tapes and records you'll buy. Such facilities will pay for themselves many times over through a longer life for the tapes.

• Don't, though, buy the many accessories available, simply because they're there. Most useful among the accessories are headphones (if other family members would be annoyed by having to listen to the selection you're playing) and outdoor antennas (sometimes necessary for good FM stereo reception).

• Stick strictly to brands of equipment which have achieved a reputation for quality and reliability. And stick to dealers with solid reputations and service facilities known to be responsible.

• Don't buy any stereo or other equipment without listening to the sound it produces. Go to a store which has a quiet area for test listening and listen to a variety of music to be sure the sound pleases you. Try to arrange to try out two or three sets for a couple of days in your own home. "Comparative" listening in your own home is probably your best way to judge quality of sound.

• If you are buying a component system, remember the system as a whole is no better than its weakest link. It would be silly to buy a set of expensive speakers and skimp on your amplifier.

• In judging quality or performance, don't let the advertised power ratings of amplifiers confuse you. All other things being equal, the higher an amplifier's power rating, the more nearly distortion-free will be the sound it produces. "Overbuying" power, though, is not a substitute for a well-engineered amplifier and is often a waste of money. Moreover, there are various ways to rate an amplifier's power—and they are not necessarily comparable. Check with a dealer you trust to avoid buying more power than you need.

How to Slash Your Household Utility Bills

Just by knowing the reasonable ways to shave the amounts you pay you can significantly reduce your over-all home ownership costs. For all of these bills are climbing fast and relentlessly.

HOW TO CUT YOUR TELEPHONE BILLS

If you dial a long-distance phone call on your own, you may slash its cost more than 50 per cent below what the same call would cost if you made it person to person.

If you call long distance from a pay phone booth or from a hotel room or you make the call collect, charge it to another number or to a credit card, you may pay a premium of as much as 50 per cent over the cost of the same call normally dialed from home.

If you make a long-distance call over the weekend or fairly late during any evening and you dial direct, your cost may be less than half what it would be if made during weekdays.

And if you organize your thoughts so you can say what you have to say in a minute, you can call coast to coast for less than a half dollar.

Telephone rates are being raised for many types of services and being simultaneously reduced for many other types of calls. The cuts—especially for direct dialing and off-hours calls—are clearly designed to help the heavily burdened telephone system make optimum use of its facilities and personnel, an understandable goal indeed.

At the same time, by knowing what Ma Bell is doing, you can save money on your phone bills and/or make more calls without spending more. Since phone bills are a major expense in millions of homes, here are key hints:

• Know how much money you can save by direct dialing.

• Know how much you can save by making your calls in off hours and on weekends.

• Take advantage of the coast-to-coast after 11 P.M. special rate if you dial and talk only one minute: (Example: "I made it home safely, Mom!"). The time difference works in your favor if you live in the East. Also try to place as many coast-to-coast personal and business calls as feasible before 8 A.M.

• Invest in an egg timer, an old but still worth-while trick to cut your telephone talk and expense.

• Organize your calls—particularly when the whole family is calling a distant relative—to avoid wasteful, costly, and irritating repetition of "How are you? I'm fine. . . ." Get each family member to make a note in advance of what he or she wants to say. Then the conversation will not drag out.

• If you reach a wrong number, ask the operator immediately to credit you for the call. And if your self-dialed call fails to go through and you are forced to get help from the operator, be sure to request that you be billed for the call at the dialed rate.

• If you need information on a long-distance number, dial the area code for that place plus 555-1212 and ask the operator for the number you want. This service is free. Then dial the call yourself. Do not call your own local operator and ask her to get you the person, for then you will be placing the most costly person-to-person type of call. Use your phone book; you'll find many of the area codes you seek.

• If you're calling an organization, find out whether it has a toll-free number you can use by dialing (800) 555-1212 and asking the toll-free information operator.

• Always report the length of time your phone is out of order. In some states the Public Service Commission requires your phone company to credit you with refunds for any extended interruption in service.

• Choose the number and type of your extensions with care, for each regular extension will probably cost you $1.00 or so a month. The monthly charges for a princess or touch tone may be 50 to 100 per cent more than the cost of a regular extension.

• Examine your telephoning habits to see if they lend themselves to less expensive categories of service.

For instance, if you do not use the phone much, you may be able to switch to a party line and save money with little inconvenience.

If you make few local calls, you might find limited local service, which results in a low monthly bill but a surcharge of 5¢ or 6¢ per local call in excess of a specified maximum (typically 50 per month), to your advantage. In some areas it might pay you to choose a limited geographical area of toll-free service to get a lower monthly bill.

Finally, if you make lots of long-distance calls, but mostly in your state, the phone company may have a way for you to save money. As an illustration, in 1974 customers in Michigan could dial direct anywhere in the state during certain hours at a 60 per cent discount for $3.00 extra per month.

• If you have children away at school, arrange specific times when you'll call them from home by direct dial—instead of having them make expensive coin phone calls to you.

• Always double-check your phone bills for possible mistakes and for evidence that others may be charging calls to your number. Report any evidence of this to the telephone business office at once—*before* you pay your bill—and ask for the company's assistance. Your basic telephone service charge should be the same from month to month. If you have any doubts, ask the telephone company business office for a rundown on the latest basic charges and check your bills against this rundown.

• If you are going on a trip, direct-dial your reservations from home. This will save you from making more costly coin phone calls en route to your various destinations.

HOW TO CUT YOUR ELECTRICITY BILLS

All of us have been bombarded, since the energy crisis exploded into our headlines in late 1973, with long lists of rules and hints on how to cut our consumption of electricity and home fuel.

Here, therefore, are not "new" guides. Here, rather, is a summary of the best and biggest moneysavers to use in cutting your electricity use in your home today. For it is only common sense to operate on the basis that the power shortages of the mid-seventies will be a way of life throughout the world for a long, long time.

• Do not buy or install more air conditioning units (or a bigger central system) than you really need. If you normally remove 40,000 BTUs an hour to air-condition your home and you are able to reduce your electricity consumption by just 10 per cent, you can save at least $25 over a period of 100 cooling days.

• When you buy an air conditioner, get an efficient model. At 1974 electric rates, such a model would save you 40 per cent of the electricity an inefficient machine would use or $40 worth in one cooling season.

• Be sure your house is properly insulated, to prevent warm air from entering the house in summer as well as cold air from coming in during the winter. Also, if you have a central air conditioning system, insulate the ducts carrying cool air to various locations around your house.

• Start your air conditioner early in the morning so you can turn it down later.

• Turn the thermostat on your air conditioner from chilly to comfortable. Even 80° is comfortable in the dehumidified atmosphere of an air-conditioned area. Just by upping the setting from 75° to 80° will slash your air conditioning load by 15 per cent or more.

• Keep your air conditioner operating as efficiently as possible by keeping air filters clean; by sealing off air leaks from the outside; by making sure the machine's condenser is clean (it's located outside the window) and free of foreign matter such as leaves, bugs, or mud; by keeping bearings on the blower and motor lubricated. Look for instructions in your owner's manual.

• Defrost your refrigerator before the ice on the coils exceeds ¼ inch, reducing its efficiency.

• Set the control switch in your refrigerator or freezer to the "economy" setting if you can. This deactivates the small heaters that prevent "sweating" around the door in humid weather, saving 15 per cent of the electricity the appliance uses.

• Don't pile things on or too close to a freezer, since the whole outside cabinet acts as a cooling condenser and must be exposed to the air.

• Restrict your cooking to a minimum in hot weather. Hot meals mean extra work for your cooling unit and there's an even greater load if your stove is electric. Keep the kitchen door closed while cooking is in progress to prevent heat from escaping into the rest of the house. Open windows and use exhaust fans to cool the kitchen instead. Don't peek in the oven unnecessarily—each time you do, 20 per cent of its heat is lost. Consider cooking two or more dishes at once even if they will be served at different times.

Avoid preheating your oven longer than necessary—most will heat up in ten minutes. Or, if you have one, do more cooking in your microwave oven. It uses about five times less electricity than the regular one.

• Reduce your power usage between the peak hours of 11 A.M. and 5 P.M. If at all possible, wash, iron, vacuum, cook, etc., during other hours.

• Use your dishwasher only when it is full.

• Keep the shades or curtains on your south and west windows drawn on hot summer days. This can cut heat penetration through the windows by as much as 50 per cent. Or, if you are building your house, use special heat-absorbing glass in your windows and glass doors—capable of reducing heat from the sun by as much as 70 per cent.

• Turn off all unnecessary lights—especially high-wattage ones.

• Reduce the size of light bulbs in places where bright light is not needed for such tasks as reading or sewing.

• Replace bulb fixtures which are used a lot with fluorescent lights— they are six times as efficient as bulbs.

• Turn off radio and TV sets when you are not listening or watching. If your TV has a fast warm-up feature, unplug the set whenever you leave the house for a few days or more.

• Turn off your hot water heater when you're away on vacation.

• If possible, confine your use of vacuum cleaners and power tools to weekends.

• Dry clothes on a line in warm weather.

• Don't buy many small electric appliances which you really don't want —e.g., curlers, can openers, knives, scissors.

• Be reasonable in your use of whatever electricity-hungry appliances you own: space heaters, electric stoves, hot water heaters, frying pans, air conditioners. Use self-cleaning cycles on ovens judiciously—they are expensive to operate.

• Prevent (or correct) errors on your electric bills by double-checking the meter reader and comparing your reading to the amount which appears on your bill. If you don't know how to do this, just ask your utility company to send you a free "how to read your meter" pamphlet.

Note: If the meter reader can't get to your meter because you're away from home you may be sent an "average" bill—an estimate based on your previous electricity usage which will be corrected later when an accurate meter reading is taken.

• You'll also save money by paying bills on time if a charge is made for late payment. A charge of only 98¢ against a $14 bill paid thirty days late amounts to an 84 per cent annual interest rate.

Consider the extra costs in electricity of upgrading your appliances. Study carefully, as you shop for and use appliances—small and large—the following rundown of typical costs of operating a variety of electrical appliances in the mid-seventies:

	ESTIMATED AVERAGE ANNUAL KWH USED	ANNUAL COST AT 3.5¢ PER KWH
Water heater (standard)	4,219	$147.67
Water heater (quick recovery)	4,811	168.39
Refrigerator-freezer (14 cu. ft.)	1,137	39.80
Refrigerator-freezer (frostless, 14 cu. ft.)	1,829	64.02
Fan	43	1.51
Dehumidifier	377	13.20
Air conditioner (window)	1,389	48.62
Microwave oven	300	10.50
Self-cleaning oven	1,146	40.11
Range	1,175	41.13
Lighting (average home)	1,050	36.75
Television (black and white)	362	12.67
Television (color)	502	17.57
Dishwasher	363	12.71
Humidifier	163	5.71
Electric blanket	147	5.15
Portable room heater	907	31.75
Clothes washer (automatic)	103	3.61
Clothes dryer	993	37.76
Vacuum cleaner	46	1.61
Toaster	39	1.37
Shaver	18	.63

Note: Appliances which heat or cool are among the hungriest.

• The 1975 Energy Policy and Conservation Act requires manufacturers to test the energy consumption of major appliances, central air conditioners, and furnaces. They also must print the results on showroom labels for you to see and use in comparison shopping.

HOW TO CUT YOUR HOME HEATING BILLS

Even in an era of chronic home heating fuel shortages and price increases year after year, you can cut your home heating bills by as much as 40 per cent. Here is a summary of the best rules for heating your home as efficiently and inexpensively as possible:

. • Insulate your exterior walls, ceilings, and floors properly. One estimate is that half of all homes fifteen years or older are not insulated—implying staggering losses in unnecessary fuel consumption. According to one study, fully 26 per cent of the heat escapes from the average two-story house in winter through windows and doors, 32 per cent seeps out through the walls, 15 per cent via the roof, 9 per cent through the floor, and 18 per cent through miscellaneous cracks and gaps in the house.

If your house is fully insulated, you can save as much as one third on fuel. Just by bringing your home insulation up to standards set by the Federal Housing Administration you can probably recoup this extra cost within two or three years via reduced fuel bills. And, of course, after that period your savings, which continue year after year, go directly into your pocket.

• New homes under construction should have a minimum of 6″ insulation in ceilings, 3″ in walls—or the equivalent in the newer, more compact insulating materials. In existing homes, where installing insulation in walls may be impractical, significant savings are still possible by installing insulation on or under the attic floor or between the roof rafters. Ask your building supplies dealer about types of insulation you can easily install yourself in less than a weekend.

• Regularly set your thermostat back at night to about 64° and turn it down to about 60° (or as low as it will go) if you're away from home for twenty-four hours or more. Each degree you turn it back at night will save you ¾ per cent of your monthly fuel bill. Turning your thermostat down 4° every night can save $1.80 on a $60-a-month heating bill.

• If you're not using certain rooms in winter, close the doors and close off the radiators in those rooms (unless the plumbing in the rooms might freeze in very cold weather).

• Don't overheat your house generally. For every degree you set your thermostat above 68°, you hike your fuel bill 3 per cent.

• Have your thermostat checked every year or so. A faulty thermostat will waste fuel and increase your costs—especially if it makes your furnace go on and off more frequently than necessary. If it needs replacement, consider a day-night thermostat which automatically sets your heat back at night and turns it up in the morning.

• Have your furnace and chimneys checked and cleaned once a year. If yours is a forced hot air system, clean your furnace filters about once a month and replace them once or twice a year to make sure you get your money's worth from the fuel you use.

• If your present insulation is inadequate, consider upgrading it. If you live in a mild climate, just increasing 3- to 4-inch insulation to a thickness of 6 inches will give you an eventual annual financial "dividend" of as much as 12 to 15 per cent.

• Insulate any heating ducts or pipes which run through a cool or cold space, such as in the basement or attic.

• Caulk around windows and eaves and weather-strip your doors to seal off cold-air leaks into the house—particularly from under the roof. A few pennies spent on weather stripping can save dollars in fuel since leaking air (warm air out and cold air in) can waste as much as 15 to 30 per cent of your heating budget.

• Despite the size of the investment, buy storm windows if you don't already own them. In areas where the average temperature during the winter months—October–April—is below 45°, storm windows will pay for themselves within a decade, including interest costs. After that, storm windows will pay an annual dividend of 13 per cent. Reason: the windows cut in half the heat loss through windows and doors which account for about one fourth of the heat loss from today's average two-story house.

In colder areas an investment in storm windows will be repaid in less than seven years, and after that the "return" on your investment will amount to 18 per cent or more.

Storm windows, incidentally, also will significantly reduce your air conditioning costs in summer if you keep them on throughout the year.

• If you cannot afford storm windows, tack, staple, or tape clear plastic inside or outside the windows and over screen doors as a substitute.

• Maintain the proper degree of humidity in your home: the dryer the air, the more heat you'll need to maintain a comfortable level. You can be comfortable with a temperature of 68° if your humidity level is between 45 and 50 per cent but you'll need a heat level of 78° if your humidity drops to less than 25 per cent. If necessary, install a humidifier which will add moisture to the dry winter air and thereby let you feel comfortable at lower temperature levels.

• Use your fireplace with restraint. When you're not using the fireplace, close the damper. If you don't have a damper, block the opening with a sheet of plywood or with an insulating board.

• Keep your blinds and curtains open during the day to get the direct sunlight but close them at night—making sure, of course, that the draperies don't cover your radiators. Don't put furniture in front of your clean radiators and warm air outlets either.

• Tack a sheet of stiff aluminum on the wall behind each radiator to reflect the heat back into the room.

• Keep opening and closing of outside doors to a minimum, especially on cold, wintry days—and lay down the law with your children on this point, too.

• If you have a gas range, make sure all burners burn with a clear blue flame, with no traces of yellow—an indication they are not burning efficiently.

If cleaning fails to restore the flame color to blue, call your stove serviceman. Note: Yellow flames produce deadly, odorless carbon monoxide.

• If you are building a house or installing a new heating system, plan your radiator enclosures so they do not trap heat and prevent it from circulating to where it is needed.

• Keep your roofs and flashings wind- and watertight.

• If your heating system is the hot-air type, periodic cleaning of the air filter every three or four months and a few drops of oil for the air blower can give you a more efficient and less expensive operation. In hot water systems, oil the circulating pump. Ask your heating dealer for the manufacturer's service pamphlet listing all the fuel-saving hints.

• Finally, take note of Consumers Union's finding that you can rarely, if ever, save money by installing a new heating system to take advantage of a cheaper fuel. But if your aged heating system needs replacement anyway, see "Heating Systems" under "How to Cut the High Cost of Building" earlier in this chapter for guides on choosing a new one.

How to Protect Your Home Against Fire

TAKE A "TRIP"

In 1973, 11,900 Americans lost their lives in fires—more than half of them in home fires. More than 600,000 home fires alone occurred and yearly dollar losses associated with home fires were close to $800 million. Many of these losses were covered by homeowners insurance, but a large percentage was not—since the majority of our homes were seriously underinsured and most still are today.

Today's leading causes of building fires, according to the National Fire Protection Association in Boston, are smoking and matches, defective or inadequate electrical wiring and other equipment, defective or careless use of electrical appliances, defective or overheated heating equipment, chimneys and flues, combustibles near hot ashes, coals, and heaters, misuse of matches by children. If all of these causes could be magically eliminated, so would more than one half of the building fires in this country.

Whether you rent or own your home, you are in the *majority* if you are permitting many of the greatest fire dangers to remain in and around your house—and thus also risking the possibility of huge financial losses.

Take a brief "inspection trip" through your house or apartment *today*. Examine every square foot of it for fire hazards and see if you can answer "yes" to all of these questions:

Do your gas and your electric appliances bear the seal of the American Gas Association and that of Underwriters Laboratories?

Is your kitchen equipped with a suitable, properly charged extinguisher for grease and/or electric fires? Does everybody in your family know how to use it? And does everyone know that such fires should *never* be doused with water?

Are your ashtrays large enough and plentiful enough for the amount of smoking which occurs in your house?

Are your small children well informed on the subject of matches and fires? For those who have developed an insatiable curiosity about them, have you taken the necessary time and patience to teach them how to use matches properly and skillfully?

Are such items as your chafing dishes and fondue pots protected by metal trays underneath to catch any alcohol overflow?

Do you have your furnaces, hot water heaters, and chimneys serviced and/or inspected regularly for safety?

Is the gas can for your lawn mower, chain saw, etc., stored properly and in a safe place? And what about those highly flammable substances with which you start barbecue fires?

Have you cleaned up and cleared out any piles of old papers and/or oil rags which may have collected in your attic, basement, garage?

Are your household cleaning fluids of the non-flammable type?

If you cannot answer *yes* to all of these questions you are taking absolutely needless risks.

FUNDAMENTAL SAFEGUARDS

• Have a specific, well-rehearsed fire escape plan, in which each member knows exactly what to do, where to go, and whom and how to call for help. If you have storm windows and screens in your windows, your children should know how to take them off in an emergency.

• Consider installing a few devices to sound a warning if a fire starts: it is all too easy to fail to awake when there is a fire.

• Be on guard against lightning and know the risks. If your house is situated on top of a hill or on a flat plain it is a dangerous lure for lightning, an important cause of home fires. It also is vulnerable if it is the tallest—or shortest—in a complex of buildings; if it has a high metal content; if it is in the suburbs or near a highway. If your house (or a house you are considering buying) fits the above description, inquire about a proper, effective lightning protection system. To be effective, the system should be capable of intercepting lightning bolts from the roof, metal equipment, antennas, power lines, and nearby trees which are taller than your house. A proper system also is marked by a "Master Label" plate, issued by Underwriters Laboratories.

• Minimize the fire risks of your roof. The fire risk of a house roofed with untreated wood shingles is far greater than that of a slate-roofed house or an asphalt-shingled house. (And homeowners insurance rates on wood shingle-roofed houses are higher in some states than the rates on houses with less dangerous types of roofing.)

• In fact, if you are buying or building or remodeling a house, inquire about the flammability characteristics of *all* materials in the house—including paints, insulation material, curtains and carpets, wood and imitation wood paneling, etc.

• Check and beware of all electrical hazards: appliance wires which continually overheat; fuses which blow repeatedly; TV pictures which contract when your refrigerator or furnace goes on. If any of these signs occur, call your electrician immediately to check into the problem.

And here are the best rules to help you prevent a disastrous home fire caused by defective electrical wiring:

Don't string inexpensive extension cords all over the place—and risk overloading your wiring system.

Don't use too light dime-store cords for heavy appliances such as electric irons, space heaters, rotisseries, and power tools.

Don't try to stretch the electrical capacity by putting in heavier and heavier fuses. "Overfusing" is a fairly common practice—but potentially a very dangerous one. (For most household circuits, the safe limit is 15 amperes.)

Don't put pennies behind your fuses to get them to carry a bigger load—because, again, what you well may end up with is overloaded wiring.

Do, particularly if you have *any* reason to suspect that your present wiring is inadequate, ask a qualified electrician (or, in many states, one who is licensed by the state) to go over your electrical system carefully. It may take as long as a full day and cost you anywhere from $50 to $150. But it will be one of the best investments you could possibly make.

Do be prepared to let the electrician remedy any problems he uncovers. Note: He won't be able to assess the condition of wires hidden behind walls and under floors, without taking your house apart and doing a complete rewiring job. But he *can* go over all the wires, switches, outlets, and fuse boxes which are visible and accessible. And, if you discuss with him the number and type of appliances you have added to the system since it was originally installed, he also can at least make an informed guess as to how much and what type of additional wiring may be necessary.

How to Baffle a Burglar

HOW SAFE IS YOUR HOUSE FROM BURGLARY?

You are a typical couple and you're now preparing for your vacation. You have just bought a new lock for your front door as extra protection while you're away. You have arranged to have deliveries of milk and newspapers stopped when you leave. You have even installed an automatic light that goes on every evening to keep would-be burglars away. Moreover, you do not own any valuable jewelry or furs that might make your house a target for burglars.

Q. *How safe is your house from burglary?*

A. Not necessarily one bit safer than the house next door where none of these precautions has been taken by your vacationing neighbors.

Any professional burglar can pick his way through the locks most of us use today. No amount of homeowners insurance can spare you the agony of having your home burgled or the losses over and above the limits of your insurance policy or the heartache which is inevitable when a thief makes off with prized personal possessions. A hep burglar also can easily spot the automatic light which goes on at sundown in the same window each night. And today's typical burglar knows that it's easier to "fence" such items as TV sets, typewriters, and cameras than it is to resell expensive jewelry or fancy fur pieces. In sum, if you have been picked as a victim, the odds are you will be hit.

Burglary is one of the most costly, pervasive, and rapidly growing crimes in the United States today. Burglaries now account for nearly one half of all serious crimes reported by the FBI and our annual losses to burglars now run into hundreds of millions. What's more, burglary is booming not only in the big cities but also in the suburbs, the exurbs, and even out in the once secure countryside. All this in the face of the fact that we spend more than $200 million a year on burglary alarm systems and protection devices.

Here, therefore, are often overlooked do's and don'ts for you, which will greatly reduce the risk of having your home burglarized while you're away:

DO'S AND DON'TS

Do, if you are installing a big plate-glass window or door, insist on reinforced glass instead of plain glass.

Do arrange to keep your lawn mowed while you're away on vacation.

Do ask the police department to check your house regularly while you're away; inform the police which friend or neighbor has your itinerary and a key to your house, and give the police the exact dates of your departure and return.

Do, if possible, leave a car conspicuously parked in your driveway, or, if you don't own a second car, at least lock your garage door to disguise the fact that there are no cars around. A non-operating junk car you are using for parts would be ideal for this purpose.

Do arrange, if possible, to keep not one but several indoor low-wattage lights burning at night. For good measure, leave a radio on near the front door as well—or have it hitched to the timer which turns on lights at night.

Do use a cylinder-type lock bolt on all outside doors, including your cellar door, with the slot protected by metal. And make sure the bolt goes far enough into the slot so that it can't be pushed back with a thin instrument such as a pocket knife or even a plastic card. Spring-type locks, also, are easily forced, and a 175-pound man can barge right through the typical lock chain. Consult an established locksmith for advice on the latest pickproof door locks—and if you're installing a new lock, put it in above eye level and put in a double-cylinder dead lock. This makes the lock picker's job that much more difficult. Don't rely on any lock which can be opened by a master key.

Do make sure your door hinges are on the inside rather than the outside of the doors, or at least make sure the pins in the hinges cannot be removed.

Do keep unused doors locked at all times.

Do realize that Christmas–New Year's—the greatest holiday week of the year—also is the period when burglaries of homes and apartments reach their peak. During this time—when gifts are scattered throughout the place, when you are visiting friends and relatives freely and on impulse, when week-long trips are commonplace—it's just natural *not* to be cautious. But instead become supercautious. Under no circumstances leave any doors unlocked even for a few minutes.

Do have locks and keys changed if you move to a new house or apartment, or if you accidentally lose your keys.

Don't put identification of any sort on your keys.

Don't leave ladders in plain sight and *don't* leave all your window shades down, a sure sign you are away.

Don't have your telephone disconnected while you're on vacation.

Don't leave notes on your front door indicating you are away.

Don't advertise the fact you're away by allowing a notice of your vacation to be published in the local newspaper social column, an excellent source of information for burglars. Other favorite sources of this information are wedding and funeral notices. Make sure your house is well protected while you're attending such occasions.

Don't assume that burglars operate only at night. There are now as many daytime burglaries as there are nighttime burglaries, and the number of daytime burglaries is soaring.

Do check the reputation and references of any new person working in or around your house.

Do invest in a peephole, so you can see who's knocking before you open the door.

Do be wary of suspicious callers who actually may be casing your house for burglary possibilities, and *don't* fall for suspicious invitations to get you out of the house. In one classic case, a burglar sent a set of free theater tickets to a suburban couple, then looted their home while his "guests" were enjoying the show.

Don't, if you have an electronic device which opens your garage doors, forget that if you can open the door by crossing a beam of light so can a thief. The best garage opener is a box with a key which, when turned, automatically opens the door for you.

Do investigate today's rapidly growing array of anti-burglar devices. But don't make any sizable investment before you have shopped carefully, checked the effectiveness of a device you're considering buying with the police—and made sure the alarm has been approved by Underwriters Laboratories.

One good place to begin shopping for advice on a burglar system is the listing for "Burglar Alarm Systems" in the Yellow Pages of your telephone book. Deal with a reputable dealer and be prepared to spend at least $200 to $250 for an alarm system. But first ask yourself: "Just what am I protecting, and against what likely type of burglar?"

Among the moderately priced devices available today are:

• "Panic buttons" next to your front door or bed, wired into the local police headquarters.

• "Seeing eyes"—infrared or ultrasonic devices which sense a person (including, possibly, *you* or a pet) entering a house and sounding an alarm.

• "Burglar pins" which can be set into big sliding glass doors to prevent entry through them.

• "Hotliners" hitched to a standard telephone jack and activated by a switch which might be mounted on a strategically located door or window, which automatically dial the police and/or fire department or neighbors and transmit a recorded announcement such as: "There is a burglary in progress at the home of John Smith at 33 Lorraine Drive, Montclair, N.J."

Pay some attention to the power source of whatever alarm system you select. Automatically recharging batteries are best, because they work even during power failures.

Do make a record of the serial numbers of cameras, guns, TV sets, typewriters, and appliances you own, to aid in recovery of these items if they are stolen. Pawnbrokers and legitimate secondhand dealers are required by law to file sales reports with the police.

Do find out whether your police department endorses an Operation Identification or a similar plan. With such a plan, the police provide forms to record the serial numbers of valuables, and rent or lend equipment to engrave an identification number (such as your driver's license number) on the items themselves. Homeowners are then given decals to warn burglars of their participation. Communities which have Operation Identification programs report burglary rates in participating homes well under the rate in nonparticipating homes.

If your community has no Operation Identification, you might suggest that one be launched by a local civic group or organization. For further information on how to go about this write Burgess Vibocrafters, Inc., Route 83, Grayslake, Ill. 60030 for a free "Action Kit."

Finally, if you can manage it, try to find a reliable "house sitter" to spend nights in your home while you're away and keep up its "lived-in" appearance: a responsible widow, a college student you know well, someone you can trust.

Your Second Home

A PLEASURE AND AN INVESTMENT

Today some 3 million American families own second homes, and the vacation home has become one of the most rapidly growing types of housing in our country. What's more, the trend is as strong among younger families and couples as among older ones.

The key force behind the powerful surge in vacation housing is our ever expanding amount of leisure time—added to our ever more desperate need to escape from congested, smoggy cities and suburbs. A spur too is the fact that a vacation home can help a family of four or five members save significantly on the costs of weekend holidays and long vacations, with all the hotel-motel-restaurant bills involved. As just one example, a two-day ski weekend for a family of four easily can cost $250. At popular summer and winter resorts, houses often rent for from $1,000 to $3,000 *per season*. (For many, many more ways to save on vacations, see Chapter 12, "How to Save on Vacations.")

A third factor is that, at a time of soaring real estate values, a second home in attractive, relaxing surroundings may be one of the best long-term investments a family can make.

Commercial bank policies on mortgages and loan terms for vacation homes vary widely. Savings and loan associations are extending loans for repairs and improvements on vacation homes in addition to regular FHA-backed home mortgages. But city banks often refuse to finance out-of-town property, so open a savings account where you plan to buy and establish a contact with a bank there. This also will give you a good source of information on reliable local real estate brokers, lawyers, accountants, insurance agents, and contractors.

Today, you can choose from among literally thousands of different prefabricated vacation home kits—ranging from A-frames to log cabins, hunting lodges, and seashore saltbox houses. Prices start at less than $2,000 and go all the way up to $30,000 or more. You can either hire a builder to put this type of house together for you or you can do it yourself—at great savings. You also can use precut sections in at least some parts of the house—as a labor saver. One reason for the big savings available on prefabs is that you are spared the 10 to 15 per cent architect's fee—but if you do invest in a prefab vacation house, it's important both aesthetically and structurally to choose one which has been designed by an architect.

Economical condominium vacation homes, too, are springing up everywhere—in many cases surrounded by golf courses, tennis courts, lakes, or seashores.

Most vacation homes, though, are still relatively small "cottage" type structures. Most are single-story. Most are valued at less than $20,000. Most are within 100 miles of their owners' primary homes. Many lack conventional plumbing and central heating.

KEY QUESTIONS

Let's say you are contemplating buying or building a second home. Ask yourselves these key questions:

How much can you really afford for a second home?

How much time do you really intend to occupy the house or cabin or cottage? Two weeks in summer? Occasional weekends? Every weekend?

During which times of the year?

How do you intend to use the house?

How much will transportation to and from your prospective vacation home cost? What about the availability of gas if you intend to travel by car?

Honestly, what is your family's idea of a pleasant vacation? Relaxing on a beach? Hiking in the woods? Fishing and hunting? Skiing? Golfing? Reading? Partying with others?

How much responsibility are you willing to take on food, upkeep, maintenance, etc.?

How important are creature comforts to you when you're on vacation?

How many of the big city conveniences do you want and need?

How near or far do you want (need) to be from your present home?

What are the chances you might decide to convert your second home later into a place for year-round retirement or vacationing?

Only after you have answered as honestly as you can all of these questions should you choose a specific place and a specific type of house. For the basic rules, simply follow the guides for buying your primary home.

YOU'RE GOING TO RENT

WHAT DO YOU WANT?

Let's switch emphasis entirely for a while and say that your reasons for renting outweigh the reasons for buying. In deciding to rent you are joining two out of every five U.S. families who now rent the homes in which they live.

But even though your decision has been made, you still have quite a few alternatives. Among them:

A house; an apartment; a duplex; a townhouse, plus the many far-out versions of the townhouse; apartments aimed at one particular category of people, such as young married people, elderly couples, singles, etc.; mobile homes which you can rent as well as buy; apartments and houses in the city or the suburbs or the country.

If you rent a house, you'll get considerably more space than if you rent an apartment, often including a yard or garden. You'll also probably have to pay a large share of the costs of maintaining and repairing the house, of utilities and yard upkeep.

The trend in apartments today, though, is strongly toward making them as much as possible like "compact houses"—with all the space and conveniences of a full-fledged house, but without the responsibilities of mortgage payments, insurance, property taxes, etc., that come with owning a big, sprawling house.

Increasingly, also, apartment building and townhouse developments are being equipped with such luxuries as swimming pools, saunas, tennis courts, social centers, gyms, golf courses, clothes-washing centers, even baby-sitting services.

Before you start hunting for a house or apartment to rent, ask yourself these questions:

Just how much space, including storage space, do you really need and want?

How dependent are you on laborsaving appliances such as dishwashers and clothes washers? These are expensive to buy yourself if you feel you must have them in your apartment. On the other hand, if they're included and you don't really care whether you have them or not, you'll be taking on needless expense, since you'll be forced to pay for them via your rent bill.

Where would be the most convenient location for you—in terms of commuting time and costs to work, as well as convenience to schools, shopping facilities, and other services you'll need?

How eager are you to do your own decorating and furniture buying? If this type of thing bores you, stick to apartments which are at least partially furnished. But if decorating interests you, don't absorb the costs, again through the monthly rent, of using somebody else's old beds, sofas, etc. Figure out what new furniture you will need for a new place. A big place may seem a bargain "at the price," until you figure out what it will cost to decorate and maintain it.

How much outdoor yard space do you really want—and would you really use? Is a small balcony worth the amount it may add to your rent?

HOW MUCH RENT CAN YOU REALLY AFFORD?

How much house and apartment can you really afford to rent?

The traditional rule is that you can afford to pay one week's take-home pay in monthly rent *and* related expenses.

There may, for example, be repairs which must be met by the tenant.

These may range from fixing a closet shelf to the purchase of a new refrigerator. And you may have to pay for gas, electricity, telephone, water, and workmen's liability insurance for men and women working on the property. (See Part IV, "Your Rights and How to Get Them," for rules on how to decide, with a landlord, who pays for what.)

There may be the cost of a garage if you rent in a city and own a car. In some big cities, garage rent is now running $100 to $150 a month and this expense has become an item next to the house rent itself. (See Chapter 9, "Your Transportation," for ways to cut your parking bills.)

There also are miscellaneous expenses that drain off the half dollars here, the dollar bills there. Tips are an example of this.

And, if you are renting a single house (or even an apartment in some parts of the country), you'll probably have to pay the heating bills. High fuel costs may throw your shelter budget out of balance.

YOUR LEASE

This is a written *or* verbal agreement between you, the tenant, and your landlord, stating all of the key terms of your occupancy. It is virtually your only form of legal protection—although you'll probably quickly find out that most landlords retain most of the rights and that you have very few. For a description of the basic rights you *do* retain under your lease, see Part IV, "Your Rights and How to Get Them."

The lease you get should be a written one, signed and dated by both you and your landlord. Before you sign it, have your lawyer look it over for you. I suggest this even though most leases in use today are standard forms and you probably don't need a lawyer's services if you have the know-how to read it yourself and you are sure you are dealing with an honest landlord.

The lease usually includes:
• the date you may move in;
• the length of time the lease is in force;
• a description of the property you are renting;
• the amount of rent to be paid;
• the dates the rent is due;
• the form in which payment of rent is to be made;
• the deposit which may be required—what it covers and under what circumstances it is forfeited;
• the conditions under which you may renew the lease;
• who pays what expenses, such as utility bills;
• the conditions under which the rent may be raised;
• the signatures of the parties to the lease.

The lease also may indicate that you are permitted to make any reasonable alterations. For other alterations you may be required to get permission from the landlord. Ordinarily, temporary alterations you make must be removed at the expiration of your lease, provided that you can do this without damage to the property.

Ordinarily the lease requires you to keep the property in good condition and to leave it in as good a state as when you moved in, with the exception of ordinary wear and tear.

Once you move in, your landlord has no right of entry, except in emergencies or to make repairs. Even then, he must check with you first if at all possible. To be safe, be sure this is spelled out in the lease.

Reading the small print in leases may be a tedious job. But every bit of that print is important to you. And the longer the lease, the more important is it that you do thoroughly understand it. Be sure all blank spaces are filled or crossed out.

A few points you might overlook:

Be sure that whatever verbal arrangements you have made with your landlord are written into your lease. Take an inspection tour with the landlord and make notes on all damage you can observe to walls, fixtures, appliances, floors. Give him one copy and keep the other yourself. Get in writing what is considered "normal" wear and tear.

Check the cancellation clause. Does it require you to give notice thirty to sixty days before a move? If you fail to give notice, is the lease automatically renewed under the old terms for another year?

Check the provisions on repairs. Otherwise you might be unpleasantly shocked when you ask who is responsible for which repairs. Normally, your landlord is responsible for periodic repainting and other major repairs and maintenance services. You, the tenant, are responsible for minor repairs.

But get the specifics: Who pays, for example, for rug and carpet cleaning, painting, window washing, electrical work, plumbing problems, fixing broken furnaces and air conditioners? If periodic painting is provided, does this mean proper scraping and preparation of the walls, window sills, etc.— or just slapping on more paint? Does it mean one coat or two coats? Who pays if an exterminator's services are needed to deal with cockroaches? If garage or parking space is provided, is it free or is it extra?

Check the regulations on subletting the property. If your circumstances change suddenly, you may have to sublet. Make sure you really have the flexibility which made you want to rent in the first place.

Watch out for restrictions—and make sure you can live with those in your lease. If you have children or pets, will they be permitted? Can you conduct a business from your home? What are the rules on noisemaking? Are there any restrictions on visitors you may have in your apartment? Extra roommates? Have stricken from the lease any restrictions the landlord says won't apply to you.

Find out what are the superintendent's duties.

Double-check on any security deposit requirement. Are you required to make one (usually amounting to one month's rent, but sometimes two or more months' rent)? How large a deposit? When and under what conditions will it be returned? Will interest be paid to you on this deposit?

What about insurance? Is the landlord responsible if his own negligence causes bodily injury to you or your family or loss of your personal property?

Look at the basic equipment—such as the heating plant, the wiring, and the plumbing. If it is not in good order, will the landlord agree in writing to have repairs made before you move in?

An increasingly important point in this era: What provisions has the landlord made to protect you against burglars—in terms of really adequate, up-to-date door locks, doorman, burglary alarm systems, tie-ins with the nearest police station?

Beware also these traps which turn up in some leases:

• An open-ended agreement by you to permit the landlord to show your apartment to prospective buyers any time he pleases, without the usual limit of only a couple of weeks or one month before you are scheduled to vacate the apartment.

• A "waiver of notice" clause which permits your landlord to evict you and literally throw your belongings out the window onto the street if you violate even some obsolete, fine-print provisions of your lease. (For instance, taking a vacation trip without notifying your landlord.)

• A "waiver of tort liability" clause which frees your landlord of any responsibility for injury or damage which may befall you on his property— even if you have repeatedly warned him about hazards such as dangerously torn stairway carpeting.

• A "confession of judgment" clause which, in effect, waives your right to defend yourself in court against summary eviction or other arbitrary actions by the landlord.

• A clause permitting the landlord to cancel your lease when he finds a buyer for the apartment.

• A requirement that *you*, the tenant, pay property taxes on the house or apartment.

CHECK LIST FOR APARTMENTS

	Yes	No
Is building sound, attractive, well built?		
Is it well managed and maintained?		
Are corridors and entranceways clean and well lighted?		
Is protection from burglars provided?		
Is there a doorman?		
Is landscaping pleasant?		
Is there enough outdoor space?		

Yes No

Are extras you want included (such as swimming pool, steam baths, a gym for men and women)?

Is there parking space, indoor or outdoor?

Is there a receiving room for packages?

Is laundry equipment available?

Are fire escapes adequate?

Are there fire extinguishers?

Is trash collected or disposed of?

Are there storage rooms or facilities?

Are there elevators?

Are mailboxes locked?

Are routine maintenance—window washing, decorating, painting—provided?

Are servicemen available for emergency repairs?

Is the floor plan convenient?

Is the apartment big enough?

Are rooms light enough?

Are wall spaces adequate for your furniture?

Is the apartment soundproof?

Is decorating (if any) attractive?

Are views attractive?

Are there enough windows, and are they well located?

Are there screens and storm windows?

Are major appliances you need installed?

Are appliances in good condition?

Is wiring sufficient?

Is ventilation adequate?

Will cleaning be easy?

Are there separate heat controls for each part of the apartment?

Are there enough electric outlets and are they well located?

Do windows and doors, including cabinet doors, open and close easily?

Is there air conditioning?

Is there a fireplace? Does it work?

Is there carpeting?

Is there a balcony?

Are there workable blinds or shades?

•

HOME IMPROVEMENTS: DO IT YOURSELF? OR DON'T?

COSTS OF COMMON IMPROVEMENTS

In 1974 we spent $15 billion just to remodel, improve, and maintain our homes. Yet home remodeling is an area in which we regularly waste billions of dollars through our own widespread ignorance. Many of us don't know how to shop for and save on materials. Many don't have even vague guidelines for dealing with contractors or tackling a major building project. We tend to be suckers when we are up against today's home improvement gypsters who continue to cash in on our conspicuous innocence.

Moreover, while we are a nation of do-it-yourselfers, millions tackle jobs for which they are utterly unqualified and, as a result, they waste huge sums of money. At the same time, millions of others don't realize that, with the help of today's "miracle" materials and gadgets for the home improvement market, there are many moneysaving jobs they *could* do easily.

At the very top of any list of rules for slashing home improvement costs must be: *Do it yourself* and save 50 per cent or more of the cost of many home improvements, here is a short list of typical cost ranges in 1974:

To give you an idea of today's high cost of some of the most common home remodeling and redecorating jobs.

JOB	COST RANGE
Replacing water pipes in basement	$200 to $400
Replacing hot air furnace (No major ductwork)	$1,500 to $2,500
Replacing concrete basement floor, rubble removal	$2.50 to $3.50 sq. ft.
Reroofing over existing asphalt shingles	$90 to $125 per 100 sq. ft.
Upgrading electrical service to 150 or 200 amperes, including circuit breakers	$1,000 to $1,500
Re-siding house	$300 to $400 per 100 sq. ft. or $2,500 to $4,000 total on average house
Sanding and refinishing wood floor	25¢ to 40¢ sq. ft.
Insulating attic floor and rafters	50¢ to 60¢ sq. ft.

Job	Cost Range
Installing new bathroom	$2,000 to $7,000
Remodeling existing bath	$1,200 to $4,000
Installing tile shower	$350 to $400
Installing complete central air conditioning system	$2,000 to $4,000 double or more with new ductwork and wiring
Removing a 15-ft. supporting wall	$2,000 to $3,000
Remodeling kitchen, including cabinets, appliances, floor, counter top, plumbing, wiring, decorating	$4,000 to $7,000
Adding a second story to a one-story house	$12,000 to $18,000
Finishing off basement into a recreation room (no plumbing)	$2,500 to $5,000
New attic room	$2,000 to $3,000
New two-car garage	$2,000 to $4,000
Exterior painting	$1,200 to $1,800
New swimming pool	$6,000 to $14,000

With these costs and with the development of so many of the miracle aids as a spur, it is not surprising that the do-it-yourself trend is so powerful.

We now do more than one third of the painting inside and outside our homes.

Of every six U.S. homeowners, one does his own home plumbing.

We do a full one fifth of the roofing work on our homes and a full two fifths of all flooring work.

We do one fourth of all outside improvements.

We do the great majority of "odd" jobs around our homes.

And, of course, the man in the house is no longer by any means the family's sole do-it-yourselfer. According to one recent study, more than three out of four wives are now doing a wide range of home repairs themselves, including painting, patio repairs, unclogging water pipes, repairing fences, installing TV antennas, putting in insulation and masonry. In all, nearly half of all repairs in households with family incomes between $7,500 and $15,000 are done by women.

Among the most obvious do-it-yourself jobs for which you are probably qualified or which you could learn fairly easily are: interior and/or exterior painting, wallpapering, window glazing, weather-stripping, installing insulation, taping and filling wallboard seams.

GUIDELINES FOR DO-IT-YOURSELFERS

Here are a few general, but fundamental, guidelines on home improvements for do-it-yourselfers:

• By all means, do as many home repair jobs as you are qualified to do yourself. While you're at it, also recruit any qualified—or at least willing—members of your family to help you. Today's expanding availability of convenient materials and supplies makes it ever simpler. Among the materials and supplies are: "miracle" glues, roll-on paints, prefabricated building materials, sophisticated power tools, caulking guns, prepasted wallpapers, "instant" lawns, and do-it-yourself fix-it kits with easy instructions on how to do just about anything around the home.

• Do not tackle the ambitious and difficult jobs, however, *unless* you are qualified: for instance, roofing, re-siding, putting in a lawn, building bookshelves or kitchen cupboards, laying a floor, sanding down and staining a floor, installing a major appliance. Also stay away from such demanding and potentially hazardous jobs as the installation of electrical wiring or fuel lines. Doing these yourself may void your fire insurance.

• Don't skimp on materials. For instance, don't buy improperly cured lumber: you may find that it buckles or contracts after it has been nailed in place.

• Pick appropriate materials. When choosing flooring and floor coverings—linoleum, carpeting, etc.—get local builders to advise you on which product grades will give you the durability you'll actually need in the area to be floored or covered. There's no sense in splurging on a super grade of hardwood or linoleum or carpeting for a room in which there will be only a minimum of traffic. At the same time, it scarcely makes economic sense to buy a light-duty grade of flooring or carpeting for a children's rumpus room—to save $50 to $100.

• Buy the most economical lengths and sizes you can of lumber, plywood, tiles, floor coverings, curtain material—to avoid costly waste. If, for example, your new garage calls for 8-foot two-by-four studs, you would do much better buying 16-foot lengths which can be cut in half than 12-foot lengths which could translate into a "waste" of one third of your lumber.

• Shop for remnants and also discontinued patterns in such items as roofing, linoleum, carpeting—for potentially big savings. And buy enough extra to use for patching later if necessary.

• In your estimate of how long a job will take you, allow plenty of time for shopping around.

• Before you embark on any major do-it-yourself construction or remodeling project, check your local zoning ordinances and/or building codes to make sure your plans and specifications conform. If a reputable local contractor is involved in the work, he will surely be fully aware of the rules—but if you're serving as your own contractor, obeying the zoning laws will be your responsibility.

• Don't buy sophisticated, costly tools unless you will use them extensively in the future. Try to rent them instead.

RULES FOR HANDLING REPAIRS

Now here are a few specifics on handling repairs for any economy-minded householder.

When an item is damaged, repair it immediately. Delay will, if anything, make the repair more costly or encourage you to throw the article away and lose your entire investment.

Give your house an annual checkup so you can anticipate trouble and slash repair costs. Winter can cause subtle damage to a house. Periodically check your gutters, window sills, drains, etc., to find damage before it becomes extensive.

Take advantage of the knowledge of any experienced owner of a hardware store: he is selling advice and service as well as products. Let him help you to train yourself to handle minor repairs and thereby save substantial sums each year.

Look into buying a "medical plan" for your house, now available in some areas. These will handle any needed repairs to plumbing, heating, electrical, or air conditioning systems for a fixed annual fee (typically $180, depending on the condition of your house). Some offer 24-hour, 365-day emergency services, too.

Also helpful to you might be a clearinghouse and referral service for household repairs, guaranteeing speed and quality—for a fee.

Financing Your Home Improvements

FUNDAMENTAL RULES FOR HOME IMPROVEMENT LOANS

Let's assume you are undertaking a home improvement and must borrow money to manage it. Be guided by these fundamental rules:

• *Do not* agree to the loan terms which may be offered by your home improvement contractor without first comparing them with terms offered by local lending institutions. Go first to your local bank, credit union, savings association, or savings bank and ask each what would be the very least expensive way for you to raise the cash you need. See Chapter 3, "How to Borrow Cash and Use Credit Wisely," for details.

• Inquire about Title I and other loans which are insured by the FHA. The maximum interest rate is significantly lower than typical lending institution charges. This type of loan is now being made for up to $15,000 repayable within fifteen years for almost any project which will improve the basic *liveability* or utility of your house and ground. Included are many major appliances but *not* luxury improvements such as swimming pools. The only key qualifications you, a borrower, must have are: you must be a good credit risk and you must own (or have a substantial interest in) the property to be improved. You can get an FHA-insured loan from dealers and contractors participating in the program as well as from the usual array of lenders.

• If you're lucky, your present mortgage may contain a clause permitting you to borrow an amount up to that you have already paid off at the same interest rate you are already paying—plus a nominal fee. Consider borrowing via this route if it's open to you.

• Consider also borrowing against the cash value of your life insurance policy. The pros and cons of this also are fully explained in Chapter 3, "How to Borrow Cash and Use Credit Wisely."

• Look too into one little-known source of home improvement loans: the so-called "little FHA" loans, available in limited numbers to lower income homeowners living in communities of less than 20,000 population. Interest rates on these federally subsidized loans are as low as you can find anywhere, and the loans are repayable over a period up to twenty-five years. You can inquire about such loans at the local Farmers Home Administration office or the U. S. Department of Agriculture.

KEY SOURCES AND TERMS OF LOANS AT A GLANCE

The following chart outlines the key sources and terms of home improvement loans available in 1975:

TYPE OF LOAN	MAXIMUM AMOUNT YOU CAN BORROW	MAXIMUM TIME FOR REPAYMENT	RELATIVE COST OF LOAN IN 1975
FHA Title I loan (Class 1a)	$15,000	15 years	12% maximum
FHA Title I loan (Class 1b)	$5,000 per dwelling unit, $25,000 for the entire structure in dwellings for 2 or more families	15 years	12% maximum

Type of Loan	Maximum Amount You Can Borrow	Maximum Time For Repayment	Relative Cost of Loan in 1975
Bank home improvement loan	$3,500 to $5,000 in some areas	5 to 7 years	11%–14%; more on small loans
Open end loan under permissive clause in present mortgage	Up to amount of mortgage already paid off	Until expiration of present mortgage	Existing mortgage rate plus nominal fee
Refinancing present mortgage (new mortgage loan with same or different source)	Depends on current appraised valuation of present property and amount of principal already paid off	Terms of new mortgage	Current mortgage rate in area plus closing costs

Your Home Improvement Contractor and Your Contract

HOW TO CHOOSE A CONTRACTOR

The primary duties of a home improvement contractor are to order and pay for materials involved in the job he has contracted to perform and to see that the materials are shipped to the site on schedule; to make sure that the appropriate workers and subcontractors are at the right place at the right time; and to direct and co-ordinate construction.

Typically you pay a contractor in one of these three ways:

• in one lump sum covering *all* costs of materials, labor, and the contractor's profits;

• on a "cost plus" arrangement—the actual cost of the project plus 10 to 15 per cent of this total as the contractor's fee;

• on a "maximum total" basis, which means that a maximum cost of the project is agreed upon by homeowner and contractor, including the contractor's profits—plus any savings he can achieve by completing the project for less than the agreed-upon maximum.

Of course, if you, the homeowner, later change your mind on design or materials or some other aspect of the project, deviating from the original plans and specifications, you should expect costs to be escalated accordingly.

Typically, you make periodic payments as work progresses and a final payment when the job has been satisfactorily completed.

In a few areas of the United States, home improvement contractors must be licensed—giving homeowners some protection against shoddy work and broken home improvement contracts. But for the vast majority of us the problems of finding honest, qualified contractors to do any major home improvements, or figuring out what should and should not go into a home improvement contract, can be truly staggering.

Here, then, are basic rules *every* homeowner or would-be homeowner should follow in choosing a contractor, drawing up a home improvement contract, and making sure the contract is properly carried out.

(1) Choose a contractor for *any* home improvement job with the utmost care.

Your key yardsticks for judging a contractor are: his credit standing with his suppliers; his reputation for reliability, fair dealing, and getting a job done on schedule; his experience, competence, and taste; his relationship with his workers, subcontractors, and suppliers; his patience and willingness to submit a reasonably detailed estimate when dealing with you.

(2) Get bids in writing on *any* sizable home improvement from two or more local contractors—with all important aspects of the work spelled out in detail. But make sure each bid is for the same building specification, the same quality of materials, the same deadlines, etc. Do all you can to double-check the bases for bids and estimates.

(3) Beware of "par selling," a practice banned by the Federal Housing Administration, in which an advance salesman rather than the home improvement contractor himself sets the price of a particular job.

(4) See earlier in this chapter for advice on choosing a contractor to build a new house, for the same guides—such as on insurance, sources of information, etc.—apply to home improvements.

HOW TO WRITE A HOME IMPROVEMENT CONTRACT

Once you have chosen a contractor, you move to the problem of drawing up a contract for your job. On this contract will hang hundreds or even thousands of dollars—your potential financial losses if the contractor fails to do the job as you want and expect it to be done. On this contract also will hang your entire legal protection against shoddy workmanship, inferior materials, non-completion of the job, many other hazards.

Under the 1969 federal Truth in Lending law, you have a "right of rescission" or "cooling-off period" lasting three business days after you sign a contract involving a home improvement loan in which you put up your home as security for the loan. A contractor must give you the appropriate "Notice of Rescission," and if you change your mind about going ahead with the work, you may cancel the contract during this period by written notice to the contractor. The contractor is not legally permitted to begin work before the end of the rescission period.

However, if the home improvement contract does *not* involve a loan, you are strictly on your own.

Here is what should be included in a home improvement contract:

• First, indisputably foremost and *clearly*, the full costs of the job. Don't haggle over the costs if the contractor is honest and his bid seems reasonable compared with other bids. You well might sacrifice quality by so doing.

• If the contractor also has arranged the financing of your job, the full financing costs of the loan and the payment schedule you'll be expected to meet.

• The specifications of all key materials, including brand names and a work completion schedule.

• If the work is guaranteed by the contractor—as many types of home improvements should be—all details of the guarantee, particularly the period during which the guarantee will remain in effect. Most important: what happens if the materials or workmanship don't hold up as the contractor said they would? And *don't* confuse a manufacturer's guarantee of his materials against defects with the guarantee you also must get from the contractor covering proper installation of the materials.

• An automatic arbitration clause—so that if cost estimates are greatly exceeded by the contractor you can submit the problem to an impartial board of arbitrators. Today such services are available in many U.S. cities.

• A clause binding the contractor to be responsible for any damage caused by his (or his workers') negligence. In some states, builders are now liable for damages from poor construction on the basis of "implied warranty." Check with your lawyer to learn what protection your state provides.

• A provision requiring the builder to do a thorough clean-up job after work is completed. Getting rid of the junk left over from any building project—interior or exterior—can be a splitting headache and a major expense.

KEY RULES AND WARNINGS

Under no circumstances sign a contract with any blank spaces left on it. Have the items which don't apply marked "Void" or crossed out.

If the contract is for repairs which are covered by insurance (e.g., fire damage), check with your insurance company on costs and terms before you sign.

Never sign any complicated deal without consulting your lawyer and, if you don't have a lawyer, get one.

Do not sign a work completion certificate before you get proof (such as duplicate bills) that the contractor has paid all subcontractors who have supplied labor or materials for your project. If you fail to do this, you could be liable for these payments and the subcontractors could legally obtain a mechanic's lien on your house—since they still "own" certain materials incorporated into it. As an alternative, you might get the contractor, subcontractors, and others involved to sign "lien waivers" before you make your final payment. This will absolve you from any further responsibility for subcontractors' bills.

Never pay a contractor in full before the work is done to your satisfaction, or as specified in your contract.

Never pay in cash.

Finally, remember that you have every right to terminate a contract if the contractor fails to carry out the terms of the contract or if he performs the job improperly. Generally, you do this by sending a written notice to the contractor. You pay for the work which has been completed—minus damages. Similarly, a contractor has the right to end a contract if you fail to pay on the schedule to which you agreed.

These may seem tedious details. But heed them, for the rules were created out of the experiences of hundreds of thousands of disappointed homeowners. They will be crucially important in protecting you in your own home improvements.

WHAT ABOUT BEING YOUR OWN CONTRACTOR?

Being your own contractor means lining up all the specialists you'll need —e.g., carpenters, electricians, masons, and plumbers—choosing and ordering materials, supervising the work as it progresses. It means timing everything so precisely that lumber is on hand when the cabinetmaker appears or there's a backlog of indoor work to do when it rains for days, etc. And it means being on the job or getting to the job often, to make decisions and changes as needed.

By doing all this yourself, you'll save the typical 10 per cent (or more) the contractor may add onto your bill for his services. You also may be able to wangle from a local building materials supplier the discount (also usually 10 per cent) he usually gives contractors.

Being your own contractor may make sense if, say, 90 per cent of the job you want done involves only one skill, such as plumbing. Here, the economical thing to do would be to call in your regular plumber, let him round up the equipment and materials he'll use—then call in an electrician or mason, etc., when the job progresses to that stage.

However, if the job involves meshing the skills of many different tradesmen and craftsmen, and you're a babe in the home improvement woods, leave the contracting job to a pro. He'll save you a lot more money in the long run than the fee he charges you.

HOUSE PAINTING GUIDELINES

If you are to avoid the house-paint and painting traps into which millions fall each year, make sure that every detail of the work done by professionals is included in a written estimate and leave nothing to "negotiations."

If the shutters must be taken off, know in advance who will do this, how much will be charged, etc. Be warned: no detail should be too small or you will find "additional labor and time charges" on your final bill and you will be able to do absolutely nothing about it.

Don't hire any paint contractor without carefully checking his qualifications and references and be immediately suspicious of any contractor who offers any long-term "guarantees"—ten, fifteen, even twenty years. The reasonable guarantee is for five years on a two-coat system exterior paint job.

If you're going to do it yourself:

Do, as in all other areas, deal only with a reputable, known merchant who will stand behind the product he sells—be it a national name of paints, a local name, or his own brand. Expect a reliable paint dealer (not just an indifferent clerk) to be prepared to consult with you before you make your decision. Tell him what you plan to paint, the present condition of the surface as you see it, the type of final finish and color you want.

Do carefully read—and reread—the label on the paint can thoroughly. "We take a lot of time, money and research to help you get the right results based on these important label instructions," says Sapolin Paints, Inc. "Read those labels and reread them. They are vital on new types of paints."

Do make sure you or the painter you hire observes the manufacturer's instructions for the proper preparation of the surface. This is more important than the paint job itself, because surface problems will prevent proper adhesion to the finish, retard drying, and cause premature failure of the paint job.

Do use the proper tools. Invest some of the savings you get as a do-it-yourselfer in a quality brush, roller, or ladder scaffold. Also investigate some of the innovations in paints and paint applications.

Don't paint outdoors if the weather turns unseasonably cold; generally for a good paint job the temperature should be above 50°. Avoid painting on any surface that is hot from direct exposure to the sun. Let the surface cool first.

Don't expect a color to look the same under different forms of lighting. Select the color in the very same light in which it will be used. And try not to buy different batches of custom-mixed colors on different days; buy enough for the job to avoid variations in color between cans and batches.

HOME IMPROVEMENT TRAPS—AND HOW TO AVOID THEM

Side by side with today's home improvement boom you will find an astonishingly wide range of gyps, misrepresentations, and come-ons—a vast swindlers' net into which you can be sucked at *any* time unless you are aware and constantly alert.

Home improvements are, in fact, among the top fields for racketeers.

You can literally lose hundreds or even thousands of dollars in one fell swoop on home *non*-improvements. By one estimate, as much as $1.00 out of every $15 we spend to remodel, repair, and refurbish our homes goes into the hands of gypsters and "miracle" materials which don't work.

This era of technical-chemical-mechanical wonders has created not only a wide array of phony "foolproof" basement sealers but also one-coat paints which are supposed to last forever; home siding which supposedly never fades, cracks, or chips; "instant" floor coating which anybody can just paint on; spray-on roofing, and on and on and on.

Of course, many of today's miracle materials *do* hold up as advertised: the epoxy glues, certain caulking compounds, and hard plastic wood finishes are three product categories which leap to mind. But as a general rule these materials *must* be applied properly and professionally. And manufacturers of such materials will *not* guarantee the final job of applying them, despite what local dealers may claim.

How, then, do you spot—and avoid—today's top home improvement gyps? Here is a short rundown and explanation to guide you.

"BAIT AND SWITCH"

In this trick, an ad holds out the bait of an unbelievably low price and the salesman then switches you, the gullible customer, to a higher-priced model.

You respond to a come-on offering, for example, floor tile at, say, 10¢ per square foot. When the salesman arrives at your door, he harshly downgrades the product advertised, refuses to sell it to you and switches you to a vastly overpriced product at 40¢, 50¢ or even 80¢ per square foot—if you let him.

DRIVEWAY RESURFACING

Itinerant gypsters will tell you they "just happen to be in the area," have just enough materials left from previous jobs to do your driveway, and offer to do the job at a "bargain" price. But their materials and workmanship will be either shoddy or totally ineffective. They may merely spray black oil on your driveway. Or they may simply make off with your advance payment —without performing any resurfacing work at all.

Among the most notorious purveyors of the driveway resurfacing swindle are the "Terrible Williamsons." The Williamsons are a clan of several hundred itinerant swindlers who have been victimizing Americans from coast to coast for two full generations. In addition to driveway resurfacing rackets they also are infamous for bilking their victims through other gyps ranging from roofing and basement waterproofing jobs to lightning-rod installation and barn painting.

If the swindle involves your roof, one of them may ring your bell and show you a handful of loose shingles which he says have dropped off your roof. Unless you sign up for a roofing job, he warns, your entire roof may cave in. If you bite, you'll pay an exorbitant price for a shoddy job. If the scheme involves chimney repairs, he will show you a loose brick which, he warns, signals the imminent collapse of your present chimney.

The Williamsons' favorite targets are naïve old ladies but they prey equally viciously on younger Americans. Better Business Bureau files are loaded with reports on the Terrible Williamsons who have charged $300 for applying an ineffective roof "sealer"; coated driveways with gunk which remained sticky for weeks; painted barns with a concoction of aluminum dust and used crankcase oil which washed off with the first rain; installed lightning rods with "conductors" consisting of nothing more than painted ropes.

The Williamsons (who also go under such Scottish names as Stewart, McMillan, and McDonald) usually work out of trucks, and usually manage to leave town before the police catch up with them—or before their victims discover they've been bilked.

There's no hard rule for spotting a Terrible Williamson or any other gypster in this area. You simply must apply the same cautions you would to *any* dealer in home improvement goods and services.

On driveway resurfacing, though, your best move is to consult established local experts and demand a contract specifying the work to be done, type and depth of asphalt to be used, type and thickness of the road base, completion date—plus a guarantee that the job will hold up for a stated period of time.

CHAIN REFERRAL

The typical come-on here is an ad for a complete home re-siding job at what is touted as a startlingly low price—with the extra provision that, if you permit the company to use your home as a model to illustrate a "before and after" advertisement of the firm's workmanship in your community, you'll get a hefty commission for each new customer you find. This commission, it is promised, will be at least enough to cover the total cost of the re-siding job. You might even make hundreds of dollars on top of the price of the job.

The gypster also may tell you the siding is unconditionally guaranteed for, say, twenty years, that it will never need repainting or repairing, and that it will be impervious to such perils as hail, storms, and fire. On top of it all, you'll be assured that by signing up for this type of siding you'll cut your heating bills by one third.

If this tempts you, beware! For you are about to become a victim of a "chain referral" sales scheme. The product being sold, almost always at an unconscionable price, may be aluminum siding, wall-to-wall carpeting, a home intercom or fire alarm system, a water softener, electric broiler, a vacuum cleaning system, etc. But the sales technique is usually the same for whatever product is being sold.

The salesman explains that the "bargain" he is offering is made possible by the fact that there are no advertising costs. You'll earn your own "savings" by participating, as an alternative to advertising, in a word-of-mouth promotion campaign. You are urged to get started at once earning commissions for your referrals. All you need do is make a modest down payment and sign a paper confirming the deal.

But the form you sign may be an ironclad contract which the salesman will sell to a financial institution. You'll be legally obligated to pay the amount stated in the contract and the amount will almost surely be several times the value of the product you are buying.

Over and beyond the pitfall of the contract, the giant hurdle is referring the required number of "qualified" prospects. The reason is simple mathematics. Assume that the first person contacted in your community is supposed to refer eight more persons. Those eight would then have to refer another eight each in order to get their "free" siding. That makes 64 referrals so far, and if each of these is supposed to get another eight . . . The numbers balloon to 512, then 4,096 on the next round, then 32,768 . . . 262,144 . . . 2,097,152 . . .

"CREW SWITCHING"

A team of high-pressure salesmen divides into two crews. "A" fans out into one part of town, selling products ranging from awnings to wall-to-wall carpeting. Crew "B," under a different company name, but selling the same products, heads for another part of town. Both quote fantastically inflated prices, almost never make a sale—and now comes the catch.

The crews switch. Crew "A" approaches the same houses Crew "B" already has visited and this time quotes much lower prices. Crew "B" goes into "A's" territory and ridicules the "other company" for its high prices.

What you don't know is that the two outfits are working together, that all the prices quoted are inflated—the second almost as much as the first—and that you are being softened up for the kill. If you do not double-check the offers and the reputations of the companies, the chances are you will be gypped on whatever you buy.

THE LEAKY BASEMENT

Not long ago an elderly Chicagoan was bilked out of $9,000 by an itinerant "engineer" who poured water into cracks in the old man's basement floor, then managed to persuade him that his house was sitting on a cesspool. The $9,000 went, of course, for utterly unneeded repairs and non-repairs performed by the "engineer."

Another homeowner, a New Yorker, paid $750 for a basement waterproofing job which failed to stem the tide of spring flooding. He was then told by the waterproofing company that the job covered "only the specific area where our process is applied, not leaks which appear elsewhere."

Damp, leaky basements are a bane to millions of homeowners, and in many cases the problem is exceedingly difficult to solve. This very difficulty is an open invitation to the unscrupulous operator with his array of miracle wet-basement cures.

Against this background, it is merely common sense to have the job done by professionals who understand such matters as soil types, water tables, etc. Be prepared for the fact that a reliable contractor may take time to solve the problem and that the work may require several treatments before it is licked. Beware of any "guarantee" that the waterproofing will be 100 per cent effective, for no claim of this sort is valid. And invalid too is any claim that a basement waterproofing method is "government-approved."

THE PHONY FURNACE "INSPECTOR"

If you have any degree of hidden fear that your heating plant may be somehow defective and that, as a result, you might be running the danger of a devastating home fire, you are probably more vulnerable than you realize to the persuasive patter of the furnace gypster.

Here are the basic earmarks by which you'll recognize this crook—and the rules for keeping out of his way:

A stranger appears at your door and offers to "inspect" your furnace. He may drop the name of your local gas and electric company, or some nationally known furnace manufacturer. If yours is an older heating plant, he may poke around the mortar holding the firebricks together, discover that it's powdery, and declare that the furnace is "dangerous." What you may not know is that in this type of installation it's perfectly normal for the mortar to be powdery.

Or he may offer you bargain-priced furnace-cleaning services—and, after dismantling your heating plant, tell you that it's a wonder you haven't already been asphyxiated by carbon monoxide or that you are extremely fortunate your house has not burned down around you. He refuses even to put the furnace back together.

These swindlers—and there are many variations—have one key goal: to scare you into buying a new furnace or expensive parts from them—whether or not you need the equipment—at prices far above the amounts which a reliable local heating contractor would charge.

Seek the advice of established local dealers on the condition of your furnace—or see if the local fire department will send somebody to check the safety aspects of your furnace for you.

THE FRAUDULENT PLUMBING AND ELECTRICAL WIRING "REPAIRMAN"

This swindler is closely related to the crooked furnace inspector, for he also deals in scare tactics and exploits the average homeowner's near total innocence on such matters as water pressure, circuit breakers, and wiring capacity.

What should you do to avoid any furnace-repair racket or similar gyp?

Beware of *anybody* who comes to your door uninvited and offers to "inspect" your electrical wiring or plumbing system. Call in your regular electrician if you have any reason to suspect wiring problems or your regular plumber if your pipes aren't working properly.

TERMITE SWINDLES

Part of the home "improvement" gyp tale—and yet so pervasive and expensive that he deserves a section all his own—is the termite swindler. Here is a typical illustration of how this gypster works:

A truck pulls into your driveway and a man introducing himself as a "termite inspector" informs you that a termite problem has cropped up in your neighborhood. He may tell you that he has found termites in the trees and shrubs around your house. Or he may offer to "inspect" your home— free—to see whether termites have moved inside. He disappears into your basement, later emerges with the frightening news that your own house has become infested. As proof, he displays a jar of live termites he says he has found downstairs.

The "inspector" may tell you that you are lucky because your termite problem has been discovered "in the nick of time" and he urges you to act immediately, "before your house collapses." He then summons a couple of men from his truck and tells them to bring a tankful of insecticide. You will pay only for the number of gallons actually sprayed in your cellar and there will be a ten-year guarantee on the job. A little later the men return to inform you that the job took 85 gallons at $4.00 a gallon—or $340.

But termites don't live in trees or shrubs. There may not be a single termite in your home either. Even if there are, the chemical spray used by the termite gypsters is probably worthless because termites generally live ten to twenty feet underground. Reputable exterminators normally do not guarantee a single termite control job for as long as ten years.

The hard facts about termites and termite control are these:

Termites are a very real menace in virtually every part of the United States. They feed primarily on wood, paper, and leather. They can indeed do extensive damage to the structural members supporting your house.

Each year 20,000,000 American homes are damaged, some severely, by colonies of voracious termites. Out of every five homes, two are under attack in every state except Alaska by these wood-chewing gluttons.

But termites work very slowly and even if they have invaded your house you can afford to take weeks or months to decide on a course of action.

Also, ridding a house of termites may involve injection of poisonous chemicals, under pressure, into the ground around infested areas and perhaps under basement floors. Termite control may involve excavation around the foundation and the construction of mechanical barriers to block entry by termites around the house or under the basement. Sometimes badly infested sills must be replaced as well.

The cost to you of termite control is generally based on the number of linear feet treated and the amount of excavation and reconstruction needed. It is not unusual for a legitimate termite-control job to cost hundreds of dollars.

Typically, the legitimate termite exterminator will guarantee his work, usually for three or more years. But the guarantees may not hold if you make additions to the house, such as a new wing or a new porch—unless you termite-proof these, too.

Here are your key guides to avoiding termite gypsters:

• If you think you have a termite problem, call one or more reputable exterminating firms, ask for expert opinions and estimates. Some firms will inspect your home free; others may charge $15 to $20.

• Investigate their references of work done in other homes.

But first do a little inspecting on your own:

• Take a screwdriver and push it into wooden beams or footings. If the screwdriver penetrates the wood and reveals it has been hollowed out from the inside, that's a bad sign. Look too for another sure visual sign: the presence of "mud tubes." These are hollow mud tunnels usually on the outside of home foundations or interior walls or support columns or even rising up unsupported from the ground to floor in crawl spaces.

• Get costs spelled out in advance—including the details and costs of post-treatment service which might involve periodic inspections to make sure construction, planting, etc., have not cracked the long-life chemical barrier used to bar termites.

If you have any doubt about a firm's reputation or control techniques, check with your Better Business Bureau, Chamber of Commerce, county agricultural agent, or state agricultural college.

• Be sure to get a guarantee. This normally will specify that if termites are detected in annual inspections (usually limited to the first three years after treatment) follow-up treatment will be provided at no extra cost. Some agreements also include insurance policies guaranteeing payment to cover repair or replacement of any part of your home damaged by termites after completion of professional treatment. The term of these policies is usually three years, with maximum coverage normally $25,000.

SWIMMING POOL GYPS

This is still another category of home improvement which has become riddled with traps and problems for the homeowner. To illustrate with a classic "bait and switch":

You see an ad in your local newspaper for a sizable above-ground swimming pool costing only $499—with all the trimmings. *But* when you look over the pool the salesman tells you that the vinyl liner is not heavy enough to hold water, that the deck is not real redwood but only redwood stain, and that maintenance will cost you more each year than the sales price. He may not even have such a pool on hand. And, of course, the cost doesn't include delivery. *However*, perhaps you'd be interested in a larger pool, costing $1,800. . . .

How do you avoid the swindlers and build a swimming pool intelligently?

• First and foremost, recognize that most swimming pools *are* expensive, so don't expect to buy a de luxe kidney-shaped model at wading-pool prices.

As a general rule, vinyl-lined above-ground pools cost $1,000 and up, and the best grades of this type of pool cost $1,500 to $2,500. Below-ground pools may be vinyl-lined, poured or sprayed concrete, steel-aluminum, or fiberglass. These generally retail for at least $5,000 and frequently up to $8,000, installed. Below-ground pools typically cost $250 to $700 a year to maintain—including electricity, repainting, patching, vacuuming, filtering, chemicals, water, heater fuel, etc.

Luxury "extras" can run into the thousands of dollars—and can include anything from special filtration systems and heating apparatus to telephone jacks and bathing cabanas with showers.

Other hidden costs of pools are property tax hikes if yours is a below-ground pool, for this is a property improvement. Also you will pay for increases in your liability insurance in your homeowners policy, for any pool is an invitation to accidents. In addition, if you finance your swimming pool, you'll pay high interest costs, of course. Then there will be increased water and electric bills.

But there is no disputing the moneysaving angles too—such as the reduced costs of going to public or club pools, the fewer trips away from home for weekend vacations. And there's no dismissing the fact that a swimming pool enhances the value of your property.

Don't buy a swimming pool from a catalog. Take time to do some basic research, since this may be a big investment. Consult the literature of local Better Business Bureaus, the National Swimming Pool Institute (2000 K Street, Washington, D.C. 20006), or your regional swimming pool association. Find out what materials are sturdiest and most appropriate for the type of pool you want.

Check your zoning regulations. Almost all communities have rules covering fences, filters, drains, etc.

Get bids on the pool you want from two or three reputable local contractors whose credentials you have checked.

Understand what's covered by each bid and, of course, by the final contract. If there is a provision for a "normal" amount of excavation, for an above-ground pool, just what does the contractor consider "normal"? Will fill be provided—or only leveling? What about the filtration and drainage systems?

Get a written timetable for the pool's construction or installation, but obey the fundamental rules on home improvements: *never* sign a completion form until all work has been completed, *never* give a pool salesman a check in his own name at the time of the sale, and *don't* pay in full before all work is completed.

Get a detailed guarantee *in writing* from the contractor and study not only what it provides but also who is responsible for fulfilling it. The guarantee should cover all labor, materials, the timetable, and optional equipment.

LANDSCAPING AND GARDENING TRAPS

In this area also the gypsters are giving homeowners an ever intensifying headache.

Tens of millions of you are now going in for home gardening and spending hundreds of millions of dollars a year on supplies alone. A single family, for instance, easily can spend hundreds (or thousands) in a year if it invests in such machinery as plows, mini tractors, rototillers, elaborate lawn and garden sprinkler systems.

As a reflection of this boom—and a spur to it too—you will find a dazzling variety of landscaping specialists (qualified or unqualified), of nursery stock (both retail and mail order), of supplies of all kinds in hardware and garden supply stores. You also will, if you are not informed, be an easy target for the important fringe of deceivers and racketeers on all sides.

For instance, "Trees of Heaven" which "grow 50 feet high in just one year" may sound great in the advertisements—and grow they do. But among botanists this particular variety is nicknamed the "stink tree"—hardly one you'd like growing in your back yard.

The "amazing climbing vine peach," a plant you're led to believe will grow a great crop of peaches, is alluring too. But actually this one bears only an inedible type of melon.

Then there are "miracle" multiple fruit trees pictured as laden with several different varieties bursting forth simultaneously. The chances of matching the ads in real life at home are minuscule.

There are legions of utterly incompetent "tree surgeons" abroad in our landscape who will come to your door and try to scare you by telling you your trees are infested with this or that insect or fungus. If you let them, they will carve up your healthy trees and spew useless pesticides on others—every move at fantastic prices.

There is the springtime humus racketeer. This swindler arrives in a truck at your door, offers an impressive-sounding topsoil to bring your garden back to life, and says that several bushels at $1.00 apiece should do the job.

You give him the go-ahead, turn back to your chores. Then he presents you with a bill for $200 to $300, claiming he has sprinkled hundreds of bushels of restorative substances on your lawn and threatening you with a lawsuit if you don't pay up. You have no way of knowing how much "humus" he actually has spread around and you're lucky if the stuff doesn't kill your lawn altogether.

And there are the gypsters who show up every year with a new miracle cure for your lawn. A typical example is one product recently marketed as a preparation to revive worn-out brown lawns. The stuff was a potion of green dye and fertilizer which streaked and washed off with the first rain.

YOUR MAJOR WEAPONS AGAINST THE HOME IMPROVEMENT RACKETEERS

To summarize your major weapons against the home improvement racketeers and fast-buck sharpsters:

• Beware of anybody who comes to your door and tells you he "just happens" to be in the neighborhood and "just happens" to have enough material left over to perform some job for you at bargain rates.

• Ask the salesman for his name and the name and address of his company. Demand his credentials. Then, in his presence, call the local banks and/or local Better Business Bureau to check out his reputation. Don't get talked into buying anything without checking your need, double-checking company prices, and triple-checking the arrangements for future servicing.

• Ask to see other jobs the company has done.

• Don't fall for any form of high-pressure sales tactics and consider them a warning to you *not* to deal with their users.

• Be extra cautious about taking merchandise "on approval" from any unknown salesman.

• Watch out for any guarantee that a product such as siding or linoleum or carpeting will last twenty to thirty years. What company can guarantee you that it will even be in business thirty years from now?

But if you discover that you have been gypped by an unscrupulous contractor or by an incompetent odd-job man, *howl*—to your local Better Business Bureau, newspapers and radio stations, the state attorney general's office, the nearest consumer protection agency. See Chapter 26, "Your Rights as a Consumer," on how to extend the range of your indignation and get action.

If you're victimized, your yells may at least save others. And possibly you'll get help in forcing the individual who bilked you to make good on your deal.

How to Cut Costs Outside Your House

Even if you manage to side-step all the landscape gyp artists and phony siding salesmen and gardening frauds, you still will be faced with the problem of how to shop for the goods and services you will need for the upkeep and beautification of the outside of your house.

HOW TO BUY LAWN AND GARDEN SUPPLIES

Here first are basic rules to guide you on buying garden supplies generally:

Plants and seeds: You won't get the gorgeous color results shown in catalogs unless you painstakingly follow directions in planting, fertilizing, thinning, and cultivating. You may not get any results if you live in a climate where certain plant varieties just can't be grown. Before you buy, read directions on packages of seeds and plants to see how much work and expertise are involved in growing them. Check, in seed catalogs, the number of days it takes each variety to mature. Ask your county agricultural agent for advice on what can be grown where.

Trees: These can run into big money and proper tree planting can take hours of your time and effort. On the other hand, improper planting easily can mean a total loss of your investment. Before you buy, make sure the tree will grow in your area. Follow directions precisely. Before you choose a type of tree, decide exactly what you want from it. Shade? Privacy? Spring blossoms? A color splash? Edible fruit? Then ask a qualified nursery which type will best fit your expectations. Or consult low-cost literature from the U. S. Department of Agriculture on various categories of trees and shrubs.

Fertilizer: Using inappropriate fertilizers can devastate your lawn or kill your vegetables and flowers. Ask your county agricultural agent for guidance on your own garden. Ask your state agricultural experiment station to test your soil and recommend a fertilizer program for you—at little or no cost.

Sprinkler systems: Since this can be a very costly investment, deal only with a reputable firm which will not only install the system according to a plan but will also service it later. Insist on standard-sized pipes, valve, and sprinkler heads in case they need to be replaced later. Be sure the system will conform to local watering restrictions in summer months. Be wary of a company which asks for advance payment—often a sign that the firm is not soundly financed.

Lawns: Seek advice from a reputable dealer or from the U. S. Department of Agriculture on which products your lawn actually needs. A key warning, though: seed your lawn properly in the first place. Seeding can be an expensive operation, perhaps involving heavy machinery for grading and rolling, plus expert assistance—but it'll be worth it if you thereby avoid having to redo the whole job later.

HOW TO BUY A POWER LAWN MOWER

The average price of the basic walk-behind power mower is well over $100—and add a zero-plus to that figure for the monster riding job. The moneysaving rules in this area are indeed important, therefore—and the number one rule of them all is:

Buy out of season if possible, timing your purchase to preseason or post-season sales. And in season or off season, look for promotions which include free accessories with your mower.

In addition, to save money no matter when you buy:

Buy the size needed for your particular lawn—enough power and width of cut to do the job and no more. To illustrate: small lawn, 19-inch hand-propelled, lightweight, easily maneuvered; large lawn, 21-inch self-propelled; extra large lawn, only then consider a riding mower or a lawn and garden tractor.

Buy from a qualified retailer who, you have assured yourself, will provide proper service and replacement parts.

Choose a reputable brand-name mower to insure quality and the service backup you'll need. Compare the quality features of various brands before you buy.

By no means buy on price alone. Comparison-shop for product and safety features too. The cheapest buy may be the most expensive because of its shorter life, more servicing, and fewer safety features—and the manufacturer and retailer guarantee must be considered a tangible part of the mower's price.

Buy only the essential features that suit your lawn's needs and yours. For instance, a self-propelled mower will be easier for older people to operate, while a mower with an electric starter will be especially appealing to women. Don't buy unnecessary attachments and thereby build up your mower's price.

Buy a mower with an Outdoor Power Equipment Institute safety seal on it. This seal, usually on the back of the mower, signifies that a model of that mower has been approved by an independent testing laboratory as meeting the power lawn mower safety specifications established by the American National Standards Institute.

Check your motor warranty with utmost care. It will be a vital factor in your long-range maintenance costs.

Curb—even slash—your maintenance costs by following closely the manufacturer's instructions in your owner's manual. Always operate the mower as prescribed. Do not abuse the mower. It is designed to cut grass, not brush, earth, or gravel.

To limit your power motor repairs, follow these rules for continuing maintenance: check the oil and fuel level before each mowing; keep the air cleaner clean; wash out the underside of the mower after each mowing; keep your entire mower clean and free of grass and dirt build-up. Follow these rules for periodic maintenance: check the blade for sharpness and balance; clean or repair spark plugs at least once a year; check belts and pulleys for adjustment; occasionally check all bolts for tightness; make repairs as soon as trouble appears; drain both oil and gas before storing your mower in the fall; have your mower tuned up annually by an authorized service center.

If you're among the millions who are buying new mowers each year, you'll get a tag giving you the basic safety operating rules. But if you're among the tens of millions of owners of older, existing mowers, go to your neighborhood store and ask for the OPEI's "A Guide for the Mowing Man."

How to Sell Your House

BASIC DO'S AND DON'TS

Selling your house, and particularly selling it at a top possible price, is not an easy job. But the efforts you, the homeowners, make—to get qualified advice on the worth of your house, to find a reputable real estate broker, to make the home repairs and improvements which will improve the terms of your sale and to avoid the ones which aren't worth it—can mean literally thousands of dollars to you when you actually sell.

Here are basic do's and don'ts on selling your house. Use them not only in selling your house but also as guidelines in repairing and remodeling it—with a view toward selling years hence.

Do consult one or more licensed real estate brokers, or Realtors, who are well informed on the values in your neighborhood and with whom you feel you can have an honest, open relationship.

There are three ways to list a home for sale: an exclusive right-to-sell listing, an open listing, and a multiple listing.

If you're in a hurry to sell, the exclusive right-to-sell listing contract is a good bet. With this kind of listing, you inform only one Realtor or broker of your home's availability and give him or her time to sell it. The broker then has the incentive to put a lot of effort into the sale.

If you are not in a hurry, you might choose an open listing, in which case you list the house with several brokers, each of whom may offer it to potential customers. The first one to find a buyer gets the commission. But with this type of listing, the incentive for each broker is lower, so the sale may take longer.

Or you may opt for the most common selling method, the multiple listing. You list the house with a single agent who in turn shares it with other co-operating brokers. He or she also shares the commission with whichever broker finds the buyer.

Don't try to sell the house yourself in order to save a broker's commission—which normally runs between 6 and 8 per cent of the sale price of the property. The sale involves a lot more time, know-how, and red tape than you think.

Do ask the Realtor to estimate the value of your house and, if you have any major disagreement on this score, check other brokers in your area for their opinions as well. (Or hire an independent appraiser whose fee may run $75 to $200 but could be well worth it if he or she can pinpoint the correct price range for your house.) Beware of the broker whose price estimate is thousands of dollars above the estimates of other brokers; he may simply be trying to get your listing and be utterly incapable of delivering a buyer at this estimated price later.

Don't make the mistake of asking a much higher price for your house than it's worth. If you do this, the salesman may lose interest in selling your house and the house may remain unsold for months or years.

According to one estimate, if the sale price you set is within 5 per cent of its actual fair market value you are ten times more likely to sell it within a reasonable period of time than if you price it 15 to 20 per cent above the fair market value. A good policy is to set your price about 5 to 10 per cent above the amount your Realtor considers fair—and bargain from there.

Do view your house with as much cold objectivity as you can muster. Try to see it—and its faults—as if you were the buyer rather than the seller. This will not only help you in arriving at a realistic price range but also give you clues on what repairs should be made.

Do invest in minor improvements both inside and outside the house, such as repairing cracks in the plaster, washing dirty walls, doing a limited amount of painting, fixing broken tiles and leaky faucets, replacing ripped screens, etc. If it's summertime and the house feels like an oven, it may be worth while to invest in a secondhand room air conditioner. Often $100 spent for such improvements can return you $1,000 in your sale price.

Don't, though, "overinvest," in, say, new additions to the house or a complete kitchen modernization job. It may turn out that prospective buyers would have designed these improvements entirely differently and your investment might go down the drain.

Do ask your Realtor to make appointments with you for showing the house to prospective buyers, so that the customer won't have to wade through an accumulation of the week's laundry or an obstacle course of children's toys. Make sure, when a prospective buyer visits, that the house is neat and clean—particularly the kitchen, living room, and bathrooms, which are the most important rooms to most buyers. Also make sure the house is well lighted when it is being inspected and keep your lawn and garden reasonably trim in summer and walkways cleared of snow and ice in winter.

Do whatever you can to warm up the atmosphere of your house—by having a fire going in the fireplace, arranging the porch or outdoor furniture attractively, putting a few flowers around.

Do prepare a couple of pages of basic facts about your house and property which you or your agent can give to would-be buyers. Sample data sheets might, for instance, mention the favorable location to schools, shopping center, bus stops or train; the number of closets, extra storage areas; special financing possibilities; landscaping; other favorable aspects.

Don't interfere with the broker and client while they're going through the house. Get lost if you can; otherwise just "sit down and shut up." *Don't* have any music playing during the inspection; your choice of music easily could distract or offend the visitor. And don't permit noisy children and dogs to accost your customer.

Do, if today's interest rates are a major barrier to a sale and you have a lower-rate mortgage, consider acting as the lender yourself by arranging to transfer the existing mortgage on your house to the buyer. Consider, too, extending a second mortgage to help make up the difference in the amount owed you at the same interest rates being charged by your local bank or other lender.

Do recognize the importance of final settlement costs on any house in the $30,000 and up range.

WHEN YOU MOVE

THE AGONIES OF MOVING

Dave was notified at Christmas of his promotion and transfer across the country to a new job. He and Kay then sold their house and in effect simply wasted time until the date he had told the company he would be ready: June 25.

By this decision, Dave and Kay wasted money as well as time, and all because they followed the outmoded U.S. tradition of summertime moving.

Of all the millions of American families who move each year, more than 60 per cent move between June 1 and September 20. To cope with this rush, the moving industry must operate on a twenty-four-hour basis and in this period it charges maximum prices.

But there's no doubt that many of these millions would be better off with a non-summer move. In spring, in fall, in winter they would get more efficient and quicker service; they would be charged a minimum, not a maximum rate; their moves would be safer too.

Although the proportion of families moving every year is one out of five, the proportion in the twenty-two to twenty-four age bracket is nearly 50 per cent; for newly married Americans, the mobility rate is a fantastic 84 per cent; and for executives in their thirties the rate soars to 97 per cent!

We are moving from city to suburb to exurb. We are congregating as never before in the nation's congested population belts along the east and west coasts. We are moving from the colder to the warmer states. We are moving from east to west.

And millions of us are moving overseas—at least temporarily—to work for the government or for the great companies and industries doing business around the world.

Many young Americans, and particularly those whose jobs involve frequent transfers, now live in a dozen or more houses and apartments over the course of their lifetimes.

Moving always has been one of the biggest and costliest agonies a family goes through. Almost always, the expenses turn out to be greater than expected; goods are often delivered late; when they are delivered, they often are damaged or important items are missing altogether. There's only a fifty-fifty chance that you'll be satisfied with your next move.

How *you*, the individual or family being transported, handle the move can make all the difference between a nightmare and a smooth, businesslike transaction.

Thus, to guide you when you move, here are basic rules for cutting costs, choosing a reliable mover, preventing and insuring losses—plus other vital and moneysaving pointers on moving.

HOW TO CUT YOUR MOVING COSTS

• Find out which costs, if any, your or your spouse's employer will pay toward the move. Some companies today offer these fringe benefits to key employees being transferred to another location—above and beyond payment of direct moving expenses:

buying a house the employee is unable to sell;

helping to track down a suitable house at the new location;

providing temporary household help at both the old and the new homes during the moving period;

paying "points" added to the basic interest rate on new mortgages;

paying the family's travel expenses to the new location—and also paying the costs of family excursions, before the move, to explore the new town or city;

even assuming the costs of moving such things as boats, second cars, cats and dogs, and other "difficult items" (although they have been known to balk at moving woodpiles, compost heaps, and flagstones from the patio).

If you are moving abroad, most major companies will pay the full costs of housing, feeding, and transporting your whole family during the usual three-to-six-week period between the time the employee must vacate his home and the time he is able to line up a house or apartment abroad.

Many companies provide special allowances to employees being transferred abroad to pay any costs above those prevailing in the United States—plus other allowances for such special expenses as storage of household belongings, foreign language courses, and the expenses of adapting appliances to electrical systems abroad.

• If at all possible avoid scheduling your move between June and the end of September. The best times to move, instead, are between mid-October and mid-May and during the second or third week of the month. Try also to give the mover at least thirty to forty-five days' notice and some choice of moving days. Try *not* to schedule your move on the first or last day of the month—the most active moving days, when many leases expire.

Simply by timing your move so it doesn't fall during peak months and days, you'll save 10 to 15 per cent on some carriers and also get far more efficient service. The tradition of the summer move dates back to an era when vacations were almost always a summer affair and the United States was an agriculture-oriented economy. It has been rooted in the belief that it is bad to transfer children during a school year.

But new staggered school terms permit far more flexibility in transfers than ever before, and there is even an argument in favor of moving children during a school year. Many educators now believe that a mid-term change can be mentally and socially stimulating, compared with having to spend a lonely summer in a strange neighborhood. Children can acquire new friends easily in a school environment, but during summer vacation there are few sources beyond next-door neighbors.

• Before getting estimates, get rid of stuff you won't need or want in your new home. This is especially important if yours is a long-distance move in which costs are based largely on weight. (Sample: heavy old appliances.)

If you are moving only to another part of town, send out your furniture for repairs or reupholstering and your rugs and drapes for cleaning, then have the articles delivered to your new home.

If your attic is loaded with junk accumulated over the years, consider advertising items of interest in the local newspaper—and see if anybody turns up to make an offer on them. If you're dubious about people's interest in what you may consider pure junk, just take a look at what's being sold today in "antique" shops, secondhand stores, and auctions.

Or, as an alternative, stage your own "garage sale." Such an event can earn you some change and can be amusing as well.

HOW TO CHOOSE A MOVER

There are four types of household moves; local, intrastate, interstate, and international. All major national carriers are usually in a position to have their local agent handle all four types.

• On a long-distance move, inquire about the reputations of moves at your destination as well as your present location. Ask friends, neighbors, and business associates who have moved recently to steer you to a reliable carrier. And your local County or State Consumer Protection Agency can at least tell you if there have been many complaints about a mover with whom you are considering doing business.

• Then ask at least two or three movers to come to your house and estimate costs. Show *each* all of your belongings to be moved. Don't forget the attic, basement, garage, or even summer cottage. Be sure to point out all the heaviest items you'll want to move. Refuse to let a mover take an inventory over the phone. A reputable mover depends on an accurate estimate to know how many shipments will fit in the van.

Find out exactly which services each mover would include in the deal—and how much each would charge.

Do *not*, however, award the job to any one mover strictly on the basis of the cost estimate. An unrealistically low estimate is a "low ball"—and it is used by unscrupulous movers as well as unreliable repairmen simply to get the job away from others who stick to more realistic figures. Similarly, a mover's vague claim that he is "bonded" or "certified" or "insured" may be no guarantee to you of his reliability.

• Make sure any mover who is making estimates for you gives you the very helpful Interstate Commerce Commission pamphlet entitled "Summary of Information for Shippers of Household Goods," outlining your rights and obligations as well as the mover's. Interstate carriers must give you a very useful booklet called "Loss and Damage of Household Goods—Prevention and Recovery."

• Normally, movers do *not* quote flat rates. In most cases, long-distance movers are regulated by federal and state law. The amount you pay depends on the amount of weight of your shipment and the distance to be shipped. A local mover may charge for his travel time between his base and your house and the number of hours it takes to perform the special services you require such as packing.

• Explore alternatives to the professional mover to reduce the cost of moving. If you have only a relatively small collection of not too valuable belongings and also have the time to supervise the move fairly closely, a one-man pickup truck variety of mover may be fine. But be on guard: this business is loaded with fly-by-nights, and if you deal with a small, unknown outfit, you do so strictly at your own risk, particularly on a long-distance move.

Every time you make a trip to inspect your new house or community, take at least a few things with you in your car—especially paintings, sculptures, lampshades, bric-a-brac which otherwise would have to be specially crated.

Of course, you can always rent a haul-it-yourself truck or trailer, which you can now get in almost any size and shape—if you have the time, energy, and skill to do the whole moving job yourself. Between 10 and 15 per cent of Americans who move do so themselves on short moves—often at savings of 50 per cent or more—and the number of do-it-yourselfers is increasing steadily.

The cost of renting a large truck ranges upward from $20 to $25 a day, plus 17¢ or so per mile, plus the cost of gas and insurance. Many rental companies today provide, for a fee, special pads, packing boxes, etc., plus instructions on how to use them to their best advantage.

Key points to check on before you rent a trailer or van include:

What surcharge, if any, will be levied at your destination for the return of the vehicle?

What type and how much insurance is provided in case of accident or damage to your belongings?

What happens if the rental van breaks down on the road?

What are the costs of "extras" you might need: the furniture pads, packing boxes, hand trucks, the like? Or are any or all of these free?

How large a deposit will you have to make at the outset and will you have to pay cash for the remainder of what you owe at your destination?

HOW TO PREVENT AND INSURE LOSSES

Interstate movers are responsible for damages or losses only up to 60¢ per pound per article. However, the 60¢-a-pound liability limit won't be much consolation if you find your set of Meissen china in smithereens when it arrives.

• So if your belongings are worth more than this, which they almost surely are, declare a realistic total value of the goods being shipped—and pay the extra charge of 50¢ for each $100 of value you declare for full added value protection.

If you neither accept the 60¢-per-pound liability limit nor declare the actual value of your shipment, the mover's liability limit is automatically $1.25 per pound—for the same 50¢ per $100.

It is quite possible, though, that your homeowners insurance policy covers your belongings while they are being moved—and if so, there may be no need to get any additional coverage for the move. Or, if your employer is absorbing the costs of your move, he may have special insurance policies to cover you. Or you may be able to have a rider added to your homeowners policy to cover your move at lower cost than the extra expense of full coverage through the mover.

• If your belongings must be stored, ask that they be held on a "storage-in-transit" basis. Otherwise, the mover may not be considered responsible for damage occurring in storage.

• Your key area in which to compare charges—and achieve savings—is in what movers call "accessorial charges." These are for such services as packing, unpacking, furnishing containers, lugging pianos up and down steps, etc. The charge for these is on a "per unit" or "per service" basis and must be separately itemized. Thus, you need not pay for unpacking unless you ordered it.

• To save time and confusion, have appropriate servicemen disconnect and service appliances such as refrigerators, room air conditioners, washing machines, stereo sets—as well as your telephone and electricity—*before* the movers arrive. Unhooking such items needs an expert hand and this is generally *your* responsibility.

Also among your responsibilities: moving small items of relatively great value, such as jewelry, coin and stamp collections, furs, the contents of your safe deposit box. Your bank may be able to advise you on special courier services specializing in transporting such valuables.

• Save money by doing at least some of the packing yourself. Movers generally will sell you containers at $2.50 or so apiece, cartons at 75¢ each, and large cardboard wardrobes for about $4.25. (Or you can get cartons free from grocery and liquor stores.) You are usually responsible if what you have packed is damaged in transit. In any event, be sure to let the movers pack such tricky items as large mirrors, appliances, and fine cabinets.

• When packing, make your own detailed inventory of your belongings. You won't have time to do it on moving day, and the one the driver makes may be incomplete. It will be a big job, but invaluable in the event of a loss.

• Make sure each carton is marked with a list of contents—or fitted with color-coded tags corresponding to each room in your new home. Try to categorize your belongings so only one or two boxes must be labeled "miscellaneous." Then, as your possessions are being unloaded, have them put as near as possible to where you ultimately will want them. Or make a sketch of the floor plan of your new home, with notations on which items should be put where—and give a copy to the mover. This will save you the energy and high cost of hiring somebody else to help you shove them around from room to room later. And mark one box "load last." This is the box containing things you'll need immediately when you arrive—e.g., sheets, towels, toiletries, light bulbs, baby food, etc.

• When your goods are picked up, the van driver or other representative of the mover will make a written inventory of everything you are having shipped—with notes on items which are "marred and scarred." Ask for a copy of the complete form, and be sure you understand the code letters on it. Check this inventory carefully and if you have any disagreement with it, note the disagreements on the inventory. (An unscrupulous mover may mark *everything* as marred and scratched at the beginning—to remove the chance of *any* blame for damage at the end.)

• Be on hand to supervise delivery. Plan to check each item as it is unpacked against the inventory. Be sure, also, that the bill of lading indicates the agreed-upon pickup and delivery dates and times, the estimated shipping costs and other charges, and any special arrangements you have made with the mover.

OTHER MONEYSAVING POINTERS

• Do not tip your mover. Tipping is illegal in any interstate move and in most states. Report any pressure for tipping to Motor Carriers Section, Interstate Commerce Commission, Washington, D.C. 20423.

• Make sure the pickup and delivery dates, and all other agreements between you and the carrier, appear on the "order for service" as well as the bill of lading. By law, interstate movers *must* deliver your goods during a span of several consecutive days to which you have agreed. Legally, they may not deliver your goods early. Fines up to $500 may be imposed for any infraction of ICC rules.

• By law each shipment must be weighed on certified scales—and if you, the customer, want to witness the weighing, you have the right to do so. The order for service must include the location of the scales. So if you have any doubts whatsoever about the weight of your shipment, request a reweigh—witnessed by you. This will cost you nothing if the mover is off target or attempting to cheat you by more than 120 pounds or 25 per cent of the estimated weight, whichever is less. At the weighing scale, be on the alert for the unethical practice of weighing the empty truck with an empty gasoline tank and the loaded truck with a full tank.

• Give the mover a telephone number and address where you can be reached if necessary while your shipment is in transit. Also, get the driver's name, van number, shipment number, and intended route in case you need to trace the shipment through the mover's home office.

• Make every effort to beat the van to your new home. Otherwise, you'll risk an extra charge for the delay beyond the "free waiting time" permitted on interstate moves.

• Be prepared to pay by cash, money order, traveler's check, certified or cashier's check when the moving van arrives at its destination. Personal checks are generally not accepted. Don't obtain the entire amount of your estimated moving charges in check form unless you know definitely what the final charge will be. You might find yourself overpaying the mover and having to wait 60 to 120 days for your change. Instead, get a cashier's check for 75 to 80 per cent of the estimated moving charges and cash for the balance. If you cannot come up quickly with the required amount of cash or an acceptable substitute, the mover *will* put all your goods in storage at *your* expense—and also charge you additional sums to transport the goods from the warehouse back to your house.

By law, movers must estimate how much money customers must have at the time of delivery. Movers may require their customers to pay no more than the estimated cost plus 10 per cent before unloading shipments. And according to the ICC rules, a mover must advise you twenty-four hours or more before the van arrives at its destination whether charges will exceed the estimate by more than 10 per cent. Then, by law, you may request, and get, fifteen business days in which to come up with the money to cover the balance due.

• Get a receipt (or "freight bill") for the amount you actually pay. This also states the weight of your shipment, mileage, the rate per 100 pounds, and the charges for transportation, added value protection, other special services which have been performed.

• If any loss or damage has occurred in transit to any of your belongings, note details on the mover's inventory of your shipment or on the delivery receipt at the time of delivery. This notation is probably your best evidence to support a claim you may later make in a letter to the home office of the carrier. Also point out the damages or missing items to the mover before he leaves your house. Check the truck yourself for any items which may have been left inside it.

In filing a claim, list lost and damaged articles separately, plus estimates of costs of repairs or replacement. Include expenses caused by delays or losses, such as hotel or motel bills. Also, give the other basic facts such as the date of the move, the weight and destination of the shipment, and the mover's order number.

Movers, incidentally, are required by law to acknowledge your claim within thirty days and to "pay, decline, or make firm compromise settlement offer" within a hundred and twenty days of the date on which the claim was received.

Normally, you may file claims up to nine months after the delivery date.

Your best bet, if a mover welches on any part of the deal he has made, is to call the nearest ICC office and ask for advice. Or get in touch with the ICC's Bureau of Operations (Washington, D.C. 20423).

Or, if your new home is in New York, take your grievances to the Office of Impartial Chairman, a sort of arbitration agency for the Moving and Storage Industry of New York (10 Columbus Circle, New York, N.Y. 10019).

Finally, remember these other points which are closely related to most moves:

Have a bank and insurance agent lined up at your new destination.

Get the rules and forms, if you are moving to another state, for switching over your automobile license and registration—and find out what the automobile insurance and inspection rules are.

Get a free "change of address kit" from any post office and use it to advise friends, banks, utilities, newspaper and magazine publishers, creditors, and other appropriate individuals of your new address and phone number—well in advance of your move.

Ask your physician and dentist for advice on physicians and dentists in your new location—or check with the local or county medical society there for names of qualified medical personnel (consult, also, Chapter 8, "The High Cost of Good Health," on how to shop for physicians, dentists, and other medical services).

Arrange for the transfer of your medical and dental records and the prescriptions for your eyeglasses.

If you are taking prescription drugs, make sure you have an ample supply when you move.

Arrange with local utilities and service people at your new home to have your telephone, electricity, appliances, etc., turned on before, or shortly after, you arrive.

IN CONCLUSION

This chapter is intended to help you make major housing decisions wisely. But your housing education shouldn't end here, for the more you learn the more you'll save. Among the best sources of additional information are government publications, and chief among these is the Department of Agriculture yearbook, "Handbook for the Home." It is available for a modest price from the Superintendent of Documents, Washington, D.C. 20402. Another source is "Houses: The Illustrated Guide to Construction, Design and Systems" ($15, National Association of Realtors, 155 East Superior Street, Chicago, Ill. 60611).

Part II

MILESTONES

14

HOW MUCH DOES A HUSBAND
AND/OR A WIFE COST?

You may think of May and June as the "marrying months"—and indeed they are. But marriage actually has become a year-round affair, with August through December an increasingly significant marrying season. In fact the first six months now account for fewer than half of each year's marriages.

To the casual observer, weddings may appear to be definitely "out" and young women may seem to be scorning legal ties and to be delighting in the illegitimate children. But well publicized as that image may be, it is just not the picture of the average young lady today. The fact is that no matter how casual (sloppy) you are in dressing, no matter how vehement and vocal you are about living according to your own ideals and goals rather than your parents' traditions, when it comes to your wedding, Miss America, you want a formal gown, attendants, and as elaborate a reception as your family can afford. Out of every five young brides, according to *Bride's Magazine*, four choose a traditional, formal wedding, a larger proportion than in 1967. Out of every five, more than four brides still receive a diamond engagement ring.

THE STAGGERING BRIDAL MARKET

"Marriage" itself is a powerful force in the U.S. economy.

• An enormous $500 million worth of engagement rings and $100 million worth of wedding rings are now being sold each year, says the Jewelry Industry Council in New York.

• The average new bride and her entourage will buy an estimated total of $2,900 worth of wedding goods and services, ranging from wedding and shower gifts to wedding clothes, and wedding reception food and drink.

• The total annual "bridal market" now tops $12 billion and even this staggering sum does not include the giant postwedding market for apartments, homes, mortgages, cars. The "furniture, home furnishings market" alone totaled $7 billion in 1974; the "honeymoon market" totaled more than $1 billion.

BREAKDOWN OF WEDDING COSTS

Although its cost is hardly the romantic part of a wedding it's of vital bread-and-butter concern to the bride and her family. (Someone has to pay the bills after the bells have rung.) Although no one could possibly estimate what it costs to translate a bachelor into a husband, there are hard facts and figures on what it costs to *tie him up legally* on the big day.

How much *does* it cost to get married today? Obviously, the costs can vary wildly. But the minimum for a church wedding, with only a few guests, is around $300 to $500—to cover the costs of a wedding dress, invitations, flowers, reception refreshments, a few other items. What the family of the bride spends depends strictly on the size of the family bank balance plus the extent of the daughter's wishes—although a key trend is for the parents of husband-to-be and wife-to-be to share expenses.

As you might suspect, a vital point is that the expense of the average wedding is much larger than most brides or their families dream until the whole thing is over. The reason is that many of the expenses are "miscellaneous," do not become obvious until, on practically the eve of the event, a member of the family or a friend realizes that a significant item has been overlooked.

You might think that the wedding gown would be among the most expensive items, for it certainly is among the most obvious. Actually, experts in the field estimate that all wedding clothes absorb only about 25 per cent of the $500 wedding, only 17 per cent of the $4,000 wedding. The average cost of the formal wedding dress and veil is about $190. In contrast, more than one fourth of the budget will be swallowed by "miscellaneous" items—such as flowers, music, photographs. Florists say that wedding flowers cost $50 in a $500 budget, $400 in a $4,000 budget.

As a further illustration of the importance of "miscellaneous" wedding expenses, a posh hotel in a major city estimates the per person cost of various wedding items as follows:

ITEM	COST PER PERSON
Music	$5.00
Flowers	2.50
Cake	1.00
Bartender	.70
Coatroom	.35
City tax	7%
Gratuities	17%

I'm taking for granted that you will check and double-check the cost of the wedding reception—its food, beverages, service, the like. Also obvious will be such items as the invitations, announcements, bridesmaids' gifts, and special transportation—in addition to the expenses in the listing above.

But not even mentioned in this wedding budget guide so far, you will note, is the bride's trousseau of lingerie, which, on *average,* runs into hundreds of dollars. Also not included in this guide is the basic trousseau of household linens which can and does run into big-time money.

Not included are hairdressers' costs.

Not included are such possible or probable items as awnings, tents, a dance floor. Incidentally, the photographs taken by specialists in bridal photography will average $3.00 to $5.00 a picture, depending on how many are purchased for the album. This expense, along with many others, will be handed to you *after* the wedding.

So, to be "safe," figure 50 per cent of your wedding budget under a miscellaneous category. Then add another 25 per cent for unanticipated extras. Or, to be realistic, at a minimum quadruple whatever total you originally estimated for the contingency fund. For this is the category which must cover all "errors and omissions."

WHAT THE GROOM PAYS FOR

Just as no one can tell you precisely what it costs a bride to lure her bachelor into matrimony, so no one can estimate what it costs a groom to court his lady. But here are the expenses usually paid for by the groom (and/or his family).

> Bride's engagement and wedding rings
> Marriage license
> Clergyman's fee (usually from $10 to $100; ask)
> Bride's flowers, including going-away corsage and bouquet
> Boutonnieres for the men of the wedding party
> Corsages for mothers
> Gloves, ties, or ascots for men of the wedding party
> Wedding gift for the bride
> Gifts for best man and ushers
> Hotel accommodations (if any) for out-of-town ushers
> Honeymoon

Practically speaking, the groom has only two major expenses—the engagement and wedding rings and the honeymoon. But, I repeat, it's becoming increasingly commonplace for the parents of the groom to help out with at least some expenses of the reception.

The vast majority of brides still get diamond engagement rings—typically costing $300 to $400 in addition to a gold wedding band costing an average of about $100. The single-stone (solitaire) as opposed to the multiple-stone ring is by far the most popular type of true engagement ring. The size of the center diamond in the ring sold by the typical jeweler is 45 points (100 points equal 1-carat diamond) or nearly ½ carat. The cost of the ring frequently is boosted by interest on installment purchases.

EXPENSES DISTRIBUTED ACCORDING TO LOCAL CUSTOM

Bride's bouquet is traditionally a gift from the groom, but it may be purchased by bride's family as part of her outfit.

Corsages for mothers and grandmothers are usually provided by the groom, but the bride may buy those for her own mother and grandmother.

Bachelor dinner is given by groom in some areas, by his attendants and male friends in other localities.

Rehearsal dinner is given by groom's family in many areas, but may be given by bride's family or friends.

Bridesmaids' luncheon is usually given by the bride, but may be given by her attendants or relatives.

Attendants' dresses are usually bought by each girl, but the bride may provide them if she wishes.

TEN RULES FOR BUYING WEDDING RINGS

Since you, the young husband-to-be, are, almost by definition, inexperienced in this field and since the occasion is in itself a temptation to splurge, you are likely to make costly errors. What rules are there to guide you?

(1) Do not spend more than three weeks' salary or 6 per cent of your annual income for the diamond ring.

(2) Just because the tendency to overspend is so great on this occasion, protect yourself by telling the jeweler your price range as soon as you enter the store. If he is a reputable merchant, he will not try to talk you into buying in a higher price category.

(3) Try to buy your jewelry for cash, but if you must buy on credit, make sure you thoroughly understand all the terms: carrying charges, legal warranties, insurance coverage. And before you accept the financing deal offered by the jeweler, check on whether you can get more favorable terms at a local bank or credit union.

(4) Insure your jewelry. Diamonds, pearls, and rubies can and do fall from their mountings and they can be lost or stolen. And whether you're buying for cash or on credit, find out the store's policy on guarantees and return of merchandise.

(5) Make sure you select a reputable and knowledgeable jewelry merchant. Ask your friends or relatives for guidance and check too with your local Chamber of Commerce or Better Business Bureau on a merchant's reputation.

(6) As soon as you enter a store, ask to speak with the expert in stones. At most stores, the manager or his assistant will be the expert.

(7) Learn the four basic characteristics of precious gems: color, clarity, cut, and weight—of which, despite common misconceptions, weight is the least important and color is the most important, followed by clarity and cut.

(8) Seek quality merchandise guaranteed by established and reputable jewelers. A precious stone should carry a written guarantee from the merchant: insist on it.

(9) Take your expensive mounted stone back to the store periodically for a mounting inspection and polishing.

(10) Steer clear of any merchant who offers ridiculous "bargains."

THE HONEYMOON AND ITS EXPENSES

After the vows are said, the husband's next major expense is the honeymoon.

There are so many variations on honeymoon expenses that to get an idea of costs I must invent a mythical couple. Okay, you're invented: you're an average groom and you're submitting typical questions.

Q. How long is the average honeymoon trip?

A. About nine days.

Q. What is the average cost?

A. It was about $650 in 1974. Outside the United States (excluding Canada and Mexico) the average cost was well over $1,000. A survey of *Bride*'s readers indicates they travel an average of 1,500 miles on a honeymoon trip.

Q. How do honeymooners in the States travel?

A. About four out of five couples go by car, about 30 per cent fly, the rest use rail or sea transportation.

Q. What about a honeymoon in Europe?

A. In this case, you should have at least two or three weeks to make it worth while. If you get in on a special cut-rate deal, though, your transportation costs will be slashed. Your expenses in Europe are subject to enormous variation.

Q. What about honeymoon costs in big cities?

A. Again, the costs of honeymooning in such cities as New York, New Orleans, San Francisco, etc., vary immensely, but if you are a typical couple spending a week or so in one of these cities, you should expect to spend between $400 and $500.

HOW TO SAVE ON YOUR WEDDING AND HONEYMOON

How can you save money and still have the wedding and honeymoon you want? Here are six tips:

(1) Consider having a home wedding, an obvious major moneysaving

area. Make your reception simple. The completely open bar is giving way to a controlled serving of wine, champagne, or punch.

(2) Have a cocktail buffet instead of a sit-down dinner. It can be just as satisfying and will be much cheaper.

(3) Or consider the services of a "wedding palace"—a professional catering establishment which provides bells-to-bonbons wedding packages at various price levels.

(4) Choose a wedding dress that you can use for other occasions later.

(5) Also select dresses for your attendants which they can use for other occasions, and the same goes for the costumes of the mothers.

(6) For your honeymoon, work with travel agents on package deals—and take advantage of bargain flights if you're going abroad. If you're renting a car, make it a compact. Plan ahead and, if feasible, make your reservations well in advance to take full advantage of any moneysaving offers.

RULES FOR BUYING WEDDING GIFTS

You need not spend nearly as much for wedding gifts as you think. Nor do you need to waste nearly as much time and effort as you do. Having learned over the years the value of expert guidance in this wedding minuet, I pass along to you my key hints on wedding gifts:

• Find out if and where the bride has registered for gifts and take advantage of the bridal registry to give her what she needs and wants. You can buy almost anything at a bridal registry now, for the concept has been broadened to include furniture, carpeting, and bedding as well as silver, china, and stemware.

• Decide at the start how much you want to spend and don't fall into the trap of spending too much in order to impress the bride's friends or to "repay" her family for a gift to your child. The gift-for-gift idea is inhibiting, costly, and in bad taste.

• Buy with an eye on the bride's life style. What are her tastes, profession, plans? Will she live on a campus, in a city or suburb? In a private home or apartment? How does she dress?

• Stay away from "the most original gift in the world," for these are the gifts most often returned or exchanged.

• If you're a relative, resist overstressing your own tastes when the bride is registering her patterns and gift choices at her favorite store.

• If you're the bridegroom, be sure you, too, respect your bride's selections.

• Find out how sophisticated a cook the bride is. Be sure that the set of gourmet cookbooks or the case of rare wine you may offer is a respectful reflection of her interest (rather than yours) in the art of cooking and dining.

• When in doubt, buy quality silver; it probably will rise substantially in value in coming years.

15

THE ECONOMICS OF CHILDREN

The High Cost of Having (or Adopting) a Baby

All signs are now pointing toward substantial and continuing moderation in procreation. A first reason is that you are postponing your marriages—and, therefore, you also are postponing starting your families. A second is that more and more women are now attending college for longer periods of time—and delaying both marriage and childbearing. And a third powerful force in our slower population growth rate is, I submit, the high cost of having babies and bringing them up.

RUNDOWN ON COSTS OF HAVING A BABY

It's not news to you that baby costs of every kind have been spiraling upward—primarily obstetricians' fees and hospital charges. In addition, we are going in for ever more and more expensive nursery supplies and other "baby equipment." So steep have been the increases that, according to the Health Insurance Institute, the total cost of having a baby has now passed the $1,600 mark. That includes only costs through the baby's first week at home.

Biggest expense of all is, of course, hospital care. In 1974 a single day in a short-term general hospital cost more than $100 and the average hospital stay in maternity cases is now about four days. Delivery room, nursery room charges, and other items count as "extras."

Next biggest cost is the layette for the baby—which easily can total more than $500. The layette includes a basic wardrobe for the baby plus a full range of nursery items, baby furniture, bathing equipment, etc.

Third biggest item is medical care—covering an obstetrician's services, usually offered as a complete package, through the delivery and hospital stay; plus a circumcision fee; plus the cost of a pediatrician's newborn baby care while the baby is in the hospital. Most obstetricians now charge about $300, but some charge $400, $500, or more.

Finally, the cost of a typical maternity wardrobe is calculated by the Health Insurance Institute at about $200.

The grand total adds up to well over $1,600. And under certain circumstances the cost can run even higher. For example:

If you stay in a private room at a fashionable big city hospital it easily might cost $150 a day in the mid-1970s, bringing this part of the cost to $600—far above the rate for a multiple-occupancy room.

If the birth is complicated, if the baby is born with special problems calling for surgery, extensive transfusion, or other special treatment, or if the birth involves caesarean section, the hospital part of the cost could skyrocket. Today about one in twenty babies is born by caesarean section, involving an average hospital stay of eight days, versus four for a normal delivery.

Hospital and physicians' services for a caesarean delivery tend to run about 50 per cent higher than the costs for a normal delivery. About one in twelve newborn babies must be temporarily confined in a glass "isolette"—involving extra charges. Rh blood factor complications at birth also can boost expenses.

If you have twins, this obviously will greatly increase your hospital bills, although some department stores promise to give you a second set of everything if you have twins.

Or you may require expensive extra drugs and medications somewhere along the line.

Or your hospital may slap on an extra fee of $75 or more for preparation of the delivery room and sharply increase its rates for nursery accommodations—in some cases to $20 or more per day.

Or if you have a boy you may find that in addition to a circumcision fee there frequently is a circumcision "setup" charge of $10 or so.

In the maternity clothes department, your costs will rise if your baby is born in winter or spring and you need to buy winter clothes instead of lightweight clothes. Or you well may decide you need more than two everyday dresses and more than one dress-up dress over the five- to six-month period when you will need special maternity clothes.

And if you insist on elegant new christening clothes, you'll have no trouble spending $50 to $150 just for a dress.

TEN WAYS TO CUT THE HIGH COSTS OF MOTHERHOOD

But aren't there some circumstances under which the costs of having a baby might be greatly reduced?

Yes. For instance, a second or third child costs a lot less than the first baby—simply because you already have most of the baby and maternity clothes, nursery things, etc., on hand. If you live in a small town or in a rural area, the expenses are likely to be a lot lower than in a big city. Mothers who breast-feed their newborn babies don't have to invest in special formulas.

Here are ten specific ways in which you can cut the high costs of motherhood:

(1) Before you make an arrangement with a specific obstetrician, discuss fees fully and frankly. In your initial consultation ask about fees for prenatal examinations and care, delivery, probable costs of such common complications as breach birth and caesarean section. If you feel you simply cannot afford the fee scale, say so. If the physician isn't willing to reduce the fee, ask him to refer you to a less expensive colleague. It's a perfectly reasonable and legitimate request, so don't be shy.

(2) Go home as soon as sensibly possible after your baby is born and alert your obstetrician to your desire to do this. You well may be more comfortable at home and the cost of hiring a practical nurse or home health aide at from $25 to $50 a day is far less than the cost of a hospital room. Although the American Hospital Association estimates that the average hospital stay for having a baby is about four days, some hospitals have shaved this to under three—and some new mothers pack up and go home after only a day or two in the hospital.

(3) Take advantage of all maternity benefits in your health insurance policies or prepaid health plan. A typical policy today contributes from $200 to $350 toward hospital and doctor bills—about half the total—and some policies also contain coverage for costly complications at birth.

(4) Check the coverage your employer (or your husband's employer) provides via group health insurance. If your company does provide group health insurance with a private insurer, chances are three out of four that maternity benefits are included. And the trend here is toward expanded maternity coverage.

(5) Carefully look into the health insurance provisions for your baby-to-be as well as yourself. Does such coverage begin at birth? When the baby is discharged from the hospital? Or when? Whatever the provisions, notify the insurer as soon as your baby is born.

(6) Investigate special maternity clinics in your neighborhood, generally associated with large teaching hospitals. Although such clinics are often geared to the needs of low-income people or special obstetrical problems, some are open to all—and these clinics almost invariably offer services at far lower costs than the typical hospital maternity service. Ask your family physician for guidance on these facilities.

(7) In selecting a hospital, find out how room rates are levied. A few hospitals do not charge maternity patients arriving late at night for a full day, but instead charge for a part day. And if you can, take a semiprivate room; it will be considerably less expensive than a private one.

(8) Eliminate the utterly unimportant but expensive at-home frills: fancy toys, nursery lamps, bottle warmers, heated plates, bath tables. Let your affluent friends and/or grandparents-to-be come up with such expensive items as dress-up baby clothes.

(9) Check secondhand stores, discount houses, and nationally recognized charities for good, used nursery furniture and other baby equipment. Tell your friends and relatives what you really *need* as baby presents—and don't hesitate to accept what relatives and friends might be happy to pass along.

(10) Explore and compare the costs of signing up for a diaper service versus buying disposable diapers versus buying cloth ones and doing them in your own washing machine. Is the convenience worth the extra money it costs you?

CHECK LIST FOR YOUR OWN BABY COSTS

You can spot other areas in which you could achieve significant savings simply by going over the following detailed check list of new-baby equipment, on which the $1,600-plus in costs is based.

HOSPITAL AND MEDICAL CARE	COST IN YOUR AREA
Four days' hospitalization	_____
Delivery-room charge	_____
Nursery charges, 4 days	_____
Circumcision setup charge	_____
Obstetrician's fees	_____
Circumcision fee	_____
Pediatrician's newborn care	_____
TOTAL	_____

BABY'S WARDROBE	
Shirts (4 to 6)	_____
Gowns (3 to 4)	_____
Sleeping bags (1 to 2)	_____
Stretch coveralls (3 to 4)	_____
Receiving blankets (4 to 6)	_____
Diapers (4 to 6 dozen) (if using diaper service)	_____
Diaper pins	_____
Sweater or shawl	_____
Waterproof panties (4)	_____

BABY'S WARDROBE (CONTD)   COST IN YOUR AREA

    Booties and bootie socks   ———————

    Bunting   ———————

    TOTAL   ———————

NURSERY ITEMS

    6 fitted crib sheets   ———————

    4 waterproof sheets   ———————

    5 waterproof pads   ———————

    3 crib blankets   ———————

    1 blanket sleeper   ———————

    Comforter or quilt   ———————

    1 mattress pad   ———————

    Bassinet or carrying basket   ———————

    Crib   ———————

    Crib mattress   ———————

    Crib bumper   ———————

    Diaper pail   ———————

    Portable baby seat   ———————

    Wicker changer with drawers   ———————

    Nursery lamp   ———————

    Vaporizer   ———————

    Baby carriage   ———————

    TOTAL   ———————

FEEDING EQUIPMENT

    8 to 12 8-oz. nursers; 2 to 4   ———————

    4-oz. nursers; extra nipples, caps;   ———————

    disposable nurser kit, sterilizer   ———————

    kit, or separate formula utensils;   ———————

    bottle and nipple brush   ———————

    Hot plate   ———————

    Bottle warmer   ———————

    2 to 3 bibs   ———————

    TOTAL   ———————

BATH ITEMS

    Bath table or tub   ———————

    4 washcloths, 2 towels   ———————

    Lotion   ———————

BATH ITEMS (CONTD)	COST IN YOUR AREA
Baby oil	_____
Cream	_____
Powder	_____
Sterile cotton and swabs	_____
Baby shampoo	_____
Bathing cream or liquid	_____
Petroleum jelly	_____
TOTAL	_____

MISCELLANEOUS	
Baby vitamins	_____
Sweater set	_____
30 disposable diapers	_____
Baby care book (Spock paperback)	_____
Diaper bag	_____
Brush and comb	_____
Diaper service (first week—70 diapers)	_____
Crib mobile	_____
Rectal thermometer	_____
Baby scissors	_____
Car bed or seat	_____
Birth announcements	_____
TOTAL	_____

MATERNITY CLOTHES	
3 dresses	_____
2 skirts	_____
4 tops	_____
2 pants	_____
2 slips	_____
3 bras	_____
1 girdle	_____
4 panties	_____
TOTAL	_____

TOTALS

Hospital and medical care	_____
Baby's wardrobe	_____

Nursery items   _____
Feeding equipment   _____
Bath items   _____
Miscellaneous   _____
Maternity clothes   _____

GRAND TOTAL   _____

Copy this table on a separate sheet of paper, study it, share it with your friends. Just having this detailed list will help you curb, cushion, and cut the costs.

One final note: *Prepare* yourself for the expenses and make up your minds right now that, no matter how much you save on these items, your baby will cost more than you anticipate. So do your best to manage your expenses properly, and you'll come through with your financial banners flying.

IF YOU ADOPT A CHILD

No rundown on the cost of a baby would be complete without at least a footnote on the costs of adopting a child. And adoption not only has become a widespread practice among childless and Zero Population Growth-conscious couples, but is being done by increasing numbers of single American women as well.

The cost of baby clothes and equipment will depend on the age of your child. But the above itemized list will guide you on how much these might run if you adopt a babe in arms.

In most states, no charge is made for adoption if you adopt a child through an approved social welfare agency, or a private one that is state-recognized. Private adoption agencies, though, charge fees ranging from $500 to $1,500, or charge on a sliding scale depending on family income. In relatively rare instances a licensed adoption agency may charge as much as 10 to 11 per cent of the husband's gross yearly income. Normally, there is no need to hire a lawyer. However, some states *require* that you hire one. In this case, fees in the mid-seventies ran between $50 and $200 and occasionally to as much as $300.

If you go the route of "black market" adoptions—usually arranged by lawyers outside normal channels and often without benefit of careful matching and screening of child and parents-to-be—you do so strictly at your own risk and probably at very high cost in dollars and cents too.

Among your best sources of information on adoption are your local community welfare council, your state or local welfare department, reputable local adoption agencies, the U. S. Department of Health, Education and Welfare in Washington, Office of Child Development.

A key source of information on adopting children from foreign countries is International Social Service, Inc., 345 East Forty-sixth Street, New York, N.Y. 10017.

The best place to inquire about children with special problems who need adoptive homes is ARENA (Adoption Resource Exchange of North America), 67 Irving Place, New York, N.Y. 10003.

THE HIGH COST OF REARING A CHILD

WHERE THE MONEY GOES

Of each child-rearing dollar now being spent by the typical moderate-income north central city family of four, the U. S. Department of Agriculture has calculated in a recent exhaustive study:

20.7¢ goes for food
11.6¢ goes for clothes
31.1¢ goes for shelter
5.1¢ goes for medical care
1.9¢ goes for education
17.2¢ goes for transportation
12.5¢ goes for "all other"

Child-rearing costs vary widely from large family to small family, from city to country, from one part of the United States to another, from income level to income level—but in general:

• The yearly cost of raising one child is approximately 15 to 17 per cent of family income.

• The costs of supporting an eighteen-year-old are 30 to 45 per cent higher than for a one-year-old.

• The costs of providing food and clothes for a growing child tend to rise at a much faster clip than other aspects of the child's support.

WHAT THE MOTHER "LOSES": THE HIDDEN COSTS

What's more, the enormous sums alone represent only the *direct* costs of rearing a child—food, clothes, schooling, etc. There also are such hidden costs as the lost earnings you, a homebound mother, accept by not taking a paying job outside the home.

The Commission on Population Growth and the American Future back in 1969 counted a full $40,000 in these lost "opportunity costs" for each mother assuming she stayed home until her youngest child reached age fourteen. These figures would be much, much higher today.

And these opportunity costs soar along with the educational level of the mother. The mother who remained at home until her youngest child reached age fourteen "lost" earnings totaling $58,904 if she had a high school diploma, $82,467 if she had a college degree, $103,023 if she had a post-college education, the Commission found. (By now, these totals are gross underestimates.)

Another fascinating point: the loss in income tends to be greatest in cases of premarital conception. (About one in three couples in the under-$3,000 bracket experiences premarital pregnancy.) Reason: If she has the baby, the mother usually has less opportunity to complete her education or job training before the child-rearing process begins, or to work and build a nest egg during the early years of marriage. Also, the husband's education or training may have to be cut short to support his family.

According to one national study, among families in the under-$15,000-a-year bracket, those who experienced premarital pregnancy averaged approximately $800 a year less in income than those whose children were conceived after marriage.

On the opposite side, your costs of child rearing will soar even more if you send your children to private schools, Ivy League colleges, to summer camps, or on summer expeditions to Europe. Or if you give your children automobiles when they reach sixteen or seventeen. Or if you must pay the high cost of orthodontia. Or even if you give your youngsters their own home encyclopedia.

Further, since the long-term trend of prices is ever upward in this century, this will be reflected in ever rising costs of rearing children. On top of this, the living *standards* of children will keep climbing along with the standards of their parents—from their preferences for food to their choices of entertainment, transportation, personal care. What "everybody else" has today is a lot more and a lot better than what anybody else ever had before.

THE LOW COST OF NOT HAVING A BABY
(OR HAVING FEWER OF THEM)

THE NEED FOR FAMILY PLANNING

Family planning permits couples to say "whether" and "when" to have a baby. Some couples have religious or other reasons that may dispose them against certain methods of family planning; but most will endorse the principle that planning of some sort is desirable, if children are to be properly cared for and families not strained to the breaking point.

COMPARATIVE COSTS OF CONTRACEPTIVE METHODS

The cost of preventing pregnancy can range from zero to more than $500, depending on the method you choose. Terminating a pregnancy also may cost you nothing, depending on your financial circumstances. However, using effective contraceptive methods is to be preferred to abortion for a variety of reasons—medical and personal as well as economic.

The method you choose to plan and space the birth of your children should depend on several factors, only one of which is cost. Your life style and tastes are important factors. Above all criteria should be: Is the method medically safe for you? Is it relatively easy for you to use? Does it have a good track record of effectiveness? The term "effectiveness" is really a statistical measurement to guide you in choosing rather than a guarantee of pregnancy prevention. In other words, a method that ranks third of fourth statistically may be the best and most effective method for you.

BIRTH CONTROL COSTS—ANNUALLY AND OVER A LIFETIME

The following chart summarizes the longer-range costs of each major type of birth control—annually and over a lifetime. Sexual activity 100 times a year is assumed, over a period of thirty years during which fertility is an issue. It also is assumed that any checkups and follow-ups related to using each method will not be counted as an "extra" cost. Gynecological exam costs not related to contraceptive use are not included in this table.

METHOD	FIRST-YEAR COST	LIFETIME COST
Rhythm and withdrawal	————	
Condom	$25.00 to $150.00	$750 to $4,500
Foam	$25.00 to $35.00	$750 to $1,050
Diaphragm	$20.00 to $60.00	$600 to $1,800*
IUD	$20.00 to $65.00	$600 to $1,950*
Pill	$45.00 to $90.00	$1,350 to $2,700*
Sterilization		male: $50 to $150
		female: $250 to $750

* Includes annual checkups after first year.

GETTING LOW COST OR FREE HELP IN FAMILY PLANNING

Where do you get family planning help?

• Your best source of clinic care is Planned Parenthood, which in the mid-1970s had 172 local affiliates operating more than 700 medically supervised clinics in forty-three states plus the District of Columbia. Fees vary around the country, and often are based on your income. However, *no one is ever turned away because of inability to pay.*

In San Francisco in the mid-1970s fees ranged from $33 down to zero for a year's services relating to contraception, including follow-up visits for any complications. A month's supply of pills cost $2.00 while other contraceptives cost much less than their usual retail price. In New York City,

Planned Parenthood's fee for pregnancy detection was $8.50. Fees are adjustable and deferred payment may be worked out. The fees are never more than the patient can afford.

• For the location of the PP affiliate nearest you, check the white pages of your telephone directory or contact the organization's national headquarters at 810 Seventh Avenue, New York, N.Y. 10019. Telephone (212) 541-7800. The telephone directory's Yellow Pages sometimes show referral or service listings under "Birth Control." And your county medical society will usually be able to give you the names of private doctors offering birth control services in your area.

• If your income is limited, you should be able to get free a low-cost service from government-subsidized family planning clinics run by PP, county health departments, county hospitals, and neighborhood health centers. Medicaid recipients are eligible to receive free family planning services and supplies in most states.

• Some private hospitals also run family planning clinics as do many community clinics and group practice plans. Inquire at facilities of this type or ask your regular physician for assistance.

Important note: An increasing number of private physicians and clinics (including Planned Parenthood) will provide birth control services, on a confidential basis, to minors upon their own request. Such physicians and clinics may offer treatment and services without charge. In some, however, parental consent is still required.

Finally, many all-purpose outpatient clinics and health centers have been opening up and offering, along with birth control services, the whole spectrum of health services for women.

STERILIZATION

Sterilization, or permanent contraception, may well be the most costly method of birth control in terms of initial outlay. However, even a payment of $500 for the procedure could be less than the cost of the pill taken over, say, a fifteen-year period. If your insurance covers sterilization, out-of-pocket costs to the patient may be only $100 or even less.

Sterilization also has the advantage of being virtually failproof. The failure rate for sterilization (male or female) is a minuscule .003 pregnancies for each 100 woman-years of use.

The male operation—the vasectomy—can be done in a doctor's office in only twenty minutes and costs about $150, although there are the usual variations above and below this. Fees at vasectomy clinics range from $150 down to zero, depending on the economic circumstances of the family involved. For the sake of the patient who may have some postoperative discomfort, doctors often schedule vasectomies on a Friday or Saturday so the patient is able to avoid missing time from work.

For a female, a common surgical procedure, tubal ligation, costs an average of $500, plus the charges for the one- to five-day hospital stay that this procedure usually entails. (The operation itself seldom takes more than twenty to thirty minutes.) With charges for a semiprivate room now averaging more than $100 a day in many cities, this could easily bring your total cost to between $600 and $1,250, not counting such "extras" as operating-room charges.

To shave some of these costs and also for convenience, you may want to have the operation performed while you are in the hospital for the delivery of what you have decided will be your last child. Your recovery from the operation should take little time more than the usual recovery time from child-birth—perhaps an additional day or two.

Increasingly, female sterilization is now being done on an outpatient basis by a technique known as laparoscopy. With total time in the hospital reduced to less than twelve hours, costs are somewhat lower. Hospitals using this technique charge from $250 to $500 for the procedure, covering both the doctor's and hospital fees.

If you want further information or if you have trouble in getting a sterilization operation, contact the Association for Voluntary Sterilization, a nationwide organization, headquartered at 708 Third Avenue, New York, N.Y. 10017. Telephone (212) 986-3880. Or contact your local Planned Parenthood affiliate.

BASIC FACTS ABOUT ABORTION

When contraceptive measures fail or are not used, abortion is the only means of stopping an unwanted pregnancy. At one time, when abortion was illegal, it often was a risky, costly procedure. Today, despite extremely vocal opposition to the operation on moral, religious and other grounds, abortion is becoming accepted as an integral part of women's health services.

The 1973 landmark U. S. Supreme Court decision, in effect, ruled that no state may restrict a woman, in consultation with her physician, from getting an abortion for any reason during her first trimester (twelve weeks) of pregnancy. The ruling also specified that states could intervene in the second trimester only to protect the health of the woman—through medical regulations requiring that the procedure be performed in a hospital setting. None of the challenges has yet reversed the fundamental trend toward abortion on request —by unmarried and married women.

In the mid-1970s an estimated 1,000,000 American women were under-going legal abortions each year, compared to only about 6,000 in 1966, the year before Colorado became the first state to rewrite its restrictive law.

Costs, however, still remain a significant factor, although they are now generally far below what people were forced to pay in years past for an illegal abortion. They range across the nation from zero to $500, depending on the span of your pregnancy, your financial status, and, of course, the type of hospital, clinic, or office in which the abortion is done.

Here were typical charges in the mid-seventies.

• At a New York state-licensed clinic or city hospital, an early abortion (done during the first twelve weeks of pregnancy, usually by vacuum aspiration, or "suction") cost $145 to $185. This was generally also the top fee at *similar facilities throughout the country,* and in some facilities, fees were even lower.

• At a New York City voluntary (non-profit) hospital, the same procedure generally cost $200 or less, while at private hospitals there, the fees were $225 to $275.

• Late abortions (fourteenth to twenty-fourth week of pregnancy, usually by saline injection, which induces labor) are not only more risky but also cost more, since they may require a few days' hospitalization. You can count on paying at least double what you would have paid for an early abortion, with all-inclusive fees generally starting at $300 to $350.

• Also available in some communities is menstrual extraction, which is really a very early abortion. It is usually performed up to fifteen days after a missed period and costs only about $50. No dilitation is necessary; thus it's faster, easier. However, simple though it is, most doctors tie it in with a positive pregnancy test and recommend strongly against its repetitive use as a substitute for contraception.

Since it may still be difficult to get an abortion in some hospitals, communities, or states, you may have to add transportation and other travel expenses involved in getting to a place where you can have the operation.

HOW TO SHOP FOR—AND REDUCE THE COSTS OF—AN ABORTION

• First, and above all, consult your family doctor or obstetrician or family planning clinic, and the sooner the better! *Avoid* profit-making abortion referral agencies which you may see advertised in your newspaper; you should *not* have to pay for a referral. Keep in mind that the cost and complexity of an abortion go up sharply after the twelfth week of pregnancy. Late abortions, it has been found, are three to four times more likely than early abortions to result in complications.

Keep in mind, too, that when you have missed one menstrual period you could be up to four weeks pregnant; if you've missed two periods, you may be as many as eight weeks pregnant. (Weeks are calculated from the last menstrual period, "LMP," so actually at a missed period the week count is four.) Also, you should wait a full two weeks after a missed period to get an accurate reading of your possible pregnancy. Tests may show a false negative before this.

If your doctor or clinic is unable or unwilling to arrange an abortion, ask for a recommendation of someone who will arrange it.

• Or call your local hospital and ask for a recommendation of a qualified physician or a specialist in obstetrics and gynecology ("OBG"). Also helpful may be your city or county public health department or medical society.

• Or you can look under "Birth Control" in the Yellow Pages of your telephone directory. In addition to local independent agencies such as women's groups or college counseling services, you also may find chapters or affiliates of such nationwide, non-profit organizations as Planned Parenthood and the Clergy Consultation Service. The referrals and pregnancy counseling services of Planned Parenthood, the Clergy Consultation Service and local chapters of Zero Population Growth (ZPG), National Organization For Women (NOW), and other women's organizations often are free.

• If none of these three organizations has an office near you, you can contact them at their central office or referral services:

Family Planning Information Service of Planned Parenthood, 300 Park Avenue South, New York, N.Y. 10010. Telephone (212) 677-3040.

National Clergy Consultation Service, 55 Washington Square South, New York, N.Y. 10012. Telephone (212) 254-6230.

A new guide, "The Abortion Clinic Directory," listing abortion facilities by state, is available from the American Civil Liberties Union Foundation, 22 East 40th Street, New York, N.Y. 10016, for 50¢.

These agencies, as well as others, also provide information on such alternatives to abortion as placing the child for adoption.

Quality is the most important factor in choosing the best abortion service. You may find you've been penny wise and pound foolish if you let cost considerations alone guide you in choosing. A phone call to any of the above organizations can help you make an informed decision or you can call the National Organization for Women (NOW) in Chicago or its local office in your area.

Here are additional tips:

Whether you are dealing with a private doctor or with a clinic, make sure that you know what your *total* cost will be, including hospitalization (if necessary), medication, lab work, and checkup exam (usually two to three weeks after the abortion). Special medication, for example, may be necessary for Rh-negative patients. Not all doctors and clinics will volunteer this information. Then you may want to compare the range of charges elsewhere.

Agree on the payment terms before the operation, especially if you have to travel. In most cases, full payment is required in advance, particularly if you are a transient. Personal checks are generally not accepted. Some hospitals, however, take BankAmericard or Master Charge.

If you are a woman in severe financial distress, ask an abortion-referral agency for suggestions of doctors and clinics who will perform abortions at reduced or no cost. Women covered by Medicaid as of 1974 could have their abortion bill paid on the same basis as their bills covering their other health care needs.

INSURANCE COVERAGE

For Abortions

Abortion coverage is generally found within the maternity provisions of group health contracts. However, the coverage may be restricted. It can be spelled out in the contract itself. Single women may be covered. Daughters of insured workers may not be covered. A waiting period may be applied to married women and daughters who are covered. Usually conception must have taken place during the contract period. The size of the benefits may be very small, etc.

So far as Blue Cross and Blue Shield are concerned, in most local plans hospital and surgical expenses for abortion are covered. But there may be conflicts in coverage by Blue Cross (for hospital expenses) and Blue Shield (for surgical costs). For example, a Blue Shield Plan may cover abortion while the Blue Cross Plan in the same area does not.

In general, however, where a local Blue Cross Plan offers obstetrical benefits, any abortions performed would be considered obstetrical benefits and covered according to the provisions of the specific contract. Where obstetrical benefits are restricted to family contracts, wives and single female dependents (usually those under nineteen years of age) would be covered.

Some Blue Cross Plans now offer such coverage to all persons—including single women and dependent children—on all contracts. In fact, the Blue Cross Association has adopted a policy requiring its Member Plans to make abortion coverage available to all subscribers (including single women and female dependents) enrolled in *national* contracts—i.e., people belonging to large groups which include employees in more than one state.

Under this expanded benefit, new women enrollees who become pregnant no longer have to wait nine months before becoming eligible for coverage for a legal abortion. This new benefit is called Rider "T." *But* it is *not* automatically included in national contracts—only to those which specifically request it. Similar riders are available on a local basis but, again, only to those groups who want to include it as a benefit.

For Sterilization

Most Blue Cross policies also cover sterilization in a hospital for contraceptive reasons or for reasons of medical necessity—including vasectomy, tubal ligation, and the newer laparoscopy method. In a few areas, however, you are covered only after a specified waiting period.

Blue Shield covers the cost of office vasectomies in most states, generally paying anywhere from one third to one half of the fee for the procedure. Blue Shield covers sterilizations performed in a hospital, for either sex. Since there are wide variations in these and other health insurance contracts, you must check your *own coverage,* to be sure of the extent to which you are protected.

Medicaid—which covers eligible low-income families and individuals—pays for sterilization for medical reasons in all states with Medicaid plans (as of 1974, Alaska and Arizona had no Medicaid plans). In most states, plus the District of Columbia, Medicaid covers sterilization for contraceptive reasons. You simply present yourself to the doctor, hospital, or clinic you usually use.

TAX TIPS ON BIRTH CONTROL PILLS, ABORTIONS, STERILIZATION

If you practice some form of birth control, virtually all your expenses now qualify as medical expenses that you can take as part of your itemized medical expense deduction. This includes: birth control pills you buy for your own personal use through a prescription provided by your physician and the costs of an operation for an abortion or sterilization, male or female, undertaken voluntarily, assuming the operation was legal under the applicable state law.

16

THE HIGH COST OF DIVORCE

FACTS ABOUT FAMILY BREAKUPS

More than 1.5 million of you are now being divorced and another 1.5 million are taking the first steps toward divorce each year—both record totals with far-reaching but little-understood financial implications. In the early 1960s there was one divorce or annulment for every four new marriages. Today, one old marriage ends in divorce or annulment for every three new marriages. To dramatize the divorce picture even more:

• One out of every five men and women getting married each year has been divorced.

• Some 15 million Americans are or have been divorced—and 4 million-plus are currently divorced.

• Nearly two out of three divorces today involve children.

Although the remarriage rates has been rising along with the divorce rate, one in five remarriages also ends in divorce. Surely the upsurge in broken marriages is related to changing American attitudes, particularly about sex; to the decline of the traditional family; to liberalized divorce laws; to the growing financial independence of women; to many other factors. Obviously influencing the figures also is the fact that the war babies of the early post-World War II years are now into the most highly divorce-prone age group, particularly among couples who married very young.

Who are the most divorce-prone?

• Nearly one in three of the marriages in which the woman's age ranges from twenty-seven to thirty-two will end in divorce.

• Blacks get divorces more frequently than whites. For every 1,000 married couples, there are 78 divorced persons among non-whites, compared to 45 divorced individuals for every 1,000 white married couples. These rates are in addition to the huge "unofficial divorce" rate among blacks.

• Divorce rates are higher in cities. On the farm, there are only 20 divorced persons for each 1,000 married couples, in contrast to 49 in non-farm areas.

• The smaller your family income and the lower your educational level, the greater the likelihood you will get divorced—contrary though this may be to popular belief.

ECONOMIC TOLL

Whatever your financial situation, a divorce is one of the most costly economic ventures you can undertake—with expenses which few to-be-divorced couples weigh in advance.

"Most Americans today live to the hilt of the breadwinner's income, and frequently even beyond it," notes a prominent New York lawyer and family law professor. "For young families with little or no financial cushion, the sudden economic toll of divorce can be catastrophic."

When can a husband financially afford a divorce? When he is prepared to cut his standard of living in half, says the professor. "My advice to anybody contemplating a divorce is to count on its costing at least twice as much as he thinks."

COSTS OF A "TYPICAL" DIVORCE

If you are considering a divorce you must be aware of all the costs—ranging from legal fees and plane fares to alimony and child support payments, division of property and other assets, tax angles, etc. What are typical divorce costs today? No divorce is "typical"—but there are general guides on the two major basic costs:

Alimony and child support (sometimes referred to as "the high cost of leaving") are usually the biggest items in any divorce settlement. Normally, a husband with two small children pays one third to one half of his after-tax income in alimony and/or child support. Thus, if your take-home pay is $9,000, you, the husband, will probably have to pay between $3,000 and $4,500 a year—often divided into half for alimony and half for child support.

How much will depend to some extent on your generosity as well as that of the particular court. If your take-home pay is $20,000, a "generous" payment for alimony and the support of two small children would total $10,000 a year; more typical, however, would be from $7,000 to $8,000. In the $30,-000 income bracket (after taxes), your payments would probably be somewhere between $10,000 and $15,000. And if you were at the $50,000 level, you might have to pay at least $20,000, although you might be able to get away with as little as $15,000.

The amount of alimony/child support will also vary, depending on your family's accustomed standard of living; whether the wife will be able to work;

the size of her independent wealth; the over-all financial status of the husband; length of the marriage; number and ages of your children.

With a take-home pay of $20,000 and three teen-age children, a "generous" combined payment for alimony and child support would be $12,000. More typical would be $9,000 to $10,000—or about 50 per cent of the husband's income. If, however, a divorcing wife has *no* children, a typical alimony allotment is one fourth to one third of her husband's income.

In some states a wealthy woman can be ordered to pay alimony to a disabled ex-husband. Because of the women's liberation movement, a growing number of divorced women now reject alimony. In general, alimony is paid only until the wife remarries, and child support payments are made only until the children reach age twenty-one, or marry, or enter military service, or get jobs. Frequently, the husband agrees to finance his children's college education *if* he is financially able.

Typically, the separation agreement, which is merged into the divorce decree, sets the amount of alimony and child support. It also may contain an "escalator clause" boosting the man's alimony and/or child support payments as his salary or other income goes up. Sometimes escalation is also geared to increases in the cost of living. If, however, there are no escalator clauses in the agreement, the alimony amount may not be changed unless it can be shown that the agreement was utterly unreasonable. Child support payments may be legally raised or decreased at any time if conditions have changed so as to alter significantly the cost of the children's support or if the amount of the payment was not or is no longer realistic, and—in all cases— if the husband is financially able to raise his contributions.

Legal fees are the second major divorce expense. Lawyers, like doctors, tend to charge clients according to their income brackets as well as according to the amount of time and work a case demands.

In the under-$10,000 bracket, fees in a divorce case will probably run at least $250 to $500 each for lawyers (the husband's and wife's), assuming negotiations are neither complex nor drawn out and actual litigation is not involved.

In the $10,000 to $20,000 bracket, the cost of drawing up a separation agreement is likely to run between $500 and $2,500 for each lawyer. The lawyer representing the spouse opposing the divorce probably will get the larger share. But, again, these amounts vary.

In the $20,000 to $40,000 bracket, total legal fees might amount to $2,000 to $5,000 if the agreement is amicable. If there is a fair amount of wrangling, this total might rise to $7,500.

In the very high income brackets, divorce lawyers tend to charge whatever the traffic will bear.

If you feel you've been overcharged, first complain to the lawyer. If he won't adjust the fee, find out if your local bar association has a table of recommended fees for divorces. If you've been charged considerably more than the recommended fee, you may have a good case to take to the bar association's grievance committee. But the best way to avoid this problem is to get a written statement of the agreed-on fee in advance.

Instead of paying a flat fee for the divorce, you might be better off finding a lawyer who will charge you for his work on an hourly basis and give you an estimate of the number of hours it will take. In some sections of the country you can pay as little as $15 an hour, but much more likely are rates of $50 to $75—and charges may run even higher per hour for lawyers in bigger, prestigious law firms.

Normally, the husband pays all legal fees. However, the wife may have to pay part or most of the fees if she is pressing the divorce or if she has considerable assets of her own.

OTHER COSTS

Who gets the family house? How are stocks, bonds, and other assets divided? Below are details on the other less obvious, indirect costs of divorce:

• *The family house.* If the house is owned by both husband and wife or even by the husband alone, the divorce settlement often provides ownership for the wife. A generous husband, or one who wants a divorce badly enough, may even be persuaded to pay off the mortgage on the property. Typically, most of the furniture in the house stays there, with the husband taking only items which he considers exclusively his. (When I asked one New York City lawyer what the husband gets in return for a house in which he may have sunk $50,000 or more, his reply was "freedom.")

But other arrangements are frequently made, too—such as giving the wife exclusive possession of the house until the children are grown. There may also be an agreement to sell the house and divide the proceeds.

• *The family car.* If there are two cars, the husband and wife each take one. If there is only one, the person who needs it most is likely to get it.

• *Stocks, bonds, cash, and other assets.* Any securities, savings accounts, and other such assets which are jointly owned are normally divided fifty-fifty between divorcing husband and wife. Otherwise, the person in whose name they are held keeps them. With jointly owned real estate, there is usually a provision for division of the proceeds of its sale. But sometimes a surrender of one spouse's joint interest in property is the price of a divorce, or may influence the amount of alimony. However, normally, inherited money is excluded from any divorce settlements.

• *Life insurance policies.* Traditionally, the husband keeps his wife and/ or children as beneficiaries of his life insurance policy until she remarries or until some agreed-upon future date. If he is not insured, or if his group policy is not sufficient to cover this part of the settlement, he may be required to take out a new life insurance policy. But details must be spelled out in the agreement—including who pays the premiums and who deals with such matters as distribution of dividends and policy loans. As a general rule, the husband may not borrow against a life insurance policy which is part of a divorce agreement or change its provisions in any way.

In the $10,000-a-year income bracket, a husband might make his ex-wife the beneficiary of a $15,000 to $20,000 life insurance policy until she remarries if he has a life insurance policy. In the $30,000 to $40,000 range, a divorcing wife would generally be fortunate if her husband made her beneficiary of a $5,000 life insurance policy.

Note: A divorcing husband who has substantial amounts of life insurance and a new wife-to-be waiting in the wings probably will try to keep at least part of the coverage and well may succeed in doing so.

• *Health insurance*. Separation agreements usually require a husband to maintain at least Blue Cross or some other hospitalization insurance for his ex-wife and children. His "family" health insurance or group policy at work probably would continue to cover his young children after a divorce, but not his ex-wife. Thus, husbands frequently are required to buy individual policies (at considerable extra cost) for their ex-wives. In a "generous" settlement, Blue Shield and major medical insurance coverage might also be included.

If the separation agreement calls for the husband to pay for any of the children's medical and dental expenses not covered by insurance, the agreement should spell out just what expenses he is responsible for. It may also specify that any really big expenses—orthodontia, cosmetic surgery, psychiatric treatment—may not be undertaken without his consent.

• *Other insurance*. Your automobile and homeowners policies are also likely to need changing when your marriage breaks up. If the ex-wife gets the car, keeps the house or continues living in the old apartment, the insurance to cover these is generally her responsibility.

• *"Hidden" costs*. There are many of these in any divorce. For instance, if the divorced wife has small children and must go to work to make ends meet—and often she must, at least part time—she'll have to pay for baby sitters or household help. Lunch money, new clothes, and other job-associated expenses also will slash her net income.

But the biggest single indirect cost lies in setting up a second household and maintaining two separate households instead of just one. This may involve considerable moving expenses for both husband and wife, if neither can afford to keep the larger house or apartment the family had lived in. It may also mean that both spouses will be forced to cut their living standard approximately in half. Therefore, unless extra income is provided by the wife working or in some way, most of you will find you cannot afford to maintain anywhere near your previous standard of living.

HOW TO CUT DIVORCE COSTS

Is there any way to cut the high costs of divorce? Perhaps the best over-all way is:

Don't be vindictive! Keep your squabbles over property, alimony, and especially children to a minimum. Obviously, the more legal infighting, the more time lawyers will have to spend and the higher will be their total charges.

More specifically:

• Each of you—but especially the spouse who may be contesting the divorce—should be as realistic as possible about the separation agreement which will be incorporated into the final divorce decree. Never forget that the biggest increase in the cost of getting a divorce comes from the breakdown in negotiations—leading to a contested action.

Probably your best guide as to how much you can realistically expect in your agreement is the record in the court in which your case would be heard. Both your lawyers should be aware of what local courts normally award in cases similar to your own. So avoid any lawyer who claims he can get you, the wife, a settlement way above the amounts your divorced friends and other lawyers in your area have told you is possible. A reputable lawyer, in settling an alimony and child support dispute, will recommend amounts he knows are in line with the amounts local courts would award if the matter were thrashed out before them.

• Try to reach an agreement out of court, particularly where children are concerned, for court litigation can be a drawn-out and costly procedure. You, the wife, almost invariably will do better by reaching a settlement out of court. Husbands generally are not the selfish characters their aggrieved wives believe them to be. A husband often will agree to valuable provisions (in a separation agreement) which a court may not be able to order—private schooling and summer camp costs, health insurance, orthodontia. The court usually will set only a dollar amount for alimony and child support—which frequently won't cover all the goods and services the husband was willing to pay for in the first place.

• Avoid court litigation over the division of *things*—litigation that can be not only costly but also utterly unsatisfactory. You, the divorcing partners, are in a much better position to divide up your belongings. And dragging the personal quarrels they entail through the courts can be expensive indeed. In fact, to save on legal fees, it may be a good idea, even before consulting lawyers, for the husband and wife—perhaps with the aid of a mutual friend—to agree not only on the division of belongings but also on alimony, child support, visitation rights, the house, insurance, and so on. The wife's lawyer can then be consulted to formalize the agreement and go ahead with the rest of the legalities.

• If there are matters on which neither you, the husband nor you, the wife, nor the lawyers can agree, consider using a professional arbitrator, available through the New York-based American Arbitration Association, 140 West Fifty-first Street, New York, N.Y. 10020, which has offices in twenty-three states—or any arbitrator whom both parties can agree to trust. Your individual lawyers might go as far as possible on working out the basic agreement and then submit the controversial points to an arbitrator to decide. The final agreement would be submitted to each spouse's own lawyer so each could decide whether it was fair.

• If your state law permits, file directly for a divorce. This is cheaper than going through the legal separation route first, for you thereby avoid two rounds of legal fees—one for the technicalities of the separation and another for the actual divorce itself.

• Try very hard to avoid a contested divorce (in which both spouses sue each other). This not only takes longer, perhaps months or even years, and opens the risk that you will be turned down, but also costs more in both legal fees and court costs. In an uncontested divorce—the least expensive way to get a divorce—one spouse brings suit on whatever grounds are acceptable, such as physical or mental cruelty, abandonment, or the like. The other spouse, who is agreeable to the divorce, does not defend the suit and the divorce occurs by default at the end of the three to six months' period when the case comes to trial. The separation agreement which has been drawn up is then incorporated into the divorce decree.

• Give at least some thought to the do-it-yourself route to a divorce if your breakup is both amicable and simple. If you live in California, you can dispense with lawyers entirely if you care to go to the trouble of filling out the various required forms including even the final dissolution decree for the judge's signature. You pay only minimal court costs. New York and the state of Washington also have court approval of a do-it-yourself divorce plan providing the instructions and legal forms necessary to file for an uncontested divorce in either of the two states.

• Finally, file joint income tax returns as long as it is legally possible for you to do so, to cut your income taxes to the minimum. And, also for tax purposes, don't schedule your divorce for late in the year. Hold it over until the following year to get the advantage of an extra year of filing a joint tax return.

HOW NEW TRENDS MAY AFFECT YOU

Many states have recently made or are contemplating changes in their laws, making possible easier, simpler, and more equitable divorces.

No-fault divorce laws. A key trend in many states is toward the so-called no-fault divorce. This eliminates the requirement, still prevalent in most states, that one spouse prove the other guilty of a specific fault, such as adultery, cruelty, non-support, or abandonment. In California a "dissolution of marriage" (the term which is now replacing the word "divorce") can be obtained on the grounds of "irreconcilable differences," leading to the "irremediable breakdown of the marriage"; you needn't prove that either partner was at fault.

Grounds for divorce. These are being broadened and liberalized. Recently added new grounds are fraud, force, impotency, and incompatibility.

Residence requirements. These also are being shortened in many states.

Alimony, child support, and custody laws. Under the proposed Equal Rights Amendment to the Constitution, requiring equality of the sexes, state laws could be extended to make men eligible for alimony under the same circumstances as women. The welfare of the child would be the criterion for child custody as it is in most states now, but court tradition in which mothers seemingly get arbitrary preference would certainly come under nationwide attack.

The terms of the long-proposed nationwide Uniform Marriage and Divorce Act are in accord with the Equal Rights Amendment. The act would demand alimony for *either* spouse (called "maintenance") based on his or her needs, child support obligations for both spouses in accordance with their means, and custody of children based on the welfare of the child. The amount and duration of maintenance payments would depend, among other things, on the ability of the spouse seeking maintenance to train for and/or find suitable employment.

This is in line with the practices already followed in the "community property" states. In California, for example, where the law holds that alimony is not the automatic right of a divorced woman, alimony payments usually are scheduled for only a short period, often less than six months if there are no children and seldom for more than a few years.

Far out as it may seem to you, also under discussion is compulsory "divorce insurance" which would cover the expenses incidental to a marital breakup. Still another proposal would create a renewable marriage contract which would make divorce obsolete. One version of this revolutionary (but not all that unrealistic) approach would transform a marriage into a three-year contract, renewable every three years if both partners consent.

But these are developments out in the distant future (if ever). Right now, you have to live with our country's patchwork of state divorce laws, all the inequities—and the excruciatingly high costs of breaking up a marriage.

17

WHAT YOU SHOULD KNOW
ABOUT WILLS, ESTATES,
AND TRUSTS

Your Will

HOW TO GUARANTEE TROUBLE FOR YOUR FAMILY

The cliché in legal circles is that "where there's a will there are relatives." But where there's no will at all there are even more. A person's death can all too easily become the opening shot in an all-out family fight over his or her possessions. Countless millions of families have been torn apart and caused immeasurable pain and expense because the income producer neglected to write a will. Every day in every city, newspapers print sordid stories of bickering and financial confusion within families, because the chief wage earner delayed too long in making a will. There even have been cases in which families have split apart over a set of soup bowls or a couple of clay pots—because a will failed to spell out how the crockery should be divided.

Take the example of the Blacks. She had wealthy parents who, on her wedding day, had given her a new house, the furnishings, and a substantial bank account with the understanding she keep them in her own name. They didn't know the bridegroom well enough to be sure of him, and they had no use for his father, a widower.

For the first baby and again for the second, the grandparents started bank accounts involving sizable deposits. Then tragedy: the young couple and children perished in a fire. It was established that the young father died last. There were no wills. Thus *his* father got all.

Most people will take just about any advice on how to expand their wealth—but these same people will fail utterly to explore the most economical ways of passing on their assets to their survivors. It's estimated that as many as one half of all Americans who own property die without leaving a will.

WHY WRITE A WILL?

Your will may be the most important single document you will sign in your lifetime. Among the sound reasons the Research Institute of America lists for having a valid will are:

• To dispose of your belongings to those whom *you* wish in the proportions that *you* choose.

• To provide for your loved ones in the best possible way.

• To let all interested relatives and/or friends know your wishes.

• To make it easier for the recipients of your bounty to obtain and use what you left and to avoid fights and irritations.

• To reveal aspects of your financial affairs that may be unknown to anybody else. (The very act of working up a will helps disclose loose ends that need to be tied up.)

• To ease the task of whoever is going to take care of minor children and influence the choice of any guardian.

• To save many types of expense. As just one illustration, if there are children under twenty-one and there is no will, the law may require the appointment of a guardian to protect these children. The guardian must be paid a fee, and that fee must come from the family's assets. A will could save that expense.

THE PITFALLS OF DYING "INTESTATE"

But the biggest single reason for having a will is to avoid the problems of dying "intestate."

If you die without leaving a will you are said to have died "intestate." In this case, your property would be distributed according to the laws of the state where you live. These laws are deeply rooted in our history and almost always assume that most of us intend to pass our property on to members of our immediate families. But these laws vary widely from state to state and they may not conform to *your* wishes.

Moreover, you could forfeit important tax advantages by leaving the distribution of your estate to the arbitrary letter of your state law, or by failing to plan ahead for the ravenous tax bite of federal estate laws. For instance, federal law permits everyone a deduction of $60,000; if your estate is valued at less than that amount, it may face no federal death taxes. In addition, the law permits you to pass on to your surviving spouse up to 50 per cent of your adjusted gross estate, also tax free. Thus, a man with an estate of $120,000 who has a will leaving half of his estate to his wife will be subject to no federal taxes because one half ($60,000) reduces his estate to only $60,000 and that is the amount of the individual personal exemption. Without the benefit of this deduction, the federal tax on a $120,000 estate under current law would be around $9,500.

If you die intestate, your close relatives will share in your estate, but most often not in the same proportions that you would have wanted. Under the laws of some states, your wife would get only one third of your assets and your child two thirds. In other states, if you die and leave a widow but not children, your property would automatically be divided equally between your wife and your parents—even though your parents might have ample financial resources and your wife might have nothing to live on but what you leave her.

Moreover, the laws of intestacy are rigid and do not allow for unusual situations. You may, for instance, have a handicapped child, or you may be supporting a widowed daughter. The court cannot give a larger share of your estate to these offspring than to any of your other children.

The *only* way to make certain that your wishes are carried out and that each member of your family is fairly protected is to leave a will stating exactly who is to get what and when.

THE FIRST "MUST": GOOD LEGAL ADVICE

Even if you want your will to be the last word in simplicity—e.g., "I just want to leave everything to my wife"—the services of an attorney are an absolute essential if you want to comply with all the technicalities and if you want your will to stand up legally. Furthermore, there are certain formalities required in the execution and witnessing of your will of which you may not even be aware. A will which conforms to your state law will save your heirs endless amounts of time and money in carrying out its provisions.

The legal fee for this service is usually modest. On average, fees may vary from $35 to $150, but by all means discuss fees in advance. The fee will be more, of course, if the provisions of the will are complicated. You can check the fee schedule at your local bar association.

Above and beyond the simple drafting of your will, a good lawyer can help you prepare an itemized list of your real and personal property and other assets. And he can guide you in tax-saving moves in the way you divide up your estate—before and after your death.

Your estate consists of all of your assets and property (real and otherwise), over which you had control, including money owed you at your death, less all your debts, death costs, and other personal expenses.

WIDESPREAD MISUNDERSTANDINGS

When you're writing your will, you don't need to make an itemized statement of your assets nor do you need to go through the process of disposing of your property item by item.

Any time you wish and as often as you wish you may change your will—reflecting changes in your assets, changes in your desires, changes in your choices of beneficiaries.

Your will is not usually recorded prior to death; no one has to know you've even made one. When it is recorded prior to death, it is sealed and not available to the public.

The existence of your will doesn't affect in any way whatsoever your ability to sell or otherwise dispose of your property. You can act as though you had never even thought of writing a will, much less had written one.

And you need not put your business into good shape in order to write your will. An excellent reason for making a will, in fact, might be that your business was in bad shape.

ASSETS WHICH CANNOT BE WILLED

Another major misconception you probably have is that you may distribute everything you own via your will. You cannot.

You cannot dispose of such assets as your life insurance, your pension benefits, your U.S. savings bonds through your will. Why not? Because, assuming you already have named the beneficiaries for these assets, you already have disposed of the assets.

You could name your estate as the beneficiary of your life insurance policy—thereby guaranteeing that the proceeds will be distributed as your will dictates. But since executors' fees are based on the gross value of your estate, you will increase the cost of administering your estate by including a fat sum of insurance in it. Usually you will find it better, faster, and less expensive to have the proceeds of your life insurance go directly to the beneficiaries you designate—particularly if life insurance is the bulk of your estate. You can eliminate any tax if you divest yourself of ownership and control.

You also cannot dispose of the following assets via your will:

property which you expect to inherit but which you did not in fact receive before your death (unless your interest had vested before your death);

assets over which you lose control after your death—such as income from a trust to be received by you only during your own lifetime.

THE INGREDIENTS OF YOUR WILL

What kind of instructions and information should your will contain? You are not legally required to draw your will in any particular form, but there are certain standard ingredients which turn up in most wills.

(1) Your will must have been written clearly enough to permit a court to determine your real intent. There is a story—perhaps apocryphal—of the man who left his favorite niece an annual income in his will for "as long as she remains above ground." When she died, her husband simply installed her in a mausoleum above ground and collected the money for the rest of *his* life.

(2) The opening paragraph of your will should identify you, the "testator," by name, give your address, and state that you are knowingly making your will. Generally included in this opening statement is a clause that makes

it clear that you are revoking any previous wills or codicils (additions or "amendments" to your will) you may have made. When you make a will, it ordinarily remains valid unless and until you revoke it.

(3) Next you would generally write a statement that directs the prompt payment of your burial expenses and all your just debts, taxes, and costs of administration. These are the first claims against your estate. Unless you specify otherwise, all the assets in your estate are regarded as a single pool of money from which these first-claim expenses are to be paid, and your executor must charge each beneficiary with a proportionate share of the cost.

(4) Then comes the core of your will—the provision for the distribution of your assets. A typical division is one half to your wife and one half to your children. Typically, you first list all the specific and general bequests you want to make. What is left in your estate after all the specific gifts of money or property have been made in your will is called your "residuary estate." This is usually given to your principal heir.

You may, for instance, want to leave a relative or friend a particular heirloom or some other part of your personal property, say 100 shares of stock. This is known as a specific legacy. A general legacy is a bequest that does not designate the particular fund out of which it is to be paid. An example would be leaving, say, $1,000 to a housekeeper or someone else who has been of particular service to you. As a rule, general and specific legacies have priority over residual legacies. Thus, there could be some danger of depriving your beneficiaries of what you want them to have if you make the legacies to others too large in proportion to the value of your estate. Probably the best way to avoid this risk is to state your general legacies as percentages of the value of your total estate.

Other major parts of your will include:

The name of one or more executors of your estate—who will manage and settle your estate according to your instructions. An executor should be someone whose competence, judgment, and integrity you trust and who has the interests of your family at heart.

Provisions for some type of trust for your wife, children, or others—if you feel such protection is necessary to keep your estate from being frittered away by financially inexperienced or irresponsible heirs. Trusts also can save on taxes. However, because trusts are subject to many laws governing their organization and administration, they should not be set up without legal help.

The name of a trustee, if your will provides for a trust, to manage and invest your estate for its beneficiaries. Your trustee can be an individual or your bank or a local trust company. The advantage of an institution is that it is sure to outlive you, it stays in one place, it can carry out any business, and it fully understands all the tax laws.

The name of a guardian for your minor children—to take care of them and their property. If you fail to name a guardian (or guardians) in your will, this responsibility falls on the court, which will almost always recognize the right of the surviving natural parent to continue as the guardian even if the two of you were not married at the time of your death. But if the court, say, names the surviving wife as guardian, she may be required to furnish a bond and account for all expenditures made from the children's property until they reach the age of maturity. You can dispense with the bond and accounting requirements in your will and thereby save these costs.

Provisions for gifts from your estate—of cash or other property—to a school, church, charity, some other organization, other people outside your family. Many wealthy people bequeath specific portions of their estates to favorite charities or educational institutions.

Rules for establishing the order of death if both husband and wife should die simultaneously—e.g., in an auto accident or plane crash. If the order of deaths cannot be clearly established, the distribution of your estate under intestacy laws could be very unfair—even if both husband and wife leave a will.

To illustrate with an actual court case the importance of rules for deciding who died first: A middle-aged couple were found dead of heart attacks in their hotel room. Each left a will. The husband's made a substantial bequest outright to a daughter. The wife's will provided a trust until the girl reached a certain age, nineteen years hence. If both husband and wife had identical provisions concerning the daughter, it wouldn't make any difference who died first. But the variation in the wills in this case *forced* the court, despite the tremendous difficulties, to decide the order of deaths.

You *and* your lawyer should ask questions such as these:

What would happen if the wife died first?

Suppose she died a few hours or days after the husband?

If no children or grandchildren survived either and both spouses died close together, would they want the whole estate to go to relatives of the one who had lived just a little longer?

These are situations that you may find hard to contemplate, but it is just this sort of thing that causes horrendously expensive lawsuits and bitter feelings. To protect yourself against such pitfalls, insert a clause in your will which provides for a "presumption of survivorship"—assuring, in effect, that your estate will be distributed as you wish.

Burial arrangements—to spare your bereaved family the effort and complications of haggling over burial costs and decisions as to what type of funeral you'll have (if any). The more specific you are in stating your funeral preferences, the less burdened will be your family with the cost of such lavish, utterly unnecessary trappings as coffins fitted with innerspring mattresses. Ponder—in advance—that a funeral director is in the most advantageous position of dealing with survivors who are under great emotional stress and he also is well aware that the estate of the deceased is responsible for paying burial costs even before it pays taxes.

Witnesses. At the end of your will is a section containing your signature, the date of your signature, followed by an "attestation clause." This clause contains the signatures and addresses of your witnesses and a statement properly certifying that they saw you sign the will. The witnesses must sign in your presence and also in the presence of each other.

Most states require two witnesses, but some require three. Even if you live in a state which requires only two witnesses, it is better to have three anyway. This will make it easier to probate your will after your death in the event, say, that you own real estate in another state which requires three witnesses to a will. A beneficiary of your will should *never* be a witness. In fact, if you do make the mistake of having a beneficiary as witness, it *could* result in this person being partially or totally disinherited.

A common procedure for getting a will witnessed is simply to snag any two people who happen to be around your house or lawyer's office when you sign your will—plus your lawyer—and ask them to serve as witnesses.

HOW ABOUT DO-IT-YOURSELF WILLS?

A young friend who was flying around the tumultuous Middle East hastily wrote her older sister as she departed: "If the Arabs blow up the plane, then I leave everything to be equally distributed between you two [her sister and her younger brother]. This includes my checking and saving accounts, my share in our property, whatever stocks are in the Merrill Lynch account, etc. Love, Mary." Hers is a do-it-yourself "will" at its utmost in simplicity—and illegality. The probable outcome if Mary's plane did blow up: a large portion of her estate would be left to her husband (from whom she is separated but not divorced) and/or her father (who has no need whatsoever for Mary's financial assets).

You surely have seen simple do-it-yourself forms for filling out wills: they are advertised for a dollar or two. You've probably also heard of people who have handwritten their own wills and had these accepted by a court— even without having been witnessed. *But!* Do it yourself only at your own risk! If you make mistakes, they may be discovered only when it's too late for anyone to fix them.

Good lawyers rarely use standard forms for a will. The courts don't like them either. Objective sources also urge you to avoid them because the forms will channel your thinking in advance and, as a result, you may overlook vital aspects of your affairs.

Of course, laymen have written wills and there are some jurisdictions that will recognize a will in your own handwriting, with no witnesses. For soldiers or sailors in active service or mariners at sea, an oral will may be accepted if it is made within hearing of two witnesses. These wills, though, will be good only for a short time after discharge. And barring the most extreme circumstances, to handwrite or speak a will is most dangerous if only because whoever has to read the will eventually may not be able to decipher the writing, or the witnesses to an oral will may not remember accurately what was said.

You may be inclined to ridicule some of the legal formalities on which lawyers insist when drafting, executing, or taking steps to keep a will intact (for instance, fastening the pages with grommets so none can be detached or replaced, initialing each page and any correction, the ceremony with witnesses, etc.). But, says the Research Institute of America, consider the consequences of omitting some of these formalities:

• Where a handwritten will is allowed, no typewritten, printed, or stamped material can appear on the paper.

• A whole will can be voided by a page missing, replaced, or out of place.

• A change, addition, or deletion, not shown to have been made before you signed your will (as could be shown by initialing), may void a provision or the entire will.

• Any doubts about the witnesses having seen the testator or each other sign may be resolved by evidence that the same pen was used for the signatures.

• A will may become entirely void if any writing that disposes of property is placed after the signature. In any case, the added provision has no effect.

• You cannot void a will by writing, "This will is void," at the end and signing your name. You must cancel with the same formality that you write the will—or destroy the documents entirely.

SHOULD A WIFE HAVE A WILL?

Definitely! Even if the wife owns absolutely no property of her own, she will probably inherit a portion of her husband's at his death and must have a will of her own for the redistribution of *that* property.

All too many families figure that, since most wives outlive their husbands, they will have plenty of time to make a will after their husbands die. But many men beat the statistical probabilities and, if the wife of one of these men dies without leaving a will, the laws of intestacy can work just as much to the disadvantage of the children as if the family breadwinner died without a will.

Another reason a wife should have a will is that she can name the guardian and/or trustee who will care for minor children and/or family property if both parents die at the same time. And this, in turn, can avoid bitter custody battles among relatives that almost always hurt the children both emotionally and financially.

Many married women fail to make a will because they feel that their property is "just not worth" drawing a will for—despite the fact that their belongings may include valuable jewelry, furs, paintings, and heirlooms, as well as insurance policies, stocks, bonds, and real estate held in their names.

Let me make the point unmistakably clear:

Every married woman should view her own will as being as important as her husband's; then, to make sure benefits end up where both the wife and husband want them to, the wife should have their lawyer prepare a will for her that does not conflict with the provisions of her husband's will.

WHERE SHOULD YOU KEEP YOUR WILL?

Your will should be kept where it can be found immediately and easily by your executor when it is needed and it should not be kept where it can be stolen, forgotten, mislaid, or lost.

Therefore, it is not wise to keep your will in your own safe deposit box because, on death, this box may be sealed—and sealed even though you hold the box jointly with another person. In this case, your executor would have to go to the court for permission to open the safe deposit box to find your will—an unnecessary annoyance at a terribly trying time. Keep your will in your attorney's safe. Or if your executor is a bank or trust company, give it to your executor for safekeeping. Keep a copy in a safe place in your home and let key beneficiaries know where it is.

"FINAL INSTRUCTIONS"

While you are deciding where to place your will for maximum convenience as well as safety, write a simple letter of "final instructions" and give this to your lawyer too. In this letter, outline the location of your will and locations of your bank accounts, vital documents, life insurance policies; special arrangements you wish followed; other points of this sort. And, particularly, remind your lawyer where your full Personal Affairs Check List is. You'll actually feel better when it's all out of the way.

HOW TO HELP YOUR LAWYER—AND YOUR FAMILY

Before your lawyer can draft a will that meets *your* needs and desires, he must have a personal "who-what-when-how" about yourself and your property. This means you must provide him with not only a breakdown of all your assets and where they are located but also a long list of personal information about yourself, your family, and others to whom you plan to give part of your estate.

This memorandum of your personal affairs will help your lawyer in drawing a will; will be extremely useful to your survivors and the executor of your estate; and will give you the vital information to figure out the size and status of your estate. So pick a quiet, relaxed moment and approach your record making in this mood.

Get a small notebook and start thinking. What do you put into a personal record to help guide you and those who must settle your affairs?

CHECK LIST FOR YOUR PERSONAL AFFAIRS

List the names, addresses, dates and places of birth of yourself, your wife or husband, your children, your father and mother, your brothers and sisters.

Write on separate lines and in clear detail the following:

• Your Social Security number and where your card is located.

• The location of your birth certificate and, if you have one, veteran's discharge certificate.

• If you have more than one residence, the address of each residence, the time you spend in each, where you vote, and where you pay income taxes.

• The date and place of your marriage and where your marriage certificate can be found.

• If you have been married previously, your deceased or former wife's or husband's name.

• If you are divorced, the place of the divorce, whether it was contested, who brought the action, where your divorce papers are. This will enable your lawyer to determine whether your former spouse has any inheritance rights remaining. If separated by agreement or court action, all the details and the place where your separation agreement can be found.

• Where a copy of any prenuptial agreement into which you entered can be found.

• Whether any of your immediate relatives are handicapped or incompetent.

• Other family information, such as the state of health of its members, whether you have any adopted children, marital problems, family feuds; "difficult" family members, if any.

• The names and addresses of others you intend to make your beneficiaries.

• If you are the beneficiary under a trust or have created a trust, where your lawyer can obtain a copy of the document.

• If you have the right to exercise a power of appointment under someone's will or under a trust, also where this document can be found.

• A statement of your approximate income and general standard of living for the past several years.

• The name and address of your accountant if you have one.

• The place where copies of your income and gift tax returns may be found and the name and address of the person who prepared them.

• Name and address of your employer.

• Details of any employment contract or stock purchase plan in which you are enrolled.

• Whether you are entitled to a pension, profit-sharing benefit, stock options, or any other employment benefits. Give the name of the person who handles your company's fringe benefits plus information on how the benefits are payable on your death.

• Any union or unions to which you belong and appropriate details.

• Life insurance policies owned by you on your life; policies owned by others on your life (stating who pays the premiums on them); and policies owned by you on the lives of others. Also list annuity policies owned by you. Include the name and address of each issuing company, name and address of your insurance agent, policy numbers, principal amount of each policy, the beneficiaries, and whether there are any outstanding loans against any of the policies.

• An itemization of all your real estate. Give the location of each property, its approximate value, the price you paid for it, any mortgages on the property and whether you own the property by yourself or jointly with others. Also give the location of deeds to any property you own.

• The location and total of stocks, bonds, and other securities you may own, the name and address of your broker or brokers.

• A complete list of all your other assets. Give the approximate value of each, its cost basis, and location of each. This would include bank accounts, any business ownership, as well as your more valuable personal effects, such as jewelry, furs, art objects, and the like. (Don't overlook details of debts due to you.)

• The location of your safe deposit box and the box key.

• A complete list of your debts, including mortgages on your house or business, leases, and other obligations. Give the names and addresses of persons to whom you are indebted and the terms under which you are supposed to repay.

• The names and addresses of whomever you wish to name as your executors, trustees, and guardians.

• The name of your lawyer, his address, telephone number, and a list of your papers in his safekeeping.

• The name and address of any person to whom you may have given power of attorney.

• The names of organizations—such as fraternal or trade societies—to which you belong. Make a special note here about any benefits which may be coming to your family from these organizations.

• If you have been in active military service, the branch and period of service.

• Funeral arrangements you prefer and any preparations you have made.

• Names and addresses of friends you wish notified of your death in any former as well as your present city.

• Names and addresses of relatives you wish notified at once.

Then, when you've completed this guide for your lawyer, your family, and yourself, put it in a safe place—but *not* your safe deposit box. Notify your family or closest friend where the list is. Forget it until you want to bring it up to date a year or so from now.

HOW TO REVISE YOUR WILL

You must give your will a checkup from time to time. As one simple illustration why, assume you have moved from New York to Arizona. If you die in Arizona, leaving a will that describes you as a resident of New York, both states might try to levy a death tax on your estate. Moreover, some states have restrictions as to who may serve as an executor—and a person eligible to serve in New York might not be eligible to serve in Arizona. In some states, foreign banks as well as non-residents who are not next of kin cannot serve as executors.

It's easy to change your will at any time either by executing a new will or by merely adding a codicil—a separate formal document that alters or adds to the provisions of the existing will. But you may *not* change a will by rewriting a provision on the original document or by scratching out the name of a beneficiary. A codicil must be written with the same formality as your original will and comply with identical rules. And when you make a new will, destroy all copies of the old one. For if a revised will is ever challenged in the court, a copy of an earlier will might be introduced as evidence of your intentions.

Ask yourself these key questions about your will:

• Has a child been born into your family since you made your will? In most states, this after-born child will receive a share of your estate—even though your will may provide nothing for children born before it was made.

• Was your will properly witnessed? A man owned property in three states, so he carefully had his will witnessed in all three. But each of his three witnesses had acted alone without either of the others being present. As a result, the will was invalid under the laws of all three states.

• Is your will easy to locate? When Smith died, no will could be found and his property was therefore distributed under the law. More than eighteen months later his will turned up. It left some real estate to a relative who hadn't received any share when Smith's estate was distributed. But the relative never got it, for though the court gave him permission to sue the present owners, this would have been a poor gamble: the chance of recovering money that might have been spent was too uncertain.

• Where is your legal residence? If you divide your time between two states, both may claim you as a resident for purposes of death taxes. If they do, your estate will be involved in expensive litigation and it may have to pay taxes in both states. Your lawyer will tell you how to avoid this problem: the first step is a will which makes your residence clear and which is drawn to conform with the laws of the state where you actually live.

• Have you married since you made your will? If so, call your lawyer, tell him so, and ask him what you should do about your will.

• If you have acquired a business interest, have you provided for its disposition at your death? No matter what the size of your interest, make a sound plan for its disposition. If your interest must be sold in a hurry to pay death taxes, it may be sacrificed—and your family may be badly hurt.

• Is the executor (or the executors) you have named appropriate for the job? Your natural inclination may be to name a member of your family or a close friend. But in view of the importance of an informed, competent executor, this move may be unwise. The commission for executing an estate is fixed by law and is the same whether done by a bank or an individual. Since the duties are complicated, a sound decision may be to avoid a relative or friend and to name an objective institution or attorney as executor. Certainly look into this matter before you select yours.

These questions are primarily designed to intrigue your interest. Your lawyer surely will bring up others. The key to all other keys is to ask yourself periodically whether your will needs revision.

HOW CAN YOU DISINHERIT MEMBERS OF YOUR FAMILY?

The idea of disinheriting your spouse or children may not even have crossed your mind. However, there are circumstances under which disinheriting a member of your family can be not only the most practical but also the most considerate thing you can do.

For instance, say one of your two children has become a huge financial success and is now worth many times the value of your estate. The other is disabled, unable to work, and badly needs all the financial protection you can offer. Your realistic decision here well might be to "cut out" the wealthy son and leave all to the dependent one.

Under certain circumstances, you may be able to disinherit one or more children simply by specifically stating so in your will and giving your reasons for cutting them off. However, you generally may *not* disinherit your wife or husband unless such surviving spouse had abandoned the deceased and such abandonment continued to date of death. Or there may be some other possible circumstance permitting disinheritance—all of which should be checked with your attorney.

Laws vary from state to state, but as a general rule a widow is entitled to one third or more of her husband's estate, and if he leaves her less than that in his will, the court may later grant it to her anyway. Moreover, many states still recognize what is called the wife's *right of dower*. This means that she is legally entitled to the use of one third of her husband's real estate so long as she lives. Some states give the husband a similar right to the real property of his deceased wife, known as the *right of curtesy*.

In some states which have abolished the old dower rights, the wife may have the choice of going along with the provisions of her husband's will or renouncing the will and claiming the share of his estate that she would have received if he had died without a will. To illustrate: a man whose estate amounts to $120,000 at his death leaves his wife only $25,000 in his will. She could, in many states, choose to reject that sum and instead take one third of the estate, or $40,000—or possibly, one half.

In still other states, however, a husband may satisfy the law by leaving his wife the minimum designated amount of his estate in trust. She is then entitled to the income from this trust during her lifetime. When she dies, though, the principal passes to whomever the husband has named in his will.

HOW TO HANDLE JOINTLY OWNED PROPERTY

You are only typical if you are befuddled by the tax aspects of jointly owned property and are in doubt about how to handle it.

To begin, it is vitally important that you determine, with the help of your lawyer, whether the property you own jointly is held as:

(1) "tenants by the entirety";

(2) "tenants in common";

(3) "joint tenants" with only a lifetime interest in the property and the survivor taking all;

(4) "community property."

To illustrate: if the names of both the husband and the wife appear on the deed to their home, they are said to own the house as *tenants by the entirety*. When one spouse dies, the other becomes the sole owner. Only real estate can be held this way and it can be held this way only by a husband and wife.

But let's say the husband and a friend of his purchase a piece of property with the idea of building vacation cottages on it. Title to the property is held in both names. In most states, this constitutes a *tenancy in common*. In this case, each man owns an undivided one-half interest in the property, and either may sell his interest or dispose of it in whatever manner he chooses when he dies. The other partner keeps only his share of the property —in this example, one half—with the balance going into the estate of the tenant in common who died, to be distributed according to the terms of his will.

Real estate and other assets—e.g., joint bank accounts, stocks, and bonds —can be held in *joint tenancy* and passed along outside the will. In this type of arrangement, two or more persons own a given property as *joint tenants*. If one of them dies, his interest in the property passes outside his will directly to the other tenant or tenants (survivor or survivors).

When the value of your property exceeds $60,000, holding all assets in joint ownership *could* actually force you to pay far greater death taxes than any amount you could save in probate costs.

Do not fall into the widespread misconception that this type of ownership always frees property from estate taxes. *It does no such thing.*

For example, under federal estate tax law, it is assumed that all property held in joint names belongs to the owner who dies first, and the burden is on the estate to prove otherwise. Say a husband buys some property and names his wife as joint owner with him. If he should die, *the full property* —not half—will be included in his taxable estate. Or, if the wife dies first, the Treasury Department *could* take the position that the wife was the original owner of the property and that it should be fully taxable in her estate.

As a further illustration of the pitfalls of jointly held property, say the wife dies first and the property consists of securities which were bought many years ago and were put in joint names. If the husband is unable to prove that he contributed the money with which to buy the securities, he might have to pay a sizable tax on the value of the securities that belonged to him in the first place. This problem of having to prove who paid for what—sometimes many years after a joint tenancy is created—is often sound reason not to create a joint tenancy in the first place.

KEY PRECAUTIONS FOR JOINTLY OWNED PROPERTY

Therefore, if you have jointly owned property, your key precautions are:

Keep accurate records showing how the property was acquired—e.g., by purchase, inheritance, or gift.

If the property was purchased, keep detailed records showing who put up the money—you, your wife, or both.

If both of you put up the money, have proof available of what proportion each of you contributed.

Go the joint ownership route only on the advice of a competent estate planner—especially if your estate is a large one.

COMMUNITY PROPERTY

Community property is another category of ownership, which is much like jointly held property. However, community property is legally recognized in only a few states. The concept behind community property laws is that all property acquired by husband and wife after marriage is considered to be owned by them fifty-fifty—no matter whose name is on the deed to a given property. So far as the law in community property states is concerned, the family home is owned jointly by husband and wife.

In some states, all community property goes automatically to the surviving spouse. In others, the property is divided fifty-fifty beween the bread-winner's wife and his estate.

Certain assets, known as "separate property," are excluded from community property. Examples: property which belonged to either spouse before marriage, or property acquired after marriage by gift or inheritance.

The laws covering community property vary widely from state to state. It is imperative to consult your lawyer on the law in your state.

PROBATING YOUR WILL

When your executor presents your will to the court to have it declared valid, this is known as probating the will. The names of courts which handle estate settlements vary from state to state and the names may give you no clue whatsoever to this important role they play. However, every state has a court which handles probate matters. In California, it's the Superior Court. In New York it's the Surrogate's Court. In Pennsylvania it's the Orphan's Court. Elsewhere, it's the Probate Court, the County Court, or the Circuit Court.

YOUR EXECUTOR—HIS FUNCTIONS AND FEES

Whom should you choose as an executor?

A first point is that, if you do *not* have a will or if you fail to name an executor in your will, the court will appoint an "administrator" to handle your estate. The duties of an executor and an administrator are roughly the same. However, your executor may have much greater latitude if you grant such flexibility in the text of your will.

If your estate is sizable, you should name an executor experienced in handling investments and familiar with the business of selling property. Or you may want to name co-executors. One might be a member of your family, to help ensure the personal interpretation of your wishes, and the other a lawyer, bank, or trust company to furnish business advice and also handle the accounting and clerical functions.

The functions of the executor are:

to submit your will to the court for probate (proof of validity);

to take title to all property owned by the deceased;

to see that all assets of the estate are inventoried and appraised;

to collect all money due the deceased;

to pay any debts owed by the deceased after allowing creditors a set, limited time to file claims against the estate;

to file estate tax returns with both federal and state authorities (or hire an accountant to do this);

to manage the estate and safeguard assets until it is time to distribute them according to the provisions of the will;

to pay out all bequests and distribute the remainder of the estate's assets according to the terms of the will;

to get receipts from all beneficiaries and file them with the court;

and to submit to the court a final accounting of all receipts and disbursements.

Only after all of these steps have been completed is the executor discharged from his or her executorship.

Commissions to be paid to your executor or administrator, and other fees paid to the attorney performing the legal work involved, are the main expenses in the administration of an estate. Although legal fees are generally left to the discretion of the court, in most states the executor's commission is fixed by state law and is based on the amount of the estate that passes through his hands.

If there are two executors, the commissions may double, and if there are more than two, the commissions may triple.

ESTATES AND TRUSTS—BRIEF ANSWERS TO BASIC QUESTIONS

JUST WHAT IS AN "ESTATE TAX"?

Under federal law, an estate tax return must be filed for every estate with gross assets of more than $60,000 by your executor (or administrator) and any tax due on this estate must be paid at the time this return is filed.

This enhances the desirability of arranging your affairs in ways that will minimize the tax burden on your estate and beneficiaries.

Although the federal estate tax is usually called an inheritance tax, death levies imposed by the states may be called inheritance tax or transfer tax, estate tax, or legacy tax. State death taxes vary so widely from state to state that there is no way to generalize on "typical" amounts—and they are imposed in every state except Nevada. The actual rate may depend, for instance, on the size of the estate or inheritance or the type of property involved or the closeness of the heir's blood relationship to the person who has died.

What's more, though some states allow roughly the same kinds of exemptions and deductions that the federal government allows, they do not necessarily allow them in the same amounts. If a state exemption is lower, for example, you may have to pay a state tax even though you are not required to pay a federal tax. On top of this, both federal and state tax rates and regulations undergo frequent changes.

HOW CAN ESTATE TAXES BE CUT BY LIFETIME GIFTS?

Probably your surest and most soul-satisfying way to reduce your estate taxes as well as your probate costs is through a gift program properly planned and faithfully carried out *during your lifetime.*

And a program of this sort will produce not only tax savings on your estate but important savings on your income tax as well. The key reason: gift tax rates are about 25 per cent lower than estate tax rates.

Our gift tax law allows you to distribute—*during your lifetime*—a total of $30,000 among any number of beneficiaries, free of federal gift tax, plus an additional sum up to $3,000 a year each to as many different people as you wish. Your lifetime exemption may be used in any one year or spread over many years.

If you give more than $3,000 to any one individual in any one tax year and have used up your lifetime exemption, you must file a gift tax return and pay the tax due. If joint gifts are made by you, as husband and wife, or if your wife technically joins you in making your gift, these limits are doubled to $6,000 and $60,000, because then each of you is entitled to the $3,000 exclusions and the $30,000 exemption.

If you leave these same amounts to family members via your will, they could be subject to the full force of federal and state estate taxes.

Another major way to reduce the federal tax bite on your estate is to make a bequest to an acceptable charitable organization or cause.

WHEN WILL YOU GET YOUR INHERITANCE?

As soon as the executor has been appointed by the court and has collected enough assets of the estate—such as cash in the bank—he can provide survivors with enough funds to meet immediate living expenses.

Certain other assets, such as proceeds from life insurance policies, also go to the beneficiaries almost immediately. If the estate is relatively small and therefore is not subject to taxation, and if there is no litigation or other complication, the proceeds can often be distributed within a year. But if it is a big estate, and if there are estate taxes to be paid, it may be several years before you can consider yourself "rich."

An executor may not distribute the proceeds of an estate until all the legal debts of the deceased have been paid. In most states, the way debts are uncovered is by giving notice to creditors and by requiring them to file their claims within a certain limited period of time. Notice is normally published in a local newspaper once a week for four weeks. And in most states the time limits for creditors to file claims against an estate range from six months to eighteen months after the decedent's death.

Frequently, an estate's value is established as the value at the date of death. However, if the estate consists mainly of securities which have shrunk in value, the executor may want to take advantage of the optional valuation date, six months from the date of death (see page 746). However, he cannot do this unless he maintains control of most of the estate's assets.

The Treasury may accept the estate tax return without audit—but the law allows it three years to audit the return. During this limbo period, the executor must retain control of at least some assets—in case additional taxes must be paid.

WHAT IS A TRUST?

A trust is an agreement whereby the person who establishes the trust gives property to a trustee to invest and manage for the advantage of the beneficiary. It is a highly flexible device that enables you to have a say in the use of your money after you have died as well as during your lifetime. Most trusts are established for the benefit of a surviving wife and children and most trusts remain in effect for some years. Trusts also can help save on taxes.

A typical provision is that only the income from the trust may go to the beneficiary. At the same time, many such trust agreements contain an emergency clause which permits the trustee to invade the principal or part of it, if necessary, to provide for the education of the children, or for other unforeseen needs such as major medical expenses.

Frequently a trust is used as a means of protecting beneficiaries against their own inexperience in managing financial assets. You may, for instance, want your wife to have the income from your property during her lifetime and your children to get the property later. Or, if you are a widower with children, you may want them to receive only the income from your property until they reach a given age (say thirty) and *then* to receive the principal outright.

Or a trust can be used to permit a desired standard of living for your family;

to educate a minor child;

to cover unexpected financial emergencies;

to provide a lifetime income for a wife or daughter or other relative;

to give a young man his inheritance in installments to keep him from squandering it all in one fell swoop;

to provide for a favorite charity;

to achieve almost any type of personal or financial objective.

The organization, purpose, administration, duration, and eventual disposition of the principal of the trust are subject to many laws, and thus the laws governing *your* prospective trust depend on the state in which you live.

There are many different types of trusts—some fairly commonplace, others not so frequently established. You will find short definitions of the various types with which you might be concerned in the section, "The Bafflegab of Wills, Estates, and Trusts," at the end of this chapter.

WHOM SHOULD YOU NAME AS TRUSTEE?

You may name a business associate or personal friend as your trustee but most people seek the advice of specialists in this field—usually a trust company or the trust department of a bank. A few states have laws that fix the amount a trustee may charge for his services, but most states rely on the competition among institutions to keep the fees generally reasonable and uniform. A local trust company or trust department of a bank will give you a schedule of its fees.

WHAT CAN BE DONE WITH LIFE INSURANCE?

If you own a considerable amount of life insurance you can create a life insurance trust and direct to whom and in what manner the policies are to be paid. The danger here is, though, that by creating a trust, or by making the insurance policy payable to your estate, you might merely increase the expense of distributing these assets.

As an alternative, you can have the proceeds of your life insurance paid promptly upon your death simply by naming the beneficiary to the policy. And you can direct your insurance company to pay the proceeds in the way you want. For instance, you can authorize the insurance company to make specific payments to your wife or children—including both the income and part of the principal—for a specific period of time. A caution, though: should you direct that payments be made to your children and should you die while they are minors, a guardian may have to be appointed by the probate court to handle these proceeds. You can avoid this by a clause in your will authorizing your executor to receive the proceeds and handle them to the best advantage of the children.

Although all life insurance proceeds must be included in computing the gross value of your estate for purposes of taxation, these proceeds must be included in the estate *only if the policy was owned and paid for by the person whose life was insured*—or if he had control of the policy.

But it is entirely possible for a man's life to be insured by his wife. Thus, if a wife takes out an insurance policy on her husband's life and has it registered in her name as owner, the policy will not have to be listed as an asset in the husband's estate and the wife will not have to share the proceeds with the tax collector.

Note: Any kind of insurance can be handled in this manner—and by either or both husband and wife.

THE BAFFLEGAB OF WILLS, ESTATES, AND TRUSTS

ACCUMULATION TRUST: Trust in which the yearly income on the capital in an estate is added to the principal for a designated period of time—e.g., usually during a young beneficiary's childhood.

ADMINISTRATOR (ADMINISTRATRIX): Individual or institution appointed by the court to handle the estate of a person who has not left a will.

ATTESTATION CLAUSE: Clause at the end of your will containing the signatures and addresses of the witnesses and a statement that they saw you sign the will.

BENEFICIARY: Person named to receive funds or property from a trust or insurance policy, or via a will.

BEQUEST (OR LEGACY): Gift of personal property via a will.

CHARITABLE TRUST: Trust in which the grantor stipulates that a certain portion of his estate be used for charitable purposes. A charitable trust may last indefinitely. All other types of trusts must have cutoff dates.

CODICIL: Addition, or "postscript," to a will, drawn up with all the formality of the will itself.

CO-EXECUTOR (-EXECUTRIX): Second person named to assist executor.

COMMUNITY PROPERTY: The concept of fifty-fifty property ownership by a married couple (see pages 738–39).

CONTEMPLATION OF DEATH: If a gift is made to a child or other person within three years of an individual's death, it may be considered by the Treasury to have been an eleventh-hour gift, made in "contemplation of death"—and therefore taxable as part of an estate instead of at lower gift tax rates. But the presumption that you made a gift in contemplation of death can be rebutted. If you're forty-nine years old and happen to drop dead on a handball court a week after giving your niece a large gift of cash, the courts would probably rule that you were not contemplating dying when you made the gift and that it therefore need not be included in your gross estate.

CONVEY: To give or sell property to someone else.

DEATH (OR ESTATE) TAXES: Taxes levied on your estate by the federal and state governments, with the amounts varying according to the size of the estate.

DECEDENT: Person who has died.

DEVISE: Give real estate through a will.

DOMICILE: Legal home, where person votes, pays taxes, etc.

ESTATE: All assets and liabilities left by a person at death.

EXECUTOR: Individual and/or institution you name in your will to safeguard the assets of your estate while it is being probated, and to distribute it according to your wishes (see pages 739–40).

EXECUTOR'S FEE: Fee paid to the person or institution handling your estate— with the amount (or percentage of the value of the estate) usually set by state law.

GUARDIAN: Person appointed to look after a person or property—e.g., a minor, until he or she is old enough to manage his or her own affairs.

HOLOGRAPHIC WILL: Handwritten will—recognized as legal only under certain circumstances and only in certain jurisdictions.

INTER VIVOS: No-strings-attached gift to which the donor during his lifetime forfeits all rights, and to which the donor gives the recipient complete control.

INTESTATE: Without leaving a will.

ISSUE: Children and direct descendants.

JOINT TENANCY WITH RIGHT OF SURVIVORSHIP: Ownership by two or more people of a piece of real estate and agreement that, if one dies, the survivor automatically gets the entire property (see pages 737–38).

LEGACY (OR BEQUEST): Gift of property—especially money or other personal property—made under a will.

LIFE INSURANCE TRUST: Type of trust in which the assets are the proceeds of life insurance policies.

MARITAL DEDUCTION: Provision in our federal tax law designed to prevent double taxation of an estate—at the death of the wife as well as at the death of the husband. It permits a husband or wife to leave up to one half of his or her estate to his spouse with this amount deductible from the taxable estate.

MARITAL DEDUCTION TRUST (See "Marital Deduction" above): A trust which makes it possible to relieve from the burden of estate taxation, in the estate of the spouse first to die, certain property interests described as "deductible interests." To the extent of not more than one half of the adjusted gross estate, these interests are not taxable as part of the estate of the first spouse, but rather as part of the estate of the surviving spouse. The surviving spouse receives all of the income from the trust; in some cases there is a right to invade the principal; and the surviving spouse must have the unqualified right to dispose of the principal of the trust in favor of himself or his estate. The residue of the estate may also be left to the surviving spouse in trust.

This *"residual trust"* may provide for the payment of income to the survivor and contain provisions for invading the principal. It will then provide for the ultimate distribution of the principal. However, the principal of this residual trust is taxable to the estate of the creator of the trust, and not to that of the surviving spouse.

MUTUAL WILLS: Common arrangement executed pursuant to an agreement in which husband and wife leave everything to each other. Frequently a further provision is that, when the second spouse has died, the estate is shared by the children. A *reciprocal will* is one which contains reciprocal gifts for and among the makers.

OPTIONAL VALUATION DATE: Date on which the size of your estate is computed for tax purposes can be either as of the date of your death or as of six months after your death—providing the assets are not disposed of in the interim—thus "optional" date. It provides a financial protection for the beneficiaries in the event of a sharp stock market slide, for if the value of the estate shrinks the tax on it will be slashed too.

POWER OF APPOINTMENT: Equivalent of absolute ownership of part or all of a trust, since the person having this power may name the ultimate recipients of the assets of the trust.

PRENUPTIAL AGREEMENT: Agreement made prior to marriage—often one in which both spouses forfeit any interest in the other's estate.

PRESUMPTION OF SURVIVORSHIP: Clause in your will establishing a way to decide the order of death if both spouses die simultaneously.

PROBATE COSTS: Costs of administering an estate.

PROBATE COURT: Court in which estate settlements are made; in some states estates are handled by a circuit court or surrogate's court.

PROBATING A WILL: Processing a will through a court in order to establish its validity.

RESIDUARY CLAUSE: Usually the key clause in your will since it covers the bulk of your "residuary estate"—typically, "all the rest, residue and remainder" of the estate—after special, individual bequests of money and/or property have been covered.

REVOCABLE LIVING TRUST: Trust in which the income from the trust is paid to the grantor during his or her lifetime, and to his or her family after he dies. This type of trust may be amended or revoked at any time during the grantor's lifetime. An *irrevocable living trust* cannot be revoked or amended without the consent of all persons mentioned in the original agreement.

RIGHT OF CURTESY: Husband's life interest in the property of his deceased wife.

RIGHT OF DOWER: Wife's life interest in the estate of her deceased husband.

SPENDTHRIFT TRUST: Trust in which only the income but not the principal may be touched by the beneficiary—no matter how urgent the demands or needs of the beneficiary.

TENANCY IN COMMON: Title held jointly by two people, usually unmarried, to a given piece of property—i.e., real estate—although each person keeps control over his individual share of the property. Either may sell or will his interest in the property independently of the other (see page 737).

TENANCY BY THE ENTIRETY: When the names of both the husband and wife appear on the deed to their home and/or other real estate (see page 737).

TESTAMENTARY TRUST: Trust established by a will to take effect after that person dies.

TESTATOR: Person making a will.

TOTTEN TRUST: Way, often used by grandparents, to leave money to their grandchildren. The donor opens a bank account in the name of one person "in trust for" the grandchild or other beneficiary but retains control over the trust during his or her lifetime.

TRUST: Property or money set aside for a certain person or persons to be managed by a trustee for the best advantage of the beneficiary.

TRUST DEPARTMENT: Department of a financial institution which is staffed with specialists in the administration of estates and in handling trust funds.

TRUSTEE: Individual or institution designated to oversee the handling and distribution of a trust fund.

WILL: Legal document—usually in writing and properly witnessed—which describes how a person wants his or her property to be distributed after death.

ONE MORE TIME

A nationally known and respected lawyer who checked this chapter for accuracy approved it with one addition.

"I know you repeatedly urged the reader to consult with and rely on his lawyer in his area," he said, "but to make sure your message is clear, say it once again." And then he dictated:

"It is not intended by this chapter to cover the law of all fifty states but merely to lay down some general rules. Consultation with your own attorney is necessary to determine whether such rules apply to your state and to your own particular set of circumstances."

18

FUNERAL EXPENSES
AND HOW TO CONTROL THEM

WOULD YOU KNOW WHAT TO DO?

Do you know what you should do if you are suddenly confronted with a death in the family? Would you know where to turn for help?

Are you aware that just the average cost of a traditional adult funeral in the United States has now risen to more than $1,500? Do you realize that if you are as utterly unprepared as most people are for the economic facts of death you easily can be victimized by a hastily chosen, unscrupulous funeral parlor? That you can easily end up deeply in debt for absolutely unnecessary and, in fact utterly frivolous "extras"?

You are almost surely totally unaware of which funeral procedures are and which are not legally required. You are almost surely equally unaware of what areas of funeral arrangements are open to negotiation and significant savings. And you probably do not realize that allowances—from, say, Social Security or union or club or veterans' benefits, the like—may cover only a fraction of the actual costs.

Death is not only a deep emotional blow. It is also a major expense. We, the living, *must* show intelligence and common sense at this bitter moment. This ultimate in emotional trouble may, if not met properly, plunge a family into deep financial trouble for years to come.

What, then, can be done to hold funeral costs within your family income range? If funeral arrangements were not made before death, those details now must be considered. Many families pay excessive funeral costs because of sheer ignorance or inexperience, because of fear of what the neighbors might think, because of a wish to honor the dead. Or because, in their grief, they are in no condition to bargain about money. The records bulge with heartbreaking tales of bewildered widows who listened to the wrong advice on funeral and financial arrangements in the wake of a death in the family.

So . . .

THE FUNDAMENTAL GUIDES

Be careful even of the advice given by your closest personal friends and dearest relatives. They may have the best intentions, but when in trouble you need help from people who have the full information and background to advise you.

If no prior arrangements have been made and if you are in a state of befuddlement, ask a sensible levelheaded friend or relative, who knows what the family can afford, to help you with the arrangements. This person or these people will help find a licensed, reasonable funeral director who will co-operate in arranging for the type of funeral you want.

If a member of the family dies in a distant place and the body is to be shipped home, investigate both railroad and plane fares for such transportation. Railroads require the purchase of two tickets, whether or not the body is accompanied. Airlines do not.

If the body is cremated near the place of death, the small container of ashes can be mailed by parcel post or carried in a suitcase.

Get advice—from your lawyer, minister, friends—on the arrangements you will make *before* you authorize any given mortician to remove the body from home or hospital. Obviously, once a mortician takes custody of a body, his bargaining power is multiplied. Note: Most large hospitals will keep a body for at least a day, and often longer, while you make arrangements.

Get a copy of "A Manual of Death Education and Simple Burial," by Ernest Morgan (Celo Press, Burnsville, N.C. 28714; $1.50). The manual gives straightforward information on costs and other vital aspects of funerals, body and organ donations to medical schools, etc.

If a bank or law firm is the executor of the deceased's estate, ask the appropriate officials to help arrange economical services.

If the funeral costs must be financed out of borrowed funds until any estate is settled, find out what interest rates will be charged by the funeral parlor or other lending source.

Check exactly what is included in the price tag on a casket. The casket alone? A complete range of services? Which? Don't permit a mortician to make you feel guilty or disrespectful if you try to economize.

Insist on an itemized list of costs for funeral services—and do not sign up for a "package" of goods or services you may not want or need. (For instance, extra limousines, use of the funeral parlor chapel, etc.) In the words of "Manual" editor Ernest Morgan: "There are important emotional and social needs to be met at the time of death, but the amount of money you spend has nothing to do with how well these needs are met."

Some states have passed laws requiring funeral directors to provide customers with a written rundown on all costs and charges and also prohibiting crematories from requiring that remains be put in a casket for cremation.

• Steer clear of expensive frills such as costly "burial vaults" to enclose the casket, costing up to $150 or even more. Unless the cemetery requires these vaults, you can omit this expense altogether.

• If your family is in a serious financial squeeze, tell the facts to the funeral director. If he's reputable, he will make allowances for your circumstances.

• If you plan to buy a cemetery plot, find out if the cemetery participates in a nationwide Lot Exchange Plan under which, if you move to another area, you can trade one plot for another.

• If you want to donate your body (or part of it) for medical teaching purposes, transplants, etc., write to the medical or dental school of your choice and ask for details on how to go about it in your area. The above-mentioned manual lists names and addresses of U.S. medical schools and their rules covering bequeathal of bodies.

• Wait a few months or even years, until the shock is dulled and you've regained your balance, before you buy expensive markers or memorials.

CREMATION

If the person who has died expressed a wish to be cremated, or to have his or her body donated to a medical school for research and/or teaching purposes, these moves could reduce costs way below those of traditional funeral procedures. One reason is that cremation may eliminate the costs of funeral formalities ranging from hearses to church services. Also, embalming is not required, nor is the increasingly expensive cemetery space.

You have the choice of a funeral service (memorial service) or utterly simple disposal of the remaining ashes almost anywhere you want (a few states prohibit the scattering of ashes—laws which are inspired not by health or aesthetic reasons but by commercial interests).

Cremation costs generally run well under $100. But a variety of crematorium rules, state laws, and funeral parlor "extras" can jack this basic cost up as far as $800 or $900.

WAYS TO CUT CREMATION COSTS

Your key ways to hold down cremation costs:

• Do not invest in a casket if one is not actually required by the crematory. If a crematorium or a funeral parlor claims a casket is required by state law, ask to see the references. State laws do *not* require caskets for cremation; some, in fact, specifically prohibit crematories from requiring them.

• Find out if state law permits private individuals or ambulance services to deliver a body directly (and inexpensively) to the crematorium.

• Do not feel under any obligation to buy a special vase or urn from the crematorium to hold the ashes. Alternatives include providing your own container—or simply scattering the ashes directly from whatever simple container (canister) is provided by the crematorium. (Incidentally, you needn't feel obliged to scatter the ashes immediately. Some people wait as long as a year or two to do so.)

• Do not, if the body is cremated some distance from home and must be returned home to be disposed of, make any special, costly arrangements for the return. The container can be mailed home by parcel post or carried in a suitcase.

• This occasion, in sum, is hardly one which calls for *any* unnecessary or unwanted extras.

PREFINANCED FUNERALS

One move that makes complete sense is the prearranged, prefinanced funeral—and prefinanced funerals can be arranged easily today. The step is just as thoughtful and appropriate as buying insurance, making a will, or choosing a cemetery lot. You should view it in the same light.

Now, while you're young, join a "Memorial Society" or similar association which has arrangements with one or more funeral parlors to provide members with a predetermined package of funeral services at a fixed cost of $150 to $350 and "simplicity, dignity, and economy in funeral arrangements." Typical family lifetime membership is about $20 and you can transfer your membership if you move.

Get details on the nearest to you of 120 such societies in the United States from the non-profit Continental Association of Funeral and Memorial Societies, 1828 L Street, N.W., Washington, D.C. 20036. Through these, hundreds of thousands of families are achieving savings running into tens of millions of dollars on an expense which, even at its best, is brutal.

Or if you decide to prearrange your funeral in some other way, here is how to go about it:

Check with local funeral directors. Choose one who will make the preferred arrangements in advance of the inevitable event. You may finance the costs now and know exactly what expenses will be involved. Or you may make the arrangements now and postpone the payment until after death. Be sure, however, that the money is put in a state-supervised trust and can be withdrawn any time you decide to cancel the arrangements.

FUNERAL BENEFITS—SOCIAL SECURITY AND VETERANS'

All Social Security beneficiaries and all those who are fully insured or who have worked at least eighteen months in the last three years with Social Security coverage are eligible for a lump-sum death benefit up to $255. If there is no surviving spouse, the benefit may be applied only toward payment of mortuary fees—or used as partial reimbursement to whoever has paid these costs.

If the deceased person is a veteran, these are the key government funeral benefits:

• A basic $250 allowance will be paid toward the burial expenses of honorably discharged war veterans—or of veterans of peacetime service who have a service-connected disability.

• Free burial will be permitted in a national cemetery in which space is available. Burial in national cemeteries is available also to an eligible veteran's wife and dependent children.

• For veterans who are not buried in a national or other U. S. Government cemetery, an additional "plot allowance" of up to $150 may be payable.

• If a veteran's death is service-connected, the total funeral expense allowance can go up to a total of $800.

• Headstone or grave markers will be available through the VA to deceased, honorably discharged veterans.

You can get complete information on government burial benefits for veterans and their families at any VA office or veterans' service organization. Most post offices and funeral parlors are familiar with the benefits also, and can assist a beneficiary in applying to the appropriate government agency.

IF YOU ARE THE DEPENDENT WIDOW

Don't make an investment of any sort until your mind is working more normally and you have had ample time to get the advice of competent, objective advisers concerned only with *your* welfare!

> *Don't* buy securities.
> *Don't* make loans.
> *Don't* convert your insurance policies.
> *Don't* buy annuities.
> *Don't* make any investment.

You have a limited amount of money. It is now more important than ever. Take your time, get the best advice available to you before you take a single step.

BEWARE: "DEATH TRAPS"

In New York a while ago police detectives nailed a young man who had been posing as an Army sergeant, had obtained the names of families of soldiers killed in Vietnam from the local Spanish-language newspaper—and had then offered to sell the grieving families special coffins with special glass windows so they could view the bodies of the slain men. As you might suspect, families who paid the $100 for this alternative to the traditional sealed military coffin never saw their purchase—or their money again.

In Palo Alto, California, a pair of hearse chasers was recently indicted on charges of mail fraud for mailing letters to families of servicemen—whose names and addresses they had found on casualty lists published by the *Army Times*—requesting payments of non-existent $10 debts which the families were told had been contracted during military service.

In Tampa, Florida, a young couple was similarly indicted for mailing C.O.D. Bibles to people whose names they found listed in newspaper obituary columns—giving the impression that the Bibles had been ordered previously by the deceased. The estimated value of each Bible was $2.00; the C.O.D. charge was $16.40.

In St. Louis two small loan company operators were found guilty in court of bilking unsuspecting widows from whom they demanded full payment on loans taken out by the deceased—although the loans had previously been fully paid by their life insurance coverage.

This is merely a sampling of one of the most savage categories of rackets in the United States today. It's vicious not only because the gypsters prey on individuals already in a state of despair but also because the victims almost surely are in the dark about the financial obligations and dealings of their deceased relatives.

To protect you from these ruthless swindlers, here are some of the guises in which they and their schemes show up:

(1) A con man moves into the area, checks into a motel under an alias, and starts reading obit columns. He telephones widows, telling them he is an insurance agent and that their deceased husbands had life insurance policies with the agent's company. If the widow mentions that she hadn't been aware of the policy, the con man glibly explains that her husband "didn't want you to know about it." He then makes an appointment to come to the widow's house to pay off, say, a $5,000 policy.

But, of course, there is a catch—which is that the policy lapsed just before her husband's death. At this point the agent becomes a good guy: he will make sure the policy is paid in full if the widow will pay the final premiums owed, perhaps $30 to $40, and that's the end of the $30 to $40—not to mention the $5,000 payoff.

Warning: If anything like this happens to anyone you know, urge the widow to check the story by phoning the home office of the company the agent claims to represent.

(2) Racketeers are spreading into the preburial insurance field I described above—in which honest operators collect funds for future funerals and deposit the collections in state-supervised trust funds. The crooks, though, don't bother with this vital formality—with the result that innocent investors often put up large sums for skimpy funeral packages which provide none of the services they expected.

Warning: Check thoroughly who administers the funds. What bank? Trust fund? Who? Be sure the cemetery is a member of the American Cemetery Association in Columbus, O., or the National Association of Cemeteries in Washington.

(3) In addition to C.O.D. Bibles and non-existent debts, unscrupulous obit-watchers send survivors many other items of C.O.D. merchandise and try to high-pressure widows into signing up for exorbitantly priced packages of lonely hearts activities.

Warning: Investigate every claim. *Take your time* acknowledging, much less paying. *Sign up for nothing* until you have recovered your balance.

(4) Finally, if you are the widow of a veteran, watch out for official-looking, direct mail burial advertising implying affiliation with the Veterans Administration. The VA does not go in for such advertising—and all too frequently it adds up to a big non-bargain rather than a low-cost burial package. Families of many veterans know only that they have some type of burial benefit; they do not know the details.

Warning: Do not accept notices of "free" benefits as being part of the government program—just because the notices are designed to resemble government correspondence. Check out the details.

Part III

MANAGING YOUR MONEY

19

PLANNING FOR YOUR FINANCIAL AND PERSONAL SECURITY

THE AGE OF THE ELDERLY

In the era now under way, the cult of youth which has so dominated our society for so long is bound to pass, and "family planning" will focus not on children and babies but on planning for our elderly population—how to accommodate them, support them, limit the numbers of dependent elderly, maximize the potential of the non-dependents.

This is just one of the probable consequences of the drastic declines in the U.S. birth rate. In 1973, for instance, our crude birth rate dropped to fewer than 16 per 1,000 population, lowest in U.S. history. Our fertility rate was down to 2.03 children per family, for the first time actually below the Zero Population Growth level of 2.1 children.

What's more, the trend is continuing. Young couples, more and more, are reporting intentions to have smaller families or no children at all. Easier abortion laws, later marriages, increased numbers of divorces, the tendency for more women to remain single—all are factors in the startling change.

The most obvious economic impact of ZPG will be on our marketing system for goods and services, for it will have to be geared to a stable rather than a soaring population. Other obvious economic implications are relief in pressures on our environment, a considerable easing of housing shortages, cutbacks in businesses catering to babies—ranging from obstetrics to diaper services, baby foods, and nursery schools. But far, far more fascinating are the implications for our elderly people. Among the specific forecasts of a major study by the Center for the Study of Democratic Institutions in Santa Barbara, Calif., co-authored by political scientist Harvey Wheeler and lawyer R. J. Carlson, are:

- A radical shift in emphasis from chronological age to "functional" age—not how old you are in years but how old you act and feel. Alongside this development will be not only tremendous new job opportunities for the elderly but actually a new dependency on the elderly to perform a wide variety of public services. In the words of the authors: "The quality of public services will deteriorate if the talents of the elderly are not utilized."

• The formation of a new class of second-class citizens—the infirm "functionally elderly."

• New standards of beauty and morality which will be based on older rather than younger models (dizzying thought: wrinkles in fashion?).

• A complete overhaul of the present exclusive youth orientation of our educational system—with the big expansion in school enrollment in the future taking place in the thirty-and-over age bracket. In fact, says the report, a new educational boom will develop in high schools and at the post-high school level. "Colleges and universities will have to be redesigned with needs of the elderly uppermost in mind."

• "A new kind of revolutionary movement,"—pressing for older Americans' rights in all spheres of life and led by the over-fifty because of their vast numbers and importance in our society.

These are just a few of the implications. I can think of dozens more: fundamental changes in both our public and private pension systems, a growing gap between young workers paying even higher Social Security taxes and the elderly retired living on Social Security taxes and the elderly retired living on Social Security benefits, an enormous expansion in government medical care programs, a surge of population to warm-weather areas, and many more. So can you think of implications, I'm sure.

But the central point is that virtually everybody, including *you,* will be elderly one day. And then you will be forever glad that you planned now for your future financial and personal security.

THE REALITIES OF RETIREMENT

Let's say you are among that infinitesimal minority of Americans able to save enough of your current income and to invest it wisely enough so that in your retirement years you'll have—along with your projected Social Security benefits—a retirement income totaling about the same as your actual earnings now.

Even if you're sufficiently informed, affluent, and thrifty to achieve this—which you almost surely are not—what you will have at your retirement will be about *half* what other Americans are then earning. With an income geared to today's living costs and living standards, you will be way, way down the scale in comparison to incomes geared to tomorrow's living costs and living standards.

There are few real-life counterparts of the contented older couples you see pictured in newspaper and magazine ads and TV commercials—basking in the sun, indulging in leisure activities, comfortably and independently enjoying family and friends; and all this paid for by their Social Security benefits, company pension benefits, the incomes they are getting on private investments they wisely made in earlier years.

For millions, the retirement dream is in reality an economic nightmare. For millions, growing old today means growing poor, being sick, living in substandard housing, and having to scrimp merely to subsist. And this is the prospect not only for the one out of every ten Americans now over sixty-five (a number and proportion increasing faster than the population as a whole) but also for the 65 million who will reach retirement age within the next thirty-three years.

Consider these facts:

• Millions of the elderly today are forced to depend solely on their Social Security benefit checks, which alone are not adequate to provide a decent standard of living. Their employers provided no pensions and their earnings were too low to permit them to save during their working lifetime.

• Even if you add the average private pension monthly benefit in the mid-seventies of $150 to the average Social Security benefit check of about $310 for a couple, the total annual income comes to only about $5,500.

• A majority of us have no pension coverage at all, and for many who are covered by private pension funds, the expected pension will turn out to be a mirage. In fact, accuse consumer advocate Ralph Nader and co-author Kate Blackwell in *You and Your Pension*, "in terms of dollar impact, the private pension system represents one of the most comprehensive consumer frauds that many Americans will encounter in their lifetime."

• As a result, one in four of the elderly lives in poverty. Poverty is, in fact, increasing among those over sixty-five and at a far more rapid rate than for those under sixty-five.

• For elderly blacks and other minority groups, the poverty ratio is one out of two, and that ratio also holds for the very elderly in general—those in the seventy-five-and-over group.

• The median income of families headed by a person sixty-five or over is *less than half* that of families headed by a younger person.

• Inflation hits older people the hardest because it erodes the value of a lifetime of retirement savings and reduces the buying power of fixed-income pension and other benefits—particularly in the areas of such necessities as home maintenance, insurance, taxes, public transportation, and medical care.

• The elderly are sicker than any other segment of our population. Two out of three Americans over sixty-five suffer from some chronic or degenerative condition—arthritis, diabetes, high blood pressure, stroke, diseases of the heart and arteries, cancer, etc. Yet as the mid-1970s approached, Medicare covered less than half of total health costs.

• When the elderly are healthy enough and willing to work in order to be self-supporting, they are hampered by the restrictions of Social Security and are denied employment opportunities. In our youth-oriented world, workers in their fifties and even in their forties face job discrimination, in spite of the federal Age Discrimination in Employment Act. (See Chapter 27, "Your Other Basic Rights," for more details on this act—and ways in which you can fight job discrimination because of age.)

PLANNING FOR YOUR RETIREMENT

How can you protect yourself against such problems? A large part of the answer lies in one four-letter word: PLAN!

If you are in your twenties or thirties, retirement may seem too far off to worry about. It's tough enough to cope with the problems of everyday living. You also may feel that any money worries you may now have will somehow disappear by the time you reach retirement age. Or you may simply put off even thinking about retirement for year after year until it finally is directly ahead of you.

But the cold fact is that retirement planning is as important to you, the younger worker, as it is to the worker now reaching retirement age. For one thing, the earlier you start planning, the less it will cost you to amass the capital and income you'll need in your retirement years. Consider, for example, the lower cost of life insurance when you are younger, or the greater flexibility you have in saving and investing your nest egg.

What's more, today's younger American will need more financial resources than a person who is retired today. You well may spend as many as twenty to twenty-five years in retirement, almost twice today's retirement span.

Even today, a man retiring at age sixty-five can look forward to a life expectancy of another thirteen years, and his slightly younger wife can expect to live an average of nearly twenty more years (see Chapter 11, "Your Job, Career, or Business"). So the sooner *you* start, the better the chance you will have of laying the groundwork for the comfortable, independent life you'll want in your retirement years.

Just how do you start planning? Begin by asking yourself two questions:

"Do I want to retire at sixty-five or sooner?"

"How much income and reserves will I need to live comfortably at that age?"

Before you can answer these two questions, you'll have to ask yourself just what kind of retirement life you want to lead, just what your future needs and wants will be.

How Much Will You Need?

How will your total estimated income fit your actual financial needs during a retirement period which easily could stretch up to twenty years or more? The answer must rest to a large extent on your family's style of living, on the things and non-things you are accustomed to and would like to continue to have. But here are some guidelines for figuring your future retirement needs, so you can later calculate how big the gap is between your projected income and your actual future needs.

Some of your expenses will be higher.

For instance, your costs for medicine, both prescription and non-prescription, will be an average two and a half times higher than they are for younger Americans. With more leisure time, you may want to increase your spending on travel, dining out, entertainment, and hobbies.

On the other hand, many of the things that now figure in your budget will either cost less or cease to be at all important to you. By the time you retire the chances are that your home mortgage will have been paid off or, if you move to a smaller place, your over-all housing expenses will be lower than they are now.

If you retire in a warm climate, your clothing needs also will be less, and your heating costs next to nothing.

When you reach age sixty-five, you will qualify for Medicare benefits, which could slash your costs for hospital and doctor bills. And these benefits are, of course, in addition to Social Security benefits.

By the time you retire, too, your life insurance policy may be paid up or, if it is not, you may find that you need less protection than you are carrying, which means a lower monthly premium cost or perhaps none.

The high cost of raising and educating your children will be behind you. And your food costs will be lower, simply because the calorie needs of older people are less than those of younger people.

You also will be eligible, in retirement, for important moneysaving tax breaks. Under the tax laws of the mid-seventies, you could claim, if you are sixty-five or older by the end of the tax year, an extra exemption plus a second exemption for your wife if she is sixty-five and files a joint return with you.

If you are sixty-five or over or are retired, you could get a retirement income credit which could cut your tax directly by a credit of up to 15 per cent of your retirement income.

If you are sixty-five or older before you sell at a profit a home in which you have lived for five of the previous eight years, you might be able to eliminate all tax on the gain, if the sale price is $20,000 or under. If the price is more than $20,000, you might be able to avoid tax on part of the gain.

If you are in this age category, you well may get significant breaks on your property taxes.

Above and beyond tax breaks on your federal income tax, most states offer some type of exemption, special deduction, or reduction for retirees. To find out the rules, check with your state tax department.

Finally, many of the expenses formerly associated with your job, ranging from eating in restaurants to commuting costs, will be sharply reduced.

The basic point remains, though: the actual dollar amount of your financial needs in retirement will depend on your expected standard of living —in housing, dining, clothes, transportation, vacationing, giving. It also will depend on the level of property and state income taxes in the area in which you decide to settle.

It also will be crucially affected—and in an adverse way to you—by the degree of inflation in our nation in coming years.

You cannot ignore this inflation factor if you are to avoid the financial panic of discovering too late how drastically you have underestimated your future needs!

PRECAUTIONS IN CALCULATING YOUR NEEDS

Obviously, no matter what your style of living, you must be coldly realistic in estimating your own needs.

• You must aim to have an emergency savings fund always on hand to take care of utterly unforeseeable emergencies (see Chapter 1, "Your Personal Money Manager").

• You must have extra health insurance to supplement Medicare.

• And you must have some kind of "inflation cushion." If pay, inflation continues to chew away at the buying power of your retirement income at an annual rate of say, 5 per cent, and you expect to retire twenty years from now, you will *need 165 per cent* more than you need today. This means that what you can buy for $3,000 a year today, you would need $7,950 in twenty years. For what your $10,000 buys today, you would need $26,500 twenty years from now.

In the same vein, here are prices for selected goods and services in 1984 at different yearly rates of inflation.

| | | ESTIMATED PRICE IN 1984 AT VARIOUS | | | |
| | ASSUMED PRICE | YEARLY RATES OF PRICE RISE | | | |
ITEM	1974	4%	5%	6%	7%
Weekly food	$ 50.00	$ 74.01	$ 81.44	$ 89.54	$ 98.36
Milk, quart	.35	.52	.57	.63	.69
Steak, pound	1.80	2.66	2.93	3.22	3.54
Subway ride	.35	.52	.57	.63	.69
Lipstick	2.50	3.70	4.07	4.48	4.92
Taxi ride	1.50	2.22	2.44	2.69	2.95
Hospital room	100.00	148.02	162.89	179.08	196.72
Cigarettes	.50	.74	.81	.90	.98
Refrigerator	275.00	407.06	447.95	492.48	540.97
Man's suit	125.00	185.03	203.61	223.86	245.89

FIGURING YOUR MONTHLY EXPENSES

Now, taking into account your own life style and needs and allowing for inflation, figure your own monthly expenses now and after retirement on a work sheet that might look something like this:

Your Monthly Expenses

ITEM	WHERE MONEY GOES NOW	AFTER RETIREMENT
Food—including meals away from home	_____	_____
Clothing	_____	_____
Laundry, cleaning	_____	_____
Transportation	_____	_____
Car expense (including operating expenses and depreciation)	_____	_____
Auto insurance	_____	_____
Train or bus, other routine travel	_____	_____

ITEM	WHERE MONEY GOES NOW	AFTER RETIREMENT
Housing	_____	_____
Rent or mortgage	_____	_____
Homeowners insurance	_____	_____
Heat	_____	_____
Gas and electric	_____	_____
Telephone	_____	_____
Repairs, maintenance	_____	_____
Lawn and garden upkeep	_____	_____
Property taxes	_____	_____
Household help	_____	_____
Furniture and furnishings	_____	_____
Medical care (not covered by insurance)	_____	_____
Medicare payments for doctor bills	_____	_____
Other health insurance premiums	_____	_____
Medicines	_____	_____
Dental care	_____	_____
Life insurance and annuity premiums	_____	_____
Vacation and travel	_____	_____
Education expenses	_____	_____
Savings	_____	_____
Newspapers, magazines, books	_____	_____

ITEM	WHERE MONEY GOES NOW	AFTER RETIREMENT
Personal allowances (including grooming, haircuts)	_____	_____
Contributions and gifts	_____	_____
Entertainment (movies, theater, etc.)	_____	_____
Hobbies and sports, club dues	_____	_____
Miscellaneous	_____	_____
Total monthly expenses	_____	_____
Total annual expenses	_____	_____

As a rule of thumb, many retired couples find that they can live comfortably on roughly two thirds of their preretirement after-tax incomes. You, though, may be able to—or have to—live on less. Or you may want to live on more.

To determine where you stand, the next step is to calculate what your retirement income is likely to be.

How Much Will You Have?

ESTIMATING YOUR RETIREMENT INCOME

If you're typical, you'll retire and start to collect your Social Security benefit checks *before* you reach sixty-five; more than half of today's beneficiaries are now electing early retirement. Many company pension plans also are encouraging early retirement. And many workers in their early sixties —and even in their fifties and late forties—become unwilling candidates for early retirement when, after leaving or being laid off a previous job, they find it difficult to get a new one.

Whatever the case, before estimating your retirement income, you have to estimate the age at which you will decide to—or think you will for some reason be ready to—retire.

What comes next will involve some arithmetic and paperwork, but this should not be difficult. The task is to make a list of all the sources from which you can anticipate retirement income.

• You can learn what you can expect in the way of Social Security benefits—most likely, the cornerstone of your retirement income program—in the section that immediately follows, called "What You Should Know About Social Security."

• Add to your expected Social Security benefits the amount of monthly income you can expect from your life insurance policies; annuities; and your company, union, or other pension program. These also are described in the sections that follow.

• Check such other key retirement income sources as cash savings, stocks, bonds, real estate. They are discussed in detail in various other chapters.

• Conservatively estimate the income you might get if you sold valuable assets you now own—art, stamp collections, your home, etc.—and reinvested the proceeds in various ways.

• Also very conservatively estimate what income you might get from a part-time job or business you are looking forward to having in retirement.

Just listing all these sources of income on the worksheet that follows will give you an idea of your expected total income. And that, along with what you have already estimated will be your future living needs, will give you a guide to how much more retirement income you should now be building to provide you with a comfortable standard of living later on.

Your Estimated Income

	MONTHLY	ANNUALLY
Social Security benefits (you and your spouse)		
Private pension		
Veteran's pension (if any)		
Any other military, civil service, or railroad retirement benefits		
Deferred profit sharing		
Income from annuities		
Income from investment of life insurance cash value		
Dividends from investments		
Interest from savings accounts		
Interest from bonds		

	MONTHLY	ANNUALLY
Capital gains from investments		
Income from property (e.g., rent)		
Payments on mortgages you hold		
Investment of capital from home sale		
Earnings from part-time job or self-employment		
Income from a business		
Other income from *any* source		
TOTAL		

GETTING THE RETIREMENT INCOME YOU NEED

Whether the estimated retirement income you arrive at will be adequate will depend, of course, on your needs. If it is not adequate, several options are open to you.

One is obviously to reduce your needs, decide what things in your original retirement plan you can manage to do without. Another is to beef up your income. Assuming you choose the second option, there are three stages in planning to get the retirement income you need.

(1) Accumulate as many resources as possible during your preretirement years. You can help bring this about, perhaps by stinting on some living expenses in this period in order to put more money in savings accounts or to invest in mutual funds or growth stocks or high-grade bonds or any of the other mediums analyzed at length in Chapter 20, on investing.

(2) Use part of your current income and the nest egg you have accumulated to buy an income for your retirement years. This income could come from life insurance, an annuity or pension program, dividends, interest, or income-producing real estate.

(3) Plan on periodically withdrawing a portion of the capital in your nest egg during your retirement.

HOW LONG WILL YOUR RETIREMENT CAPITAL LAST?

How long will your nest egg last? That will depend on the rate of return it is earning and the amount you withdraw each year. Conceivably, your fund could last indefinitely, as the following chart* indicates.

* Copyright 1971 by Medical Economics Company, Oradell, N.J. 07649. Reprinted by permission.

If you retire with a nest egg of $100,000, you can make it last for one decade, two, three, or even longer. Just how long will be determined by the rate of return on your capital and the amount you withdraw for living expenses each year. Suppose, for example, you need $9,000 a year and your fund is earning a 7 per cent return; then your money will last twenty-two years. If your return equals or exceeds your withdrawals, your fund will last indefinitely, as indicated by the symbol ∞. (Always keep in mind that the dollars will buy less in the marketplace than they are buying as you read this.)

ANNUAL WITHDRAWAL	YEARS YOUR FUND WILL LAST AT THESE ANNUAL RATES OF RETURN*					
	5%	6%	7%	8%	9%	10%
$6,000	36	∞	∞	∞	∞	∞
7,000	25	33	∞	∞	∞	∞
8,000	20	23	30	∞	∞	∞
9,000	16	18	22	28	∞	∞
10,000	14	15	17	20	26	∞
11,000	12	13	14	16	19	25
12,000	11	11	12	14	15	18

* Copyright 1971 by Medical Economics Company, Oradell, N.J. 07649. Reprinted by permission.

Of course, if your nest egg amounts to just $50,000, you simply cut the annual withdrawal amounts in half and your money will last the same number of years shown in the chart.

What You Should Know About Social Security

FOUNDATION OF YOUR RETIREMENT PROGRAM

About nine out of ten of all working Americans are now covered under Social Security.

By itself Social Security today is not sufficient to support any retired American in dignity and comfort.

At last, however, Social Security is taking on the shape of a real public pension program—providing an ever broader base of retirement income on which you can build from your own activities and investments and thereby create adequate funds to support you in dignity and decency during your older years.

What's more, Social Security is much more than a retirement program and a source of Medicare benefits. If you die, the program also provides for your survivors. And it takes care of you and your family if you become disabled, even before you reach sixty-five.

Social Security always has been a highly complicated and confusing subject. But in recent years the Social Security law has so vastly expanded the list of benefits and beneficiaries that many newly eligible beneficiaries aren't even aware that they qualify, and many prospective beneficiaries don't know what they may qualify for or when. Thus, many Americans are losing out on benefits they desperately need.

WHO IS ELIGIBLE FOR SOCIAL SECURITY?

You qualify if you work or have worked a required length of time at any job which is covered by the Social Security law—and that now includes most jobs. You also may qualify if you're self-employed. Railroad workers are, in effect, jointly covered by Social Security and their own separate retirement system. Most federal civilian employees, those who are covered by the civil service retirement program or other staff retirement systems, are not covered by Social Security, although they may be protected under Social Security as dependents of other workers. Other occupations (such as farm labor, domestic employment, and state and local government employment), and some types of earnings (such as tips and wages in kind) may be affected by special provisions of the law.

If you're not sure you qualify, inquire at your local Social Security office.

YOUR WORK CREDITS

To qualify for benefits, you also must build up a certain number of work credits. If you are a non-farm worker, you get credit for a "quarter of coverage"—for each calendar quarter in which you are paid $50 or more in covered wages. If you are a farm worker, you get one quarter of coverage for each $100 of covered wages you receive in a year up to a maximum of four quarters for the year.

If you're self-employed, you need net earnings from self-employment of only $400 for a whole year to get credit for all four quarters. Military service during the World War II and postwar periods may give you additional wage credits for each month of active duty.

Note: If you served in the armed forces during 1957–67 or are a survivor of someone who did, and are now getting monthly Social Security benefit checks, contact your Social Security office. You may under amendments passed in recent years, be eligible for a higher monthly benefit.

In order for your widow and children to be eligible for survivor benefits, you must have at least one and a half years of work credits within three years before your death, unless you are fully insured on the basis of earlier work.

To be fully insured so that you and your family are entitled to retirement and all other benefits, you must, depending on your age, have anywhere from one and a half to ten years of work credits, as indicated in the following tables:

FOR WORKERS BORN BEFORE 1929

If you were born before 1929, reach 62, become disabled, or die in	You will need credit for this much work to be fully insured
1973	5½ years (for women)*
1975	6
1977	6½
1979	7
1981	7½
1983	8
1987	9
1991 or later	10

* Men who reached age 62 in 1973 or 1974 need six years of credit.

FOR WORKERS BORN AFTER 1928

If you die when you are	You will be fully insured with credit for this much work
28 or younger	1½ years
30	2
32	2½
34	3
36	3½
38	4
40	4½
42	5
46	6
50	7
54	8
58	9
62 or older	10

Note: A person is fully insured if he has credit for a quarter year of work for each year after 1950 or, if later, the year in which he reached age twenty-one up to the year he reaches retirement age, becomes disabled, or dies—whichever event occurs earlier.

To be eligible for disability benefits when you are thirty-one or older, you must be fully insured and must have credit for five years of work in the ten-year period ending with the time you become disabled. If you become disabled between the ages of twenty-four and thirty-one, you need credit for only one half the time between age twenty-one and the time you become unable to work. If disability starts before age twenty-four, you need credit for one and a half years of work in the three-year period before you became disabled.

You should know, too, that you do not automatically receive Social Security benefits as soon as you retire, become disabled, or a working member of your family dies or becomes disabled.

You must apply for these benefits at the nearest Social Security office. For retirement benefits, apply a few months before you expect to retire. A long delay in applying for benefits might cause you to lose some.

HOW MUCH YOU WILL PAY IN

The work credits you accumulate determine only the particular *type* of benefits for which you qualify, not the amount. The amount depends on your average monthly wage during the years that have elapsed between 1955 and when you reach age sixty-two.

The amount of Social Security tax you pay is based on two things: the current tax rate applied to your wages (matched by your employer) and the current "wage base"—the maximum dollar amount of your wages which may be taxed.

Back in 1950, the employee Social Security tax was 1.5 per cent on the first $3,000 of earnings, or a maximum of $45 a year—a sum matched by the employer. Over the years, this tax has gradually risen to the point where a worker in 1976 paid 5.85 per cent on all his wages up to $15,300 or a maximum of $895.05, with the employer contributing the same percentage. For the self-employed, for whom there is, of course, no matching contribution, the tax in 1976 was 7.9 per cent on everything earned up to $15,300 or a maximum of $1,208.70.

In the years to come, both the tax rate and/or the amount of wages subject to tax are scheduled by law to continue to rise.

As of the mid-1970s, unless Congress changes the rules, the taxable "wage base"—the maximum amount of your wages to which the Social Security tax may be applied—may, by law, be automatically increased to keep up with increases in our taxable wages and to help finance benefit hikes to blunt the effect of our climbing cost of living. Such an increase can be made only when there is an automatic rise in Social Security benefits which also are legally tied to increases in our living costs.

Even if the wage base were to be raised only gradually over the years, your Social Security tax would be based on a maximum wage of more than $30,000 by the next decade, more than $50,000 by the 1990s, etc. It will go up much, much faster than that—spectacularly so.

Similarly, as of 1974, the Social Security tax was legally scheduled to go to 6.05 per cent each on employee and employer (8.10 per cent on the self-employed) in 1978, then climb to 6.30 per cent in 1981, and so on, reaching a maximum of 7.45 per cent in 2011. The tax bite in dollars will get heavier and heavier—and heavier.

HOW MUCH YOU WILL GET AS A RETIREE OR DEPENDENT

Spectacular as these taxes you will pay may seem, you, a young worker, also can look forward to getting (eventually) retirement benefits worth considerably more than the total you will pay into Social Security.

• A man retiring at age sixty-five in 1974 after paying at the top level through his working years, received a monthly pension of $305. But a thirty-five-year-old retiring at sixty-five in the year 2003 can now count on a maximum pension of $1,479 a month, as the table below indicates. And since benefits are now tied to increases in the cost of living, tracked by the Consumer Price Index from year to year, pensions could be much higher. The cost of living boosts also apply to those already retired.

And how will benefits grow in the years between now and 2011?

If you assume that our living costs will rise at the rate of 3 per cent a year (unrealistically conservative) and that national average taxable wages (and the wage base as well) will rise at 5 per cent a year from now on (also unrealistically conservative), here are some projections:

Year	Maximum Monthly Benefit for Worker Retiring at Age 65	Maximum for Retired Worker and Dependent Spouse (if wife is 65)
1980	465	697
1981	487	731
1982	512	768
1983	537	806
1984	564	846
1985	591	887
1986	620	930
1987	650	975
1988	682	1,023
1989	713	1,070
1990	748	1,122
1991	783	1,175
1992	822	1,233
1993	860	1,290
1994	901	1,352

Year	Maximum Monthly Benefit for Worker Retiring at Age 65	Maximum for Retired Worker and Dependent Spouse (if wife is 65)
1995	953	1,430
1996	1,007	1,511
1997	1,064	1,597
1998	1,125	1,688
1999	1,189	1,734
2000	1,256	1,885
2001	1,327	1,991
2002	1,400	2,101
2003	1,479	2,219
2004	1,560	2,340
2005	1,645	2,467
2006	1,734	2,602
2007	1,829	2,744
2008	1,930	2,895
2009	2,034	3,051
2010	2,141	3,211
2011	2,254	3,381
2012	2,374	3,561
2013	2,499	3,748
2014	2,631	3,947
2015	2,769	4,153
2016	2,913	4,370
2017	3,068	4,602
2018	3,228	4,843
2019	3,396	5,095
2020	4,612	5,363

• Your wife can get a pension check equal to 50 per cent of yours if she is sixty-five, or somewhat lower benefits as early as age sixty-two. (If the wife, because of her own earnings, is entitled to more than 50 per cent of her husband's benefit, she gets the bigger benefit.)

• Your wife also can collect that extra 50 per cent if she is younger, if she has in her care dependent children under eighteen (or over eighteen but disabled before age twenty-two).

• Each unmarried child under eighteen (or over eighteen, but disabled), or a full-time student aged eighteen to twenty-two, also is eligible for a benefit equal to 50 per cent of your full benefit. However, the maximum amount of benefits payable to a family for a man retiring at sixty-five in 1976 was $648.40 a month.

• If you retire at age sixty-two you can collect a pension check amounting to 80 per cent of your full benefit. At age sixty-three and sixty-four, these amounts will rise to 86⅔ and 93⅓ per cent, respectively.

• A divorced woman is entitled to benefits based on her former husband's earnings if the marriage lasted at least twenty years.

• As of 1974, a special minimum payment for certain low-paid retirees at age sixty-five who had thirty years or more of coverage was $180 a month, and with twenty-five years of coverage the special minimum was $135 a month.

• If you want to continue working after sixty-five, you can, under the law as it read in 1976, earn as much as $2,760 a year without having any benefits withheld; however, if you earn more than $2,760 your monthly benefit is reduced $1.00 for every $2.00 you earn. After you reach age seventy-two, you can earn as much as you want without penalty.

YOUR NON-RETIREMENT BENEFITS

In addition to these pension benefits, monthly allowances will go to your survivors in the event of your death. You and certain members of your family also can collect important benefits if you become disabled. Or, if your income is very limited, you may qualify for benefits under the supplemental security income program. To illustrate the survivors' benefits:

• A widow who was first entitled to benefits at age sixty-five can receive a pension equal to the one her deceased husband would be collecting if he were still alive. If a widow begins drawing benefits at age sixty, her allowance will start at 71.5 per cent and then range upward each year. Widows may not start collecting benefits until they are sixty—unless they are disabled and aged fifty to fifty-nine or have dependent children.

And to illustrate the disability and survivor's benefits:

• If a widow is under sixty-five, with a young or disabled child in her care, she can receive 75 per cent of her deceased husband's age sixty-five benefits. Each dependent child, if unmarried, under eighteen (or eighteen to twenty-two if they are full-time students), or disabled before age twenty-two, also may receive 75 per cent of the deceased husband's full benefit, up to the current family maximum allowance. For families in which the breadwinner earned relatively little, however, the total family allowance can be as low as $152.10.

• Benefits also may be paid to a surviving dependent parent or to a dependent husband aged sixty-two or over or dependent widower aged sixty or over, or a disabled dependent widow or widower aged fifty or over.

• If you yourself are disabled—that is, suffering from a condition, physical or mental, which is serious enough to prevent you from working for twelve months or more—you can collect a disability benefit while you are under age sixty-five. The payments would be equal to your age-sixty-five retirement benefits. Your wife and each of your young, dependent, unmarried children also could collect amounts equal to 50 per cent of your allowance, subject to a family maximum.

• Rehabilitation costs and services are available to disabled workers in the form of paid job training, counseling and placement, physical therapy, and money to buy work tools and equipment.

• If you are blind as defined by the law, you can qualify for disability benefits without having to meet the requirement of substantial recent work. Under Social Security regulations, a worker considered "industrially blind" —that is, with visual acuity of 20-200 or less in the better eye, with corrective lens—is considered totally blind. So is a person whose visual field is limited to 20°.

SUPPLEMENTAL SECURITY INCOME

The federal supplemental security income program (SSI) is designed for aged, blind, and disabled persons with very limited income and resources. It replaces the state-federal programs of Old Age Assistance, Aid to the Blind, and Aid to the Permanently and Totally Disabled. SSI is administered by the Social Security Administration but is financed from general revenues rather than from Social Security trust funds.

The program guarantees a standard, nationwide monthly income floor for eligible individuals. If your present income is below the levels set by the program and you are otherwise eligible you will get a monthly benefit raise to bring your total benefit up to at least these minimums. In some cases, this SSI payment is augmented by an extra state supplement. This extra sum is either paid separately by the state or included in the federal supplement check.

To qualify for SSI benefits, individual beneficiaries may have cash assets of up to $1,500 and, for couples, up to $2,250. You may own your home, household goods and other personal effects, and an automobile—so long as these are only of "reasonable value"—and still qualify. Your relatives' income and assets do *not* count as yours; your eligibility for SSI benefits is determined without regard for their assets. If, however, you are married to an ineligible spouse, his or her possessions *do* count as yours. If you think you—or a relative or friend—may be eligible, contact your nearest Social Security office.

THE BAFFLEGAB OF SOCIAL SECURITY

DISABILITY INSURANCE BENEFIT—Monthly benefit payable to a worker and his family if he has a severe physical or mental condition which prevents him from working and the condition is expected to last for at least twelve months. He also must have a certain required number of work credits.

LUMP-SUM DEATH BENEFIT—Benefit paid at the death of a worker covered under Social Security.

QUARTER OF COVERAGE—See Work Credits.

RETIREMENT BENEFITS—Monthly benefits payable to a man or woman at age sixty-two (reduced benefits) or age sixty-five (full benefits) who has stopped working or whose annual earnings are limited to $2,760 or less (as of 1976).

RETIREMENT TEST—Known also as the "annual earnings test" under the Social Security Act. This test is used to determine how much of a beneficiary's annual Social Security benefit will be paid. A beneficiary can earn $2,760 in a calendar year and collect all of his Social Security benefits for that year.

SOCIAL SECURITY CONTRIBUTIONS (TAXES)—Percentage of your earnings paid into the Social Security trust funds—matched by your employer. In 1976 the contribution rate was 5.85 per cent each for worker and employer on the first $15,300 of earnings during the year.

SOCIAL SECURITY TRUST FUNDS—The three funds into which Social Security contributions are paid: Old Age and Survivors Insurance Trust Fund, Disability Insurance Trust Fund, and Hospital Insurance Trust Fund. Social Security benefit costs are met out of these funds on a pay-as-you-go basis. The amounts kept in each fund are adjusted periodically by a special board of trustees.

SURVIVORS' INSURANCE BENEFITS—Monthly benefits are paid to your survivors in the event of your death if you have had the required number of work credits. Other survivors' benefits include lump sum death benefits.

WAGE BASE—Amount of a worker's annual earnings which is taxed for Social Security. The wage base for 1976 was $15,300.

WORK CREDITS—Also known as "quarters of coverage." To get monthly Social Security benefits a person must have worked under Social Security for a certain period of time. An employee earns credit for one quarter year of work if he is paid $50 during that calendar quarter. A self-employed person earns four quarters of coverage for any full year in which he earns at least $400 in self-employment income.

YOUR PRIVATE PENSION PLAN

If you have been in the private work force, your financial independence in retirement rests on three foundations: Social Security benefits, individual savings from all sources, and private pensions.

It well may be that your fringe benefits include a relatively generous retirement pension plan promising to provide you and your spouse with a decent living standard—when added to your expected Social Security benefits, private savings, and insurance.

It also is probable that at least part of your accumulated pension coverage is "vested" if you go to another job after you reach a certain age and/or number of years of service in that plan.

And your pension plan well may offer some kind of monthly benefit if you become disabled before retirement age.

The probability also remains, though, that millions of you are either uninformed or misinformed about your pension rights and coverage. Many of you are drifting along under the dangerous illusion that your private pension will serve as the bulk of your retirement income—when, in reality, it won't.

Many know little or nothing about the vital new kinds of protection they are now getting as a result of the 1974 Employee Retirement Income Security Act.

OUR HUGE PRIVATE PENSION SYSTEM

Are you aware of how huge the private "pension industry" in the United States has become in recent years?

• Already set aside in pension funds in the mid-1970s was $180 billion and this total was slated to double by the early 1980s.

• About 25 to 30 million Americans—roughly 45 per cent of our private labor force—were covered by pension plans.

• Each year some $10 billion was being distributed to some 5½ million retirees and/or their surviving spouses in the form of pension benefits.

• Today virtually every major U.S. corporation, financial institution, and labor union is heavily involved in pension planning, funding, and investing.

Great? Yes, but . . .

Many pension plans do *not* provide survivors' benefits for dependent widows or widowers—or they provide only very limited benefits.

Hundreds of thousands of businesses change owners every year and, in cases where there is a pension plan, the plan is likely to be terminated. Many workers in businesses which fail never get pension benefits, and hundreds of thousands of businesses, large as well as small, fail in the United States each year.

What's more, typically, pension plans give the biggest benefits and broadest coverage to top-paid executives; almost none offer protection against inflation after retirement; most bar part-time workers, temporary workers, those at the bottom of the pay scale. Yet the central point is that pensions are not viewed as "gifts" from employers. They have become part of a worker's basic pay package, a form of deferred wage which millions consider their due.

THE 1974 PENSION REFORM LAW

Under the 1974 pension reform law, pension plan administrators must make available to you, the participants, a special summary of the plan—and also a special supplement explaining the plan in "easy-to-understand" language, including the conditions under which a participant will *not* be eligible to receive benefits.

In plain English, you *must* be told such vital points as:

Is *all* your compensation counted toward figuring your benefits?

When will benefit payments begin and how will they be paid?

Does the time you worked for other employers count toward the term of service?

How much does your employer contribute to the plan?

How are your employer's contributions figured? A fixed rate per hour? Or week? Or month you work? A lump monthly sum? Other?

If you, the employee, contribute toward your pension benefits, is this contribution mandatory or voluntary?

What happens to *your* contribution if you quit—or die—before retirement age?

What will happen to your benefits if your company is merged or company contributions are suspended or terminated?

Under the law's provisions, each year your employer must file up-to-date, detailed financial data and a complete plan description with the Labor Department. At your request, he must furnish you with this same information.

In addition, each year you may request a statement indicating the total benefits you personally have accrued and your nonforfeitable ("vested") benefit rights that have accrued.

Furthermore, if you should quit or otherwise leave your job with a vested right, your employer must tell you how much and what nature of benefits are due you. The same information is sent to the Social Security Administration which will remind you (or your survivors) of any benefits to which you're entitled when you apply for Social Security benefits.

NOW GIVE YOUR PENSION A CHECKUP!

The 1974 pension reform law, finally, gave you solid assurance that you will actually get the benefits you think you will get, and eliminated a lot of the fine print which prevents so many from collecting their benefits.

But it will be years before this law is fully in effect and until then many pension benefits will remain needlessly uncollected simply because an employee fails to meet some condition for being awarded benefits.

You *must not* overlook a crucial detail because of ignorance or apathy! Here, therefore, to help you avoid making disastrous errors are key questions to ask about your own pension based on a list put together by Kate Blackwell and Ralph Nader, co-authors of *You and Your Pension*.

Your Eligibility:

How many years must you work for your employer before you qualify for a pension? How old must you be to collect benefits? How is a "break in service" defined? Could a layoff eliminate your chances of receiving a benefit? What total of years of "credited service" must you have? Must these years be continuous or may they be broken by a leave or layoff?

Must you be a member of a union or union local at retirement to get the benefits you've earned?

What must you do to collect your benefit rights if you quit your job before retirement age?

What must you do before you retire to apply?

Your Vesting Rights:

What are the conditions for establishing a "claim" to your pension rights in the event you quit, or change employers, or are the victim of an extended layoff, or are fired?

Do your benefits "vest" only after you've worked a certain number of years or reach a certain age, or what?

Under the 1974 law, employers will be able to choose between these minimum vesting standards: (1) full vesting after ten years of employment, or (2) vesting of 25 per cent of accrued benefits after five years, with an increase each year until full vesting occurs after fifteen years on the job, or, (3) the "rule of 45"—providing 50 per cent vesting after an employee's age and years of service total forty-five, and increasing vesting by 10 per cent a year until 100 per cent vesting has occurred. In any case, if you have ten years of service, you are vested in at least 50 per cent of your benefit.

Your Benefits:

What benefits does your plan promise you if you work until official retirement age? Quit? Get laid off or fired tomorrow?

What's the status of your pension now?

How is your benefit figured? Is it a fixed amount? Based on the number of years you've worked? Or based on your salary? Or both?

Will the years you worked before the plan was started count if the benefit is based on the years you've worked?

How many employees in your company or division or plant are slated to get pensions?

What are typical amounts for workers like you? Do lower-paid workers get a fair share of the benefits?

Does the plan have any provision to hike postretirement benefits along with living cost increases?

What benefits, if any, will you get if you retire early or if you become disabled?

Survivors' Benefits:

If you die before normal retirement age, will your spouse get any benefits?

Is the benefit in the form of a "survivors' option"—under which you may elect, while you're still working, to accept a reduced pension benefit in exchange for a guarantee that your spouse will continue to receive some proportion of your benefit if you die?

Under what circumstances does this option go into effect if you die before—or after—you retire?

How much of a pension cut must you agree to take if you elect the survivors' option? And if you die after you retire, how much will your survivors' monthly benefit be? For how many years?

Is there a cutoff point for your widow to receive benefits—e.g., for only X number of years, or only until she starts getting Social Security benefits?

Under the law's provisions, a plan *must* provide for a joint and survivor option. The survivor benefit must not be less than 50 per cent of the benefit payable to the retiree. The joint and survivor provision applies *unless* the employee elects not to participate.

Also under the law, pensions are insured by the Pension Benefit Guarantee Corporation. This insurance protects survivors—as well as the pensioners themselves—against total loss of their benefits should their plan collapse for any reason. If this happens the corporation will pay up to $750 in monthly retirement benefits.

PENSIONS FOR THE SELF-EMPLOYED: THE KEOGH PLAN

If you are a self-employed person or professional, by all means consider whether you should set up a retirement plan for yourself under the Keogh Act of 1962, as amended in 1974. It may have dramatic tax advantages for you.

In essence, as of the mid-seventies, an approved self-employed retirement plan would allow you, a self-employed person, to set aside and deduct on your income tax return up to the lesser of 15 per cent of your earned income or $7,500 each year. The amounts you set aside earn income tax-free until they are distributed to you on your retirement. You can invest this money in various ways—including mutual funds, plans offered by banks, insurance companies, etc. You pay tax on these amounts and on the income that until then they have earned tax-free only when you begin to collect the funds on retirement.

With such a program, you, the self-employed individual, can build up a fund for your retirement at a faster pace and at a smaller tax cost than you could without the tax deduction for your contributions and the tax exemption of the income of your fund. Here are some basics on how such a plan can work.

Q. *Who can have a self-employed plan?*

A. Generally, anyone who is a self-employed individual and who has earned income. You may have a plan whether you conduct your business or profession as a sole proprietorship or as a partnership and whether or not you have any other employees. Your plan must be set up by you, the individual who owns the business, or by the partnership, if you are a partner. An individual partner cannot set up a Keogh plan for himself.

Q. *Is there any age limit?*

A. Not on setting up a plan.

Q. *How much can be put into a plan each year?*

A. Up to 15 per cent of the self-employed person's earnings or $7,500, whichever is less. In any event, the self-employed individual may contribute each year an amount equal to his or her earnings up to $750. There is no over-all lifetime limit.

Q. *How do you set up a plan?*

A. For most of you, the simple, practical thing to do is to tie in with an already existing plan offered by a bank, mutual fund, savings institution, etc., you have selected for long-term investment. In the mid-seventies, more than 200 mutual funds alone were offering such Keogh programs and there were well over 150,000 mutual fund Keogh plans in force, covering more than 200,000 individuals. What's more, the prospect was for a period of spectacular growth in the plans by all the major plan administrators because of the increase in the maximum limits on investment.

Q. *What if you want to set up a plan of your own?*

A. You must go through the same cumbersome, difficult steps needed to set up a regular employee benefit plan and furnish all the information required by the Treasury. It's far, far easier to tie in with an approved master or prototype plan.

Q. *When should you set up a plan?*

A. If you're seeking the full tax reduction now and want to start to build tax-free earnings on your contribution as soon as possible, begin at once.

Q. *When can retirement benefits be paid out?*

A. Most self-employed persons cannot draw benefits before age fifty-nine and a half without incurring a penalty. Benefits *must* be distributed starting with the year in which the self-employed person reaches seventy and a half.

Q. *What are some pros and cons?*

A. If you are a successful self-employed person, the odds are you'll find a Keogh plan an excellent idea.

If this program intrigues you, talk it over with your lawyer and accountant to make sure all the angles are covered. If they agree, the Keogh plan could be a real tax shelter for you.

PENSIONS FOR THOSE NOT COVERED BY ANY OTHER PLAN

Finally, in the 1974 law, Congress gave some real tax breaks to the millions of us who have been completely left out of the private pension system—if we use our own money to create our own retirement plans.

There are as many as 35 million of us with no pension coverage at all who can start to set up our own retirement plans—whether we are employed or self-employed, in a low-, middle-, or high-income bracket, in a trade, business, or profession. To be specific, under the law you can:

contribute up to 15 per cent of your wages and earnings each year to your own retirement plan—but no more than $1,500 a year;

accumulate your annual contributions until your retirement—through a bank endowment policy, etc.;

earn *tax free* all interest and dividends during your years of accumulation;

receive your pension payments after age 59½, but no later than age seventy, in annual installments taxed as ordinary income to you each year.

KEY: GREAT TAX BREAKS

The key to this whole deal for us lies in the tax breaks which let our savings grow much more and much faster.

For instance, say you begin in 1975 to contribute $1,500 each year under a tax-sheltered retirement plan and say your investment accumulates 5 per cent interest a year tax free. Here is the *lifetime* pension you would get at age sixty-five if you began your retirement plan at the following ages:

If you began your plan at age forty, your annual pension starting at age sixty-five would be $7,500.

If you began at age forty-five, your annual pension at age 65 would be $4,800.

If you began at fifty, your annual pension would be $3,400.

If you began at fifty-five, it would be $2,000.

And even if you began as late as age sixty, you would build up a lifetime pension starting at sixty-five of $900 a year.

This law could set off an explosive expansion in tax-deductible retirement plans.

The Bafflegab of Pensions

BENEFIT FORMULA—Formula which your employer uses to determine what size your pension actually will be.

DEATH BENEFITS—Payments, usually in a lump sum or a short series of payments, made to the surviving spouse of a worker in the event of his or her death. Sometimes, payments are made to the surviving spouse of a worker already retired.

DISABILITY BENEFITS—Pension paid to a worker who becomes disabled and is forced to retire but before normal retirement age.

DISCLOSURE RULES—Federal regulations requiring full and clear explanation to the employees covered by a pension plan of provisions which might affect them. Disclosure rules also inform would-be beneficiaries of the plan's financial condition.

EARLY RETIREMENT BENEFITS (or actuarially reduced benefits)—Reduced pension which some employees may get upon early retirement.

FIDUCIARY RESPONSIBILITY—Obligation of the trustees of a pension plan to act strictly for the benefit of the employees under the plan, and to be accountable to their "clients"—the funds' beneficiaries.

FINAL PAY PENSION FORMULA—Type of benefit formula which computes the amount of your pension as a portion of your average pay during the last few years before retirement, rather than your average pay over your entire term of service.

FUNDING—Setting aside pension money in advance of actually paying it to retirees. A pension fund is fully funded when it has enough money in the till to meet *all* expected future obligations to employees. A pension is *underfunded* when reserves are insufficient to meet anticipated demands without additional contributions. A pension plan is *unfunded* if benefits are paid directly from the company's operating budget as claims arise.

MULTI-EMPLOYER PENSION PLANS—Plans in which more than one employer pool pension contributions in a single fund which is run by union and employer representatives. Employees can transfer between the participating employers in a plan without losing pension credits.

NORMAL COSTS—Cost of providing for future pension benefits based on earnings and/or number of years worked from the time at which the pension plan is established. *Past service costs* are costs of providing for pension benefits based on service a worker has put in before the plan goes into affect.

PENSION—Regular income provided to a retired worker who has put in a certain number of years of service by retirement age, and in many cases to his (or her) survivor after he dies.

PENSION FUNDS—An insured pension fund is pension money paid to an insurance company, which guarantees a rate of return on the investment *and* payment of the benefits, providing the employer continues to make payments. A *non-insured pension fund* is pension money set aside in a fund with its own management (typically turned over to a bank trust department), which invests the money according to its own judgment and pays out the benefits as well.

PORTABILITY—Feature of a pension plan which permits a worker to "carry" whatever pension credits he has earned from one job to another or from one industry to another.

REINSURANCE—Pension benefit protection by a government agency called the Pension Benefit Guarantee Corporation—similar to today's federal insurance on your checking and savings accounts—against loss of expected benefits because of insufficient funds in your pension plan if it terminates.

SURVIVORS' BENEFITS—Payments made to the designated survivors of a deceased pensioned employee who has not waived the survivors' option. Survivors' benefits are usually lower than the pension benefits.

SURVIVORS' OPTION—Provision of a pension plan allowing an employee to designate a person (usually his or her spouse) to receive benefits if the worker dies. The survivors' option results in a lower pension to the retiree while he or she is alive.

VESTING—Giving an employee the right to claim the pension benefits he has earned during his period of employment—typically based on his number of years of service—even if he quits or is fired or laid off before his normal retirement age.

WHAT YOU SHOULD KNOW ABOUT LIFE INSURANCE

DO YOU NEED LIFE INSURANCE?

Make no mistake about it: the main purpose of life insurance—*and nothing does it better*—is to create an "instant estate" for your family in the event of your death.

It's not difficult to argue that you don't need any life insurance if:

you have no children or other dependent relatives;

your wife is working—or is perfectly capable of returning to work tomorrow, as she did before you were married;

you are in the maximum Social Security bracket providing substantial monthly benefits to your widow in the event of your death;

your company promises to provide you with a good-sized pension when you retire, with adequate benefits for your survivor when you die;

you have fairly comfortable savings or other assets;

you are in a position to put your money in other *safe* as well as high-yielding investments from which you can earn a far bigger return than the meager dividends which a life insurance policy accumulates over the years.

If you are such a person, you represent a distinct minority. And the fact remains that nine out of ten U.S. families and seven out of ten individuals in this country—both young and old—have life insurance today. The average insured American family in the mid-seventies had policies of one type or another giving the family about $27,000 of protection—or the equivalent of two years of take-home pay.

With what else but life insurance could you—on a relatively modest salary and little chance to save—provide the sizable estate that would enable your survivors to maintain some semblance of their accustomed standard of living, perhaps even assure your children of college educations?

Or, after the children are grown, give your wife a life income and help her pay off the mortgage on the family home?

Consider, too, these key advantages life insurance offers the survivors of the average policyholder:

• Unlike the returns from many other assets, death payments from life insurance, under almost all circumstances, are not subject to federal income taxes to the beneficiary.

• If you die, the processing of your estate may take months, even years before the proceeds can be distributed. The value of your life insurance, though, becomes available immediately to your beneficiaries upon your death.

• It does not cost you a cent, as it may in the case of a will, to change the beneficiary of your life insurance or to revise the terms under which the proceeds will be paid.

Life insurance has certain other attractive features—what insurance men call "living values"—although they should be regarded as secondary to the primary purpose of protection.

• One value, though not inherent in all types of insurance, is savings. There are more rewarding ways to save than via life insurance. But many families find that the only way they can be disciplined into saving any money at all is through regular forced payments of life insurance premiums.

• Increases in the cash value of your policy contributed from the insurance company's earnings are usually tax free—so long as you keep your policy in force.

• No matter how bad your credit rating, you are guaranteed the right to use the cash value of your policy as collateral for a relatively low-interest loan from your insurance company. And you can take as long as you like to repay this loan.

• If you get in trouble with your creditors, they'll have a lot harder time laying hands on the cash value of your life insurance than, say, the money you have in securities or bank accounts. This is simply because creditors' rights under the law are considerably weaker vis-à-vis life insurance than toward most other types of investments.

• As an investment, life insurance has obvious drawbacks—but it does promise to yield a stated total of dollars, whereas stock investments involve fluctuating totals of dollars.

• And certain types of life insurance will pay you a guaranteed specified lump sum or a specified income for life when you are ready to retire.

You cannot, in sum, reasonably argue that there are *no* good reasons why you should buy and hold life insurance. Much more to the point is how you, as a young family, should shop for life insurance—or how you can make sure your existing coverage is all you think it is.

HOW TO FIGURE YOUR LIFE INSURANCE NEEDS

To reach a proper decision on just how much coverage you need for your wife and children, answer these key questions:

(1) How much income would your family need for living expenses if you were to die tomorrow?

Many experts say that a young family with children would need 60 to 75 per cent of its present after-tax income. If you have no children or your children are grown, your wife might be able to get by on as little as 40 per cent of what you earned.

Another pertinent question here: If the wife of the family breadwinner died, how much would it cost to hire others to perform her duties?

(2) What resources are there to produce this income?

Add up your total assets, including equity in your home or business, savings accounts, stocks, bonds, property, etc., and estimate how much income all this could produce.

(3) What would your family receive from Social Security?

To find out just what your family would receive on the basis of your earnings, fill out and mail the card available at Social Security offices to get a record of your income credits together with instructions on how to estimate your expected future annual benefits.

(4) How much pension income—including veterans' pension—can you expect when you retire, and would any of this income be available to your spouse if you were to die?

(5) Do you have a group life insurance policy?

If so, what amount of benefits will it produce? Will it continue past retirement from your job, and could you afford to convert it into an individual policy if you left your present employer?

(6) Will your wife have any income of her own?

Does she now work or could she get a job and at what salary? A wife who has not held a job for several years might have to invest a period of time in training before she could qualify for a well-paying job. While working she might have to deduct considerable amounts for child care expenses, commuting costs, restaurant lunches, etc.

(7) Is there a mortgage on your home?

If your family sold the home, the proceeds could be used for their other needs. Otherwise, your insurance should also be enough to cover the mortgage payments—unless you have credit life insurance to pay off the mortgage in the event of your death.

(8) How much will your children need for their college education?

With college costs today averaging $3,000 to $4,000 annually and going up year after year, enough money must be set aside or otherwise made available to cover this expense. See Chapter 10, "A College Education and How to Finance It."

(9) Do you have any large debts outstanding?

Include in your calculations any money you may owe on auto or personal loans, installment payments, etc. These, too, would have to be paid off after your death.

(10) What cash would be needed immediately?

Your family may need money for "final expenses"—medical bills, funeral costs, minor debts.

Now add up everything your family will need for living expenses, your mortgage, college costs, debt clearance, other expenses. From this total, subtract the money that will be coming in from Social Security and other pensions, salaries, savings, investments and other assets, as well as any outstanding life insurance. The difference is the amount of insurance needed to enable your survivors to reach that income level of 60 to 75 per cent after tax, or to provide adequately for their needs.

Family needs differ depending on age and number of children. A reputable life insurance agent also may be able to offer you helpful advice on the amount—and types—of life insurance you need. But one industry rule of thumb is that a family needs at least enough life insurance to cover four or five times its yearly income. More specifically, the average family with a typical annual income of $10,000 needs a total of $40,000 to $50,000 of life insurance.

WHAT KIND OF LIFE INSURANCE FOR YOU?

With hundreds of different life insurance policy types, combinations, and options available today, deciding just what kind of insurance may be best for you can be a confusing experience. Some policies are designed purely for protection; others stress savings; still others retirement benefits; and many give you a combination of these features.

It will help if you think of life insurance as falling into one of four basic categories:

(1) *Term insurance.* This is the simplest, least costly type of coverage. As the name indicates, it gives you protection for a specific term or period of time. Naturally, the shorter the period of coverage and the younger you are, the lower the yearly premium. At age thirty-five, a typical five-year $10,000 term policy cost you about $65 a year in 1974, although premium costs vary from company to company, according to the special features of the policy.

Term policies pay off only if you die during the period covered by the policy. Like fire insurance, these policies generally have no cash or loan value. However, for young families with limited funds, they provide the best means of getting a maximum of protection. If you get *convertible term,* you have the option of swapping the policy for one of the higher-premium permanent protection plans without having to take another medical exam.

With *level term* insurance, the amount of insurance and your premium rate remain the same as long as your policy is in force or until it is renewed. This insurance is usually issued on a renewable basis for five or ten years, or on a non-renewable basis for longer periods or to age sixty, sixty-five, or seventy. At each renewal, the premium goes up to reflect the policyholder's increased age.

With *decreasing term* insurance—often used to cover such large debts as a mortgage—the amount of insurance declines a small amount from year to year until the policy finally expires.

(2) *Straight life (also called "ordinary life" or "whole life").* This type of policy is sometimes called a "bank account in an insurance policy," and costs considerably more than term because straight life must pay off, whereas a term policy may or may not pay off. At age thirty-five, a $10,000 policy would cost you about $190 a year. However, the premium does not go up as you grow older, and you get permanent protection for your entire lifetime. In addition, your policy's cash value increases from year to year.

By the time the policyholder reaches age sixty-five, the cash value usually amounts to more than half the face value of the policy. A key advantage of whole life insurance is that you, the owner of the policy, may borrow against its increasing cash value at any time at comparatively very favorable interest rates.

Moreover, a reasonably priced whole life policy is a useful device for those who require the mechanism of "forced savings."

You also have a number of other options with this particular type of policy. If you stop paying premiums, you can elect to continue to be covered in full for a specified period of time, or for a reduced amount of the policy's face value for the rest of your life. Or you can later cancel the policy and receive a cash settlement either in one lump sum or in the form of an income for a limited period of time, perhaps even for the rest of your life.

(3) *Limited-payment life.* In this variation of straight life, you pay premiums for only a specified number of years—usually ten, twenty or thirty, or until you reach a certain age, such as sixty or sixty-five. Because of the limited premium-paying period, premiums are higher than for straight life policies. At age thirty-five, a twenty-payment $10,000 policy would cost you about $300 a year. However, the higher premium builds up cash values correspondingly faster. Policies of this sort are favored by professional men, athletes, entertainers, and others whose earnings tend to be concentrated during a relatively short period.

(4) *Endowment.* This type of policy emphasizes savings and is designed for those who need not only protection for their dependents but, perhaps equally important, a specific sum of money—say, to provide funds for a child's college education or for a retirement income. Because of the emphasis on savings, cash value builds up most quickly in this type of policy. Consequently, it is also the most expensive. At age thirty-five, a typical $10,000 endowment policy that pays off twenty years later would cost about $450 a year.

There also are many variations and combinations of these basic types. A "family income" policy, for example, is a combination of permanent policy, usually straight life, and decreasing term insurance, and is a favorite of many couples with young children. With such a fifteen-year, $10,000 policy, the family will receive $10,000 *plus* $100 a month (1 per cent of $10,000) for ten years if the breadwinner dies five years after the policy is written. If the breadwinner outlives the fifteen-year family protection, the family still has a permanent policy for $10,000.

The "family plan" policy, which also combines straight life for the father with term insurance protection for the mother and children, simply covers the life of everybody in the family in varying amounts—all for one basic premium.

PRACTICAL EXAMPLES OF WHO NEEDS WHAT

For more guidance on how to pick the policies best suited to your needs, consider these case histories:

Let's say you're twenty-five and just married. You started work a year ago after you finished college and your wife also is employed. Your income is $7,000 and your wife's income is $5,250 a year. You, the breadwinner, have a group life insurance policy through your employer which would pay your wife $7,000—one year's salary—in the event of your death. (You have no children yet, but plan to start a family soon.)

How much individual life insurance should you have—if any? What type? For what reasons?

Even though you are just starting out on limited resources, some life insurance experts say, you should invest in a $10,000 straight life insurance policy with an option permitting you to buy up to $60,000 in additional insurance at later dates with no medical examination. The initial cost of this program would be well under $150 a year, would give you a means of continually increasing your insurance coverage as your family needs increase—and would at the same time provide a growing financial reserve in the form of increasing cash values. You may, if you need to, borrow against these cash values.

Or let's say you are a medical student, aged twenty-five, with a young wife, an infant child—and practically no income outside your summer earnings. The most practical type of insurance for you probably would be convertible term insurance covering the few years before you start to earn a big income, at which time you might convert to straight life, which covers you as long as you live and builds cash values as well.

Or let's say you are thirty, married, and have two children, ages one and four. Your income is $12,500 a year. Your group insurance policy would pay a year's income, and you also have a $10,000 straight life policy which you bought five years ago, prior to the birth of your first child.

Your primary need is for immediate insurance protection which would provide income for your wife in the event of your death while the children are dependent and would pay for your children's later education. You also should be creating some form of nest egg for emergencies.

To achieve these goals you should consider buying a $15,000 straight life policy with a twenty-year family income rider which would provide $250 a month to your widow, from the date of your death to twenty years from the issue date. This income, when combined with your Social Security benefits (see earlier in this chapter), would provide for most of the average income needs of a young widow with children.

Also, under this policy your wife would receive, in the event of your death, the face amount of the policy ($15,000)—plus your previous insurance coverage amounting to $22,500, which could fairly easily be translated into an additional $140 monthly income supplement. The total annual cost of the extra $15,000 policy would be about $340 a year.

Or say you're the type who is simply incapable of saving to supplement your anticipated retirement income. A more expensive retirement income or endowment policy, with limited life insurance protection in the meantime, might be your best means of forced savings.

Or say you want to be sure your children can afford college should you, the breadwinner, die in the interim. A life policy on your life—not theirs—would be the best bet.

Or say you're a disciplined investor capable of building a hefty nest egg and protection for your family. You might find sufficient protection in a straight life policy providing a death benefit just covering immediate cash needs and death taxes.

Or finally, say you have no dependents, you don't intend to marry, and you do have liquid assets more than adequate to cover death expenses, small debts, and probable death taxes. Then it's hard to justify any life insurance program for you at all.

If any rules can be formulated from all this, it would be these:

• As a young family, your vital interest is in immediate protection—not in the amount of life insurance you might be able to carry in your older years or in building retirement income or whatever. So buy life insurance as early as you can, but of the kind that will give you the most protection, even if it is only temporary.

• If your funds are limited, buy term insurance. At age twenty-five, with an initial premium of about $230 a year, you can buy $50,000 of term insurance. To get that full $50,000 coverage under a straight life policy would cost you nearly $600 a year—much more than most young people can afford.

• Buy term insurance that is renewable and convertible. Later on, when you can afford the larger premiums, you can explore the advantages, disadvantages, and ways of converting your term policy to permanent insurance.

• If you're in your middle years, you might be best off starting with straight life for at least your long-run needs. But don't go for this higher-priced policy if it means straining your budget and cutting down on your regular savings program.

Instead of paying a high premium for straight life, what about buying a term insurance policy for a fraction of that premium amount and investing the difference in some other form of savings? Calculate how much interest or other income you would have to earn on such an account to outperform a straight life "savings account."

HOW TO FIND A "STRONG" INSURANCE COMPANY

• *Do not* assume all life insurance companies are financially sound! Instead, shop among the best 20 per cent of the companies available to you. That's not being too choosy at all.

• To find a financially strong company, consult *Best's Insurance Guide* or *Best's Insurance Reports*. Best's is the most authoritative insurance rating service available and you can find these publications in most public libraries.

Best's has four recommended ratings for life insurance companies: (1) "most substantial"; (2) "very substantial"; (3) "substantial"; (4) "considerable." In one recent edition of *Best's,* 126 companies were rated "most substantial," 54 companies were rated "very substantial," 110 companies were rated "substantial," and 169 companies got a "considerable" rating. More than 1,300 out of the 1,800 insurance companies received no rating at all.

• If you buy a low-cost insurance policy from one of the top companies, you will not necessarily have to pay higher premiums. In fact, many of the low-cost companies are among the financially strongest and many of the high-cost companies are among the financially weakest.

• And of course, also take into account the services and professional advice the company offers you.

HOW TO SAVE ON YOUR INSURANCE

If you are paying higher than standard rates for your life insurance because of medical considerations, and if your health has improved since your policy was issued, call your insurance agent, tell him you want your policies reviewed, and then apply to your insurance company for a reduction or elimination of the extra-risk premiums. Even if your health hasn't improved, you might be able to get a lower risk rating.

This is just one way to save significant sums on your life insurance premiums. But there are other ways either to slash your over-all insurance costs or to free funds to buy extra, needed coverage. Here are some of them:

• Find out whether any club, association, union, professional or fraternal organization to which either you or your spouse belong offers any low-cost group life insurance plan. In some group term insurance plans you can save as much as 40 per cent over the cost of individual coverage. Most of these plans taper off coverage as you grow older, and the insurance may end at age sixty or sixty-five.

Another big advantage of group coverage is that medical exams are waived.

• Consider reducing or even dropping some or all of your present life insurance coverage—and thus also your premiums—*if* your children have grown up and are self-supporting, *if* the beneficiary you originally desig-nated for your policy has died or become financially independent, *if* you have built up a substantial outside nest egg, *if* you have no debts. But before you drop any life insurance, be sure you're not likely to need the coverage again, for if you're forced to rebuy a policy later, you'll pay a considerably higher premium and, should your health deteriorate, you may not be able to get any coverage at all. (See "Handling Your Insurance at Retirement," directly below.)

• *Shop* for whatever individual life insurance coverage you decide on—not only among local agents but also, in certain states, at savings banks, which generally offer over the counter lower-priced policies than insurance companies.

• Pay your premiums in as few installments as possible to avoid extra charges. A policy with a $150 annual premium might cost you $156 if you paid it in two semi-annual installments. If paid quarterly, it might cost you a total of $159, and monthly, $162 for the year, or $12 more than the one-time annual payment.

• If you have several policies, reduce the frequency of payment on all of them and make it easier for yourself by staggering your payments so that they aren't bunched near each other.

• If there is some special reason why you prefer to pay your premiums monthly, ask your agent about a cost-saving "pre-authorized check" plan under which your bank automatically deducts the appropriate amount each month to the life insurance company from your regular checking account.

• If you are paying a higher-than-usual premium because of the nature of your occupation when you bought the policy, and have changed occupa-tions, inform your insurance agent of this fact and request a reclassification.

Only recently, millions of Americans were regarded as virtually un-insurable—including wild animal trainers, steeplechase riders, car racers, deep sea divers, test pilots, submariners, and mine police. But all of these today are insurable. Today, even armored car drivers and chemists in nitro-glycerin plants are regarded as "standard risks." And premium rates for workers in almost all "dangerous" trades have sharply declined. Key reasons: improved job safety and successful trials by the insurance companies which offered coverage to workers in these occupations.

Admittedly, if you are a steeplechase rider, trapeze artist, or a Grand Prix race car driver, you'll have to pay a somewhat higher premium to get life insurance. Similarly, private avocations are taken into account in cal-culating insurance rates. "A sky diver who won't open his parachute until he reaches treetop level would be rated as a pretty bad risk," says one top industry spokesman. But the key point is that almost all workers are in-surable and almost all at a reasonable cost.

• It may be cheaper for you to add to an existing policy than to buy a completely new one. A decreasing term or family income policy, for example, will cost less as a rider to your regular policy than if bought separately.

• If you are a World War II veteran and have a GI term insurance policy, consider converting it to permanent government insurance, one of the best bargains ever offered veterans, even though the premium will be higher. Check with the nearest Veterans Administration office to see if the conversion is still possible in your case. (See Part IV, in "Your Rights and How to Get Them" and Chapter 10, "A College Education and How to Finance It," for details on other veterans' rights and benefits.)

HANDLING YOUR INSURANCE AT RETIREMENT

When you reach retirement age—*and that's the latest date for doing this*—review and re-evaluate all your life insurance policies in terms of your need for them and of your personal goals.

Do not be the least surprised to discover you *no longer need* your life insurance—for you no longer have a young family to protect. Your whole way of life has been drastically changed and straight life insurance simply doesn't fit into it.

When you took out your life insurance policies, you were forcing yourself to save out of your current income, but continuing to save after retirement is inconsistent with that concept. When you began your insurance program, you were intent on creating an instant estate for the benefit of your dependents in the event of your premature death. But when there's no need for protecting dependents this way, it's all wrong for any older person to deprive himself of a dollar to finance this protection.

You might cash in your policies and put the released funds to work earning more money for you—in a simple savings account or high-grade bonds or high-grade common or preferred stocks. Or you might put your insurance on a paid-up basis and relieve yourself of all further premium obligations.

Only if you are in the wealthier income brackets—in which life insurance could be an excellent way to pass on an estate or to provide cash for estate taxes—will you be told that it could be unwise to drop your policies. But this gets into a different area altogether.

IS YOUR LIFE INSURANCE UP TO DATE?

Now let's assume you already have adequate amounts of insurance—both group and individual.

As the preceding section on handling your insurance in retirement dramatized, it is vitally important for you to review your coverage at least every two or three years to make sure it is appropriate for your financial needs, geared to your rising or falling standard of living, realistic in terms of the number and ages of your children, and properly tied into your other savings and investments.

Do both husband and wife know, for example, where all of your various family life insurance policies are now kept? The total value of all your life insurance protection—including veterans', fraternal organizations, group policies, credit life insurance, individual policies? The name and address of your insurance agent? Which members of the family are covered and for approximately how much? Are there children not covered? The amount and due date of premiums? Who are the beneficiaries of each policy? And the "secondary" or contingent beneficiaries—in the event both husband and wife are killed in a single accident? How benefits would be paid? The amount of cash values which have accumulated so far—against which loans could be made? If you've moved, does the insurance company have your new address?

Once you have the answers to these basic questions, explore these other important questions concerning your life insurance—and determine just where and just how big are the gaps in coverage:

What, if any, provision is there to cover the possibility that the family breadwinner might become disabled over a long period of time? Does your policy include a "waiver of premium" clause—a waiver of the obligation to pay further premiums in the event of total and permanent disability?

Does your policy contain a provision under which, if you for any reason fail to pay your premiums within the specified grace period (usually thirty-one days), the premium will automatically be paid by a loan against the cash value of the policy?

Does it also contain an "accidental death benefit" provision, often called "double indemnity," that doubles the amount payable if the insured dies accidentally? (Triple indemnity also is offered by some companies.)

Are your term policies renewable and convertible without your having to take another medical examination?

How much has the upsurge in the U.S. cost of living shrunk the actual buying power of your policies since you bought them? Have you made or can you make any provisions to offset this erosion?

Do you meet the rule of thumb that you should have the equivalent of four to five years' pay in life insurance? You may need more of a cushion if you have several children, if you are loaded with debt, if your non-insurance financial protection is limited, and if you simply can't discipline yourself into saving. You may need less if your group coverage is extensive, if your wife is well trained for a job, if your debts are paid off, if your children have left the nest, if you have substantial savings and other investments.

How much income would all of your present life insurance policies provide when you retire—assuming you are using life insurance for this purpose at all? Add this income, figured on a monthly basis, to the amount you can expect from Social Security retirement benefits, from income on all your other savings and investments, and from your company pension.

If you own your business, is your life insurance adequate to keep it going should you die before you've trained a successor?

Is your designated beneficiary still the correct one—or should other dependents be added or substituted?

Should the wife be listed as the policy owner, even though it is written on the husband's life? In this case, the premium payments should be made from her funds. If done validly, this could result in considerable savings in estate taxes. Get advice on this from your insurance agent, tax adviser, or lawyer.

Only when you have the answers to these questions will you know how much financial protection you and your family actually have. In this period of steep inflation, having these answers is absolutely vital to your financial security—now *and* later.

SHOULD YOU SWITCH INSURANCE POLICIES?

If any insurance agent suggests you switch a policy you own—life or accident and health—for "a better one," the law in most states requires the agent to explain fully and clearly the differences between the policy the agent says you should cancel and the new one. If the agent doesn't make this "full disclosure" about the policies, he (or she) is breaking the law and could forfeit his license.

But even if the agent does tell you the differences there are many, many shadings to full disclosure—and you well may not understand what is being recommended. Even if you would be better off in some ways by switching, the disadvantages of changing might far outweigh the advantages the agent is stressing.

And even if you are persuaded by the arguments heed this blunt warning: *In very few cases can changing insurance policies be advantageous to the policyholder.*

Unscrupulous insurance agents still do exist—although not on the scale of the past, when they thrived in the ghettos particularly. They still do sell to the poor and uninformed, then coax the ignorant policyholder into switching to other policies after only a couple of years—so that the buyer pays the front-end costs over and over again. There is still a real danger that you'll make a serious error in this area—if only because so many millions of you own so many more insurance policies and in such a wider variety than ever before.

There are, of course, many reasons why you might change a life (or accident and health) policy. But the most likely reason is that an agent advises you that another policy from another insurance company is a better buy. Here, therefore, are basic guides to weigh if and when a switch is suggested:

(1) Realize that with any new policy you are paying the full front-end

costs all over again—just as you did when you bought your original policy. Most agents' commissions and company administrative costs come out of your first-year premium. If you've had your policy for several years, you've already paid these costs once. Don't duplicate them without extraordinarily sound reasons.

(2) Also be fully aware of the importance of the contestability clause in most life insurance contracts—under which your insurance contract can't be broken because of statements you made on the application after the policy has been in force for a period, usually two years (except, of course, for a misstated age). With a new contract, you start a new two-year contestability period. The person who switches policies frequently not only pays the front-end costs over again but rarely gets out of the contestable period.

(3) Find out precisely what will be the premium payments for your new policy and compare them with what you are paying. If the benefits are similar, your premiums probably will be higher—merely because you are older than when you bought the first policy.

(4) Be wary about the waiting period involved when a new policy is issued. All too often people apply for a new policy and let the old one lapse before the new policy becomes effective. The tragedy here is that the person may die in the meantime, with no insurance at all in force.

(5) As your best protection, deal with an insurance agent who represents a reputable company. If you're thinking about changing policies, ask his advice. If you're not satisfied with what he recommends, ask the company. Throughout the entire process, do not forget that it is the agent's duty under the law to disclose clearly all the facts to you before you switch any policy.

If, after all this, you feel you've been unfairly treated by the company or its agents, you do have a recourse. You can lodge a complaint with your state insurance commissioner's office at the state capital.

WHAT ABOUT WIFE INSURANCE?

Assuming you are convinced that you, the breadwinner, must have some life insurance to protect your family against loss of your income, the next question is: Should the life of your wife also be insured?

Do you, Mr. America, realize how great would be the added expenses to you, should the lady of your house not be around to share, plan, cook, clean, mother, drive, take care?

And do you recognize what would be the financial impact of the loss—if she also is a working mother who contributes substantially to the household's total income?

Today, three out of four wives are covered by life insurance and the proportion is growing steadily. As a guide on whether or not the wife in *your* household should have life insurance, the key functions of "wife insurance" are to:

(1) Cover final expenses in the event of her death. Expenses of final medical and hospital care, funeral costs, and all other incidentals can now total $5,000 or more—enough to wipe out most family nest eggs and even put the surviving mate quite deeply in debt. (See Chapter 18, "Funeral Expenses and How to Control Them.")

(2) Help care for the young children, for a fair period at least, and perform the other tasks that go with running a home. The cost of a competent housekeeper, or even regular cleaning help, can run into hundreds of dollars a month.

(3) Help meet the increase in income taxes which results from the husband's loss of his wife's personal exemption and the joint-return privilege. After a grace period, this increase in income taxes for a man in the $10,000 bracket with two children will amount to more than $200 a year.

(4) Cover the loss of the wife's contribution to the family income, if it represents a vital part of the family budget.

What sort of policy would be best?

In most cases a term policy should fill the bill.

A young wife with a young child might take out a $10,000 five-year renewable term policy—enough to cover final expenses and to tide the family over for a year until the husband gets his bearings. The annual premium cost of one such policy for a twenty-five-year-old woman in 1974 was $35.

A second alternative would be a twenty-year family income term policy which can be bought separately or tacked on as a rider to a whole life policy (if the wife happens to have one). The yearly premium cost of such a policy, which would provide survivors with a monthly income of $100 for the balance of the twenty-year span of the policy, would be $55, and less if it were added as a rider.

The fundamental point is that the loss of a wife and mother is a financial blow to the family as real—although not as readily measurable—as the loss of the husband and breadwinner. Wife insurance is one way to safeguard the family against this loss.

AND WHAT ABOUT INSURANCE FOR CHILDREN?

On their grandson's fifth birthday recently, a smart couple we know bought him as a gift a $10,000 straight life insurance policy—with the pledge that they will pay the premiums until the boy reaches twenty-five and will arrange to have the policy paid up immediately should they die before that date.

Young Dick's parents were less than delighted. "If any life insurance is to be taken out," grumbled the disappointed father, "it should be on my life, not Dick's."

"I gave that boy the best present I could think of," said the equally disappointed grandfather, "and neither my daughter nor her husband understood it at all."

Actually, both grandfather and father were right and wrong. The first and top priority in life insurance must go to adequate coverage for the breadwinner. And since Dick's mother hasn't earned a penny since he was born and the family is having a tough struggle on one pay check in today's inflation, our friends could have been a little less original in their gift to Dick. And if they were determined to give a life insurance policy, it should have been to their twenty-five-year-old son-in-law.

On the other hand, our friends are doing their daughter, son-in-law, and grandson a tremendous favor by buying that policy so early in Dick's life. Since millions of you will be directly or indirectly affected by this tale, here are the key reasons why.

• You can buy basic insurance coverage on a child's life at extremely low rates.

• The basic $10,000 policy is set. On top of this, you can guarantee the child the right to continue and add to his life insurance starting at age twenty-five—despite any illnesses or accidents in the interim which might otherwise disqualify him.

For instance, for an extra $7.50 a year, you could guarantee the child the right to buy $10,000 of life insurance at age twenty-five plus an additional $10,000 every three years after that until age forty—a total of $60,000 in additional insurance.

• The insurance establishes an important savings habit for the child.

In this case, our friend plans to pay the premiums until the boy is twenty-five. He also has taken out an inexpensive "pay or benefit" coverage which will waive the premiums until the boy is twenty-five should our friend die or become disabled. (You have to be under fifty-five years old to be eligible for this.) At twenty-five, though, the boy knows he must take over and start paying for his protection.

• This policy might be particularly valuable in times of emergency or to help finance the child's education.

The $10,000 policy will have a cash value of $2,550 when Dick reaches twenty-five. He could borrow this amount at the low guaranteed rates charged on life insurance policies whenever he wished and could set his own repayment schedule.

• And, of course, this life insurance is protection for the parents should their child die.

How you apply this tale is up to you entirely. But at least you should know what's available and what others are doing, so you can reach an intelligent, informed decision.

One basic caution, though:

Don't invest in this type of coverage—or even in wife insurance—*unless and until* the family breadwinner is adequately insured.

WHAT YOU SHOULD KNOW ABOUT ANNUITIES

WHAT THEY ARE

Annuities are sold by life insurance companies, but they should *not* be confused with life insurance. You buy life insurance primarily because, if you die, you want to have provided for those you leave behind. You buy an annuity primarily because you assume you will live and you want to have some sort of steady income to supplement what you'll get from Social Security, and perhaps your company pension, savings, other investments during your retirement years.

An annuity is a contract or agreement under which an insurance company accepts a given sum of money from you and in return guarantees to pay you a regular (usually monthly) income for a stated period or, more typically, for as long as you live. The size of the payments are based on your life expectancy, according to the mortality tables and how much money you put in. Since women tend to live longer than men, they normally receive smaller monthly incomes from annuities than do men for the same dollar input, but over a longer period of time.

PROS AND CONS OF ANNUITIES

An annuity program frees you from the responsibility of money management or investment decisions, guarantees you a fixed monthly payment, and assures you that you will never outlive your capital. But it *must* not be your entire retirement program in an era of inflation.

Although an annuity can generate a good monthly return, you may be able to do much, much better by investing at a young age in, say, real estate, stocks, or other mediums.

For all the "cons," turn back to the section "The Realities of Retirement," and what today's standards will mean in terms of tomorrow's incomes.

It's simply not *that* easy.

THE BAFFLEGAB OF LIFE INSURANCE AND ANNUITIES

ACCIDENTAL DEATH BENEFIT: Extra benefit, often added to life insurance policies, which is paid in the event of death by accident. Often called "double indemnity," sometimes "triple indemnity."

ANNUITY: Contract under which you pay the life insurance company a given sum of money and receive in return a regular (usually monthly) income for the remainder of your life. A *deferred annuity* provides for the income payments to begin at some future date—e.g., after a certain number of years or when you reach a certain age. A *variable annuity* is one in which payments may fluctuate, often reflecting stock price changes.

BENEFICIARY: Person you name in your life insurance policy to receive the policy's proceeds in the event of your death. Also called "primary beneficiary."

BUSINESS LIFE (OR "KEY MAN") INSURANCE: Life insurance bought by a corporation or partnership on the life of a key executive.

CASH SURRENDER VALUE: Amount of money for which you can cash in your life insurance policy before it becomes payable by death or maturity.

CONTINGENT BENEFICIARY: One or more additional persons you name in your policy to receive all or part of its proceeds in the event the primary beneficiary dies before you.

CREDIT LIFE INSURANCE: Life insurance offered (and sometimes required) by lenders, providing for full payment of a home mortgage or other loan in the event the borrower dies.

DIVIDEND: Refund of part of premium on a participating policy not needed by the company. Since it actually represents the refund of an overpayment, it is not taxable.

ENDOWMENT INSURANCE: Insurance in which the face value is payable at maturity to the policyholder if he is still living, or to his beneficiary if he dies before the policy matures.

FACE AMOUNT: Amount, stated on the face of the policy, that will be paid on the death of the insured or at maturity of the contract.

FAMILY INCOME POLICY: Policy which combines whole life insurance with decreasing term insurance and which pays your beneficiary a regular income for a specified period of time if you die before the end of that period. It also pays the full face amount of the policy at the death of the policyholder.

FAMILY POLICY: Life insurance contract covering all members of your family. Generally, such a policy provides whole life insurance on the family bread-winner and limited amounts of term insurance on his wife and also on present and future children.

GRACE PERIOD: Time span, usually thirty or thirty-one days after a premium is due, during which you may delay payment of your insurance premium without any penalty and without losing your coverage.

GROUP LIFE INSURANCE: Low-priced life insurance usually issued to employees by employers, or to members by their unions or professional groups, without a medical examination.

INDUSTRIAL LIFE INSURANCE: Insurance sold to individuals, usually in low income brackets, in amounts of less than $1,000. Weekly or monthly premiums collected by an agent. Traditionally used to pay funeral expenses.

INSURED: Person on whose life insurance policy is issued.

LEVEL PREMIUM INSURANCE: A form of insurance in which the annual premium stays the same throughout the period over which premiums are payable.

LIMITED-PAYMENT LIFE INSURANCE: Whole life insurance on which premiums are fully paid in a limited, specified number of years.

MATURITY: Date when the face value of a policy becomes payable.

ORDINARY LIFE INSURANCE: Individual life insurance, either or whole, which is sold in amounts of $1,000 or more. The proceeds can be in the form of a lump sum or as income or your policy can be converted to an annuity.

PAID-UP INSURANCE: Insurance on which you have paid all required premiums. With reduced paid-up insurance, the plan for which you originally signed up remains in force, but the benefit amount is reduced, with no further premiums to pay.

PARTICIPATING INSURANCE: Insurance on which the premium is somewhat higher than the actual cost of protection, but on which the company returns any amount it does not need in the form of policy dividends. Mostly sold by "mutual" life insurance companies. On *non-participating* life insurance, the premium you pay is calculated as closely as possible to the actual cost of the protection, and on this type of policy you receive no dividends. Sold by "stock" life insurance companies.

PERMANENT LIFE INSURANCE: Any form of life insurance except term insurance. This type builds a cash value, which you can use as collateral to borrow from the insurance company, or which you may withdraw entirely by giving up the policy.

POLICY: Printed document stating the terms of the contract with the life insurance company. This document should *not* be kept in your safety deposit box, but rather in a safe place at home where your wife or other survivor can get at it quickly if and when she needs to.

POLICY LOAN: Money you borrow from your life insurance company, at relatively low interest cost, using as security the cash value of your policy.

PREMIUM: Amount you pay periodically, usually once or twice or four times a year, or monthly (perhaps as a payroll deduction), for your life insurance coverage.

RENEWABLE TERM INSURANCE: Temporary insurance which you may renew, for another limited period of time if you wish, when the original term of coverage runs out—even though you may have become "uninsurable" in the interim. However, your premium rates increase each time you renew your term insurance because you are older.

STRAIGHT LIFE (OR ORDINARY OR WHOLE LIFE) INSURANCE: Insurance on which premiums are payable during your entire life.

TERM INSURANCE: Relatively low-cost insurance which remains in force for a limited, specified period of time—usually five or ten years, or until you reach a certain age. Benefits are paid only if you die within this period of time. *Convertible* term insurance is guaranteed to be exchangeable for some other type of coverage, even if you, the policyholder, would not ordinarily be eligible for such coverage.

WHOLE LIFE (OR ORDINARY OR STRAIGHT) INSURANCE: Insurance on which a lump-sum benefit is paid on your death. Also builds up a cash value based on premiums you have paid, and you may borrow against this amount at any time. Premiums are payable either during your entire life (straight life) or over limited number of years (limited-payment whole life insurance).

VETERANS' PENSIONS

Another major category of retirement benefits is veterans' pensions. The conditions and amounts tend to change from year to year, as new legislation boosts and liberalizes these pensions. Pensions vary according to a veteran's income, the number of dependents he has, how severe his disability is, and his net worth.

But, basically, VA pensions are reserved for veterans who are in considerable financial need, and so disabled that they are unable to pursue "substantially gainful employment."

Pension amounts are scaled according to need (as measured by the amount of other income available to the veteran). *No* pension benefits are payable if the veteran has sizable assets to draw on.

As of 1975, a veteran without dependents could have an income of no more than $3,000 a year to be eligible for a pension or, if he had a wife and/or other dependents, no more than $4,200 a year.

For a veteran alone, the basic pension ranged from $5 to $160 a month in 1975, depending on the veteran's other income. For a veteran with one dependent, the range was $14 to $172; with two dependents, $19 to $177; and with three or more dependents, $24 to $182. Extra payments are made if the veteran is in a nursing home or needs the regular help of another person (an extra $123 per month), or if he is housebound (an extra $49 per month).

WHAT EVERY WIDOW SHOULD KNOW

BASIC FACTS FOR WIDOWS

The thirty-nine-year-old husband of a young friend was recently killed in an automobile accident, leaving his widow with two preschool children. The husband, a dentist, had life insurance policies which paid his widow $60,000; credit life insurance which completed mortgage payments on the family's home; automobile insurance which bought a new car to replace the wreck in which the husband was killed, as well as funeral expenses. His dental practice was put on the market at $25,000.

The young widow received Social Security and veterans' benefits amounting to about $450 per month. She was confident she could manage on $800 per month. Her cash reserve of $85,000 would, therefore, be able to earn the extra $350 per month she would need and would contribute toward the education of her children.

This is not a typical set of financial circumstances for the nation's 500,000 young widowed mothers. Few young husbands have this much protection (including a salable professional practice) for their families.

Yet if you, an American wife, are typically five years younger than your husband, the chances are three out of four that you will wind up as a widow. Because females have a seven-year greater life expectancy than males, even if you are the same age as your spouse, there is a two-out-of-three chance that you will outlive your husband. And if you happen to be five years older than your husband, you have a 50 per cent chance of becoming a widow.

For your protection, you should be aware of the ways to handle the expenses that go with a final illness and funeral costs, and also with estates, wills, probates, and taxes. (See Chapter 18, "Funeral Expenses and How to Control Them," and Chapter 17, "What You Should Know About Wills, Estates, and Trusts.") Equally important, you should take steps now to find out what Social Security, life insurance, and other survivor benefits your family could automatically count on and how to go about getting them. It is never too early for a wife and husband to talk about the financial resources that would be available if the breadwinner were no longer around.

HOW MUCH WOULD YOU GET?

If you are typical, chances are it wouldn't be very much. So, to make sure that you overlook nothing, run down this list of possible sources of funds for you:

Social Security

There is a tremendous general ignorance of how Social Security protects women and young people in our country.

• The maximum family Social Security benefit being paid to young widows with two children in 1974 was $785 a month. This means that if your children are very young your family might receive an "inheritance" of benefits totaling as much as $125,000 during the entire period in which the benefits are payable. The minimum monthly check was $141.

• The full Social Security benefit is *tax free* and continues to be paid until you remarry or until your children reach the age of eighteen unless a disabled child remains in your care, in which case your benefits may continue.

• If and when you remarry, your benefits ordinarily stop—but the children's benefits continue to be paid and these benefits may amount to more than one half of the total.

• The total benefit begins to be reduced as each child reaches the age of eighteen (unless the child is disabled and has been before the age of twenty-two). After all children have reached this age, both widow's and children's benefits cease, unless there is a disabled child in the mother's care, in which case benefits for both may continue. However, if the children are full-time students, the children's benefits continue until they reach age twenty-two.

• Social Security also pays a lump-sum death benefit of $255 to all widows covered by the system who were living in the same household with the worker at the time of his death.

• For other categories of benefits that may apply to you or the children, see earlier in this chapter or contact the nearest Social Security office.

• *Caution: all* Social Security benefits must be applied for—*none* is automatic. And delay in applying can cause the loss of some benefits because back payments cannot be made for periods exceeding twelve months. To save valuable time, contact the nearest Social Security office as soon as possible after the death of your husband. Take with you:

(1) A certified copy of the death certificate.
(2) Your husband's Social Security number.
(3) A record of his approximate earnings in the year previous to his death and his employer's name (the W-2 form that accompanies the U.S. income tax form should suffice).
(4) Your marriage certificate.
(5) Your Social Security numbers and those of your dependent children.
(6) Proof of your age and the ages of any dependent children under age twenty-three.

Veterans' Benefits

The Veterans Administration pays a dependency and indemnity compensation to widows of veterans who died while in service or from a service-connected disability, based on the husband's pay grade while he was in service. In 1975 this ranged from $215 to $549 a month for a widow, with an additional $26 a month for each child under age eighteen.

If your husband died while on active duty (including training) or within 120 days after discharge and from a service-connected cause, there also is an award of a six months' death gratuity. This is a lump-sum payment of six times the veteran's monthly pay, but not more than $3,000 or less than $800, payable by his military service.

If your husband was a war veteran who died from non-service-related causes you also might qualify for a Veterans Administration "death pension." In 1975 these survivors' benefits ranged from $5 to $108 a month for a widow alone and $49 to $128 a month for a widow with one child, plus $20 for each additional child. An extra $64 per month is added to the basic benefit amounts if the widow is in a nursing home or needs regular help at home.

To be eligible for death pension benefits your income may not exceed $3,000 if you are a widow alone, or $4,200 if you have one or more dependent children.

There also is a burial expense grant of $250 for veterans whose death was not service-connected, and up to $800 if the death was service-connected. (See Chapter 18 "Funeral Expenses and How to Control Them," for more details on veterans' death benefits.)

If the funeral director does not alert the VA insurance division of your husband's death, contact the nearest VA center.

Unremarried widows of men who served in World War II, the Korean war, or the Vietnam war and who died in service or from service-connected disabilities also may qualify for GI home loans and educational benefits. (See Chapter 13, "A Roof Over Your Head," for more on the GI home loan program, and also Chapter 10, "A College Education and How to Finance It.")

In addition, widows are entitled, until they remarry, to special preference when applying for Civil Service positions. If the widow is the mother of a veteran who lost his life or became totally disabled, she also is entitled to special preference.

For answers to other questions you may have, or assistance you may need, write, phone, or visit your nearest VA regional office.

Civil Service and Railroad Workers' Benefits

You also may be eligible for a survivor annuity benefit under the civil service retirement system *if* you are a widow or widower of a person who completed at least eighteen months of civilian service and, at the time of death:

the widow or widower held a position covered by the retirement system; or

had accepted a reduced annuity with survivor benefits to his or her spouse.

If you are a widow or disabled dependent widower of a person covered by the civil service retirement system, you must have been married to this person at least two years before his or her death *or* be the parent of a child born of the marriage.

As a general rule, the amount of your widow's or widower's annuity is based on the number of years your spouse worked and on the salary your spouse earned during this period. Your annuity ceases if you remarry before age sixty.

Any unmarried children of your deceased spouse who are under age eighteen (or under age twenty-two if they are full-time students) or who are incapable of supporting themselves because of a disability which began before age eighteen also are entitled to annuities.

If you are the widow or widower of a person who worked for the nation's railroads for fewer than ten years, the railroad retirement credits earned by your spouse will be transferred to and counted toward your survivor's benefits under the Social Security program.

If your spouse had more than ten years of railroad employment, his railroad retirement credits will be combined with his Social Security credits (if any) and counted toward survivor's benefits under either the Social Security program or the railroad retirement program, depending on whether he had a "current connection" with the railroad industry when he died.

For further details on railroad retirement benefits, contact your nearest Social Security office or your nearest Railroad Retirement office.

Other Employee Benefits

If your husband worked for a private company or had his own business, he probably had group life insurance and perhaps was covered by a profit-sharing or pension plan. Most likely your husband's employer will notify you about benefits to which you are entitled. If not, contact the employer.

Be sure to check out: any accrued vacation and sick pay; terminal pay allowances; unpaid commissions; service recognition awards; disability income; credit union balance; and anything else that also may be due your husband. At the same time, ask whether you and the children are still eligible for benefits under your husband's hospital, surgical, and disability coverage and, if so, for how long.

Life Insurance

Your husband's insurance agent or company will tell you what information you have to supply with your claim. If your husband did not already decide on whether you were to get a lump-sum settlement or monthly income payments and if you have no immediate need for all of the cash you would get in a lump-sum payment, you have a number of settlement options. Generally, your options fall into these categories:

You may leave all of the money with the company and draw interest on it, with a provision that gives you the right to withdraw as much as you want at any time.

Or you may arrange to receive fixed installments on set dates over your lifetime or over an agreed-on period of time. Your insurance agent can discuss the pros and cons of these possibilities with you.

Finally, make sure to apply for any Medicare benefits due your husband —hospital or doctor bills he may have incurred and paid directly before he died but for which he did not apply for Medicare reimbursement.

A useful 40-page guide for widows and those who may be called to help widows in their financial affairs—covering everything from contacting the funeral director to life insurance, estate taxes, and probate matters—is "What Does She Do Now?" put out by the Life Insurance Management Research Association. If your insurance agent cannot give you a copy, write the Association directly at 170 Sigourney Street, Hartford, Conn. 06105.

BEWARE: GYPS AIMED AT THE ELDERLY

Would you believe that a special tablet could be "effective for the treatment of run-down and weak conditions . . . loss of enjoyment of life . . . inability to be the man or woman formerly possible" as well as make it easier for you to endure noisy children, coated tongue, and gas?

Would you lay out money to buy mail order "electronic pulsators," "special stimulants," "geriatric elixirs," or any other chemical or mechanical product advertised as capable of restoring "lost vigor," reviving sexual activity, or even rebuilding sex organs?

I hope you wouldn't. As the late Dr. Alfred Kinsey put it: "Good health, sufficient exercise and plenty of sleep still remain the most effective aphrodisiacs known to man."

But, as an elderly American, you are now the major target of an endless variety of fountain-of-youth promoters in this country. You also are the target of an endless variety of other types of gypsters attempting to bilk you out of your limited retirement income.

For tips on how to recognize health quackery, see Chapter 8, "The High Cost of Good Health."

Even if you are not yet retired, you probably have elderly friends or relatives. Surely you want to help them avoid the gyps which could seriously deplete their modest savings or slash their monthly benefit checks.

Here is a sampling of other widespread gyps and exaggerations aimed at our elderly population:

• In the dance studio racket, con men seduce lonely, elderly women into buying oversize packages of dancing lessons, payable in advance. In some cases, confused elderly widows agree to buy "lifetime memberships" in a dance studio, at a cost of thousands, even tens of thousands, of dollars.

• In the "vitamins forever" scheme, mail order houses of questionable reputation persuade the elderly to buy "subscriptions" to geriatric preparations but refuse to act on instructions to stop the cascade of pills.

• In another gyp, a phony "Social Security representative" offers to take over your benefit check and in return to prepare your taxes, pay your bills, etc. All too often, though, those offering such services take an unconscionable cut of cash for themselves—or even accept money for payment of income taxes but never file a return.

• In the sphere of often essential physical supports, hearing aids, eyeglasses, and dentures are advertised and sold through the mails to the elderly, without benefit of doctors' prescriptions or other data necessary for proper purchases. Or these vital aids are peddled by utterly unqualified, unlicensed promoters.

• In the world of finance, there always are the stock racketeers, who frequently are able to high-pressure older people into buying worthless securities just because the elderly are so pressed for money and eager to make an extra dollar.

CAN YOU FIND THE FOUNTAIN OF YOUTH?

One day fairly soon the intensive research now going on in the field of aging will make it possible for you to feel and look "young" into your oldest years. Imaginative experiments in the field of genetics are at last promising exhilarating answers to some of the most depressing—and unaesthetic—problems of old age.

When that day comes, the cures for face wrinkles and crows' feet in women, for baldness and other embarrassing failings in men, will cease to be "secrets" and "miracles." Then the cures will be promoted and sold on the basis of their own proven worth. There will be no reason for phony testimonials and faked photographs. Then the real cures will cost only a fraction of what the worthless or near worthless treatments cost today.

It will come. And I hope it will come in time to matter to me. In the meantime, though, I (along with American women from coast to coast) will spend an all-time record total of tens of millions of dollars for a fabulous array of cosmetic gadgets, creams, and secret "methods" to turn back the clock. Simultaneously, it's quite possible that you, along with American men from coast to coast, also will spend record amounts for cures, rejuvenators, and other gimmicks to "slow" the aging process.

And we will spend these fortunes despite this brutally cold observation recently by a respected dermatologist at the University of Southern California in Los Angeles:

"With time and exposure to light, the skin loses its tensile strength—

like an old worn girdle. No amount of massage has ever been shown to restore an old girdle."

Here, therefore, are warnings and guidelines to help you not waste money in two important areas of aging today: face wrinkles and balding.

• None of the facial creams, hormone creams, or so-called rejuvenating creams being sold today has been proven capable of safely preventing or removing wrinkles. This is because wrinkles are the result of permanent changes in and under the skin.

• Facial massage can temporarily improve circulation of blood to the skin but it cannot remove wrinkles.

• Facial saunas also may temporarily improve skin appearance by promoting hydration. But so will applying hot towels or coating your face with oily cream.

• Exotic-sounding face cream ingredients may slow evaporation of water from the skin and thereby temporarily improve its appearance too—but they cannot remove wrinkles either.

• Chemosurgery—or face peeling—can, though, in a limited number of cases, bring about a real improvement in the appearance of aging skin. But the treatment can be exceedingly dangerous. Like plastic surgery (which *can* successfully remove wrinkles), it should be attempted only by qualified physicians—not unqualified "wrinkle farms."

• On balding, the key fact is that 95 per cent of male baldness is of the "male pattern baldness" type, for which there is no known massage or special preparation cure. However, at least one effective, if tedious and costly, treatment has emerged for this type of baldness: hair transplants performed by dermatologists specializing in this field. In the other 5 per cent of baldness cases (called alopecia areata) regrowth occurs by itself in almost all instances. The "before" and "after" pictures promoting baldness cures, incidentally, are often of this type of baldness.

WARNINGS ON BUYING A RETIREMENT HOMESITE

Thousands of Americans are being lured by newspaper and magazine ads to invest *now* in a retirement homesite in California, Florida, Texas, New Mexico, Arizona, Nevada. Thousands are being invited and flown to retirement home developments by the developers, put up in motels for a weekend, wined and dined, bused around the developed parts of the development, shown "then and now" movies of the area to prove how rapidly it is growing, and subjected to a grueling hard sell.

Thousands are being persuaded to pay anywhere from $2,000 to $5,000 for a fraction of an acre, very often on or at the edge of the desert, at enticingly low monthly terms. I have no argument with your paying $2,000 or $3,000 or whatever for a homesite in surroundings which are likely to enrich your later years. I will even salute the farsightedness of the land tycoons who bought up huge tracts of land fifteen or twenty years ago for $50 an acre and who now can sell it for $8,000 to $10,000 or more an acre. I will argue, though, with touting these tiny parcels as great "investments."

There are millions of land parcels on the market today, so scarcity certainly won't be a factor driving up prices in the foreseeable future. In many cases all of the "investment" value—and then some—is being reaped by the developers. Whenever credit gets tight, many real estate development operations are forced to a halt, and then it's anybody's guess when the promised improvements will be completed.

Moreover, because of high-pressure sales techniques, a lot of people buy land they can't really afford. Included in the price are the promoters' high costs of advertising, bringing buyers in for the weekend, etc.

If you—or a friend or relative—are in the market for a piece of ground on which to build a retirement home, here are important rules to follow:

(1) Ask the Better Business Bureau in the area in which you are considering buying for a report on the promoter. Also ask for material to help you determine whether the price being asked is fair in comparison with the deals others are offering.

(2) Be sure the land seller gives you a "property report," not unlike a stock prospectus. The Interstate Land Sales Full Disclosure Act of 1968 requires anyone who is selling or leasing 50 or more unimproved lots smaller than five acres in interstate commerce (e.g., through the mails or advertised in nationally circulated magazines or newspapers) to furnish each customer with a statement giving "all material facts" about the land, including (but not limited to) the following:

• Name and location of developer and development.
• Date or property report.
• The distance to nearby communities over paved or unpaved roads.
• Taxes and special assessments you must pay.
• Existence of liens on the land.
• Whether the payments you make will be placed in escrow until you get clear title to the land.
• Existing and planned utilities and services, and their costs.
• The number of homes occupied at the time of the statement.
• Details of any obstacles to building on the land.
• The type of title you will ultimately get.

The development must file a similar statement with the Office of Interstate Land Sales Registration, an agency of Housing and Urban Development in Washington which can help you get your money back if any part of the property report proves to be fiction.

You, the buyer, have a "cooling off" period after signing the contract to change your mind about buying. The law permits you to waive this right if you personally inspected the property, so read the contract carefully to be sure you do not do so unintentionally. If you discover the facts have been mis-represented, you may sue for damages in a federal court. HUD can halt sales of land if it finds a property statement misleading, and if the courts find a promoter guilty of fraud, the penalty can be stiff.

If a developer who is covered by this act fails to give you the legally required property report, be on guard.

(3) In addition to getting this property report, find out if the state in which you are considering buying can give you the property report it requires developers to file covering subdivisions or land sold by mail. California and Florida are two such states. A responsible developer will be willing to provide a report even if not required to by state or federal law.

(4) Find out how near or far the land is from roads, public transportation, churches, hospitals, refuse removal services, etc. If these are merely promised by the developer, make sure they are described in the sales contract.

(5) Before you sign any contract, have a lawyer or the local legal aid society go over it carefully.

(6) Inspect *any* retirement homesite personally—perhaps by combining this tour with a vacation—since you may spend ten, twenty, or thirty years of your life there.

(7) Most important, ask yourself these questions:

How do you envision your retirement home—surrounded by wide-open space and plenty of quiet and privacy, or in the middle of a busy community, surrounded by a lot of nearby neighbors?

How are you likely to spend your time? Hiking and fishing? Traveling frequently to other places? Attending theater, concerts, other cultural events?

How near do you want to be to old friends, children, and grandchildren in your retirement years?

A sunny climate, a big sky, and a patch of ground are *not* enough to make a happy retirement.

20

HOW TO INVEST IN STOCKS

INTRODUCTION

Let's say that tomorrow you receive the news that you have a sweepstakes combination which gives you a chance to win from $50,000 to $200,000 net after taxes. Let's say your dream is to turn this into a million. How much of your possible winnings would you have to invest, for how long, and in what ways, to reach this magic mark?

(1) You could invest as little as $69,000 and be a millionaire within thirty years, if you could earn the 9.3 per cent a year which was the average rate of return on all common stocks listed on the New York Stock Exchange between 1926 and 1965. (The assumption was that you invested an equal sum of money in each stock each year and reinvested all your dividends.)

(2) You would have to put up $75,000 to become a millionaire in the thirty-year period if, instead, you put it into certificates of deposit or corporate bonds paying 9 per cent (the mid-point of the range in the early 1970s).

(3) Or you would have to put up your entire $200,000 winnings plus $6,000 more—$206,000—to become a millionaire three decades hence if you invested in a passbook savings account paying the 5½ per cent rate prevailing in the 1960s, or $114,000 in the deposit certificates offered in the early 1970s.

But let's come back down to earth: you're not due to win any wild contests or to get any financial windfall soon.

You may be, however, approaching your peak earning years, or actually in them, and thus you may be ready to set aside fairly substantial sums. How much would you have to invest each year at 6 per cent to become a millionaire in one decade, two decades, three?

You could become a millionaire within thirty years by setting aside $12,649 a year if you could achieve the relatively commonplace yearly rate of return of 6 per cent—in stocks or bonds or real estate or some other investment medium.

You could become a millionaire within twenty years if you set aside $27,185 each year at 6 per cent.

Or you could become a millionaire in ten years if you invested $75,868 each year at 6 per cent.

These are statistics the American Bankers Association and the New York Stock Exchange developed for me on their computers. They're drastically simplified, of course. Neither of the computer programs took into account the inevitable tax bite on capital gains, dividends, or interest. And it's unrealistic to assume any set rate of return on stock or bond investments will continue indefinitely.

Nevertheless, a first key point is that, in today's society and at today's available rates of return on investments, it is within the realm of possibility that you can become the fabled millionaire. Right now, hundreds of thousands of American families have $1 million in assets. And there are several hundred families in the United States with assets of well over that.

A second key point is that the vast majority of these very wealthy have invested not with the goal of safety or liquidity or dividend income, but instead with the consistent aim of long-term capital gains. Most of the very wealthy look for returns of at least 10 per cent and usually 15 to 20 per cent a year in various types of enterprises, securities or real estate, or in the farther-out mediums of art works, antiques, commodities, etc.

A third key point underlined by the computations is that the faster you want to make your million the higher the return you must seek—which means the greater risk you must be willing to assume. The implication of this third fundamental point is that you must be able to afford to take the chance.

And a fourth point: Not everybody aspires to be a millionaire. What most people want is an investment program that can help them reach some of their long-term family financial objectives: a comfortable retirement, a college education for the youngsters, perhaps a second home. For them, investing successfully can bring peace of mind and successful attainment of their goals even if they never come close to being millionaires.

WHY INVEST IN STOCKS?

You should invest part of your nest egg in the stock market for five fundamental reasons:

(1) *The long-term trend of stock prices is up.* According to the now famous study by the Center for Research and Security Prices at the University of Chicago, an investment in a random cross section of stocks on the New

York Stock Exchange over a forty-year period would have increased in value to a degree giving you an average rate of return (before taxes) equal to 9.3 per cent a year compounded annually. To translate, an investment of $1,000 compounded annually at 9.3 per cent would have grown to $35,000 in the forty years.

(2) *The long-term trend of consumer prices in general is up,* meaning that inflation has become a way of life in the United States. Stocks often are abysmal hedge against inflation (witness the 1969–74 period) but they have been over the long-term as good as or better than most other mediums.

(3) *The long-term growth trend of the United States economy is up.* Real Gross National Product (adjusted for price increases) has been increasing at the rate of 3 per cent a year for a substantial number of years and by 1980 the total of all goods and services produced in the United States (GNP) will probably be, in 1974's prices, 100 per cent higher than it was in 1970. Stocks are a basic way for you to participate in this long-term economic growth.

(4) *New packages of investments are being developed to give you protection against inflation* and savings for retirement as well as appreciation. These packages are being offered by a growing number of institutions including investment firms, mutual funds, banks, and insurance companies. Nearly all these packages involve stocks.

(5) *There is a continuing demand for stocks* from major institutions— although the gap between institutional demand for and new supplies of stocks has been narrowing in recent years. Purchasers include the huge pension funds, insurance companies, mutual funds, universities, and endowment funds. In addition, there is a continuing, though erratic, demand for American securities from foreign investors who often prefer investing in American securities because of the liquidity and the depth of the U.S. securities markets.

When you buy stocks you will be joining an enormous minority of Americans who are using stocks to build long-term financial security. The total number of shareholders in the United States approximated 31 million in the mid-seventies and, despite intermittent dips, is undoubtedly headed upward in the years ahead. This means that by 1980 more than one in four adults will be holders of stock and the proportion among higher- and middle-income groups will be far bigger than this. The base of Wall Street has broadened to a point where it literally reaches every Main Street in the nation.

Now, let's go!

WHAT ARE STOCKS?

When you buy stock of a company you buy part of the ownership of that company. If, say, you buy a share of—let's call it the Widget Company, in effect you buy a part of Widget's plant, its output, and everything that company owns.

If the Widget Company has 10,000 shares of stock outstanding and you own 100 shares, you own 100/10,000 or 1 per cent. As a stockholder you are normally entitled to vote in the election of directors and to participate in other company affairs. Each share has one vote and big companies have millions of shares outstanding and many thousands of stockholders. For example, the American Telephone & Telegraph Company in the mid-1970s had 3 million shareholders; General Motors had almost 1.3 million; International Business Machines had more than 550,000; and General Electric had more than 530,000. If the company whose stock you hold grows and increases its earnings per share, the price of your stock should rise over the long run. The price will also fluctuate day by day based on ever changing supply and demand trends. It is a rare stock that stands still.

WHAT CAUSES PRICES OF STOCKS TO CHANGE?

Once a company has sold its original stock to the public and the stock is freely traded in the market, the price of the stock will be set solely by what buyers are willing to pay for it and what sellers are willing to take. This is a classic case of how supply and demand operates in action.

Thus the price a stock sells for is the reflection of all the opinions of all the people who are buying or selling it. Among the key factors influencing what people are willing to pay for a stock will be the company's earnings. The more money a company earns, presumably the more value will be attached to its shares. Obviously, selecting a profitable stock involves knowledge and judgment of the company behind it. How aggressive is its management? How popular are its products and services? What new products is it offering or planning? What about the industry in which it operates? Does it have a bright future? (The trolley car industry once was hot.) What about its competitors? How many and how strong are they?

Finally, what about the general business trend? Is it favorable or unfavorable to the industry in general and your company in particular?

WHAT ARE DIVIDENDS?

When a company earns money it usually pays out a part of its earnings in dividends to its owners or stockholders. This is a certain amount for every share of stock. For example, if you own 100 shares of the company's stock and the dividend is $1.00 a share, you will get $100 in dividends. The rest of the company's earnings will be put back in the business.

Whether a dividend should be paid on common stock and what the amount of the dividend should be are determined by the directors of the company, who are elected by the stockholders. Many things, including how much the company earned and how much should be retained in the business, influence the directors' decision about the dividend. Usually, most companies pay out about 50 per cent of their earnings in dividends. A study made earlier in this decade by the New York Stock Exchange showed that the 1,400 companies then listed on the Exchange paid out 51 per cent of earnings in the form of dividends.

There are many companies which have paid dividends over a long span of years. In fact, on the New York Stock Exchange there are 23 companies which have paid out some cash dividends to their stockholders every year for more than a hundred years. J. P. Morgan & Co. has been paying dividends since 1840, the Singer Company has paid dividends since 1863. Also the New York Stock Exchange lists 150 companies which have paid cash dividends quarterly for forty years or more.

HOW BIG ARE DIVIDENDS?

The size of a dividend will depend on what a company earns in any given year. Most companies try to pay dividends regularly each year at a fixed annual rate such as $1.00 or $1.50 or $2.00 for each share of stock. In good years the rate may be increased or an extra dividend declared at the end of the year. In bad years a company may reduce its dividend or eliminate it completely. Interestingly enough, there are some major companies with fine records which don't pay any dividends. They plow back all the earnings they generate for future developments of new products and services. So, while the dividend payment is important for many who are looking for a yield every year on their investment, it does not carry so much weight with other investors.

One important term used in connection with dividends is yield. The yield of a stock is the yearly dividend divided by the cost of the stock. For example, if you paid $60 for a stock that pays $3.00 a year in dividends, your yield is 3/60 or 5 per cent. If you bought a $50 stock and it pays $1.00 a year in dividends, your yield is 2 per cent.

On an over-all basis, dividends in modern times have provided yields from as high as 7.8 per cent in 1948 to as low as 2.6 per cent in 1968. This is the median yield on dividend-paying common stocks listed on the New York Stock Exchange, but the range of yields on individual stocks can be very sizable in a given year. For example, in 1973 when the median yield on all NYSE stocks was 5.0 per cent, 239 stocks were paying yields of 8 per cent or better while 226 stocks were paying yields of less than 2 per cent.

HOW DO YOU FIND OUT WHAT STOCKS ARE DOING?

That's easy! Just look in the financial section of your newspaper for the latest daily reading of any stock market indicator it publishes and see whether that indicator is up or down. The Dow Jones averages and Standard & Poor's indexes are the most familiar of these market "thermometers." The New York Stock Exchange also publishes a composite index that includes all its listed common stocks. The American Stock Exchange publishes one too and the over-the-counter market has a composite NASDAQ index (see page 828) which indicates the movement of stocks traded in this system. These indexes will tell you at once the price trends of large groups of stocks. In addition to these broad indicators, there are special indexes indicating how special industry groups—such as utilities stocks—have moved as a group.

If you are interested in finding out how a specific stock that you own or may want to buy is doing, you will find that most major newspapers publish detailed price information every day on the most popular and widely held stocks. Many print the entire list of stocks traded on the New York Stock Exchange and the American Stock Exchange. They also print at times condensed lists of stocks traded on regional stock exchanges and the over-the-counter market.

A chart showing you how to read a financial table follows.

If the newspaper doesn't print price information on the stock you are interested in, chances are the stock is not popular or widely held. In that case, call your broker and ask the price of the stock. He will have a wide variety of reference materials from which he can get the answer.

HOW DO YOU GET INFORMATION ABOUT STOCKS?

Whether you are among the tens of millions of us who already hold shares of publicly owned corporations and mutual funds or among the men and women who become stockholders for the first time each year, most of you share this one characteristic: you want to learn more about the stock market and about individual stocks but you don't know how to go about getting the information.

Okay, here are ten simple guidelines on how to inform yourself.

(1) Make an excellent start by enrolling in one of the primer or advanced courses offered through New York Stock Exchange member firms in major U.S. cities from coast to coast. Under this program, brokers offer three series of nine-course lectures: elementary, intermediate, and advanced. These securities and investing lectures cover such subjects as: your investment objectives, investing for income, investing for growth, and methods of investing. Many of the larger brokerage firms offer their own lecture programs too. Check with your local brokerage houses to find out what they have available and when they plan their next series.

(2) Take courses on investing at adult education institutions across the country. Investigate the sources in your neighborhood. Colleges and junior colleges in your area well may offer special credit and non-credit courses in investment. In New York, the New York Institute of Finance offers broad training in finance to both amateurs and professionals. Some of these courses can be taken by correspondence.

(3) Ask your own broker or investment firm for literature on specific companies and industries as well as on the general stock market. Several hun-

Reading Newspaper Stock Tables

NEW YORK STOCK EXCHANGE TRANSACTIONS – DAY OF WEEK, DATE, YEAR

YEAR HIGH	YEAR LOW	STOCKS	DIV.	P.E. RATIO	SALES 100's	HIGH	LOW	CLOSE	NET CHG.
55	49¼	AM T&T[1]	2.80	11	1362	51¾	51¼	51¾	....
9⅝[2]	6⅛[2]	AT&T wt[2]	....	.....	1221	6⅜	6⅛	6⅜	....
75⅞	59½	Gen Elec	1.40[3]	19	1231	60½	57¾	59¼	– 1¼
84⅝	70⅜	Gen Mot	4.45e[4]	9	797	71⅝	70⅝	71⅜	+ ½
78½	74⅝	Gen Mot pf[5]	5	.....	15	75⅝	75	75⅝	+ ⅝
76⅞	59	McDonalds	....	63[6]	1048	60	58	59⅜	+ ¼
88⅞	77⅝	M.M.M.	1	34	444[7]	78⅜	77½	78⅛	– ⅛
91	68¾	RCAcv.pf[8]	4	.....	30	69⅞[8]	68¾[8]	69¾	+ ½
123¼	94⅞	SEARS	1.40a	24	389	97⅝	94½	97[9]	+ 1⅝[9]

1. Abbreviated name of the corporation issuing the stock. The stocks listed are common stocks unless an entry after the name indicates otherwise.
2. Wt stands for warrant. As with stocks, the price range indicates the highest and lowest prices per share paid for this warrant on the Exchange during the year–in this case, $9.62½ and $6.12½.
3. Rate of annual dividend–for this stock, $1.40. This amount is an estimation based on the last quarterly or semi-annual payment.
4. Letters following the dividend number indicate additional information. Here, for example, the "e" designates the stated amount as declared or paid so far this year. Other symbols are explained in tables appearing in newspapers.
5. "pf" following the name indicates a preferred stock.
6. The price of a share of stock divided by earnings per share for a 12-month period.
7. This column shows the number of shares reported traded for the day, expressed in hundreds – for this stock, 44,400. This number does not include stocks bought in odd-lot quantities, that is, in quantities less than 100 shares for most stocks. The letter "z" preceding an entry indicates the actual number of shares traded.
8. The highest price paid for this security during the day's trading session was $69.87½ – the lowest, $68.75. Cv. pf. stands for convertible preferred.
9. The closing price or last sale of the day in this stock was at $97.00 per share. And this, the closing price, is $1.62½ more than the closing price of the previous day – as indicated by the "+1⅝."

dred New York Stock Exchange firms alone are now turning out more than 400,000 pages of investment research a year—much of it exceedingly helpful.

(4) Get free copies from a local NYSE firm of the Big Board's basic educational pamphlets. You will learn plenty from such publications as "The Language of Investing" and "How to Get Help When You Invest."

(5) Write to the New York Stock Exchange, 11 Wall Street, New York, N.Y. 10005, for an "Investors Information Kit" providing basic booklets for $2.00.

(6) Use your public library. You will find dozens of useful books written for the amateur as well as for the more sophisticated investor. On pages 868–69 there is a bibliography of good books on investing that you might want to read.

(7) Read the business and investment news in your newspapers and subscribe to one or more specialized business publications—such as *Barron's, Forbes, Financial World,* and the *Wall Street Journal.* Keep up with trends in the economy as well as with developments in individual industries and companies.

(8) Learn by doing. For instance, you might begin learning through an investment club. These clubs are groups of people who share a common interest, who get together usually once a month to discuss securities and invest small sums contributed by each club member in stocks selected by the group. Brokers often serve as advisers to these clubs and many of the best clubs are members of the National Association of Investment Clubs. Write this association for advice on forming a club. (A separate section on investment clubs follows.

(9) Ask an organization to which you belong to show films on investing. The New York Stock Exchange no longer supplies films at no charge, but you may get guidance on what's available by writing to the Investors Service Department, New York Stock Exchange, 11 Wall Street, New York, N.Y. 10005.

(10) Check your local educational television stations to see whether any are offering, as some do, a program or programs on general business news and on the stock market.

Any of these moves will help you. All of them will help make you well informed and ready to continue your education on your own. When you make decisions based on facts and your study of available information—plus the help of a qualified broker or adviser—you have gone through the process which distinguishes investing in stocks from gambling.

Your decisions will not always be correct, far from it, but you will at least have acted in a mature, intelligent way. And, being intelligent, you'll not only learn from your mistakes but also translate them into successes.

WHAT IS THE NEW YORK STOCK EXCHANGE?

Although there are tens of thousands of different stocks, the ones bought and sold most frequently were in the mid-seventies traded on the floor of the New York Stock Exchange. The New York Stock Exchange has a history going back to 1792, well over a hundred and eighty years ago, when a group of brokers gathered under a buttonwood tree on lower Wall Street to make up rules of conduct as to how the business of trading in stocks could be done.

Since that humble beginning, the New York Stock Exchange has become the leading securities exchange not only in the United States but also in the world—and many of the world's other exchanges are patterned after its activities.

As of 1974, the Exchange was located in a historic building at 11 Wall Street at the corner of Broad and Wall streets in New York and physically encompassed a trading floor about the size of a football field. On that floor, more than 2,000 common and preferred stocks were traded, worth more than $500 billion in market value. In these stocks alone, the number of transactions often equaled 50,000 in a day. To handle these transactions, about 2,700 people were involved on the floor of the Exchange.

Functionally, the Exchange was an organization consisting of 1,366 members who had bought memberships (commonly called seats) on the Exchange for prices that have varied in the last ten years from under $100,000 to over $500,000. Most of these 1,366 members represented brokerage firms whose primary business was carrying out the orders of other people to buy and sell securities. These brokers were paid commissions for executing the orders placed by their customers. There were in this country a dozen exchanges ranging from the largest, NYSE, to the second-ranking American Stock Exchange (Amex), also located in New York City, at 86 Trinity Place, to small exchanges in such cities as Seattle and Honolulu.

Among the other exchanges in the mid-seventies were the National Stock Exchange, New York City; the Boston Stock Exchange; the PBW (Philadelphia-Baltimore-Washington) Stock Exchange; the Midwest Stock Exchange in Chicago; the Pacific Exchange in San Francisco and Los Angeles.

The "Big Board" (the NYSE) did the bulk of the trading in listed securities because of the high caliber of the corporations it lists: AT&T, IBM, General Motors, General Electric, etc., and because, to be listed there, companies had to meet the highest existing standards. These standards involved earnings, assets, number of shares outstanding, number of stockholders, and number of stockholders who held at least 100 shares. The standards for listing on the New York Stock Exchange also are raised periodically.

The listing standards of the American Stock Exchange were deliberately lower—and to the Amex went many young, smaller corporations not yet seasoned enough to reach the NYSE criteria.

Most regional exchanges traded in stocks that also were listed on the New York Stock Exchange. In fact, 90 per cent of their volume came from issues listed on the NYSE. In addition, the regional stock exchanges traded in a few local stocks. For instance, stocks of Chicago-based companies were traded on the Midwest Stock Exchange.

WHAT ARE UNLISTED SECURITIES?

Stocks listed on recognized exchanges are called listed stocks. Huge numbers of stocks and bonds, however, aren't listed on any exchange at all and are bought and sold in what is called the over-the-counter market.

The vast over-the-counter market is not a place. It is a method of doing business: by private negotiation among securities broker/dealers who communicate via an immense communications network rather than use a trading floor on which to buy and sell securities.

It is a market which in volume and variety of transactions dwarfs all the listed exchanges combined. And it is a market which not only has no market place; it also has no ticker tape and not even any rigidly fixed hours of trading.

Most of the broker/dealers do a large part of their buying and selling of securities over the NASDAQ system—a broad communications system linked together by computers. Most offices of over-the-counter broker/dealers* have a NASDAQ terminal which looks like a television set and which shows on the screen bid and asked quotes in O-T-C stocks. These quotes keep the broker/dealers current on the prices at which other dealers throughout the country are willing to buy or sell the specific stocks. The actual buying and selling, though, is done through phone conversations between the dealers in which they come to an agreement as to the price.

Most of the dealers who transact billions of dollars' worth of business with each other every year never meet face to face. They are "voices." Their word over a phone is accepted with complete trust.

In contrast to the exchange market places, which are primarily auction markets, the over-the-counter market is mostly a dealer market. This means that a dealer makes the market in securities as a principal (he's the owner) and, when you buy the security, generally you are buying it from his inventory. Prices are quoted as bid (the price a dealer is willing to pay) and as asked (the price a dealer is willing to take), and the transaction may be at a price somewhere in between.

You, the public, will either buy at the asked or sell at the bid price.

Most bank and insurance company stocks are traded in this market. So are U. S. Government bonds, municipal bonds, and as of the mid-seventies,

* Most over-the-counter dealers also may act as brokers.

the securities of some giant companies (American Express, Anheuser-Busch). But unlisted securities in general are those of small companies.

The over-the-counter market offers investors a broad variety of issues ranging from the most conservative to the most speculative. Here investors will find many attractive growth stocks of companies which have not yet become popular because they operate in a regional area rather than on the national scene. Here the stocks are given time to "mature" before they are listed on one of the exchanges.

WHAT COMMISSIONS DO YOU PAY TO TRADE STOCKS?

As this decade rolls on, you, the individual investor, will buy and sell securities via an entirely new range of methods costing you an entirely new range of fees.

To give you a glimpse of what might be ahead, let's imagine you as an investor in four different roles:

(1) On your own, you decide to buy a particular stock. You don't need or want any advice from your broker. You wish merely to place an order to buy, say, 100 shares of your choice. You will do precisely this with a securities representative trained only to execute your buy (or sell) orders. You will pay this order-taker a modest fee for his minimum service.

It well may be that all your orders in the 100-share range will be executed automatically—fed through a machine just as your purchase of an airplane ticket with a charge plate is now fed through a machine.

(2) Or say you ask to have some research done for you on certain securities and you seek advice on what to buy or sell. You will go to a securities representative trained to handle your requests and advise you. You will pay this man or woman a higher fee for what is obviously more service.

(3) Or say you want your securities representative to assume complete charge of your securities account and buy and sell for you. You will go to a securities representative with the credentials testifying to his or her training for this skilled work and you will understandably pay a still higher fee for this higher service.

(4) Or say you want to go even beyond this and want one single firm to take responsibility for all aspects of your family financial life: your mortgage payments, insurance, liquid savings, mutual fund shares, individual stocks and bonds, wills, etc. You will go to what might be called a "certified financial planner," a firm employing many different experts trained in the different fields to serve you. And for these services altogether, you'll pay the highest fee.

By the early 1980s the make-up of the markets easily could be unrecognizable to the observer of the mid-1970s. Even the conventional floor of the New York Stock Exchange, as a physical place where securities are bought and sold, may cease to exist.

Among the other changes that will create a new "Wall Street":

• A central market system with a tickertape showing prices of securities in all markets;

• An industrywide clearance and depository system to reduce processing costs and increase service to investors;

• A major improvement of the protection provided by the Securities Investor Protection Corp. for investors with accounts at brokerage firms that go bankrupt.

• An eventual revision in the capital gains tax so that the tax rate on securities profits on truly long-term holdings would be lower than the capital gains tax rate on stocks held a year or two.

It's useless, therefore, to give details on specific commissions when convulsive changes are clearly in the making.

Institutions now freely negotiate the commissions they'll pay on large blocks of stocks they buy or sell. Individuals are able to negotiate rates too.

But no matter how "Wall Street" finally is restructured, it's likely that you will invest via the diversified ways pinpointed here and fees will be "unbundled." And you will pay a schedule of fees determined by the size of your order and the level of service you get.

WHAT ARE BULL AND BEAR MARKETS?

When a lot of people decide at about the same time to buy stocks, this increase in buying interest tends to push up the average price of stocks. If the price rise of these stocks over all is substantial and prolonged it is called a bull market.

When a lot of people decide at about the same time to sell stocks, their more or less simultaneous selling tends to push down the average price of stocks. If the price decline is substantial and prolonged it is called a bear market. If the price decline is both substantial and precipitous, we run into the possibility of a panic.

To be bullish or bearish, then, simply means to think that stocks will go up or down. The reason the term "bull" is linked with those who expect an uplift in prices is probably the tendency of a bull to lift and throw up an object with his horns. The bear is usually more cautious in his fighting tactics and tries to knock down his opponent.

HOW DO YOU CHOOSE A BROKER?

If you are to do your buying and selling of stocks through a broker, it is obviously of vital importance to you to choose one who can service your account properly. But *don't* create a tough and unnecessary problem for yourself by expecting the broker you choose to be right all the time. For he won't be—and when he is wrong, you may be tempted to follow the tips of amateurs who intrigue you by claiming they are making fortunes. This way often leads to disaster and every day a dismally large percentage of Americans do take this course. Even the most astute professional will not be right all of the time. In fact, in some periods, his advice will range from indifferent to downright bad.

Choosing and recommending stocks is not a science. It is an art. Your broker should be right enough of the time to help guide you toward your investment objectives and help you to enhance your assets. You should be able to trust his experience, research, and judgment and you should feel comfortable with him. That's all. It's *your* money, *your* investment program. And basically your nest egg is *your responsibility*.

Here are four key rules to follow in selecting a broker.

(1) Choose a firm which is a member of the New York Stock Exchange. Of course there are non-member firms which also rank at the top but you are a beginner and you probably have no sound information on these. The New York Stock Exchange in the mid-1970s had about 500 firms including nearly all the important firms doing business with the public, for an estimated 90 per cent of all the securities business in the country. Moreover, a member of the New York Stock Exchange must meet the highest standards established to date—fulfill minimum capital requirements, undergo both an annual surprise audit by an independent CPA firm and spot financial checks by the Exchange. The member firm's employees must complete a minimum training period of six months, pass an Exchange examination, and work at their jobs full time. These requirements give you at least some protection and it is only common sense to accept it.

(2) Shop around as you would shop around for any service as important as this. Ask your friends, business acquaintances, and local banker for recommendations on which broker might be the best for you—particularly important in the uncertain conditions of the mid-1970s. Call at least three or four brokerage firms in your area and talk to the manager of each. Tell each one about your investment goals, the amounts of money you can invest, and ask whether he can assign someone to your account with whom he thinks you will have good rapport.

(3) Ask each firm for its recommendations of investments for a person in your financial position and for its research reports on the companies suggested. Incidentally, the person who will eventually be assigned to you may be variously called a registered representative, a customer's man, or an account executive—but you will call him your broker.

(4) Select your broker on the basis of your comparisons of the firms and their advice to you. Then give the broker all the pertinent facts about your financial circumstances and goals. The more he knows about your situation, the better he can advise you. Be frank and honest. Ask what you should reasonably expect in terms of capital gains and over what period of

time. Find out how much service he can provide, how often you should expect him to call you, and how often he expects you to call him for information.

BUT WHERE DO YOU FIND A BROKER WHO WANTS YOU?

But let's say you don't know three or four firms in your area with which you might open an account, you don't want to follow the herd and simply open an account with a world-famous firm—and you don't know where else to turn. What do you do?

You send a postcard with your name and address on it to Directory, New York Stock Exchange, P. O. Box 1971, Radio City Station, New York, N.Y. 10019. You will receive by return mail and without charge a small pamphlet giving you the names and headquarters addresses of hundreds of New York Stock Exchange member firms which say they are willing and able to handle your small account—and listing what minimum requirements and criteria each firm may have.

In the mid-1970s these firms had several thousand branch offices in more than 800 cities in all fifty states, of which more than 1,000 or 33 per cent were located in 24 major U.S. cities. More than nine out of ten of them say they do not have a minimum dollar requirement for the size of any buy or sell order they will accept from you. More than eight out of ten (or about 2,000 branch offices) say they will buy for or sell to you any stock traded on the major stock exchanges at any price—with no minimum price-per-share limitations either.

What the NYSE is obviously trying to do with this free pamphlet is to counter in part at least the very negative publicity Wall Street has received for its attitude toward and treatment of the small investor in the past several years.

HOW DO YOU DETECT A SWINDLER?

Another key rule to follow in selecting a broker is: Explore each of the following questions about any person who suggests stocks to you, even a broker at what you believe is a highly reputable firm—and *if any answer is "yes," beware, for these are frequently the earmarks of a swindler.*

Does he plug one certain stock and refuse to sell you anything else? The crook always has a specific stock to sell and he'll not bother with you if you request another stock or ask for written information about the company he's plugging.

Does he promise a quick, sure profit? The legitimate broker never guarantees that the price of any given stock will go up. Nor will he attempt to guarantee you against losses.

Does he claim to have inside information? Second only to outright fraud, alleged "inside information" has cost investors more money than anything else. Most tips are phony and furthermore, if he truly does have inside information, there is always the possibility that at some future date he might be sued by other investors because he improperly obtained inside information and you too might be liable in a lawsuit if you use inside information.

Is he in a hurry and does he urge you to buy "before the price goes up"? The legitimate broker doesn't try to stampede you into action.

Can you check his reputation? The crook will have no references except perhaps forged ones which won't stand checking.

SHOULD YOU GO INTO THE STOCK MARKET?

Certainly! But before you do, be sure that:

(1) You realize there is always an element of risk in stockownership. Some of the top stock performers of the late 1960s were among the worst performers in the early 1970s. Some of the most glamorous companies of the 1960s, with corporate names that included the lures of "tronics," "aero," "computer," "photocopy" were among the most unglamorous stock issues in the first half of the 1970s. And some of the most spectacular mutual fund performers in one year can become the most spectacular no-go performers the next year.

(2) *You are investing money you do not need for regular living expenses,* have adequate life insurance, and have sufficient liquid savings to help you through an unexpected financial emergency. (See Chapter 1, "Your Personal Money Manager," for details on the appropriate size of this emergency cash reserve.)

(3) *You determine a specific investment goal suited to your needs before you invest,* and you are prepared to stick to that goal until your circumstances change. If your goal is income, you'll want one type of stock; if it is growth, you'll want another; and if it is, above all, security of principal, you'll want a third.

If you're a young man earning more than enough to meet your family's current expenses and have set aside funds to cope with financial emergencies, your objective normally will be growth. Therefore, you'll buy stocks that promise to grow in price along with the economy's growth over the years. You may take greater-than-average risks in the hope of getting higher-than-average profits. Although you may lose on a stock in which you speculate, you can afford the risk at your age; you have time to recoup.

(4) *You have the emotional temperament to own stocks.* As the New York State Exchange itself says, "Many persons should never buy stocks. The individual who can be seriously upset by a slight decline in price or who goes off on a spending spree when prices rise is better off out of the stock market."

That leads into the confession that one of the most embarrassing questions frequently put to me is, "What do you think the stock market is going to do?" And, usually before I can open my mouth, the questioner adds, "Boy,

I bet you get plenty of inside tips! In your position, you probably clean up. . . ."

When I answer that (a) I don't get many tips and the ones I do get I invariably ignore, and (b) I don't clean up, and what's more, have absolutely no desire to—the mildest reaction is disappointment.

It is true, though, for because of my temperament—my emotional attitude toward speculating in the stock market—I don't feel comfortable taking stock tips. I haven't the temperament to be a gambler in Wall Street. I don't clean up because I don't even try to. But I don't go broke either.

Without my being particularly aware of it, my activities in the stock market reflect my own personality. And the purpose of this confession is to emphasize to you the vital point that if your aim is to be a serene as well as a successful investor the first thing you must do is analyze your own personality.

To be even more specific, don't buy—or sell—stocks because it seems the thing to do: in the stock market, "conforming" doesn't pay off.

Don't buy stocks of a type or in amounts that give you anxiety and concern. If you are so nervous about owning stocks that you can't take a trip without worrying about what is happening to your stocks, stay out of the market.

Don't try to beat the professional traders unless you are willing to study enough to become a pro yourself.

In short, follow the fundamental rule: "Know thyself."

(5) *You are willing to take the time to become informed* about the stocks which interest you and are determined not to act on the basis of tips or rumors no matter how intriguing they are.

You wouldn't dream of buying a house simply on the basis of how it looks from the outside. You would examine the inside thoroughly, check on the reputation of the builder, the quality of the construction, and a hundred other things. The same thoroughness must be applied to buying stocks for, along with buying a house, investing in the stock market may be among the most important financial decisions you make.

You also probably wouldn't dream of trying to trade in and out of real estate and pit yourself against the real professionals in this field. Again, the same rule must apply to stocks. In the long run, you, as a novice investor, will almost surely make out better than an in-and-out trader.

One of the best ways to select a stock is on the basis of your own familiarity with (and respect for) the company's products or services.

(6) *You have the advice of an experienced and reputable broker* to help guide you.

(7) *You don't expect too much too soon.* Many inexperienced investors become fidgety when their stocks rise only a little or decline soon after they buy them. They refuse to allow time for their stocks to perform as expected. Millions who have taken short-term losses would have shown handsome

profits if they had had more confidence in their own judgment and were willing to give their stocks a chance to move.

The over-all caliber of hundreds of the stocks listed on the NYSE is sufficiently high to bail you out of your errors most of the time, assuming you have the courage and capacity to hold on. The odds on gain are heavily against the individual trading blindly in and out of the market and heavily for the individual investing for the long term.

(8) *You stick to your investment objectives.* Many investors pay lip service to the objective of long-term growth and ask their brokers to recommend stocks to them that meet this criterion. Then they hear rumors and read stories about stocks that have doubled and tripled in a period of months. In envy and greed, they soon are badgering their broker to recommend speculative stocks in the hopes of also making tremendous gains. Be honest about your objectives. If you want long-term growth, buy and hold stocks that promise long-term appreciation. Don't be sidetracked into dangerously risky, speculative situations.

(9) *You are aware that you buy stocks, not the stock averages.* A common error of the amateur is to justify the holding of a "cat or dog" issue because the over-all economy is growing or the stock averages are climbing. Even in the biggest bull markets, many stocks slide and, in this era's viciously selective and for so long deeply depressed market, what you own has been critical.

(10) *You have an over-all family investment plan to* protect you from falling into "hit or miss" investing. Most new investors overlook the importance of a diversified financial program which allocates funds to major types of investments—real estate (a home), stocks, bonds, etc., in addition to savings in cash or its equivalent, life insurance, and similar mediums.

There is no formula under which you can automatically put a proper percentage in each type of investment. The key point, though, is to avoid the error of "hit or miss" by diversification of your financial program.

EMPLOYEE SAVINGS PLANS

An excellent way to enter the stock market and start creating your securities nest egg is via your company's employee savings plan—if it offers one.

The fundamental mechanism of an employee savings plan is simple.

(1) A participant voluntarily contributes part of his or her salary through payroll deductions. The most common contribution is 3 to 6 per cent of one's salary.

(2) The company then matches all or part of the participant's savings with a company contribution. The average is 50¢ by the company for each $1.00 the employee saves, but in some companies the corporation contribution is higher.

(3) The company and employee contributions are put into an employee

trust fund to be invested and later paid out to the employees. In some cases, part of the funds are placed in the company's own common stock, but usually the investments are in a wide selection of stocks similar to the range of a mutual fund portfolio. And, generally speaking, the company turns over the management of these investments to a professional management company which oversees them.

A majority of employees in companies offering these plans take advantage of them. Most save at the maximum rate their plan permits. And most stay in their plan until they leave their jobs or retire. There are many benefits. First, the company is automatically boosting the chances you will get a profit from the savings program by the amount of money it has put in to match your contributions. Second, you get professional management of your funds at no cost to you and you also get a diversification of a portfolio which helps make sure that, over the long term, the over-all fund will grow. And, third, there are tax advantages arising from the fact that your employer's contribution to you is not taxable income to you in the year in which it is made. You pay no taxes on this money and only pay taxes on the contributions when you finally draw out your nest egg on leaving the company or retirement.

A variation on this program are company stock purchase plans. Under these, the company helps encourage employees to buy stock in the company. In the simplest version, an employee signs up to purchase stock in the company through payroll deductions every month and is credited over the period of his or her participation with buying shares of the stock. The company usually picks up the bill for any commissions or other fees involved in the purchase of the stock and keeps all the records indicating how many shares of stock the employee owns. Obviously, if you are having $50 or $100 a month deducted from your pay check to buy stock, you will wind up with fractional shares of stock and this is permissible under these company stock purchase plans.

Use one of these plans if you get the opportunity. They are a superb plus for any employee eligible to save and invest this way.

HOW TO START AN INVESTMENT CLUB

Let's say you feel that the only way you'll get started in the stock market is by being forced to invest a certain amount every month or so—and you want to do this via an investment club.

If so, you have plenty of company. In the mid-1970s there were about 60,000 investment clubs across the nation with an estimated membership of more than a million. The majority of the clubs in operation for several years have been profitable, reports the non-profit National Association of Investment Clubs in Royal Oak, Mich. Some 200,000 people belonged to clubs that were members of the NAIC and the track record on the investing of these clubs has in a surprising percentage of cases surpassed the Dow Jones averages

—not bad at all considering the fact that many professional managers of money didn't do nearly as well.

Basically, investment clubs are groups of ten, fifteen, or twenty people who work together, know each other socially, or belong to the same fraternal or business organization—and who then meet once a month to invest money regularly. In a sense, each club is akin to a small mutual fund with each club's members contributing $10, $15, $20, $25, or perhaps as much as $50 a month apiece into the club kitty for investment in stocks. Before stocks are purchased the club's members must make extensive investigations on the choices to be made.

If you are thinking of or are at the point of trying to start an investment club, you must recognize that you will be inviting a financial fiasco unless you know and manage your group according to the basic rules. Here are your ten guidelines:

(1) Limit your initial membership to ten or fifteen people. An investment club should be a long-term proposition and your members must be compatible not only personally but also in their attitudes toward investment.

(2) Understand, from the outset, that an investment club offers no avenue to instant riches. Instead, a get-rich-quick philosophy frequently is the cause for a club's failure.

(3) In an exploratory meeting with prospective members, try to arrive at an over-all investment policy. For instance, what growth rate of your funds will you try to achieve? Will you invest every month?

(4) Set a reasonable goal for growth of your investments, including dividends and capital appreciation.

(5) Plan to invest a given sum each month no matter what the over-all market conditions are. By buying shares of a selected company at both higher and lower prices, you average out the per-share cost over the long term.

(6) Plan also to reinvest dividends as they are issued.

(7) Aim for a diversified portfolio as protection against major swings in one segment of the economy or another. Strive, say, for shares in a dozen different companies per $10,000 invested.

(8) Seek guidance from well-qualified brokers, economists, security analysts, and established business publications. The amount of research and self-education members are willing to do and share with each other can mark the difference between a successful and an unsuccessful club.

(9) Before you formally establish your club, consult a qualified lawyer or tax adviser on how to get the biggest tax advantage for your club. Your club should have some legal status because brokers may refuse to do business with an informal organization. Usually, a partnership is the most economical form. If there are earnings in any given year, all members must report this on their income tax returns, of course.

(10) Also at the start, draw up a written agreement covering the club's investment policy; the maximum share any one member may own; which member will deal with the club's broker; how much information each will be expected to present monthly; what happens if a member wants to leave and wants to be paid out for his or her shares. Also make sure when you establish your club how much each will be expected to contribute monthly—and make sure, too, that the amount is a comfortable sum for each member.

Follow these rules, consult the NAIC for more detailed guidelines—and the likelihood is that your club will be profitable. Incidentally, there are many NAIC publications that you will find useful when trying to decide which stocks to buy. For illustration, the NAIC has and will send you samples of a 50-page investment club manual, stock selection guides, and a portfolio management guide.

The NAIC's address is 1515 East Eleven Mile Road, Royal Oak, Mich. 48068.

HOW TO BEAT THE STOCK MARKET THROUGH "DOLLAR COST AVERAGING"

One way you can beat any viciously fluctuating stock market, put your money to work, and sleep well at night is through "dollar cost averaging"—a stock-buying method which many institutional as well as individual investors use in a logical attempt to acquire a stock at a reasonable price.

First, let's assume you don't have any convictions about where the stock market is heading in the next several months—but you feel strongly that the long-term trend of the U.S. economy is upward and stock prices will be much higher on average ten years, fifteen years from now.

Let's also assume you've accumulated some extra cash and you earn enough to be able to accumulate cash for investment from time to time. Okay:

(1) Decide now how much money you can comfortably invest at regular intervals.

(2) Plan to invest the same fixed amount at regular intervals in the future—say, the fifteenth of each month or the fifteenth of every third month or the fifteenth of every sixth month, etc. Don't get fainthearted and hold back purchases if the market drops.

(3) Keep this up over the long term, so your shares can grow with the economy's growth over five or ten or more years.

(4) Ignore the day-to-day fluctuations in the market, for you aren't trying to guess the bottom. You're averaging out your costs and the fundamental uptrend of the market over the long term should carry you with it.

Here's an easy example of dollar cost averaging with a hypothetical investment of $50 a month. The price swings have been exaggerated and commissions have been eliminated to make the illustration stand out.

Date	Invested	Price per share	Shares bought
Jan. 15, 1976	$50	$25	2
Feb. 15	50	20	2½
Mar. 15	50	15	3⅓
Apr. 15	50	15	3⅓
May 15	50	20	2½
June 15	50	25	2
July 15	50	30	1⅔

What you have done is buy fewer shares at the higher prices, more shares at the lower prices—with equal amounts of money. Your average price on your shares on the seven dates is $21.43 per share. But with your $350 you have purchased 17⅓ shares, so each share has cost you $20.19.

In this hypothetical case, you would be showing a paper loss in April 1976 but you would be nicely ahead by July 15 (your cost per share, $20.19; the market, $30).

You can, of course, lose even with this system if your judgment is so bad that you buy a stock that doesn't realize its growth potential or if you are forced to sell out when the market value of your accumulated shares is less than your actual cost. So you can't commit funds to dollar cost averaging that may be needed for other purposes.

But I'm assuming that you'll follow these easy—but absolutely essential —rules. If so, history shouts that over the long term you'll come out well ahead.

REINVESTING DIVIDENDS

If you have a savings account you know how interest you leave in the account adds to your deposit and then, as your interest earns its own interest, the compounding accelerates the building of your nest egg of cash.

If you own mutual fund shares, you know that you have the option of having the dividends you earn automatically reinvested in more shares of the mutual fund and you know that, as the new shares earn dividends too, this compounding speeds the building of your nest egg of mutual fund shares.

Or if you are buying your company's stock under an employee payroll deduction plan and are regularly plowing back the dividends to buy more of your own company's stock, you know how this compounding enhances your nest egg of these company shares.

How, then, would you like to have any cash dividends you earn on any stocks you own automatically reinvested for you?

This automatic reinvestment would be a superb method of forced savings

—for you would never get your hands on the dividends and thus wouldn't be able to dribble the money away. This would be a way to compound your dividend income as you compound your interest income—about as sure a way as there is to make a sound investment grow steadily. This would be a way to get the advantage of dollar cost averaging on your reinvestment of dividends for your dividends would be invested regularly through bear and bull markets, and thus your costs would average out.

A plan to permit you to do precisely this is spreading rapidly to an impressive list of corporations and banks across the country. It's a common-sense concept which is particularly geared to the small investor. Here are the key details.

Q. How does the plan work?

A. Say the company in which you own stock is a member of the dividend reinvestment plan of a major bank and you've signed up. As your dividends are declared, the bank will invest them in your company's stock along with the dividends of other participating shareholders.

All prices paid will be averaged and all stockholders will pay the identical price for the new shares. You will be credited with ownership of your additional shares. You will receive a statement of the dividends you were paid, the price of your new shares, the total amount you own.

The bank will also keep your stock certificate for you.

Q. How do you enroll in the program?

A. If your company is a member of the plan, it will send you information. Or you can write the treasurers of companies in which you own shares and request data on any automatic dividend reinvestment program. You can also urge your companies to offer the service.

Q. What are the charges for reinvestment?

A. This is a crucial point, for because the bank is combining dividends from all participating shareholders it buys in big amounts, pays lower commission charges as a result—and is able to pass along the lower commissions to you. Your commissions will usually be less than 1 per cent. The bank will also charge you a small fee for its service.

It's an intelligent program, good for the companies, healthy for the markets, and well worth your consideration.

(Note: In a few cases, a company will run its own dividend reinvestment program for shareholders and charge no fees at all.)

HOW TO INVEST ON A BUDGET

Small investors also may buy shares of leading stocks via periodic purchases and have the privilege of automatic reinvestment of dividends through plans being offered by stock exchange firms and many major banks throughout the country. The first of the bank plans was established in 1973 and the idea since then has spread rapidly.

This is a way to invest on a budget which you may find attractive, economical, and suited to your needs. Check stock exchange firms and banks in your area to find out which ones offer plans of this sort and the specific details.

INVESTMENT ADVICE——WHERE DO YOU GET IT?

Most investors expect, ask for, and get advice on buying and selling stocks from their stockbrokers. Most brokerage firms have research department or access to professional research staffs and constantly feed their clients (you) with a stream of buy and sell recommendations. Some firms will even manage your portfolio on a non-discretionary basis——meaning you give the broker authority (discretion) to buy and sell without checking back for your approval. (Many brokers, though, shy away from such accounts.)

All you have traditionally paid for such services has been your commission fees——nothing more. But this is in the process of change——and this is just one of many great new changes taking place in the field of investment advice. Read on . . .

PROFESSIONAL INVESTMENT MANAGEMENT——TREND OF THE FUTURE

When my husband and I accumulated a nest egg to invest in securities some years back, we entrusted it to a small, little-known, but top-notch investment counsel firm in Wall Street. We paid the firm an annual fee based on a small percentage of our portfolio's over-all total value each year. In return, the firm took over all investment decisions and worked to increase the size of the portfolio and, thus, the size of its fee. When the firm was dissolved about a decade later and we reluctantly terminated our relationship, we were spectacularly ahead of the Dow Jones average. We couldn't possibly have done as well devoting a few hours (if that) a week to managing our money.

This type of professional management for a fee is now in a renaissance and breaking into entirely new areas. The investment manager who supervises the funds of the small investor for a fee is one of the financial trends of the future in our country. Brokerage companies have taken over or set up investment management subsidiaries which are wooing accounts in the up to $25,000 range. Some established investment advisers are cutting the minimum account they'll manage for a fee to $10,000. And a growing number of banks are taking accounts as small as $10,000 (and even under) to manage. Until fairly recently banks were interested only in $100,000-and-up accounts.

Also new on the scene are a growing number of small investment counsel firms which accept accounts as low as $5,000. These are the so-called "mini counselors" and the likelihood is there will be hundreds servicing the small investor in a few years.

The reasons for this unexpected movement to serve the small investor aren't hard to find. The market declines of 1969–74 made millions of small investors brutally aware of how atrociously unprepared they were to manage their own money. They were also bitterly disillusioned by the performance of their go-go mutual fund shares. Simultaneously, many brokerage firms found out just how unprofitable were many transactions for individuals—and trading in and out of stock to make commissions on small accounts came in for universal condemnation.

Here are several key characteristics of the investment counsel firms.

• The firm will take over responsibility for your entire investment portfolio, will buy and sell on your behalf to achieve whatever goals are consistent with your needs, and will generally aim for enhancement of your portfolio's value. These firms make no commissions on your transactions. Their earnings come from the set percentage fee—usually 1½ or 2 per cent or a minimum dollar amount—you pay on your total portfolio and thus they profit most when you profit.

• Your fee will be tied to the size of your account. A typical fee might be 2 per cent of the total, or 2 per cent on the first $10,000 and a smaller percentage on amounts above $10,000. Others might charge a yearly minimum of $250. Fees are usually payable annually, although you may arrange otherwise. Of course, the fees are deductible on your federal tax return if you itemize.

• You pay your own brokerage commissions in addition to the fee you pay. Sometimes you can ask the investment adviser to put your trades through your own broker, but generally you open a brokerage account with a firm suggested by your investment adviser.

• You receive a statement—usually monthly—of all transactions and a list of securities you own and a periodic report on the progress of your account.

• You may open your account with cash or securities or both. You usually give your adviser a limited power of attorney so he can make discretionary investment decisions for you. All securities are bought in your name and only you can withdraw capital or securities from your account. You may cancel the power of attorney at any time.

• Generally, you give your investment adviser discretion to make investments for you without consulting you every time he wants to buy or sell something for your portfolio. Some advisers, however, do consult with clients in advance of taking action, and still others do not want a discretionary account setup.

• You may close out your account at any time on written notice. You may have dividends credited to your account or sent to you. You may withdraw a given percentage of your funds on a regular basis and you may also tell your adviser what stocks or industries you want to avoid.

But the central point of this is that in most cases you have no control over what securities are bought and sold for you. Your adviser takes over once your objectives are set. He's paid a fee to help you achieve your investment goals.

Of course, there are many variations in the way investment counseling is developing. Under the usual bank setup, the bank sends you a list of its recommendations on securities to be bought and sold. You then indicate if you agree and send the buy and sell order documents to your broker for execution.

Under the way most mini counselors operate, each client has his own account with an average of from 5 to 10 or 12 stocks, depending on the size of the account. Thus, if the mini counselor has given you some very good advice and you hold a cross section of excellent securities in your portfolio, your whole portfolio can grow rapidly in value.

Obviously, you can't expect the fancy treatment given someone with a million-dollar account. You will not have long personal interviews; you may talk to your counselor only on the phone and even then not too much; you will not receive a portfolio designed just for you; you will find that your portfolio is quite similar to other accounts that the mini counselor manages.

But there is nothing wrong with any of this, for presumably the stocks recommended to you are the stocks the firm has confidence in.

HOW DO YOU CHOOSE THE RIGHT ADVISER FOR YOU?

(1) Decide at the very beginning what *your* investment objectives are: Long-term growth? Current income? Maximum safety? Compare your objectives with the stated investment philosophy (if any) of each of the investment management firms you are considering.

(2) Explore the credentials of each firm's officers and research staff (if any). This is particularly important if the firm is a one- or two-man operation, as many of those catering to small investors are. If it doesn't have its own research staff, where does it get its investment research? Investment counseling has been an unregulated field in the past with no established standards for the counselors. It's only recently that the SEC has moved to set up some sort of standards.

(3) Ask the firm to provide you with references against which you can check these credentials—and follow up on them. Check with local banks and brokerage firms. Do not hesitate to query other clients to whom you are referred. Question any friends or acquaintances who may have been clients or may have information.

(4) Pay particular attention to the performance records of the firm. How have the organization's actual accounts made out during the past five or ten years? (*Not* a selected "model" account!) If the firm hasn't been in existence that long, check back on the previous performance records of its individual members with other organizations. If the firm refuses to divulge its performance records, be skeptical about any of its claims.

(5) See what you can find out about the firm's performances in bear as well as bull markets. A firm should be able to demonstrate it has at least lost less than average in bear markets and surely gained more than average in bull markets.

(6) Make sure you differentiate between a firm's stated investment goal of a growth rate per account of, say, 10 to 15 per cent a year and its actual achievement.

(7) Try to interview personally at least one or two of the firm's officers and use this interview to discuss your investment goals and to ask such questions as these:

Are you permitted to specify the securities you want to invest in? The answer should be *no*, or why pay your money for professional advice?

What is the procedure for withdrawing part or all of your funds to, say, meet an emergency? Can you do so immediately? How much, if any, of the fee is refundable if you cancel before completing a year?

How many different companies are in the portfolio of a typical account of the same size as yours? How often is your account reviewed?

At what intervals do you receive financial statements covering trading activity and progress reports on your portfolio? Who will have custody of your account?

(8) Before you make your decision among firms, compare the fees charged as well as their services and investment philosophies.

(9) Beware of any manager who pushes you to sign up. No reputable firm will use this type of hard sell. Take your time.

(10) But once you have selected a firm you consider competent, alert, and geared to your needs, don't try to second-guess the manager or push in turn. Let your investment counsel exercise the judgment you're paying for during a reasonable time span. Then reconsider, if need be.

WAY OUT ON THE HORIZON—FINANCIAL SUPERMARKETS AND FINANCIAL PLANNERS

When the "financial supermarket" finally comes, it will be one of the most exciting developments on the U.S. financial scene: most, if not all, the major financial services you need available to you under one roof. And surely several emerging trends are telegraphing what is ahead.

• Commercial banks are not only expanding their activities in the management of investment portfolios for both the little and the big fellow. They also are preparing income tax returns for a fee, aggressively promoting their extensive estate planning services, pushing innovations in paying of customer bills, creating new savings methods, and maintaining leadership in the overall lending field. Many banks are moving fairly close to one-stop financial centers even now.

• Similarly, insurance companies are expanding the forms of insurance sold under one roof: life, homeowners, health, etc. They are increasingly powerful factors in the making of personal as well as institutional loans. The insurance salesman who sells mutual funds is commonplace. Now an increasing number of insurance companies are planning stock brokerage subsidiaries.

• Stock brokerage firms are studying the concept with utmost seriousness. Some brokers are diversifying by buying real estate and investment management companies. Many brokers now sell life insurance, some handle tax shelters (real estate, oil, and cattle deals). Although no brokerage firm is anything like a one-stop center, the giants are known to be working on it.

Still way out on the horizon is the organization which offers in one place *truly professional, high-caliber* assistance on services of such scope as: investment advice on stocks, bonds, mutual funds, other mediums; guidance on a sound over-all insurance program; help in making out your income tax; financial planning for retirement; assistance in planning your estate and drawing up your will; bill paying; on and on.

Why is the financial supermarket so easy to explain, so difficult to achieve?

The key stumbling block is the need for truly high-caliber professional experts. For such supermarkets can come into existence only when they are staffed by experts trained in each area, capable of giving you the assistance you want and guiding you, the individual. Although we have independent experts in each area, bringing them together in a constructive, profitable arrangement is something else again.

Another stumbling block is the establishment of standards for such a group, for in the long run this is imperative to protect the public. Several organizations are now at work to develop a professional category of "financial planner" and this should be a reality by the end of the 1970s.

Meanwhile, though, all over the country new small organizations are springing up to service on a completely different basis the over-all financial needs of individuals. Their business takes a wholly different approach to the financial supermarket concept. These firms provide a broad range of financial counseling and advice to their clients but they usually *don't* offer any products.

What they do is analyze an individual's needs for insurance, savings, stocks, bonds, mutual funds; plan tax and estate strategy; and then come up with an integrated package of recommendations touching on about every aspect of the client's financial needs. But their work generally stops right there. If the client wants to follow the firm's recommendations, he does it through his own broker, insurance agent, banker, accountant, and lawyer.

The financial planning organization gets a fee for the master financial program it presents and doesn't try to make any commissions from the stocks or mutual funds the client buys or legal or accounting fees the client pays to implement the recommendations on estate planning and tax strategy.

So far, only a handful of organizations provide such services and their fees are steep. It is not unusual for a plan tailored to an individual's requirements and needs to cost $2,000 to $4,000. As a result, most customers for this service are wealthy individuals; in some cases corporations pay the costs of such programs for their executives and consider it an additional fringe benefit.

However, these new-breed financial planning organizations are working on ways to cut the cost of their services so they can serve the needs of the many millions of you who need professional help but can't pay such staggering fees.

On one side, there is growing interest by major financial institutions in developing financial supermarkets. On the other, there is the growth of professional financial planning firms offering comprehensive financial programs.

Between these, it seems clear that the professional assistance and variety of financial services available to you in the future will be vastly superior to any existing today.

STOCK MARKET LETTERS

If you don't want to go the investment adviser route, but want another source of investment advice besides your own broker, you might consider subscribing to one of the many stock market letters that are available. The letters range in quality from excellent to awful so check with some of your business associates to get an idea of those that are highly regarded. The price tags on such letters can run from $25 to $1,000 a year and no one has yet proven that the price tag for such a market letter and the value of its advice go hand in hand.

One thing you should know: Most market letter writers make their money from the *subscriptions they sell and not by using their own investment advice.*

SHOULD YOU BUY NEW STOCK ISSUES?

With almost frightening regularity over the years, speculators are caught up in "new issue" crazes during which they feel that all they have to do is buy shares in a company just going on the market and they'll be in a stock that may double or triple in a matter of weeks or months. Or they believe that, if they hold the new stock, in a couple of years they'll own another IBM or Xerox.

Informed speculation in "hot" new stocks issues can be intelligent and worth while; get-rich-quick gambling in new stock issues is dangerous and usually ends in disaster for the greedy.

To illustrate, in 1961, a historic year for new stock issues, many new stocks skyrocketed 100 to 500 per cent in a matter of hours. Then came the cleanout. Scores of the companies went bankrupt. New issues prices were brutally shaved in the market collapse of 1962. Countless numbers of greedy gamblers were wiped out. Today, some of the hottest stock issues of 1961–62 are still trading at a mere fraction of their initial prices.

The same boom-bust pattern was repeated in 1967–68 and 1969–70. And during these more recent periods investing institutions joined individuals in a search for the hot stocks which soared and then crashed—first swelling and then slashing the value of their portfolios. The threat of other blowoffs cannot be shrugged off at any time.

Not all new issues are "hot" new issues, of course—and not all are gambles. Some of the issuers are well-known corporations offering new shares simply to raise additional capital; these stocks are immediately listed on the exchanges and should not be considered part of the hot new issue scene. Another group also doesn't really fit the hot new issue category. These issuers are well-established, well-known companies which have been privately owned and which have decided to become publicly owned. Behind these new issues is a substantial record of company past performance, and you can analyze these companies in the same way you analyze companies with stock on the market for years.

But the type of new issues I'm discussing and those which have caused the excitement—and trouble—in the past are the small, so-called "promotional" or "concept" companies which usually don't have *any* history of past operations. Often they are hoping to put a new product or service on the market and at the time of issue they have no tangible business. They need the money that will be raised from the sale of their stock actually to *get* into business. If they can't raise money through selling stock to the public, they will have *no* business.

Much of the history of these promotional companies has been dismal. An SEC study showed that, of all the "promotional"-type companies that offered securities to the public between 1959 and 1962, 55 per cent were in liquidation by the end of 1962. Another study showed that, of 49 firms that went public between January 1, 1968 and June 30, 1969, and that sold stock which jumped 100 per cent or more in the first month following issue, 16 per cent were bankrupt by 1972, most of the others were close to it, and only 20 per cent showed any profit.

To understand the new issue market, you must know some basics about how companies go public. First, the stock is usually sold through an underwriter or group of underwriting firms. It's the job of the underwriter to help the firm sell its stock to the public, and sometimes the underwriting group will even guarantee the firm that the issue will be sold out at a fixed price no matter how difficult a time the underwriters have unloading it on the public.

In most cases, the firm has to register and file a prospectus with the SEC as well as state regulatory agencies before it can sell shares to the public. The prospectus describes in considerable detail facts about the company, its management, products, problems, and other key data.

Filing a prospectus with the SEC and with other regulatory agencies does *not* mean that the SEC is saying the stock of the firm is a good investment. It simply means that the SEC feels all the relevant facts about the company are disclosed in the prospectus that must be given to prospective buyers.

If you are trying to pick a new issue that will turn out to be a real winner, you will find a careful reading of the prospectus a major help. Yet despite the fact that the prospectus is a key aid in evaluating the company, few investors bother to read it at all! If they did, they probably would be stunned by some of the disclosures. Here, for instance, are just two excerpts from prospectuses selected at random over the past several years.

"This offering involves special risks concerning the company: substantial potential profits to nine officers, directors, founders, and other persons who . . . received 203,300 shares at no cost. . . . In view of the substantial elements of risk, it is possible the company's operations will prove unsuccessful." This from the prospectus of a small industrial company.

"The Dallas warehouse-showroom has remained open for business on consecutive days of Saturday and Sunday despite a Texas statute which forbids sales on such consecutive days. The company contends that the statute is unconstitutional. . . . In the event the company's appeal . . . is unsuccessful . . . it may have to remain closed on Sundays and also pay damages to the State of Texas. . . ." Prospectus from a retail firm.

These tidbits indicate that the prospectus can be the most revealing piece of literature issued by a corporation—often containing information seldom discussed outside the closed doors of a company's boardroom. What's more, the disclosures—even the most damaging—usually are stated in language you can understand.

The fact that prospective buyers don't read prospectuses delights most new companies. They would rather you *not* know the complete, unadulterated truth about them. If you are seriously considering buying a new issue, though, get and read the prospectus. Ask the company for a copy or ask an underwriting firm managing its public offering. You should have no problem obtaining one.

What should you look for? Concentrate on four key sections: "Company Business," "Recent Developments," "Use of Proceeds," and "Litigation." With these, you should have enough information to turn you on or permanently off the stock.

Also, when you get the prospectus check what the underwriting fee is for handling the issue. The underwriters receive their compensation out of the proceeds of the sale of the stock. Buyers don't pay separate commissions on new issues as they do on buying shares of stock listed on an exchange. The more the underwriter receives, the less the company issuing the stock has left to help produce the profits to make the stock a sound investment. The underwriters' compensation can run 12 to 18 per cent of the over-all issue. If an issuing company is in a strong position, it can usually hold the underwriting fees low.

Reading the prospectus is a fundamental way to a wise decision on the type of investment the company represents. Many speculators who wouldn't consider disobeying this fundamental guide when buying seasoned stocks completely forget it when buying new stock issues.

In addition, to protect yourself from blind gambling, heed these *don'ts:*

Don't buy any new issues on the basis of information not contained in the prospectus—for if the information is true and if it's valuable you may be sure it will be in the prospectus covering the stock sale. You might be hearing rumors deliberately circulated to whirl up the price of the stock so those spreading the stories can unload on you.

Don't fail to check into the reputation of the underwriter—one of the best safeguards you could have.

Don't buy a stock because it represents a company in a current favorite glamor industry or a current favorite industry of the speculators.

HOW TO AVOID THE "GARBAGE" STOCKS

It is not only in so-called hot new issues that you find "garbage" stocks that should intrigue only the wildest gamblers—who know what they are doing and can afford the risks. You can find these unknown "growth" stocks outstanding in the over-the-counter markets and listed on the smaller stock exchanges too.

How do you, an average speculator-gambler, protect yourself from this garbage? How do you speculate-gamble intelligently?

Here are ten questions to ask yourself which, when answered honestly, will be a superb guide to this sort of speculation:

(1) Is this a high-quality stock in its own industry? It should be. It could be a dominant company in a small industry. Or it could be the number one but still a small company in a big, fragmented industry. Whatever, it should be at the top.

(2) Does it have a record of solid earnings even in adverse times? How, for instance, did it make out in 1969–70 and in 1973–74?

(3) Has it a history of steady, solid growth? Buy a company with a history unless you're willing to admit you're in a wild gamble.

(4) Is the company's product or service sufficiently appealing to make

customers willing to pay a good price for it? You can check this one out by your own willingness to pay for the products or services.

(5) Is the company saddled with long-term debt? It's okay for it to be aggressive in sales, but it should be conservative in finance. A well-managed, growing company should be able to pay off its debts.

(6) Is it paying a dividend? It probably should *not* be. A strongly growing company can use that dividend money more profitably than you can. A no-dividend policy usually is a plus.

(7) Has it a high degree of profitability? Its per-share earnings should be rising each year by at least 9 per cent. Some professionals put the level for professional selections much higher than that, but for you, the amateur, 9 per cent should be the yardstick.

(8) Is the stock already popular or its product or service already a fad? Then beware: the stock is probably fully priced by now, and you want to beat the mob, not follow it.

(9) Is the company subject to government regulation? If so, avoid it. Regulatory agencies generally limit a company's gains, but they let it chalk up all the losses.

(10) Are you risking too much of your money in this speculation? Don't. The time-honored rule against putting all your eggs in one basket applies particularly to high-risk growth stocks. You could be wrong in your decision. Protect yourself by diversifying.

WHAT ABOUT REGIONAL STOCKS?

Most investors are interested in the big national companies with well-known products and names that are household bywords. And in the past the big brokerage firms concentrated their research efforts on analyzing these firms.

But beginning in the late sixties, attention turned to the so-called "regional" stocks—issues of companies that basically serve a small geographic area. Regional stocks, as their name implies, may be well known locally but their products and services aren't known nationally.

What the security analysts discovered—and so did the public—is that many regional firms had the makings to become major national firms, yet they were undervalued in price just because not many investors knew about them. In fact, many firms that have become fairly well known in recent years started out as regional stocks. As a result, Wall Street firms try now to discover the regional companies that might become the IBMs or Xeroxes of tomorrow.

So, as an investor, do not downgrade a recommendation to buy a stock just because it represents a company you never heard about before. It well may be easier for you to find a real growth stock among the outstanding regional firms than on the lists of the national firms which have been carefully and repeatedly studied by countless numbers of analysts.

HOW TO READ AN ANNUAL REPORT

Each year American shareholders receive more than 100 million annual reports from 40,000 to 50,000 publicly owned U.S. corporations. But a shocking proportion of you will throw away these valuable documents without even opening the envelopes and many others of you will simply skim over the highlights.

If you are among these millions, you are junking the single most important account of the financial health of your company and your single best measure of how well (or how poorly) your savings now are invested. If you are also an employee of the company in which you own stock, your indifference is really inexcusable.

Why do so many stockholders, as many as 40 per cent according to one study, ignore this key document? What are corporations doing to win stockholders' confidence in their annual reports and to make the reports more readable?

Only a couple of decades ago the typical annual report did not contain even a table of contents to guide you through its maze of facts and figures. The typical report told the shareholder how the company did the previous year but gave no figures for other years to help you measure its long-term trends. The untrained shareholder was at the mercy of the professional corporation statisticians and accountants and considerable imagination went into the preparation of the balance sheets.

Now this has changed dramatically. Virtually all major corporations today provide not only detailed indexes in their annual reports but usually also a generous assortment of easy-to-read charts and summaries so you can judge at a glance your company's and its industry's progress. The crucially important ten-year summary of financial highlights, rare ten to fifteen years ago, is now commonplace. A growing number of corporations are printing financial highlights on the covers of their annual reports, to lure more readers to look inside and delve further into their figures.

In Europe, corporation financial reports frequently omit key figures, use outdated information, or fudge statistics beyond semblance of reality. In this country, though, today's shareholder can, with few exceptions, trust every fact, figure and footnote in every annual report he receives. Helping to assure the accuracy and completeness of financial reports are the rules of the major U.S. stock exchanges, the regulations of the Securities and Exchange Commission, and the auditing procedures of the American Institute of Certified Public Accountants. Virtually all annual reports now contain a "stamp of approval" of a reputable outside auditing firm or a statement by this firm that it takes issue with some aspect of the report—and why.

Today, even the unsophisticated investor can see through most efforts a company may still make to obscure bad financial news. In the words of one expert, "When the President's letter to shareholders begins with 'The year was a period of adjustment for your company,' you can assume it was a bad year." Or you can simply turn to the record itself and judge.

Despite the progress, though, it's not easy (and never will be) to understand a corporation annual report. Thus, here is a glossary of key items and the basic rules for interpreting them intelligently.

(1) *The President's letter to stockholders* is the first place to look for a summary of your company's financial highlights for the previous year, plus the reasons why profits were up or down. This letter or the subsequent text also should give you the company's own assessment of its short- and long-term outlook, with supporting facts.

(2) *The "income statement" or "earnings report"* is a summary of the year's sales volume, other income, costs, net profits or losses with comparative figures for the previous year. The crucial figure is the company's net income or net profit and this figure should be compared to profits over the previous five or ten years (usually summarized separately).

(3) *The "price-earnings ratio"* is a measure of how the over-all investment community views your company. The ratio won't appear in an annual report, but you can calculate it by dividing the current market price of a share of your stock by the company's per-share earnings noted in the earnings report. A ratio well below the average for the company's industry or for business in general may reflect investor wariness of the future profit potential of the company and/or for the industry.

(4) *The "retained earnings statement"* tells you what share of company profits is being returned to you in the form of dividends and what share is being held back. If the proportion going to you in dividends declines sharply, look for an explanation of how the extra funds are being reinvested.

(5) *Footnotes often reveal important information.* A footnote, for instance, might tell you that an unusually high profit stemmed from a one-shot ("non-recurring") financial windfall. It may be tedious, but read those footnotes!

If the annual report you receive does not contain at least these basic items of information, or the facts from which to calculate them yourself, ask your stockbroker for further details. Your broker also can provide you with the industry-wide record. This is the minimum you should know about the company and the industry in which you are investing your savings.

WHAT IS A "BLUE CHIP"?

Ask a dozen stock market experts to define a "blue chip" and you may get a dozen different answers. I, though, stick to the original rules for spotting a blue chip—for they are basic, time-tested, and always have value.

To begin with, the name "blue chip" is traced easily to the game of poker in which there are three colors of chips: blue, the highest value; red, next in rank; white, the lowest value.

Now here are four yardsticks for a blue chip:

(1) A long history of good earnings performance in recessions as well as in booms. This does not mean the company's earnings must be skyrocketing. It does mean the company must be turning in a record of solid profits year after year.

(2) A long history of cash dividend payments and, again, the record must be consistent in bad times as well as good.

(3) Recognition as an established leader in an established industry. There can be several leaders in an established industry. For instance, General Motors and Ford in the auto industry or Eastman Kodak and Polaroid in the camera industry.

(4) A clear prospect for continued earnings growth and dividend payments in the years ahead: A solid—but not flashy—outlook.

Of course, today's red chip can become tomorrow's blue and today's blue can fade into tomorrow's white. The dividend yardstick alone produces some arbitrary divisions. It leaves out many solid and promising corporations operating in the United States today—in terms of recent earnings and dividend payments—simply because they don't have the "ancestry."

These very requirements may make a blue chip stock a dull investment. But, dull or not, the blue chip represents solidity, security, steady growth—precisely what millions of investors cherish most.

WHAT IS A "GROWTH" STOCK?

Several times I have suggested that you buy "growth" stocks for capital gains—but how do you define a "growth" stock? How do you find and invest in this type of stock?

Grasp one point from the start: a growth stock is *not* merely a stock that has gone up in price. A growth stock *is:*

(1) The stock of a company which has shown and is likely to continue to show a record of both consistent and *superior* growth in its earnings per share of stock.

Consistency means year after year, even in the face of business reverses. For instance, many years back the demand for color TV sets was so much larger than the supply that even the marginal producers were prospering. But if that sales pace had continued, there would have been four or five TV sets in every home! When the inevitable slowdown occurred, the stronger companies survived while the sales and earnings of the secondary ones collapsed.

Consistency means a year-in, year-out market for the company's products. Superior growth, in the opinion of many professional investment advisers, means a growth of better than 8 or 9 per cent a year in earnings per share. This on a consistent basis certainly narrows the field from the start.

(2) The stock of a company which dominates its market or is a leading company in a fast-growing field. One expert says he would rather have the stock of the number one company breeding tropical fish than that of a little firm trying to make a better transistor.

(3) The stock of a company in an emerging field or a company developing new concepts in an established field.

(4) The stock of a company you are convinced is under strong management. You might buy IBM without personally knowing its management, but you should not buy stock in a tiny electronics firm without knowing something about the people running it. The smaller the company, the more crucial is its management's ability.

(5) And it is the stock of a company offering a high return on equity— meaning the company's net profit related to its stockholders' equity is high in comparison to that earned by other firms in the same industry. On an average in the United States today, for every dollar committed in a corporation, the stockholder gets a return on his investment of about 11¢. The owner of a true growth stock might do better than this.

Admittedly, this merely touches the various aspects of a growth stock and there will be many disagreements with the definitions. But these rules are fundamental, and I trust you notice that each rule assumes that the company has a *record* to analyze and compare. This last hint alone will help protect you from a lot of "garbage" stock that will be touted under the banner of "growth" stocks in the years ahead.

WHAT IS A "SPECIAL SITUATION" STOCK?

Attractive as a "growth" stock is, a "special situation" stock has even more potential for substantial appreciation. But again how do you define, find, and invest in a "special situation"? These questions and answers will guide you:

Q. *What is a special situation?*

A. In the modern sense, it is a stock in which you're likely to make a profit as a result of a new or impending specific and unusual development either within the company or in the outside environment affecting the company. What makes this special is that few investors recognize the impending change, and the improvement has not yet been reflected in the price of the stock. In either case, the development is setting the stage for a substantial upsurge in the company's earnings—and usually you'll be able to make your profit no matter what the short-term swings in the general stock market.

Q. *How do you identify special situations?*

A. Although they can occur in almost any industry and kind of company, the overriding characteristic of them all is *change*.

The changes within the company itself might include: a new technological breakthrough; a major new process, product, or service; a shift in ownership control; a major acquisition; a fundamental switch in the management philosophy of a previously poorly run company.

The changes in the company's external environment might include: new favorable government action (such as tax breaks); favorable court rulings; new favorable legislation; a significant shift in technological or market trends in the company's industry or related fields; any change which could lead to a dramatic rise in demand for the company's product or service.

Q. *What are the dangers?*

A. You might not be able to analyze the new development or be reasonably sure of its outcome. If you can't do either, it's a sheer speculation, not a special situation.

Also, often, an external environmental change may not produce the expected outcome. If, for instance, you had bought stock of a land development company which had bought raw land cheap hoping to cash in on the land boom but saw your hopes of a rise in the price of the stock disappear because of accounting practices, your purchase of this "special situation" would have been an expensive mistake.

Or a seemingly great new product may fail in the market place. As one expert points out, "Most potential Xeroxes turn out to be nothing more than an idea for 3-D motion pictures."

Q. *How can you avoid the dangers?*

A. Extreme selectivity and obviously intensive study of the nature of the external or internal changes are vital.

If it's a new management, look for a demonstrated record of superior previous achievement and whether the new managers have competence in the area involved. If it's a new product or service or process, look for some kind of previous track record by the company in introducing such products.

Some of the country's top investment research firms, for instance, rarely even bother to analyze a development until the product's commercial feasibility has been proven.

And whatever the development, it's truly a special situation only when the earnings breakthrough which results is of major proportions and is sustainable for at least several years.

OIL AND GAS SPECULATIONS

One not surprising spinoff of the emergence of energy shortages was an upsurge in the popularity of oil and gas investments—among the riskiest but also, if they pay off, among the most spectacularly rewarding of all speculations.

The economic reasons spurring the boomlet began with our shortages of fuel, of course. But there were more reasons than this behind the spurt.

• Oil and gas investments are topflight tax shelters of special value to taxpayers in high income brackets.

• The payoff for finding new reserves of oil and gas before the oil crisis had been big enough, but it became dazzling as prices soared in the mid-seventies.

The fact that these are high-risk ventures cannot be overemphasized, however. The following questions and answers give basic guides:

Q. *Is there any key technique that an amateur speculator in oil and gas properties can use to give himself an edge in an oil deal?*

A. Yes, get into a deal that, say, two or three other oil companies also are investing in. This immediately improves the odds in your favor because, instead of getting the advice of one set of oil professionals, you get the advice of several experts.

Q. *Does this mean that all one-company deals are riskier investments than multi-company deals?*

A. Some are, some aren't. But if a company asks unsophisticated, independent investors to put up all the money for a well, perhaps the chances for making money in that deal aren't as hot as represented to you.

Q. *Realistically, how good a chance does the amateur investor have at striking it rich in oil?*

A. The chances of making money in the second half of the 1970s are probably better than ever. But a lot depends on the kind of drilling program involved—development or exploratory.

One kind of drilling program is development drilling, done in proven oil- and gas-producing areas. Here the odds are the sponsoring company will hit oil in three out of four wells or even better—but there's little chance of hitting the big payoff. You shoot for getting back twice your investment and that payoff usually will be spread out over a period of years. The other kind is exploratory or wildcat drilling conducted in areas that may yield oil or gas but have yet to prove productive. Here, you're looking for the big killing and, if you hit, you'll probably hit big. But wildcatters on average hit oil in only about one in ten wells. The other nine wells are dry holes.

Q. *How can an investor go after the big payoff without putting all his investment dollars on 10-to-1 shots?*

A. By investing in a program that combines development and exploratory drilling. Development drilling will keep you in the game, and wildcat drilling will give you a chance at the big money. And make sure the people running the program make their money from the discovery of oil and gas. Ask the sponsor the same tough, straightforward questions you would ask about any other business deal. Find out where the money will go and why. Determine the percentage of dollars that will actually go into the search for oil. Ask to see just how the sponsor or the promoter will make his profit. Make sure it's necessary for the sponsoring oil company to bring in oil and gas to make its money.

Q. *What else should an amateur investor do?*

A. Before you put down a penny, know throughly whom you're in business with. Make sure the people running the deal are oil men—not salesmen. The whole program will be in trouble unless those responsible for bringing in the oil and gas are real oil pros—preferably a combination of pros—and unless these professionals will be supervising the entire program.

SHOULD YOU BUY ON MARGIN?

Most of the country's millions of investors buy their shares outright and hold them for the long term—that is, they put up 100 per cent cash and hold on no matter what the market does. But there is a sizable minority of active investors and professional traders who use credit from their brokers to help finance their purchases. This, of course, gives the investor a lot more leverage and thus a bigger potential for profits—and losses too.

In the mid-seventies there were probably 700,000 to 800,000 individuals who had margin accounts with their brokers. The amount of credit customers were receiving from their brokers for this purpose was as high as $8 billion in the early 1970s.

Just how much credit you can receive from your broker depends on several key elements. First, the Federal Reserve Board sets initial margin requirements. This requirement has ranged from 50 to 100 per cent in the post-World War II period. Say the initial margin rate is 70 per cent. It means if you want to buy $10,000 worth of stock you have to put up $7,000 in cash to buy the stock; you can receive credit for the rest from your broker. Or you have to deposit securities with a loan value of $7,000 in order to purchase $10,000 worth of a listed stock. You must deposit the required cash or securities with your broker within five business days after the purchase to conform to Regulation T of the Federal Reserve Board.

The New York Stock Exchange also has a set of rules covering buying on margin. To open a margin account with an NYSE broker you must deposit at least $2,000 or its equivalent in marginable securities. And on top of this, individual brokerage firms may—and often do—set initial margin requirements higher than those of the Federal Reserve or the Exchange.

Q. *What do you pay for the money you borrow?*

A. The going interest rates vary from time to time but usually were in the 7 to 13 per cent range in the early 1970s. The amount of interest will show up in the monthly or periodic statement you receive on your margin account.

Q. *How do you open a margin account?*

A. If you have the $2,000 cash deposit or equivalent in securities—or meet the higher standards that your broker sets—there is little problem or paper work in opening an account. You simply sign a margin agreement and a securities loan consent form. The agreement gives your broker the power to pledge or lend securities carried for your account. All securities purchased on margin will be held by your broker in "street name." However, you'll be credited with all dividends received on them. Your broker will also send along to you all annual and quarterly reports on the company whose stock you are holding and he will vote your stock in proxy matters the way you direct him.

Once you open a margin account, you must abide by another set of regulations—margin maintenance requirements. The New York Stock Exchange requires that the margin equity of customers be at least 25 per cent of the market value of securities held in the account and some brokerage firms insist on percentages higher than 25 per cent. For example, say you bought that $10,000 worth of stock with an initial margin requirement of 70 per cent. You put up $7,000 and received credit of $3,000 from your broker. Now say the price of the stock drops to the point where it is worth $4,000. Since you owe your broker $3,000, your equity in the securities is only $1,000 and you are right at the 25 per cent limit.

Q. *What happens if the value of your stock approaches the minimum requirement line?*

A. You will get what is termed a margin call. The brokerage firm usually has a squad of margin clerks whose job is to keep track of the firm's margin accounts and to send out warning phone calls and letters if the value of your account is approaching the minimum requirement line. You'll be asked to put more cash into your account or to put up more marginable securities as collateral. Instead of doing either of these things, you might choose to sell some of the stock in your margin account and pay your broker back part of the money for which he gave you credit.

Q. *What is an undermargined account?*

A. Your account is undermargined when it has definitely fallen below the minimum requirements. If you don't move fast to put it back in order by a transfusion of more cash or securities, your broker has the right to sell the securities in your margin account to replace the credit he advanced to you.

Q. *Should you open a margin account?*

A. Probably not. Margin accounts are generally for individuals who are sophisticated investors, who are active in the market, and who understand the risks as well as the rewards of this type of account.

Also it is difficult to make a profit on small margin purchases. The amount of interest you pay on the borrowed money in your account, plus odd-lot differential charges and commission rates, easily can eat up small trading profits.

And though the leverage in purchasing power you get in a margin account can produce increased profits for you, it also can result in bigger losses if you have guessed wrong on the direction of either the market or an individual stock.

SELLING SHORT

Once you start investing, somewhere along the line the question of whether you should sell short will come up.

What is short selling? It's a technique that reverses most normal attitudes about buying stocks. It starts off on the assumption that you think a certain stock is going to drop in value. So what you do is sell the shares at the current market price, borrow shares of the stock from your broker, and then wait in the hope that the price of the stock will go down. If it does, you buy the same number of shares at a lower price and use these shares to "cover" the stock you borrowed from your broker.

Obviously, the bigger the drop in the price of the stock, the more potential profit you can make. Sounds good? Well, don't jump into short selling, at least until you read on.

Actually, short selling has earned a bad name, mainly because questionable practices of short selling were used by such market manipulators as Dan Drew and Jay Gould in the nineteenth century. They deliberately drove down the prices of stocks in the hopes of buying them back cheap. And short selling still carries a bad connotation, even seems unpatriotic. But as a result of some of these shady practices, there are several rules that now govern short selling, the most important of which is the so-called "up-tick" rule.

This means you can sell short only after the previous sale in the stock was one eighth point or more higher than the last sale price. No short sale is permitted except on a rising price. The goal is to make sure that repeated selling waves don't force prices into a down spiral.

At best, though, selling short is a risky business, better left to coldly sophisticated investors. To be specific, the risk is this: You can make money if the stock you are selling short takes a big drop. But what if, instead of dropping, the stock's price takes off in a sharp upturn?

Say you sell short 100 shares at $50 a share, hoping the stock drops, but instead it goes up to $70. You then have a $20-a-share loss which you must take if you then buy shares to cover the stock you've borrowed. And there's no limit at least in theory as to how large your losses can become—whereas in normal trading your loss can never exceed 100 per cent of your investment. Say the stock soars to $100 or $200 a share! Your losses could be catastrophic —200 per cent, 400 per cent . . .

Best bet: Don't be tempted to sell short.

WHAT ARE RIGHTS?

A few years ago one of the world's major enterprises, American Telephone & Telegraph Company, raised $1.2 billion in new capital. This was a goodly sum even for AT&T: many governments would have trouble raising as much.

Telephone raised the money through the offering of rights—a common technique employed by a wide range of corporations but, unfortunately, often overlooked by share owners.

A right, in essence, is a privilege given by the issuing corporation to buy its common or preferred stock or bonds or debentures, usually at a favorable price in relation to the price of the outstanding security.

The Telephone offering was a classic illustration of rights. Its several million share owners were informed that they could buy one additional share for each 20 shares they owned. They would receive one "right" for each share they presently owned. To buy one share, the share owner would have to have 20 "rights" and pay $100—although at the time of the announcement Telephone was selling at about $146 a share. The rights, of course, immediately acquired a value. (If you have the right to buy a security below its market value, this right has a value.) Theoretically, the rights were worth $46/20 or $2.30 apiece.

Telephone's share owners had several choices. A shareholder could exercise his rights by paying the company $100 plus giving AT&T 20 rights for each share he wanted and was entitled to. Or he could sell his rights. Or if he owned, say, 15 shares, and had 15 rights, he could buy 5 additional rights, which would allow him to purchase 1 more share of AT&T at the favorable price.

When it issued the rights, Telephone went on the basis of the privileged subscription or pre-emptive right. Translated, this bafflegab means the company felt its share owners should have the privilege of buying the additional shares before the stock was offered to the general public. Selling additional shares, of course, dilutes the proportionate equity of the original share owners —unless the original share owner has the opportunity to maintain his equity by buying the additional shares.

Rights are often confused with warrants and, admittedly, the difference is a bit hazy. In the broadest terms, a right is a short-term privilege to buy a security at a favorable price; the privilege derives from the security you already own. A warrant is the privilege, usually of a longer term, to buy a security at a specific price. This privilege is usually offered to facilitate the sale of a stock or bond which you do not own. You, the buyer, get the stock or bond plus the warrant.

Caution: Check your broker before you ignore your rights or sell them.

ARE YOU BETTER OFF WITH STOCK SPLITS?

If you buy stocks, you probably will find that over a period of time one of the stocks you own will split and soon you will be receiving additional shares from the company. Will these shares make you any richer? In theory, no. In fact, maybe.

To explain just what a stock split means, say you own 100 shares of the 1 million outstanding shares of the ABC Company. The company votes to split its stock 2 for 1, increasing the number of shares to 2 million. Since you own 100, you get an additional 100 shares—one for each you own—raising your stake to 200 shares. Before the split you owned 100 shares out of 1 million of the ABC firm. After the split you own 200 out of 2 million shares of the company. Obviously, in terms of percentage ownership, your position hasn't changed one bit and generally speaking, since company ABC hasn't increased its assets in any way, the value of your holdings shouldn't be affected.

If the shares sold at $1.00 each before the split the price should drop to 50¢, making the 200 shares you now have after the split equal to the $100 market value of the 100 shares you owned before the stock split. Theoretically this would be true no matter what the ratio of the split—2 for 1, 3 for 1, 5 for 1, 6 for 1. Yet speculators and investors often respond with enthusiastic buying to news that companies plan to split their stock—and following are the two key reasons why:

(1) It is commonplace for a company to combine a stock split with an increase in its dividend rate. If company A pays 4¢ a year on each of your 100 shares before the split and now pays 3¢ on the split shares you are getting a 50 per cent increase in dividend—6¢ in place of 4¢.

(2) Usually working to boost the value of split shares to more than the value of the shares before the split is the fact that many investors would rather buy lower-priced stocks than higher-priced stocks. Say, for instance, that you own 10 shares of a stock selling for $150 a share. Many investors will not buy a stock with that high a price simply for psychological reasons. But if your company splits its shares 2 for 1, you now have 20 shares at a market price of $75 per share. Historically, many more investors are interested in buying a stock at $75 than at $150.

And the increased investor demand alone well may help push up the price of the stock beyond its initial $75 level.

WHAT PRICE/EARNINGS RATIOS ARE ALL ABOUT

An old Wall Street adage holds that a stock is worth what somebody is willing to pay for it. In stiffer words, the price at which a stock sells represents the buyer's opinion of its value at a particular time.

Investors use a wide range of yardsticks to try to arrive at this judgment on the worth of a stock. Among them are such factors as book value, net income per share, cash flow, dividend rate, several others. But probably the most widely used measurement is the price/earnings ratio, better known as the P/E ratio.

Q. *What is the price/earnings ratio?*
A. It is the ratio of the current price of the stock to its earnings over the

past twelve months. Sometimes experts try to figure price/earnings ratios based on predicted earnings for the next twelve months, but that introduces a speculative element that just complicates matters for the average investor.

Putting an even greater emphasis on price/earnings ratio is the fact that, starting in early 1973, newspapers added price/earnings ratios to the New York and American Stock Exchange tables.

Q. *How do you calculate the price/earnings ratio?*

A. While you can get the ratios in the newspaper stock tables, it also is a simple do-it-yourself task. The current price is in the newspaper tables, and the earnings for the last twelve months are usually available in a Standard & Poor's or other reference work. Divide the current price by the earnings, and you get the P/E ratio. For example, a stock that currently sells for $40 and that earned $2.00 a share over the past twelve months has a P/E ratio of 20.

Another way of saying it is that an investor is paying $20 for each $1.00 of the company's most recent annual earnings.

Q. *How much do price/earnings ratios fluctuate?*

A. Although they don't fluctuate much for stocks in general, they do fluctuate tremendously for individual issues. In the 1960s the average price/earnings ratio for stocks traded on the New York Stock Exchange ran about 18×. By the early 1970s this figure had dropped to 14×. But even as the average P/E ratio fell, ratios on some individual stocks soared and there have been stocks with P/E ratios above 100×.

Q. *What can P/E ratios tell you?*

A. As you study price/earnings ratios, several points will soon become clear:

• Stocks in a given industry tend to have about the same P/E ratio. For example, most auto companies or international oil companies have the same price/earnings ratios.

• In broad market movements, the price/earnings ratios of stocks in an industry group tend to move up and down together. If chemical stocks become depressed, say, the P/E ratio of nearly all chemical stocks will move down.

• Companies in growth industries—photographic equipment, computers —tend to have higher price/earnings ratios than firms in such established industries as utilities.

• Cyclical stocks in general tend to have lower P/E ratios than companies with more stable earnings.

Obviously, the P/E ratio fluctuates with each change in price and earnings. It also depends on what people active in the market think of the industry's and the company's future earnings prospects.

Q. *Can P/E ratios help you spot bargains in stocks?*

A. Yes. Many analysts and experienced investors use P/E ratios as a tool to find undervalued situations in which they might want to invest.

As an illustration, say that you are interested in a machine tool company. You notice that when the machine tool business is in the doldrums this company's stock (as well as others in its industry) sells for a price/earnings ratio of 9. You also notice that when the industry moves into a favorable business cycle the price/earnings ratio for the company and the group runs around 14. Say the stock is currently selling for $18 and has earned $2.00 a share. You read that prospects for the machine tool industry are bright, and the earnings of the company you are watching are expected to move up to $2.50 next year. So you figure that even with the low P/E average the price of the stock could move up (based on $2.50 earnings) to $22.50. But based on the high P/E ratio of 14×, and with $2.50 earnings, it could move as high as $35. Certainly, you now have one very helpful clue to the possible price potential of the stock.

By studying a company's pattern of earnings and P/E ratios you may ultimately see a pattern that will help tell you if you should invest in the stock —and when.

Q. *What about stocks selling at low P/E ratios?*

A. P/E ratios may also give you some idea of the relative profit/loss pattern in an investment. If a stock has historically never had a P/E ratio lower than 5×, and its earnings seem headed up, you would seem to be taking little risk in buying the stock when its P/E ratio was 5×. The likelihood that the stock will go down further seems fairly slim. On the other hand, the potential upward movement of the stock would seem very promising.

Now take the reverse situation. You are looking at a company which has never had a P/E ratio below 5× or higher than 18×. Its earnings outlook appears modestly good, and it presently is selling at a P/E of 18×. If you buy that stock when its P/E ratio is at its high point, you obviously are taking a bigger risk, for the likelihood that it will go up depends almost entirely on a sharp increase in its future earnings. On the other hand, the stock could slump before it reaches its historic P/E ratio low.

Huge numbers of investors and speculators have been badly hurt in recent years by buying growth stocks with astronomical P/E ratios. Only a handful of these stocks have been able to maintain their high P/E ratios over the years. The majority with ratios in the 40× to 80× category eventually slide down to realistic levels—but the slide is more akin to a crash for the many who paid fancy prices for the shares.

Q. *What's the safest policy then?*

A. It usually is safest to spot stocks which are selling at low P/E ratios and which are headed for substantial earnings growth. Your downside risk tends to be smaller and your upside opportunities can be very good.

DO OPTIONS MAKE SENSE FOR YOU?

The use of put and call options has been soaring in popularity—with the volume of option business up a sensational 300 per cent just in the past ten years and obviously heading much higher. Yet, if you're typical, you've either never heard of "puts and calls" or you shrink from them as among the most esoteric of trading devices, with an utterly confusing jargon.

You probably have dealt with or heard about options of other types, however. As one illustration, if you want to buy a piece of land or a house, you may be asked to take an option on it. This means you pay a set amount of money for the option to buy the property for a given price within a pre-scribed period of time. Say you are interested in buying a $50,000 property but you are not quite sure you want to go ahead with the deal. For $1,000 you might buy an option which gives you four weeks' time to make up your mind whether or not to buy the house. If you don't buy in the four weeks' time you lose your option money.

As another illustration, options are a way of life when baseball and bas-ketball teams try to acquire players.

Q. *What is a call? And a put?*

A. In the securities business, a "call" option is a contract which gives you the right to buy 100 shares of a given stock at a fixed price (usually the price of the stock on the day the option contract is made) for a fixed period of time. The period of time usually runs six months and ten days (for tax reasons) but can run thirty, ninety, a hundred twenty days, or some other length.

You pay a premium for the option, usually running to about 10 to 15 per cent of the value of the stock. If you want an option on 100 shares of a $50 stock, you might pay a premium of $500 to $750.

A "put" option is the reverse of a call option. Here you have the privilege of selling 100 shares of stock at a fixed price within the option period. Put op-tions usually cost a few percentage points less than call options and are not nearly as popular.

Q. *Why do people buy options?*

A. There are many reasons, but the main one is that it gives an investor who thinks a stock will move sharply up or down a chance to make a sizable profit on the move while limiting the amount of possible loss.

Say you think that Ajax Mousetrap Company stock, selling for $50, may surge to $100 in six months. It would cost you $5,000 to buy 100 Ajax shares, and you may not want to risk $5,000 or you may not have $5,000 to invest. Still, you would like to take the chance that Ajax will jump and as a result will make you a large profit.

In this case, you might go the option route. You ask your broker to get you a call on 100 shares of Ajax. Your broker comes back with a report that for a premium of $500 you can get a call option on Ajax for six months and ten days. You buy the option.

Q. *How does the call option work?*

A. Here are some of the various things that then can happen:

(1) Ajax stock takes off as anticipated, and it hits $90 within the option period. Now you exercise your option, buy the 100 shares at $50, turn around and sell the shares you acquired on the market for $90.

You have received $9,000 from the sale of the shares. From this subtract the $5,000 you paid for them, the $500 premium for the option and about $150 in brokerage commissions, and you wind up with a profit of $3,350.

(2) Now look at another scenario. You buy the option and three months later Ajax nosedives to $40. What do you do? You do nothing, and simply let your option expire. You are out $500. Your loss is limited to the cost of your option. And you thank your lucky stars that you didn't buy 100 shares of Ajax for $5,000 and watch your investment shrink.

(3) Or say the price of Ajax moves up to $54. You decide to exercise your option because even if you haven't made a profit you can cut down on your option cost. Here's the mathematics. You exercise your option to buy at $50, then sell the stock for $54. You have received $5,400, and your expenses are $5,000 to buy the stock, $500 for the premium for the option, and $150 in broker's commissions. In this example, you come out with a loss of $250, which is better than letting your option expire and being out $500.

Q. *What about puts?*

A. Put options work the same way but in reverse. There are also some very fancy devices, such as "straddles," which are a combination of a put and call option, "strips," which are two puts and one call, and "straps," which are one put and two calls. But don't get involved in them unless you are a truly sophisticated investor.

Q. *In what other situations might you use options?*

A. You might have a short position in a stock you can protect by buying a call option, or you might protect a profit in a long position by the purchase of a put option.

Q. *Where do you get puts and calls?*

A. They are available from roughly 20 dealers who make up the membership of the Put and Call Brokers Association. Many of these dealers advertise in the financial sections of newspapers, giving a sampling of some of the puts and calls available. Or more likely you will deal with your own broker. More than 70 member firms of the New York Stock Exchange have put and call departments.

Q. *What factors decide the premium you pay?*

A. Option premiums are negotiable and depend on the volatility of the stock and length of the option contract. The longer the contract, the higher the premium, and the more volatile the stock, the costlier the premium. Other factors such as the number of option writers who are interested in offering the stock, the quality and number of shares outstanding, also help determine the premium price you pay.

Q. What is the Options Exchange?

A. The Chicago Board Options Exchange—the first organized and the first continuous exchange market for put and call options in this country—opened in 1973. Subsequently, other option markets were opened at the American and Philadelphia exchanges and more are being organized.

The markets establish one central point where many options can be traded and prices can be disseminated daily. They also provide an active resale market for those who already have bought options.

FOR YOUR PROTECTION—"SIPC"

The 1967–70 crisis in Wall Street came perilously close—far closer than was ever publicly acknowledged—to wiping out huge numbers of innocent investors who had entrusted their securities to the safekeeping of their brokers. But as a direct result of that nightmare the Securities Investor Protection Act of 1970 went on the statute books.

This law gives you protection against being hurt by the liquidation of the brokerage firm to which you have entrusted securities and cash almost in the same way that the Federal Deposit Insurance Corporation gives you protection against being hurt by the liquidation of the bank to which you have entrusted your deposits. The difference is that SIPC is a federally chartered membership organization and FDIC is an agency of the government.

SIPC is one of the most important pieces of securities legislation of the past generation and of direct meaning to you. You must know its general outlines, so here goes:

Q. What is SIPC?

A. The Securities Investor Protection Corporation is a federally chartered membership corporation created by Congress to provide financial protection for you—the customers of an over-the-counter broker/dealer or of a member of a national securities exchange. It is not, however, an agency of the U. S. Government.

Q. What protection does it give you?

A. Should a member of SIPC go into liquidation, SIPC would have advanced as of the mid-seventies up to $50,000 per account on customer claims —with the $50,000 limit taking effect after the return of your fully paid securities to you, the customer. For cash, though, your protection was limited at that time to $20,000 per account.

Q. Is there any way I can get more than $50,000 protection?

A. As of the mid-1970s, you could have obtained more than $50,000 in SIPC protection if you had set up your accounts in different ways. For example, if you had an account with several brokers, *each* was covered up to $50,000. Or you might have had several accounts with one broker but one might have been in your name, another in your wife's name, and a third might have been in a joint account. In each case, the account was covered up to the $50,000 limit. For the more information on SIPC, ask your broker for the special SIPC booklet.

Q. *Who are members of SIPC?**

A. Automatically, members are all registered broker/dealers and members of national securities exchanges, including specialists. Firms excluded from membership are those doing only a mutual fund, insurance, or investment company advisory business—but they can apply for membership in SIPC if they wish.

Q. *Who puts up the insurance funds for SIPC?*

A. The securities industry itself, through assessments on SIPC member organizations, finances the SIPC fund. The fund is created by assessment of ½ of 1 per cent of the gross security business of the member firms that belong. The fund is targeted to reach a total of $150 million in cash. In addition, SIPC has a $1 billion line of credit with the United States Treasury in case it ever needs it. However, if this occurs, the brokerage firms who are members of SIPC will eventually have to repay the Treasury for the loan.

Q. *How does SIPC work?*

A. When it appears that an SIPC member firm is in danger of failing to meet its obligations to customers, SIPC will apply to the appropriate court for appointment of a trustee. Once appointed, the trustee will liquidate the firm, complete open securities transactions, deliver out customers' fully paid securities to the extent that they are on hand and can be identified, and then settle any customer claims up to a limit of $50,000 per account and a limit of $20,000 in cash.

Q. *Who manages SIPC?*

A. A seven-man board of directors including two representatives of the general public, three of the securities industry appointed by the President of the United States, and one each named by the Secretary of the Treasury and the Federal Reserve Board.

Q. *What does that $1 billion line of Treasury credit mean?*

A. It's an ultimate resource aimed at meeting a crisis far beyond any ever yet experienced. It is to provide for even the most remote danger of financial disaster. SIPC is indeed for your protection—make sure the firm with which you are dealing is a member.

Q. *What other protection do I have for my account at a brokerage firm?*

A. Early in 1973 the Securities and Exchange Commission implemented a series of rules adopted in turn by the New York Stock Exchange providing

---

* All of the following as of 1974 but changes and refinements are certain to come in the years ahead.

even further safeguards for investors. The key rule is nicknamed the "Needham rule" after James Needham, chairman of the New York Stock Exchange at that time, who helped formulate this rule when he was a commissioner of the SEC.

Q. *What does the Needham rule do?*

A. It makes sure that your securities and cash are kept separate from the firm's own operating funds. Your broker can use your funds only in those areas of his business which are related to servicing customers—for instance, in financing loans to other customers. He cannot use your funds to finance his own activities, such as trading for his firm's own account or underwriting.

Q. *How does the rule achieve this?*

A. There are several safeguards, including required reports from brokers to the stock exchanges and other regulatory bodies and periodic checkups by exchange examiners and independent public accountants.

Q. *Has the customer any obligation under the new rule?*

A. Yes. When you, a customer (individual or institutional), sell securities, you must deliver them to your broker promptly, and, in any event, you are expected to deliver your securities by the settlement date for the transaction. If you have not completed delivery by ten business days after the settlement date, your broker is required to close out your sale and you are responsible for any loss he suffers as a result.

Q. *In sum, what do these changes mean to you?*

A. They mean that in the process of development is the most comprehensive regulatory program ever devised for the safekeeping of customers' funds and securities by brokerage houses.

Q. *Then can customers be confident of 100 per cent protection against brokerage firm failures?*

A. No, there is no system that is foolproof. For the vast majority of brokerage accounts, though, the $50,000 and $20,000 limits do amount to 100 per cent protection. And this is certainly a spectacular improvement over the defenses of only a few years ago.

NOTE: Several large incorporated brokerage firms also provide insurance of their own that raises the limit on payments to customers—some to as much as $300,000 per account.

INVESTMENT BIBLIOGRAPHY

The Stock Market and How It Works

Bernstein, Peter L. *Economist on Wall Street.* New York: Macmillan, 1970.

Brooks, John. *Once in Golconda.* New York: Harper & Row, 1969.

Goodman, George ("Adam Smith").   *The Money Game.* New York: Random House, 1968.

Mayer, Martin. *The New Breed on Wall Street.* New York: Macmillan, 1969.

Rosen, Lawrence R.   *Go Where the Money Is*. Homewood, Illinois: Dow Jones-Irwin, 1969.

Schwartz, Robert J.   *You and Your Stockbroker*. New York: Macmillan, 1967.

Sobel, Robert.   *The Big Board: A History of the New York Stock Market*. New York: Free Press, 1965.

Learning to Invest

Engel, Louis.   *How to Buy Stocks*. 5th ed. rev. Boston: Little, Brown, 1971.

Finley, Harold M.   *The Logical Approach to Investing*. Chicago: Regnery, 1971.

Graham, Benjamin.   *The Intelligent Investor*. 3rd ed. rev. New York: Harper & Row, 1965.

Loeb, Gerald M.   *The Battle for Stock Market Profits*. New York: Simon & Schuster, 1971.

Lohman, Philipp H.   *The Art of Investing*. New York: Hawthorn, 1972.

Merritt, Robert D.   *Financial Independence Through Common Stocks*. Rev. ed. New York: Simon & Schuster, 1969.

Phelps, Thomas W.   *100 To 1 In the Stock Market*. New York: McGraw-Hill, 1972.

Rosenberg, Claude N., Jr.   *Stock Market Primer*. Rev. ed. New York: World, 1969.

Sederberg, Arelo.   *The Stock Market Investment Club Handbook*. Los Angeles: Sherbourne Press, 1971.

Stabler, C. Norman.   *How to Read the Financial News*. Rev. ed. New York: Harper & Row, 1965.

Newspapers and Periodicals

Barron's: National Business and Financial Weekly (weekly newspaper). New York.

Commercial and Financial Chronicle (semi-weekly newspaper). New York.

The Exchange (New York Stock Exchange monthly magazine). New York.

Financial Analysts Journal (bimonthly magazine). New York.

Financial World (weekly magazine). New York.

Forbes (semimonthly magazine). New York.

Wall Street Journal (daily newspaper). New York.

Wall Street Transcript (weekly newspaper). New York.

THE BAFFLEGAB OF STOCKS

The language of Wall Street is colorful and enriched by many idioms. Some of the words and phrases go back more than a century; others are as up to date as this year's music. Here is a guide through the bafflegab. I have selected only terms which you will come across fairly frequently and, thus, which you should understand.

ARBITRAGE: A technique which takes advantage of a temporary price difference between a security traded on both a U.S. exchange and a foreign exchange; or a temporary price difference between new and old securities of the same company; or a temporary price difference between convertible securities and the securities into which they are convertible. The arbitrageur's profit lies in taking almost simultaneous opposite action in two markets to take advantage of the price differentials. You must have detailed technical knowledge of the different prices, excellent communications, be able to take major risks, and be fairly sophisticated in finance to be an arbitrageur. It's not for amateurs. Rather, it is practiced mostly by brokers who are members of exchanges and not subject to their customers' usual commission costs.

AT THE MARKET: An order to buy or sell a stated number of shares at the most advantageous price your broker can get when the order is executed. You are ordering immediate execution of your order "at the market," not specifying any price. Also called a "market order."

AVERAGES: Yardsticks for measuring broad trends in stock prices. The best known is the Dow Jones average of the prices of 30 outstanding industrial stocks listed on the New York Stock Exchange. Other widely used market indicators, known as indexes, are issued by Standard & Poor's and the New York Stock Exchange.

The Dow Jones average generally gives you the trends in well-established blue chip stocks but *not* in stocks of service companies, smaller companies, or glamor issues. The New York Stock Exchange index includes *all* common stocks listed on the NYSE and is most representative of the market. The Standard & Poor's indexes of 425 industrial stocks and of 500 stocks (including utilities and rails)—all listed on the NYSE—are also excellent yardsticks.

BEAR: An investor who thinks that a stock's price, or the market as a whole, will fall. A bear market is a sharply declining market.

BID AND ASKED: The "bid" price for a stock is the highest price that anyone has declared he is willing to pay for a share of the stock at a given time. The "asked" price is the lowest price at which anyone has declared he is willing to sell this same share at a given time. The actual price at which you buy or sell the share usually will be somewhere between the bid and the asked price. "Bid and asked" is usually called a quote.

BIG BOARD: Wall Street nickname for the New York Stock Exchange, Inc.

BLOOD BATH: In the stock market, this means a horrendous loss suffered by many investors due to a sharp market decline. "Taking a bath" means taking a terrific loss, usually a personal loss but not necessarily a widespread market drop.

BLUE CHIPS: Stocks which, like poker chips, have the highest "rank" in terms of: a long history of earnings in both good times and bad times; an unbroken history of paying quarterly cash dividends, for twenty-five years or more, in recessions as well as booms; established leadership in an established industry; a clear, solid prospect for continued earnings, growth, and dividend payments.

BLUE SKY LAWS: A securities industry expression for the laws of various states designed to protect the public against securities frauds. These state regulations prescribe the requirements which must be met for intrastate issue and sale of securities. The term is said to have come into being when a judge ruled that a particular stock had the value of a patch of blue sky.

BOOK VALUE: A company's total assets (exclusive of such intangibles as good will) less its liabilities and the liquidating value of its preferred stock divided by the number of shares of common stock outstanding to put the figure on a per-share basis. Book value is not the same as market value and generally has little or no relation to it.

BROAD TAPE: Wall Street slang for the Dow Jones & Co. news ticker displayed in many brokerage houses as a large rectangular screen with lines of copy rolling upward, while the American and Big Board tickertapes are displayed as narrow rectangles with copy running horizontally from right to left.

BROKER: An agent who executes your orders to buy and sell shares of stock, other securities or commodity futures contracts for a commission. The word "broker" can refer to the partnership or corporation with whom investors have accounts and, by extension, to its sales employees. A securities salesman is more accurately known as a registered representative, account executive, or customer's man. See above.

BULL: A person who thinks a stock's price, or the market as a whole, will go up. A bull market is a sharply advancing market. See page 830.

CALLABLE: Stock, usually preferred shares, which may be bought back (redeemed) or called by the company, at the option of the company's board of directors, at a certain price within a certain time span and under certain agreed-upon conditions. It is much more usual for bonds and debentures to be callable than stocks. Shares traded on exchanges are usually non-callable.

CAPITAL GAIN (OR LOSS): Profit (or loss) on the sale of any capital asset, including securities. A long-term capital gain is a gain achieved after the securities have been held for a set period under the law: as of 1974 the period was "more than six months." Long-term gains are taxed at a lower federal rate than short-term gains, which in 1974 were gains achieved in "six months or less." A capital loss occurs when you sell stock (or other capital assets) at a loss. This loss also can be short-term or long-term, and each type is treated differently in income tax reporting.

CATS AND DOGS: Highly speculative and usually very low-priced stocks.

CHURNING: An extraordinary, excessive—and therefore suspicious—amount of trading in a customer's account without adequate or proper justification and probably done only to generate additional commissions for an unscrupulous broker. Such improper conduct is subject to disciplinary action by various regulatory organizations.

CLOSED-END INVESTMENT COMPANY: First, let's define an investment company. This is a company which invests in the securities of other companies, holds a diversified list of these securities, and buys and sells them for the purpose of making profits and earning income. It is, in short, a mutual fund.

Now, the closed-end investment company is an investment company which has a fixed capitalization, and usually a fixed number of shares outstanding which may be traded on a securities exchange. You buy shares of a closed-end investment company in the open market from another owner and sell your shares to another buyer exactly as you would trade in other stocks. In contrast, the familiar open-end investment company (or mutual fund) constantly issues new shares and its capitalization is "open." You buy new shares from the mutual fund itself and redeem them by selling them back to the mutual fund. See Chapter 21, "How to Invest in Mutual Funds," for details on both types.

COMMISSION: The broker's basic fee for purchasing or selling securities or property as an agent.

COMMISSION BROKER: An agent who executes the public's orders for the purchase or sale of securities or commodities.

CONFIRMATION: A form you receive from your brokerage house after you buy or sell securities informing you that your buy or sell order has been executed, the number of shares traded, at what price, in what market, the standing of your account, and the settlement date.

CONGLOMERATE: A corporate "supermarket" which has grown externally by rapidly acquiring many unrelated companies primarily through the use of borrowed money and the exchange of securities. In one sense, buying stock in a conglomerate is similar to buying an entire portfolio of different stocks—but at the top a conglomerate, like any other company, is run by a single management team. Basically, therefore, this team's competence and the ability of a conglomerate to grow in size and in earnings per share through both good and bad economic times will determine the prospects for the company as a whole.

CONVERTIBLE: A bond or debenture or preferred stock which not only provides a fixed rate of return (in interest or dividends) but which you can also convert into shares of the same company's common stock at a later date if it is to your advantage to do so. Conversion terms often change and are governed by the indenture (contract) covering the original underwriting.

CORNER: Buying of a stock or commodity on a scale large enough to give the buyer, or buying group, control over the price. A person who must buy that stock or commodity—for example one who is short—is forced to do business at an arbitrarily high price with those who obtained the corner. Corners are rare these days, since registered exchanges have the power to prevent them.

COVERING A SHORT POSITION: What happens when a person who has sold short buys shares of the stock he has "shorted" so he can deliver the shares to the broker from whom he has borrowed the shares. He thereby "covers" his short position. See page 859.

CURB EXCHANGE: Former name of the American Stock Exchange. Now known as the Amex.

CURRENT YIELD: The dividends or interest paid on a security by a company expressed as a percentage of the current price. A stock with a current market price of $40 a share which has paid $2.00 in dividends in the preceding twelve months is said to return 5 per cent ($2.00÷$40.00). The current yield (also called return) on a bond is figured the same way. A 3 per cent $1,000 bond selling at $600 offers a return of 5 per cent ($30÷$600). Figuring the yield of a bond to maturity calls for a bond yield table.

Yields vary tremendously from stock to stock and often they may be misleading. To illustrate, a very low yield may be a good, not bad, sign for it may reflect the fact that a company is putting most of its earnings into its own future business and buyers of its stock are banking on that future. A high yield, on the other hand, may be a bad sign for it may suggest that the company may in time cut the dividend and that investors question its future growth potential.

CUSTOMER'S MAN: Another name for a registered representative, account executive, or securities salesman. See Broker, above.

CYCLICAL STOCKS: Stocks which go up and down with the trend of business (the business cycle)—climbing fast in periods of rapidly improving business conditions and sliding fast when business conditions deteriorate. However, cyclical stocks might also follow special cycles related to their own industry which might not parallel the business cycle.

DEALER: An individual in the securities business who acts as a principal in contrast to a broker who acts as an agent. A dealer buys securities for his own account and then sells to you, the customer, from his own holdings. His profit or loss is the difference between the price he paid for a security and the price at which he sells the security to you. At different times, an individual or firm may act either as a broker or as a dealer. But he has to alert you to the capacity in which he is acting.

DEBENTURE: A promissory note backed by the general credit of a company and usually not secured by a mortgage or lien on any specific property. See Convertible, above.

DEFENSIVE STOCKS: Stocks which tend to be more stable, in terms of dividends, earnings, and market performance in periods of recession or economic uncertainty, than a general cross section of the market. When the market seems to be entering a major bear phase, portfolio managers and experienced investors attempt to switch from high-growth and speculative stocks to quality stocks, hence the term "defensive."

DISCOUNT: A reduction in market price from the face value or original price of a security. In contrast, a premium means an increase in market price above the face value or original price of a security. Much more commonly used in the bond than the stock markets. For instance, a bond selling at a discount is selling below its face value or original price while a bond selling at a premium is selling above its face value or original price. See Chapter 22, "How to Invest in Bonds."

DISCOUNTING THE NEWS: When the price of a stock or the level of a major market indicator rises or falls in anticipation of a specific development— good or bad—and then scarcely moves when the actual development takes place and is announced; this stock, or the market, has "discounted the news." Sometimes the stock or the market moves in a direction opposite to the bullish or bearish news when it is actually published.

DISCRETIONARY ACCOUNT: An account in which you, the investor, give your stockbroker or other agent full or partial authority in writing to buy and sell securities or commodities for you without requiring your specific approval on each transaction. The discretion will include selection, timing, and price to be paid or received for the securities.

DIVIDENDS: A payment distributed to share owners on a proportional basis in amounts and at times voted by a company's board of directors. A dividend may be in cash, additional shares of the company's own stock, or in the securities of another company it owns.

On preferred stock, the dividend amounts are usually fixed but can be reduced or skipped at the discretion of the directors. On common stock, dividends may vary throughout a year and from year to year—or may not be paid at all depending on the company's earnings and the decisions of its directors. See preceding pages.

DOLLAR COST AVERAGING: A system in which you invest a fixed amount of money regularly in a given stock or stocks and thereby, due to price fluctuations, always have an average purchase cost that is lower than the average market price of the stocks bought. See above.

DOW THEORY: A theory of market analysis based upon the performance of the Dow Jones industrial and transportation stock price averages. The theory says that the market is in a basic upward trend if one of these averages advances above a previous important high, accompanied or followed by a similar advance in the other. When the averages both dip below previous important lows, this is regarded as confirmation of a basic downward trend. The theory does not attempt to predict how long either trend will continue, although it is widely misinterpreted as a method of forecasting future action. Whatever the merits of the theory, it is sometimes a strong factor in the market because many people believe in the theory—or believe that a great many others do.

EARNINGS (OR INCOME) STATEMENT: A company's statement to share owners which may appear in an annual, semi-annual, or quarterly report, of its net profits (or "net income") or losses after taxes and expenses, for the period covered by the report.

EQUITY FINANCING: Since stock represents ownership or equity in a company, equity financing is the obtaining of funds by a company through the sale of stock.

EX-DIVIDEND: Means "without dividend" and is usually indicated by the symbol "X" after the company's name in the stock tables. If you buy a stock when it is selling ex-dividend, it means you will not receive a just-declared dividend. Instead, that dividend will go to the previous owner (the seller) who was the stockholder of record.

EX-RIGHTS: Means "without rights" that a corporation may have offered stockholders to subscribe to new or additional stock. If you buy a stock selling "ex-rights," you are not entitled to the rights; these remain the property of the seller.

EXTRA: The short form of "extra dividend." A dividend in the form of stock or cash in addition to the regular or usual dividend the company has been paying.

FALL OUT OF BED: A crash in stock prices. For instance, "The market fell out of bed on the news" means the market declined very sharply.

FISCAL YEAR: A company's accounting year, which may coincide with the calendar year or may span some other period—typically July 1 through June 30.

FLOOR: The trading area of any of the world's stock exchanges; as of the mid-seventies, most particularly the huge trading area, about the size of a football field, where common and preferred stocks were bought and sold on the New York Stock Exchange. Bonds were traded on the New York Stock Exchange in a separate small Bond Room adjacent to the floor.

FLOOR BROKER: A member of an exchange who in the mid-1970s executed orders to buy or sell listed securities on that floor.

FOREIGN EXCHANGES: Refers to securities exchanges operating in other countries. For instance, the London Stock Exchange is a foreign (securities) exchange.

FORMULA INVESTING: An investment technique. One formula calls for the shifting of funds from common shares to preferred shares or bonds as the market, on average, rises above a certain predetermined point—and the return of funds to common share investments as the market average declines.

GOING PUBLIC: The underwriting process whereby a privately owned company offers its own stock for sale to the public for the first time and makes it available for trading in the over-the-counter market or on an organized exchange.

GROWTH STOCKS: Stock in a company with superior prospects of growth in earnings which historically have exceeded the growth rate of the economy or of corporations on average. See above.

HEDGE: In the securities and commodities markets, to hedge means to try to minimize or eliminate a risk by taking certain steps to offset the risk.

HOLDING COMPANY: A non-operating company which owns the securities, and usually holds voting control, of another company which does sell products or services. Hence, "holding company."

IN-AND-OUT: Buying and selling a stock within a short period of time. In-and-out speculators strive for profits resulting from hour-to-hour and day-to-day stock price changes.

INSIDER: Directors, officers, and principal securities holders of a corporation. The latter can be companies or individuals who are beneficial shareholders of 10 per cent or more of a publicly traded company's stock. The Securities and Exchange Commission requires insiders to report their initial position and details of any significant change in their holdings.

INSTITUTIONAL INVESTOR: An organization or company with substantial funds invested in securities—i.e., a bank, insurance company, mutual fund, university, labor union, pension plan.

INVESTMENT ADVISER OR COUNSEL: Individual (or firm) who supervises or manages funds of investors for a fee. See above.

INVESTMENT BANKER (OR UNDERWRITER): Middlemen between companies needing capital and the investing public. To illustrate, when a company wants capital for expansion or modernization, it may sell its securities to an investment banker or underwriter; this firm, in turn, will sell the securities to the public.

INVESTMENT CLUB: See earlier in this chapter.

INVESTMENT COMPANY: Current meaning refers usually to an open-end or a closed-end mutual fund. See Chapter 21, "How to Invest in Mutual Funds."

INVESTOR: An individual, owning securities, whose main goals are relatively long-term growth of his principal and/or dividend income. He differs from a speculator in his goals, expectations, risks, and temperament.

LAMB: An amateur speculator who blindly follows the flock, buying or selling on tips and rumors, and is easily "fleeced" by the pros or by his own naïveté and greed.

LETTER STOCK: A type of unregistered stock—often issued by new small companies to avoid the cost of a formal underwriting—that is sold at a presumed discount to mutual funds and experienced investors specializing in such speculative investments. Letter stock usually carries a proviso that it may not be resold for a considerable period of time.

LIMIT ORDER: An order to buy or sell a stated amount of a security at a specified price, or a better price if obtainable, after the order has been placed.

LIQUIDATION: Dissolution of a company; process of converting securities and other assets into cash.

LIQUIDITY: Capacity of the market in a particular security to absorb a reasonable amount of buying or selling at reasonably limited price changes. An "illiquid" market in a security means you cannot buy or sell with reasonable freedom at reasonable price changes.

LISTED STOCK: Stock traded on a national securities exchange. Both the stock and the exchange have been registered with the Securities and Exchange Commission. Detailed information on such stock has been filed with the SEC and the issuing company has met the listing standards of the exchange upon which it is being traded.

LOAD: Sales charge which a buyer of mutual funds must pay on top of the actual net asset value of the shares—unless the mutual fund is a no-load fund (meaning the fund is sold without any sales charge to the buyer). See Chapter 21, "How to Invest in Mutual Funds."

LOCKED IN: An investor who will not sell stocks in which he has a substantial profit because he would have to pay capital gains tax on the profit. He has a "paper" profit which he is reluctant to take because the tax will consume a good part of it and thus he is "locked in."

LONG: Means simply that you have bought a certain number of shares of a stock and hold it in anticipation of higher prices (are "long" of it) or for whatever other goals you have in mind.

MAKE A KILLING: Make a spectacular profit.

MANIPULATION: Illegal buying and selling of securities in order to create false impression of active trading, or to drive prices up or down as a lure for others to buy or sell while the manipulators are taking profits.

MARGIN: Minimum proportion of the purchase price you must pay when you wish to use your broker's credit to buy a security. Initial margins are regulated by the Federal Reserve Board and have ranged in recent years from 50 per cent to 100 per cent of the stock purchase price. A 100 per cent margin means no borrowing is permitted.

You buy on margin when you want to purchase more stock than your cash on hand would permit. You get credit for the balance from your broker at current interest rates because obviously you are hoping to increase your gains. A 50 per cent margin means you put up only 50 per cent of your cash to buy a stock; you get credit for the rest. The New York Stock Exchange also has strict margin maintenance rules that its member organizations are expected to enforce in customer accounts.

MARGIN CALL: A call from your broker asking you to put up additional cash (or collateral) in order to bring your equity in your account at least up to the margin maintenance requirements stipulated by the exchange. You might get this call if your stock declines sharply instead of rising. If you don't meet the call and bring up your equity to the requirement, your stock will be liquidated by your broker.

MARKET ORDER: Order to buy or sell a stated amount of a security at the best price obtainable in the market at the time.

MARKET PRICE: The last reported transaction price of a security.

MEMBER FIRM: A securities brokerage firm organized either as a corporation or a partnership and having at least one executive or general partner who is a member of the exchange.

NASD: The National Association of Securities Dealers, Inc., an association of brokers and dealers in the over-the-counter securities business. The association has the power to expel members who have been declared guilty of unethical practices. NASD is dedicated to—among other objectives—"adopt, administer and enforce rules of fair practice and rules to prevent fraudulent and manipulative acts and practices, and in general to promote just and equitable principles of trade for the protection of investors."

NET ASSET VALUE: Most often used by mutual funds which report their net asset value per share every day. The NAV represents the market value of the securities the fund owns on that day plus the cash it holds divided by the total number of the shares the mutual fund has outstanding. "Load" mutual funds charge a sales charge in addition to their net asset value per share. "No load" mutual funds simply sell their shares at the NAV per share.

NEW ISSUE: New stocks or bonds sold for the first time to raise money for just about any purpose. The issuers range from the U. S. Government and great foreign governments to the most risky small corporations and cities. If a new issue is in heavy demand and its price rises to a premium over the issue price immediately after the offering, it is called "hot." See above.

NEW YORK STOCK EXCHANGE: The nation's largest securities exchange in the mid-1970s was the New York Stock Exchange.

The NYSE is a not-for-profit corporation which does not own the securities traded and does not set prices. Nor does it make or lose money when securities prices rise or fall. It provides a market place for the purchase and sale of securities.

ODD LOT: An amount of stock normally less than the 100 shares which make up a "round lot." In seldom-traded "inactive" stocks, 10 shares make up a round lot, and 1 to 9 shares make up an odd lot.

ODD-LOT DEALER: A member firm of the exchange which buys and sells odd lots of stocks—1 to 9 shares in the case of stocks traded in 10-share units and 1 to 99 shares for 100-share units. The odd-lot dealer's customers are commission brokers acting on behalf of their customers.

OPTION: A right to buy or sell specific securities, commodities, or properties at a specified price within a specified time.

OVER-THE-COUNTER: By far the biggest securities market in the world, where stocks and bonds which are not listed on securities exchanges are traded. It is the principal area for the trading of U. S. Government securities and municipal bonds. The O-T-C is not a place but mostly a communications network of stock and bond dealers doing business chiefly on a principal basis. This area is supervised by the National Association of Securities Dealers, Inc., which has the power to expel members who have been declared guilty of unethical practices.

PAPER PROFIT: Amount of profit you, the holder of a security, have "on paper" and *would* make *if* you sold this security. Paper loss is the amount of loss you *would* take *if* you sold the security.

PAR VALUE: In a common stock, its nominal value. But many common stocks today are issued without par value, and par value has little meaning to buyers of common stock. Although it has no relation at all to market value or book value, par value for common stock does have legal and corporate significance. In a preferred stock, par value has meaning to the investor because dividends are normally paid on the basis of par value. (A 5 per cent preferred stock might pay that percentage on a par of $100 or a $5.00 dividend.) In a bond, par value is also important to the investor, because par is its face value, the principal on which interest is paid. (A 5 per cent bond might pay that percentage [or $50] every year, usually on a par value of $1,000.) Par value is also the amount usually repaid at the maturity of a bond by the borrower.

PENNY STOCKS: Superspeculative stocks, often of mining companies, which usually sell for $1.00 a share or less.

POINT: In stock prices, one point equals a change of $1.00 and a one-point rise or fall means a $1.00 rise or fall in the stock's price. A half-point rise or fall means a 50¢ change; one quarter means 25¢, etc.

In bond prices, though, one point equals a change of $10 and a one-point rise or fall in the price per $1,000 face value of bond means a $10 rise or fall in the price of that bond. A 2-point change means a $20 change per bond, etc. See Chapter 22, "How to Invest in Bonds."

PORTFOLIO: The collection of securities held by an individual or institutional investor (such as a mutual fund). Term is especially applicable when these securities have been carefully researched and assembled in a deliberate fashion, regarding proportions of: bonds to stocks, growth to income, cyclical to non-cyclical, and speculative to conservative issues.

PREFERRED STOCK: A category of stock which is subordinate to the debt a company owes but which has a claim ahead of the company's common stock upon the payment of dividends or the assets of the company in the event the company is liquidated. (Hence the name "preferred stock.") Preferred stock is usually called a "senior" security and its dividend usually is at a set rate—both characteristics similar to those of bonds.

A key difference between preferred stock and bonds is that bonds almost always have a final maturity date (when a bond becomes due and payable) while preferreds do not because these stocks represent ownership. A preferred stock will remain outstanding indefinitely unless called for redemption at a price fixed by the company at the date the stock was issued. Most preferred stocks also are cumulative—meaning that if their dividends are omitted they build up in arrears and then the company must pay these arrears plus current preferred stock dividends before it can pay common stock dividends.

Some preferred stocks are convertible into common stocks just as some bonds are.

PREMIUM: The amount by which a preferred stock or bond may sell above the par value. See Discount, above.

PRICE/EARNINGS RATIO: The relationship between the price at which a stock is selling and the company's earnings per share.

PROFIT TAKING: Selling stock which has appreciated in value since purchase in order to realize the profit. The term is often used to explain a downturn in the market following a period of rising prices.

PROSPECTUS: One of the documents filed with the Securities and Exchange Commission by a company when it is planning an issue of securities for public sale totaling $500,000 or more. It is a selling circular containing highlights from the full registration statement, subject to the SEC's disclosure rules, and used by brokers to help investors evaluate the new securities before or at the time of purchase. See above.

PROXY: Authorization you give to a company official or other representative to vote your shares for you at a shareholders' meeting.

PUTS AND CALLS: Options to buy or sell a fixed amount of a specific stock at a specified price within a specified period of time, usually thirty to ninety days or six months and ten days. A call is an option to buy a certain number of shares of stock within a certain period of time at a certain price. A call is bought by a bullish investor. A put is an option to sell a certain number of shares of stock within a certain period at a certain price. It is bought by a bearish investor. These are expensive and sophisticated forms of speculation and hedging and are not for the amateur. See above.

QUOTATION: Often shortened to "quote." The highest bid to buy and the lowest offer to sell a security in a given market at a given time. If you ask your broker for a "quote" on a stock, he may come back with something like "45¼ to 45½." This means that $45.25 was the highest price any buyer wanted to pay at the time the quote was given and that $45.50 was the lowest price which any seller would take at the same time.

RALLY: A sharp rapid rise in stock prices or in the price of one particular stock, following a decline.

RED HERRING: A preliminary prospectus. It carries a cautionary statement on the first page, printed in red, which gives rise to the term "red herring."

REGISTERED REPRESENTATIVE: A securities salesman employed by a brokerage firm who has passed certain tests and met certain standards set by the New York Stock Exchange and/or the National Association of Securities Dealers. Also called an account executive, customer's man, a stock broker, or simply a broker.

REGISTRATION: Before a public offering may be made of new securities by a company, or of outstanding securities by controlling stockholders—through the mails or in interstate commerce—the securities must be registered under the Securities Act of 1933 and a registration statement must be filed with the SEC by the issuer. This statement must disclose pertinent information relating to the company's operations, securities, management, and purpose of the public offering. Securities of railroads under jurisdiction of the Interstate Commerce Commission, and certain other types of securities, are exempted. On securities offerings involving less than $500,000, less information is required.

Before a security may be admitted to dealings on a national securities exchange, it must be registered under the Securities Exchange Act of 1934. The application for registration must be filed with the exchange and the SEC by the company issuing the securities. It must disclose pertinent information relating to the company's operations, securities, and management. Registration may become effective thirty days after receipt by the SEC of the certification by the exchange of approval of listing and registration, or sooner by special order of the commission.

RIGHT: A short-term privilege to buy additional shares at a specified, advantageous price for a short, limited time given to the shareholders on a proportional basis by the issuing company. Rights are often offered by a company seeking to raise additional capital, and may involve bonds, especially debentures. Rights are offered to existing shareholders so that they will continue to hold the same equity position after the change in capitalization has taken place. You, the shareholder receiving rights, have two choices: (a) to buy the security on the terms offered (for example, 1 share for each 20 shares owned); (b) to sell the rights which, because of the favorable price of the offer, have a value of their own. Failure to exercise or sell your rights results in a loss—through dilution of the value of your existing holdings by the issuance of the additional stock. Therefore, you should either exercise your rights or sell them during the allotted time span. See above.

ROUND LOT: A unit of trading in a security. Usually 100 shares for active stocks; 10 shares for inactive stocks.

SEAT: Membership in a stock exchange which entitles the owner to buy and sell securities on that exchange. Big Board seat prices have ranged from $40,-000 to $515,000 in recent years.

SEC: The Securities and Exchange Commission, the federal agency established by Congress to help protect investors. The SEC administers the Securities Act of 1933, the Trust Indenture Act, the Investment Company Act, the Investment Advisers Act, and the Public Utility Holding Company Act.

SECONDARY DISTRIBUTION: (also known as a secondary offering). The redistribution of a block of stock some time after it has been sold by the issuing company. The sale is handled off the NYSE by a securities firm or group of firms and the shares are usually offered at a fixed price which is related to the current market price of the stock. Usually the block is a large one, such as might be involved in the settlement of an estate. The security may be listed or unlisted.

SETTLEMENT DAY: The deadline by which a buyer of securities must pay for securities he has purchased and a seller must deliver certificates for securities he has sold. In regular trading, settlement day is the fifth business day after execution of an order.

SHORT POSITION: Stocks sold short and not covered as of a particular date. On the NYSE, a tabulation is issued once a month listing all issues on the exchange in which there was a short position of 5,000 or more shares and issues in which the short position had changed by 2,000 or more shares in the preceding month. Short position or interest also means the total amount of stock an individual has sold short and has not covered, as of a particular date. See Short Selling, below.

SHORT SELLING: The reverse of the usual transaction, for instead of buying a stock first and selling it later, the short seller sells it first, then borrows the stock and buys it back later to complete the transaction. See above.

"SMART MONEY": Refers to the so-called professional and sophisticated traders who supposedly exploit alleged "inside" information to make profits at the expense of other investors. In other words, the term implies exceptional contacts, knowledge, timing and forecasting ability, the special knack of finding the most profitable deals, and using the newest financing or investing techniques and media.

SPECIALIST: A member of an exchange who has two functions. The first is to maintain an orderly market, as far as reasonably practicable, in the stocks in which he is registered as a specialist. In order to maintain an orderly market, the exchange expects the specialist to buy or sell for his own account, to a reasonable degree, when there is a temporary disparity between supply and demand. The second function of the specialist is to act as a broker's broker.

When a commission broker on the exchange floor receives a limit order, say, to buy at $50 a stock then selling at $60—he cannot wait at the post where the stock is traded until the price reaches the specified level. So he leaves the order with the specialist, who will try to execute it in the market if and when the stock declines to the specified price. There were hundreds of specialists on the NYSE alone in the mid-1970s.

SPECULATOR: A person whose goal in buying and selling securities is to multiply his capital quickly and who is willing to take greater risks than an investor to attain this objective. Differs from an investor in goals, risks temperament. See In-and-Out, above.

SPLIT: A division of a company's outstanding stock: i.e., if a company has 1 million shares outstanding, currently priced at $50 per share, and splits its stock two for one, it has 2 million shares outstanding which will sell at $25 per share. If you own 100 "old" shares at $50, after the split you own 200 "new" shares at $25. Theoretically, the new shares are worth only half the amount of the old shares, but in actual practice prices tend to rise when a stock is split—at least temporarily. Reason: investors generally are more interested in buying relatively lower-priced stocks than high-priced stocks, hence buying frequently increases after a stock is split.

SPREAD: The difference between two prices, between bid and asked or between purchase and sale price.

STOCK DIVIDEND: A dividend paid by a company to its stockholders in the form of additional shares of the company's stock instead of in the form of cash (when it is a cash dividend).

STOCK OPTION: A privilege, often conferred as a fringe benefit by a company to its executive and key employees, to buy stock in the company at a specified presumably favorable price, within a specified period of time and on advantageous terms.

STOP ORDER: Standing instructions to your broker to sell your shares automatically if the price drops to a specified level. The aim is to assure yourself that profits don't disappear or your losses don't exceed a given amount. There is no guarantee that a stop order will be executed exactly at its "trigger" price, because when a stop is activated it becomes a market order and allows the broker to get the best possible price then available in a market. Stops can be used for buy orders too.

STREET: The New York financial community in the Wall Street area.

STREET NAME: Securities left by the owner in his broker's name and custody. Often investors leave all their securities in street name as a matter of choice and convenience but securities bought on margin must be left in street name.

SYMBOL: The single capital letter or combination of letters given to a company when it is listed on an exchange and by which it is thereafter identified on the tape. For instance, U. S. Steel is "X"; General Motors is "GM"; American Telephone & Telegraph is "T"; Radio Corp. of America is "RCA."

TAKEN TO THE CLEANERS: In the stock market, this means the same thing as taking a bath or blood bath. In short, it means being hit by one or many whopping losses.

TENDER: In stock market language, a tender means an offer to acquire a security you own or to exchange stock which you own for stock in another company. Usually a tender is made by a corporation or individual to gain control of a company or to simplify the corporate structure of the company.

THE STREET: Wall Street. But "Wall Street" is not just a street in New York City bounded at one end by a river and at the other by a graveyard. It has been broadened to include all the financial institutions, securities and money markets, and investors on all the Main Streets of the United States from coast to coast.

THIN MARKET: A market in which there are comparatively few bids to buy or offers to sell or both—or an illiquid market. The phrase may apply to a single security or to the entire stock market. In a thin market, price fluctuations between transactions are usually larger than when the market is liquid. A thin market in a particular stock may reflect lack of interest in that issue or a limited supply of stock in the market.

TICKER: The instrument which prints prices and volume of security transactions in cities and towns throughout the United States and Canada within minutes after each trade on the floor. In recent years it has been complemented by thousands of visual display units on top of brokers' desks.

TIPS: Recommendations of stocks to buy or sell often given to novices by other novices on the false basis of alleged "inside" information about the stock. Tips may be accurate too, and given in entirely good faith—but these are in a slim minority as far as the general public is concerned. Tipping could be illegal. A tipster, of course, is a person who gives tips.

TRANSFER AGENT: A transfer agent keeps a record of the name of each registered share owner, his or her address, the number of shares owned, and sees that certificates presented to his office for transfer are properly canceled and new certificates issued in the name of the transferee.

TURNOVER: The volume of trading on a stock exchange—or in a particular security, or in the entire securities market—on a given day or in a given period.

UNDERWRITER: See Investment Banker, above.

WARRANT: A privilege to buy a security at a specified price—within a specified time limit or perpetually. Usually a long-term offer made by a corporation to pave the way for the eventual sale of stocks or bonds to persons who do not already own its securities. As a rule, it is offered as an inducement to get investors to buy the other securities. A warrant is similar to a right but it normally has a much longer life. See above.

"WHEN ISSUED": Term used to describe a new issue of securities that has been authorized but not actually issued to purchasers and that is being bought and sold in the market with all transactions settled only when, as, and if the securities are finally issued. "WI" is the label for these issues in the newspaper stock tables.

YIELD: The percentage of return per year on a security. To find the current yield on a stock, you divide the current annual dividend rate by the current price of the stock. (If you bought the stock at $100, and it is paying $3.00 a year in dividends, your current yield is 3 per cent.) Figuring yields on bonds is more complex and determining yields to maturity requires the use of bond tables. See above.

YO-YO STOCKS: Volatile, usually high-priced specialty issues, which fluctuate wildly.

21

HOW TO INVEST IN
MUTUAL FUNDS

WHAT ARE MUTUAL FUNDS?

Mutual funds are a medium through which you invest your money in a diversified list of stocks and bonds chosen by professional investment managers. You buy shares in a mutual fund which in turn uses your money to buy the securities of other companies. You can buy and sell mutual fund shares at prices that are calculated once or twice a day on any days that the securities markets are open.

There are "load" and "no-load" funds. There are also the closed-end funds which are discussed separately at the end of this section. The load funds are sold by salesmen through elaborate marketing systems and on these shares there is a sales charge (load). The no-load funds have no salesmen, no elaborate distribution systems, and no sales charge. You are not "sold" these shares; you must "buy" them. You usually learn about a no-load fund from another investor, from a banker, a lawyer, an investment adviser, an inconspicuous ad in a financial news section, or from a discussion such as this.

Q. *How many mutual funds are there?*

A. In the mid-1970s there were about 600, of which about 150 were no-load funds.

Q. *Who buys mutual funds?*

A. Individuals. Also many institutional investors have in recent years become large holders of fund shares.

Q. *Where are the prices on mutual funds quoted?*

A. In the financial pages of the major daily newspapers, which usually have a section giving bid and asked prices on mutual funds. On the no-load funds, you will find the same price quoted under "bid" and "asked." On the load funds you will find a higher price under "asked" than under "bid" because the "asked" price will reflect the sales charge. For example, if the bid on Fund A is $10.50 and the asked is $11.20, the sales charge is 70 cents. Also many major newspapers use the designation "NL" (no-load) next to this type of fund, thereby making it easy to find the no-load funds.

Q. *Do you recommend mutual funds for a new young investor?*

A. In most cases, yes, if you don't have the time or inclination to select individual stocks. However, the key to success is to select the right mutual fund for yourself, one which meets your investment objectives and performs well over a long period of time.

WHY SHOULD YOU BUY MUTUAL FUNDS?

If I were to tell you that the investment advice given to the small investor in the United States is far inferior to that given to the Big Guy, and that the men and women who *give* that advice agree the above is true, wouldn't you be deeply disturbed? Okay, I'm telling you that this is the opinion of an overwhelming percentage of the nation's security analysts. According to a recent survey:

• A shocking seven out of ten security analysts have "reservations about the advice available to the small investor as compared with that given the large one."

• Only one in three believes that "the quality of investment advice now available adequately serves all types of investors."

• Nearly half favor "some form of blanket registration of security analysts" (in short, greater control).

This is a serious indictment of investment advice by the advice industry itself.

By itself, this report would be sobering enough. It becomes even more so in view of the forecasts dramatized in the previous chapter on investing in stocks: first, that the fees you pay for Wall Street's service will be "unbundled" in the years ahead and you'll pay a schedule of commissions determined in part by the level of the investment advice you request; and, second, the emergence of the investment manager who supervises the funds of the small investor for a fee on top of the commissions the investor must pay to buy and sell.

What does all this mean to *you?*

It means you must recognize that you will not get the same high-quality research and advice as an institutional investor and certainly not at the same time the pro gets it—unless you pay extra for it. This in turn means that one possible solution for you lies in joining the pros via buying mutual fund shares.

Here are some of the major advantages of mutual fund ownership versus personal selection by the amateur of a portfolio of stocks and bonds.

Diversification. In general, the greater variety of stocks, bonds, and other types of investments selected by mutual funds lessens the risk of loss due to your making one big mistake in selecting individual stocks.

Mutual funds have to diversify. By federal law, except in instances of special exemption disclosed in the prospectus, they may not invest more than 5 per cent of their assets in the securities of any single issuer. Funds may not own more than 10 per cent of any class of securities issued by a single company.

Professional management. All of the major mutual funds are managed by professionals backed by substantial facilities for research, statistical analysis, and economic research.

Federal regulation. By law, mutual funds ordinarily must distribute at least 90 per cent of their net income to share owners each year. Moreover, there are tight federal restrictions on the amounts of money a mutual fund may borrow.

Convenience. Obviously it's much simpler for you, the share owner, to have one single certificate—representing your ownership (through a mutual fund) in 100 or more stocks. Mutual funds have a fine record in handling the paper work of their customers. Many take care of the paper work completely.

Easy purchase plans. There are many different, easy, and new ways in which you can buy—and enjoy the proceeds of—mutual funds today. This includes automatic reinvestment plans, periodic purchase plans, withdrawal plans, and the like.

Liquidity. It's very easy to sell a mutual fund. Nearly all funds will repurchase fund shares at the bid price and the sell order can be conveniently arranged.

Variety of funds. There are dozens of different types of mutual funds to choose from—including stock, bond, and money market funds, as well as growth, balanced, income, speculative funds—which means there's probably at least one fund that can meet your specific needs.

WHAT IS THE INVESTMENT RECORD OF MUTUAL FUNDS?

Of course, the performance varies from fund to fund—depending on the objective of the fund (growth versus income, for instance) and on the excellence of management. But over the long term, the records of mutual funds compare favorably with the familiar stock averages.

Over the short term, though, the performances of mutual funds can be abysmally poor. In fact, in the 1969–74 period, many of the fund shares chalked up dreadful records. Their performance came in for particular criticism in view of the fact that the funds are managed by professionals at a handsome fee and the fact that at a minimum their goal is preservation of capital plus income while, at a maximum, their aim is significant enhancement of capital plus income.

This was the period in which the "go-go" performance funds went into their downward spin. Some of the star fund performers of the 1960s—such as the Manhattan Fund, Mates Investment Fund, Enterprise Fund, and Neuwirth Fund—plummeted from the list of top performers to the also-ran category. It was painful testimony of the extent to which so many of the funds had changed from being a safe, sane haven for the small investor wanting long-term growth into a playground for the fast-moving speculator seeking instant performance. I repeat, however, that this is short-term. In contrast the long-term record of the funds shapes up impressively in the investor's favor.

In the decade of the 1960s, for instance, there were three major stock market breaks. Here is how the record of mutual funds compared with other forms of investing and saving and with key stock market indexes in the ten-year period. The mutual fund average was compiled by FundScope.

	ORIGINAL INVESTMENT (JAN. 1, 1960)	AFTER 10 YEARS (JAN. 1, 1970)
Growth mutual fund average	$10,000	$25,022
All mutual fund average	10,000	21,255
Standard & Poor's 500 Stock index	10,000	20,950
Dow Jones Industrial Average	10,000	16,450
5% interest, compounded quarterly	10,000	16,436
Savings and loan associations	10,000	15,230
Government savings bonds (Series E)	10,000	14,580
Commercial bank time and savings deposits	10,000	14,273

TYPES OF MUTUAL FUNDS

Today you can buy shares in literally dozens of different types of mutual funds—many of them new and little known and many of them highly specialized. These, of course, are in addition to the "old" types of funds, which have been part of the scene from the start of the industry's expansion.

For instance, you can invest your money in shares of a mutual fund specializing in chemical stocks or energy companies. You can choose a fund which gambles in ultrarisky speculative securities—or you can settle for a fund with a conservative investment philosophy. You can also buy shares in funds specializing in tax-exempt bonds or in foreign securities. You can even buy shares in a mutual fund carrying built-in insurance against any loss in your investment—assuming you're willing to pay an insurance premium cost in addition to the sales charge.

Mutual funds have now diversified to the point where you can actually lose your way in this financial industry without a guide. Quietly but rapidly, whole new classes of mutual funds have been developed. For example, it has been only since 1970 that bond and money market (or cash reserve) funds have become very popular.

To the old-line definitions, it is thus essential to add explanations of some of the new types of funds. In alphabetical order, here is a guide through "old" and "new":

Balanced funds: Among the more conservative funds, with investment portfolios "balanced" at all times among bonds, preferred stocks and common stocks—as a protection against a roller-coastering stock market. This type of fund is for a person who is seeking safety of principal plus a regular income and who, to get this, is willing to settle for relatively modest growth of his investment.

Bond and money market instrument funds: Funds which invest in portfolios of various types of bonds and short-term money market securities to produce high yields. In recent years, the yields on such funds have often substantially outstripped those of savings accounts or even large certificates of deposit. Another attraction of such funds is the possibility of eventual capital gains if some of the bonds in the portfolio were bought at discounts below face value. Among the popular types have been the tax-exempt bond funds. Here the portfolios consist entirely of tax-exempt bonds, which means holders of these mutual funds pay no income tax on the income they receive from these funds. Also popular have been the funds holding only U. S. Government securities, certificates of deposit issued by banks in denominations of $100,000 or more, commercial paper, other short-term paper of high quality. See "How To Invest in Bonds."

Closed-end funds: Operate like open-end mutual funds except that they issue only a fixed number of shares and will not usually buy shares back. Shares are bought and sold on the stock market but hardly ever at a price equal to the net asset value per share. As a result, they either sell at a "premium" over their asset price or at a "discount" below it.

Common stock funds: Funds which have limited their portfolios to common stocks. They range from ultraconservative funds investing primarily in the highest-quality blue chip common stocks to ultrarisky funds investing in speculative stocks.

Convertible funds: Are aimed at producing current income and capital gains by investing in convertible preferred stocks and convertible bonds.

Dual-purpose funds: Type of funds offering two kinds of shares: income shares and capital shares. In most dual-purpose funds, each class of investor at the outset stands to get double his money's worth. The capital shareholder will reap gains (or losses) on the income shareholder's money as well as his own. The income shareholder collects the capital shareholder's dividends. To obtain this form of leverage, the income shareholder must usually give up all claim to capital appreciation and the capital shareholder must forfeit all income. So far there have been only a handful of such funds and they haven't operated long enough to get a good reading on their performance. They have a long and successful history in England and Holland.

Growth funds: Funds concentrating on purchase of growth stocks. Growth funds involve relatively more risk than income or balanced funds. A growth fund should give you a return ranging from at least 8 per cent to 12 per cent annually over a five-year period or it's not worth the risk.

Hedge funds: Began as private pools of speculative funds formed by groups of wealthy investors but now there are hedge funds for anyone who wants them. These funds use such unorthodox (for mutual funds) techniques as borrowing against their own stocks in order to buy more shares, speculating in put and call options, and selling shares short in order to profit from stock price declines as well as rises (thus, "hedge" funds). Their major objective is capital gains.

Billions of dollars were put into hedge funds in the 1960s, and until 1969 some turned in dazzling performances. But in the 1969–70 crash, many of the leading hedge funds lost as much as 40 to 50 per cent in value and their reputations were seriously tarnished. Many went out of business. Hedge funds are usually *not* for the small investor.

Income funds: The principal goal of these is income to be achieved by investment in high-yielding stocks and bonds. Only an incidental objective is capital gains. These funds tend to be the most conservative—and their popularity swings up and down depending on shifting investor interest in income versus long-term growth.

Letter stock funds: Highly speculative funds which invest your money in stocks of companies not yet registered with the Securities and Exchange Commission. This stock is called "letter stock" because a buyer (in this case, the mutual fund) must sign an "investment letter" promising not to resell the stock for a specified short-term period and pledging instead to hold it for a longer term. This type of stock is generally sold by small, fledgling companies to finance research, development, expansion.

Look upon any investment in mutual funds specializing in letter stock as sheer speculation. This is definitely too risky for most mutual fund buyers and the funds virtually disappeared in the market breaks of the early 1970s.

Money-market funds: Funds which invest in short-term money-market securities in periods of high short-term interest rates. Investors can buy these shares in comparatively small amounts and thus get the same advantages of the high rates on these instruments that big investors get when they buy large blocks in the open market.

Open-end funds: This is the broad classification of mutual fund which will sell its own new shares to you whenever you want to buy and stands ready to buy back at any time, and usually at no charge, shares it has issued to you for the current net asset value of the shares. There is no limit to the number of shares which an open-end fund can issue. In short, its capitalization is open at both ends and hence the term "open-end."

Special purpose funds: Aren't new but their number is multiplying. These funds invest primarily in one specific type of stock or bond or in one particular industry to take advantage of the faster growth in that area or industry. For example, there are funds which invest heavily in chemicals, energy, also in other mutual funds—or only in United States Government securities. Within this special purpose category, too, there are funds adhering to a special stock market forecasting theory or technique.

If you invest in a special purpose stock fund, a wise precaution would be to seek a fund with an investment portfolio widely diversified among key beneficiaries of any major advance in its chosen area or industry.

Venture capital funds: Funds which usually invest in securities of companies that are little known and with stock usually not yet registered with the Securities and Exchange Commission. These restricted securities cannot be sold publicly until they have been registered. Other funds provide new companies with seed capital. Nowhere is an investor betting more on a manager's ability and judgment than in venture capital funds. Most of the funds are still too young to have proved themselves.

LOAD AND NO-LOAD FUNDS

As I wrote earlier, a load fund will usually be sold to you by a salesman or selling organization and, for this, you will pay a sales charge, or a "load." A no-load fund you will have to seek out and buy on your own. There are no salesmen, no sales charges—and thus the description "no-load." This is the sole distinction.

Among the no-load funds you will find the same wide selection as among the load funds—in investment goals, in size, in investment record, in quality of management, etc. You can get the same services on no-loads as on loads: systematic purchasing plans, withdrawal plans, and insurance plans. You can sell them easily simply by telling the fund's home office you want to redeem your shares. (A few have a redemption charge, usually of 1 per cent.) The tax status is the same in both cases and so are the SEC's regulations.

When you buy a load fund, you pay the net asset value plus the sales charge. This is generally around 8½ per cent, which translates into something over 9 per cent above the asset value. The charge, however, can range from 1 per cent to more than 9½ per cent. In short, the minute you buy a load fund the worth of your holdings is less than what you put in. For example, if you buy $1,000 worth of a load fund, you may only get $910 in asset value; $90 went for commission.

The long-term records of the no-load funds compare favorably with those of the load funds. The lack of a sales charge has nothing to do with the caliber of the fund's management.

In recent years, no-load funds have become increasingly popular as investors have become aware that they are around and that they provide a savings in commissions. But you well may decide that a specific load fund is right for you and thus you'll ignore the sales charge. The crucial thing is that the specific fund meets your investment goals. Moreover, in time the amount of commissions on "load" funds will go down—in response to the competitive pressure from the "no-loads" plus increasing pressure from the SEC and Congress.

Since this could be your biggest single investment medium for now and the future, the only sensible move is to explore the whole field of loads and no-loads.

WAYS TO BUY AND USE MUTUAL FUNDS

There are not only many different types of mutual funds to choose among, there are also many easy and new ways in which you can buy mutual funds. Just how you buy them depends in part on the way you plan to use them ultimately, for, say, extra regular income, building a retirement fund, or creating a college education fund.

Here's a simple guide through some of the buying programs now available:

Automatic dividend reinvestment. Under this program all dividend and capital gains distributions are automatically reinvested. In the mid-seventies, roughly 3 million dividend reinvestment plans were in force.

Group plans. With these, typically, ten or more investors may pool funds for periodic investments in a mutual fund—often on a monthly or quarterly basis. These groups also may authorize the fund to reinvest all proceeds automatically—including dividends, interest, and capital gains distributions—in additional fund shares.

Periodic purchase (or accumulation) plans. Under these, you simply authorize your bank to invest regularly (usually monthly but sometimes bimonthly or quarterly) in mutual fund shares for you and to deduct the costs from your monthly bank statement. In the mid-seventies there were about 5 million such plans in force. The minimum deduction under these plans is typically between $25 and $50; also, in most plans, you can change the dollar amount at any time or stop investing altogether, if you so decide. Another way is for you to send in checks monthly or quarterly to pay for your mutual fund shares.

A key point here is that, while you're investing via these periodic purchase plans, you are also getting the advantage of dollar cost averaging—meaning you get more shares when stock prices are depressed and less shares when they are rising. Thus, you average out your costs, which is, as I have stressed, an excellent way to invest in stocks over the long term.

Payroll deduction plans. These are among the most rapidly growing fringe benefits offered by U.S. corporations—and, as you might suspect, the payroll plans are being aggressively pushed by the mutual fund industry. Often, by investing this way through your company you will pay a lower load charge.

Life insurance-mutual fund plans. You use the proceeds of your mutual fund investment to buy life insurance. Under this expanding type of plan, a single monthly check will buy X number of shares of a given mutual fund and then the dividends plus capital gains on your shares will pay your life insurance premiums. If, however, the value of your mutual fund shares drops substantially, you may have to pay your life insurance premium costs out of capital you have invested—or out of your pocket.

Now, just to suggest some other uses:

• You can buy shares for your children under the "uniform gifts to minors" act and arrange to have dividends and capital gains automatically reinvested to build a college fund. There are significant tax angles, so check them. One major advantage is that you usually have to pay taxes on your fund dividends and capital gains distributions and your youngster doesn't.

• You can use mutual funds (among other investments) to create a retirement nest egg for yourself, if you are self-employed. As of the mid-seventies, you could contribute up to $7,500 a year under the Keogh law—with the total amount deductible for income tax purposes—and until you retire you need not pay any income tax on any dividends or capital gains distribution paid into your account.

• You can arrange for a second income from your mutual fund shares by setting up a voluntary withdrawal plan. Typically, users of these plans have shares valued at a minimum of $7,500 to $10,000. If you own $10,000 worth of shares and elect to withdraw a typical 6 per cent a year, you'll get about $50 a month. If your shares grow by more than 6 per cent a year, you'll be able to withdraw $50 a month and keep your assets intact.

• You can switch programs. Often so-called "families" of mutual funds, several of which are run by the same management, permit the owner of one fund to switch to another without paying additional load charges. For example, if a young man buys a growth fund and continues investing in it and then wants to switch to an income fund as he reaches retirement age, he could do this without paying additional load charges to acquire the income fund. The restriction is that the income fund be in the same "family" as the growth fund. Federal income taxes, though, are applicable on such a switch.

HOW TO BUY MUTUAL FUNDS PROFESSIONALLY

There is far more to the purchase of mutual funds than a simple decision that this is the prudent way for you to invest. There is much more to the wise selection of a fund than a cursory comparison of records and a quick look at a fund's portfolio of investments. Behind a fund's investment record, portfolio make-up, investment philosophy, and investment objectives are many crucial considerations and facts with which you should be thoroughly familiar before you can reach a decision on which fund is the most suitable for you.

Most of the selling of mutual funds focuses on points which *all* funds have in common: management, diversification, services, etc. No one fund has anything unique here. Most mutual fund literature you will see contains similarly persuasive text, photos, and charts. What I'm trying to do in this section is help you become professional in your selection of a fund—so you can, in fact as well as theory, choose the right fund for your needs. You won't get this sort of talk from the average mutual fund salesman; he probably doesn't even know it. Nor will you get it in the average mutual fund literature; it isn't there.

Here are six basic factors in addition to the sales charge to consider before choosing a fund.

(1) *Your own situation.* Don't be deceived by the seeming simplicity of this, for it is the most fundamental consideration of all. Too often, mutual fund salesmen pay only lip service to your circumstances—financial and otherwise. And don't mislead yourself in your eagerness for quick and big profits. Keep in mind that if you pick a fund with the wrong objective and then decide to switch to another fund it can be costly.

Analyze your own needs and objectives. Do you want a fund for forced savings? College tuition for your child? Long-term financial security? A monthly income supplement? What? Based on these factors, decide on your investment strategy and stick with it in good times and bad.

(2) *Your investment objectives.* This isn't as simple as it sounds either. It's much more complex than finding a fund which has objectives matching yours.

Size of a fund, for instance, can be crucial to whether and how your investment objectives are achieved. A small fund may be less successful in achieving the goals of stability of income than a large fund, for the large fund can buy a more diversified and extensive portfolio and may be able to grow in a more orderly way than the smaller fund. On the other hand, a large fund is likely to be less successful in achieving the goal of big capital gains than a small fund, for it cannot concentrate as a small fund can on a few small companies which have explosive growth potentials. In a small portfolio, say of $10 million to $25 million, two or three hot stocks can do wonders for performance.

Comparative risk is another factor crucial to which of the many funds— all with the same investment objectives—is right for you. A fund which diversifies its holdings among many industries and companies is likely to have a less spectacular short-term record than one which concentrates on relatively few industries and companies with spectacular possibilities. The diversified fund's longer-term record, though, can be far superior—particularly if the limited fund's management runs into a period of bad judgment. To illustrate, in 1968 some of the smaller growth funds chalked up superb records—but in the devastating bear markets which followed, these very same funds faded away.

To capsulize, the lesson of the tortoise and the hare should be required reading for mutual fund investors! Size and portfolio make-up are vital in analyzing performance.

(3) *The time factor.* The original idea of the mutual fund was to provide a means by which the small investor could acquire a diversified investment portfolio under constant management. A fund can produce large gains—or losses—over any short-term period but it *never* was intended for short-term speculation and if you try to so use it you are misusing it. Funds are meant for long-term investing objectives.

This leads to the key point that, in buying mutual funds, "timing" of your investments to catch tops or bottoms is much less significant than "consistency" in making your investments. Since the fund's managers are investing to produce continuing results over the long term, whether prices are high or low at a given moment is far less important than your ability to maintain a buying program through good times and bad. (This, again, is the professional approach to dollar cost averaging.)

Another point on timing: a fund which raises lots of money from new investors during a bull market will have a hoard of cash which it will feel compelled to invest. This can become a minus factor the instant the markets dip. Thus, "timing" ranks with earlier points as a far more complex and subtle factor than most investors suspect.

(4) *The structure of the management.* Some funds are pretty much one-man operations—and, as with any one-man business, the built-in risks are obvious. Other funds have created strong management teams with diversified brains at the top and with a strong backup in research and other tools essential for successful management of a securities portfolio. You owe it to yourself to find out precisely what sort of management you are buying when you buy mutual fund shares. Since you're buying your shares for the long term, you should make sure your fund has a management structure which can operate successfully over the long term.

In short, an investment program worthy of the name does not consist of just "name" personalities! Many of the famous portfolio managers of the late 1960s have left the business. Also you may buy into a fund because you understand it has top portfolio managers and find they have left to go to another firm. If you're a truly professional investor in mutual fund shares, you'll do your homework in areas such as this.

(5) *The investment record.* On the face of it, it seems simple enough

to say that Fund X has performed better than Fund Y and therefore you should buy X. But as any professional would tell you (and remember, you're trying to become a professional too) there is far more to an investment record than the simple comparison of percentage gains or losses (which salesmen love to stress when the comparison is in their favor).

To illustrate, for what periods are the investment records being compared? If it is a short-term period, what was the market environment? Was it a market in which speculative issues dominated on the upside? If so, was Fund X, as opposed to Fund Y, in a position to take advantage of this environment?

In recent years, much has been made of the short-term investment record of a limited number of mutual funds. But ask: What actually produced the results? Was it, for instance, the fact that the fund had a very small portfolio with a limited number of holdings and a couple of these happened to be star performers? Or did the fund come on the scene just when a bull market was starting? Was it because the fund emphasized a given "hot" industry which may soon cool? Was the fund using borrowed capital? Was it invested in highly speculative—and to a great extent unmarketable—securities?

If the answer to any of these questions is in part or in whole "yes," proceed with caution. For you must avoid being deluded by short-term percentage figures. Ask and get clear, unqualified answers to such hard questions as I've posed here. The central question is: What has been the fund's long-term record? The importance of this cannot be overemphasized, for you want to see how the fund performs through bad markets as well as good. To the extent that your fund produces relatively favorable results through down markets as well as up markets, you can feel reasonably confident in the management's ability. Figure on a ten-year performance record as a minimum to compare it with another.

And what about the age of the fund? The benefit of a long life is that the fund has had the obvious advantages of navigating through both down and up markets. Its management has become seasoned. A fund which has prospered only in "up" markets is unseasoned. The acumen of its management must remain open to question. It's generally a good bet to stay clear of mutual funds which have been in business less than five years.

(6) *Make-up of the portfolio.* This point will give you vital clues to the operating philosophy of the fund's management as well as to its investment goals. Among the factors which you should analyze in this area are: whether the portfolio includes a great many holdings or just a limited number; the fields of investment in which the fund is primarily involved; the relative emphasis on investments in each of these fields; the size of companies in which the fund invests; the balance between seasoned companies and unseasoned companies; the holdings (or lack) of bonds, preferred stocks, cash.

It is this knowledge and understanding of the portfolio make-up of a fund which will help you assure yourself that this is indeed the fund in which you wish to invest your nest egg and current earnings.

If you'll abide just by the guidance in these pages, you'll be on your way to investing successfully the way the real pros do. You'll also sleep well at night.

OPEN-END FUNDS VERSUS CLOSED-END FUNDS

Closed-end funds have been around a long time but they have never been as popular as the open-end funds—even though these funds operate the same way as open-end mutual funds in terms of diversified portfolio, professional management, and various investment objectives.

The difference is that there are a fixed number of shares in a closed-end fund and their price fluctuates up and down (past its net asset value) just as ordinary common stocks fluctuate up and down on the stock exchanges or in the over-the-counter market. Many closed-ends, in fact, have sold historically at discounts from their net asset value. This has made them at times attractive to some investors who felt they would profit if the discount eventually disappeared.

What are the pros and cons of closed-ends as compared to open-end funds?

• If you buy open-end shares you know precisely on a given day that you can sell your shares to the mutual fund for the net asset value. If you own closed-end shares you don't know what price you'll get for your shares on any given day. The price you get can be higher or lower than the net asset value.

• Because closed-end funds do not have to worry about investors redeeming their outstanding shares, they can invest for the long term without some of the concerns that an open-end fund may have.

• On the other hand, the fixed number of shares makes it difficult for closed-end funds to trade their portfolios as aggressively as some open-end mutual funds. Before buying a new stock, a closed-end fund must frequently sell a current holding.

• No one has really solved the mystery of why most closed-end funds sell at a discount. The explanation could be merely that securities salesmen push open-end mutual funds on which they can earn perhaps an 8½ per cent commission rather than closed-end funds on which there is only a 1 or 2 per cent brokers' commission.

• Open-end funds offer investors a greater flexibility and range in buying options. For instance, more of them offer such programs as automatic reinvestment and withdrawal plans than do closed-end funds.

• As for whether a closed-end fund selling at a large discount from its asset value is a real bargain, yes, in many cases this is true. However, if you buy a fund for this reason, there is no guarantee that when you sell it other investors will realize it is such a bargain and you might have to sell your shares at the same discount at which you bought them. Moral of the story: a "bargain" is only a bargain if other investors think it is and ultimately push its price up.

SOURCES OF INFORMATION ON MUTUAL FUNDS

Also to help you with your homework on mutual funds and to prepare you to discuss your goals intelligently with any mutual fund salesman, here are top sources of detailed information on the industry and individual funds. Check what is available in your local library.

(1) Wiesenberger Services Inc. (1 New York Plaza, New York, N.Y. 10005), which publishes each year a voluminous book on mutual funds performance—past and present—entitled *Investment Companies*. It also publishes Wiesenberger's *Mutual Fund Performance Monthly Yearend* issue which can be very helpful.

(2) Moody's Investors Service, Inc. (99 Church Street, New York, N.Y. 10004), which publishes *Moody's Bank and Finance Manual*—a compendium of details on the 100 largest mutual funds in the United States.

(3) Hugh A. Johnson (Rand Building, Buffalo, N.Y. 14203), publisher of the yearly *Johnson's Investment Company Charts*—giving the long-term performance records of all major funds, plus other details.

(4) The Investment Company Institute (1775 K Street, N.W., Washington, D.C. 20006)—trade organization of the majority of the funds, which publishes industry statistics and *Mutual Funds Forum*, a bimonthly news magazine.

(5) No-Load Mutual Fund Association, Inc. (475 Park Avenue South, New York, N.Y. 10016)—trade organization of the no-load mutual fund industry.

(6) *Forbes Magazine* (60 Fifth Avenue, New York, N.Y. 10011)— annual mutual fund performance issues.

(7) *Mutual Funds Scoreboard*, a quarterly published by Yale Hirsch of Old Tappan, N.J.

(8) *FundScope*, a monthly published by FundScope, Suite 700, 1900 Avenue of the Stars, Los Angeles, Calif. 90067.

In addition, there are other weekly, biweekly, and monthly publications devoted to mutual funds which are written for the public and which often contain valuable data. They are frequently advertised in your daily newspaper's financial pages.

THE BAFFLEGAB OF MUTUAL FUNDS

ACCUMULATION PLAN: An increasingly popular arrangement under which you may buy mutual fund shares on a regular basis in small or large amounts

—either on your own or through an automatic payroll deduction plan such as a company employee savings plan. Automatic reinvestment of dividends and distributions is commonplace. Many investors are using this type of plan to accumulate funds for retirement, for emergencies, or for the college education of their children.

ASSET VALUE PER SHARE: The worth of a share—as you see it quoted in the newspaper financial pages—based on the market value of the fund's entire portfolio of stocks and other financial assets, minus the fund's expenses and liabilities, divided by the number of shares which have been issued by the fund. Same as net asset value per share or NAU. See above.

CAPITAL GAINS DISTRIBUTION: A distribution to shareholders by the mutual fund from the net long-term capital gains the fund has taken on the sale of securities from its portfolio. Many investors choose to have such distributions, if in cash, automatically reinvested in additional shares of the fund.

CLOSED-END INVESTMENT COMPANY: See above.

CONTRACTUAL PLAN: A type of accumulation plan under which the total amount you intend to invest is stated and you commit yourself to invest regular amounts monthly or quarterly for a specified pay-in period until you reach the total. A substantial amount of the sales charge covering the entire total is sometimes deducted from the first year's payments; this is called a front-end load.

DISTRIBUTIONS: Payments to shareholders from capital gains realized by the fund or dividends paid from the fund's net investment income.

EXCHANGE PRIVILEGE: The right to exchange the shares of one mutual fund for shares of another fund under the same sponsorship at either no cost or a reduced sales charge. However, you are liable to federal taxes on profits of first fund.

INVESTMENT COMPANY: A company which invests the funds it obtains from buyers of its shares in a diversified list of securities. See above.

INVESTMENT COMPANY ACT OF 1940: The basic federal law governing the registration and regulation of investment companies.

INVESTMENT TRUST: Same as Investment Company.

KEOGH PLAN: A retirement program for self-employed persons and their employees under which these persons can save on income taxes while regularly investing funds for their retirement via mutual funds, savings bonds, savings accounts, insurance, etc. One of the services offered by most mutual funds. Formally known as the Self-Employed Individuals Tax Retirement Act of 1962 but familiarly known by the name of the congressman who sponsored the law. See Chapter 19, "Planning for Your Financial and Personal Security."

LOAD: The sales charge imposed on a mutual fund investor to cover the costs of the elaborate sales organizations maintained by the majority of the funds. Added to the asset value of the fund's shares (the offering price).

MANAGEMENT FEE: The amount which the managers of mutual fund portfolios charge for their management services—in both load and no-load funds.

PERIODIC PAYMENT PLAN: Same as Accumulation Plan.

PORTFOLIO: The stocks, bonds, and other assets held by a mutual fund at any given time—and thus, held indirectly by the fund's share owners.

REDEMPTION PRICE: The price at which a holder of mutual fund shares may redeem his shares. In most cases of open-end shares, it's the current net asset value per share. Sometimes there is a redemption charge of about 1 per cent. In the closed-end companies, this would be the highest price offered for the shares in the exchange market, which may be either a premium over of a discount from the net asset value per share. See above.

REINVESTMENT PRIVILEGE: A privilege under which your mutual fund dividends may be automatically invested in additional shares of the fund, sometimes without a sales charge.

TURNOVER RATIO: The extent to which the portfolio of securities owned by a mutual fund is changed (traded or turned over) within the course of a single year.

WITHDRAWAL PLAN: An arrangement under which investors in mutual funds can regularly receive monthly or quarterly payments of a specified amount. This may be more or less than the actual investment income.

22

HOW TO INVEST IN BONDS

In the early part of this decade a profoundly important new force entered the outlook for stock prices. It was the historically high interest rates which investors—big and small, institutions and individuals—could earn on bonds, even the highest-quality bonds. This development created competition of the toughest caliber for the stock market. In the early 1970s many investors switched out of common stocks and growth mutual funds and put their money into corporate bonds, tax-exempt bonds, new bond and money market funds. Money in savings accounts, too, was shifted into money market instruments and bonds on an impressive scale. And professional investment managers returned to what was a once fashionable investment technique of "balanced" portfolios with both stock and bond holdings.

To understand this fascinating turnabout, you must realize that thirty years ago yields on stocks were about twice those of bonds. By the early 1970s yields on bonds were about twice those of common stocks!

High interest rates have an understandable appeal to investors. If you can invest your money in a bond that pays 8 per cent and if you let the interest accumulate, your nest egg will double in about nine years. If you invest it at 7 per cent, it will double in about ten years. This assumes that you will be reinvesting at the same interest rate and omits tax factors.

These fixed annual returns have been available in the bond and money markets of the United States in recent years. Obviously, at these interest rates, high-quality fixed-income investments—in the obligations of the U. S. Treasury, federal agencies, our states and cities, U.S. corporations—take on some of the characteristics of "growth" securities. You can also buy discount bonds and make long-term capital gains as the bonds rise to their par value at maturity.

An investment that can double in nine or ten years is growing by any definition. At the same time this type of investment retains the advantages of its fixed annual return and offers greater protection against adverse economic conditions than do stocks. (It is not without hazards, though, as witness the defaults on some of the Turnpike Authority bonds in the 1960s. And of course, steep inflation rates can offset and even eliminate the "growth" entirely.)

If buyers can get these high rates, they can count on them every year until their bonds are called or finally mature and that can be five, ten, fifteen, twenty or even thirty years from purchase date.

Let me be more specific. If a high-grade corporate bond provides an 8 per cent return, it is rivaling the long-term return record for common stocks. Not so many years ago typical interest rates on top-rated corporate bonds were 3½ to 4 per cent.

What will be the level of interest rates on fixed-income securities when *you* are reading this chapter I do not know, of course—and only a fool would pretend to have the capacity to forecast precisely—for the forces which determine interest rate trends are varied and exceedingly complex. However, it is reasonable to assume that in the decade of the 1970s we will maintain a level of interest rates which, regardless of temporary market fluctuations, should be high enough to provide a "living wage" to all investors—meaning the coupons should cover the anticipated annual rise in living costs as well as the income tax bite out of the interest. Under these circumstances, you will need basic information on the fixed-income securities markets so you can carry on to get whatever additional facts you want. And so the following is your *primer on bonds.*

BASIC FACTS ON BONDS AND MONEY MARKET INSTRUMENTS

Q. *What's a coupon interest rate on a bond?*

A. This is the specified amount of money the issuer promises to pay you during the life of the bond in return for the use of your money throughout the period. The issuers (borrowers) may be: the federal government, federal agencies, state and local governments, corporations.

The interest may be payable to you every six months or every year and in a few cases every month. Or, as in U. S. Government Series E savings bonds, the interest may accumulate during the life of the bond and be payable to you only when you cash in the bond or when it reaches final maturity date.

Q. *What's the difference between a bond and a stock?*

A. When you buy a bond you are lending your money to its issuer and thus you become a lender. When you buy shares of common stock in a corporation you are becoming a part owner of the corporation.

When you buy bonds you expect to earn a fixed rate of return (the interest) as long as you own this type of obligation. When you buy common stocks, you expect to share in the company's profits via the dividends the company pays you—which may vary from year to year. You also get retained earnings, which can lead to capitalization of earnings, hopefully leading to higher prices for your stocks—but you can make capital gains on bonds as well as on stocks.

Q. *What's the key to bond prices?*

A. Interest rate levels. Interest rates doubled in the last five years of the decade of the 1960s and reached the highest levels in more than a century. They spiraled even higher in 1974. This drove down the prices of bonds issued in earlier years at much lower interest rates. Those prices in turn reached historically low levels.

Q. *What moves interest rates up or down?*

A. What usually determines the price of any product or service? The demand for and supply of it. When the demand for loans is greater than the available supply of credit, the price for loans (the interest rate) goes up; when the supply of credit is greater than the demand for loans, the price (interest rate) goes down. Expectations of higher or lower interest rates also influence the direction of rates—meaning psychology plays a major role too.

But this is by no means the whole story, for a key factor determining the supply of credit in the United States is the monetary policy of the Federal Reserve System (the central bank) of the United States, which regulates the flow of money and credit into our economy.

There is no point in this primer in going into the enormously complicated, technical details on how the Federal Reserve System attains its credit goals. Suffice it to say that through various devices and operations the Federal Reserve pursues its objective of trying to put just enough credit into the economic stream to promote orderly, sustained growth over the years.

Q. *Why have interest rates risen so much in recent years?*

A. Because, starting in the mid-1960s, the demand for credit exploded —reflecting the prolonged business boom, the Vietnam war, the development of a deep inflation psychology.

At the same time the Federal Reserve tried to curb inflation via the orthodox means of limiting the supply of credit available for expansion. With the demand for loans soaring and the supply of credit restricted, interest rates had to skyrocket.

Q. *Should we all own bonds?*

A. It would be ridiculous for me to claim that bonds are an appropriate investment for all of you: there are so many different types of fixed-income securities, so many different maturities, so many different grades that even the single word "bonds" becomes a misleading generality. It also would be utterly out-of-character folly for me to make so superficial a recommendation.

Nevertheless, the money and bond markets since the start of this decade have appealed to an extraordinarily broad cross section of income and age groups. Many individuals in the $15,000 to $30,000-a-year income brackets have for the first time ventured into bonds. In fact, in the first half of the 1970s many stock brokerage salesmen made a good part of their income selling bonds and money market securities of all types rather than stocks to individuals. That's why this chapter is giving you the fundamentals so you can find out the details on your own.

Q. *What about the income tax factor?*

A. This is vitally important, for you must pay income taxes on interest you earn. Of course, this cuts into your net return and the higher your income bracket the more the cut—except on tax-exempt bonds. For example, if you are in the 40 per cent tax bracket and collect $100 a year in interest on your bonds, you'll pay out $40 of the $100 in taxes, will keep only $60.

Q. *What about inflation?*

A. In judging what your real net rate of return will be on a fixed-income security, you also must consider the erosion in your dollar's buying power caused by the likely annual rate of rise in living costs in coming years.

To illustrate, let's say you buy a $1,000 bond carrying an interest rate of 8¾ per cent and that the annual rate of inflation in the years ahead turns out to be 4¾ per cent. Your "real" rate of return—bond interest rate less rate of inflation—would be 4 per cent.

The following table shows the "real" rates of return on high-grade corporate bonds over the years. (Note that in years of severe inflation in the past [1920, 1943], real rates of return become *negative*. And in years of severe deflation [1922, 1932], they have become extraordinarily *positive*.)

YEAR	BOND YIELD	"REAL" RATES OF RETURN (BOND YIELD LESS RATE OF INFLATION)
1970	8.75%	4.75%
1965	4.49	3.35
1961	4.35	3.21
1958	3.81	0.65
1951	3.03	−2.17
1943	2.55	−6.27
1939	2.77	4.39

YEAR	BOND YIELD	"REAL" RATES OF RETURN (BOND YIELD LESS RATE OF INFLATION)
1932	4.61	13.71
1928	4.19	5.71
1922	4.49	12.71
1920	5.27	−11.37

Q. *What about your age?*

A. Again, this is a vital consideration, for if you are young and can look forward to many years in which you can recoup losses on your investments, you can properly assume more risks in the stock market and speculate for big long-term capital gains. But if you are in the older age brackets, bonds yielding 8 to 10 per cent have indisputable appeal.

Q. *How are bonds quoted?*

A. As a percentage of their par value or face amount—usually in denominations of $1,000. However, many U. S. Government and federal agency issues are now issued with minimum denominations of $5,000 and $10,000. A price of 98 for a $1,000 par value bond means that $980 would be the actual cost (plus any accrued interest).

Since interest is paid on the par value of the bond, your actual percentage return may be more or less than the interest rate specified on the coupon by the issuer of the bond.

To illustrate, say you buy a bond just issued that pays 9 per cent interest or $90 at a price of exactly $1,000. That gives you $90 a year interest on a $1,000 investment or an actual yield of 9 per cent.

But say the bond has already been issued and has been on the market some time and you buy it at 95, or $950. This means your current yield is more than 9 per cent. Current yield is determined by dividing the interest by the price paid for the bond. This means 90/950 or 9.47 per cent.

Or say you bought the same bond for 105, or $1,050. This means your yield is less than 9 per cent. It would be 90/1050, or 8.57 per cent.

Q. *Is this what is meant by yield?*

A. Yes, this is what is meant by current yield. It is interest divided by the price you paid for the bond—the rate of return you receive on the amount of money it cost you to buy the security.

Q. *What's the difference between current yield and yield to maturity?*

A. Yield to maturity takes into consideration the price at which your bond is paid off (redeemed) at maturity as well as the interest coupon it bears and the price at which you bought the obligation.

For example, suppose you bought the 9 per cent bond at a premium, say 105, or $1,050. In figuring yield to maturity it is necessary to amortize this premium until the maturity date. In this case, the yield to maturity will be less than the 9 per cent coupon rate.

In the case of a bond purchased for $950, or at a discount, the yield to maturity will be the coupon rate of 9 per cent, plus the $50 additional money the holder will receive when the bond matures. In this case, the yield to maturity will be greater than 9 per cent. A reference volume, generally referred to as the *Basis Book,* accurately computes yield to maturity.

Q. *How do you collect interest on your bonds?*

A. There are two major ways you collect your interest. If you own a coupon bond or "bearer" bond you clip a coupon attached to the bond and collect the money due from the issuer's paying agency or your own bank. If you own a registered bond, your name appears on the bond and also is registered with the issuer. Interest is usually paid by check. Registered bonds offer greater protection from theft than coupon bonds.

Q. *Why are you using the term "fixed-income" instead of just calling them "bonds"?*

A. This is deliberate, I assure you, for a large percentage of the obligations available to you aren't bonds at all. By definition, they're "notes" or "bills." And a large percentage aren't traded in the bond markets either. They are bought and sold in the money markets—which are part of the vast over-the-counter markets to start with.

Q. *What are money market securities?*

A. They are the short-term obligations of various borrowers: the U. S. Treasury, federal agencies, state and local government, corporations of all types.

In general, these are the most marketable, the most liquid, the least risky of fixed-income obligations. Among the obligations you might be interested in and which you can readily buy and sell in the money markets are:

U. S. Treasury bills, due in up to one year and considered the virtual equivalent of cash;

Short-term federal agency issues, which next to Treasury bills are the most marketable of securities;

Short-term tax-exempt obligations, highly liquid too.

Also traded in the money markets are large ($100,000 and over) commercial bank certificates of deposit; large ($100,000 and more) denominations of commercial paper notes of corporations; bankers' acceptances in denominations of $25,000 and up; federal funds and Eurodollars.

Q. *How can small investors buy in such big amounts?*

A. The smaller investor was effectively barred from the often higher-yielding money market instruments and restricted to the lower-paying "consumer" certificates available from commercial banks and savings institutions for many years, but as interest rates on large certificates of deposit spiraled upward in the mid-1970s, enterprising firms found ways to get around this patently unfair discrimination against the little fellow.

The concept was simple: the funds of many small investors were "pooled" until the amounts in the pools were large enough to meet the minimums imposed. The "pools" took various forms. Also, as short-term interest rates hit historic peaks in the mid-1970s new mutual funds came into existence to specialize in these money market instruments and offer small investors a way to share in the juicy returns by purchase of fund shares. The funds were of both no-load and load variety and they lured hundreds of millions of dollars out of savings institutions.

Q. *What are bond markets?*

A. In the bond markets, longer-term obligations of various issuers are traded. In turn, the bond markets subdivide into the market for corporate bonds; for U. S. Government bonds and notes and for longer-term federal agency issues; and for municipal bonds.

In only a few places, such as the Bond Trading Room of the New York Stock Exchange, can you visit and watch bond trading in action. Most bonds are handled in the over-the-counter market where securities are bought and sold by dealers and brokers located all over the nation, communicating with each other via an intricate and immense telephone network and video display terminals.

Q. *What is meant by underwriting syndicates?*

A. These are groups of investment bankers (syndicates) which commit their capital to buy new issues of securities from borrowers at set prices. By doing this, the bankers "underwrite" the issue—provide the funds to the corporation, state, city, or other type of borrower. Then the group re-offers the securities at a higher price to institutional and individual investors. The difference (spread) between what the underwriting syndicate pays for the securities and the higher price at which the group re-offers the securities to you represents the bankers' or syndicate's profit after expenses. Of course, the underwriting syndicate loses money when the bankers misjudge the market and are forced to resell the securities at a lower price than they paid the issuer.

Now let's say you are thinking for the first time about buying fixed-income securities as an investment. . . .

HOW TO BUY BONDS

Q. *How do you buy outstanding fixed-income securities?*

A. Go to your broker, place your order, and pay the principal amount plus the required commission. It usually will run about $5.00 per $1,000 face value bond, but it can be more, particularly if you buy just one or two bonds. If you don't have a broker, establish a relationship with a reputable brokerage firm which maintains a retail bond department. Ask questions about commissions and which types of fixed-income securities would be right for you. Often you can buy bonds through your bank but you'll probably pay more in commissions and fees.

Q. *How do you buy* new *fixed-income securities?*

A. You can subscribe to new issues of corporation or municipal bonds through a firm which is a member of the underwriting group distributing the new issue to the public. If your order is accepted, you'll pay no commission. As I wrote earlier, the investment banking house gets its profit from the "spread."

You can subscribe through your broker or banker to new U. S. Treasury issues and pay a small service charge for the convenience. Or you can subscribe to new U. S. Treasury issues through your district Federal Reserve Bank and pay no commission. You'll have to learn the details about forms, minimum deposits required, etc., but they're not difficult.

And you can subscribe to new federal agency issues through the firms which belong to the selling group customarily distributing new agency securities. You'll pay no commission but you'll probably have to pay a service charge if yours is a small subscription.

Check out the details with a broker, bank, or bond dealer who knows you and who will give you a fair deal.

Q. *What firms might you go to?*

A. Some of the great, world-famous investment banking firms won't take your orders. They deal only with institutional investors or with wealthy individuals. But many major brokerage firms do maintain bond departments and readily accept individual orders. If you're already a customer of one of these firms, ask your own broker about the firm's policy before you go elsewhere. In some areas, however, you might find it more convenient to do business through banks.

THE CORPORATE BOND MARKET

The corporate bond market is where a lot of the action has been in recent years. Here is where our nation's leading industrial and utility corporations, finance companies, and real estate enterprises have borrowed tens of billions of dollars for modernization, expansion, and working capital too. Here is where, during the early 1970s, interest rates spiraled up to the highest levels in more than a hundred years. And here is where individual investors began in 1970 to invest aggressively for the first time in decades.

Q. *How many types of corporate bonds are there?*

A. At least a dozen. But the types which will be of most interest to you are:

First mortgage bonds. These are bonds secured by a mortgage on all or a portion of the fixed property of the issuing corporation. These are among the highest-grade of corporate bonds because they provide a prime, clear, and indisputable claim on the company's assets and earnings. Most utilities issue mortgage bonds.

Debenture bonds. These are bonds backed by the general credit and full faith of the issuing corporation. In short, they represent a pure I.O.U., a promise to pay. Many of the nation's big, well-established industrial corporations issue debentures. Under the classification of debentures are *subordinated debentures,* which have a claim on a corporation's assets only after senior debt claims have been met, and *income debentures,* on which interest is payable only if it is earned.

Convertible debentures. These are bonds which give the owner the extra privilege of converting the debenture into a certain number of shares of common stock of the same corporation under specified conditions. In other words this is a hybrid, combining some of the features of both a stock and a bond. Convertible bonds are not as safe as straight bonds but the conversion sweetener adds speculative appeal because the owner has the chance of making an additional profit if the stock of the issuing company goes up. This makes the conversion privilege more valuable. Of course, the stock can also go down.

Q. *Should I buy only first mortgage bonds, then?*

A. Of course not. The over-all strength of a corporation is the key. A debenture of a great, prosperous industrial corporation is far more desirable than a first mortgage bond of a shaky third-rater.

Q. *How can I find out about the quality of bonds?*

A. The quality of bonds ranges from the very highest to the riskiest—with the judgments on the credit worthiness of the various obligations being made by various independent services, such as Moody's and Standard & Poor's. The ratings starting from the top are: Aaa (Moody's) or AAA (Standard & Poor's); Aa or AA; A; Baa or BBB; Ba or BB; B; Caa or CCC; Ca or CC; C. If you're anxious to avoid any risks of default, you'll not go below ratings of A. Most dealers will quote the bond ratings along with prices and yields.

Q. *What about call provisions?*

A. This is a key point—for if interest rates decline sharply below the levels at which corporations have sold their bonds they will try to call them in and replace them with new issues bearing lower rates. Thus, you want to make certain that your bond will be protected against redemption by the corporation for a specified period. Usually you can get protection against a call for five years from issue date on industrial bonds.

Also check with care the price at which the corporation reserves the right to call in its bonds, for this will place an effective ceiling on the price to which your bond can rise in the open market. One way of beating this is to buy bonds that are non-callable.

THE TAX-EXEMPT MUNICIPAL MARKETS

The great factor favoring purchase of municipal bonds or other tax-exempts is that interest on these obligations is exempt from federal income tax—and if you are a resident of the issuing locality, often from state and local taxes as well. That's the major reason why individuals now own about one third of all the tax-exempt bonds outstanding. A second reason is that tax-exempts of top-rated issuers have a high degree of safety.

Even if you're only in the 30 per cent tax bracket, a 7 per cent tax-free return is equal to a taxable rate of 10 per cent. And in the 70 per cent bracket, it's the equivalent of a 23.34 per cent return!

There's no doubt that new municipal bonds will be pouring into the market in coming years, for the borrowing needs of states, cities, and towns across our land are and will be enormous. There's no doubt too that this will help place a floor under the rates you can earn and that you'll have a wide variety of types of bonds, of quality of bonds, and of maturity dates from which to choose.

Q. *What are municipal bonds?*

A. These include any obligation issued by a city, town, or village and also by states, territories, U.S. possessions. In addition, they include obligations issued by housing authorities, port authorities, and local government agencies providing and maintaining community services ranging from schools to waterworks. They are all tax-exempt and are all nicknamed "municipals."

Q. *What sets the interest rates on municipals?*

A. First, the general level of interest rates. After that, the credit rating of the issuer—determined by the rating services. Triple A, of course, is the best. I repeat: if you wish to avoid risks of default, don't go below their ratings of A.

Q. *What types of municipals are there?*

A. GENERAL OBLIGATION BONDS, secured by the full faith and credit and general unlimited taxing power of the municipal authority. Many bonds of big cities are in this category.

LIMITED TAX OR SPECIAL TAX BONDS, backed by a limited portion of the issuer's taxing power, or payable only from the proceeds of a single tax.

REVENUE BONDS, secured by the revenue of a particular municipal department or a special authority created to operate a self-supporting project. The best known of these are toll road and turnpike authority bonds.

HOUSING AUTHORITY BONDS, issued by local authorities to finance construction of low-rent housing projects and secured by the pledge of annual contributions by the Federal Housing Assistance Administration. This federal backing gives these bonds top (AAA) rating.

INDUSTRIAL REVENUE BONDS, issued by a municipality or authority but secured by the lease payments made by the industrial corporation using the facilities financed by the revenue bond issue.

Q. *What are the special characteristics of municipals?*

A. Most are in denominations of $1,000 and up—although the $5,000 denomination is highly popular. Most are bearer bonds. The owner's name is not on record with the issuer and if you *hold* the bond the presumption is you *own* it. Usually you'll clip a coupon every six months and collect interest from a paying agency or your own bank.

You must safeguard bearer bonds as you would cash, for if "your" bonds are in someone else's possession, how can you prove they are yours? If your bearer bonds are stolen, you may be completely out of luck—just as you would be if your cash was stolen.

Most are serial bonds. A certain number will mature each year, will be paid off and retired. The range of maturities may be five, ten, fifteen, twenty years or perhaps thirty or forty years, which means you can decide the date on which you want your capital back and then choose a maturity that fits.

Q. *What about the tax exemption?*

A. You may be able to get eye-popping rates of return—tax free—on low-quality municipal bonds. But I will not suggest anything second class—particularly since in the mid-seventies you could buy top-rated municipals at comparatively high interest rates.

The tax advantages are not just for the wealthy! Tax exemption can benefit you to a lesser extent in the lower tax brackets as well. The returns are far more attractive than you probably realize, particularly if you're among the millions of us who are subject to state and local as well as federal income taxes.

To the individual in a moderate 30 per cent income bracket (including state and local taxes), a tax-free 5 per cent bond equals 7.14 per cent on taxable interest; 6 per cent equals 8.57 per cent on taxable interest; 6½ per cent equals 9.29 per cent; and 7 per cent equals 10 per cent.

Or say you're in the 60 per cent bracket. Then 5 per cent tax-free equals 12½ per cent taxable; 6 per cent equals 15; 6½ equals 16¼; and 7 per cent equals 17½.

The following table highlights it for you. It assumes the income tax rate bracket includes federal, state, and local income taxes.

IF YOUR TAX BRACKET IS	A TAX-FREE RATE OF	EQUALS A TAXABLE RATE OF
20%	5%	6.25%
30	5	7.14
40	5	8.33
50	5	10.00
60	5	12.50

IF YOUR TAX BRACKET IS	A TAX-FREE RATE OF	EQUALS A TAXABLE RATE OF
20%	6%	7.50%
30	6	8.57
40	6	10.00
50	6	12.00
60	6	15.00

IF YOUR TAX BRACKET IS	A TAX-FREE RATE OF	EQUALS A TAXABLE RATE OF
20%	7%	8.75%
30	7	10.00
40	7	11.67
50	7	14.00
60	7	17.50

Q. *What is a "moratorium" on municipal securities?*

A. Suspension (postponement) by a state or municipality of repayment of principal on a maturing debt. Moratoriums are declared when a debtor hasn't the cash to pay off its obligations when due, even though it continues to pay interest owed on time. New York City declared a moratorium on repayment of notes due December, 1975.

Q. *Is the tax-exempt feature of these bonds safe?*

A. New federal legislation almost surely will authorize states and localities to issue taxable bonds—if they so desire—with the federal government providing subsidies to offset the added interest cost to them. The goal: to attract investors who have no incentive now to buy tax-exempts.

But this will not disturb the tax-exempt status of outstanding securities or any new tax-exempts the issuers prefer to sell instead of taxables.

THE UNITED STATES GOVERNMENT SECURITIES MARKETS

One fixed-income securities market in which the question of quality doesn't even come up is the market for U. S. Government securities. Default on U. S. Treasury's issues is unthinkable.

Q. *What about U.S. savings bonds?*

A. These are non-marketable bonds and are covered in the following pages.

Q. *What are the marketable types of U.S. securities?*

A. (1) U. S. TREASURY BILLS, the most marketable fixed-income securities in the world, are issued on a discount (sold at less than face value) basis with maturities of three, six, nine, and twelve months and are redeemed at face value at the specified maturity dates. The difference between the lower issue price and the higher maturity price represents your interest. Or if you sell them in the open market before maturity, your income is the difference between the issue price and your sale price.

There are also tax-anticipation bills (TAB), which are attractive to investors with large incomes.

(2) U. S. TREASURY NOTES, by definition, securities with maturities of one to ten years. These carry specified coupons and pay interest semi-annually.

(3) U. S. TREASURY BONDS, by definition, obligations maturing in more than ten years. Most treasury bonds outstanding today were sold many years ago at much, much lower than prevailing interest rates. Because of their comparatively low coupons—3½ to 4¼ per cent—they sell at deep discounts from par value. Some long-term Treasury bonds issued in recent years, though, carry coupons up to 8½ per cent.

Q. *Is buying discount bonds a good idea?*

A. It's a way of helping to guarantee yourself a capital gain if you hold the bond to maturity. You run a risk of loss if interest rates rise sharply in the meantime and the price of your bonds is down to an even deeper discount when you sell. Also, a limited number of U. S. Treasury bonds which can be bought at a discount from par and which are held at death of the owner can be redeemed at par and accrued interest for payment of estate taxes. Of course, you can't have it both ways: These so-called "flower bonds" will be valued in the estate at par for inheritance tax purposes too. (See page 926.)

Q. *How are Treasury securities issued?*

A. Treasury bills are issued only in bearer form, meaning the owner's name is not recorded, and if you hold them you are presumed to own them. (Refer back to page 917 and above for fuller explanation.)

Q. *How do you buy U. S. Treasury issues?*

A. As you buy other outstanding bonds, you can buy them through your broker or banker and pay the principal amount plus the current commission or service charge.

Q. *How do you buy the new U.S. issues which the Treasury offers to raise cash?*

A. You can subscribe through your broker or banker and pay whatever service charge is asked. Or you can subscribe through your district Federal Reserve Bank—filling out the appropriate forms and putting up the required down payment—and pay no commission.

Q. *What are the minimums you can buy?*

A. In 1970 the Treasury raised the minimum purchase on Treasury bills to $10,000 in an obvious move to eliminate the nuisance of the small investor. The minimum on most Treasury notes and on bonds was still $1,000 in the mid-1970s, although higher minimums were fixed on selected issues.

Q. *If you have the $10,000 minimum, how do you buy U. S. Treasury bills?*

A. You subscribe directly through the Federal Reserve Bank or bank branch in your district. Assuming you're buying less than $200,000 worth, you'll buy at the non-competitive tender (bid)—meaning you won't compete with the professionals but will accept the *average* price. The non-competitive bid is the best for you.

Either go in person to your Federal Reserve Bank or branch or write and ask for a "non-competitive tender" covering the bill maturity you want: three, six, nine, or twelve months. Fill out the total you want ($10,000 minimum) and enclose payment in full (face amount). Pay either by certified personal check, bank check, cash, or through Treasury bills you own which mature by the new issue date. Indicate whether you'll pick up the bills in person or want the bills mailed to you at Treasury expense by registered mail.

The discount on the bills—the difference between the *average* bid submitted (and the price at which you will therefore buy your bills) and the $10,000 you sent—is your interest. It will be refunded to you on the date on which the bills are issued. On the maturity date of your bills, when they are worth $100 or $10,000, you'll either redeem them for cash or exchange them —"roll them over"—for more new bills.

From time to time the Treasury also offers tax-anticipation bills at a discount from face value which you may use at face value to pay income taxes. Once you learn the technique of buying ordinary Treasury bills, you'll find it a cinch to buy the TABs—if you can use them.

Q. *Where do you find a Federal Reserve Bank?*

A. Here are the 12 Federal Reserve Banks and their 24 branches. Choose yours. You'll find the exact address in Part IV, "Your Rights and How to Get Them."

BOSTON, MASS. 02106

NEW YORK, N.Y. 10045
   Buffalo, 14240

PHILADELPHIA, PA. 19101

CLEVELAND, O. 44101
   Cincinnati, 45201
   Pittsburgh, 15230

RICHMOND, VA. 23213
   Baltimore, Md., 21203
   Charlotte, 28201

ATLANTA, GA. 30303
   Birmingham, Ala., 35202
   Jacksonville, Fla., 32203
   Nashville, Tenn., 37203
   New Orleans, La., 70160

CHICAGO, ILL. 60690
   Detroit, Mich., 48231

ST. LOUIS, MO. 63166
   Little Rock, Ark., 72203
   Louisville, Ky., 40201
   Memphis, Tenn., 38101

MINNEAPOLIS, MINN. 55480
    Helena, Mont., 59601

KANSAS CITY, MO. 64198
    Denver, Colo., 80217
    Oklahoma City, Okla., 73125
    Omaha, Nebr., 68102

DALLAS, TEX. 75222
    El Paso, 79999
    Houston, 77001
    San Antonio, 78295

SAN FRANCISCO, CALF. 94120
    Los Angeles, 90051
    Portland, Oreg., 97208
    Salt Lake City, Ut., 84110
    Seattle, Wash., 98124

THE MARKET FOR FEDERAL AGENCY SECURITIES

Ranking a mere step below the direct obligations of the U. S. Treasury are the obligations of the federal agencies. They are not direct obligations of the U. S. Treasury itself but in one way or another they involve federal government guarantees or sponsorship. They are not outstanding in anywhere near the volume of U. S. Treasury issues but tens of billions of dollars of agency issues already are being traded in the open market and the volume keeps climbing.

What's more, just because they are *not* direct Treasury obligations, the returns available on federal agency issues are usually higher than on Treasuries. As a general rule, at any given time the yield on an agency issue will be above the yield on a Treasury issue of similar maturity.

Q. *Just what are federal agency issues?*

A. They are securities issued by federal agencies created by Congress over the years and operating under federal charter and supervision.

Among the federal agencies concerned with financing the agricultural industry are: the Federal Intermediate Credit Banks (FIC); the District Banks for Cooperatives (Coops); and the Federal Land Banks.

Among the agencies concerned with the housing industry are the Federal Home Loan Bank; the Federal National Mortgage Association (FNMA or Fannie Mae); the Government National Mortgage Association (GNMA or Ginnie Mae).

Also, to illustrate the variety and scope among other agencies, there are the Tennessee Valley Authority (TVA) and the Export-Import Bank (ExIm). And this is far, far from a complete list. What's more, new agencies are created from time to time and they too will sell their obligations in the open market—or will have their securities sold for them by the Federal Financing Bank, created by law in 1974.

Q. *What are the minimums on purchases and maturities of the agency issues?*

A. A $10,000 minimum was set in 1970 on some federal agency issues also to eliminate the small "nuisance" subscriber. A $5,000 denomination is still fairly typical among the agencies, though, and the minimum on Federal

Land Bank issues is $1,000. The maturities of agency issues generally run from a few months to over fifteen years.

Q. *What do federal agency and Treasury issues yield?*

A. Check your daily newspaper for the bid and asked quotes and yields available or call your broker or bank. The quotations and yields change from day to day.

Q. *How do you subscribe to new issues of federal agencies?*

A. Each of the federal agencies has a fiscal agent in New York City which puts together a nationwide selling group when it has a new issue to sell. In the group will be securities dealers, brokerage houses, and dealer banks and the sale will be publicly announced in the newspapers and other media at the time.

Each of the firms which is a member of the selling group will accept subscriptions from investors on the established terms—and assuming your order is accepted, you will pay no commission on your purchase. You will pay a clearing fee or service charge, however, and this will cut your net return. You must check these details, as I've stressed over and over in this chapter, with a broker, dealer, or banker who knows *you* and will give you a *fair* deal.

Q. *How do you buy outstanding federal agency issues?*

A. The same way you buy other fixed-income securities trading in the open market: through a broker or banker with whom you have an established relationship. If you buy in the open market, you'll pay the prevailing commission or the offered price.

Q. *In what form are agency securities issued?*

A. Usually in bearer form. You have to assume the responsibility of safeguarding them, collecting interest, and redeeming them at maturity. This can be done through your broker or bank.

LOWER-QUALITY BONDS

On these, you can really earn some juicy returns. The rate just below A is Baa according to Moody's and BBB according to Standard & Poor's. And these are not low ratings, for those categories go down to Ba or BB; Caa or CCC; Ca or CC; C. In some of these areas, bonds will return a yield ranging up from 10 per cent. But I warn you. Bonds of this caliber *can* turn out to be very risky and you may deeply regret reaching for the rich returns.

In fact, the Penn Central Railroad bankruptcy in mid-1970 spurred a substantial widening of the spread (differential) between the returns you can earn on top-rated obligations and the rates you can earn on second- or third-grade issues. Investors have been turning their backs on the lower-quality securities, despite their high-interest coupons.

At the same time, there has been powerful demand for top-rated obligations, which has forced down rates on this grade of bond. This spread in interest rates represents the consensus among investors on the safety of the various obligations.

There has been no mistaking the message: investors clearly prefer the safety of top-caliber obligations at lower rates to the higher incomes available on lower-quality bonds.

PITFALLS FOR THE SMALL INVESTOR

Q. *But what if you don't have a big account or working relationship with a bank?*

A. Unless you have a most extraordinary relationship with your bank, you'll not be able to buy outstanding short-term issues of the U. S. Treasury and federal agencies without meeting some rigid requirements. Specifically:

• You must have a hefty total of cash in your account and be a regular customer. You can't just walk into any bank with a check.

• You must invest at least $100,000 or you'll be considered an odd-lot buyer and have to pay a service charge. You must make sure this service charge doesn't eliminate the interest rate advantage.

• You must meet the minimums—$10,000 on Treasury bills; $5,000 to $10,000 on federal agency issues. The usual minimum for commercial paper you buy through your bank is $25,000.

• You must keep track of your maturity dates, for if you fail to reinvest your money when your obligations mature, you lose future interest.

Q. *And what about brokers?*

A. You'll have to meet the same rigid requirements. Most brokers also consider you a nuisance to avoid and will slap on a service charge of $20 or more per order. This can more than offset your interest rate advantage.

In short, these are sophisticated markets. You have to seek them out, you have to do your homework, you have to have money, and you have to assume responsibilities.

If you are not only small but also remain uninformed and unknown, forget it.

A BANK OR A BOND? WHICH FOR YOU?

What should you do if you have a fair-sized sum to invest and what you primarily want is safety and income?

Should you simply put your money in a corner bank or savings institution, take no risks of the market place at all, and get whatever returns the financial institutions offer?

Or should you go into the open market, accept some risks of price fluctuation, and freeze for yourself some of the returns available there?

To get your answer, ask yourself:

• How long do you want to freeze your savings in fixed-income mediums? You will certainly not buy long-term bonds if you plan to keep the money invested in the bonds for only a short time—not unless you're trading in and out for quick profits. And that kind of trading is an entirely different matter from what I'm covering in this section.

• What are your investment goals? If all you want is absolute safety and a fair interest rate, you might as well put your money in a nearby savings institution. It's simple and satisfactory.

• What is your age? You can afford to take more risks at a young age.

• What is your judgment on the future pace of inflation? You will want to feel confident that your interest coupon will more than cover the annual loss in the purchasing power of the dollars you have invested.

• Do you have enough money to go into the open market? You must consider the commission charges on buying a few bonds and, of course, there also are the minimums required on many investments.

• How willing are you to accept responsibility for managing your savings in the market? Investing in any of the securities I have discussed in the preceding pages takes more knowledge and responsibility on your part than does a simple deposit in a local bank or savings institution.

These questions will guide you to the proper decision for yourself.

WHAT SHOULD BE *your* POLICY ON BONDS?

Let me put it bluntly: unless you know your way around the bond markets, and can afford to take the risks, go and stay first class.

Don't go into these sophisticated markets blindly.

Don't buy low-grade bonds which might default and wipe you out.

Unless you have at least $5,000 to invest *don't* buy individual bond issues even where there are no minimums. (An exception here would be buying a bond fund, described earlier.)

Don't try to diversify too much when you are buying just a few bonds. Commission charges on buying or selling one or two bonds can be pretty steep and in addition the spread on the bid and asked when you are buying just one or two bonds can also be sizable. Some brokers might quote you a spread as much as 5 points ($50 on a $1,000 par value) if you buy a single bond. If you can, buy several of one issue. You'll probably get a better price and pay less in commissions.

Don't try to make a killing by trading on thin margins.

Do get guidance from a broker or banker you respect and who knows you and your circumstances.

Do make sure you are dealing with a reputable firm. In the early 1970s there were several scandals in connection with high-pressure bond salesmen including quite a few operating in the Memphis, Tenn., area. Among the shoddy as well as illegal sales tactics were quoting misleading prices, maturities, and ratings.

Do learn the basics of bond yield, maturity, discounts, and ratings before taking the plunge.

Do use your head and curb your greed.

The bond markets are great for wise and cool investors. They can be murder for fools.

THE BAFFLEGAB OF BONDS

ACCRUED INTEREST: Interest which has accumulated on a bond from the last interest payment to the present day. When you buy a bond, you must pay the interest which has accrued from the last interest payment to the seller of the bond. When you in turn sell a bond, the buyer must pay you the interest accrued from the last interest payment. Not all bonds trade with accrued interest. Those in default trade *flat,* and income bonds usually pay interest only when and if it is earned.

AMORTIZE: Reduction or elimination of a bond issuer's debt by fixed periodic payments scheduled for the specific purpose of such debt reduction. See Sinking Fund, below.

BASIS: This is another word for yield. The basis of a bond is its yield to maturity.

BASIS POINT: 1/100 of 1 per cent or 0.01. Used in finely calculating the yield to maturity of a bond and found in mathematical tables used by brokers and bankers in bond transactions.

BEARER BOND: Bond on which the owner's name is not registered with the issuer and thus, in some ways, is equivalent to cash in your possession. See earlier in this chapter.

BLUE LIST: Daily trade publication for dealers in municipal bonds listing the names and amounts of municipal bonds that dealers all over the country are offering for sale. Printed in blue ink on blue paper, hence Blue List. The Blue List also includes coupon price, yield, and bond ratings on offerings.

BOND: Promissory instrument to obtain credit on which principal is to be repaid in usually more than ten years (shorter period for U. S. Government bonds) after the loan is made and interest is to be paid periodically. Bonds are issued by federal, state, and municipal governments as well as corporations and are usually marketable. All non-government bonds are covered by a contract (trust indenture) held by a trustee who—in case of serious violation of the indenture by the bond issuer—can take action to protect the rights of all the bondholders.

BOND MARKETS: Markets in which longer-term debt securities of various borrowers are traded. See above.

CALLABLE BOND: Bonds which include a call provision stating that the issuer may redeem them before their maturity date under specified conditions. Usually the call price is at a premium over par. For example: a corporation has a $10 million bond issue outstanding which carries a 9 per cent coupon maturing in twenty-four years and which is callable at 105. If interest rates drop to, say, 6½ per cent, and the corporation can be assured by its investment bankers that this lower rate is available, it is obvious that the corporation can benefit by paying the slightly additional cost involved in calling the bonds at 105 and floating another loan at a coupon rate so much lower than 9 per cent.

COMPOUND INTEREST: Interest paid on accumulated interest as well as on the principal and computed on both the accumulated interest and the principal. Over the life of a bond, compounding interest can be equal to more than half the total of realized return.

CONVERTIBLE DEBENTURE: Bond issued on the general credit of the corporation which may be converted into common and sometimes the preferred stock of the same corporation at a specified price under stated conditions. See page 914.

CORPORATES: Corporation bonds. See above in this chapter.

COUPON: The piece of paper attached to a bearer (or coupon) bond which is evidence that interest is payable on the bond, usually every six months. The coupon rate is the rate of interest which the issuer has pledged to pay you, the bondholder, annually. The coupon amount is the dollar amount you will receive when this paper is submitted to a bank or through your broker for collection.

CURRENT YIELD: The interest paid by a bond expressed as a percentage of the current market price. Example: A 3 per cent $1,000 bond selling at $600 offers a current return of 5 per cent ($30/$600).

DEBENTURE BOND: A type of corporate bond which is backed only by the general credit of the issuing corporation and not by any pledge of property.

DISCOUNT: Difference between the lower price at which a bond may be trading and its higher value (par value) at issuance or normally at maturity. (See also "U. S. Savings Bonds" below.)

DISCOUNT BOND: Bonds quoted at a price below their face (or par) value. For example: a bond selling at par would be shown in a newspaper bond table at 100, a discount bond would be shown below that (99, 62, 73, etc.).

DISCOUNT RATE: The interest rate the Federal Reserve System charges banks belonging to the Federal Reserve System for loans. It is considered a basic interest rate of the nation because it is the rate banks themselves pay to borrow money. As a result, changes in the discount rate by the Federal Reserve affect all other interest rates in the nation.

EASY MONEY: See Tight Money below.

FEDERAL AGENCY ISSUES: Securities issued by federal agencies created by Congress over a long span of years and ranking in caliber right below U. S. Government securities themselves. See above.

FEDERAL RESERVE SYSTEM: Established under the Federal Reserve Act of 1913 to regulate the banking system of the United States and to set monetary policy of country. See Monetary Policy, below, and elsewhere in this chapter.

FIRST MORTGAGE BOND: A type of corporate bond which is secured by a mortgage on all or part of the fixed property of the issuing corporation. See above.

FIXED-INCOME SECURITIES: Securities which return a fixed income over a specified period. Fixed-income securities may be bonds, notes, bills, or preferred stocks.

FLOWER BOND: Nickname for certain U. S. Treasury bonds which, as of the mid-1970s, can be turned in at par or face value ($1,000 per bond) for payment of federal estate taxes if the bonds are actually owned by the decedent at the time of death. However, the bonds lose some of their tax advantage if they are bought in "contemplation of death."

If these bonds can be bought at a deep discount from par and placed in the portfolio of an extremely ill person, the bonds can be helpful in estate planning. Under a recent law, no more bonds with the special par redemption provision for estate tax purposes will be issued, so the supply of the bonds is limited and growing smaller as the bonds mature or are turned in. Here are flower bonds still outstanding and their maturities as of the mid-seventies:

COUPON	MATURITY
4	2/80
3½	11/80
3¼	6/83
3¼	5/85
4¼	5/85
3½	2/90
4¼	8/92
4	2/93
4⅛	5/94
3	2/95
3½	11/98

GENERAL OBLIGATION BOND: The major type of municipal bond backed by the full faith and credit of the issuer. These differ from limited obligation bonds, which rely upon special assessments and specific sources of revenue. See above.

HOUSING AUTHORITY BOND: Type of municipal bond which often has the highest-quality rating because the bonds rely on federal, state, or municipal government grants for debt service and not directly on collectible rents. Usually guaranteed by the federal government.

INTEREST: Money paid for the use of money. See pages 907–8, 911–12.

INTEREST RATE: A percentage determined by the amount of money the borrower pledges to pay to the lender of money for the use of the total borrowed. If you pay $80 interest per year on a loan of $1,000, you are paying an 8 per cent interest rate.

INVESTMENT BANKERS: Financial organizations, but usually not commercial banks, raising funds for various types of borrowers often by buying all of the securities and selling them through a selling group of broker-dealers to institutional and individual investors. See elsewhere, this chapter.

LIMITED TAX OR SPECIAL TAX BOND: Also a type of municipal bond. See above.

MATURITY: Specified date on which the stated value of a bond—the principal—becomes payable in full to the bond's owners. Also called due or maturity date.

MONETARY POLICY: Set by the Federal Reserve Board, acting through its Open Market Committee, to influence the supply of bank credit and other monetary conditions in the U.S. economy. Monetary policy, therefore, is a key factor in the trend of interest rates and the direction of the entire U.S. economy. Since interest rate changes send the bond and money markets up or down, monetary policy is also obviously a crucial force in these markets. See Federal Reserve System, above.

MONEY MARKETS: Markets in which the short-term securities of various borrowers are traded. See above.

MORTGAGE BOND: See First Mortgage Bond, above.

MUNICIPAL BONDS: Any obligations issued by a city, town, village, state, territory, U.S. possession, etc., etc. All are exempt from federal income taxation as of the laws in 1974 (and under certain conditions sometimes from state and local taxes too), and all are called municipals. See above.

NATIONAL ASSOCIATION OF SECURITIES DEALERS, INC.: A non-profit membership corporation, established in 1938 by Congress and including thousands of securities dealers and brokers throughout the United States. The NASD is responsible for self-regulation of the over-the-counter securities markets and also, in turn, to the Securities and Exchange Commission.

OBLIGATION: In Wall Street, an I.O.U., a bond, a note, or a bill.

OFFERING: Principal amount of an obligation or the face value at which an obligation is issued and on which interest is paid. Usually $1,000 per bond.

POINT: In bonds, one point represents a $10 change in the price per $1,000 (face value) bond—in contrast to stocks, where one point is a $1.00 change in price. The reason a point is $10 is that a bond price is quoted as a percentage of $1,000: 1 per cent of $1,000 is $10, 5 per cent is $50, etc., and so 1 point is $10, 5 points is $50, etc. To illustrate further, a quotation of 92 is $920 and a 5-point rise to 97 would be equal to $50 or a rise to $970.

PREMIUM: Difference between higher price above par at which a bond may be selling and the lower price recorded at the time it was issued or to be received at maturity date.

PRINCIPAL: Face value of a bond on which interest is paid. (Also see other meaning under definition of Dealer.)

PRUDENT-MAN RULE: A standard for investments. Under this standard, states having "prudent-man laws" permit trustees managing other people's money to diversify their investments and include high-quality stocks as well as the highest-quality bonds in the portfolios they manage.

RATINGS: The informed judgments of independent rating services (the two major ones are Moody's and Standard & Poor's) on the quality of various obligations. Obligations are ranked from the very highest Aaa (Moody's) and AAA (S & P's) to C and even lower. The ratings of these two services play a key role in evaluating the quality of bonds to investors. See above.

REAL RATE OF RETURN: Annual yield derived from fixed-income securities reduced by per cent of yearly rise in cost of living. Sometimes quoted on a pretax basis and sometimes on an after-tax basis. See above.

REDEEM: Repayment of the par value of a bond at maturity or at the price that has to be paid if the bond is being redeemed at the call date.

REFUNDING: The replacement of an outstanding and redeemed obligation with a new obligation. When interest rates decline, an issuer may in advance of maturity date decide to call in securities it sold at higher interest rates and refund them into new lower-interest bonds.

REGISTERED BOND: A bond registered in the name of the owner with either the issuer of the bond or the issuer's agent. The owner is mailed a check when interest is due and the bond can be transferred only by endorsement of the certificate. See Bearer Bond, above.

RETURN: Also known as yield. The rate of income derived from an investment—interest in the case of bonds, dividends in the case of stocks.

REVENUE BOND: A limited obligation type of municipal bond relying upon revenues generated by some public facility (bridges, tunnels, roads, transit, etc.) rather than taxes. See above.

ROLLOVER: Another word for refund, commonly used when the Treasury replaces its short-term bills at their maturity dates with new short-term bills.

SELLING AT A DISCOUNT: A bond selling at a price below its face value. See definition of Discount, above.

SELLING AT A PREMIUM: A bond selling at a price above its face value. See definition of Premium, above.

SERIAL BONDS: Issues which are redeemed on an installment basis in sequential order. A certain predetermined amount of the bonds falls due every period until the full amount is paid up.

SIMPLE INTEREST: Interest that is paid only on the principal and computed only on the principal.

SINKING FUND: A pool of money created through periodic payments by an issuer of bonds that must be used to retire (call in) a certain fixed (or variable) amount of its outstanding bonds at specified intervals. See Amortize, above.

SPREAD: Difference between two prices. Between bid and asked; or between the price at which an investment banking syndicate buys an issue from the issuer and the price at which the syndicate sells the issue to the public; or between the prices at which top-rated bonds are quoted and the prices at which second-quality bonds are quoted; or just between different types of bonds.

SYNDICATES: Groups of investment bankers formed to underwrite and distribute issues of securities. See above.

TAX-ANTICIPATION BILLS: A type of short-term U. S. Treasury security. See above.

TAX-EXEMPTS: Slang name for all types of municipal obligations which are exempt from federal income tax and sometimes from state and local taxation. See above.

TERM: Length of time that a bond is outstanding. A term bond, in comparison with a serial bond, has only a single maturity date.

TIGHT MONEY: Financial conditions that develop when the Federal Reserve adopts a monetary policy under which it restrains the supply of credit and thereby encourages higher interest rates. As the supply of credit becomes more limited while demand remains unaffected, the availability of the credit to would-be borrowers shrinks and there is a feeling of "tightness" in the markets. Easy Money describes financial conditions that develop when the Federal Reserve adapts a monetary policy under which it expands the supply of credit and thereby encourages lower interest rates. The policy usually follows a decline in demand for funds, reflecting a slowdown in business activity.

TREASURY BILLS: Short-term marketable U. S. Treasury obligations maturing from ninety days to one year and offered on a discount basis. T-bills are considered in the investment community almost as liquid as cash or as savings in the bank.

TREASURYS: Nickname for the securities of the United States Government: bonds, notes, and bills.

UNDERWRITING SYNDICATES: Groups of investment bankers who buy and market new issues to public. See above.

UNITED STATES GOVERNMENT SECURITIES MARKET: Generally speaking, the vast over-the-counter market in which bills, notes, and bonds of the U. S. Treasury are bought and sold. (Some are listed on the New York Stock Exchange too.) See above.

YIELD TO MATURITY: Total, true rate of return you are slated to receive on a debt instrument, taking into consideration the price you paid, the interest to be received, and the price at which your bond will be paid off at its maturity date. This is an exact calculation that must be worked out with aid of specially prepared mathematical tables. See above.

UNITED STATES SAVINGS BONDS

INTRODUCTION

"On New Year's morning, my husband and I vowed to save $50 a month, about 10 per cent of his take-home pay. But in the past few weeks an unexpected bunch of expenses has wiped it all out. This has happened over and over again to us, with the result that we haven't accumulated one extra dollar in the past five years. Is there any cure for the habitual non-saver?"

This typed plea for help, sent to me, is far more typical of Americans than any figures on total savings suggest. This is the sort of letter, in fact, which highlights the fact that, despite our ever rising volume of over-all savings, a full one third or more of U.S. families have no savings at all—in the form of bank deposits, stocks, bonds, etc.—and for millions of other families the savings total is less than $500.

If you are among the millions who feel unable to stick to voluntary savings plans, your best answer will be a form of "forced savings." There are literally dozens of different ways to discipline yourself into saving and I've analyzed many of the techniques in these pages. But among the very, very best ways to force yourself to save is to buy United States savings bonds under a payroll savings plan at the place where you work—or via a bond-a-month plan at your corner bank. And in fact a fantastic total of nearly 10 million Americans in the mid-1970s were buying bonds via these savings plans at their offices or plants or factories.

This advantage is not to be underestimated in any way! By buying savings bonds via these plans, you discipline yourself into saving money you otherwise might easily fritter away. By authorizing regular small deductions from your pay check, you build over the years a sizable total of savings. By enrolling in a payroll savings or bond-a-month plan you tend to become "frozen" to the savings program and to keep building your nest egg through good times and bad.

This is the "heart" of the United States savings bond program. This is the "magic" by which a few dollars put aside regularly every week becomes hundreds of dollars saved over a year. This is the secret of the program's continuing popularity, for as one of the leading industrialists of the country said to me a while ago:

"Many employees wouldn't save at all unless they were enrolled in a payroll savings plan. It is a lot better to get only a mediocre interest rate on something than a sensational interest rate on nothing!"

To put it another way, there may be better ways to invest—and there are—but there is no better way to save. It's a subtle but significant distinction.

Okay, the above explains why the savings bond program has survived so long. Now what are these bonds?

KEY QUESTIONS ON SAVINGS BONDS

There are two series of U.S. savings bonds currently on sale—Series E and Series H. Since savings bonds were originally issued more than thirty years ago, the Treasury has raised the interest they pay in successive stages and you can now earn 6 per cent on the bonds if you hold them to maturity.

Q. *What are the characteristics of savings bonds?*

A. The familiar E bond is an appreciation-type security. This means you buy it at a discount from its face amount and the gradual increase in the value of the bond, from your purchase price to its face amount (or redemption price), represents your interest. For instance, as of the mid-1970s, you can buy a Series E savings bond for $18.75, which matures at $25.20; you can buy an E bond for $75, which matures at $100.80. Series E bonds now mature five years from their issue date.

The less familiar Series H bond is a current-income security. This means you buy it at par (face value) and you receive interest in the form of semi-annual checks from the U. S. Treasury. Series H bonds mature ten years from their issue date.

Both Series E and H bonds are non-marketable bonds—non-negotiable, not acceptable as collateral for loans. Series E bonds may be redeemed by the Treasury or one of its authorized paying agents (most banks and other financial institutions are authorized paying agents and will redeem your bonds). H bonds may be redeemed only by the Treasury or any Federal Reserve Bank branch.

Q. *How do you earn the 6 per cent rate?*

A. Series E bonds return 6 per cent interest, compounded semi-annually, when held to maturity of five years. They earn 4.54 per cent for the first year; from that point on, interest increases on a graduated scale to 6 per cent at maturity.

The following table shows you your return on E bonds—with issue dates beginning December 1, 1973—if you cash them in before or at original maturity.

E BONDS CASHED IN AFTER:	YIELD
2 months	4.00% (annual)
1 year	4.54
1½ year	4.69
2 years	4.76
2½ years	4.86
3 years	4.95
3½ years	5.03
4 years	5.14
4½ years	5.25
5 years	6.00

Series H bonds also return 6 per cent when held to a maturity of ten years. They earn 4.99 per cent the first year; thereafter, their interest increases too, until, at maturity date, they have returned 6 per cent a year over the ten-year span.

The following table shows you your return on H bonds—with issue dates beginning December 1, 1973—if you cash them in before or at original maturity.

H BONDS CASHED IN AFTER:	YIELD
½ year	4.20%
1 year	4.99
1½ year	5.25
2 years	5.38
2½ years	5.46
3 years	5.51
3½ years	5.55
4 years	5.58
4½ years	5.60
5 years	5.62
5½ years	5.69
6 years	5.75
6½ years	5.80
7 years	5.84
7½ years	5.87
8 years	5.91
8½ years	5.93
9 years	5.96
9½ years	5.98
10 years (maturity)	6.00

Q. *What are the denominations of savings bonds?*

A. For the E bond: $25; $50; $75; $100; $200; $500; $1,000; $10,-000. These are the values at which the bonds mature. You buy them, I repeat, at a discount from their face amount. Thus—

DENOMINATION	PURCHASE PRICE
$25	$ 18.75
50	37.50
75	56.25
100	75.00
200	150.00
500	375.00
1,000	750.00
10,000	7,500.00

Actual values at maturity are $25.20; $50.40; $75.60; $100.80; $201.60; $504.00; $1,008.00; $10,080.00.

For the H bond, the denominations are: $500; $1,000; $5,000; $10,000.

Q. *Are there limits on how many bonds you can buy?*

A. Yes. The annual limit on the amount of Series E bonds you are permitted to buy is currently $10,000, face amount, $7,500, issue price. The annual limit on the amount of H bonds you can buy is also $10,000, face amount. In computing these limits, though, bonds registered in the names of co-owners may be applied to the holdings of either one of you or apportioned between you.

For instance, two of you, as co-owners, may hold $20,000, face amount, of Series E and also $20,000 of Series H bonds, provided neither of you has other savings bonds purchased during the same calendar year.

Q. *Has the rate been increased for older bonds?*

A. Yes. Beginning with 1959, the yields on outstanding savings bonds have been improved several times, bringing them in line with current issues.

The latest increase was effective December 1, 1973 or at the beginning of the first semi-annual interest period thereafter.

Q. *How do the various extensions of maturity apply to E and H bonds?*

A. E bonds, with original maturities ranging from five years and ten months to ten years, have been granted one or more ten-year extensions:

DATE OF ISSUE		EXTENDED MATURITY		LIFE OF BOND
May 1941–Apr.	1952	May 1981–Apr.	1992	40 years
May 1952–Jan.	1957	Jan. 1982–Sep.	1986	29 years, 8 months
Feb. 1957–May	1959	Jan. 1976–Apr.	1978	18 years, 11 months
June 1959–Nov.	1965	Mar. 1977–Aug.	1983	17 years, 9 months
Dec. 1965–May	1969	Dec. 1982–May	1986	17 years
June 1969–Nov.	1973	Apr. 1985–Sep.	1989	15 years, 10 months
Beginning December 1973		———		15 years

For H bonds, the extended maturities are as follows:

DATE OF ISSUE		EXTENDED MATURITY		LIFE OF BOND
June 1952–Jan.	1957	Feb. 1982–Sep.	1986	29 years, 8 months
Feb. 1957–Nov.	1965	Feb. 1977–Nov.	1985	20 years
Beginning December 1965		10 year extension published February 1974.*		

Q. *Is there any advantage in redeeming older E or H bonds to buy new bonds?*

A. Absolutely none. They all pay the same interest rate schedule and pay off at the same price at maturity. And in fact there is a good reason *not*

* All H bonds now being issued carry an automatic ten-year extension beyond original maturity.

to cash in—if the interest has not been reported each year as it accrued—for then you would be required to report the accumulated interest (the gain in value) for federal income tax purposes during the year you cash in. In addition, the new bonds purchased with the proceeds would initially accrue interest at a lower rate than the bonds that were cashed.

Q. *Are the rates guaranteed?*

A. Yes. The bonds are backed by the full faith and credit of the U. S. Government and the rates are guaranteed to maturity. You can, though, cash in your bonds as you wish after a short time. You can never get back less than you pay in. Interest may be increased but not decreased, once the rate for an extension has been published.

Q. *How do I sell my bonds?*

A. You don't sell savings bonds. You cash them in or redeem them at guaranteed values. Specifically, at your, the owner's, option, E bonds may be redeemed at any time after two months from issue date at most banks and other financial institutions at their current redemption value.

At your, the owner's, option, H bonds may be redeemed at par at any Federal Reserve Bank or Branch, or at the Bureau of the Public Debt, Securities Transactions Branch, Washington, D.C. 20226, at any time after six months from issue date. H bonds received during the month preceding an interest payment date will be held for redemption until that date.

Q. *What about cash-in restrictions?*

A. Savings bonds are, I repeat, liquid assets which may be cashed in after their minimal holding periods—two months for E bonds and six months for H bonds.

Q. *What if a bond is lost or stolen?*

A. Savings bonds are "indestructible." Any bond which is lost, stolen, mutilated, or destroyed will be replaced by the U. S. Treasury upon your application without charge to you. A record of each bond sold is maintained by serial number and name and address of owner—and by Social Security account number for those issued on or after October 1, 1973.

The record is kept by the Bureau of Public Debt. More than 2.8 million U.S. savings bonds, valued at more than $240 million—either lost, stolen, damaged, or destroyed—have been replaced by the Treasury, over the past three decades, without charge to their owners.

Q. *You mean all bonds are registered?*

A. Yes. And you have a choice of registration. The bonds may be issued in one name only, in the names of two persons as co-owners, or in the name of one person with a second person as beneficiary (payable on death).

If bonds are registered in co-ownership form, during co-owner's lifetime either of you may cash the bonds, but a co-owner's name cannot be removed without his or her consent. If registered in beneficiary form, during owner's lifetime only he or she may cash the bond and beneficiary's name cannot be removed without the beneficiary's consent.

Savings bonds cannot be transferred, sold, or used as collateral.

Q. *How do I make a claim if my bonds are lost?*

A. Write to the Bureau of Public Debt, Box 509, Parkersburg, W. Va., 26101. Provide as much information as you can about the lost, stolen, damaged, or destroyed bonds: serial numbers, issue dates, names and addresses on bonds. The Bureau of Public Debt will send you a special form to execute to receive your "duplicate" bonds. Keep your bonds in a secure place, such as a safe deposit box. *In another location,* maintain a list of your bonds, with their serial numbers, denominations, and dates issued.

Q. *What about taxation of savings bonds?*

A. Interest on savings bonds is exempt from all state and local income or personal property taxes. Interest on savings bonds is subject to federal income tax, but the tax may be deferred on E bonds until the bonds are cashed, otherwise disposed of, or finally mature. This tax-deferral privilege permits you to create and build up education, retirement, disability funds (or funds for whatever your objective) which—under certain circumstances—may be tax-free. This aspect is also a major "plus" for E bonds.

You cannot similarly postpone paying income tax on interest you earn on marketable Treasury obligations or other taxable obligations. H bond interest, paid semi-annually by Treasury check, must be reported annually for federal income tax purposes.

Q. *Any other important characteristics?*

A. Yes. Unless administration is required for other purposes, probate is not required in order to dispose of a decedent's savings bonds. The Treasury provides special forms, depending on the amount involved, which may be used for the purpose. Bonds registered in co-owner or beneficiary form belong to the survivor and are not a part of the decedent's probate estate; their value may be includable in computing the size of the estate for estate and inheritance tax purposes, whether federal or state.

HOW TO USE THE TAX ADVANTAGES OF SAVINGS BONDS TO CREATE A TAX-FREE EDUCATION FUND

The fact that you need not report the interest you receive on E bonds until you cash in the bonds is a vital tax benefit for you. And you can increase these tax savings when you buy the bonds as gifts for your children.

For instance, as a means of saving for your child's education, buy E bonds in your child's name and designate yourself as beneficiary (*not* co-owner). At the end of the first year, file a federal income tax return in your child's name and state thereon that the child elects to report the interest annually. Then list the increase in the value of the bonds as his or her income. This establishes your child's "intent" and you need file no further returns as long as the interest on the bonds plus your child's other investment income is *less than $750 a year.* * Nor will any tax be due on your child's income unless the total of the investment income exceeds $750 a year.

Thus, when your child cashes his or her bonds to meet the costs of college, all the accrued interest on the bonds will be free from federal income tax. And the interest is also exempt from all state and local income taxes and personal property taxes.

Or you might buy the bonds in your child's name, with yourself as beneficiary, and not file a federal income tax return until your child starts college and begins to cash in the bonds for his or her educational expenses. Your child then would file a tax return each year and report the full amount of interest on the redeemed bonds as income.

As of the tax laws of the mid-1970s, if the total amount of your child's investment income was less than $750 a year, no income tax would be due. (The tax-free income of the child could increase to as much as $2,050 if the child had "earned income" in addition to his investment income. In this regard, earned income does not include interest or dividends.)

If you use the first Tax-Free Education Plan, be sure you keep a copy of the tax return you file to prove "intent."

Here's how your "Dollars for Education" grow in Series E bonds:

CHILD'S AGE	VALUE* OF E BONDS AT AGE 18 THROUGH MONTHLY INVESTMENTS OF:			
	$18.75	$37.50	$56.25	$75.00
0	$7,125	$14,249	$21,374	$28,498
1	6,497	12,995	19,492	25,990
2	5,906	11,813	17,719	23,626
4	4,824	9,648	14,472	19,297
6	3,863	7,725	11,588	15,450
8	3,008	6,016	9,024	12,033
10	2,249	4,498	6,747	8,996
12	1,575	3,149	4,724	6,299

* Assuming an interest rate of 6 per cent, if held for five years, and 6 per cent annum compounded semi-annually thereafter. The interest rate on *new* issues of U.S. savings bonds is subject to continuous review by the Treasury, and may be increased or decreased, in accordance with changes in economic and financial conditions. The interest on *outstanding* bonds *cannot* be decreased; over the years, it has been increased several times.

HOW TO USE THE TAX ADVANTAGES OF SAVINGS BONDS TO CREATE A TAX-BREAK RETIREMENT FUND

Buy E bonds regularly during your working years and at a rate geared to your income. After you retire, cash in the bonds as you need them, reporting the interest as income on your federal income tax return.

* Tax laws as of mid-1970s.

Since your income usually is lower in your retirement years, and since you have double tax exemptions after the age of sixty-five, you'll either pay a sharply reduced tax or you'll eliminate your tax entirely.

Or buy the bonds during your working years and then at retirement exchange your E bonds for H bonds—which pay you interest semi-annually by Treasury check. The accumulated interest on your E bonds can be applied to the purchase of your H bonds and, again, you have the privilege of deferring your tax liability on your E-bond interest until you cash in your H bonds, otherwise dispose of them, or they reach final maturity.

Thus, the tax money you still owe on your E-bond interest enables you to earn more money in H-bond interest. To illustrate, if you buy a $100 E bond (for $75) a month for fifteen years, you accumulate $21,397, assuming the interest rate for the extended period continues at 6 per cent. At that point, you exchange the Es for $21,500 in H bonds (which requires adding $103 in cash to bring the amount exchanged up to the next higher $500 multiple). Of this total, $7,897 represents accrued interest, which is not taxable at exchange. From your $21,500 in H bonds, you receive $1,075 in interest the first year, $1,247 each year for the next four years, and $1,400.08 each year for the next five years. Average monthly income for ten years would be $108.86, compared to the original monthly investment of $75 (plus the lump-sum payment of $103, at time of exchange), leaving the $21,500 principal sum intact. Tax on the accumulated E-bond interest would be due, of course, when the H bonds reach final maturity or are redeemed—but at your lower post-retirement rate.

Here's how this Tax-Break Retirement Plan works:

Buy an E bond each month for 15 years at a cost of	Your original investment	Interest from E bonds	In 15 years your 190 bonds will be worth	Exchange your E bonds for H bonds*	Average monthly H-bond interest for 10 years**
$ 18.75	$ 3,375	$ 1,974	$ 5,349	$ 5,500	$ 27.85
37.50	6,750	3,949	10,699	11,000	55.70
56.25	10,125	5,923	16,048	16,500	83.54
75.00	13,500	7,897	21,397	21,500	108.86
150.00	27,000	15,794	42,794	43,000	217.72

* Adding necessary cash to bring total amount exchanged to next multiple of $500.
** And your principal is still intact (table assumes 6 per cent interest rate, if held for five years, per annum compounded semi-annually thereafter, and that present E-for-H exchange offer continues).

HOW SAVINGS GROW THROUGH SMALL WEEKLY DEDUCTIONS VIA
A PAYROLL SAVINGS PLAN

Say you start a regular weekly savings plan the first day of the New Year. And say you put up the following small amounts toward a $25 savings bond. Here is how your savings would build up over the years:

WEEKLY SAVINGS AMOUNTS	ACCUMULATED VALUE AT THE END OF:				
	1 YR.	3 YRS.	5 YRS.	10 YRS.	15 YRS.*
$ 1.25	$ 66	$ 207	$ 364	$ 864	$ 1,538
2.50	131	414	729	1,735	3,088
3.75	198	622	1,096	2,608	4,641
5.00	263	831	1,462	3,478	6,190
6.25	329	1,038	1,828	4,351	7,742
7.50	395	1,246	2,194	5,222	9,292
12.50	659	2,077	3,659	8,709	15,496
18.75	988	3,117	5,492	13,071	23,258

* Assuming continuation of 6 per cent interest rate.

A FINANCIALLY INTELLIGENT ATTITUDE TOWARD BUYING
AND HOLDING SAVINGS BONDS

If you buy the bonds via payroll savings, they are a superb way to force yourself to save small amounts regularly and, by so doing, to accumulate a basic reserve. But a rate of 6 per cent does not cover the erosion in your return from spiraling living costs and steep income taxes in the mid-seventies.

If inflation is to be our way of life in the rest of the twentieth century as it has been in the past, the Treasury will not be fair to buyers of its bonds until it offers a purchasing power guarantee—e.g., a bond with a dollar value that would rise as the cost-of-living index rose.

This is not a new idea—and, in fact, in the United States in recent years we have been moving closer and closer to purchasing-power guarantees to give major segments of our population some automatic protections against steadily rising prices. Social Security benefits are now automatically tied to increases in the Consumer Price Index. Cost-of-living escalator clauses have become commonplace in union wage contracts. The record high interest rates of the 1970s reflect, in part at least, efforts to protect investors in marketable fixed-income securities from the erosion of inflation.

The very least the Treasury should do is give the subject the exhaustive study it demands but since even the study is still in the future, once you've accumulated your nest egg, maintain only a modest proportion in savings bonds.

Divide the balance among sound investments which will grow as our economy grows and, thereby, put and keep you well ahead.

In essence, savings bonds will help you create a nest egg. Other investments will help you enhance it.

THE BAFFLEGAB OF SAVINGS BONDS

ACCRUAL-TYPE SECURITIES: This is the E-bond type. A bond sold at about a 25 per cent discount, and which gradually increases to above its face amount at maturity. The difference between the purchase price and the amount received for the bond when you redeem it is your interest.

ACCRUED INTEREST: Interest that has been earned on savings bonds but has not been collected, because the bond has not been redeemed by holder.

APPRECIATION-TYPE SECURITY: Same as Accrual-type Security, above.

CHAIN-LETTER SCHEMES: Illegal get-rich quick schemes which frequently are built around Series E savings bonds. If you purchase savings bonds as an innocent participant in a fraudulent chain-letter deal, you may request a refund of your money. Get and use Treasury Form PD-2966.

COLLATERAL: Securities or other property pledged by a borrower against the payment of a loan. Savings bonds cannot be used as collateral for loans.

CURRENT-INCOME SECURITY: This is the H-bond type. A bond sold at face value (par value) on which a specified amount of interest is paid semi-annually. See page 932.

DENOMINATION: Face amount of various savings bonds. The E bond now has seven denominations, from $25 to $10,000. The H bond has three, from $500 to $10,000.

EXTENDED MATURITIES: Extension by the U. S. Treasury of original maturity date on savings bonds for an additional ten-year period. All E and H bonds now on sale carry an automatic ten-year extension. Owners need do nothing to take advantage of the extension of maturity. Just hold the bonds.

FREEDOM SHARES: U.S. savings notes sold from 1967 through mid-1970. No longer on sale. However, the original savings notes have been granted a ten-year extension beyond their initial four-and-a-half-year maturity date at the 6 per cent current interest rate.

H-BOND EXCHANGE: All E bonds and Freedom Shares are eligible for exchange for current-income H bonds, under specified conditions. Payment of income tax on the interest from E bonds/shares exchanged may be deferred.

ISSUE PRICE: Price actually paid for bond by the buyer. Differs from denomination in E bonds and Freedom Shares, because issue price is at a discount from the denomination, and that difference is the interest which accrues on the bond or share until it finally matures or is redeemed, in advance of final maturity.

NON-MARKETABLE BONDS: Non-negotiable securities which cannot be sold or bought in the open market. Savings bonds are non-marketable securities.

PURCHASE LIMIT: Maximum of savings bonds which can be bought by one owner in a single year. At present, the limit is $10,000 face amount.

REGISTERED BOND: Bond with its owner's name recorded on the books of the issuer. With savings bonds, the owner's name is recorded by the United States Treasury.

SAVINGS STAMPS: No longer issued by the U. S. Treasury. If you have or find any of these 10¢ to $5.00 stamps, cash them in at your post office or bank (if it will redeem stamps) or add enough cash to acquire a small-denomination E bond.

TAX DEFERMENT: Postponement of taxes. Payment of federal income tax on interest accrued on E bonds may be deferred to redemption, other disposition, or final redemption of the bonds.

WAR BONDS: Also called Defense Bonds. Series A, B, C, D, F, G, J, K or any other letter of the alphabet, except E and H, are no longer being issued and are no longer earning interest. If you hold or find any of these series, redeem them at once. Send them by registered mail to the Federal Reserve Bank or branch in your district or to the Bureau of the Public Debt, Securities Transactions Branch, Washington, D.C. 20226. Many banks are not qualified to handle this redemption for you.

23

HOW TO SPECULATE
IN COMMODITIES

How would you like to buy 28,000 pounds of iced broilers or 69,120 square feet of plywood, or 36,000 pounds of pork bellies, or 100 tons of soybean meal? How do you like this contrasted with investing in, say, American Telephone and Telegraph, or in a savings certificate?

If you *would* like to "invest" in such exotic products via the buying or selling of commodity futures contracts—you would be joining many thousands of other Americans who are now actively speculating in a wide variety of commodities on more than a dozen exchanges in this country and abroad. For commodity futures speculating has been booming ever since the late 1960s. Much of it is due to the fact that more and more business firms buy (or sell) commodity futures to *protect* themselves against price fluctuations: these firms trade in commodity contracts to reduce some of the speculative elements of their normal business. This kind of trading is called "hedging," and it is done by professionals. But many thousands of individuals—doctors, lawyers, engineers, countless others in a wide variety of occupations—are buying commodity futures as pure speculation: these individuals are trying to get big profits from a small investment. (They also sell short.)

There are four powerful forces behind the commodity boom:

• Prices of many agricultural and industrial commodities are being spurred upward by world population growth and global inflation.

• This is a wildly speculative era and the small-time speculator is crowding into the commodity markets. According to authoritative estimates, a large number of speculators today are amateurs, dabblers, and small investors who have just recently learned how easily commodities can be traded.

• Huge profits can be made on tiny margins. If you are a successful and lucky speculator, you could multiply your own nest egg by 1,000 per cent within a matter of months. A mere penny price hike for a pound of sugar in the market place translates into a rise of $1,120 for a 112,000-pound sugar futures contract. (Of course, you can also roll up big losses if you are wrong.)

• Almost uncontrolled forces of supply and demand at work in the world today make for gyrating price moves in commodities.

Those who trade are motivated by either greed or fear. The amateur who is seeking a quick profit on a small outlay is motivated by greed. But a large part of current trading is attributed to those motivated by fear—primarily fear for the purchasing power of their paper currency. Such traders often are very wealthy. They trade—i.e., buy commodities—as a hedge against inflation.

Intriguing, isn't it? But you can't jump into the complex commodity market without first getting a better picture of what makes it tick. So here goes.

HOW COMMODITIES ARE TRADED

Speculating in commodities is basically done on commodity exchanges. There are about a dozen such exchanges in this country. The biggest is the Chicago Board of Trade, where the trading accounts for about half of the trading done in all commodities in the United States. Then there are other big ones: the Chicago Mercantile Exchange, the New York Cotton Exchange, the Commodity Exchange, Inc., the New York Cocoa Exchange, the New York Coffee and Sugar Exchange. And there are lesser-known exchanges, too: the Kansas City Board of Trade, the Minneapolis Grain Exchange. Then there are also the foreign exchanges: the London Metal Exchange, London Cocoa Terminal Market, the London Sugar Exchange, and other less important markets in Paris and Hamburg.

Under federal legislation passed in 1974, the Commodity Futures Trading Commission now imposes strict regulations on trading in all commodities.

The actual trading on the exchanges is normally done by brokers who are members of the various exchanges. In some cases member firms of the commodity exchanges are major factors in the stock brokerage business as well. But even if you are a sophisticated investor in stocks, you'll find it doesn't help much if you want to speculate in commodities. Commodity trading is a different world.

As an illustration, say you want to trade in wheat, the world's most widely cultivated grain. Here the trading unit is 5,000 bushels, and it is quoted in cents and quarters of a cent per bushel, with a minimum fluctuation of $1/4 ¢$ per bushel, or $12.50 per contract. The daily limit is 20¢ above or below the previous day's settlement price. But if the market closes up or down the limit for three consecutive days in three or more contract months during the crop year, it is subject to variable limits. The trading hours for wheat on the Chicago Board of Trade are between 9:30 A.M. and 1:15 P.M., Central Time.

This is just the tip of the iceberg of information you need if you are to know how to trade commodities.

To suggest the mechanics of a specific trade, let's say you want to buy a contract for 30,000 pounds of cocoa (a standard contract) for delivery to you during a specific month next spring. This is like going to an automobile dealer and making a commitment to buy a Ford car when next year's models arrive. As you might with the car, you make a "down payment" on your cocoa contract amounting to a few hundred dollars or about 10 per cent of the total value of the cocoa you have agreed to buy.

As spring approaches (if you haven't already), you must decide whether to take your 30,000 pounds of cocoa and pay for the total shipment plus storage charges—or whether to sell the contract at a price which may be more or less than the amount for which the cocoa was originally selling. (Chances are you would take the latter course. Only an insignificant portion of commodity futures contracts traded today are ever actually delivered, and then primarily to professional dealers or processors. After all, what would you do with 30,000 pounds of cocoa?

Commissions you pay your broker for commodity trades are relatively small. For most commodities, commissions are between $30 and $60 for a "round turn"—covering both purchase and sale of a contract. (In contrast, in stock trading, you pay two commissions.)

The following five points will put the commodity trading background in realistic perspective:

(1) Commodity futures contracts are traded on a "margin" (deposit), typically around 10 per cent of the value of the contract. (Additional margin must be put up if the market goes against you.) This is a very low margin compared to the margins required when you purchase stocks—running usually between 50 and 80 per cent.

(2) The commodity market is not a market for ordinary investment. Rather, it is a market for speculative funds—funds an individual can afford to lose, without any danger to his over-all financial security. In order to enter the commodity markets, experienced brokers recommend that you should have at least $10,000 in "pure risk" capital to play with. There is no room in the commodity market for the uninformed speculator or a person who can't afford to risk his money.

(3) Today, a key reason why many small-time commodity traders lose their shirts is because they do not start out with enough capital. It's estimated that of all speculators in commodities an estimated 85 per cent are losers. Only 15 per cent are winners.

(4) Speculating in commodities successfully seems to require a special type of personality—a willingness to recognize mistakes which any specula-

tor invariably makes, a philosophical attitude about accepting losses quickly while they are still small, and a "cold" unemotional attitude toward previous commitments.

(5) You must have a clear understanding of the risks involved in trading commodity futures. Profits in commodity trading can be very large considering the small sums you actually have to put down. But losses can also be enormous, particularly if you have a tendency to overextend or overtrade.

THE IMPACT OF SMALL PRICE CHANGES ON COMMODITIES

One point that is hard for newcomers to commodity trading to understand is the impact of small price changes on commodity prices. It is not unusual for an individual commodity to undergo a 25 per cent change in price in a couple of months.

The daily price changes can be severe—because even though there are usually limits set by each exchange on the amount of change per day, you can be "locked in." For instance, you may want to sell if the market declines the limit, but there may be no buyers. So the market can go down day after day—without giving you an opportunity to sell. If you are whipsawed by a price change of merely a few pennies, you can lose a substantial amount of money on your contract. For example, as the chart below shows, if the price of soybean oil drops 2¢ per pound and you have a standard 60,000-pound contract, this 2¢ change amounts to $1,200. For sugar, a penny-a-pound change is $1,120.

Here are specific examples to show you how far a penny-a-pound price change can move the value of a single commodity futures contract—up *or* down.

COMMODITY	EXCHANGE	CONTRACT UNIT	EFFECT OF A 1¢ PRICE CHANGE
Boneless Beef	N. Y. Mercantile	30,000 ℔	$300
Cattle (live)	Chicago Mercantile	40,000 ℔	$400
Orange juice (frozen)	N. Y. Cotton	15,000 ℔	$150
Cocoa	N. Y. Cocoa	30,000 ℔	$300
Copper	Commodity (N.Y.)	25,000 ℔	$250
Cotton	N. Y. Cotton	50,000 ℔	$500
Eggs (fresh)	Chicago Mercantile	22,500 doz.	$225
Hogs (live)	Chicago Mercantile	30,000 ℔	$300
Silver	Chicago Board of Trade	5,000 troy oz.	$50
Silver coins	N. Y. Mercantile	$10,000 (face amt.)	$100
Soybeans	Chicago Board of Trade	5,000 bu.	$50
Wheat	Chicago Board of Trade	5,000 bu.	$50

BASIC RULES FOR TRADING

But let's say you remain undaunted by all the pitfalls that you face in speculating in commodities. What intrigues you is the knowledge that some people have been making huge profits on small investments. You are well aware of the risks, you have at least $10,000 of pure risk capital to spare, and you are determined to speculate with this sum in the commodity market. If this is you, here are basic rules to follow. They should give you at least a fighting chance to make a profit.

(1) Before you put down a single dollar in trading, make a list of several commodities whose prices you believe are likely to change and whose movements you would like to follow. Find out everything you can about these —via research from reputable brokerage houses and research advisory firms, reports from the U. S. Department of Agriculture, the major commodity exchanges. Keep abreast of all basic forces affecting the price of each commodity—the weather, crop forecasts, inflation, international market developments, government subsidies and policies, currency changes.

Also study the specifics on each—wheat, frozen orange juice, silver, beef, etc. For example, if it's live cattle, become thoroughly familiar with government reports covering the number of cattle on feed, beef production and consumption trends, weather conditions in livestock-producing states.

(2) Choose a brokerage firm which has had extensive experience in commodity futures trading, which covers the specific markets in which you plan to speculate, and which can provide you with facts on the commodities which interest you. You'll find that most of the major stock brokerage firms have substantial commodity departments.

(3) *Before* you invest, decide exactly how much money you can afford to commit. Do *not* wait for a market crisis to make this decision. Set a profit goal. Determine if and how much you will add to any given position in the event of a prolonged price rise. In essence, make a plan, in advance, designed to limit your losses and to achieve maximum profits.

(4) Plan to place stop orders, instructing your broker to sell if losses reach a certain predetermined level—and ask him to guide you on where your stop orders should realistically be placed. As a general rule, you should limit losses to a maximum of one fourth to one third of the profits you hope to achieve. *Don't* change your stop order one penny in the direction of further risk.

(5) Be faithful to the old rule: "Cut your losses short and let your profits run." About the only way to make a long-range profit in commodities is to hold out for a few very substantial price rises to offset the many small losses you'll surely suffer. The typical savvy speculator achieves success with profitable trades in only one third of his transactions.

The following illustrates how four successful speculators actually reaped substantial profits despite a startling number of losses:

SPECULATOR	NUMBER OF TRADES AT A PROFIT	NUMBER OF TRADES AT A LOSS	PROFITABLE TRADES (%)	ACTUAL NET PROFITS ($)
A	17	27	39%	$ 3,593
B	25	32	44	9,992
C	19	36	35	510
D	29	68	30	16,177

And below shows how much you can lose—even if a majority of your trades are profitable—if you settle for small gains.

SPECULATOR	NUMBER OF TRADES AT A PROFIT	NUMBER OF TRADES AT A LOSS	PROFITABLE TRADES (%)	ACTUAL NET LOSSES ($)
E	124	27	82%	$— 21
F	26	2	93	— 1,328
G	20	10	67	— 3,149
H	19	6	76	—19,758
I	43	16	73	— 3,060

(6) *Don't* commit the bulk of your funds to any one trade, no matter how convinced you are of a price rise. Any number of unforeseen events ranging from weather to war can abruptly change the price outlook for the commodity involved. There is no "sure" thing.

(7) Instead, see if you can spread your funds among contracts in at least a couple of commodities.

(8) *Don't* trade on the basis of tips or rumors—which might be aimed at tricking you into buying or selling. Trade on the best factual information you can obtain.

(9) Look upon commodity trading as an avocation and *not* a one-shot deal. Realize that commodity speculation is an exceedingly complex business and view the first few years as "education." Pace your trades so you'll still have capital left after you have learned from your own errors. Start your education program early and stick with it.

Trading even in commodities regulated by the Commodity Futures Trading Commission is risky, as this short analysis must have dramatized to you. The key to your own protection lies in selecting a responsible, well-established, well-recommended broker.

WHERE TO GET INFORMATION ON COMMODITY TRADING

Among your best sources of information on commodities are financial publications, trade publications, reputable commodity research organizations, up-to-date books on commodity speculation, your own brokerage firm's booklets, and lectures offered by a number of firms.

The Chicago Board of Trade offers many different booklets and pamphlets on commodity trading. Its basic manual on commodity trading sells for $17.50, but there are many small brochures available in the 50¢ range too and single copies may be free. The Board of Trade also offers twenty-five- to forty-five-minute tape cassettes which include lectures on various aspects of commodity trading. You can obtain these by writing to the Educational Department of the Board at its Chicago address listed below.

Merrill Lynch offers extensive materials on commodities. Write the firm at 1 Liberty Plaza, New York, N.Y. 10006.

A popular book in the field is *Modern Commodity Futures Trading* by Gerald Gold, available through the Commodity Research Bureau, 1 Liberty Plaza, New York, N.Y. 10006. The Commodity Research Bureau, Inc., also publishes other materials for beginners. Write the Bureau for its list of publications.

Another source of information is the Association of Commodity Exchange Firms, Inc. (1 World Trade Center, New York, N.Y. 10005).

Here are the addresses of the major exchanges to which you might write for additional material:

New York Mercantile Exchange
6 Harrison Street
New York, N.Y. 10013

New York Cocoa Exchange, Inc.
127 John Street
New York, N.Y. 10038

Chicago Mercantile Exchange
444 West Jackson Boulevard
Chicago, Ill. 60606

New York Cotton Exchange
37 Wall Street
New York, N.Y. 10005

Chicago Board of Trade
141 West Jackson Boulevard
Chicago, Ill. 60604

New York Coffee and Sugar
  Exchange, Inc.
79 Pine Street
New York, N.Y. 10005

Commodity Exchange, Inc.
81 Broad Street
New York, N.Y. 10004

THE BAFFLEGAB OF COMMODITIES

ACCUMULATION: Building up of either a long or short position in a given commodity by buying or selling contracts over a period of time.

ACTUALS: (*Spot commodities*): Physical commodities. Goods available for immediate delivery following sale, as opposed to future contracts.

ARBITRAGE: Simultaneous buying and selling of the same commodity in two different markets to profit from a temporary price discrepancy.

AT THE MARKET: Order to buy or sell a contract at whatever is the best price available at the time the order reaches the pit (or market). Also called "Market Order."

BID: Price offer made by a buyer for a specific quantity of a commodity.

BOT: Abbreviation for "bought," widely used in the stock and bond as well as commodity markets.

BREAK: Sharp price decline for a given commodity.

BULGE: Sharp price advance.

BUY IN: To cover or liquidate a sale.

BUY ON CLOSE: To buy at close of a trading session at a price prevailing at that time. *Buy on opening* means to buy at a price within the range at the opening of a trading session.

BUYER'S MARKET: Market in which more goods are available than buyers wish to buy, thus giving buyers the upper hand and hence buyer's market. Usually results in lower prices.

CARRYING CHARGE: Charges incurred in carrying the actual commodity including interest, insurance, and storage.

CCC: Commodity Credit Corporation. Wholly government-owned corporation established in 1933 to assist agriculture through price support programs and other measures.

CFTA: Commodity Futures Trading Commission. The federal agency which regulates trading on the commodity exchanges in this country and also administers the Commodity Exchange Act.

CONTRACT: A unit of the commodity being traded. The amount of the unit is set for each commodity by the exchange where it is traded.

CORNER: To get control over readily available supply of a commodity (or stock) so that the individuals who have obtained the corner can manipulate the commodity's price.

COVER: Shorts are said to "cover" when they buy back the contracts they had previously sold, thereby liquidating their position.

CURRENT DELIVERY: Delivery during the current month.

DAY ORDERS: Limited orders that are to be executed the day for which they are effective and are automatically canceled at the close of that day.

DELIVERY MONTH: The calendar month during which a futures contract matures.

DISCRETIONARY ACCOUNT: Account under which you specifically authorize your broker to place buy and sell orders for you—without your having to give the broker your consent prior to each order. Your broker, in short, has "discretion" over your account.

FILL OR KILL ORDER: Order which requires that it be either executed at once or that it be canceled.

FUTURES CONTRACT: Agreement to buy and receive or to sell and deliver a commodity at a future date and in accord with established rules.

HARD SPOT: Period of strength in a commodity market usually due to heavy buying.

HEDGE: In its simplest form, a hedge is a sale of a commodity futures contract against a purchase of spots, or vice versa. It is a medium through which offsetting commitments are employed to eliminate or minimize the impact of an adverse price movement on inventories or other previous commitments.

LIMIT: Maximum fluctuation in the price of a futures contract permitted during one trading session as fixed by the rules of a contract market.

LONG: Person who is on the buying side of an unhedged futures contract.

MARGIN: The amount which you deposit with your broker as a guarantee that you will fulfill your financial obligation in cases of losses on contracts being carried or to be carried by the brokers. In the commodity market, margins generally range between 5 and 20 per cent of the actual value of the contract.

MARGIN CALL: Demand by your broker for additional funds to cover losses in the event of a price decline in the commodity for which you own a contract—in order to restore your deposit to original level required or maintenance requirements. Or a margin call may be the demand to deposit the original margin at the time of the transaction.

MARKET ORDER: Order to your broker to buy or sell a futures contract at the best possible price as soon as received.

OPEN ORDER: Buy or sell order which is considered good unless and until you cancel it.

OPEN OUTCRY: Method of registering all bids and offers to buy or sell commodities in the pits.

PAPER PROFIT: Profit on paper that holder of the commodity contract has and that can be realized on sale of the commodities.

PITS: Platforms (locations) on the trading floor of a commodity exchange on which traders and brokers stand as they trade in particular commodities.

POSITION: Your stake in the commodity market—via long or short ownership of a futures contract.

PYRAMIDING: Using profits of open or unliquidated positions to add to your original position.

RING: Same as "Pit," above.

ROUND TURN: Completion of your order to buy a futures contract and, later, to sell it as well. Or, vice versa, completion of both a sale and purchase order.

SELLER'S MARKET: Market in which amount of goods available is less than amount buyers want to purchase—hence, favoring the seller (seller's market) and resulting in better sale conditions or higher prices.

SPOT COMMODITIES: Same as "Actuals," above.

STOP LOSS ORDER: Order to buy or to sell a futures contract when the market reaches a given price. Primarily used as a protection to limit your losses or protect profits.

VISIBLE SUPPLY: Amount of a particular commodity in store at loading centers.

24

HOW TO INVEST IN LAND

WHERE TO FIND IT . . . CONDOMINIUMS, CO-OPS, MOBILE HOMES, ETC.

The following pages are devoted to the fundamental rules for successful investing in land and nothing else. You will find the guides you want on investing in condominiums and co-ops—primarily as homes for yourselves—in Chapter 13, "A Roof Over Your Head," particularly pages 565–69. You will find the rules on mobile homes and similar housing in the same chapter. You also will find the details you need on mortgages and other points about financing of homes in that chapter. And you'll find a rundown on the Bafflegab of Real Estate at the end of that chapter.

Any investment in commercial real estate is far too complex a subject for treatment here. If this is the sort of investment or speculation you are seeking, you will of course go beyond the basics in this chapter on how to invest in land and will obtain thoroughly professional advice.

As for investments in single-family homes or small apartment complexes, these can be very risky, disappointing ventures indeed. A vacancy in a one-family house of a couple of months can wipe out your profit for a year. In a small apartment complex, if you aren't a handyman and can't handle all the servicing work on your own, you're "dead" anyway.

Apartments can be good investments under the right circumstances but if they are under 20 units yours has to be a Mom and Pop operation. You will have to work around the clock and count your labor as given for love only in order to service the frills your tenants will demand—ranging from laundry rooms to swimming pools. If you hire a handyman, he could take care of a 30-apartment unit as easily as a 20-apartment unit, but then you are getting into the problems of major labor expenses and inadequate caliber of help. For all these reasons and more, these forms of real estate investment are beyond the scope of this chapter, which will give you only the basics on buying land.

"Of all millionaires, 90 per cent became so through owning real estate. More money has been made in real estate than in all industrial investments combined. The wise young man or wage earner should invest his money in real estate," Andrew Carnegie, the great steel tycoon, once remarked.

The value of raw land in this country has risen in recent years at an *average* of 10 to 20 per cent a year. Between 1950 and 1970, the value of a single acre of U.S. farm land *on average* more than tripled. In the early 1970s some 50,000 to 100,000 farms were being sold each year.

Prices of homesites for single-family houses and prices paid for industrial sites also have been rising on a similar scale throughout the United States.

Over the years, fortunes, large and small, have been made in land—for suburban housing developments, vacation resorts, shopping centers, industrial plant sites, even in reclaimed swamp and desert land. What's more, many different types of investors have become involved—individuals, partnerships, other groups of individuals, syndicates, corporations, land developers, etc.

So let's say you've been watching your friends, neighbors, and associates invest sizable chunks of their nest eggs in raw, undeveloped land—as a long-term hedge against inflation. Let's say you've also been watching these people chalk up much bigger profits than you have been able to make elsewhere, and you know that the interest earned on your dollars in a savings account hasn't even offset what those dollars have lost in buying power in recent years. But how can you, the amateur investor, get a piece of the action in land? To guide you, here are both sides of the story of real estate as an investment today.

DISADVANTAGES OF BUYING LAND

(1) In all parts of the country, property taxes have soared—and taxes, of course, are a major part of the cost of landownership. Moreover, property taxes tend to leap with each sale.

(2) High interest rates add heavily to the cost of real estate you buy with borrowed money.

(3) To invest in real estate, you generally must be prepared to commit a sizable sum of money—say $10,000 or more—in order to turn any significant profit. You can obtain a stake in securities with much less.

(4) Real estate is one of the least liquid of all investments, and it may take months or years to dispose of a property at a price you approve. Realtors' commissions, when you sell, can cost 10 per cent or more of the selling price.

(5) Some forms of real estate—such as land slated for recreational purposes—are highly vulnerable in any period of business recession. So an investor in this type of land must be prepared to accept such risks and be prepared to sit out a prolonged downturn. In the depression of the 1930s there

was simply *no* market at all and in 1974, the market became exceedingly "sticky." (The "advantage" side of this was that you could pick up tremendous bargains at tax auctions.)

(6) There is no formal market for buying and selling real estate, as there is for trading securities. And there is no really solid way for the small investor to investigate and compare values in various parts of the country.

ADVANTAGES OF BUYING LAND

(1) The key advantage, of course, is the relatively high return you can achieve over the long term on any sound investment in real estate.

(2) By investing in real estate and making your profit on land, you can get favorable tax treatment when you sell because your land profits are treated as capital gains.

(3) You can get the great benefit of "leverage," for you may be able to borrow between 60 and 75 per cent of the cost of the property and thus tie up only a small amount of your own capital. To illustrate how leverage works, let's say you invest in a $10,000 parcel of land with a $3,000 down payment; you get a ten-year mortgage for the remaining $7,000 at 8 per cent interest a year. And let's say you're able to resell at $15,000 after two years, which isn't an unrealistic achievement. Your monthly mortgage payments on the $7,000 loan are $85 and after two years you've paid off $1,000 in principal and $1,040 in interest (tax-deductible). Your net profit on the deal is $3,960 ($15,000 less $11,040)— but your total outlay has been just $5,040. That's an 80 per cent profit in only two years!

(4) Finally, debt in itself is a hedge against inflation because you borrow "expensive" dollars, repay with increasingly "cheap" dollars over the years.

Let's assume you feel the advantages win. Let's assume, therefore, that even though you're a complete amateur you have decided to try a modest investment in land.

WHERE ARE THE BARGAINS?

If you're an amateur, a good place to begin your search for sound investments in land is in your own "back yard." The reasons are obvious. You've been living with local trends in real estate. Here is where you've watched the process of buying and selling among neighbors, friends, and outsiders. You undoubtedly know quite a bit about prices now being paid and about how those prices dwarf those paid five or ten years ago. You have a good idea of what is and what isn't a bargain.

If you live in any major suburb, you almost surely have seen prices climb steeply to levels often double or triple those of the early 1960s (the prices are astronomical in some wealthy suburbs, and thus the dollar totals don't mean much). What's more, there is no sign of anything more than an interruption in these trends in the years directly ahead.

Here, according to the National Association of Real Estate Boards and other key sources, are some of the best places to shop for reasonably priced raw land with a good profit potential:

(1) In the suburbs. Although prices in many areas seem dreadfully inflated, reasonable buys still do exist—and with more than 70 per cent of our expanding population continuing to congregate in the nation's major metropolitan areas, the likelihood is for sustained price advances in the years ahead. Consult local real estate agents on going prices for various types of land in this category; on zoning matters affecting property which appeals to you; on current population growth trends; plans for new or expanded public services, schools, hospitals, bus lines, recreational facilities, etc.

(2) Areas just beyond the suburbs.

(3) Exurbs—areas beyond the suburbs but still accessible to major city facilities—into which increasing numbers of corporations have moved, followed, of course, by the movement of employees and their families, with obvious impact on land values. If you are investing in land with the objective of later resale for industrial use, though, be warned: *musts are adequate transportation facilities,* appropriate utilities, labor sources.

(4) Recreational areas—particularly "water-oriented" land near lakes, rivers, fishing brooks and streams, shore lines within three to five hours' drive of major metropolitan areas.

(5) Commercially zoned real estate near airports and with good accessibility to the airports. Industrial parks are burgeoning in these areas as reliance on air freight increases.

(6) Any land within the boundaries of any U.S. megalopolis with some very special attribute: a beautiful view, woodlands, a tempting body of water, a very attractive location. You'll have to pay extra for these special aspects. But the future profit potential also is likely to be much greater than the potential for an ordinary parcel of land.

(7) Properties already in the process of change and upgrading by others —through the installation of new public facilities, planned new roads or highway interchanges, parking facilities, an urban renewal or rural beautification project, a new town, a reservoir or park or man-made lake.

TEN RULES FOR INVESTING IN LAND

What I have given you in this short chapter is only a primer—for if you are going into investing in land in a serious way, what you need most at this beginning stage is an easy-to-read guide outlining the most basic points for you in broad strokes. Then you can carry on to find the facts which will tell you whether your specific investment is the right one for you.

What, then, are the fundamental rules for investing in land for you, an amateur?

(1) *Before* you invest, get answers to this key question: How can the land actually be used when you sell it? For housing? Fishing? Hunting? Swimming? Enjoying a good climate? Skiing? Shopping center? Retirement homes? Summer vacations? Winter vacations? Industrial parks? Your profit when you resell the land will depend largely on the uses to which the buyer can put it.

(2) Also *before* you invest, find out from local census statistics, local realtors, gossipy individual citizens, other sources in the area: Are there local shortages of housing and available land? How fast is the section which interests you growing? (This rate could be obscured by the growth rate for the area as a whole.) Is the land suitable for building? What have similar properties been selling for?

(3) Calculate how much money you would have to invest to turn the property into one which you could resell at a maximum profit. Or will time alone probably bring you adequate profits on a resale? An investment could be brutally costly, entail bringing in telephone lines, building a road, cutting views, clearing, finding and drilling for water, on and on.

(4) Study the possibilities of making the land earn money during the period in which you are waiting to resell. Among the choices: planting trees, raising some other crop, selling timber rights, charging admissions to hunters and campers, renting pasture land. Other ideas will be suggested by what nearby owners do.

(5) If you intend to resell a part of the property right away, sell the less valuable parts first. The more desirable parts of the land tend to grow more rapidly in value.

(6) Be on guard if a property is advertised as a "distress sale." However, notes Don G. Campbell, author of *The Handbook of Real Estate Investment,* "hell hath no fury like a property owner whose love affair with a piece of real estate has flagged"—so at least investigate the "distress."

(7) Try to gauge what the effect of various national economic developments will be on the value or salability of any land you buy. For instance, if a business recession, fuel shortages, or similar misfortunes dampened sales of vacation properties, could you hold on until the nation was again in a strong upturn?

(8) Shop for the best possible financing deal—a fundamental point which becomes particularly important in any period of high or rising interest rates. If you can arrange a comparatively favorable mortgage rate and if you can pass on this mortgage to a future buyer, this could be a real "plus."

(9) Avoid ultra-cheap, undeveloped land in the middle of nowhere—especially if it's being pushed in high-pressure promotions. There are millions

of acres of raw land that are just as unwanted and undeveloped now as they were two hundred years ago.

(10) And study books about land as an investment. Get the most expert advice you can find (and be willing to pay for it). Treat this investment with the respect it demands!

25

HOW TO INVEST
"FAR OUT"

Now let's say you're more venturesome and want to go beyond the traditional areas of investment—to probe other channels for profit. Let's say that it's the unlikely risk which challenges your imagination, the unusual purchase which appeals to your investment sense.

If so, you're not nearly as out of step as you might think. You are, in fact, in harmony with tens of billions of dollars of "smart money" which has been and is being poured into what I call the "far-out investments"— books which are not for reading, paintings and sculptures which are not for viewing, cattle herds and citrus groves which are never even seen by their owners.

There's more than a whit of fact to the old gag which has a wheeler-dealer trying to unload a railroad car full of sardines on a skeptical buyer who soon discovers that the sardines are rotten. "But these are not *eating* sardines," protests the fast-talking salesman, "these are just *buying* and *selling* sardines!"

Okay, let's say it, then. You have this sort of investment sense, you are intrigued by unusual purchases, you have a modest sum to play with, and you are willing to study the basics of the far-out investments of the late twentieth century. This chapter is for *you*.

COINS

How would you like to buy an ordinary 1964 50¢ piece for twice its face value?

Or a 1940 quarter for $7.50—30 times its face value?
Or a 1950 nickel for $10.00—200 times its face value?
Or a 1909 penny for $5.00—500 times its face value?

These were actual prices paid for these coins, as the mid-1970s approached, by collectors, investors, and speculators the nation over.

The reason why the 50¢ piece brought $1.00 was that it was minted in honor of President John F. Kennedy the year after he was assassinated and immediately became a much sought-after sentimental coin.

The reason why the quarter sold for $7.50 was that it was all silver, had never been circulated, and was in excellent condition.

The explanation for the $10 nickel was that this batch of Jefferson nickels was minted in Denver in very limited quantities.

And the explanation for the high-priced penny was that 1909 was the first year the Lincoln penny was issued and thus it carried the initials of its designer, Victor D. Brenner.

There has been a phenomenal upsurge in recent years in the values of many types of coins—and some astute collectors among the nation's estimated 10 million have seen the value of their holdings double or triple.

HOW TO APPRAISE A COLLECTION OF COINS

What are the chances that the cigar box full of collected coins left by one of your ancestors is worth millions? The chances are small. Your "collection" is probably nothing more than an "accumulation." But if you have reason to believe you may own valuable pieces:

(1) Take the collection to two or three respected dealers in your area and ask what each would pay *for the entire collection,* not just the best pieces. Dealers may legitimately charge for this appraisal—it takes time and expertise—5 to 10 per cent of the collection's value.

(2) Do not make your own inventory of the coins in order to present it to a dealer for appraisal. He wants to see the coins themselves.

(3) And do not attempt to clean the coins. A poor job can drastically reduce a coin's value.

HOW TO BUY COINS AS AN INVESTMENT

What, though, if you want to buy coins as an investment?

Then, since the general price trend of well-selected coins is strongly up, the odds are you'll make money in coins if you follow the following fundamentals.

Don't, especially as a beginner, try to collect every type of coin. Instead, specialize—say, in ancient Greek or Roman coins, or gold coins, or U.S. nickels. Read extensively on your specialty. Before making any major investment, consult a known specialist in the field.

Do buy the best examples of coins you can. As a general rule, choose one coin costing $10 over 10 coins costing $1.00 apiece. One reason is that dealers' profit margins on many less expensive coins are greater than on a single higher-priced coin. And, over the long range, the better coins are the ones most likely to rise the most in value.

Don't fall for the coin "fads" or for new, publicly touted foreign sets of coins. One runaway fad was the 1964 Kennedy proof set (a specially packaged penny, nickel, dime, quarter, and half dollar, issued by the U.S. mint) which sold for as much as $26 in 1965, then dropped back to a fraction of its high. In recent years several foreign governments have been selling virtually worthless proof sets of coins in fancy leather cases for $30 or more to small-time dealers and unsophisticated collectors. One such set, which speculators bid up to $30 or more, slid right back to $5.00.

Do guard against counterfeit coins and forgeries—by dealing strictly with well-established dealers. There are counterfeits for every type of valuable coin, but a knowledgeable dealer can almost always detect the phonies. And a reputable dealer will give you a written guarantee that he'll rebuy any coin from you if it isn't genuine.

Don't, as a small investor, count on turning a quick profit in coins. Be prepared to hold for the long term. Keep accurate records of your purchases and check the coin market regularly so you'll know whether you're making or losing money on your holdings.

Do beware of coins which appear to be grossly underpriced; there's probably something wrong with them. Chances of finding colossal bargains are small unless you know a lot more than the dealer. However, bargains do occur simply because there are so many different types of coins and so many millions of individual coins and sets available.

Don't deal with unknown mail order coin dealers or fly-by-nights. Not long ago one mail order swindler pleaded guilty to a scheme in which the public paid him more than $37,000 for coins they never received.

Do beware of hoarding on the basis of rumors—e.g., that the Treasury plans to withdraw a certain type of currency from circulation, and thus it might multiply in value.

Do remember, finally, these most basic rules on coins:

Value depends *not* on the age of the coin, its face value, the price originally paid.

Value *does* depend on the coin's rarity, its condition, collectors' demand for it, its date and mint mark—and its legitimacy.

RARE BOOKS AND MANUSCRIPTS

The soaring values of rare books and manuscripts have not made front-page or financial-page news and you, a new investor, almost surely have not thought of this as an appropriate field for your funds.

But the price rises are indisputable. And the likelihood is overwhelming that values will continue to climb in the years immediately ahead.

As one striking illustration of the long-term trend, a thirteenth-century English illuminated Bible sold in the late 1960s for $500,000, up from $180,000 in ten years.

Also in the 1960s prices of handwritten (by monk-scribes) books from the period around A.D. 1400, especially those containing illuminated miniatures, tripled.

Between the early 1950s and the early 1970s, single pages of the Gutenberg Bible rose in value from $600 to $3,500 or more, with pages of exceptional interest going for as much as $10,000.

Not long ago a "first edition" of the United States Constitution sold for $150,000 and an original copy of the Declaration of Independence went for $404,000.

PITFALLS IN RARE BOOK INVESTING

Can you, an amateur, cash in on today's rare book boom? Are there basic rules to guide you? When I put these questions to one of the world's leaders in this field, his first reaction was: "The book business is strictly for the connoisseur. An amateur would be a complete fool to try to make a killing in this game." And here's why:

Let's say a neophyte buys a prize first edition for $10,000. But he then finds that the "errata" page or the fly leaf (before the title page) is missing. Suddenly the book's value plunges to $6,000.

Or he buys a rare book and finds it has been rebound, slashing it to one fourth of its value if it were in its original "boards." (On the other hand, if it is the *only* copy of a rare book in its original boards, it may be worth twenty times the value of other copies.)

Notes this dealer: "Even many experts don't know some of these fine points, so how can the amateur be expected to know?"

Another problem is that there are very, very few hard, universal rules on rare book values. (One exception: any book printed in Boston before 1700 is valuable because these were the earliest Anglo-American books.) In addition, though the most valuable books and manuscripts (in the $3,000 to $300,000 range) are virtually recession proof, even a minor economic downturn can glut the market with "weakly held" lesser-valued books and manuscripts and force their prices down.

Finally, the "real diamonds" of rare books today are exceedingly rare, primarily because they are all traveling a one-way street into the world's great libraries, museums, universities, or the hands of enormously wealthy collectors who, for tax purposes, plan to leave their libraries to such institutions. Examples are Gutenberg Bibles, first editions of Shakespeare, Dante, Chaucer, the illuminated manuscripts of the ninth to sixteenth centuries, original copies of the U. S. Declaration of Independence and the U. S. Constitution.

THREE KEY FIELDS FOR PROFITABLE INVESTING

Nevertheless, there are always a few fields in which you, the amateur, can invest modest sums in the expectation that your investment can swell significantly. Here are some guidelines:

As a general rule, rare book values are based on rarity, beauty, importance, and condition. But the value of any rare book can vary widely. Therefore, if your personal library contains a volume which you have reason to believe is exceedingly valuable, seek the advice of a rare book specialist (for example, in American history, English literature, etc.). The specialist could be a library or museum curator, a university professor, or a reputable dealer.

More specifically, here are three fields in which you might invest a portion of your savings with a reasonable expectation of seeing your investment grow in the years ahead:

(1) *Medical and scientific papers* on important discoveries and inventions. In this category, values have been soaring. All the great breakthroughs of modern times have appeared as articles in scientific or medical journals, generally available at very low cost when published. All you, the collector, need do is read the newspapers to learn of the important developments. As an indication of what is happening: as recently as the 1950s, a copy of the journal in which Einstein's *Theory of Relativity* appeared (published in Leipzig in 1916) was worth $40 to $50; in the mid-seventies it was worth $750. In the mid-1950s a copy of Newton's *Principia Mathematica* sold for $600 to $800; less than two decades later, it sold for as much as $14,000. Also in this period, Copernicus' *De Revolutionibus* (1543) soared from $1,500 to $35,000.

A similar trend is logical for the original papers on such breakthroughs as penicillin, polio vaccine, the transistor, tranquilizers, atomic fission, jet propulsion, the synthesis of DNA, birth control innovations, etc. A $3.00 investment in a well-chosen scientific article can turn into a $50 to $100 value in less than a decade. *Your key rule: keep the entire issue* of the journal in which the article appears—in perfect condition.

(2) *First editions of modern young authors and playwrights who show great literary promise.* Since 1950 well-selected examples of modern literature have more than quintupled in value. Between the early 1960s and mid-1970s, one edition of James Joyce's *Ulysses,* illustrated by Matisse, soared in value from $165 to $1,200.

But if you try collecting first editions, handle with utmost care! If the pages are uncut, don't cut them. Don't even open or read them. Don't remove the dust jacket. Just wrap them in plastic and put them carefully aside.

(3) *Children's books with "a certain eternity."* In the early 1970s a first edition of *Pinocchio* (Carlo Lorenzini, 1880) was selling for $500 to

$800; Heinrich Hoffman's *Slovenly Peter* (*Struwwelpeter,* 1846) was selling for $25,000 to $30,000; Lewis Carroll's *Alice in Wonderland* for $10,000 to $20,000. One reason for these high values is that perfect copies of *any* children's books are rare. My own choices for more recent children's books which could become classics are the Dr. Seuss books, the Hobbit books, *Peter Rabbit,* and *Stuart Little.*

Incidentally, *comic books* fall into this category. But if you want to stash some of these away, make sure they're in perfect condition and also have that "aura of eternity."

If you follow these basic rules, if you're willing and able to hold the "growth" volumes you buy, if you keep them in perfect condition—your chances of seeing your investment grow substantially are excellent.

POSTAGE STAMPS

Would you pay $380,000 for two tiny chits of paper measuring less than one inch square each? This is precisely what a New Orleans stamp dealer did not long ago for a couple of 1847 1¢ stamps from the Indian Ocean island of Mauritius. "But why?" I asked the well-known international stamp auctioneer who sold them. "Why would anybody bid $380,000 for a couple of postage stamps?"

"Because," explained he, "the Mauritius stamps combine just about every element of value in stamps today."

(*1*) *Rarity.* Only 14 of these 1847 Mauritius stamps, all hand-printed with primitive printing techniques, are known to exist. Of the few letters existing with these stamps on them the letter with these "two tiny chits of paper" is considered by far the finest in quality.

(*2*) *Demand.* Stamps from Mauritius always have been a favorite of collectors. Interest by U.S. collectors goes back to 1860, only two decades after stamps were first issued in Great Britain.

(*3*) *Condition of the Stamps.* In the case of these two stamps, there were no tears or creases, no defects or thin spots, no heavy cancellation marks. Margins around the design were wide and even, a factor which can spell a difference of thousands or even tens of thousands of dollars in value.

The Mauritius stamps would be even more valuable if they contained a *typographical error.* As a classic example of the effect of printing errors on stamp values, a 1918 24¢ U.S. airmail stamp with an upside-down airplane was worth some $35,000 to $40,000 in the mid-1970s—while the same stamp with a right-side-up plane was worth only $10 or so.

Another important prop for stamp values is the economic condition of the country in which the stamps are collected.

Yearly world-wide spending by collectors for stamps was recently calculated in the hundreds of millions of dollars and it's climbing sharply as more and more millions of people turn to stamps as an investment medium.

One reason is that postage stamps are a traditional hedge against inflation. Over the years, stamp values have held up better than most investments tied to an individual country (savings accounts, bonds, insurance, cash).

Another is that they have successfully ridden out national economic crises, primarily because the market for stamps is international.

A third is that the value of stamps can be extraordinarily high in relation to their tiny size. Hence they are easy to store and very portable.

And, finally, there are few national restrictions against buying and selling stamps, or taking them from one country to another—probably because such restrictions would be nearly impossible to enforce.

During the early 1970s U.S. stamp values rose an average of about 20 per cent a year and in many cases the increases were even more spectacular. In one unusual instance, a British Guiana 1¢ stamp which was bought in 1940 for $45,000 was auctioned in 1970 for $280,000!

DO'S AND DON'TS FOR INVESTING IN STAMPS

How then can you, the amateur, intelligently invest a portion of your capital in stamps to protect your savings against inflation and probably to make substantial profits too?

(1) *Do* start as a general collector, investing only small sums. Then develop a specialty—such as stamps of one type—air mail stamps or classic stamps, stamps from a particular country or region, stamps from a particular era. Study as much reliable literature as possible and attend as many auctions in your area as you can. Join a local stamp club and learn from experienced collectors.

(2) *Don't* waste your money on cheap packets of stamps. The odds that you'll find a valuable one are virtually nil because these packets are put together by experts who almost surely have snagged any valuable stamps before they get into the packet. The wholesale price of a typical collection of 5,000 stamps may be only $12.50.

(3) *Don't* buy up whole sheets of ordinary new stamps from this or that country—where a currency devaluation could slash their value. This goes for the United States too: the value of post-1943 U.S. stamps as collectors' items has remained at or below their face value and their sole use is as postage.

(4) *Do* stick to the higher-price specimens and avoid the typical 50 per cent retail markup on inexpensive examples. The big increases in values are taking place today in this high-priced category—particularly, nineteenth-century quality stamps and early air mail stamps.

(5) *Do*, if you find an old stamp collection in the attic and want to sell it, take it to one or two reputable stamp dealers and/or auctioneers. Ask

each how much he considers the whole collection to be worth. If the stamps are attached to the original letters, *don't* remove them, or you may slash their value to virtually nothing. A stamp professional may legitimately charge you for an assessment of your collection, if you do not end up selling it to him. Typically an auctioneer will charge you a commission of 20 per cent of the sale price of the collection for auctioning it, less if the collection is *very* valuable.

To make sure a stamp dealer is reputable (and quite a few aren't), check names with the American Stamp Dealers Association in New York City or one of its chapters in other big cities.

(6) *Do,* if you know nothing about stamps but still want to invest for profit, employ a knowledgeable dealer or other expert to advise you, to buy stamps for you at auction, or simply to sell you stamps he deems investment-worthy. Such agents today are representing increasing numbers of investors; their fees generally run about 5 to 10 per cent of the cost price of stamps bought. Serious collectors and top stamp auctioneers can steer you to good advisers or, in the case of some auctioneers, advise you.

(7) *Do* beware of improbable "bargains" of any sort. Errors and varieties can be manufactured and apparent quality improved by a "stamp doctor" for the sole purpose of fleecing the unwary. On such "bargains," get advice from a reputable dealer, a trusted expert friend, or a reputable committee of stamp experts (usually part of the large philatelic societies) which issue certificates of stamp authenticity.

In the words of Milton Ozaki, a Colorado stamp broker and author of *How to Play the Stamp Market:* "The stamp market is . . . an exciting investment frontier, very similar to the commodity markets of thirty years ago."

DIAMONDS

Large, top-quality diamonds also have in recent years outrun many traditional investments. And the temptation to make this traditional gift also a superb investment is very great. Since diamonds have been celebrated in song and folklore through the ages, the across-the-board appeal of this medium is undeniable. On top of this, in cities across the land and in New York especially, there are well-defined areas in which "secondhand" diamonds reputedly bought from estates, impoverished owners, etc., are daily advertised as "bargains"!

Diamonds are widely considered a hedge against inflation and against currency devaluation because diamond supplies are limited (De Beers Consolidated Mines in South Africa controls an estimated 85 to 95 per cent of

the world production); no government can effectively control diamond ownership or diamond exports although many countries impose controls on exports
of currencies; buying and selling diamonds can be a tax dodger's dream if
the transactions are carried out in cash; diamonds also can be passed on from
generation to generation "tax-free."

But at the same time a key drawback to buying diamonds for profit is
the cold fact that the people who make profits in diamonds are primarily
dealers in the gems who buy and sell at wholesale prices. The rest of us
generally must buy at retail and sell at wholesale—a disadvantage indeed,
considering that, typically, the diamond retailer's markup is a minimum of
30 per cent and often as high as 50 to 100 per cent.

And a new possible drawback is that future processes for producing
imitation diamonds may undercut the demand for and thus depress the
prices of real diamonds.

BUY—BUT ONLY "IF . . ."

Under the circumstances and in view of the trends would it be wise for
you to invest part of your nest egg in diamonds or other gems which have
been skyrocketing in price? In the opinion of a cross section of experts on
inflation hedges, precious metals, and exotic investments of many types, the
answer is a very highly qualified "Yes—but only if . . ."

(1) *If* you are willing and able to keep the gems—diamonds, sapphires,
emeralds, rubies, etc.—ten years. Big price fluctuations occur from year to
year and if you are forced to resell your diamond after a year or two you
easily can take a licking on the deal.

(2) *If* you stick to highest-priced, largest diamonds. Specifically, diamonds under one and one half to two carats, costing under $1,500 to
$2,000 per carat, should not even be considered as an investment. When you
are investing, you should aim at the four-carat-and-up range, costing more
than $5,000 per carat.

(3) *If* you restrict your buying to the highest-quality diamonds, classified as truly colorless and flawless. As one diamond expert put it: "Simply
the best quality is not good enough." This rule—buy only the highest
quality—also applies to sapphires, emeralds, and rubies: to be meaningful as
an investment, these should cost in the tens of thousands of dollars.

(4) *If* you avoid paying for special settings and other decorations adorn-
ing a diamond. These drastically raise the retail price of a gem and tend to
have little or no investment value.

(5) *If* you deal only with a top, highly reputable, big-city jeweler on
whose investment advice you can rely and in whose appraisal of a gem
you have implicit trust. Another factor favoring big-city jewelers or diamond

dealers is that small-town stores often do not carry the size and quality gems required for a worth-while investment.

HOW TO SHOP FOR DIAMOND "BARGAINS"

Now, what about the diamond "bargains"? How real are they and where are they to be found? How do you shop for the best possible deal in diamonds?

There are no "bargains" in diamonds and a chase after one may lead you to a distinct non-bargain. As for the diamonds which are advertised at "drastically reduced prices" in retail stores, no retailer—even one forced to go out of business—needs to slash his diamond prices to the public when he can simply put in a telephone call or two to a wholesaler who will pay him just what his stock is actually worth. The "reduced" price you pay is just what the stone is worth.

There are no diamond "bargains" at estate auctions either. Not in the stones themselves. At an auction there are not only professional diamond dealers but also government appraisers for inheritance tax purposes, insurance company appraisers, and often appraisers representing the estate itself. Against such an array of experts, how could you, the amateur, expect to find a hidden bargain?

What about the auctions put on by the U. S. Customs Service, which intercepts diamonds from smugglers? Here again you're up against an army of professionals. Before a customs auction, notice goes out to diamond wholesalers and others in the trade. The bidding may start low but, by the time it stops, prices offered will almost surely be at or very near the actual value of the stone. You're an amateur. You can't expect to walk into a diamond auction and outsmart men whose livelihoods depend on their ability to judge diamond values.

What are the strictly financial facts about stolen diamonds which find their way back into commercial channels? No bargains here either—not to mention the fact that if you buy a stolen diamond you're party to an illegal transaction. Here, you're dealing with a black marketeer whose merchandise may have traveled a long, devious underground route before it gets to you— with price markups at each stop. No reputable dealer will touch a stolen diamond, and any buyer will have to trust the word of an unscrupulous seller on the stone's worth. Moreover, since diamonds are individual and often can be traced, crooks will frequently try to disguise the stones by recutting—and often they botch the job.

The fundamental point about shopping for bargains in diamonds is that the gem's value is directly dependent on the "four C's"—carat (weight), color, cut, and clarity. There are standard yardsticks throughout the trade, and generally each reputable dealer will evaluate a given diamond at around the same price.

HOW TO SPOT A DIAMOND GYP

No agency of the law—federal, state, or local—or any Better Business Bureau or any jewelers' trade association can possibly stringently police the individual sale of diamonds through retail outlets. Even so-called "reputable" jewelers have been known to palm off inferior diamonds to an unknowledgeable consumer, hiding the deception by incorrect and collusive appraisals. Your fundamental guide is obvious: buy only from an established jeweler whose reputation you can trust.

You also may be able to detect an unscrupulous dealer if he tries to sell you:

(1) A perfect blue-white diamond, unless it is truly colorless and flawless. Because the term "blue-white" has been misused so much, most reputable dealers do not use it.

(2) An artificially colored diamond. This is a genuine diamond of poor color. The diamond may be painted or coated to disguise its yellowish color. In either case, a jeweler must state in writing before the diamond is sold what treatment was used, under penalty of fine and jail.

(3) A piggyback diamond. This is a small diamond placed in close proximity to another, with the mounting hiding the separations of the stones and making the two small diamonds look like one large one. Dishonest jewelers will try to sell this as, say, "one carat in diamonds" or some other deceptive advertising.

(4) An imitation or simulated diamond which will look like the real thing. Its chemical term, though, will be "colorless synthetic sapphire," or "synthetic rutile," or "strontium titanite."

A PERSONAL OPINION

Even assuming the long-term potential for profit in diamonds is good, I would be cool—for I dislike the wide retail-wholesale gap, the fact that an investor must tie up large sums of money for five, ten, or more years, the "taste" of the dealing, all the warnings I've felt compelled to give you here.

But that's a personal opinion. If you can follow the rules of the game as underlined and summarized above, diamonds could be the ideal far-out investment for you.

ART

A gag making the rounds of the Madison Avenue art gallery world has an aggressive dowager accosting a gallery director with the demand: "I'd like to see your growth paintings." The gag isn't far off.

An Edinburgh art teacher made world-wide headlines a few years ago when she sold for $537,600 a picture which had hung unrecognized in her modest living room for fifteen years and which had once been valued at $50.

New York's Metropolitan Museum of Art made even bigger headlines in late 1970 when it bought a Velazquez portrait for $5,544,000.

Sales of paintings of major importance in the $1 million range are becoming increasingly common. A Van Gogh sold for $1,300,000 and a Rembrandt self-portrait for $1,519,200—in both instances, hundreds of thousands of dollars more than these works might have brought a few years earlier.

Prices of French Impressionist paintings also have multiplied, along with British eighteenth- and nineteenth-century paintings, twentieth-century European paintings, seventeenth-century Italian paintings.

Among individual artists, the upsurge also has been spectacular, particularly for Renoirs, Monets, Picassos, and Braques. The year-to year increases in Utrillos and Vlamincks have been almost unbelievable.

Prices in many art categories have risen so dramatically that it has been suggested that art prices be published daily in the newspapers—like stock quotations. Big-city department stores have opened art departments to offer original art works. Franchised art galleries have been set up from coast to coast. Art investment funds—mutual funds—have been organized to invest in works of art strictly for profit. In New York and Paris investment counselors, too, are offering advisory services in investment in art works. Young Americans are increasingly spending their extra money on paintings and sculptures—in many cases by their contemporaries—for the investment value as well as the aesthetic pleasure. Many wealthier young Americans are budgeting $10,000 and up a year for art works, along with their other profit-seeking investments. Big and small corporations are sinking substantial sums in paintings and sculptures—and not just for decoration. The objective is profits ultimately, as well.

What's behind the art boom?

As in the case in every one of the far-out investments detailed in this chapter, an obvious force is inflation. In a time of inflation, tangible, rare, valuable objects—ranging from rare books to nickelodeons, early farm implements, old wines, and early computers—are favorite investment media for so-called smart money.

A second factor is that we in this nation have reached unprecedented peaks of education achievement. We travel regularly to the world's cultural centers. We have developed the desire for art and obtained the means to satisfy the desire. At the same time tens of millions of us have become regular museum-goers. Before World War II there were only about 20 major art museums in the United States; today there are about 200. The museums—along with the universities—are not only stimulating our interest in buying art but also are helping to drive up prices through their own purchases of art works.

Finally, there are the basic forces of a steadily shrinking supply and a relentlessly growing long-term demand for the finest art works.

TEN RULES TO GUIDE YOU IN ART INVESTING

Let's say "art" is your choice of the areas covered in this chapter. Here are ten rules to guide you.

(1) Before you lay out a penny, invest as much time as you can reading art auction catalogs in a field which interests you, visiting galleries to see what works are available and how much they cost, inspecting art works before auctions, attending auctions to get the feel of them. You might even *subscribe* to art auction catalogs published by major galleries in the field of your interest. Many of these catalogs will give you, after each auction, prices paid for each item which appeared in the pre-auction catalog. *Keep* these catalogs for later comparisons of prices for various items.

Try to read all the scholarly books you can on your subject of specialization to help give you a feel for "good," "better," and "best" in quality and value.

(2) When you decide to buy, do so cautiously at first. Don't spend all you have on one item you think is a good buy.

(3) Make sure you have, also before you buy, a really special feeling about a painting or sculpture—a sense which tells you it has quality. Or have somebody who has this type of instinctive feeling represent you as a buyer or bidder at an art auction.

(4) Deal with a top gallery or art dealer. Don't be afraid to frequent the very best. Also, a top dealer is interested in holding your patronage. If you are not satisfied, he will make every effort to resell anything you bought for at least what you paid. Some dealers and major galleries will guarantee the authenticity of the art works they sell, in fact, so check this point as well.

(5) Have an understanding with your dealer or gallery about trading up—so he'll repurchase or resell your works as you have more money to invest in high-quality art. Also find out whether he'll let you and your prospective purchase have a "trial marriage"—by taking a picture home for a week or so before you make a final decision.

(6) Be wary of works by modern artists in current fashion. Inflated prices can easily be the result of an exhibit by a single major museum. But after the excitement of the show has subsided, prices tend to drop as well. Buying art works because they are a current rage is akin to buying stocks on tips at a cocktail party.

(7) If there is a museum director or curator in your community, ask for his advice on buying. Or use the services of specially assigned personnel at large art galleries whose job is to guide you.

(8) Decide, before you buy, how much money you can afford to invest

and stick to that ceiling. If you find a more expensive work irresistible, arrange to pay for it over a period of time.

(9) Unless you are an expert, spread your financial risks by investing in the works of a *variety* of different artists. Try at the same time however, to maintain a theme or unifying force in your collection.

(10) Buy the best examples you can afford in any category.

For buyers with limited funds, a *good* drawing by a given artist may be a better buy than a poor painting. You well may find artists who were overshadowed by the greats in the era in which they lived a better buy than new artists who have not been tested by time.

FIVE TYPES OF ART FOR RAPID "GROWTH"

The first essential, of course, is to learn and to obey the fundamental rules on how to shop for art works with profit in mind. But what types of art should you shop for? What types are likely to grow at a relatively rapid rate in the years ahead? These, according to top officials of one of the nation's leading galleries were some of the best bets as of the mid-seventies:

(1) *Almost any fine old master painting or drawing* is virtually certain to continue rising in value—even from today's lofty price levels—although probably at a slower rate than other art categories. As a major dealer says, "A good work of art is a good investment at the going price for its category. By the same token, a poor work of art, even at a very low price, is a bad investment."

You can get excellent original old master drawings for prices ranging up to $50,000 and more, but a surprising number are available for only a fraction of this amount. Get the advice of a reputable dealer on what *good* drawings by superb artists are available at reasonable prices.

(2) *Almost any good American painting* of a subject of unusual historical, social, or geographical interest also is likely to be a good investment. Some dealers feel there are bargains to be had in late nineteenth- and early twentieth-century paintings by respected American artists of the Hudson River School (Thomas Cole, Thomas Doughty, Asher Durand, and their associates) and in good marine paintings by a variety of American artists. The price range for a large proportion of these is $1,000 to $10,000.

(3) *Artists of the nineteenth-century French Barbizon School* have been making a comeback. Good examples of their works are said to be good buys —at prices often in the $600 to $6,000 range.

(4) *Primitive art works,* such as authentic African wood carvings, pre-Columbian works such as sculptured figures, vessels, ceramics, are considered good investments. Patronize only the top-rated galleries for these, and expect to pay from a few hundred to a few thousand dollars. Primitive oceanic carvings (from the Southwest Pacific islands) cost as little as $50 to $100 or up to several thousands for large, elaborate carvings.

(5) *Classical antiquities* (small bronzes, pottery, and sculptures from the Mediterranean) are bound to rise in price, the dealers agree. Today you can build a fairly large and significant collection for about $30,000. Most individual art objects in this category cost only a few hundred dollars, if that much. A key rule is to specialize in a specific field.

ANTIQUES

I'll wager you never considered porcelain paperweights, pewter tableware, or old drugstore fittings as "just the place!" for your nest egg, but small fortunes are being made by sophisticated collectors of these as well as antique furniture, snuffboxes, many other objets d'art. To give you intriguing examples of soaring prices for antiques:

A pair of carved seventeenth-century English silver tankards (drinking mugs) which went for $47,700 in 1963 was auctioned late in 1968 in London for $134,400.

A few years ago an eighteenth-century American Paul Revere tea set brought $70,000 at New York's Sotheby Parke-Bernet Galleries art auction house—double the amount experts predicted—and a 5-inch sugar tongs fetched a staggering $5,250. The prices of some antique American silver pieces more than doubled during the 1960s.

Exceptional pieces of eighteenth-century French furniture were being sold in the early 1970s for more than $100,000. Single eighteenth-century French chairs brought $5,000 to $10,000.

Between 1950 and 1970 Chinese porcelain multiplied more than fifteen times in value, and continued to skyrocket into the early 1970s.

So it goes—and it is going this way in almost every class, period, and price range of antiques. The reasons are simple and apparently fundamental: first, the supply of antiques—technically defined as having been made more than a hundred years ago—is strictly limited; second, the investing public has concluded that antiques are an attractive haven for savings and has begun to stampede toward them.

In this atmosphere, you—either as the would-be investor in antiques or as the relatively naïve owner of potentially valuable items trying to decide whether or not to hold on or to sell now—stand to win or lose big. Which it is and to what extent will depend on whether you know and follow the basic rules for investing in antiques.

THE BASIC RULES FOR INVESTING IN ANTIQUES

If you are a beginner, concentrate on a specific category that interests you—such as American silver or African carvings or English glass or French tapestries. Subscribe to and *collect* literature and catalogs in your field. Study and watch prices in your field by surveying the dealers and by attending auctions.

If you buy at auction—and you often can save 25 per cent or more by buying at auction against retail—be sure to attend previews or showings of items before the auction. Examine each item that interests you—including inside drawers of furniture, hardware, etc.—and ask a lot of questions. Remember, anything you buy is returnable only if it has been misrepresented.

Note: A country auction may *not* be the place to find a bargain. Typically, plenty of real junk is offered at these auctions, side by side with better pieces. So don't become hypnotized into bidding fantastic amounts for things you neither want nor need. Don't be among the many who get stuck with wagonloads of white elephants.

If you are completely uninformed, hire a dependable dealer or connoisseur for a fee to represent you at an auction. No matter whether you buy at auction or at retail, keep in mind that the value depends on these key aspects of an antique:

Quality. How good an example is it?

Authenticity. Can the item's origin be properly verified?

Condition. What is the extent of repairs, restorations, and missing areas?

Rarity. Is it unique?

Age. Is the piece dated and can the date be verified?

Era and area. Is it from a period and country considered valuable by connoisseurs?

Buy the best examples you can afford.

FOUR CATEGORIES FOR BARGAINS IN ANTIQUES

Here are four categories in which experts at New York's Sotheby Parke-Bernet Galleries believed bargains still existed in the mid-1970s:

(1) *Late American Federal (or "Empire") furniture*—from the 1830–50 period. In pre-1830 early fine American Federal furniture, too, relatively lower-priced pieces still are available.

(2) *Mid-Victorian furniture* made in 1845–70, an often ugly, ornate category which goes in and out of fashion. As of the early 1970s, it was out of fashion and therefore inexpensive, but the statistical likelihood is that it will come into fashion again and values will rise.

(3) *Early American* textiles, including quilts and flags with some unique historic association.

(4) *Other Americana*, such as early hand-carved duck decoys, New England tinware, utensils of the post-Civil War period; late nineteenth-century decorative objects such as candelabra, fixtures, art pottery, and porcelains.

That you are a small investor isn't the drawback you might think. The great majority of the items sold by Sotheby Parke-Bernet went for under $1,000 in the mid-seventies and a very significant proportion went for $50 to $200.

Of course, there are disadvantages to antiques as an investment. Among them: they are perishable; they may be costly to maintain properly; the retail markup may be 100 per cent or more; they are subject to price fluctuations based on fashion; and they cannot necessarily be sold quickly at top prices.

But the key advantages of investing in antiques are that—aside from the strong chance of substantial increase in values—you can also develop a happy hobby of collecting and you can decorate your home at least temporarily with the antiques you buy.

PRINTS

Among the far-out investments which always have held up remarkably well through bad times as well as good are the graphic arts: prints, etchings, engravings.

Specifically, in the early sixties, an original signed Matisse lithograph entitled "Seated Odalisque," from an edition of 50, was priced at $350. Only ten years later the quote for this print was $5,000.

In recent years a well-known Rembrandt etching known as the "Hundred Guilder" print has sold for $40,000 and other Rembrandts have sold for as much as $77,000. Prices of old master prints multiplied thirty-seven times between 1951 and 1969, far outpacing even the spectacular rises for old master paintings.

One signed Mary Cassatt color etching which sold in 1959 for $150 brought $7,500 in the early 1970s. In the early 1960s, a Picasso linoleum cut entitled "After Cranach" was priced at $600. An example of this edition (of 50) more recently sold for $50,000.

This illustrates the "print explosion." What are the forces behind this boom?

(1) The numbers of print dealers have been multiplying and as these have bought up prints to build their inventories they have had an obvious impact on prices. In the early sixties, there were no more than 20 top print dealers in the United States. Today there are hundreds of "outlets," including not only galleries and print shops but also department store boutiques, bookstores, picture frame and gift shops.

(2) The numbers of collectors, particularly young Americans who cannot afford the prices asked for paintings and sculptures by major artists, also have been multiplying. These have added to the demand and in the process have lifted prints out of a second-class status and into an artistic niche of their

own. In fact, one leading print dealer notes, "It has now become a status symbol to have a collection of fine prints."

(3) And art investors along with art investment funds have begun to flock to the print market. These are now openly competing with the collectors of art for art's sake.

BASIC RULES FOR BUYING PRINTS

The print market—like other similar markets—is plagued by its share of fly-by-nights, forgers, and unscrupulous dealers. Hundreds of Chagall "original" lithographs have been clipped out of books and French publications, dressed up with fake signatures and "limited edition" numbers, and sold for ridiculously inflated prices.

High-pressure auctioneers have been known to offer examples from large editions (300 to 400 impressions) by artists who are described as fabulous and famous by the auctioneers—but who are, in fact, unknown to the rest of the art world. How then can *you* avoid paying big sums for forged prints and other non-originals? How can *you* find etchings, engravings, lithographs, or other types of prints to adorn your living-room walls and at the same time see your purchases grow in value in coming years?

A fundamental first point is that prints can be either originals or reproductions. An original print, as defined by the prestigious Print Council of America, comes from a plate, block, stone, or other medium on which an image has been created *by the artist himself*. A reproduction, however, is a *copy* of a print or other art work made by photographic techniques, seldom under supervision by the artist.

Here are basic rules for buying prints, both for their artistic rewards and for their profit potential:

(1) Before buying, consult established sources of information, including auction catalogues, art books, and *catalogues raisonnés* which are comprehensive, well-annotated compilations of all the prints of various artists. Also, to get a basic education, visit museum print cabinets. Often you must make an appointment to do so but don't fail to do this, for many of the finest examples of prints are to be found today in museums.

(2) Browse in galleries and shops, both in the United States and abroad, to get an idea of the range of prints available and prices being charged by various outlets for similar works. Try to find an era or an artist or a school of artists really attractive to you and then focus your interests and attention on your choices.

(3) When you are ready to buy, stick to established print dealers—preferably those who have been in business at least five years. Seek their guidance on the quality and authenticity of the prints you are considering purchasing.

(4) *Avoid* one-shot print exhibitions in hotel suites and sales by un-

known auctioneers. Frequently, experts say, fly-by-night auctioneers will hold up a page which has been torn out of an art book, announce flatly, "This is worth $150 but let's start the bidding at $15"—and succeed in selling it for a distinctly non-bargain price of $30.

"Small-time auctions," the dealers warn, "can be a great place to buy prints, but *only* if you know exactly what you are doing." A cardinal rule on this type of auction is to attend the exhibition beforehand and examine the prints, since they are generally sold "as is."

(5.) Also avoid the "bargains" advertised in your neighborhood picture frame shop unless the dealer has an established reputation in the field of prints and you know what you want.

(6) Be on the lookout for "restrikes"—which are reruns of the original plates. These plates may have been rediscovered long after an artist's death, sometimes with cancellation lines drawn through them by the artist so that further prints supposedly could not be made.

(7) Finally, examine catalogs at auctions and at print exhibitions. Descriptions of individual prints should include whether or not they are signed by the artist, the condition and quality of each print, the number of impressions in the entire edition (for modern prints), the print's size and date, the process or processes used. Reputable dealers also should be happy to put whatever descriptive data you wish on the invoice or give a certificate of authenticity.

FOUR CATEGORIES FOR INVESTING

Armed with the basic rules for shopping with profit in mind, what might you find the most provocative areas for investing in the print market? Here are four specific categories underlined by leading dealers:

(1) *French nineteenth-century artists* such as Jean Baptiste Camille Corot, Jean François Millet, Adolphe Appia, Albert Besnard, Félix Buhot, and Charles François Daubigny. In the mid-1970s, you could buy good Corots and Millets for $300 to $600 and good examples of others for $20 to $200—a fraction of the prices which were paid for other major artists of this era such as Toulouse-Lautrec, Manet, Cézanne, Renoir.

(2) *American early twentieth-century artists* and especially those who worked in the 1930s. Good prints by Thomas Hart Benton, John Steuart Curry, Grant Wood, George Bellows, John Sloan, and Reginald Marsh could be bought for $150 to $750.

(3) *The celebrated British "triumvirate"* of the 1920s—D. Y. Cameron, Muirhead Bone, and James McBey. Works by these once fantastically popular artists were available until just recently for only 10 per cent of the prices they commanded a half century ago ($200 to $3,000 in the expensive dollars of the 1920s). "Whether the prices for works by these artists will ever come back to the levels of the 1920s is anybody's guess," says one print

dealer. "But they might possibly be an interesting school to explore." Similarly, works by Seymour Haden, Whistler's brother-in-law, well may start to rise on Whistler's coattails. Prices of major Whistler prints have passed the $3,000 mark.

(4) *High-quality works by lesser-known printmakers of the fifteenth, sixteenth, and seventeenth centuries*—e.g., Lievens, Goudt, Hollar, Waterloo, to name just a few. Outstanding examples of prints by these artists could be bought in the mid-seventies for $50 to $500. *But* choosing among these lesser-knowns takes a lot of expert knowledge and if you don't possess it, consult someone who does.

FACTORS DETERMINING VALUES OF PRINTS

Print values in all categories are based on these four factors: the artist, the image or subject of the print, the rarity of the print, and the print's condition.

But an artist's standing as an oil painter or a sculptor has little to do with his stature as a print maker. Aristide Maillol, for instance—whose sculptures are valued in the tens of thousands of dollars—is considered a minor print maker.

Rarity is the key to the upswing in prices for fine examples of prints by such artists as Rembrandt, Dürer, Cranach, Callot. And a print from an edition of only 50 may cost four times the price of an example from an edition of 200, everything else being equal.

As an illustration of the importance of a print's condition, a Toulouse-Lautrec poster which normally would sell for $5,000 might fetch less than $1,000 if it were torn or wrinkled or otherwise in poor condition.

A final guide: if you do decide to choose prints as an investment medium as well as a source of great personal pleasure, avoid the hottest print fads and concentrate on the temporarily less fashionable but still high-quality artists and epochs. In fact here—among the less fashionable eras and less fashionable artists—is where you will find the real price bargains.

ANTIQUE CARS

How would you like to buy a 1934 Rolls-Royce boat-tail roadster for a mere $65,000? Or a Mercedes-Benz SS tourer for just $90,000? Or a 1930 Duesenberg Model SJ roadster for $125,000? A 1912 Mercer raceabout for $45,000? A Stutz Bearcat, Locomobile, or Stanley Steamer—for from $10,000 to $40,000?

You could have, in 1974.

Even if you are among the millions who remember these names with nostalgia, are you aware how dazzling has been the boom in antique and classic cars or how astronomical have been their prices? While tens of thousands of car hobbyists have appeared on the American automotive scene, these have in the past few years been joined by growing numbers of investors spending large amounts in the antique car business strictly for profit.

This has become a true far-out investment and prices of car antiques have soared so high, in fact, that a new breed of car counterfeiters has begun clandestine operations, both in the United States and in England. The counterfeiters will copy, say, original parts from a prized old Mercedes, add fake manufacturer's identification plates, construct a counterfeit body—and sell the final product for $25,000 or more. Or they'll simply use counterfeit parts to convert a less desirable Rolls-Royce sedan into a very expensive, and seemingly rare, exotic model.

Like Rembrandts in the art world, the greats among antique cars have become so rare that people were paying as much as $25,000 in the mid-seventies for completely unrestored examples with tattered upholstery, flat tires, rusted fenders, etc. For example, a 1927 Hispano-Suiza tourer which you could have bought for $4,500 in 1964 sold in 1974 *unrestored* for $25,000.

One major force behind the antique car boom is our continuing love affair with the automobile coupled with our national nostalgia for early Americana of all kinds. And millions of American men, particularly those who wear white collars all day, aspire to be their own automobile mechanics, or at least successful tinkerers.

A second force is the fact that antique cars have become an "in" hobby for the very wealthy—and some collect them literally by the hundreds. When a millionaire gets his eye on a supercharged Mercedes SS phaeton or an Isotta Fraschini, he'll pay whatever the asking price—thus "pegging" a "fair market value" for future similar cars coming into the market at that lofty level. Certainly the intense organization which has taken place—clubs, regional and national car meets, slick periodicals, etc.—has helped to spur demand and thus to drive up the prices. Finally, certain antique cars have reached the point where they are widely regarded as art works and, as such, have ridden the wave of rising prices for art works of all kinds.

Antique car auctions are on a steep increase—including auctions held by prestigious art galleries. Big art museums, too, are exhibiting ancient cars with increasing frequency as works of art. Antique car "museums" are springing up all over the country.

HOW TO INVEST IN ANTIQUE CARS

Should you be tempted to try your hand at investing in this fast-growing field, here are the rules on how to do it—and how not to:

(1) Read antique car magazines, catalogs, and books to find out what models are available at what prices. Study such "bibles" as Hemming's Motor News and Old Cars.

(2) Join local antique-classic car clubs and attend meets at which seasoned enthusiasts bring their prizes to hobnob and to horse-trade. These colorful events are held all over the country at various times of the year.

(3) Learn the basic ingredients of value in antique (pre-1940) and classic cars (generally speaking, the bigger, grander ones, built between 1925 and 1942). Specifically, this means the car's make and model, its rarity, condition, engineering and aesthetic excellence.

Open cars—tourers, roadsters—tend to be many times more valuable than sedans and coupés. Convertibles fall somewhere in between these two categories. Any classic car which was considered a masterpiece when it was built still is considered so by sophisticated antique car collectors.

A car's model is all-important: in the mid-1970s, you could buy a fully restored 1903 curved-dash Oldsmobile runabout for $3,500, but a 1908 Mercedes tourer would have cost $50,000. However, a car's age has relatively little to do with its value. Many pre-1915 cars could be bought for less than $4,000, while many of the greats which were manufactured during the 1920s and '30s were unavailable, no matter what the condition, for less than $20,000 to $30,000.

(4) Avoid antique car auctions—until you learn your way around this field. Says one leading antique car dealer: "I've seen people bid more than $10,000 for ugly, mass-produced cars with no historical interest—cars which would bring no more than $3,000 if they were put back on the open market the next day." Antique and classic car auctions—which have experienced an explosive boom in the past decade or so—can be a disastrous financial trap for the unwary.

The following classification made by one seasoned dealer will help you protect yourself against the fraudulent fringe:

• A "natural" antique car auction is put on by a competent, reputable dealer, art-antique gallery, or auctioneer when an important collector dies or decides to sell his automobiles. This type of auction is spontaneous and cars are generally sold at fair prices—particularly if the collection is an important one and if the auction house is known to have dignity, integrity, and competence. Both collector and auctioneer want to preserve their good names as well as make a profit.

• A "contrived" (or artificial) auction is put together by one or more car collectors or dealers strictly for profit, is set in a carnival atmosphere, and is widely and loudly advertised—through every available medium—to car owners who might want to sell their specimens. The ads may guarantee a "gate" (audience) of 3,000 or 5,000 or 6,000, the amount a given car will bring— in fact, says one expert, "everything but the weather." Among the dangers in this type of emotionally heated auction are the "shills"—people who are planted in the audience to bid up prices and then disappear, leaving whoever gets caught up in this sort of auction frenzy stuck with the grossly inflated tab which the "successful" bidder has been lured into offering for the vehicle.

(5) Get the advice of established dealers on types and prices before you spend your money—or, if you have a particular car in mind, get a professional appraisal.

(6) Before you hire a professional car restorer, consider the fact that many charge from $10,000 to $40,000 for a "ground up" restoration—frequently more than you're likely to get back in a resale.

(7) Don't attempt a major restoration job yourself on an expensive antique or classic car unless you are highly experienced at it, and unless you have the near infinite patience to tear the thing apart nut by nut and put it back together—replacing or reproducing every single part as authentically as is humanly possible. (Some buffs go so far as to buy old-fashioned automotive upholstery sewing machines which themselves need restoration before they can be used.) And, naturally, only authentic vintage color schemes are permissible.

(8) Recognize that to restore a car properly you must have not only the ability but also the costly facilities—a garage and the proper tools.

WHERE THE BARGAINS ARE

Okay. Let's say you're willing to go slow, to learn the above rules, to abide by them. Where are you, the eager amateur wanting to dabble in the antique car business, likely to locate a bargain which hasn't already been snapped up by the pros?

The supply of antique and classic cars may not be nearly so limited as is generally believed. Many are still sitting idle in old barns—including, possibly, that barn right down the road from you. So ask around, and if you can spare the time, tour back roads in rural areas of northern New England, Pennsylvania, and Long Island, and such once fashionable summer resorts as Bar Harbor, Me., and Saratoga Springs, N.Y. Stop along the way in villages and towns and simply chat with local people about old cars which may still be around.

Second, you'll find a source of old cars at reasonable prices in the rather large volume of half-restored cars which their owners have never finished fixing up.

Third, one marvelous suggestion from a dealer on how to find vintage cars is "Load an old car, any old car, on a trailer and begin towing it cross country, stopping at every possible opportunity at service stations, etc. Talk to as many people as possible; many men want to talk about old cars." If you do this, eventually somebody will say, "I know where there is a 1917 Cadillac" or "I know where you can get an old Ford for $200."

A lot of work? Of course—but then, you must be prepared to make such an investment of your time and interest if you want to invest profitably in antique cars—just as you must study any investment, far out or far in, to make money from it.

In the $2,500-and-under price range, Pontiacs, Plymouths, Dodges, and Reos were still available in the early 1970s. Also, most makes of closed cars, which are less fashionable, may still be available in this lower price range. For example, Buick models of the late twenties and 1930s.

Now here are more specific suggestions for the antique car investor: Pre-1935 Plymouth roadsters; Buick, Ford and Chevrolet convertibles of the 1930s; big Packard and Cadillac sedans of any era; Pierce-Arrow sedans and coupés.

All of these (and many others) are available at prices ranging from $300 to $5,000. *But*—if you want to speculate by buying these (or if you're lucky enough to have one sitting around in your garage), remember that the best-looking, the most elegantly designed ones, and the ones which were originally manufactured in the smallest numbers are the cars which are most likely to grow in value over the long run.

NEW FRONTIERS

Trucks are another type of vehicle in which price appreciation well may take place in the years ahead—specifically pre-1920 U.S. mail trucks, beer trucks, flower delivery wagons, Black Marias, and fire trucks. In some cases you can get these in junk yards and elsewhere for less than $500—but be prepared to put a lot of elbow grease into restoring them.

Among trucks, look for very early chain-drive models with huge engines which are especially amusing and attractive. In old fire trucks, look for pre-1915 models which are loaded with brass ornamentation and other pizzazz.

NEW-NEW FRONTIERS

What if you can't find any vehicles you consider bargains in these categories? Then look to the new-new frontiers. And where are these? . . .

Old private railroad cars, early steam locomotives (or *anything* with a steam engine) . . . Racing cars with a documented racing history . . . Antique aircraft . . . Old speedboats and schooners. . . . For a mere $4,500 you could pick up a dilapidated pre-World War II open-cockpit biplane and if you could figure out how to restore it, you might be able to sell it to somebody else for $20,000 . . . or more.

Part IV

YOUR RIGHTS AND
HOW TO GET THEM

26

YOUR RIGHTS
AS A CONSUMER

WHAT ARE YOUR RIGHTS AS A CONSUMER?

YOUR BASIC RIGHTS IN THE MARKET PLACE

Are you aware that if you can prove that a used car dealer has turned back the odometer of a car you have bought from him you can recover treble damages (three times the amount of loss you suffered because of this deception), with a minimum recovery of $1,500—in addition to lawyers' fees and any court costs you may incur?

Or that if you sign a contract to buy a used car and can't get it off the lot the contract is not binding—even if you agreed to buy the car "as is"?

Did you know that if a toy or other product you buy turns out to be patently unsafe you have reasonable grounds to sue its manufacturer for negligence—and that if you're injured by a product you have rented you may have grounds to sue the rental company?

Or have you been informed that if you have signed a sales contract in which the seller has used fraudulent tactics you may (in most cases) cancel such a contract?

Or that you have a right to take legal action against a dealer in any type of merchandise who unjustifiably threatens to do anything which would damage your credit rating?

There are many rules and laws guaranteeing you a long list of legal rights in today's vast and immensely complex society. You have—as a tenant, a share owner, a taxpayer, a borrower, a worker—an ever lengthening and broadening list of "unwritten" as well as written rights which are backed up by many avenues of redress and recourse.

President John F. Kennedy's special 1962 consumer message to Congress was, in many senses, the beginning of today's consumer movement.

What has happened since can be ranked as no less than revolutionary change in the U.S. market place. In Kennedy's message he proclaimed these four basic consumer rights:

The right to safety—to be protected against the marketing of goods which are hazardous to your health, life, or limb.

The right to be informed—to be protected against fraudulent advertising, labeling, or grossly misleading information about products, and to be given the facts you need to make an informed choice in the market place.

The right to choose—to have, as far as possible, access to a variety of products and services at reasonable prices.

The right to be heard—to be assured that your interests as a consumer will get a sympathetic hearing by the government, and that the laws which are supposed to protect you will be enforced.

Other rights that also have been widely mentioned, if not actually blessed by legal sanction:

Your right to pay only a "fair price" for the goods and services you buy and to get "full value" for what you buy; the right to quality and integrity in the market place; the right of legal redress of complaints and grievances.

PROTECTION PROVIDED BY THE FEDERAL GOVERNMENT

Here are the key federal laws that have been passed over the years to help assure you of your rights as consumers:

The *1906 Pure Food and Drug Act* prohibited mislabeling of the contents of food, liquor, and medicine containers—a highly significant first step, in an age of laissez-faire government, toward the more comprehensive protection we now take for granted.

The *1907 Agricultural Meat Inspection Act* provided for federal regulation and inspection of meat packing plants engaged in interstate commerce for sanitary plant conditions and meat cleanliness. "Engaged in interstate commerce" meant that at least some aspect of business stretched across state lines; today almost all businesses and industries are considered to be in "interstate commerce." This law was originally inspired by Upton Sinclair's classic muckraking book *The Jungle,* which exposed horrifying examples of filthy conditions in meat processing plants.

The *1914 Federal Trade Commission Act* and later amendments state broadly that "unfair methods of competition in commerce are hereby declared unlawful" and "unfair or deceptive acts or practices in commerce also are illegal." These statements laid the foundation for much of the consumer protection legislation now in effect—e.g., product labeling.

The *1938 Food, Drug, and Cosmetic Act* strengthened food labeling requirements and extended strict requirements to advertising and labeling of cosmetics. The act also required that drug advertising and labels include "all material facts" about a drug, such as instructions for use, medical conditions making its use unwise, and differences of established medical opinion on its effectiveness.

The *1939 Wool Products Labeling Act* required disclosure of the true composition of all types of wool products at every step along their way from the sheep to the user.

The *1951 Fur Products Labeling Act* protected the public against false labeling and advertising of furs.

The *1953 Flammable Fabrics Act,* and especially later amendments, empowered the Secretary of Commerce to ban the sale of certain items of clothes and household furnishings—ranging from flame-prone scarves to flammable bedding—if the Secretary determines that a particular product presents an "unreasonable risk of death, personal injury or significant property damage." This law has led to the development of flameproof children's sleepwear and other items of clothing.

The *1958 Textile Fiber Products Indentification Act* established comprehensive standards for labeling and advertising clothes and other textile products. These standards enable you to compare the characteristics of materials when you shop. (To learn how this act and related laws listed above benefit you, see Chapter 7, "The Now-and-Then Necessity of Clothes," pages 217–18.)

The *1960 Federal Hazardous Substances Labeling Act* and later amendments established a list of hazardous household substances subject to stringent labeling standards. You can now instantly identify extremely flammable, corrosive, or highly toxic substances by the designation "DANGER" on the label. The words "WARNING" or "CAUTION" alert you to less extreme chemical hazards.

The *1966 National Traffic and Motor Vehicle Safety Act* was inspired by consumer advocate Ralph Nader's now classic critique of the U.S. automobile, *Unsafe at Any Speed.* The goals of this law are to eliminate unsafe automobile manufacturing practices, to establish safety standards in the design of automobiles, and to require the development and installation of certain lifesaving equipment in motor vehicles. This act also created the National Highway Safety Bureau, which is concerned with all aspects of automobile safety. Amendments in 1974 further required auto manufacturers to repair safety defects promptly and without charge, and required them to set safety standards for school buses.

The *1966 Child Protection Act* and the *1970 Toy Safety Act* prohibited the sale of products that are dangerous to the health and safety of your children—even if such products have warnings on their labels. Among the key products affected: toys that are toxic, corrosive, or flammable, and toys that present mechanical, thermal, or electrical hazards to life or limb.

The *1966 Fair Packaging and Labeling Act* required manufacturers of a wide variety of consumer products to state clearly the net quantity of contents on the package's principal display panel. It called for the elimination of packages of consumer goods (e.g., breakfast cereals) that are unnecessarily slack filled (the product does not fill the package, or the package has too much "air") and required that the name and address of the product's manufacturer or distributor be included on the package. It also banned the use of such meaningless terms as "Giant Quart" and "Jumbo Gallon"—as well as phony "cents off" come-ons and non-economical "economy size" packages. If such terms are almost unknown to you today, it's because of this Truth in Packaging law.

The *1966 Freedom of Information Act,* and 1974 amendments, established the principle that the public has a *right*—with certain exceptions—to information collected and kept by federal government agencies.

The *1967 Wholesome Meat Act* required states to regulate meat processors in their jurisdictions at least as strictly as the federal government does, and authorized federal aid to states for inspecting meat plants doing intrastate (within the state) business only.

The *1968 Wholesome Poultry Products Act* extended strict federal poultry inspection standards to poultry processing plants not doing interstate business.

The *1968 Radiation Control for Health and Safety Act* set performance standards for certain electronic products and limits on the amount of radiation that may be emitted by such products as microwave ovens and color television sets.

The *1968 Natural Gas Pipeline Safety Act* set safety standards for transmitting, or shipping gas through interstate pipelines—as the public's protection against explosions.

The *1968 Consumer Credit Protection Act* (*popularly called the Truth in Lending law*) required most categories of lenders to disclose the true annual interest rate on virtually all types of loans and credit sales as well as the total dollar cost and other terms of a loan. (See Chapter 3, "How to Borrow Money and Use Credit Wisely," pages 110–15, for details on interest rates and how to compare costs of various types of loans.) The law also prohibited a variety of cruel and deceptive lending practices and gave you, the borrower, the right to cancel most types of credit transactions in which your home is used as collateral for a loan. (See "What You Should Know About Contracts," pages 1014–17, for your rights under this provision.)

The act prohibited anyone from sending you a credit card you have not requested—and provided other kinds of protection against card thieves running up bills in your name.

Finally, an important provision of the act limited the amount of your wages which may be garnished (withheld by your employer at the order of a court for repayment of an overdue debt). (See pages 1033–35 for more details on the provisions of the Truth in Lending law.)

The *1968 Interstate Land Sales Full Disclosure Act* required all large land sales promoters to furnish prospective buyers a detailed and meaningful report on the land, and spelled out buyers' rights in the transaction. For more details on this law, see Chapter 19, "Planning for Your Financial and Personal Security," page 815.

The *1970 Poison Prevention Packaging Act* required childproof packaging for medicine and household chemicals to reduce your child's risk of accidental poisoning.

The *1971 Fair Credit Reporting Act* gave you, the user of credit, the buyer of insurance, or the applicant for a job, the right to learn the contents of your file at any credit bureau. In addition, you have the specific rights to:

be told the name and address of the credit bureau or similar agency any time you are denied credit, insurance, or employment;

find out who has received information from your file;

have your file treated confidentially, except for legitimate purposes;

force changes in the file if it is inaccurate, and have the credit bureau notify, at no cost to you, recipients of false reports that have been made;

sue anyone infringing on these rights.

The *1972 Motor Vehicle Information and Cost Savings Act,* also known as the "Better Bumper law," established standards for car bumpers to reduce damage in low-speed collisions, provided for federal diagnostic centers to promote better auto diagnostic facilities, and directed the Transportation Department to conduct research on the comparative fragility of automobiles —and to give the results of that research to you, the public.

The act also prohibited used car dealers or private individuals from turning back odometers to hide the true mileage a car has been driven and required dealers to give each buyer a written "verification" of the mileage if the mileage is known. This information gives you, the used car buyer, an important way to compare the value of one car versus another.

The *1972 Consumer Product Safety Act* established a five-member Consumer Product Safety Commission. The commission collects, investigates, and disseminates information relating to death, illness, and injuries associated with consumer products, conducts studies on consumer product safety, develops safety test methods and devices, tests products, and assists public and private organizations in developing and enforcing product safety standards and test methods. In addition, it promotes research into the causes of product-related deaths, injuries, and illnesses.

The *1974 Fair Credit Billing Act,* an amendment to the Truth in Lending law, effective in late 1975, protects charge account customers against billing errors. It also permits credit card customers to use the same legal defenses against banks or other "third party" credit card companies as they previously had against merchants in the event an item bought on a credit card and costing more than $50 turns out to be defective.

The 1974 Consumer Product Warranty and Federal Trade Commission Improvement Act requires that all provisions of *any* warranty be explained clearly and in simple language on (or close to) the product when you purchase it. The explanation must include: what the warrantor will do if something fails; who will pay for what; exactly how you can get the warranty honored.

PROTECTION PROVIDED BY YOUR STATE OR CITY

Various states and cities also have various laws and regulations protecting consumers against such practices as:

charging usurious interest rates on loans (the rates that are considered usurious vary from state to state);

charging you for extra weight in meat and poultry which has been injected with water;

shutting off your gas or electricity or telephone over a weekend because of late payment of your bill;

changing the terms of an advertised guarantee when you come to the store to look over the item;

failing to post prices of prescription drugs in drugstores;

stating that an item has been "marked down" when it normally has been priced at its current level;

presenting you with non-itemized repair bills;

selling used goods (such as demonstrator cars and worn furniture floor models) as new.

How to Complain—and Get Action!

The fact that we in the United States are the owners of more than one *billion* home appliances, small and large, is convenience carried to a new dimension. But the miseries of repairing and servicing all these appliances also can be agony in a new dimension.

When was the last time *you* brought home some brand-new gadget, found it to be a lemon—then struggled through the utterly frustrating experience of having the dealer who sold it to you pass the buck to some huge and distant manufacturer, who maintained a stony silence for weeks before even acknowledging your complaint, much less fixing the appliance?

When was the last time you registered a complaint during the warranty period—then watched the dealer welch out of the warranty because *he* failed to cope with the problem before the warranty ran out?

But do you know *what* to do about these infuriating situations? Do you know how to complain—and get action?

BASIC RULES ON COMPLAINING

Here's what—and how:

(1) Go back to the dealer who sold you the product, or to the service agency to which he directs you, and complain—*loudly*. Take the ailing product with you (unless it's a refrigerator or a stove or some other monolith) and the original sales slip. Give the dealer all the pertinent details—such as the date of the purchase, the date on which the problem arose, a description of the problem and, if you could not take the appliance for any reason, the identification number of the machine. Don't threaten; this will only turn people off. Let the facts speak for themselves. And don't accost an innocent sales girl who has neither the know-how nor the authority to handle your problem. If you document your case well, the normal channels of complaint usually will work.

(2 If the dealer or service agency refuses to help, *then* write or telephone the manufacturer's customer relations department. Again, state the key facts clearly—including dates, serial numbers, place of purchase, amount paid, what went wrong. Send photocopies of canceled checks and previous correspondence if you can. Never, never send your only and original documents.

(3) If this doesn't produce results, write to the company's president, again coldly stating the facts. Indicate at the bottom of your letter that copies are being sent to a variety of consumer organizations. If you do not know the name of the company president or the address of the company, ask your state or local consumer protection agency how and where you can find this information. Or go to your local library and look them up in *Poor's Register of Corporations, Directors and Executives* or *Moody's Industrial Manual.* If these directories are not available in your local library, ask for the "directory" issues of such business publications as *Fortune, Business Week,* or *Forbes.*

(4) Send copies of your letter to your local consumer protection organization and also to such organizations as the Office of Consumer Affairs in Washington; Consumers Union; and your local Better Business Bureau. (See Chapter 28, "Where to Get Help," for addresses of agencies and organizations which are eager to hear about your problems and in some cases prepared to assist you.)

(5) Be sure to use the Better Business Bureau, for this well may be your most effective local consumer advocate. In many cases it—or the local Chamber of Commerce—is the *only* one there is. When it receives a complaint, the Better Business Bureau contacts the company involved and tries

to arrange a settlement. In some cases, arbitration is used. Because the Better Business Bureau makes contact with a company's top managers, reasonable complaints are almost always settled satisfactorily.

However, there are limits to what the BBBs can or will do.

A BBB can only be a negotiator—not a judge.

It cannot force a firm to make an equitable settlement.

It can rarely even negotiate a settlement of a complaint with an unscrupulous enterprise, and it cannot force it out of business.

It will *not* handle complaints involving legal matters, credit matters, collection of accounts, or wages owed.

It will *not* pass judgment on prices or quality of goods or services.

To make the best use of a Better Business Bureau, request a Bureau report on a company—summarizing its past methods of operation—*before* committing yourself to any expensive proposition.

(6) Be constructive all along the line. If you have a suggestion on how the company or the dealer or the manufacturer could avoid the problems you are complaining about, include this suggestion in your correspondence. Propose a specific remedy. Do you want a refund? Repairs? Replacement? An apology? Be fair and realistic about what you propose.

(7) *Don't* try to be an amateur lawyer or insist on your "rights." The company or person to whom you are complaining probably knows a lot more about your rights than you do.

(8) If you are complaining in writing for the umpteenth time, give the dates of previous complaints.

(9) If you have bought the unsatisfactory or undelivered merchandise on a charge account, tell the store you don't intend to pay for it until a fair adjustment has been made.

(10) If it's an appliance, and if the manufacturer is unresponsive, send all pertinent information to the Major Appliance Consumer Action Panel or "complaint exchange" operated by the Association of Home Appliance Manufacturers in Chicago. MACAP has a staff of consumer specialists equipped to get action on your complaints on both small and large appliances. Also appeal directly to a local consumer organization, and if no such organization exists, ask the Consumer Federation of America in Washington for help in locating one.

(11) Tell your problem to your local newspaper in the form of a letter to the editor, a tip to the city desk, a telephoned request for help. Don't exaggerate, don't dramatize: just tell it the way it is. If your problem is real and other consumers also are victims, most newspapers or TV or radio stations will rise to your defense. There is no more powerful weapon than publicity.

Above all: *Don't* fail to complain if you feel you have a valid gripe—not only about a money loss but also about rude salespeople, deceptive advertising, late deliveries, confusing warranties, or outright gyps. It may be embarrassing to admit you've been had, but your complaints—if you make them fairly and coolly—will win better products and better service over the long range not only for yourself but also for other shoppers.

HOW TO FILE A FORMAL COMPLAINT

If you are filing a formal complaint with a government agency—say the Food and Drug Administration—be reasonably sure there is a violation of a law for which that agency has responsibility to avoid wasting your and the agency's time. (See Chapter 28, "Where to Get Help," for the addresses of all key federal agencies you might want to write or call.)

To be effective, your complaint should be prompt and should contain the following information:

• Your name, address, phone number, and directions to your home or where you work.

• A clear description of the problem.

• A description of the label on the product and any code marks on it (such as the numbers stamped on a tin can).

• The name and address of the store which sold you the product, and the date you bought it.

Save whatever is left of the offending product, and save any unopened containers, for your doctor's use or for possible inspection by the agency.

Also report the suspect product to its manufacturer, the packer or distributor shown on the product label, and to the store where you bought it.

HOW TO WRITE YOUR REPRESENTATIVES

Finally, you may strongly support current consumer legislation to protect you and others in the future. If so, the first thing to do is to write your representatives—both in your state legislature and in Washington. Good, thoughtful, constructive letters may have a great impact on your senator's or congressman's thinking, and ultimately on legislation.

Here are five key rules for writing your representative:

(1) Identify the issue or bill that concerns you—by either its official or its popular title.

(2) Write as soon as possible after a bill has been introduced—but in any event before it comes out of the committee that is holding hearings on it and is responsible for shaping it into the form in which it will be put before the entire Senate or House.

(3) Make your comments constructive: if you oppose a bill, offer sound alternatives; if you approve, say why.

(4) If you are especially knowledgeable in the area about which you are writing, or if you have significant personal experience related to the legislation to report, share your knowledge and your experience.

(5) Keep your letter short—and clearly written.

The addresses at which you write (or telegraph) all senators and representatives are:

The Honorable _____ _____   The Honorable _____ _____
Senate Office Building   House Office Building
Washington, D.C. 20510   Washington, D.C. 20515

How to Avoid Mail Order Agonies

One of the convenient but also potentially the most agony-laden ways to shop is by mail—either from mail order catalogs or in response to advertisements. Among the worst agonies are late deliveries, non-deliveries, broken merchandise, and refusal to honor warranties on products.

But as of February 2, 1976, some relief came to you through a Federal Trade Commission rule requiring a mail order seller who is unable to ship merchandise within the stated time to notify you, the buyer, 30 days after receiving your order that there will be a delay and giving you the option to cancel. (The seller also must do this in 30 days if no delivery time is stated.) You must be furnished with an adequate cost-free means to notify the seller, such as a postage paid card. If you so request, the seller must cancel your order and refund your money.

RULES FOR SHOPPING BY MAIL

• Order at least three to four weeks before the date on which you want delivery—particularly during the Christmas season. Look in the catalog for a notation on the deadline for guaranteed delivery for Christmas.

• Be explicit in your instructions. Be sure to include your name and address, and any other information required. Also tell the store how to include your name if the gift is being sent by you to a friend.

• Stick to mail order houses familiar to you. Is it a member of the Direct Mail Marketing Association, Inc., the New England Mail Order Association, or some other recognized trade group? If in doubt, check your local Better Business Bureau.

• Don't rely solely on the picture of the merchandise you want to order. Read the description of its size, dimensions, weight, contents.

• Look into the conditions of sale and/or guarantees. Are all sales final? Are products guaranteed to satisfy? To grow? To work? What will the company do if you are not satisfied—especially with expensive items?

• Pay by check or money order—not cash. If you are ordering from a department store, charge the order if you can. If you must return an item, do so promptly, stating your reasons in a letter attached to the package. Give your name, address, account number, date of your order, description and cost of the item. If you complain "properly," most reliable companies will replace unsatisfactory merchandise or refund your money. And if your order does not arrive until after the time when you need it, the company will almost always accept return of the merchandise.

• Inspect mail order packages as soon as you receive them to be sure no parts are missing and to confirm the contents.

• If your complaints don't get a response within a reasonable period of time, write the Postal Inspection Service of the U. S. Postal Service in Washington to start an investigation into possible fraud, your local Better Business Bureau, and the Direct Mail Marketing Association Consumer Service Director, 230 Park Avenue, New York, N.Y. 10017. This trade association will bring pressure on any member violating its standards of ethics.

In sum, be at least as wise a shopper by mail as you are in a store.

WHAT TO DO WITH UNORDERED MERCHANDISE

What should you do if you receive, say, a clutch of ugly neckties either through the mail or delivered to your door, which you have not ordered, do not want, and certainly do not wish to pay for? You also do not want to go to the trouble of rewrapping them, trundling them to the post office, and paying return postage to return them to their sender.

You have no obligation to accept the merchandise, return it, pay for it, or give it any special care. So feel free to ignore any dunning letters for payment for any unordered merchandise you may receive. If you receive any such merchandise C.O.D. through the mail this is a postal violation and should be reported immediately to your post office.

Of course, first be sure that the merchandise was not sent to you by a merchandiser—such as a book or record club—which has signed you up for "negative option" selling. Under this arrangement you, the member of the "club," must return a reply card to the company if you do *not* want the merchandise, and are obligated to pay for the items if you fail to return the card within the allotted time. Under a Federal Trade Commission "Trade Regulation Rule," effective mid-1974, you have at least ten days in which to return the form rejecting an offer of merchandise. The FTC also requires the merchandiser to tell you "clearly and conspicuously" on all promotion materials:

how to reject the offer of a selection;

whether you are required by your agreement to buy a certain number of items in a certain time;

that you have the right to cancel your membership in the plan at any time.

If you would like to reduce the volume of unsolicited mail you receive, write to the Direct Mail Marketing Association and request a form to remove your name from the mailing lists of their 1,600 member firms.

HOW TO ARGUE WITH A COMPUTER

The computer at the local department store bills you repeatedly for goods you have long since returned to the store. How do you get that computer to listen to reason?

Your company's paymaster, also a computer, short-changes you on your weekly pay check by miscalculating your deductions. How should you approach this problem?

Or the amount of your Social Security check is suddenly and unexplainably slashed. Or the telephone company's electronic billing brain suddenly jacks your monthly bill from $12 to $1,200.

COMMON BILLING ERRORS

Billing errors can be not only a major nuisance, in terms of the time and energy you must spend sorting them out, but also a major expense to you if you do not detect the errors and as a result go ahead and pay such hidden charges. Moreover, a single computer error ultimately can lead to a nightmare of past-due notices, telephone calls from collection agencies, and threats of damage to your credit rating. To cite just a few real-life cases of gross billing errors which have occurred in recent years:

One man gave twenty magazine subscriptions to friends as Christmas gifts, but the donor got all the magazines and his friends got the bills!

Another man wanted two subscriptions at the same address, but a well-educated computer had been instructed never to send a duplicate subscription to anybody—and determinedly rejected the second subscription.

In a classic case, a lady was repeatedly billed for a balance of $0.00. After her repeated failure to "pay up" her account, the matter was turned over to a collection agency. She finally solved the matter—by sending a check for $0.00.

A young Arizona pneumonia patient received a bill from a hospital computer charging him not only for his chest ailment but also for delivery room and nursery costs—alleging that he had given birth to a baby girl.

More than one half of all retail purchases we make today are being made with charge accounts and credit cards—thus, in most cases, a computer bills us. The likelihood now is that these—and many more—types of bills and checks are being calculated and printed out with the help of computers and related electronic devices:

• Your weekly pay check, including a dozen or more deductions for Social Security, unemployment compensation insurance, etc.

- Your telephone, gas, and electricity bills.
- Your income tax returns.
- Your insurance bills.
- Charges on your bank credit cards, travel and entertainment cards, and oil company charge cards.
- Any government checks you are receiving—including veterans' benefits, Social Security benefits, and welfare checks.
- The monthly statement of your stock and bond account.
- Your monthly bank statement.
- Your hospital and medical bills and, in many cases, your doctor's bills as well.

HOW TO AVOID THEM

Against this background, take these precautions to help *avoid* billing errors:

Use your department store charge card or other credit card plate whenever possible. This at least will assure you that your own account number will turn up on your sales slip.

Check *all* sales slips to make sure they're correct—and compare them to figures appearing on your monthly statement. This is particularly important if you are dealing with stores that have switched from including copies of individual sales slips to computerized "descriptive" billing in which you are sent only a summary of your purchases and billings.

Each time you pay a department store bill, return the portion of the bill identifying the transaction along with your payment. Include your account number on the face of your check.

When you receive your monthly statement, go over it carefully. Report to the store promptly any errors you uncover or questions you have.

Don't include a letter of complaint with your payments. Send it separately to the complaint department or the credit department or customer relations department. In this letter, identify the bill that is in error by number or, if possible, include an identifying number of your account.

If you complain by phone, take down the name of the person to whom you complained—so you can mention the person if you need to follow up the complaint.

If you find you are arguing with a computer your key rule is to be as polite as you possibly can. Remember, it is the programer or whoever else may have fed information into it who is at fault. Be sure to include your bill number or sales slip number when you ask a computer for a correction.

If, after a few rounds of this type of gentle pleading, you get nothing but a big electronic silence, *then* start getting human. One way is to send the next letter to the company president, noting that you plan to send extra copies to all board members.

Review in your letter all pertinent facts *briefly* and objectively. Send a copy to the credit bureau as a protection for your credit rating. Point out that the store has no legal right to dun you for bills you don't owe or have already paid—and that if the dunning persists you'll take appropriate legal action against the errant creditor as well as the collection agency. Send this letter by registered mail—and save the receipt as a legal document you may need later. (Note: The law is increasingly on the consumer's side on this type of complaint, so don't hesitate at least to hint at the possibility of legal action *by you*.)

Under federal legislation effective in late 1975, retailers, lenders, and purveyors of credit cards are legally required to acknowledge within thirty days and resolve within sixty more days, in clear and definitive terms, customers' written inquiries on possible billing errors. And until there is a resolution the customer is not required to pay any service charges. During this period the creditor is barred from taking action to collect the account or even from reporting it as delinquent to a credit bureau.

Finally, remember that the error just *might* be *your* error. I know of a case, for example, in which a department store customer paid off a $41.50 charge account balance with a check for the balance of her checking account—some $1,600. She wrote a half dozen furious letters before she had a chance to balance her checkbook and discover her own error.

How to Use a Small Claims Court

WHAT IS A SMALL CLAIMS COURT?

Let's say the dry cleaner has ruined your favorite coat and refuses to compensate you for the damage . . . or the TV repairman has charged you for fixing your set but has failed to do so . . . or someone owes you money—for whatever reason—and refuses to pay you back.

If the sum involved is relatively small, it would hardly be worth while for you to hire a lawyer and take the trouble of going through the involved, time-consuming—and often costly—court procedure necessary in order to get back the money you feel is due you. However, today, in most areas, an often overlooked, easy avenue for quick redress in disputes of this sort is the small claims court.

In such courts, which exist in almost every state, the procedures are so simple and informal that you don't need a lawyer; in fact, some courts don't even allow lawyers. Court fees are low. Cases seldom take more than a month to come to trial; in some areas you may have to wait only from ten days to two weeks after your claim is entered. Most judges will usually render a decision on the spot or within a day or two after the trial.

How much you can sue for depends on where you live, but the maximum limits across the country in the mid-1970s usually ranged from $100 to

$1,000—with the courts in a few places imposing higher ceilings of from $1,500 to $3,500.

WHO MAY SUE WHOM?

Generally you can use a small claims court only to sue for *money* (but not in such cases as assault or libel). You may not sue for the furnishing of goods or services, for the return of property, or for negligence, unless you can fix a money value to these claims.

Most claims involve run-of-the-mill disputes with local tradesmen, landlords, service firms, and neighbors: inability to recover rent security deposits from landlords (a frequent complaint); defective or undelivered merchandise; minor personal injury or property damage (including those due to auto accidents); unsatisfactory appliance, auto, or house repairs; clothing ruined or lost by dry cleaners and laundries; breaches of warranties; wage claims; damage by movers; and unpaid loans and insurance claims.

To give a few examples:

In Washington, D.C., an irate consumer sued the local power company for damage to his air conditioner, claiming that the company had suddenly reduced its power without advance notice. The consumer won $61.60 for repairs and court costs.

A Californian won a $300 judgment against the Chrysler Corporation and one of its dealers for hotel and travel expenses incurred when his brand-new Dodge developed motor trouble during a trip to Nevada.

One woman brought suit to get back the money she paid for a dog that died three days after she had bought it. Another sued for the damage done to her patio by a tree service.

HOW TO START A SUIT

To sue on your own behalf, you must meet your state's legal age minimum, which is usually eighteen or twenty-one. If you are under this age you usually must file your claim through a parent, relative, legal guardian, or friend, and have this adult appear with you at the trial. If you yourself are unable to appear, whatever your age, you can give an adult power of attorney to sue or act in your behalf. In some states, corporations, partnerships, associations, and businesses such as collection agencies are not allowed to sue in small claims courts—although they can be sued there.

To start a suit:

• First, locate the court in the territory where the person or company you are suing lives, has an office, or does business. In a large city, such as New York, you can sue either in the borough where you live or the borough in which the party you are suing lives or works.

To find the small claims court in most towns, check the telephone book for the courts listed under your local, county, or state governments. In some places the small claims courts are part of the civil court, magistrate's court, district court, county court, justice court, municipal court, or other regular court system. Or their functions may be filled by the local justice of the peace.

• Once you have located the court, ask the clerk whether it can handle your type of claim and whether it has jurisdiction over the party you want to sue. (If the party lives or works in another state, you may have to contact your state government to learn what procedures to follow.)

• Assuming your claim is appropriate, you will be asked to pay the modest court fee (usually between $3.00 and $15) to cover the cost of the complaint and summons. The forms filled out by you or the clerk usually include your name and address, the *complete* name and address of the person you are suing, the reason you are suing, and the amount you are suing for.

Accuracy is important. If, for instance, you list the store you are suing as "XYZ Store" or "XYZ" instead of by its complete *legal* name of "XYZ Store, Inc.," or by its wrong address, you may not be able to get your money, even though you win your suit. Also, a person whom you know as Bob Smith should be sued as Robert Smith (with his middle initial too). To find out a company's complete name, inquire at the company itself or, better still, ask the court clerk where you can look up the name of the company.

• Once your complaint is filed, the clerk will tell you when to return for the trial and will send out the summons notifying the defendant of the date and place of the hearing and the nature of the claim against him.

WHAT TO DO WHILE AWAITING TRIAL

Very often the party you are suing, upon receiving the summons, will realize that you mean business and will offer to settle out of court. If you agree to the settlement (try to have it include your court fee) and are paid, tell the court that you have settled the matter. However, if the trial date is approaching and you haven't yet been paid, ask the other party to put the terms you've agreed on in written form and have a copy signed by both of you filed with the court.

Otherwise, to prepare for the trial, collect all relevant documents—such as bills of sale, invoices, receipts, canceled checks, guarantees, written estimates and appraisals—you may need to substantiate your claim. For some claims, photographs may be helpful. If the actual item is small, be prepared to take to court the item itself that figures in your claim—for example, the article of apparel you feel your dry cleaner or laundry has ruined.

Contact all witnesses who might back up your story and arrange for them to appear in court with you. If any will not appear voluntarily—say, a garage attendant who saw someone scratch your car but does not want to get involved—you can have the court clerk subpoena him. To get a so-called expert witness, such as a physician, to testify, you might have to pay him as much as $100 for his time. If a witness can't appear in person, a written statement probably would be acceptable as evidence.

If possible, try to watch a session of the court before your trial date so that you will know what to expect. Perhaps a lawyer friend also will give you some free advice on how to prepare for your appearance in court. Some courts also provide free legal advice and counsel, including help with filing the claim.

WHAT TO DO IN COURT

Get to court early and make sure you have brought *all* your evidence with you.

Tell your side of the story and present your evidence and witnesses. Stick simply to the facts and don't impugn the defendant's honesty or motives. Then the other party will tell his side of the story. The judge or arbitrator may break in to question you and the other party. You, the litigants, also will be given the opportunity to question each other. Above all, don't sound contentious or argue with the judge or arbitrator or your opponents.

After everyone has been heard from, a decision may be made immediately favoring you or the defendant. However, the judge or arbitrator may need a day or two to come to a decision. In that event, you'll have to call the court clerk to learn if you've won and, if so, how much. (You may find that you've been awarded less than the full amount you've sued for.)

If the defendant fails to show up at the trial, the judge or arbitrator probably will find in your favor, assuming you are able to give him enough proof of the truth of your story.

GETTING YOUR MONEY

Winning a judgment is one thing but collecting the money is another. In most cases, as soon as the other party has been informed he has lost the case he'll probably send you a check or money order to avoid any more trouble. In at least one out of five cases, though, according to a Consumers Union survey—you won't be able to collect the money you win.

The party you've sued may be penniless or bankrupt, may have gone out of business or left town, or may simply be unwilling to pay. In cases where the defendant is able to pay but stubbornly refuses, you may be able to collect by using a city marshal or sheriff—but since these local government officials usually get a percentage of whatever judgments they collect, they do not like to bother with small cases and prefer to concentrate on the big ones. As other alternatives, you might try to have the court place a lien on the defendant's property or bank account, or you might take steps to attach his wages.

If you can't collect, a judgment in your favor may turn out to be a hollow victory. Thus, along with the time and trouble of bringing a suit, also weigh the possibility of collecting.

BUT WHAT IF YOU ARE BEING SUED IN SMALL CLAIMS COURT?

If you wind up as the person being sued, here are tips you may find helpful:

• If you feel the claim is justified, contact the plaintiff and pay the money you owe. This will save you the time you would have to waste in court, which would probably find for the plaintiff anyway. If you can't pay everything you owe at once and would like to pay in installments, you'll probably have to appear in court on the trial date and show the judge the *written* settlement terms you've worked out. These are usually filed with the court.

• If you disagree with the charges or the amount of money claimed by the plaintiff, gather the pertinent documents and other evidence that will help back up your side of the story in court. Also arrange to take any witnesses to help you prove your case.

• Upon receiving the summons, find out whether your local court requires you to file an answer—an oral or written statement explaining your reasons for not paying the money claimed. (However, most small claims courts do not require an answer.)

• In some states you also can initiate a counterclaim against the plaintiff, either by mail or by phone—or, in some places, orally at the time of the hearing. If the plaintiff is not prepared to defend the counterclaim on short notice, the court may set a new future trial date.

• If the date set for the trial turns out to be inconvenient, you usually can have the court change it. You can do this with a registered letter mailed so that it is received by the court before the original date set for the trial. (Courts usually specify the number of days in advance it should be received.) Some courts allow you to have a friend ask for the postponement on the day of the trial. Make sure your excuse for a delay is a good one.

• If the person suing you does not show up, the court may dismiss the case. However, with the court's permission, the plaintiff may be able to file suit again.

• If you do not understand the charges against you, are puzzled about the proceedings, or have any other questions, ask the court clerk for help.

• If you feel that you need special legal assistance, the money claimed is relatively high, and the case is complicated, it may pay you to hire a lawyer— the particular court permitting. This may be advisable if the plaintiff has legal counsel. If you cannot afford a lawyer, your local legal aid society, neighborhood law office, or some social service organization may be able to help you.

What Is a Warranty Worth?

WHAT IS A WARRANTY?

You buy a new TV set from a neighborhood store, the set is "guaranteed," and it breaks down within the guarantee's time limit. Who is responsible for repairs—the store or the manufacturer? Will the entire set be replaced, or will it simply be patched up? Will you have to pay labor costs and other charges which could amount to the bulk of the repair bill?

If you are promised "satisfaction or your money back," how dissatisfied do you have to be to get a refund and how much red tape do you have to go through before you get it? If an appliance is guaranteed only for "normal" use, how much and what kind of use is "normal"? If it's guaranteed for a "lifetime," what does "lifetime" mean?

These are just a few of the annoying, often frustrating questions facing you when one of those sixteen appliances in your "average" household quits, collapses, goes up in flames, starts shooting sparks at you, or otherwise dreadfully misbehaves. It's merely common sense to inform yourself on the basic general provisions of warranties and on the fundamental rule for protecting yourself against worthless ones.

However, consumer product warranty legislation is now giving you a basic floor of federal warranty coverage and requiring that warranties on virtually all types of products "mean what they say and say what they mean."

For practical purposes, a warranty is the same thing as a guarantee, but there are two main types of warranties: an "express" warranty and an "implied" warranty. An express warranty is one in writing—the type you see on most automobiles, small and large appliances, other household and around-the-house equipment. An implied warranty, which goes with most purchases you make, is the *unwritten* protection *implied* by the seller when he offers to sell to you. It is created by law. It simply says that when you buy something it should operate as it is supposed to, whether there is a written warranty or not. *If* it doesn't work, it's up to the dealer to repair it or replace it or give you a refund. (See Chapter 9, "Your Transportation," for details on automobile warranties, expressed and implied. Also see below.)

With any guarantee or warranty, what is *not* covered often tends to be far more significant than what *is* covered. In one study by the Federal Trade Commission, no fewer than 34 different types of disclaimers were found on appliance warranties! For instance, a toaster you buy may have a single defective part which ruins the entire machine. The warranty, though, may provide *only* for the replacement of the defective part and *not* for replacement or repair of the entire toaster.

There is no such thing as a guarantee without conditions. Thus, be automatically skeptical about products advertised as covered by an "unconditional guarantee" or a "lifetime guarantee." In the case of "lifetime" guarantees, the fascinating question is: *whose* lifetime? What assurance do you have that the company guaranteeing a product will still be in existence even ten or twenty years hence? What would happen if the guarantor company merged or went bankrupt? Read the fine print on a lifetime guarantee; you'll probably find it actually is a lifetime disclaimer.

KEY QUESTIONS TO ASK ABOUT WARRANTIES

Here are the key questions you should ask about *any* warranty or guarantee:

Does it cover the entire product—or only certain parts?

Is labor included—or only replacement of parts?

Who will be responsible for repairing the product? The dealer? A service agency? The manufacturer? A repairman designated by the manufacturer?

For how long a period is the warranty or guarantee in effect?

Is there a provision for prorating the guarantee—e.g., paying only an allowance toward replacement of an item such as the motor of a year-old food blender which has depreciated somewhat?

If the product you have bought is defective and must be removed from your home for repair, will the dealer or manufacturer substitute an equivalent appliance in the interim?

How and by whom would the warranty or guarantee be honored if you should move to another location? Is there an authorized service agency at your destination which would be capable of performing needed repairs?

Just what is covered for which periods of time? Note: In five-year warranties offered on many appliances, there often are two different sets of rules —one set covering the first year and the other set covering the remaining four years.

WHAT YOU MUST DO TO MAKE YOUR WARRANTY WORK

You, the buyer, must protect your warranty coverage by informing yourself thoroughly and *before you buy* what a product's warranty does and does not cover, and by doing *your* part to keep the warranty valid.

If you must mail in a special warranty card before the warranty is valid, do so. Keep any guarantee you may have seen in an advertisement, too. If you must keep the original box in which the appliance arrived, do so. If you must use the product for only certain purposes, do so. If you must submit the product for special inspections or servicing to make the guarantee good, do so.

Also be sure to keep a written record of the dates you request service so that if your warranty period runs out before repairs are performed you'll at least be able to establish the fact that the problem started while the warranty was still in effect. Keep the bill of sale and receipts of service.

And remember:

"Do-it-yourself" repairs on an appliance within the warranty period will probably make the warranty invalid. So leave such work strictly to the seller or his authorized service company.

Put in a file the exact name and address of the company or individual who is making the guarantee.

Above all, *heed* this ancient rule on guarantors and guarantees: a guarantee is no better than the person or company making the guarantee. Frequently, in fact, a verbal guarantee by a reputable, reliable dealer can be worth more than a sheaf of fine-print bafflegab which shirks more responsibility than it accepts.

How to Get the Most Out of Your Car Warranty

In 1972 a Florida court handed down a precedent-setting decision: the buyer of a new car is entitled to have it perform as it should. In Maryland, by law, auto manufacturers must post a $100,000 bond in order to sell cars in that state—and they must forfeit funds if they fail to honor the warranty. In other states, car manufacturers must pay dealers the same rate for warranty work as customers pay for regular work—a requirement which encourages them to give warranty service equal priority.

This *is* progress, but there is still a long way to go before warranty protection is what it is claimed to be. Meanwhile, here is how to get your money's worth while your car is under warranty.

NEW CAR WARRANTIES

Once you have bought a car, do your part by maintaining it according to the schedule in the owner's manual. Have the shop doing the work note it in the schedule and keep copies of work orders and receipts.

Then, if you have a problem which you believe is covered under the warranty, take the car to the dealer from whom you bought it. Get a written estimate on what must be done and on whether or not the work will be covered by the warranty—*before* you authorize the dealer to proceed with it. And give him adequate time to do the necessary work.

If you do not get satisfaction, write to the manufacturer's zone manager or factory zone service manager. You can get his name and address from the dealer (and simply asking him for this may make him more co-operative). If the zone manager doesn't get results, write directly to the car's manufacturer. A courteous and objective letter—giving full, appropriate details—will have the best chance of success. Or use the manufacturer's toll-free "action line" (Chapter 28) for complaints.

In a few places, you can take your problem to a small claims court—where you do not need to be represented by a lawyer—to get a settlement for substantial manufacturing defects. A settlement may even include reimbursement for your lost pay, time, and for the cost of renting alternative transportation—depending on the state in which you live. (See Chapter 26.)

You can work through a local consumer group to spur a dealer to action by, say, running an ad in your local newspaper detailing how the dealer short-changed you. But *don't* attempt this on your own without legal advice.

You also can write to the Office of Consumer Affairs, Washington, D.C. 20506, asking the OCA to write to the appropriate authorities on your behalf.

Send copies of your warranty complaint letters to one or more of the organizations listed in Chapter 28.

When you write, include: your name, address, and telephone number; the name and address of the dealer from whom you bought the car; the vehicle make, model, identification number; year and date of purchase; a description of the problem; what measures the dealer says he has taken to solve the problem, the odometer mileage, when the problem arose and the present mileage.

Inform the dealer that you are doing all this.

Court action is your last resort.

USED CAR WARRANTIES

In New Jersey, used car dealers must offer a guarantee that their cars will pass state inspection. In some other states, used cars must pass inspection before they leave the lot. But most states leave the condition of a used car offered for sale pretty much up to the dealer. And since manufacturers do not put pressure on used car dealers, it is difficult to force a reluctant dealer to honor his warranty. Most of the steps outlined above should improve your chances of fair treatment, though.

Shopping for Legal Services

It wasn't so many years ago that only the well to do, the individual with a large estate to distribute, the accident victim, and the divorcing couple used the services of a law firm. Today, however, only a fraction of us—rich, poor, in between—can survive legally or financially without the services of a lawyer. Today, not only are rapidly mounting numbers of middle-income Americans becoming clients of lawyers but hundreds of thousands of the lowest-income brackets also are routinely using neighborhood legal facilities for a wide variety of problems.

BASIC RULES ON CHOOSING A LAWYER

The best time to decide who will be your family lawyer is *before* you need one. If you are new in town or have never used the services of a lawyer before, find out through the Yellow Pages if the local bar association has a Lawyer's Referral Service. Or you can write directly to the American Bar Association, 1155 East 60th Street, Chicago, Ill. 60637, which runs this service.

More than 260 cities now have such services and they are used annually by hundreds of thousands of Americans. For only $5.00 to $10 this service can advise you whether a particular problem you have actually requires legal help—and, if so, who can handle it. In a majority of cases, problems are resolved within an hour or so—at very modest cost. Cases needing more attention are referred to competent private lawyers.

Check each prospective lawyer's reputation—for competence, responsiveness, and reliability—with friends, bank officers, real estate agents, your company lawyer, or others. The Martindale-Hubbell directory, which should be available in your library, lists and rates lawyers throughout the United States.

Don't be lured by any lawyer who holds out to you the hope of an unusually fat court settlement in, say, a negligence case. Look, instead, for evidence that a lawyer's key interest is in *preventing* major legal confrontations and in making all reasonable efforts to keep you *out* of court.

Be sure that both husband and wife *like* and *trust* the person you are considering as a family lawyer.

WHICH LEGAL SERVICES DO YOU NEED?

Inquire about what services and specialties are and are not provided by the law firm as a whole. If services important to you are not provided, ask whether the lawyer or firm has access to top-notch outside legal specialists.

Here's a partial list of the various legal services a family lawyer should be able to provide:

• Deed preparation, title searches and other details of a real estate transaction. (See Chapter 13, "A Roof Over Your Head," for a description of the legal mechanics of home buying.)

• Drawing up a will and perhaps later serving as executor or legal adviser for your estate. (See Chapter 17, "What You Should Know About Wills, Estates, and Trusts.")

• Representing you in and out of court if you should be arrested or sued, or if you should decide to sue someone else.

• Preparing a separation agreement and other documents associated with a divorce and, if necessary, representing you in a divorce court. (See Chapter 16, "The High Cost of Divorce.")

• Steering you to a competent insurance agent, tax adviser, and other experts whose fees are much lower or who will make a special arrangement for you. But the key point is to discuss fees before you hire *any* lawyer. Find out, in advance, not only the hourly rate for routine office work but also the cost of specific legal jobs you want performed and how small legal questions you ask over the phone will be handled.

HOW TO SLASH LEGAL COSTS

But what if you cannot afford to pay anywhere near what a lawyer asks to help you solve a serious legal problem? Then . . .

• Go to one of the nation's 500-plus Legal Aid Society offices. Check the Yellow Pages under "Legal Aid" or "Attorneys" or call the local bar association for the address and phone. These societies are backed by community funds and offer legal aid at low or no cost. (In criminal cases, the best source of free help is the Public Defender.)

• Or go to one of the 1,000-plus Neighborhood Legal Service agencies, staffed by more than 2,000 lawyers specializing in poverty law.

• Check if any law schools in your area have set up legal service facilities for ordinary consumers or low-income groups.

• Find out if your company or labor union offers free legal advice or group "lawyer insurance" (a few do) with premiums deducted from your pay check. You also may be able to buy a prepaid legal plan on the open market.

• Ask a lawyer to charge you at the regular hourly rate for all services he performs for you; this is almost always cheaper.

• Determine which local law firms are using less costly "paraprofessional" help (law students, etc.) to prepare certain types of routine legal documents; you'll be charged less too.

• If you and your spouse are drawing up wills, do it at the same time. You may get the second will at a 50 per cent discount (see Chapter 17, "What You Should Know About Wills, Estates and Trusts").

• Consult "A Shopper's Guide to Lawyers." Available free to Pennsylvanians: send a self-addressed 9×12-inch envelope with two postage stamps to the Pennsylvania Insurance Department, Finance Building, Harrisburg, Pa. 17120. For residents of other states: send $1.00 to Consumer News, Inc., 813 National Press Building, Washington, D.C. 20045.

WHAT YOU SHOULD KNOW ABOUT CONTRACTS

Under most circumstances, any contract you sign legally compels you to abide by its provisions, including the fine print. To protect yourself against being stuck with a contract you'll regret, therefore, the fundamental rule is to avoid being a legal party to any agreement binding you to do anything you do not wish to do, are not able to do, or cannot afford to do. Learn how to spot the key pitfalls which tend to turn up in the kind of contract you'll wish you hadn't signed.

In Chapter 13, "A Roof Over Your Head," you'll find the key guide on several major types of contracts: deeds and real estate sales agreements, home improvement contracts, and apartment leases. But these are very special categories. Going far beyond all special points are these two guides applying to contracts in general:

Do be sure you really need, want, and can afford the product or service for which you are signing the contract.

Do be sure you understand every word a contract contains—or hire a lawyer to understand it for you, or ask a friend who you think may know more about such matters than you know, or go to your local Legal Aid office.

TYPES OF CONTRACTS

Here are examples of contracts, many of which you almost surely will have occasion to sign at some time:

a sales agreement to buy a house, a car, or some other major item;

a marriage (in some states even an engagement is a legal contract);

a separation agreement preceding a divorce decree and the divorce contract itself;

a loan contract with a bank or finance company;

a partnership agreement to launch a new business;

a contract establishing a corporation of any kind, profit or non-profit;

an insurance policy;

an agreement to employ the services of a real estate agent, an employment agency, a literary agent, a service company;

an agreement covering the terms of your employment, used by many types of employers.

THE CONDITIONAL SALES CONTRACT

A conditional sales contract is probably the most common type of contract being used in connection with purchases of automobiles, appliances, or other items you are buying on time. The key provision of such a contract is that the seller retains legal title to the goods he is selling until you have made the last payment. Meanwhile you, the buyer, assume full responsibility for any loss or damage to the goods. So, in cases where large amounts of money are involved, definitely consider life insurance coverage during the repayment period.

Similarly, with a chattel mortgage you, the buyer of a car, or a refrigerator, a TV set, or similar item on time, transfer title to the item you are buying to the seller-lender until the entire loan, including interest, has been paid off.

HOW TO SAFEGUARD YOURSELF

So, *do* be sure to get a copy of any contract you have signed.

Do, where contracts are involved, deal only with a reputable individual or company. The fly-by-night door-to-door huckster who persuades you to sign a contract to purchase whatever he happens to be selling may disappear from town, taking his promises with him—but leaving the contract in force until *you* have fulfilled *your* part of the deal.

Do find out if there are any provisions for cancellation of the contract, and understand the circumstances under which you may cancel.

Do be sure that you understand exactly what (if anything) the seller is agreeing to do for *you*—e.g., in terms of guaranteeing his product or service. Note: As a general rule, contracts are written primarily to protect the seller, not you.

Do remember that a contract does not have to be "legal-looking" in order to be binding. Contracts come in all shapes and sizes, long and short, written simply or loaded with bafflegab.

Do be sure, if a salesman promises you verbally that goods and services in addition to those provided for in the contract also will be provided, that the details on these extras are written into the agreement.

Do be sure that any goods or services or obligations for which you do not wish to sign up, but which are mentioned in the contract, are stricken from all copies of the contract.

Do be prepared to live up to every aspect of any contract you sign. This is your part of the deal, whatever a salesman may have told you verbally. If you do *not* do so, you may risk losing the entire investment you may already have made in the product or service covered by the contract.

Don't make the mistake of signing a sales contract for an appliance in the mistaken belief that it is a receipt for a "free trial."

Don't sign any contract unless blank spaces have been filled in or crossed out in permanent ink. Signing a blank or penciled contract is like signing a blank check.

Don't permit yourself to be pressured into signing any contract.

Don't overlook tricky clauses which may appear in a contract, often in the fine print. If you cannot have the clauses eliminated, at least make sure you know what they mean. (See Chapter 3, "How to Borrow Cash and Use Credit Wisely," for details on credit traps.)

HOW TO CANCEL A CONTRACT

If you find that you have been tricked into signing an installment sales contract that obligates you beyond your means, check into your rights via your state attorney general's office, your state and/or local consumer protection agency.

You may be able to have a contract which is flagrantly deceptive canceled—if you can persuade a court that the contract involved fraud or a major breach of warranty (e.g., a TV set which is dead on arrival and which the seller can't or won't fix).

You may be able to get it canceled if you can prove to a court that you were forced to sign a contract.

Also, a contract that is for an illegal purpose—such as gambling in a state where gambling is illegal—is not legally binding.

And under some circumstances an unmarried minor is permitted by law to cancel a contract that a person of legal majority age could not cancel.

A reputable, well-established home improvement contractor in your community probably would permit you to duck out of a contract you signed if work on your project had not begun and if you could persuade the contractor that you simply were not financially able to go through with the deal.

And the federal Truth in Lending law gives you a "cooling-off" period of three business days after you have signed a contract involving a credit transaction in which your house is being used as collateral. This cooling-off period is usually your last chance to change your mind and cancel the contract. (See Chapter 27, "Your Other Basic Rights," for a rundown on the cooling-off period.)

Federal Trade Commission rules also give you a three-day cooling-off period to cancel any contract you have signed with a door-to-door salesman for more than $25. This rule does not apply to the relatively few firms with no interstate business, though. Note: Your cancellation *must* be in writing.

Other protections for you are under consideration or on the way but, in total, the safeguards offered you as of the mid-1970s by federal or state laws were still limited. And getting that protection on your own—via lawyers or court claims—may be a costly ordeal.

So, where contracts are concerned, you must still fall back on the oldest rule of the market place: "Caveat emptor" or "let the buyer beware."

LEGAL BAFFLEGAB GUIDE

BAR ASSOCIATION: State or local association of lawyers who also may be members of the American Bar Association.

CAVEAT EMPTOR: "Let the buyer beware." (A variation on this theme is former Pennsylvania Insurance Commissioner Herbert Denenberg's motto— "Populus Iamdudum Defutatus Est," or "The public has been screwed long enough.")

CLAIM: A demand for something due or believed to be owed; or, a right to something of value.

CLASS ACTION: Legal action in which one or more individuals move against a racketeer, polluter of public waterways, government agency, stock market manipulator, or other individual, agency, or business on behalf of an aggrieved group or "class" of citizens.

CONDEMNATION: Procedure used by federal, state, or local governments to take a part of your property (e.g., land) for public use (e.g., a new highway).

CONDITIONAL SALES CONTRACT: Usual type of sales agreement, in which the seller keeps legal title to goods you are buying until you have paid in full.

CONFESSION OF JUDGMENT: Tricky clause appearing in some contracts and leases in which the purchaser or tenant forfeits his right—in advance—to challenge legally a salesman or landlord (or other purveyor of goods or services) who fails to live up to *his* part of the deal; illegal in most states.

CONSUMER LAW: Relatively large body of law designed to protect the ordinary consumer against such threats as: hazardous foods, drugs, and other products; mislabeling and misrepresentation of goods and services; meaningless or unfulfilled warranties; gyps and frauds.

CONTINGENCY FEE: Form of payment to a lawyer often used in personal injury and liability cases in which the lawyer gets a certain fixed percentage of the court award if he wins the case, nothing if he loses.

CONTRACT: Legal agreement, usually (but not necessarily) in writing between two or more people (or corporations or other such legal entities) binding each party to abide by its provisions.

DEFAULT: Failure to comply with a legal agreement (especially a sales agreement, a home mortgage, or an installment loan).

DEFICIENCY JUDGMENT: Determination by a court order (e.g., following mortgage foreclosure) of amount of money owed to a creditor, and how the outstanding balance on the loan will be repaid after the collateral has been repossessed and sold.

ESCROW: An aid in securing a deal—such as a real estate sale—in which the buyer turns over part or all of the purchase price to a bank or other third party, which in turn delivers the payment to the seller after certain conditions have been met.

LEGAL AID SOCIETY: Nationwide network of publicly supported legal agencies that provide low-cost legal services for those who cannot afford to pay for such services, often including court costs.

LEGAL INSURANCE: Prepaid group insurance, available through some employers and unions, covering fees for certain specified legal procedures.

LIABILITY: Financial responsibility based on a contractual obligation you (or a company) have assumed, arising from negligence on the part of this person or company or other party—especially in the event of accident or personal injury.

LIEN: Claim against a property used as security for payment of a debt. A *mechanic's lien* is one in which your house is used as security by carpenters and others who are involved in a construction or home improvement project at your house.

NEIGHBORHOOD LEGAL SERVICE CENTERS: Network of federally subsidized law offices in poverty areas of the United States, such as big-city ghettos, offering low-cost or no-cost legal help.

OMBUDSMAN: Term, originating in Sweden, used to describe the individual citizen's own publicly supported representative who pleads the citizen's cause against unfair or illegal actions by government officials or agencies. Now broadened in the United States to include "ombudsmen" who are employed by corporations and others in private life to represent and plead the consumer's cause within the organization. Legal Aid and Neighborhood Legal Service lawyers often perform the ombudsman's function.

PERSONAL PROPERTY: Cash, stocks and bonds, insurance policies, jewelry, furs, automobiles, and similar tangible personal belongings.

POWER OF ATTORNEY: Legal power which you may convey to a broker, bank, friend, or other individual to execute certain transactions—e.g., purchase stock or sign checks on your behalf at that person's (or institution's) own discretion.

PUBLIC DEFENDER: Publicly supported lawyer or legal group offering free legal representation to the needy in criminal cases.

REAL PROPERTY: Land, including any buildings such as a house, garage, or barn that are attached to it.

RIGHT OF RESCISSION OR "COOLING OFF" PERIOD: Your right, as a consumer, backed by federal and state law under many circumstances, to cancel a sales contract within a given period of time if you change your mind.

SMALL CLAIMS COURT: Court in which an ordinary citizen may "be his own lawyer" and prosecute his own case so long as his claim involves only a relatively small amount of money.

WAIVER: Forfeiture of certain legal rights or responsibilities via a written clause in a deed, contract, or other legal agreement.

WARRANTY: There are two key types: an *express warranty,* the common type, covering automobiles and household equipment, is in writing and states what the manufacturer promises to do if the product fails to perform as represented; an *implied warranty* is unwritten and says that something you have bought should operate as it is supposed to.

27

YOUR OTHER BASIC RIGHTS

Your Rights as a Worker

Today, there are federal and state laws covering just about every aspect of work: minimum wage laws, equal pay for equal work laws, overtime rules, on-the-job safety and health laws, child labor laws, and many more. But gross neglect and flagrant violation of these laws still exist. Moreover, employee protection laws and rules are made, revised, and enforced by literally dozens of separate federal and state agencies, divisions, and departments. Thus you, the employee, must remain the "policeman" of your own workplace. What are your rights? How do you make sure you get them?

YOUR RIGHT TO A JOB

The *Employment Act of 1946* makes it a continuing responsibility of the federal government to foster economic and financial conditions which will promote high employment and offer useful employment opportunities for those able, willing, and seeking to work.

YOUR RIGHT TO A MINIMUM WAGE

The *Fair Labor Standards Act of 1938* and its long string of amendments require employers to pay a minimum hourly rate to workers in covered employment. ($2.10 in 1975 for most covered employment.) Virtually all types of workers were covered by the mid-1970s.

The Fair Labor Standards Act is administered by the Wage and Hour Division, Employment Standards Administration, of the U. S. Department of Labor in Washington. (See Chapter 28, "Where to Get Help," for the addresses of this and other public and private agencies concerned with enforcement of your rights in dozens of different areas.)

In some states, these occupations are covered by state minimum wage laws. In addition, this act provides for extra pay for overtime work for the majority of workers. The lowest overtime pay must be at least one and one half times the regular rate after forty hours a week.

This act also rides herd over U.S. child labor laws—of which the key provision is that children under age sixteen may not be employed in most types of work. The minimum age for occupations defined as hazardous by the Secretary of Labor (e.g., mining, warehousing, logging) is eighteen.

YOUR RIGHT TO JOIN A UNION

The *National Labor Relations Act of 1934* and amendments to it guarantee the right of employees in private industry to organize and bargain collectively—including the right to strike.

YOUR RIGHT TO EQUAL EMPLOYMENT OPPORTUNITY

Another major category of protection you, the employee, have today is equal access to jobs, pay, promotion, training, fringe benefits. Here are the key federal laws offering the guarantee of equal employment opportunity:

(1) The equal protection clause of the Fourteenth Amendment to the United States Constitution prohibits discrimination by federal, state, or local governments against *any* category of citizens involved in any government-connected activity.

(2) The *1870 Civil Rights Act* provides that all Americans shall have the same right as "white citizens, to enter into contracts." Under this historic law, you have the right to sue in federal or state court if you are the victim of job discrimination by unions or by employers on account of race. Unions, for example, may not be granted the support of the government if they are practicing discrimination. Employers may not do business as government contractors if they practice job discrimination.

(3) The *1964 Civil Rights Act* specifically bans job discrimination in private employment on account of race, sex, religion, or national origin. This law also prohibits discrimination against anyone who wants to join a union or who is seeking the services of an employment agency. It bars discrimination across the board—not just against a worker who is applying for a job but also discrimination in help wanted ads, pay scales, promotions, training programs, seniority rules, pension plans and other fringe benefits, many other aspects of employment. This law applies to all employers with fifteen or more employees, and also covers employees of state and local government and educational institutions.

Apprenticeship and training programs that are registered with the Federal Bureau of Apprenticeship and Training are subject to special non-discrimination requirements with regard to race, creed, color, sex, and national origin. These rules cover all phases of the program, including initial selection of trainees and employment during the program.

YOUR WORK RIGHTS AS A WOMAN

The *only* legal grounds for job discrimination on the basis of sex as of the mid-seventies is if sex is a "bona fide occupational qualification" (e.g., as it is for fashion models), if hiring a woman would violate our basic morals (e.g., as a men's rest-room attendant), or if this would imply unreasonable extra expenses for an employer.

Since many companies today still are practicing both subtle and direct forms of illegal discrimination, here is a rundown on women's rights in the job market place under the 1964 Civil Rights Act:

• Unless state law prohibits it, women must now be considered for jobs requiring the lifting of heavy loads—if they want such jobs and are capable of doing the lifting.

• If a woman applies for a job in an all-male shop and doesn't mind hearing four-letter words, an employer must now give her a fair chance for employment—assuming it doesn't involve installing costly facilities to accommodate her. Similarly, if a man wants to work in an all-female office and is qualified for the job, it's up to him—not the employer—to decide whether he's "out of place."

• Women must be considered for jobs as "salesmen," even if the job involves traveling alone. The premise is that if a woman is twenty-one (or, in some states, eighteen) she's old enough to look out for her own welfare.

• A company also must admit qualified women to executive training programs, provided the women state they would be willing to relocate later, if necessary.

• Specifically banned under the Civil Rights Act: setting waiting periods before a woman becomes eligible for maternity benefits and labeling job advertisements "men wanted" or "women wanted"—when sex is not a "bona fide occupational qualification."

WOMEN'S RIGHT TO EQUAL PAY

The worst form of discrimination against women is our abysmally wide "pay gap."

According to the Census Bureau, as of the mid-seventies American women were earning less than 60 per cent of the amounts men did—a proportion which had actually dropped since 1955, when it was 64 per cent.

There are two important sides of the pay gap:

First, the jobs most women hold are not in fact "equal" to the jobs that men hold; even in a professional field such as elementary school teaching, most classroom teachers are women, while most principals are men. In institutions of higher education, women are much less likely than men to be full or even associate professors. In the technical fields, women are usually in the lowest categories—e.g., draftsmen or engineering technicians. These inequalities in the *kinds* of jobs men and women hold are partly a reflection of real differences in educational qualifications but they also are—in many instances —sheer discrimination.

Second, even when men and women hold jobs that *are* in fact equal in the skills and experience required, the pay they get for their work often is *not* equal. In some occupations the pay gap is much wider than the 60 per cent average.

Your key defense against the "pay gap" is the federal Equal Pay for Equal Work law. The 1963 Equal Pay Act went into effect in June 1964 and was quickly followed by "equal pay" laws in most states. This law is administered by the Wage and Hour Division, Employment Standards Administration, U. S. Department of Labor.

YOUR RIGHTS AS AN OLDER WORKER

The *1967 Age Discrimination in Employment Act,* administered by the Department of Labor's Wage and Hour Division:

bans employers of twenty or more workers from firing or refusing to hire an individual aged forty to sixty-five simply because of his or her age —unless age is a bona fide qualification, such as modeling dresses for teen-agers;

forbids employment agencies to refuse to refer a job applicant for a job opening because of his or her age;

prohibits any statement of age preferences—e.g., "Boy," "Girl," "under twenty"—by employers or employment agencies in help-wanted ads.

prohibits favoring younger workers in pay, promotion, and fringe benefits, or similar practices;

bars unions with twenty-five or more members from denying membership to older persons or refusing to refer an older member to a job.

Your rights to your earned pension benefits, closely related to your rights as an older worker, are described in Chapter 19, "Planning for Your Financial and Personal Security."

YOUR UNEMPLOYMENT INSURANCE RIGHTS

And if you lose your job?

As an executive, your contract with your former employer almost surely provides for some amount of severance pay (often a substantial amount). Or the company which plans to lay you off may permit you to continue working until you have located a suitable new job.

Another vitally important source of between-job financial assistance for workers in all pay brackets is unemployment insurance benefits. These could be a significant financial life jacket until you land a new job—whatever your income bracket. And these benefits are yours by law. The minimums and maximums vary from state to state, according to your marital status and also the number of your dependents, but in the early 1970s covered unemployed workers were getting minimum benefits from $5.00 to $25 a week while maximums ranged from $49 to $147. In the past the maximum span of time during which benefits are paid has been 26 weeks, but all states in the mid-seventies had provisions to stretch this to 39 weeks as long as the national jobless rate persisted at 4.5 per cent or more—and in some states with even higher rates, the span was 52 weeks.

The size of your savings nest egg has nothing to do with your eligibility for unemployment compensation. You may collect unemployment benefits if you're on welfare—although the amount of your welfare is based on the amount of your other income, including unemployment benefits.

Workers in virtually all occupations are covered except those working for religious institutions, for the public school system, in agriculture, and for certain very small businesses and most household workers.

Who pays for unemployment compensation?

Employers pay a fixed percentage of each covered worker's wage up to $4,200 a year. The percentage varies from state to state and in many cases from firm to firm.

YOUR RIGHTS TO SAFE AND HEALTHFUL WORKING CONDITIONS

The *1970 Occupational Safety and Health Act* was designed to "assure so far as possible every working man and woman in the nation safe and healthful working conditions." It eventually could turn out to be the most important new source of protection for the U.S. worker in this half of the twentieth century.

About three out of four civilian workers in 5 million workplaces throughout the country are covered. Everybody, in fact, is covered except workers (such as public employees and coal miners) covered by other federal job safety programs. The safety law provisions also apply to workers in training.

The Occupational Safety and Health Administration (OSHA) of the U. S. Department of Labor, based in Washington, sets the rules and enforces this law. The National Institute for Occupational Safety and Health within the U. S. Department of Health, Education and Welfare acts as a research agency, investigates working conditions and complaints, explores specific threats to workers' health and safety, and develops safety information used in formulating health and safety standards.

OSHA has several hundred inspectors in the field, and if you report a complaint it is up to these inspectors to visit your plant or office, explore the details, and set the machinery in motion to right the situation. Inspectors are supposed to arrive unannounced, and you can ask to have your complaint kept confidential.

If an employer is found violating the law, he may be fined and required to eliminate the hazards. The law provides for fines up to $10,000 for willful or repeated violations and/or six months' imprisonment. The law permits OSHA to go to the courts to have a dangerous workplace or a given dangerous operation within a company closed down until violations are cleaned up.

Here are obvious potential hazards for which you should be on the lookout in your workplace:

Dust, fumes, gases, vapors, and mists that you breathe; radioactive materials, asbestos, microwaves, lasers, drugs and hormones; molds, parasites, or bacteria from animals or animal products; materials that irritate your skin; excessive noise.

Your Rights as a Renter or Homeowner

NEW PROTECTION FOR RENTERS

As long ago as 1949 the *Housing Act of 1937* was amended to set as its objective "a decent home and a suitable living environment for every American family."

However, so medieval are our landlord-tenant laws that only a handful of states now require landlords even to provide "a place fit for the occupation of human beings." Local penalties for violations of housing and health codes are still so frequently minuscule that badly needed repairs may be held up for months or even years.

But this bleak picture is now brightening perceptibly and steadily. In New York State landlords are now legally required to keep rent security deposits made by tenants in interest-bearing accounts. In a landmark decision, a United States Court of Appeals in the District of Columbia upheld the right of striking tenants to put their rent in escrow while housing code violations by their landlords were being settled in court. And this merely suggests what is building up.

Across the nation petitions and rent strikes were becoming daily affairs in the mid-1970s. Tenants' unions were being formed everywhere and were bargaining militantly with their landlords for more and better services ranging from cleaner halls to tighter security measures. Tenant complaints against landlords now include gripes not only about soaring rents but also about lack of heat and hot water, harassment of many kinds, refusal to make needed repairs, etc.

Behind the new militancy are these reasons:

According to the 1970 census, one in fifteen houses and apartments (4.7 million) was minus "basic plumbing facilities," and among Negro households the proportion was one in six. The typical tenant is helpless to get his landlord to make needed repairs. Many landlords still reserve the right to evict their tenants for a wide range of good and bad reasons, to hike rents virtually whenever and by whatever amounts they choose, to enter rented houses or apartments more or less when the spirit moves them, to refuse to re-pay security deposits if they so wish, to refuse to perform certain repairs even in defiance of the lease. In short, the attitude is "What are you going to do about it?"

In big city slums one of the biggest categories of legal problems being tackled by neighborhood law offices is tenant-landlord problems. Even the neighborhood health centers are finding that many health problems with which they are daily confronted—such as lead poisoning from peeling paint—result directly from outright negligence by landlords.

But even at this early stage you, the tenant, do have certain rights and certain ways of enforcing those rights.

If you are threatened by rats, bugs, or similar health hazards, and if your landlord ignores your protests, you have a right to appeal at once to your city's Housing Authority and/or Health Department and to insist on corrective action. Your state and local health laws almost surely also protect you against such dangerous structural defects as faulty wiring and falling plaster. Health codes also protect you against persistent plumbing problems (sewage backups, overflowing septic tanks) and garbage pile-ups.

If you feel there is a fire hazard in your rented house or apartment, your state or local fire laws must protect you against these too. You can easily find out the names of the local authorities: complain and demand enforcement of the fire codes.

If you live in any type of public housing and have a legal complaint—for example, in connection with your lease or for sudden eviction without a rea-son, or for being charged for breakage in your apartment which you did not cause—you are protected by a standard set of rights and grievance procedures issued by the Federal Department of Housing and Urban Development and administered by the public housing authority.

As a tenant you have a right to demand that your landlord perform those repairs which have been agreed upon in the lease. And if he fails to live up to his lease you might even simply have the repairs done and deduct the costs from your rent check. Such a course of action has been upheld by at least one state Supreme Court—so long as sufficient notice is given to the landlord be-fore the repairs are ordered. It is advisable to consult a lawyer before taking such a step, however.

A rent strike is a more drastic—but increasingly common—course of ac-tion being taken by tenants at all income levels, as a defense against exorbi-tant rent hikes, shoddy building maintenance by landlords, inadequate heat-ing, and leaky plumbing. Another of this era's powerful trends, in fact, is toward collective bargaining between tenants' groups and their landlords. This trend affects not just low-income groups but all socioeconomic classes including the inhabitants of luxury apartments.

YOUR RIGHTS AS A HOME BUYER

If you are among the many who have bought or are considering buying a house which the contractor has not yet built, you have a legal right to sue the builder if your house turns out to have been built improperly. The courts are becoming increasingly sympathetic to such actions as development housing continues its explosive growth and alarming numbers of buyers find that the houses they have agreed to buy are seriously defective. Such sales, the courts are ruling, carry an implied warranty that the completed house will be reasonably fit for human habitation.

Thus, if you find that the air conditioner duct work has been improperly installed, or the foundation has cracked because the soil beneath your house has settled and your new roof leaks, you may have cause for recovery of damages connected with the dwelling's shortcomings.

AND YOUR "FAIR HOUSING" RIGHTS

Finally, if you, a single woman, a family with children, or a member of a minority group, find that you are being discriminated against in buying or renting a house or apartment, understand fully that this discrimination is illegal under almost all circumstances.

If you find that a lease or an advertisement contains any racially discriminating clauses, you have a right to have them stricken from the lease. Such clauses violate federal civil rights laws.

Title VIII of the *1968 Civil Rights Act*—our key federal "fair housing" statute—specifically guarantees equal access to housing by all U.S. citizens. It prohibits discrimination in almost all housing—rental or purchase—on the basis of race, color, religion, or national origin.

If you believe you have been a victim of discrimination in housing you can do one or both of the following:

(1) File a complaint, giving details of the discrimination, with the Secretary of Housing and Urban Development, Washington, D.C. 20410. Address your complaint to "Fair Housing."

(2) Take your complaint directly to the United States District Court or to a state or local court—in the form of a private civil action. If you go this route, get the advice of a lawyer.

YOUR RIGHTS AS A TAXPAYER

You have just come home from an infuriating afternoon at the local office of the Internal Revenue Service—during which you tried with increasing desperation to convince an IRS agent that you *do not* owe an extra $300 on your latest income tax return. But the IRS agent won't concede a dollar, even though you are convinced of your right to deduct $1,000 of disputed contributions to your church. Further appeals within the IRS have been abysmal failures.

You are incensed. You want to fight the IRS, not to give in with a whimper. What do you do? Your basic right, as a taxpayer, is to pay *only* the federal income tax which you actually owe—and to pay not one cent more. To protect this basic right, you, as a taxpayer, have a distinct and formal set of legal procedures you can use.

HOW TO FIGHT THE IRS

You may fight the IRS—via the Small Tax Case Division of the U. S. Tax Court, the court which Congress created specifically to help you, the taxpayer, and which came into existence in 1971 under a minor provision of the Tax Reform Act of 1969.

This provision authorized the Tax Court to appoint tax commissioners (rather than judges) to hear and decide small claims—now defined as any dispute about income, gift, or estate taxes involving not more than $1,500. You argue your own case without a lawyer and without filing any technical and time-consuming forms. In the Small Tax Case Division, the technical rules of evidence are off and the dominant rule instead is informality. However, if you wish, you may hire a lawyer or file a brief or do both.

You have no worries about strangulating red tape or masses of paper work. Both are at a minimum. You will not be placed at an immediate disadvantage by being forced to travel far from your home for your informal hearing and the decision. A hearing on your case will be held as near your home as the court finds possible, and you'll get advance notice of when your case is coming up. The Small Tax Case commissioners hold hearings in more than 100 cities across the nation each year. You won't have to wait long for a decision either. The commissioner hearing your case probably will decide whether you win or lose against the IRS within thirty days.

Of course, since this is a division of the Tax Court, you can fight your own case there without first paying the tax deficiency claimed by the IRS. Only if and when you lose or settle will you have to pay up. If you were to use the other courts—a district court or the Court of Claims—you would have to pay the deficiency claimed by the IRS first and then bring suit for a refund to get that money back.

You can be relaxed when telling your side of the dispute, trusting the commissioner hearing you to give you any benefit of the doubt. In fact the commissioner probably will help you to bring out points in your own favor which, in your innocence, you might overlook or shrug off on your own.

Moreover, the decisions of the commissioner are not subject to review by any other court. This means that neither party—neither the taxpayer nor the IRS—can appeal the decision to any higher court. This encourages the commissioners to rule more speedily and freely, for they do not face the possibility of being overthrown by another court.

And the fact that the decisions set no precedents means that a commissioner's ruling in one case will have no effect on future cases in any court. This encourages the commissioners to be more lenient with taxpayers, for they need not fear that their rulings will open the way for cases which would cost the Treasury countless tens of millions of dollars.

So, what if you are the reasonable taxpayer described above and you want to fight the IRS's claim that you owe $300 more on your last year's taxes?

WHAT TO DO

Here's what you do:

(1) Get a ninety-day letter (its official name is a "notice of deficiency") from the IRS office that is handling your case. You must start your case in the Tax Court within ninety days after the date on which that ninety-day letter is mailed to you. If you do not, you lose your right to litigate in the Tax Court.

(2) Write to the Clerk of the Court, U. S. Tax Court, Washington, D.C. 20217, and ask for four copies each of these two forms:

Form 2 Petition (Small Tax Case).

Form 4 Request for Place of Trial.

(3) Fill out the forms. They are very simple.

In paragraph one of Form 2 Petition fill in the taxable year or years for which the deficiency is claimed and the city and state of the IRS office that sent you the ninety-day letter.

To illustrate, in your case it would read: "John and Mary Doe, Petitioners v. Commissioner of Internal Revenue, Respondent. Petitioners request the court to redetermine the tax deficiency for the year 197 . . . , as set forth in the notice of deficiency, dated (blank), a copy of which is attached. The notice was issued by the Office of the Internal Revenue Service at 120 Church Street, New York, N.Y. 10007."

In paragraph two, fill in your Social Security number and your spouse's if a joint return is involved. In your case, it would read: "Petitioners' taxpayer identification [e.g., Social Security] numbers are 012-34-5678 and 876-54-3210."

In paragraph three, tell how you disagree with the IRS deficiency notice. If your case, it would read: "Year, 197 . . . Amount of deficiency disputed, $300."

In paragraph four, state briefly where you think the IRS agent went wrong in claiming you owe more taxes. In your case, you might write: "The commissioner of Internal Revenue made the following error in determining this tax deficiency: he mistakenly disallowed the entire $1,000 amount that I deducted as a charitable contribution."

Also, give facts to support your claim that the commissioner was wrong. In your case, you might write: "We have witnesses who saw me give $1,000 in cash to my church as part of a special fund-raising drive on May 6, 197 . . ."

Now you sign the petition, with your spouse if it is a joint return, and give your present address. For example:

"John Doe, 105 Main Street, New York, N.Y. 10010.

"Mary Doe, 105 Main Street, New York, N.Y. 10010."

The official form has this paragraph about your signatures: "Petitioners request that the proceedings in this case be conducted as a 'small tax case' under section 7463 of the Internal Revenue Code of 1954, as amended, and Rule 172 of the Rules of Practice of the United States Tax Court."

There also is room for the signature and address of your lawyer if you retain one—but I'm assuming you're battling the IRS in this instance all on your own with a minimum of expense and red tape. For that's the central idea of this Small Tax Case Division.

Now make three identical copies of the Petition and set them aside.

(4) Turn to Form 4 Request for Place of Trial, of which you also have four copies. Fill out one form by listing the city and state in which you would like to have your trial and by signing it where required.

To illustrate in your case, the form would read: "John and Mary Doe, Petitioners v. Commissioner of Internal Revenue, Respondent Petitioners hereby request that trial of this case be held at New York City, New York State. (Signed) John Doe, husband. Mary Doe, wife." And that's all there is to it!

Make three identical copies of this form too.

(5) Make out a check or money order for $10 payable to "Clerk, U. S. Tax Court."

(6) Mail this check together with the original and two copies of your Petition and the original and two copies of your Request for Place of Trial to: United States Tax Court, Washington, D.C. 20217.

Keep one copy of each form for yourself.

(7) The commissioner will answer your petition and, almost surely, will make some concession or compromise suggestion—assuming you have a fairly reasonable case.

If there is still a disagreement between the IRS and you after the commissioner's answer, your case will be set for trial at a time and place of which you will be notified by the court.

(8) The size and location of the city you have selected for your trial will determine whether the Tax Court will be able to comply with your request in your Form 4. (New York City is a cinch.) But, if the court cannot comply,

it will pick a place that is as close and convenient to your choice as possible and it will then notify you.

A crucial point is that the commissioner will try to persuade you to settle the case without going to trial, if your case has any validity. If you are satisfied with any settlement offer, that will end the case. A fat majority of taxpayers, incidentally, do settle before trial.

A caution, however: even though the Small Tax Case Division is informal, easygoing, relaxed, and designed to help *you*, the taxpayer, you still must have a reasonable case to win.

YOUR RIGHTS AS A BORROWER

The 1969 Truth in Lending law requires virtually all lenders to spell out clearly and boldly the true interest costs and other finance charges you are paying for any given loan. In essence, this historic legislation gives you superb ways to compare the *real* costs of a loan from Lender A versus a loan from Lender B.

The list of items of information that must be spelled out—both on the loan contract itself and in any lender's advertisement of loan terms—is long and detailed. Here's a sampling of the information you *must* be given:

• The amount of your loan and amount of your down payment.

• The total dollar "amount financed" and true annual rate of the finance charge, expressed as the "annual percentage rate." The "amount financed" is to include all charges, individually itemized, which are included in the amount of credit extended but which are not part of the finance charge.

• The number, amount, and dates of payments.

• The date on which the finance charge begins to accrue, if different from the date of the transaction.

• The total amount of the finance charge, using the term "finance charge," *except* in the case of a loan secured by a first lien or equivalent security interest on a dwelling and made to finance the purchase of that dwelling.

• A description or identification of any security interest.

• A description of any penalty charge for prepayment along with a description of the method of computation of such charge and the conditions under which such charges may be imposed.

• The amount, or method of computing the amount, of any delinquency or similar charges payable in the event of late payments.

• The sum of all payments, using the term "total of payments" except in the case of a loan secured by a first lien.

The Truth in Lending law applies to virtually all consumer credit transactions—whether you are borrowing cash directly, charging a purchase, or financing a car. The law specifies the conditions of the credit agreement which must be disclosed to you before you open a charge account. For example, the creditor must tell you: how the creditor determines the amount of the finance charge; how long you can postpone paying without having to pay a finance charge; the minimum periodic payment required. It also lists the information which must be included in your monthly statement: including your previous balance on the account, the date and amount of each of your purchases, a recognizable description of each item you have charged, credits for returns, other adjustments, the amount of the finance charge for the month, and many more items. And it spells out how credit on charge accounts may be advertised.

The Truth in Lending law also protects you from illegal use of your credit cards. You are liable for a maximum of $50 in losses in the case of unauthorized use of any credit card which has been stolen from you. This maximum—per card—holds even if you fail to discover the loss for a considerable period of time, and even if you fail to notify the issuer promptly. However, if the issuer has failed to provide a self-addressed, prestamped notice for you to use in the event you lose the card, you have no liability at all. You also have no liability if the credit card issued to you has a photograph of you or other method of identification of you as the person authorized to use the card.

The key point for you to remember is that if there is a $50 liability limit it applies to each card you have which is subject to this limit.

Under Truth in Lending, it's also illegal to mail unsolicited credit cards—a major protection against credit card thieves snatching, and using, credit cards you didn't even know you had.

Home improvement contractors also are covered under this law. Any home improvement contractor who has made a deal under which you get credit as well as home improvements, and under which your home would be security for a loan, must not only give you detailed information on credit costs in his installment contract but also inform you that you have a right to a three-day rescission—or "cooling-off"—period during which you may change your mind about having the improvements performed and cancel the contract you may have signed.

Note: In any credit transaction in which you put up your home to secure a loan, the lender is legally required to give you two copies of a "Notice of the Right of Rescission," one of which you may use to cancel the loan contract if you so decide.

Other types of loans to which this three-day cooling-off period applies are: most second mortgages, loan refinancings, repair bills with finance charges or involving payments in more than four installments or in which there are mechanics' and similar liens (see Chapter 13, "A Roof Over Your Head," for a description of mechanics' liens). You should assume that such a lien exists unless it is specifically waived in your home improvement contract. Such liens, although not mentioned in most contracts, are automatically effective in most states for the protection of home improvement contractors and their employees.

The advertising of credit terms is regulated by Truth in Lending too. If a seller or lender advertises any specific credit term, he also must include in the ad all other pertinent credit terms. Thus he may not simply advertise "no down payment" or "36 months to pay" without saying no down payment for what, for how large a monthly payment schedule, and under what other important conditions. Exception: advertisements of certain revolving charge accounts.

"Advertising" includes commercial messages in newspapers, magazines, catalogs, leaflets, flyers, radio and television broadcasts, public address announcements, and direct mail literature. Any printed promotional materials available at the store, bank, or other lender's establishment are covered and so are price tags on merchandise.

If a creditor fails to make these disclosures to you, you may sue for twice the amount of the finance charge (but no less than $100 or no more than $1,000). Also, you can be reimbursed for court costs and attorney's fees if you win the lawsuit.

However, even if you do win, you still have to pay off the debt, including the finance charges. For lenders who deliberately violate the law, the government may impose criminal penalties including fines up to $5,000 or up to one year in prison, or both.

Several federal agencies share responsibility for enforcing the Truth in Lending law. You'll find all of their names, addresses, and areas of jurisdiction in Chapter 28, "Where to Get Help."

Still another area in which you now have legal protection as a borrower is wage garnishment (the legal withholding of a part of your wages by your employer to repay a creditor whom you have failed to repay). The Truth in Lending law limits the amount of your wages which may be subject to garnishment to whichever is less of the following formulas: your after-tax earnings above thirty times the federal minimum hourly wage or 25 per cent of your weekly pay check. In states where wage garnishment laws provide the borrower with more protection than the federal law, the state rules hold.

The law also makes it illegal for an employer to fire you simply because your wages are being withheld under garnishment (if you are behind in only one debt).

Finally, the Truth in Lending law forbids underworld—or merely heavy-handed—lenders to threaten your life or limb in order to collect a loan.

YOUR RIGHTS TO AN HONEST CREDIT RATING

In Chapter 3, "How to Borrow Money and Use Credit Wisely," you read the fundamental rules for maintaining or restoring a good credit rating. But what if you are turned down for credit and believe the turndown is unwarranted? For the first time, you have the right under the law to obtain information—except medical—in your file and also on the sources of this information.

Under the *Fair Credit Reporting Act,* effective 1971, you have a great new array of defenses against abuse of your credit status by credit bureaus, credit granters, and the like. To illustrate, you are now able to:

• obtain, upon your own request and proper identification of yourself, from any consumer credit reporting agency that issues a report on you, disclosure of all the information in your credit file—including the sources of that information on you;

• get the names of all who have received from any consumer credit reporting agency employment reports on you within the past two years and the names of all others who have received credit reports about you within the past six months;

• arrange for a reinvestigation of any item about you which you question;

• have that item deleted from your record if the reinvestigation finds it to be inaccurate or if the item can no longer be verified;

• file a statement of about 100 words reporting your side of the story if the reinvestigation does not settle the matter—so that your side will be included in any future reports containing the item;

• see to it, if an item is deleted or a statement added to your file, that the credit bureau gives this information to those who have received employment reports about you within the past two years or regular credit reports about you in the past six months;

• have your record explained to you in detail and have it reviewed without charge if in the past thirty days you have been denied credit because of information in a credit report or if you have received a notice from a collection department affiliated with the credit bureau; and under the same circumstances, have previous recipients of information about you notified without charge if an item is deleted or a statement from you is added. The law also forbids credit bureaus to send out adverse information which is more than seven years old, although bankruptcies may be reported for fourteen years, and there are no time limits on information on you if you apply for a loan or insurance policy of $50,000 or more or apply for a job with a salary of $20,-000 or more.

There are weaknesses in the law—particularly involving enforcement—but it is an indisputable advance for you.

Never forget that, once you establish credit, the credit bureaus will keep your payment record up to date. And this will apply not only to your payment record but also to any reports about your activities printed in the newspapers or broadcast by radio or television—assuming the data can be verified.

Your performance in all transactions involving credit will become part of your credit record. The amount of credit you use in relation to your income, your respect for your commitments, no matter how small or seemingly unimportant—all these will become part of your permanent credit file.

Your credit record will follow you all over the country through the member bureaus of Associated Credit Bureaus, Inc. This can be a great service to you when you move to a new town and are applying for credit. It also can be a dark shadow if the record contains erroneous black marks.

Take your credit bureau problems to the nearest office of the Federal Trade Commission.

YOUR CREDIT RIGHTS AS A WOMAN

The *1974 Equal Credit Opportunity Act*, effective in late 1975, is an amendment to the Federal Truth in Lending law. It makes it illegal for a bank or other lender to deny you personal or commercial credit on the basis of sex or marital status. As a married woman, you owe it to yourself to establish credit—and a credit rating—in your own name (e.g., as Mrs. Mary Smith rather than as Mrs. Sam Smith). You thus will avoid being left without a credit rating should you be separated, divorced, or widowed. The same agencies which enforce Truth in Lending are enforcing this law.

AND MORE CREDIT RIGHTS

Even more extensive, legislation effective March 23, 1977, prohibits banks, retailers and others from discriminating on the basis of your age, race, color, religion or national origin in the granting of credit. This is in addition to the ban on discrimination based on your sex or marital status, and amends provisions in the earlier acts. Credit also may not be denied simply because an applicant is on welfare.

YOUR RIGHTS AS A VETERAN

In the mid-1970s, about 100 million Americans, including veterans, their families, and survivors of deceased veterans, were eligible for benefits distributed by the Veterans Administration—ranging from low-cost life insurance to VA hospital and medical care, VA-guaranteed home loans, GI Bill benefits for education and training, disability and death compensation, pension payment.

Details on most of these are in other sections of this book and you'll find a full range of veterans' benefits spelled out in a VA booklet entitled "Federal Benefits for Veterans and Dependents." Listed too are the locations of VA offices, hospitals, and drug treatment centers, and veterans' programs administered by other government agencies. Copies of the booklet are available for a small sum from the Superintendent of Documents, Washington, D.C. 20420.

Every eligible veteran (man or woman) has a right to these benefits. But among the most important rights a veteran has are those connected with the job he or she left to enter military service.

If you are a veteran now re-entering the job market, it will be crucially important for you to be thoroughly aware of these rights to your former job, as well as to promotions, fringe benefits, seniority, etc.

Under the law, you are entitled to get back the job you left to go into service—with the same pay, seniority, and status you would have had if you had never gone—up to a time limit of four years (or five years if the government requests the extra year).

If your old job has been abolished, you are entitled to the nearest similar job in pay, seniority, and status. This rule also applies if you can't do your old job because of physical disability or because the job has been changed. It doesn't matter if the company has been sold, as long as the business still goes on.

If your employer has a seniority system—in a contract or in practice—you must be credited with seniority for your time in service. If there has been a general pay raise or increase in benefits, you are entitled to these too. If promotions are automatic, based on length of employment, you are entitled to any promotion you would have received if you hadn't been in service. If fringe benefits depend on length of service, you must be credited for the time you were away. If your right to a pension or a longer vacation depends on the period of your employment, your military service must be counted. For other benefits, you're like any other employee who has been on leave. You also share in pay losses or changes in working conditions which occurred while you were away.

You can't be fired or demoted for one year, except for misconduct or other good reason. Your seniority and other rights last as long as you stay on the job.

If your employer refuses to rehire you, you can bring a lawsuit in a federal district court and ask the United States Attorney to represent you. You can get help or further information at the Office of Veterans' Reemployment Rights, which is part of the United States Labor Department and has offices in cities all over the United States. Also, you can go to the local VA, state employment service, or any veterans' organization for guidance. To make sure you know and get all your job rights, register with one of the state employment service offices throughout the country. By law, you will get preference and priority in both job counseling and placement.

Check with your nearest Veterans Administration regional office on your rights and eligibility for a wide range of education, employment, and training programs. These change frequently; keep up to date.

And most important: do not ignore or downgrade the full range of benefits available. Make sure you explore all the possibilities.

YOUR RIGHTS AS A HOSPITAL PATIENT

The American Hospital Association a few years ago adopted the first nationwide "Patient's Bill of Rights"—a milestone for you in view of the probability that sooner or later you'll be hospitalized for one reason or another and, if you're unlucky, you'll be confronted with a long series of unnecessary indignities, confusion, secrecy, arrogance, and frustrating lack of responsiveness to *your* needs.

Yet *you,* the patient, are the one paying the nation's multibillion-a-year health care bill—with a huge share of this for hospital services. *Your* life and limb and comfort are at stake—not anybody else's. You, therefore, have every right to insist on certain basic rights while you're hospitalized—even if they are not specifically spelled out in any lawbook.

According to the American Hospital Association's Bill of Rights you, the patient, should have the right:

(1) To considerate and respectful care.

(2) To get complete information from your physician concerning your diagnosis, treatment, and prognosis, in terms you understand.

(3) To receive whatever information is necessary for you to give your informed advance consent for any procedure and/or treatment.

(4) To every consideration for your privacy concerning your medical care program.

(5) To refuse treatment to the extent permitted by law, and to be informed of the medical consequences of your action. (This would mean that, as an adult, you have the right to die if your condition is hopeless.)

(6) To expect that all communications and records pertaining to your care will be treated as confidential.

(7) To expect a hospital to respond, within reason, to your request for services.

(8) To get information about any relationship between your hospital and other health care and educational institutions in so far as your care is concerned and to get information (including names) on the existence of any professional relationship between individuals who are treating you. (This means that you, the patient, have the right to know whether you are being treated by a member of a university hospital or by your physician's student.)

(9) To be advised if the hospital proposes to engage in or perform human experimentation on you in the course of your care or treatment.

(10) To expect reasonable continuity of care.

(11) To examine and receive an explanation of your bill, regardless of the source of payment.

(12) To know what hospital rules and regulations apply to your conduct as a patient.

YOUR RIGHTS TO A CLEAN ENVIRONMENT

Suppose that in your town there is a plant that discharges stinking, poisonous chemical wastes into a lake. This well may be the cheapest way out for the company. But it is ruining your property values—not to mention your water supply, swimming and fishing facilities, and the over-all quality of your life. What can you do about it?

LOOK TO THE LAW

Under the critically important *1899 Refuse Act,* you can sue the polluter, if other forms of pressure exerted on him to obey federal, state, or local laws are unsuccessful. You may, though, be able to get the company to filter its junk out of the lake and dispose of it simply by writing or phoning the president or getting in touch with your state's water resources agency.

The Refuse Act says, essentially, that *nobody*—person, corporation, factory, ship, or municipality—may dump refuse into any navigable waterway without first getting permission from the U. S. Army Corps of Engineers, which may not grant such permission until after it has determined that the refuse is safe to dump. "Refuse" includes "all foreign substances and pollutants apart from those flowing from streets and sewers and passing therefrom in a liquid state into the watercourse." A "navigable waterway" means any body of water that will float a log or a canoe.

In practice, very few permits to dump such "refuse" have actually been granted to date. Moreover, since 1970, new permits have been required where existing permits had been granted without adequate consideration in the first place of the nature of the pollutants.

Here is a rundown on other key federal laws designed to protect you against polluted surroundings:

The *1969 National Environmental Policy Act* made environmental quality a matter of government policy, creating the Council on Environmental Quality to advise the President on national policy. The Council was charged with devising ways to prevent environmental problems rather than patching up past damage and was authorized to direct research and surveys relevant to ecology, natural resources, and the quality of life.

The act directed all federal government agencies to consider the environmental and social cost of their major activities, and to investigate all feasible ways of accomplishing their aims to be sure of choosing the cleanest one. Agencies must submit evaluations of the environmental impact of their decisions and activities for comment by the public, the Council on Environmental Quality, and all affected government agencies. Thus, the act provides an opportunity for you to participate in decisions affecting your environment.

The *1970 Clean Air Act* established national air quality standards and deadlines for meeting them. This act set steadily lower limits on automo-

bile emissions, with a table of deadlines, and authorized states and municipalities to regulate land use and transportation if necessary to meet air
quality standards.

The law required new factories and power plants to install the latest
air pollution control technology and authorized the administrator of the Environmental Protection Agency to reduce air emission limits to zero for very
dangerous pollutants.

Under this act you have the right to sue in federal court to force air
polluters to adhere to the law and also to sue lax federal enforcement agencies.

The *1972 Federal Water Pollution Control Act* set as a goal the total
elimination of water pollution by 1985. By 1983, all the water in the
country is to be safe for fish, shellfish, wild life, and *your* recreation.

To meet this goal, industries must install the "best practicable" water
pollution control equipment, and cities and towns must install secondary
sewage treatment plants, by 1977. To ease the burden on municipalities,
three quarters of the cost of the required sewage treatment plants will be
met by the federal government (and therefore by you, the taxpayer). By
1983 industries must use the "best available" waste treatment methods, regardless of cost, and municipal sewage treatment plants must be substantially upgraded to achieve better results than primary and secondary treatment.

Exact water pollution limits will be specified in permits granted to each
discharger by the EPA or the state. The public must be notified of each application for a permit and you can request a hearing where you can express
your views. You also have the right to sue water polluters or enforcers if
they fail to meet their obligations.

The *1972 Noise Control Act* directed the Environmental Protection
Agency to set noise limits for virtually all noisy products manufactured in
the United States. It also gave the Environmental Protection Agency authority to act jointly with the Federal Aviation Agency in establishing noise
control standards for aircraft.

The *1972 Federal Environmental Pesticide Control Act* set up a system
of classification and regulations for using pesticides safely. Dangerous pesticides may be declared illegal, and misusing pesticides is prohibited.

In the next section of this chapter, you will find the names and addresses
of the agencies and organizations to which you can appeal for help in protecting our environment.

YOUR RIGHT TO PRODUCT SAFETY

The Consumer Product Safety Commission was created by the *1972
Consumer Product Safety Act* to reduce unreasonable risk of injury due to
consumer products.

Among the products covered are: stairs, cleaning agents, sports equipment, swimming pools, baby furniture, flammable fabrics, household appliances, tools, heaters, matches.

Not covered are: food, drugs, cosmetics, automobiles, insecticides, tobacco, aircraft, boats. All of these are regulated by other federal agencies.

The commission has the power to investigate any or all consumer product hazards, to conduct safety tests, help develop safety standards, and ban the sale of unnecessarily unsafe products which have been found to present an "imminent hazard."

If you have bought a product which has been banned by the commission, you have a right to a refund of the purchase price *plus* the cost to you of returning it.

If you want to know whether a given product has been banned, call the CPSC's hot line: (800) 638-2666, or, in Maryland (301) 492-2937.

If you want to report an unsafe product, you can either call the hot line or write to the commission's headquarters (Washington, D.C. 20207) or to one of its regional offices. Only one copy of a written complaint is necessary, and an answer is guaranteed.

Similarly, the federal Food and Drug Administration is charged with protecting the public against unsafe foods and drugs (including veterinary products), cosmetics, biologics (blood and blood substitutes), and radiological products (e.g., X rays, microwave ovens, TV sets). The FDA's key source of leads and information on unsafe, or mislabeled, or misrepresented, or contaminated, products is *you*.

So, if you want to report, inquire, or complain, do so to your nearest FDA office. Or call your local health agency. Keep the product to show investigators.

A key private organization you can notify if you find a serious food or drug or medical device safety hazard is: Health Research Group, 7th Floor, 2000 P Street, N.W., Washington, D.C. 20036.

28

WHERE TO GET HELP

Never before have you had so many allies to assist you in finding your way through our endlessly complex market place and in dealing with your complaints of every description. Never before could it be said that getting help is simply a matter of knowing where to take your gripes.

To learn where, leaf through the pages which follow. Listed first are the nationwide government agencies and major private groups concerned with many types of consumer rights or environmental matters—the broadly based groups. Then there is a list of agencies, groups, and organizations which concentrate on one or a few categories of products or services, broken down so you easily can find the subjects which concern you. Each list is alphabetically arranged—the first by organization name, the second by category or subject area.

Nationwide Organizations

Bureau of Consumer Protection, Federal Trade Commission, Washington, D.C. 20580. Rides herd over deceptive advertising, illegal sales tactics, violations of the Truth in Lending law, and a host of other categories of consumer frauds, misrepresentations, and unfair trade practices.

Center for Concerned Engineering, Room 1224, 1346 Connecticut Avenue, N.W., Washington, D.C. 20036. Research in technical aspects of all types of consumer issues. Original research group started by Ralph Nader.

Center for the Study of Responsive Law, P.O. Box 19367, Washington, D.C. 20036. Subjects of study range from mental health to aviation, coal mining to land grant colleges. This is also Ralph Nader's working address.

Citizen Action Group, 133 C Street, S.E., Washington, D.C. 20003. Helps students and citizens organize state and local consumer action groups and public interest research groups.

Common Cause, 2030 M Street, N.W., Washington, D.C. 20036. Largest citizens' lobby in the country; concentrates on "structure and process" issues to improve function and accountability of government; also, in mid-1970s, key issues were tax reform, energy policy, consumer and environmental protection.

Congress Watch, 133 C Street, S.E., Washington, D.C. 20003. Lobby group which keeps tabs on voting records, committee performance, and responsiveness by senators and representatives to their constituents and to the public generally.

Consumer Federation of America, Suite 406, 1012 14th Street, N.W., Washington, D.C. 20005, Telephone: (202)737-3732. Private, non-profit national federation of hundreds of state and local consumer groups which helps groups organize and act, testifies and lobbies on any proposed consumer legislation, and publicizes important issues.

Consumers Union, 256 Washington Street, Mt. Vernon, N.Y. 10550, Telephone: (914) MO 4-6400. Publishes *Consumer Reports* magazine, the classic shopper's guide, which includes results of Consumers Union tests of products ranging from cars to contraceptives—for safety, convenience, effectiveness. Also participates in lawsuits on behalf of consumers.

Corporate Accountability Research Group, Suite 101, 1832 M Street, N.W., Washington, D.C. 20036. Contests corporate power, violation of anti-trust laws, seeks to make corporations accountable to share owners and the public.

Council of Better Business Bureaus, 1150 17th Street, N.W., Washington, D.C. 20036. Headquarters of the well-known Better Business Bureaus; can put you in touch with the right local Bureau.

Office of Consumer Affairs, Washington, D.C. 20201, Telephones: Consumer complaints (202)245-6093, State and local programs (202) 245-9890. The consumer's "man in Washington"; government agency concerned with all kinds of consumer problems, consumer education and legislation.

Public Citizen Litigation Unit, 7th Floor, 2000 P Street, N.W., Washington, D.C. 20036. Initiates lawsuits against corporations, government agencies on behalf of the public.

STATE AND LOCAL CONSUMER PROTECTIVE ORGANIZATIONS

All states—and many cities and counties as well—now have a central department or agency to deal with consumer fraud and also with less dramatic problems and gripes. Frequently this office is a part of the state attorney general's office. Or it may be listed under such names as:

Department (or Division) of Consumer Protection; Consumer Affairs Bureau; Consumer Protection Agency; Department of Weights and Measures, or perhaps some other name.

Every state also has at least one privately sponsored consumer organization. It may be called a Consumers Council or Consumer Association or Consumer Information Center. Most states have a Ralph Nader-affiliated Public Interest Research Group, which may be called CALPIRG (in California) or VPIRG (in Vermont)—depending on the state.

Look for the agencies and organizations in your city or state—both government and non-government—under "Consumer . . ." in the government agencies section of your telephone book and in "Information" for your state capital, as well as in the regular telephone listings.

In addition to seeking help from these organizations, you may find it helpful to get in touch with:

your city department of consumer affairs (see the telephone directory, or call City Hall to find out whether there is such an agency);

your local Chamber of Commerce;

your local Better Business Bureau;

the "Action Line" of your local newspaper, radio, or TV station;

the Consumer Education Department of a local college or university;

the Extension Service of the U. S. Department of Agriculture.

WHERE TO TAKE YOUR PROBLEM: BY CATEGORY OR SUBJECT

Aging. See "Retirement."

Air Travel. If you have a complaint which you have been unable to resolve with an airline—about mishandled baggage, or failure to deliver you to your destination, or being illegally "bumped" off a flight, or being over-charged on a fare—write: Office of Consumer Affairs, Civil Aeronautics Board, 1825 Connecticut Avenue, N.W., Washington, D.C. 20428.

Or you may use the CAB hot line (202) 382-7735 at any hour of the day or night. You will be billed for a three-minute call, but after that the CAB will call back to finish discussing your problem.

To help eliminate the "bumping" problem so you or other air travelers won't have to face it repeatedly, contact Aviation Consumer Action Panel (ACAP), 1346 Connecticut Avenue, Washington, D.C. 20036.

ACAP works on problems in air carrier safety and regulation as well as passenger treatment.

Appliances. First try to settle your complaint with the dealer or the manu-facturer. Several toll-free lines that you may be able to use are Whirlpool: (800)253-1301; Westinghouse: (800)245-0600; Admiral: (800)447-1350.

If the appliance dealer, manufacturer, or serviceman fails to act on any legitimate complaint you have, write:

Major Appliance Consumer Action Panel (MACAP), Complaint Ex-change, Room 1514, 20 North Wacker Drive, Chicago, Ill. 60606.

Or telephone MACAP collect at: (312) 236-3165.

Auto Insurance. See Insurance.

Automobiles. American Motors provides several toll-free lines to handle warranty complaints: (800) 572-9570 from within Michigan; (800) 521-7500 from the rest of the United States; and (800) 261-0800 from Canada.

Owners also can write:

American Motors Corporation, 14250 Plymouth Road, Detroit, Mich. 48232; or, in Canada, 350 Kennedy Road South, Brampton, Ont.

Chrysler Corporation, P.O. Box 1086, Detroit, Mich.; in Canada, the Chrysler Center, Windsor, Ont.

Ford Marketing Corporation, Ford Customer Service Division, Box 1514, 19855 West Outer Drive, Dearborn, Mich. 48121, about warranty problems.

General Motors car owners should contact the appropriate division's Owner-Relations Manager. Division addresses are:

Buick Motor Division, 902 East Hamilton Avenue, Flint, Mich. 48550;

Cadillac Motor Car Division, 2860 Clark Avenue, Detroit, Mich. 48232;

Chevrolet Motor Division, GM Building, Detroit, Mich. 48202;

Oldsmobile Division, 920 Townsend Street, Lansing, Mich. 48921;

Pontiac Motor Division, 1 Pontiac Plaza, Pontiac, Mich. 48053.

Auto Safety. If your complaint has to do with automobile safety (or lack of safety)—which may affect other car owners as well—address your question, gripe, or suggestion to:

National Transportation Safety Board, U. S. Department of Transportation, Washington, D.C. 20591;

Office of Defects Investigation, Department of Transportation, Washington, D.C. 20590;

Center for Auto Safety, Box 7250, Ben Franklin Station, Washington, D.C. 20044.

If you are a truck or bus driver and would like to contribute information and ideas for improved truck or bus safety, contact: Professional Driver (PROD), 7th Floor, 2000 P Street, N.W., Washington, D.C. 20036.

Borrowing. If you suspect a store, a dealer, finance company, or a small loan company of violating the federal Truth in Lending law—for example, by not clearly stating the true simple annual interest rate on an installment loan or a purchase agreement on time—call or write the nearest regional office of the Federal Trade Commission. National headquarters of the FTC is Washington, D.C. 20580 (address complaints and inquiries to the Bureau of Consumer Protection).

The FTC's regional offices are at these addresses:

John F. Kennedy Federal
   Building
Government Center
Boston, Mass. 02203

Federal Bldg.
26 Federal Plaza
New York, N.Y. 10007

Gelman Building
2120 L Street, N.W.
Washington, D.C. 20037

Federal Office Bldg.
1240 East Ninth St.
Cleveland, O. 44199

730 Peachtree Street
Atlanta, Ga. 30308

55 East Monroe Street
Chicago, Ill. 60603

Federal Office Bldg.
911 Walnut Street
Kansas City, Mo. 64106

500 South Ervay Street
Dallas, Texas 75201

450 Golden Gate Ave.
Box 36005
San Francisco, Calif. 94102

Federal Building
11000 Wilshire Blvd.
Los Angeles, Calif. 90024

1511 Third Ave.
Seattle, Wash. 98101

If you have any reason to believe that your *bank* is not clearly spelling out full details of the loan you are negotiating, and if it's a national bank, check with Comptroller of the Currency, United States Department of the Treasury, Washington, D.C. 20220.

Or if it's a state-chartered bank which is a member of the Federal Reserve System get in touch with the Truth-in-Lending Officer of the Federal Reserve Bank in the city closest to you. Federal Reserve Banks are located at these addresses:

30 Pearl Street Boston, Mass. 02106	230 South LaSalle Street Chicago, Ill. 60690
33 Liberty Street New York, N.Y. 10045	411 Locust Street St. Louis, Mo. 63166
925 Chestnut Street Philadelphia, Penna. 19101	250 Marquette Avenue Minneapolis, Minn. 55480
1455 East Sixth Street Cleveland, O. 44101	925 Grand Avenue Kansas City, Mo. 64198
100 North Ninth Street Richmond, Va. 23261	400 South Akard Street Dallas, Tex. 75222
104 Marietta Street, N.W. Atlanta, Ga. 30303	400 Sansome Street San Francisco, Calif. 94120

NON-MEMBER INSURED BANKS. If it's a bank which is not a member of the Federal Reserve System but is federally insured contact the Division of Examination, Federal Deposit Insurance Corporation, 550 Seventeenth St., N.W., Washington, D.C. 20429.

Or call the FDIC Supervising Examiner for the district in which bank is located.

If it is a *federally insured savings and loan association* get in touch with the Federal Home Loan Bank Board's Supervisory Agent in the district in which association is located. Or write Office of the General Counsel, Federal Home Loan Bank Board, 101 Indiana Avenue, N.W., Washington, D.C. 20552.

Addresses of the FHLBB's twelve districts are:

(Connecticut, Maine, Massachusetts, New Hampshire, Rhode Island, and Vermont): 1 Union Street, Boston, Mass. 02108.

(New Jersey, New York, Puerto Rico, and Virgin Islands): 60 Broad Street, New York, N.Y. 10004.

(Delaware, Pennsylvania, and West Virginia): 4th Floor, 11 Stanwix Street, Gateway Center, Pittsburgh, Pa. 15222.

(Alabama, District of Columbia, Florida, Georgia, Maryland, North Carolina, South Carolina, and Virginia): Coastal States Building, 260 Peachtree Street, N.W., Atlanta, Ga. 30303.

(Kentucky, Ohio, Tennessee): 2500 DuBois Tower, Cincinnati, O. 45202.

(Indiana and Michigan): 2900 Indiana Tower, 1 Indiana Square, Indianapolis, Ind. 46204.

(Illinois and Wisconsin): 111 East Wacker Drive, Chicago, Ill. 60601.

(Iowa, Minnesota, Missouri, North Dakota, and South Dakota): Second Avenue at Center Street, Des Moines, Ia. 50309.

(Arkansas, Louisiana, Mississippi, New Mexico, and Texas): 1400 Tower Building, Little Rock, Ark. 72201.

(Colorado, Kansas, Nebraska, and Oklahoma): Seventh and Harrison Streets, Topeka, Kan. 66601.

(Arizona, Nevada, and California): 600 California Street, Post Office Box 7948, San Francisco, Calif. 94120.

(Alaska, Hawaii and Guam, Idaho, Montana, Oregon, Utah, Washington, and Wyoming): 600 Stewart Street, Seattle, Wash. 98101.

FEDERAL CREDIT UNIONS. If it is a federally chartered credit union, write National Credit Union Administration, Office of Examination and Insurance, 2025 M Street, N.W., Washington, D.C. 20456.

Or contact the NCUA's regional office serving the area in which the federal credit union is located. Regional offices are located in Boston, Atlanta, Toledo, San Francisco, Harrisburg, and Austin.

If it is a state-chartered credit union, get in touch with the appropriate state supervising agency—either the Department of Banking or the Finance Department or the state agency covering credit unions.

Another federal agency enforcing various aspects of the Truth in Lending law is the Civil Aeronautics Board, Bureau of Enforcement, 1825 Connecticut Avenue, N.W., Washington, D.C. 20428.

And if the problem involves interstate transportation (trucking companies and railroads that cross state lines), write the Office of Proceedings, Interstate Commerce Commission, Washington, D.C. 20523.

Finally, if you believe you have been illegally fired or otherwise harmed because your wages have been garnisheed—a possible violation of the Truth in Lending law—contact the Labor Department's Wage and Hour Division, which is in charge of enforcing this part of the law.

Broadcasting. Send your complaints about radio or television broadcasting or business practices to: Federal Communications Commission, 1919 M Street, N.W., Washington, D.C. 20554.

Civil Liberties. If you believe there has been a serious infringement of your civil liberties, contact: American Civil Liberties Union, 22 East Fortieth Street, New York, N.Y. 10016. (See also Discrimination.)

Counseling. If you need counseling on subjects ranging from wage garnishment to problems in your child's school to psychiatric needs, call a local voluntary Family Service agency. For names and other specifics on such agencies in the area where you live, write: Family Service Association of America, 44 East Twenty-third Street, New York, N.Y. 10010.

Or contact: Community Services Administration, Social and Rehabilitation Service, Department of Health, Education and Welfare, 330 C Street, S.W., Washington, D.C. 20201.

Or get in touch with your local YMCA or YWCA. For the address of the branch nearest you write: Young Men's Christian Association, 291 Broadway, New York, N.Y. 10007, or the Young Women's Christian Association of the U.S.A., 600 Lexington Avenue, New York, N.Y. 10022.

Credit Rating. If you are unfairly rated a bad credit risk, write for help directly to: Associated Credit Bureaus, Inc., 6767 Southwest Freeway, Houston, Tex. 77036. Or appeal to the nearest office of the Federal Trade Commission, which enforces the Fair Credit Reporting Act.

Discrimination. If you believe you are the victim of illegal discrimination—on the basis of race, age, sex, or national origin—at your job, in your pay, in your search for housing, in trying to borrow money, in the courts, or in any aspect of your constitutional rights, there are a number of organizations ready to help you.

If your problem is racial discrimination:

National Association for the Advancement of Colored People, 1790 Broadway, New York, N.Y. 10019.

NAACP Legal Defense and Education Fund, 10 Columbus Circle, New York, N.Y. 10019.

American Civil Liberties Union, 22 East Fortieth Street, New York, N.Y. 10016 (or your state's branch of the ACLU).

If the problem is sex discrimination, in jobs, credit, pay:

Women's Bureau, United States Department of Labor, Washington, D.C. 20210.

Center for Women's Policy Studies, 2000 P Street, N.W., Washington, D.C. 20036.

National Organization for Women, Suite 1615, 5 South Wabash, Chicago, Ill. 60603. (312)332-1954.

If your problem is discrimination in housing: "Fair Housing," Secretary of Housing and Urban Development, Washington, D.C. 20410.

If your problem is employment discrimination:

Equal Employment Opportunity Commission, Washington, D.C. 20506 (or any of the EEOC field offices).

Wage and Hour Division, Employment Standards Administration, U. S. Department of Labor, Washington, D.C. 20210 (or any of the 350-plus field or regional offices listed under "United States Government—Department of Labor, Wage and Hour Division" in the telephone book).

If you are an applicant, trainee, or apprentice in a program covered by federal regulations, and you believe you have been discriminated against: Bureau of Apprenticeship and Training, United States Department of Labor, Washington, D.C. 20210.

If your employer is a federal government contractor or subcontractor: Office of Federal Contract Compliance, Employment Standards Administration, United States Department of Labor, Washington, D.C. 20210, or: Assistant Attorney General, Civil Rights Division, United States Department of Justice, Washington, D.C. 20530.

If you believe you have suffered from job discrimination by the federal government, complain to: The U. S. Civil Service Commission, 1900 E Street, N.W., Washington, D.C. 20415.

You can also address a complaint to your state Fair Employment Commission or Human Rights Agency or your city's Commission on Civil Rights.

If you feel immediate action is in order, report the matter to the nearest office of the Federal Bureau of Investigation or to your nearest United States Attorney.

If your complaint goes unanswered or if you don't get satisfactory action, write or call: United States Commission on Civil Rights, Washington, D.C. 20425.

Door-to-door Sales. If your problem or dispute involves a door-to-door salesperson, or the goods or services he is selling: Direct Selling Association, 1730 M Street, N.W., Washington, D.C. 20036.

Drugs. See Food and Drugs.

Environment. If you believe court action is warranted against a person or corporation destroying some aspect of your environment, go first to your local environmental board or agency. If you fail to get satisfaction, get in touch with one of these groups of lawyers and scientists dedicated to preserving a healthful environment through court action: Environmental Defense Fund, 162 Old Town Road, East Setauket, N.Y. 11733,
or: Natural Resources Defense Council, Inc., 15 West Forty-fourth Street, New York, N.Y. 10036.

For help in finding technical expertise to press your case before a bureaucracy or a court: Center for Science in the Public Interest, 1779 Church Street, N.W., Washington, D.C. 20036.

For advice on how to change your buying habits to minimize their adverse environmental effects: Concern, Inc., 2233 Wisconsin Avenue, N.W., Washington, D.C. 20007.
or: Consumer Alliance, Inc., P.O. Box 11773, Palo Alto, Calif. 94306.

If you want to do your share to prevent further pollution or depletion of the earth's natural resources, among the leading national environmental and conservation organizations you can join:

Environmental Action, Inc., 1346 Connecticut Avenue, N.W., Washington, D.C. 20036. Publishes biweekly *Environmental Action*. Lobbies and educates for stronger laws and enforcement.

A good source of environmental news is the weekly *Environmental Action Bulletin* (Rodale Press, Emmaus, Pa. 18049).

Friends of the Earth, 529 Commercial Street, San Francisco, Calif. 94111. Publishes monthly *Not Man Apart*, publicizes issues, lobbies, brings suits.

National Audubon Society, 950 Third Avenue, New York, N.Y. 10022. Publishes monthly *Audubon* magazine, educates, researches environmental problems.

National Wildlife Federation, 1412 16th Street, N.W., Washington, D.C. 20036. Publishes bimonthly *National Wildlife* and *International Wildlife*. Concerned with all environmental problems affecting wildlife.

Sierra Club, 1050 Mills Tower, San Francisco, Calif. 94104. Publishes monthly *Sierra Club Bulletin*. Local chapters sponsor outdoor activities, lobbying, legal action.

Wilderness Society, 1901 Pennsylvania Avenue, N.W., Washington, D.C. 20006. Publishes quarterly *Living Wilderness*, lobbies, educates, sues, conducts outings.

Flammable Fabrics. Use the Consumer Product Safety Commission's hot line (800) 638-2666 to report cases of dangerously flammable fabrics on the market or to get safety-related information on fabrics you suspect of being dangerously flammable—including names of offending brands and retailers.

Food and Drugs. If you find you have bought any contaminated or otherwise harmful food, drugs, or cosmetics, report it to your nearest FDA regional or district office or resident post.

The FDA's national headquarters is: Food and Drug Administration, 5600 Fishers Lane, Rockville, Md. 20852.

The FDA's district offices are:

DISTRICT OFFICE	ADDRESS	AREA CODE & NUMBER
Atlanta, Ga. 30309	60 Eighth Street, N.E.	(404) 526-5265
Baltimore, Md. 21201	900 Madison Avenue	(301) 962-4012
Boston, Mass. 02109	585 Commercial Street	(617) 223-4425

District Office	Address	Area Code & Number
Brooklyn, N.Y. 11232	Room 700 850 Third Avenue	(212) 788-1300
Buffalo, N.Y. 14202	599 Delaware Avenue	(716) 842-6906
Chicago, Ill. 60607	Room 1222, Main Post Office 433 West Van Buren Street	(312) 353-7379
Cincinnati, O. 45202	Paul B. Dunbar Building 1141 Central Parkway	(513) 684-3503
Dallas, Tex. 75204	3032 Bryan Street	(214) 749-2735
Denver, Colo. 80202	513 New Customhouse	(303) 837-4915
Detroit, Mich. 48207	1560 East Jefferson Avenue	(313) 226-6260
Kansas City, Mo. 64106	1009 Cherry Street	(816) 374-5521
Los Angeles, Calif. 90015	John L. Harvey Building 1521 West Pico Boulevard	(213) 688-3776
Minneapolis, Minn. 55401	240 Hennepin Avenue	(612) 725-2121
Newark, N.J. 07102	Room 831 970 Broad Street	(201) 645-3023
New Orleans, La. 70130	423 Canal Street Room 222 U. S. Customhouse Building	(504) 527-2401
Philadelphia, Pa. 19106	Room 1204 U. S. Customhouse Building 2nd and Chestnut	(215) 597-4173
San Francisco, Calif. 94102	Room 518 50 Fulton Street	(415) 556-0318
San Juan, Puerto Rico 00905	P. O. Box 4427 Old San Juan Station	(809) 723-1982
Seattle, Wash. 98104	Room 5003 Federal Office Building 901 First Avenue	(206) 442-5304

(Also see "Health Care.")

If you have reason to believe that your butcher or supermarket or grocer's scales are rigged to show a heavier weight for meats, fruits, vegetables, or other products—or that the weight of a product you have bought is misstated on the label—alert your state Bureau of Weights and Measures or: Office of Weights and Measures, National Bureau of Standards, Washington, D.C. 20234.

Furniture. If you cannot clear up a dispute with a furniture dealer within a reasonable time:

Furniture Industry Consumer Advisory Panel (FICAP), P. O. Box 951, High Point, N.C. 27261. Telephone: (919) 885-5065.

Health Care. If you have a problem or question or serious complaint about medical service, tell it to:

- your state's office of Consumer Health Affairs (if there is one);
- your local and/or state Health Department;
- your state or county Medical Society;
- the local private Health and Welfare Council (in major cities);
- the local chapter of the Medical Committee for Human Rights based at P. O. Box 7155, Pittsburgh, Pa. 15213 (but with chapters in other major cities);
- the nearest Comprehensive Health Planning agency;
- your state insurance commissioner;
- state or local consumer protection agencies (see page 1046 for names and addresses of these);
- your state's Public Interest Research Group;
- the local offices of the Blue Cross and Blue Shield organizations, Social Security Administration, the Welfare Department;

Or to one of these key national organizations:

American Medical Association
535 North Dearborn Street
Chicago, Ill. 60610

National Medical Association
2109 E Street, N.W.
Washington, D.C. 20006

American Dental Association
211 East Chicago Avenue
Chicago, Ill. 60611

United States Public Health Service
5600 Fishers Lane
Rockville, Md. 20852

American Psychiatric Association
1700 18th Street, N.W.
Washington, D.C. 20009

American Hospital Association
840 North Lake Shore Drive
Chicago, Ill. 60611

American Public Health Association
1015 18th Street, N.W.
Washington, D.C. 20036

Health Research Group*
7th Floor
2000 P Street, N.W.
Washington, D.C. 20036

Find out whether the hospital has a patient advocacy system or any other type of grievance mechanism.

Get a copy of the American Hospital Association's Patient's Bill of Rights (see page 1039 and show it to hospital authorities).

A few states have special "grievance panels" which function as alternatives to malpractice suits. Inquire about whether your problem could be handled by such a panel.

Letters to the editors of newspapers covering your area may help speed the resolution of your problem.

* Also works with food additives, flammable fabrics, toy safety, cosmetics, occupational health, health care delivery.

Finally, you can get a variety of excellent "Shopper's Guides"—to surgery, dentistry, and health insurance—published by the Pennsylvania Insurance Department. If you are a Pennsylvania resident, send a self-addressed 9×12-inch envelope with 20¢ postage per guide to the Pennsylvania Insurance Department, Harrisburg, Pa. 17120. Non-residents can get copies of these and other guides for $1.00 each from Consumer News, Inc., 813 National Press Building, Washington, D.C. 20045.

Information. For help in prying loose government information under the Freedom of Information Act: Freedom of Information Clearinghouse, P. O. Box 19267, Washington, D.C. 20036.

If you need advice or information on such close-to-home matters as child care, gardens, nutrition, health, clothes care, food storage, "do-it-yourself" projects, farm subsidies, financial problems, or dozens of other subjects, two superb sources of pamphlets, instructions, and guidance are: Extension Service, U. S. Department of Agriculture, 14th Street and Independence Avenue, S.W., Washington, D.C. 20250,
and Superintendent of Documents, U. S. Government Printing Office, Washington, D.C. 20402.

Of the two, the United States Government Printing Office offers the wider range of subjects covered by its publications. You can read anything from "Controlling Wasps" to a "Directory of Information Sources in the U.S." Indexes to publications within a given field are available free. You can get a biweekly list of selected government publications free, and for $7.00 a year you can subscribe to a monthly list of *all* government publications. You must pay for publications from the United States Government Printing Office, but the prices are so low that you'll be unable to find a more economical bookstore. In most cases you'll get the publications you want more quickly by ordering from one of these GPO field bookstores:

Birmingham Bookstore
Room 102A
2121 Eighth Avenue North
Birmingham, Ala. 35203

Los Angeles Bookstore
Room 1015
Federal Office Building
300 North Los Angeles Street
Los Angeles, Calif. 90012

San Francisco Bookstore
Room 1023
Federal Office Building
450 Golden Gate Avenue
San Francisco, Calif. 94102

Denver Bookstore
Room 1421
Federal Building, U. S. Courthouse
1961 Stout Street
Denver, Colo. 80202

Pueblo Bookstore
PDDC
P. O. Box 713
Pueblo, Colo. 81001

Atlanta Bookstore
Room 100
Federal Building
275 Peachtree Street, N.E.
Atlanta, Georgia 30303

Chicago Bookstore
Room 1463-14th Floor
Everett McKinley Dirksen Building
219 South Dearborn Street
Chicago, Ill. 60604

Boston Bookstore
Room G25
John F. Kennedy Federal Building
Sudbury Street
Boston, Mass. 02203

Detroit Bookstore
Room 229
Federal Building
231 West Lafayette Boulevard
Detroit, Mich. 48226

Kansas City Bookstore
Room 135
Federal Office Building
601 East 12th Street
Kansas City, Mo. 64106

New York Bookstore
Room 110
26 Federal Plaza
New York, N.Y. 10007

Canton Bookstore
Federal Office Building
201 Cleveland Avenue, S.W.
Canton, O. 44702

Philadelphia Bookstore
Main Lobby
U. S. Post Office
9th and Chestnut Streets
Philadelphia, Pa. 19107

Dallas Bookstore
Room 1C46
Federal Building-U. S. Courthouse
1100 Commerce Street
Dallas, Tex. 75202

For information on many types of consumer products, services, and concerns, compiled by federal agencies, write: Consumer Information, Pueblo, Colo. 81009.

Ask for the free "Consumer Information Index" to pamphlets. Many pamphlets are free, and some are available in Spanish.

One good source of more addresses of organizations which stand ready to help you and accept your help is the *Directory of Consumer Protection and Environmental Agencies* (available from Academic Media, 32 Lincoln Avenue, Orange, N.J. 07050, or at a reference library), which lists and describes hundreds of private and government agencies across the country. A detailed guide to what you can *do* to secure your rights is *A Public Citizen's Action Manual,* by Donald Ross ($1.95 from Grossman Publishers, 625 Madison Avenue, New York, N.Y. 10022).

Insurance. If your question is about insurance, an insurance agency, or insurance salesman, direct it to the State Insurance Department in your state capital, or to one of these private trade associations:

FOR LIFE INSURANCE:

The Institute of Life Insurance
and Health Insurance Institute
277 Park Avenue
New York, N.Y. 10017

FOR AUTOMOBILE AND LIABILITY INSURANCE:

Insurance Information Institute
110 William Street
New York, N.Y. 10038

1266 National Press Building
529 14th Street, N.W.
Washington, D.C. 20004

400 Montgomery Street
San Francisco, Calif. 94104

You can get excellent, no-nonsense advice on how to buy insurance by sending small sums for "Shopper's Guide to Term Insurance"; "Shopper's Guide to Cash Value Life Insurance"; "Shopper's Guide to Health Insurance"; and "Shopper's Guide to Mobile Home Insurance" (Consumer News, Inc., 813 National Press Building, Washington, D.C. 20045), "The Shopper's Guidebook" by Herbert Denenberg also is available from this source ($3.50).

Job Safety. If you think you are being exposed to a hazardous substance or other dangerous condition in your workplace, contact the nearest field office of the Occupational Safety and Health Administration, listed in the phone book under United States Government, Department of Labor.

Or contact one of the following OSHA regional offices:

REGION I (Connecticut, Maine, Massachusetts, New Hampshire, Rhode Island, Vermont): 18 Oliver Street, Boston, Mass. 02110. Telephone: (617) 223-6712.

REGION II (New Jersey, New York, Puerto Rico, Virgin Islands): 1515 Broadway (1 Astor Plaza), New York, N.Y. 10036. Telephone: (212) 971-5941.

REGION III (Delaware, District of Columbia, Maryland, Pennsylvania, Virginia, West Virginia), 15220 Gateway Center, 3535 Market Street, Philadelphia, Pa. 19104. Telephone: (215) 597-1201.

REGION IV (Alabama, Florida, Georgia, Kentucky, Mississippi, North Carolina, South Carolina, Tennessee), Suite 587, 1375 Peachtree Street, N.E., Atlanta, Ga. 30309. Telephone: (404) 526-3573.

REGION V (Illinois, Indiana, Minnesota, Michigan, Ohio, Wisconsin), Room 1201, 300 South Wacker Drive, Chicago, Ill. 60606. Telephone: (312) 353-4716.

REGION VI (Arkansas, Louisiana, New Mexico, Oklahoma, Texas), 7th

Floor, Texaco Building, 1512 Commerce Street, Dallas, Tex. 75201. Telephone: (214) 749-2477.

REGION VII (Iowa, Kansas, Missouri, Nebraska), 911 Walnut Street, Room 3000, Kansas City, Mo. 64106. Telephone: (816) 374-5861.

REGION VIII (Colorado, Montana, North Dakota, South Dakota, Utah, Wyoming), Room 15010, Federal Building, 1961 Stout Street, Denver, Colo. 80202. Telephone: (303) 837-3883.

REGION IX (Arizona, California, Hawaii, Nevada), 9470 Federal Building, 450 Golden Gate Avenue, Box 36017, San Francisco, Calif. 94102. Telephone: (415) 556-0586.

REGION X (Alaska, Idaho, Oregon, Washington), 1808 Smith Tower Building, 506 Second Avenue, Seattle, Wash. 98104. Telephone: (206) 442-5930.

Also, see Health Care.

Life Insurance. See Insurance.

Mail Order. If you suspect mail fraud of any description or if you receive unordered merchandise through the mails, or even if you simply receive a piece of highly deceptive advertising, ask your local post office whether a formal complaint is in order, or write: Office of the Chief Postal Inspector, U. S. Postal Service, Washington, D.C. 20260.

If you have complaints about postal service (e.g., packages lost or damaged, surly clerks, long lines), take them first to your local postmaster. If he can't help you, write: Consumer Advocate, at the United States Postal Service, 475 L'enfant Plaza West, S.W., Washington, D.C. 20260.

If you have an unresolved disagreement with a mail order house, or would like to reduce the amount of junk mail you get, write: Consumer Service Director, Direct Mail Marketing Association, 230 Park Avenue, New York, N.Y. 10017.

Mortgages. If you have problems about a home mortgage insured by the Veterans Administration or the Federal Housing Administration, or a home improvement contractor who is working on a project involving a federally guaranteed loan, ask your bank for the address of the nearest office of the VA or FHA. The FHA's national headquarters are: Federal Housing Administration, Department of Housing and Urban Development, 451 7th Street, S.W., Washington, D.C. 20410.

And the VA's headquarters are: Veterans Administration, 810 Vermont Avenue, Washington, D.C. 20420.

Moving. Send your complaints about movers to: Bureau of Operations, Interstate Commerce Commission, Washington, D.C. 20423, or call the ICC on its hot line: (202) 343-4761.

Occupational Health. See Health Care and Job Safety.

Pensions. The Department of Labor keeps tabs on pension plans and has legal responsibility, under the 1974 pension reform law to initiate action to correct abuses. If you have a complaint about your pension plan, send it to the Office of Employee Benefit Security which has a representative at your nearest area office of the Labor-Management Services Administration:

1371 Peachtree Street, N.E.
Atlanta, Ga. 30309

110 Tremont Street
Boston, Mass. 02108

111 West Huron Street
Buffalo, N.Y. 14202

219 South Dearborn Street
Chicago, Ill. 60604

1240 East Ninth Street
Cleveland, O. 44199

Bryan and Ervay Streets
Dallas, Tex. 75221

1020-15th Street
Denver, Colo. 80202

234 State Street
Detroit, Mich. 48226

1833 Kalakaua Avenue
Honolulu, Hawaii 96815

911 Walnut Street
Kansas City, Mo. 64106

300 North Los Angeles Street
Los Angeles, Calif. 90012

18350 Northwest 2nd Avenue
Miami, Fla. 33169

110 South Fourth Street
Minneapolis, Minn. 55401

1808 West End Building
Nashville, Tenn. 37203

9 Clinton Street
Newark, N.J. 07102

600 South Street
New Orleans, La. 70130

26 Federal Plaza
New York, N.Y. 10007

600 Arch Street
Philadelphia, Pa. 19106

1000 Liberty Avenue
Pittsburgh, Pa. 15222

100 McAllister Street
San Francisco, Calif. 94102

605 Condado Avenue
Santurce, Puerto Rico 00907

506 Second Avenue
Seattle, Washington 98104

210 North Twelfth Boulevard
St. Louis, Mo. 63101

1111 20th Street, N.W.
Washington, D.C. 20036

or send your complaint to: The Office of Employee Benefit Security, Washington, D.C. 20044.

The Internal Revenue Service also regulates pension plans and can terminate a plan and split its assets among the participants if it is being improperly administered. So send a copy of your complaint to: Office of Employee Plans and Exempt Organizations, Internal Revenue Service, Constitution Avenue, N.W., Washington, D.C. 20224.

If you're thinking of taking a pension case to court, you or your lawyer may want to contact: National Senior Citizens Law Center, Suite 600, 1709 West Eighth Street, Los Angeles, Calif. 90017,
or: National Senior Citizens Law Center, Suite 212–216, 910 17th Street, N.W., Washington, D.C. 20006.

Other groups concerned with your pension rights are: Association of Private Pension and Welfare Plans, Inc., 1028 Connecticut Avenue, N.W., Washington, D.C. 20036,
and: American Pension Conference, 358 Fifth Avenue, New York, N.Y. 10001.

See also Social Security and Veterans' Benefits.

Pollution. If you believe that a local industry or individual is illegally polluting the air or water in your community, check with one or all of these agencies:

The state or local or Environmental Control Board or pollution control board;

The state or local Health Department;

The U. S. Environmental Protection Agency, Washington, D.C. 20460;

Fisherman's Clean Water Action Project, Box 19367, Washington, D.C. 20036;

Consumer Protection and Environmental Health Service, Public Health Service, Department of Health, Education and Welfare, 5600 Fishers Lane, Rockville, Md. 20852.

Product Labeling. See Food and Drugs.

Product Safety. If you have found an unsafe product of almost any kind, get in touch with the Consumer Product Safety Commission, Washington, D.C. 20207.

Addresses and phone numbers of the commission's regional offices are:

1330 West Peachtree Street, N.W.
Atlanta, Ga. 30309
  (404) 526-2231

408 Atlantic Avenue
Boston, Mass. 02110
  (617) 223-5576

1 North Wacker Drive, Fifth Floor
Chicago, Ill. 60606
  (312) 353-8260

Room 410-C
500 South Ervay
P. O. Box 15035
Dallas, Tex. 75201
  (214) 749-3871

Suite 938
Guaranty Bank Building
817-17th Street
Denver, Colo. 80202
c/o Food and Drug Administration
  (303) 837-2904

Room 1905,
911 Walnut Street
Kansas City, Mo. 64106
  (816) 374-2034

Continental Building, 10th Floor
400 Market Street
Philadelphia, Pa. 19106
  (215) 597-9105

Suite 1100,
3660 Wilshire Boulevard
Los Angeles, Calif. 90010
  (213) 688-7272

Room 558,
50 Fulton Street
San Francisco, Calif. 94102
  (415) 556-1816

Room 650,
Federal Building, Fort Snelling
Twin Cities, Minn. 55111
  (612) 725-3424

1131 Federal Building
909 First Avenue
Seattle, Wash. 98104
  (206) 442-5276

International Trade Mart, Suite 414
2 Canal Street
New Orleans, La. 70013
  (504) 527-2102

DEB Annex 21046
Brookpark Road
Cleveland, O. 44135
  (216) 522-3886

Building 1, 8th Floor, Bay 7
830 Third Avenue
Brooklyn, N.Y. 11232
  (212) 788-5000, Ext. 1166

You also can contact the commission via a toll-free hot line: (800) 638-2666, except in Maryland, where it is (301) 492-2937.

Retirement. Here are key organizations and agencies concerned with the special needs of elderly citizens:

Your state's Commission on Aging

United States Administration on Aging

Social and Rehabilitation Service
Department of Health, Education
  and Welfare
Washington, D.C. 20201

National Council on the Aging, Inc.
200 Park Avenue South
New York, N.Y. 10010

National Council of Senior Citizens
1511 K Street, N.W.
Washington, D.C. 20005

Senate Special Committee on Aging
Senate Office Building
Washington, D.C. 20510

American Association of Retired
  Persons
1909 K Street, N.W.
Washington, D.C. 20006

Social Security. For any problem with Social Security benefits, contact your local Social Security office first (look for it in the phone book under "United States Government"). If the local office cannot or will not resolve your problem, contact: Social Security Administration, 6401 Security Boulevard, Baltimore, Md. 21235.

See Retirement for other potential sources of information or help.

Stocks and Securities. If you are the victim (or even suspect you may be the victim) of a shady deal involving a transaction in securities, get in touch with the nearest regional office of the Securities and Exchange Commission, or write: Securities and Exchange Commission, 500 North Capitol Street, N.W., Washington, D.C. 20549.

Taxes. If you have a question or complaint about your federal income tax, call your local Internal Revenue Service office. To learn where this office is, check your Form 1040 Instructions, or contact: Internal Revenue Service, Washington, D.C. 20224.

Or use one of the IRS's toll-free information numbers. These are listed on the Form 1040 Instructions, and in many telephone books under "United States Government." You also can get the number for your area by calling "Information."

For information on tax court procedures, contact: Clerk of the Court, United States Tax Court, Washington, D.C. 20217.

If you feel you have been the victim of inequities or abuse in any aspect of the tax system—sales, property, income, etc.—contact: Tax Reform Research Group, 133 C Street, S.E., Washington, D.C. 20003.

Tenants' Rights. If you are, for any reason, served with an eviction notice, consult your lawyer. Or, if you don't have a lawyer and can't afford to hire one, go to the local tenants' association for advice on what to do about it. Or get in touch with: National Tenants Organization, 425 13th Street, N.W., Washington, D.C. 20004.

Toy Safety. See Health Care and Product Safety.

Unemployment Insurance. To sign up for benefits or to resolve a problem concerning benefits, go to the nearest state employment service office (look for the address in the telephone book under the listing for your state government).

Utilities. If you are dissatisfied with the service or business policies of your phone, gas, water, or electricity company and cannot resolve the matter with the company itself, complain to your state utility regulating body. This may be called the public utility commission, the public service board, or some similar name; its address will be under the state government listing in the capital phone book.

Veterans' Benefits. If your local Veterans Administration office cannot resolve your difficulty with veterans' benefits, contact: Veterans Administration, 810 Vermont Avenue, N.W., Washington, D.C. 20420.

Weights and Measures. See Food and Drugs.

INDEX

Coupon bonds, 907, 911, 916, 925

Coupon credit plan, 109

"Courtesy days," clothes buying and, 223

Courts (*see also* Law; Lawyers; Legal procedures): and divorce and settlements, 719, 720–21; and small claims suits, 1004–8; and wills, 736–37, 739

Craft occupations (craftsmen), 417, 420, 428–29; job training and, 439–43

"Cream," auto insurance, 339

Credit, 108ff. (*see also* Borrowing; Charge accounts; Credit cards; Debts; Installment buying; Loans); advantages of, 80–82; and auto loans, 318–20; and bankruptcy, 131–32; banks and, 43, 45–46, 49, 52 (*see also* Banks); basic do's and don'ts of, 82–85; bonds and, 102–3, 908; borrowing and (*see* Borrowing); cards and use of, 115–20 (*see also* Credit cards); and consumer protection and rights, 994–96, 1002–4, 1033–37, 1051; credit and investigative reports, 88, 134 (*see also* Credit bureaus); definitions and terms, 132–38; establishing credit rating, 85–88; how much is too much?, 128–30; interest rate charges, 82, 110–15 (*see also* Interest rates, borrowing and credit and); loans in cash and, 90–96; pitfalls of, 121–28; "ready," 96–97, 121; sources of cash loans, 90–96; types, interest rates, and maturities (loans), 88–107; types and sources of, 108ff.

Credit application, defined, 134

Credit bureaus, 85, 88, 134; consumer rights and, 995–96, 1035–37, 1051

Credit cards, 102–3, 111, 115–20; bank, 102–3; billing errors, 1002–4; care and protection of, 119–20; and car rentals, 361, 362–63; consumer rights and, 994, 1002–4, 1034; costs, 115; differences between types of, 115–17; liability and, 119; and loans, 94; and rail travel, 366–67; sources of, 110; use of, 117–19; using to best advantage, 118–19

"Credit Card Use in the U.S." (study), 117

Credit contract, defined, 134

Credit counselors, 130

Credit investigation, 88, 134. *See also* Credit bureaus

Credit life insurance, 134, 319–20, 790, 805

Credit lines, defined, 134

Creditors (lenders), defined, 134

Credit rate, defined, 135

Credit rating, 85–88; consumer rights and, 1035–37, 1051; credit investigative reports and, 88; defined, 135; establishing, 85–87; maintaining or restoring, 87–88

Credit risk, defined, 135

Credit sale, defined, 135

Credit sale disclosure statement, defined, 135

Credit unions, 45–46; and life insurance, 62; and loans, 98–99, 397, 401–3; and student loans, 397, 401–3

Credit-worthy, defined, 135

Cremation, 750, 751–52; cutting costs of, 751–52

"Crew switching," home improvement gyps and, 666

Crime insurance: homeowners and, 604–9; small businesses and, 496–97

Cruise-ship tipping guide, 527–28

CUNA International, Inc., 99

Cures, health hoaxes and, 280–88

Current-income security, 932, 940

Current yield, 910, 925

Curtains, when to buy, 147

Curtesy rights, 737, 746

Custodians, building (jobs), 428

Customs duties, vacation shopping and, 517–18

Cryogenics field, 412

Cyclical stocks, 873

Dance studios, 812–13; gyps, 812–13

Data processors (jobs), 423–24, 446

Dating of checks, 55

Dating of food, "open," 176–77

Dauer, Dr. Ernst, 7

Day Care and Child Development Council of America, 473

Day care centers (day care facilities), working women and, 472–76; employment and, 446; financial value of, 474–76; finding, 472–74; guide to, 474

Day care workers (jobs), 446

Day hospital and treatment centers, the elderly and, 270

Day-to-day expenses, budgeting of, 17–20, 24; main categories of, 18

Dealers (*see also* specific kinds): antique cars, 984–85; art, 974–76; automobiles (*see* Dealers, automobile); coins, 964; complaints and, 996–1000; consumer protection and rights and, 989–1042; diamonds, 970–71; mobile homes, 576–78; prints, 978, 979–80; rare books, 965; securities, 828, 874; stamps, 968–69; warranties and, 1009–12

Dealers, automobile, 296–98; and financing, 318–20; franchises, 296–97; and insurance, 333; new cars, 296–98; and optional equipment, 311–15; and rentals, 360–63; and service and repairs, 317, 343–50; and tires, 328–32; and trade-ins, 298–300; and used cars, 300–11; and warranties, 297, 298, 303, 311, 315–17

Death: funeral and burial expenses, 749–55; life insurance and, 788–804; "presumption of survivorship" and, 729; survivors' benefits and, 784, 787, 788, 810 (*see also* Survivors; specific kinds, plans); and taxes, 725, 736, 737, 738, 744; wills, estates, and trusts and, 727–47

Debenture bonds, 914, 925; income, 914; subordinated, 914

Debentures, 874

Debts (debt payments, in-

SCORE (Service Corps of Retired Executives), 510, 512
Service credit, 109
Service occupations, 411, 416
Services and goods, *See* Goods and services; specific items, kinds, problems
Service stations, auto repairs and, 344, 345, 347–49; avoiding dirty tricks away from home, 348
Sewage protection, 1040, 1041
"Sewer service" technique, credit and, 123
Sewer system: house building and, 583; house buying and, 557
Sewing, saving on clothing and, 224. *See also* Sewing machines, buying
Sewing machines, buying, 225–29; care, maintenance, and use of, 228–29; features to look for, 228; portable and cabinet models, 227; testing, 227–28; traps to avoid, 229; zigzag and stretch stitch attachments, 226–27
Sheet-metal workers, 427
Shelter (homes, housing), 535–685; advantages and disadvantages of ownership, 544–45; advantages and disadvantages of renting, 545; bargains, 554–55; building, 581–93 (*see also* Building a house); burglary prevention, 643–47; buying or renting, 542, 543–45; condominiums, 567–69; co-ops, 565–66; costs, 543–44; developments, 569–71; divorce and disposition of, 717; do's and don'ts in house shopping, 555–56; fire prevention, 641–43; home improvements and, 654–75; house equipment buying and, 609–33; house hunting and buying, 553–64 (*see also* House hunting and buying); income and, 594–95; income and rent costs and, 649–50; insurance and, 604–9; investing in real estate, 954–59; kinds and factors in choosing, 540–41; leases, 650–52; mobile

homes, 572–78; mortgages and interest rates, 543–44, 593–601; neighborhoods (communities) and, 547–53; new towns, 570–71; new *vs.* old houses, 541; property taxes and, 548–49; real estate terminology, 601–4; renters' and homeowners' rights, 1027–29; renting, 648–53; second (vacation) homes, 647–48; selling, 675–77; suitable type for you, 542–43; utility bills, slashing, 633–41
Sheriff's deed, 580
Shingles, house buying and, 559
Shirts, buying, 148, 217, 221
Shoes, buying, 219–20, 231–32; care of, 230; sizes and fit, 231–32; ways to reduce bills, 231–32; when to buy, 149, 221, 232
"Shop at home" plan, banks, and, 50
Shop manual, automobile, 324
"Shopper's Guides," 1056
"Shopper's Guide to Dentistry, A," 266
"Shopper's Guide to Hospitals," 259
"Shopper's Guide to Lawyers, A," 1014
Shopping, duty-free, vacations and, 517–18
Shopping and saving, 140–51, 152–53ff. (*see also* specific aspects, items, problems); air travel, 363–64; automobiles, 292–363; bus travel, 364–66; calendar for bargains, 144, 146–49 (*see also* Bargains; Seasonal Buying); clothing, 213–32; college education and, 375–404; and doctors and dentists, 260, 264–66, 267; and drugs (medications), 263–64; and food, 152–53, 154–212; general information on, 140–51, 152–53; and health and medical care and services, 233ff.; and "house equipment," 609ff.; and household equipment, 618–33; key weapons against rising costs, 143–44; and nursing homes, 271–72; planning, 163; quiz on buying

wisely, 145; and rail travel, 366–67; and recreational vehicles, 367–68; rules for, 144–45, 162ff.; and shelter, 535–685 (*see also* Shelter); and transportation, 289–372; and vacations, 515–34
Short selling of stock, 859, 883; covering, 873
Short-term credit, defined, 138
Short-term loan, 89
Siding: do-it-yourself, 654, 656; gyps, 665
Sierra Club, 532–33, 1053
Signatures, endorsing checks and, 53–54
Silver, antique, 976–78
Silverware, when to buy, 149
Single-payment loan, 88–89, 97; costs of, 112, 115
Single-plan ("comprehensive") major medical insurance, 240
Single-purpose credit cards, 116
Sizes: clothing range, 215–17, 221–22, 223; shoe, 232
Skates, when to buy, 149
Skiing, 515, 516; costs, 647; equipment, when to buy, 149
Skin aging, gyps and, 813–14
Skirts, buying, 223
Sleeping equipment, buying, 610
Small business(es), going into, 489–508. *See also* Self-employment; specific kinds
Small Business Administration, 490, 491, 496
Small Business Guidance and Development Center, 496
Small Claims Court, 1004–8; being sued in, 1008; collecting judgments, 1007; suing in, 1005–7
Small loans companies, 87, 97–98
Smithsonian-Peace Corps Environmental Program, 512
Smoking, 277; stopping, 282–83
Snacks, cost of, 157, 161, 162, 163
Snow tires, 331
Social and environmental jobs, 412, 423, 445, 455, 456. *See also* specific kinds